Lecture Notes in Computer Science   11921

More information about this series at http://www.springer.com/series/7410

Steven D. Galbraith · Shiho Moriai (Eds.)

Advances in Cryptology – ASIACRYPT 2019

25th International Conference on the Theory
and Application of Cryptology and Information Security
Kobe, Japan, December 8–12, 2019
Proceedings, Part I

 Springer

Editors
Steven D. Galbraith (ID)
University of Auckland
Auckland, New Zealand

Shiho Moriai (ID)
Security Fundamentals Lab
NICT
Tokyo, Japan

ISSN 0302-9743   ISSN 1611-3349   (electronic)
Lecture Notes in Computer Science
ISBN 978-3-030-34577-8   ISBN 978-3-030-34578-5   (eBook)
https://doi.org/10.1007/978-3-030-34578-5

LNCS Sublibrary: SL4 – Security and Cryptology

This Springer imprint is published by the registered company Springer Nature Switzerland AG
The registered company address is: Gewerbestrasse 11, 6330 Cham, Switzerland

Preface

ASIACRYPT 2019, the 25th Annual International Conference on Theory and Application of Cryptology and Information Security, was held in Kobe, Japan, during December 8–12, 2019.

The conference focused on all technical aspects of cryptology, and was sponsored by the International Association for Cryptologic Research (IACR).

We received a total of 307 submissions from all over the world. This was a significantly higher number of submissions than recent Asiacrypt conferences, which necessitated a larger Program Committee (PC) than we had originally planned. We thank the seven additional PC members who accepted our invitation at extremely short notice. They are Gorjan Alagic, Giorgia Azzurra Marson, Zhenzhen Bao, Olivier Blazy, Romain Gay, Takanori Isobe, and Daniel Masny.

The PC selected 71 papers for publication in the proceedings of the conference. The two program chairs were supported by a PC consisting of 55 leading experts in aspects of cryptology. Each submission was reviewed by at least three Program Committee members (or their sub-reviewers) and five PC members were assigned to submissions co-authored by PC members. The strong conflict of interest rules imposed by the IACR ensure that papers are not handled by PC members with a close working relationship with authors. There were approximately 380 external reviewers, whose input was critical to the selection of papers.

The review process was conducted using double-blind peer review. The conference operated a two-round review system with a rebuttal phase. After the reviews and first-round discussions the PC selected 193 submissions to proceed to the second round. The authors of those 193 papers were then invited to provide a short rebuttal in response to the referee reports. The second round involved extensive discussions by the PC members. Indeed, the total number of text items in the online discussion (including reviews, rebuttals, questions to authors, and PC member comments) exceeded 3,000.

The three volumes of the conference proceedings contain the revised versions of the 71 papers that were selected, together with 1 invited paper. The final revised versions of papers were not reviewed again and the authors are responsible for their contents.

The program of Asiacrypt 2019 featured excellent invited talks by Krzysztof Pietrzak and Elaine Shi. The conference also featured a rump session which contained short presentations on the latest research results of the field.

The PC selected the work "Wave: A New Family of Trapdoor One-Way Preimage Sampleable Functions Based on Codes" by Thomas Debris-Alazard, Nicolas Sendrier, and Jean-Pierre Tillich for the Best Paper Award of Asiacrypt 2019. Two more papers were solicited to submit a full version to the *Journal of Cryptology*. They are "An LLL Algorithm for Module Lattices" by Changmin Lee, Alice Pellet-Mary, Damien Stehlé, and Alexandre Wallet, and "Numerical Method for Comparison on Homomorphically Encrypted Numbers" by Jung Hee Cheon, Dongwoo Kim, Duhyeong Kim, Hun Hee Lee, and Keewoo Lee.

The Program Chairs are delighted to recognize the outstanding work by Mark Zhandry and Shweta Agrawal, by awarding them jointly the Best PC Member Award.

Many people have contributed to the success of Asiacrypt 2019. We would like to thank the authors for submitting their research results to the conference. We are very grateful to the PC members and external reviewers for contributing their knowledge and expertise, and for the tremendous amount of work that was done with reading papers and contributing to the discussions.

We are greatly indebted to Mitsuru Matsui, the general chair, for his efforts and overall organization.

We thank Mehdi Tibouchi for expertly organizing and chairing the rump session.

We are extremely grateful to Lukas Zobernig for checking all the latex files and for assembling the files for submission to Springer.

Finally we thank Shai Halevi and the IACR for setting up and maintaining the Web Submission and Review software, used by IACR conferences for the paper submission and review process. We also thank Alfred Hofmann, Anna Kramer, Ingrid Haas, Anja Sebold, Xavier Mathew, and their colleagues at Springer for handling the publication of these conference proceedings.

December 2019   Steven Galbraith
                                                                        Shiho Moriai

ASIACRYPT 2019

The 25th Annual International Conference on Theory and Application of Cryptology and Information Security

Sponsored by the International Association for Cryptologic Research (IACR)

Kobe, Japan, December 8–12, 2019

General Chair

Mitsuru Matsui   Mitsubishi Electric Corporation, Japan

Program Co-chairs

Steven Galbraith   University of Auckland, New Zealand
Shiho Moriai   NICT, Japan

Program Committee

Shweta Agrawal   IIT Madras, India
Gorjan Alagic   University of Maryland, USA
Shi Bai   Florida Atlantic University, USA
Zhenzhen Bao   Nanyang Technological University, Singapore
Paulo S. L. M. Barreto   UW Tacoma, USA
Lejla Batina   Radboud University, The Netherlands
Sonia Belaïd   CryptoExperts, France
Olivier Blazy   University of Limoges, France
Colin Boyd   NTNU, Norway
Xavier Boyen   Queensland University of Technology, Australia
Nishanth Chandran   Microsoft Research, India
Melissa Chase   Microsoft Research, USA
Yilei Chen   Visa Research, USA
Chen-Mou Cheng   Osaka University, Japan
Nils Fleischhacker   Ruhr-University Bochum, Germany
Jun Furukawa   NEC Israel Research Center, Israel
David Galindo   University of Birmingham and Fetch AI, UK
Romain Gay   UC Berkeley, USA
Jian Guo   Nanyang Technological University, Singapore
Seokhie Hong   Korea University, South Korea
Andreas Hülsing   Eindhoven University of Technology, The Netherlands
Takanori Isobe   University of Hyogo, Japan
David Jao   University of Waterloo and evolutionQ, Inc., Canada

Jérémy Jean	ANSSI, France
Elena Kirshanova	ENS Lyon, France
Virginie Lallemand	CNRS, France
Jooyoung Lee	KAIST, South Korea
Helger Lipmaa	Simula UiB, Norway
Feng-Hao Liu	Florida Atlantic University, USA
Atul Luykx	Swirlds Inc., USA
Hemanta K. Maji	Purdue, USA
Giorgia Azzurra Marson	NEC Laboratories Europe, Germany
Daniel Masny	Visa Research, USA
Takahiro Matsuda	AIST, Japan
Brice Minaud	Inria and ENS, France
David Naccache	ENS, France
Kartik Nayak	Duke University and VMware Research, USA
Khoa Nguyen	Nanyang Technological University, Singapore
Svetla Nikova	KU Leuven, Belgium
Carles Padró	UPC, Spain
Jiaxin Pan	NTNU, Norway, and KIT, Germany
Arpita Patra	Indian Institute of Science, India
Thomas Peters	UCL, Belgium
Duong Hieu Phan	University of Limoges, France
Raphael C.-W. Phan	Monash University, Malaysia
Carla Ràfols	Universitat Pompeu Fabra, Spain
Ling Ren	VMware Research and University of Illinois, Urbana-Champaign, USA
Yu Sasaki	NTT laboratories, Japan
Junji Shikata	Yokohama National University, Japan
Ron Steinfeld	Monash University, Australia
Qiang Tang	New Jersey Institute of Technology, USA
Mehdi Tibouchi	NTT Laboratories, Japan
Hoeteck Wee	CNRS and ENS, France
Mark Zhandry	Princeton University, USA
Fangguo Zhang	Sun Yat-sen University, China

Local Organizing Committee

General Chair
Mitsuru Matsui	Mitsubishi Electric Corporation, Japan

Honorary Advisor
Tsutomu Matsumoto	Yokohama National University, Japan

External Reviewers

Masayuki Abe
Parhat Abla
Victor Arribas Abril
Divesh Aggarwal
Martin Albrecht
Bar Alon
Prabhanjan Ananth
Elena Andreeva
Yoshinori Aono
Daniel Apon
Toshinori Araki
Seiko Arita
Tomer Ashur
Nuttapong Attrapadung
Man Ho Allen Au
Benedikt Auerbach
Saikrishna
  Badrinarayanan
Vivek Bagaria
Josep Balasch
Gustavo Banegas
Laasya Bangalore
Subhadeep Banik
Achiya Bar-On
Manuel Barbosa
James Bartusek
Carsten Baum
Arthur Beckers
Rouzbeh Behnia
Francesco Berti
Alexandre Berzati
Ward Beullens
Shivam Bhasin
Nina Bindel
Nicolas Bordes
Jannis Bossert
Katharina Boudgoust
Christina Boura
Florian Bourse
Zvika Brakerski
Anne Broadbent
Olivier Bronchain
Leon Groot Bruinderink

Megha Byali
Eleonora Cagli
Ignacio Cascudo
Pyrros Chaidos
Avik Chakraborti
Donghoon Chang
Hao Chen
Jie Chen
Long Chen
Ming-Shing Chen
Qian Chen
Jung Hee Cheon
Céline Chevalier
Ilaria Chillotti
Wonhee Cho
Wonseok Choi
Wutichai Chongchitmate
Jérémy Chotard
Arka Rai Choudhuri
Sherman Chow
Michele Ciampi
Michael Clear
Thomas De Cnudde
Benoît Cogliati
Sandro Coretti-Drayton
Edouard Cuvelier
Jan Czajkowski
Dana Dachman-Soled
Joan Daemen
Nilanjan Datta
Gareth T. Davies
Patrick Derbez
Apporva Deshpande
Siemen Dhooghe
Christoph Dobraunig
Rafael Dowsley
Yfke Dulek
Avijit Dutta
Sébastien Duval
Keita Emura
Thomas Espitau
Xiong Fan
Antonio Faonio

Oriol Farràs
Sebastian Faust
Prastudy Fauzi
Hanwen Feng
Samuele Ferracin
Dario Fiore
Georg Fuchsbauer
Thomas Fuhr
Eiichiro Fujisaki
Philippe Gaborit
Tatiana Galibus
Chaya Ganesh
Daniel Gardham
Luke Garratt
Pierrick Gaudry
Nicholas Genise
Esha Ghosh
Satrajit Ghosh
Kristian Gjøsteen
Aarushi Goel
Huijing Gong
Junqing Gong
Alonso González
Dahmun Goudarzi
Rishabh Goyal
Jiaxin Guan
Aurore Guillevic
Chun Guo
Kaiwen Guo
Qian Guo
Mohammad Hajiabadi
Carmit Hazay
Jingnan He
Brett Hemenway
Nadia Heninger
Javier Herranz
Shoichi Hirose
Harunaga Hiwatari
Viet Tung Hoang
Justin Holmgren
Akinori Hosoyamada
Kexin Hu
Senyang Huang

Yan Huang
Phi Hun
Aaron Hutchinson
Chloé Hébant
Kathrin Hövelmanns
Ilia Iliashenko
Mitsugu Iwamoto
Tetsu Iwata
Zahra Jafargholi
Christian Janson
Ashwin Jha
Dingding Jia
Sunghyun Jin
Charanjit S. Jutla
Mustafa Kairallah
Saqib A. Kakvi
Marc Kaplan
Emrah Karagoz
Ghassan Karame
Shuichi Katsumata
Craig Kenney
Mojtaba Khalili
Dakshita Khurana
Duhyeong Kim
Hyoseung Kim
Sam Kim
Seongkwang Kim
Taechan Kim
Agnes Kiss
Fuyuki Kitagawa
Michael Klooß
François Koeune
Lisa Kohl
Stefan Kölbl
Yashvanth Kondi
Toomas Krips
Veronika Kuchta
Nishant Kumar
Noboru Kunihiro
Po-Chun Kuo
Kaoru Kurosawa
Ben Kuykendall
Albert Kwon
Qiqi Lai
Baptiste Lambin
Roman Langrehr

Jason LeGrow
ByeongHak Lee
Changmin Lee
Keewoo Lee
Kwangsu Lee
Youngkyung Lee
Dominik Leichtle
Christopher Leonardi
Tancrède Lepoint
Gaëtan Leurent
Itamar Levi
Baiyu Li
Yanan Li
Zhe Li
Xiao Liang
Benoît Libert
Fuchun Lin
Rachel Lin
Wei-Kai Lin
Eik List
Fukang Liu
Guozhen Liu
Meicheng Liu
Qipeng Liu
Shengli Liu
Zhen Liu
Alex Lombardi
Julian Loss
Jiqiang Lu
Xianhui Lu
Yuan Lu
Lin Lyu
Fermi Ma
Gilles Macario-Rat
Urmila Mahadev
Monosij Maitra
Christian Majenz
Nikolaos Makriyannis
Giulio Malavolta
Sogol Mazaheri
Bart Mennink
Peihan Miao
Shaun Miller
Kazuhiko Minematsu
Takaaki Mizuki
Amir Moradi

Kirill Morozov
Fabrice Mouhartem
Pratyay Mukherjee
Pierrick Méaux
Yusuke Naito
Mridul Nandi
Peter Naty
María Naya-Plasencia
Anca Niculescu
Ventzi Nikov
Takashi Nishide
Ryo Nishimaki
Anca Nitulescu
Ariel Nof
Sai Lakshmi Bhavana
    Obbattu
Kazuma Ohara
Emmanuela Orsini
Elena Pagnin
Wenlun Pan
Omer Paneth
Bo Pang
Lorenz Panny
Jacques Patarin
Sikhar Patranabis
Alice Pellet-Mary
Chun-Yo Peng
Geovandro Pereira
Olivier Pereira
Léo Perrin
Naty Peter
Cécile Pierrot
Jeroen Pijnenburg
Federico Pintore
Bertram Poettering
David Pointcheval
Yuriy Polyakov
Eamonn Postlethwaite
Emmanuel Prouff
Pille Pullonen
Daniel Puzzuoli
Chen Qian
Tian Qiu
Willy Quach
Håvard Raddum
Ananth Raghunathan

Somindu Ramanna
Kim Ramchen
Shahram Rasoolzadeh
Mayank Rathee
Divya Ravi
Joost Renes
Angela Robinson
Thomas Roche
Miruna Rosca
Mélissa Rossi
Mike Rosulek
Yann Rotella
Arnab Roy
Luis Ruiz-Lopez
Ajith Suresh
Markku-Juhani
    O. Saarinen
Yusuke Sakai
Kazuo Sakiyama
Amin Sakzad
Louis Salvail
Simona Samardjiska
Pratik Sarkar
Christian Schaffner
John Schanck
Berry Schoenmakers
Peter Scholl
André Schrottenloher
Jacob Schuldt
Sven Schäge
Sruthi Sekar
Srinath Setty
Yannick Seurin
Barak Shani
Yaobin Shen
Sina Shiehian
Kazumasa Shinagawa
Janno Siim
Javier Silva
Mark Simkin

Boris Skoric
Maciej Skórski
Yongsoo Song
Pratik Soni
Claudio Soriente
Florian Speelman
Akshayaram Srinivasan
François-Xavier Standaert
Douglas Stebila
Damien Stehlé
Patrick Struck
Valentin Suder
Bing Sun
Shifeng Sun
Siwei Sun
Jaechul Sung
Daisuke Suzuki
Katsuyuki Takashima
Benjamin Hong Meng
    Tan
Stefano Tessaro
Adrian Thillard
Yan Bo Ti
Jean-Pierre Tillich
Radu Țițiu
Yosuke Todo
Junichi Tomida
Viet Cuong Trinh
Rotem Tsabary
Hikaru Tsuchida
Yi Tu
Nirvan Tyagi
Bogdan Ursu
Damien Vergnaud
Jorge Luis Villar
Srinivas Vivek
Christine van Vredendaal
Satyanarayana Vusirikala
Sameer Wagh
Hendrik Waldner

Alexandre Wallet
Michael Walter
Han Wang
Haoyang Wang
Junwei Wang
Mingyuan Wang
Ping Wang
Yuyu Wang
Zhedong Wang
Yohei Watanabe
Gaven Watson
Weiqiang Wen
Yunhua Wen
Benjamin Wesolowski
Keita Xagawa
Zejun Xiang
Hanshen Xiao
Shota Yamada
Takashi Yamakawa
Kyosuke Yamashita
Avishay Yanai
Guomin Yang
Kan Yasuda
Masaya Yasuda
Aaram Yun
Alexandros Zacharakis
Michal Zajac
Bin Zhang
Cong Zhang
En Zhang
Huang Zhang
Xiao Zhang
Zheng Zhang
Chang-An Zhao
Raymond K. Zhao
Yongjun Zhao
Yuanyuan Zhou
Jiamin Zhu
Yihong Zhu
Lukas Zobernig

Contents – Part I

E-cash and Blockchain

Invited Talk

Streamlined Blockchains: A Simple and Elegant Approach (A Tutorial and Survey)

Elaine Shi[✉]

Cornell University, Ithaca, USA
runting@gmail.com

Abstract. A blockchain protocol (also called state machine replication) allows a set of nodes to agree on an ever-growing, linearly ordered log of transactions. The classical consensus literature suggests two approaches for constructing a blockchain protocol: (1) through composition of single-shot consensus instances often called Byzantine Agreement; and (2) through direct construction of a blockchain where there is no clear-cut boundary between single-shot consensus instances. While conceptually simple, the former approach precludes cross-instance optimizations in a practical implementation. This perhaps explains why the latter approach has gained more traction in practice: specifically, well-known protocols such as Paxos and PBFT all follow the direct-construction approach.

In this tutorial, we present a new paradigm called "streamlined blockchains" for directly constructing blockchain protocols. This paradigm enables a new family of protocols that are extremely simple and natural: every epoch, a proposer proposes a block extending from a notarized parent chain, and nodes vote if the proposal's parent chain is not too old. Whenever a block gains enough votes, it becomes *notarized*. Whenever a node observes a notarized chain with several blocks of consecutive epochs at the end, then the entire chain chopping off a few blocks at the end is *final*.

By varying the parameters highlighted in blue, we illustrate two variants for the partially synchronous and synchronous settings respectively. We present very simple proofs of consistency and liveness. We hope that this tutorial provides a compelling argument why this new family of protocols should be used in lieu of classical candidates (e.g., PBFT, Paxos, and their variants), both in practical implementation and for pedagogical purposes.

1 Introduction

In a blockchain protocol, a set of nodes seek to reach agreement on an ever-growing, linearly ordered log. It is helpful to think of this log as an ordered chain of blocks where each block may contain application-specific payload as well as metadata pertaining to the consensus protocol, and hence the name *blockchain*.

In this tutorial, we consider how to construct a blockchain protocol in a "permissioned" setting, assuming the existence of a public-key infrastructure

© International Association for Cryptologic Research 2019
S. D. Galbraith and S. Moriai (Eds.): ASIACRYPT 2019, LNCS 11921, pp. 3–17, 2019.
https://doi.org/10.1007/978-3-030-34578-5_1

and that the public key of every consensus node is common knowledge. This is the also the classical setting under which consensus has been studied for more than three decades. Classically, this problem was often called "State Machine Replication" [12,13,15] or "Byzantine Fault Tolerance" [3,9]. In this work, we also refer to it as "consensus" for short.

Such permissioned blockchains can serve as the cornerstone not only for a private, consortium blockchain, but also for building open-access "proof-of-stake" systems. In a proof-of-stake setting, a set of nodes (called a committee) are elected based on their stake in the system to vote in the consensus protocol. The election is typically repeated over time, using the blockchain protocol itself to agree on the next committee (and assuming the existence of an initial committee that is common knowledge).

The goal of this tutorial is to illustrate a new paradigm called "streamlined blockchains" that enables extremely simple and natural blockchain constructions. This new paradigm emerged as a result of the community's joint push at building better consensus protocols in the past few years, motivated by large-scale cryptocurrency applications. Elements of this idea were developed and improved in a sequence of works, including Casper-FFT [16], Dfinity [8], Hotstuff [1], Pili [5] and Pala [4], but understanding of this line of work still appears somewhat "scattered".

In this tutorial, we hope to describe the simplest possible embodiments of this idea, with concise and clean proofs that are suitable for pedagogy. We hope that this tutorial helps to illustrate the most compelling advantage of this new paradigm, i.e., its conceptual simplicity, making the resulting protocols desirable for practical implementation. We also contrast this new paradigm with classical blockchain constructions represented by Paxos [9], PBFT [3], and their variants. We hope that this will shed light on how the community's push in the past few years has enabled a leap: we now have practical blockchain constructions that are significantly simpler and fundamentally better than classical approaches.

1.1 Problem Statement

Slightly informally, we would like to construct a blockchain protocol satisfying two properties for all but a negligible fraction of executions:

- *Consistency*: if two blockchains chain and chain′ are ever considered *final* by two honest nodes, it must be that chain $\preceq$ chain′ or chain′ $\preceq$ chain where $\preceq$ means "is a prefix of or equal to".
- *Liveness*: if an honest node receives a transaction, the transaction will appear in every honest node's finalized blockchain in a bounded amount of time.

In a cryptocurrency application, all transactions contained in a *final* chain are considered confirmed and the merchant may ship the product. If all nodes are honest and always correctly follow the prescribed protocol, then designing a blockchain protocol is trivial. We consider a setting where a subset of the nodes can be corrupt; corrupt nodes are controlled by a single adversary and they can deviate from the protocol arbitrarily—such a fault model is commonly referred to as Byzantine Faults in the classical distributed consensus literature.

In general, we can construct a blockchain protocol in two ways: (1) through composition of single-shot consensus instances; and (2) direct construction of a blockchain protocol where there is no clearly defined boundary between consensus instances. From a historical perspective, the study of distributed consensus in fact originated from the study of one-shot consensus protocols, often called Byzantine Agreement [10]. While composing single-shot instances is a conceptually clean approach towards building a blockchain, cross-instance performance optimizations are often challenging. This is arguably why later approaches such as Paxos and PBFT and their variants—also coinciding with most deployed systems—adopt the direct-construction approach. In this tutorial we will also focus on the direct-construction approach.

1.2 Classical Blockchain Protocols: A Bi-modal Approach

Most approaches in the classical consensus literature adopt a bi-model approach. We illustrate the idea assuming that fewer than $n/3$ nodes are corrupt where n denotes the total number of nodes[1].

1.2.1 Normal Mode: A Natural Voting Protocol

The normal mode is simple and natural and works by super-majority voting. We shall explain the idea semi-formally, since this is the nice part of the protocol we would like to preserve in our new paradigm. Recall that every block is part of a blockchain and henceforth its index within the blockchain is called its position. We assume that every block encodes its own position.

Imagine that a designated proposer proposes blocks, and nodes vote on the proposed blocks by signing the block's hash. Whenever a block gains votes from at least $2n/3$ distinct nodes, it becomes final. If in a blockchain every block is final, then the chain is considered final too.

An important invariant is that *an honest node never votes for two distinct blocks at the same position* (even if the proposer is corrupt and proposes multiple blocks at the same position). This enforces consistency at every position, i.e., at each position, there cannot be two different blocks both gaining at least $2n/3$ votes. The proof of consistency is extremely simple: suppose that two different blocks at the same position both gain at least $2n/3$ votes. It must be that a set of at least $2n/3$ distinct nodes denoted S_1 have voted for one, and a set of at least $2n/3$ distinct nodes denoted S_2 have voted for the other. Obviously $|S_1 \cap S_2| \geq 2n/3 + 2n/3 - n = n/3$. Since fewer than $n/3$ nodes are corrupt, it must be that an honest node lives in the intersection $S_1 \cap S_2$ and has voted for

---

[1] Our exposition in spirit illustrates the ideas behind most classical blockchain constructions although our exposition is not necessarily faithful to any particular protocol. In fact, we give a simplified exposition of the technical ideas to maximally aid understanding.

both blocks at the same position—but this is ruled out by the aforementioned invariant.

Such a normal-mode protocol is extremely simple and natural, and it gives consistency as long as fewer than $n/3$ nodes are corrupt; and moreover, consistency does not rely on the proposer being honest. However, if the proposer is corrupt, e.g., if it stops making proposals or makes different proposals to different nodes, then liveness can be stalled and the blockchain can stop growing. We note also that here, consistency is guaranteed without having to make any network timing assumptions such as synchrony assumptions.

1.2.2   Recovery Mode: Ensuring Liveness

Given the aforementioned normal-mode protocol, the only remaining problem is how to achieve liveness when the proposer is corrupt. We informally explain how classical protocols deal with this problem without going into details, since this is the complicated part of classical approaches that we would ideally like to get rid of.

Most classical protocols such as Paxos, PBFT and their variants solve this problem by falling back to a recovery mode (often called "view change") whenever liveness is stalled. Typically the view change implements a mechanism to rotate to the next proposer such that progress can be resumed. Thus a view can be regarded as a phase of the protocol in which a specific node acts as the proposer. Without going into details, and perhaps unsurprisingly, from a technical standpoint the view change protocol must be a full-fledged consensus protocol offering both consistency and liveness (*c.f.* the normal mode guarantees only consistency assuming fewer than $n/3$ corrupt).

At an intuitive level, this perhaps explains why in most classical consensus approaches, the view change is often much more complicated to understand and subtle to implement correctly than the normal mode. In fact, the need for such a recovery mode often imposes more requirements on the normal mode too—and this is why most actual instantiations of this bi-modal idea such as Paxos and PBFT introduce more iterations of voting in the normal mode (unlike our earlier description that has only one iteration of voting). Very roughly, the additional iterations of voting in the normal mode give amplified properties that the recovery mode can make use of.

1.3   Streamlined Blockchains: A New Paradigm

Classical approaches are somewhat undesirable because most of the time we expect that the protocol should operate in the normal mode (since faults should not happen very often); however, the conceptual complications and the heavy-lifting in implementation stem from the complicated recovery path. Ideally, we would like to achieve the following holy grail:

> Can we have a blockchain protocol that is (almost) *as simple as the normal mode?*

Amazingly, it turns out that this is in fact possible! All the protocols we describe in this tutorial, for different settings, can be obtained by making small tweaks to the aforementioned normal-path voting protocol. Through these tweaks we now offer not just consistency but also liveness and thus there is no need for a separate recovery mode! Specifically, the entire protocol always follows a unified propose-vote paradigm as described below:

- Every epoch, a proposer proposes a block extending from a parent chain. Every block encodes its own epoch.
- Nodes vote on the proposed block if they have seen the parent chain's notarization and if the parent chain is not too old (where "old" means that the block contains a small epoch number, and we will specify the concrete parameter in the later sections).
- Whenever a block gains sufficiently many votes, it becomes *notarized*.
- Notarized does not mean *final*. Finality is determined as follows: if all blocks in a blockchain are notarized and the chain ends at several blocks of consecutive epochs, then the entire chain chopping off the trailing few blocks are considered final.

We show how to use this simple paradigm to obtain protocols under various network assumptions, by modifying the parameters highlighted in blue, and by slightly varying a couple other details such as how epochs are determined for different settings.

So What Became of the View Change? As mentioned earlier, in classical approaches the view change was necessary to attain liveness under a corrupt proposer. So technically, how can we achieve both consistency and liveness without the view change? In the streamlined blockchain paradigm described in this tutorial, basically every epoch embeds a proposer-rotation opportunity, and thus an implicit view change mechanism is already inherently baked in the protocol everywhere. This is arguably the coolest feature of this new paradigm: we show that the traditionally complicated view change can be embedded into an extremely simple paradigm by small tweaks to the normal-path voting protocol.

For this reason, another advantage of our streamlined blockchain protocols is that they readily support two distinct proposer-rotation policies: the *democracy-favoring* policy where one wishes to rotate proposer every block; and the classical *stability-favoring* policy (adopted by classical approaches such as Paxos and PBFT) where we stick to the same proposer until it starts to misbehave. In new cryptocurrency applications, the democracy-favoring policy may be more desired due to better decentralization; however, a stability-favoring policy is likely more friendly towards performance optimizations.

Throughout this paper, we use the democracy-favoring policy for exposition. Some recent works [4, 5] have shown how minor tweaks to the protocol can support a stability-favoring policy[2].

---

[2] Author's note: even if the syntactical changes to the protocol are minor, it is important that they be done correctly since some additional subtleties arise in the liveness proof for a stability-favoring policy. See the recent works [4,5] for more explanation.

2   A Blockchain Tolerating <1/3 Corruptions

Recall that we consider a network consisting of n nodes numbered $0, 1, \ldots, n-1$ respectively. We assume that there is a public-key infrastructure such that all nodes' public keys are common knowledge. In this section we shall assume that fewer than $n/3$ nodes are corrupt. In our protocol, whenever a node *multicasts* a message to everyone, it means it sends this message to every node.

Delay Parameter Δ. The protocol is parametrized with a parameter Δ which captures our a-priori guess of the maximum message delay. We will prove that *consistency holds regardless even if our guess of Δ is wrong and network delays are arbitrary*. However, liveness only holds during "periods of synchrony", i.e., periods in which honest messages are delivered in at most Δ rounds.

Remark 1. Although we assume that time progresses in discrete *rounds* in this tutorial, all the results still hold if the round is infinitesimally small, i.e., if time is continuous. We assume that all nodes have local clocks that increment per round. Since clock offsets can be absorbed by the network delay, our consistency proof holds even if clock offsets between nodes are arbitrarily large. However, unsynchronized clocks may stall liveness by preventing a period of synchrony from happening.

2.1   Valid Blockchain and Freshness

Our protocol will progress in epochs where each epoch contains 2Δ rounds, i.e., long enough for honest nodes to make a round trip during a period of synchrony.

Valid Blockchain. A blockchain, often denoted chain, is an ordered sequence of blocks. Each block chain$[\ell]$ where $\ell \geq 0$ is of the format $(e, \mathsf{TXs}, h_{-1})$, where e encodes the epoch number, TXs is application-specific payload (e.g., a set of transactions to confirm), and h_{-1} is the parent block's hash. In a valid blockchain chain, the 0-th block must be a special genesis block of the form $(0, \bot, \bot)$.

When we define a chain's length denoted |chain|, *it does not count the genesis block.* This way, the chain's length is the same as the index of the last block. Henceforth for $\ell \geq 0$, we use the notation chain$[: \ell]$ to denote the prefix of the blockchain up to the ℓ-th block and chain$[: -\ell]$ is an alias for chain$[: m - \ell]$ where $m := $ |chain| denotes the length of the blockchain. Similarly, chain$[-\ell]$ is an alias for chain$[m - \ell]$.

For a blockchain chain to be valid, all the blocks must have strictly increasing epoch numbers, and moreover for every $\ell \geq 0$, the block chain$[\ell].h_{-1}$ must be equal to $H(\text{chain}[: \ell - 1])$. In our protocol, all protocol messages containing ill-formed blockchains are immediately discarded.

Freshness. For a blockchain chain, the larger chain$[-1].e$ is the fresher chain is. Formally, we say that chain is fresher than chain$'$ if chain$[-1].e > $ chain$'[-1].e$. For a blockchain chain, chain$[-1].e$ is also said to be the blockchain chain's epoch number.

2.2   Protocol

Now, imagine that the protocol proceeds in *epochs* numbered $1, 2, \ldots$. Each epoch is 2Δ rounds, i.e., the maximum round-trip delay during a period of synchrony. In each epoch $e \in \{1, 2, \ldots, \}$, we use a hash function H^* (i.e., a random oracle) to select a random node ($H^*(e) \mod n$) to be the designated proposer—note that here we are using a democracy-favoring proposer-rotation policy as an example.

The protocol proceeds as follows where we assume that a node always signs every message it wants to send, and that every valid message must be tagged with the purported sender; further, nodes discard messages with invalid signatures. The notation "_" denotes a wildcard field.

Notarization: A valid vote for chain from node i is a valid signature from node i on $H(\text{chain})$ where H is a global hash function chosen at random from a collision-resistant hash family upfront. A collection of at least $2n/3$ votes from distinct nodes on some chain is said to be a notarization for chain.

For each epoch $e = 1, 2, \ldots$:

- **Propose:** At the beginning of the epoch, node ($H^*(e) \mod n$) proposes a new block $\mathsf{B} := (e, \mathsf{TXs}, h_{-1})$ extending the freshest notarized chain in its view denoted chain. Here TXs denotes a set of outstanding transactions to confirm and $h_{-1} = H(\text{chain})$. The proposal, containing chain$\|$B and a notarization for chain, is signed and multicast to everyone—here chain is referred to as the parent chain of B.
- **Vote:** Every node performs the following: when the *first* valid proposal of the form chain$\|(e, \_, \_)$ is received from node ($H^*(e) \mod n$) with a valid notarization on chain, vote on the proposal iff chain is at least as fresh as the freshest notarized chain the node has observed *at the beginning of the previous* epoch or if the current epoch $e = 1$.
  To vote on chain$\|$B, simply multicast a signature on the value $H(\text{chain}\|\mathsf{B})$ to everyone.

Finalization: At any time, if a notarized chain has been observed ending at three consecutive epochs, then chain$[: -2]$ is considered final.

Remark 2 (Block and chain as aliases of each other). Suppose that there are no hash collisions, then due to the structure of the blockchain where every block must refer to its parent's hash, in fact a block chain$[\ell]$ and the chain chain$[: \ell]$ can be used interchangeably, since the block chain$[\ell]$ uniquely defines the entire prefix chain$[: \ell]$. Therefore, henceforth whenever convenient, we use "a vote or a notarization for chain$[\ell]$" and "a vote or notarization for chain$[: \ell]$" interchangeably.

Remark 3 (Practical considerations). The above protocol is described in a way that maximizes conceptual simplicity. In practice, a couple of obvious optimizations can be made. First, the hash H can be computed incrementally by hashing the parent block's hash and the current block's contents. Second, the proposer need not include the entire parent chain in the proposal, it suffices to include the hash $h_{-1} = H(\text{chain})$. When a proposal is received, if the recipient has not received a parent chain consistent with h_{-1}, it buffers this proposal until it has received a consistent parent chain.

2.3 Consistency Proof

We now present a very simple consistency proof. Recall that the adversary controls strictly fewer than $n/3$ nodes. Throughout, we assume that the signature and hash schemes are ideal, i.e., the adversary cannot forge honest nodes' signatures or find hash collisions. Technically we are removing from our consideration the negligible fraction of bad executions in which an honest node's signature is forged or hash collisions are found—all the lemmas and theorems below hold for all but the negligible fraction of such bad executions.

We say that some string is *in honest view* iff some honest node observes it at some point during the execution. The following simply lemma is in fact already proven in Sect. 1, but we restate it for completeness.

A simple fact is the following: if there is a notarization for chain in honest view, there must be a notarization chain[: -1] in honest view since if not, no honest node would have voted for chain and chain cannot gain notarization in honest view. Applying this argument inductively, if there is a notarization of chain in honest view then there must be a notarization of every prefix of chain in honest view.

Lemma 2.1 (Uniqueness per epoch). *There cannot be two different blocks of epoch e both notarized in honest view.*

Proof. Suppose that two different blocks B_1 and B_2 of epoch e both gained notarization in honest view. Let S_1 be the set of at least $2n/3$ nodes who have signed B_1 and let S_2 be the set of at least $2n/3$ nodes who have signed B_2. It must be that $|S_1 \cap S_2| \geq 2n/3 + 2n/3 - n = n/3$. This means that at least one honest node is in $S_1 \cap S_2$, and this honest node must have signed both B_1 and B_2 in epoch e. By our protocol definition, every honest node signs only one epoch-e block in each epoch e. Thus we have reached a contradiction. □

Theorem 2.2 (Consistency). *Suppose that chain and chain$'$ are notarized chains in honest view both ending at three consecutive epochs, it must be that chain[: -2] $\preceq$ chain$'$[: -2] or chain$'$[: -2] $\preceq$ chain[: -2].*

Proof. Suppose that chain ends with three blocks of epochs $e - 2$, $e - 1$, and e, and chain$'$ ends with three blocks of epochs $e' - 2$, $e' - 1$, and e'. Without loss of generality, assume that $e' \geq e$. For the sake of reaching a contradiction, suppose that chain[: -2] and chain$'$[: -2] are not prefixes of each other. Due to Lemma 2.1, chain$'$ cannot have a block at epochs $e - 2$, $e - 1$, or e; since otherwise chain$'$[: -2] must contain the prefix chain[: -2] which ends at a block of epoch $e - 2$. Therefore, there is some block in chain$'$ with an epoch number greater than e. Let $e'' > e$ be the smallest epoch number greater than e in chain$'$, and let chain$'[\ell]$ be the block in chain$'$ with epoch number e''. It must be that chain$'[\ell - 1]$ has epoch smaller than $e - 2$.

Since (every prefix of) chain gained notarization in honest view, it must be that at least $2n/3$ distinct nodes have signed the block chain$[-1]$ of epoch $e - 1$, meaning that more than $n/3$ honest nodes have signed this block. Moreover, honest nodes can only sign this block in epoch $e - 1$. This means that more than $n/3$ honest nodes have observed a notarization for chain$[: -2]$ of epoch $e - 2$ in epoch $e - 1$, i.e., before the beginning of epoch e—let S denote this set of more than $n/3$ honest nodes. The set S therefore will not vote for chain$'[\ell]$ in epoch $e'' > e$ which extends from a parent chain of epoch less than $e - 2$; and thus chain$'[\ell]$ cannot have gained notarization in honest view. $\qquad\square$

2.4   Liveness Proof

Message Delivery Assumption During Periods of Synchrony. As mentioned earlier, a period of synchrony is a period with good network conditions such that all messages sent by honest nodes are delivered to the recipients within at most Δ rounds.

Without loss of generality, we shall assume that every honest node always echos (i.e., multicasts) every fresh message as soon as it is observed. Thus, during a period of synchrony, the following holds:

If an honest node has observed a message m *n round* t, *then all honest nodes must have observed* m *by the beginning of round* $t + \Delta$ *if not earlier.*

Liveness Proof. Suppose a period of synchrony eventually takes place. We now prove liveness during such a period of synchrony. Specifically, we prove that during a period of synchrony, honest nodes' finalized blockchains will grow whenever there are 3 consecutive epochs with honest proposers (note that under random proposer election, this takes $O(1)$ number of epochs in expectation).

To see this, it suffices to show that every honest node will vote on the proposal of an honest proposer—since an honest proposer makes a proposal at the beginning of the epoch e, as long as every honest node votes on it, the honest votes will have been received by all honest nodes by the beginning of epoch $e+1$; and thus epoch $(e + 1)$'s proposer, if honest, will propose to extend a notarized chain ending at epoch $e + 1$. We now prove this.

If an honest node i rejects a proposal from an honest proposer j, it must be that the proposed block extends from a parent chain that is less fresh than the freshest notarized chain (denoted chain*) observed at the beginning of the *previous* epoch. However, if i has observed chain* at the beginning of the previous epoch, then due to the message delivery assumption during a period of synchrony, by the beginning of this epoch, node j must have observed it and thus j cannot have proposed to extend from a less fresh parent chain.

Remark 4. Alternatively, we can modify the proposer rotation policy for the same node to serve as a proposer for three consecutive epochs. In this case, progress will be made whenever an honest proposer makes proposals for 3 consecutive epochs.

3   A Synchronous Blockchain Tolerating Minority Corruptions

In the previous section, we presented a streamlined blockchain protocol whose consistency guarantee holds with arbitrary network delays, but whose liveness guarantee may hold only during periods of synchrony—such protocols are said to be secure in a "partially synchronous" network [6]. Due to a well-known lower bound by Dwork et al. [6], no partially synchronous protocol can tolerate $n/3$ or more corruptions, and therefore the protocol in the previous section is in fact optimal in resilience.

In this section we illustrate another streamlined blockchain protocol that tolerates up to minority corruptions. To achieve this, however, we must make a synchrony assumption even for the consistency proof. Recall that earlier in Sect. 2.4 we made the following synchrony assumption for proving liveness:

> *If an honest node has observed a message* m *in round* t, *then all honest nodes must have observed* m *by the beginning of round* $t + \Delta$ *if not earlier.*

In this section, we shall make this assumption for proving both consistency and liveness.

Remark 5. The consensus problem would be trivial if all honest nodes must observe every message m in the same round. In fact, in the synchronous setting, the crux of the consensus problem is essentially to overcome the Δ difference in the timing at which honest nodes observe the same message m.

3.1   Protocol

The protocol is almost identical as the one in Sect. 2 except for two modifications: (1) the parameters for forming a notarization and for finalizations are chosen differently; and (2) the finalization rule makes an additional check for conflicting proposals. The protocol is described below and the difference from the earlier protocol in Sect. 2 is highlighted in blue.

Notarization: A valid vote for chain from node i is a valid signature from node i on $H(\text{chain})$ where H is a hash function chosen at random from a collision-resistant hash family. A collection of at least $n/2$ votes from distinct nodes on some chain is said to be a notarization for chain.

For each epoch $e = 1, 2, \ldots$:

- **Propose:** At the beginning of the epoch, node $(H^*(e) \bmod n)$ proposes a new block $\mathsf{B} := (e, \mathsf{TXs}, h_{-1})$ extending the freshest notarized chain in its view denoted chain. Here TXs denotes a set of outstanding transactions to confirm and $h_{-1} = H(\text{chain})$. The proposal, containing chain$\|\mathsf{B}$ and a notarization for chain, is signed and multicast to everyone—here chain is referred to as the parent chain of B.
- **Vote:** Every node performs the following: when the *first* valid proposal of the form chain$\|(e, \_, \_)$ is received from node $(H^*(e) \bmod n)$ with a valid notarization on chain, vote on the proposal iff chain is at least as fresh as the freshest notarized chain the node has observed *at the beginning of the previous* epoch or if the current epoch $e = 1$.
  To vote on chain$\|\mathsf{B}$, simply multicast a signature on the value $H(\text{chain}\|\mathsf{B})$ to everyone.

Finalization: At any time, if a notarized chain has been observed ending at 6 blocks with consecutive epoch numbers, and moreover for each these 6 epoch numbers, no conflicting proposal (from an eligible proposer) for a different block has been seen, then the prefix chain$[: -5]$ is final.

3.2 Consistency Proof

In comparison with Sect. 2.3, under minority corruption, the "uniqueness per epoch" lemma (Lemma 2.1) no longer holds. Consistency now crucially relies on the new finalization rule which additionally checks for conflicting proposals. We thus present a different but nonetheless simple consistency proof. Henceforth we use the notation chain$\langle e \rangle$ to denote the block at epoch e in chain, and we use chain$\langle : e \rangle$ to denote the prefix of chain up to and including the block of epoch e.

Lemma 3.1 (No contiguous skipping). *Suppose that a notarized chain with two consecutive epoch numbers e and $e+1$ appear in honest view. Then, no notarized chain in honest view whose ending epoch at least e can skip all of the epochs $e, e+1, e+2, e+3$ (i.e., one of these epochs must be contained in the notarized chain).*

Proof. Let chain be the notarized chain in honest view with two consecutive epochs e and $e + 1$. It must be that at least one honest node i has voted for chain$\langle : e + 1 \rangle$ during epoch $e + 1$, and thus i has observed a notarization for chain$\langle : e \rangle$ in epoch $e + 1$. Therefore all honest nodes must have observed a notarization for chain$\langle : e \rangle$ in epoch $e + 2$, i.e., *by the beginning of* epoch $e + 3$.

Thus in any epoch $e' > e + 3$ no honest node will vote to extend a parent chain whose epoch is smaller than e.

Suppose chain$'$ is a notarized chain in honest view whose ending epoch is at least $e + 4$ and moreover chain$'$ does not contain the epochs $e, e + 1, e + 2, e + 3$. Let e' be the smallest epoch in chain$'$ that is greater than $e + 3$. It must be that at least one honest node voted on chain$'\langle: e'\rangle$ during epoch e' but this is impossible because chain$'\langle: e'\rangle$'s parent has epoch smaller than e.   □

Theorem 3.2 (Consistency). *Suppose that an honest node i triggered the finalization rule on* chain *and an honest node j triggered the finalization rule on* chain$'$, *then it must be that either* chain$[: -5] \preceq$ chain$'[: -5]$ *or* chain$'[: -5] \preceq$ chain$[: -5]$.

Note that i and j can be the same or different node in the above theorem.

Proof. Suppose that chain ends at 6 consecutive epochs $e - 5, e - 4, \ldots, e$ and chain$'$ ends at 6 consecutive epochs $e' - 5, e' - 4, \ldots, e'$. Without loss of generality, assume that $e' \geq e$.

Since chain contains two consecutive epochs $e - 5$ and $e - 4$, due to Lemma 3.1, chain$'$ cannot skip all of epochs $e - 5, e - 4, e - 3, e - 2$. Therefore there must be a block in chain$'$ at epoch $\tilde{e} \in \{e - 5, e - 4, e - 3, e - 2\}$. Thus, at least one honest node must have voted for chain$'\langle\tilde{e}\rangle$ in epoch $\tilde{e}$, and this honest node must have observed a proposal for chain$'\langle\tilde{e}\rangle$ from an eligible proposer in epoch $\tilde{e}$. This means that all honest nodes must have observed a proposal for chain$'\langle\tilde{e}\rangle$ from an eligible proposer by the beginning of $\tilde{e} + 2 \leq e$.

Notice that a notarization for chain cannot appear in honest view before epoch e since honest nodes will only vote for chain in epoch e. Thus the finalization rule for chain must be triggered after epoch e starts, but by this time all honest nodes have observed a proposal for chain$'\langle: \tilde{e}\rangle$. Therefore it must be that chain$'\langle: \tilde{e}\rangle =$ chain$\langle: \tilde{e}\rangle$ since otherwise the finalization rule cannot trigger on chain due to seeing a conflicting proposal for $\tilde{e}$.   □

3.3   Liveness Proof

We can show that honest nodes' finalized chains must grow whenever there are 6 consecutive epochs all with honest proposers. The proof follows almost identically as in Sect. 2.4, where we can prove that an honest proposer's proposal never gets rejected by honest recipients. The liveness claim therefore follows by observing that an honest proposer does not propose two blocks of the same epoch.

4   Additional Improvements and References

Optimistic Responsiveness. The protocols described earlier are preconfigured with an anticipated delay parameter Δ, and a new block can only be confirmed per $\Theta(\Delta)$ rounds (also called an epoch earlier). In practice, if and whenever the actual network delay δ is much smaller than Δ, it would be desirable to confirm transactions as fast as the network makes progress, i.e., the confirmation time should be dependent only on the actual delay δ and not on the a-priori upper bound Δ. Protocols that achieve this property are said to be *optimistically responsive* [14].

In Pala [4] and Pili [5], the authors show that with very minor tweaks to protocols described in this tutorial, one can achieve optimistic responsiveness in the partial synchronous and synchronous settings respectively. Later versions of the Hotstuff [1] paper and subsequently Sync Hotstuff [2] also achieved optimistic responsiveness.

Synchronous and Yet Partition Tolerant. The synchronous, honest-majority protocol described in Sect. 3 makes a strong network synchrony assumption for its consistency proof. Specifically, every honest node's messages must be delivered within Δ delay. In other words, if an honest node ever temporarily drops offline and violates the Δ bound, it is treated as corrupt by the model and the consensus protocol is no longer required to provide consistency and liveness guarantees for this node. In practice, typically no one can deliver 100% uptime—since blockchains are long running, every node may become offline at some point, and thus at the end time, the classical synchronous model will treat everyone as corrupt! This means that protocols proven secure in the classical synchronous model do not necessarily offer strong enough robustness for practical deployment. A symptom of this is that almost all known *synchronous* consensus protocols appear *under-specified* and *unimplementable*: typically these protocols do not fully specify what a node should do if it receives messages out of sync, e.g., after coming back online after a short outage (and it is dangerous to leave this decision entirely to an ordinary implementer).

Recently, Guo, Pass, and Shi [7] propose a new model that allows one to capture a notion of "best-possible partition tolerance" while making mild network timing assumptions. Specifically, in their model, a secure consensus protocol must provide both consistency and liveness to all honest nodes, even those who might have suffered from temporary outages but have come back online, as long as at any point of time, there exists a set of honest and online nodes that are majority in size. Moreover, this honest and online set may even churn rapidly over time. Given Guo et al.'s model, a recent work called Pili showed how to achieve this notion of best-possible partition tolerance through very minor tweaks to the protocol described in Sect. 3 (and at the same time offering optimistic responsiveness too).

Reference Implementation. We refer the reader to an open-source implementation of Pala (https://github.com/thundercore/pala). This implementation adopted a doubly-streamlined, and optimistically responsive variant of the protocol described in Sect. 2. We briefly explain the "doubly-streamlined" idea: in the protocol in Sect. 2, a node must have received the parent chain's notarization to vote on the next block—this can lead to pipeline stalls in settings with long delay and large bandwidth. Double streamlining is a generalization of the protocol in Sect. 2 such that nodes can propose and vote on a block as long as its k-th ancestor's notarization has been received; however, for finalization, one has to chop off roughly k blocks too.

Acknowledgments. We gratefully acknowledge Kartik Nayak, Ling Ren, Robbert van Renesse, and Steven Galbraith for helpful feedback on improving the writeup. The author would like to thank T-H. Hubert Chan and Rafael Pass for inspiring discussions.

A   Notations

Variable	Meaning
chain	Blockchain
chain$[: \ell]$	Prefix of chain upto and including the ℓ-th block
chain$[: -\ell]$	Prefix of chain after removing the trailing ℓ blocks
Δ	maximum network delay between honest nodes (during a period of synchrony)
e	Epoch number, i.e., a collection of 2Δ rounds
n	Number of nodes
h_{-1}	Parent hash encoded in a block
TXs	Application-specific payload in a block, e.g., a set of transactions to confirm
H	Collision-resistant hash function for hashing blockchains
H^*	A random oracle for proposer election

References

1. Abraham, I., Gueta, G., Malkhi, D.: Hot-stuff the linear, optimal-resilience, one-message BFT devil. CoRR, abs/1803.05069 (2018)
2. Abraham, I., Malkhi, D., Nayak, K., Ren, L., Yin, M.: Sync HotStuff: simple and practical synchronous state machine replication. Cryptology ePrint Archive, Report 2019/270 (2019). https://eprint.iacr.org/2019/270
3. Castro, M., Liskov, B.: Practical Byzantine fault tolerance. In: OSDI (1999)
4. Hubert Chan, T.-H., Pass, R., Shi, E.: Pala: a simple partially synchronous blockchain. Manuscript (2018). https://eprint.iacr.org/2018/981
5. Hubert Chan, T.-H., Pass, R., Shi, E.: Pili: a simple, fast, and robust family of blockchain protocols. Cryptology ePrint Archive, Report 2018/980 (2018). https://eprint.iacr.org/2018/980
6. Dwork, C., Lynch, N., Stockmeyer, L.: Consensus in the presence of partial synchrony. J. ACM **35**, 288–323 (1988)
7. Guo, Y., Pass, R., Shi, E.: Synchronous, with a chance of partition tolerance. Cryptology ePrint Archive (2018)

8. Hanke, T., Movahedi, M., Williams, D.: Dfinity technology overview series: consensus system. https://dfinity.org/tech
9. Lamport, L.: The part-time parliament. ACM Trans. Comput. Syst. **16**(2), 133–169 (1998)
10. Lamport, L., Shostak, R., Pease, M.: The Byzantine generals problem. ACM Trans. Program. Lang. Syst. **4**(3), 382–401 (1982)
11. Nakamoto, S.: Bitcoin: a peer-to-peer electronic cash system (2008)
12. Pass, R., Shi, E.: Hybrid consensus: efficient consensus in the permissionless model. In: DISC (2017)
13. Pass, R., Shi, E.: Rethinking large-scale consensus. In: CSF (2017)
14. Pass, R., Shi, E.: Thunderella: blockchains with optimistic instant confirmation. In: Nielsen, J.B., Rijmen, V. (eds.) EUROCRYPT 2018. LNCS, vol. 10821, pp. 3–33. Springer, Cham (2018). https://doi.org/10.1007/978-3-319-78375-8_1
15. Schneider, F.B.: Implementing fault-tolerant services using the state machine approach: a tutorial. ACM Comput. Surv. **22**(4), 299–319 (1990)
16. Griffith, V., Buterin, V.: Casper the friendly finality gadget. https://arxiv.org/abs/1710.09437

Best Paper

Wave: A New Family of Trapdoor One-Way Preimage Sampleable Functions Based on Codes

Thomas Debris-Alazard[1,2]([✉]), Nicolas Sendrier[2], and Jean-Pierre Tillich[2]

[1] Sorbonne Université, Collège Doctoral, 75005 Paris, France
[2] Inria, Paris, France
{thomas.debris,nicolas.sendrier,jean-pierre.tillich}@inria.fr

Abstract. We present here a new family of trapdoor one-way functions that are Preimage Sampleable on Average (PSA) based on codes, the Wave-PSA family. The trapdoor function is one-way under two computational assumptions: the hardness of generic decoding for high weights and the indistinguishability of generalized $(U, U + V)$-codes. Our proof follows the GPV strategy [28]. By including rejection sampling, we ensure the proper distribution for the trapdoor inverse output. The domain sampling property of our family is ensured by using and proving a variant of the left-over hash lemma. We instantiate the new Wave-PSA family with ternary generalized $(U, U + V)$-codes to design a "hash-and-sign" signature scheme which achieves *existential unforgeability under adaptive chosen message attacks* (EUF-CMA) in the random oracle model.

1 Introduction

Code-Based Signature Schemes. It is a long standing open problem to build an efficient and secure digital signature scheme based on the hardness of decoding a linear code which could compete with widespread schemes like DSA or RSA. Those signature schemes are well known to be broken by quantum computers and code-based schemes could indeed provide a valid quantum resistant replacement. A first answer to this question was given by the CFS scheme proposed in [15]. It consisted in finding parity-check matrices $\mathbf{H} \in \mathbb{F}_2^{r \times n}$ such that the solution $\mathbf{e}$ of smallest weight of the equation

$$\mathbf{e}\mathbf{H}^{\mathsf{T}} = \mathbf{s}. \tag{1}$$

could be found for a non-negligible proportion of all $\mathbf{s}$ in $\mathbb{F}_2^r$. This task was achieved by using high rate Goppa codes. This signature scheme has however two drawbacks: (i) for high rates Goppa codes the indistinguishability assumption used in its security proof has been invalidated in [22], (ii) security scales only

---

This work was supported by the ANR CBCRYPT project, grant ANR-17-CE39-0007 of the French Agence Nationale de la Recherche.

S. D. Galbraith and S. Moriai (Eds.): ASIACRYPT 2019, LNCS 11921, pp. 21–51, 2019.
https://doi.org/10.1007/978-3-030-34578-5_2

weakly superpolynomially in the keysize for polynomial time signature generation. A crude extrapolation of parallel CFS [23] and its implementations [10,35] yields for 128 bits of classical security a public key size of several gigabytes and a signature time of several seconds. Those figures even grow to terabytes and hours for quantum-safe security levels, making the scheme unpractical.

This scheme was followed by other proposals using other code families such as for instance [4,29,36]. All of them were broken, see for instance [40,42]. Other signature schemes based on codes were also given in the literature such as for instance the KKS scheme [33,34], its variants [7,27] or the RaCoSS proposal [25] to the NIST. But they can be considered at best to be one-time signature schemes and great care has to be taken to choose the parameters of these schemes in the light of the attacks given in [13,31,41]. Finally, another possibility is to use the Fiat-Shamir heuristic. For instance by turning the Stern zero-knowledge authentication scheme [46] into a signature scheme but this leads to rather large signature lengths (hundred(s) of kilobits). There has been some recent progress in this area for another metric, namely the rank metric. A hash and sign signature scheme was proposed, RankSign [26], that enjoys remarkably small key sizes, but it got broken too in [20]. On the other hand, following the Schnorr-Lyubashevsky [37] approach, a new scheme was recently proposed, namely Durandal [2]. This scheme enjoys small key sizes and managed to meet the challenge of adapting the Lyubashevsky [37] approach for code-based cryptography. However, there is a lack of genericity in its security reduction to a rather convoluted problem, namely PSSI^+ (see [2, §4.1]).

One-Way Preimage Sampleable Trapdoor Functions. There is a very powerful tool for building a hash-and-sign signature scheme. It is based on the notion of *one-way trapdoor preimage sampleable function* [28, §5.3]. Roughly speaking, this is a family of trapdoor one-way functions $(f_a)_a$ such that with overwhelming probability over the choice of f_a (i) the distribution of the images $f_a(e)$ is very close to the uniform distribution over its range (ii) the distribution of the output of the trapdoor algorithm inverting f_a samples from all possible preimages in an appropriate way. This trapdoor inversion algorithm should sample its outputs e for any x in the domain of f_a such that the distribution of e is indistinguishable in a statistical sense from the input distribution of f_a conditioned by $f_a(e) = x$. This notion and its lattice-based instantiation was used in [28] to give a full-domain hash (FDH) signature scheme with a tight security reduction based on lattice assumptions, namely that the Short Integer Solution (SIS) problem is hard on average. Furthermore, this approach also allowed to build the first identity based encryption scheme that could be resistant to a quantum computer. We will refer to this approach for obtaining a FDH scheme as the GPV strategy. This strategy has also been adopted in Falcon [24], a lattice based signature submission to the NIST call for post-quantum cryptographic primitives that was recently selected as a second round candidate.

This preimage sampleable primitive is notoriously difficult to obtain when the functions f_a are not trapdoor permutations but many-to-one functions. This is typically the case when one wishes quantum resistant primitives based on lattice based assumptions. The reason is the following. The hard problem on which this primitive relies is the SIS problem where we want to find for a matrix $\mathbf{A}$ in $\mathbb{Z}_q^{n \times m}$ (with $m \geq n$) and an element $\mathbf{s} \in \mathbb{Z}_q^n$ a short enough (for the Euclidean norm) solution $\mathbf{e} \in \mathbb{Z}_q^m$ to the equation

$$\mathbf{e}\mathbf{A}^\mathsf{T} = \mathbf{s} \mod q. \tag{2}$$

$\mathbf{A}$ defines a preimage sampleable function as $f_\mathbf{A}(\mathbf{e}) = \mathbf{e}\mathbf{A}^\mathsf{T}$ and the input to $f_\mathbf{A}$ is chosen according to a (discrete) Gaussian distribution of some variance σ^2. Obtaining a nearly uniform distribution for the $f_\mathbf{A}(\mathbf{e})$'s over its range requires to choose σ^2 so large so that there are actually *exponentially many* solutions to (2). It is a highly non-trivial task to build in this case a trapdoor inversion algorithm that samples appropriately among all possible preimages, *i.e.* oblivious to the trapdoor.

The situation is actually exactly the same if we want to use another candidate problem for building this preimage sampleable primitive for being resistant to a quantum computer, namely the decoding problem in code-based cryptography. Here we rely on the difficulty of finding a solution $\mathbf{e}$ of Hamming weight *exactly* w with coordinates in a finite field $\mathbb{F}_q$ for the equation

$$\mathbf{e}\mathbf{H}^\mathsf{T} = \mathbf{s}. \tag{3}$$

where $\mathbf{H}$ is a given matrix and $\mathbf{s}$ (usually called a syndrome) a given vector with entries in $\mathbb{F}_q$. The weight w has to be chosen large enough so that this equation has always exponentially many solutions (in n the length of $\mathbf{e}$). As in the lattice based setting, it is non-trivial to build trapdoor candidates with a trapdoor inversion algorithm for $f_\mathbf{H}$ (defined as $f_\mathbf{H}(\mathbf{e}) = \mathbf{e}\mathbf{H}^\mathsf{T}$) that is oblivious to the trapdoor.

Our Contribution: A Code-Based PSA Family and a FDH Scheme. Our main contribution is to give here a code-based one way trapdoor function that meets the preimage sampleable property in a slighty relaxed way: it meets this property on average. We call such a function Preimage Sampleable on Average, PSA in short. This property on average turns out to be enough for giving a security proof for the signature scheme built from it. Our family relies here on the difficulty of solving (3). We derive from it a FDH signature scheme which is shown to be existentially unforgeable under a chosen-message attack (EUF-CMA) with a tight reduction to solving two code-based problems: one is a distinguishing problem related to the trapdoor used in our scheme, the other one is a multiple targets version of the decoding problem (3), the so called "Decoding One Out of Many" problem (DOOM in short) [44]. In [28] a signature scheme based on preimage sampleable functions is given that is shown to be strongly existentially unforgeable under a chosen-message attack if in addition the preimage sampleable functions are also collision resistant. With our choice of w and $\mathbb{F}_q$, our preimage sampleable functions are not collision resistant. However, as observed in [28], collision resistance allows a tight security reduction but is not necessary: a security proof could also be given when the function is "only" preimage sampleable. Here we will show that it is even enough to have such a property on average. Moreover, in contrast with the lattice setting where the size of the alphabet q grows with n, our alphabet size will be constant in our proposal, it is fixed to $q = 3$.

Our Trapdoor: Generalized $(U, U+V)$-Codes. In [28] the trapdoor consists in a short basis of the lattice considered in the construction. Our trapdoor will be of a different nature, it consists in choosing parity-check matrices of generalized $(U, U + V)$-codes. In our construction, U and V are chosen as random codes. The number of such generalized $(U, U + V)$-codes of dimension k and length n is of the same order as the number of linear codes with the same parameters, namely $q^{\Theta(n^2)}$ when $k = \Theta(n)$. A generalized $(U, U + V)$ code $\mathcal{C}$ of length n over $\mathbb{F}_q$ is built from two codes U and V of length $n/2$ and 4 vectors $\mathbf{a}, \mathbf{b}, \mathbf{c}$ and $\mathbf{d}$ in $\mathbb{F}_q^{n/2}$ as the following "mixture" of U and V:

$$\mathcal{C} = \{(\mathbf{a} \odot \mathbf{u} + \mathbf{b} \odot \mathbf{v}, \mathbf{c} \odot \mathbf{u} + \mathbf{d} \odot \mathbf{v}) : \mathbf{u} \in U, \ \mathbf{v} \in V\}$$

where $\mathbf{x} \odot \mathbf{y}$ stands for the component-wise product, also called the Hadamard or Schur product. It is defined as: $\mathbf{x} \odot \mathbf{y} \overset{\triangle}{=} (x_1 y_1, \cdots, x_{n/2} y_{n/2})$. Standard $(U, U+V)$-codes correspond to $\mathbf{a} = \mathbf{c} = \mathbf{d} = \mathbf{1}_{n/2}$ and $\mathbf{b} = \mathbf{0}_{n/2}$, the all-one and the all-zero vectors respectively.

The point of introducing such codes is that they have a natural decoding algorithm D_{UV} solving the decoding problem (3) that is based on a generic decoding algorithm D_{gen} for linear codes. D_{gen} will be here a very simple decoder, namely a variation of the Prange decoder [43] that is able to easily produce for *any* parity-check matrix $\mathbf{H} \in \mathbb{F}_q^{r \times n}$ a solution of (3) for any w in the range $[\![\frac{q-1}{q} r, n - \frac{r}{q}]\!]$. Note that this algorithm works in polynomial time and that the complexity of the best known algorithms is exponential in n for weights w of the form $w = \omega n$ where ω is a constant that lies outside the interval $[\frac{q-1}{q}\rho, 1 - \frac{\rho}{q}]$ with $\rho \overset{\triangle}{=} \frac{r}{n}$. D_{UV} works by combining the decoding of V with D_{gen} with the decoding of U by D_{gen}. The nice feature is that D_{UV} is more powerful than D_{gen} applied directly on the generalized $(U, U + V)$-code: the weight of the error produced by D_{UV} in polynomial time can be made to lie outside the interval $[\![\frac{q-1}{q} r, n - \frac{r}{q}]\!]$. This is in essence the trapdoor of our signature scheme. A tweak in this decoder consisting in performing only a small amount of rejection sampling (with our choice of parameters one rejection every 10 or 12 signatures, see the full paper [18]) allows to obtain solutions that are uniformly distributed over the words of weight w. This is the key for obtaining a PSA family and a signature scheme from it.

Finally, a variation of the proof technique of [28] allows to give a tight security proof of our signature scheme that relies only on the hardness of two problems, namely

Decoding Problem: Solving at least one instance of the decoding problem (1) out of multiple instances for a certain w that is outside the range $[\![\frac{q-1}{q} r, n - \frac{r}{q}]\!]$

Distinguishing Problem: Deciding whether a linear code is a permuted generalized $(U, U + V)$ code or not.

Hardness of the Decoding Problem. All code-based cryptography relies upon that problem. Here we are in a case where there are multiple solutions of (3) and the adversary may produce any number of instances of (3) with the same matrix $\mathbf{H}$ and various syndromes $\mathbf{s}$ and is interested in solving only one of them. This relates to the, so called, Decoding One Out of Many (DOOM) problem. This problem was first considered in [32]. It was shown there how to adapt the known algorithms for decoding a linear code in order to solve this modified problem. This modification was later analyzed in [44]. The parameters of the known algorithms for solving (3) can be easily adapted to this scenario where we have to decode simultaneously multiple instances which all have multiple solutions.

Hardness of the Distinguishing Problem. This problem might seem at first sight to be ad-hoc. However, even in the very restricted case of $(U, U + V)$-codes, deciding whether a code is a permuted $(U, U + V)$-code or not is an NP-complete problem. Therefore the Distinguishing Problem is also NP-complete for generalized $(U, U+V)$-codes. This theorem is proven in the case of binary $(U, U + V)$-codes in [17, §7.1, Thm 3] and the proof carries over to an arbitrary finite field $\mathbb{F}_q$. However as observed in [17, p. 3], these NP-completeness reductions hold in the particular case where the dimensions k_U and k_V of the code U and V satisfy $k_U < k_V$. If we stick to the binary case, i.e. $q = 2$, then in order that our $(U, U + V)$ decoder works outside the integer interval $[\![\frac{r}{2}, n - \frac{r}{2}]\!]$ it is necessary that $k_U > k_V$. Unfortunately in this case there is an efficient probabilistic algorithm solving the distinguishing problem that is based on the fact that in this case the hull of the permuted $(U, U + V)$-code is typically of large dimension, namely $k_U - k_V$ (see [16, §1 p. 1–2]). This problem can not be settled in the binary case by considering generalized $(U, U + V)$-codes instead of just plain $(U, U + V)$-codes, since it is only for the restricted class of $(U, U + V)$-codes that the decoder considered in [16] is able to work properly outside the critical interval $[\![\frac{r}{2}, n - \frac{r}{2}]\!]$. This explains why the ancestor Surf [16] of the scheme proposed here that relies on binary $(U, U + V)$-codes can not work.

This situation changes drastically when we move to larger finite fields. In order to have a decoding algorithm D_{UV} that has an advantage over the generic decoder $\mathsf{D}_{\mathrm{gen}}$ we do not need to have $\mathbf{a} = \mathbf{c} = \mathbf{d} = \mathbf{1}_{n/2}$ and $\mathbf{b} = \mathbf{0}_{n/2}$ (i.e. $(U, U + V)$-codes) we just need that $\mathbf{a} \odot \mathbf{c}$ and $\mathbf{a} \odot \mathbf{d} - \mathbf{b} \odot \mathbf{c}$ are vectors with only non-zero components. This freedom of choice for the $\mathbf{a}, \mathbf{b}, \mathbf{c}$ and $\mathbf{d}$ thwarts completely the attacks based on hull considerations and changes completely the nature of the distinguishing problem. In this case, it seems that the best approach for solving the distinguishing problem is based on the following observation. The generalized $(U, U + V)$-code has codewords of weight slightly smaller than the minimum distance of a random code of the same length and dimension. It is very tempting to conjecture that the best algorithms for solving the Distinguishing Problem come from detecting such codewords. This approach can be easily thwarted by choosing the parameters of the scheme in such a way that the best algorithms for solving this task are of prohibitive complexity. Notice that the best algorithms that we have for detecting such codewords are in essence precisely the generic algorithms for solving the Decoding Problem. In some sense, it seems that we might rely on the very same problem, namely solving the Decoding Problem, even if our proof technique does not show this.

Large Weights Decoding and $q = 3$. In terms of simplicity of the decoding procedure used in the signing process, it seems that defining our codes over the finite field $\mathbb{F}_3$ is particularly attractive. In such a case, the biggest advantage of D_{UV} over $\mathsf{D}_{\mathrm{gen}}$ is obtained for large weights rather than for small weights (there is an explanation for this asset in Sect. 4.3). This is a bit unusual in code-based cryptography to rely on the difficulty of finding solutions of large weight to the decoding problem. However, it also opens the issue of whether or not it would be advantageous to have (non-binary) code-based primitives rely on the hardness of solving the decoding problem for large weights rather than for small weights. Of course these two problems are equivalent in the binary case, i.e. $q = 2$, but this is not the case for larger alphabets anymore and still everything seems to point to the direction that large weights problem is by no means easier than its small weight counterpart.

All in all, this gives the first practical signature scheme based on ternary codes which comes with a security proof and which scales well with the parameters: it can be shown that if one wants a security level of 2^λ, then the signature size is of order $O(\lambda)$, the public key size is of order $O(\lambda^2)$, and the computational effort is of order $O(\lambda^3)$ for generating a signature and $O(\lambda^2)$ for verifying it. It should be noted that contrarily to the current thread of research in code-based or lattice-based cryptography which consists in relying on structured codes or lattices based on ring structures in order to decrease the key-sizes we did not follow this approach here. This allows for instance to rely on the NP-complete Decoding Problem which is generally believed to be hard on average rather that on decoding in quasi-cyclic codes for instance whose status is still unclear with a constant number of circulant blocks. Despite the fact that we did not use the standard approach for reducing the key sizes relying on quasi-cyclic codes for instance, we obtain acceptable key sizes (about 3.2 megabytes for 128 bits of security) which compare very favorably to unstructured lattice-based signature schemes such as TESLA for instance [1]. This is due in part to the tightness of our security reduction.

2   Notation

General Notation. The notation $x \stackrel{\triangle}{=} y$ defines x to be equal to y. We denote by $\mathbb{F}_q$ the finite field with q elements and by $S_{w,n}$, or S_w when n is clear from the context, the subset of $\mathbb{F}_q^n$ of words of weight w. For a and b integers with

$a \leq b$, we denote by $[\![a, b]\!]$ the set of integers $\{a, a+1, \ldots, b\}$. Furthermore, h_3 will denote the function: $h_3(x) \overset{\triangle}{=} -x \log_3(x) - (1-x) \log_3(1-x)$ defined on $[0, 1]$.

Vector and Matrix Notation. Vectors will be written with bold letters (such as $\mathbf{e}$) and uppercase bold letters are used to denote matrices (such as $\mathbf{H}$). Vectors are in row notation. Let $\mathbf{x}$ and $\mathbf{y}$ be two vectors, we will write $(\mathbf{x}, \mathbf{y})$ to denote their concatenation. We also denote by $\mathbf{x}_{\mathcal{I}}$ the vector whose coordinates are those of $\mathbf{x} = (x_i)_{1 \leq i \leq n}$ which are indexed by $\mathcal{I}$, i.e. $\mathbf{x}_{\mathcal{I}} = (x_i)_{i \in \mathcal{I}}$. We will denote by $\mathbf{H}_{\mathcal{I}}$ the matrix whose columns are those of $\mathbf{H}$ which are indexed by $\mathcal{I}$. We may denote by $\mathbf{x}(i)$ the i-th entry of a vector $\mathbf{x}$, or by $\mathbf{A}(i, j)$ the entry in row i and column j of a matrix $\mathbf{A}$. We define the support of $\mathbf{x} = (x_i)_{1 \leq i \leq n}$ as $\mathrm{Supp}(\mathbf{x}) \overset{\triangle}{=} \{i \in \{1, \cdots, n\}$ such that $x_i \neq 0\}$. The Hamming weight of $\mathbf{x}$ is denoted by $|\mathbf{x}|$. By some abuse of notation, we will use the same notation to denote the size of a finite set: $|S|$ stands for the size of the finite set S. For a vector $\mathbf{a} \in \mathbb{F}_q^n$, we denote by $\mathbf{Diag}(\mathbf{a})$ the $n \times n$ diagonal matrix $\mathbf{A}$ with its entries given by $\mathbf{a}$, i.e. $\mathbf{A}(i, i) = a_i$ for all $i \in [\![1, n]\!]$ and $\mathbf{A}(i, j) = 0$ for $i \neq j$.

Probabilistic Notation. Let S be a finite set, then $x \hookleftarrow S$ means that x is assigned to be a random element chosen uniformly at random in S. For two random variables X, Y, $X \sim Y$ means that X and Y are identically distributed. We will also use the same notation for a random variable and a distribution $\mathcal{D}$, where $X \sim \mathcal{D}$ means that X is distributed according to $\mathcal{D}$. We denote the uniform distribution on S_w by $\mathcal{U}_w$. The statistical distance between two discrete probability distributions over a same space $\mathcal{E}$ is defined as: $\rho(\mathcal{D}_0, \mathcal{D}_1) \overset{\triangle}{=} \frac{1}{2} \sum_{x \in \mathcal{E}} |\mathcal{D}_0(x) - \mathcal{D}_1(x)|$. Recall that a function $f(n)$ is said to be negligible, and we denote this by $f \in \mathrm{negl}(n)$, if for all polynomials $p(n)$, $|f(n)| < p(n)^{-1}$ for sufficiently large n.

Coding Theory. For any matrix $\mathbf{M}$ we denote by $\langle \mathbf{M} \rangle$ the vector space spanned by its rows. A q-ary linear code $\mathcal{C}$ of length n and dimension k is a subspace of $\mathbb{F}_q^n$ of dimension k. A *parity-check matrix* $\mathbf{H}$ over $\mathbb{F}_q$ of size $r \times n$ is such that $\mathcal{C} = \langle \mathbf{H} \rangle^{\perp} = \{\mathbf{x} \in \mathbb{F}_q^n : \mathbf{x}\mathbf{H}^{\mathsf{T}} = \mathbf{0}\}$. When $\mathbf{H}$ is of full rank we have $r = n - k$. The code rate, usually denoted by R, is defined as the ratio k/n. An *information set* of a code $\mathcal{C}$ of length n is a set of k coordinate indices $\mathcal{I} \subset [\![1, n]\!]$ such that its complement indexes $n - k$ independent columns on any parity-check matrix. For any $\mathbf{s} \in \mathbb{F}_q^{n-k}$, $\mathbf{H} \in \mathbb{F}_q^{(n-k) \times n}$, and any information set $\mathcal{I}$ of $\mathcal{C} = \langle \mathbf{H} \rangle^{\perp}$, for all $\mathbf{x} \in \mathbb{F}_q^n$ there exists a unique $\mathbf{e} \in \mathbb{F}_q^n$ such that $\mathbf{e}\mathbf{H}^{\mathsf{T}} = \mathbf{s}$ and $\mathbf{x}_{\mathcal{I}} = \mathbf{e}_{\mathcal{I}}$.

3   The Wave-family of Trapdoor One-Way Preimage Sampleable Functions

3.1   One-Way Preimage Sampleable Code-Based Functions

In this work we will use the FDH paradigm [9,14] using as one-way the syndrome function:

$$f_{\mathbf{H}} : \mathbf{e} \in S_w \longmapsto \mathbf{e}\mathbf{H}^{\mathsf{T}} \in \mathbb{F}_q^{n-k}$$

The corresponding FDH signature uses a trapdoor to choose $\boldsymbol{\sigma} \in f_{w,\mathbf{H}}^{-1}(\mathbf{h})$ where $\mathbf{h}$ is the digest of the message to be signed. Here, the signature domain is S_w and its range is the set of syndromes $\mathbb{F}_q^{n-k}$ according to $\mathbf{H}$, an $(n-k) \times n$ parity check matrix of some q-ary linear $[n,k]$ code. The weight w is chosen such that the one-way function $f_{w,\mathbf{H}}$ is surjective but not bijective. Building a secure FDH signature in this situation can be achieved by imposing additional properties [28] to the one-way function (we will speak of the GPV strategy). This is mostly captured by the notion of Preimage Sampleable Functions, see [28, Definition 5.3.1]. We express below this notion in our code-based context with a slightly relaxed definition dropping the collision resistance condition and only assuming that the preimage sampleable property holds on average and not for any possible element in the function range. This will be sufficient for proving the security of our code-based FDH scheme.

Definition 1 (Trapdoor One-way Preimage Sampleable on Average Code-based Functions). *It is a pair of probabilistic polynomial-time algorithms* (Trapdoor, InvAlg) *together with a triple of functions* $(n(\lambda), k(\lambda), w(\lambda))$ *growing polynomially with the security parameter λ and giving the length and dimension of the codes and the weights we consider for the syndrome decoding problem, such that*

- Trapdoor *when given λ, outputs $(\mathbf{H}, T)$ where $\mathbf{H}$ is an $(n-k) \times n$ matrix over $\mathbb{F}_q$ and T the trapdoor corresponding to $\mathbf{H}$.*
- InvAlg *is a probabilistic algorithm which takes as input T and an element $\mathbf{s} \in \mathbb{F}_q^{n-k}$ and outputs an $\mathbf{e} \in S_{w,n}$ such that $\mathbf{e}\mathbf{H}^{\mathsf{T}} = \mathbf{s}$.*

The following properties have to hold for all but a negligible fraction of $\mathbf{H}$ output by Trapdoor.

1. Domain Sampling with uniform output:

$$\rho(\mathbf{e}\mathbf{H}^{\mathsf{T}}, \mathbf{s}) \in \mathrm{negl}(\lambda), \ where \ \mathbf{e} \hookleftarrow S_{w,n} \ and \ \mathbf{s} \hookleftarrow \mathbb{F}_q^{n-k}.$$

2. Preimage Sampling on Average (PSA) with trapdoor:

$$\rho\left(\mathrm{InvAlg}(\mathbf{s}, T), \mathbf{e}\right) \in \mathrm{negl}(\lambda), \ where \ \mathbf{e} \hookleftarrow S_{w,n} \ and \ \mathbf{s} \hookleftarrow \mathbb{F}_q^{n-k}.$$

3. One wayness without trapdoor: *for any probabilistic poly-time algorithm $\mathcal{A}$ outputting an element $\mathbf{e} \in S_{w,n}$ when given $\mathbf{H} \in \mathbb{F}_q^{(n-k) \times n}$ and $\mathbf{s} \in \mathbb{F}_q^{n-k}$, the probability that $\mathbf{e}\mathbf{H}^{\mathsf{T}} = \mathbf{s}$ is negligible, where the probability is taken over the choice of $\mathbf{H}$, the target value $\mathbf{s}$ chosen uniformly at random, and $\mathcal{A}$'s random coins.*

Remark 1. 1. The preimage property as defined in [28] would translate in our setting in the following way. For any $\mathbf{s} \in \mathbb{F}_q^{n-k}$ we should have

$$\rho\left(\mathrm{InvAlg}(\mathbf{s}, T), \mathbf{e}_s\right) \in \mathrm{negl}(\lambda), \ where \ \mathbf{e}_s \hookleftarrow \left\{\mathbf{e} \in S_{w,n} : \mathbf{e}\mathbf{H}^{\mathsf{T}} = \mathbf{s}\right\}.$$

As observed by an anonymous reviewer, we have

$$\rho\left(\texttt{InvAlg}(\mathbf{s},T),\mathbf{e}\right) = \sum_{\mathbf{s}}\sum_{\mathbf{e}\in f_{\mathbf{H}}^{-1}(\mathbf{s})}\left|\frac{1}{|S_w|} - \frac{1}{q^{n-k}}\mathbb{P}(\texttt{InvAlg}(\mathbf{s},T) = \mathbf{e})\right|$$

$$= \sum_{\mathbf{s}}\sum_{\mathbf{e}\in f_{\mathbf{H}}^{-1}(\mathbf{s})}\left|\frac{1}{|S_w|} - \frac{1}{q^{n-k}|f_{\mathbf{H}}^{-1}(\mathbf{s})|} + \frac{1}{q^{n-k}|f_{\mathbf{H}}^{-1}(\mathbf{s})|} - \frac{1}{q^{n-k}}\mathbb{P}(\texttt{InvAlg}(\mathbf{s},T) = \mathbf{e})\right|$$

$$\geq \sum_{\mathbf{s}}\frac{1}{q^{n-k}}\sum_{\mathbf{e}\in f_{\mathbf{H}}^{-1}(\mathbf{s})}\left|\frac{1}{|f_{\mathbf{H}}^{-1}(\mathbf{s})|} - \mathbb{P}(\texttt{InvAlg}(\mathbf{s},T) = \mathbf{e})\right| - \sum_{\mathbf{s}}\left|\frac{|f_{\mathbf{H}}^{-1}(\mathbf{s})|}{|S_w|} - \frac{1}{q^{n-k}}\right|$$

$$= \sum_{\mathbf{s}\in\mathbb{F}_q^{n-k}}\frac{1}{q^{n-k}}\rho\left(\texttt{InvAlg}(\mathbf{s},T),\mathbf{e}_s\right) - \rho(\mathbf{e}\mathbf{H}^{\mathsf{T}},\mathbf{s}).$$

Therefore with the domain sampling property and our definition of the preimage sampling property the average of the $\rho\left(\texttt{InvAlg}(\mathbf{s},T),\mathbf{e}_s\right)$'s is negligible too, whereas [28] requires that all terms $\rho\left(\texttt{InvAlg}(\mathbf{s},T),\mathbf{e}_s\right)$ are negligible. Note that our property that holds for the average implies that this property holds for all but a negligible fraction of $\mathbf{s}$'s. Indeed, if we have

$$\frac{1}{q^{n-k}}\sum_{\mathbf{s}\in\mathbb{F}_q^{n-k}}\rho\left(\texttt{InvAlg}(\mathbf{s},T),\mathbf{e}_s\right) = \varepsilon,$$

then

$$\frac{\#\left\{\mathbf{s}:\rho\left(\texttt{InvAlg}(\mathbf{s},T),\mathbf{e}_s\right)\geq\sqrt{\varepsilon}\right\}}{q^{n-k}} \leq \sqrt{\varepsilon}.$$

As noted by the anonymous reviewer, this relaxed property is enough to apply the GPV proof technique.

2. It turns out that this relaxed definition of preimage sampleable function is enough to prove the security of the associated signature scheme using a salt as given in the next paragraph. This relaxed definition is of independent interest, since it can be easier to find trapdoor one-way functions meeting this property than the more stringent definition given in [28].

Given a one-way preimage sampleable code-based function $(\texttt{Trapdoor},\texttt{InvAlg})$ we easily define a code-based FDH signature scheme as follows. We generate the public/secret key as $(\mathrm{pk},\mathrm{sk}) = (\mathbf{H},T) \leftarrow \texttt{Trapdoor}(\lambda)$. We also select a cryptographic hash function $\texttt{Hash}: \{0,1\}^* \to \mathbb{F}_q^{n-k}$ and a salt $\mathbf{r}$ of size λ_0. The algorithms $\texttt{Sgn}^{\mathrm{sk}}$ and $\texttt{Vrfy}^{\mathrm{pk}}$ are defined as follows

$\texttt{Sgn}^{\mathrm{sk}}(\mathbf{m})$:	$\texttt{Vrfy}^{\mathrm{pk}}(\mathbf{m},(\mathbf{e}',\mathbf{r}))$:
$\mathbf{r} \leftarrow \{0,1\}^{\lambda_0}$	$\mathbf{s} \leftarrow \texttt{Hash}(\mathbf{m},\mathbf{r})$
$\mathbf{s} \leftarrow \texttt{Hash}(\mathbf{m},\mathbf{r})$	if $\mathbf{e}'\mathbf{H}^{\mathsf{T}} = \mathbf{s}$ and $|\mathbf{e}'| = w$ return 1
$\mathbf{e} \leftarrow \texttt{InvAlg}(\mathbf{s},T)$	else return 0
return$(\mathbf{e},\mathbf{r})$	

A tight security reduction in the random oracle model is given in [28] for the associated signature schemes. It requires collision resistance. Our construction uses a ternary alphabet $q = 3$ together with large values of w and collision resistance is not met. Still, we achieve a tight security proof [18, §7] by considering a reduction to the multiple target decoding problem.

3.2   The Wave Family of PSA Functions

The trapdoor family of codes which gives an advantage for inverting $f_{w,\mathbf{H}}$ is built upon the following transformation:

Definition 2. *Let* $\mathbf{a}$, $\mathbf{b}$, $\mathbf{c}$ *and* $\mathbf{d}$ *be vectors of* $\mathbb{F}_q^{n/2}$. *We define*

$$\varphi_{\mathbf{a},\mathbf{b},\mathbf{c},\mathbf{d}} : (\mathbf{x},\mathbf{y}) \in \mathbb{F}_q^{n/2} \times \mathbb{F}_q^{n/2} \to (\mathbf{a} \odot \mathbf{x} + \mathbf{b} \odot \mathbf{y}, \mathbf{c} \odot \mathbf{x} + \mathbf{d} \odot \mathbf{y}) \in \mathbb{F}_q^{n/2} \times \mathbb{F}_q^{n/2}$$

We will say that $\varphi_{\mathbf{a},\mathbf{b},\mathbf{c},\mathbf{d}}$ *is UV-normalized if*

$$\forall i \in [\![1,n/2]\!], \quad a_i d_i - b_i c_i = 1, \ a_i c_i \neq 0.$$

For any two subspaces U *and* V *of* $\mathbb{F}_q^{n/2}$, *we extend the notation*

$$\varphi_{\mathbf{a},\mathbf{b},\mathbf{c},\mathbf{d}}(U,V) \overset{\triangle}{=} \{\varphi_{\mathbf{a},\mathbf{b},\mathbf{c},\mathbf{d}}(\mathbf{u},\mathbf{v}) : \mathbf{u} \in U, \mathbf{v} \in V\}$$

Proposition 1 (Normalized Generalized $(U, U + V)$-code). *Let* n *be an even integer and let* $\varphi = \varphi_{\mathbf{a},\mathbf{b},\mathbf{c},\mathbf{d}}$ *be a UV-normalized mapping. The mapping* φ *is bijective with* $\varphi^{-1}(\mathbf{x},\mathbf{y}) = (\mathbf{d} \odot \mathbf{x} - \mathbf{b} \odot \mathbf{y}, -\mathbf{c} \odot \mathbf{x} + \mathbf{a} \odot \mathbf{y})$.

For any two subspaces U *and* V *of* $\mathbb{F}_q^{n/2}$ *of parity check matrices* $\mathbf{H}_U$ *and* $\mathbf{H}_V$, *the vector space* $\varphi(U,V)$ *is called a* normalized generalized $(U, U+V)$-*code. It has dimension* $\dim U + \dim V$ *and admits the following parity check matrix*

$$\mathcal{H}(\varphi, \mathbf{H}_U, \mathbf{H}_V) \overset{\triangle}{=} \left(\begin{array}{c|c} \mathbf{H}_U \mathbf{D} & -\mathbf{H}_U \mathbf{B} \\ \hline -\mathbf{H}_V \mathbf{C} & \mathbf{H}_V \mathbf{A} \end{array} \right)$$

where $\mathbf{A} \overset{\triangle}{=} \mathbf{Diag}(\mathbf{a})$, $\mathbf{B} \overset{\triangle}{=} \mathbf{Diag}(\mathbf{b})$, $\mathbf{C} \overset{\triangle}{=} \mathbf{Diag}(\mathbf{c})$ *and* $\mathbf{D} \overset{\triangle}{=} \mathbf{Diag}(\mathbf{d})$.

In the sequel, a UV-normalized mapping φ implicitly defines a quadruple of vectors $(\mathbf{a},\mathbf{b},\mathbf{c},\mathbf{d})$ such that $\varphi = \varphi_{\mathbf{a},\mathbf{b},\mathbf{c},\mathbf{d}}$. We will use this implicit notation and drop the subscript whenever no ambiguity may arise.

Remark 2. – This construction can be viewed as taking two codes of length $n/2$ and making a code of length n by "mixing" together a codeword $\mathbf{u}$ in U and a codeword $\mathbf{v}$ in V as the vector formed by the set of $a_i u_i + b_i v_i$'s and $c_i u_i + d_i v_i$'s.

– The condition $a_i c_i \neq 0$ is here to ensure that coordinates of U appear in all the coordinates of the normalized generalized $(U, U + V)$ codeword. This is essential for having a decoding algorithm for the generalized $(U, U + V)$-code that has an advantage over standard information set decoding algorithms for linear codes. The trapdoor of our scheme builds upon this advantage. It can really be viewed as the "interesting" generalization of the standard $(U, U+V)$ construction.

– We have fixed $a_i d_i - b_i c_i = 1$ for every i to simplify some of the expressions in what follows. It is readily seen that any generalized $(U, U + V)$-code that can be obtained in the more general case $a_i d_i - b_i c_i \neq 0$ can also be obtained in the restricted case $a_i d_i - b_i c_i = 1$ by choosing U and V appropriately.

Defining `Trapdoor` **and** `InvAlg`. From the security parameter λ, we derive the system parameters n, k, w and split $k = k_U + k_V$ (see [18, §5.4] for more details). The secret key is a tuple sk $= (\varphi, \mathbf{H}_U, \mathbf{H}_V, \mathbf{S}, \mathbf{P})$ where φ is a UV-normalized mapping, $\mathbf{H}_U \in \mathbb{F}_q^{(n/2-k_U) \times n/2}$, $\mathbf{H}_V \in \mathbb{F}_q^{(n/2-k_V) \times n/2}$, $\mathbf{S} \in \mathbb{F}_q^{(n-k) \times (n-k)}$ is non-singular with $k = k_U + k_V$, and $\mathbf{P} \in \mathbb{F}_q^{n \times n}$ is a permutation matrix. Each element of sk is chosen randomly and uniformly in its domain.

From $(\varphi, \mathbf{H}_U, \mathbf{H}_V)$ we derive the parity check matrix $\mathbf{H}_{\text{sk}} = \mathcal{H}(\varphi, \mathbf{H}_U, \mathbf{H}_V)$ as in Proposition 1. The public key is $\mathbf{H}_{\text{pk}} = \mathbf{S}\mathbf{H}_{\text{sk}}\mathbf{P}$. Next, we need to produce an algorithm $D_{\varphi, \mathbf{H}_U, \mathbf{H}_V}$ which inverts $f_{w, \mathbf{H}_{\text{sk}}}$. The parameter w is such that this can be achieved using the underlying $(U, U + V)$ structure while the generic problem remains hard. In Sect. 5 we will show how to use rejection sampling to devise $D_{\varphi, \mathbf{H}_U, \mathbf{H}_V}$ such that its output is uniformly distributed over S_w when $\mathbf{s}$ is uniformly distributed over $\mathbb{F}_q^{n-k}$. This enables us to instantiate algorithm `InvAlg`. To summarize:

$$\text{sk} \leftarrow (\varphi, \mathbf{H}_U, \mathbf{H}_V, \mathbf{S}, \mathbf{P}) \qquad \begin{aligned} &\texttt{InvAlg(sk, s)} \\ &\quad \mathbf{e} \leftarrow D_{\varphi, \mathbf{H}_U, \mathbf{H}_V}(\mathbf{s}(\mathbf{S}^{-1})^{\mathsf{T}}) \end{aligned}$$
$$\text{pk} \leftarrow \mathbf{H}_{\text{pk}}$$
$$(\text{pk}, \text{sk}) \leftarrow \texttt{Trapdoor}(\lambda) \qquad \qquad \texttt{return } \mathbf{e}\mathbf{P}$$

As in [28], putting this together with a domain sampling condition –which we prove in Sect. 6 from a variation of the left-over hash lemma– allows us to define a family of trapdoor preimage sampleable functions, later referred to as the Wave-PSA family.

4 Inverting the Syndrome Function

This section is devoted to the inversion of $f_{w, \mathbf{H}}$ which amounts to solve:

Problem 1 (Syndrome Decoding with fixed weight). Given $\mathbf{H} \in \mathbb{F}_q^{(n-k) \times n}$, $\mathbf{s} \in \mathbb{F}_q^{n-k}$, and an integer w, find $\mathbf{e} \in \mathbb{F}_q^n$ such that $\mathbf{e}\mathbf{H}^{\mathsf{T}} = \mathbf{s}$ and $|\mathbf{e}| = w$.

We consider three nested intervals $[\![w_{\text{easy}}^-, w_{\text{easy}}^+]\!] \subset [\![w_{\text{UV}}^-, w_{\text{UV}}^+]\!] \subset [\![w^-, w^+]\!]$ for w such that for $\mathbf{s}$ randomly chosen in $\mathbb{F}_q^{n-k}$:

- $f_{w, \mathbf{H}}^{-1}(\mathbf{s})$ is likely/very likely to exist if $w \in [\![w^-, w^+]\!]$ (Gilbert-Varshamov bound)
- $\mathbf{e} \in f_{w, \mathbf{H}}^{-1}(\mathbf{s})$ is easy to find if $w \in [\![w_{\text{easy}}^-, w_{\text{easy}}^+]\!]$ for all $\mathbf{H}$ (Prange algorithm)
- $\mathbf{e} \in f_{w, \mathbf{H}}^{-1}(\mathbf{s})$ is easy to find if $w \in [\![w_{\text{UV}}^-, w_{\text{UV}}^+]\!]$ and $\mathbf{H}$ is the parity check matrix of a generalized $(U, U + V)$-code. This is the key for exploiting the underlying $(U, U + V)$ structure as a trapdoor for inverting $f_{w, \mathbf{H}}$.

4.1 Surjective Domain of the Syndrome Function

The issue is here for which value of w we may expect that $f_{w, \mathbf{H}}$ is surjective. This clearly implies that $|S_w| \geq q^{n-k}$. In other words we have:

Fact 1. *If $f_{w,\mathbf{H}}$ is surjective, then $w \in [\![w^-, w^+]\!]$ where $w^- < w^+$ are the extremum of the set $\left\{ w \in [\![0, n]\!] \mid \binom{n}{w}(q-1)^w \geq q^{n-k} \right\}$.*

For a fixed rate $R = k/n$, let us define $\omega^- \stackrel{\triangle}{=} \lim_{n \to +\infty} w^-/n$ and $\omega^+ \stackrel{\triangle}{=} \lim_{n \to +\infty} w^+/n$. Note that the quantity ω^- is known as the asymptotic Gilbert-Varshamov distance. A straightforward computation of the expected number of errors $\mathbf{e}$ of weight w such that $\mathbf{e}\mathbf{H}^\mathsf{T} = \mathbf{s}$ when $\mathbf{H}$ is random shows that we expect an exponential number of solutions when w/n lies in (ω^-, ω^+). However, coding theory has never come up with an efficient algorithm for finding a solution to this problem in the whole range (ω^-, ω^+).

4.2   Easy Domain of the Syndrome Function

The subrange of (ω^-, ω^+) for which we know how to solve efficiently Problem 1 is given by the condition $w/n \in [\omega_{\mathrm{easy}}^-, \omega_{\mathrm{easy}}^+]$ where

$$\omega_{\mathrm{easy}}^- \stackrel{\triangle}{=} \frac{q-1}{q}(1 - R) \quad \text{and} \quad \omega_{\mathrm{easy}}^+ \stackrel{\triangle}{=} \frac{q-1}{q} + \frac{R}{q}, \tag{4}$$

where R is the code rate k/n. This is achieved by a slightly generalized version of the Prange decoder [43]. Prange algorithm is able to complement any word whose coordinates are fixed on an information set into a word of prescribed syndrome. In practice, it outputs in polynomial time using linear algebra, a word $\mathbf{e}$ of prescribed syndrome and of the form $(\mathbf{e}'', \mathbf{e}')$ up to a permutation. The word $\mathbf{e}' \in \mathbb{F}_q^k$ has its support on an information set and can be chosen. The word $\mathbf{e}'' \in \mathbb{F}_q^{n-k}$ is random, thus of average weight $\frac{q-1}{q}(n-k)$. By properly choosing $|\mathbf{e}'|$ the algorithm average output relative weight can thus take any value between $\frac{q-1}{q}\frac{n-k}{n} = \omega_{\mathrm{easy}}^-$ and $k + \frac{q-1}{q}\frac{n-k}{n} = \omega_{\mathrm{easy}}^+$. This procedure, that we call PRANGEONE·, is formalized in Algorithm 1.

Proposition 2. *When $\mathbf{H}$ is chosen uniformly at random in $\mathbb{F}_q^{(n-k) \times n}$ and $\mathbf{s}$ uniformly at random in $\mathbb{F}_q^{n-k}$, for the output $\mathbf{e}$ of PRANGEONE$(\mathbf{H}, \mathbf{s})$ we have $|\mathbf{e}| = S + T$ where S and T are independent random variables, $S \in [\![0, n-k]\!]$, $T \in [\![0, k]\!]$, S is the Hamming weight of a vector that is uniformly distributed over $\mathbb{F}_q^{n-k}$ and $\mathbb{P}(T = t) = \mathcal{D}(t)$. Let $\overline{\mathcal{D}} = \sum_{t=0}^{k} t\mathcal{D}(t)$, we have:*

$$\mathbb{P}(|\mathbf{e}| = w) = \sum_{t=0}^{w} \frac{\binom{n-k}{w-t}(q-1)^{w-t}}{q^{n-k}} \mathcal{D}(t), \mathbb{E}(|\mathbf{e}|) = \overline{\mathcal{D}} + \frac{q-1}{q}(n-k) = \overline{\mathcal{D}} + n\omega_{\mathrm{easy}}^-$$

From this proposition, we deduce that any weight w in $[\![\omega_{\mathrm{easy}}^- n, \omega_{\mathrm{easy}}^+ n]\!]$ can be reached by this Prange decoder with a probabilistic polynomial time algorithm that uses a distribution $\mathcal{D}$ such that $\overline{\mathcal{D}} = w - \omega_{\mathrm{easy}}^- n$ and which is sufficiently concentrated around its expectation. It will be helpful in what follows to be able to choose a probability distribution $\mathcal{D}$ as this gives a rather large degree of freedom in the distribution of $|\mathbf{e}|$ that will come very handy to simulate an

---

Algorithm 1. PRANGEONE($\mathbf{H}, \mathbf{s}$) — One iteration of the Prange decoder

---

Parameters: $q, n, k, \mathcal{D}$ a distribution over $[\![0, k]\!]$

Require: $\mathbf{H} \in \mathbb{F}_q^{(n-k) \times n}$, $\mathbf{s} \in \mathbb{F}_q^{n-k}$
Ensure: $\mathbf{eH}^\mathsf{T} = \mathbf{s}$
  1: $t \hookleftarrow \mathcal{D}$
  2: $\mathcal{I} \leftarrow$ INFOSET($\mathbf{H}$) ▷ INFOSET($\mathbf{H}$) *returns an information set of* $\langle \mathbf{H} \rangle^\perp$
  3: $\mathbf{x} \hookleftarrow \{ \mathbf{x} \in \mathbb{F}_q^n \mid |\mathbf{x}_\mathcal{I}| = t \}$
  4: $\mathbf{e} \leftarrow$ PRANGESTEP($\mathbf{H}, \mathbf{s}, \mathcal{I}, \mathbf{x}$)
  5: **return e**

---

function PRANGESTEP($\mathbf{H}, \mathbf{s}, \mathcal{I}, \mathbf{x}$) — Prange vector completion

---

Require: $\mathbf{H} \in \mathbb{F}_q^{(n-k) \times n}$, $\mathbf{s} \in \mathbb{F}_q^{n-k}$, $\mathcal{I}$ an information set of $\langle \mathbf{H} \rangle^\perp$, $\mathbf{x} \in \mathbb{F}_q^n$
Ensure: $\mathbf{eH}^\mathsf{T} = \mathbf{s}$ and $\mathbf{e}_\mathcal{I} = \mathbf{x}_\mathcal{I}$
  $\mathbf{P} \leftarrow$ any $n \times n$ permutation matrix sending $\mathcal{I}$ on the last k coordinates
  $(\mathbf{A} \mid \mathbf{B}) \leftarrow \mathbf{HP}$; $(* \mid \mathbf{e}') \leftarrow \mathbf{xP}$ ▷ $\mathbf{A} \in \mathbb{F}_q^{(n-k) \times (n-k)}$; $\mathbf{e}' \in \mathbb{F}_q^k$
  $\mathbf{e} \leftarrow \left(\left(\mathbf{s} - \mathbf{e}'\mathbf{B}^\mathsf{T} \right) \left(\mathbf{A}^{-1} \right)^\mathsf{T}, \mathbf{e}' \right) \mathbf{P}^\mathsf{T}$
  return e

---

output distribution that is uniform over the words of weight w in the generalized $(U, U + V)$-decoder that we will consider in what follows.

Enlarging the Easy Domain $[\![w_{\text{easy}}^-, w_{\text{easy}}^+]\!]$. Inverting the syndrome function $f_{w,\mathbf{H}}$ is the basic problem upon which all code-based cryptography relies. This problem has been studied for a long time for relative weights $\omega \overset{\triangle}{=} \frac{w}{n}$ in $(0, \omega_{\text{easy}}^-)$ and despite many efforts the best algorithms [6, 8, 11, 19, 21, 38, 39, 45] for solving this problem are all exponential in n for such fixed relative weights. In other words, after more than fifty years of research, none of those algorithms came up with a polynomial complexity for relative weights ω in $(0, \omega_{\text{easy}}^-)$. Furthermore, by adapting all the previous algorithms beyond this point we observe for them the same behaviour: they are all polynomial in the range of relative weights $[\omega_{\text{easy}}^-, \omega_{\text{easy}}^+]$ and become exponential once again when ω is in $(\omega_{\text{easy}}^+, 1)$. All these results point towards the fact that inverting $f_{w,\mathbf{H}}$ in polynomial time on a larger range is fundamentally a hard problem.

4.3 Solution with Trapdoor

Let us recall that our trapdoor to invert $f_{w,\mathbf{H}}$ is given by the family of normalized generalized $(U, U + V)$-codes (Proposition 1 in Sect. 3.2). As we will see, this family comes with a simple procedure which enables to invert $f_{w,\mathbf{H}}$ with errors of weight which belongs to $[\![w_{\text{UV}}^-, w_{\text{UV}}^+]\!] \subset [\![w^-, w^+]\!]$ but with $[\![w_{\text{easy}}^-, w_{\text{easy}}^+]\!] \subsetneq [\![w_{\text{UV}}^-, w_{\text{UV}}^+]\!]$. We summarize this situation in Fig. 1. We wish to point out here, to avoid any misunderstanding that the procedure we give here is not the one we use at the end to instantiate Wave, but is merely here to give the underlying idea of the trapdoor. Rejection sampling will be needed as explained in the following section to avoid any information leakage on the trapdoor coming from the outputs of the algorithm given here.

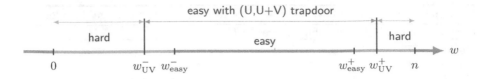

Fig. 1. Hardness of $(U, U + V)$ Decoding

It turns out that in the case of a normalized generalized $(U, U + V)$-code, a simple tweak of the Prange decoder will be able to reach relative weights w/n outside the "easy" region $[\omega_{\text{easy}}^-, \omega_{\text{easy}}^+]$. It exploits the fundamental leverage of the Prange decoder : it consists in choosing the error $\mathbf{e}$ satisfying $\mathbf{e}\mathbf{H}^{\mathsf{T}} = \mathbf{s}$ as we want in k positions when the code that we decode is random and of dimension k. When we want an error of low weight, we put zeroes on those positions, whereas if we want an error of large weight, we put non-zero values. This idea leads to even smaller or larger weights in the case of a normalized generalized $(U, U+V)$-code. To explain this point, recall that we want to solve the following decoding problem in this case.

Problem 2 (decoding problem for normalized generalized $(U, U+V)$-codes). Given a normalized generalized $(U, U + V)$ code $(\varphi, \mathbf{H}_U, \mathbf{H}_V)$ (see Proposition 1) of parity-check matrix $\mathbf{H} - \mathcal{H}(\varphi, \mathbf{H}_U, \mathbf{H}_V) \in \mathbb{F}_q^{(n-k)\times n}$, and a syndrome $\mathbf{s} \in \mathbb{F}_q^{n-k}$, find $\mathbf{e} \in \mathbb{F}_q^n$ of weight w such that $\mathbf{e}\mathbf{H}^{\mathsf{T}} = \mathbf{s}$.

The following notation will be very useful to explain how we solve this problem.

Notation 1. *For a vector $\mathbf{e}$ in $\mathbb{F}_q^n$, we denote by $\mathbf{e}_U$ and $\mathbf{e}_V$ the vectors in $\mathbb{F}_q^{n/2}$ such that $(\mathbf{e}_U, \mathbf{e}_V) = \varphi^{-1}(\mathbf{e})$.*

The decoding algorithm will recover $\mathbf{e}_V$ and then $\mathbf{e}_U$. From $\mathbf{e}_U$ and $\mathbf{e}_V$ we recover $\mathbf{e}$ since $\mathbf{e} = \varphi(\mathbf{e}_U, \mathbf{e}_V)$. The point of introducing such an $\mathbf{e}_U$ and a $\mathbf{e}_V$ is that

Proposition 3. *Solving the decoding Problem 2 is equivalent to find an $\mathbf{e} \in \mathbb{F}_q^n$ of weight w satisfying*

$$\mathbf{e}_U\mathbf{H}_U^{\mathsf{T}} = \mathbf{s}^U \text{ and } \mathbf{e}_V\mathbf{H}_V^{\mathsf{T}} = \mathbf{s}^V \tag{5}$$

where $\mathbf{s} = (\mathbf{s}^U, \mathbf{s}^V)$ with $\mathbf{s}^U \in \mathbb{F}_q^{n/2-k_U}$ and $\mathbf{s}^V \in \mathbb{F}_q^{n/2-k_V}$.

Remark 3. We have put U and V as superscripts in $\mathbf{s}^U$ and $\mathbf{s}^V$ to avoid any confusion with the notation we have just introduced for $\mathbf{e}_U$ and $\mathbf{e}_V$.

Proof. Let us observe that $\mathbf{e} = \varphi(\mathbf{e}_U, \mathbf{e}_V) = (\mathbf{a}\odot\mathbf{e}_U + \mathbf{b}\odot\mathbf{e}_V, \mathbf{c}\odot\mathbf{e}_U + \mathbf{d}\odot\mathbf{e}_V) = (\mathbf{e}_U\mathbf{A} + \mathbf{e}_V\mathbf{B}, \mathbf{e}_U\mathbf{C} + \mathbf{e}_V\mathbf{D})$ with $\mathbf{A} = \mathbf{Diag}(\mathbf{a}), \mathbf{B} = \mathbf{Diag}(\mathbf{b}), \mathbf{C} = \mathbf{Diag}(\mathbf{c}), \mathbf{D} = \mathbf{Diag}(\mathbf{d})$. By using this, $\mathbf{e}\mathbf{H}^{\mathsf{T}} = \mathbf{s}$ translates into

$$\begin{cases} \mathbf{e}_U\mathbf{A}\mathbf{D}^{\mathsf{T}}\mathbf{H}_U^{\mathsf{T}} + \mathbf{e}_V\mathbf{B}\mathbf{D}^{\mathsf{T}}\mathbf{H}_U^{\mathsf{T}} - \mathbf{e}_U\mathbf{C}\mathbf{B}^{\mathsf{T}}\mathbf{H}_U^{\mathsf{T}} - \mathbf{e}_V\mathbf{D}\mathbf{B}^{\mathsf{T}}\mathbf{H}_U^{\mathsf{T}} = \mathbf{s}^U \\ -\mathbf{e}_U\mathbf{A}\mathbf{C}^{\mathsf{T}}\mathbf{H}_V^{\mathsf{T}} - \mathbf{e}_V\mathbf{B}\mathbf{C}^{\mathsf{T}}\mathbf{H}_V^{\mathsf{T}} + \mathbf{e}_U\mathbf{C}\mathbf{A}^{\mathsf{T}}\mathbf{H}_V^{\mathsf{T}} + \mathbf{e}_V\mathbf{D}\mathbf{A}^{\mathsf{T}}\mathbf{H}_V^{\mathsf{T}} = \mathbf{s}^V \end{cases}$$

which amounts to $e_U(\mathbf{AD} - \mathbf{BC})\mathbf{H}_U^\mathsf{T} = s^U$ and $e_V(\mathbf{AD} - \mathbf{BC})\mathbf{H}_V^\mathsf{T} = s^V$, since $\mathbf{A}, \mathbf{B}, \mathbf{C}, \mathbf{D}$ are diagonal matrices, they are therefore symmetric and commute with each other. We finish the proof by observing that $\mathbf{AD} - \mathbf{BC} = \mathbf{I}_{n/2}$.   □

Performing the two decoding in (5) independently with the Prange algorithm gains nothing. However if we first solve in V with the Prange algorithm, and then seek a solution in U which properly depends on e_V we increase the range of weights accessible in polynomial time for e. It then turns out that the range $[\omega_{\mathsf{UV}}^-, \omega_{\mathsf{UV}}^+]$ of relative weights w/n for which the $(U, U + V)$-decoder works in polynomial time is larger than $[\omega_{\mathsf{easy}}^-, \omega_{\mathsf{easy}}^+]$. This will provide an advantage to the trapdoor owner.

Tweaking the Prange Decoder for Reaching Large Weights. When $q = 2$, small and large weights play a symmetrical role. This is not the case anymore for $q \geq 3$. In what follows we will suppose that $q \geq 3$. In order to find a solution e of large weight to the decoding problem $e\mathbf{H}^\mathsf{T} = s$, we use Proposition 3 and first find an arbitrary solution e_V to $e_V\mathbf{H}_V^\mathsf{T} = s^V$. The idea, now for performing the second decoding $e_U\mathbf{H}_U^\mathsf{T} = s^U$, is to take advantage of e_V to find a solution e_U that maximizes the weight of $e = \varphi(e_U, e_V)$. On any information set of the U code, we can fix arbitrarily e_U. Such a set is of size k_U and on those positions i we can always choose $e_U(i)$ such that this induces *simultaneously* two positions in e that are non-zero. These are e_i and $e_{i+n/2}$. We just have to choose $e_U(i)$ so that we have simultaneously $a_i e_U(i) + b_i e_V(i) \neq 0$ and $c_i e_U(i) + d_i e_V(i) \neq 0$. This is always possible since $q \geq 3$ and it gives an expected weight of e:

$$\mathbb{E}(|e|) = 2\left(k_U + \frac{q-1}{q}(n/2 - k_U)\right) = \frac{q-1}{q}n + \frac{2k_U}{q} \tag{6}$$

The best choice for k_U is to take $k_U = k$ up to the point where $\frac{q-1}{q}n + \frac{2k}{q} = n$, that is $k = n/2$ and for larger values of k we choose $k_U = n/2$ and $k_V = k - k_U$.

Why Is the Trapdoor More Powerful for Large Weights than for Small Weights? This strategy can be clearly adapted for small weights. However, it is less powerful in this case. Indeed, to minimize the final error weight we would like to choose $e_U(i)$ in k_U positions such that $a_i e_U(i) + b_i e_V(i) = 0$ and $c_i e_U(i) + d_i e_V(i) = 0$. Here as $a_i d_i - b_i c_i = 1$ and $a_i c_i \neq 0$ in the family of codes we consider, this is possible if and only if $e_V(i) = 0$. Therefore, contrarily to the case where we want to reach errors of large weight, the area of positions where we can gain twice is constrained to be of size $n/2 - |e_V|$. The minimal weight for e_V we can reach in polynomial time with the Prange decoder is given by $\frac{q-1}{q}(n/2 - k_V)$. In this way the set of positions where we can double the number of 0 will be of size $n/2 - \frac{q-1}{q}(n/2 - k_V) = \frac{n}{2q} + \frac{q-1}{q}k_V$. It can be verified that this strategy would give the following expected weight for the final error we get:

$$\mathbb{E}(|e|) = \frac{q-1}{q}n - 2\frac{q-1}{q}k_U \text{ if } k_U \leq \frac{n}{2q} + \frac{q-1}{q}k_V \text{ and } \frac{2(q-1)^2}{(2q-1)q}(n-k) \text{ else.}$$

5 Preimage Sampling with Trapdoor: Achieving a Uniformly Distributed Output

We restrict our study to $q = 3$ but it can be generalized to larger q. To be a trapdoor one-way preimage sampleable function, we have to enforce that the outputs of our algorithm, which inverts our trapdoor function, are very close to be uniformly distributed over S_w. The procedure described in the previous section using directly the Prange decoder, does not meet this property. As we will prove, by changing it slightly, we will achieve this task by still keeping the property to output errors of weight w for which it is hard to solve the decoding problem for this weight. However, the parameters will have to be chosen carefully and the area of weights w for which we can output errors in polynomial time decreases. Figure 2 gives a rough picture of what will happen. A calculation available in [18] shows that leakage immunity can be efficiently achieved by rejection sampling for $w > w_{\text{easy}}^+$. At this moment, we do not know how to achieve this efficiently for $w < w_{\text{easy}}^-$.

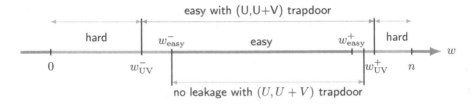

Fig. 2. Hardness of $(U, U + V)$ Decoding with no leakage of signature

5.1 Rejection Sampling to Reach Uniformly Distributed Output

We will tweak slightly the generalized $(U, U + V)$-decoder from the previous section by performing in particular rejection sampling on $\mathbf{e}_U$ and $\mathbf{e}_V$ in order to obtain an error $\mathbf{e}$ satisfying $\mathbf{e}\mathbf{H}^{\mathsf{T}} = \mathbf{s}$ that is uniformly distributed over the words of weight w when the syndrome $\mathbf{s}$ is randomly chosen in $\mathbb{F}_3^{n-k}$. Solving the decoding problem 2 of the generalized $(U, U+V)$-code will be done by solving (5) through an algorithm whose skeleton is given in Algorithm 2. $\text{DECODEV}(\mathbf{H}_V, \mathbf{s}^V)$ returns a vector satisfying $\mathbf{e}_V\mathbf{H}_V^{\mathsf{T}} = \mathbf{s}^V$, whereas $\text{DECODEU}(\mathbf{H}_U, \varphi, \mathbf{s}^U, \mathbf{e}_V)$ returns a vector satisfying $\mathbf{e}_U\mathbf{H}_U^{\mathsf{T}} = \mathbf{s}^U$ *and such that* $|\varphi(\mathbf{e}_U, \mathbf{e}_V)| = w$. Here $\mathbf{s} = (\mathbf{s}^U, \mathbf{s}^V)$ with $\mathbf{s}^U \in \mathbb{F}_3^{n/2-k_U}$ and $\mathbf{s}^V \in \mathbb{F}_3^{n/2-k_V}$. What we want to achieve by rejection sampling is that the distribution of $\mathbf{e}$ output by this algorithm is the same as the distribution of $\mathbf{e}^{\text{unif}}$ that denotes a vector that is chosen uniformly at random among the words of weight w in $\mathbb{F}_3^n$. This will be achieved by ensuring that:

1. the $\mathbf{e}_V$ fed into $\text{DECODEU}(\cdot)$ at Step 5 has the same distribution as $\mathbf{e}_V^{\text{unif}}$,
2. the distribution of $\mathbf{e}_U$ surviving to Condition 2 at Step 7 conditioned on the value of $\mathbf{e}_V$ is the same as the distribution of $\mathbf{e}_U^{\text{unif}}$ conditioned on $\mathbf{e}_V^{\text{unif}}$.

Algorithm 2. DECODEUV($\mathbf{H}_V, \mathbf{H}_U, \varphi, \mathbf{s}$)

1: **repeat**
2:    $\mathbf{e}_V \leftarrow$ DECODEV($\mathbf{H}_V, \mathbf{s}^V$)
3: **until** Condition 1 is met
4: **repeat**
5:    $\mathbf{e}_U \leftarrow$ DECODEU($\mathbf{H}_U, \varphi, \mathbf{s}^U, \mathbf{e}_V$)   ▷ We assume that $|\varphi(\mathbf{e}_U, \mathbf{e}_V)| = w$ here.
6:    $\mathbf{e} \leftarrow \varphi(\mathbf{e}_U, \mathbf{e}_V)$
7: **until** Condition 2 is met
8: **return e**

There is a property of the decoders DECODEV($\cdot$) and DECODEU($\cdot$) derived from Prange decoders that we will consider that will be very helpful here.

Definition 3. DECODEV($\cdot$) *is said to be weightwise uniform if the output* $\mathbf{e}_V$ *of* DECODEV($\mathbf{H}_V, \mathbf{s}^V$) *is such that* $\mathbb{P}(\mathbf{e}_V)$ *is a function of the integer* $|\mathbf{e}_V|$ *when* $\mathbf{s}^V$ *is chosen uniformly at random in* $\mathbb{F}_3^{n/2-k_V}$. DECODEU($\cdot$) *is* m_1-*uniform if the outputput* $\mathbf{e}_U$ *of* DECODEU($\mathbf{H}_U, \varphi, \mathbf{s}^U, \mathbf{e}_V$) *is such that the conditional probability* $\mathbb{P}(\mathbf{e}_U|\mathbf{e}_V)$ *is a function of the pair of integers* $(|\mathbf{e}_V|, m_1(\varphi(\mathbf{e}_U, \mathbf{e}_V))$ *where*

$$m_1(\mathbf{x}) \triangleq \left| \left\{ 1 \leq i \leq n/2 : |(x_i, x_{i+n/2})| = 1 \right\} \right|.$$

It is readily observed that $\mathbb{P}(\mathbf{e}_V^{\text{unif}})$ and $\mathbb{P}(\mathbf{e}_U^{\text{unif}}|\mathbf{e}_V^{\text{unif}})$ are also only functions of $|\mathbf{e}_V^{\text{unif}}|$ and $(|\mathbf{e}_V^{\text{unif}}|, m_1(\mathbf{e}^{\text{unif}}))$ respectively. From this it is readily seen that we obtain the right distributions for $\mathbf{e}_V$ and $\mathbf{e}_U$ conditioned on $\mathbf{e}_V$ by just ensuring that the distribution of $|\mathbf{e}_V|$ follows the same distribution as $|\mathbf{e}_V^{\text{unif}}|$ and that the distribution of $m_1(\mathbf{e})$ conditioned on $|\mathbf{e}_V|$ is the same as the distribution of $m_1(\mathbf{e}^{\text{unif}})$ conditioned on $|\mathbf{e}_V^{\text{unif}}|$. This is shown by the following lemma.

Lemma 1. *Let* $\mathbf{e}$ *be the output of Algorithm 2 when* $\mathbf{s}^V$ *and* $\mathbf{s}^U$ *are uniformly distributed in* $\mathbb{F}_3^{n/2-k_V}$ *and* $\mathbb{F}_3^{n/2-k_U}$ *respectively. Assume that* DECODEU($\cdot$) *is* m_1-*uniform whereas* DECODEV($\cdot$) *is weightwise uniform. If for any possible* y *and* z, $|\mathbf{e}_V| \sim |\mathbf{e}_V^{\text{unif}}|$ *and* $\mathbb{P}(m_1(\mathbf{e}) = z \mid |\mathbf{e}_V| = y) = \mathbb{P}(m_1(\mathbf{e}^{\text{unif}}) = z \mid |\mathbf{e}_V^{\text{unif}}| = y)$, *then* $\mathbf{e} \sim \mathbf{e}^{\text{unif}}$. *The probabilities are taken here over the choice of* $\mathbf{s}^U$ *and* $\mathbf{s}^V$ *and over the internal coins of* DECODEU($\cdot$) *and* DECODEV($\cdot$).

Proof. We have for any $\mathbf{x}$ in S_w

$$\begin{aligned}
\mathbb{P}(\mathbf{e} = \mathbf{x}) &= \mathbb{P}(\mathbf{e}_U = \mathbf{x}_U \mid \mathbf{e}_V = \mathbf{x}_V)\mathbb{P}(\mathbf{e}_V = \mathbf{x}_V) \\
&= \mathbb{P}(\text{DECODEU}(\mathbf{H}_U, \varphi, \mathbf{s}^U, \mathbf{e}_V) = \mathbf{x}_U \mid \mathbf{e}_V = \mathbf{x}_V) \\
&\qquad \mathbb{P}(\text{DECODEV}(\mathbf{H}_V, \mathbf{s}^V) = \mathbf{x}_V) \\
&= \frac{\mathbb{P}(m_1(\mathbf{e}) = z \mid |\mathbf{e}_V| = y)}{n(y, z)} \frac{\mathbb{P}(|\mathbf{e}_V| = y)}{n(y)} \triangleq P
\end{aligned}$$

(7)

where $n(y)$ is the number of vectors of $\mathbb{F}_3^{n/2}$ of weight y and $n(y, z)$ is the number of vectors $\mathbf{e}$ in $\mathbb{F}_3^n$ such that $\mathbf{e}_V = \mathbf{x}_V$ and such that $m_1(\mathbf{e}) = z$ (this last number only depends on $\mathbf{x}_V$ through its weight y). Equation (7) is here a consequence of the weightwise uniformity of $\mathrm{DECODEV}(\cdot)$ on one hand and the m_1-uniformity of $\mathrm{DECODEU}(\cdot)$ on the other hand. We conclude by noticing that

$$P = \frac{\mathbb{P}(m_1(\mathbf{e}^{\mathrm{unif}}) = z \mid |\mathbf{e}_V^{\mathrm{unif}}| = y)}{n(y,z)} \frac{\mathbb{P}(|\mathbf{e}_V^{\mathrm{unif}}| = y)}{n(y)} \tag{8}$$

$$= \mathbb{P}(\mathbf{e}_U^{\mathrm{unif}} = \mathbf{x}_U \mid \mathbf{e}_V^{\mathrm{unif}} = \mathbf{x}_V)\mathbb{P}(\mathbf{e}_V^{\mathrm{unif}} = \mathbf{x}_V) = \mathbb{P}(\mathbf{e}^{\mathrm{unif}} = \mathbf{x})$$

Equation (8) follows from the assumptions on the distribution of $|\mathbf{e}_V|$ and of the conditional distribution of $m_1(\mathbf{e})$ for a given weight $|\mathbf{e}_V|$. $\qquad\square$

This shows that in order to reach a uniformly distribution for $\mathbf{e}$ over S_w it is enough to perform a rejection sampling based on the weight $|\mathbf{e}_V|$ for $\mathrm{DECODEV}(\cdot)$ and based on the pair $(|\mathbf{e}_V|, m_1(\mathbf{e}))$ for $\mathrm{DECODEU}(\cdot)$. In other words, our decoding algorithm with rejection sampling will use a rejection vector $\mathbf{r}_V$ indexed by the weights of $\mathbf{e}_V$ for $\mathrm{DECODEV}(\cdot)$ and a two-dimensional rejection vector $\mathbf{r}_U$ indexed by $(|\mathbf{e}_V|, m_1(\mathbf{e}))$ for $\mathrm{DECODEU}(\cdot)$. This is described in Algorithm 3.

Algorithm 3. $\mathrm{DECODEUV}(\mathbf{H}_V, \mathbf{H}_U, \varphi, \mathbf{s})$

1: **repeat**
2:     $\mathbf{e}_V \leftarrow \mathrm{DECODEV}(\mathbf{H}_V, \mathbf{s}^V)$
3: **until** $\mathrm{rand}([0,1]) \leq \mathbf{r}_V(|\mathbf{e}_V|)$
4: **repeat**
5:     $\mathbf{e}_U \leftarrow \mathrm{DECODEU}(\mathbf{H}_U, \varphi, \mathbf{s}^U, \mathbf{e}_V)$
6:     $\mathbf{e} \leftarrow \varphi(\mathbf{e}_U, \mathbf{e}_V)$
7: **until** $\mathrm{rand}([0,1]) \leq \mathbf{r}_U(|\mathbf{e}_V|, m_1(\mathbf{e}))$
8: **return** $\mathbf{e}$

Standard results on rejection sampling yield the following proposition:

Proposition 4. *For any $i, t \in [\![0, n/2]\!]$ and $s \in [\![0, t]\!]$, let*

$$q_1(i) \stackrel{\triangle}{=} \mathbb{P}\left(|\mathbf{e}_V| = i\right) \; ; \; q_1^{\mathrm{unif}}(i) \stackrel{\triangle}{=} \mathbb{P}\left(|\mathbf{e}_V^{\mathrm{unif}}| = i\right) \tag{9}$$

$$q_2(s,t) \stackrel{\triangle}{=} \mathbb{P}\left(m_1(\mathbf{e}) = s \mid |\mathbf{e}_V| = t\right) \; ; \; q_2^{\mathrm{unif}}(s,t) \stackrel{\triangle}{=} \mathbb{P}\left(m_1(\mathbf{e}^{\mathrm{unif}}) = s \mid |\mathbf{e}_V^{\mathrm{unif}}| = t\right) \tag{10}$$

$$\mathbf{r}_V(i) \stackrel{\triangle}{=} \frac{1}{M_V^{\mathrm{rs}}} \frac{q_1^{\mathrm{unif}}(i)}{q_1(i)} \quad and \quad \mathbf{r}_U(s,t) \stackrel{\triangle}{=} \frac{1}{M_U^{\mathrm{rs}}(t)} \frac{q_2^{\mathrm{unif}}(s,t)}{q_2(s,t)} \quad with$$

$$M_V^{\mathrm{rs}} \stackrel{\triangle}{=} \max_{0 \leq i \leq n/2} \frac{q_1^{\mathrm{unif}}(i)}{q_1(i)} \quad and \quad M_U^{\mathrm{rs}}(t) \stackrel{\triangle}{=} \max_{0 \leq s \leq t} \frac{q_2^{\mathrm{unif}}(s,t)}{q_2(s,t)}$$

Then if $\mathrm{DECODEV}(\cdot)$ is weightwise uniform and $\mathrm{DECODEU}(\cdot)$ is m_1-uniform, the output $\mathbf{e}$ of Algorithm 3 satisfies $\mathbf{e} \sim \mathbf{e}^{\mathrm{unif}}$.

5.2 Application to the Prange Decoder

To instantiate rejection sampling, we have to provide here (i) how $\textsc{DecodeV}(\cdot)$ and $\textsc{DecodeU}(\cdot)$ are instantiated and (ii) how $q_1^{\text{unif}}, q_2^{\text{unif}}, q_1$ and q_2 are computed. Let us begin by the following proposition which gives q_1^{unif} and q_2^{unif}.

Proposition 5. *Let n be an even integer, $w \leq n$, $i,t \leq n/2$ and $s \leq t$ be integers. We have,*

$$q_1^{\text{unif}}(i) = \frac{\binom{n/2}{i}}{\binom{n}{w}2^{w/2}} \sum_{\substack{p=0 \\ w+p\equiv 0 \mod 2}}^{i} \binom{i}{p}\binom{n/2-i}{(w+p)/2-i}2^{3p/2} \tag{11}$$

$$q_2^{\text{unif}}(s,t) = \frac{\binom{t}{s}\binom{n/2-t}{\frac{w+s}{2}-t}2^{\frac{3s}{2}}}{\sum_p \binom{t}{p}\binom{n/2-t}{\frac{w+p}{2}-t}2^{\frac{3p}{2}}} \quad if\ w+s \equiv 0 \mod 2 \quad and \quad 0\ else \tag{12}$$

Algorithm 4. $\textsc{DecodeV}(\mathbf{H}_V, \mathbf{s}^V)$ the Decoder outputting an $\mathbf{e}_V$ such that $\mathbf{e}_V \mathbf{H}_V^{\mathsf{T}} = \mathbf{s}^V$.

1: $\mathcal{J}, \mathcal{I} \leftarrow \textsc{FreeSet}(\mathbf{H}_V)$
2: $\ell \hookleftarrow \mathcal{D}_V$
3: $\mathbf{x}_V \hookleftarrow \left\{ \mathbf{x} \in \mathbb{F}_3^{n/2} \mid |\mathbf{x}_{\mathcal{J}}| = \ell, \text{Supp}(\mathbf{x}) \subseteq \mathcal{I} \right\}$ ▷ $(\mathbf{x}_V)_{\mathcal{I}\setminus\mathcal{J}}$ is random
4: $\mathbf{e}_V \leftarrow \textsc{PrangeStep}(\mathbf{H}_V, \mathbf{s}^V, \mathcal{I}, \mathbf{x}_V)$
5: **return** $\mathbf{e}_V$

---
function $\textsc{FreeSet}(\mathbf{H})$

Require: $\mathbf{H} \in \mathbb{F}_3^{(n-k)\times n}$
Ensure: $\mathcal{I}$ an information set of $\langle\mathbf{H}\rangle^{\perp}$ and $\mathcal{J} \subset \mathcal{I}$ of size $k-d$
1: **repeat**
2:     $\mathcal{J} \hookleftarrow [\![1,n]\!]$ of size $k-d$
3: **until rank** $\mathbf{H}_{\overline{\mathcal{J}}} = n-k$
4: **repeat**
5:     $\mathcal{J}' \hookleftarrow [\![1,n]\!]\setminus\mathcal{J}$ of size d
6:     $\mathcal{I} \leftarrow \mathcal{J} \sqcup \mathcal{J}'$
7: **until** $\mathcal{I}$ is an information set of $\langle\mathbf{H}\rangle^{\perp}$
8: **return** $\mathcal{J}, \mathcal{I}$

Algorithms $\textsc{DecodeV}(\cdot), \textsc{DecodeU}(\cdot)$ are described in Algorithms 4 and 5. These two algorithms both use the Prange decoder in the same way as we did with the procedure described in Sect. 4.3 to reach large weights, except that here we introduced some internal distributions $\mathcal{D}_V$ and the $\mathcal{D}_U^t$'s. These distributions are here to tweak the weight distributions of $\textsc{DecodeV}(\cdot)$ and $\textsc{DecodeU}(\cdot)$ in order to reduce the rejection rate. We have:

Algorithm 5. DECODEU($\mathbf{H}_U, \varphi, \mathbf{s}^U, \mathbf{e}_V$) the U-Decoder outputting an $\mathbf{e}_U$ such that $\mathbf{e}_U \mathbf{H}_U^\mathsf{T} = \mathbf{s}^U$ and $|\varphi(\mathbf{e}_U, \mathbf{e}_V)| = w$.

1: $t \leftarrow |\mathbf{e}_V|$
2: $k_{\neq 0} \hookleftarrow \mathcal{D}_U^t$
3: $k_0 \leftarrow k_U' - k_{\neq 0}$ $\triangleright\ k_U' \overset{\triangle}{=} k_U - d$
4: **repeat**
5:     $\mathcal{J}, \mathcal{I} \leftarrow$ FREESETW($\mathbf{H}_U, \mathbf{e}_V, k_{\neq 0}$)
6:     $\mathbf{x}_U \hookleftarrow \{\mathbf{x} \in \mathbb{F}_3^{n/2} \mid \forall j \in \mathcal{J},\ \mathbf{x}(j) \notin \{-\frac{b_i}{a_i} \mathbf{e}_V(i), -\frac{d_i}{c_i} \mathbf{e}_V(i)\}$ and $\mathrm{Supp}(\mathbf{x}) \subseteq \mathcal{I}\}$
7:     $\mathbf{e}_U \leftarrow$ PRANGESTEP($\mathbf{H}_U, \mathbf{s}^U, \mathcal{I}, \mathbf{x}_U$)
8: **until** $|\varphi(\mathbf{e}_U, \mathbf{e}_V)| = w$
9: **return** $\mathbf{e}_U$

---
function FREESETW($\mathbf{H}, \mathbf{x}, k_{\neq 0}$)

Require: $\mathbf{H} \in \mathbb{F}_q^{(n-k) \times n}, \mathbf{x} \in \mathbb{F}_q^n$ and $k_{\neq 0} \in [\![0, k]\!]$.
Ensure: $\mathcal{J}$ and $\mathcal{I}$ an information set of $\langle \mathbf{H} \rangle^\perp$ such that $|\{i \in \mathcal{J} : x_i \neq 0\}| = k_{\neq 0}$ and $\mathcal{J} \subset \mathcal{I}$ of size $k - d$.
1: **repeat**
2:     $\mathcal{J}_1 \hookleftarrow \mathrm{Supp}(\mathbf{x})$ of size $k_{\neq 0}$
3:     $\mathcal{J}_2 \hookleftarrow [\![1, n]\!] \backslash \mathrm{Supp}(\mathbf{x})$ of size $k - d - k_{\neq 0}$.
4:     $\mathcal{J} \leftarrow \mathcal{J}_1 \sqcup \mathcal{J}_2$
5: **until** $\mathrm{rank}\, \mathbf{H}_{\overline{\mathcal{J}}} = n - k$
6: **repeat**
7:     $\mathcal{J}' \hookleftarrow [\![1, n]\!] \backslash \mathcal{J}$ of size d
8:     $\mathcal{I} \leftarrow \mathcal{J} \sqcup \mathcal{J}'$
9: **until** $\mathcal{I}$ is an information set of $\langle \mathbf{H} \rangle^\perp$
10: **return** $\mathcal{J}, \mathcal{I}$

Proposition 6. *Let n be an even integer, $w \leq n$, $i, t, k_U \leq n/2$ and $s \leq t$ be integers. Let d be an integer, $k_V' \overset{\triangle}{=} k_V - d$ and $k_U' \overset{\triangle}{=} k_U - d$. Let X_V (resp. X_U^t) be a random variable distributed according to $\mathcal{D}_V$ (resp. $\mathcal{D}_U^t$). We have,*

$$q_1(i) = \sum_{t=0}^{i} \frac{\binom{n/2 - k_V'}{i-t} 2^{i-t}}{3^{n/2 - k_V'}} \mathbb{P}(X_V = t) \tag{13}$$

$$q_2(s, t) = \begin{cases} \displaystyle\sum_{k_{\neq 0} \in \mathcal{K}} \frac{\binom{t - k_{\neq 0}}{s} \binom{n/2 - t - k_0}{\frac{w+s}{2} - t - k_0} 2^{\frac{3s}{2}}}{\sum_p \binom{t - k_{\neq 0}}{p} \binom{n/2 - t - k_0}{\frac{w+p}{2} - t - k_0} 2^{\frac{3p}{2}}} \mathbb{P}(X_U^t = k_{\neq 0}) & \text{if } w - s \text{ even.} \\ 0 & \text{else} \end{cases} \tag{14}$$

with $\mathcal{K} = \{k_{\neq 0} \mid t + k_U' - n/2 \leq k_{\neq 0} \leq t\}$ and $k_0 \overset{\triangle}{=} k_U' - k_{\neq 0}$

A parameter d is introduced in Proposition 6 and in Algorithms 4 and 5. When d is large enough $\rho(\mathbf{e}, \mathbf{e}^{\mathrm{unif}})$ will be typically very small as shown by

Theorem 1. *Let* e *be the output of Algorithm 3 based on Algorithms 4,5 where the entry* s *is chosen uniformly at random in* $\mathbb{F}_3^{n-k}$ *and* e^{unif} *be a uniformly distributed error of weight w. We have*

$$\mathbb{P}_{\mathbf{H}_U, \mathbf{H}_V} \left(\rho(\mathbf{e}, \mathbf{e}^{\mathrm{unif}}) > 3^{-d/2} \right) \leq 3^{-d/2}.$$

A much stronger result showing that $\rho(\mathbf{e}, \mathbf{e}^{\mathrm{unif}})$ is typically smaller than $n^2 3^{-d}$ will be given in the full paper [18]. It will be helpful to consider now the following definition.

Definition 4 (Bad and Good Subsets). *Let* $d \leq k \leq n$ *be integers and* $\mathbf{H} \in \mathbb{F}_3^{(n-k) \times n}$. *A subset* $\mathcal{E} \subseteq [\![1, n]\!]$ *of size* $k - d$ *is defined as a good set for* $\mathbf{H}$ *if* $\mathbf{H}_{\overline{\mathcal{E}}}$ *is of full rank where* $\overline{\mathcal{E}}$ *denotes the complementary of* $\mathcal{E}$. *Otherwise,* $\mathcal{E}$ *is defined as a bad set for* $\mathbf{H}$.

The proof of this theorem relies on introducing a variant of the decoder based on variants of the U and V decoders VARDECODEV$(\cdot)$ and VARDECODEU$(\cdot)$ of algorithms DECODEV$(\cdot)$ and DECODEU$(\cdot)$ respectively that work as DECODEV$(\cdot)$ and DECODEU$(\cdot)$ when $\mathcal{J}$ is a good set and depart from it when $\mathcal{J}$ is a bad set. In the later case, the Prange decoder is not used anymore and an error is output that simulates what the Prange decoder would do with the exception that there is no guarantee that the error $\mathbf{e}_V$ that is output by VARDECODEV$(\cdot)$ satisfies $\mathbf{e}_V \mathbf{H}_V = \mathbf{s}_V$ or that the $\mathbf{e}_U$ that is output by VARDECODEU$(\cdot)$ satisfies $\mathbf{e}_U \mathbf{H}_U = \mathbf{s}_U$. The $\mathbf{e}_V$ and $\mathbf{e}_U$ that are output are chosen on the positions of $\mathcal{J}$ as DECODEV$()$ and DECODEU$()$ as would have done it, but the rest of the positions are chosen uniformly at random in $\mathbb{F}_3$. It is clear that in this case

Fact 2. VARDECODEV$(\cdot)$ *is weightwise uniform and* VARDECODEU$(\cdot)$ *is* m_1-*uniform.*

The point of considering VARDECODEV$(\cdot)$ and VARDECODEU$(\cdot)$ is that they are very good approximations of DECODEV$(\cdot)$ and DECODEU$(\cdot)$ that meet the uniformity conditions that ensure by using Lemma 1 that the output of Algorithm 3 using VARDECODEV$(\cdot)$ and VARDECODEU$(\cdot)$ instead of DECODEV$(\cdot)$ and DECODEU$(\cdot)$ produces an error $\mathbf{e}$ that is uniformly distributed over the words of weight w. The outputs of VARDECODEV$(\cdot)$ and VARDECODEU$(\cdot)$ only differ from the output of DECODEV$(\cdot)$ and DECODEU$(\cdot)$ when a bad set $\mathcal{J}$ is encountered. These considerations can be used to prove the following proposition.

Proposition 7. *Algorithm 3 based on* VARDECODEV$(\cdot)$ *and* VARDECODEU$(\cdot)$ *produces uniformly distributed errors* $\mathbf{e}^{\mathrm{unif}}$ *of weight w. Let* $\mathbf{e}$ *be the output of Algorithm 3 with the use of* DECODEV$(\cdot)$ *and* DECODEU$(\cdot)$. *Let* J^{unif} *be uniformly distributed over the subsets of* $[\![1, n/2]\!]$ *of size* $k_V - d$ *whereas* $J^{\mathbf{H}_V}$ *is uniformly distributed over the same subsets that are good for* $\mathbf{H}_V$. *Let* $I_{\mathbf{x}_V, \ell}^{\mathrm{unif}}$ *be uniformly distributed over the subsets of* $[\![1, n/2]\!]$ *of size* $k_U - d$ *such that their* *intersection with* $\mathbf{x}_V$ *is of size* ℓ *whereas* $I^{\mathbf{H}_U}_{\mathbf{x}_V,\ell}$ *is the uniform distribution over the same subsets that are good for* $\mathbf{H}_U$. *We have:*

$$\rho\left(\mathbf{e}; \mathbf{e}^{\text{unif}}\right) \leq \rho\left(J^{\mathbf{H}_V}; J^{\text{unif}}\right)$$
$$+ \sum_{\mathbf{x}_V,\ell} \rho\left(I^{\mathbf{H}_U}_{\mathbf{x}_V,\ell}; I^{\text{unif}}_{\mathbf{x}_V,\ell}\right) \mathbb{P}\left(k_{\neq 0} = \ell \mid \mathbf{e}_V = \mathbf{x}_V\right) \mathbb{P}\left(\mathbf{e}^{\text{unif}}_V = \mathbf{x}_V\right)$$

Proof. The first statement about the output of Algorithm 3 is a direct consequence of Fact 2 and Lemma 1. The proof of the rest of the proposition relies on the following proposition [30, Proposition 8.10]:

Proposition 8. *Let* X, Y *be two random variables over a common set* A. *For any randomized function* f *with domain* A *using internal coins independent from* X *and* Y, *we have:*
$$\rho\left(f(X); f(Y)\right) \leq \rho\left(X; Y\right).$$

Let us define for $\mathbf{x}_V \in \mathbb{F}_3^{n/2}$ and $\mathbf{x}_U \in \mathbb{F}_3^{n/2}$,

$$p(\mathbf{x}_V) \stackrel{\triangle}{=} \mathbb{P}\left(\mathbf{e}_V = \mathbf{x}_V\right)$$
$$q(\mathbf{x}_V) \stackrel{\triangle}{=} \mathbb{P}\left(\mathbf{e}^{\text{unif}}_V = \mathbf{x}_V\right)$$
$$p(\mathbf{x}_U|\mathbf{x}_V) \stackrel{\triangle}{=} \mathbb{P}\left(\mathbf{e}_U = \mathbf{x}_U \mid \mathbf{e}_V = \mathbf{x}_V\right)$$
$$q(\mathbf{x}_U|\mathbf{x}_V) \stackrel{\triangle}{=} \mathbb{P}\left(\mathbf{e}^{\text{unif}}_U = \mathbf{x}_U \mid \mathbf{e}^{\text{unif}}_V = \mathbf{x}_V\right)$$

We have,

$$\rho\left(\mathbf{e}; \mathbf{e}^{\text{unif}}\right) = \rho\left(\mathbf{e}_U, \mathbf{e}_V; \mathbf{e}^{\text{unif}}_U, \mathbf{e}^{\text{unif}}_V\right)$$
$$= \sum_{\mathbf{x}_V,\mathbf{x}_U} |p(\mathbf{x}_V)p(\mathbf{x}_U|\mathbf{x}_V) - q(\mathbf{x}_V)q(\mathbf{x}_U|\mathbf{x}_V)|$$
$$= \sum_{\mathbf{x}_V,\mathbf{x}_U} |(p(\mathbf{x}_V) - q(\mathbf{x}_V))p(\mathbf{x}_U|\mathbf{x}_V) + (p(\mathbf{x}_U|\mathbf{x}_V) - q(\mathbf{x}_U|\mathbf{x}_V))q(\mathbf{x}_V)|$$
$$\leq \sum_{\mathbf{x}_V,\mathbf{x}_U} |(p(\mathbf{x}_V) - q(\mathbf{x}_V))p(\mathbf{x}_U|\mathbf{x}_V)| + |(p(\mathbf{x}_U|\mathbf{x}_V) - q(\mathbf{x}_U|\mathbf{x}_V)q(\mathbf{x}_V)|$$
$$= \sum_{\mathbf{x}_V} |(p(\mathbf{x}_V) - q(\mathbf{x}_V))| + \sum_{\mathbf{x}_V,\mathbf{x}_U} |p(\mathbf{x}_U|\mathbf{x}_V) - q(\mathbf{x}_U|\mathbf{x}_V)| \, q(\mathbf{x}_V) \qquad (15)$$

where in the last line we used that $\sum_{\mathbf{x}_U} |p(\mathbf{x}_U|\mathbf{x}_V)| = 1$ for any $\mathbf{x}_V$. Thanks to Proposition 8:

$$\sum_{\mathbf{x}_V} |p(\mathbf{x}_V) - q(\mathbf{x}_V)| \leq \rho\left(J^{\mathbf{H}_V}; J^{\text{unif}}\right) \qquad (16)$$

as the internal distribution $\mathcal{D}_V$ of DECODEV($\cdot$) is independent of $J^{\mathbf{H}_V}$ and J^{unif}. Let us upper-bound the second term of the inequality. The distribution of $k_{\neq 0}$ is only function of the weight of the vector given as input to DECODEU($\cdot$) or VARDECODEU($\cdot$). Therefore,

$$\mathbb{P}\left(k_{\neq 0} = \ell \mid \mathbf{e}_V = \mathbf{x}_V\right) = \mathbb{P}\left(k_{\neq 0} = \ell \mid \mathbf{e}^{\text{unif}}_V = \mathbf{x}_V\right) \qquad (17)$$

From (17), using the notation $p(\mathbf{x}_U | \mathbf{x}_V, \ell) \triangleq \mathbb{P}(\mathbf{e}_U = \mathbf{x}_U \mid k_{\neq 0} = \ell, \mathbf{e}_V = \mathbf{x}_V)$ and $q(\mathbf{x}_U | \mathbf{x}_V, \ell) \triangleq \mathbb{P}(\mathbf{e}_U^{\mathrm{unif}} = \mathbf{x}_U \mid k_{\neq 0} = \ell, \mathbf{e}_V^{\mathrm{unif}} = \mathbf{x}_V)$, we obtain

$$p(\mathbf{x}_U | \mathbf{x}_V) - q(\mathbf{x}_U | \mathbf{x}_V) = \sum_{\ell} \left(p(\mathbf{x}_U | \mathbf{x}_V, \ell) - q(\mathbf{x}_U | \mathbf{x}_V, \ell) \right) \mathbb{P}\left(k_{\neq 0} = \ell \mid \mathbf{e}_V = \mathbf{x}_V \right)$$

(18)

The internal coins of $\mathrm{DECODEU}(\cdot)$ and $\mathrm{VARDECODEU}(\cdot)$ are independent of $I_{\mathbf{x}_V, \ell}^{\mathbf{H}_U}$ and $I_{\mathbf{x}_V, \ell}^{\mathrm{unif}}$ and by using Proposition 8 we have for any $\mathbf{x}_V$ and ℓ:

$$\sum_{x_U} |p(\mathbf{x}_U | \mathbf{x}_V, \ell) - q(\mathbf{x}_U | \mathbf{x}_V, \ell)| \leq \rho\left(I_{\mathbf{x}_V, \ell}^{\mathbf{H}_U}; I_{\mathbf{x}_V, \ell}^{\mathrm{unif}} \right)$$

(19)

Combining Equations (15), (16), (18) and (19) concludes the proof.   □

The expectations of $\rho\left(J^{\mathbf{H}_V}; J^{\mathrm{unif}} \right)$ and $\rho\left(I_{\mathbf{x}_V, \ell}^{\mathbf{H}_U}; I_{\mathbf{x}_V, \ell}^{\mathrm{unif}} \right)$ are upperbounded by

Lemma 2. *We have*

$$\rho\left(J^{\mathbf{H}_V}; J^{\mathrm{unif}} \right) = \frac{\#\{subsets\ of\ [\![1, n/2]\!]\ of\ size\ k - d\ bad\ for\ \mathbf{H}\}}{\binom{n/2}{k-d}}$$

(20)

$$\rho\left(I_{\mathbf{x}_V, \ell}^{\mathbf{H}_U}; I_{\mathbf{x}_V, \ell}^{\mathrm{unif}} \right) = \frac{N_{\mathbf{x}, \ell}}{\binom{|\mathbf{x}|}{\ell}\binom{n/2 - |\mathbf{x}|}{k - d - \ell}}$$

(21)

$$\mathbb{E}\left\{ \rho\left(J^{\mathbf{H}_V}; J^{\mathrm{unif}} \right) \right\} \leq \frac{3^{-d}}{2}$$

(22)

$$\mathbb{E}\left\{ \rho\left(I_{\mathbf{x}_V, \ell}^{\mathbf{H}_U}; I_{\mathbf{x}_V, \ell}^{\mathrm{unif}} \right) \right\} \leq \frac{3^{-d}}{2\binom{|\mathbf{x}|}{\ell}\binom{n/2 - |\mathbf{x}|}{k - d - \ell}},$$

(23)

where $N_{\mathbf{x}, \ell}$ is the number of subsets of $[\![1, n/2]\!]$ of size $k - d$ such that their intersection with $\mathrm{Supp}(\mathbf{x})$ is of size ℓ and that are bad for $\mathbf{H}$.

Proof. (20) and (21) follow from the fact that the statistical distance between the uniform distribution over $[\![1, s]\!]$ and the uniform distribution over $[\![1, t]\!]$ (with $t \geq s$) is equal to $\frac{t-s}{t}$. Let us index from 1 to $\binom{n/2}{k-d}$ the subsets of size $k-d$ of $[\![1, n/2]\!]$ and let X_i be the indicator of the event "the subset of index i is bad". We have $N = \sum_{i=1}^{\binom{n/2}{k-d}} X_i$. For integers $d < m$ we have (see [18, Lemma 6]) $\mathbb{P}(\mathrm{rank}\,\mathbf{M} < m - d) \leq \frac{1}{2 \cdot 3^d}$ when $\mathbf{M}$ is chosen uniformly at random in $\mathbb{F}_3^{(m-d) \times m}$. This implies $\mathbb{P}(X_i = 1) \leq \frac{1}{2 \cdot 3^d}$ and $\mathbb{E}\left\{ \rho\left(J^{\mathbf{H}_V}; J^{\mathrm{unif}} \right) \right\} = \mathbb{E}\left\{ \frac{N}{\binom{n/2}{k-d}} \right\} = \sum_{i=1}^{\binom{n/2}{k-d}} \frac{\mathbb{P}(X_i = 1)}{\binom{n/2}{k-d}} \leq \frac{1}{2 \cdot 3^d}$. This proves (22). (23) follows from similar arguments.   □

Proof (of Theorem 1). By using Markov's inequality we have, by Proposition 7 and Lemma 2

$$\mathbb{P}\left(\rho(\mathbf{e}, \mathbf{e}^{\mathrm{unif}}) > 3^{-d/2}\right) \leq 3^{d/2}\mathbb{E}\left\{\rho(\mathbf{e}, \mathbf{e}^{\mathrm{unif}})\right\}$$

$$\leq 3^{d/2}\mathbb{E}\left\{\rho\left(J^{\mathbf{H}_V}; J^{\mathrm{unif}}\right) + \sum_{\mathbf{x}_V,\ell} \rho\left(I^{\mathbf{H}_U}_{\mathbf{x}_V,\ell}; I^{\mathrm{unif}}_{\mathbf{x}_V,\ell}\right)\mathbb{P}\left(k_{\neq 0} = \ell \mid \mathbf{e}_V = \mathbf{x}_V\right)\right.$$

$$\left.\mathbb{P}\left(\mathbf{e}^{\mathrm{unif}}_V = \mathbf{x}_V\right)\right\} \leq 3^{d/2}\left\{\frac{3^{-d}}{2} + \sum_{\mathbf{x}_V,\ell} \frac{3^{-d}}{2\binom{|\mathbf{x}|}{\ell}\binom{n/2-|\mathbf{x}|}{k-d-\ell}}\right\} \leq 3^{-d/2}.$$

$\square$

6 Achieving Uniform Domain Sampling

$\mathbf{H}_{\mathrm{pk}}$ denotes the public parity-check matrix of a normalized generalized $(U, U + V)$-code as described in Sect. 3.2. The random structure of $\mathbf{H}_{\mathrm{pk}}$ makes the syndromes associated to $\mathbf{H}_{\mathrm{pk}}$ indistinguishable in a very strong sense from random syndromes as the following proposition shows. This achieves the Domain Sampling property of Definition 1. The following definition will be useful.

Definition 5 (number of V blocks of type I). *In a normalized generalized $(U, U + V)$ code of length n associated to $(\mathbf{a}, \mathbf{b}, \mathbf{c}, \mathbf{d})$, the number of V blocks of type I, which we denote by n_I, is defined as:* $n_I \triangleq |\{1 \leq i \leq n/2 : b_i d_i = 0\}|$.

Proposition 9. *Let $\mathcal{D}^{\mathbf{H}}_w$ be the distribution of $\mathbf{e}\mathbf{H}^{\mathsf{T}}$ when $\mathbf{e}$ is drawn uniformly at random among S_w and let $\mathcal{U}$ be the uniform distribution over $\mathbb{F}_3^{n-k}$. We have*

$$\mathbb{E}_{\mathbf{H}_{\mathrm{pk}}}\left(\rho(\mathcal{D}^{\mathbf{H}_{\mathrm{pk}}}_w, \mathcal{U})\right) \leq \frac{1}{2}\sqrt{\varepsilon} \quad \text{with,}$$

$$\varepsilon = \frac{3^{n-k}}{2^w\binom{n}{w}} + \sum_{j=0}^{\frac{n}{2}} \frac{3^{\frac{n}{2}-k_V}\binom{\frac{n}{2}}{j}\left(\sum\limits_{p=0:p\equiv w \pmod 2}^{j} \binom{j}{p}\binom{\frac{n}{2}-j}{\frac{w+p}{2}-j}2^{\frac{3p}{2}}\right)^2}{2^{w+j}\binom{n}{w}^2}$$

$$+ 3^{\frac{n}{2}-k_U}\left(\sum_{j=0}^{n_I} \frac{\binom{n_I}{j}\binom{n-n_I}{w-j}^2}{\binom{n}{w}^2 2^j}\right).$$

This bound decays exponentially in n in a certain regime of parameters:

Proposition 10. *Let $R_U \triangleq \frac{2k_U}{n}$, $R_V \triangleq \frac{2k_V}{n}$, $R \triangleq \frac{k}{n}$, $\omega \triangleq \frac{w}{n}$, $\nu \triangleq \frac{n_I}{n}$, then under the same assumptions as in Proposition 9, we have as n tends to infinity*

$$\mathbb{E}_{\mathbf{H}_{\mathrm{pk}}}\left(\rho(\mathcal{D}^{\mathbf{H}_{\mathrm{pk}}}_w, \mathcal{U})\right) \leq 2^{(\alpha+o(1))n}$$

where $\alpha \overset{\triangle}{=} \frac{1}{2}\min\left((1-R)\log_2(3) - w - h_2(w), \alpha_1, \alpha_2\right)$ and

$$\alpha_1 \overset{\triangle}{=} \min_{(x,y)\in\mathcal{R}} \frac{1}{2}(1-R_V)\log_2 3 - w - 2h_2(w) + \frac{h_2(x)}{2} + x\left(h_2(y) + \frac{3}{2}y - \frac{1}{2}\right)$$

$$+(1-x)h_2\left(\frac{w - x(1-y)}{1-x}\right)$$

$$\mathcal{R} \overset{\triangle}{=} \{(x,y) \in [0,1) \times [0,1] : 0 \le w - x(1-y) \le 1 - x\}$$

$$\alpha_2 \overset{\triangle}{=} \min_{\max(0,w+\nu-1)\le x\le\min(\nu,w)} \frac{1}{2}(1-R_U)\log_2 3 - 2h_2(w) + \nu h_2\left(\frac{x}{\nu}\right)$$

$$+2(1-\nu)h_2\left(\frac{w-x}{1-\nu}\right) - x.$$

Remark 4. For the set of parameters suggested in [18], we have $\varepsilon \approx 2^{-354}$ and $\alpha \approx -0.02135$. Note that the upper-bound of Proposition 9 is by no means sharp, this comes from the $3^{\frac{n}{2}-k_U}\left(\sum_{j=0}^{n_I} \frac{\binom{n_I}{j}\binom{n-n_I}{w-j}^2}{\binom{n}{w}^2 2^j}\right)$ term which is a very crude upper-bound which is given here to avoid more complicated terms. It is straightforward to come up with a much sharper bound by improving this part of the upper-bound.

The proof of this proposition relies among other things on a variation of the left-over hash lemma [5] that is adapted to our case: here the hash function to which we apply the left-over hash lemma is defined as $\mathcal{H}(\mathbf{e}) = \mathbf{e}\mathbf{H}_{\mathrm{pk}}^{\mathsf{T}}$. $\mathcal{H}$ does not form a universal family of hash functions (essentially because the distribution of the $\mathbf{H}_{\mathrm{pk}}$'s is not the uniform distribution over $\mathbb{F}_3^{(n-k)\times n}$).

Lemma 3. *Consider a finite family $\mathcal{H} = (h_i)_{i\in I}$ of functions from a finite set E to a finite set F. Denote by ε the bias of the collision probability, i.e. the quantity such that*

$$\mathbb{P}_{h,e,e'}(h(e) = h(e')) = \frac{1}{|F|}(1 + \varepsilon)$$

where h is drawn uniformly at random in $\mathcal{H}$, e and e' are drawn uniformly at random in E. Let $\mathcal{U}$ be the uniform distribution over F and $\mathcal{D}(h)$ be the distribution of the outputs $h(e)$ when e is chosen uniformly at random in E. We have

$$\mathbb{E}_h\left\{\rho(\mathcal{D}(h),\mathcal{U})\right\} \le \frac{1}{2}\sqrt{\varepsilon}.$$

To use this lemma we observe that

Lemma 4. *Assume that $\mathbf{x}$ and $\mathbf{y}$ are random vectors of S_w that are drawn uniformly at random in this set. We have*

$$\mathbb{P}_{\mathbf{H}_{\mathrm{pk}},\mathbf{x},\mathbf{y}}\left(\mathbf{x}\mathbf{H}_{\mathrm{pk}}^{\mathsf{T}} = \mathbf{y}\mathbf{H}_{\mathrm{pk}}^{\mathsf{T}}\right) \le \frac{1}{3^{n-k}}(1+\varepsilon) \quad \text{with } \varepsilon \text{ given in Proposition 9.}$$

Proof. By Proposition 3, the probability we want to compute for is given by $\mathbb{P}\left((\mathbf{x}_U - \mathbf{y}_U)\mathbf{H}_U^{\mathsf{T}} = \mathbf{0} \text{ and } (\mathbf{x}_V - \mathbf{y}_V)\mathbf{H}_V^{\mathsf{T}} = \mathbf{0}\right)$ where the probability is taken over $\mathbf{H}_U, \mathbf{H}_V, \mathbf{x}, \mathbf{y}$. To compute this, we use a standard result [18, Lemma 6] that gives

$$\mathbb{P}\left(\mathbf{y}\mathbf{H}^{\mathsf{T}} = \mathbf{s}\right) = \frac{1}{3^r}, \tag{24}$$

when $\mathbf{y}$ is a non-zero vector of $\mathbb{F}_3^n$, $\mathbf{s}$ an arbitrary element in $\mathbb{F}_3^r$ and when $\mathbf{H}$ is chosen uniformly at random in $\mathbb{F}_3^{r \times n}$. We distinguish between the events:

$$\mathcal{E}_1 \overset{\triangle}{=} \{\mathbf{x}_U = \mathbf{y}_U \text{ and } \mathbf{x}_V \neq \mathbf{y}_V\}; \quad \mathcal{E}_2 \overset{\triangle}{=} \{\mathbf{x}_U \neq \mathbf{y}_U \text{ and } \mathbf{x}_V = \mathbf{y}_V\}$$

$$\mathcal{E}_3 \overset{\triangle}{=} \{\mathbf{x}_U \neq \mathbf{y}_U \text{ and } \mathbf{x}_V \neq \mathbf{y}_V\}; \quad \mathcal{E}_4 \overset{\triangle}{=} \{\mathbf{x}_U = \mathbf{y}_U \text{ and } \mathbf{x}_V = \mathbf{y}_V\}$$

Under these events we get thanks to (24) and $k = k_U + k_V$:

$$\mathbb{P}_{\mathbf{H}_{\mathrm{sk}},\mathbf{x},\mathbf{y}}\left(\mathbf{x}\mathbf{H}_{\mathrm{sk}}^{\mathsf{T}} = \mathbf{y}\mathbf{H}_{\mathrm{sk}}^{\mathsf{T}}\right)$$

$$= \sum_{i=1}^{4} \mathbb{P}_{\mathbf{H}_{\mathrm{sk}}}\left(\mathbf{x}\mathbf{H}_{\mathrm{sk}}^{\mathsf{T}} = \mathbf{y}\mathbf{H}_{\mathrm{sk}}^{\mathsf{T}} | \mathcal{E}_i\right) \mathbb{P}_{\mathbf{x},\mathbf{y}}\left(\mathcal{E}_i\right)$$

$$= \frac{\mathbb{P}_{\mathbf{x},\mathbf{y}}\left(\mathcal{E}_1\right)}{3^{n/2 - k_V}} + \frac{\mathbb{P}_{\mathbf{x},\mathbf{y}}\left(\mathcal{E}_2\right)}{3^{n/2 - k_U}} + \frac{\mathbb{P}_{\mathbf{x},\mathbf{y}}\left(\mathcal{E}_3\right)}{3^{n-k}} + \mathbb{P}_{\mathbf{x},\mathbf{y}}\left(\mathcal{E}_4\right)$$

$$\leq \frac{1}{3^{n-k}}\left(1 + 3^{n/2 - k_U}\mathbb{P}\left(\mathcal{E}_1\right) + 3^{n/2 - k_V}\mathbb{P}\left(\mathcal{E}_2\right) + 3^{n-k}\mathbb{P}(\mathcal{E}_4)\right),$$

where we used for the last inequality the trivial upper-bound $\mathbb{P}\left(\mathcal{E}_3\right) \leq 1$. Let us now upper-bound (or compute) the probabilities of the events $\mathcal{E}_1, \mathcal{E}_2$ and $\mathcal{E}_4$. For $\mathcal{E}_4$, recall that from the definition of normalized generalized $(U, U+V)$-codes $\mathbb{P}_{\mathbf{x},\mathbf{y}}\left(\mathcal{E}_4\right) = \mathbb{P}(\mathbf{x} = \mathbf{y}) = \frac{1}{2^w\binom{n}{w}}$. For $\mathcal{E}_2$ we observe that $\mathbb{P}\left(\mathcal{E}_2\right) \leq \mathbb{P}\left(\mathbf{x}_V = \mathbf{y}_V\right)$. To upper-bound this probability, we first observe that for any error $\mathbf{e} \in S_{j,n/2}$

$$\mathbb{P}(\mathbf{x}_V = \mathbf{e}) = \mathbb{P}\left(\mathbf{x}_V = \mathbf{e} \mid |\mathbf{x}_V| = j\right) \mathbb{P}(|\mathbf{x}_V| = j) = \frac{1}{2^j\binom{n/2}{j}} q_1(j)$$

where $q_1^{\mathrm{unif}}(j)$ denotes $\mathbb{P}(|\mathbf{e}_V^{\mathrm{unif}}| = j)$ and is computed in Proposition 5. From this we deduce that

$$\mathbb{P}(\mathbf{x}_V = \mathbf{y}_V) = \sum_{j=0}^{n/2} \sum_{\mathbf{e} \in \mathbb{F}_3^{n/2}: |\mathbf{e}|=j} \mathbb{P}_{\mathbf{x}}(\mathbf{x}_V = \mathbf{e})^2 = \sum_{j=0}^{n/2} \frac{1}{2^j\binom{n/2}{j}} q_1^{\mathrm{unif}}(j)^2$$

which gives:

$$\mathbb{P}\left(\mathcal{E}_2\right) \leq \sum_{j=0}^{n/2} \frac{q_1^{\mathrm{unif}}(j)^2}{2^j\binom{n/2}{j}}.$$

The upper-bound on $\mathcal{E}_1$ is obtained in a similar way by using first that $\mathbb{P}(\mathcal{E}_1) \leq \mathbb{P}(\mathbf{x}_U \neq \mathbf{y}_U)$ and then the following bound

$$\mathbb{P}(\mathbf{x}_U \neq \mathbf{y}_U) \leq \sum_{j=0}^{n_I} \binom{n_I}{j} 2^{-j} \left(\frac{\binom{n-n_I}{w-j}}{\binom{n}{w}} \right)^2.$$

proven in [18, §C.2].   □

7   Concluding Remarks and Further Work

We have presented Wave the first code-based "hash-and-sign" signature scheme which follows the GPV strategy [28]. It allows to reduce the security of our scheme to only two assumptions from coding theory. Both of those assumptions relate closely to hard decoding problems. In the full paper [18], we provide a precise quantification of the security of the scheme and provide parameters for it. Note that the GPV strategy provides a very high level of security, but because of the multiple constraints it imposes, very few schemes managed to comply to it. For instance, only one such scheme based on hard lattice problems [24] was proposed to the recent NIST standardization effort. The main purpose of our work was to propose this new scheme and assess its security. Still, it has a few issues and extensions that are of interest.

The Far Away Decoding Problem. The message security of Wave relates to the hardness of finding a codeword *far* from a given word. A recent work [12] adapts the best ISD techniques for low weight [8,38] and goes even further with a higher order generalized birthday algorithm [47]. Interestingly enough, in the non-binary case, this work gives a worst case exponent for the far away codeword that is significantly larger than the close codeword worst case exponent. This suggest that one could design code-based primitives with better parameters by considering the far away codeword problem rather than the usual close codeword problem.

Distinguishability. Deciding whether a matrix is a parity check matrix of a generalized $(U, U+V)$-code is also a new problem. As shown in [17] it is hard in the worst case since the problem is NP-complete. In the binary case, $(U, U+V)$ codes have a large hull dimension for some set of parameters which are precisely those used in [17]. In the ternary case the normalized generalized $(U, U + V)$-codes do not suffer from this flaw. The freedom of the choice on vectors $\mathbf{a}, \mathbf{b}, \mathbf{c}$ and $\mathbf{d}$ is very likely to make the distinguishing problem much harder for generalized $(U, U + V)$-codes than for plain $(U, U + V)$-codes. Coming up with non-metric based distinguishers in the generalized case seems a tantalizing problem here.

On the Tightness of the Security Reduction. It could be argued that one of the reasons of why we have a tight security-reduction comes from the fact that we reduce to the multiple instances version of the decoding problem, namely DOOM, instead of the decoding problem itself. This is true to some extent, however this problem is as natural as the decoding problem itself. It has already been studied in some depth [44] and the decoding techniques for linear codes have a natural extension to DOOM as noticed in [44]. We also note that with our approach, where a message has many possible signatures, we avoid the tightness impossibility results given in [3] for instance.

Rejection Sampling. Rejection sampling in our algorithm is relatively unobtrusive: a rejection every few signatures with a crude tuning of the decoder. We believe that it can be further improved. Our decoding has two steps. Each step is parametrized by a weight distribution which conditions the output weight distribution. We believe that we can tune those distributions to reduce the probability of rejection to an arbitrarily small value and thus to avoid the rejection phase.

Improving Parameters. In order to predict accurately enough the output distribution of the signature algorithm, we had to restrict the decoders by excluding d positions from the information sets. Our result almost certainly applies when $d = 0$. By either proving it or stating it as a conjecture we may reduce the block size by more than 10%.

Instantiation. The scheme is instantiated in [18, §5,§8]. For 128 bits of security, a signature takes 13 kilobits and a public key 3 megabytes. The rejection rate is under 10%. An implementation is also available at http://wave.inria.fr.

Acknowledgements. We wish to thank the anonymous reviewers. In particular, our warmest gratitude goes to the last of them whose work went much beyond what can be found in a standard review. This includes the link clarifying our definition of "preimage sampleable on average" with the GPV definition [28] given in Sect. 3.1, a reorganization of the paper focusing on the main theoretical contribution, and simplifications and/or clarifications that all helped a great deal to improve this paper. We are also indebted to André Chailloux, Léo Ducas and Thomas Prest for their early interest, insightful suggestions, and unwavering support.

References

1. Alkim, E., et al.: Revisiting TESLA in the quantum random oracle model. In: Lange, T., Takagi, T. (eds.) PQCrypto 2017. LNCS, vol. 10346, pp. 143–162. Springer, Cham (2017). https://doi.org/10.1007/978-3-319-59879-6_9
2. Aragon, N., Blazy, O., Gaborit, P., Hauteville, A., Zémor, G.: Durandal: a rank metric based signature scheme. IACR Cryptology ePrint Archive (2018), Report 2018/1192, December 2018
3. Bader, C., Jager, T., Li, Y., Schäge, S.: On the impossibility of tight cryptographic reductions. In: Fischlin, M., Coron, J.-S. (eds.) EUROCRYPT 2016. LNCS, vol. 9666, pp. 273–304. Springer, Heidelberg (2016). https://doi.org/10.1007/978-3-662-49896-5_10
4. Baldi, M., Bianchi, M., Chiaraluce, F., Rosenthal, J., Schipani, D.: Using LDGM codes and sparse syndromes to achieve digital signatures. In: Gaborit, P. (ed.) PQCrypto 2013. LNCS, vol. 7932, pp. 1–15. Springer, Heidelberg (2013). https://doi.org/10.1007/978-3-642-38616-9_1

5. Barak, B., et al.: Leftover hash lemma, revisited. In: Rogaway, P. (ed.) CRYPTO 2011. LNCS, vol. 6841, pp. 1–20. Springer, Heidelberg (2011). https://doi.org/10.1007/978-3-642-22792-9_1

6. Barg, A.: Complexity issues in coding theory. Electronic Colloquium on Computational Complexity, October 1997. https://eccc.weizmann.ac.il/eccc-reports/1997/TR97-046/Paper.pdf

7. Barreto, P.S., Misoczki, R., Simplicio, M.A.J.: One-time signature scheme from syndrome decoding over generic error-correcting codes. J. Syst. Softw. **84**(2), 198–204 (2011)

8. Becker, A., Joux, A., May, A., Meurer, A.: Decoding random binary linear codes in $2^{n/20}$: How $1 + 1 = 0$ improves information set decoding. In: Pointcheval, D., Johansson, T. (eds.) EUROCRYPT 2012. LNCS, vol. 7237, pp. 520–536. Springer, Heidelberg (2012). https://doi.org/10.1007/978-3-642-29011-4_31

9. Bellare, M., Rogaway, P.: The exact security of digital signatures-how to sign with RSA and Rabin. In: Maurer, U. (ed.) EUROCRYPT 1996. LNCS, vol. 1070, pp. 399–416. Springer, Heidelberg (1996). https://doi.org/10.1007/3-540-68339-9_34

10. Bernstein, D.J., Chou, T., Schwabe, P.: McBits: fast constant-time code-based cryptography. In: Bertoni, G., Coron, J.-S. (eds.) CHES 2013. LNCS, vol. 8086, pp. 250–272. Springer, Heidelberg (2013). https://doi.org/10.1007/978-3-642-40349-1_15

11. Both, L., May, A.: Decoding linear codes with high error rate and its impact for LPN security. In: Lange, T., Steinwandt, R. (eds.) PQCrypto 2018. LNCS, vol. 10786, pp. 25–46. Springer, Cham (2018). https://doi.org/10.1007/978-3-319-79063-3_2

12. Bricout, R., Chailloux, A., Debris-Alazard, T., Lequesne, M.: Ternary syndrome decoding with large weights. preprint, arXiv:1903.07464, February 2019. To appear in the proceedings of SAC 2019

13. Cayrel, P.-L., Otmani, A., Vergnaud, D.: On Kabatianskii-Krouk-Smeets signatures. In: Carlet, C., Sunar, B. (eds.) WAIFI 2007. LNCS, vol. 4547, pp. 237–251. Springer, Heidelberg (2007). https://doi.org/10.1007/978-3-540-73074-3_18

14. Coron, J.-S.: Optimal security proofs for PSS and other signature schemes. In: Knudsen, L.R. (ed.) EUROCRYPT 2002. LNCS, vol. 2332, pp. 272–287. Springer, Heidelberg (2002). https://doi.org/10.1007/3-540-46035-7_18

15. Courtois, N.T., Finiasz, M., Sendrier, N.: How to achieve a McEliece-based digital signature scheme. In: Boyd, C. (ed.) ASIACRYPT 2001. LNCS, vol. 2248, pp. 157–174. Springer, Heidelberg (2001). https://doi.org/10.1007/3-540-45682-1_10

16. Debris-Alazard, T., Sendrier, N., Tillich, J.P.: A new signature scheme based on $(U|U + V)$ codes. preprint, arXiv:1706.08065v1, June 2017

17. Debris-Alazard, T., Sendrier, N., Tillich, J.P.: The problem with the surf scheme. preprint, arXiv:1706.08065, November 2017

18. Debris-Alazard, T., Sendrier, N., Tillich, J.P.: Wave: A new family of trapdoor one-way preimage sampleable functions based on codes. Cryptology ePrint Archive, Report 2018/996, May 2019. Full version of the current paper. All statement and section numbers quoted in this paper refer specifically to the May 2019 version

19. Debris-Alazard, T., Tillich, J.P.: Statistical decoding. preprint, arXiv:1701.07416, January 2017

20. Debris-Alazard, T., Tillich, J.-P.: Two attacks on rank metric code-based schemes: ranksign and an IBE scheme. In: Peyrin, T., Galbraith, S. (eds.) ASIACRYPT 2018. LNCS, vol. 11272, pp. 62–92. Springer, Cham (2018). https://doi.org/10.1007/978-3-030-03326-2_3

21. Dumer, I.: On minimum distance decoding of linear codes. In: Proceedings of 5th Joint Soviet-Swedish International Workshop Information Theory, pp. 50–52. Moscow (1991)
22. Faugère, J.C., Gauthier, V., Otmani, A., Perret, L., Tillich, J.P.: A distinguisher for high rate McEliece cryptosystems. In: Proceedings of IEEE Information Theory Workshop- ITW 2011, pp. 282–286. Paraty, Brasil, October 2011
23. Finiasz, M.: Parallel-CFS- strengthening the CFS McEliece-based signature scheme. In: Biryukov, A., Gong, G., Stinson, D.R. (eds.) SAC 2010. LNCS, vol. 6544, pp. 159–170. Springer, Heidelberg (2011). https://doi.org/10.1007/978-3-642-19574-7_11
24. Fouque, P.A., et al.: Falcon: fast-fourier lattice-based compact signatures over NTRU
25. Fukushima, K., Roy, P.S., Xu, R., Kiyomoto, S., Morozov, K., Takagi, T.: RaCoSS (random code-based signature scheme). first round submission to the NIST postquantum cryptography call, November 2017
26. Gaborit, P., Ruatta, O., Schrek, J., Zémor, G.: New results for rank-based cryptography. In: Pointcheval, D., Vergnaud, D. (eds.) AFRICACRYPT 2014. LNCS, vol. 8469, pp. 1–12. Springer, Cham (2014). https://doi.org/10.1007/978-3-319-06734-6_1
27. Gaborit, P., Schrek, J.: Efficient code-based one-time signature from automorphism groups with syndrome compatibility. In: Proceedings IEEE International Symposium Information Theory - ISIT 2012, pp. 1982–1986. Cambridge, MA, USA, July 2012
28. Gentry, C., Peikert, C., Vaikuntanathan, V.: Trapdoors for hard lattices and new cryptographic constructions. In: Proceedings of the Fortieth Annual ACM Symposium on Theory of Computing, pp. 197–206. ACM (2008)
29. Gligoroski, D., Samardjiska, S., Jacobsen, H., Bezzateev, S.: McEliece in the world of Escher. IACR Cryptology ePrint Archive, Report 2014/360 (2014)
30. Goldwasser, S., Micciancio, D.: Complexity of lattice problems: a cryptographic perspective. In: Kluwer International Series in Engineering and Computer Science, vol. 671. Kluwer Academic Publishers, Dordrecht, March 2002
31. Huelsing, A., Bernstein, D.J., Panny, L., Lange, T.: Official NIST comments made for RaCoSS, official NIST comments made for RaCoSS (2018)
32. Johansson, T., Jönsson, F.: On the complexity of some cryptographic problems based on the general decoding problem. IEEE Trans. Inform. Theory $48(10)$, 2669–2678 (2002)
33. Kabatianskii, G., Krouk, E., Semenov, S.: Error Correcting Coding and Security for Data Networks: Analysis of the Superchannel Concept. Wiley, Hoboken (2005)
34. Kabatianskii, G., Krouk, E., Smeets, B.: A digital signature scheme based on random error-correcting codes. In: Darnell, M. (ed.) Cryptography and Coding 1997. LNCS, vol. 1355, pp. 161–167. Springer, Heidelberg (1997). https://doi.org/10.1007/BFb0024461
35. Landais, G., Sendrier, N.: Implementing CFS. In: Galbraith, S., Nandi, M. (eds.) INDOCRYPT 2012. LNCS, vol. 7668, pp. 474–488. Springer, Heidelberg (2012). https://doi.org/10.1007/978-3-642-34931-7_27
36. Lee, W., Kim, Y.S., Lee, Y.W., No, J.S.: Post quantum signature scheme based on modified Reed-Muller code pqsigRM. first round submission to the NIST postquantum cryptography call, November 2017
37. Lyubashevsky, V.: Fiat-shamir with aborts: applications to lattice and factoring-based signatures. In: Matsui, M. (ed.) ASIACRYPT 2009. LNCS, vol. 5912, pp.

598–616. Springer, Heidelberg (2009). https://doi.org/10.1007/978-3-642-10366-7_35

38. May, A., Meurer, A., Thomae, E.: Decoding random linear codes in $\tilde{\mathcal{O}}(2^{0.054n})$. In: Lee, D.H., Wang, X. (eds.) ASIACRYPT 2011. LNCS, vol. 7073, pp. 107–124. Springer, Heidelberg (2011). https://doi.org/10.1007/978-3-642-25385-0_6

39. May, A., Ozerov, I.: On computing nearest neighbors with applications to decoding of binary linear codes. In: Oswald, E., Fischlin, M. (eds.) EUROCRYPT 2015. LNCS, vol. 9056, pp. 203–228. Springer, Heidelberg (2015). https://doi.org/10.1007/978-3-662-46800-5_9

40. Moody, D., Perlner, R.: Vulnerabilities of McEliece in the world of Escher. In: Takagi, T. (ed.) PQCrypto 2016. LNCS, vol. 9606, pp. 104–117. Springer, Cham (2016). https://doi.org/10.1007/978-3-319-29360-8_8

41. Otmani, A., Tillich, J.-P.: An efficient attack on all concrete KKS proposals. In: Yang, B.-Y. (ed.) PQCrypto 2011. LNCS, vol. 7071, pp. 98–116. Springer, Heidelberg (2011). https://doi.org/10.1007/978-3-642-25405-5_7

42. Phesso, A., Tillich, J.-P.: An efficient attack on a code-based signature scheme. In: Takagi, T. (ed.) PQCrypto 2016. LNCS, vol. 9606, pp. 86–103. Springer, Cham (2016). https://doi.org/10.1007/978-3-319-29360-8_7

43. Prange, E.: The use of information sets in decoding cyclic codes. IRE Trans. Inf. Theory $\mathbf{8}$(5), 5–9 (1962)

44. Sendrier, N.: Decoding one out of many. In: Yang, B.-Y. (ed.) PQCrypto 2011. LNCS, vol. 7071, pp. 51–67. Springer, Heidelberg (2011). https://doi.org/10.1007/978-3-642-25405-5_4

45. Stern, J.: A method for finding codewords of small weight. In: Cohen, G., Wolfmann, J. (eds.) Coding Theory 1988. LNCS, vol. 388, pp. 106–113. Springer, Heidelberg (1989). https://doi.org/10.1007/BFb0019850

46. Stern, J.: A new identification scheme based on syndrome decoding. In: Stinson, D.R. (ed.) CRYPTO 1993. LNCS, vol. 773, pp. 13–21. Springer, Heidelberg (1994). https://doi.org/10.1007/3-540-48329-2_2

47. Wagner, D.: A generalized birthday problem. In: Yung, M. (ed.) CRYPTO 2002. LNCS, vol. 2442, pp. 288–304. Springer, Heidelberg (2002). https://doi.org/10.1007/3-540-45708-9_19

Lattices (1)

Middle-Product Learning with Rounding Problem and Its Applications

Shi Bai[1]([⊠]), Katharina Boudgoust[2]([⊠]), Dipayan Das[3]([⊠]),
Adeline Roux-Langlois[2]([⊠]), Weiqiang Wen[2]([⊠]), and Zhenfei Zhang[4]([⊠])

[1] Department of Mathematical Sciences, Florida Atlantic University,
Boca Raton, USA
shih.bai@gmail.com
[2] Univ Rennes, CNRS, IRISA, Rennes, France
[3] Department of Mathematics, National Institute of Technology, Durgapur, India
[4] Algorand, Boston, USA

Abstract. At CRYPTO 2017, Roşca et al. introduce a new variant of
the *Learning With Errors* (LWE) problem, called the *Middle-Product*
LWE (MP-LWE). The hardness of this new assumption is based on the
hardness of the *Polynomial* LWE (P-LWE) problem parameterized by a
set of polynomials, making it more secure against the possible weakness
of a *single* defining polynomial. As a cryptographic application, they also
provide an encryption scheme based on the MP-LWE problem. In this
paper, we propose a deterministic variant of their encryption scheme,
which does not need Gaussian sampling and is thus simpler than the
original one. Still, it has the same quasi-optimal asymptotic key and
ciphertext sizes. The main ingredient for this purpose is the *Learning
With Rounding* (LWR) problem which has already been used to deran-
domize LWE type encryption. The hardness of our scheme is based on
a new assumption called *Middle-Product Computational Learning With
Rounding*, an adaption of the computational LWR problem over rings,
introduced by Chen et al. at ASIACRYPT 2018. We prove that this new
assumption is as hard as the decisional version of MP-LWE and thus
benefits from worst-case to average-case hardness guarantees.

Keywords: LWE · LWR · Middle-Product · Public key encryption

1 Introduction

Lattice-based cryptosystems attracted considerable research interest in recent
years due to their versatility, assumed quantum-resilience and efficiency. The
Learning With Errors problem, introduced by Regev [Reg05] in his pioneering
work, serves as a fundamental computational problem in lattice-based cryptography. Informally, the LWE problem asks for the solution of a system of noisy
linear modular equations: Given positive integers n and q, an LWE sample con-
sists of $(\mathbf{a}, b = \langle \mathbf{a}, \mathbf{s} \rangle + e \bmod q)$ for a fixed vector $\mathbf{s} \in \mathbb{Z}^n$, where $\mathbf{a}$ is sampled

© International Association for Cryptologic Research 2019
S. D. Galbraith and S. Moriai (Eds.): ASIACRYPT 2019, LNCS 11921, pp. 55–81, 2019.
https://doi.org/10.1007/978-3-030-34578-5_3

from the uniform distribution over $\mathbb{Z}_q^n$ and e is sampled from a probability distribution χ over $\mathbb{R}$. The LWE problem exists in two versions: The *search* version asks to recover the secret $\mathbf{s}$ given arbitrarily many LWE samples; The *decision* version asks to distinguish between LWE samples and samples drawn from the uniform distribution over $\mathbb{Z}_q^n \times \mathbb{R}$.

As an very attractive property for cryptography, LWE enjoys worst-case to average-case reductions [Reg05, Reg09, Pei09, BLP+13] from well-studied problems such as finding a set of short independent vectors (SIVP) or the decisional variant of finding short vectors (GapSVP) in Euclidean lattices. A standard conjecture is to assume that there is no polynomial-time algorithm that solves these problems (and their mildly approximated versions), even on quantum computers. Thus, any solver of the average-case problems can be transformed into a solver for any instance of the worst-case problem, which is presumed to be difficult.

The protocols relying on the hardness of LWE are inherently inefficient due to the size of the public keys which usually contain m elements of $\mathbb{Z}_q^n$, where m is the number of samples which is usually larger than $n \log(n)$. To improve the efficiency, structured variants of LWE have been proposed [SSTX09, LPR10, LS15]. One promising variant is the *Polynomial Learning With Errors* (P-LWE) problem, introduced by Stehlé et al. [SSTX09]. Given a monic irreducible polynomial $f \in \mathbb{Z}[x]$ and an integer $q \geq 2$, a P-LWE sample is given by $(a, b = a \cdot s + e \bmod q)$ for a fixed polynomial $s \in \mathbb{Z}_q[x]/f$, where a is sampled from the uniform distribution over $\mathbb{Z}_q[x]/f$ and e is sampled from a probability distribution χ over $\mathbb{R}[x]/f$. The P-LWE problem also admits worst-case to average-case connections from well-studied lattice problems. Whereas the hardness reductions for LWE start from the lattice problem in the class of general Euclidean lattices, the class has to be restricted to *ideal lattices* in the case of P-LWE. These ideal lattices correspond to the ideals in the polynomial ring $\mathbb{Z}[x]/f$. Lyubashevsky et al. [LPR10] propose another promising variant, namely the *Ring Learning With Errors* (R-LWE) problem, where polynomial rings are replaced by the ring of integers of some number fields. In the case of cyclotomic fields, the P-LWE and R-LWE problems coincide up to some parameter losses. As a recent result, Roşca et al. [RSW18] show that P-LWE and R-LWE are equivalent for a larger class of polynomials. In addition, they also investigate other relations between these structured variants.

Hedging Against Possible Weak Instances. Gaining in efficiency on the positive side comes with a potential decrease in the security level guarantees on the negative side. There are concrete examples of polynomials f on which the P-LWE becomes computationally easy: for instance when f has a linear factor over $\mathbb{Z}$ [CIV16]. Note that this case is excluded by restricting to irreducible polynomials. A review on the known weak instances of P-LWE and R-LWE is given by Peikert [Pei16]. To the best of our knowledge, it is still not fully understood how to choose a *good* polynomial for instantiating P-LWE.

Motivated by the question of how to choose a good polynomial, Lyubashevsky introduces the so-called $R^{<n}$-SIS problem [Lyu16], a variant of the *Short Integer Solution* (SIS) problem, whose hardness does not depend only on a *single*

polynomial, but on a set of polynomials. Inspired by this, Roşca et al. [RSSS17] propose its LWE counterpart: the *Middle-Product Learning With Errors* (MP-LWE) problem. The MP-LWE problem is defined as follows: Taking two polynomials a and s over $\mathbb{Z}_q$ of degrees less than n and $n+d-1$, respectively, the middle-product $a \odot_d s$ is the polynomial of degree less than d given by the middle d coefficients of $a \cdot s$. In other words, $a \odot_d s = \lfloor (a \cdot s \bmod x^{n+d-1})/x^{n-1} \rfloor$, where the floor rounding $\lfloor \cdot \rfloor$ denotes deleting all those terms with negative exponents on x. Instead of choosing a and s from the ring $\mathbb{Z}_q[x]/f$ as in the P-LWE setting, they are now elements of $\mathbb{Z}_q^{<n}[x]$ and $\mathbb{Z}_q^{<n+d-1}[x]$. Here, $\mathbb{Z}_q^{<n}[x]$ denotes the set of all polynomials with coefficients in $\mathbb{Z}_q$ of degree less than n for $n \geq 1$. For integers d, n and q with $q \geq 2$ and $0 < d \leq n$ as parameters, an MP-LWE sample is given by $(a, b = a \odot_d s + e \bmod q)$, where s is a fixed element of $\mathbb{Z}_q^{<n+d-1}[x]$, a is sampled from the uniform distribution over $\mathbb{Z}_q^{<n}[x]$ and e is sampled from a probability distribution χ over $\mathbb{R}^{<d}[x]$. As for the hardness of MP-LWE, Roşca et al. [RSSS17] establish a reduction from the P-LWE problem parametrized by a polynomial f to the MP-LWE problem defined independently of any such f. Thus, as long as the P-LWE problem defined over some f (belonging to a huge family of polynomials) is hard, the MP-LWE problem is also guaranteed to be hard. As a cryptographic application, Roşca et al. [RSSS17] propose a public-key encryption (PKE) scheme that is IND-CPA secure under the MP-LWE hardness assumption, with keys of size $\tilde{O}(\lambda)$ and running time $\tilde{O}(\lambda)$, where λ is the security parameter.

Learning With Rounding (LWR). In the worst-to-average case reduction of LWE [Reg05] and P-LWE [SSTX09] the error e is sampled from discrete Gaussian distributions. Such sampling procedure is in general costly, difficult to implement and vulnerable to side-channel attacks, e.g. [DB15, BHLY16, Pes16, Saa18]. In 2012, Banerjee et al. [BPR12] introduce a deterministic variant of LWE, namely the *Learning With Rounding* (LWR) problem. It is used to construct efficient pseudorandom functions [BPR12], lossy trapdoor functions and deterministic encryption schemes [AKPW13].

An LWR sample is given by $(\mathbf{a}, b = \lfloor \langle \mathbf{a}, \mathbf{s} \rangle \rceil_p)$, where $\mathbf{s} \in \mathbb{Z}_q^n$ is fixed and $\mathbf{a}$ is sampled from the uniform distribution over $\mathbb{Z}_q^n$. The rounding operator $\lfloor x \rceil_p$ denotes multiplying x by p/q and then rounding the result to the nearest integer modulo p. Informally, this rounding operator corresponds to dividing the set of elements of $\mathbb{Z}_q$ into p chunks, each containing approximately q/p elements. The definition can be adapted to a ring setting, denoted by R-LWR.

In the full version of their paper, published on the IACR Cryptology ePrint Archive, Banerjee et al. [BPR11] show a reduction from LWE to LWR with arbitrarily many samples, which also works for the ring counterpart. Unfortunately, the reduction requires q/p to be larger than the error size B (where B bounds the magnitude of the LWE error with high probability) by a super-polynomial factor, thus leading to a large modulus paired with a small error bound. This in turn implies that the underlying worst-case lattice-problems are assumed to be hard with super-polynomial approximation factors, which stands for a stronger assumption. In practice, this also leads to inefficient protocols.

Subsequent studies propose new reductions that work for a larger range of parameters. Alwen et al. [AKPW13] give a reduction that allows a polynomial modulus and modulus-to-error ratio. However, the modulus q in the reduction depends on the number of LWR samples, thus the number of samples needs to be fixed in prior by some polynomials. Further, the reduction imposes certain number theoretical restrictions on the modulus q. For example, power-of-two moduli are not covered. In a recent work, Bogdanov et al. [BGM+16] use the Rényi divergence to show a sample preserving reduction. The reduction is also dimension preserving for the special case that the modulus is prime. They also provide a reduction from the search variant of R-LWE to the search variant of R-LWR. In another work, Alperin-Sheriff and Apon [AA16] further improve the parameter sets for the reduction. In particular, the reduction is dimension-preserving with a polynomial-sized modulus. However, the ring setting analogue, a reduction from decisional R-LWE to decisional R-LWR with a polynomial-sized modulus, is still an open problem. Nevertheless, due to the simplicity and efficiency of R-LWR, several schemes as SABER [DKRV18] and Round5 [BBF+19] basing their hardness on R-LWR are currently participating in the NIST standardization process [NIS].

To overcome the lack of provable hardness for decisional R-LWR with practical parameters, Chen et al. [CZZ18] propose a new assumption, called the *Computational Learning With Rounding Over Rings* (R-CLWR) assumption. They show a reduction from decisional R-LWE to R-CLWR, where the secret in the R-LWE sample is drawn uniformly at random from the set of all invertible ring elements whose coefficients are small. They also show that one can construct an efficient PKE scheme based on the hardness of R-CLWR in the random oracle model.

Our Contributions. Our first main contribution is a new hardness assumption which we refer to as the *Middle Product Computational Learning With Rounding* (MP-CLWR) problem. On the one hand, the MP-CLWR problem uses rounding in a similar way to R-LWR and hence avoids the error sampling. On the other hand, the MP-CLWR problem is analogue to the MP-LWE problem whose hardness does not depend on a specific polynomial. Thus, the MP-CLWR assumption enjoys the desired properties from both, the security advantage of MP-LWE and the simplicity advantage of LWR. We show that the MP-CLWR problem is at least as hard as the decisional MP-LWE problem parametrized over a set of polynomials (Sect. 4). To complete the reduction, we also bring in some new results on random Hankel matrices which might be of independent interest (Sect. 3). As a typical application, we propose a PKE scheme based on this MP-CLWR assumption which is IND-CPA secure in the random oracle model (Sect. 5). The attractiveness of our encryption scheme stems from the fact that we only have to round the middle-product of two polynomials instead of sampling Gaussian error during public key generation while guaranteeing the same security and having the same asymptotic key and ciphertext sizes as [RSSS17] (Sect. 6). Furthermore, we provide at the end of Sect. 6 a study of the concrete security of our scheme by looking at the currently best known attacks against it.

In the following, we give a brief overview of the MP-CLWR problem and our proof for its hardness. An MP-CLWR sample is given by $(a, b = \lfloor a \odot_d s \rceil_p)$, where a is sampled from the uniform distribution over $\mathbb{Z}_q^{<n}[x]$ and s is a fixed element in $\mathbb{Z}_q^{<n+d-1}[x]$. We define the MP-CLWR problem as the following game, where we embed the MP-CLWR samples into two experiments. In both experiments, three different parties appear: A challenger $\mathcal{C}$, an adversary $\mathcal{A}$ and a source $\mathcal{S}$. The source $\mathcal{S}_1$ of the first experiment provides t different MP-CLWR samples $(a_i, \lfloor a_i \odot_d s \rceil_p)_{i \in [t]}$ and the source $\mathcal{S}_2$ of the second experiment provides t rounded uniform samples $(a_i, \lfloor b_i \rceil_p)_{i \in [t]}$, where all a_i and b_i are independently sampled from the corresponding uniform distribution. The challenger $\mathcal{C}$ now uses these samples to compute an Input and a Target. It sends the Input to the adversary $\mathcal{A}$ which itself computes an Output. The adversary wins the experiment if Target = Output. The important point in this setting is that the challenger $\mathcal{C}$ and the adversary $\mathcal{A}$ are in both experiments the same. The MP-CLWR assumption captures that an adversary has no more advantage to compute the correct output if it receives rounded middle-product samples than if it gets rounded uniform samples. A formal definition of MP-CLWR is given in Sect. 4.1.

Our reduction from MP-LWE to MP-CLWR, shown in Theorem 2, is dimension-preserving and works for polynomial-sized modulus q. In more details, let d, n, p, q and t be positive integers with $0 < d \leq n$ and $q \geq p \geq 2$. The parameters d and n describe the order of the middle-product, t denotes the number of samples and p defines the rounding. Let χ be an error distribution over $\mathbb{R}^{<d}[x]$. We show the following sequence of reductions:

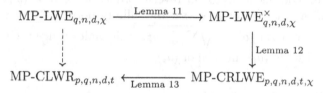

The first part of this sequence, Lemma 11, gives a reduction from decisional MP-LWE to decisional MP-LWE$^\times$, where the latter one denotes the MP-LWE problem where the secret is sampled uniformly at random from the set of elements having full rank Hankel matrix. The Hankel matrix plays an important role during the reductions as one can use it to represent the middle-product. In Sect. 3 we prove new results on random Hankel matrices, which might be of independent interest. We give a lower bound of the probability that the Hankel matrix of a random element has full rank and prove a uniformity property of the middle-product. This property is used in Lemma 13, where we show a reduction from the rounded middle-product LWE problem to the middle-product LWR problem, for their computational versions. Note that using the Rényi divergence asks for fixing the requested number of samples t a priori. This is a necessary requirement which is also imposed in [BPR12, BGM+16, CZZ18].

Similarly to the encryption scheme of Chen et al. [CZZ18], we make use of the reconciliation mechanism of Peikert [Pei14]. In order to show the correctness of our scheme, we have to guarantee that the reconciliation method succeeds.

We also use a probabilistic lifting function to lift elements from $\mathbb{Z}_p[x]$ to elements in $\mathbb{Z}_q[x]$. To prove the IND-CPA security of our scheme, we use the general leftover hash lemma from [RSSS17]. We show that a lifted version of their family of hash functions is still universal (Lemma 8).

Open Problems. As mentioned above, a reduction from decisional R-LWE to decisional R-LWR with a polynomial-sized modulus is still an open problem. This carries over to the middle-product setting, where it would also be of interest to show a reduction from decisional MP-LWE to decisional MP-LWR. Such a hardness result would help to build a secure encryption scheme based on the decisional MP-LWR in the standard model. A search-to-decision reduction for R-LWR or MP-LWR would be an alternative way to promise the security of such protocols.

2   Preliminaries

Let q be a positive integer, then $\mathbb{Z}_q$ denotes the ring of integers modulo q. For any natural number n, we represent the set $\{1, \ldots, n\}$ by $[n]$. In order to ease readability, a vector $\mathbf{a}$ will be denoted in a bold small letter and a matrix $\mathbf{A}$ in a bold capital letter. By $\mathbf{a}^t$ and $\mathbf{A}^t$ we denote the transpose of the vector $\mathbf{a}$ and the matrix $\mathbf{A}$, respectively. For a positive integer n, we write $\mathbb{Z}^{<n}[x]$ to describe the set of all polynomials in $\mathbb{Z}[x]$ with degree less than n. We identify each polynomial a in $\mathbb{Z}^{<n}[x]$ with its coefficient column vector $\mathbf{a} = (a_0, \ldots, a_{n-1})^t$. Further, we denote by $\overline{\mathbf{a}}$ its coefficient vector in reverse order, hence $\overline{\mathbf{a}} = (a_{n-1}, \ldots, a_0)^t$. For any n-dimensional vector $\mathbf{a}$, we set the infinity norm $\|\mathbf{a}\|_\infty = \max_{i \in [n]} |a_i|$ and the Euclidean norm $\|\mathbf{a}\|_2 = \sqrt{\sum_{i \in [n]} a_i^2}$. If the index range is clear from the context, we will write $(a_i)_i$ instead of $(a_i)_{i \in [n]}$.

2.1   Rounding

Let p and q be integers both larger than 1. We define the *modular rounding function* $\lfloor \cdot \rceil_p : \mathbb{Z}_q \to \mathbb{Z}_p$ as $\lfloor x \rceil_p = \left\lfloor \left(\frac{p}{q}\right) \cdot x \right\rceil \bmod p$. The rounding function extends component-wise to vectors over $\mathbb{Z}_q$ and coefficient-wise to polynomials in $\mathbb{Z}_q[x]$. Note that we use the same notation as Banerjee et al. [BPR12] for the purpose of coherence. It is also possible to use the floor rounding function $\lfloor \cdot \rfloor$, where each element is rounded down to the next smaller integer, as for instance done by Chen et al. [CZZ18].

2.2   Reconciliation

Reconciliation is a method used by two parties to agree on a secret bit, where they only share a common value up to an approximation factor. A first reconciliation mechanism was presented by Ding et al. [DXL12] followed by other proposals (e.g., [Pei14, ADPS16]). We use the notation of Peikert and exert the nearest integer rounding. For this purpose, we need the rounding function $\lfloor \cdot \rceil_2 : \mathbb{Z}_q \to \mathbb{Z}_2$ for $p = 2$ and define the *reconciliation cross-rounding function* $\langle \cdot \rangle_2 : \mathbb{Z}_q \to \mathbb{Z}_2$ as

$$\langle x \rangle_2 = \left\lfloor \left(\frac{4}{q} \right) \cdot x \right\rceil \bmod 2.$$

For q even, the reconciliation algorithm REC takes as input two values $y \in \mathbb{Z}_q$ and $b \in \{0,1\}$ and outputs $\lfloor x \rceil_2$, where x is the closest element to y such that $\langle x \rangle_2 = b$. A concrete definition of REC is given as follows. Define two disjoint intervals $I_0 = \{0, \ldots, \lfloor \frac{q}{4} \rfloor - 1\}$ and $I_1 = \{-\lfloor \frac{q}{4} \rfloor, \ldots, -1\}$. Let E be the set given by $[-\frac{q}{8}, \frac{q}{8}) \cap \mathbb{Z}$. Further, let y be an element of $\mathbb{Z}_q$ and b be a bit. Then,

$$\mathtt{REC}(y, b) = \begin{cases} 0, & y \in I_b + E \bmod q, \\ 1, & \text{else.} \end{cases}$$

We recall the following results about the cross-rounding function and the reconciliation mechanism from Peikert [Pei14].

Lemma 1. *For q even, if $x \in \mathbb{Z}_q$ is uniformly random, then is $\lfloor x \rceil_2$ uniformly random given $\langle x \rangle_2$.*

Lemma 2. *For q even and $x, y \in \mathbb{Z}_q$ such that $|x - y| < \frac{q}{8}$, then*

$$\mathtt{REC}(y, \langle x \rangle_2) = \lfloor x \rceil_2 .$$

In the case of q odd, thus $2 \nmid q$, the output bit of the reconciliation method is biased. That is why Peikert [Pei14] introduced a randomized doubling function

$$\mathtt{DBL} : \mathbb{Z}_q \to \mathbb{Z}_{2q}, \quad \mathtt{DBL}(x) = 2x - e,$$

where $e \leftarrow \{-1, 0, 1\}$ with probabilities $p_{-1} = p_1 = \frac{1}{4}$ and $p_0 = \frac{1}{2}$.

Lemma 3. *For q odd, if $x \in \mathbb{Z}_q$ is uniformly random, $\bar{x} \leftarrow \mathtt{DBL}(x)$, then is $\lfloor \bar{x} \rceil_2$ uniformly random given $\langle \bar{x} \rangle_2$.*

Lemma 4. *For q odd and $x, y \in \mathbb{Z}_q$ such that $|x - y| < \frac{q}{8}$, let $\bar{x} \leftarrow \mathtt{DBL}(x)$, then*

$$\mathtt{REC}(y, \langle \bar{x} \rangle_2) = \lfloor \bar{x} \rceil_2 .$$

We extend all functions $\langle \cdot \rangle_2$, $\lfloor \cdot \rceil_2$ and $\mathtt{DBL}(\cdot)$ component-wise to vectors over $\mathbb{Z}_q$ and coefficient-wise to polynomials in $\mathbb{Z}_q[x]$, as well as the mechanism REC to vectors over $\mathbb{Z}_q \times \{0,1\}$ and to polynomials in $\mathbb{Z}_q[x] \times \{0,1\}[x]$.

Let p and q be integers such that $2 \leq p \leq q$. We define a probabilistic lifting function $\mathtt{INV}(\cdot) : \mathbb{Z}_p \to \mathbb{Z}_q$ that takes $x \in \mathbb{Z}_p$ as input and chooses uniformly at random an element u from the set $\{u \in \mathbb{Z}_q : \lfloor u \rceil_p = x\}$. As usual, $\mathtt{INV}(\cdot)$ can be extended coefficient-wise to $\mathbb{Z}_q^{<n}[x]$. This lifting function becomes important in the encryption scheme in Sect. 5. There, we use $\mathtt{INV}(\cdot)$ to lift rounded polynomials in $\mathbb{Z}_p[x]$ to $\mathbb{Z}_q[x]$ such that $\left\lfloor \mathtt{INV}(\lfloor a \rceil_p) \right\rceil_p = \lfloor a \rceil_p$. Note that $\mathtt{INV}(\lfloor a \rceil_p) = a + e$ with $\|e\|_\infty \leq \frac{q}{p}$.

2.3 Probabilities

For a set S and a distribution χ over S, we denote by $x \leftarrow \chi$ the process of sampling $x \in S$ according to χ. With $x \leftarrow U(S)$ we denote sampling x according to the uniform distribution over S. In this work, the support S is sometimes a subset of $\mathbb{R}$. In such a case, we say a distribution χ is *B-bounded with probability at least* δ for a real number $B \geq 0$, if $\mathrm{Pr}_{x \leftarrow \chi}[|x| \leq B] \geq \delta$. We say a B-bounded distribution χ is *balanced* if $\mathrm{Pr}_{x \leftarrow \chi}[|x| \leq 0] \geq \frac{1}{2}$ and at the same time $\mathrm{Pr}_{x \leftarrow \chi}[|x| \geq 0] \geq \frac{1}{2}$. For the parameter $s > 0$, we define the *Gaussian function* $\rho_s \colon \mathbb{R}^n \to (0, 1]$ as $\rho_s(x) = \exp(-\pi \langle x, x \rangle / s^2)$. Normalizing this function yields the density function of the *continuous Gaussian distribution* D_s of standard deviation s. A (finite) family H of hash functions $h \colon X \to Y$ is called *universal* if

$$\mathrm{Pr}_{h \leftarrow U(H)}\left[h(x_1) = h(x_2)\right] = \frac{1}{|Y|},$$

for all $x_1 \neq x_2 \in X$. Roşca et al. [RSSS17] introduced the following variant of the leftover hash lemma.

Lemma 5 (Generalized Leftover Hash Lemma). *Let X, Y and Z be finite sets, H be a universal family of hash functions $h \colon X \to Y$ and $f \colon X \to Z$ be an arbitrary function. Then, for any random variable T taking values in X we have*

$$\Delta\left((h, h(T), f(T)), (h, U(Y), f(T))\right) \leq \frac{1}{2} \cdot \sqrt{\gamma(T) \cdot |Y| \cdot |Z|},$$

where $\gamma(T) = \max_{t \in X} \mathrm{Pr}\left[T = t\right]$.

Definition 1 (Statistical distance). *Let P and Q be two discrete probability distributions on a discrete domain E. Their* statistical distance *is defined as*

$$\Delta(P; Q) = \frac{1}{2} \sum_{x \in E} |P(x) - Q(X)|.$$

The *Rényi divergence* [R61, vEH14] defines another measure of distribution closeness and was first used in cryptography as a powerful alternative for the statistical distance measure by Bai et al. [BLL+15]. In this paper, it suffices to use the Rényi divergence of order 2.

Definition 2 (Rényi divergence of order 2). *Let P and Q be two discrete probability distributions such that $\mathrm{Supp}(P) \subset \mathrm{Supp}(Q)$. The* Rényi divergence of order 2 *is defined as*

$$\mathrm{RD}_2(P \| Q) = \sum_{x \in \mathrm{Supp}(P)} \frac{P(x)^2}{Q(x)}.$$

The Rényi divergence admits the following properties, proved in [vEH14].

Lemma 6. *Let P, Q be two discrete probability distributions with $\mathrm{Supp}(P) \subset \mathrm{Supp}(Q)$. Further, let $(P_i)_i, (Q_i)_i$ be two families of independent discrete probability distributions with $\mathrm{Supp}(P_i) \subset \mathrm{Supp}(Q_i)$ for all i. Then, the following properties are fulfilled:*

1. *(**Data Processing Inequality**) $\mathrm{RD}_2(P^f \| Q^f) \leq \mathrm{RD}_2(P \| Q)$ for any function f, where P^f (resp. Q^f) denotes the distribution of $f(y)$ induced by sampling $y \leftarrow P$ (resp. $y \leftarrow Q$),*
2. *(**Multiplicativity**) $\mathrm{RD}_2\left(\prod_i P_i \| \prod_i Q_i\right) = \prod_i \mathrm{RD}_2(P_i \| Q_i)$,*
3. *(**Probability Preservation**) Let $E \subset \mathrm{Supp}(Q)$ be an arbitrary event, then*

$$Q(E) \cdot \mathrm{RD}_2(P \| Q) \geq P(E)^2.$$

2.4   Middle-Product Learning With Errors

The use of the middle-product in lattice-based cryptography was introduced by Roşca et al. [RSSS17] in the form of the so-called *Middle-Product Learning With Errors* (MP-LWE) problem.

Definition 3 (Middle-Product). *Let d_a, d_b, d, k be integers fulfilling the equation $d_a + d_b - 1 = d + 2k$. The middle-product of $a \in \mathbb{Z}^{<d_a}[x]$ and $b \in \mathbb{Z}^{<d_b}[x]$ is defined as*

$$a \odot_d b = \left\lfloor \frac{a \cdot b \bmod x^{k+d}}{x^k} \right\rfloor,$$

where the floor rounding in this case means removing all terms with negative exponents on x.

The middle-product fulfills additivity if one of its inputs is fixed. Associativity is generally not achieved, instead only the following weaker associativity property is guaranteed.

Lemma 7. *Let d, k and n be positive integers. For all $r \in \mathbb{Z}^{<k+1}[x]$, $a \in \mathbb{Z}^{<n}[x]$ and $s \in \mathbb{Z}^{<n+d+k-1}[x]$, we have*

$$r \odot_d (a \odot_{d+k} s) = (r \cdot a) \odot_d s.$$

In order to prove the security of the encryption scheme in Sect. 5, we need the following hash function family to be universal. Recall that $\mathrm{INV}(\cdot)$ denotes the probabilistic lifting function from $\mathbb{Z}_p[x]$ to $\mathbb{Z}_q[x]$ for two integers p and q with $2 \leq p \leq q$.

Lemma 8. *Let q, k, d, p and t be integers such that $k, d \geq 2$ and $2 \leq p \leq q$. For $(b_i)_{i \in [t]} \in (\mathbb{Z}_p^{<d+k}[x])^t$, we define*

$$h_{(b_i)_i} \colon \left(\{0,1\}^{<k+1}[x]\right)^t \to \mathbb{Z}_q^{<d}[x]$$

to be the map that sends

$$(r_i)_i \mapsto \sum_{i \in [t]} \mathrm{INV}(b_i) \odot_d r_i.$$

The hash function family $(h_{(b_i)_i})_{(b_i)_i}$ is universal.

Proof. The proof is very similar to the one of [RSSS17, Lemma 4.2]. We simply replace b_i by $\mathrm{INV}(b_i)$, using the same argument to show that

$$\mathrm{Pr}_{(b_i)_i \leftarrow U\left(\left(\mathbb{Z}_p^{\leq d+k}[x]\right)^t\right)} \left[\sum_{i \in [t]} \mathrm{INV}(b_i) \odot_d r_i = \sum_{i \in [t]} \mathrm{INV}(b_i) \odot_d r_i' \right] = \frac{1}{q^d},$$

with $(r_i)_i \neq (r_i')_i$. $\qquad\square$

We now recall the Learning With Errors (LWE) problem in the polynomial and middle-product setting, together with the hardness result of the latter one. The reader is referred to the original paper by Roşca et al. [RSSS17] for more details.

Definition 4 (Decisional P-LWE). *Let q and m be integers fulfilling $q \geq 2$ and $m > 0$. Let f be a polynomial in $\mathbb{Z}[x]$ of degree m and χ be a distribution over $\mathbb{R}[x]/f$. The decisional P-LWE$_{q,\chi}^{f}$ problem asks to distinguish arbitrary many samples of the form $(a_i, b_i = a_i \cdot s + e_i \bmod q)$, where $e_i \leftarrow \chi$ and $a_i \leftarrow U(\mathbb{Z}_q[x]/f)$, from the same number of samples chosen uniformly from $\mathbb{Z}_q[x]/f \times \mathbb{R}_q[x]/f$ with non-negligible success probability over the choices of $s \leftarrow U(\mathbb{Z}_q[x]/f)$.*

Definition 5 (Decisional MP-LWE). *Let q, d and n be integers with $q \geq 2$ and $0 < d \leq n$. Further, let χ be a distribution over $\mathbb{R}^{<d}[x]$. The decisional MP-LWE$_{q,n,d,\chi}$ problem asks to distinguish arbitrary many samples of the form $(a_i, b_i = a_i \odot_d s + e_i \bmod q)$ where $e_i \leftarrow \chi$ and $a_i \leftarrow U(\mathbb{Z}_q^{<n}[x])$, from the same number of samples chosen uniformly from $\mathbb{Z}_q^{<n}[x] \times \mathbb{R}_q^{<d}[x]$ with non-negligible success probability over the choices of $s \leftarrow U(\mathbb{Z}_q^{<n+d-1}[x])$.*

If instead the secret s is chosen uniformly at random from the set of all elements in $\mathbb{Z}_q^{<n+d-1}[x]$ having a Hankel matrix (see Sect. 3) of order $d + n - 1$ of full rank d, denoted by $s \leftarrow U\left((\mathbb{Z}_q^{<n+d-1}[x])^\times\right)$, we call the corresponding problem MP-LWE$_{q,n,d,\chi}^{\times}$. Note that the main difference is the imposed full-rank condition, which plays an important role in Sect. 4.

Theorem 1 (Hardness of MP-LWE [RSSS17, Thm. 3.6]). *Let q, d and n be integers with $0 < d \leq n$ and $q \geq 2$. Further, let $\alpha \in (0,1)$. For $S > 0$, let $\mathcal{F}(S, d, n)$ denote the set of all monic polynomials f in $\mathbb{Z}[x]$ whose constant coefficient is coprime to q, having degree $m \in [d, n]$ and $\mathrm{EF}(f) < S$. Then, there exists a probabilistic polynomial-time reduction from P-LWE$_{q,D_{\alpha q}}^{f}$ for any polynomial $f \in \mathcal{F}(S, d, n)$ to MP-LWE$_{q,n,d,D_{\alpha' q}}$ with $\alpha' = \alpha dS$.*

Recall that $D_{\alpha q}$ (resp. $D_{\alpha' q}$) denotes the Gaussian distribution of width αq (resp. $\alpha' q$). Further, $\mathrm{EF}(f)$ is the expansion factor of f, introduced by Lyubashevsky and Micciancio [LM06] and defined as

$$\mathrm{EF}(f) = \max\left(\frac{\|g \bmod f\|_\infty}{\|g\|_\infty} : g \in \mathbb{Z}^{2m-1}[x] \setminus \{0\} \right).$$

3   Random Hankel Matrices

In this section, we show new results on the distribution of random Hankel matrices. First, we recall the definition of Hankel and Toeplitz matrices for a given polynomial, which we interpret as usual as a vector. We prove a lower bound for the probability that the Hankel matrix of a polynomial which is chosen uniformly at random has full rank. Finally, this result leads to a uniformity property of the middle-product which plays a crucial part in the hardness reduction of the new middle-product learning with rounding assumption in Sect. 4.2.

Hankel and Toeplitz matrices are not only used in the context of the middle-product of two polynomials. More generally, as pointed out by Kaltofen and Lobo [KL96], Toeplitz matrices are used as pre-conditioners in the process of solving linear systems of equations having unstructured coefficient matrices. The attractiveness of these structured matrices is twofold: First, it suffices to store the first column and first row, in order to rebuild the whole matrix. Second, the product of a Toeplitz matrix and a vector is in fact a convolution and can be computed in superlinear time using the fast Fourier transformation.

Other than that, large-dimensional random matrices with additional algebraic structure, as Hankel and Toeplitz matrices, play an important role in statistics, in particular in multivariate analysis. More concretely, Hankel matrices arise in polynomial regressions and Toeplitz matrices appear as covariance of stationary processes. In particular, the spectral distribution for their eigenvalues is important and was studied by Bryc et al. [BDJ06].

Let q be any positive integer and $a \in \mathbb{Z}_q^{<n+d-1}[x]$ be a polynomial over $\mathbb{Z}_q$ with coefficient vector $\mathbf{a} = (a_0, \dots, a_{n+d-2})^t$. We define the *Hankel matrix* of a of *order* $d + n - 1$ as

$$
\mathbf{Hank}(a) = \begin{pmatrix} a_0 & a_1 & \dots & a_{d-1} & \dots & a_{n-1} \\ a_1 & a_2 & \dots & a_d & \dots & a_n \\ & & \ddots & & \vdots & \\ a_{d-1} & a_d & \dots & a_{2d-2} & \dots & a_{n+d-2} \end{pmatrix} \in \mathbb{Z}_q^{d \times n}.
$$

The Hankel matrix is fully determined by its first row and its last column. Its rank is at most d. If it has full rank d we write $\mathrm{rank}(\mathbf{Hank}(a)) = d$. Further, we recall the definition of Toeplitz matrices. Let $a \in \mathbb{Z}_q^{<n+d-1}[x]$ be a polynomial over $\mathbb{Z}_q$ with coefficient vector $\mathbf{a} = (a_0, \dots, a_{n+d-2})^t$. The *Toeplitz matrix* of a of *order* $d + n - 1$ is given by

$$
\mathbf{Toep}(a) = \begin{pmatrix} a_0 & a_1 & a_2 & \dots & \dots & a_{n-1} \\ a_n & a_0 & a_1 & \ddots & & \vdots \\ a_{n+1} & a_n & \ddots & \ddots & \ddots & \vdots \\ \vdots & \ddots & \ddots & \ddots & a_1 & a_2 \\ \vdots & & \ddots & a_n & a_0 & a_1 \\ a_{n+d-2} & \dots & \dots & a_{n+1} & a_n & a_0 \end{pmatrix} \in \mathbb{Z}_q^{d \times n}.
$$

The Toeplitz matrix is fully determined by its first row and its first column. There exists a special relation between the Toeplitz matrix and the Hankel matrix. Let $\mathbf{J}_n$ be the reflection matrix of order n defined as

$$
\mathbf{J}_n = \begin{pmatrix} 0 \cdots 0\,0\,1 \\ 0 \cdots 0\,1\,0 \\ 0 \cdots 1\,0\,0 \\ \vdots \ddots \vdots \vdots \vdots \\ 1 \cdots 0\,0\,0 \end{pmatrix} \in \mathbb{Z}_q^{n \times n}.
$$

Then, for any polynomial $a \in \mathbb{Z}_q^{<n+d-1}[x]$ with coefficient vector $\mathbf{a} = (\mathbf{a'}, \mathbf{a''})$ in $\mathbb{Z}_q^n \times \mathbb{Z}_q^{d-1}$ it yields $\mathbf{Toep}(a) \cdot \mathbf{J}_n = \mathbf{Hank}(\tilde{a})$, where $\tilde{a}$ is the polynomial given by the coefficient vector $\tilde{\mathbf{a}} = (\overline{\mathbf{a'}}, \mathbf{a''})$ with $\overline{\mathbf{a'}}$ denoting the vector $\mathbf{a'}$ in reverse order. Thus, we can use the result of Kaltofen and Lobo [KL96] about random Toeplitz matrices to calculate the probability of a random Hankel matrix to have full rank.

Lemma 9. *Let q be a positive integer with unique prime power factorization given by $q = \prod_{i \in [l]} p_i^{\alpha_i}$, where p_i are primes and $\alpha_i > 0$. Let d and n be integers with $0 < d \le n$ and choose $b \leftarrow U(\mathbb{Z}_q^{<n+d-1}[x])$. Then,*

$$
\Pr\left[\mathrm{rank}(\mathbf{Hank}(b)) = d\right] \ge \prod_{i \in [l]} \left(1 - \frac{1}{p_i}\right).
$$

Proof. Case 1 (q is prime). Any Hankel matrix of order $d + n - 1$ can be represented as the matrix product of the corresponding Toeplitz matrix of order $d + n - 1$ times the non-singular reflection matrix $\mathbf{J}_n$ of order n whose anti-diagonal elements are 1's and all other entries are 0's. Thus, the rank of a given Hankel matrix will be the same as the one of the corresponding Toeplitz matrix. For the case $d = n$, it follows from Theorem 4 of [KL96] that the total number of Hankel matrices of full rank d is exactly $(q - 1)q^{2d-2}$. If we choose $b \leftarrow U(\mathbb{Z}_q^{<n+d-1}[x])$, then

$$
\Pr\left[\mathrm{rank}(\mathbf{Hank}(b)) = d\right] = \frac{(q-1)q^{2d-2}}{q^{2d-1}} = 1 - \frac{1}{q}.
$$

For $d < n$, the $d \times n$ Hankel matrix has full rank d if at least the left $d \times d$ submatrix, which is naturally a $d \times d$ Hankel matrix as well, has rank d. This happens with probability at least $1 - \frac{1}{q}$.

Case 2 (q = p^α). Initially, consider the case $d = n$. Any Hankel matrix $\mathbf{A}$ can be represented as $\mathbf{A} = p\mathbf{Q} + \mathbf{R}$, where both $\mathbf{R}$ and $\mathbf{Q}$ are Hankel matrices with coefficients in $\mathbb{Z}_p$ and $\mathbb{Z}_{p^{\alpha-1}}$, respectively. This formula follows from integer division by p with remainder, i.e., Euclidean division. Any element from $\mathbb{Z}_{p^\alpha}$, when divided by p, has a reminder in $\mathbb{Z}_p$ and quotient in $\mathbb{Z}_{p^{\alpha-1}}$. This representation is unique, thus preserves the structure of the matrix $\mathbf{A}$. Since $\mathbf{A}$ is a Hankel matrix, so are $\mathbf{Q}$ and $\mathbf{R}$. The matrix $\mathbf{A}$ has full rank in $\mathbb{Z}_{p^\alpha}$ if and only if $\mathbf{R}$ has full rank in $\mathbb{Z}_p$. Hence, we can deduce from the previous case that the number of Hankel matrices of full rank equals $(p-1)p^{(\alpha-1)(2d-1)+(2d-2)}$. If we choose $b \leftarrow U(\mathbb{Z}_q^{<n+d-1}[x])$, then

$$\Pr\left[\text{rank}(\mathbf{Hank}(b)) = d\right] = \frac{(p-1)p^{(\alpha-1)(2d-1)+(2d-2)}}{p^{\alpha(2d-1)}} = 1 - \frac{1}{p}.$$

For $d < n$, using the same argument as before, the probability is at least $1 - \frac{1}{p}$.

Case 3 $(q = \prod_{i\in[l]} p_i^{\alpha_i})$. For the case $d = n$, it follows from the Chinese remainder theorem that the number of Hankel matrices of full rank d modulo q equals the product of the number of Hankel matrices of full rank d modulo $p_i^{\alpha_i}$ which is given by

$$\prod_{i\in[l]} (p_i - 1)p_i^{(\alpha_i-1)(2d-1)+(2d-2)}.$$

Thus, if we choose $b \leftarrow U(\mathbb{Z}_q^{<n+d-1}[x])$, then

$$\Pr\left[\text{rank}(\mathbf{Hank}(b)) = d\right] = \prod_{i\in[l]} \left(1 - \frac{1}{p_i}\right).$$

Similarly as before, for $d < n$ and $b \leftarrow U(\mathbb{Z}_q^{<n+d-1}[x])$, then

$$\Pr\left[\text{rank}(\mathbf{Hank}(b)) = d\right] \geq \prod_{i\in[l]} \left(1 - \frac{1}{p_i}\right).$$

$\square$

We denote by $(\mathbb{Z}_q^{<n+d-1}[x])^\times$ the set of polynomials of $\mathbb{Z}_q^{<n+d-1}[x]$ with Hankel matrix of full rank d. Note that for $a \in \mathbb{Z}_q^{<n}[x]$ and $b \in \mathbb{Z}_q^{<n+d-1}[x]$, the middle-product can be represented as a matrix-vector product

$$a \odot_d b = \mathbf{Hank}(b) \cdot \overline{a}.$$

Lemma 10. *Let d and n be two integers with $0 < d \leq n$ and b a fixed element of $(\mathbb{Z}_q^{<n+d-1}[x])^\times$. If we choose $a \leftarrow U(\mathbb{Z}_q^{<n}[x])$, then $a \odot_d b$ is uniformly random in $\mathbb{Z}_q^{<d}[x]$.*

Proof. We can write $a \odot_d b = \mathbf{Hank}(b) \cdot \overline{a}$. For any $d \leq n$ and full rank matrix $\mathbf{A} \in \mathbb{Z}_q^{d\times n}$, the mapping from $\mathbb{Z}_q^n$ to $\mathbb{Z}_q^d$ given by multiplication with $\mathbf{A}$ is surjective. As a is chosen uniformly at random and the Hankel matrix of b has full rank d, the middle-product is also uniformly distributed. $\square$

4 Middle-Product Learning with Rounding

In this section, we define in the first subsection the new assumption and then show in the second subsection its hardness by reducing the MP-LWE problem to it.

4.1 Definition of the MP-CLWR Assumption

In the following, we define the *Middle-Product Computational Learning With Rounding* (MP-CLWR) assumption which is an adaption of the *Ring Computational Learning With Rounding* (R-CLWR) assumption from Chen et al. [CZZ18] to the middle-product setting. For a detailed introduction and motivation of this computational notion, see [CZZ18, Section 3].

In order to define this computational assumption, we need to introduce our experiment setting. Within the experiment, three different parties in form of algorithms appear: A challenger $\mathcal{C}$ interacting with an adversary $\mathcal{A}$ who is receiving its samples from a source $\mathcal{S}$. All three algorithms are restricted to be probabilistic and polynomial-time (PPT). As a first step, the source $\mathcal{S}$ generates a sample (X, aux) using two sets called var and con. It then sends this sample to the challenger $\mathcal{C}$, which computes, with the help of this sample, a tuple $(\mathsf{Input}, \mathsf{Target})$. The adversary only receives the Input part of the tuple to compute Output. The adversary wins the experiment if Output equals Target (Fig. 1).

$\mathsf{Exp}(\mathcal{C}, \mathcal{A}, \mathcal{S})$

1 : $(X, \mathsf{aux}) \leftarrow \mathcal{S}(\mathsf{var}, \mathsf{con})$

2 : $(\mathsf{Input}, \mathsf{Target}) \leftarrow \mathcal{C}(X, \mathsf{aux})$

3 : $(\mathsf{Output}) \leftarrow \mathcal{A}(\mathsf{Input})$

4 : **return** $\mathsf{Output} = \mathsf{Target}$

Fig. 1. The experiment $\mathsf{Exp}(\mathcal{C}, \mathcal{A}, \mathcal{S})$.

The idea of the computational assumption is to consider two different experiments with the same challenger $\mathcal{C}$ and adversary $\mathcal{A}$ but with different sources $\mathcal{S}_1$ and $\mathcal{S}_2$, which differ in the distribution var but have the same distribution con, motivating the notation var for variable and con for constant. The new notion guarantees that if $\mathcal{A}$ cannot compute Target from X_1 generated by $\mathcal{S}_1$, then it is not able to compute Target from X_2 generated by $\mathcal{S}_2$ either.

We illustrate the new notion in Fig. 2 below. Let $\mathcal{C}$ be an arbitrary challenger. If the success probability of any adversary $\mathcal{A}$ outputting the correct answer in $\mathsf{Exp}_1(\mathcal{C}, \mathcal{A}, \mathcal{S}_1)$ is negligible, then it is in $\mathsf{Exp}_2(\mathcal{C}, \mathcal{A}, \mathcal{S}_2)$ as well.

$\mathsf{Exp}_1(\mathcal{C}, \mathcal{A}, \mathcal{S}_1)$	$\mathsf{Exp}_2(\mathcal{C}, \mathcal{A}, \mathcal{S}_2)$
1 : $(X_1, \mathsf{aux}) \leftarrow \mathcal{S}_1(\mathsf{var}_1, \mathsf{con})$	1 : $(X_2, \mathsf{aux}) \leftarrow \mathcal{S}_2(\mathsf{var}_2, \mathsf{con})$
2 : $(\mathsf{Input}_1, \mathsf{Target}_1) \leftarrow \mathcal{C}(X_1, \mathsf{aux})$	2 : $(\mathsf{Input}_2, \mathsf{Target}_2) \leftarrow \mathcal{C}(X_2, \mathsf{aux})$
3 : $\mathsf{Output}_1 \leftarrow \mathcal{A}(\mathsf{Input}_1)$	3 : $\mathsf{Output}_2 \leftarrow \mathcal{A}(\mathsf{Input}_2)$
4 : **return** $\mathsf{Output}_1 = \mathsf{Target}_1$	4 : **return** $\mathsf{Output}_2 = \mathsf{Target}_2$

Fig. 2. Experiment setting of the computational assumption.

Now, we define our new MP-CLWR assumption which is an adaption of the R-CLWR assumption from [CZZ18] to the middle-product setting. As an analog of the notion of units in the original paper, we define $(\mathbb{Z}_q^{<n+d-1}[x])^{\times}$ as the set of all polynomials over $\mathbb{Z}_q$ having degree less than $n+d-1$ and a Hankel matrix of order $d \times n$ of full rank d. The integers d and n define the parameters of the middle-product, q defines the general and p the rounding modulus. The number of samples has to be fixed beforehand and is given by t.

Definition 6 (MP-CLWR assumption). *Let d, n, p, q and t be positive integers fulfilling $0 < d \leq n$ and $q \geq p \geq 2$. Choose s uniformly at random over $(\mathbb{Z}_q^{<n+d-1}[x])^{\times}$. Denote by $\mathcal{X}_s$ the distribution of $(a, \lfloor a \odot_d s \rfloor_p)$, where $a \leftarrow U(\mathbb{Z}_q^{<n}[x])$, and denote by $\mathcal{U}$ the distribution of $(a, \lfloor b \rfloor_p)$, where $a \leftarrow U(\mathbb{Z}_q^{<n}[x])$ and $b \leftarrow U(\mathbb{Z}_q^{<d}[x])$. For $i \in \{1, 2\}$ define the input for $\mathcal{S}_i$ as $(\mathsf{var}_i, \mathsf{con})$, where var_1 denotes the distribution $\mathcal{X}_s^t$, and var_2 the distribution $\mathcal{U}^t$, and con is an arbitrary distribution over $\{0, 1\}^*$ which is independent from var_1 and var_2. For a fixed challenger $\mathcal{C}$ let $\mathcal{P}_{\mathcal{C},\mathcal{A}}$ be the probability for an adversary $\mathcal{A}$ to win $\mathsf{Exp}_1(\mathcal{C}, \mathcal{A}, \mathcal{S}_1)$, while $\mathcal{Q}_{\mathcal{C},\mathcal{A}}$ be that for $\mathcal{A}$ to win $\mathsf{Exp}_2(\mathcal{C}, \mathcal{A}, \mathcal{S}_2)$.*

The MP-CLWR$_{p,q,n,d,t}$ assumption states that for any challenger $\mathcal{C}$ if $\mathcal{Q}_{\mathcal{C},\mathcal{A}}$ is negligible for any adversary $\mathcal{A}$, so is $\mathcal{P}_{\mathcal{C},\mathcal{A}}$. We call the difference $|\mathcal{P}_{\mathcal{C},\mathcal{A}} - \mathcal{Q}_{\mathcal{C},\mathcal{A}}|$ the advantage of the adversary $\mathcal{A}$.

Correspondingly, we also define the *Middle-Product Computational Rounded Learning With Errors* (MP-CRLWE) assumption which is important in the hardness reduction in Sect. 4.2 below.

Definition 7 (MP-CRLWE assumption). *Let d, n, p, q and t be positive integers fulfilling $0 < d \leq n$ and $q \geq p \geq 2$. Choose s uniformly at random over $(\mathbb{Z}_q^{<n+d-1}[x])^{\times}$. Let χ_e be the error distribution over $\mathbb{R}^{<d}[x]$. Denote by $\mathcal{Y}_{s,\chi_e}$ the distribution of $(a, \lfloor a \odot_d s + e \rfloor_p)$, where $a \leftarrow U(\mathbb{Z}_q^{<n}[x])$ and $e \leftarrow \chi_e$ and denote by $\mathcal{U}$ the distribution of $(a, \lfloor b \rfloor_p)$ where $a \leftarrow U(\mathbb{Z}_q^{<n}[x])$ and $b \leftarrow U(\mathbb{Z}_q^{<d}[x])$. For $i \in \{1, 2\}$ define the input for $\mathcal{S}_i$ as $(\mathsf{var}_i, \mathsf{con})$, where var_1 denotes the distribution $\mathcal{Y}_{s,\chi_e}^t$, and var_2 the distribution $\mathcal{U}^t$, and con is an arbitrary distribution over $\{0, 1\}^*$ which is independent from var_1 and var_2. For a fixed challenger $\mathcal{C}$ let $\mathcal{P}'_{\mathcal{C},\mathcal{A}}(\chi_e)$ be the probability for an adversary $\mathcal{A}$ to win $\mathsf{Exp}_1(\mathcal{C}, \mathcal{A}, \mathcal{S}_1)$, while $\mathcal{Q}_{\mathcal{C},\mathcal{A}}$ be that for $\mathcal{A}$ to win $\mathsf{Exp}_2(\mathcal{C}, \mathcal{A}, \mathcal{S}_2)$.*

The MP-CRLWE$_{p,q,n,d,t,\chi_e}$ assumption related to the error distribution χ_e states that for any challenger $\mathcal{C}$ if $\mathcal{Q}_{\mathcal{C},\mathcal{A}}$ is negligible for any adversary $\mathcal{A}$, so is $\mathcal{P}'_{\mathcal{C},\mathcal{A}}(\chi_e)$. We call the difference $|\mathcal{P}'_{\mathcal{C},\mathcal{A}}(\chi_e) - \mathcal{Q}_{\mathcal{C},\mathcal{A}}|$ the advantage of the adversary $\mathcal{A}$.

4.2   Hardness of MP-CLWR

We now prove the hardness of MP-CLWR with the help of a reduction from the decisional MP-LWE problem to the MP-CLWR problem. The decisional version of MP-LWE itself can be reduced from the decisional P-LWE problem for a large class of defining polynomials, see Theorem 1. As P-LWE benefits from worst-case to average-case reductions from lattice problems, our new MP-CLWR assumption also enjoys the worst-case hardness.

Theorem 2 (Hardness of MP-CLWR). *Let d, n, p, q and t be positive integers with $0 < d \leq n$ and $q \geq p \geq 2$. Further, let $q = \prod_{i \in [l]} p_i^{\alpha_i}$ be the prime power factorization of q with some $l > 0$, where p_i is prime and $\alpha_i > 0$ for all $i \in [l]$. Let χ be an error distribution over $\mathbb{R}^{<d}[x]$ which is balanced and B-bounded with probability at least δ, fulfilling $q > 2pBdt$ and $\delta \geq 1 - \frac{1}{td}$. There is a reduction from the decisional MP-LWE$_{q,n,d,\chi}$ problem to the MP-CLWR$_{p,q,n,d,t}$ problem, with t the number of samples fixed beforehand.*

Assume that the advantage of an MP-CLWR solver is ε. Then, there is an MP-LWE solver with advantage at least

$$\left(\frac{1}{e^2} \left(\varepsilon + \mathcal{Q}_{\mathcal{C},\mathcal{A}} \right)^2 \right) \cdot \prod_{i \in [l]} \left(1 - \frac{1}{p_i} \right).$$

In order to prove the theorem, we show the following sequence of reductions:

$$\text{MP-LWE}_{q,n,d,\chi} \xrightarrow{\text{Lemma 11}} \text{MP-LWE}^{\times}_{q,n,d,\chi}$$

$$\downarrow \qquad\qquad\qquad\qquad\qquad \Big\downarrow \text{Lemma 12}$$

$$\text{MP-CLWR}_{p,q,n,d,t} \xleftarrow[\text{Lemma 13}]{} \text{MP-CRLWE}_{p,q,n,d,t,\chi}$$

The first reduction is achieved by a standard technique.

Lemma 11. *Let d, n, p, q and t be positive integers, such that it yields $0 < d \leq n$ and $q \geq p \geq 2$. Let χ_e be the error distribution over $\mathbb{R}^{<d}[x]$. Further, let the unique prime power factorization of q be given by $q = \prod_{i \in [l]} p_i^{\alpha_i}$ with some $l > 0$, where p_i is prime and $\alpha_i > 0$ for all $i \in [l]$. If there is a PPT algorithm solving MP-LWE$^{\times}_{q,n,d,\chi}$ with non-negligible advantage ε, then there is a PPT algorithm solving MP-LWE$_{q,n,d,\chi}$ with non-negligible advantage at least*

$$\varepsilon \cdot \prod_{i \in [l]} \left(1 - \frac{1}{p_i} \right).$$

Proof. Let $(a_i, b_i)_{i \in [t]}$ be the given input tuple of samples of MP-LWE$_{q,n,d,\chi}$, where $s \leftarrow U(\mathbb{Z}_q^{n+d-1}[x])$. An adversary can take this tuple of samples $(a_i, b_i)_i$ and query an oracle of MP-LWE$^{\times}_{q,n,d,\chi}$ on it. As showed in Lemma 9, the probability that the Hankel matrix of s has full rank d is at least $\prod_{i \in [l]} \left(1 - \frac{1}{p_i} \right)$. Assuming that the oracle succeeds with non-negligible probability ε in general, it will now succeed with probability at least $\varepsilon \cdot \prod_{i \in [l]} \left(1 - \frac{1}{p_i} \right)$, which completes the proof.   □

The following lemma is an adaption of Lemma 12 in [CZZ18] into our context.

Lemma 12 (MP-LWE to MP-CRLWE). *Assume that the advantage of any PPT algorithm to solve the decisional* MP-LWE$_{q,n,d,\chi}^{\times}$ *problem is less than ε, then we have*

$$\left| \mathcal{P}'_{\mathcal{C},\mathcal{A}}(\chi) - \mathcal{Q}_{\mathcal{C},\mathcal{A}} \right| < \varepsilon,$$

for any PPT adversary $\mathcal{A}$ and PPT challenger $\mathcal{C}$. Thus, there is a reduction from MP-LWE$_{q,n,d,\chi}^{\times}$ *to* MP-CRLWE$_{p,q,n,d,t,\chi}$, *with t the number of samples fixed beforehand.*

Proof. In order to show this reduction, we will construct an adversary $\mathcal{B}$ to solve the decisional MP-LWE$_{q,n,d,\chi}$ problem. This adversary $\mathcal{B}$ will at the same time play the role of the challenger $\mathcal{C}$ in the MP-CRLWE experiment. At the beginning, $\mathcal{B}$ receives a tuple of samples $(x_i, y_i)_{i \in [t]}$. It sets $a_i = x_i$ and $b_i = \lfloor y_i \rceil_p$ for all $i \in [t]$ and $X = (a_i, b_i)_{i \in [t]}$. As a challenger of the experiment, $\mathcal{B}$ can compute the corresponding Input and Target. $\mathcal{B}$ also verifies if the Output of $\mathcal{A}$ equals the Target. If this is the case, $\mathcal{B}$ outputs 1, otherwise 0.

If $(x_i, y_i)_i$ are MP-LWE samples, then are $(a_i, b_i)_i$ samples from $\mathcal{Y}_{s,\chi}$, used in the MP-CRLWE assumption. Thus, $\Pr(\mathcal{B}((x_i, y_i)_i) = 1) = \mathcal{P}'_{\mathcal{C},\mathcal{A}}(\chi)$. On the other hand, if $(x_i, y_i)_i$ is a tuple of uniform samples, then is $(a_i, b_i)_i$ also uniformly distributed. Hence, $\Pr(\mathcal{B}((x_i, y_i)_i) = 1) = \mathcal{Q}_{\mathcal{C},\mathcal{A}}$. Assuming the hardness of decisional MP-LWE, we have $\left| \mathcal{P}'_{\mathcal{C},\mathcal{A}}(\chi) - \mathcal{Q}_{\mathcal{C},\mathcal{A}} \right| < \varepsilon$, for negligible ε and for any adversary $\mathcal{A}$. In particular, the MP-CRLWE assumption holds: If $\mathcal{Q}_{\mathcal{C},\mathcal{A}}$ is negligible, so is $\mathcal{P}'_{\mathcal{C},\mathcal{A}}$ for the same challenger $\mathcal{C}$ and adversary $\mathcal{A}$ using the equation above. □

The following reduction is an adaption of Lemmas 8 and 9 in [CZZ18], based on the results of [BGM+16], together with our results about random Hankel matrices of Sect. 3.

Lemma 13 (MP-CRLWE to MP-CLWR). *Let $s \in (\mathbb{Z}_q^{<n+d-1}[x])^{\times}$. Let $\mathcal{X}_s$ and $\mathcal{Y}_s$ denote the random variables of a single MP-CLWR sample $(a, \lfloor a \odot_d s \rceil_p)$ and a single MP-CRLWE $(a, \lfloor a \odot_d s + e \rceil_p)$ sample, respectively. Further, let χ be an error distribution which is balanced and B-bounded with probability at least δ over $\mathbb{Z}_q^{<d}[x]$, where $q > 2pBdt$ and $\delta \geq 1 - \frac{1}{td}$. Then we have*

$$(\mathcal{P}_{\mathcal{C},\mathcal{A}})^2 \leq \mathcal{P}'_{\mathcal{C},\mathcal{A}}(\chi) \cdot e^2,$$

where e is the Euler's number.

Hence, there is a reduction from MP-CRLWE$_{p,q,n,d,t,\chi}$ *to* MP-CLWR$_{p,q,n,d,t}$.

Proof. Using Lemma 6 about the multiplicativity and the probability preservation property from the Rényi divergence, we have

$$(\mathcal{P}_{\mathcal{C},\mathcal{A}})^2 \leq \mathcal{P}'_{\mathcal{C},\mathcal{A}}(\chi) \cdot \mathrm{RD}_2(\mathcal{X}_s \| \mathcal{Y}_s)^t.$$

In the following we show that the Rényi divergence of $\mathcal{X}_s$ and $\mathcal{Y}_s$ fulfills

$$\mathrm{RD}_2(\mathcal{X}_s \| \mathcal{Y}_s) \leq \frac{(1 + 2pB/q)^d}{\delta^d}.$$

Following the definition of the Rényi divergence it yields

$$RD_2(\mathcal{X}_s \| \mathcal{Y}_s) = E_{a \leftarrow U(\mathbb{Z}_q^{<n}[x])} \frac{\Pr\left[\mathcal{X}_s = (a, \lfloor a \odot_d s \rceil_p)\right]}{\Pr\left[\mathcal{Y}_s = (a, \lfloor a \odot_d s \rceil_p)\right]}$$

$$= E_{a \leftarrow U(\mathbb{Z}_q^{<n}[x])} \frac{1}{\Pr_{e \leftarrow \chi}\left[\lfloor a \odot_d s + e \rceil_p = \lfloor a \odot_d s \rceil_p\right]}.$$

First, we define the border elements in $\mathbb{Z}_q$ with regard to B and p by

$$Bor_{p,q}(B) = \left\{ x \in \mathbb{Z}_q \colon \lfloor x + B \rceil_p \neq \lfloor x \rceil_p \right\}.$$

These are the elements in $\mathbb{Z}_q$ which are close to the rounding boundary. It yields $|Bor_{p,q}(B)| \leq 2Bp$. For $0 \leq t \leq d$, let us also define

$$Bad_{s,t} = \left\{ a \in \mathbb{Z}_q^{<n}[x] \colon |\{i \in [d] \colon (a \odot_d s)_i \in Bor_{p,q}(B)\}| = t \right\}.$$

In other words, $Bad_{s,t}$ defines, for a given polynomial s and number of coefficients t, the set of polynomials a in $\mathbb{Z}_q^{<n}[x]$ such that the middle-product $a \odot_d s$ has exactly t coefficients close to the rounding boundary. Now we fix t and assume $a \in Bad_{s,t}$. For any $i \in [d]$ with $(a \odot_d s)_i \notin Bor_{p,q}(B)$, it yields

$$\Pr_{e_i}\left[\lfloor (a \odot_d s)_i + e_i \rceil_p = \lfloor (a \odot_d s)_i \rceil_p\right] \geq \delta,$$

as e_i is sampled from the distribution χ which is B-bounded with probability at least δ. If $(a \odot_d s)_i \in Bor_{p,q}(B)$, then

$$\Pr_{e_i}\left[\lfloor (a \odot_d s)_i + e_i \rceil_p = \lfloor (a \odot_d s)_i \rceil_p\right] \geq \frac{1}{2},$$

because e_i is sampled from a balanced distribution. Thus, the probabilities of $e_i \in [-B, 0]$ or in $[0, B]$ are each greater or equal to $\frac{1}{2}$ and $\lfloor (a \odot_d s)_i + e_i \rceil_p \neq \lfloor (a \odot_d s)_i \rceil_p$ happens in exactly one of the two cases. Since each coefficient of e is independently distributed and $a \odot_d s$ has exactly t coefficients in $Bor_{p,q}(B)$, it yields

$$\Pr_{e \leftarrow \chi}\left[\lfloor a \odot_d s + e \rceil_p = \lfloor a \odot_d s \rceil_p\right] \geq \frac{1}{2^t} \cdot \delta^{d-t} \geq \frac{1}{2^t} \cdot \delta^d.$$

By Lemma 10, we know that if a is uniform in $\mathbb{Z}_q^{<n}[x]$, so is $a \odot_d s \in \mathbb{Z}_q^{<d}[x]$. Thus, it yields

$$\Pr\left[a \in Bad_{s,t}\right] \leq \binom{d}{t} \left(1 - \frac{|Bor_{p,q}(B)|}{q}\right)^{d-t} \left(\frac{|Bor_{p,q}(B)|}{q}\right)^t.$$

Hence,

$$\mathrm{RD}_2(\mathcal{X}_s \| \mathcal{Y}_s) \leq \delta^{-d} \sum_{t \in [d]} 2^t \cdot \Pr\left[a \in Bad_{s,t}\right]$$

$$= \delta^{-d} \sum_{t \in [d]} \binom{d}{t} \left(1 - \frac{|Bor_{p,q}(B)|}{q}\right)^{d-t} \left(2 \cdot \frac{|Bor_{p,q}(B)|}{q}\right)^t$$

$$= \delta^{-d} \left(1 + \frac{|Bor_{p,q}(B)|}{q}\right)^d$$

$$\leq \delta^{-d} \left(1 + \frac{2pB}{q}\right)^d.$$

From the results above, we can derive

$$\mathrm{RD}_2(\mathcal{X}_s \| \mathcal{Y}_s)^t \leq \frac{(1 + 2pB/q)^{td}}{\delta^{td}} \leq \frac{(1 + 1/td)^{td}}{(1 - 1/td)^{td}} \approx e^2,$$

where $\delta \geq 1 - \frac{1}{td}$ and $q > 2pBdt$. □

5 A Public Key Encryption Scheme Based on MP-CLWR

In this section, we present a Public Key Encryption (PKE) scheme whose security is based on the hardness of the middle-product computational learning with rounding problem (MP-CLWR, see Sect. 4.1). Its design is inspired by the PKE scheme from Roşca et al. [RSSS17] based on the hardness of the middle-product learning with errors (MP-LWE, see Sect. 2.4) problem and by the PKE scheme from Chen et al. [CZZ18] based on the hardness of the ring computational learning with rounding problem. As a first step, we define the scheme and show its correctness in Sect. 5.1. Subsequently, we prove its security based on the hardness of MP-CLWR in Sect. 5.2.

5.1 Definition and Correctness

In this section, we define the PKE scheme and show its correctness under a proper choice of parameters. We use the reconciliation rounding function $\lfloor \cdot \rceil_2 : \mathbb{Z}_q \to \mathbb{Z}_2$, the reconciliation cross-rounding function $\langle \cdot \rangle_2 : \mathbb{Z}_q \to \mathbb{Z}_2$, the randomized doubling function $\mathrm{DBL} : \mathbb{Z}_q \to \mathbb{Z}_{2q}$ and the reconciliation algorithm REC from Sect. 2.2. As we only need the randomized doubling function DBL for q odd, we set it to be the identity function for q even.

Recall that $\mathrm{INV}(\cdot)$ denotes the probabilistic lifting function from $\mathbb{Z}_p[x]$ to $\mathbb{Z}_q[x]$ for two integers p and q with $2 \leq p \leq q$. We need $\mathrm{INV}(\cdot)$ to lift rounded polynomials in $\mathbb{Z}_p[x]$ to $\mathbb{Z}_q[x]$ such that $\left\lfloor \mathrm{INV}(\lfloor a \rceil_p) \right\rceil_p = \lfloor a \rceil_p$. Note that $\mathrm{INV}(\lfloor a \rceil_p) = a + e$ with $\|e\|_\infty \leq \frac{q}{p}$.

Let H denote a random oracle $H : \{0,1\}^d \to \{0,1\}^k$. Further, let k, d, n, p, q and t be positive integers with $d + k \leq n$ and $q \geq p \geq 2$. The plaintext space is $\{0,1\}^{<k}[x]$.

1. KGen(1^λ). Sample $s \leftarrow U\left((\mathbb{Z}_q^{<n+d+k-1}[x])^\times\right)$ such that **Hank**(s) has full rank[1]. For $i \in [t]$, choose $a_i \leftarrow U(\mathbb{Z}_q^{<n}[x])$ and compute $b_i = \lfloor a_i \odot_{d+k} s \rceil_p$. Return pk $= (a_i, b_i)_{i \in [t]}$ and sk $= s$.
2. Enc(pk, μ). For $i \in [t]$, sample $r_i \leftarrow U(\{0,1\}^{<k+1}[x])$ and set the first part of the ciphertext as

$$c_1 = \sum_{i \in [t]} r_i a_i \bmod q.$$

Compute $v = \sum_{i \in [t]} r_i \odot_d \text{INV}(b_i) \bmod q$. Set the second and third part of the ciphertext as

$$c_2 = \langle \text{DBL}(v) \rangle_2 \text{ and } c_3 = H(\lfloor \text{DBL}(v) \rceil_2) \oplus \mu.$$

Return $c = (c_1, c_2, c_3)$.
3. Dec(sk, c). Compute $w = c_1 \odot_d s$ and return $\mu' = c_3 \oplus H(\text{REC}(w, c_2))$.

Lemma 14 (Correctness). *Assume that $p > 8t(k+1)$. For every plaintext μ and key pair* (pk, sk) $\leftarrow$ KGen(1^λ)*, we have*

$$\Pr(\text{Dec}(\text{sk}, \text{Enc}(\text{pk}, \mu)) = \mu) = 1.$$

Proof. In order to prove the correctness of the scheme, we need to guarantee that the reconciliation mechanism succeeds. Following Lemma 4 we have to show that $\|w - v\|_\infty < q/8$. Notice that we have

$$v = \sum_{i \in [t]} r_i \odot_d \text{INV}(b_i) = \sum_{i \in [t]} r_i \odot_d (a_i \odot_{d+k} s + e_i) = \sum_{i \in [t]} (r_i a_i) \odot_d s + \sum_{i \in [t]} r_i \odot_d e_i$$

$$= c_1 \odot_d s + \sum_{i \in [t]} r_i \odot_d e_i = w + \sum_{i \in [t]} r_i \odot_d e_i,$$

where $\|e_i\|_\infty < q/p$ for $i \in [t]$ is determined by the lifting function $\text{INV}(\cdot)$. Thus it suffices to have

$$\left\| \sum_{i \in [t]} r_i \odot_d e_i \right\|_\infty < q/8.$$

For $i \in [t]$ each coefficient of $r_i \odot_d e_i$ can be seen as the inner product $\langle u, v \rangle$ of a binary vector u of dimension $k+1$ and a vector v also of dimension $k+1$, where each coefficient has magnitude $\leq q/p$. Notice that we have

$$|\langle u, v \rangle| \leq \|u\|_2 \cdot \|v\|_2 \leq \sqrt{k+1} \cdot \sqrt{(k+1) \cdot q^2/p^2} = (k+1)q/p.$$

Hence, it yields

$$\left\| \sum_{i \in [t]} r_i \odot_d e_i \right\|_\infty \leq \sum_{i \in [t]} \|r_i \odot_d e_i\|_\infty \leq t(k+1)q/p.$$

As $p > 8t(k+1)$, we have $t(k+1)q/p < q/8$ which guarantees that the reconciliation mechanism succeeds. $\qquad\square$

---

[1] This can be done by sampling $s \leftarrow U\left(\mathbb{Z}_q^{<n+d+k-1}[x]\right)$ uniformly at random and rejecting it if its Hankel matrix is not full rank.

5.2   Provable Security

In this section, we prove the security of the PKE scheme defined above based on the hardness of MP-CLWR.

Lemma 15 (Security). *Let λ be the security parameter. Further, let k, d, n, p, q and t be positive integers such that it yields $d + k \leq n$ and $q \geq p \geq 2$. Assume that $t \geq (2 \cdot \lambda + (k + d + n) \cdot \log q)/(k + 1)$. The PKE scheme above is IND-CPA secure under the MP-CLWR$_{p,q,n,d+k,t}$ hardness assumption.*

Proof. The IND-CPA security game is the following: A challenger $\mathcal{C}$ generates a key pair (pk, sk), samples a random bit b and sends the public key pk to the adversary $\mathcal{A}$. The adversary chooses two messages m_0, m_1 and sends them to the challenger $\mathcal{C}$, which in turn encrypts m_b and sends the corresponding ciphertext c back to $\mathcal{A}$. The adversary outputs a bit b' as a guess of b and wins the game if $b = b'$. The game is illustrated in Fig. 3.

$$\underline{\text{IND-CPA}_{\mathsf{Enc}}^{\mathcal{A}}}$$

1 : $b \xleftarrow{\$} \{0, 1\}$

2 : $(\mathsf{pk}, \mathsf{sk}) \leftarrow \mathsf{KGen}(1^{\lambda})$

3 : $(m_0, m_1) \leftarrow \mathcal{A}(1^{\lambda}, \mathsf{pk})$

4 : $c \leftarrow \mathsf{Enc}(\mathsf{pk}, m_b)$

5 : $b' \leftarrow \mathcal{A}(1^{\lambda}, \mathsf{pk}, c)$

6 :   **return** $b = b'$

Fig. 3. The IND-CPA security game.

If H was not queried on the value of $\lfloor \mathrm{DBL}(v) \rceil_2 \in \{0, 1\}^d$ during the game, the adversary $\mathcal{A}$ can only guess the (randomly chosen) bit b with success probability $1/2$. In particular, we can use a successful adversary $\mathcal{A}$ of the IND-CPA security game to construct a successful adversary $\mathcal{A}'$ which outputs $\lfloor \mathrm{DBL}(v) \rceil_2$, given the first two parts (c_1, c_2) of any ciphertext $c = (c_1, c_2, c_3)$. These first two parts are independent of the message to encrypt. We will call this the COMP-DBL game.

During the IND-CPA game, $\mathcal{A}'$ answers the random oracle queries of $\mathcal{A}$ by maintaining an input-output table for H. For each query, $\mathcal{A}'$ first checks if H was already programmed on the queried input. If yes, it outputs the corresponding hash value, otherwise it chooses a fresh random value and sets H accordingly. Assuming $\mathcal{A}$ has non-negligible advantage to win the IND-CPA security game, it must have queried H on $\lfloor \mathrm{DBL}(v) \rceil_2$, hence $\mathcal{A}'$ can look up the pair $(\lfloor \mathrm{DBL}(v) \rceil_2, r)$ with $r = H(\lfloor \mathrm{DBL}(v) \rceil_2)$ in the random oracle table. The procedure is illustrated in Fig. 4 below.

Protocol for $\mathcal{C}$, $\mathcal{A}$ and $\mathcal{A}'$

$\mathcal{C}'_{\text{COMP-DBL}}$	$\mathcal{A}'_{\text{COMP-DBL}}/\mathcal{C}_{\text{IND-CPA}}$	$\mathcal{A}_{\text{IND-CPA}}$

$(\mathsf{pk},\mathsf{sk}) \leftarrow \mathsf{KGen}(1^\lambda)$

$(c_1, c_2, *) \leftarrow \mathsf{Enc}(\mathsf{pk}, *)$

$\xrightarrow{\quad 1^\lambda, pk, c_1, c_2 \quad}$

$\xrightarrow{\quad 1^\lambda, pk \quad}$

$m_0, m_1 \leftarrow \{0,1\}^k$

$\xleftarrow{\quad m_0, m_1 \quad}$

$b \leftarrow \{0,1\}$

$r \leftarrow \{0,1\}^k$

$\xrightarrow{\quad c=(c_1, c_2, r \oplus m_b) \quad}$

$\xleftarrow{\quad b' \quad}$

$\xleftarrow{\quad [\text{DBL}(v)]_2 \quad}$

Fig. 4. Using $\mathcal{A}$ of the IND-CPA security game to win the COMP-DBL game.

As a next step, we need to show that the advantage of $\mathcal{A}'$ to win is negligible under the MP-CLWR assumption. We will consider the following sequence of games, where in all games $a_i \leftarrow U(\mathbb{Z}_q^{<n}[x])$ for $i \in [t]$ and the secret s is chosen via $s \leftarrow U\left((\mathbb{Z}_q^{<n+d+k-1}[x])^\times\right)$. Further, we sample $r_i \leftarrow U(\{0,1\}^{<k+1}[x])$ for $i \in [t]$ and set the first part of the ciphertext as $c_1 = \sum_{i \in [t]} r_i a_i \bmod q$.

The adversary $\mathcal{A}'$ receives in each game the tuple $(1^\lambda, \mathsf{pk}, c_1, c_2)$ and its target is to compute $\lfloor \text{DBL}(v) \rceil_2$, where v is specified by each game separately. Game 1 corresponds to the COMP-DBL game above.

G1 : Set $b_i = \lfloor a_i \odot_{d+k} s \rceil_p$, $\mathsf{pk} = (a_i, b_i)_i$, $v = \sum_i \text{INV}(b_i) \odot_d r_i \bmod q$, and $c_2 = \langle \text{DBL}(v) \rangle_2$,

G2 : Set $b_i \leftarrow \lfloor U(\mathbb{Z}_q^{<d+k}[x]) \rceil_p$, $\mathsf{pk} = (a_i, b_i)_i$, $v = \sum_i \text{INV}(b_i) \odot_d r_i \bmod q$, and $c_2 = \langle \text{DBL}(v) \rangle_2$,

G3 : Set $b_i \leftarrow \lfloor U(\mathbb{Z}_q^{<d+k}[x]) \rceil_p$, $\mathsf{pk} = (a_i, b_i)_i$, $v \leftarrow U(\mathbb{Z}_q^{<d}[x])$, and $c_2 = \langle \text{DBL}(v) \rangle_2$.

Note that in the last game, c_1 and c_2 are independent and hence the probability that $\mathcal{A}'$ outputs $\lfloor \text{DBL}(v) \rceil_2 \in \{0,1\}^d$ is exactly $1/2^d$, using Lemma 3.

Furthermore, the second and third game are within exponentially small statistical distance, using the generalized leftover hash lemma. In more detail, the statistical distance of the two distributions of $((a_i, b_i)_i, c_1, v)$ in Game 2 and 3 is given by

$$\Delta\left[\left((a_i, b_i)_i, \sum_{i \in [t]} r_i a_i, \sum_{i \in [t]} r_i \odot_d \text{INV}(b_i)\right), \left((a_i, b_i)_i, \sum_{i \in [t]} r_i a_i, v\right)\right] \le 2^{-\lambda},$$

where for all $i \in [t]$ the polynomials a_i, b_i, r_i and v are chosen uniformly at random in $\mathbb{Z}_q^{<n}[x]$, $\lfloor \mathbb{Z}_q^{<d+k}[x] \rfloor_p$, $\{0,1\}^{<k+1}[x]$ and $\mathbb{Z}_q^{<d}[x]$, respectively. Note that the randomness of $(h_{(b_i)_i})_{(b_i)_i}$ comes from the randomness of $(b_i)_i$ and since Lemma 8 shows that $(h_{(b_i)_i})_{(b_i)_i}$ is universal we can use Lemma 5. Thus, the statistical distance is bounded above by

$$\frac{1}{2} \cdot \sqrt{2^{-(k+1)t} \cdot q^{k+n+d}}.$$

Recall the data processing inequality of the statistical distance

$$\Delta(P^f, Q^f) \leq \Delta(P, Q)$$

for any function f, where P^f (resp. Q^f) denotes the distribution of $f(y)$ induced by sampling $y \leftarrow P$ (resp. $y \leftarrow Q$). Setting $f = \langle \mathrm{DBL}(\cdot) \rangle$, we get

$$\Delta\left(((a_i, b_i)_i, c_1, c_2), ((a_i, b_i)_i, c_1, u)\right) \leq 2^{-\lambda}.$$

The first and second game differ only in the way how the b_i are computed. In the first game, b_i is a rounded middle-product sample and in the latter on, it is a rounded uniform sample. We can interpret this situation as two different experiments, see Fig. 5.

$\mathrm{Exp}_1(\mathcal{C}, \mathcal{A}, \mathcal{S}_1)$	$\mathrm{Exp}_2(\mathcal{C}, \mathcal{A}, \mathcal{S}_2)$
1 : $((a_i, \lfloor a_i \odot_d s \rceil_p)_i, \mathsf{aux}) \leftarrow (\mathcal{X}_s^t, \mathsf{con})$	1 : $((a_i, b_i)_i, \mathsf{aux}) \leftarrow (\mathcal{U}^t, \mathsf{con})$
2 : $(\mathsf{Input}_1, \lfloor \mathrm{DBL}(v) \rceil_2) \leftarrow \mathcal{C}((a_i, b_i)_i, \mathsf{aux})$	2 : $(\mathsf{Input}_2, \lfloor \mathrm{DBL}(v) \rceil_2) \leftarrow \mathcal{C}((a_i, b_i)_i, \mathsf{aux})$
3 : $\mathsf{Output}_1 \leftarrow \mathcal{A}(\mathsf{Input}_1)$	3 : $\mathsf{Output}_2 \leftarrow \mathcal{A}(\mathsf{Input}_2)$
4 : **return** $\mathsf{Output}_1 = \lfloor \mathrm{DBL}(v) \rceil_2$	4 : **return** $\mathsf{Output}_2 = \lfloor \mathrm{DBL}(v) \rceil_2$

Fig. 5. Experiment setting of the security proof.

Recall from Definition 6 that $\mathcal{X}_s^t$ denotes the distribution of $(a_i, \lfloor a_i \odot_d s \rceil_p)_i$, where we choose the $a_i \leftarrow U(\mathbb{Z}_q^{<n}[x])$ independently and sample a fixed secret $s \leftarrow U\left((\mathbb{Z}_q^{<n}[x])^\times\right)$. Further, we denote by $\mathcal{U}^t$ the distribution of $(a_i, \lfloor b_i \rceil_p)_i$, where we choose the $a_i \leftarrow U(\mathbb{Z}_q^{<n}[x])$ and the $b_i \leftarrow U(\mathbb{Z}_q^{<d}[x])$ independently. In addition, con is an arbitrary distribution over $\{0,1\}^*$ which is independent from $\mathcal{X}_s^t$ and $\mathcal{U}^t$. The Input_1 of the first experiment $\mathrm{Exp}_1(\mathcal{C}, \mathcal{A}, \mathcal{S}_1)$ is given by $(1^\lambda, \mathsf{pk}, c_1, \langle \mathrm{DBL}(v) \rangle_2)$, where $v = \sum_i \mathrm{INV}(b_i) \odot_d r_i$ with $b_i = \lfloor a_i \odot_{d+k} s \rceil_p$. On the other hand, the Input_2 of the second experiment $\mathrm{Exp}_2(\mathcal{C}, \mathcal{A}, \mathcal{S}_2)$ is defined by $(1^\lambda, \mathsf{pk}, c_1, \langle \mathrm{DBL}(v) \rangle_2)$, where we still have $v = \sum_i \mathrm{INV}(b_i) \odot_d r_i$ but this time with $b_i \leftarrow \lfloor U(\mathbb{Z}_q^{<d+k}[x]) \rceil_p$. The Target is in both cases the same, namely $\lfloor \mathrm{DBL}(v) \rceil_2$.

According to the MP-CLWR assumption, if the success probability for any $\mathcal{A}$ to output the requested $\lfloor \mathrm{DBL}(v) \rceil_2$ is negligible when $b_i \leftarrow \lfloor U(\mathbb{Z}_q^{<d+k}[x]) \rceil_p$, it is also negligible when b_i is an MP-LWR instance.

Combining the arguments above shows that the success probability of $\mathcal{A}'$ is negligible under the MP-CLWR assumption, completing the security proof of our PKE scheme. $\square$

6   Parameters and Comparison

As example parameters we set the dimension $n \geq \lambda$, $k = d = n/2$, $t = \Theta(\log(n))$, $q = \Theta(n^{4+c} \log(n)^2)$ and $p = \Theta(n \log(n))$, where c is an arbitrary positive constant and λ the underlying security parameter. Using these parameters, the scheme is correct (Lemma 14) and secure under the MP-CLWR$_{p,q,n,d+k,t}$ assumption (Lemma 15). This allows us to rely on the MP-LWE$_{q,n,d+k,\chi}$ problem (Theorem 2), where the error distribution χ is B-bounded with $B = O(n^{2+c})$. Using the P-LWE$^f_{q,D_{\beta q}}$ to MP-LWE$_{q,n,d+k,D_{\alpha q}}$ reduction (Theorem 1), this in turn prevents attack as [AG11], where $\beta = \Omega(\sqrt{n}/q)$ for any f monic of degree n with constant coefficient coprime with q and expansion factor at least n^c.

We now compare our encryption scheme with the one of [RSSS17]. Figure 6 shows the asymptotic parameters, key sizes and ciphertext sizes for both schemes. The most important parameter is the value $\log(q)$ as it dominates the key and ciphertext sizes of both schemes. Asymptotically, in both cases this value is $\Theta(\log(n))$. For concrete parameters and security analysis, the interested reader may refer to the full version[2].

Parameter	[RSSS17]	Our work
n	$\geq \lambda$	$\geq \lambda$
c	> 0	> 0
k	$n/2$	$n/2$
d	$n/2$	$n/2$
t	$\Theta(\log(n))$	$\Theta(\log(n))$
q	$\Theta(n^{2.5+c}\sqrt{\log(n)})$	$\Theta(n^{4+c}\log(n)^2)$
$\log(q)$	$\Theta(\log(n))$	$\Theta(\log(n))$
α	$\Theta\left(\frac{1}{n\sqrt{\log(n)}}\right)$	-
p	-	$\Theta(n\log(n))$
B	-	$O(n^{2+c})$
Key size		
sk	$(n+d+k-1) \cdot \log(q)$	$(n+d+k-1) \cdot \log(q)$
pk	$t \cdot ((n+d+k)\log(q))$	$t \cdot (n\log(q) + (d+k)\log(p))$
Ciphertext size		
c_1	$(n+k)\log(q)$	$(n+k)\log(q)$
c_2	$d\log(q)$	d
c_3	-	k

Fig. 6. Comparison of asymptotic parameters, key sizes and ciphertext sizes

In general, the sampling cost is one of the intense operations of an encryption scheme. In the encryption scheme of [RSSS17], we need $2 \cdot t + 1$ sampling subroutines, including t from a rounded Gaussian distribution, during key generation

[2] The full version of this paper can be found in the Cryptology ePrint Archive with link: https://eprint.iacr.org/2019/1001.

and t sampling subroutines during encryption. In contrast, in our case we only need $t+1$ sampling subroutine during key generation and t sampling subroutines during encryption. Additionally, in our case all sampling is performed over some uniform distribution which is more efficient than Gaussian type sampling.

Further, in our encryption scheme we don't need to restrict the modulus q to be prime. Unlike [RSSS17], it works for all integer moduli which are sufficiently large. This gives an advantage on the choice of parameters.

Acknowledgments. This work is supported by the European Union PROMETHEUS project (Horizon 2020 Research and Innovation Program, grant 780701). This work has also received a French government support managed by the National Research Agency in the "Investing for the Future" program, under the national project RISQ P141580-2660001/DOS0044216, and under the project TYREX granted by the Comin-Labs excellence laboratory with reference ANR-10-LABX-07-01. This work is also supported through NATO SPS Project G5448 and through NIST awards 60NANB18D216 and 60NANB18D217.

Katharina Boudgoust is funded by the Direction Générale de l'Armement (Pôle de Recherche CYBER). Dipayan Das is funded by MHRD, India.

We also thank our anonymous referees for their helpful and constructive comments.

References

[AA16] Alperin-Sheriff, J., Apon, D.: Dimension-preserving reductions from LWE to LWR. IACR Cryptology ePrint Archive, 2016:589 (2016)

[ADPS16] Alkim, E., Ducas, L., Pöppelmann, T., Schwabe, P.: Post-quantum key exchange - a new hope. In: 25th USENIX Security Symposium, USENIX Security 16, Austin, TX, USA, 10–12 August 2016, pp. 327–343 (2016)

[AG11] Arora, S., Ge, R.: New algorithms for learning in presence of errors. In: Aceto, L., Henzinger, M., Sgall, J. (eds.) ICALP 2011. LNCS, vol. 6755, pp. 403–415. Springer, Heidelberg (2011). https://doi.org/10.1007/978-3-642-22006-7_34

[AKPW13] Alwen, J., Krenn, S., Pietrzak, K., Wichs, D.: Learning with rounding, revisited. In: Canetti, R., Garay, J.A. (eds.) CRYPTO 2013. LNCS, vol. 8042, pp. 57–74. Springer, Heidelberg (2013). https://doi.org/10.1007/978-3-642-40041-4_4

[BBF+19] Baan, H., et al.: Round5: compact and fast post-quantum public-key encryption. In: Ding, J., Steinwandt, R. (eds.) PQCrypto 2019. LNCS, vol. 11505, pp. 83–102. Springer, Cham (2019). https://doi.org/10.1007/978-3-030-25510-7_5

[BDJ06] Bryc, W., Dembo, A., Jiang, T.: Spectral measure of large random Hankel, Markov and Toeplitz matrices. Ann. Probab. **34**(1), 1–38 (2006)

[BGM+16] Bogdanov, A., Guo, S., Masny, D., Richelson, S., Rosen, A.: On the hardness of learning with rounding over small modulus. In: Kushilevitz, E., Malkin, T. (eds.) TCC 2016. LNCS, vol. 9562, pp. 209–224. Springer, Heidelberg (2016). https://doi.org/10.1007/978-3-662-49096-9_9

[BHLY16] Groot Bruinderink, L., Hülsing, A., Lange, T., Yarom, Y.: Flush, gauss, and reload - a cache attack on the BLISS lattice-based signature scheme. In: Cryptographic Hardware and Embedded Systems - CHES 2016–18th International Conference, Santa Barbara, CA, USA, 17–19 August 2016, Proceedings, pp. 323–345 (2016)

[BLL+15] Bai, S., Langlois, A., Lepoint, T., Stehlé, D., Steinfeld, R.: Improved security proofs in lattice-based cryptography: using the Rényi divergence rather than the statistical distance. In: Iwata, T., Cheon, J.H. (eds.) ASIACRYPT 2015. LNCS, vol. 9452, pp. 3–24. Springer, Heidelberg (2015). https://doi.org/10.1007/978-3-662-48797-6_1

[BLP+13] Brakerski, Z., Langlois, A., Peikert, C., Regev, O., Stehlé, D.: Classical hardness of learning with errors. In: Symposium on Theory of Computing Conference, STOC 2013, Palo Alto, CA, USA, 1–4 June 2013, pp. 575–584 (2013)

[BPR11] Banerjee, A., Peikert, C., Rosen, A.: Pseudorandom functions and lattices. IACR Cryptology ePrint Archive, 2011:401 (2011)

[BPR12] Banerjee, A., Peikert, C., Rosen, A.: Pseudorandom functions and lattices. In: Pointcheval, D., Johansson, T. (eds.) EUROCRYPT 2012. LNCS, vol. 7237, pp. 719–737. Springer, Heidelberg (2012). https://doi.org/10.1007/978-3-642-29011-4_42

[CIV16] Castryck, W., Iliashenko, I., Vercauteren, F.: Provably weak instances of ring-LWE revisited. In: Fischlin, M., Coron, J.-S. (eds.) EUROCRYPT 2016. LNCS, vol. 9665, pp. 147–167. Springer, Heidelberg (2016). https://doi.org/10.1007/978-3-662-49890-3_6

[CZZ18] Chen, L., Zhang, Z., Zhang, Z.: On the hardness of the computational ring-LWR problem and its applications. In: Peyrin, T., Galbraith, S. (eds.) ASIACRYPT 2018. LNCS, vol. 11272, pp. 435–464. Springer, Cham (2018). https://doi.org/10.1007/978-3-030-03326-2_15

[DB15] Du, C., Bai, G.: Towards efficient discrete Gaussian sampling for lattice-based cryptography. In: 25th International Conference on Field Programmable Logic and Applications, FPL 2015, London, United Kingdom, 2–4 September 2015, pp. 1–6 (2015)

[DKRV18] D'Anvers, J.-P., Karmakar, A., Sinha Roy, S., Vercauteren, F.: Saber: module-LWR based key exchange, CPA-secure encryption and CCA-secure KEM. In: Joux, A., Nitaj, A., Rachidi, T. (eds.) AFRICACRYPT 2018. LNCS, vol. 10831, pp. 282–305. Springer, Cham (2018). https://doi.org/10.1007/978-3-319-89339-6_16

[DXL12] Ding, J., Xie, X., Lin, X.: A simple provably secure key exchange scheme based on the learning with errors problem. IACR Cryptology ePrint Archive 2012:688 (2012)

[KL96] Kaltofen, E., Lobo, A.: On rank properties of Toeplitz matrices over finite fields. In: ISSAC, vol. 96, pp. 241–249 (1996)

[LM06] Lyubashevsky, V., Micciancio, D.: Generalized compact knapsacks are collision resistant. In: Bugliesi, M., Preneel, B., Sassone, V., Wegener, I. (eds.) ICALP 2006. LNCS, vol. 4052, pp. 144–155. Springer, Heidelberg (2006). https://doi.org/10.1007/11787006_13

[LPR10] Lyubashevsky, V., Peikert, C., Regev, O.: On ideal lattices and learning with errors over rings. In: Gilbert, H. (ed.) EUROCRYPT 2010. LNCS, vol. 6110, pp. 1–23. Springer, Heidelberg (2010). https://doi.org/10.1007/978-3-642-13190-5_1

[LS15] Langlois, A., Stehlé, D.: Worst-case to average-case reductions for module lattices. Des. Codes Cryptogr. **75**(3), 565–599 (2015)

[Lyu16] Lyubashevsky, V.: Digital signatures based on the hardness of ideal lattice problems in all rings. In: Cheon, J.H., Takagi, T. (eds.) ASIACRYPT 2016. LNCS, vol. 10032, pp. 196–214. Springer, Heidelberg (2016). https://doi.org/10.1007/978-3-662-53890-6_7

[NIS]   NIST: Post-quantum cryptography standardization. https://csrc.nist.gov/
            Projects/Post-Quantum-Cryptography/Post-Quantum-Cryptography-
            Standardization
[Pei09]   Peikert, C.: Public-key cryptosystems from the worst-case shortest vec-
            tor problem: extended abstract. In: Proceedings of the 41st Annual ACM
            Symposium on Theory of Computing, STOC 2009, Bethesda, MD, USA,
            31 May–2 June 2009, pp. 333–342 (2009)
[Pei14]   Peikert, C.: Lattice cryptography for the internet. In: Mosca, M. (ed.)
            PQCrypto 2014. LNCS, vol. 8772, pp. 197–219. Springer, Cham (2014).
            https://doi.org/10.1007/978-3-319-11659-4_12
[Pei16]   Peikert, C.: How (Not) to instantiate ring-LWE. In: Zikas, V., De Prisco,
            R. (eds.) SCN 2016. LNCS, vol. 9841, pp. 411–430. Springer, Cham (2016).
            https://doi.org/10.1007/978-3-319-44618-9_22
[Pes16]   Pessl, P.: Analyzing the shuffling side-channel countermeasure for lattice-
            based signatures. In: Dunkelman, O., Sanadhya, S.K. (eds.) INDOCRYPT
            2016. LNCS, vol. 10095, pp. 153–170. Springer, Cham (2016). https://doi.
            org/10.1007/978-3-319-49890-4_9
[R61]   Rényi, A.: On measures of entropy and information. In: Proceedings 4th
            Berkeley Symposium Mathematical Statistics and Probability, vol. I, pp.
            547–561. University California Press, Berkeley (1961)
[Reg05]   Regev, O.: On lattices, learning with errors, random linear codes, and
            cryptography. In: Proceedings of the 37th Annual ACM Symposium on
            Theory of Computing, Baltimore, MD, USA, 22–24 May 2005, pp. 84–93
            (2005)
[Reg09]   Regev, O.: On lattices, learning with errors, random linear codes, and
            cryptography. J. ACM 56(6), 34:1–34:40 (2009)
[RSSS17]   Roşca, M., Sakzad, A., Stehlé, D., Steinfeld, R.: Middle-product learning
            with errors. In: Katz, J., Shacham, H. (eds.) CRYPTO 2017. LNCS, vol.
            10403, pp. 283–297. Springer, Cham (2017). https://doi.org/10.1007/978-
            3-319-63697-9_10
[RSW18]   Rosca, M., Stehlé, D., Wallet, A.: On the ring-LWE and polynomial-LWE
            problems. In: Nielsen, J.B., Rijmen, V. (eds.) EUROCRYPT 2018. LNCS,
            vol. 10820, pp. 146–173. Springer, Cham (2018). https://doi.org/10.1007/
            978-3-319-78381-9_6
[Saa18]   Saarinen, M.-J.O.: Arithmetic coding and blinding countermeasures for
            lattice signatures - engineering a side-channel resistant post-quantum sig-
            nature scheme with compact signatures. J. Cryptographic Eng. 8(1), 71–84
            (2018)
[SSTX09]   Stehlé, D., Steinfeld, R., Tanaka, K., Xagawa, K.: Efficient public key
            encryption based on ideal lattices. In: Matsui, M. (ed.) ASIACRYPT 2009.
            LNCS, vol. 5912, pp. 617–635. Springer, Heidelberg (2009). https://doi.
            org/10.1007/978-3-642-10366-7_36
[vEH14]   van Erven, T., Harremoës, P.: Rényi divergence and kullback-leibler diver-
            gence. IEEE Trans. Inf. Theory 60(7), 3797–3820 (2014)

A Novel CCA Attack Using Decryption Errors Against LAC

Qian Guo[1,2](✉), Thomas Johansson[2](✉), and Jing Yang[2]

[1] Department of Informatics, University of Bergen,
Box 7803, 5020 Bergen, Norway
qian.guo@uib.no
[2] Department of Electrical and Information Technology, Lund University,
P.O. Box 118, 221 00 Lund, Sweden
{qian.guo,thomas.johansson,jing.yang}@eit.lth.se

Abstract. Cryptosystems based on Learning with Errors or related problems are central topics in recent cryptographic research. One main witness to this is the NIST Post-Quantum Cryptography Standardization effort. Many submitted proposals rely on problems related to Learning with Errors. Such schemes often include the possibility of decryption errors with some very small probability. Some of them have a somewhat larger error probability in each coordinate, but use an error correcting code to get rid of errors. In this paper we propose and discuss an attack for secret key recovery based on generating decryption errors, for schemes using error correcting codes. In particular we show an attack on the scheme LAC, a proposal to the NIST Post-Quantum Cryptography Standardization that has advanced to round 2.

In a standard setting with CCA security, the attack first consists of a precomputation of special messages and their corresponding error vectors. This set of messages are submitted for decryption and a few decryption errors are observed. In a statistical analysis step, these vectors causing the decryption errors are processed and the result reveals the secret key. The attack only works for a fraction of the secret keys. To be specific, regarding LAC256, the version for achieving the 256-bit classical security level, we recover one key among approximately 2^{64} public keys with complexity 2^{79}, if the precomputation cost of 2^{162} is excluded. We also show the possibility to attack a more probable key (say with probability 2^{-16}). This attack is verified via extensive simulation.

We further apply this attack to LAC256-v2, a new version of LAC256 in round 2 of the NIST PQ-project and obtain a multi-target attack with slightly increased precomputation complexity (from 2^{162} to 2^{171}). One can also explain this attack in the single-key setting as an attack with precomputation complexity of 2^{171} and success probability of 2^{-64}.

Keywords: Chosen-ciphertext security · Decryption errors ·
Lattice-based cryptography · NIST post-quantum standardization ·
LAC · LWE · Reaction attack

© International Association for Cryptologic Research 2019
S. D. Galbraith and S. Moriai (Eds.): ASIACRYPT 2019, LNCS 11921, pp. 82–111, 2019.
https://doi.org/10.1007/978-3-030-34578-5_4

1   Introduction

Lattice-based cryptography and the learning with errors problem (LWE) [24] is now one of the main research areas in cryptography. Factoring and the discrete logarithm problem have always been the fundamental basis in modern cryptography, but due to the threat of quantum computers, this will change. Lattice-based cryptography is the enabler for a rich collection of cryptographic primitives, ranging from key exchange, KEMs, encryption and digital signature to more advanced constructions like fully homomorphic encryption.

There are several reasons for using LWE or related problems as the underlying problem in cryptographic constructions. One is that constructions can be computationally very efficient compared to existing solutions. Another motivation is that LWE-based constructions may be resistant to quantum computers. It is also potentially the way how one can best provide constructions of fully homomorphic encryption [5,7].

An important problem is to establish the difficulty of solving various LWE-like problems, as it directly determines an upper bound on the security for a construction. One can use reductions for LWE to worst-case lattice problems [6,23,24], but it may not always be applicable or it may not give useful help in choosing optimal parameters. As of today, the security of a primitive is often estimated from the computational complexity of lattice-basis reduction algorithms like BKZ and its different versions.

Recent developments in several areas where problems may potentially be difficult even for a quantum computer, motivated several standardization projects, and some time ago the NIST post-quantum standardization project [2] started. In the specification of the analysis of submitted proposals, the most important aspect was said to be their security. Typically, the computational complexity for solving problems like LWE through lattice basis reduction is the guide when explicitly suggesting parameters in the different constructions. Most proposals have some proof of security, relating to some well known and difficult problems in lattice theory, such as the shortest vector problem. Most lattice-based schemes include also the possibility of having decryption errors with some small probability. Making this probability zero has a price, as the parameters should be adjusted accordingly, resulting in a performance loss. So many schemes tolerate a very small probability of decryption error, say something of size 2^{-128}.

An approach used by some schemes to enhance the performance is to allow a larger error probability in each position and then use error-correcting codes to correct the errors that occurred. In essence, part of the message information are parity-check bits that enable correction of up to a fixed number of errors. Such schemes can thus have a larger error probability in each bit position, as it requires that a number of them are in error for a decryption error to occur. Still, the possibility of having decryption errors can be used in cryptanalysis and the motivation for this paper is to further examine such possibilities.

We specifically focus on the proposal LAC, a scheme that has now advanced to round 2 in the NIST project. LAC is perhaps the most extreme scheme among the LWE-based schemes in the NIST project. It has a very small modulus, $q = 251$, which makes it very interesting. It leads to a rather large probability of error in a single position ($2^{-7.4}$), but then it uses a strong error correcting code to correct up to 55 errors, resulting in a small overall probability of decryption error (2^{-115}). LAC has excellent performance and is indeed an elegant design.

In our attack we consider CCA (chosen-ciphertext attacks) security for PKE (public-key encryption) schemes and use the algorithms as specified in the LAC design document.

1.1 Related Works

The use of decryption errors in cryptanalysis has been frequently used in all areas of cryptography, e.g., [4]. For lattice-based encryption systems and NTRU, some works in this direction are listed [12, 16–18].

More recently, Fluhrer [11] showed an attack on key-exchange protocols in a key reuse setting and [9] extended the attack. In [3] a chosen-ciphertext attack on the recent proposal HILA5 [25] was described, using decryption errors. These attacks can be described as CCA type attacks on proposals without CCA transforms.

Here we will only consider CCA attacks on schemes proposed for CCA security. For such a case, an attack model for LWE-based schemes and a specific attack on ss-ntru-pke, another NIST submission, was given in the recent paper [8]. We base the attack in this paper on the same model. For the specific case of LAC, there has also been some discussion on the NIST forum, on how to increase the probability of decryption errors [1].

For code-based schemes, Guo, Johansson and Stankovski [14] proposed a key-recovery attack against the CCA-secure version of QC-MDPC. They used a property that 'colliding pairs' in the noise and the secret can change the decryption failure rate. In the statistical analysis in this paper, we use some kind of similar idea, identifying similar patterns between a part of the secret key and error vectors.

1.2 Contributions

In this paper we describe an attack for secret key recovery based on generating decryption errors, where error correcting codes are used. It is applied on the CCA version of the proposal LAC and it is a chosen-ciphertext attack. The attack is described as a sequence of steps. The first step is a precomputation phase where messages generating special error vectors are found. In the second step we send these encrypted messages for decryption and some decryption errors are observed. Finally, the major part of the attack is the last step, in which a statistical analysis of the messages/errors causing the decryption errors are analyzed. In particular, we identify a correlation between consecutive positions in the secret key and consecutive positions in error vectors that can be used to restore the secret vector. The attack success is conditioned on a certain weight-property of the secret key, causing the decoding error probability to be significantly higher than that in the average case. In particular, we describe the details of an attack to LAC256 with success probability[1] larger than 2^{-64} with complexity less than 2^{79}, assuming a single precomputation of complexity 2^{162} encryptions. The statistical analysis is supported by extensive simulation results[2].

We also extend our approach to attacking a new version of LAC256 in round 2 of the NIST PQ-project. We design a new desired noise pattern that can lead to a high decryption error probability. For instance, with the precomputation of about 2^{120} for one chosen message/error, the error probability is simulated to be $2^{-12.74}$, for a key with probability 2^{-64}. Using this error pattern, one could classically solve LAC256-v2 with complexity far less than that of the claimed security level by our estimation.

1.3 Organization

The remaining of the paper is organized as follows. In Sect. 2 we describe the LAC proposal from the NIST Post-Quantum standardization process. In Sect. 3, we present the main attack procedure, which is followed by a section elaborating the statistical analysis step, i.e., how to reconstruct the secret key from the decryption failures. Section 5 shows how to apply the proposed attack to the new LAC version in round 2 of the NIST PQ-project, and Sect. 6 includes related discussions. Finally, we present the conclusion in Sect. 7.

2 Description of LAC

LAC [19] is a proposal in the NIST Post-Quantum competition, including three versions for different security levels, i.e., LAC128, LAC192, and LAC256. We focus in this paper only on attacking LAC256. Also, we consider only CCA security as a CPA-version is almost trivially broken in a reaction attack model.

2.1 Some Basic Notation

Let $\mathbb{Z}_q$ be the ring of integers modulo q represented in $(-q/2, q/2]$ and let $\mathcal{R}$ denote the ring $\mathbb{Z}_q[X]/(X^n+1)$. Consider the one-to-one correspondence between polynomials in $\mathcal{R}$ and vectors in $\mathbb{Z}_q^n$. Vectors will be represented with bold lower-case letters, while matrices are written in uppercase. For a vector $\mathbf{a}$, the transpose vector is written $\mathbf{a}^T$.

The Euclidean norm of a polynomial $a \in \mathcal{R}$ is written as $\|a\|_2$ and defined as $\sqrt{\sum_i a_i^2}$, which is extended to vectors as $\|\mathbf{a}\|_2 = \sqrt{\sum_i \|\mathbf{a}_i\|_2^2}$. The notation $a \xleftarrow{\$} \chi(\mathcal{R})$ will be used to represent the sampling of $a \in \mathcal{R}$ according to the

---

[1] Assuming for 2^{64} users in the system is considered as a reasonable setting in the NIST PQC project discussion forum [1].

[2] The implementation is available at: https://github.com/MelodyJuly/A-Novel-CCA-Attack-using-Decryption-Errors-against-LAC.

distribution χ. Writing $\mathsf{Samp}(\chi; \mathsf{seed})$ means computing an output following the distribution χ using seed as the seed.

A distribution used in LAC is the centered binomial distribution, denoted Ψ_σ^n. In particular, in LAC256 one uses Ψ_1, which is the distribution on $\{-1, 0, 1\}$, where $P(X = 0) = 1/2$ and $P(X = -1) = P(X = 1) = 1/4$ for $X \xleftarrow{\$} \Psi_1$. Note that the mean is 0 and the variance is $1/2$, so for Ψ_1^n the variance is $n/2$. We also denote $U(\mathcal{R})$ the uniform distribution on $\mathcal{R}$.

For cryptographic schemes of this type, the definition of security is to (at least) fulfill the concept of indistinguishability under adaptive chosen ciphertext attacks, denoted IND-CCA2. This is usually described through the *advantage* of a certain security game where the adversary may adaptively ask for decryptions of various ciphertexts, except the one that is given as the challenge. As our attack is more direct and simply tries to recover the secret key, we do not further introduce notions of security. We note however that all results given can be translated to corresponding results in the form of advantage of security games in the IND-CCA2 model.

2.2   The LAC Scheme

LAC is a concrete instantiation of a general construction proposed in [22] where the novelty lies in the combination of a very small q together with a very strong error correcting procedure, which allows to have many errors in different positions and still be able to correctly decrypt to the message used in encryption with a very large probability.

The key generation algorithm of LAC is shown in Algorithm 1. The encapsulation algorithm Enc is shown in Algorithm 2, and the decapsulation algorithm Dec is shown in Algorithm 3. These algorithms call the CPA-secure schemes described in Algorithms 4–5. For more details we refer to the original design document [19].

Algorithm 1. LAC.KeyGen()

Output: A pair of public key and secret key (pk, sk).

1) $\mathsf{seed_a} \xleftarrow{\$} \mathcal{S}$;
2) $\mathbf{a} \leftarrow \mathsf{Samp}(U(\mathcal{R}); \mathsf{seed_a}) \in \mathcal{R}$;
3) $\mathbf{s} \xleftarrow{\$} \Psi_\sigma^n$;
4) $\mathbf{e} \xleftarrow{\$} \Psi_\sigma^n$;
5) $\mathbf{b} \leftarrow \mathbf{as} + \mathbf{e} \in \mathcal{R}$;
6) **return** $(pk := (\mathsf{seed_a}, \mathbf{b}), sk := \mathbf{s})$;

Recall that our prime target LAC256, uses Ψ_1, a distribution that is 1 (or -1) with probability $1/4$ and 0 with probability $1/2$. We assume that $l_v = n$.

Algorithm 2. LAC.CCA.Enc(pk; seed_m)

Output: A ciphertext and encapsulation key pair $(\mathbf{c}, K)$.

1) $\mathbf{m} \leftarrow \text{Samp}(U(\mathcal{M}); \text{seed}_m) \in \mathcal{M}$;
2) $\text{seed} \leftarrow G(\mathbf{m}) \in \mathcal{S}$;
3) $\mathbf{c} \leftarrow \text{LAC.CPA.Enc}(pk, \mathbf{m}; \text{seed})$;
4) $K \leftarrow H(\mathbf{m}, \mathbf{c}) \in \{0, 1\}^{l_k}$;
5) **return** $(\mathbf{c}, K)$;

Algorithm 3. LAC.CCA.Dec(sk; $\mathbf{c}$)

Output: An encapsulation key (K).

1) $\mathbf{m} \leftarrow \text{LAC.CPA.Dec}(sk, \mathbf{c})$;
2) $K \leftarrow H(\mathbf{m}, \mathbf{c})$;
3) $\text{seed} \leftarrow G(\mathbf{m}) \in \mathcal{S}$;
4) $\mathbf{c}' \leftarrow \text{LAC.CPA.Enc}(pk, \mathbf{m}; \text{seed})$;
5) **if** $\mathbf{c}' \neq \mathbf{c}$ **then**
   $\quad \lfloor \; K \leftarrow H(H(sk), \mathbf{c})$;
6) **return** K;

The underlying ring is of the form $\mathcal{R} = \mathbb{Z}_q[x]/(x^n + 1)$, where $n = 1024$ and $q = 251$. One important selling point of this scheme is its much smaller alphabetic size, compared with other lattice-based proposals; this, however, also leads to the main obstacle regarding to its decryption success probability. This scheme targets the highest NIST security level of V, corresponding roughly to 256-bit classical security.

An important part of the scheme is the use of the ECCEnc($\mathbf{m}$) subroutine. This part uses a BCH code with length 1023 and dimension 520, which is capable of decoding up to 55 errors and is employed for correcting errors. We assume a decoder for the BCH code that will fail if the number of erroneous positions is 56 or more. All parameters are summarized in Table 1.

A characterizing property of the scheme (as for many other schemes) is the fact that decryption may fail. A main question is to examine the probability of such an event. This is done in the design document [19] and we briefly summarize the results. The error term in LAC, denoted $\mathbf{W}$, is of the form[3]

$$\mathbf{W} = \mathbf{e}_1 \mathbf{s} - \mathbf{e} \mathbf{r} + \mathbf{e}_2,$$

since the computation $\mathbf{c}'_m \leftarrow \mathbf{c}_2 - \mathbf{c}_1 \mathbf{s}$ gives

$$\mathbf{c}'_m = (\mathbf{br}) + \mathbf{e}_2 + \lfloor \tfrac{q}{2} \rfloor \cdot \mathbf{c}_m - (\mathbf{ar} + \mathbf{e}_1)\mathbf{s} = \lfloor \tfrac{q}{2} \rfloor \cdot \mathbf{c}_m + \mathbf{W}.$$

---

[3] The noise term is equivalent to the representation in [19] due to symmetry.

Algorithm 4. LAC.CPA.Enc($pk = (\mathrm{seed_a}, b), m \in \mathcal{M}; \mathrm{seed} \in \mathcal{S}$)

Output: A ciphertext c.

1) $a \leftarrow \mathsf{Samp}(U(\mathcal{R}); \mathrm{seed_a}) \in \mathcal{R}$;
2) $c_m \leftarrow \mathsf{ECCEnc}(m) \in \{0,1\}^{l_v}$;
3) $(r, e_1, e_2) \leftarrow \mathsf{Samp}(\Psi_\sigma^n, \Psi_\sigma^n, \Psi_\sigma^{l_v}; \mathrm{seed})$;
4) $c_1 \leftarrow ar + e_1 \in \mathcal{R}$;
5) $c_2 \leftarrow (br)_{l_v} + e_2 + \lfloor \frac{q}{2} \rfloor \cdot c_m \in \mathbb{Z}_q^{l_v}$;
6) **return** $c := (c_1, c_2) \in \mathcal{R} \times \mathbb{Z}_q^{l_v}$;

Algorithm 5. LAC.CPA.Dec($sk = s; c = (c_1, c_2)$)

Output: A plaintext m.

1) $u \leftarrow c_1 s \in \mathcal{R}$;
2) $c_m' \leftarrow c_2 - (u)_{l_v} \in \mathbb{Z}_q^{l_v}$;
3) **for** $i = 0$ to $l_v - 1$ **do**
   if $\frac{q}{4} \le c_{mi}' < \frac{3q}{4}$ then
   $\quad c_{mi} \leftarrow 1$
   else
   $\quad c_{mi} \leftarrow 0$
4) $m \leftarrow \mathsf{ECCDec}(c_m)$;
5) **return** m;

Now a single position in **W** is essentially a sum of $2n$ random variables, each drawn from a distribution obtained by multiplying two random variables from Ψ_1. The variance for such a random variable is $1/4$. The sum is then approximated by a Gaussian distribution with mean 0 and variance $2n/4$. A single position is in error if the contribution from **W** in that position is larger than $\lfloor \frac{q}{4} \rfloor$ in absolute value, so this gives an error probability in a single position which is roughly

$$\delta = 1 - \mathrm{erf}(62/\sqrt{1024}) \approx 2^{-7.44}.$$

Now, since the error correction procedure corrects up to 55 errors, it is argued in [19] that one can then approximate the overall probability of a decryption error as

$$\sum_{i=56}^{1024} \binom{1024}{i} \delta^i (1-\delta)^{1024-i} \approx 2^{-115}.$$

Table 1. Proposed parameters of LAC256.

n	q	$\mathcal{R}$	Distribution	BCH$[n_e, l_e, d_e, t_e]$	Security
1024	251	$\frac{\mathbb{Z}_q[x]}{\langle x^n+1 \rangle}$	Ψ_1	$[1023, 520, 111, 55]$	V

Since the stated decryption error probability is very small, the scheme does appear to be quite safe against attacks trying to use the possibility of having decryption errors.

3   The Attack

We first note that LAC is a scheme without protection against multi-target attacks, meaning that precomputed information can be used on any public key. This is because the public key is not included when the seed is computed for generating the noise vectors in encryption. In the code, this is visible in the step 2) $\text{seed} \leftarrow G(\mathbf{m}) \in \mathcal{S}$; of Algorithm 2. It is also a bit unclear how to consider the computational complexity of the precomputation part, as it is something that only needs to be performed once and then never again. At least, as long as the complexity is below 2^{256} encryptions (or 2^{128} in a quantum setting) it should not violate the limits of a successful attack.

We will now present the attack on LAC256 and it is described in three steps; a first step of precomputation; a second step of getting precomputed ciphertexts decrypted and checking the decryption error probability; and a last phase of performing a statistical analysis to recover the secret key.

3.1   Attack Step 1 - Precomputation

We construct a special set $\mathcal{S}$ of messages/error vectors by precomputation. To be precise, we pick a random message $\mathbf{m}$ ($\text{seed}_\mathbf{m}$) and compute the seed through the two steps from Algorithm 2:

$$1) \ \mathbf{m} \leftarrow \text{Samp}(U(\mathcal{M}); \text{seed}_\mathbf{m}) \in \mathcal{M};$$
$$2) \ \text{seed} \leftarrow G(\mathbf{m}) \in \mathcal{S};$$

Then compute the noise vectors according to step 3 of Algorithm 4:

$$3) \ (\mathbf{r}, \mathbf{e}_1, \mathbf{e}_2) \leftarrow \text{Samp}(\Psi_\sigma^n, \Psi_\sigma^n, \Psi_\sigma^{l_v}; \text{seed});$$

We are now only interested in keeping messages that give rise to noise vectors of special form. In our attack we target only special properties of the $\mathbf{e}_1$ vector. Let us first consider messages/errors including any combination where the error vector $\mathbf{e}_1$ contains an interval of consecutive l_1 all positive or all negative entries. Assuming a randomly selected error vector, the probability of finding such an interval starting in the first position is then

$$p = 2 \times (1/4)^{l_1}.$$

As we can start from any position, the probability that a random message/noise vector fulfills the condition for $\mathcal{S}$ can be lower-bounded by

$$p_0 = 2 \times (1/4)^{l_1} \times 3/4 \cdot n. \tag{1}$$

The reason is that if one searches for a desired pattern, an erroneous sequence will on average use $3/4 \cdot 1 + 1/4 \cdot 3/4 \cdot 2 + (1/4)^2 \cdot 3/4 \cdot 3 + \ldots \approx 4/3$ positions until there is a possibility for a new desired sequence. We then know Eq. (1) by $p_0 = p \times 3/4 \cdot n$. The precomputation complexity is thus less than $|\mathcal{S}|/p_0$ runs of the steps above. We denote the type of noise vectors of the above kind as *TYPE 1* noise vectors. In particular, we will consider the length[4] $l_1 \in \{65, 85\}$ when describing the attack by examples.

We note that there are many other special forms of the noise that can be useful in an attack. We define one more such set of special noise vectors related to the $\mathbf{e}_1$ vector, being the case when $\mathbf{e}_1$ contains an interval of length $l_0 + l_1$ with at least l_1 either all positive or all negative entries and the remaining entries all-zero. The probability of finding such an interval in $\mathbf{e}_1$ starting in the first position is then

$$p' = 2 \sum_{i=l_1}^{l_0+l_1} \binom{l_0 + l_1}{i} \times (1/4)^i \cdot (1/2)^{l_1+l_0-i}.$$

Determining the probability of having such a subsequence starting from any position is more complicated to compute, but would roughly result in a probability $c \cdot n \cdot p'$ for some not too small constant c. We denote the type of noise vectors of the above kind as *TYPE 2* noise vectors.

Basically, *TYPE 2* noise vectors are much more likely to appear compared to *TYPE 1* noise vectors, so the required precomputation complexity will be smaller, but at the same time it will give a smaller contribution to the correlation used in the later statistical analysis part of the attack, for the same length.

After finishing this step, we have a stored set $\mathcal{S}$ of precomputed messages/error vectors with some special property for the $\mathbf{e}_1$ part.

3.2   Attack Step 2 - Submit Ciphertexts for Decryption

We now map the messages in $\mathcal{S}$ to ciphertexts and give them to the decryption algorithm for each public key. We record the decryption error rate and keep track of the set of error vectors creating a decryption error, denoted $\mathcal{S}'$. We will attack and recover the secret key for keys[5] where the decryption error rate is large.

As the enabling property for $\mathbf{s}$ to have a large decryption error rate, we assume the property

$$\left| \sum_{i=0}^{n-1} s_i \right| \geq \delta_0,$$

---

[4] We choose $l_1 \in \{65, 85\}$ to balance the complexity of precomputation and simulations. One can definitely choose a smaller l_1 to achieve a lower precomputation complexity at the cost of increasing the attack effort.

[5] In the real case, one can start with the key with the largest decryption error rate, and then try different keys with error rates in the decreasing order.

for δ_0 a positive integer. One can approximate $\sum_{i=0}^{n-1} s_i$ by a Gaussian distribution with mean 0 and variance $n/2$. With this approximation, if we set $\delta_0 = 208$ as an example, the secret $\mathbf{s}$ will have this property with probability about 2^{-64}.

We now need to examine the decryption error probability for such a condition on $\mathbf{s}$. The error term in LAC is of the form

$$\mathbf{W} = \mathbf{e_1 s} - \mathbf{er} + \mathbf{e_2}.$$

The decryption error occurs if among all the coefficients of $\mathbf{W}$, at least 56 of them are with absolute value larger than $\lfloor q/4 \rfloor = 62$. In polynomial form, the error $w(x)$ is computed as

$$w(x) = e_1(x)s(x) - e(x)r(x) + e_2(x).$$

We only target the $e_1(x)s(x)$ term and consider the remaining as additional contributing noise in each position, denoted $\hat{N}(x)$, for the moment. For simplicity, we assume that all error vectors are of *TYPE 1* and have the assumed consecutive ones in their first positions, i.e., $e_1(x)$ is of the form $(e_0, e_1, \ldots, e_{n-1}) = (1, 1, \ldots, 1, e_{l_1}, \ldots, e_{n-1})$. In vector form, the multiplication $e_1(x)s(x)$ can be written as

$$(s_0, s_1, \ldots, s_{n-1}) \cdot \begin{bmatrix} e_0 & e_1 & e_2 & \cdots & e_{n-1} \\ -e_{n-1} & e_0 & e_1 & \cdots & e_{n-2} \\ \vdots & \vdots & \vdots & \ddots & \vdots \\ -e_1 & -e_2 & -e_3 & \cdots & e_0 \end{bmatrix}.$$

Since we assume $(e_0, e_1, \ldots, e_{l_1-1}) = (1, 1, \ldots, 1)$, the above is written

$$(s_0, s_1, \ldots, s_{n-1}) \cdot \begin{bmatrix} 1 & 1 & \cdots & 1 & e_{l_1} & e_{l_1+1} & \cdots & e_{n-1} \\ -e_{n-1} & 1 & 1 & \cdots & 1 & e_{l_1} & \cdots & e_{n-2} \\ -e_{n-2} & -e_{n-1} & 1 & \cdots & 1 & 1 & \cdots & e_{n-3} \\ \vdots & \vdots & \ddots & \ddots & \vdots & \vdots & \ddots & \vdots \\ -e_{l_1} & -e_{l_1+1} & \cdots & -e_{n-1} & 1 & 1 & \cdots & 1 \\ -1 & -e_{l_1} & -e_{l_1+1} & \cdots & -e_{n-1} & 1 & \cdots & 1 \\ \vdots & \ddots & \ddots & \ddots & \cdots & \ddots & \ddots & \vdots \\ -1 & \cdots & -1 & -e_{l_1} & -e_{l_1+1} & \cdots & -e_{n-1} & 1 \end{bmatrix}.$$

We model the $\hat{N}(x) = -\mathbf{er} + \mathbf{e_2}$ part of the noise as a sum of randomly generated variables (as also done in the LAC submission). Instead, we focus on the $\mathbf{e_1 s}$ part, where we now have both $\mathbf{e_1}$ and $\mathbf{s}$ of special forms. We see that for a particular key $\mathbf{s}$, the contribution from the fixed part $(e_0, e_1, \ldots, e_{l_1-1}) = (1, 1, \ldots, 1)$ to the multiplication $\mathbf{e_1 s}$ is a vector defined as follows.

Definition 1 (Contribution vector). *The contribution vector* $\mathbf{cv(s)}$ *of* $(e_0, e_1, \ldots, e_{l_1-1}) = (1, 1, \ldots, 1)$ *for a secret key* $\mathbf{s}$ *is defined as*

$$(cv_0, cv_1, \ldots, cv_{n-1}),$$

where

$$cv_i = \begin{cases} \sum_{k=0}^{i} s_{i-k} - \sum_{k=n-l_1+1+i}^{n-1} s_k, & \text{if } 0 \le i < l_1 - 1, \\ \sum_{k=0}^{l_1-1} s_{i-k}, & \text{if } l_1 - 1 \le i \le n - 1. \end{cases} \tag{2}$$

The basic idea in the attack is that the contribution vector is a fixed contribution that is the same for all $\mathbf{e_1}$ vectors of *TYPE 1*. Furthermore, assuming the secret vector $\mathbf{s}$ of the form $\left| \sum_{i=0}^{n-1} s_i \right| \ge \delta_0$, it is easily verified that most coefficients in the contribution vector $cv(\mathbf{s})$ are quite large. With a large fixed contribution in most coefficients, the probability of having a decryption error will drastically increase.

It seems difficult to derive an accurate estimation on the error probability due to the dependence between different positions in the error. One may try to use experiments to determine the variance and have a Gaussian approximation. But this distribution could be key-dependent and therefore somewhat unhelpful in a general sense.

Example 1: We have two choices for l_1 in implementation, i.e., $l_1 = 85$ or 65. In the first case, if we collect errors with 85 consecutive 1's or -1's, then this event happens with probability about

$$2^{-85 \times 2} \times n \times \frac{3}{2} \ge 2^{-160}.$$

In the latter case, the probability is about 2^{-120}. To collect $|\mathcal{S}|$ messages/error vectors, we need $2^{160}|\mathcal{S}|$ (or $2^{120}|\mathcal{S}|$) precomputation work. If we bound the number of decryption oracle calls by 2^{64}, as suggested by NIST, then the overall precomputation complexity is bounded by 2^{224} (or 2^{184}).

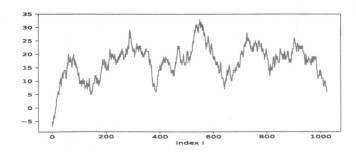

Fig. 1. The contribution vector $cv(\mathbf{s})$ for a key $\mathbf{s}$ with $\delta_0 = 208$ when $l_1 = 85$.

Assume we target a secret key $\mathbf{s}$ having $\delta_0 = 208$ more 1 (-1) than -1 (1). For a randomly chosen secret key $\mathbf{s}$ of this type we have plotted the contribution vector in Fig. 1. In Fig. 2 the corresponding histogram for $cv(\mathbf{s})$ is given. We see that many coefficients in the contribution vector are quite large. Thus, the

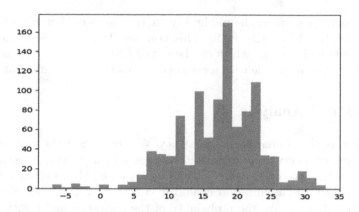

Fig. 2. The histogram of the contribution vector depicted in Fig. 1.

overall probability of having more than 56 coefficients with large absolute value can be much larger than that in the official analysis of decryption errors.

The error probability is difficult to predict and requires further investigation. In simulation, as shown in Table 2, we obtained decryption error probabilities of $2^{-6.6}$ for $l_1 = 85$ and $2^{-12.2}$ for $l_1 = 65$. This should be compared to the general decryption error probability of 2^{-115}!

Table 2. Decryption error probability P_e for a key s with $\delta_0 = 208$.

l_1	P_e
85	$2^{-6.6}$
65	$2^{-12.2}$

To conclude this part of the attack, we submit a limited number of ciphertexts of *TYPE 1* (say with $l_1 = 65$) for decryption (say 2^{15}) and if we detect several errors (say around $2^{15} \cdot 2^{-12.2}$) we assume that δ_0 is large. We then get many more decryption failures in $\mathcal{S}'$ for this weak key and move to the statistical analysis part. If few errors are detected, we move on to another public key.

3.3 Attack Step 3 - Statistical Analysis

This step assumes that we have identified a weak public key in the previous step. After receiving the errors, caused by the vectors in $\mathcal{S}'$, we need to reconstruct the secret key s. Since the reconstruction step is the most difficult task for attacking LAC, we write it in the next section for fully describing the details.

Last, suppose that we have a guessed secret vector denoted by (s', e'). If $(\Delta s, \Delta e) = (s, e) - (s', e')$ is small, we can recover it using lattice reduction efficiently. Thus, we obtain the correct value of (s, e). To be more specific, we want to recover $(\mathbf{s}, \mathbf{e})$ from the public key $(\mathbf{a}, \mathbf{b} = \mathbf{as} + \mathbf{e})$. Let $\mathbf{b}' = \mathbf{as}' + \mathbf{e}'$. We have that $\mathbf{b} - \mathbf{b}' = \mathbf{a}\Delta\mathbf{s} + \Delta\mathbf{e}$. This is a new lattice problem with same dimension but smaller noise, which can be solved with less computational effort. In conclusion, we can handle with some small errors from the statistical testing.

4   Statistical Analysis

Assume that we have determined a weak key. We now collect the vectors $(\mathbf{e_1}, \mathbf{r})$ in $\mathcal{S}'$ that caused decryption errors and average all the collected vectors. Our observation is that the parts $\mathbf{e_1}\mathbf{s}$, $-\mathbf{er}$, and $\mathbf{e_2}$ are all highly correlated with the contribution vector. The intuition behind it is that for a larger absolute value in the contribution vector, the probability of the corresponding position in $\mathbf{W}$ exceeding 62 is larger, thereby implying that the values of $\mathbf{e_1}\mathbf{s}$, $-\mathbf{er}$, and $\mathbf{e_2}$ should be all larger.

We next derive two different approaches for the statistical analysis. The first one is a theoretical approach that is easy to analyze, where we recover the secret $\mathbf{s}$ by observing the correlation between $\mathbf{e_2}$ and the contribution vector. The second one is a heuristic approach exploiting the fact that $-\mathbf{er}$ has a positive contribution on almost all the coefficients. We then try to recover the $\mathbf{e}$ vector. This heuristic approach shows stronger correlation in implementation.

4.1   Theoretical Arguments for Statistical Recovery of the Contribution Vector

This subsection contains a recovery procedure which uses more theoretical arguments. We first note that if we recover the contribution vector (or something close to the contribution vector) then we can also almost trivially recover the secret key. The procedure to be given uses the dependence between $\mathbf{cv}(\mathbf{s})$ and the given $\mathbf{e_2}$ vector. We know from before that the probability of error in a particular position i depends on the value of the contribution vector in this position, which is here simply denoted cv_i. The good thing for analysis is that $\mathbf{e_2}$ is independent of the other parts involved in the error $\mathbf{W}$. Now denote the value of $\mathbf{e_2}$ in position i as E_i for simplicity. The observation we will examine is that the larger the value of cv_i is, the more likely it is that $E_i = 1$.

We denote the event of decryption error by $\mathcal{D}$, meaning no less than 56 positions are in error. We know that the probability for an error in position i in the set of vectors causing decryption failure is $P(cv_i + N_i + E_i > 62|\mathcal{D})$, where N_i denotes the non-fixed part of $\mathbf{W}$ excluding E_i, that can be numerically computed via the convolution of probability distributions.

Now let us examine $P(E_i = 1|\mathcal{D})$ through

$$P(E_i = 1|\mathcal{D}) = P(\text{error in pos. } i|\mathcal{D})P(E_i = 1|\text{error in pos. } i, \mathcal{D})$$
$$+ P(\text{no error in pos. } i|\mathcal{D})P(E_i = 1|\text{no error in pos. } i, \mathcal{D}).$$

We assume that $P(E_i = 1|\text{no error in pos. } i, \mathcal{D}) \approx P(E_i = 1|\text{no error in pos.} i)$. Also, $P(E_i = 1|\text{error in pos. } i, \mathcal{D}) \approx P(E_i = 1|\text{error in pos. } i)$. Then we can rewrite as

$$P(E_i = 1|\mathcal{D}) = P(\text{error in pos. } i|\mathcal{D})P(E_i = 1|\text{error in pos. } i) \quad (3)$$
$$+ P(\text{no error in pos.} i|\mathcal{D}) \cdot P(E_i = 1|\text{no error in pos. } i).$$

Finally, we note that $P(E_i = x|\text{error in pos. } i) = P(\text{error in pos. } i|E_i = x) \cdot P(E_i = x)/P(\text{error in pos. } i)$, and compute $P(E_i = 1|\text{error in pos. } i)$ by

$$\frac{P(N_i > 61 - cv_i)}{P(N_i > 61 - cv_i) + 2P(N_i > 62 - cv_i) + P(N_i > 63 - cv_i)}. \quad (4)$$

Similarly, $P(E_i = x|\text{no error in pos. } i) = P(\text{no error in pos. } i|E_i = x) \cdot P(E_i = x)/P(\text{no error in pos. } i)$, and we compute $P(E_i = 1|\text{no error in pos. } i)$ by

$$\frac{P(N_i \leq 61 - cv_i)}{P(N_i \leq 61 - cv_i) + 2P(N_i \leq 62 - cv_i) + P(N_i \leq 63 - cv_i)}.$$

We get

$$P(E_i = 1|\mathcal{D}) = P(\text{error in pos. } i|\mathcal{D})P(E_i = 1|\text{error in pos. } i)$$
$$+ (1 - P(\text{error in pos.} i|\mathcal{D})) \cdot P(E_i = 1|\text{no error in pos. } i).$$

The probability $P(\text{error in pos.} i|\mathcal{D})$ is difficult to derive analytically, as one has to consider all combinations of error patterns with ≥ 56 errors. However, it can be determined from simulation results quite efficiently, since its dependence on cv_i is strong. Figure 3 plots this correlation and shows that a bigger $|cv_i|$ leads to a larger $P(\text{error in pos.} i|\mathcal{D})$ in almost all the cases.

Let us now examine the difference between $P(E_i = 1|\mathcal{D})$ for two different positions where the cv_i values are close, say 10 and 11. Examining $P(\text{error in pos.} i|\mathcal{D})$ for $cv_i = 10$ in simulation gives $P(\text{error in pos.} i|\mathcal{D}) \approx 0.023587$ and the same for $cv_i = 11$ gives $P(\text{error in pos.} i|\mathcal{D}) \approx 0.027138$.

With these values, one can compute the absolute difference ϵ of $P(E_i = 1|\mathcal{D})$ for $cv_i = 10$ and $cv_i = 11$, respectively. It would then require no more than $4/\epsilon^2$ decryption failures to distinguish between different cv_i values counting only the frequency of $E_i = 1$, with high probability. For larger cv_i values the difference between probabilities for consecutive cv_i values is increasing, so almost all entries of $\mathbf{cv}(\mathbf{s})$ can be determined through the frequency of $E_i = 1$.

Note that we need to determine the cv_i values for multiple positions, so we conservatively choose the following formula to estimate the data complexity,

$$\frac{8 \ln(n_t)}{\epsilon^2}, \quad (5)$$

where n_t is the number of tests bounded by n. Setting $n_t = n$, we numerically compute that it requires about $2^{34.0}$ errors to distinguish all the cv_i values larger than 11 with probability close to 1, if $l_1 = 85$.

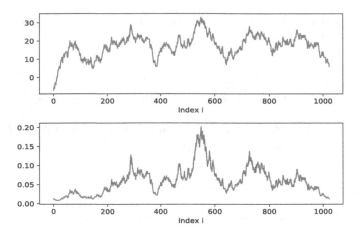

Fig. 3. The correlation of cv_i v.s. $P(\text{error in pos}.i|\mathcal{D})$. $700{,}000$ $TYPE$ 1 errors are collected and $l_1 = 85$. The x axis represents the index i, for $0 \leq i < n$.

Now assume that we have recovered about 870 cv_i values[6] for all $cv_i \geq 11$. We can then trivially recover the secret by using the inherent algebraic equations in the definition of cv_i, i.e., Eq. (2). We first notice that if two consecutive values of cv_i are with an absolute difference 2, then two positions in the secret $\mathbf{s}$ are known. Based on these known positions, we then iteratively recover more positions in $\mathbf{s}$ using the differences of known consecutive values of cv_i. We last fully recover the secret using a small number of guesses or other post-processing procedures like lattice reduction algorithms.

This recovery approach works well in our simulation[7]. In the simulation, we directly recover 594 positions using the algebraic structures discussed before. We then use the obtained 877 equations corresponding to the 877 positions with cv_i value no less than 11, and write them into a mixed integer linear programming model to maximize the value of $\left| \sum_{i=0}^{n-1} s_i \right|$. After running the optimization procedure for around 100 seconds using a desktop with an Intel(R) Core(TM) i7-7700 CPU, we successfully recover 995 positions among the 1024 unknown entries of $\mathbf{s}$. After guessing a few positions, it is easy to recover the key as most of the remaining errors are located in the first 100 positions.

For $l_1 = 65$, we similarly compute that it requires about $2^{29.8}$ errors to distinguish all the cv_i values larger than 9 with probability close to 1. We can then do a full key recovery similar to the approach discussed above.

---

[6] For a key we chose in simulation, 877 positions are with a cv_i value no less than 11.

[7] In simulation, we assume that cv_i is totally unknown for all $cv_i \leq 10$, which is pessimistic for an attacker. Actually, when the required decryption errors are obtained, we can have good knowledge of the values cv_i even if $cv_i \leq 10$.

Table 3. Success probability P_s of estimating $\mathbf{cv(s)}$ for a key $\mathbf{s}$ with $\delta_0 = 208$.

Number of *TYPE 1* errors	P_s
$2^{28.0}$	0.47
$2^{29.5}$	0.58
$2^{30.3}$	0.65

Experimental Verification. We have launched extensive simulation (of about 40,000 CPU core hours) to obtain $2^{30.3}$ *TYPE 1* errors when setting $l_1 = 85$. Firstly, we verify that the correlation between the probability $P(E_i = 1|\mathcal{D})$ and the value cv_i is very strong (see Fig. 4). Secondly, the experimental results match our theoretical prediction well. For instance, as shown in Table 3, one can recover 47% of the values cv_i with $2^{28.0}$ *TYPE 1* errors. The ratio increased to 65% (or 58%) when using $2^{30.3}$ (or $2^{29.5}$) *TYPE 1* errors.

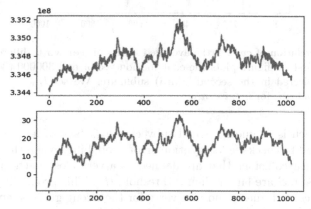

Fig. 4. The correlation of the frequency of $(E_i = 1|\mathcal{D})$ v.s. cv_i. $2^{30.3}$ *TYPE 1* errors are collected and $l_1 = 85$. The x axis represents the index i, for $0 \leq i < n$.

4.2 A Heuristic Approach

We have presented a simple key-recovery approach with theoretical arguments and also experimental validation. We next propose an alternative heuristic method, to demonstrate that better ways for key-recovery can probably be found.

We now look at the averaged values of $-\mathbf{er}$ for all the vectors in $\mathcal{S}'$ causing errors. The strong correlation between this averaged vector and the contribution vector is shown in Fig. 5. Considering *TYPE 1* errors and $l_1 = 85$, we see that the correlation is much stronger if ten times more (i.e., 300000 v.s. 30000) decryption errors are provided, and the correlation is already very strong for 300000 error samples. Comparing Figs. 5 and 6, we also see that with a similar number of decryption failures the correlation between the contribution vector and the averaged vector is stronger if the error probability is smaller.

The remaining problem is to have an accurate estimation $\mathbf{e}'$ of $\mathbf{e}$.

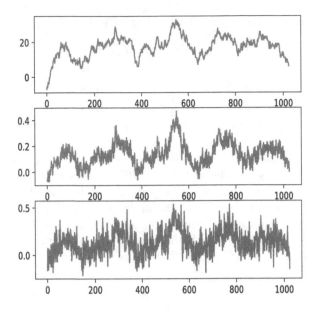

Fig. 5. The correlation of cv_i v.s. the averaged values of $-\mathbf{er}$ w.r.t. different positions for a key. The first subfigure plots the contribution vector and 300000 (30000) $TYPE$ 1 errors are collected in the second (third) subfigure. We set $l_1 = 85$. The x axis represents the index i, for $0 \leq i < n$.

One approach is to guess a small subvector $\mathbf{e_{sec}}$ (say of length $l_s = 12$) of the $\mathbf{e}$ vector and to check the decryption error probability when the occurrences of $-\mathbf{e_{sec}}$ (or near-collisions that are defined as a very close pattern) in part of the ciphertexts in $\mathcal{S}$ are larger than a threshold th_0. This probability should be higher for the correct guess, and vice versa for the wrong guesses, among all the guesses with the same numbers of '-1', '1', and '0'.

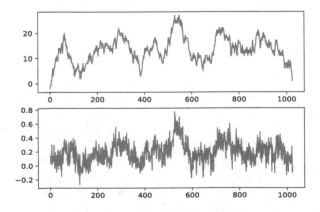

Fig. 6. The correlation of cv_i v.s. the averaged values of $-\mathbf{er}$ w.r.t. different positions for a key. 36690 $TYPE$ 1 errors are collected and $l_1 = 65$. The x axis represents the index i, for $0 \leq i < n$.

This idea is similar to that of colliding 'ones' from the key and the collected ciphertexts proposed in [14]. The intuition behind it is that it is more probable to show multiple (near-)collisions for a right guess because in a decryption error from $\mathcal{S}'$, more than 56 positions are of a large positive value.

Let us for instance guess the first $l_s = 12$ entries $\mathbf{e_{sec}}$ of $\mathbf{e}$. We then record the number of the ciphertexts in $\mathcal{S}'$ that more than th_0 (near-)collisions to its negative $-\mathbf{e_{sec}}$ in each chosen ciphertext $\mathbf{r}$ with index from $l_1 - l_s$ to n are found. We next need to know the number for the ciphertexts in $\mathcal{S}$ that the same condition holds and compute the likelihood by the ratio of the two numbers. In simulation, we can instead sample at random a large number (say 10,000,000) of ciphertexts in $\mathcal{S}$ since the size of $\mathcal{S}$ could be too large. We then rank all the guesses by these likelihood values. Note that the index interval should be adjusted if the guessed consecutive entries start from a different position. We select this index interval $[l_1 - l_s, n]$ since the starting entries of the contribution vector could be (with a high probability) negative.

We now have a list of subkeys near a certain position sorted according to their key-ranks. We then shift to a nearby starting position and produce a new list of subkeys with respect to the new position. Since the guessed subkeys with respect to nearby positions could have large overlaps and the correlation becomes stronger if the guessed length is longer, we can combine different subkeys to generate a list of longer subkeys. We iteratively combine the subkeys to have an estimation on the full $\mathbf{e}$ vector.

If we accurately recovered the $\mathbf{e}$ vector, then the secret $\mathbf{s}$ can be solved from the public key $(\mathbf{seed_a}, \mathbf{b})$. Even if some errors occur in the statistical test step, they can be corrected by a further lattice reduction step.

Implementation Results. We present the implementation results with the test interval $[l_1 - l_s, n]$, where $l_s = 12$ and $l_1 = 65$. Thus, the starting positions of the guessed keys with a high rank should be close to the initial position. We checked all possible key patterns with length 12, five nonzero positions and nonzero starting and end entries. The threshold th_0 is set to be 18 and a near-collision is found if in a ciphertext a pattern of length 12 whose inner product with the guessed pattern is smaller than -4 occurs.

We use the collected 36690 decryption errors and test the ranks of 5 subvectors in $\mathbf{e}$ of the select form and also of a starting position close to the initial position. From Table 4 we see, among the 5 tested 'true' keys, that four keys are with a relatively high rank. For example, the first row in the table states that a key with two minus ones and three ones is ranked fourth among all the 1200 possible key patterns.

Table 4. Key ranks of the 'true' keys.

Type	Rank
[2, 3]	4/1200
[2, 3]	109/1200
[1, 4]	34/600
[1, 4]	87/600

We notice that most of the guesses with a high rank are a subvector of $\mathbf{e}$ with the starting position (left or right) shifted[8] for less than 30 positions. Thus, we can reconstruct a longer (than length 12) subkey near the initial position with high confidence. The further combination of the subkey patterns is straightforward but requires much more implementation effort.

The correlation would be much stronger if more decryption failures are collected, as shown in Fig. 5. We conjecture that increasing the used number of errors in implementation by a reasonable constant factor (say 10 or 20) would lead to a full attack, and then the required number of data in the heuristic approach could be much smaller than that of the theoretical approach.

4.3 The Complexity Analysis

As claimed in Sect. 4.1, when setting $l_1 = 65$, the secret $\mathbf{s}$ can be fully recovered using no more than $2^{29.8}$ decryption failures in the theoretical approach. Thus, the precomputation cost can be estimated as $2^{120+29.8}/2^{-12.2} \approx 2^{162}$. The heuristic approach may reduce the precomputation cost further. For both approaches, one needs to submit 2^{15} ciphertexts to 2^{64} decryption algorithms (public keys) to determine the weak key, with complexity about 2^{79}. He also needs to perform the statistical test whose complexity is negligible. It is common to exclude the precomputation effort in the complexity analysis since the precomputation will be done only once; therefore, we claim an overall attacking complexity of 2^{79}.

4.4 Discussions

In this part, we discuss possible extension of the new attack.

Increase the Weak-Key Probability. In implementation, weak keys with probability of 2^{-64} are targeted. Based on the simulation results, we in Table 5 show the precomputation cost for generating a ciphertext regarding weak keys of various probability p. If the *TYPE 2* errors are chosen, then one can achieve an error rate of about 2^{-12} for weak keys with a fairly large probability, say 2^{-16}, having the precomputation effort below the claimed 256-bit (classical) security

---

[8] This shift operation can be viewed as being multiplied by x^j for $j \in \mathbb{Z}$ over the ring $\frac{\mathbb{Z}_q[x]}{(x^n+1)}$.

level of LAC256. These keys can be risky, under the assumption that a similar level of key information (correlation) can be extracted for a fixed number of errors with similar error rates.

Table 5. Precomputation cost of generating a ciphertext for random keys with probability p to achieve an error rate of about 2^{-12}.

p	$\log_2(C)$	l_1	l_0	δ_0
2^{-64}	$120^\dagger$	65	0	208
2^{-32}	140	145	135	143
2^{-16}	220	225	215	98

†This complexity can be lower if $l_0 \neq 0$

5   Attacking the LAC Version in Round 2 of the NIST PQ-Project

The authors very recently revised the LAC proposal when it entered the round 2 of the NIST post-quantum standardization effort, see [20,21]. The introduced modifications are a few:

- They employed a new coding scheme where the message is firstly encoded with BCH codes and the codeword is further encoded with the D2 error correcting codes. The BCH code now corrects much less number of errors (16 errors can be corrected), but the addition of the D2 encoder makes the overall error probability roughly the same as before. Also, the message/key size is decreased to 256 bits.
- The noise distribution is changed to have a constant weight and the same number of ones as minus ones. For instance, the vectors of $\mathbf{s}, \mathbf{e}, \mathbf{e_1}, \mathbf{r}$ are now sampled from $\Psi_1^{n,h}$, containing exactly $h/2$ ones and $h/2$ minus ones, and the distribution of $\mathbf{e_2}$ is unchanged. The authors[9] made this change to resist against the high Hamming weight CCA attacks [1,8], in which higher decryption error rates are achieved via choosing high Hamming weight messages/errors through precomputation.
- Some 4 bits of each position in the second part of the ciphertext are dropped, bringing some ciphertext compression. This however adds an additional noise term uniformly distributed in $[-7, 7]$.

Table 6 shows the concrete parameters of LAC256-v2 proposed in the NIST round 2 submission. In LAC256-v2, l_v is equal to 800; thus only the first 800 positions matter, and the D2 encoding/decoding combines two positions of distance 400 apart[10]. The decryption error probability is estimated to be 2^{-122}.

---

[9] In the round 2 submission [20], they also argued that 'it is difficult to get any information about the private key from these decryption failures'.

[10] This part is verified from the reference implementation.

Table 6. Proposed parameters of LAC256-v2 in round 2.

n	q	$\mathcal{R}$	h	l_v	Distribution	ecc	DER	Security
1024	251	$\frac{Z_q[x]}{\langle x^n+1\rangle}$	512	800	$\Psi_1, \Psi_1^{n,h}$	BCH$[511, 256, 33]$ + D2	2^{-122}	V

We shortly present the steps of generalizing the previous attack to the new version. The basic idea is that we split the enabling error patterns in two parts, one part being the even positions having a positive contribution and the second part being the odd positions having a negative contribution. The same goes for the desired pattern in the secret vector **s**. We expect the contribution of the two parts to have the same sign and the sum to be roughly doubled.

5.1   Attack Step 1 - Precomputation

We again construct a special set $\mathcal{S}$ of messages/error vectors by precomputation. We are only interested in keeping messages that give rise to noise vectors of special form of the $\mathbf{e}_1$ vector. Let us include combinations where the error vector $\mathbf{e}_1$ contains an interval of consecutive l_1 entries, where every even position in the interval contains a 1 and every odd position contains a -1 (or vice versa). Thus, l_1 is even. The starting position of this interval is chosen from $[801, n - l_1]$, leading to the largest contribution to the first $l_v = 800$ positions[11] of $\mathbf{e}_1\mathbf{s}$.

Assuming a randomly selected error vector from the error distribution $\Psi_1^{n,h}$, the probability of finding such an interval starting from a fixed position in $[801, n - l_1]$ is then

$$p = 2 \times \frac{\binom{h/2}{l_1/2} \cdot \binom{h/2}{l_1/2}}{\binom{n}{l_1} \cdot \binom{l_1}{l_1/2}}.$$

The overall probability can be approximated by

$$p_0 \approx (n - 800 - l_1)p. \tag{6}$$

We denote the type of noise vectors of the above kind as *TYPE 1b* noise vectors.

Just as before, we can consider many other special forms of the noise that can be useful in an attack, for example noise vectors similar to what we previously defined as *TYPE 2* noise vectors but split in even and odd parts. We also define *TYPE 2b* errors that the error vector $\mathbf{e}_1$ contains an interval of consecutive $l_1 + l_0$ entries, where all the even positions include $l_1/2$ ones and $l_0/2$ zeros, and all the odd positions include $l_1/2$ minus-ones and $l_0/2$ zeros (or vice versa). The starting position of this interval is chosen from $[801, n - l_1 - l_0]$. With the same precomputation effort, this error pattern can lead to a much larger decryption error probability compared with *TYPE 1b* errors.

---

[11] Due to the mod $(x^n + 1)$ operation, the controlled interval is split into two consecutive parts in $(l_1 - 1)$ columns of the matrix generated by shifting $\mathbf{e}_1$. These two parts will be multiplied by 1 or -1, respectively, leading to a reduced absolute contribution.

After finishing this step, we assume that we have a stored set $\mathcal{S}$ of precomputed messages/error vectors with the *TYPE 1b* (or *TYPE 2b*) property for the e_1 part. We could describe a *TYPE 1b* error as a *TYPE 2b error* with $l_0 = 0$.

5.2   Attack Step 2 - Submit Ciphertexts for Decryption

Similar to the procedure in Sect. 3.2, we map the messages in $\mathcal{S}$ to ciphertexts and submit them to the decryption algorithm for each public key. We keep track of the set of error vectors causing a decryption error, denoted $\mathcal{S}'$, and record the decryption error rate. We then attempt to recover the public key for keys where the decryption error rate is large i.e., targeting users with error rates in a decreasing order.

The weak key property for **s** that gives a large decryption error rate, is the property

$$\left| \sum_{i=0}^{n/2-1} s_{2i} \right| + \left| \sum_{i=0}^{n/2-1} s_{2i+1} \right| \geq \delta_0.$$

For a noise distribution with fixed $n/4$ ones and $n/4$ minus ones, it is easy to compute the probability for the above condition. For example, if we set $\delta_0 = 206$, the secret **s** will have the above property with probability about 2^{-64}. Since $\sum_{i=0}^{n} s_i = 0$, we further have

$$\left| \sum_{i=0}^{n/2-1} s_{2i} \right| = \left| \sum_{i=0}^{n/2-1} s_{2i+1} \right| = \frac{\delta_0}{2} = 103.$$

We now examine the decryption error probability for such a weak secret **s**. The error term in the new LAC is of the form

$$\mathbf{W} = \mathbf{e_1 s} - \mathbf{er} + \mathbf{e_2} + \mathbf{e_3},$$

where $\mathbf{e_3}$ is a new error term due to the ciphertext compression.

We now get a decryption error occurring if among all 400 values after the D2 encoding/decoding of $\mathbf{W}$, at least 17 of them are in error.

The D2 encoding/decoding means that the same binary value (message/key bit) is encoded in two different code positions and the decoding means adding the two positions together and checking if the sum is around 0 or around q. For an error to occur, the sum of the noise in the two positions must have an absolute value larger than $\lfloor q/2 \rfloor = 125$.

In polynomial form, the error $w(x)$ is computed as

$$w(x) = e_1(x)s(x) - e(x)r(x) + e_2(x) + e_3(x).$$

We focus on $e_1(x)s(x)$ and consider the remaining as noise.

For simplicity, we assume that all error vectors are of *TYPE 1b* and have the assumed sequence of even ones and odd minus ones in their last positions, i.e., $e_1(x)$ is of the form $(e_0, e_1, \ldots, e_{n-1}) = (e_0, \ldots, e_{n-l_1-1}, 1, -1, \ldots, 1, -1)$. We examine the $\mathbf{e_1}$s part, where we again have both $\mathbf{e_1}$ and $\mathbf{s}$ of special forms. For a particular key $\mathbf{s}$, the contribution from the fixed part $(e_{n-l_1}, \ldots, e_{n-1}) = (1, -1, \ldots, 1, -1)$ to the multiplication $\mathbf{e_1 s}$ is the contribution vector now defined as follows.

Definition 2 (Contribution vector for TYPE 1b errors). *The contribution vector* $\mathbf{cv(s)}$ *of* $(e_{n-l_1}, \ldots, e_{n-1}) = (1, -1, \ldots, 1, -1)$ *for a secret key* $\mathbf{s}$ *is defined as*

$$(cv_0, cv_1, \ldots, cv_{n-1}),$$

where

$$cv_i = \begin{cases} \sum_{k=i+1, k \text{ odd}}^{i+l_1} s_k - \sum_{k=i+1, k \text{ even}}^{i+l_1} s_k, & \text{if } 0 \leq i < n - l_1, i \text{ even}, \\ \sum_{k=i+1, k \text{ even}}^{i+l_1} s_k - \sum_{k=i+1, k \text{ odd}}^{i+l_1} s_k, & \text{if } 0 \leq i < n - l_1, i \text{ odd}, \\ \sum_{k=i+1, k \text{ odd}}^{n-1} s_k - \sum_{k=i+1, k \text{ even}}^{n-1} s_k \\ \quad -(\sum_{k=0, k \text{ odd}}^{i+l_1-n} s_k - \sum_{k=0, k \text{ even}}^{i+l_1-n} s_k), & \text{if } n - l_1 \leq i \leq n - 1, i \text{ even}, \\ \sum_{k=i+1, k \text{ even}}^{n-1} s_k - \sum_{k=i+1, k \text{ odd}}^{n-1} s_k \\ \quad -(\sum_{k=0, k \text{ even}}^{i+l_1-n} s_k - \sum_{k=0, k \text{ odd}}^{i+l_1-n} s_k), & \text{if } n - l_1 \leq i \leq n - 1, i \text{ odd}. \end{cases} \tag{7}$$

The new idea in this attack is that the contribution vector is a fixed contribution as before for all $\mathbf{e_1}$ vectors of *TYPE 1b*, but now it will shift in sign depending on whether i is even or odd.

Assuming the secret vector $\mathbf{s}$ of the form $\left| \sum_{i=0}^{n/2-1} s_{2i} \right| + \left| \sum_{i=0}^{n/2-1} s_{2i+1} \right| \geq \delta_0$, we can verify that most coefficients in the contribution vector $\mathbf{cv(s)}$ are quite large, but with shifting signs (see Fig. 7 for an instance). Again, with a large fixed contribution in most coefficients, the probability of a decryption error will be much larger than expected.

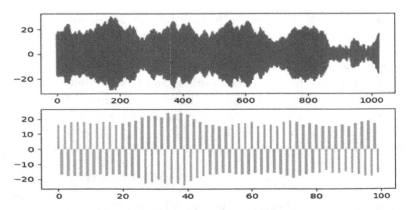

Fig. 7. The contribution vector $\mathbf{cv(s)}$ of a key $\mathbf{s}$ with $\delta_0 = 206$ when $l_1 = 86$, for *TYPE 1b* errors. The first figure plots the whole vector and the second one plots its first 100 positions.

Table 7. Decryption error probability P_e for a key **s** with $\delta_0 = 206$.

$\log_2(C_{\text{pre}})$	l_1	l_0	P_e
170	86	0	$2^{-21.03}$
128	66	0	$2^{-28.42}$
120	114	80	$2^{-12.74}$

In LAC256-v2, the D2 encoding/decoding combines two positions of distance 400 apart, which means that the fixed contribution is of the same sign in both positions and we have a large fixed contribution when summing the two positions.

Example 2: For LAC256-v2 we tested three choices for l_1 and l_0 in implementation, i.e., for *TYPE 1b* errors with $l_1 = 86$ and 66, and for *TYPE 2b* errors with $l_1 = 114$ and $l_0 = 80$. We targeted a secret key **s** having $\delta_0 = 206$, and the key probability can be estimated as 2^{-64}. The simulated decryption error probabilities (no less than 17 positions in error) are shown in Table 7, where the first column describes the computational efforts (in $\log_2(\cdot)$) of finding one desired message/noise. We see that the decryption error probability can be higher than 2^{-13} with complexity of about 2^{120} for one message/noise.

We note that the error performance of the new LAC256-v2 in round 2 with respect to our attack is slightly better than that of the old version, but is still far from preventing this attack.

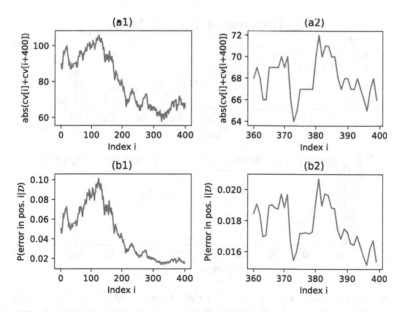

Fig. 8. The correlation of **cv** w.r.t. the *TYPE 1b* errors with $l_1 = 194$ v.s. $P(\text{error in pos}.i|\mathcal{D})$. About $6,500,000$ *TYPE 2b* errors are collected with $l_1 = 114$ and $l_0 = 80$.

5.3   Attack Step 3 - Recovering S

This final step assumes an identified weak public key in the previous step. After receiving the decryption errors, caused by the vectors in $\mathcal{S}'$, we reconstruct the secret key $\mathbf{s}$. The procedure is analogue to the procedure described in the previous section. Throughout the section, we focus on *TYPE 2b* errors as they can lead to a higher decryption error probability. Note that the distributions of the i-th and the $(i + 400)$-th positions (of say $\mathbf{e}_2$) should be studied jointly due to the implementation of the D2 error correcting codes.

The interesting main observation is that for *TYPE 2b* errors with $l_1 = 114$ and $l_0 = 80$, the distribution of $P(E_i|\mathcal{D})$ is a function of the sum of the i-th and the $(i + 400)$-th positions of the contribution vector for *TYPE 1b* errors with $l_1 = 194$, where E_i is the random variable representing the sum of the the i-th and the $(i + 400)$-th positions of $\mathbf{e}_2$.

We plot the simulation results for verifying this correlation in the first and the second subfigures of Fig. 9. Since about 2^{38} encryptions have been performed,

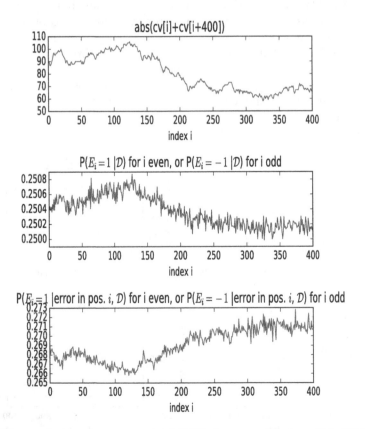

Fig. 9. The correlation of $\mathbf{cv}$ w.r.t. the *TYPE 1b* errors with $l_1 = 194$, $P(E_i|\mathcal{D})$ and $P(E_i|\text{error in pos.}i, \mathcal{D})$. About $2^{25.09}$ *TYPE 2b* errors are collected with $l_1 = 114$ and $l_0 = 80$.

it is beyond our computational capability to run an even larger experiment. However, the correlation between the sum of two positions in the contribution vector w.r.t. the *TYPE 1b* errors with $l_1 = 194$ and $P(\text{error in pos.}i|\mathcal{D})$ is much stronger and can be verified with fewer decryption errors. This strong correlation explains our main observation.

We show the latter strong correlation in Fig. 8 where the plots are obtained from about $6,500,000$ *TYPE 2b* errors. The left two subfigures, (a1) and (a2), plot the correlation for the whole vector of length 400, and the right two, (b1) and (b2), plot the last 40 entries.

We can now use the theory from Sect. 4.1 to study the data complexity for this attack on LAC256-v2. We first obtain an equation with the same form as Eq. (3), and the difficulty is then to numerically compute $P(E_i = 1|\text{error in pos. } i)$ (or $P(E_i = 1|\text{no error in pos. } i)$). Since we include l_0 zeros in the controlled interval to form *TYPE 2b* errors, the contribution (denoted by a random variable CV) from the controlled intervals (of the i-th and $(i+400)$-th positions) is no longer a constant. We could approximate the distribution of CV by using a typical choice, i.e., assuming half of the positions of $\mathbf{s}$ corresponding to the controlled intervals are 0, and then compute the distribution via convolution. Then, $P(E_i = 1|\text{error in pos. } i)$ can be computed as

$$ \sum_{cv} P(\text{CV} = cv)P(E_i = 1|\text{error in pos. } i, \text{CV} = cv), $$

where similarly to Eq. (4), $P(E_i = 1|\text{error in pos. } i, \text{CV} = cv)$ can be computed as $\frac{4P(N_i > 124 - cv)}{f(cv)}$, and $f(cv) = P(N_i > 123 - cv) + 4P(N_i > 124 - cv) + 6P(N_i > 125 - cv) + 4P(N_i > 126 - cv) + P(N_i > 127 - cv)$. Here N_i is defined, similar to that in Sect. 4.1, as the noise term after the D2 decoding excluding the CV part and the E_i part. We compute $P(E_i = 1|\text{no error in pos. } i)$ similarly, and finally apply Eq. (5) to estimate the data complexity[12]. With this analysis, the complexity to distinguish the sum of the i-th and the $(i+400)$-th positions of the contribution vector for *TYPE 1b* errors with $l_1 = 194$ to be 89 or 90 is $2^{34.73}$.

If we test $P(E_i|\text{error in pos.}i, \mathcal{D})$ empirically, as shown in the last subfigure of Fig. 9, we obtain a data complexity estimation of about $2^{33.42}$, to distinguish the sum to be 89 or 90. This empirical estimation verifies our theoretical estimation to which we will stick in our later analysis.

In simulation, we obtained 151 equations corresponding to the index set $\mathcal{I}_{90}$ with size 151, where for $i \in \mathcal{I}_{90}$ the sum of the i-th and the $(i+400)$-th positions of the contribution vector for *TYPE 1b* errors with $l_1 = 194$ is no less than 90. We do more rounds to collect more linear equations using error patterns derived from *TYPE 2b* errors, i.e., replacing one position in the controlled interval by an carefully selected position outside the interval. We ask the two positions to be both even or odd and assign corresponding values of the same sign. Since only a single index of the controlled positions is changed, the contribution vector or the

---

[12] The analysis is conservative because we only consider one value of E_i conditioned on the collected errors. In fact, we can use the full distribution, i.e., the probabilities of $E_i|\mathcal{D}$ being 5 different possible values, to reduce the data complexity further.

error probability keeps (or has a small difference) but more linear equations of entries from s are obtained. One then performs about $n/151 \approx 7$ times to collect enough linear equations for a full recovery. In summary, the required number of decryption errors is bounded by 2^{38} and the overall precomputation complexity is estimated to be 2^{171}.

6 Discussions

On Multi-target Protection. Many proposals to the NIST post-quantum standardization process have a multi-target protection technique, i.e., including the public key as an input to a hash function for generating the noise seeds. We see that for LAC256, the multi-target protection cannot thwart this attack because this attack can work in the single-key setting that is independent of the multi-target protection technique. Actually, this attack recovers the key with precomputation complexity 2^{162} and success probability 2^{-64}, when only a single key is assumed.

Using the adaptive attack model in [13], for LAC256 with the multi-target protection, one can prepare 2^{15} ciphertexts for 2^{64} users with complexity $2^{120+64+15} = 2^{199}$ if $l_1 = 65$, to determine the weak keys. The dominant part in the complexity analysis is a precomputation of 2^{199}, far below the 2^{256} bound. We can further reduce the complexity by balancing the computational efforts in different steps.

Similar analysis applies to LAC256-v2.

On Other LAC Parameter Settings. On LAC128-v2 having a key with probability 2^{-64}, with precomputation of 2^{58} for one chosen ciphertext, we simulated a decryption failure probability of around 2^{-28}. This experimental data demonstrate that LAC128-v2 could be vulnerable to the newly proposed attack in the multi-target setting. This multi-target attack can be prevented via including the multi-target protection technique discussed before. We believe that LAC192-v2 is more vulnerable to the multi-target attack than LAC128-v2 since one has a less restricted bound for precomputation.

7 Conclusions and Future Works

We have presented a CCA attack on the scheme LAC256, a proposal to the NIST Post-Quantum Cryptography Standardization project that has passed the first round selection. This attack exploits the decryption failures and recovers one weak key among about 2^{64} public keys. This attack has two versions due to the two different approaches to reconstruct the secret key from the decryption failures. With the first approach, we present an attack with complexity of 2^{79}, i.e., the cost of determining a weak key, if the required precomputation cost is bound by 2^{162} encryptions. One can definitely achieve different trade-offs between the attacking complexity and the precomputation cost via choosing suitable parameters. The second approach is similar to the reaction attacks [10,14,15] on the MDPC and LDPC based cryptosystems, which could heuristically decrease the precomputation effort further. We also discuss the possibility of attacking a key with a much larger probability, say 2^{-16}. Last, we discuss the attack on a new version of LAC256 in round 2 of the NIST PQC project. We claim a multi-target attack with complexity bounded by 2^{80} and precomputation of about 2^{171} to recover a weak key among about 2^{64} public keys. This attack also means a CCA attack on LAC256-v2 with precomputation of 2^{171}, and success probability 2^{-64}, in the single-key setting.

This attack can also be applied to other schemes. It is interesting future work to check the performance of the attack with respect to different proposals in the NIST Post-Quantum Cryptography Standardization project.

Acknowledgments. The authors would like to thank Xianhui Lu and the anonymous reviewers from Asiacrypt 2019 for their helpful comments. This work was supported in part by the Swedish Research Council (Grant No. 2015-04528), by the Swedish Foundation for Strategic Research (Grant No. RIT17-0005), and by the Norwegian Research Council (Grant No. 247742/070). Jing Yang was also supported by the scholarship from the National Digital Switching System Engineering and Technological Research Center, China. The computations/simulations were performed on resources provided by UNINETT Sigma2 - the National Infrastructure for High Performance Computing and Data Storage in Norway, and by Swedish National Infrastructure for Computing.

References

1. NIST Post-Quantum Cryptography Forum. https://groups.google.com/a/list.nist.gov/forum/#!forum/pqc-forum. Accessed 11 Jan 2019
2. NIST Post-Quantum Cryptography Standardization. https://csrc.nist.gov/Projects/Post-Quantum-Cryptography/Post-Quantum-Cryptography-Standardization. Accessed 24 Sept 2018
3. Bernstein, D.J., Groot Bruinderink, L., Lange, T., Panny, L.: HILA5 pindakaas: on the CCA security of lattice-based encryption with error correction. In: Joux, A., Nitaj, A., Rachidi, T. (eds.) AFRICACRYPT 2018. LNCS, vol. 10831, pp. 203–216. Springer, Cham (2018). https://doi.org/10.1007/978-3-319-89339-6_12
4. Boldyreva, A., Degabriele, J.P., Paterson, K.G., Stam, M.: On symmetric encryption with distinguishable decryption failures. In: Moriai, S. (ed.) FSE 2013. LNCS, vol. 8424, pp. 367–390. Springer, Heidelberg (2014). https://doi.org/10.1007/978-3-662-43933-3_19
5. Brakerski, Z., Gentry, C., Vaikuntanathan, V.: (Leveled) fully homomorphic encryption without bootstrapping. In: Goldwasser, S. (ed.) ITCS 2012: 3rd Innovations in Theoretical Computer Science, Cambridge, MA, USA, 8–10 January 2012, pp. 309–325. Association for Computing Machinery (2012)
6. Brakerski, Z., Langlois, A., Peikert, C., Regev, O., Stehlé, D.: Classical hardness of learning with errors. In: Boneh, D., Roughgarden, T., Feigenbaum, J. (eds.) 45th Annual ACM Symposium on Theory of Computing, Palo Alto, CA, USA, 1–4 June 2013, pp. 575–584. ACM Press (2013)

7. Brakerski, Z., Vaikuntanathan, V.: Efficient fully homomorphic encryption from (standard) LWE. In: Ostrovsky, R. (ed.) 52nd Annual Symposium on Foundations of Computer Science, Palm Springs, CA, USA, 22–25 October 2011, pp. 97–106. IEEE Computer Society Press (2011)
8. D'Anvers, J.-P., Guo, Q., Johansson, T., Nilsson, A., Vercauteren, F., Verbauwhede, I.: Decryption failure attacks on IND-CCA secure lattice-based schemes. In: Lin, D., Sako, K. (eds.) PKC 2019. LNCS, vol. 11443, pp. 565–598. Springer, Cham (2019). https://doi.org/10.1007/978-3-030-17259-6_19
9. Ding, J., Alsayigh, S., Saraswathy, R.V., Fluhrer, S., Lin, X.: Leakage of signal function with reused keys in RLWE key exchange. Cryptology ePrint Archive, Report 2016/1176 (2016). http://eprint.iacr.org/2016/1176
10. Fabšič, T., Hromada, V., Stankovski, P., Zajac, P., Guo, Q., Johansson, T.: A reaction attack on the QC-LDPC McEliece cryptosystem. In: Lange, T., Takagi, T. (eds.) PQCrypto 2017. LNCS, vol. 10346, pp. 51–68. Springer, Cham (2017). https://doi.org/10.1007/978-3-319-59879-6_4
11. Fluhrer, S.: Cryptanalysis of ring-LWE based key exchange with key share reuse. Cryptology ePrint Archive, Report 2016/085 (2016). http://eprint.iacr.org/2016/085
12. Gama, N., Nguyen, P.Q.: New chosen-ciphertext attacks on NTRU. In: Okamoto, T., Wang, X. (eds.) PKC 2007. LNCS, vol. 4450, pp. 89–106. Springer, Heidelberg (2007). https://doi.org/10.1007/978-3-540-71677-8_7
13. Guo, Q., Johansson, T., Nilsson, A.: A generic attack on lattice-based schemes using decryption errors with application to ss-ntru-pke. IACR Cryptology ePrint Archive 2019, 43 (2019). https://eprint.iacr.org/2019/043
14. Guo, Q., Johansson, T., Stankovski, P.: A key recovery attack on MDPC with CCA security using decoding errors. In: Cheon, J.H., Takagi, T. (eds.) ASIACRYPT 2016, Part I. LNCS, vol. 10031, pp. 789–815. Springer, Heidelberg (2016). https://doi.org/10.1007/978-3-662-53887-6_29
15. Guo, Q., Johansson, T., Wagner, P.S.: A key recovery reaction attack on QC-MDPC. IEEE Trans. Inf. Theory 65(3), 1845–1861 (2019). https://doi.org/10.1109/TIT.2018.2877458
16. Hall, C., Goldberg, I., Schneier, B.: Reaction attacks against several public-key cryptosystem. In: Varadharajan, V., Mu, Y. (eds.) ICICS 1999. LNCS, vol. 1726, pp. 2–12. Springer, Heidelberg (1999). https://doi.org/10.1007/978-3-540-47942-0_2
17. Hoffstein, J., Silverman, J.H.: NTRU Cryptosystems Technical Report Report# 016, Version 1 Title: Protecting NTRU Against Chosen Ciphertext and Reaction Attacks (2000)
18. Howgrave-Graham, N., et al.: The impact of decryption failures on the security of NTRU encryption. In: Boneh, D. (ed.) CRYPTO 2003. LNCS, vol. 2729, pp. 226–246. Springer, Heidelberg (2003). https://doi.org/10.1007/978-3-540-45146-4_14
19. Lu, X., Liu, Y., Jia, D., Xue, H., He, J., Zhang, Z.: LAC. Technical report, National Institute of Standards and Technology (2017). https://csrc.nist.gov/projects/post-quantum-cryptography/round-1-submissions
20. Lu, X., et al.: LAC. Technical report (2019). https://csrc.nist.gov/Projects/Post-Quantum-Cryptography/Round-2-Submissions
21. Lu, X., et al.: LAC: practical ring-LWE based public-key encryption with byte-level modulus. Cryptology ePrint Archive, Report 2018/1009 (2018). https://eprint.iacr.org/2018/1009

22. Lyubashevsky, V., Peikert, C., Regev, O.: On ideal lattices and learning with errors over rings. In: Gilbert, H. (ed.) EUROCRYPT 2010. LNCS, vol. 6110, pp. 1–23. Springer, Heidelberg (2010). https://doi.org/10.1007/978-3-642-13190-5_1
23. Peikert, C.: Public-key cryptosystems from the worst-case shortest vector problem: extended abstract. In: Mitzenmacher, M. (ed.) 41st Annual ACM Symposium on Theory of Computing, Bethesda, MD, USA, 31 May–2 June 2009, pp. 333–342. ACM Press (2009)
24. Regev, O.: On lattices, learning with errors, random linear codes, and cryptography. In: Gabow, H.N., Fagin, R. (eds.) 37th Annual ACM Symposium on Theory of Computing, Baltimore, MA, USA, 22–24 May 2005, pp. 84–93. ACM Press (2005)
25. Saarinen, M.J.O.: Hila5. Technical report, National Institute of Standards and Technology (2017). https://csrc.nist.gov/projects/post-quantum-cryptography/round-1-submissions

Towards Attribute-Based Encryption for RAMs from LWE: Sub-linear Decryption, and More

Prabhanjan Ananth[1(✉)], Xiong Fan[2], and Elaine Shi[2]

[1] MIT CASIL, Boston, MA, USA
prabhanjan@csail.mit.edu
[2] Cornell University, Ithaca, NY, USA
{xfan,elaine}@cs.cornell.edu

Abstract. Attribute based encryption (ABE) is an advanced encryption system with a built-in mechanism to generate keys associated with functions which in turn provide restricted access to encrypted data. Most of the known candidates of attribute based encryption model the functions as circuits. This results in significant efficiency bottlenecks, especially in the setting where the function associated with the ABE key is represented by a random access machine (RAM) and a database, with the runtime of the RAM program being sublinear in the database size. In this work we study the notion of attribute based encryption for random access machines (RAMs), introduced in the work of Goldwasser, Kalai, Popa, Vaikuntanathan and Zeldovich (Crypto 2013). We present a construction of attribute based encryption for RAMs satisfying sublinear decryption complexity assuming learning with errors; this is the first construction based on standard assumptions. Previously, Goldwasser et al. achieved this result based on non-falsifiable knowledge assumptions. We also consider a dual notion of ABE for RAMs, where the database is in the ciphertext and we show how to achieve this dual notion, albeit with large attribute keys, also based on learning with errors.

1 Introduction

Attribute-based encryption (ABE) [54] is a powerful paradigm that provides a controlled access mechanism to encrypted data. Unlike a traditional encryption scheme, in an attribute-based encryption scheme, an authority can generate a constrained key sk_P for a program P such that it can decrypt an encryption of message μ, associated with attribute x, only if the condition $P(x) = 0$ is satisfied. The last decade of research in this area [13,21,26,28,36,37,39,41,42, 45,50,54,56–58] has led to several useful applications including verifiable computation [51] and reusable garbled circuits [35]. Special cases of ABE, such as identity-based encryption [12,18,24,55], and generalizations of ABE, such as functional encryption [14,25,49], have also been extensively studied.

Current known constructions of ABE offer different flavors of efficiency guarantees and can be based on various cryptographic assumptions. Barring few

S. D. Galbraith and S. Moriai (Eds.): ASIACRYPT 2019, LNCS 11921, pp. 112–141, 2019.
https://doi.org/10.1007/978-3-030-34578-5_5

exceptions, all these constructions [13,38,39,42,46,56] model the program, associated with the constrained keys, as circuits. Real-world programs, however, are composed in the so-called Random Access Machine (RAM) model. In this paper, we consider the natural question of constructing attributed-based encryption scheme for RAM programs.

As in the circuit setting, an attribute-based encryption scheme for RAM programs consists of the setup, key generation, encryption and decryption algorithms. The key generation algorithm takes as input the master secret key, program P, database D and produces an attribute key associated with (P, D). The encryption algorithm takes as input attribute x, secret message μ and produces a ciphertext. Decrypting this ciphertext using the key of (P, D) yields the secret message μ if and only if $P^D(x) = 0$.

Towards constructing attribute-based encryption for RAMs, a naïve approach is to convert RAM programs generically to circuits: a RAM program initialized with N words of memory and running in time T can be converted to a circuit of size $O((N + T) \cdot T)$ and depth T. Thus, the approach via naïve RAM-to-circuit conversion would incur a $(N+T) \cdot T$ multiplicative factor in the decryption time. In this paper, we are interested in the common case when T is *sublinear* in N, e.g., imagine that the RAM is initialized with a large database with N entries and the RAM program models a binary search on the database. Goldwasser et al. [36] gave the first feasibility result of ABE for RAM programs with sub-linear decryption time based on the existence of extractable witness encryption and succinct non-interactive arguments of knowledge (SNARK). Recent works [10, 15,27], however, have brought into question the veracity of the assumptions of extractable witness encryption and SNARKs.

Since building ABE for RAMs on solid cryptographic foundations is an important problem, we ask the following natural question:

Is there an ABE for RAMs scheme with sublinear decryption overhead based on standard assumptions? More specifically, we would like the decryption overhead to be $o(N) \cdot \mathsf{poly}(T, \lambda)$ where λ is the security parameter.

1.1 Our Results and Contributions

ABE for RAMs with Sub-linear Decryption Efficiency. We construct an ABE scheme for RAMs with sub-linear decryption overhead from the Learning With Errors (LWE) assumption. Henceforth we assume that the scheme is parameterized with N and T which denote the size of the database and the upper bound on the runtime of the RAM respectively, and a security parameter denoted by λ. Our construction achieves the following:

- There is an initial setup phase that generates a global public parameter of size $\mathsf{poly}(T, \lambda)$ and master secret key of size $\mathsf{poly}(T, \lambda)$.
- Anyone that has access to the public parameters can encrypt a message μ to an attribute x of size λ (For simplicity, we set the size of attribute x to be λ. However, the size of the attribute can be set in advance and of any fixed

polynomial in λ) — later x will serve as an input to a RAM program. The encryption time and ciphertext size is upper bounded by $\mathsf{poly}(T, \lambda)$.

– An authority with master secret key can generate a decryption key $\mathsf{sk}_{P,D}$ given the description of a RAM program P (where the description will include the RAM's next instruction circuit) and a long attribute vector denoted by D of size N, and the size of the secret key $\mathsf{sk}_{P,D}$ is upper bounded $\mathsf{poly}(T, N, \lambda)$.

– Finally, given the ciphertext ct_x that is associated with the attribute x, anyone with the public parameters and the decryption key $\mathsf{sk}_{P,D}$ can decrypt the plaintext message μ if $P^D(x) = 0$; and importantly decryption time is $\mathsf{poly}(T, \lambda)$, i.e., independent of the RAM's initial memory size N. For security, we show that an adversary learns nothing about the encrypted plaintext μ if he does not possess any sk_P such that $P^D(x) = 0$.

More formally, our main theorem is the following:

Theorem 1.1 (ABE for RAMs). *Assuming the hardness of the Learning With Errors problem (with sub-exponential modulus)[1], there exists an ABE scheme for RAMs with $\mathsf{poly}(T, \lambda)$ decryption efficiency, i.e., independent of N.*

Moreover, (i) the cost of generating public parameters is $\mathsf{poly}(T, \lambda)$, i.e., independent of N, (ii) the cost of generating secret keys is $\mathsf{poly}(N, T, \lambda)$ and, (iii) the cost of generating ciphertexts is $\mathsf{poly}(T, \lambda)$.

Input-Specific Runtime. While the construction in the above theorem has decryption complexity proportional to the worst case running time of the RAM programs, we can transform this scheme into another scheme where the decryption complexity is *input-specific*. This is performed by running $\log T$ copies of the scheme by setting the worst case runtime of the first scheme to be 2, second scheme to be 2^2, so on and the runtime of the $(\log T)$-th scheme is set to be T. This idea has been used in prior works (for instance [36]). Note that this increases the size of the public parameters, keys and ciphertexts by a multiplicative factor of $\log T$.

On Fixing the Attribute Length. In our construction, the length of the attribute is fixed at the time of setup. In particular, both the public parameters and the attribute keys grow with the length of the attribute. Note that the attribute keys already grow proportional to the length of the database and the database size is typically larger than the attribute length. However, achieving public key sizes independent of the attribute length would be interesting, especially given that there are works [21] that have achieved this in the context of ABE for circuits.

Comparison with [36]. As mentioned earlier, [36] also achieves ABE for RAMs with sub-linear decryption complexity from exotic assumptions. The only drawback in our scheme in comparison with [36] is that the parameters in the construction of [36], specifically the public parameters, ciphertext size and the key sizes do not grow with the maximum time bound. On the other hand, our parameters do grow with the maximum time bound T. There is evidence to suggest

---

[1] All known lattice-based ABE for circuits [13] are based on the same assumption.

that an ABE for RAMs scheme whose parameters do not grow with the maximum time bound can only be based on strong cryptographic assumptions. In particular such a notion would imply succinct randomized encodings for Turing machines [6,11][2]; a notion, despite numerous attempts, we don't yet know how to build from well-studied assumptions.

Comparison with Circuit-Based Schemes. We compare the parameters we obtain in our scheme with the parameters obtained in the naive approach of RAM-to-circuit conversion and then applying previously known ABE for circuits schemes. Refer to Fig. 1.

Schemes	# of $\mathbb{Z}_q^{n \times m}$ Public key	# of $\mathbb{Z}_q^m$ Ciphertext of (x, μ)	Size of Key of (P, D)	Decryption complexity
Via ABE for circuits [13]	$\tilde{O}(\lvert x \rvert)$	$\tilde{O}(\lvert x \rvert)$	$\lvert P \rvert + N + \left(\underset{\# \text{ of } \mathbb{Z}_q^{n \times m}}{\tilde{O}(1)} \right)$	$\tilde{O}((T + N)T)$
Via ABE for circuits [21]	$\tilde{O}(1)$	$\tilde{O}(\lvert x \rvert)$	$\lvert P \rvert + N + \left(\underset{\# \text{ of } \mathbb{Z}_q^{n \times m}}{\tilde{O}(1)} \right)$	$\tilde{O}((T + N)T)$
Our Work for RO-RAMs	$\tilde{O}(\lvert x \rvert + T)$	$\tilde{O}(\lvert x \rvert + T)$	$\lvert P \rvert + \left(\underset{\# \text{ of } \mathbb{Z}_q^{n \times m}}{\tilde{O}(TN)} \right)$	$\tilde{O}(T)$
Our Work for RAMs	$\tilde{O}(\lvert x \rvert + T)$	$\tilde{O}(\lvert x \rvert + T)$	$\lvert P \rvert + \left(\underset{\# \text{ of } \mathbb{Z}_q^{n \times m}}{\tilde{O}(T(N+T))} \right)$	$\tilde{O}(T)$

Fig. 1. We compare the parameters in our work with previous works. The lattice dimension (n, m, q) is asymptotically the same in all three approaches. The $\tilde{O}$ notation suppresses poly-logarithmic factors (in N and T). The encryptor takes an auxiliary input x and the key generator takes as input a program P and a database D of size N. The decryption complexity is calculated in terms of vector-matrix multiplication over $\mathbb{Z}_q$. The attribute key is generated for a RAM program P with worst case runtime to be T and it takes time t to compute on D. In previous works, an attribute key for P is generated by first transforming it into a circuit of size $(T + N)$ and depth T and then generating an attribute key for the resulting circuit.

While the key sizes in our scheme are larger than the ones obtained via circuit ABE schemes, our scheme has the following advantage over ABE for circuit schemes: since the same decryption keys, once generated, can be applied to (unbounded polynomially) many ciphertexts, the cost of key generation and its size can be *amortized over multiple decryption queries*. This is especially useful in scenarios, where a client can perform a one-time cost of generating keys and sending it over to the server during the offline phase and during the online phase, can verifiably delegate multiple computations by suitably sending

---

[2] The works [6,11] show implication of ABE for Turing machines (as defined in [6]) to succinct randomized encodings (Appendix A.5 in [11]).

encryptions of its inputs; note that in this scenario, we are only interested in verifying whether the server has performed the computation correctly and not hiding the computation itself.

Dual ABE for RAMs. We also consider an alternate notion of ABE for RAMs, that we call dual ABE for RAMs. In this notion, the database is part of the ciphertext and not the key. That is, the key generation procedure now only takes as input the master secret key and the RAM program P while the encryption procedure takes as input the database D, the auxiliary input x (in the technical section, we consider x to be part of D) and the secret message μ. As before, we require that it should be possible to recover μ if indeed $P^D(x) = 0$.

We demonstrate a construction of dual ABE for RAMs, also based on the learning with errors problem with the same decryption efficiency as stated in Theorem 1.1. In more detail,

Theorem 1.2 (Dual ABE for RAMs). *Assuming the hardness of the Learning With Errors problem (with sub-exponential modulus)[3], there exists a dual ABE scheme for RAMs with* $\mathsf{poly}(T, \lambda)$ *decryption efficiency, i.e., independent of N.*

Moreover, (i) the cost of generating public parameters is $\mathsf{poly}(N, T, \lambda)$, *(ii) the cost of generating secret keys is* $\mathsf{poly}(N, T, \lambda)$ *and, (iii) the cost of generating ciphertexts is* $\mathsf{poly}(N, T, \lambda)$.

On Large Attribute Keys. Unlike our construction of ABE for RAMs (Theorem 1.1), our construction of dual ABE for RAMs has public keys that grow proportional to the size of the database. Moreover, even the size of our attribute keys depends on the database size. While this is not inherent and an undesirable feature of our scheme, we see our work as a first step in achieving dual ABE schemes beyond circuits; note that none of the previous ABE schemes achieved sub-linear decryption property and our dual ABE construction is the first to do so.

1.2 Technical Overview

We give an overview of the techniques employed in our main construction. We later reuse some of the techniques used in our main construction to obtain a construction in the dual setting.

Starting Point: Garbled RAMs. A natural idea to build ABE for RAMs is to use garbled RAMs [29,30,32]. A garbled RAM allows for separately encoding a RAM program[4]-database pair (P, D) and encoding an input x such that the encodings only leak the output $P^D(x)$; computing both the encodings requires a private key not revealed to the adversary. Notice that a garbled RAM scheme implies a *one-time, secret key* ABE for RAM scheme; meaning that the adversary

---

[3] All known lattice-based ABE for circuits [13] are based on the same assumption.

[4] The formal definition of a RAM program can be found in the preliminaries.

only gets to make a single ciphertext query and a single attribute key query. Indeed, it is unclear how to remove the one-time restriction while simultaneously achieve a public-key ABE for RAMs scheme by generically using garbled RAMs. Hence, we circumvent this conundrum by diving into the innards of the existing garbled RAMs schemes. The hope would be to adopt some of the techniques used in constructing garbled RAMs to build an ABE for RAMs scheme.

Most of the current known constructions of garbled RAMs have the following blueprint: to garble a RAM program P (associated with a step circuit C), database D, generate T garbled circuits, where T is an upper bound on the running time of P. The ith garbled circuit performs the execution of the ith time step of P. Also, every entry of the database D is suitably encoded using an appropriate encoding scheme (for instance, in [32], an IBE (identity-based encryption) key is associated with every entry of the database). The garbling of P consists of all the T garbled circuits and the encoding of the database D. The encoding of input x consists of wire labels of the first garbled circuit corresponding to the input x.

To evaluate a garbling of P on an encoded database D and wire labels of x, perform the following operations for $i = 1, \ldots, T - 1$:

- If $i = 1$, evaluate the first garbled circuit on wire labels of x.
- If $i > 1$, evaluate the ith garbled circuit to obtain output encodings of the ith step of execution of P^D on x.
- Next, we compute the *recoding step* that converts the output encodings of the ith step into the input encodings of the $(i + 1)^{th}$ step. These input encodings will be fed to the $(i + 1)^{th}$ garbled circuit.

The output of the Tth garbled circuit determines the output of execution of $P^D(x)$.

From Garbled RAMs to ABE for RAMs: Challenges. Towards realizing our hope of using garbled RAMs techniques to build an ABE for RAMs scheme, we encounter the following fundamental issues:

- The garbling and encoding operations in a garbled RAM scheme are inherently secret-key operations; they require a shared secret-key to compute garbled program and database encodings respectively. Since our goal is to construct public-key ABE for RAMs, the encryptor can perform neither the garbling nor the encoding procedures.
- Garbling schemes typically do not offer any reusability property[5]; they are useful only when a single computation needs to be hidden. It is unclear how to use garbled circuits, an integral part of current garbled RAM constructions, in the ABE setting, where multiple attribute keys need to be issued.

---

[5] An exception is the reusable garbling scheme of Goldwasser et al. [35], however their scheme only offers one-sided reusability: that is, their scheme only allows the adversary to get a single garbled circuit which can be reused across multiple input encodings. This is not useful in our setting since the adversary gets to query multiple keys. Moreover, just like any garbling scheme, even reusable garbled circuits require secret-key to perform the encoding operations.

– Tied to the issue of using garbled circuits is also the issue of implementing the recoding step. We need to implement a recoding step that can be reused across different computations.

Our Solution in a Nutshell. The main technical contribution of this paper is to identify a template to solve this problem and instantiate this template using a novel combination of existing lattice-based techniques.

We describe our template of ABE for RAMs. This will be an over-simplifcation of our actual scheme and is intended to help the reader towards understanding our final construction. For now, focus on the setting when the keys are only associated with read-only RAMs (i.e., they only read from the memory and never write into the memory). This template can be easily adapted to the setting where the program can also write to the memory.

– A key for a program P and a database D will consist of two parts: the first part, denoted by sk_D, is associated with the database and the second part, denoted by $(\mathsf{StepKey}_1, \ldots, \mathsf{StepKey}_T)$, consists of T sets of **recoding** keys with T being the maximum running time of $P^D(\cdot)$.
– A ciphertext for an input x and a secret message μ consists of two parts $(\mathsf{ct}_x^{(1)}, \mathsf{ct}_x^{(2)})$ and an encryption of μ, namely ct_μ (we will need a scheme that satisfies some specific properties): the first part $\mathsf{ct}_x^{(1)}$ serves as encoding of the initial input to the step circuit of the RAM program. We describe the role of the second part $\mathsf{ct}_x^{(2)}$ when we describe the decryption operation below.
– The decryption of a ciphertext of (x, μ) using a key of (P, D) proceeds in the following steps:
  • **Translation Step**: First, using the second part of the ciphertext, i.e., using $\mathsf{ct}_x^{(2)}$, and using the key associated with the database sk_D in the attribute key, obtain a probabilistic encoding of D.
  • The following operations are executed for time steps $t = 1, \ldots, T$:
    * **Evaluation Step**: Homomorphically evaluate on the input encodings of the tth step to obtain the output encodings of the tth step. This is akin to the evaluation of the tth garbled circuit in the garbled RAM constructions.
    * **Recoding Step**: Recode the output encodings of the tth step to obtain the input encodings of the $(t+1)^{th}$ step. This is akin to the recoding step of the garbled RAM constructions.
    The tth evaluation and the recoding steps are performed using the key $\mathsf{StepKey}_t$. Moreover, they interact with the probabilistic encoding of D produced in the translation step.
    If the output of the final T^{th} step is an encoding of 0 then this is used to decrypt the encryption of μ, given as part of the ciphertext, to obtain the result μ.

We now show how to implement the above template using lattice-based techniques. The starting point to our construction is the work of [13].

Implementation of Our Template: Read-Only RAMs. We implement our template using lattice-based techniques; as before, we first consider the read-only setting. We start with the high level description of the encryption procedure: let $(\mathsf{ct}_x^{(1)}, \mathsf{ct}_x^{(2)}, \mathsf{ct}_\mu)$ be the ciphertext associated with the input x and secret message μ. The first part $\mathsf{ct}_x^{(1)}$ consists of lattice-based encodings of x, initial state, initial read address and the initial read value of the RAM program. A lattice-based encoding of a bit b is computed using $\mathbf{s} \cdot (\mathbf{A} + b \cdot \mathbf{G}) + \mathbf{e}$, where $\mathbf{s} \xleftarrow{\$} \mathbb{Z}_q^{1 \times n}, \mathbf{A} \xleftarrow{\$} \mathbb{Z}_q^{n \times m}$ and $e \in \mathbb{Z}_q^{1 \times m}$ is drawn from a suitable error distribution; such lattice-based encodings has been studied by many works in the past [13,38]. We generate ct_μ to be $\langle \mathbf{s}, \mathbf{u} \rangle + \mu \lceil q/2 \rceil + e^*$, where $\mathbf{u}, \mathbf{s} \xleftarrow{\$} \mathbb{Z}_q^{1 \times n}$ and $e^* \in \mathbb{Z}_q$ is drawn from a suitable error distribution.

We will postpone the discussion on the generation of $\mathsf{ct}_x^{(2)}$ and the attribute keys. Instead, we first mention the main ideas incorporated in the translation, evaluation and the recoding steps; this will then guide us towards identifying the attribute keys and also $\mathsf{ct}_x^{(2)}$ that will let us execute these steps.

- **Implementing the translation step:** The goal of this step is to obtain a lattice-based encoding of the database D; in particular, this encoding should be computed with respect to the same secret $\mathbf{s}$ used in the lattice-based encoding in $\mathsf{ct}_x^{(1)}$. To do this, we generate $\mathsf{ct}_x^{(2)}$ and sk_D (belonging to the attribute key) such that evaluating sk_D on $\mathsf{ct}_x^{(2)}$ yields encodings of the form $(\{\mathbf{s} \cdot (\mathbf{A}_i^* + D[i]\mathbf{G}) + e_i\})^6$. In more detail, $\mathsf{ct}_x^{(2)}$ contains auxiliary encodings of many Boolean matrices such that given any matrix, using these auxiliary encodings, we can compute an encoding of this specific matrix. That is, $\mathsf{ct}_x^{(2)}$ will consist of encodings of the form $\mathbf{s} \cdot (\mathbf{B}_{jk\ell} + 2^\ell \mathbf{M}_{jk}) + e_{jk\ell}$ and $\mathbf{s} \cdot \mathbf{B}'_{jk\ell} \mid c'_{jk\ell}$, where $\mathbf{s} \xleftarrow{\$} \mathbb{Z}_q^{1 \times n}, (\mathbf{B}_{jk\ell}, \mathbf{B}'_{jk\ell}) \xleftarrow{\$} \mathbb{Z}_q^{n \times m}$ for $j \in [n], k \in [m], \ell \in [\log(q)]$ and $(e_{jk\ell}, e'_{jk\ell}) \in \mathbb{Z}_q^{1 \times m}$ is drawn from a suitable error distribution. Here, $\mathbf{M}_{jk}$ is a matrix with 1 in the $(j,k)^{th}$ entry and zeroes everywhere else. Now, observe that using the additive homomorphic properties, we can compute an encod-

$$\text{ing that is approximately } \mathbf{s} \cdot \left(\underbrace{\sum_{jk\ell} a_{jk\ell} \mathbf{B}_{jk\ell} + (1 - a_{jk\ell}) \mathbf{B}'_{jk\ell} + \mathbf{A}'_i}_{\mathbf{A}_i^*} + D[i] \cdot \mathbf{G} \right),$$

where $a_{jk\ell}$ denotes the ℓth bit in the bit decomposition of the $(j,k)^{th}$ entry in the matrix $\mathbf{A}'_i + D[i] \cdot \mathbf{G}$, with $\mathbf{A}'_i + D[i] \cdot \mathbf{G}$ being part of sk_D. Finally, we note that $\mathsf{ct}_x^{(2)}$ is independent of the size of the database D; this is necessary since we require that the ciphertext is of of size independent of the database length. We note that this technique of transforming encodings of bit decomposition of matrices into encodings of matrices have been studied in the past albeit for different reasons (see [19] for example).

---

^{6} $\mathbf{A}_i^* + D[i]\mathbf{G}$ will be denoted by $\mathbf{E}_i$ in the technical sections.

An astute reader would notice that the translation step takes time proportional to the database size and thus, would violate the sub-linear decryption property! We avoid this problem by *only* translating only those database entries that are going to read during the evaluation of $P^D(x)$; note that P, D and x are public and hence, the entries that are going to be read can be correctly identified.

- **Implementing the evaluation step**: This step would be a direct adaptation of the lattice-based evaluation procedure of [13]. Given approximate encodings $(\{\mathbf{s} \cdot (\mathbf{A}_i + b_i\mathbf{G})\})$, for bits $b_1, \ldots, b_n$, and for any circuit C with a single-bit output, the evaluation procedure of [13] (we will use the notation later for this procedure as CtEval) allows for obtaining $(\{\mathbf{s} \cdot (\mathbf{A}_C + C(b_1, \ldots, b_n)\mathbf{G})e_i\})$. The matrix $\mathbf{A}_C$ is obtained by homomorphically evaluating the matrices $(\mathbf{A}_1, \ldots, \mathbf{A}_n)$ using the circuit C (later, we will refer to this procedure as PubEval). We use the procedure of [13] to homomorphically evaluate the step circuit.
- **Implementing the recoding step**: We use lattice trapdoors [33] to convert output encodings of one time step into input encodings of the next time step. To give a flavor of how the lattice trapdoors are generated, we will take a simple case: suppose we need to translate an encoding of the read address $i \in [N]$ output by the τth evaluation step, we first sample a matrix $\mathbf{A}^{\mathsf{val}, \tau}$ and then generate $\mathbf{T}_i^{\mathsf{rd}, \tau}$ such that the following holds:

$$[\mathbf{A}^{\mathsf{rd}, \tau} + i\mathbf{G}\|\mathbf{A}_i^* + D[i] \cdot \mathbf{G}]\begin{pmatrix}\mathbf{T}_i^{\mathsf{rd}, \tau}\\\mathbf{I}\end{pmatrix} = \mathbf{A}^{\mathsf{val}, \tau} + D[i] \cdot \mathbf{G} \qquad (1)$$

where $\mathbf{A}^{\mathsf{rd}, \tau}$ is the matrix computed during the τth evaluation step. Recall that $\mathbf{A}_i^* + D_i \cdot \mathbf{G}$ is output by encryptor. Moreover, $\mathbf{A}^{\mathsf{val}, \tau} + b\mathbf{G}$ will serve as the matrix that is used to encode the read value for the $(\tau + 1)^{th}$ step. (Later we will see that in order to make the security proof work, we also additionally need an anchor matrix $\mathbf{A}$ and this will be taken into account when we generate the trapdoor matrices; see the technical sections for more details). All the lattice trapdoors generated during the tth step will be part of StepKey$_t$.

Implementation of Our Template: Handling Write Operations. To handle RAM programs that also write to the memory, we do the following: first, we view the database as an append-only data structure, with initial size to be N. That is, every time the program wishes to write to some memory location i, it instead appends this value to the end of the database, say at the $(N+\tau)^{th}$ location. However, this procedure introduces an additional issue. Before we describe the issue, we point out that the current lattice-based techniques disallow us from rewriting to the same location twice[7] and thus, our only other option is to use the append-only data structure.

---

[7] This would tantamount to obtaining two approximate encodings of the form $\mathbf{s}(\mathbf{A}_i + b_i \cdot \mathbf{G})$ and $\mathbf{s}(\mathbf{A}_i + b_i' \cdot \mathbf{G})$, where b_i is the old value and b_i' is the newly written value; assuming $b_i' \neq b_i$, having these two encodings is sufficient to break LWE.

Suppose the ith location is written during the τth step. This means that the $(N + \tau)^{th}$ location would now encode the latest value corresponding to the ith location. If at a later point in time, i.e., in time step $\gg \tau$, the ith location needs to be read, there is no mechanism in place that prevents an adversarial evaluator to use the old encoding of the ith memory location to perform an illegal evaluation.

To solve this problem, we introduce an auxiliary circuit C^{up} which keeps track of all the writes done so far and thus, for any given location i, can correctly identify the latest encoding to be used. In particular, the evaluation step from the read-only setting needs to be revised to also take into account the circuit C^{up}. That is, first the step circuit is homomorphically evaluated to obtain the location i to be read next and then the circuit C^{up} is executed to correctly identify the $(N + \tau)^{th}$ encoding that contains the value associated with location i, where τ is the time step where the ith memory location was last written to. The translation and the recoding steps will be defined along the same lines as that of the read-only setting; we defer the details to the technical sections.

Careful readers may notice that the run-time of circuit C^{up} is $O(T)$, which implies the decryption time would additionally incur a multiplicative overhead of T. However, we can resolve this issue by first compiling a RAM into a last-write-aware RAM. Given a RAM P, we can compile it into another machine denoted RAM P' where the next-instruction circuit is replaced with a "next-instruction RAM" that not only emits the next address to access, but also when the next address was last written. We show such a compilation algorithm that incurs only logarithmic overhead. The idea is to maintain a balanced search tree (e.g., a 2–3 tree) that records for each logical address, when the last write was. Moreover, in this balanced search tree, each parent also keeps track of the last written times of its children. Now, when the next-instruction circuit of RAM P decides to access some logical address addr, P' would search for addr in this search tree to find out when addr was last written. Note that every search-tree operation touches constant number of tree-paths, and since the parent knows the last-written times of the children, during the search-tree operation, every memory access always knows its last-written time.

The construction for the dual setting, where the database is part of the ciphertext as against the attribute key, is obtained by a simple modification of the above template. In particular, the translation step is not necessary for the dual setting and hence, will be removed. The other steps, evaluation and recoding steps, will be defined along the same lines as the above template.

1.3 Related Work

The constructions of ABE systems has a rich literature. The seminal result of Goyal, Pandey, Sahai and Waters [42] presented the first construction of ABE for boolean formulas from bilinear DDH assumption. Since then, several prominent works achieved stronger security guarantees [46], better efficiency or design guarantees [1,9,58] and achieving stronger models of ABE for a restricted class of functions [43]. The breakthrough work of Gorbunov, Vaikuntanathan and Wee [38] presented the first construction of ABE for all polynomial-sized circuits assuming learning with errors. Following this, several works [13,21] improved this result in terms of efficiency and also considering stronger security models [38]. In addition to [36], there are a few works that consider ABE in other models of computation. Waters [57] proposed a construction of functional encryption for regular languages and subsequently, Agarwal and Singh [4] constructed reusable garbled finite automata from LWE. Ananth and Sahai [8] construct functional encryption for Turing machines assuming sub-exponentially secure functional encryption for circuits; later this assumption was weakened to polynomially secure functional encryption by [3,7,31,44]. Deshpande et al. [23] present an alternate construction of attribute based encryption for Turing machines under the same assumptions.

2   Preliminaries

Notations. Let λ denote the security parameter, and ppt denote probabilistic polynomial time. Bold uppercase letters are used to denote matrices $\mathbf{M}$, and bold lowercase letters for vectors $\boldsymbol{v}$ (row vector). We use $[n]$ to denote the set $\{1, ..., n\}$. We say a function $\mathsf{negl}(\cdot) : \mathbb{N} \to (0,1)$ is negligible, if for every constant $c \in \mathbb{N}$, $\mathsf{negl}(n) < n^{-c}$ for sufficiently large n. Let X and Y be two random variables taking values in Ω. Define the statistical distance, denoted as $\Delta(X, Y)$ as

$$\Delta(X, Y) := \frac{1}{2} \sum_{s \in \Omega} |\Pr[X = s] - \Pr[Y = s]|$$

Let $X(\lambda)$ and $Y(\lambda)$ be distributions of random variables. We say that X and Y are statistically close, denoted as $X \overset{s}{\approx} Y$, if $d(\lambda) := \Delta(X(\lambda), Y(\lambda))$ is a negligible function of λ. We say two distributions $X(\lambda)$ and $Y(\lambda)$ are computationally indistinguishable, denoted as $X \overset{c}{\approx} Y$ if for any ppt distinguisher D, it holds that $|\Pr[D(X(\lambda)) = 1] - \Pr[D(Y(\lambda)) = 1]| = \mathsf{negl}(\lambda)$.

2.1   Random Access Machines

We recall the definition of RAM program from [32]. A RAM computation consists of a RAM program P and a database D. The representation size of P is independent of the length of the database D. P has random access to the database D and we represent this as P^D. On input x, $P^D(x)$ outputs the answer y. In more detail, the computation proceeds as follows.

The RAM program P is represented as a step-circuit C. It takes as input internal state from the previous step, location to be read, value at that location and it outputs the new state, location to be written into, value to be written and the next location to be read. More formally, for every $\tau \in T$, where T is the upper running time bound

$$(\mathsf{st}^\tau, \mathsf{rd}^\tau, \mathsf{wt}^\tau, \mathsf{wb}^\tau) \leftarrow C(\mathsf{st}^{\tau-1}, \mathsf{rd}^{\tau-1}, b^\tau)$$

where we have the following:

- $\mathsf{st}^{\tau-1}$ denotes the state from the $(\tau-1)$-th step and st^{τ} denotes the state in the τ-th step.
- $\mathsf{rd}^{\tau-1}$ denotes the location to be read from, as output by the $(\tau-1)$-th step.
- b^{τ} denotes the bit at the location $\mathsf{rd}^{\tau-1}$.
- rd^{τ} denotes the location to be read from, in the next step.
- wt^{τ} denotes the location to be written into.
- wb^{τ} denotes the value to be written at τ-th step at the location wt^{τ}.

At the end of the computation, denote the final state to be $\mathsf{st_{end}}$. If the computation has been performed correctly, $\mathsf{st^{end}} = y$. In this work, we are interested only in RAM programs with boolean outputs.

2.2 Attribute-Based Encryption for RAMs

We state the syntax and security definition of (key-policy) public-key attribute-based encryption (ABE) for RAMs. It consists of a tuple of ppt algorithms $\Pi = (\mathsf{Setup}, \mathsf{KeyGen}, \mathsf{Enc}, \mathsf{Dec})$ with details as follows:

- **Setup**, $\mathsf{Setup}(1^{\lambda}, 1^{T})$: On input security parameter λ and upper time bound T, setup algorithm outputs public parameters pp and master secret key msk.
- **Key Generation**, $\mathsf{KeyGen}(\mathsf{msk}, P, D)$: On input a master secret key msk, a RAM program P and database D, it outputs a secret key $\mathsf{sk}_{P,D}$.
- **Encryption**, $\mathsf{Enc}(\mathsf{pp}, x, \mu)$: On input public parameters pp, an input x and a message μ, it outputs a ciphertext ct_x.
- **Decryption**, $\mathsf{Dec}(\mathsf{sk}_{P,D}, \mathsf{ct}_x)$: This is modeled as a RAM program. In particular, this algorithm will have random access to the binary representations of the key $\mathsf{sk}_{P,D}$ and the ciphertext ct_x. It outputs the corresponding plaintext μ if $P^D(x) = 0$; otherwise, it outputs $\bot$.

Definition 2.1 (Correctness). *We say that the ABE for RAMs scheme described above is correct, if for any message μ, any RAM program P, any database D and any input x where $P^D(x) = 0$, we have $\mathsf{Dec}(\mathsf{sk}_{P,D}, \mathsf{ct}_x) = \mu$, where $(\mathsf{msk}, \mathsf{pp}) \leftarrow \mathsf{Setup}(1^{\lambda}, 1^{T})$, $\mathsf{sk}_{P,D} \leftarrow \mathsf{KeyGen}(\mathsf{msk}, P, D)$ and $\mathsf{ct}_x \leftarrow \mathsf{Enc}(\mathsf{pp}, x, \mu)$.*

We define the efficiency and security properties below.

Efficiency. We define two efficiency properties associated with an ABE for RAMs scheme: namely sub-linear decryption and input-specific runtime property. The latter property implies the former.

SUB-LINEAR DECRYPTION: This property states that the complexity of decryption is $p(\lambda, T)$ for some fixed polynomial p, where T is the maximum runtime bound specified as part of the setup. We call this sub-linear decryption for the following reason: suppose T is *sufficiently* sublinear in $|D|$ (for instance, poly-logarithmic in $|D|$) then the decryption time is sub-linear in $|D|$. More specifically, suppose $p(\lambda, T) = \lambda^{c'} \cdot T^c$ and if $T << |D|^{\frac{1}{c}}$, for some constants $c', c \in \mathbb{N}$, then the decryption complexity is sub-linear in $|D|$.

Definition 2.2 (Sublinear Decryption). *An ABE for RAMs scheme* ABE *is said to satisfy sublinear decryption property if the following holds: for any database D, message μ, program P, input x, (i)* $(\mathsf{msk}, \mathsf{pp}) \leftarrow \mathsf{Setup}(1^\lambda, 1^T)$*, (ii)* $\mathsf{sk}_{P,D} \leftarrow \mathsf{KeyGen}(\mathsf{msk}, P, D)$*, (iii)* $\mathsf{ct}_x \leftarrow \mathsf{Enc}(\mathsf{pp}, x, \mu)$ *and, (iv) the decryption* Dec *of the functional key* $\mathsf{sk}_{P,D}$ *on input the ciphertext* ct_x *takes time* $poly(T, \lambda)$*, where T is the running time of $P^D(x)$.*

INPUT-SPECIFIC RUNTIME: This property states that the time to decrypt a ciphertext ct of (D, μ) using an attribute key of sk_P is $p(\lambda, t)$ for some fixed polynomial p, where t is the execution time of P on input database D. Note that t could be much smaller than T, where T is the maximum bound on the running time of the P.

Definition 2.3 (Input-specific Runtime). *An ABE for RAMs scheme* ABE *is said to satisfy input-specific runtime property if the following holds: for any database D, message μ, program P, input x, (i)* $(\mathsf{msk}, \mathsf{pp}) \leftarrow \mathsf{Setup}(1^\lambda, 1^T)$*, (ii)* $\mathsf{sk}_{P,D} \leftarrow \mathsf{KeyGen}(\mathsf{msk}, P, D)$*, (iii)* $\mathsf{ct}_x \leftarrow \mathsf{Enc}(\mathsf{pp}, x)$ *and, (iv) the decryption* Dec *of the functional key* $\mathsf{sk}_{P,D}$ *on input the ciphertext* ct_x *takes time* $poly(t, \lambda)$*, where t is the running time of $P^D(x)$.*

Remark 2.4. While the above properties focus on the decryption complexity, we can also correspondingly define efficiency measures for setup, key generation and encryption. Since the focus of this work is on decryption complexity, we postpone the discussion of these properties to future works.

Security. Our definition of security for ABE for RAMs will be simulation-based and in the selective setting; along the same lines as that of ABE for circuits. Informally speaking, the adversary is allowed to make multiple RAM program and database queries and submit an input query x^* such that for every program/database (P, D) queried, we have $P^D(x^*) \neq 0$. The adversary is also allowed to submit the challenge message μ. We require that the adversary cannot distinguish the two worlds: (i) when the attribute keys and ciphertext are computed as per the scheme, (ii) when the attribute keys and ciphertext can be simulated even without given μ.

Definition 2.5. *An ABE scheme Π for RAMs is simulation-based selectively secure if there exists ppt simulator $\mathcal{S} = (\mathcal{S}_1, \mathcal{S}_2, \mathcal{S}_3)$ such that for any ppt admissible adversary $\mathcal{A} = (\mathcal{A}_1, \mathcal{A}_2)$, the two distributions $\{\mathsf{Expt}_{\mathcal{A}}^{\mathsf{real}}(1^\lambda)\}_{\lambda \in \mathbb{N}} \overset{c}{\approx} \{\mathsf{Expt}_{\mathcal{S}}^{\mathsf{ideal}}(1^\lambda)\}_{\lambda \in \mathbb{N}}$ are computationally indistinguishable*

1. $x^* \leftarrow \mathcal{A}_1(1^\lambda)$
2. $(\mathsf{pp}, \mathsf{msk}) \leftarrow \mathsf{Setup}(1^\lambda, 1^T)$
3. $\mu \leftarrow \mathcal{A}_2^{\mathsf{KeyGen}(\mathsf{msk}, \cdot, \cdot)}(\mathsf{pp})$
4. $\mathsf{ct}_{x^*} \leftarrow \mathsf{Enc}(\mathsf{pp}, x^*, \mu)$
5. $\alpha \leftarrow \mathcal{A}_2^{\mathsf{KeyGen}(\mathsf{msk}, \cdot, \cdot)}(\mathsf{pp}, \mathsf{ct}_{x^*})$
6. Output $(\mathsf{pp}, \mu, \alpha)$

$$\textbf{(a) } \mathsf{Expt}_{\mathcal{A}}^{\mathsf{real}}(1^\lambda)$$

1. $x^* \leftarrow \mathcal{A}_1(1^\lambda)$
2. $\mathsf{pp} \leftarrow \mathcal{S}_1(1^\lambda, 1^T, x^*)$
3. $\mu \leftarrow \mathcal{A}_2^{\mathcal{S}_3(x^*, \cdot, \cdot)}(\mathsf{pp})$
4. $\mathsf{ct}_{x^*} \leftarrow \mathcal{S}_2(\mathsf{pp}, x^*, 1^{|\mu|})$
5. $\alpha \leftarrow \mathcal{A}_2^{\mathcal{S}_3(x^*, \cdot, \cdot)}(\mathsf{pp}, \mathsf{ct}_{x^*})$
6. Output $(\mathsf{pp}, \mu, \alpha)$

$$\textbf{(b) } \mathsf{Expt}_{\mathcal{S}}^{\mathsf{ideal}}(1^\lambda)$$

We call adversary $\mathcal{A} = (\mathcal{A}_1, \mathcal{A}_2)$ admissible, if the query (P_i, D_i) made by $\mathcal{A}_2$ satisfies $P_i^{D_i}(x^*) \neq 0$. In the ideal experiment $\mathsf{Expt}_{\mathcal{S}}^{\mathsf{ideal}}(1^\lambda)$: $\mathcal{S}_1$ is used to generate simulated public parameters, $\mathcal{S}_2$ generates challenge ciphertext, and $\mathcal{S}_3$ answers secret key queries.

Dual Setting. We also consider the dual setting of the syntax described above, where the database is associated with ciphertext. We term this notion as *dual ABE for RAMs*. As in the above definition, the dual scheme consists of algorithms $(\mathsf{Setup}, \mathsf{KeyGen}, \mathsf{Enc}, \mathsf{Dec})$. The algorithms Setup and Dec are defined the same way as above. We define KeyGen and Enc as follows.

– $\mathsf{KeyGen}(\mathsf{msk}, P)$: On input a master secret key msk, a RAM program P, it outputs a secret key sk_P.
– $\mathsf{Enc}(\mathsf{pp}, D, x, \mu)$: On input public parameters pp, a database D, an input x and a message μ, it outputs a ciphertext $\mathsf{ct}_{D,x}$.

We omit the descriptions of the correctness, efficiency and security properties of dual ABE for RAMs as they are defined analogously. Due to space limit, the construction and its security proof are presented in the full version.

2.3 Learning with Errors

The learning with errors assumption was introduced by Regev [53]. This assumption has been influential in basing the security of many cryptographic primitives and most notably, fully homomorphic encryption.

Definition 2.6 (LWE). *For an integer $q = q(n) \geq 2$, and an error distribution $\chi = \chi(n)$ over $\mathbb{Z}_q$, the Learning With Errors problem $\mathsf{LWE}_{n,q,\chi}$ is to distinguish between the following pairs of distributions (e.g. as given by a sampling oracle $\mathcal{O} \in \{\mathcal{O}_s, \mathcal{O}_\$\}$):*

$$\{\mathbf{A}, s\mathbf{A} + \boldsymbol{x}\} \text{ and } \{\mathbf{A}, \boldsymbol{u}\}$$

where $\mathbf{A} \xleftarrow{\$} \mathbb{Z}_q^{n \times m}$, $s \xleftarrow{\$} \mathbb{Z}_q^n$, $\boldsymbol{u} \xleftarrow{\$} \mathbb{Z}_q^m$, and $\boldsymbol{x} \leftarrow \chi^m$.

In this work we only consider the case where the modulus $q \leq 2^n$. Recall that GapSVP$_\gamma$ is the (promise) problem of distinguishing, given a basis for a lattice and a parameter d, between the case where the lattice has a vector shorter than d, and the case where the lattice does not have any vector shorter than $\gamma \cdot d$.

There are known reductions between LWE$_{n,q,\chi}$ and those problems, which allows us to appropriately choose the LWE parameters for our scheme. We summarize in the following corollary (which addresses the regime of sub-exponential modulus-to-noise ratio).

Theorem 2.7 ([17,47,48,52,53]). *For any function $B = B(n) \geq \tilde{O}(\sqrt{n})$ there exists a B-bounded distribution ensemble $\chi = \chi(n)$ over the integers s.t. for all $q = q(n)$, letting $\gamma = \tilde{O}(\sqrt{b}q/B)$, it holds that LWE$_{n,q,\chi}$ is at least as hard as the quantum hardness of GapSVP$_\gamma$. Classical hardness GapSVP$_\gamma$ follows if $q(n) \geq 2n/2$ or for other values of q for $\tilde{\Omega}(\sqrt{n})$ dimensional lattices and approximation factor $q/B \cdot \mathsf{poly}(n\lceil \log q \rceil)$.*

2.4 Trapdoors and Discrete Gaussians

Let $n, q \in \mathbb{Z}$, and $m = n\lceil \log q \rceil$ and $\boldsymbol{g} = (1, 2, 4, \ldots, 2^{\lceil \log q \rceil - 1})$. The *gadget matrix* [48] $\mathbf{G}$ is defined as the diagonal concatenation of vector $\boldsymbol{g}$ n times. Formally, $\mathbf{G} = \boldsymbol{g} \otimes \mathbf{I}_n \in \mathbb{Z}_q^{n \times m}$. For any $t \in \mathbb{Z}$, the function $\mathbf{G}^{-1} : \mathbb{Z}_q^{n \times t} \to \{0,1\}^{m \times t}$ expands each entry $a \in \mathbb{Z}_q$ of the input matrix into a column of size $\lceil \log q \rceil$ consisting of the bit-representation of a. For any matrix $\mathbf{A} \in \mathbb{Z}_q^{n \times l}$, it holds that $\mathbf{G} \cdot \mathbf{G}^{-1}(\mathbf{A}) = \mathbf{A} \bmod q$.

The (centered) discrete Gaussian distribution over $\mathbb{Z}^m$ with parameter τ, denoted $\mathcal{D}_{\mathbb{Z}^m, \tau}$, is the distribution over $\mathbb{Z}^m$ where for all $\boldsymbol{x}$, $\Pr[\boldsymbol{x}] \propto e^{-\pi \|\boldsymbol{x}\|^2 / \tau^2}$.

The following lemmas have been established in a sequence of works.

Lemma 2.8 (Trapdoor Generation [33,48]). *Let q, n, m be positive integers with $q \geq 2$ and sufficiently large $m = \Omega(n \log q)$. There exists a ppt algorithm $\mathsf{TrapGen}(1^n, q, m)$ that with overwhelming probability outputs a pair $(\mathbf{A} \in \mathbb{Z}_q^{n \times m}, \mathbf{T_A} \in \mathbb{Z}^{m \times m})$ such that the distribution of $\mathbf{A}$ is statistically close to uniform distribution over $\mathbb{Z}_q^{n \times m}$ and $\|\mathbf{T_A}\| \leq O(\sqrt{n \log q})$.*

Lemma 2.9 ([2,22,33]). *Given integers $n \geq 1, q \geq 2$ there exists some $m = m(n, q) = O(n \log q)$ There are sampling algorithms as follows:*

- *There is a ppt algorithm $\mathsf{SampleLeft}(\mathbf{A}, \mathbf{B}, \mathbf{T_A}, \boldsymbol{u}, s)$, that takes as input: (1) a rank-n matrix $\mathbf{A} \in \mathbb{Z}_q^{n \times m}$, and any matrix $\mathbf{B} \in \mathbb{Z}_q^{n \times m_1}$, (2) a "short" basis $\mathbf{T_A}$ for lattice $\Lambda_q^\perp(\mathbf{A})$, a vector $\boldsymbol{u} \in \mathbb{Z}_q^n$, (3) a Gaussian parameter $s > \|\widetilde{\mathbf{T_A}}\| \cdot \omega(\sqrt{\log(m + m_1)})$; then outputs a vector $\boldsymbol{r} \in \mathbb{Z}^{m+m_1}$ distributed statistically close to $\mathcal{D}_{\Lambda_q^u(\mathbf{F}), s}$ where $\mathbf{F} := [\mathbf{A} \| \mathbf{B}]$.*
- *There is a ppt algorithm $\mathsf{SampleRight}(\mathbf{A}, \mathbf{B}, \mathbf{R}, \mathbf{T_B}, \boldsymbol{u}, s)$, that takes as input: (1) a matrix $\mathbf{A} \in \mathbb{Z}_q^{n \times m}$, and a rank-n matrix $\mathbf{B} \in \mathbb{Z}_q^{n \times m}$, a matrix $\mathbf{R} \in \mathbb{Z}_q^{m \times m}$, where $s_\mathbf{R} := \|\mathbf{R}\| = \sup_{\boldsymbol{x}: \|\boldsymbol{x}\| = 1} \|\mathbf{R}\boldsymbol{x}\|$, (2) a "short" basis $\mathbf{T_B}$ for lattice $\Lambda_q^\perp(\mathbf{B})$, a vector $\boldsymbol{u} \in \mathbb{Z}_q^n$, (3) a Gaussian parameter $s > \|\widetilde{\mathbf{T_B}}\| \cdot s_\mathbf{R} \cdot$*

$\omega(\sqrt{\log m})$; then outputs a vector $r \in \mathbb{Z}^{2m}$ distributed statistically close to $\mathcal{D}_{\Lambda_q^u(\mathbf{F}),s}$ where $\mathbf{F} := [\mathbf{A}||\mathbf{AR} + \mathbf{B}]$.

Based on the above sampling algorithms, we have the following lemma:

Lemma 2.10 ([40]). *Given integers $n \geq 1, q \geq 2$ there exists some $m = m(n,q) = O(n \log q)$, $\beta = \beta(n,q) = O(n\sqrt{\log q})$ and $s > ||\widetilde{\mathbf{T_A}}|| \cdot \omega(\sqrt{\log(m)})$ such that for all $m \geq m^*$ and all k, we have the following two distributions are statistically close*

$$(\mathbf{A}, \mathbf{T_A}, \mathbf{B}, \mathbf{U}, \mathbf{V}) \approx (\mathbf{A}, \mathbf{T_A}, \mathbf{B}, \mathbf{U}', \mathbf{V}')$$

where $(\mathbf{A}, \mathbf{T_A}) \leftarrow \mathsf{TrapGen}(q, n, m), (\mathbf{A}', \mathbf{B}) \xleftarrow{\$} \mathbb{Z}_q^{n \times m}$ and $\mathbf{U} \leftarrow \mathcal{D}_{\mathbb{Z}^{2m \times k}}, \mathbf{V} = \mathbf{A} \cdot \mathbf{U}, \mathbf{V}' \xleftarrow{\$} \mathbb{Z}_q^{n \times k}$ and $\mathbf{U}' \leftarrow \mathsf{SampleLeft}(\mathbf{A}, \mathbf{B}, \mathbf{T_A}, \mathbf{V}', s)$.

We conclude with a variant of Leftover Hash Lemma [2,13]:

Lemma 2.11. *Suppose that $m > (n+1)\log q + \omega(\log n)$ and that $q > 2$ is prime. Let $\mathbf{S}$ be an $m \times k$ matrix chosen uniformly in $\{0,1\}^{m \times k}$ where $k = k(n)$ is polynomial in n. Let $\mathbf{A}$ and $\mathbf{B}$ be matrices chosen uniformly in $\mathbb{Z}_q^{n \times m}$ and $\mathbb{Z}_q^{n \times k}$ respectively. Then, for all vectors e in $\mathbb{Z}_q^m$, the distribution $(\mathbf{A}, \mathbf{AS}, e\mathbf{S})$ is statistically close to the distribution $(\mathbf{A}, \mathbf{B}, e\mathbf{S})$.*

2.5 Homomorphic Evaluation Procedures

The following is an abstraction of the evaluation procedure in recent LWE based FHE and ABE schemes that developed in a long sequence of works [2,5,13,34,40,48]. We use a similar formalism as in [16,19,20].

Theorem 2.12. *There exist efficient deterministic algorithms $\mathsf{PubEval}$ and CtEval such that for all $n, q, \ell \in \mathbb{N}$, and for any sequence of matrices $(\mathbf{D}_1, \ldots, \mathbf{D}_\ell) \in (\mathbb{Z}_q^{n \times n\lceil \log q \rceil})^\ell$, for any depth-d Boolean circuit $f : \{0,1\}^\ell \to \{0,1\}$ and for every $x = (x_1, \ldots, x_\ell) \in \{0,1\}^\ell$, the following properties hold:*

- $\mathsf{PubEval}(f, \{\mathbf{D}_i \in \mathbb{Z}_q^{n \times n\lceil \log q \rceil}\}_{i \in [\ell]})$: *On input matrices $\{\mathbf{D}_i\}_{i \in [d]}$ and a function $f \in \mathcal{F}$, the public evaluation algorithm outputs $\mathbf{D}_f \in \mathbb{Z}_q^{n \times n\lceil \log q \rceil}$ as the result.*
- $\mathsf{TrapEval}(f, x, \mathbf{A} \in \mathbb{Z}_q^{n \times \lceil \log q \rceil}, \{\mathbf{R}_i\}_{i \in [\ell]})$: *the trapdoor evaluation algorithm outputs $\mathbf{R}_f$, such that*

$$\mathsf{PubEval}(f, \{\mathbf{AR}_i + x_i\mathbf{G}\}_{i \in [\ell]}) = \mathbf{AR}_f + f(x)\mathbf{G}$$

Furthermore, we have $||\mathbf{R}_f|| \leq \delta \cdot \max_{i \in [\ell]} ||\mathbf{R}_i||$.
- $\mathsf{CtEval}(f, x, \{c_i\}_{i=1}^\ell)$: *On input vectors $\{c_i\}_{i=1}^\ell \in \mathbb{Z}_q^m$, an attribute x and function f, the ciphertext evaluation algorithm outputs $c_{f(x)} \in \mathbb{Z}_q^{n\lceil \log q \rceil}$, such that*

$$\mathsf{CtEval}(f, x, \{s^\top(\mathbf{D}_i + x_i\mathbf{G}) + e_i\}_{i \in [\ell]}) = s^\top(\mathbf{D}_f + f(x)\mathbf{G}) + e'$$

where $x = (x_1, \ldots, x_\ell)$ and $\mathbf{D}_f = \mathsf{PubEval}(f, \{\mathbf{D}_i \in \mathbb{Z}_q^{n \times n\lceil \log q \rceil}\}_{i \in [\ell]})$. Furthermore, we require $||e'|| \leq \delta \cdot \max_{i \in [\ell]} ||e_i||$.

3   ABE for RAMs: Read-Only Case

In this part, we describe our ABE construction for read-only RAMs. A RAM program P, with random access to database D and input x, is said to be read-only if it only reads from D and never writes to it. The step circuit for read-only RAM will be defined as follows:

$$(\mathsf{st}^\tau, \mathsf{rd}^\tau) \leftarrow C(\mathsf{st}^{\tau-1}, \mathsf{rd}^{\tau-1}, b^\tau)$$

where st^τ denotes the state information at τ-th step, rd^τ denotes the read address at τ-th step and b^τ is the read value.

Parameters of the Scheme. In the description below, the parameters we use are specified in Table 1.

Table 1. Read-only ABE parameters

Parameters	Description	Setting
N	Maximum database length	$\mathsf{poly}(\lambda)$
T	Maximum running time	$\mathsf{poly}(\lambda)$
L_{st}	State bit-length	$\mathsf{poly}(\lambda)$
L_{rd}	Address bit-length	$\log N$

We use notation $\{\mathsf{rd}_i^\tau\}_{i \in [L_{\mathsf{rd}}]}$ to denote the bit representation of read address $\mathsf{rd}^\tau \in [N]$.

3.1   Subroutines TranslatePK, StepEvalPK and StepEvalCT

Before proceeding to our ABE construction, we first describe the syntax of three following subroutines that are used in the construction:

- $\mathsf{ListMxDB} \leftarrow \mathsf{TranslatePK}\,(\mathsf{MxPK}_{\mathsf{aux}},\, D)$: On input auxiliary encoding public key $\mathsf{MxPK}_{\mathsf{aux}}$ and database $D = \{D_i\}_{i \in [N]}$, the translation algorithm outputs encoding matrices $\mathsf{ListMxDB}$ for the database.
- $(\mathsf{StepKey}_\tau, \mathsf{ListMxPK}_\tau) \leftarrow \mathsf{StepEvalPK}\,(C, \tau, \mathsf{ListMxPK}_{\tau-1}, \mathsf{msk}, D)$: On input the step circuit C, step index τ, matrices $\mathsf{ListMxPK}_{\tau-1}$ for the $(\tau-1)$-th step and master secret key msk, the key evaluation outputs the τ-th step key $\mathsf{StepKey}_\tau$ and encoding matrices $\mathsf{ListMxPK}_\tau$ for the τ-th step.
- $\mathsf{ListVecCT}_\tau \leftarrow \mathsf{StepEvalCT}\,(C, \tau, \mathsf{ListVecCT}_{\tau-1}, \mathsf{StepKey}_\tau, D)$: On input the step circuit C, step index τ, ciphertext $\mathsf{ListVecCT}_{\tau-1}$ of the $(\tau-1)$-th step, τ-th attribute key and databae D, the ciphertext evaluation outputs the ciphertext $\mathsf{ListVecCT}_\tau$ of the τ-th step.

In the following description, we set function $f : \{0,1\}^{L_{st}} \to \mathbb{Z}$ to be $f\left(\{x_i\}_{i=1}^{L_{st}}\right) = \sum x_i \cdot 2^i$. The construction of StepEvalPK and StepEvalCT with respect to step circuit C are as follows:

TranslatePK $(\mathsf{MxPK}_{\mathsf{aux}}, D)$: the translation algorithm does the following:

- Parse $\mathsf{MxPK}_{\mathsf{aux}}$ as $\left\{\mathbf{B}_{jk\ell}, \mathbf{B}'_{jk\ell}\right\}_{j\in[n],k\in[m],\ell\in\lceil\log q\rceil}$.
- Sample N random matrices $\{\mathbf{A}'_i\}_{i\in[N]}$ from uniform distribution over $\mathbb{Z}_q^{n\times m}$.
- For $i \in [N]$, set $\mathbf{A}_i = \mathbf{A}'_i + D[i]\mathbf{G}$.
- For $i \in [N]$, compute the encoding of i-th entry $\mathbf{E}_i$ as

$$\mathbf{E}_i = \sum_{j,k,\ell}\left(a_{jk\ell}\left(\mathbf{B}_{jk\ell} + 2^\ell\mathbf{M}_{j,k}\right) + \bar{a}_{jk\ell}\mathbf{B}'_{jk\ell}\right) = \mathbf{A}_i + \sum_{j,k,\ell}\left(a_{jk\ell}\mathbf{B}_{jk\ell} + \bar{a}_{jk\ell}\mathbf{B}'_{jk\ell}\right)$$

where $\mathbf{M}_{j,k} \in \{0,1\}^{n\times m}$ is matrix with 1 on the (j,k)-th element and 0 elsewhere, $a_{jk\ell}$ is ℓ-th bit of the bit-decomposition of (j,k)-th element a_{jk} in matrix $\mathbf{A}_i$, and $\bar{a}_{jk\ell}$ is its complement. For ease of notation, we set $\mathbf{B}_i = \sum_{j,k,\ell}\left(a_{jk\ell}\mathbf{B}_{jk\ell} + \bar{a}_{jk\ell}\mathbf{B}'_{jk\ell}\right)$.

Output matrices $\mathsf{ListMxDB} = \{(\mathbf{A}'_i, \mathbf{B}_i, \mathbf{E}_i)\}_{i\in[N]}$.

StepEvalPK $(C, \tau, \mathsf{ListMxPK}_{\tau-1}, \mathsf{msk} = \mathbf{T_A}, D)$: the key evaluation algorithm does the following:

- Parse the encoding matrices $\mathsf{ListMxPK}_{\tau-1}$ as

$$\left(\mathbf{A}, \mathsf{ListMxPK}, \left\{\mathbf{A}_i^{st,\tau-1}\right\}_{i\in[L_{st}]}, \left\{\mathbf{A}_i^{rd,\tau-1}\right\}_{i\in[L_{rd}]}, \mathbf{A}^{val,\tau-1}\right)$$

- Compute $\left(\left\{\mathbf{A}_i^{st,\tau}\right\}_{i\in[L_{st}]}, \left\{\mathbf{A}_i^{rd,\tau}\right\}_{i\in[L_{rd}]}\right) = \mathsf{PubEval}\left(\mathsf{ListMxPK}_{\tau-1}, C\right)$, where algorithm PubEval is defined in Theorem 2.12.
- Sample $\mathbf{A}^{val,\tau} \stackrel{\$}{\leftarrow} \mathbb{Z}_q^{n\times m}$. For $i \in [N]$, compute $\mathbf{T}_i^{rd,\tau}$ as

$$\mathbf{T}_i^{rd,\tau} \leftarrow \mathsf{SampleLeft}(\mathbf{A}, \mathbf{T_A}, \mathbf{A}^{rd,\tau} + i\mathbf{G}, \mathbf{A}^{val,\tau} - \mathbf{A}'_i - \mathbf{B}_i, s)$$

where $\mathbf{A}^{rd,\tau} = \mathsf{PubEval}\left(f, \left\{\mathbf{A}_i^{rd,\tau}\right\}_{i\in[L_{rd}]}\right)$, and $\mathsf{ListMxPK} = \{\mathbf{A}'_i, \mathbf{B}_i, \mathbf{E}_i\}_{i\in[N]}$ is computed from algorithm TranslatePK $(\mathsf{MxPK}_{\mathsf{aux}}, D)$. We have that

$$\left[\mathbf{A} \| \mathbf{A}^{rd,\tau} + i\mathbf{G} \| \mathbf{A}'_i + \mathbf{B}_i + D[i]\mathbf{G}\right]\begin{pmatrix}\mathbf{T}_i^{rd,\tau}\\\mathbf{I}\end{pmatrix} = \mathbf{A}^{val,\tau} + D[i]\mathbf{G}$$

- Set $\mathsf{StepKey}_\tau = \left\{\mathbf{T}_i^{rd,\tau}\right\}_{i\in[N]}$ and

$$\mathsf{ListMxPK}_\tau = \left(\mathbf{A}, \mathsf{ListMxPK}, \left\{\mathbf{A}_i^{st,\tau}\right\}_{i\in[L_{st}]}, \left\{\mathbf{A}_i^{rd,\tau}\right\}_{i\in[L_{rd}]}, \mathbf{A}^{val,\tau}\right)$$

Output $(\mathsf{StepKey}_\tau, \mathsf{ListMxPK}_\tau)$.

$\underline{\mathsf{StepEvalCT}\ (C, \tau, \mathsf{ListVecCT}_{\tau-1}, \mathsf{StepKey}_\tau, D)}$: the ciphertext evaluation algorithm does the following:

- Parse the ciphertext $\mathsf{ListVecCT}_{\tau-1}$ as

$$
\left(\{\mathsf{ct}_{ijk}, \mathsf{ct}'_{ijk}\}_{\substack{i\in[n],j\in[m],\\k\in[\log q]}}, \left\{\mathsf{ct}_i^{\mathsf{st},\tau-1}\right\}_{i\in[L_{\mathsf{st}}]}, \left\{\mathsf{ct}_i^{\mathsf{rd},\tau-1}\right\}_{i\in[L_{\mathsf{rd}}]}, \mathsf{ct}^{\mathsf{val},\tau-1} \right)
$$

along with its associated value $\mathsf{ListST}_{\tau-1} = (\{\mathsf{st}^{\tau-1}\}_{i\in[L_{\mathsf{st}}]}, \{\mathsf{rd}^{\tau-1}\}_{i\in[L_{\mathsf{rd}}]}, \mathsf{val}^{\tau-1})$.

- **Ciphertext evaluation**: Compute

$$
\left(\left\{\mathsf{ct}_i^{\mathsf{st},\tau}\right\}_{i\in[L_{\mathsf{st}}]}, \left\{\mathsf{ct}_i^{\mathsf{rd},\tau}\right\}_{i\in[L_{\mathsf{rd}}]} \right) = \mathsf{CtEval}\,(\mathsf{ListMxPK}_{\tau-1}, \mathsf{ListST}_{\tau-1}, C), \text{ where}
$$

algorithm CtEval is defined in Theorem 2.12.

- **Ciphertext translation and recoding steps**: Compute

$$
\mathsf{ct}^{\mathsf{val},\tau} = \left(\widehat{\mathsf{ct}}, \mathsf{ct}^{\mathsf{rd},\tau}, \mathsf{ct}_{\mathsf{rd}^\tau}\right) \begin{pmatrix} \mathbf{T}_{\mathsf{rd}^\tau}^{\mathsf{rd},\tau} \\ \mathbf{I} \end{pmatrix}
$$

where $\mathsf{ct}^{\mathsf{rd},\tau} = \mathsf{CtEval}\left(\left\{\mathsf{ct}_i^{\mathsf{rd},\tau}\right\}_{i\in[L_{\mathsf{rd}}]}, \{\mathsf{rd}_i^\tau\}_{i\in[L_{\mathsf{rd}}]}, f \right)$ and

$$
\mathsf{ct}_{\mathsf{rd}^\tau} = \sum_{j,k,\ell} \left(a_{jk\ell}\mathsf{ct}_{jk\ell} + \bar{a}_{jk\ell}\mathsf{ct}'_{jk\ell} \right)
$$

$a_{jk\ell}$ is ℓ-th bit of the bit-decomposition of (j,k)-th element a_{jk} in matrix $\mathbf{A}_{\mathsf{rd}^\tau} = \mathbf{A}'_{\mathsf{rd}^\tau} + D[\mathsf{rd}^\tau]\mathbf{G}$.

Output $\mathsf{ListVecCT}_\tau = \left(\{\mathsf{ct}_{ijk}, \mathsf{ct}'_{ijk}\}_{\substack{i\in[n],j\in[m],\\k\in[\log q]}}, \left\{\mathsf{ct}_i^{\mathsf{st},\tau}\right\}_{i\in[L_{\mathsf{st}}]}, \left\{\mathsf{ct}_i^{\mathsf{rd},\tau}\right\}_{i\in[L_{\mathsf{rd}}]}, \mathsf{ct}^{\mathsf{val},\tau} \right)$.

We note that $\mathsf{StepEvalCT}$ incorporates the translation, evaluation and the recoding steps described in the technical overview.

3.2   Construction

In our construction below, we assume the initial states are all 1, the initial read address is always the first index of database.

Our read-only ABE for RAMs construction $\Pi = (\mathsf{Setup}, \mathsf{KeyGen}, \mathsf{Enc}, \mathsf{Dec})$ can be described as follows:

Setup, $\mathsf{Setup}(1^\lambda, T)$: On input security parameter λ and time bound T, the setup algorithm computes:

- $(\mathbf{A}, \mathbf{T_A}) \leftarrow \mathsf{TrapGen}(1^n, 1^q, m)$, the anchor matrix and its associated trapdoor.

- $\forall i \in [L_{st}]$, sample $\mathbf{A}_i^{st,0} \xleftarrow{\$} \mathbb{Z}_q^{n \times m}$, encoding matrix for the initial state.
- $\forall i \in [L_{rd}]$, sample $\mathbf{A}_i^{rd,0} \xleftarrow{\$} \mathbb{Z}_q^{n \times m}$, encoding matrix for the initial read address.
- $\forall j \in [n], k \in [m], \ell \in \lceil \log q \rceil$, sample $\left(\mathbf{B}_{jk\ell}, \mathbf{B}'_{jk\ell} \right) \xleftarrow{\$} \mathbb{Z}_q^{n \times m}$, encoding matrix for the database.
- For $i \in [\lambda]$, sample $\mathbf{A}_i^{val,0} \xleftarrow{\$} \mathbb{Z}_q^{n \times m}$, encoding matrix for the initial read value.
- Sample $\boldsymbol{u} \xleftarrow{\$} \mathbb{Z}_q^n$, encoding vector for the plaintext.

Set $\mathsf{MxPK_{aux}} = \left\{ \left(\mathbf{B}_{jk\ell}, \mathbf{B}'_{jk\ell} \right) \right\}_{j\in[n],k\in[m],\ell\in\lceil\log q\rceil}$. Output $\mathsf{msk} = (\mathsf{pp}, \mathbf{T_A})$
and

$$\mathsf{pp} = \left(\mathbf{A}, \mathsf{MxPK_{aux}}, \left\{ \mathbf{A}_i^{st,0} \right\}_{i\in[L_{st}]}, \left\{ \mathbf{A}_i^{rd,0} \right\}_{i\in[L_{rd}]}, \left\{ \mathbf{A}_i^{val,0} \right\}_{i\in[\lambda]}, \boldsymbol{u} \right)$$

Key Generation, $\mathsf{KeyGen}(\mathsf{msk}, P, D)$: On input master secret key msk, RAM program P with step circuit C and database D, it does the following:

- First compute the translation algorithm

$$\mathsf{ListMxDB} \leftarrow \mathsf{TranslatePK}\left(\mathsf{MxPK_{aux}}, D \right)$$

where $\mathsf{ListMxDB} = \{(\mathbf{A}'_i, \mathbf{B}_i, \mathbf{E}_i)\}_{i\in[N]}$. Set

$$\mathsf{ListMxPK_0} = \left(\mathbf{A}, \mathsf{ListMxDB}, \left\{ \mathbf{A}_i^{st,0} \right\}_{i\in[L_{st}]}, \left\{ \mathbf{A}_i^{rd,0} \right\}_{i\in[L_{rd}]}, \left\{ \mathbf{A}_i^{val,0} \right\}_{i\in[\lambda]} \right).$$

- For $\tau \in [T]$, compute

$$(\mathsf{ListMxPK_\tau}, \mathsf{StepKey_\tau}) \leftarrow \mathsf{StepEvalPK}\left(C, \tau, \mathsf{ListMxPK_{\tau-1}}, \mathbf{T_A}, D \right)$$

- Compute $\boldsymbol{t}^{st,T}$ as

$$\boldsymbol{t}^{st,T} \leftarrow \mathsf{SampleLeft}(\mathbf{A}, \mathbf{T_A}, \mathbf{A}_1^{st,T}, \boldsymbol{u}, s)$$

such that

$$\left[\mathbf{A} || \mathbf{A}_1^{st,T} \right] \cdot \boldsymbol{t}^{st,T} = \boldsymbol{u}$$

Output $\mathsf{sk}_{P,D} = \left(P, D, \mathsf{ListMxDB}, \{\mathsf{StepKey_\tau}\}_{\tau\in[T]}, \boldsymbol{t}^{st,T} \right)$.

Encryption, $\mathsf{Enc}(\mathsf{pp}, x, \mu)$: On input public parameters pp, input $\boldsymbol{x} \in \{0,1\}^\lambda$, message μ, the encryption algorithm does the following:

- Sample vector $\boldsymbol{s} \xleftarrow{\$} \mathbb{Z}_q^n$ and error vectors $\widehat{\boldsymbol{e}}, \boldsymbol{e}^*$ from Gaussian distribution $\mathcal{D}_{\mathbb{Z}^m}$.
- $\forall i \in [L_{st}]$, compute $\mathsf{ct}_i^{st,0} = \boldsymbol{s} \left(\mathbf{A}_i^{st,0} + \mathbf{G} \right) + \widehat{\boldsymbol{e}} \mathbf{R}_i^{st,0}$, encoding of the initial state, where $\mathbf{R}_i^{st,0} \leftarrow \{0,1\}^{m \times m}$.

- $\forall i \in [L_{rd}]$, compute $\mathsf{ct}_i^{rd,0} = s\left(\mathbf{A}_i^{rd,0} + rd_i^0\mathbf{G}\right) + \widehat{\mathbf{e}}\mathbf{R}_i^{rd,0}$, encoding of the initial read address, where $\mathbf{R}_i^{rd,0} \leftarrow \{0,1\}^{m\times m}$ and $\{rd_i^0\}_{i\in[L_{rd}]}$ is the bit representation of 1.
- For $i \in [\lambda]$, compute $\mathsf{ct}_i^{val,0} = s\left(\mathbf{A}_i^{val,0} + \boldsymbol{x}[i]\mathbf{G}\right) + \widehat{\mathbf{e}}\mathbf{R}_i^{val,0}$, encoding of the initial read value, where $\mathbf{R}_i^{val,0} \leftarrow \{0,1\}^{m\times m}$.
- $\forall j \in [n], k \in [m], \ell \in \lceil \log q \rceil$, compute

$$\mathsf{ct}_{jk\ell} = s\left(\mathbf{B}_{jk\ell} + 2^\ell \mathbf{M}_{j,k}\right) + \widehat{\mathbf{e}}\mathbf{R}_{jkl}, \quad \mathsf{ct}'_{jk\ell} = s\mathbf{B}'_{jk\ell} + \widehat{\mathbf{e}}\mathbf{R}'_{jkl}$$

  auxiliary encodings, where $\mathbf{R}_{jk\ell}, \mathbf{R}'_{jk\ell} \leftarrow \{0,1\}^{m\times m}$.
- Compute $\widehat{\mathsf{ct}} = s\mathbf{A} + \widehat{\mathbf{e}}$ and $\mathsf{ct}^* = s\boldsymbol{u}^\mathsf{T} + \mu\lceil q/2 \rceil + e^*$.
- Set

$$\mathsf{ListVecCT}_0 = \left(\left\{\mathsf{ct}_i^{st,0}\right\}_{i\in[L_{st}]}, \left\{\mathsf{ct}_i^{rd,0}\right\}_{i\in[L_{rd}]}, \left\{\mathsf{ct}_i^{val,0}\right\}_{i\in[\lambda]} \{\mathsf{ct}_{ijk}, \mathsf{ct}'_{ijk}\}_{\substack{i\in[n], j\in[m], \\ k\in[\log q]}}\right)$$

Output ciphertext $\mathsf{ct}_{\boldsymbol{x}} = \left(\widehat{\mathsf{ct}}, \mathsf{ct}^*, \mathsf{ListVecCT}_0, \boldsymbol{x}\right)$.

Decryption, $\mathsf{Dec}(\mathsf{sk}_{P,D}, \mathsf{ct}_{\boldsymbol{x}})$: On input secret key $\mathsf{sk}_{P,D}$, ciphertext $\mathsf{ct}_{\boldsymbol{x}}$, the decryption algorithm does the following:

- Output $\bot$ if $P^D(\boldsymbol{x}) \neq 0$.
- For $\tau \in [T]$, compute,

$$\mathsf{ListVecCT}_\tau \leftarrow \mathsf{StepEvalCT}\left(C, \tau, \mathsf{ListVecCT}_{\tau-1}, \mathsf{StepKey}_\tau, D\right)$$

Check if $\left\|\left([\widehat{\mathsf{ct}}\|\mathsf{ct}_1^{st,T}] \cdot (\boldsymbol{t}^{st,T})^\mathsf{T}\right) - \mathsf{ct}^*\right\|_\infty < q/4$ and if so, output 0, otherwise output 1.

3.3 Analysis of Correctness, Efficiency and Parameters

In this part, we show that the ABE construction described above is correct (c.f. Definition 2.1), then analysis decryption time and set lattice parameters afterwards.

Lemma 3.1. *The ABE construction for read-only RAMs satisfies correctness as defined in Definition 2.1.*

Proof. Let the ciphertext be $\mathsf{ct}_{\boldsymbol{x}}$ and secret key be $\mathsf{sk}_{P,D}$, such that $P^D(\boldsymbol{x}) = 0$. At the τ-th step, by evaluating the ciphertext using algorithm $\mathsf{StepEvalCT}$ with respect to the step circuit, we have $\left\{\mathsf{ct}_i^{st,\tau}\right\}_{i\in[L_{st}]}$, $\left\{\mathsf{ct}_i^{rd,\tau}\right\}_{i\in[L_{rd}]}$ are encryption of state and read address at the τ-th step respectively. Unfolding ciphertext $\mathsf{ct}^{val,\tau}$ (ignoring the error terms), we obtain

$$\mathsf{ct}^{val,\tau} = \left(\widehat{\mathsf{ct}}, \mathsf{ct}^{rd,\tau}, \mathsf{ct}_{rd^\tau}\right)\begin{pmatrix}\mathbf{T}_k^{rd,\tau} \\ \mathbf{I}\end{pmatrix}$$

$$\approx s\left[\mathbf{A}\|\mathbf{A}^{rd,\tau} + rd^\tau\mathbf{G}\|\mathbf{E}_{rd^\tau}\right]\begin{pmatrix}\mathbf{T}_i^{rd,\tau} \\ \mathbf{I}\end{pmatrix}$$

$$\approx \mathbf{A}^{val,\tau} + D[rd^\tau]\mathbf{G}$$

Thus, ciphertext $\mathsf{ct}^{\mathsf{val},\tau}$ encodes the read value of database at rd^τ index, which can be used in the next step evaluation.

Suppose at step $\hat{T}$, we have $P^D = 0$, then $\mathsf{ct}_1^{\mathsf{st},t}$ encrypts state value 0. Thus,

$$([\hat{\mathsf{ct}}\|\mathsf{ct}_1^{\mathsf{st},t}] \cdot \boldsymbol{t}^{\mathsf{st},t}) - \mathsf{ct}^* = \boldsymbol{s}\left[\mathbf{A}\|\mathbf{A}_1^{\mathsf{st},\tau}\right] \cdot (\boldsymbol{t}^{\mathsf{st},t})^\mathsf{T} + \mathbf{e}^t - \mathsf{ct}^*$$
$$= \mathbf{e}^t - \mu\lceil q/2\rceil - \mathbf{e}^*$$

By setting parameters appropriately as below, our ABE scheme is correct.   □

Parameters Setting. If the step circuit being evaluated has length d, then the noise in ciphertext grows in the worst case by a factor of $O(m^d)$. Thus, to support a RAM program with maximum running time T (the unit of time corresponds to one step), we set (n, m, q) as

- Lattice dimension n is an integer such that $n \geq (Td\log n)^{1/\epsilon}$, for some fixed $0 < \epsilon < 1/2$.
- Modulus q is set to be $q = 2^{n^\epsilon}$, since the noise in the ciphertexts grows by a factor of $O(m^{Td})$. Hence, we need q to be on the order of $\Omega(Bm^{Td})$, where $B = O(n)$ is the maximum magnitude of noise (from discrete Gaussian distribution) added during encryption. To ensure correctness of decryption and hardness of LWE, we set $q = 2^{n^\epsilon}$.
- Lattice column parameter m is set to be $m = \Theta(n\log q)$ to make the leftover hash lemma hold.

The parameter s used in algorithms SampleLeft and SampleRight are set as $s > \sqrt{n\log q} \cdot \omega(\sqrt{\log m})$, as required by Lemma 2.9.

For security we rely on the hardness of the LWE problem, which requires that the ratio q/B is not too large, where $B = O(n)$ is the maximum magnitude of noise (from discrete Gaussian distribution) added during encryption. In particular, the underlying problem is believed to be hard even when q/B is 2^{n^ϵ}.

Efficiency Analysis. The (space/time) complexity of our construction can be analyzed by the following aspects. The polynomial $n(\cdot, \cdot)$ denotes the lattice dimension.

- The public parameters contain $(L_{\mathsf{st}} + L_{\mathsf{rd}} + nmT)$ random $n \times m$ matrices in $\mathbb{Z}_q$, which is $\tilde{O}(n(\lambda, T)^2 \cdot n^2 T^2)$ in bit complexity. The master secret key is one $m \times m$ matrix.
- The secret key for program and database pair (P, D) contains $T(N+1)$ small $m \times m$ matrices, which is $\tilde{O}(n(\lambda, T)^2 \cdot NT)$ in bit complexity.
- The ciphertext for input $\boldsymbol{x}$ contains $(L_{\mathsf{st}} + L_{\mathsf{rd}} + nmT + \lambda)$ dimension-m vectors in $\mathbb{Z}_q$, which is $\tilde{O}(n(\lambda, T) \cdot \lambda n^2 T^2)$ in bit complexity.
- Decryption involves matrix-vector multiplication. The time complexity of decryption is $\tilde{O}(T)$.

Next, we would like to show the following: if a program P^D on input $\boldsymbol{x}$ takes time at most T then correspondingly, the decryption of secret key for P^D on input an encryption of message μ associated with attribute input x takes time $p(\lambda, T)$, for a fixed polynomial p.

We analyze the time to decrypt an encryption of database x associated with message μ using a key of RAM program/database with runtime bounded by T. The essential algorithm StepEvalCT, which may be computed T times, in decryption algorithm can be divided into two steps, as analyzed below

- **Step circuit**: The runtime of CtEval with respect to step circuit C is a polynomial in $(\lambda, L_{st}, L_{rd})$. Observe that L_{st} is the length of the state, which is independent of the input length, and $L_{rd} = \log N$. Thus, the runtime of CtEval is upper bounded by a polynomial in (λ, L_{st}).
- **Recoding part**: In this step, we compute CtEval with respect to the gadget circuit f, then the translation part, and last multiplication. This part is upper bounded by a polynomial in (λ, L_{rd}).

From the above observations, it follows that the runtime of the decryption algorithm is a polynomial in (λ, T), where the polynomial is independent of the length of the database. In particular, notice that if T is polylogarithmic in the input length then the decryption time is sub-linear in the input length.

3.4   Security Proof

In this part, we show the security of our ABE for read-only RAM construction, assuming the hardness of LWE assumption. We first describe algorithms (Sim.Setup, Sim.Enc, Sim.StepEvalPK) in the following:

- Sim.Setup produces "programmed" public parameters. That is, every pubic matrix produced as part of algorithm Sim.Setup has hardwired in it, a bit of the challenge ciphertext, initial state, read address, etc.
- Sim.Enc produces a simulated encryption of the message.
- Sim.StepEvalPK takes as input the $(\tau - 1)$-th layer of simulated public keys Sim.ListMxPK$_{\tau-1}$ and produces the τ-th layer of simulated public keys Sim.ListMxPK$_\tau$ and τ-th layer of step keys Sim.StepKey$_\tau$.

These simulated algorithms can be constructed as follows:

Sim.Setup($1^\lambda, x^*$): On input the challenge input x^*, the simulated setup algorithm does:

- Compute $(\mathbf{A}, \mathbf{T_A}) \leftarrow$ TrapGen$(1^n, 1^q, m)$ and sample $\boldsymbol{u} \xleftarrow{\$} \mathbb{Z}_q^n$.
- $\forall i \in [L_{st}]$, set $\mathbf{A}_i^{st,0} = \mathbf{A}\mathbf{R}_i^{st,0} - \mathbf{G}$, where $\mathbf{R}_i^{st,0} \leftarrow \{0,1\}^{m \times m}$.
- $\forall i \in [L_{rd}]$, set $\mathbf{A}_i^{rd,0} = \mathbf{A}\mathbf{R}_i^{rd,0} - \mathbf{G}$, where $\mathbf{R}_i^{rd,0} \leftarrow \{0,1\}^{m \times m}$.
- $\forall j \in [n], k \in [m], \ell \in \lceil \log q \rceil$, set

$$\mathbf{B}_{jk\ell} = \mathbf{A}\mathbf{R}_{jk\ell} - 2^\ell \mathbf{M}_{j,k}, \quad \mathbf{B}'_{jk\ell} = \mathbf{A}\mathbf{R}'_{jk\ell}$$

  where $(\mathbf{R}_{jk\ell}, \mathbf{R}'_{jk\ell}) \leftarrow \{0,1\}^{m \times m}$.
- $\forall i \in [\lambda]$, set $\mathbf{A}^{val,0} = \mathbf{A}\mathbf{R}_i^{val,0} - x^*[i]\mathbf{G}$, where $\mathbf{R}_i^{val,0} \leftarrow \{0,1\}^{m \times m}$.

Let $\mathsf{Sim.MxPK_{aux}} = \left(\mathbf{B}_{jk\ell}, \mathbf{B}'_{jk\ell}\right)_{j\in[n],k\in[m],\ell\in\lceil\log q\rceil}$, and denote trapdoor matrix for initial step as

$$\mathsf{ListMxTD}_0 = \left(\left\{\mathbf{R}_i^{\mathsf{st},0}\right\}_{i\in[L_{\mathsf{st}}]}, \left\{\mathbf{R}_i^{\mathsf{rd},0}\right\}_{i\in[L_{\mathsf{rd}}]}, \mathbf{R}^{\mathsf{val},0}\right)$$

Output $\mathsf{msk} = (\mathsf{pp}, \mathbf{T_A})$ and

$$\mathsf{Sim.pp} = \left(\mathbf{A}, \mathsf{Sim.MxPK_{aux}}, \left\{\mathbf{A}_i^{\mathsf{st},0}\right\}_{i\in[L_{\mathsf{st}}]}, \left\{\mathbf{A}_i^{\mathsf{rd},0}\right\}_{i\in[L_{\mathsf{rd}}]}, \left\{\mathbf{A}_i^{\mathsf{val},0}\right\}_{i\in[\lambda]}, \boldsymbol{u}\right)$$

$\underline{\mathsf{Sim.Enc}(\mathsf{Sim.pp}, \boldsymbol{x}^*, 1^{|\mu|}, (\mathbf{A}, \boldsymbol{u}), (\boldsymbol{b}, b'))}$: On input simulated public parameters $\mathsf{Sim.pp}$, challenge input $\boldsymbol{x}^*$ and message length $|\mu|$ and LWE instance $((\mathbf{A}, \boldsymbol{u}), (\boldsymbol{b}, b'))$, the simulated encryption algorithm does

- $\forall i \in [L_{\mathsf{st},0}]$, compute $\mathsf{ct}_i^{\mathsf{st},0} = \boldsymbol{b}\mathbf{R}_i^{\mathsf{st},0}$, where $\mathbf{R}_i^{\mathsf{st},0}$ is generated in $\mathsf{Sim.Setup}$.
- $\forall i \in [L_{\mathsf{rd},0}]$, compute $\mathsf{ct}_i^{\mathsf{rd},0} = \boldsymbol{b}\mathbf{R}_i^{\mathsf{rd},0}$, where $\mathbf{R}_i^{\mathsf{rd},0}$ is generated in $\mathsf{Sim.Setup}$.
- $\forall i \in [\lambda]$, compute $\mathsf{ct}_i^{\mathsf{val},0} = \boldsymbol{b}\mathbf{R}_i^{\mathsf{val},0}$, where $\mathbf{R}_i^{\mathsf{val},0}$ is generated in $\mathsf{Sim.Setup}$.
- $\forall j \in [n], k \in [m], \ell \in \lceil\log q\rceil$, compute $\mathsf{ct}_{jk\ell} = \boldsymbol{b}\mathbf{R}_{jk\ell}$, $\mathsf{ct}'_{jk\ell} = \boldsymbol{b}\mathbf{R}'_{jk\ell}$ where $\left(\mathbf{R}_{jk\ell}, \mathbf{R}'_{jk\ell}\right)$ is generated in $\mathsf{Sim.Setup}$.
- Set $\widehat{\mathsf{ct}} = \boldsymbol{b}$ and $\mathsf{ct}^* = b'$.
- Define $\mathsf{ListVecCT}_0$ in the same way as the real scheme.

Output challenge ciphertext $\mathsf{ct}_{\boldsymbol{x}^*} = \left(\widehat{\mathsf{ct}}, \mathsf{ct}^*, \mathsf{ListVecCT}_0, \boldsymbol{x}^*\right)$.

$\underline{\mathsf{Sim.StepEvalPK}(C, \tau, \mathsf{Sim.ListMxPK}_{\tau-1}, \mathsf{Sim.pp}, D)}$: On input the step circuit C of program P satisfying $P^D(\boldsymbol{x}^*) = 1$, step index τ, simulated $(\tau - 1)$-th layer of simulated public keys $\mathsf{Sim.ListMxPK}_{\tau-1}$, simulated public parameters $\mathsf{Sim.pp}$ and database query D, if $\tau = 1$, compute the translation algorithm

$$\mathsf{ListMxDB} \leftarrow \mathsf{TranslatePK}\left(\mathsf{MxPK_{aux}}, D\right)$$

where $\mathsf{ListMxDB} = \{(\mathbf{A}'_i, \mathbf{B}_i, \mathbf{E}_i)\}_{i\in[N]}$. Set

$$\mathsf{ListMxPK}_0 = \left(\mathbf{A}, \mathsf{ListMxDB}, \left\{\mathbf{A}_i^{\mathsf{st},0}\right\}_{i\in[L_{\mathsf{st}}]}, \left\{\mathbf{A}_i^{\mathsf{rd},0}\right\}_{i\in[L_{\mathsf{rd}}]}, \left\{\mathbf{A}_i^{\mathsf{val},0}\right\}_{i\in[\lambda]}\right)$$

Otherwise, it does:

- Compute $\left(\left\{\mathbf{A}_i^{\mathsf{st},\tau}\right\}_{i\in[L_{\mathsf{st}}]}, \left\{\mathbf{A}_i^{\mathsf{rd},\tau}\right\}_{i\in[L_{\mathsf{rd}}]}\right) = \mathsf{PubEval}\left(\mathsf{Sim.ListMxPK}_{\tau-1}, C\right)$, and then $\mathbf{A}^{\mathsf{rd},\tau} = \mathsf{PubEval}\left(f, \left\{\mathbf{A}_i^{\mathsf{rd},\tau}\right\}_{i\in[L_{\mathsf{rd}}]}\right)$, where $\mathbf{A}^{\mathsf{rd},\tau}$ encodes the actual read address rd^τ of $P^D(\boldsymbol{x}^*)$ at τ-th step.

- Sample $\mathbf{T}_{\mathsf{rd}^\tau}^{\mathsf{rd},\tau} = \left(\mathbf{T}_{\mathsf{rd}^\tau,0}^{\mathsf{rd},\tau}, \mathbf{T}_{\mathsf{rd}^\tau,1}^{\mathsf{rd},\tau} \right) \leftarrow \mathcal{D}_{\mathbb{Z}^{m \times m}}$ and set $\mathbf{A}^{\mathsf{val},\tau} = \mathbf{A}\left(\mathbf{T}_{\mathsf{rd}^\tau,0}^{\mathsf{rd},\tau} + \mathbf{R}^{\mathsf{rd},\tau} \right.$
  $\left. \mathbf{T}_{\mathsf{rd}^\tau,1}^{\mathsf{rd},\tau} + \mathbf{R}_i \right)$, where $\mathbf{R}^{\mathsf{rd},\tau} = \mathsf{TrapEval}\left(f \circ C, \mathsf{Sim.ListMxPK}_{\tau-1}, \mathsf{ListMxTD}_{\tau-1} \right)$
  and $\mathbf{R}_i = \sum_{jk\ell} \left(d_{jk\ell} \mathbf{R}_{jk\ell} + \bar{d}_{jk\ell} \mathbf{R}'_{jk\ell} \right)$ and algorithm $\mathsf{TrapEval}$ is defined in
  Theorem 2.12.
- For $i \in [N] - \{\mathsf{rd}^\tau\}$, compute $\mathbf{T}_i^{\mathsf{rd},\tau}$ as

$$\mathbf{T}_i^{\mathsf{rd},\tau} \leftarrow \mathsf{SampleRight}\left(\mathbf{A}, (i - \mathsf{rd}^\tau)\mathbf{G}, \mathbf{R}^{\mathsf{rd},\tau}, \mathbf{T}_\mathbf{G}, \mathbf{A}^{\mathsf{val},\tau} - \mathbf{A}'_i - \mathbf{B}_i, s \right)$$

such that

$$\left[\mathbf{A} \| \mathbf{AR}^{\mathsf{rd},\tau} + (i - \mathsf{rd}^\tau)\mathbf{G} \| \mathbf{E}_i \right] \begin{pmatrix} \mathbf{T}_i^{\mathsf{rd},\tau} \\ \mathbf{I} \end{pmatrix} = \mathbf{A}^{\mathsf{val},\tau} + D[i]\mathbf{G}$$

where $\{\mathbf{A}'_i, \mathbf{B}_i, \mathbf{E}_i\}$ is computed by algorithm $\mathsf{TranslatePK}$.
- As $P^D(\boldsymbol{x}^*) = 1$, so $\mathbf{A}_1^{\mathsf{st},T}$ is the encoding of 1, i.e. $\mathbf{A}_1^{\mathsf{st},T} = \mathbf{AR}_1^{\mathsf{st},T} - \mathbf{G}$.
  Compute $\boldsymbol{t}^{\mathsf{st},T}$ as

$$\boldsymbol{t}^{\mathsf{st},T} \leftarrow \mathsf{SampleRight}(\mathbf{A}, \mathbf{G}, \mathbf{R}_1^{\mathsf{st},T}, \mathbf{T}_\mathbf{G}, \boldsymbol{u}, s)$$

such that

$$\left[\mathbf{A} \| \mathbf{AR}_1^{\mathsf{st},T} - \mathbf{G} \right] \cdot \boldsymbol{t}^{\mathsf{st},T} = \boldsymbol{u}$$

Set $\mathsf{Sim.StepKey}_\tau = \left\{ \mathbf{T}_i^{\mathsf{rd},\tau} \right\}_{i \in [N]}$. Output $(\mathsf{Sim.StepKey}_\tau, \mathsf{Sim.ListMxPK}_\tau)$.

Theorem 3.2. *Assuming the hardness of LWE assumption (with parameters as specified above), our ABE construction is secure (c.f. Definition 2.5).*

Proof. Let Q be the number of key queries made by the adversary. We first describe a sequence of hybrids in the following:

Hybrid Hyb_1: This corresponds to the real experiment:
 - $\mathcal{A}$ specifies challenge attribute input $\boldsymbol{x}^*$ and message μ.
 - Challenger computes $\mathsf{Setup}(1^\lambda)$ to obtain the public parameters pp and secret key msk. Then challenger generates the challenge ciphertext $\mathsf{ct}^* \leftarrow \mathsf{Enc}(\mathsf{pp}, \boldsymbol{x}^*, \mu)$. It sends ct^* and pp to $\mathcal{A}$.
 - For $\gamma \in [Q]$, adversary $\mathcal{A}$ specifies the programs/database (P_γ, D_γ) such that $P_\gamma^{D_\gamma}(\boldsymbol{x}^*) = 1$. Challenger generates the attribute keys for (P_γ, D_γ), for $\gamma \in [Q]$, $\mathsf{sk}_{P_\gamma, D_\gamma} \leftarrow \mathsf{KeyGen}(\mathsf{msk}, P_\gamma, D_\gamma)$.
 - Let b be the output of adversary. Output b.

Hybrid Hyb_2: Hyb_2 is the same as Hyb_1 except that it uses $\mathsf{Sim.Setup}(1^\lambda, \boldsymbol{x}^*)$ to generate $\mathsf{Sim.pp}$.

Hybrid $\{\mathsf{Hyb}_{3,i,j}\}_{i \in [Q], j \in [T]}$: Simply put, in hybrid $\mathsf{Hyb}_{3,i,j}$, for $\gamma < i$, the secret key for query (P_γ, D_γ) is simulated. For query (P_i, D_i), upto the j-th step, the step keys are simulated. For $\tau > j$, the step keys are normally generated. For query (P_γ, D_γ), where $\gamma > i$, the secret key is normally generated. We describe it in details below:

- Adversary specifies challenge attribute input x^* and message μ.
- Challenger computes $\mathsf{Sim.Setup}(1^\lambda)$ to obtain the public parameters pp and secret key msk. Then challenger generates the challenge ciphertext $\mathsf{ct}^* \leftarrow \mathsf{Enc}(\mathsf{pp}, x^*, \mu)$. It sends ct^* and pp to $\mathcal{A}$.
- For $\gamma \in [Q]$, adversary $\mathcal{A}$ specifies the program/database (P_γ, D_γ) such that $P_\gamma^{D_\gamma}(x^*) = 1$. Challenger generates the secret key $\mathsf{sk}_{P_\gamma, D_\gamma}$ as

$$\mathsf{sk}_{P_\gamma, D_\gamma} = (P_\gamma, D_\gamma, \{\mathsf{StepKey}_\tau\}_{\tau \in [T]}, t^{\mathsf{st}, T})$$

- For $\gamma < i$, answer secret key query P_γ as
  1. For every $\tau \in [T]$, compute

  $$(\mathsf{Sim.ListMxPK}_\tau, \mathsf{Sim.StepKey}_\tau)$$
  $$\leftarrow \mathsf{Sim.StepEvalPK}(C, \mathsf{Sim.ListMxPK}_{\tau-1}, \mathsf{Sim.pp})$$

  2. Set $\mathsf{sk}_\gamma = (\{\mathsf{Sim.StepKey}_\tau\}_{\tau \in [T]})$.
- For $\gamma = i$, answer secret key query (P_i, D_i) as
  1. For $\tau < j$, generate

  $$(\mathsf{Sim.ListMxPK}_\tau, \mathsf{Sim.StepKey}_\tau)$$
  $$\leftarrow \mathsf{Sim.StepEvalPK}(C, \mathsf{Sim.ListMxPK}_{\tau-1}, \mathsf{Sim.pp})$$

  2. For $\tau \geq j$, generate

  $$(\mathsf{ListMxPK}_\tau, \mathsf{StepKey}_\tau) \leftarrow \mathsf{StepEvalPK}(C, \mathsf{Sim.ListMxPK}_{\tau-1}, \mathsf{Sim.pp})$$

  Set $\mathsf{sk}_i = (\{\mathsf{Sim.StepKey}_\tau\}_{\tau < i}, \{\mathsf{StepKey}_\tau\}_{\tau \geq i})$.
- For $\gamma > i$, answer secret key query (P_γ, D_γ) as
  1. For every $\tau \in [T]$, generate

  $$(\mathsf{ListMxPK}_\tau, \mathsf{StepKey}_\tau) \leftarrow \mathsf{StepEvalPK}(C, \mathsf{Sim.ListMxPK}_{\tau-1}, \mathsf{Sim.pp})$$

  2. Set $\mathsf{sk}_\gamma = (\{\mathsf{StepKey}_\tau\}_{\tau \in [T]})$.

Hybrid Hyb_4: Hyb_4 is the same as $\mathsf{Hyb}_{3,Q,T}$ except that the anchor public key $\mathbf{A}$ is sampled randomly from $\mathbb{Z}_q^{n \times m}$. In $\mathsf{Hyb}_{3,Q,T}$ the secret keys for all queries are simulated without using $\mathsf{msk} = \mathbf{T_A}$.

Hybrid Hyb_5: Hyb_5 is the same as Hyb_4 except that it uses algorithm $\mathsf{Sim.Enc}$ to generate the challenge ciphertext.

Due to the space limit, we show the indistinguishability proof between adjacent hybrids in the full version. ☐

Acknowledgements. We would like to thank the anonymous reviewers of Asiacrypt 2019 and Jiaxin Pan for helpful suggestions to improve the presentation of the paper. Xiong Fan is supported in part by IBM under Agreement 4915013672 and NSF Award CNS-1561209. Elaine Shi is supported by NSF Award CNS-1617676.

References

1. Agrawal, S., Chase, M.: A study of pair encodings: predicate encryption in prime order groups. In: Kushilevitz, E., Malkin, T. (eds.) TCC 2016. LNCS, vol. 9563, pp. 259–288. Springer, Heidelberg (2016). https://doi.org/10.1007/978-3-662-49099-0_10

2. Agrawal, S., Boneh, D., Boyen, X.: Efficient lattice (H)IBE in the standard model. In: Gilbert, H. (ed.) EUROCRYPT 2010. LNCS, vol. 6110, pp. 553–572. Springer, Heidelberg (2010). https://doi.org/10.1007/978-3-642-13190-5_28

3. Agrawal, S., Maitra, M.: FE and iO for turing machines from minimal assumptions. In: Beimel, A., Dziembowski, S. (eds.) TCC 2018. LNCS, vol. 11240, pp. 473–512. Springer, Cham (2018). https://doi.org/10.1007/978-3-030-03810-6_18

4. Agrawal, S., Singh, I.P.: Reusable garbled deterministic finite automata from learning with errors. In: LIPIcs-Leibniz International Proceedings in Informatics, vol. 80. Schloss Dagstuhl-Leibniz-Zentrum fuer Informatik (2017)

5. Alperin-Sheriff, J., Peikert, C.: Faster bootstrapping with polynomial error. In: Garay, J.A., Gennaro, R. (eds.) CRYPTO 2014. LNCS, vol. 8616, pp. 297–314. Springer, Heidelberg (2014). https://doi.org/10.1007/978-3-662-44371-2_17

6. Ananth, P., Jain, A., Sahai, A.: Indistinguishability obfuscation from functional encryption for simple functions. Cryptology ePrint Archive, Report 2015/730 (2015). http://eprint.iacr.org/2015/730

7. Ananth, P., Lombardi, A.: Succinct garbling schemes from functional encryption through a local simulation paradigm. In: Beimel, A., Dziembowski, S. (eds.) TCC 2018. LNCS, vol. 11240, pp. 455–472. Springer, Cham (2018). https://doi.org/10.1007/978-3-030-03810-6_17

8. Ananth, P., Sahai, A.: Functional encryption for turing machines. In: Kushilevitz, E., Malkin, T. (eds.) TCC 2016. LNCS, vol. 9562, pp. 125–153. Springer, Heidelberg (2016). https://doi.org/10.1007/978-3-662-49096-9_6

9. Attrapadung, N.: Dual system encryption via doubly selective security: framework, fully secure functional encryption for regular languages, and more. In: Nguyen, P.Q., Oswald, E. (eds.) EUROCRYPT 2014. LNCS, vol. 8441, pp. 557–577. Springer, Heidelberg (2014). https://doi.org/10.1007/978-3-642-55220-5_31

10. Bellare, M., Stepanovs, I., Waters, B.: New negative results on differing-inputs obfuscation. In: Fischlin, M., Coron, J.-S. (eds.) EUROCRYPT 2016. LNCS, vol. 9666, pp. 792–821. Springer, Heidelberg (2016). https://doi.org/10.1007/978-3-662-49896-5_28

11. Bitansky, N., Goldwasser, S., Jain, A., Paneth, O., Vaikuntanathan, V., Waters, B.: Time-lock puzzles from randomized encodings. In: Sudan, M. (ed.) ITCS 2016, pp. 345–356. ACM, January 2016

12. Boneh, D., Franklin, M.: Identity-based encryption from the weil pairing. In: Kilian, J. (ed.) CRYPTO 2001. LNCS, vol. 2139, pp. 213–229. Springer, Heidelberg (2001). https://doi.org/10.1007/3-540-44647-8_13

13. Boneh, D., et al.: Fully key-homomorphic encryption, arithmetic circuit ABE and compact garbled circuits. In: Nguyen, P.Q., Oswald, E. (eds.) EUROCRYPT 2014. LNCS, vol. 8441, pp. 533–556. Springer, Heidelberg (2014). https://doi.org/10.1007/978-3-642-55220-5_30

14. Boneh, D., Sahai, A., Waters, B.: Functional encryption: definitions and challenges. In: Theory of Cryptography, pp. 253–273 (2011)

15. Boyle, E., Pass, R.: Limits of extractability assumptions with distributional auxiliary input. In: Iwata, T., Cheon, J.H. (eds.) ASIACRYPT 2015. LNCS, vol.

9453, pp. 236–261. Springer, Heidelberg (2015). https://doi.org/10.1007/978-3-662-48800-3_10

16. Brakerski, Z., Cash, D., Tsabary, R., Wee, H.: Targeted homomorphic attribute-based encryption. In: Hirt, M., Smith, A. (eds.) TCC 2016. LNCS, vol. 9986, pp. 330–360. Springer, Heidelberg (2016). https://doi.org/10.1007/978-3-662-53644-5_13

17. Brakerski, Z., Langlois, A., Peikert, C., Regev, O., Stehlé, D.: Classical hardness of learning with errors. In: Boneh, D., Roughgarden, T., Feigenbaum, J. (eds.) 45th ACM STOC, pp. 575–584. ACM Press, June 2013

18. Brakerski, Z., Lombardi, A., Segev, G., Vaikuntanathan, V.: Anonymous ibe, leakage resilience and circular security from new assumptions. Technical report, Cryptology ePrint Archive, Report 2017/967 (2017). https://eprint.iacr.org/2017/967, 2017

19. Brakerski, Z., Tsabary, R., Vaikuntanathan, V., Wee, H.: Private constrained PRFs (and More) from LWE. In: Kalai, Y., Reyzin, L. (eds.) TCC 2017. LNCS, vol. 10677, pp. 264–302. Springer, Cham (2017). https://doi.org/10.1007/978-3-319-70500-2_10

20. Brakerski, Z., Vaikuntanathan, V.: Constrained key-homomorphic PRFs from standard lattice assumptions. In: Dodis, Y., Nielsen, J.B. (eds.) TCC 2015. LNCS, vol. 9015, pp. 1–30. Springer, Heidelberg (2015). https://doi.org/10.1007/978-3-662-46497-7_1

21. Brakerski, Z., Vaikuntanathan, V.: Circuit-ABE from LWE: unbounded attributes and semi-adaptive security. In: Robshaw, M., Katz, J. (eds.) CRYPTO 2016. LNCS, vol. 9816, pp. 363–384. Springer, Heidelberg (2016). https://doi.org/10.1007/978-3-662-53015-3_13

22. Cash, D., Hofheinz, D., Kiltz, E., Peikert, C.: Bonsai trees, or how to delegate a lattice basis. In: Gilbert, H. (ed.) EUROCRYPT 2010. LNCS, vol. 6110, pp. 523–552. Springer, Heidelberg (2010). https://doi.org/10.1007/978-3-642-13190-5_27

23. Deshpande, A., Koppula, V., Waters, B.: Constrained pseudorandom functions for unconstrained inputs. In: Fischlin, M., Coron, J.-S. (eds.) EUROCRYPT 2016. LNCS, vol. 9666, pp. 124–153. Springer, Heidelberg (2016). https://doi.org/10.1007/978-3-662-49896-5_5

24. Döttling, N., Garg, S.: Identity-based encryption from the Diffie-Hellman assumption. In: Katz, J., Shacham, H. (eds.) CRYPTO 2017. LNCS, vol. 10401, pp. 537–569. Springer, Cham (2017). https://doi.org/10.1007/978-3-319-63688-7_18

25. Garg, S., Gentry, C., Halevi, S., Raykova, M., Sahai, A., Waters, B.: Candidate indistinguishability obfuscation and functional encryption for all circuits. SIAM J. Comput. 45(3), 882–929 (2016)

26. Garg, S., Gentry, C., Halevi, S., Sahai, A., Waters, B.: Attribute-based encryption for circuits from multilinear maps. In: Canetti, R., Garay, J.A. (eds.) CRYPTO 2013. LNCS, vol. 8043, pp. 479–499. Springer, Heidelberg (2013). https://doi.org/10.1007/978-3-642-40084-1_27

27. Garg, S., Gentry, C., Halevi, S., Wichs, D.: On the implausibility of differing-inputs obfuscation and extractable witness encryption with auxiliary input. In: Garay, J.A., Gennaro, R. (eds.) CRYPTO 2014. LNCS, vol. 8616, pp. 518–535. Springer, Heidelberg (2014). https://doi.org/10.1007/978-3-662-44371-2_29

28. Garg, S., Gentry, C., Halevi, S., Zhandry, M.: Fully secure attribute based encryption from multilinear maps. Cryptology ePrint Archive, Report 2014/622 (2014). http://eprint.iacr.org/2014/622

29. Garg, S., Lu, S., Ostrovsky, R.: Black-box garbled ram. In: 2015 IEEE 56th Annual Symposium on Foundations of Computer Science (FOCS), pp. 210–229. IEEE (2015)
30. Garg, S., Lu, S., Ostrovsky, R., Scafuro, A.: Garbled ram from one-way functions. In: Proceedings of the Forty-Seventh Annual ACM Symposium on Theory of Computing, pp. 449–458. ACM (2015)
31. Garg, S., Srinivasan, A.: A simple construction of iO for turing machines. In: Beimel, A., Dziembowski, S. (eds.) TCC 2018. LNCS, vol. 11240, pp. 425–454. Springer, Cham (2018). https://doi.org/10.1007/978-3-030-03810-6_16
32. Gentry, C., Halevi, S., Lu, S., Ostrovsky, R., Raykova, M., Wichs, D.: Garbled RAM revisited. In: Nguyen, P.Q., Oswald, E. (eds.) EUROCRYPT 2014. LNCS, vol. 8441, pp. 405–422. Springer, Heidelberg (2014). https://doi.org/10.1007/978-3-642-55220-5_23
33. Gentry, C., Peikert, C., Vaikuntanathan, V.: Trapdoors for hard lattices and new cryptographic constructions. In: Ladner, R.E., Dwork, C. (eds.) 40th ACM STOC, pp. 197–206. ACM Press, May 2008
34. Gentry, C., Sahai, A., Waters, B.: Homomorphic encryption from learning with errors: conceptually-simpler, asymptotically-faster, attribute-based. In: Canetti, R., Garay, J.A. (eds.) CRYPTO 2013. LNCS, vol. 8042, pp. 75–92. Springer, Heidelberg (2013). https://doi.org/10.1007/978-3-642-40041-4_5
35. Goldwasser, S., Kalai, Y., Popa, R.A., Vaikuntanathan, V., Zeldovich, N.: Reusable garbled circuits and succinct functional encryption. In: Proceedings of the Forty-Fifth Annual ACM Symposium on Theory of Computing, pp. 555–564. ACM (2013)
36. Goldwasser, S., Kalai, Y.T., Popa, R.A., Vaikuntanathan, V., Zeldovich, N.: How to run turing machines on encrypted data. In: Canetti, R., Garay, J.A. (eds.) CRYPTO 2013. LNCS, vol. 8043, pp. 536–553. Springer, Heidelberg (2013). https://doi.org/10.1007/978-3-642-40084-1_30
37. Gorbunov, S., Vaikuntanathan, V., Wee, H.: Attribute-based encryption for circuits. In: Boneh, D., Roughgarden, T., Feigenbaum, J. (eds.) 45th ACM STOC, pp. 545–554. ACM Press, June 2013
38. Gorbunov, S., Vaikuntanathan, V., Wee, H.: Attribute-based encryption for circuits. J. ACM (JACM) **62**(6), 45 (2015)
39. Gorbunov, S., Vaikuntanathan, V., Wee, H.: Predicate encryption for circuits from LWE. In: Gennaro, R., Robshaw, M. (eds.) CRYPTO 2015. LNCS, vol. 9216, pp. 503–523. Springer, Heidelberg (2015). https://doi.org/10.1007/978-3-662-48000-7_25
40. Gorbunov, S., Vaikuntanathan, V., Wichs, D.: Leveled fully homomorphic signatures from standard lattices. In: Servedio, R.A., Rubinfeld, R. (eds.) 47th ACM STOC, pp. 469–477. ACM Press, June 2015
41. Goyal, V., Jain, A., Pandey, O., Sahai, A.: Bounded ciphertext policy attribute based encryption. In: Aceto, L., Damgård, I., Goldberg, L.A., Halldórsson, M.M., Ingólfsdóttir, A., Walukiewicz, I. (eds.) ICALP 2008. LNCS, vol. 5126, pp. 579–591. Springer, Heidelberg (2008). https://doi.org/10.1007/978-3-540-70583-3_47
42. Goyal, V., Pandey, O., Sahai, A., Waters, B.: Attribute-based encryption for fine-grained access control of encrypted data. In: Proceedings of the 13th ACM Conference on Computer and Communications Security, pp. 89–98. ACM (2006)
43. Katz, J., Sahai, A., Waters, B.: Predicate encryption supporting disjunctions, polynomial equations, and inner products. In: Smart, N. (ed.) EUROCRYPT 2008. LNCS, vol. 4965, pp. 146–162. Springer, Heidelberg (2008). https://doi.org/10.1007/978-3-540-78967-3_9

44. Kitagawa, F., Nishimaki, R., Tanaka, K., Yamakawa, T.: Adaptively secure and succinct functional encryption: improving security and efficiency, simultaneously. Cryptology ePrint Archive, Report 2018/974 (2018). https://eprint.iacr.org/2018/974

45. Lewko, A., Waters, B.: Decentralizing attribute-based encryption. In: Paterson, K.G. (ed.) EUROCRYPT 2011. LNCS, vol. 6632, pp. 568–588. Springer, Heidelberg (2011). https://doi.org/10.1007/978-3-642-20465-4_31

46. Lewko, A., Okamoto, T., Sahai, A., Takashima, K., Waters, B.: Fully secure functional encryption: attribute-based encryption and (hierarchical) inner product encryption. In: Gilbert, H. (ed.) EUROCRYPT 2010. LNCS, vol. 6110, pp. 62–91. Springer, Heidelberg (2010). https://doi.org/10.1007/978-3-642-13190-5_4

47. Micciancio, D., Mol, P.: Pseudorandom knapsacks and the sample complexity of LWE search-to-decision reductions. In: Rogaway, P. (ed.) CRYPTO 2011. LNCS, vol. 6841, pp. 465–484. Springer, Heidelberg (2011). https://doi.org/10.1007/978-3-642-22792-9_26

48. Micciancio, D., Peikert, C.: Trapdoors for lattices: simpler, tighter, faster, smaller. In: Pointcheval, D., Johansson, T. (eds.) EUROCRYPT 2012. LNCS, vol. 7237, pp. 700–718. Springer, Heidelberg (2012). https://doi.org/10.1007/978-3-642-29011-4_41

49. O'Neill, Adam: Definitional issues in functional encryption. IACR Cryptology ePrint Archive 2010, 556 (2010)

50. Ostrovsky, R., Sahai, A., Waters, B.: Attribute-based encryption with non-monotonic access structures. In: Proceedings of the 14th ACM Conference on Computer and Communications Security, pp. 195–203. ACM (2007)

51. Parno, B., Raykova, M., Vaikuntanathan, V.: How to delegate and verify in public: verifiable computation from attribute-based encryption. In: Cramer, R. (ed.) TCC 2012. LNCS, vol. 7194, pp. 422–439. Springer, Heidelberg (2012). https://doi.org/10.1007/978-3-642-28914-9_24

52. Peikert, C.: Public-key cryptosystems from the worst-case shortest vector problem: extended abstract. In: Mitzenmacher, M. (ed.) 41st ACM STOC, pp. 333–342. ACM Press, May/June 2009

53. Regev, O.: On lattices, learning with errors, random linear codes, and cryptography. In: Gabow, H.N., Fagin, R. (eds.) 37th ACM STOC, pp. 84–93. ACM Press, May 2005

54. Sahai, A., Waters, B.: Fuzzy identity-based encryption. In: Cramer, R. (ed.) EUROCRYPT 2005. LNCS, vol. 3494, pp. 457–473. Springer, Heidelberg (2005). https://doi.org/10.1007/11426639_27

55. Waters, B.: Efficient identity-based encryption without random oracles. In: Cramer, R. (ed.) EUROCRYPT 2005. LNCS, vol. 3494, pp. 114–127. Springer, Heidelberg (2005). https://doi.org/10.1007/11426639_7

56. Waters, B.: Dual system encryption: realizing fully secure IBE and HIBE under simple assumptions. In: Halevi, S. (ed.) CRYPTO 2009. LNCS, vol. 5677, pp. 619–636. Springer, Heidelberg (2009). https://doi.org/10.1007/978-3-642-03356-8_36

57. Waters, B.: Functional encryption for regular languages. In: Safavi-Naini, R., Canetti, R. (eds.) CRYPTO 2012. LNCS, vol. 7417, pp. 218–235. Springer, Heidelberg (2012). https://doi.org/10.1007/978-3-642-32009-5_14

58. Wee, H.: Dual system encryption via predicate encodings. In: Lindell, Y. (ed.) TCC 2014. LNCS, vol. 8349, pp. 616–637. Springer, Heidelberg (2014). https://doi.org/10.1007/978-3-642-54242-8_26

Symmetric Cryptography

4-Round Luby-Rackoff Construction is a qPRP

Akinori Hosoyamada[1,2]($\boxtimes$) and Tetsu Iwata[2]

[1] NTT Secure Platform Laboratories, Tokyo, Japan
hosoyamada.akinori@lab.ntt.co.jp
[2] Nagoya University, Nagoya, Japan
{hosoyamada.akinori,tetsu.iwata}@nagoya-u.jp

Abstract. The Luby-Rackoff construction, or the Feistel construction, is one of the most important approaches to construct secure block ciphers from secure pseudorandom functions. The 3- and 4-round Luby-Rackoff constructions are proven to be secure against chosen-plaintext attacks (CPAs) and chosen-ciphertext attacks (CCAs), respectively, in the classical setting. However, Kuwakado and Morii showed that a quantum superposed chosen-plaintext attack (qCPA) can distinguish the 3-round Luby-Rackoff construction from a random permutation in polynomial time. In addition, Ito et al. recently showed a quantum superposed chosen-ciphertext attack (qCCA) that distinguishes the 4-round Luby-Rackoff construction. Since Kuwakado and Morii showed the result, a problem of much interest has been how many rounds are sufficient to achieve provable security against quantum query attacks. This paper answers to this fundamental question by showing that 4-rounds suffice against qCPAs. Concretely, we prove that the 4-round Luby-Rackoff construction is secure up to $O(2^{n/12})$ quantum queries. We also give a query upper bound for the problem of distinguishing the 4-round Luby-Rackoff construction from a random permutation by showing a distinguishing qCPA with $O(2^{n/6})$ quantum queries. Our result is the first to demonstrate the security of a typical block-cipher construction against quantum query attacks, without any algebraic assumptions. To give security proofs, we use an alternative formalization of Zhandry's compressed oracle technique.

Keywords: Symmetric-key cryptography · Post-quantum cryptography · Provable security · Quantum security · The compressed oracle technique · Quantum chosen plaintext attacks · Luby-Rackoff constructions

1 Introduction

Post-quantum public-key cryptography has been one of the most actively researched areas in cryptography since Shor developed the polynomial-time integer factoring quantum algorithm [30]. NIST is working on a standardization

© International Association for Cryptologic Research 2019
S. D. Galbraith and S. Moriai (Eds.): ASIACRYPT 2019, LNCS 11921, pp. 145–174, 2019.
https://doi.org/10.1007/978-3-030-34578-5_6

process for post-quantum public-key schemes such as public-key encryption, key-establishment, and digital signature schemes [27].

On the other hand, for symmetric key cryptography, it was said that the security of symmetric-key schemes would not be much affected by quantum computers. However, a series of recent results has shown that some symmetric key schemes are also broken in polynomial time by using Simon's algorithm [31] if quantum adversaries have access to quantum circuits that implement keyed primitives [6,8,11–13,17,18,20,21,29], though they are proven or assumed to be secure in the classical setting. Thus, the post-quantum security of symmetric-key schemes also needs to be studied.

Although many quantum query attacks on symmetric-key schemes have been proposed, post-quantum provable security of symmetric-key schemes has attracted little attention. There are two possible post-quantum security notions for symmetric-key schemes: *standard security* and *quantum security* [33]. The standard security assumes adversaries have quantum computers, but have access to keyed oracles in a classical manner. On the other hand, the quantum security assumes adversaries can make queries to keyed primitives in quantum superpositions. If a scheme is proven to have quantum security, then it will remain secure even in a far future where all computations and communications are done in quantum superpositions. Therefore, it is a problem of much interest whether a classically secure symmetric-key scheme also has quantum security.

The Luby-Rackoff Construction. The Luby-Rackoff construction, or the Feistel construction, is one of the most important approaches to construct efficient and secure block ciphers, which are pseudorandom permutations (PRPs), from efficient and secure pseudorandom functions (PRFs). A significant number of block ciphers including commonly used ones such as DES [25] and Camellia [3] has been designed on the basis of this construction.

For families of functions $f_i := \{f_{i,k} : \{0,1\}^{n/2} \to \{0,1\}^{n/2}\}_{k \in \mathcal{K}}$ that are parameterized by k in a key space $\mathcal{K}$ ($1 \le i \le r$), the r-round Luby-Rackoff construction $\mathsf{LR}_r(f_1, \ldots, f_r)$ is defined as follows: First, keys $k_1, \ldots, k_r$ are chosen independently and uniformly at random from $\mathcal{K}$. For each input $x_0 = x_{0L} \| x_{0R}$, where $x_{0L}, x_{0R} \in \{0,1\}^{n/2}$, the state is updated as

$$x_{(i-1)L} \| x_{(i-1)R} \mapsto x_{iL} \| x_{iR} := x_{(i-1)R} \oplus f_{i,k_i}(x_{(i-1)L}) \| x_{(i-1)L} \tag{1}$$

for $i = 1, \ldots, r$ in a sequential order (see Fig. 1). The output is the final state $x_r = x_{rL} \| x_{rR}$. Then the resulting function becomes a keyed permutation over $\{0,1\}^n$ with keys in $(\mathcal{K})^r$.

In the classical setting, if each f_i is a secure PRF, LR_r becomes a secure PRP against chosen-plaintext attacks (CPAs) for $r \ge 3$ and a secure PRP against chosen-ciphertext attacks (CCAs) for $r \ge 4$ [23], i.e., LR_r becomes a strong PRP. However, in the quantum setting, Kuwakado and Morii showed that LR_3 can be distinguished in polynomial time from a truly random permutation

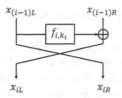

Fig. 1. The i-th round state update.

by a quantum superposed chosen-plaintext attack [20] (qCPA).[1] Moreover, Ito et al. recently showed that LR_4 can be distinguished in polynomial time by a quantum superposed chosen-ciphertext attack (qCCA) [17]. On the other hand, for any r, no post-quantum security proof of LR_r is known. A very natural question is then whether such a proof is feasible for some r, and if so, the minimum number of r such that we can prove the post-quantum security of LR_r needs to be determined.

1.1 Our Contributions

As the first step to giving post-quantum security proofs for the Luby-Rackoff constructions, this paper shows that the 4-round Luby-Rackoff construction LR_4 is secure against qCPAs. In particular, we give a security bound of LR_4 against qCPAs when all round functions are truly random functions. We also give a query upper bound for the problem of distinguishing LR_4 from a random permutation by showing a distinguishing attack. Concretely, we show the following theorems (see Table 1 for comparing security proofs and attacks for LR_4).

Theorem 1 (Lower bound and upper bound, informal). *If all round functions are truly random functions, then the following claims hold.*

1. *LR_4 cannot be distinguished from a truly random permutation by qCPAs up to $O(2^{n/12})$ quantum queries.*
2. *A quantum algorithm exists that distinguishes LR_4 from a truly random permutation with a constant probability by making $O(2^{n/6})$ quantum chosen-plaintext queries.*

Theorem 2 (Construction of PRP from PRF, informal). *Suppose that each f_i is a secure PRF against efficient quantum query attacks, for $1 \le i \le 4$. Then $LR_4(f_1, f_2, f_3, f_4)$ is a secure PRP against efficient qCPAs.*

Technical Details. To give a quantum security proof for LR_4 in the case that all round functions are truly random, we use the *compressed oracle technique*

---

[1] Strictly speaking, the attack by Kuwakado and Morii works only when all round functions are keyed permutations. Kaplan et al. [18] showed that the attack works for more general cases.

developed by Zhandry [37]. To be precise, we give an alternative formalization of the technique and use it.

One challenging obstacle to giving security proofs against quantum superposed query adversaries is that we cannot record *transcripts* of quantum queries and answers. Although it is trivial to store query-answer records in the classical setting, it is highly non-trivial to store them in the quantum setting, since measuring or copying (parts of) quantum states will lead to perturbing them, which may be detected by adversaries.

Table 1. Comparison of security proofs and attacks for the 4-round Luby-Rackoff construction LR_4 when all round functions are truly random. In the quantum CPA/CCA settings, adversaries can make quantum superposed queries.

Attack setting	Classical CPA	Classical CCA	Quantum CPA	Quantum CCA
Security proof	Secure up to $O(2^{n/4})$ queries [23]	Secure up to $O(2^{n/4})$ queries [23]	Secure up to $O(2^{n/12})$ queries **[Ours]** (Sect. 4)	No proofs (Insecure)
Distinguishing attack	$O(2^{n/4})$ queries [28]	$O(2^{n/4})$ queries [28]	$O(2^{n/6})$ queries **[Ours]** (Sect. 5)	$O(n)$ queries [17]

Zhandry's compressed oracle technique enables us to overcome the obstacle when oracles are truly random functions. The technique is so powerful that it can be used to show quantum indifferentiability of the Merkle-Damgård domain extender and quantum security for the Fujisaki-Okamoto transformation [37], in addition to the (tight) lower bounds for the multicollision-finding problems [22]. His crucial observation is that we can record queries and answers without affecting quantum states by appropriately forgetting previous records. In addition, he observed that transcripts of queries can be recorded in an compressed manner, which enables us to simulate random functions (random oracles) extremely efficiently.

The compressed oracle technique is a powerful tool, although the formalization of the technique is (necessarily) somewhat complex. A simpler alternative formalization would be better to have when we apply the technique to complex schemes that use multiple random functions, such as the Luby-Rackoff construction.

Zhandry's formalization enables us to both record transcripts and compress recorded data. We need the compression to efficiently simulate random functions but not when we focus on information theoretic security of cryptographic schemes.

With this in mind, we modify the construction of Zhandry's *compressed standard oracle* and give an alternative formalization of Zhandry's technique without compression of the database. Moreover, we scrutinize the properties of our modified oracle and observe that its behaviors can be described in an intuitively clear manner by introducing some *errors*. We also explicitly describe error terms, which enables us to give mathematically rigorous proofs. We name our alternative oracle the *recording standard oracle with errors*, because it records transcripts of queries and its behavior is described with errors. We believe that our alternative formalization and analyses for our oracle's behavior help us understand Zhandry's technique better, which will lead to the technique being applied even more widely. See Sect. 3 for details on our alternative formalization.

By heavily using our recording standard oracle with errors, we complete the security proof of LR_4 against quantum superposed query attacks, taking advantage of classical proof intuitions to some extent. First, we consider LR_3, the 3-round Luby-Rackoff construction, which is easy to distinguish from a truly random permutation, and a slightly modified version of it, where the last-round state update of LR_3 is modified. Our observation is that even quantum (chosen-plaintext) query adversaries seem to have difficulty noticing the modification, and we are actually able to show that this is indeed the case. Intuitively, the proof is possible since even quantum query adversaries cannot feasibly produce collisions on the input of the third round. Second, we prove that a family of random permutations (i.e., a function $P : \{0,1\}^{n/2} \times \{0,1\}^{n/2} \rightarrow \{0,1\}^{n/2}$ such that $P(x, \cdot)$ is a truly random permutation over $\{0,1\}^{n/2}$ for each x) is hard to distinguish from a truly random function. To show the first hardness result, we use our recording standard oracle with errors. On the other hand, for the second hardness result, we can show it by just combining some previous results. Once we prove these two hardness results, the rest of the proof can be done easily without any argument specific to the quantum setting. Our proof is much more complex than the classical one, though, we give rigorous and careful analyses. See Sect. 4 for details on the security proof of LR_4.

In contrast to the high complexity of the provable security result, our quantum distinguishing attack is a simple quantum polynomial speed-up of existing classical attacks. See Sect. 5 for details on the quantum distinguishing attack.

1.2   Related Works

Other than the ones introduced above, security proofs against quantum query adversaries for symmetric key schemes include a proof for standard modes of operations by Targhi et al. [2], one for the Carter-Wegman message authentication codes (MACs) by Boneh and Zhandry [5], one for NMAC by Song and Yun [32], and one for Davies-Meyer and Merkle-Damgård constructions by Hosoyamada and Yasuda [16]. Zhandry showed the PRP-PRF switching lemma in the quantum setting [35] and demonstrated that quantum-secure PRPs can be constructed from quantum-secure PRFs by using a technique of format preserving encryption [36]. Czajkowski et al. showed that the sponge construction is *collapsing* (collapsing is a quantum extension of the classical notion of collision-resistance) when round functions are one-way random permutations or functions [9].[2] Alagic and Russell proved that polynomial-time attacks against

---

[2] Note that the condition in which the round function of the sponge construction is one-way is unusual in the context of classical symmetric-key provable security.

symmetric-key schemes that use Simon's algorithm can be prevented by replacing XOR operations with modular additions on the basis of an algebraic hardness assumption [1]. However, Bonnetain and Naya-Plasecia showed that the countermeasure is not practical [7]. For standard security proofs (against quantum adversaries that make only classical queries) for symmetric-schemes, Mennink and Szepieniec proved security for XOR of PRPs [24]. Czajkowski et al. [10] recently showed that the compressing technique can be extended to quantum oracles with non-uniform distributions such as a random permutation, and showed quantum indifferentiability of the sponge construction.

2   Preliminaries

This section describes notations and definitions. In this paper, all algorithms (or adversaries) are assumed to be quantum algorithms, and make quantum superposed queries to oracles. For any finite sets X and Y, let $\mathsf{Func}(X, Y)$ denote the set of all functions from X to Y. For any n-bit string x, we denote the left-half $n/2$-bits of x by x_L and the right-half $n/2$-bits by x_R, respectively. We identify the set $\{0, 1\}^m$ with the set of the integers $\{0, 1, \ldots, 2^m - 1\}$.

2.1   Quantum Computation

Throughout this paper, we assume that readers have basic knowledge about quantum computation and finite dimensional linear algebra (see textbooks such as [19,26] for an introduction). We use the computational model of quantum circuits. We measure complexity of quantum algorithms by the number of queries, and the number of basic gates in addition to oracle gates. In this paper, *basic gates* denote the gates in the standard basis of quantum circuits $\mathcal{Q}$ [19]. Let $\| \cdot \|$ and $\| \cdot \|_{\mathsf{tr}}$ denote the norm of vectors and the trace norm of operators, respectively. In addition, let $\mathsf{td}(\cdot, \cdot)$ denote the trace distance. For Hermitian operators ρ, σ on a Hilbert space $\mathcal{H}$, $\mathsf{td}(\rho, \sigma) = \frac{1}{2} \| \rho - \sigma \|_{\mathsf{tr}}$ holds. For a mixed state ρ of a joint quantum system $\mathcal{H}_A \otimes \mathcal{H}_B$, let $\mathsf{tr}_B(\rho)$ (resp., $\mathsf{tr}_A(\rho)$) denote the partial trace of ρ over $\mathcal{H}_B$ (resp., $\mathcal{H}_A$). Moreover, for a pure state $|\psi\rangle$ of the joint quantum system $\mathcal{H}_A \otimes \mathcal{H}_B$, we write $\mathsf{tr}_B(|\psi\rangle)$ (resp., $\mathsf{tr}_A(|\psi\rangle)$) instead of $\mathsf{tr}_B(|\psi\rangle \langle\psi|)$ (resp., $\mathsf{tr}_A(|\psi\rangle \langle\psi|)$), for simplicity. Similarly, for a pure state $|\psi\rangle$ and a mixed state ρ of a quantum system $\mathcal{H}$, we write $\mathsf{td}(|\psi\rangle, \rho)$ and $\mathsf{td}(\rho, |\psi\rangle)$ instead of $\mathsf{td}(|\psi\rangle \langle\psi|, \rho)$ and $\mathsf{td}(\rho, |\psi\rangle \langle\psi|)$, respectively. For an integer $n \geq 1$, I_n and $H^{\otimes n}$ denote the identity operator on n-qubit systems and the n-qubit Hadamard operator, respectively. If n is clear from the context, we just write I instead of I_n, for concision. By abuse of notation, for an operator V, we sometimes use the same notation V to denote $V \otimes I$ or $I \otimes V$ for simplicity, when it will cause no confusion. In addition, for a vector $|\phi\rangle$ and a positive integer m, we sometimes use the same notation $|\phi\rangle$ to denote $|\phi\rangle \otimes |0^m\rangle$ or $|0^m\rangle \otimes |\phi\rangle$ for simplicity, when it will cause no confusion.

Quantum Oracle Query Algorithms. Following previous works (see [4], for example), any quantum oracle query algorithm $\mathcal{A}$ that makes at most q queries to oracles is modeled as a sequence of unitary operators $(U_0, \ldots, U_q)$, where each U_i is a unitary operator on an ℓ-qubit quantum system, for some integer ℓ. Here, U_0 can be regarded as the initialization process, and for $1 \leq i \leq q - 1$, U_i is the process after the i-th query. U_q can be regarded as the finalization process. We only consider quantum algorithms that take no inputs and assume that the initial state of $\mathcal{A}$ is $|0^\ell\rangle$.

Stateless Oracles. For a function $f : \{0,1\}^m \to \{0,1\}^n$, the quantum oracle of f is defined as the unitary operator $O_f : |x, y\rangle \mapsto |x, y \oplus f(x)\rangle$. When we run $\mathcal{A}$ relative to the oracle O_f, the unitary operators $U_0, O_f, \ldots, U_{q-1}, [3]O_f, U_q$ act sequentially on the initial state $|0^\ell\rangle$. (We consider that O_f acts on the first $(m + n)$-qubits of $\mathcal{A}$'s quantum register.) Finally, $\mathcal{A}$ measures the resulting quantum state $U_q O_f U_{q-1} \cdots O_f U_0 |0^\ell\rangle$, and returns the measurement result as the output. f may be chosen in accordance with a distribution at the beginning of each game. Let us denote the event that $\mathcal{A}$ runs relative to the oracle O_f and returns an output α by $\alpha \leftarrow \mathcal{A}^{O_f}()$ or by $\mathcal{A}^{O_f}() \to \alpha$.

Stateful Oracles. In this paper, we also consider more general cases in which quantum oracles are stateful, i.e., oracles have ℓ'-qubit quantum states for an integer $\ell' \geq 0$.[3] In these cases, an oracle $\mathcal{O}$ is modeled as a sequence of unitary operators $(\mathcal{O}_1, \ldots, \mathcal{O}_q)$ that acts on the first $(m + n)$-qubits of $\mathcal{A}$'s quantum register in addition to $\mathcal{O}$'s quantum register. When we run $\mathcal{A}$ relative to the oracle $\mathcal{O}$, the unitary operators $U_0 \otimes I_{\ell'}, \mathcal{O}_1, \ldots, (U_{q-1} \otimes I_{\ell'}), \mathcal{O}_q, (U_q \otimes I_{\ell'})$ act in a sequential order on the initial state $|0^\ell\rangle \otimes |\mathsf{init}_\mathcal{O}\rangle$, where $|\mathsf{init}_\mathcal{O}\rangle$ is the initial state of $\mathcal{O}$. Finally, $\mathcal{A}$ measures the resulting quantum state $(U_q \otimes I_{\ell'})\mathcal{O}_q(U_{q-1} \otimes I_{\ell'}) \cdots \mathcal{O}_1(U_0 \otimes I_{\ell'}) |0^\ell\rangle \otimes |\mathsf{init}_\mathcal{O}\rangle$, and returns the measurement result as the output. If $\mathcal{O}$ has no state and $\mathcal{O}_i = O_f$ holds for each i, the behavior of $\mathcal{A}$ relative to $\mathcal{O}$ precisely matches that of $\mathcal{A}$ relative to the stateless oracle O_f. Thus, our model of stateful oracles is an extension of the typical model of stateless oracles described above. $\mathcal{O}$ may be chosen in accordance with a distribution at the beginning of each game. We denote the event that $\mathcal{A}$ runs relative to the oracle $\mathcal{O}$ and returns an output α by $\alpha \leftarrow \mathcal{A}^{\mathcal{O}}()$ or by $\mathcal{A}^{\mathcal{O}}() \to \alpha$.

Quantum Distinguishing Advantages. Let $\mathcal{A}$ be a quantum algorithm that makes at most q queries and outputs 0 or 1 as the final output, and let $\mathcal{O}_1$ and $\mathcal{O}_2$ be some oracles. We consider the situation in which $\mathcal{O}_1$ and $\mathcal{O}_2$ are

---

[3] Here we do not mean that our model captures all reasonable stateful quantum oracles. We use our model of stateful quantum oracles just for intermediate arguments to prove our main results, and the claims of the main results are described in the typical model of stateless oracles.

chosen randomly in accordance with some distributions. We define the *quantum distinguishing advantage* of $\mathcal{A}$ by

$$\mathbf{Adv}^{\mathrm{dist}}_{\mathcal{O}_1,\mathcal{O}_2}(\mathcal{A}) := \left| \Pr_{\mathcal{O}_1} \left[\mathcal{A}^{\mathcal{O}_1}() \to 1 \right] - \Pr_{\mathcal{O}_2} \left[\mathcal{A}^{\mathcal{O}_2}() \to 1 \right] \right|. \tag{2}$$

When we are interested only in the number of queries and do not consider other complexities such as the number of gates (i.e., we focus on information theoretic adversaries), we use the notation

$$\mathbf{Adv}^{\mathrm{dist}}_{\mathcal{O}_1,\mathcal{O}_2}(q) := \max_{\mathcal{A}} \left\{ \mathbf{Adv}^{\mathrm{dist}}_{\mathcal{O}_1,\mathcal{O}_2}(\mathcal{A}) \right\}, \tag{3}$$

where the maximum is taken over all quantum algorithms that make at most q quantum queries.

Quantum PRF Advantages. RF denotes the quantum oracle of random functions, i.e., the oracle such that a function $f \in \mathsf{Func}(\{0,1\}^m, \{0,1\}^n)$ is chosen uniformly at random, and an oracle access to O_f is given to adversaries.

Let $\mathcal{F} = \{F_k : \{0,1\}^m \to \{0,1\}^n\}_{k \in \mathcal{K}}$ be a family of functions. Let us use the same symbol $\mathcal{F}$ to denote the oracle such that k is chosen uniformly at random, and an oracle access to O_{F_k} is given to adversaries. In addition, let $\mathcal{A}$ be an oracle query algorithm that outputs 0 or 1. Then we define the quantum pseudorandom-function (qPRF) advantage by $\mathbf{Adv}^{\mathrm{qPRF}}_{\mathcal{F}}(\mathcal{A}) := \mathbf{Adv}^{\mathrm{dist}}_{\mathcal{F},\mathsf{RF}}(\mathcal{A})$. Similarly, we define $\mathbf{Adv}^{\mathrm{qPRF}}_{\mathcal{F}}(q)$ by $\mathbf{Adv}^{\mathrm{qPRF}}_{\mathcal{F}}(q) := \max_{\mathcal{A}} \left\{ \mathbf{Adv}^{\mathrm{qPRF}}_{\mathcal{F}}(\mathcal{A}) \right\}$, where the maximum is taken over all quantum algorithms $\mathcal{A}$ that make at most q quantum queries.

Quantum PRP Advantages. By RP we denote the quantum oracle of random permutations, i.e., the oracle such that a permutation $P \in \mathsf{Perm}(\{0,1\}^n)$ is chosen uniformly at random, and an oracle access to O_P is given to adversaries.

Let $\mathcal{P} = \{P_k : \{0,1\}^n \to \{0,1\}^n\}_{k \in \mathcal{K}}$ be a family of permutations. We use the same symbol $\mathcal{P}$ to denote the oracle such that k is chosen uniformly at random, and an oracle access to O_{P_k} is given to adversaries. Let $\mathcal{A}$ be an oracle query algorithm that outputs 0 or 1, and we define the quantum pseudorandom-permutation (qPRP) advantage by $\mathbf{Adv}^{\mathrm{qPRP}}_{\mathcal{P}}(\mathcal{A}) := \mathbf{Adv}^{\mathrm{dist}}_{\mathcal{P},\mathsf{RP}}(\mathcal{A})$. Similarly, we define $\mathbf{Adv}^{\mathrm{qPRP}}_{\mathcal{P}}(q)$ by $\mathbf{Adv}^{\mathrm{qPRP}}_{\mathcal{P}}(q) := \max_{\mathcal{A}} \left\{ \mathbf{Adv}^{\mathrm{qPRP}}_{\mathcal{P}}(\mathcal{A}) \right\}$, where the maximum is taken over all quantum algorithms $\mathcal{A}$ that make at most q quantum queries.

Security Against Efficient Adversaries. An algorithm $\mathcal{A}$ is called *efficient* if it can be realized as a quantum circuit that has a polynomial number of basic gates and oracle gates in n. A set of functions $\mathcal{F}$ (resp., a set of permutations $\mathcal{P}$) is a *quantumly secure PRF* (resp., a *quantumly secure PRP*) if the following properties are satisfied:

1. Uniform sampling $f \xleftarrow{\$} \mathcal{F}$ (resp., $P \xleftarrow{\$} \mathcal{P}$) and evaluation of each f (resp., each P) can be implemented on quantum circuits that have a polynomial number of basic gates in n.
2. $\mathbf{Adv}_{\mathcal{F}}^{\mathrm{qPRF}}(\mathcal{A})$ (resp., $\mathbf{Adv}_{\mathcal{P}}^{\mathrm{qPRP}}(\mathcal{A})$) is *negligible* (i.e., for any positive integer c, it is upper bounded by n^{-c} for all sufficiently large n) for any efficient algorithm $\mathcal{A}$.

2.2   The Luby-Rackoff Constructions

The Luby-Rackoff construction [23] is a construction of n-bit permutations from $n/2$-bit functions by using the Feistel network.

Fix $r \geq 1$, and for $1 \leq i \leq r$, let $f_i := \{f_{i,k} : \{0,1\}^{n/2} \to \{0,1\}^{n/2}\}_{k \in \mathcal{K}}$ be a family of functions parameterized by key k in a key space $\mathcal{K}$. Then, the Luby-Rackoff construction for $f_1, \ldots, f_r$ is defined as a family of n-bit permutations $\mathsf{LR}_r(f_1, \ldots, f_r) := \{\mathsf{LR}_r(f_{1,k_1}, \ldots, f_{r,k_r})\}_{k_1, \ldots, k_r \in \mathcal{K}}$ with the key space $(\mathcal{K})^r$. For each fixed key $(k_1, \ldots, k_r)$, $\mathsf{LR}_r(f_{1,k_1}, \ldots, f_{r,k_r})$ is defined by the following procedure: First, given an input $x_0 \in \{0,1\}^n$, divide it into $n/2$-bit strings x_{0L} and x_{0R}. Second, iteratively update n-bit states as

$$(x_{(i-1)L}, x_{(i-1)R}) \mapsto (x_{iL}, x_{iR}) := (x_{(i-1)R} \oplus f_{i,k_i}(x_{(i-1)L}), x_{(i-1)L}) \quad (4)$$

for $1 \leq i \leq r$. Finally, return the final state $x_r := x_{rL} \| x_{rR}$ as the output (see Fig. 2).

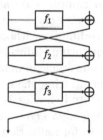

Fig. 2. The 3-round Luby-Rackoff construction.

The resulting function $\mathsf{LR}_r(f_{1,k_1}, \ldots, f_{r,k_r}) : x_0 \mapsto x_r$ becomes an n-bit permutation owing to the property of the Feistel network. Each f_{i,k_i} is called the i-th round function. When we say that an adversary is given an oracle access to $\mathsf{LR}_r(f_1, \ldots, f_r)$, we consider the situation in which keys $k_1, \ldots, k_r$ are first chosen independently and uniformly at random, and then the adversary runs relative to the stateless oracle $O_{\mathsf{LR}_r(f_{1,k_1}, \ldots, f_{r,k_r})} : |x\rangle |y\rangle \mapsto |x\rangle |y \oplus \mathsf{LR}_r(f_{1,k_1}, \ldots, f_{r,k_r})(x)\rangle$. When each round function is chosen from $\mathsf{Func}([3]\{0,1\}^{n/2}, \{0,1\}^{n/2})$ uniformly at random (i.e., each f_i is the set of all functions $\mathsf{Func}(\{0,1\}^{n/2}, \{0,1\}^{n/2})$ for all i), we use the notation LR_r for short.

3   An Alternative Formalization for the Compressed Oracle Technique

Many security proofs in the *classical* random oracle model (ROM), implicitly rely on the fact that transcripts of queries and answers can be recorded. However, such proofs do not necessarily work in the *quantum random oracle model* (QROM) [4], since recording transcripts may significantly perturb quantum states, which might be detected by adversaries. To solve this issue, Zhandry introduced the "compressed oracle technique" [37] to enable us to record transcripts of queries and answers even in QROM. In addition to recording transcripts, Zhandry's technique enables us to simulate the random oracle extremely efficiently by compressing databases of transcripts.

Zhandry's technique was originally developed for QROM, in which adversaries can make direct queries to random functions, but it can also be applied when adversaries can make queries to random functions only indirectly. In particular, one may think that the technique is applicable to giving a security proof for the Luby-Rackoff constructions when all round functions are truly random.

The compressed oracle technique is very insightful and promising, but its formal description is somewhat (necessarily) complex. A simpler formalization would be better to have when we want to apply the technique to complex schemes that use multiple random functions, such as the Luby-Rackoff construction.

In provable security, especially for symmetric-key mode of operations, we often focus on security against information theoretic adversaries. When we are interested in such security, we do not care about efficient simulation of a random oracle, and thus do not have to compress databases. With this in mind, we modify the construction of Zhandry's *compressed standard oracle* and give an alternative formalization of his technique without compressing databases that can be used when we focus on (quantum) information theoretic security.

We also study the behavior of our oracle in detail and show that its properties can be described intuitively by introducing the notion of errors. Since our oracle records transcripts of queries and its behavior is described with errors, we call our oracle *recording standard oracle with errors* and denote it by RstOE.

We believe that our alternative formalization and analyses for its behavior help us understand Zhandry's technique better, which will lead to the technique begin applied even more widely.

In Sect. 3.1 we give an overview of the original technique by Zhandry, and describe which part of it can be improved. Then, in Sect. 3.2 we describe our alternative formalization for the technique.

3.1   An Overview of the Original Technique

First, Zhandry observed that the oracle O_f can be implemented with an encoding of f and an operator stO that is independent of f. In this subsection, we consider that each function $f : \{0,1\}^m \to \{0,1\}^n$ is encoded into the $(n2^m)$-qubit state $|f\rangle = |f(0)\|f(1)\| \cdots \|f(2^m - 1)\rangle$. The operator stO is the unitary operator that acts on $(n + m + n2^m)$-qubit states defined as

$$\mathsf{stO} : |x\rangle \, |y\rangle \otimes |\alpha_0\rangle \cdots |\alpha_{2^m-1}\rangle \mapsto |x\rangle \, |y \oplus \alpha_x\rangle \otimes |\alpha_0\rangle \cdots |\alpha_{2^m-1}\rangle, \qquad (5)$$

where $\alpha_x \in \{0,1\}^n$ for each $0 \leq x \leq 2^m - 1$. We can easily confirm that $\mathsf{stO} \, |x\rangle \, |y\rangle \, |f\rangle = |x\rangle \, |y \oplus f(x)\rangle \, |f\rangle$ holds. Here, we consider that $|x\rangle \, |y\rangle$ corresponds to the first $(m + n)$-qubits of adversaries' registers.

When f is chosen uniformly at random and $\mathcal{A}$ runs relative to stO and $|f\rangle$ (i.e., $\mathcal{A}$ runs relative to the quantum oracle of a random function), the whole quantum state before $\mathcal{A}$ makes the $(i + 1)$-st quantum query becomes

$$|\phi_{f,i+1}\rangle = (U_i \otimes I)\mathsf{stO}(U_{i-1} \otimes I)\mathsf{stO} \cdots \mathsf{stO}(U_0 \otimes I) \, |0^\ell\rangle \, |f\rangle \qquad (6)$$

with probability $1/2^{n2^m}$. Here, we assume that $\mathcal{A}$ has ℓ-qubit quantum states.

Random choice of f can be implemented by first making the uniform superposition of functions $\sum_f \frac{1}{\sqrt{2^{n2^m}}} |f\rangle = H^{\otimes n2^m} |0^{n2^m}\rangle$ and then measuring the state with the computational basis. So far we have considered that a random function f is chosen at the beginning of games, but the output distribution of $\mathcal{A}$ will not be changed even if we measure the $|f\rangle$ register at the same time as $\mathcal{A}$'s register. Thus, below we consider that all quantum registers including those of functions are measured only once at the end of each game.

Then the whole quantum state before $\mathcal{A}$ makes the $(i+1)$-st quantum query becomes

$$|\phi_{i+1}\rangle = \sum_f |\phi_{f,i+1}\rangle = (U_i \otimes I)\mathsf{stO} \cdots \mathsf{stO}(U_0 \otimes I) \left(|0^\ell\rangle \otimes \sum_f \frac{1}{\sqrt{2^{n2^m}}} |f\rangle \right).$$

$$(7)$$

Next, we change the basis of the y register and α_i registers in (5) from the standard computational basis $\{|u\rangle\}_{u \in \{0,1\}^n}$ to one called the *Fourier basis* $\{H^{\otimes n} |u\rangle\}_{u \in \{0,1\}^n}$[4] by Zhandry [37]. In what follows, we use the symbol "$\,\widehat{}\,$" to denote the encoding of classical bit strings into quantum states by using the Fourier basis instead of the computational basis, and we ambiguously denote $H^{\otimes n} |u\rangle$ by $|\widehat{u}\rangle$ for each $u \in \{0,1\}^n$. Then, it can be easily confirmed that

$$\mathsf{stO} \, |x\rangle \, |\widehat{y}\rangle \otimes |\widehat{\alpha_0}\rangle \cdots |\widehat{\alpha_{2^m-1}}\rangle = |x\rangle \, |\widehat{y}\rangle \otimes |\widehat{\alpha_0}\rangle \cdots |\widehat{\alpha_x \oplus y}\rangle \cdots |\widehat{\alpha_{2^m-1}}\rangle \qquad (8)$$

holds. Intuitively, the direction of data writing changes when we change the basis: When we use the standard computational basis, data is written from the function registers to adversaries' registers as in (5). On the other hand, when we use the Fourier basis, data is written in the opposite direction as in (8). With the Fourier basis, $|\phi_{i+1}\rangle$ can be written as

$$|\phi_{i+1}\rangle = (U_i \otimes I)\mathsf{stO}(U_{i-1} \otimes I)\mathsf{stO} \cdots \mathsf{stO}(U_0 \otimes I) \left(|0^\ell\rangle \otimes |\widehat{0^{n2^m}}\rangle \right). \qquad (9)$$

---

[4] Note that the Hadamard operator $H^{\otimes n}$ corresponds to the Fourier transformation over the group $(\mathbb{Z}/2\mathbb{Z})^{\oplus n}$.

Here, note that $\sum_f |f\rangle = H^{\otimes n2^m} |0^{n2^m}\rangle = |\widehat{0^{n2^m}}\rangle$ holds. In particular, the register of the functions are initially set as $|\widehat{0^{n2^m}}\rangle$, and at most one data is written (in superpositions) when an adversary makes a query. Thus

$$|\phi_{i+1}\rangle = \sum_{xyz\widehat{D}} a'_{xyz\widehat{D}} |xyz\rangle \otimes |\widehat{D}\rangle \tag{10}$$

holds for some complex numbers $a'_{xyz\widehat{D}}$ such that $\sum_{xyz\widehat{D}} |a'_{xyz\widehat{D}}|^2 = 1$, where each x is an m-bit string that corresponds to $\mathcal{A}$'s query register, y is an n-bit string that corresponds to $\mathcal{A}$'s answer register, z corresponds to $\mathcal{A}$'s remaining register, and $\widehat{D} = \widehat{\alpha_0}\|\cdots\|\widehat{\alpha_{2^m-1}}$ is a concatenation of 2^m many n-bit strings.

Zhandry's key observation is that, since stO adds at most one data to the $\widehat{D}$-register in each query, $\widehat{\alpha_x} \neq 0^n$ holds for at most i many x, and thus $\widehat{D}$ can be regarded as a database with at most i many non-zero entries. (Note that $\widehat{D}$ may contain fewer than i non-zero entries. For example, if a state $|x\rangle|\widehat{y}\rangle$ is successively queried to stO twice, then the database will remain unchanged since $\mathsf{stO} \cdot \mathsf{stO} = I$.) We use the same notation $\widehat{D}$ to denote the database and call it the *Fourier database* since now we are using the Fourier basis for $\widehat{D}$. Each entry of the database $\widehat{D}$ has the form $(x, \widehat{\alpha_x})$, where $x \in \{0,1\}^m$, $\widehat{\alpha_x} \in \{0,1\}^n$, and $\widehat{\alpha_x} \neq 0^n$.

Intuitively, if the Fourier database $\widehat{D}$ contains an entry $(x, \widehat{\alpha_x})$, it means that $\mathcal{A}$ has queried x to a random function f and holds some information about the value $f(x)$. Hence $\widehat{D}$ can be seen as a record of transcripts for queries and answers. However, it is still not clear what kind of information $\mathcal{A}$ has about the value $f(x)$, since we are now using the Fourier basis. To clarify this information, let the Hadamard operator $H^{\otimes n}$ act on each $\widehat{\alpha_x}$ in $\widehat{D}$ and obtain another (superposition of) database D. Then, intuitively, D satisfies the condition in which "$(x, \alpha_x) \in D$ corresponds to the condition that $\mathcal{A}$ has queried x to the oracle and received the value α_x in response." We call D a *standard database*.

In summary, Zhandry observed that the quantum random oracle can be described as a stateful quantum oracle CstO. The whole quantum state of an adversary $\mathcal{A}$ and the oracle just before the $(i+1)$-st query is

$$|\phi_{i+1}\rangle = \sum_{xyzD} a_{xyzD} |xyz\rangle \otimes |D\rangle, \tag{11}$$

where each D is a standard database that contains at most i entries. Initially, the database D is empty. Intuitively, when $\mathcal{A}$ makes a query $|x, y\rangle$ to the oracle, CstO does the following three-step procedure.[5]

The three-step procedure of CstO.

1. Look for a tuple $(x, \alpha_x) \in D$. If one is found, respond with $|x, y \oplus \alpha_x\rangle$.

---

[5] Note that this three-step procedure is a quoted verbatim from the original paper [37] of version 20180814:183812, except that the symbol y' and 0 are used instead of α_x and 0^n, respectively, in the original procedure.

2. If no tuple is found, create new registers initialized to the state $\frac{1}{\sqrt{2^n}} \sum_{\alpha_x} |\alpha_x\rangle$.
   Add the registers (x, α_x) to D. Then respond with $|x, y \oplus \alpha_x\rangle$.
3. Finally, regardless of whether the tuple was found or added, there is now a tuple (x, α_x) in D, which may have to be removed. To do so, test whether the registers containing α_x contain 0^n in the Fourier basis. If so, remove the tuple from D. Otherwise, leave the tuple in D.

Intuitively, the first and second steps correspond to the classical *lazy sampling*, which do the following procedure: When an adversary makes a query x to the oracle, look for a tuple (x, α_x) in the database. If one is found, respond with α_x (this part corresponds to the first procedure of CstO). If no tuple is found, *choose α_x uniformly at random from* $\{0,1\}^n$ (this part corresponds to creating the superposition $\frac{1}{\sqrt{2^n}} \sum_{\alpha_x} |\alpha_x\rangle$ in the second step of CstO), respond with α_x, and add (x, α_x) to the database.

The third "test and forget" step is crucial and specific to the quantum setting. Intuitively, the third step forgets data that is no longer used by the adversary from the database. By appropriately forgetting information, we can record transcripts of queries and answers without perturbing quantum states.

Formalization with Compression. On the basis of above clever intuitions, Zhandry gave a formalized description of the compressed standard oracle CstO (although we do not give the explicit description here). Note that, since each database D has at most i entries before the $(i+1)$-st query, D can be encoded in a compressed manner by using only $O(i(m+n))$ qubits. With this observation, CstO is formalized in such a way that it has $O(i(m+n))$-qubit states before the $(i+1)$-st query for each i, which enables us to simulate a random oracle very efficiently on the fly, without an a priori bound on the number of queries (which required computational assumption before Zhandry's work).

3.2 Our Alternative Formalization

Next we give our alternative formalization. The original oracle CstO maintains only a $O(i(m+n))$-qubit state by compressing databases. On the other hand, in our alternative formalization, we do not consider any compression to focus on recording transcripts of queries, and our oralce always has $(n+1)2^m$-qubit states.

From now on, we represent each function $f : \{0,1\}^m \to \{0,1\}^n$ as $(n+1)2^m$-bit strings $(0\|f(0))\|(0\|f(1))[3]\|\cdots\|(0\|f(2^m - 1))$. Remember that the whole quantum state before $\mathcal{A}$ makes the $(i+1)$-st query is described as

$$|\phi_{i+1}\rangle = (U_i \otimes I)\mathsf{stO}(U_{i-1} \otimes I)\mathsf{stO} \cdots \mathsf{stO}(U_0 \otimes I) \left(|0^\ell\rangle \otimes \sum_f \frac{1}{\sqrt{2^{n2^m}}} |f\rangle \right). \quad (12)$$

At each query, unlike the original technique that adds/deletes at most one entry to/from each database, we first "decode" superpositions of databases to superpositions of functions when an adversary makes a query, then respond to the adversary, and finally "encode" again superpositions of functions to superpositions of databases. Below we describe our encoding.

Encoding Functions to Databases: Intuitive Descriptions. Modifying the idea of Zhandry, we apply the following operations to the $|f\rangle$-register of $|\phi_{i+1}\rangle$.

1. Let the Hadamard operator $H^{\otimes n}$ act on the $f(x)$ register for all x. Now the state becomes

$$\sum_{xyz\widetilde{D}} a'_{xyz\widetilde{D}} |xyz\rangle \otimes |\widetilde{D}\rangle \qquad (13)$$

   for some complex numbers $a'_{xyz\widetilde{D}}$, where each $\widetilde{D} = (0\|\widehat{\alpha}_0)\| \cdots \|(0\|\widehat{\alpha}_{2^m-1})$ is a concatenation of 2^m many $(n+1)$-bit strings, and $\widehat{\alpha}_x \neq 0^n$ at most i-many x.
2. For each x, if $\widehat{\alpha}_x \neq 0^n$, flip the bit just before $\widehat{\alpha}_x$. Now each $\widetilde{D}$ changes to the bit strings $(b_0\|\widehat{\alpha}_0)\| \cdots \|(b_{2^m-1}\|\widehat{\alpha}_{2^m-1})$, where $b_x \in \{0,1\}$, and $b_x = 1$ if and only if $\widehat{\alpha}_x \neq 0^n$.
3. For each $x \in \{0,1\}^n$, let the n-bit Hadamard transformation $H^{\otimes n}$ act on $|\widehat{\alpha}_x\rangle$ if and only if $b_x = 1$. Then the quantum state becomes

$$|\psi_{i+1}\rangle := \sum_{xyzD} a_{xyzD} |xyz\rangle \otimes |D\rangle \qquad (14)$$

   for some complex numbers a_{xyzD}, where each D is a concatenation of 2^m many $(n+1)$-bit strings $(b_0\|\alpha_0)\| \cdots \|(b_{2^m-1}\|\alpha_{2^m-1})$ such that $b_x \neq 0$ holds for at most i many x, and intuitively $b_x \neq 0$ means that $\mathcal{A}$ has queried x to a random function f and has information that $f(x) = \alpha_x$.

Encoding Functions to Databases: Formal Descriptions. The above three operations can be formally realized as actions of unitary operators on $|f\rangle$-registers. The first one is realized as $\mathsf{IH} := (I_1 \otimes H^{\otimes n})^{\otimes 2^m}$. The second one is realized as $U_{\text{toggle}} := (I_1 \otimes |0^n\rangle \langle 0^n| + X \otimes (I_n - |0^n\rangle \langle 0^n|))^{\otimes 2^m}$, where X is the 1-qubit operator such that $X|0\rangle = |1\rangle$ and $X|1\rangle = |0\rangle$. The third one is realized by the operator $\mathsf{CH} := (CH^{\otimes n})^{\otimes 2^m}$, where $CH := |0\rangle \langle 0| \otimes I_n + |1\rangle \langle 1| \otimes H^{\otimes n}$.

We call the action of unitary operator $U_{\text{enc}} := \mathsf{CH} \cdot U_{\text{toggle}} \cdot \mathsf{IH}$ and its conjugate U_{enc}^* *encoding* and *decoding*, respectively. By using our encoding and decoding, the recording standard oracle with errors is defined as follows.

Definition 1 (Recording standard oracle with errors). *The* recording standard oracle with errors *is the stateful quantum oracle such that queries are processed with the unitary operator* RstOE *defined by* $\mathsf{RstOE} := (I \otimes U_{\text{enc}}) \cdot \mathsf{stO} \cdot (I \otimes U_{\text{enc}}^*)$.

Note that $|\psi_{i+1}\rangle = (U_i \otimes I)\mathsf{RstOE}(U_{i-1} \otimes I)\mathsf{RstOE} \cdots \mathsf{RstOE}(U_0 \otimes I)(|0^\ell\rangle \otimes |0^{(n+1)2^m}\rangle)$ and $|\phi_{i+1}\rangle = (I \otimes U_{\text{enc}}^*)|\psi_{i+1}\rangle$ hold for each i.

Next, we introduce notations related to our recording standard oracle with errors that are required to describe properties of RstOE.

Notations Related to RstOE. We call a bit string $D = (b_0\|\alpha_0)\|\cdots\|$ $[5](b_{2^m-1}\|\alpha_{2^m-1})$, where $b_x \in \{0,1\}$ and $\alpha_x \in \{0,1\}^n$ for each $x \in \{0,1\}^m$, is a *valid database* if $\alpha_x \neq 0^n$ holds only if $b_x \neq 0$. We call D an *invalid database* if it is not a valid database. Note that, in a valid database, b_x can be 0 or 1 if $\alpha_x = 0^n$. We identify a valid database D with the partially defined function from $\{0,1\}^m$ to $\{0,1\}^n$ of which the value on $x \in \{0,1\}^m$ is defined to be y if and only if $b_x \neq 0$ and $\alpha_x = y$. We use the same notation D for this function. Moreover, we identify D with the set $\{(x, D(x))\}_{x\in\text{dom}(D)} \subset \{0,1\}^m \times \{0,1\}^n$. We say that *an entry of x is in D* if $(x, y) \in D$ for some y. Unless otherwise noted, we always assume that D is valid.

We say that a valid database D is compatible with a function $f : \{0,1\}^m \to \{0,1\}^n$ if $D(x) = f(x)$ holds for each x in the domain of D. For each valid database D, let $\text{comp}(D)$ denote the set of functions that are compatible with D.

If $\|\,|\psi\rangle - |\psi'\rangle\,\|$ is in $O(\epsilon)$ for two vectors $|\psi\rangle, |\psi'\rangle$, and some parameter ϵ (which will be a function of n in later applications), then we say that $|\psi\rangle$ is *equal to $|\psi'\rangle$ with an error in $O(\epsilon)$*, or just write $|\psi\rangle = |\psi'\rangle$ *with an error in $O(\epsilon)$*.

The following proposition describes the core properties of RstOE.

Proposition 1 (Core Properties). *Let D be a valid database. Then, the following properties hold.*

1. Suppose that $|D| \leq i$ holds. Then

$$U_{\text{enc}}^* |D\rangle = \sum_{f\in\text{comp}(D)} \sqrt{\frac{1}{|\text{comp}(D)|}} |f\rangle \tag{15}$$

holds with an error in $O(\sqrt{i^2/2^n})$.
2. Suppose that there is no entry of x in D. Then, for any y and α,

$$\text{RstOE}\,|x\rangle\,|y\rangle \otimes |D \cup (x, \alpha)\rangle = |x\rangle\,|y \oplus \alpha\rangle \otimes |D \cup (x, \alpha)\rangle$$

with an error in $O(1/\sqrt{2^n})$. More precisely,

$$\begin{aligned}
&\text{RstOE}\,|x, y\rangle \otimes |D \cup (x, \alpha)\rangle \\
&= |x, y \oplus \alpha\rangle \otimes |D \cup (x, \alpha)\rangle \\
&\quad + \frac{1}{\sqrt{2^n}} |x, y \oplus \alpha\rangle \left(|D\rangle - \left(\sum_{\gamma\in\{0,1\}^n} \frac{1}{\sqrt{2^n}} |D \cup (x, \gamma)\rangle\right)\right) \\
&\quad - \frac{1}{\sqrt{2^n}} \sum_{\gamma} \frac{1}{\sqrt{2^n}} |x, y \oplus \gamma\rangle \otimes \left(|D \cup (x, \gamma)\rangle - |D_\gamma^{\text{invalid}}\rangle\right) \\
&\quad + \frac{1}{2^n} |x\rangle |\widehat{0^n}\rangle \otimes \left(2 \sum_{\delta\in\{0,1\}^n} \frac{1}{\sqrt{2^n}} |D \cup (x, \delta)\rangle - |D\rangle\right)
\end{aligned} \tag{16}$$

holds, where $|D_\gamma^{\text{invalid}}\rangle$ is a superposition of invalid databases for each γ, and $|\widehat{0^n}\rangle = H^{\otimes n} |0^n\rangle$.

3. *Suppose that there is no entry of x in D. Then, for any y,*

$$\mathsf{RstOE}\,|x\rangle\,|y\rangle\otimes|D\rangle = \sum_{\alpha\in\{0,1\}^n}\frac{1}{\sqrt{2^n}}\,|x\rangle\,|y\oplus\alpha\rangle\otimes|D\cup(x,\alpha)\rangle$$

with an error in $O(1/\sqrt{2^n})$. To be more precise,

$$\mathsf{RstOE}\,|x\rangle\,|y\rangle\otimes|D\rangle = \sum_{\alpha\in\{0,1\}^n}\frac{1}{\sqrt{2^n}}\,|x,y\oplus\alpha\rangle\otimes|D\cup(x,\alpha)\rangle$$

$$+\frac{1}{\sqrt{2^n}}\,|x\rangle\,|\widehat{0^n}\rangle\otimes\left(|D\rangle - \sum_{\gamma\in\{0,1\}^n}\frac{1}{\sqrt{2^n}}\,|D\cup(x,\gamma)\rangle\right)$$

(17)

holds, where $|\widehat{0^n}\rangle = H^{\otimes n}\,|0^n\rangle$.

Proposition 1 can be shown by straightforward calculations. For completeness, a proof of Proposition 1 is given in Section A in this paper's full version [14].

An Intuitive Interpretation of Proposition 1. The first property is a subsidiary one, which will be useful in later applications. When we ignore error terms, the second and third properties correspond to the first and second procedures of CstO, respectively: When an adversary makes a query x to the oracle, RstOE looks for a tuple (x,α) in the database. If one is found, respond with α (the second property in the above proposition). If no tuple is found, create the superposition $\frac{1}{\sqrt{2^n}}\sum_{\alpha_x}|\alpha_x\rangle$, respond with α_x, and add (x,α_x) to the database (the third property in the above proposition).

Note that we do not need any "test and forget" step to describe the second and third properties in Proposition 1. Thus we can intuitively capture time evolutions of databases with only the (classical) lazy-sampling-like arguments.

To get rid of the "test and forget" step, we have to introduce some errors. The error increases as the number of adversaries' queries q increases, but it remains negligible as long as $q \ll 2^{n/2}$. Thus the error will not be problematic when we focus on the situation $q \ll 2^{n/2}$, which is the case for showing the security bound of the 4-round Luby-Rackoff construction.

In later applications, similarly to classical proofs, we introduce *good* and *bad* transcripts. The explicit formulas of the second and third properties will be used to show that, intuitively, adversaries cannot distinguish two oracles if transcripts are "good". Moreover, the first property and the descriptions with errors of the second and third properties will be used to show that the probability that transcripts become "bad" is negligible.

4   Security Proofs

The goal of this section is to show the following theorem, which gives the quantum query lower bound for the problem of distinguishing the 4-round Luby-Rackoff construction LR_4 from random permutations RP, when all round functions are truly random functions.

Theorem 3. *Let q be a positive integer. Let $\mathcal{A}$ be an adversary that makes at most q quantum queries. Then, $\mathbf{Adv}_{\mathsf{LR}_4}^{\mathrm{qPRP}}(\mathcal{A})$ is in $O\left(\sqrt{q^6/2^{n/2}}\right)$.*

Since we can efficiently simulate truly random functions against efficient quantum algorithms [34], the following corollary follows from Theorem 3.

Corollary 1. *Let f_i be a quantumly secure PRF for each $1 \leq i \leq 4$. Then, the 4-round Luby-Rackoff construction $\mathsf{LR}_4(f_1, f_2, f_3, f_4)$ is a quantumly secure PRP.*

In the rest of this section, we assume that all round functions in the Luby-Rackoff constructions are truly random functions, and we focus on the number of queries when we consider computational resources of adversaries. To have a good intuition on our proof in the quantum setting, it would be better to intuitively capture how LR_3 is proven to be secure against classical CPAs, how the quantum attack on LR_3 works, and what problem will be hard even for quantum adversaries. Thus, before giving a formal proof for the above theorem, in what follows we give some observations about these questions, and then explain where to start.

An Overview of a Classical Security Proof for LR_3. Here we give an overview of a *classical* proof for the security of LR_3 against chosen plaintext attacks in the classical setting. For simplicity, we consider a proof for PRF security of LR_3.

Let bad_2 be the event that an adversary makes two distinct plaintext queries (x_{0L}, x_{0R})[3] $\neq (x_{0L}', x_{0R}')$ to the real oracle LR_3 such that the corresponding inputs x_{1L} and x_{1L}' to the second round function f_2 are equal, i.e., inputs to f_2 collide. In addition, let bad_3 be the event that inputs to f_3 collide, and define $\mathsf{bad} := \mathsf{bad}_2 \vee \mathsf{bad}_3$.

If bad_2 (resp., bad_3) does not occur, then the right-half (resp., left-half) $n/2$ bits of LR_3's outputs cannot be distinguished from truly random $n/2$-bit strings. Thus, unless the event bad occurs, adversaries cannot distinguish LR_3 from random functions.

If the number of queries of an adversary $\mathcal{A}$ is at most q, we can show that the probability that the event bad occurs when $\mathcal{A}$ runs relative to the oracle LR_3 is in $O(q^2/2^{n/2})$. Thus we can deduce that LR_3 is indistinguishable from a random function up to $O(2^{n/4})$ queries.

Quantum Chosen Plaintext Attack on LR_3. Next, we give an overview of the quantum chosen plaintext attack on LR_3 by Kuwakado and Morii [20]. Note that we consider the setting in which adversaries can make quantum superposition queries. The attack distinguishes LR_3 from a random permutation with only $O(n)$ queries.

Fix $\alpha_0 \neq \alpha_1 \in \{0,1\}^{n/2}$ and for $i = 0, 1$, define $g_i : \{0,1\}^{n/2} \to \{0,1\}^{n/2}$ by $g_i(x) = (\mathsf{LR}_3(\alpha_i, x))_R \oplus \alpha_i$, where $(\mathsf{LR}_3(\alpha_i, x))_R$ denote the right half $n/2$-bits of $\mathsf{LR}_3(\alpha_i, x)$. In addition, define $G : \{0,1\} \times \{0,1\}^{n/2} \to \{0,1\}^{n/2}$ by $G(b, x) = g_b(x)$. Then, $g_0(x) = g_1(x \oplus s)$ can be easily confirmed to hold for any

$x \in \{0,1\}^{n/2}$, where $s = f_1(\alpha_0) \oplus f_1(\alpha_1)$. Thus $G(b,x) = G((b,x) \oplus (1,s))$ holds for any b and x, i.e., the function G has the period $(1,s)$.

If we can make quantum superposed queries to G, then we can find the period $(1,s)$ by using Simon's period finding algorithm [31], making $O(n)$ queries to G. In fact G can be implemented on an oracle-querying quantum circuit $\mathcal{C}^{\mathsf{LR}_3}$ by making $O(1)$ queries to LR_3.[6]

Roughly speaking, Simon's algorithm outputs the periods with a high probability by making $O(n)$ queries if applied to periodic functions, and outputs the result that "this function is not periodic" if applied to functions without periods.

If we are given the oracle of a random permutation RP, the circuit $\mathcal{C}^{\mathsf{RP}}$ will implement an almost random function, which does not have any period with a high probability. Thus, if we run Simon's algorithm on $\mathcal{C}^{\mathsf{RP}}$, with a high probability, it does not output any period. Therefore, we can distinguish LR_3 from RP by checking if Simon's period finding algorithm outputs a period.

Observation: Why the Classical Proof Does Not Work? Here we give an observation about why quantum adversaries can distinguish LR_3 from random permutations even though LR_3 is proven to be indistinguishable from a random permutation in the classical setting.

We observe that quantum adversaries can make the event bad_2 occur: Once we find the period $1\|s = 1\|f_1(\alpha_0) \oplus f_2(\alpha_1)$ given the real oracle LR_3, we can force collisions on the input of f_2. Concretely, take $x \in \{0,1\}^{n/2}$ arbitrarily and set $(x_{0L}, x_{0R}) := (\alpha_0, x)$, $(x'_{0L}, x'_{0R}) := (\alpha_1, x \oplus s)$. Then the corresponding inputs to f_2 become $f_1(\alpha_0) \oplus x$ for both plaintexts. Thus the classical proof idea does not work in the quantum setting.

Quantum Security Proof for LR_4: The Idea. As we explained above, the essence of the quantum attack on LR_3 is finding collisions for inputs to the second round function f_2. On the other hand, finding collisions for inputs to the third round function f_3 seems difficult even for quantum (chosen-plaintext) query adversaries.

Having these observations, our idea is that even quantum adversaries would have difficulty in noticing that the third state update $(x_{2L}, x_{2R}) \mapsto (x_{2R} \oplus f_3(x_{2L}), x_{2L})$ of LR_3 is modified as $(x_{2L}, x_{2R}) \mapsto (F(x_{2L}, x_{2R}), x_{2L})$, where $F : \{0,1\}^{n/2} \times \{0,1\}^{n/2} \to \{0,1\}^{n/2}$ is a random function. We denote this modified function by LR'_3 (see Fig. 3) and begin by showing that it is hard to distinguish LR'_3 from LR_3.

We will show this by combining the classical proof idea and our recording standard oracle with errors. Roughly speaking, we define "bad" databases as the ones that contain "collisions at left-half inputs to the third round function". Then we show that the probability that we measure bad databases is very small, and that adversaries cannot distinguish LR'_3 from LR_3 when databases are not bad.

---

[6] Here we have to truncate outputs of $\mathcal{O}$ without destroying quantum states, which is pointed out to be non-trivial in the quantum setting [18]. However, this "truncation" issue can be overcome by using a technique described in [15].

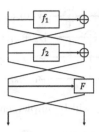

Fig. 3. LR_3'

Next, let $\mathsf{FamP}(\{0,1\}^{n/2})$ be the set of functions $F : \{0,1\}^{n/2} \times \{0,1\}^{n/2} \to \{0,1\}^{n/2}$ such that $F(x, \cdot)$ is a permutation for each x. If P is chosen uniformly at random from $\mathsf{FamP}(\{0,1\}^{n/2})$, we say that P is a *family of random permutations* (FRP). Then, we intuitively see that FRP is hard to distinguish from a random function RF from $\{0,1\}^n$ to $\{0,1\}^{n/2}$.

Once we show the above two properties, i.e.,

1. LR_3' is hard to distinguish from LR_3, and
2. FRP is hard to distinguish from RF,

we can prove Theorem 3 with simple and easy arguments. In other words, those two properties are technically the most difficult parts to show in our proof for Theorem 3. To show the first property, we use our recording standard oracle with errors. On the other hand, to show the second property, we can just combine some previous results.

Organization of the Rest of Section 4. Section 4.1 shows that LR_3' is hard to distinguish from LR_3. Section 4.2 shows that FRP is hard to distinguish from RF. Section 4.3 proves Theorem 3 by combining the results in Sects. 4.1 and 4.2.

4.1 Hardness of Distinguishing LR_3' from LR_3

Here we show the following proposition.

Proposition 2. *Let q be a positive integer. Let $\mathcal{A}$ be an adversary that makes at most q quantum queries. Then,* $\mathbf{Adv}_{\mathsf{LR}_3,\mathsf{LR}_3'}^{\mathrm{dist}}(\mathcal{A})$ *is in* $O\left(\sqrt{q^3/2^{n/2}}\right)$.

First, let us discuss the behavior of the quantum oracles of LR_3 and LR_3'.

Quantum Oracle of LR_3. Let O_{f_i} denote the quantum oracle of each round function f_i. In addition, let us define the unitary operator $O_{\mathrm{UP}.i}$ that computes the state update of the i-th round by

$$O_{\mathrm{UP}.i} : |x_{(i-1)L}, x_{(i-1)R}\rangle\, |y_L, y_R\rangle$$
$$\mapsto |x_{(i-1)L}, x_{(i-1)R}\rangle\, |(y_L, y_R) \oplus (f_i(x_{(i-1)L}) \oplus x_{(i-1)R}, x_{(i-1)L})\rangle.$$

$O_{\mathrm{UP}.i}$ can be implemented by making one query to f_i (see Fig. 4).

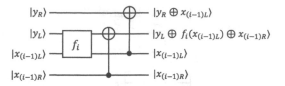

Fig. 4. Implementation of $O_{\text{UP}.i}$. f_i will be implemented by using the recording standard oracle with errors.

Now O_{LR_3} can be implemented as follows by using $\{O_{\text{UP}.i}\}_{1 \le i \le 3}$:

1. Take $|x\rangle\,|y\rangle = |x_{0L}, x_{0R}\rangle\,|y_L, y_R\rangle$ as an input.
2. Compute the state (x_{1L}, x_{1R}) by querying $|x_{0L}, x_{0R}\rangle\,|0^n\rangle$ to $O_{\text{Up}.1}$, and obtain

$$|x_{0L}, x_{0R}\rangle\,|y_L, y_R\rangle \otimes |x_{1L}, x_{1R}\rangle\,. \tag{18}$$

3. Compute the state (x_{2L}, x_{2R}) by querying $|x_{1L}, x_{1R}\rangle\,|0^n\rangle$ to $O_{\text{Up}.2}$, and obtain

$$|x_{0L}, x_{0R}\rangle\,|y_L, y_R\rangle \otimes |x_{1L}, x_{1R}\rangle \otimes |x_{2L}, x_{2R}\rangle\,. \tag{19}$$

4. Query $|x_{2L}, x_{2R}\rangle\,|y_L, y_R\rangle$ to $O_{\text{Up}.3}$, and obtain

$$|x\rangle\,|y \oplus \text{LR}_3(x)\rangle \otimes |x_{1L}, x_{1R}\rangle \otimes |x_{2L}, x_{2R}\rangle\,. \tag{20}$$

5. Uncompute Steps 2 and 3 to obtain

$$|x\rangle\,|y \oplus \text{LR}_3(x)\rangle\,. \tag{21}$$

6. Return $|x\rangle\,|y \oplus \text{LR}_3(x)\rangle$.

The above implementation is illustrated in Fig. 5.

Quantum Oracle of LR_3'. The quantum oracle of LR_3' is implemented in the same way as LR_3, except that the third round state update oracle $O_{\text{UP}.3}$ is replaced with another oracle $O_{\text{UP}.3}'$ defined as

$$O_{\text{UP}.3}' : |x_{2L}, x_{2R}\rangle\,|y_L, y_R\rangle \mapsto |x_{2L}, x_{2R}\rangle\,|(y_L, y_R) \oplus (F(x_{2L}, x_{2R}) \oplus x_{2R}, x_{2L})\rangle\,.$$

$O_{\text{UP}.3}'$ is implemented by making one query to O_F, i.e., the quantum oracle of F (see Fig. 6).

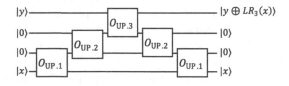

Fig. 5. Implementation of LR_3.

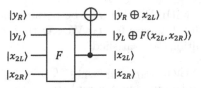

Fig. 6. Implementation of $O'_{\text{UP.3}}$. F will be implemented by using the recording standard oracle with errors.

Below, we show the claim of the proposition by using the recording standard oracle with errors for f_1, f_2, f_3, and F. We consider that the oracles of these functions are implemented as the recording standard oracle with errors, and we use D_1, D_2, D_3, and D_F to denote (valid) databases for f_1, f_2, f_3, and F, respectively. In particular, after the i-th query of an adversary to LR_3, the joint quantum states of the adversary and functions can be described as

$$\sum_{xyzD_1D_2D_3} a_{xyzD_1D_2D_3} |xyz\rangle \otimes |D_1\rangle |D_2\rangle |D_3\rangle \tag{22}$$

for some complex numbers $a_{xyzD_1D_2D_3}$ such that $\sum_{xyzD_1D_2D_3} |a_{xyzD_1D_2D_3}|^2 = 1$. Here, x, y, and z correspond to the adversary's query, answer, and output registers, respectively. (If the oracle is LR'_3, then the register $|D_3\rangle$, which corresponds to f_3, is replaced with $|D_F\rangle$, which corresponds to F.)

Next, we define good and bad databases for LR_3 and LR'_3. Intuitively, we say that a tuple (D_1, D_2, D_3) (resp., (D_1, D_2, D_F)) for LR_3 (resp., LR'_3) is bad if and only if it contains the information that some inputs to f_3 (resp., the left halves of some inputs to F) collide. Roughly speaking, we define good and bad databases in such a way that a one-to-one correspondence exists between good databases for LR_3 and those for LR'_3, so that adversaries will not be able to distinguish LR'_3 from LR_3 as long as databases are good.

Good and Bad Databases for LR_3. Here we introduce the notion of *good* and *bad* for each tuple (D_1, D_2, D_3) of valid database for LR_3. We say that (D_1, D_2, D_3) is good if, for each entry $(x_{2L}, \gamma) \in D_3$, there exists exactly one pair $((x_{0L}, \alpha), (x_{1L}, \beta)) \in D_1 \times D_2$ such that $\beta \oplus x_{0L} = x_{2L}$. We say that (D_1, D_2, D_3) is bad if it is not good.

Good and Bad Databases for LR'_3. Next we introduce the notion of *good* and *bad* for each tuple (D_1, D_2, D_F) of valid database for LR'_3. We say that a valid database D_F is *without overlap* if each pair of distinct entries (x_{2L}, x_{2R}, γ) and $(x'_{2L}, x'_{2R}, \gamma')$ in D_F satisfies $x_{2L} \neq x'_{2L}$. We say that (D_1, D_2, D_F) is good if D_F is without overlap, and for each entry $(x_{2L}, x_{2R}, \gamma) \in D_F$, there exists exactly one pair $((x_{0L}, \alpha), (x_{1L}, \beta)) \in D_1 \times D_2$ such that $\beta \oplus x_{0L} = x_{2L}$ and $x_{2R} = x_{1L}$. We say that (D_1, D_2, D_F) is bad if it is not good.

Compatibility of D_F with D_3. Let D_F be a valid database for F without overlap and D_3 be a valid database for f_3. We say that D_F is compatible with D_3 if the following conditions are satisfied:

1. If $(x_{2L}, x_{2R}, \gamma) \in D_F$, then $(x_{2L}, x_{2R} \oplus \gamma) \in D_3$.
2. If $(x_{2L}, \gamma) \in D_3$, there is a unique x_{2R} and $(x_{2L}, x_{2R}, x_{2R} \oplus \gamma) \in D_F$.

For each valid D_F without overlap, the unique valid database exists for f_3, which we denote by $[D_F]_3$.

Remark 1. For each good database (D_1, D_2, D_3) for LR_3, a unique D_F without overlap exists such that $[D_F]_3 = D_3$ and (D_1, D_2, D_F) is a good database for LR_3', by the definition of good databases. Similarly, for each good database (D_1, D_2, D_F) for LR_3', $(D_1, D_2, [D_F]_3)$ becomes a good database for LR_3.

Next we define regular and irregular quantum states for the oracles O_{LR_3} and $O_{\mathsf{LR}_3'}$. Roughly speaking, we will treat irregular states as some small error terms, and focus on regular states.

Regular and Irregular States of Oracles. Recall that, in addition to database registers, the quantum oracle O_{LR_3} uses ancillary $2n$-qubit registers to compute the intermediate state after the first and second rounds (see (19) and (20)). We say that a state vector $|D_1\rangle |D_2\rangle |D_3\rangle \otimes |x_1\rangle \otimes |x_2\rangle$ for O_{LR_3}, where $|x_1\rangle \otimes |x_2\rangle$ is the ancillary $2n$ qubits, is *irregular* if $x_1 \neq 0^n \vee x_2 \neq 0^n$ holds, or at least one of the three databases (D_1, D_2, or D_3) is invalid. We say that the state vector is *regular* if it is not irregular. We define regular and irregular states for $O_{\mathsf{LR}_3'}$ similarly.

Next we define some modified versions of LR_3 and LR_3', which we denote by LR_3-det and LR_3'-det, respectively ("det" is an abbreviation of "detection of bad database").

The oracles LR_3-det and LR_3'-det. The oracle LR_3-det is defined in the same way as LR_3, except that the oracle checks whether the database is bad (or the state of the oracle is irregular) after each query, and writes the result to an additional qubit. Note that we define regular and irregular states for LR_3-det in the same way as for LR_3. Additional qubits are prepared before an adversary $\mathcal{A}$ runs (q additional qubits are sufficient if $\mathcal{A}$ is a q query adversary). If $i \neq j$, the results of "detection of bad database" for the i-th and j-th queries are written in distinct qubits.

Intuitively, LR_3-det behaves as follows when $\mathcal{A}$ makes the i-th query:

1. Check if the j-th additional qubit is 1 for $1 \leq j \leq i - 1$ (i.e., check if the database has been bad before the i-th query). If so, do nothing. If not, go to the next step.
2. Make a query to O_{LR_3}.
3. Check if the database is bad, or the quantum state of O_{LR_3} is irregular. If so, flip the i-th additional qubit.

Next, we formally explain how the above procedures can be realized as a unitary operator. Let Π_{bad} be the projection to the space spanned by the vectors of *bad* databases, and irregular state vectors. In addition, let $\Pi_{\text{flipped}}^{[i-1]}$ be the projection onto the space spanned by the vectors such that the j-th additional qubit is 1 for some $1 \leq j \leq i - 1$.

Formally, for the i-th query, the behavior of the quantum oracle of LR_3-det is described by the unitary operator

$$
O_{\text{LR}_3\text{-det}} := \Big((\Pi_{\text{bad}} \otimes I_{i-1} \otimes X + (I - \Pi_{\text{bad}}) \otimes I_{i-1} \otimes I_1)
$$

$$
\cdot (O_{\text{LR}_3} \otimes I_{i-1} \otimes I_1) \Big) \cdot ((I - \Pi_{\text{flipped}}^{[i-1]}) \otimes I_1) + \Pi_{\text{flipped}}^{[i-1]} \otimes I_1, \quad (23)
$$

where I_{i-1} is the identity operator which acts on the first $(i-1)$ additional qubits. In addition, I_1 and X are the identity operator and the operator such that $X|0\rangle = |1\rangle$ and $X|1\rangle = |0\rangle$, respectively, which act on the i-th additional qubit.

LR_3'-det is constructed from LR_3' in the same way as LR_3-det is constructed from LR_3-det as above. The behaviors of the oracles of LR_3'-det and LR_3-det depend on i, though for simplicity, we always use the notations $O_{\text{LR}_3'\text{-det}}$ and $O_{\text{LR}_3\text{-det}}$ without i.

Below we first show that LR_3-det is hard to distinguish from LR_3'-det, and second show that LR_3-det (resp., LR_3'-det) is hard to distinguish from LR_3 (resp., LR_3').

Hardness of Distinguishing LR_3-det from LR_3'-det. Let $|\psi_i\rangle$ and $|\psi_i'\rangle$ be the state just before the i-th query to LR_3-det and LR_3'-det, respectively. By abuse of notation, we let $|\psi_{(q+1)}\rangle, |\psi_{(q+1)}'\rangle$ denote the quantum states $(U_q \otimes I)O_{\text{LR}_3\text{-det}} |\psi_q\rangle$ and $(U_q \otimes I)O_{\text{LR}_3'\text{-det}} |\psi_q'\rangle$, respectively.

We need the following lemma. Intuitively, the lemma claims that no adversary can distinguish LR_3-det from LR_3'-det if databases are "good".

Lemma 1. *For each j, let $|\psi_j^{\text{good}}\rangle$ and $|\psi_j'^{\,\text{good}}\rangle$ denote $(I - \Pi_{\text{flipped}}^{[i-1]})|\psi_j\rangle$ and $(I - \Pi_{\text{flipped}}^{[i-1]})|\psi_j'\rangle$, respectively. Let $\text{tr}_{\mathcal{D}_{123}}$ and $\text{tr}_{\mathcal{D}_{12F}}$ denote the partial trace over databases and additional qubits for LR_3-det and LR_3'-det, respectively. Then,*
$$
\text{tr}_{\mathcal{D}_{123}}\left(|\psi_i^{\text{good}}\rangle \right) = \text{tr}_{\mathcal{D}_{12F}}\left(|\psi_i'^{\,\text{good}}\rangle \right) \text{ holds for } 1 \leq i \leq q+1.
$$

Proof Intuition. Lemma 1 can be shown by straightforward algebraic calculations using the strict formulas of the second and third properties in Proposition 1. The equality holds owing to the one-to-one correspondences between good databases for LR_3 and those for LR_3' (see Remark 1). More precisely, for every $x, y, x', y' \in \{0,1\}^n$ and for every good databases $(D_1, D_2, D_F), (D_1', D_2', D_F')$ for LR_3', the "probability" (in the quantum meaning) that

$$
O_{\text{LR}_3'} \text{ changes the vector } |x, y\rangle |D_1, D_2, D_F\rangle \text{ to } |x', y'\rangle |D_1', D_2', D_F'\rangle \quad (24)
$$

is equal to the probability that

$$O_{\mathsf{LR}_3} \text{ changes the vector } |x, y\rangle\, |D_1, D_2, [D_F]_3\rangle \text{ to } |x', y'\rangle\, |D_1', D_2', [D_F']_3\rangle\,, \quad (25)$$

where $(D_1, D_2, [D_F]_3)$ and $(D_1', D_2', [D_F']_3)$ are the good databases for LR_3 that correspond to (D_1, D_2, D_F) and (D_1', D_2', D_F'), respectively. By linearity of unitary operations, this equality shows that if $\mathrm{tr}_{\mathcal{D}_{123}}\left(|\psi_j^{\text{good}}\rangle\right) = \mathrm{tr}_{\mathcal{D}_{12F}}\left(|\psi_j^{'\text{good}}\rangle\right)$ (i.e., the good probabilities before the j-th queries are equal) then $\mathrm{tr}_{\mathcal{D}_{123}}\left(|\psi_{j+1}^{\text{good}}\rangle\right) = \mathrm{tr}_{\mathcal{D}_{12F}}\left(|\psi_{j+1}^{'\text{good}}\rangle\right)$ (i.e., the good probabilities are still equal after the j-th queries) holds. A complete proof of Lemma 1 is given in Section B in this paper's full version [14].

We also need the following lemma, which intuitively claims that "good" states change to "bad" states only with a negligible probability.

Lemma 2. *For each j,* $\left\| \Pi_{\mathsf{bad}} \cdot O_{\mathsf{LR}_3} |\psi_j^{\text{good}}\rangle \right\|$ *and* $\left\| \Pi_{\mathsf{bad}} \cdot O_{\mathsf{LR}_3'} |\psi_j^{'\text{good}}\rangle \right\|$ *are in* $O(\sqrt{j/2^{n/2}})$.

Proof Intuition. Here we give a proof intuition for LR_3. Owing to the second and third properties of Proposition 1 with errors, we can use classical lazy-sampling intuition (see explanations below Proposition 1). Roughly speaking, good databases change to bad if and only if a fresh query is made to f_1 or f_2, and the corresponding input to f_3 collides with some existing record in the database for f_3.

Since each database of $|\psi_j^{\text{good}}\rangle$ has at most $(j-1)$ entries and outputs of f_1 and f_2 are $(n/2)$-bits, the input to f_3 that corresponds to a fresh input to f_1 or f_2 collides with one of the existing records in D_3 with a probability at most $O(j/2^{n/2})$. This corresponds to the claim that $\left\| \Pi_{\mathsf{bad}} \cdot O_{\mathsf{LR}_3} |\psi_j^{\text{good}}\rangle \right\|^2 \leq O(j/2^{n/2})$ holds. This argument actually ignores some errors, but the errors will be in $O(\sqrt{1/2^{n/2}})$ due to Proposition 1. The claim for LR_3' can be shown similarly. A complete proof of Lemma 2 is given in Section C in this paper's full version [14].

The following proposition guarantees that $\mathsf{LR}_3\text{-det}$ is hard to distinguish from $\mathsf{LR}_3'\text{-det}$.

Proposition 3. $\mathbf{Adv}_{\mathsf{LR}_3\text{-det}, \mathsf{LR}_3'\text{-det}}^{\text{dist}}(\mathcal{A})$ *is in* $O\left(\sqrt{q^3/2^{n/2}}\right)$.

Proof Intuition. Due to Lemma 1, $\mathcal{A}$ cannot distinguish $\mathsf{LR}_3\text{-det}$ from $\mathsf{LR}_3'\text{-det}$ as long as databases are good. Thus, intuitively, the distinguishing advantage is upper bounded by the square root of the probability that databases become bad while $\mathcal{A}$ makes q queries, which is further upper bounded by $\sum_{1 \leq j \leq q} \| \Pi_{\mathsf{bad}} \cdot O_{\mathsf{LR}_3\text{-det}} |\psi_j^{\text{good}}\rangle \| + \sum_{1 \leq j \leq q} \| \Pi_{\mathsf{bad}} \cdot O_{\mathsf{LR}_3'\text{-det}} |\psi_j^{'\text{good}}\rangle \|$. From Lemma 2, this can be upper bounded by $\sum_{1 \leq j \leq q} O(\sqrt{j/2^{n/2}}) + \sum_{1 \leq j \leq q} O(\sqrt{j/2^{n/2}}) = O(\sqrt{q^3/2^{n/2}})$. A complete proof of Proposition 3 is given in Section D in this paper's full version [14].

Hardness of Distinguishing LR_3-det and LR_3'-det from LR_3 and LR_3'.
The following proposition guarantees that LR_3-det and LR_3'-det are hard to distinguish from LR_3 and LR_3', respectively.

Proposition 4. $\mathbf{Adv}^{\mathrm{dist}}_{\mathsf{LR}_3,\mathsf{LR}_3\text{-det}}(\mathcal{A})$ *and* $\mathbf{Adv}^{\mathrm{dist}}_{\mathsf{LR}_3',\mathsf{LR}_3'\text{-det}}(\mathcal{A})$ *are*   *in*
$O\left(\sqrt{q^3/2^{n/2}}\right)$.

Proof Intuition. We give a proof intuition for LR_3-det and LR_3. Since the databases of round functions for LR_3-det are the same as those for LR_3, $\mathcal{A}$ cannot distinguish LR_3-det from LR_3'-det as long as databases are good. Thus, roughly speaking, the distinguishing advantage is upper bounded by the square root of the probability that databases become bad while $\mathcal{A}$ makes q queries. Owing to Lemma 2, we can show the claim in the same way as the proof intuition for Proposition 3. The claim for LR_3'-det and LR_3' can be shown in a similar way. A complete proof of Proposition 4 is given in Section E in this paper's full version [14].

Proof of Proposition 2. Finally, we show Proposition 2.

Proof (of Proposition 2). $\mathbf{Adv}^{\mathrm{dist}}_{\mathsf{LR}_3,\mathsf{LR}_3'}(\mathcal{A})$ is upper bounded by $\mathbf{Adv}^{\mathrm{dist}}_{\mathsf{LR}_3,\mathsf{LR}_3\text{-det}}$ $(\mathcal{A})[3] + \mathbf{Adv}^{\mathrm{dist}}_{\mathsf{LR}_3\text{-det},\mathsf{LR}_3'\text{-det}}(\mathcal{A}) + \mathbf{Adv}^{\mathrm{dist}}_{\mathsf{LR}_3'\text{-det},\mathsf{LR}_3'}(\mathcal{A})$. Thus, the claim of Proposition 2 follows from Propositions 3 and 4.   □

4.2   Hardness of Distinguishing FRP from RF

Recall that $\mathsf{FamP}(\{0,1\}^{n/2})$ is the set of functions $F : \{0,1\}^{n/2} \times \{0,1\}^{n/2} \to \{0,1\}^{n/2}$ such that $F(x,\cdot)$ is a permutation for each x, and if P is chosen uniformly at random from $\mathsf{FamP}(\{0,1\}^{n/2})$, we say that P is a *family of random permutations* (FRP). The following proposition claims that FRP is hard to distinguish from RF.

Proposition 5. *For any quantum adversary $\mathcal{A}$ that makes at most q quantum queries, $\mathbf{Adv}^{\mathrm{dist}}_{\mathsf{FRP},\mathsf{RF}}(\mathcal{A}) \leq O\left(\sqrt{q^6/2^{n/2}}\right)$ holds.*

Proof Intuition. This proposition can be proven by just combining the two previous results: The first one is the indistinguishability of a random function and a random permutation shown by Zhandry [35], and the second one is the equivalence of oracle-indistinguishability and indistinguishability, which was first shown by Zhandry [33] and later generalized by Song and Yun [32]. If a function $F : \{0,1\}^{n/2} \times \{0,1\}^{n/2} \to \{0,1\}^{n/2}$ is a random function RF (resp., a family of random permutations FRP), $F(x,\cdot)$ is a random function (resp., a random permutation) for each $x \in \{0,1\}^{n/2}$. Roughly speaking, F can be regarded as an "oracle" that returns a random function (resp., random permutation) for each x. Then, from the equivalence of indistinguishability and oracle-indistinguishability, indistinguishability of RF and FRP (which is, intuitively, "oracle"-indistinguishability of a random function and a random permutation) follows from the indistinguishability of a random function and a random permutation from $\{0,1\}^{n/2}$ to $\{0,1\}^{n/2}$, which is already shown as the first result above. See Section F in this paper's full version [14] for a formal proof.

4.3 Proof of Theorem 3

This subsection finishes our proof of Theorem 3, by using the results given in Sects. 4.1 and 4.2.

Proof (of Theorem 3). First, let us modify LR_4 in such a way that the state updates of the third and fourth rounds are replaced with $(x_{2L}, x_{2R}) \mapsto (x_{3L}, x_{3R}) := (F(x_{2L}, x_{2R}), x_{2L})$ and $(x_{3L}, x_{3R}) \mapsto (x_{4L}, x_{4R}) := (F'(x_{3L}, x_{3R}), x_{3L})$, respectively, where $F, F' : \{0,1\}^{n/2} \times \{0,1\}^{n/2} \to \{0,1\}^{n/2}$ are random functions. Let us denote the modified function by LR_4''. In addition, by $\mathsf{LR}_2''(F, F')$ we denote the function defined by $(x_L, x_R) \mapsto (F'(F(x_L, x_R), x_L), F(x_L, x_R))$ (see Fig. 7).

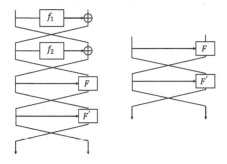

Fig. 7. LR_4'' and $\mathsf{LR}_2''(F, F')$.

Then, by applying Proposition 2 twice we can show that

$$\mathbf{Adv}^{\text{dist}}_{\mathsf{LR}_4, \mathsf{LR}_4''}(q) \le O\left(\sqrt{\frac{q^3}{2^{n/2}}}\right) \tag{26}$$

holds.

Let us modify $\mathsf{LR}_2''(F, F')$ in such a way that F is replaced with a family of random permutations P, and denote the resulting function by $\mathsf{LR}_2''(P, F')$. Then, from Proposition 5 it follows that $\mathbf{Adv}^{\text{dist}}_{\mathsf{LR}_2''(F,F'), \mathsf{LR}_2''(P,F')}(q) \le O(\sqrt{q^6/2^{n/2}})$ holds. Next, let us define a function G by $G(x_L, x_R) = F'(x_L, x_R) \| P(x_L, x_R)$, where F' is a random function and P is a family of random permutations (see Fig. 8). Then, the function distribution of $\mathsf{LR}_2''(P, F')$ is the same as that of G. (Note that $P(x_L, x_R) \ne P(x_L, x_R')$ always holds if $x_R \ne x_R'$. Thus, if $(x_L, x_R) \ne (x_L', x_R')$, the corresponding inputs to F' will be distinct.) Therefore we have that $\mathbf{Adv}^{\text{dist}}_{\mathsf{LR}_2''(P,F'), G}(q) = 0$ holds. Moreover, from Proposition 5 $\mathbf{Adv}^{\text{dist}}_{\mathsf{RF}, G}(q) \le$

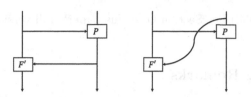

Fig. 8. $\mathsf{LR}_2''(P, F')$ and G.

$O\left(\sqrt{q^6/2^{n/2}}\right)$ holds. Therefore $\mathbf{Adv}^{\mathrm{dist}}_{\mathsf{LR}_2''(P,F'),\mathsf{RF}}(q) \leq O\left(\sqrt{q^6/2^{n/2}}\right)$ follows, which implies that

$$\mathbf{Adv}^{\mathrm{dist}}_{\mathsf{LR}_4'',\mathsf{RF}}(q) \leq O\left(\sqrt{\frac{q^6}{2^{n/2}}}\right) \tag{27}$$

holds.

Hence, from (26) and (27), it follows that $\mathbf{Adv}^{\mathrm{dist}}_{\mathsf{LR}_4,\mathsf{RF}}(\mathcal{A}) \leq O\left(\sqrt{q^6/2^{n/2}}\right)$ holds for any quantum adversary $\mathcal{A}$ that makes at most q quantum queries. In addition, $\mathbf{Adv}^{\mathrm{dist}}_{\mathsf{RP},\mathsf{RF}}(\mathcal{A}) \leq O(q^6/2^n)$ follows from a quantum version of the PRP-PRF switch [35]. (See Proposition 7 in this paper's full version [14] for details.) Therefore $\mathbf{Adv}^{\mathrm{dist}}_{\mathsf{LR}_4,\mathsf{RP}}(\mathcal{A}) \leq O\left(q^6/2^{n/2}\right)$ follows for any quantum adversary $\mathcal{A}$ that makes at most q quantum queries, which completes the proof of the theorem. □

Remark 2. In the above proof, we went back and forth between random functions and (families of) random permutations, which may seem unnatural. The motivation for our proof strategy was to avoid complex arguments that are specific to the quantum setting as much as possible.

5   A Query Upper Bound

Here we give a query upper bound for the problem of distinguishing LR_4 from a random permutation by showing a distinguishing attack. Again, we consider the case that all round functions of LR_4 are truly random functions, and show the following theorem.

Theorem 4. *A quantum algorithm $\mathcal{A}$ exists that makes $O(2^{n/6})$ quantum queries and satisfies $\mathbf{Adv}^{\mathrm{qPRP}}_{\mathsf{LR}_4}(\mathcal{A}) = \Omega(1)$.*

Proof Intuition. Intuitively, our distinguishing attack is just a quantum version of a classical collision-finding-based distinguishing attack [28]. A classical attack distinguishes LR_4 from a random permutation by finding a collision of a function that takes values in $\{0,1\}^{n/2}$, which requires $O(\sqrt{2^{n/2}}) = O(2^{n/4})$ queries in the quantum setting. However, finding a collision of the function requires only $O(\sqrt[3]{2^{n/2}}) = O(2^{n/6})$ queries in the quantum setting, which enables us to make a $O(2^{n/6})$-query quantum distinguisher. (Note that, we can generally find a collision of random functions from $\{0,1\}^{n/2}$ to $\{0,1\}^{n/2}$ with $O(\sqrt[3]{2^{n/2}}) = O(2^{n/6})$

quantum queries [35].) See Section G in this paper's full version [14] for a complete proof.

6 Concluding Remarks

This paper showed that $\Omega(2^{n/12})$ quantum queries are required to distinguish the (n-bit block) 4-round Luby-Rackoff construction from a random permutation by qCPAs. In particular, the 4-round Luby-Rackoff construction becomes a quantumly secure PRP against qCPAs if round functions are quantumly secure PRFs. We also gave a qCPA that distinguishes the 4-round Luby-Rackoff construction from a random permutation with $O(2^{n/6})$ quantum queries. To give security proofs, we gave an alternative formalization of the compressed oracle technique by Zhandry and applied it.

An important future work is to give the tight bound for the problem of distinguishing the 4-round Luby-Rackoff construction from a random permutation.[7] It would be interesting to see if the provable security bound improves when we increase the number of rounds. Also, analyzing the security of the Luby-Rackoff constructions against qCCAs is left as an interesting open question. It would be a challenging problem since we have to treat inverse (decryption) queries to quantum oracles. Oracles that allow inverse quantum queries are usually much harder to deal with than the ones that allow only forward quantum queries, and some other new techniques would be required for the analysis.

Acknowledgments. The authors thank Qipeng Liu and anonymous reviewers for pointing out an issue of Proposition 5 in a previous version of this paper.

References

1. Alagic, G., Russell, A.: Quantum-secure symmetric-key cryptography based on hidden shifts. In: Coron, J.-S., Nielsen, J.B. (eds.) EUROCRYPT 2017. LNCS, vol. 10212, pp. 65–93. Springer, Cham (2017). https://doi.org/10.1007/978-3-319-56617-7_3
2. Anand, M.V., Targhi, E.E., Tabia, G.N., Unruh, D.: Post-quantum security of the CBC, CFB, OFB, CTR, and XTS modes of operation. In: Takagi, T. (ed.) PQCrypto 2016. LNCS, vol. 9606, pp. 44–63. Springer, Cham (2016). https://doi.org/10.1007/978-3-319-29360-8_4
3. Aoki, K., et al.: *Camellia*: a 128-bit block cipher suitable for multiple platforms — design and analysis. In: Stinson, D.R., Tavares, S. (eds.) SAC 2000. LNCS, vol. 2012, pp. 39–56. Springer, Heidelberg (2001). https://doi.org/10.1007/3-540-44983-3_4
4. Boneh, D., Dagdelen, Ö., Fischlin, M., Lehmann, A., Schaffner, C., Zhandry, M.: Random Oracles in a quantum world. In: Lee, D.H., Wang, X. (eds.) ASIACRYPT 2011. LNCS, vol. 7073, pp. 41–69. Springer, Heidelberg (2011). https://doi.org/10.1007/978-3-642-25385-0_3

---

[7] See Section H in this paper's full version [14] for the reason that closing the gap is important.

5. Boneh, D., Zhandry, M.: Quantum-secure message authentication codes. In: Johansson, T., Nguyen, P.Q. (eds.) EUROCRYPT 2013. LNCS, vol. 7881, pp. 592–608. Springer, Heidelberg (2013). https://doi.org/10.1007/978-3-642-38348-9_35

6. Bonnetain, X.: Quantum key-recovery on full AEZ. In: Adams, C., Camenisch, J. (eds.) SAC 2017. LNCS, vol. 10719, pp. 394–406. Springer, Cham (2018). https://doi.org/10.1007/978-3-319-72565-9_20

7. Bonnetain, X., Naya-Plasencia, M.: Hidden shift quantum cryptanalysis and implications. In: Peyrin, T., Galbraith, S. (eds.) ASIACRYPT 2018. LNCS, vol. 11272, pp. 560–592. Springer, Cham (2018). https://doi.org/10.1007/978-3-030-03326-2_19

8. Bonnetain, X., Naya-Plasencia, M., Schrottenloher, A.: On quantum slide attacks, Appeared at SAC (2019)

9. Czajkowski, J., Groot Bruinderink, L., Hülsing, A., Schaffner, C., Unruh, D.: Post-quantum security of the sponge construction. In: Lange, T., Steinwandt, R. (eds.) PQCrypto 2018. LNCS, vol. 10786, pp. 185–204. Springer, Cham (2018). https://doi.org/10.1007/978-3-319-79063-3_9

10. Czajkowski, J., Majenz, C., Schaffner, C., Zur, S.: Quantum lazy sampling and game-playing proofs for quantum indifferentiability. IACR Cryptology ePrint Archive 2019, p. 428 (2019)

11. Dong, X., Dong, B., Wang, X.: Quantum attacks on some Feistel block ciphers. IACR Cryptology ePrint Archive, Report 2018/504 (2018)

12. Dong, X., Li, Z., Wang, X.: Quantum cryptanalysis on some generalized Feistel schemes. Sci. China Inf. Sci. **62**(2), 22501:1–22501:12 (2019)

13. Dong, X., Wang, X.: Quantum key-recovery attack on Feistel structures. Sci. China Inf. Sci. **61**(10), 102501:1–102501:7 (2018)

14. Hosoyamada, A., Iwata, T.: 4-Round Luby-Rackoff Construction is a qPRP. IACR Cryptology ePrint Archive, Report 2019/243 (2019)

15. Hosoyamada, A., Sasaki, Y.: Quantum Demiric-Selçuk meet-in-the-middle attacks: applications to 6-round generic Feistel constructions. In: Catalano, D., De Prisco, R. (eds.) SCN 2018. LNCS, vol. 11035, pp. 386–403. Springer, Cham (2018). https://doi.org/10.1007/978-3-319-98113-0_21

16. Hosoyamada, A., Yasuda, K.: Building quantum-one-way functions from block ciphers: Davies-Meyer and Merkle-Damgård constructions. In: Peyrin, T., Galbraith, S. (eds.) ASIACRYPT 2018. LNCS, vol. 11272, pp. 275–304. Springer, Cham (2018). https://doi.org/10.1007/978-3-030-03326-2_10

17. Ito, G., Hosoyamada, A., Matsumoto, R., Sasaki, Y., Iwata, T.: Quantum chosen-ciphertext attacks against Feistel ciphers. In: Matsui, M. (ed.) CT-RSA 2019. LNCS, vol. 11405, pp. 391–411. Springer, Cham (2019). https://doi.org/10.1007/978-3-030-12612-4_20

18. Kaplan, M., Leurent, G., Leverrier, A., Naya-Plasencia, M.: Breaking symmetric cryptosystems using quantum period finding. In: Robshaw, M., Katz, J. (eds.) CRYPTO 2016, Part II. LNCS, vol. 9815, pp. 207–237. Springer, Heidelberg (2016). https://doi.org/10.1007/978-3-662-53008-5_8

19. Kitaev, A.Y., Shen, A.H., Vyalyi, M.N.: Classical and Quantum Computation. American Mathematical Society, Boston (2002)

20. Kuwakado, H., Morii, M.: Quantum distinguisher between the 3-round Feistel cipher and the random permutation. In: ISIT 2010, Proceedings, pp. 2682–2685. IEEE (2010)

21. Kuwakado, H., Morii, M.: Security on the quantum-type Even-Mansour cipher. In: ISITA 2012, Proceedings, pp. 312–316. IEEE (2012)

22. Liu, Q., Zhandry, M.: On finding quantum multi-collisions. In: Ishai, Y., Rijmen, V. (eds.) EUROCRYPT 2019, Part III. LNCS, vol. 11478, pp. 189–218. Springer, Cham (2019). https://doi.org/10.1007/978-3-030-17659-4_7

23. Luby, M., Rackoff, C.: How to construct pseudo-random permutations from pseudo-random functions (abstract). In: Williams, H.C. (ed.) CRYPTO 1985. LNCS, vol. 218, pp. 447–447. Springer, Heidelberg (1986). https://doi.org/10.1007/3-540-39799-X_34

24. Mennink, B., Szepieniec, A.: XOR of PRPs in a quantum world. In: Lange, T., Takagi, T. (eds.) PQCrypto 2017. LNCS, vol. 10346, pp. 367–383. Springer, Cham (2017). https://doi.org/10.1007/978-3-319-59879-6_21

25. National Bureau of Standards: Data encryption standard. FIPS 46, January 1977

26. Nielsen, M.A., Chuang, I.L.: Quantum Computation and Quantum Information: 10th Anniversary Edition (2010)

27. NIST: Announcing request for nominations for public-key post-quantum cryptographic algorithms. National Institute of Standards and Technology (2016)

28. Patarin, J.: New results on pseudorandom permutation generators based on the des scheme. In: Feigenbaum, J. (ed.) CRYPTO 1991. LNCS, vol. 576, pp. 301–312. Springer, Heidelberg (1992). https://doi.org/10.1007/3-540-46766-1_25

29. Santoli, T., Schaffner, C.: Using Simon's algorithm to attack symmetric-key cryptographic primitives. Quantum Inf. Comput. 17(1&2), 65–78 (2017)

30. Shor, P.W.: Algorithms for quantum computation: discrete logarithms and factoring. In: FOCS 1994, Proceedings, pp. 124–134. IEEE (1994)

31. Simon, D.R.: On the power of quantum computation. SIAM J. Comput. 26(5), 1474–1483 (1997)

32. Song, F., Yun, A.: Quantum security of NMAC and related constructions - PRF domain extension against quantum attacks. In: Katz, J., Shacham, H. (eds.) CRYPTO 2017, Part II. LNCS, vol. 10402, pp. 283–309. Springer, Cham (2017). https://doi.org/10.1007/978-3-319-63715-0_10

33. Zhandry, M.: How to construct quantum random functions. In: FOCS 2012, Proceedings, pp. 679–687. IEEE (2012)

34. Zhandry, M.: Secure identity-based encryption in the quantum random oracle model. In: Safavi-Naini, R., Canetti, R. (eds.) CRYPTO 2012. LNCS, vol. 7417, pp. 758–775. Springer, Heidelberg (2012). https://doi.org/10.1007/978-3-642-32009-5_44

35. Zhandry, M.: A note on the quantum collision and set equality problems. Quantum Inf. Comput. 15(7&8), 557–567 (2015)

36. Zhandry, M.: A note on quantum-secure PRPs. IACR Cryptology ePrint Archive 2016, p. 1076 (2016)

37. Zhandry, M.: How to record quantum queries, and applications to quantum indifferentiability. In: Boldyreva, A., Micciancio, D. (eds.) CRYPTO 2019, Part II. LNCS, vol. 11693, pp. 239–268. Springer, Cham (2019). https://doi.org/10.1007/978-3-030-26951-7_9

Indifferentiability of Truncated Random Permutations

Wonseok Choi[✉], Byeonghak Lee[✉], and Jooyoung Lee[✉]

KAIST, Daejeon, Korea
{krwioh,lbh0307,hicalf}@kaist.ac.kr

Abstract. One of natural ways of constructing a pseudorandom function from a pseudorandom permutation is to simply truncate the output of the permutation. When n is the permutation size and m is the number of truncated bits, the resulting construction is known to be indistinguishable from a random function up to $2^{\frac{n+m}{2}}$ queries, which is tight.

In this paper, we study the indifferentiability of a truncated random permutation where a fixed prefix is prepended to the inputs. We prove that this construction is (regularly) indifferentiable from a public random function up to $\min\{2^{\frac{n+m}{3}}, 2^m, 2^\ell\}$ queries, while it is publicly indifferentiable up to $\min\{\max\{2^{\frac{n+m}{3}}, 2^{\frac{n}{2}}\}, 2^\ell\}$ queries, where ℓ is the size of the fixed prefix. Furthermore, the regular indifferentiability bound is proved to be tight when $m + \ell \ll n$.

Our results significantly improve upon the previous bound of $\min\{2^{\frac{m}{2}}, 2^\ell\}$ given by Dodis et al. (FSE 2009), allowing us to construct, for instance, an $\frac{n}{2}$-to-$\frac{n}{2}$ bit random function that makes a single call to an n-bit permutation, achieving $\frac{n}{2}$-bit security.

Keywords: Random permutation · Random function · Truncation · Indifferentiability · Chi-square method

1 Introduction

A block cipher is typically modeled as a pseudorandom permutation in a provable security setting: no distinguisher should be able to distinguish the block cipher from a truly random permutation by making a certain number of encryption and decryption queries in a black-box manner. However, for some modes of operation, one might want the block cipher to behave like a pseudorandom function. A variety of cryptographic protocols (such as signature schemes, random number generators, key derivation schemes, etc.) provide provable security in the random oracle model. This observation motivates the problem of constructing a pseudorandom function from pseudorandom permutations. Sometimes this

Jooyoung Lee was supported by a National Research Foundation of Korea (NRF) grant funded by the Korean government (Ministry of Science and ICT), No. NRF-2017R1E1A1A03070248.

S. D. Galbraith and S. Moriai (Eds.): ASIACRYPT 2019, LNCS 11921, pp. 175–195, 2019.
https://doi.org/10.1007/978-3-030-34578-5_7

problem is called "Luby-Rackoff backward" [2]: the Feistel network transforms a set of (not necessarily one-to-one) functions into a permutation, and this problem considers its opposite direction. In this direction, two approaches are natural and straightforward; one is to xor multiple independent random permutations and the other is to simply truncate the output of the permutation.

In this work, we will focus on the security of a truncated random permutation. One advantage of this construction (over xoring multiple permutations) is its minimality; it is based on a single permutation, using only a single call to the permutation. We will study the security of a truncated random permutation in the indifferentiability framework. In this framework, we will fix some of the input bits to the permutation, since otherwise one can easily differentiate the construction from a public random function F by making a backward query v to the simulator S, and then checking out if $F(S^{-1}(v)) = v$. Later we will discuss this attack in more detail.

TRUNCATED PERMUTATION. Let n, ℓ, m be positive integers such that $\ell, m < n$. Our construction is precisely defined as

$$\mathsf{TRP}[\mathsf{P}] \overset{\text{def}}{=} \mathsf{Tr}_m(\mathsf{P}(c \parallel \cdot)),$$

where $c \in \{0,1\}^\ell$ is an ℓ-bit prefix, P is an n-bit permutation (modeled as a random permutation oracle), and

$$\mathsf{Tr}_m : \{0,1\}^n \longrightarrow \{0,1\}^{n-m}$$

$$x \longmapsto x_R,$$

when $x \in \{0,1\}^n$ is written as $x_L \parallel x_R$ for $x_L \in \{0,1\}^m$ and $x_R \in \{0,1\}^{n-m}$. (So Tr_m truncates the first m bits of the input.) In this way, we obtain an $(n-\ell)$-to-$(n-m)$ bit function from an n-bit permutation.

In order to prove that this construction is indifferentiable from a public random function F, one should present a simulator S that emulates P having access to F so that it is infeasible to distinguish two systems $(F, S[F])$ and $(\mathsf{TRP}[\mathsf{P}], \mathsf{P})$.

As far as we know, the indifferentiability of TRP has been studied only in [6], where the adversarial differentiating advantage is upper bounded by

$$\frac{(q_F + q_S)^2}{2^n} + \frac{q_F q_S}{2^m} + \frac{q_S}{2^\ell},$$

where q_F and q_S denote the number of function queries and the number of simulator queries, respectively.

OUR CONTRIBUTION. In the indifferentiability framework, we consider two different notions; (regular) indifferentiability and public indifferentiability. With respect to regular indifferentiability, we present a simulator S such that any distinguisher is able to distinguish $(F, S[F])$ and $(\mathsf{TRP}[\mathsf{P}], \mathsf{P})$ with probability at most

$$\left(\frac{(q_F + q_S)^3}{2^{n+m-1}} \right)^{\frac{1}{2}} + \frac{(3 \ln q_F + 3(n-m) + 1) q_S}{2^{m-1}} + \frac{5 q_S}{2^{\ell-1}}.$$

We also prove that the regular indifferentiability bound is tight when $m + \ell \ll n$.

With respect to public indifferentiability, we present a simulator S such that any distinguisher is able to distinguish $(\mathsf{F}, \mathsf{S}[\mathsf{F}])$ and $(\mathsf{TRP}[\mathsf{P}], \mathsf{P})$ with probability at most

$$\left(\frac{(q_F + q_S)^3}{2^{n+m-1}}\right)^{\frac{1}{2}} + \frac{q_S}{2^{\ell - 1}}$$

if $q_F + q_S < 2^m$, and

$$\left(\frac{5(q_F + q_S)^2}{2^{n+1}}\right)^{\frac{1}{2}} + \frac{q_S}{2^{\ell - 1}},$$

otherwise. Figure 1 compares our bounds and the bound from [6] in terms of the threshold number of queries q (in log base 2), where $q = q_F + q_S$; TRP is regularly indifferentiable (resp. publicly indifferentiable) from a public random function up to $\min\{2^{\frac{n+m}{3}}, 2^m, 2^\ell\}$ (resp. $\min\{\max\{2^{\frac{n+m}{3}}, 2^{\frac{n}{2}}\}, 2^\ell\}$) queries, improving upon the previous bound of $\min\{2^{\frac{m}{2}}, 2^\ell\}$.

Our results allow us to construct an n-to-n bit random function that makes a single call to a wider $2n$-bit permutation, achieving n-bit security. This construction is comparable to the sum of two independent permutations, $\mathsf{P}_1 \oplus \mathsf{P}_2$, that makes two calls to the underlying n-bit permutations P_1 and P_2 to achieve n-bit security. For each simulator query, our simulator makes at most one call to the public random function F, while the simulator for $\mathsf{P}_1 \oplus \mathsf{P}_2$ (given in [3]) might possibly make n calls to F.

By letting $q_S = 0$, an indifferentiability bound of TRP is reduced to an indistinguishability bound of TRP. Without any simulator query, we can make our computation even tighter, recovering the optimal indistinguishability bound of TRP given in [8]. See Appendix A.

We remark that efficient and secure construction of a fixed-input-length random oracle (FIL-RO) can be of practical relevance. As a FIL-RO, TRP founds various applications; a public finalization function for MACs, a non-compressing primitive for compression functions [21], a key derivation function, etc. A key derivation function in GCM-SIV was also proposed to use TRP [9,10], although later studies offered alternatives [12,21]. We already have large and secure permutations at hand, including KECCAK and GIMLI, that can be used to construct a FIL-RO with reasonable size and security.

RELATED WORK. The sum of two random permutations was first considered by Bellare et al. [2] in the indistinguishability framework. Subsequently, a series of works improved this seminal result [1,4,14,19,20], culminating with the proof by Dai et al. [5] that the sum of two n-bit random permutations is (fully) secure up to 2^n queries.

In the indifferentiability model, Mandal et al. [15] proved that the sum of two public random permutations is secure up to $2^{\frac{2n}{3}}$ queries, and later Mennink and Preneel [19] pointed out a flaw in their security proof and fixed it. Lee [13] proved that the sum of k independent random permutations is secure up to $2^{\frac{(k-1)n}{k}}$ queries. Finally, Bhattacharya and Nandi [3] proved that the sum of two random permutations is secure up to 2^n queries.

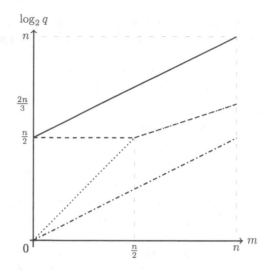

Fig. 1. Our regular and public indifferentiability bounds for TRP as a function of m (ignoring ℓ). For all parameters below the dashed line (resp. the dotted line), TRP is regularly indifferentiable (resp. publicly indifferentiable) from a public random function. The solid and dash-dotted lines represent the indistinguishability bound [8] and the previous indifferentiability bound [6], respectively.

Truncating a random permutation was first considered by Hall et al. [11], where they proved the security of TRP (with $\ell = 0$) up to $\min\{2^{\frac{n+m}{2}}, 2^{\frac{2(n-m)}{3}}\}$ queries in terms of indistinguishability. Bellare and Impagliazzo [1] improved this bound up to $\min\{2^{2m}, 2^{\frac{n+m}{2}}\}$. Recently, Gilboa et al. [8] proved that TRP is indistinguishable from a random function up to $2^{\frac{n+m}{2}}$ queries. This bound turns out to be tight as they also present matching attacks. Mennink [18] generalized truncation functions used in TRP, and showed that the security of such constructions (in terms of indistinguishability) cannot exceed that of the original TRP.

As mentioned before, Dodis et al. [6] proved the security of TRP up to $\min\{2^{\frac{m}{2}}, 2^{\ell}\}$ queries in terms of indifferentiability, and used it to build the MD6 hash function. Precisely, the MD6 hash function uses TRP with $n = 5696$, $\ell = 960$ and $m = 4672$.

2   Preliminaries

NOTATION. Throughout this work, we fix positive integers n, m, ℓ such that $m, \ell < n$ to denote the size of the underlying permutation P, the number of truncated bits and the prefix size of TRP, respectively. We also fix $c \in \{0, 1\}^{\ell}$ to denote the prefix of TRP. We will write $\mathcal{C} = \{c \parallel x : x \in \{0, 1\}^{n-\ell}\}$.

REGULAR AND PUBLIC INDIFFERENTIABILITY. In the indifferentiability framework, a distinguisher is given two systems (C[P], P) and (F, S[F]), where P is an ideal primitive, C[P] is a bigger construction using P as a building block, F is another ideal primitive with the same interface as C[P], and S[F] is a probabilistic Turing machine with the same interface as P that has oracle access to F. The goal of the *simulator* S[F] is to emulate the ideal primitive P so that no distinguisher can tell apart the two systems (F, S[F]) and (C[P], P) with a significant probability, based on their responses to queries that the distinguisher may send. We say that the construction C[P] is indifferentiable from the ideal primitive F if the existence of such a simulator is proved. The indifferentiability guarantees universal composability of C[P]: if C[P] is indifferentiable from F, then C[P] can replace F in any cryptosystem, and the resulting cryptosystem is at least as secure under the assumption that P is ideal as under the assumption that F is ideal.

More precisely, in an information-theoretic sense, a construction C with oracle access to an ideal primitive P is said to be (q_F, q_S, ε)-*regular indifferentiable from an ideal primitive* F if there exists a simulator S with oracle access to F such that for any distinguisher $\mathcal{A}$ making exactly q_F queries to the outer construction ($C[P]$ or F) and exactly q_S queries to the inner primitive (P or S[F]),[1] it holds that

$$\mathbf{Adv}^{\text{reg}}_{C,S}(\mathcal{A}) \stackrel{\text{def}}{=} \left| \Pr\left[1 \leftarrow \mathcal{A}^{C[P],P}\right] - \Pr\left[1 \leftarrow \mathcal{A}^{F,S[F]}\right] \right| < \varepsilon.$$

See [17] for more detail on indifferentiability.

Public indifferentiability has been introduced in [7,22] and formalized in [16] as a variant of indifferentiability, where the simulator knows all queries made by the distinguisher to the primitive it tries to simulate. This weaker notion is useful to argue the security of cryptosystems where all the queries to the ideal primitive are public (as e.g., in many digital signature schemes). The adversarial public-differentiating advantage $\mathbf{Adv}^{\text{pub}}_{C,S}(\mathcal{A})$ is similarly defined for any distinguisher $\mathcal{A}$, and hence (q_F, q_S, ε)-*public indifferentiability*.

THE χ^2 METHOD. We give here all the necessary background on the χ^2 method [5] that we will use throughout this paper.

We fix a set of random systems, a deterministic distinguisher $\mathcal{A}$ that makes q oracle queries to one of the random systems, and a set Ω that contains all possible answers for oracle queries to the random systems. For a random system S and $i \in \{1, \ldots, q\}$, let $Z_{S,i}$ be the random variable over Ω that follows the distribution of the i-th answer obtained by $\mathcal{A}$ interacting with S. Let

$$\mathbf{Z}^i_S \stackrel{\text{def}}{=} (Z_{S,1}, \ldots, Z_{S,i}),$$

and let

$$\mathsf{p}^i_S(\mathbf{z}) \stackrel{\text{def}}{=} \Pr\left[\mathbf{Z}^i_S = \mathbf{z}\right]$$

for $\mathbf{z} \in \Omega^i$. For $i < q$ and $\mathbf{z} = (z_1, \ldots, z_{i-1}) \in \Omega^{i-1}$ such that $\mathsf{p}^{i-1}_S(\mathbf{z}) > 0$, the probability distribution of $Z_{S,i}$ conditioned on $\mathbf{Z}^{i-1}_S = \mathbf{z}$ will be denoted $\mathsf{p}^{\mathbf{z}}_{S,i}(\cdot)$,

---

[1] We can assume that $\mathcal{A}$ is deterministic since it is computationally unbounded.

namely for $z \in \Omega$,

$$\mathsf{p}_{\mathcal{S},i}^{\mathbf{z}}(z) \overset{\text{def}}{=} \Pr\left[Z_{\mathcal{S},i} = z \mid \mathbf{Z}_{\mathcal{S}}^{i-1} = \mathbf{z}\right].$$

For two random systems $\mathcal{S}_0$ and $\mathcal{S}_1$, and for $i < q$ and $\mathbf{z} = (z_1, \ldots, z_{i-1}) \in \Omega^{i-1}$ such that $\mathsf{p}_{\mathcal{S}_0}^{i-1}(\mathbf{z})$, $\mathsf{p}_{\mathcal{S}_1}^{i-1}(\mathbf{z}) > 0$, the χ^2-*divergence* for $\mathsf{p}_{\mathcal{S}_0,i}^{\mathbf{z}}(\cdot)$ and $\mathsf{p}_{\mathcal{S}_1,i}^{\mathbf{z}}(\cdot)$ is defined as follows.

$$\chi^2\left(\mathsf{p}_{\mathcal{S}_1,i}^{\mathbf{z}}(\cdot), \mathsf{p}_{\mathcal{S}_0,i}^{\mathbf{z}}(\cdot)\right) \overset{\text{def}}{=} \sum_{\substack{z \in \Omega \text{ such that} \\ \mathsf{p}_{\mathcal{S}_0,i}^{\mathbf{z}}(z) > 0}} \frac{\left(\mathsf{p}_{\mathcal{S}_1,i}^{\mathbf{z}}(z) - \mathsf{p}_{\mathcal{S}_0,i}^{\mathbf{z}}(z)\right)^2}{\mathsf{p}_{\mathcal{S}_0,i}^{\mathbf{z}}(z)}.$$

We will simply write $\chi^2(\mathbf{z}) = \chi^2\left(\mathsf{p}_{\mathcal{S}_1,i}^{\mathbf{z}}(\cdot), \mathsf{p}_{\mathcal{S}_0,i}^{\mathbf{z}}(\cdot)\right)$ when the random systems are clear from the context. If the support of $\mathsf{p}_{\mathcal{S}_1}^{i-1}(\cdot)$ is contained in the support of $\mathsf{p}_{\mathcal{S}_0}^{i-1}(\cdot)$, then we can view $\chi^2\left(\mathsf{p}_{\mathcal{S}_1,i}^{\mathbf{z}}(\cdot), \mathsf{p}_{\mathcal{S}_0,i}^{\mathbf{z}}(\cdot)\right)$ as a random variable, denoted $\chi^2\left(\mathbf{Z}_{\mathcal{S}_1}^{i-1}\right)$, where $\mathbf{z}$ follows the distribution of $\mathbf{Z}_{\mathcal{S}_1}^{i-1}$.

Then $\mathcal{A}$'s distinguishing advantage is upper bounded by the *total variation distance* of $\mathsf{p}_{\mathcal{S}_0}^{q}(\cdot)$ and $\mathsf{p}_{\mathcal{S}_1}^{q}(\cdot)$, denoted $\|\mathsf{p}_{\mathcal{S}_0}^{q}(\cdot) - \mathsf{p}_{\mathcal{S}_1}^{q}(\cdot)\|$, and we also have

$$\|\mathsf{p}_{\mathcal{S}_0}^{q}(\cdot) - \mathsf{p}_{\mathcal{S}_1}^{q}(\cdot)\| \leq \left(\frac{1}{2}\sum_{i=1}^{q}\mathbf{Ex}\left[\chi^2\left(\mathbf{Z}_{\mathcal{S}_1}^{i-1}\right)\right]\right)^{1/2}. \tag{1}$$

See [5] for the proof of (1).

3   Indifferentiability of TRP

We will assume that a distinguisher $\mathcal{A}$ has access to an oracle $\mathcal{O}$ with three types of queries; $\mathcal{O}(x, 0)$ for $x \in \{0,1\}^{n-\ell}$, $\mathcal{O}(u, +)$ and $\mathcal{O}(v, -)$ for $u, v \in \{0,1\}^n$, which are called a *function query*, a *forward query* and a *backward query*, respectively. Forward and backward queries will be also called *simulator queries*. In the real world, an n-bit permutation P is chosen uniformly at random, and queries $\mathcal{O}(u, +)$ and $\mathcal{O}(v, -)$ are answered with $\mathsf{P}(u)$ and $\mathsf{P}^{-1}(v)$, respectively, and a query $\mathcal{O}(x, 0)$ is answered with $\mathsf{TRP}[\mathsf{P}](x)$. In the simulated world, an $(n - \ell)$-to-$(n - m)$ bit function F is chosen uniformly at random, and a query $\mathcal{O}(x, 0)$ is answered with $\mathsf{F}(x)$ for any $x \in \{0,1\}^{n-\ell}$. On the other hand, queries $\mathcal{O}(u, +)$ and $\mathcal{O}(v, -)$ will be answered by a simulator S that has oracle access to F.

3.1   Regular Indifferentiability of TRP

We define a simulator S without using any information on the adversarial queries of type $\mathcal{O}(\cdot, 0)$. Simulator S is stateful, keeping variables $\mathcal{O}(u)$ and $\mathcal{O}^{-1}(v)$ for every u and $v \in \{0,1\}^n$, all initialized as $\bot$, meaning "undefined",[2] as well as sets $\mathcal{D}$, $\mathcal{R}$, and $\mathcal{R}_y$ for each $y \in \{0,1\}^{n-m}$, all initialized as empty. It behaves as follows.

---

[2] We uses $\mathcal{O}$ to denote both oracle interfaces and variables by slight abuse of notation.

– On a forward query $\mathcal{O}(u, +)$, S does the following.
1. If $\mathcal{O}(u) = \bot$, then
   (a) obtain $y = \mathsf{F}(x)$ via an oracle query to F if $u = c \parallel x$ for some $x \in \{0,1\}^{n-\ell}$, and choose y uniformly at random from $\{0,1\}^{n-m}$ otherwise;
   (b) choose w uniformly at random from $\{0,1\}^m \setminus \mathcal{R}_y$;
   (c) assign $w \parallel y$ and u to $\mathcal{O}(u)$ and $\mathcal{O}^{-1}(w \parallel y)$, respectively;
   (d) update $\mathcal{D}$, $\mathcal{R}$ and $\mathcal{R}_y$ as $\mathcal{D} \cup \{u\}$, $\mathcal{R} \cup \{w \parallel y\}$ and $\mathcal{R}_y \cup \{w\}$, respectively.
2. Return $\mathcal{O}(u)$.
– On a backward query $\mathcal{O}(v, -)$, S does the following.
1. If $\mathcal{O}^{-1}(v) = \bot$, then
   (a) choose u uniformly at random from $\{0,1\}^n \setminus (\mathcal{D} \cup \mathcal{C})$;
   (b) assign u and v to $\mathcal{O}^{-1}(v)$ and $\mathcal{O}(u)$, respectively;
   (c) update $\mathcal{D}$, $\mathcal{R}$ and $\mathcal{R}_y$ as $\mathcal{D} \cup \{u\}$, $\mathcal{R} \cup \{v\}$ and $\mathcal{R}_y \cup \{w\}$, respectively, where $v = w \parallel y$ for $w \in \{0,1\}^m$ and $y \in \{0,1\}^{n-m}$.
2. Return $\mathcal{O}^{-1}(v)$.

By definition, our simulator consistently answers redundant queries. So we can assume that $\mathcal{A}$ makes no redundant query; if $\mathcal{A}$ obtains $\mathcal{O}(u, +) = v$ (resp. $\mathcal{O}(v, -) = u$), then it would not make a query $\mathcal{O}(v, -)$ (resp. $\mathcal{O}(u, +)$). $\mathcal{A}$ will not make a function query $\mathsf{F}(x)$ once it has made a forward query $\mathcal{O}(c \parallel x, +)$. On the other hand, $\mathcal{A}$ is allowed to make a forward query $\mathcal{O}(c \parallel x, +)$ after it obtains $\mathsf{F}(x)$.

Theorem 1. *Let* S *be the simulator defined as above, and let* q_F *and* q_S *be positive integers such that* $q_F + q_S \leq 2^{n-1}$. *Then for any distinguisher* $\mathcal{A}$ *making* q_F *queries to the outer construction and* q_S *queries to the inner primitive,*

$$Adv_{\mathsf{TRP,S}}^{\mathsf{reg}}(\mathcal{A}) \leq \left(\frac{(q_F + q_S)^3}{2^{n+m-1}} \right)^{\frac{1}{2}} + \frac{(3 \ln q_F + 3(n-m) + 1)q_S}{2^{m-1}} + \frac{5q_S}{2^{\ell-1}}.$$

Proof. We can assume that $q_S \leq 2^{m-1}$ since otherwise the upper bound trivially holds.

Let $\mathcal{S}_0 = (\mathsf{F}, \mathsf{S}[\mathsf{F}])$ and $\mathcal{S}_2 = (\mathsf{TRP}[\mathsf{P}], \mathsf{P})$ denote the simulated world and the real world, respectively. We cannot directly apply the χ^2 method to $\mathcal{S}_0$ and $\mathcal{S}_2$ since the support of $\mathsf{p}_{\mathcal{S}_2}^{i-1}(\cdot)$ is not contained in the support of $\mathsf{p}_{\mathcal{S}_0}^{i-1}(\cdot)$ (and vice versa) for any $i = 1, \ldots, q$; S does not return any element of $\mathcal{C}$ on a backward query $\mathcal{O}(\cdot, -)$. For this reason, we introduce an intermediate world, denoted $\mathcal{S}_1$, that has the same oracle interface as $\mathcal{S}_0$ and $\mathcal{S}_2$.

This random system uses two flags, denoted bad_1 and bad_2, all initialized as false, and a sampling procedure P^* as a subroutine. The procedure P^* keeps variables $\mathsf{P}^*(u)$ and $(\mathsf{P}^*)^{-1}(v)$ for every u and $v \in \{0,1\}^n$, all initialized as $\bot$, meaning "undefined", and also keeps sets $\mathcal{D}^*$ and $\mathcal{R}^*$, all initialized as empty. This procedure accepts oracle queries of types $\mathsf{P}^*(\cdot, +)$ and $\mathsf{P}^*(\cdot, -)$.

- On a query $\mathsf{P}^*(u, +)$, P^* does the following.
  1. If $\mathsf{P}^*(u) = \bot$, then
     (a) choose v uniformly at random from $\{0, 1\}^n \setminus \mathcal{R}^*$;
     (b) assign v and u to $\mathsf{P}^*(u)$ and $(\mathsf{P}^*)^{-1}(v)$, respectively;
     (c) update $\mathcal{D}^*$ and $\mathcal{R}^*$ as $\mathcal{D}^* \cup \{u\}$ and $\mathcal{R}^* \cup \{v\}$, respectively.
  2. Return $\mathsf{P}^*(u)$.
- On a query $\mathsf{P}^*(v, -)$, P^* does the following.
  1. If $(\mathsf{P}^*)^{-1}(v) = \bot$, then
     (a) choose u uniformly at random from $\{0, 1\}^n \setminus \mathcal{D}^*$;
     (b) if $u \in \mathcal{C}$, then set bad_1 to true, and choose u uniformly at random from $\{0, 1\}^n \setminus (\mathcal{D}^* \cup \mathcal{C})$;
     (c) assign v and u to $\mathsf{P}^*(u)$ and $(\mathsf{P}^*)^{-1}(v)$, respectively;
     (d) update $\mathcal{D}^*$ and $\mathcal{R}^*$ as $\mathcal{D}^* \cup \{u\}$ and $\mathcal{R}^* \cup \{v\}$, respectively.
  2. If $(\mathsf{P}^*)^{-1}(v) = u'(\neq \bot)$ where $v = w \| y$ for $w \in \{0, 1\}^m$ and $y \in \{0, 1\}^{n-m}$, then
     (a) set bad_2 to true;
     (b) choose u uniformly at random from $\{0, 1\}^n \setminus (\mathcal{D}^* \cup \mathcal{C})$;
     (c) assign v and u to $\mathsf{P}^*(u)$ and $(\mathsf{P}^*)^{-1}(v)$, respectively;
     (d) choose v' uniformly at random from

     $$\{w \| y : w \in \{0, 1\}^m\} \setminus \mathcal{R}^*;$$

     (e) assign v' and u' to $\mathsf{P}^*(u')$ and $(\mathsf{P}^*)^{-1}(v')$, respectively;
     (f) update $\mathcal{D}^*$ and $\mathcal{R}^*$ as $\mathcal{D}^* \cup \{u\}$ and $\mathcal{R}^* \cup \{v'\}$, respectively.
  3. Return $(\mathsf{P}^*)^{-1}(v)$.

Note that $\{0, 1\}^n \setminus (\mathcal{D}^* \cup \mathcal{C})$ is always nonempty since $q_F + q_S + 2^{n-\ell} \leq 2^n$. Using this sampling procedure, oracle queries to $\mathcal{S}_1$ are answered as follows.

- On a function query $\mathcal{O}(x, 0)$, $\mathcal{S}_1$ obtains $w \| y = \mathsf{P}^*(c \| x, +)$ where $w \in \{0, 1\}^m$ and $y \in \{0, 1\}^{n-m}$, and returns y.
- On a forward query $\mathcal{O}(u, +)$, $\mathcal{S}_1$ obtains $v = \mathsf{P}^*(u, +)$ and returns v.
- On a backward query $\mathcal{O}(v, -)$, $\mathcal{S}_1$ obtains $u = \mathsf{P}^*(v, -)$ and returns u.

So $\mathcal{S}_1$ behaves like the real world $\mathcal{S}_2$ with the inner permutation replaced by the sampling procedure P^*. Again, P^* behaves like a truly random permutation except that it never samples any element of $\mathcal{C}$ on a backward query $\mathsf{P}^*(\cdot, -)$.

Note that $\mathsf{P}^*(v, -)$ is queried on an element v such that $(\mathsf{P}^*)^{-1}(v) \neq \bot$ only when $(\mathsf{P}^*)^{-1}(v)$ is fixed via a function query $\mathcal{O}(x, 0)$ for some $x \in \{0, 1\}^{n-\ell}$ (since we are assuming that a distinguisher never makes redundant queries). When $\mathsf{P}^*(c \| x) = v$ is fixed via a function query, a distinguisher would not obtain any information on the leftmost m bits of v. Namely, when $v = w \| y$ for $w \in \{0,1\}^m$ and $y \in \{0,1\}^{n-m}$, the distinguisher has $\mathsf{P}^*(u) = \star \| y$ for unknown $\star$. When a backward query $\mathsf{P}^*(v,-)$ is made later during the attack, w is replaced by a new element w' and $(\mathsf{P}^*)^{-1}(v)$ is also given a new element u' outside $\mathcal{D}^*$. In this way, every oracle query will add a new element to $\mathcal{D}^*$ and $\mathcal{R}^*$.

Let $q = q_F + q_S$ denote the total number of queries. Then we have

$$\mathbf{Adv}_{\mathsf{TRP},\mathsf{S}}^{\mathsf{reg}}(\mathcal{A}) \leq \| \mathsf{p}_{\mathcal{S}_0}^q (\cdot) - \mathsf{p}_{\mathcal{S}_2}^q (\cdot) \|$$
$$\leq \| \mathsf{p}_{\mathcal{S}_0}^q (\cdot) - \mathsf{p}_{\mathcal{S}_1}^q (\cdot) \| + \| \mathsf{p}_{\mathcal{S}_1}^q (\cdot) - \mathsf{p}_{\mathcal{S}_2}^q (\cdot) \|. \qquad (2)$$

Once $\mathcal{A}$ obtains the first $i - 1$ answers $\mathbf{z} = (z_1, \ldots, z_{i-1})$ via oracle queries, they (partially) determine all the corresponding evaluations of P^*. For a fixed $j \in \{1, \ldots, i-1\}$, the j-th query is associated with (u_j, v_j, σ_j), where

- if z_j has been obtained by a function query on x, then $\sigma_j = 0$, $u_j = c \| x$, and $v_j = \star \| z_j$ (with $\star$ meaning "unknown").
- if z_j has been obtained by a forward query on u, then $\sigma_j = +$, $u_j = u$, and $v_j = z_j$.
- if z_j has been obtained by a backward query on v, then $\sigma_j = -$, $u_j = z_j$, and $v_j = v$.

With this notation, we will consider random variables V_y, S_y, F_y for each $y \in \{0,1\}^{n-m}$, where

$$V_y = |\{u_j : v_j = w \| y \text{ for some } w \in \{0,1\}^m\}|,$$
$$S_y = |\{u_j : \sigma_j \in \{+,-\} \text{ and } v_j = w \| y \text{ for some } w \in \{0,1\}^m\}|,$$
$$F_y = V_y - S_y.$$

In words,

- V_y counts the number of elements u where $\mathsf{P}^*(u)$ has been determined by $\mathcal{A}$'s function/simulator queries and $\mathsf{P}^*(u) = w \| y$ for some $w \in \{0,1\}^m$,
- S_y counts the number of elements u where $\mathsf{P}^*(u)$ has been determined by $\mathcal{A}$'s *simulator* queries and $\mathsf{P}^*(u) = w \| y$ for some $w \in \{0,1\}^m$,
- F_y counts the number of elements u where $\mathsf{P}^*(u)$ has been partially determined only by $\mathcal{A}$'s *function* queries and $\mathsf{P}^*(u) = \star \| y$ with *unknown* $\star \in \{0,1\}^m$.

Let $V = \sum_{y \in \{0,1\}^{n-m}} V_y$. At any point during the attack, $V = |\mathcal{D}^*| = |\mathcal{R}^*|$. Suppose that $\mathbf{z}$ determines $\mathsf{P}^*(u) = \star \| y$ for $u \in \{0,1\}^n$ and $y \in \{0,1\}^{n-m}$ (with unknown $\star$). Then for $w \in \{0,1\}^m$ such that $\mathbf{z}$ does not determine $(\mathsf{P}^*)^{-1}(w \| y)$, the conditional probability that $\star = w$ given $\mathbf{z}$ is $1/S_y$. (Note that we can define a set of candidate permutations which are compatible with (u_j, v_j, σ_j) for all $j < i$; the distribution of the next query answer $\mathbf{z}$ from $\mathcal{S}_1$ is the same as the distribution one would get by drawing one of those compatible permutations uniformly at random conditioned on backward queries not falling in $\mathcal{C}$, and using it to answer the query in the obvious way.

UPPER BOUNDING $\|p_{\mathcal{S}_1}^q(\cdot) - p_{\mathcal{S}_2}^q(\cdot)\|$. The procedure P^* behaves exactly like a truly random permutation without any of the bad flags being set to true. So we can upper bound $\|p_{\mathcal{S}_1}^q(\cdot) - p_{\mathcal{S}_2}^q(\cdot)\|$ by the probability that either bad_1 or bad_2 is set to true.

For $i = 1, \ldots, q_S$, let $\mathsf{E}_{1,i}$ (resp. $\mathsf{E}_{2,i}$) be the event that the i-th simulator query set bad_1 (resp. bad_2) to true. Since $|\mathcal{C}| = 2^{n-\ell}$ and $|\mathcal{D}^*| \le q \le 2^{n-1}$, we have

$$\Pr\left[\mathsf{E}_{1,i}\right] = \frac{|\mathcal{C}|}{2^n - |\mathcal{D}^*|} \le \frac{2^{n-\ell}}{2^{n-1}} = \frac{1}{2^{\ell-1}}$$

for each $i = 1, \ldots, q_S$.

When the i-th simulator query $\mathcal{O}(v, -)$ is made (in the backward direction) with $v = w \| y$, the conditional probability that bad_2 is set to true (conditioned on the previous queries) is upper bounded by

$$\frac{F_y}{2^m - S_y},$$

where F_y and S_y can be viewed as random variables determined by the previous queries. Since y can be chosen adversarially and $S_y \le 2^{m-1}$, the conditional probability that the i-th simulator query sets bad_2 to true is upper bounded by

$$\frac{\max_{y \in \{0,1\}^{n-m}} F_y}{2^{m-1}}.$$

Therefore, we have

$$\Pr\left[\mathsf{E}_{2,i}\right] \le \frac{\mathbf{Ex}_i\left[\max_{y \in \{0,1\}^{n-m}} F_y\right]}{2^{m-1}},$$

where the expectation is taken over the interaction of $\mathcal{A}$ and $\mathcal{S}_1$ until the i-th simulator query is made. We also have

$$\mathbf{Ex}_i\left[\max_y F_y\right] \le \frac{q_F}{2^{n-m-2}} + 3\ln q_F + 3(n-m) + 1. \tag{3}$$

The proof of (3) is deferred to the end of this section. Overall, we have

$$\|p_{\mathcal{S}_1}^q(\cdot) - p_{\mathcal{S}_2}^q(\cdot)\| \le \Pr\left[\bigvee_{i=1}^{q_S} (\mathsf{E}_{1,i} \vee \mathsf{E}_{2,i})\right]$$

$$\le \sum_{i=1}^{q_S} \Pr\left[\mathsf{E}_{1,i}\right] + \sum_{i=1}^{q_S} \Pr\left[\mathsf{E}_{2,i}\right]$$

$$\le \frac{q_S}{2^{\ell-1}} + \frac{q_F q_S}{2^{n-3}} + \frac{(3\ln q_F + 3(n-m) + 1)q_S}{2^{m-1}}$$

$$\le \frac{5q_S}{2^{\ell-1}} + \frac{(3\ln q_F + 3(n-m) + 1)q_S}{2^{m-1}}, \tag{4}$$

where the last inequality holds since $q_F \le 2^{n-\ell}$.

UPPER BOUNDING $\|p_{\mathcal{S}_0}^q(\cdot) - p_{\mathcal{S}_1}^q(\cdot)\|$. For the intermediate system $\mathcal{S}_1$, we can easily check that the support of $p_{\mathcal{S}_1}^{i-1}(\cdot)$ is contained in the support of $p_{\mathcal{S}_0}^{i-1}(\cdot)$ for $i = 1, \ldots, q$, allowing us to use the χ^2 method.

Let $\Omega = \{0,1\}^n \cup \{0,1\}^{n-m}$. For fixed $i \in \{1, \ldots, q\}$ and $\mathbf{z} \in \Omega^{i-1}$ such $p_{\mathcal{S}_1}^{i-1}(\mathbf{z}) > 0$, we will compute

$$\chi^2(\mathbf{z}) = \sum_{\substack{z \in \Omega \text{ such that} \\ p_{\mathcal{S}_0,i}^{\mathbf{z}}(z) > 0}} \frac{\left(p_{\mathcal{S}_1,i}^{\mathbf{z}}(z) - p_{\mathcal{S}_0,i}^{\mathbf{z}}(z)\right)^2}{p_{\mathcal{S}_0,i}^{\mathbf{z}}(z)}.$$

The previous queries $\mathbf{z} \in \Omega^{i-1}$ will determine the type of the next query. We will distinguish four cases: a function query, a "fresh" forward query, a forward query on an element where a function query already has been made, and a backward query.

Suppose that the i-th query is a function query. For any $z \in \{0,1\}^{n-m}$, we have

$$p_{\mathcal{S}_0,i}^{\mathbf{z}}(z) = \frac{1}{2^{n-m}},$$

$$p_{\mathcal{S}_1,i}^{\mathbf{z}}(z) = \frac{2^m - V_z}{2^n - V}$$

since $V = |\mathcal{R}^*|$ and $V_z = |\{v \in \mathcal{R}^* : v = w \,\|\, z \text{ for some } w \in \{0,1\}^m\}|$. Therefore we have

$$\chi^2(\mathbf{z}) = \sum_{z \in \{0,1\}^{n-m}} \frac{(2^{n-m} V_z - V)^2}{2^{n-m}(2^n - V)^2}. \tag{5}$$

Suppose that the i-th query is a forward query $\mathcal{O}(u, +)$, where either $u \notin \mathcal{C}$ or $u = c \,\|\, x$ for some $x \in \{0,1\}^{n-\ell}$ and $\mathcal{O}(x, 0)$ has not been queried. Let $z = w \,\|\, y$ for $w \in \{0,1\}^m$ and $y \in \{0,1\}^{n-m}$, where $(P^*)^{-1}(w \,\|\, y)$ is not fixed by $\mathbf{z}$. Then it is easy to see that

$$p_{\mathcal{S}_0,i}^{\mathbf{z}}(z) = \frac{1}{2^{n-m}} \cdot \frac{1}{2^m - S_y}.$$

In $\mathcal{S}_1$, $\perp \,\|\, y$ is chosen with probability $(2^m - V_y)/(2^n - V)$ conditioned on $\mathbf{z}$ (with $\perp$ meaning "undetermined"), and then $\perp$ becomes w with probability $1/(2^m - S_y)$. Therefore we have

$$p_{\mathcal{S}_1,i}^{\mathbf{z}}(z) = \frac{2^m - V_y}{2^n - V} \cdot \frac{1}{2^m - S_y},$$

and hence,

$$\chi^2(\mathbf{z}) = \sum_{y \in \{0,1\}^{n-m}} \frac{(2^{n-m} V_y - V)^2}{2^{n-m}(2^n - V)^2}, \tag{6}$$

since the number of $w \in \{0,1\}^m$ such that $(P^*)^{-1}(w \,\|\, y)$ is fixed by $\mathbf{z}$ is S_y for each $y \in \{0,1\}^m$.

Suppose that the i-th query is a forward query $\mathcal{O}(u,+)$, where $u = c \,\|\, x$ for some $x \in \{0,1\}^{n-\ell}$ and $y = \mathcal{O}(x,0)$ has been obtained by a previous function query. Let $z = w \,\|\, y$ where $w \in \{0,1\}^m$. Then we have

$$\mathsf{p}^{\mathbf{z}}_{\mathcal{S}_0,i}(z) = \mathsf{p}^{\mathbf{z}}_{\mathcal{S}_1,i}(z) = \frac{1}{2^m - S_y},$$

and hence

$$\chi^2(\mathbf{z}) = 0. \tag{7}$$

Suppose that the i-th query is a backward query $\mathcal{O}(v,-)$. It is easy to see that

$$\mathsf{p}^{\mathbf{z}}_{\mathcal{S}_0,i}(z) = \mathsf{p}^{\mathbf{z}}_{\mathcal{S}_1,i}(z) = \frac{1}{2^n - |\mathcal{D}^* \cup \mathcal{C}|}$$

for any $z \in \{0,1\}^n \setminus (\mathcal{D}^* \cup \mathcal{C})$, and hence

$$\chi^2(\mathbf{z}) = 0. \tag{8}$$

By (5), (6), (7), (8), we have

$$
\|\mathsf{p}^q_{\mathcal{S}_0}(\cdot) - \mathsf{p}^q_{\mathcal{S}_1}(\cdot)\| \le \left(\frac{1}{2} \sum_{i=1}^{q} \mathbf{Ex}\left[\chi^2(\mathbf{z})\right] \right)^{\frac{1}{2}}
$$

$$
\le \left(\frac{1}{2} \sum_{i=1}^{q} \mathbf{Ex}\left[\sum_{y \in \{0,1\}^{n-m}} \frac{(2^{n-m}V_y - V)^2}{2^{n-m}(2^n - V)^2} \right] \right)^{\frac{1}{2}}. \tag{9}
$$

Since $\sum_{y \in \{0,1\}^{n-m}} V_y = V \le q_F + q_S$ and $V \le 2^{n-1}$, we have

$$
\sum_{y \in \{0,1\}^{n-m}} \frac{(2^{n-m}V_y - V)^2}{2^{n-m}(2^n - V)^2} = \sum_{y \in \{0,1\}^{n-m}} \frac{2^{2n-2m}V_y^2 - 2^{n-m+1}V_y V + V^2}{2^{n-m}(2^n - V)^2}
$$

$$
= \frac{2^{n-m}}{(2^n - V)^2}\left(\sum_{y \in \{0,1\}^{n-m}} V_y^2 - \frac{V^2}{2^{n-m}} \right)
$$

$$
\le \frac{1}{2^{n+m-2}}\left(\sum_{y \in \{0,1\}^{n-m}} V_y \right)^2
$$

$$
\le \frac{(q_F + q_S)^2}{2^{n+m-2}},
$$

and by (9),

$$
\|\mathsf{p}^q_{\mathcal{S}_0}(\cdot) - \mathsf{p}^q_{\mathcal{S}_1}(\cdot)\| \le \left(\sum_{i=1}^{q} \frac{(q_F + q_S)^2}{2^{n+m-1}} \right)^{\frac{1}{2}} = \left(\frac{(q_F + q_S)^3}{2^{n+m-1}} \right)^{\frac{1}{2}}. \tag{10}
$$

By (2), (4), (10), the proof is complete. □

When $q_S = 0$, we can obtain a tighter upper bound on $\|\mathsf{p}_{\mathcal{S}_0}^q(\cdot) - \mathsf{p}_{\mathcal{S}_1}^q(\cdot)\|$ than the one obtained above, recovering the optimal indistinguishability bound of TRP given in [8]. See Appendix A.

PROOF OF (3). For any function query $\mathcal{O}(x,0)$ and for any $y \in \{0,1\}^{n-m}$, the probability that $\mathcal{O}(x,0) = y$ is upper bounded by

$$\frac{2^m}{2^n - (q_F + q_S)} \leq \frac{1}{2^{n-m-1}}.$$

Let X be a random variable that follows the binomial distribution with parameters q_F and $p = 1/2^{n-m-1}$, namely,

$$\Pr[X = j] = \binom{q_F}{j} p^j (1-p)^{q_F - j}$$

for $j = 0, \ldots, q_F$. Then for any $y \in \{0,1\}^{n-m}$, we have

$$\Pr[F_y \geq j] \leq \Pr[X \geq j].$$

By the Chernoff bound, we have

$$\Pr[X \geq j] \leq e^{-\frac{j - p q_F}{3}} \leq \frac{p}{2q_F}$$

for any $j \geq 2p q_F + 3 \ln \frac{2q_F}{p}$. Therefore we have

$$\mathbf{Ex}\left[\max_y F_y\right] = \sum_{j \geq 1} \Pr\left[\max_y F_y \geq j\right]$$

$$\leq 2p q_F + 3 \ln \frac{2q_F}{p} + \sum_{j > 2p q_F + 3 \ln \frac{2q_F}{p}} \Pr\left[\max_y \Gamma_y \geq j\right]$$

$$= 2p q_F + 3 \ln \frac{2q_F}{p} + \sum_{j > 2p q_F + 3 \ln \frac{2q_F}{p}} \Pr\left[\bigvee_{y \in \{0,1\}^{n-m}} F_y \geq j\right]$$

$$\leq 2p q_F + 3 \ln \frac{2q_F}{p} + \sum_{y \in \{0,1\}^{n-m}} \sum_{j > 2p q_F + 3 \ln \frac{2q_F}{p}} \Pr[X \geq j]$$

$$\leq 2p q_F + 3 \ln \frac{2q_F}{p} + 2^{n-m} \cdot q_F \cdot \frac{p}{2q_F}$$

$$\leq \frac{q_F}{2^{n-m-2}} + 3 \ln q_F + 3(n-m) + 1.$$

3.2   Public Indifferentiability of TRP

We define a simulator S which is stateful, keeping variables $\mathcal{O}(u)$ and $\mathcal{O}^{-1}(v)$ for every u and $v \in \{0,1\}^n$, all initialized as $\bot$, meaning "undefined", as well as sets $\mathcal{D}$, $\mathcal{R}$, and $\mathcal{R}_y$ for each $y \in \{0,1\}^{n-m}$, all initialized as empty. It also uses a special symbol ⊛ (not in $\{0,1\}^{n-m}$). We will call oracle queries $\mathcal{O}(u,+)$ (resp. $\mathcal{O}(v,-)$) *fresh* if $\mathcal{O}(u) = \bot$ (resp. $\mathcal{O}^{-1}(v) = \bot$).

- On a fresh forward query $\mathcal{O}(u, +)$, S does the following.

  1. If $u = c \,\|\, x$ for some $x \in \{0,1\}^{n-\ell}$ (i.e., $u \in \mathcal{C}$), then obtain $y = \mathsf{F}(x)$ via an oracle query to F.

     (a) If $\mathcal{R}_y \neq \{0,1\}^m$, then

         i. choose w uniformly at random from $\{0,1\}^m \setminus \mathcal{R}_y$;

         ii. assign $w \,\|\, y$ and u to $\mathcal{O}(u)$ and $\mathcal{O}^{-1}(w \,\|\, y)$, respectively;

         iii. update $\mathcal{D}$, $\mathcal{R}$ and $\mathcal{R}_y$ as $\mathcal{D} \cup \{u\}$, $\mathcal{R} \cup \{w \,\|\, y\}$ and $\mathcal{R}_y \cup \{w\}$, respectively;

         iv. return $\mathcal{O}(u)$.

     (b) If $\mathcal{R}_y = \{0,1\}^m$, then return $\circledast \,\|\, y$.

  2. If $u \notin \mathcal{C}$, then

     (a) choose v uniformly at random from $\{0,1\}^n \setminus \mathcal{R}$;

     (b) assign v and u to $\mathcal{O}(u)$ and $\mathcal{O}^{-1}(v)$, respectively;

     (c) update $\mathcal{D}$, $\mathcal{R}$ and $\mathcal{R}_y$ as $\mathcal{D} \cup \{u\}$, $\mathcal{R} \cup \{v\}$ and $\mathcal{R}_y \cup \{w\}$, respectively, where $v = w \,\|\, y$ for $w \in \{0,1\}^m$ and $y \in \{0,1\}^{n-m}$;

     (d) return $\mathcal{O}(u)$.

- On a fresh backward query $\mathcal{O}(v, -)$, S does the following.

  1. Choose u uniformly at random from $\{0,1\}^n \setminus (\mathcal{D} \cup \mathcal{C})$.

  2. Assign v and u to $\mathcal{O}(u)$ and $\mathcal{O}^{-1}(v)$, respectively.

  3. Update $\mathcal{D}$, $\mathcal{R}$ and $\mathcal{R}_y$ as $\mathcal{D} \cup \{u\}$, $\mathcal{R} \cup \{v\}$ and $\mathcal{R}_y \cup \{w\}$, respectively, where $v = w \,\|\, y$ for $w \in \{0,1\}^m$ and $y \in \{0,1\}^{n-m}$.

  4. Return $\mathcal{O}^{-1}(v)$.

- On a forward query $\mathcal{O}(u, +)$ (resp. a backward query $\mathcal{O}(v, -)$) which is not fresh, S returns $\mathcal{O}(u)$ (resp. $\mathcal{O}^{-1}(v)$).

In the public indifferentiability model, the simulator knows all queries made by the distinguisher to F. When a distinguisher makes a function query $\mathcal{O}(x, 0)$, S will behave exactly in the same manner as it would have done with a forward query $\mathcal{O}(c \,\|\, x, +)$, except returning the response.

Theorem 2. *Let S be the simulator defined as above, and let q_F and q_S be positive integers such that $q_F + q_S \leq 2^{n-1}$. Then for any distinguisher $\mathcal{A}$ making q_F queries to the outer construction and q_S queries to the inner primitive,*

$$\boldsymbol{Adv}_{\mathrm{TRP,S}}^{\mathrm{pub}}(\mathcal{A}) \leq \begin{cases} \left(\frac{(q_F + q_S)^3}{2^{n+m-1}} \right)^{\frac{1}{2}} + \frac{q_S}{2^{\ell - 1}} & \text{if } q_F + q_S < 2^m, \\ \left(\frac{5(q_F + q_S)^2}{2^{n+1}} \right)^{\frac{1}{2}} + \frac{q_S}{2^{\ell - 1}} & \text{otherwise.} \end{cases}$$

Proof. By the definition of the simulator, we can assume that $\mathcal{A}$ makes a forward query $\mathcal{O}(c \,\|\, x, +)$ and then truncates the leftmost m bits (or $\circledast$) of the response when it wants to obtain $\mathcal{O}(x, 0)$; this modification would not degrade the adversarial distinguishing advantage. So we can remove the oracle interface $\mathcal{O}(\cdot, 0)$ in both the simulated world and the real world. Instead, the number of forward queries and backward queries should be upper bounded by $q_F + q_S$ and q_S, respectively. We can still assume that $\mathcal{A}$ does not make redundant queries.

Let $\mathcal{S}_0 = \mathsf{S}[\mathsf{F}]$ and $\mathcal{S}_2 = \mathsf{P}$ denote the simulated world and the real world, respectively. As in the regular indifferentiability proof, we introduce an intermediate world, denoted $\mathcal{S}_1$, that has the same oracle interface as $\mathcal{S}_0$ and $\mathcal{S}_2$. This random system uses a flag, denoted bad and initialized as false, and keeps sets $\mathcal{D}$ and $\mathcal{R}$, all initialized as empty. Oracle queries to $\mathcal{S}_1$ are answered as follows.

– On a forward query $\mathcal{O}(u, +)$, $\mathcal{S}_1$ does the following.
  1. Choose v uniformly at random from $\{0, 1\}^n \setminus \mathcal{R}$.
  2. Update $\mathcal{D}$ and $\mathcal{R}$ as $\mathcal{D} \cup \{u\}$ and $\mathcal{R} \cup \{v\}$, respectively.
  3. Return v.
– On a backward query $\mathcal{O}(v, -)$, $\mathcal{S}_1$ does the following.
  1. Choose u uniformly at random from $\{0, 1\}^n \setminus \mathcal{D}$.
  2. if $u \in \mathcal{C}$, then set bad to true, and choose u uniformly at random from $\{0, 1\}^n \setminus (\mathcal{D} \cup \mathcal{C})$.
  3. Update $\mathcal{D}$ and $\mathcal{R}$ as $\mathcal{D} \cup \{u\}$ and $\mathcal{R} \cup \{v\}$, respectively.
  4. Return u.

So $\mathcal{S}_1$ behaves like a truly random permutation except that it does not sample any element of $\mathcal{C}$ on a backward query $\mathcal{O}(\cdot, -)$. Let $q = q_F + q_S$ denote the total number of queries. Then we have

$$\mathbf{Adv}^{\mathsf{pub}}_{\mathsf{TRP}, \mathsf{S}}(\mathcal{A}) \le \| \mathsf{p}^q_{\mathcal{S}_0}(\cdot) - \mathsf{p}^q_{\mathcal{S}_2}(\cdot) \|$$
$$\le \| \mathsf{p}^q_{\mathcal{S}_0}(\cdot) - \mathsf{p}^q_{\mathcal{S}_1}(\cdot) \| + \| \mathsf{p}^q_{\mathcal{S}_1}(\cdot) - \mathsf{p}^q_{\mathcal{S}_2}(\cdot) \|. \tag{11}$$

We will consider a random variable V_y for each $y \in \{0, 1\}^{n-m}$, where

$$V_y = |\{v \in \{0, 1\}^n : v = w \,\|\, y \in \mathcal{R} \text{ for some } w \in \{0, 1\}^m\}|.$$

We also define random variables

$$V = \sum_{y \in \{0,1\}^{n-m}} V_y,$$
$$H = |\{y : V_y = 2^m\}|.$$

It is easy to see that $V = |\mathcal{D}| = |\mathcal{R}|$ at any point during the attack.

UPPER BOUNDING $\| \mathsf{p}^q_{\mathcal{S}_1}(\cdot) - \mathsf{p}^q_{\mathcal{S}_2}(\cdot) \|$. The system $\mathcal{S}_1$ behaves exactly like the real world $\mathcal{S}_2$ without the bad flag bad being set to true. So we can upper bound $\| \mathsf{p}^q_{\mathcal{S}_1}(\cdot) - \mathsf{p}^q_{\mathcal{S}_2}(\cdot) \|$ by the probability that bad is set to true.

For $i = 1, \ldots, q_S$, let E_i be the event that the i-th backward query sets bad to true. Since $|\mathcal{C}| = 2^{n-\ell}$ and $|\mathcal{D}| \le q \le 2^{n-1}$, we have

$$\Pr[\mathsf{E}_i] = \frac{|\mathcal{C}|}{2^n - |\mathcal{D}|} \le \frac{2^{n-\ell}}{2^{n-1}} = \frac{1}{2^{\ell-1}}$$

for each $i = 1, \ldots, qs$. Therefore, we have

$$\|\mathsf{p}_{\mathcal{S}_1}^q(\cdot) - \mathsf{p}_{\mathcal{S}_2}^q(\cdot)\| \leq \Pr\left[\bigvee_{i=1}^{qs} \mathsf{E}_i\right] \leq \sum_{i=1}^{qs} \Pr\left[\mathsf{E}_i\right] \leq \frac{qs}{2^{\ell-1}}. \tag{12}$$

UPPER BOUNDING $\|\mathsf{p}_{\mathcal{S}_0}^q(\cdot) - \mathsf{p}_{\mathcal{S}_1}^q(\cdot)\|$. For the intermediate system $\mathcal{S}_1$, we can easily check that the support of $\mathsf{p}_{\mathcal{S}_1}^{i-1}(\cdot)$ is contained in the support of $\mathsf{p}_{\mathcal{S}_0}^{i-1}(\cdot)$ for $i = 1, \ldots, q$, allowing us to use the χ^2 method. Any element of $\{\circledast\} \times \{0,1\}^{n-m}$ is returned only in $\mathbf{S}_0$.

Let $\Omega = \{0,1\}^n \cup (\{\circledast\} \times \{0,1\}^{n-m})$. For fixed $i \in \{1, \ldots, q\}$ and $\mathbf{z} \in \Omega^{i-1}$ such $\mathsf{p}_{\mathcal{S}_1}^{i-1}(\mathbf{z}) > 0$, we will compute

$$\chi^2(\mathbf{z}) = \sum_{\substack{z \in \Omega \text{ such that} \\ \mathsf{p}_{\mathcal{S}_0,i}^{\mathbf{z}}(z) > 0}} \frac{\left(\mathsf{p}_{\mathcal{S}_1,i}^{\mathbf{z}}(z) - \mathsf{p}_{\mathcal{S}_0,i}^{\mathbf{z}}(z)\right)^2}{\mathsf{p}_{\mathcal{S}_0,i}^{\mathbf{z}}(z)}.$$

The previous queries $\mathbf{z} \in \Omega^{i-1}$ determine random variables H, $V(= i - 1)$ as well as the type of the next query. We will distinguish three cases: a forward query $\mathcal{O}(u, +)$ for $u \in \mathcal{C}$, a forward query $\mathcal{O}(u, +)$ for $u \notin \mathcal{C}$, and a backward query $\mathcal{O}(v, -)$.

Suppose that the i-th query is a forward query $\mathcal{O}(u, +)$, where $u \in \mathcal{C}$. If $z = \circledast \parallel y$ for $y \in \{0,1\}^{n-m}$ such that $|\mathcal{R}_y| = 2^{n-m}$, then

$$\mathsf{p}_{\mathcal{S}_0,i}^{\mathbf{z}}(z) = \frac{1}{2^{n-m}},$$

$$\mathsf{p}_{\mathcal{S}_1,i}^{\mathbf{z}}(z) = 0.$$

If $z \in \{0,1\}^n \setminus \mathcal{R}$, then

$$\mathsf{p}_{\mathcal{S}_0,i}^{\mathbf{z}}(z) = \frac{1}{2^{n-m}} \cdot \frac{1}{2^m - V_y},$$

$$\mathsf{p}_{\mathcal{S}_1,i}^{\mathbf{z}}(z) = \frac{1}{2^n - V}.$$

Since the number of elements $y \in \{0,1\}^{n-m}$ such that $|\mathcal{R}_y| = 2^{n-m}$ is H, we have

$$\chi^2(\mathbf{z}) = \frac{H}{2^{n-m}} + \sum_{z \in \{0,1\}^n \setminus \mathcal{R}} \frac{(2^{n-m} V_y - V)^2}{(2^n - V)^2 (2^n - 2^{n-m} V_y)}. \tag{13}$$

For each $y \in \{0,1\}^{n-m}$, the number of elements $w \in \{0,1\}^m$ such that $w \parallel y \in \{0,1\}^n \setminus \mathcal{R}$ is $2^m - V_y$. Furthermore, $\sum_{y \in \{0,1\}^{n-m}} V_y = V$ and $V_y \leq 2^m$ for every $y \in \{0,1\}^{n-m}$. Therefore we have

$$\sum_{z\in\{0,1\}^n\setminus\mathcal{R}} \frac{(2^{n-m}V_y - V)^2}{(2^n - V)^2(2^n - 2^{n-m}V_y)} = \sum_{y\in\{0,1\}^{n-m}} \frac{(2^{n-m}V_y - V)^2}{2^{n-m}(2^n - V)^2}$$

$$= \frac{2^{n-m}}{(2^n - V)^2}\left(\sum_{y\in\{0,1\}^{n-m}} V_y^2 - \frac{V^2}{2^{n-m}}\right)$$

$$\leq \frac{1}{2^{n+m-2}} \sum_{y\in\{0,1\}^{n-m}} V_y^2$$

$$\leq \frac{\min\{V^2, 2^m V\}}{2^{n+m-2}}$$

$$\leq \frac{\min\{q^2, 2^m q\}}{2^{n+m-2}}. \tag{14}$$

Since $H \leq \lfloor \frac{V}{2^m} \rfloor$ and $V \leq q$, we have $\frac{H}{2^{n-m}} = 0$ if $q < 2^m$, and $\frac{H}{2^{n-m}} \leq \frac{q}{2^n}$ otherwise. By (13) and (14), we conclude that

$$\chi^2(\mathbf{z}) \leq \begin{cases} \frac{q^2}{2^{n+m-2}} & \text{if } q < 2^m, \\ \frac{5q}{2^n} & \text{otherwise.} \end{cases} \tag{15}$$

Suppose that the i-th query is a forward query $\mathcal{O}(u, +)$, where $u \notin C$. For any $z \in \{0,1\}^n \setminus \mathcal{R}$ we have

$$p_{\mathcal{S}_0,i}^{\mathbf{z}}(z) = p_{\mathcal{S}_1,i}^{\mathbf{z}}(z) = \frac{1}{2^n - V},$$

and hence

$$\chi^2(\mathbf{z}) = 0. \tag{16}$$

Suppose that the i-th query is a backward query $\mathcal{O}(v, -)$. For any $z \in \{0,1\}^n \setminus (\mathcal{D} \cup \mathcal{C})$ we have

$$p_{\mathcal{S}_0,i}^{\mathbf{z}}(z) = p_{\mathcal{S}_1,i}^{\mathbf{z}}(z) = \frac{1}{2^n - |\mathcal{D} \cup \mathcal{C}|},$$

and hence

$$\chi^2(\mathbf{z}) = 0. \tag{17}$$

By (15), (16), (17), we have

$$\|p_{\mathcal{S}_0}^q(\cdot) - p_{\mathcal{S}_1}^q(\cdot)\| \leq \left(\frac{1}{2}\sum_{i=1}^{q} \mathbf{Ex}\left[\chi^2(\mathbf{z})\right]\right)^{\frac{1}{2}}$$

$$\leq \begin{cases} \left(\frac{q^3}{2^{n+m-1}}\right)^{\frac{1}{2}} & \text{if } q < 2^m, \\ \left(\frac{5q^2}{2^{n+1}}\right)^{\frac{1}{2}} & \text{otherwise.} \end{cases} \tag{18}$$

By (11), (12), (18), the proof is complete. □

4   Tightness of Regular Indifferentiability

We can prove that our regular indifferentiability bound is tight with respect to the total number of queries $q = q_F + q_S$ when $m + \ell \ll n$. Note that if $m + \ell \ll n$ then $\min\{m, \ell\} \leq \frac{n+m}{3}$. We will assume that the number of F-queries that a simulator makes for each query of the distinguisher is a polynomial in n, denoted $\texttt{poly}(n)$.

First, suppose that $m \leq \ell$. In this case, we consider a distinguisher $\mathcal{A}$ that begins the attack by obtaining $y = F(x)$ for a random element x via a function query to F. Then $\mathcal{A}$ makes 2^m backward queries at $w \parallel y$, where $w \in \{0, 1\}^m$. With high probability, $\mathcal{A}$ should be able to obtain $c \parallel x$ for some $x \in \{0, 1\}^{n-\ell}$ as a response if the simulator faithfully reproduces $(\mathsf{TRP}[\mathsf{P}], \mathsf{P})$. Furthermore, it should be the case that $F(x) = y$, while it is infeasible for the simulator to find a preimage of y under F (without any information of the adversarial function query) using at most 2^m queries to F if $\texttt{poly}(n) \cdot 2^m \ll 2^{n-\ell}$. So we conclude that if $m + \ell \ll n$ then there is no simulator which is secure against any distinguisher that makes about 2^m simulator queries.

Next, suppose that $\ell \leq m$. In this attack, a distinguisher $\mathcal{A}$ randomly chooses an element $y \in \{0, 1\}^{n-m}$, and makes 2^ℓ backward queries at $w \parallel y$, where $w \in \{0, 1\}^m$. With high probability, $\mathcal{A}$ will obtain $c \parallel x$ for some $x \in \{0, 1\}^{n-\ell}$ as a response if the simulator behaves like a random permutation. Furthermore, it should be the case that $F(x) = y$. In this way, $\mathcal{A}$ is able to find a preimage of y under F using at most 2^ℓ queries to F, which is infeasible if $\texttt{poly}(n) \cdot 2^\ell \ll 2^{n-m}$. So we conclude that if $m + \ell \ll n$ then there is no simulator which is secure against any distinguisher that makes about 2^ℓ simulator queries. Note that the second attack holds even in the public indifferentiability setting.

A   Indistinguishability of TRP

A *hypergeometric random distribution* $\mathsf{HG}_{N,M,q}$, parameterized by N, M, and q, is a probability distribution that describes the probability that exactly k elements are selected from a subset of M "good" elements when q elements are selected from the universe of N elements without replacement; this probability is precisely $\binom{M}{k}\binom{N-M}{n-k}/\binom{N}{n}$.

If a distinguisher makes no simulator query (namely, $q_S = 0$) when it interacts with $\mathcal{S}_1$ in the regular indifferentiability setting, then V_y would follow the hypergeometric distribution with $N = 2^n$, $M = 2^m$ and $q = i - 1(= V)$. In this case, it is well known that

$$\mathbf{Ex}[V_y] = \frac{V}{2^{n-m}},$$

$$\mathbf{Var}[V_y] = \frac{2^m(2^n - 2^m)(2^n - V)V}{2^{2n}(2^n - 1)}.$$

Since

$$\mathbf{Var}[V_y] = \mathbf{Ex}[V_y^2] - \mathbf{Ex}[V_y]^2,$$

and

$$\sum_{y \in \{0,1\}^{n-m}} \mathbf{Var}[V_y] \leq 2^{n-m} \left(\frac{2^m(2^n - 2^m)(2^n - V)V}{2^{2n}(2^n - 1)} \right)$$

$$\leq \frac{2^m(2^n - 2^m)V}{2^{n+m}}$$

$$\leq V \leq q_F,$$

we have

$$\mathbf{Ex}\left[\sum_y \frac{(2^{n-m}V_y - V)^2}{2^{n-m}(2^n - V)^2} \right] \leq \frac{1}{2^{n+m-2}} \sum_{y \in \{0,1\}^{n-m}} \left(\mathbf{Ex}\left[V_y^2\right] - \mathbf{Ex}\left[V_y\right]^2 \right)$$

$$\leq \frac{q_F}{2^{n+m-2}}.$$

Plugging this into (9), we obtain the indistinguishability bound of TRP as follows.

$$\mathbf{Adv}_{\mathsf{TRP}}^{\mathsf{ind}}(\mathcal{A}) \leq \frac{q}{2^{\frac{n+m-1}{2}}},$$

for any distinguisher $\mathcal{A}$ making q queries.

References

1. Bellare, M., Impagliazzo, R.: A tool for obtaining tighter security analyses of pseudorandom function based constructions, with applications to PRP to PRF conversion. In: IACR Cryptology ePrint Archive 1999/024 (1999)
2. Bellare, M., Krovetz, T., Rogaway, P.: Luby-Rackoff backwards: increasing security by making block ciphers non-invertible. In: Nyberg, K. (ed.) EUROCRYPT 1998. LNCS, vol. 1403, pp. 266–280. Springer, Heidelberg (1998). https://doi.org/10.1007/BFb0054132
3. Bhattacharya, S., Nandi, M.: Full indifferentiable security of the Xor of two or more random permutations using the χ^2 method. In: Nielsen, J.B., Rijmen, V. (eds.) EUROCRYPT 2018. LNCS, vol. 10820, pp. 387–412. Springer, Cham (2018). https://doi.org/10.1007/978-3-319-78381-9_15
4. Cogliati, B., Lampe, R., Patarin, J.: The indistinguishability of the XOR of k permutations. In: Cid, C., Rechberger, C. (eds.) FSE 2014. LNCS, vol. 8540, pp. 285–302. Springer, Heidelberg (2015). https://doi.org/10.1007/978-3-662-46706-0_15
5. Dai, W., Hoang, V.T., Tessaro, S.: Information-theoretic indistinguishability via the chi-squared method. In: Katz, J., Shacham, H. (eds.) CRYPTO 2017. LNCS, vol. 10403, pp. 497–523. Springer, Cham (2017). https://doi.org/10.1007/978-3-319-63697-9_17

6. Dodis, Y., Reyzin, L., Rivest, R.L., Shen, E.: Indifferentiability of permutation-based compression functions and tree-based modes of operation, with applications to MD6. In: Dunkelman, O. (ed.) FSE 2009. LNCS, vol. 5665, pp. 104–121. Springer, Heidelberg (2009). https://doi.org/10.1007/978-3-642-03317-9_7

7. Dodis, Y., Ristenpart, T., Shrimpton, T.: Salvaging Merkle-Damgård for practical applications. In: Joux, A. (ed.) EUROCRYPT 2009. LNCS, vol. 5479, pp. 371–388. Springer, Heidelberg (2009). https://doi.org/10.1007/978-3-642-01001-9_22

8. Gilboa, S., Gueron, S., Morris, B.: How many queries are needed to distinguish a truncated random permutation from a random function? J. Cryptol. **31**(1), 162–171 (2018)

9. Gueron, S., Langley, A., Lindell, Y.: AES-GCM-SIV: Specification and Analysis. IACR Cryptology ePrint Archive 2017:168 (2017)

10. Gueron, S., Lindell, Y.: GCM-SIV: full nonce misuse-resistant authenticated encryption at under one cycle per byte. In: Proceedings of the 22nd ACM SIGSAC Conference on Computer and Communications Security, pp. 109–119 (2015)

11. Hall, C., Wagner, D., Kelsey, J., Schneier, B.: Building PRFs from PRPs. In: Krawczyk, H. (ed.) CRYPTO 1998. LNCS, vol. 1462, pp. 370–389. Springer, Heidelberg (1998). https://doi.org/10.1007/BFb0055742

12. Iwata, T., Seurin, Y.: Reconsidering the security bound of AES-GCM-SIV. IACR Transactions on Symmetric Cryptology, pp. 240–267 (2017)

13. Lee, J.: Indifferentiability of the sum of random permutations toward optimal security. IEEE Trans. Inf. Theory **63**(6), 4050–4054 (2017)

14. Lucks, S.: The sum of PRPs is a secure PRF. In: Preneel, B. (ed.) EUROCRYPT 2000. LNCS, vol. 1807, pp. 470–484. Springer, Heidelberg (2000). https://doi.org/10.1007/3-540-45539-6_34

15. Mandal, A., Patarin, J., Nachef, V.: Indifferentiability beyond the Birthday Bound for the Xor of Two public random permutations. In: Gong, G., Gupta, K.C. (eds.) INDOCRYPT 2010. LNCS, vol. 6498, pp. 69–81. Springer, Heidelberg (2010). https://doi.org/10.1007/978-3-642-17401-8_6

16. Mandal, A., Patarin, J., Seurin, Y.: On the public indifferentiability and correlation intractability of the 6-round Feistel construction. In: Cramer, R. (ed.) TCC 2012. LNCS, vol. 7194, pp. 285–302. Springer, Heidelberg (2012). https://doi.org/10.1007/978-3-642-28914-9_16

17. Maurer, U., Renner, R., Holenstein, C.: Indifferentiability, impossibility results on reductions, and applications to the random oracle methodology. In: Naor, M. (ed.) TCC 2004. LNCS, vol. 2951, pp. 21–39. Springer, Heidelberg (2004). https://doi.org/10.1007/978-3-540-24638-1_2

18. Mennink, B.: Linking Stam's bounds with generalized truncation. In: Matsui, M. (ed.) CT-RSA 2019. LNCS, vol. 11405, pp. 313–329. Springer, Cham (2019). https://doi.org/10.1007/978-3-030-12612-4_16

19. Mennink, B., Preneel, B.: On the XOR of multiple random permutations. In: Malkin, T., Kolesnikov, V., Lewko, A.B., Polychronakis, M. (eds.) ACNS 2015. LNCS, vol. 9092, pp. 619–634. Springer, Cham (2015). https://doi.org/10.1007/978-3-319-28166-7_30

20. Patarin, J.: A proof of security in $O(2^n)$ for the Xor of two random permutations. In: Safavi-Naini, R. (ed.) ICITS 2008. LNCS, vol. 5155, pp. 232–248. Springer, Heidelberg (2008). https://doi.org/10.1007/978-3-540-85093-9_22

21. Shrimpton, T., Stam, M.: Building a collision-resistant compression function from non-compressing primitives. In: Aceto, L., Damgård, I., Goldberg, L.A., Halldórsson, M.M., Ingólfsdóttir, A., Walukiewicz, I. (eds.) ICALP 2008. LNCS, vol. 5126, pp. 643–654. Springer, Heidelberg (2008). https://doi.org/10.1007/978-3-540-70583-3_52

22. Yoneyama, K., Miyagawa, S., Ohta, K.: Leaky random oracle (Extended Abstract). In: Baek, J., Bao, F., Chen, K., Lai, X. (eds.) ProvSec 2008. LNCS, vol. 5324, pp. 226–240. Springer, Heidelberg (2008). https://doi.org/10.1007/978-3-540-88733-1_16

Anomalies and Vector Space Search: Tools for S-Box Analysis

Xavier Bonnetain[1,2], Léo Perrin[1(✉)], and Shizhu Tian[1,3,4]

[1] Inria, Paris, France
{xavier.bonnetain,leo.perrin}@inria.fr
[2] Collège Doctoral, Sorbonne Université, Paris, France
[3] State Key Laboratory of Information Security, Institute of Information Engineering, Chinese Academy of Sciences, Beijing, China
tianshizhu@iie.ac.cn
[4] School of Cyber Security, University of Chinese Academy of Sciences, Beijing, China

Abstract. S-boxes are functions with an input so small that the simplest way to specify them is their lookup table (LUT). How can we quantify the distance between the behavior of a given S-box and that of an S-box picked uniformly at random?

To answer this question, we introduce various "anomalies". These real numbers are such that a property with an anomaly equal to a should be found roughly once in a set of 2^a random S-boxes. First, we present statistical anomalies based on the distribution of the coefficients in the difference distribution table, linear approximation table, and for the first time, the boomerang connectivity table.

We then count the number of S-boxes that have block-cipher like structures to estimate the anomaly associated to those. In order to recover these structures, we show that the most general tool for decomposing S-boxes is an algorithm efficiently listing all the vector spaces of a given dimension contained in a given set, and we present such an algorithm.

Combining these approaches, we conclude that all permutations that are *actually* picked uniformly at random always have essentially the same cryptographic properties and the same lack of structure.

Keywords: S-box · Vector space search · BCT · Shannon effect · Anomaly · Boolean functions

1 Introduction

S-boxes are small functions with an input small enough that they can be specified by their lookup tables. If F is an S-box with an n-bit input then it is feasible to describe it using only the sequence $F(0), F(1), ..., F(2^n - 1)$ since, in the vast majority of the cases, $3 \leq n \leq 8$. S-boxes can therefore correspond to arbitrarily

---

The full version of this paper is available on **eprint** (report 2019/528) [10].

ⓒ International Association for Cryptologic Research 2019
S. D. Galbraith and S. Moriai (Eds.): ASIACRYPT 2019, LNCS 11921, pp. 196–223, 2019.
https://doi.org/10.1007/978-3-030-34578-5_8

complex functions. In practice, such components are the only source of non-linearity of many symmetric primitives. Most prominently, the AES [1] uses an 8-bit bijective S-box.

The aim of a block cipher is to simulate a *pseudo-random permutation (PRP)*, meaning that it should not be possible for an attacker given a black box access to a block cipher with a secret key and to a permutation picked uniformly at random to figure out which is which. In this context, it might a priori make intuitive sense for block cipher designers to use (pseudo-)random components to design their algorithm. However, this approach would have substantial short-comings in practice. For example, a random S-box is a priori hard to implement in hardware, random components are unlikely to yield an easy to analyze cipher, their mediocre properties may imply a higher number of rounds (which would slow the cipher down), and the seeds used to generate its random components would have to be published.

Instead, in practice, S-boxes are *constructed* taking multiple design require-ments into account. For example, the mathematical properties of this compo-nent can be leveraged to prove that an algorithm is safe from differential [2] or linear [29] cryptanalysis. At the same time, the S-box may be intended to be implemented in hardware or in a bit-sliced fashion, in which case it is necessary to give it a specific structure that will ease such implementations.

While it is easy to compare the properties of two given S-boxes (we can simply compute them and then rank them), it is not trivial to quantify how different they are from an S-box picked uniformly at random with regard to each of their properties. Informally, the comparison with such an "ideal" object will quantify the *distance* between an S-box and random ones: if the property of the studied S-box is unlikely to occur by chance, then it means that the S-box is much better (or much worse) than average. In this paper, we build upon a framework introduced in [6] to provide both definitions and practical means to compute such probabilities.

Let $\mathfrak{S}_{2^n}$ be the set of all n-bit permutations and let $F \in \mathfrak{S}_{2^n}$. As mentioned above, there are two sets of properties that are relevant when investigating S-boxes: how good their cryptographic properties are and whether or not they have some structure. Hence, in order to compare F with a random S-box, we need to be able to answer the following two questions.

1. What is the probability that an S-box picked uniformly in $\mathfrak{S}_{2^n}$ has differen-tial/linear properties at least as good as those of F?
2. How can we recover the structure of F (if it has any)?

Answering the first question can also help us better understand the properties of random permutations and thus to better estimate the advantage of an adversary trying to distinguish a (round-reduced) block cipher from a random permutation.

On the other hand, the second one is related to so-called *white-box cryptog-raphy*, i.e. to implementation techniques that will hide a secret from an attacker with a total access to the implementation of the algorithm. In practice, in order to try and hide for instance an AES key, the attacker will only be given access to an implementation relying on big lookup tables that hide the details of the computations. Recovering the original structure of these tables can also be seen as a particular case of S-box reverse-engineering in the sense of [6].

1.1 Our Contributions

A Key Concept: Anomalies. We answer the two questions asked above using different variants of a unique approach based on what we call *anomalies.* Intuitively, an anomaly is a real number that quantifies how unlikely a property is. For example, there are very few differentially-6 uniform 8-bit permutations,[1] meaning that the anomaly of this property should be high. However, we could argue that what matters in this case is not just the number of differentially-6 uniform permutations but the number of permutations with a differential uniformity *at most* equal to 6. In light of this, we define anomalies as follows.

Definition 1 (Anomaly). *Let $F \in \mathfrak{S}_{2^n}$ and let P be a function mapping $\mathfrak{S}_{2^n}$ to a partially ordered set. The* anomaly *of $P(F)$ is defined as $\mathsf{A}\left(P(F)\right) = -\log_2\left(\Pr\left[P(G) \le P(F)\right]\right)$, where the probability is taken over $G \in \mathfrak{S}_{2^n}$. We can equivalently write*

$$\mathsf{A}\left(P(F)\right) \;=\; -\log_2\left(\frac{\left|\{G \in \mathfrak{S}_{2^n}, P(G) \le P(F)\}\right|}{|\mathfrak{S}_{2^n}|}\right).$$

The negative anomaly *of $P(F)$ is $\overline{\mathsf{A}}\left(P(F)\right) = -\log_2\left(\Pr\left[P(G) \ge P(F)\right]\right)$.*

Regardless of P, we always have $2^{-\mathsf{A}(P(F))} + 2^{-\overline{\mathsf{A}}(P(F))} = 1 + \Pr\left[P(G) = P(F)\right]$.

In the example given above, P is simply the function returning the differential uniformity of a permutation. The anomaly of the differential uniformity then gets higher as the differential uniformity of F decreases under the median differential uniformity as there are fewer permutations with a low differential uniformity. At the same time, the *negative anomaly* of the differential uniformity increases as the differential uniformity increases above its median value. To put it differently, the anomaly of $P(F)$ quantifies how many S-boxes are at least as good[2] as F in terms of P, and the negative one how many are at least as bad as F. In this paper, we study different anomalies and design new tools that allow their estimation for any S-box.

A property with a high anomaly can be seen as distinguisher in the usual sense, i.e. it is a property that differentiates the object studied from one picked uniformly at random. However, unlike usual distinguishers, we do not care about the amount of data needed to estimate the probabilities corresponding to the anomalies.

---

[1] We formally define differential uniformity later. All that is needed in this discussion is that the differential uniformity is an integer which is better when lower.

[2] In this paper, the properties P considered are better when lower.

Statistical Anomalies. In [6] and [34], the notions of "differential" and "linear" anomalies were introduced. Definition 1 is indeed a generalization of them. They are based on properties P that correspond to how good the differential and linear properties are. In Sect. 2, we generalize this analysis to take into account the corresponding negative anomalies, and we introduce the use of the so-called *Boomerang Connectivity Table (BCT)* [17] for this purpose. To this end, we establish the distribution of the coefficients of the BCT of a random permutation. As an added bonus, this new result allows a better estimation of the advantage of an adversary in a boomerang attack.

Structural Anomalies. Anomalies can also be related to the presence of a structure. For example, for n-bit Boolean functions, the existence of a simple circuit evaluating a function is unlikely:

> "almost all functions" of n arguments have "an almost identical" complexity which is asymptotically equal to the complexity of the most complex function of n arguments.

This statement of Lupanov [28] summarizes the so-called *Shannon effect* [39]. In other words, the existence of a short description is an unlikely event for a Boolean function. Here, we generalize this observation to permutations of $\mathbb{F}_2^n$ and construct anomalies that capture how "structured" an S-box is.

In Sect. 3, we present an estimation of the number of permutations that can be constructed using common S-box generation methods (multiplicative inverse, Feistel networks...) and derive the corresponding anomalies. In order to identify these anomalies, it is necessary to recover said structures when they are unknown. We present a simple approach applicable to inversion-based S-boxes that we successfully apply to the 8-bit S-box of the leaked German cipher Chiasmus. In other cases, we show that the detection of structures with a high anomaly can be performed using a vector space search.

Vector Space Search. We provide an efficient algorithm performing this search: given a set S of elements of $\{0,1\}^n$ and an integer d, this algorithm returns all the vector spaces of dimension d that are fully contained in S. We present it in Sect. 4. While such an algorithm is needed when looking for a structure in an S-box, we expect it to find applications beyond this area.

1.2 Mathematical Background

Boolean Functions. Let $\mathbb{F}_2 = \{0,1\}$. In what follows, we consider the following subsets of the set of all functions mapping $\mathbb{F}_2^n$ to itself.

- Recall that the set of all n-bit permutations is denoted $\mathfrak{S}_{2^n}$. It contains $2^n!$ elements. The compositional inverse of $F \in \mathfrak{S}_{2^n}$ is denoted F^{-1}.
- The set of all n-bit linear permutations is denoted $\mathcal{L}_{2^n}$. Its size is such that $|\mathcal{L}_{2^n}| = \prod_{i=0}^{n-1}(2^n - 2^i)$.

For elements of $\mathbb{F}_2^n$, "+" denotes the characteristic-2 addition, i.e. the XOR. In cases that might be ambiguous, we use "$\oplus$" to denote this operation.

Let $F \in \mathfrak{S}_{2^n}$ be an S-box. Many of its cryptographic properties can be described using $2^n \times 2^n$ tables: the LAT, DDT and BCT. They are defined below.

The *Linear Approximation Table (LAT)* of F is the table $\mathcal{W}_F$ with coefficients $\mathcal{W}_F(a, b) = \sum_{x \in \mathbb{F}_2^n} (-1)^{a \cdot x + b \cdot F(x)}$ where $x \cdot y = \bigoplus_{i=0}^{n-1} x_i \times y_i$ is the scalar product of two elements $x = (x_0, ..., x_{n-1}), y = (y_0, ..., y_{n-1}) \in \mathbb{F}_2^n$. Its maximum for $b \neq 0$ is the *linearity* of F and is denoted $\ell(F)$. The LAT is used to study linear cryptanalysis [29,40]. The set of the coordinates of the coefficients equal to 0 plays a special role, as shown in [15]. It is called the *Walsh zeroes* of F and is denoted $\mathcal{Z}_F = \{(a, b) \in (\mathbb{F}_2^n)^2 \mid \mathcal{W}_F(a, b) = 0\} \cup \{(0,0)\}$.

The *Difference Distribution Table (DDT)* of F is the table δ_F with coefficients $\delta_F(a, b) = \#\{x \in \mathbb{F}_2^n, F(x + a) + F(x) = b\}$. Its maximum for $a \neq 0$ is the *differential uniformity* of F and is denoted $u(F)$. The DDT is needed to study differential cryptanalysis [3].

Recently, Cid et al. introduced a new tool which they called *Boomerang Connectivity Table (BCT)* [17]. It is again a $2^n \times 2^n$ table $\mathcal{B}_F$ defined by

$$\mathcal{B}_F(a, b) = \#\{x \in \mathbb{F}_2^n, F^{-1}(F(x) + b) + F^{-1}(F(x + a) + b) = a\} .$$

Its maximum value for $a, b \neq 0$ is the *boomerang uniformity* of F and is denoted β_F. As hinted by its name, the BCT is relevant when studying boomerang attacks [41]. Unlike the DDT and LAT, it is necessary that F is a permutation for the BCT to be well defined.

Statistics. Some of our results rely on both the binomial and Poisson distribution. We denote with Binomial(n, p) the binomial distribution with parameters p and n which correspond respectively to the probability of an event and to the number of trial. It is defined as follows:

$$\Pr[X = i] = \text{Binomial}(i; n, p) = p^i (1 - p)^{n-i} \binom{n}{i} .$$

It has a mean equal to np and a variance of $np(1 - p)$. The Poisson distribution with parameter λ is defined by

$$\Pr[X = i] = \text{Poisson}(i; \lambda) = \frac{e^{-\lambda} \lambda^i}{i!} .$$

The mean value and variance of this distribution are both λ. A binomial distribution with small p can be closely approximated by a Poisson distribution with $\lambda = np$.

2   Statistical Properties

Let us consider a permutation F that is picked uniformly at random from $\mathfrak{S}_{2^n}$ and let us consider one of its tables, i.e. its DDT, LAT or BCT. The coefficients in this table may be connected to one another: for example the sum of the coefficients in a row of the DDT have to sum to 2^n. Yet, in practice, the coefficients act like independent and identically distributed random variables. In Sect. 2.1), we recall what the distributions of the DDT and LAT coefficients are and we establish the distribution of the BCT coefficients.

Then, Sect. 2.2 presents how the knowledge of these distributions can be used to bound the probability that a random permutation has differential/linear/boomerang properties at least as good as those of the S-box investigated. Additionally, we explain in Sect. 2.3 how our newly gained knowledge of the distribution of the BCT coefficients allows a better estimation of the advantage of the attacker in a boomerang attack.

2.1 Coefficient Distributions

In [18], the authors established and experimentally verified the distribution followed by the DDT and LAT coefficients. The distribution of the LAT coefficients was first established in [33] and then provided a different expression in [18]. A more thorough study of the DDT coefficient can be found in [32]. We recall these results in the following two theorems.

Proposition 1 (DDT coefficient distribution *[18]*). *The coefficients in the DDT of a random S-Box of $\mathfrak{S}_{2^n}$ with $n \geq 5$ are independent and identically distributed random variables following a Poisson distribution Poisson(2^{-1}).*

Proposition 2 (LAT coefficient distribution *[18,33]*). *The coefficients in the LAT of a random permutation[3] of $\mathfrak{S}_{2^n}$ are independent and identically distributed random variables with the following probability distribution:*

$$\Pr\left[\mathcal{W}_F(i,j) = 4z\right] = \frac{\binom{2^{n-1}}{2^{n-2}+z}^2}{\binom{2^n}{2^{n-1}}} \ .$$

The situation is the same for the BCT. In order to establish the distribution of the non-trivial coefficients of the BCT of a random permutation, we first recall an alternative definition of the BCT that was introduced in [26].

Proposition 3 (Alternative BCT definition *[26]*). *Let $F \in \mathfrak{S}_{2^n}$ be a permutation. For any $a, b \in \mathbb{F}_2^n$, the entry $\mathcal{B}_F(a,b)$ of the BCT of F is given by the number of solutions in $\mathbb{F}_2^n \times \mathbb{F}_2^n$ of the following system of equations*

$$\begin{cases} F^{-1}(x+b) + F^{-1}(y+b) = a \\ F^{-1}(x) + F^{-1}(y) = a \ . \end{cases} \tag{1}$$

We use this theorem to obtain the distribution of the coefficients in the BCT.

---

[3] The distribution of the coefficients in the LAT of random functions (not permutations) is also provided in [18].

Theorem 1 (BCT coefficient distribution). *If F is picked uniformly at random in $\mathfrak{S}_{2^n}$, then its coefficients with $a, b \neq 0$ can be modeled like independent and identically distributed random variables with the following distribution:*

$$\Pr\left[\mathcal{B}_F(a, b) = c\right] = \sum_{2i_1 + 4i_2 = c} P_1(i_1) P_2(i_2) ,$$

where P_1 and P_2 are stochastic variable following binomial distributions: $P_1(i) = $ Binomial $\left(i; 2^{n-1}, \frac{1}{2^n - 1}\right)$ and $P_2(i) = $ Binomial $\left(i; 2^{2n-2} - 2^{n-1}, \frac{1}{(2^n - 1)^2}\right)$.

Proof. For any $x, y \in \mathbb{F}_2^n$ such that $x \neq y$, we define

$$S_{x,y} = \{(x, y), (y, x), (x + b, y + b), (y + b, x + b)\} ,$$

which is of cardinality 4 unless $x + y = b$, in which case it only contains 2 elements. These sets are such that a pair (x, y) is a solution of System (1) if and only if all the elements in $S_{x,y}$ are as well. In order to prove this theorem, we will partition the set of all pairs of elements of $\mathbb{F}_2^n$ into such sets $S_{x,y}$.

To this end, we consider the following equivalence relation: $(x, y) \sim (x', y')$ if and only if the multisets $S_{x,y}$ and $S_{x',y'}$ are identical. The corresponding equivalence classes are of size 4 except when $x + y = b$, in which case they contain only 2 elements. There are in total 2^{n-1} classes of size 2. As there are $2^n(2^n - 1)$ ordered pairs of elements in $\mathbb{F}_2^n$, we deduce that there are $\left(2^n(2^n - 1) - 2 \times 2^{n-1}\right)/4$ classes of cardinality 4, i.e. $2^{2n-2} - 2^{n-1}$.

Then, in order for System (1) to have exactly c solutions, we need that there exists i_1 solutions in classes of size 4 and i_2 in classes of size 2, where $2i_1 + 4i_2 = c$. We deduce that

$$\Pr\left[\mathcal{B}_F(a, b) = c\right] = \sum_{2i_1 + 4i_2 = c} P_1(i_1) P_2(i_2) ,$$

where $P_1(i_1)$ (respectively $P_2(i_2)$) is the probability that there exists i_1 classes of size 4 (resp. 2) that are solutions of System (1). Let us now prove that the distributions of $P_1(i_1)$ and $P_2(i_2)$ are as stated in the theorem.

Size 2. In this case, it holds that $y = x + b$ so that the lines of System (1) are identical. We assume that $F^{-1}(x) + F^{-1}(x + b) = a$ holds with probability $1/(2^n - 1)$ as $F^{-1}(x) + F^{-1}(x + b)$ can take any value in $\mathbb{F}_2^n \backslash \{0\}$. Since there are 2^{n-1} such pairs, $P_1(i_1)$ corresponds to a binomial distribution with 2^{n-1} repetitions of a Bernoulli trial that succeeds with probability $(2^n - 1)^{-1}$.

Size 4. The two equations of System (1) are now independent. Using the same reasoning as above, we assume that each line holds with probability $1/(2^n - 1)$. Since there are $2^{2n-2} - 2^{n-1}$ such pairs, $P_2(i_2)$ corresponds to a binomial distribution with parameters $2^{2n-2} - 2^{n-1}$ and $(2^n - 1)^{-2}$. $\qquad\square$

2.2   Anomalies in Table Coefficients Distributions

Building upon the general approach presented in [6], we can define several anomalies using the distribution of the coefficients in the tables of a permutation $F \in \mathfrak{S}_{2^n}$. We will then be able to estimate the values of the corresponding anomalies using the distributions derived in the previous section.

Maximum Value. For any table, the maximum absolute value of all coefficients is a natural property to use to construct an anomaly as the integers are ordered. Let $\max_T : \mathfrak{S}_{2^n} \to \mathbb{N}$ be the function mapping a permutation $F \in \mathfrak{S}_{2^n}$ to the maximum absolute value of the non-trivial coefficients in a table T. Then we can use the distributions in Propositions 1 and 2 as well as Theorem 1 to estimate the associated anomalies:

$$\mathsf{A}\left(\max_T(F)\right) = -(2^n - 1)^2 \log_2 \left(\sum_{i=0}^{\max_T(F)} p_i \right) ,$$

where p_i is the probability that $T(a, b) = i$. Indeed, there are only $(2^n - 1)^2$ non-trivial coefficients in the DDT, LAT and BCT as the first row and column are fixed in each case. The (negative) anomalies corresponding to the differential uniformity, linearity and boomerang uniformity for $n = 8$ are given in the appendix of the full version of this paper [10].

Maximum Value and Number of Occurrences. In $\mathfrak{S}_{2^8}$, the anomaly of a differential uniformity of 8 is equal to 16.2 but, for a differential uniformity of 6, it is 164.5. In order to have a finer grained estimate of how unlikely the properties of an S-box are, we combine the maximum coefficient in one of its tables with its number of occurrences as was first done in [6]. For a $2^n \times 2^n$ table of integers T, let MO be the function such that $\mathsf{MO}(T) = (c, m)$ where c is the maximum absolute value in T and m is its number of occurrences (where the first row and column are ignored). The set $\mathbb{N} \times \mathbb{N}$ in which the output of MO lives can be ordered using the lexicographic ordering, i.e. $(x, y) \le (x', y')$ if and only if $x < x'$ or $x = x'$ and $y \le y'$. We then define the differential, linear and boomerang anomalies of F as respectively

$$\mathsf{A}^{\mathsf{d}}(F) = \mathsf{A}\left(\mathsf{MO}(\delta_F)\right), \ \mathsf{A}^{\ell}(F) = \mathsf{A}\left(\mathsf{MO}(\mathcal{W}_F)\right), \ \text{and} \ \mathsf{A}^{\mathsf{b}}(F) = \mathsf{A}\left(\mathsf{MO}(\mathcal{B}_F)\right) .$$

This definition of the differential and linear anomalies matches with the one given in [34]. The boomerang anomaly was not used before. We also introduce the *negative* differential, linear and boomerang anomalies as the corresponding negative anomalies.

We estimate these anomalies for a table T using the following expression:

$$\mathsf{A}\big(\mathsf{MO}(T) \le (c, m)\big) = -\log_2 \left(\sum_{k=0}^{m} \binom{(2^n - 1)^2}{k} \times p_c^k \times \left(\sum_{j=0}^{c-1} p_j \right)^{(2^n - 1)^2 - k} \right) ,$$

where p_i is the probability that $T(a,b) = |i|$. For the corresponding negative anomaly, we use the following relation:

$$2^{\mathsf{A}(\mathsf{MO}(T)\leq(c,m))} + 2^{\overline{\mathsf{A}}(\mathsf{MO}(T)\leq(c,m))} = 1 + \left(\frac{(2^n-1)^2}{m}\right)p_c^m \left(\sum_{j=0}^{c-1} p_j\right)^{(2^n-1)^2 - m}.$$

2.3   Tighter Advantage Estimations for Boomerang Attacks

The coefficient distribution we established in Theorem 1 can also be used to compute the expected value of a BCT coefficient. This in turn implies a better understanding of the advantage an adversary has in a boomerang attack.

Theorem 2. *The expected value for each BCT coefficient of a random permutation of $\mathfrak{S}_{2^n}$ converges towards 2 as n increases.*

Proof. Let $F \in \mathfrak{S}_{2^n}$ be picked uniformly at random. The expected value E of $\mathcal{B}_F(a,b)$ is $\sum_{c=0}^{2^n} \Pr[\mathcal{B}_F(a,b) = c]\,c$. Using Theorem 1, we express $\Pr[\mathcal{B}_F(a,b) = c]$ using two binomial distributions P_1 and P_2 so that

$$E = \sum_{c=0}^{2^n} c \times \left(\sum_{2i_1 + 4i_2 = c} P_1(i_1)P_2(i_2)\right)$$

$$= \sum_{c=0}^{2^n}\sum_{i_1=0}^{2^{n-1}}\sum_{i_2=0}^{2^{n-2}} (2i_1 + 4i_2)P_1(i_1)P_2(i_2) \times [2i_1 + 4i_2 = c] ,$$

where the expression between the brackets is equal to 1 if $2i_1 + 4i_2 = c$, and 0 otherwise. Reordering the sums, we obtain the following expected value:

$$E = \underbrace{\sum_{i_1=0}^{2^{n-1}}\sum_{i_2=0}^{2^{n-2}} (2i_1 + 4i_2)P_1(i_1)P_2(i_2)}_{E(n)} \underbrace{\sum_{c=0}^{2^n} [2i_1 + 4i_2 = c]}_{\leq 1} . \qquad (2)$$

We then approximate the binomial distributions P_1 and P_2 by Poisson distributions, namely $P_1(i) \approx \text{Poisson}(i; 2^{-1}) = e^{-\frac{1}{2}}2^{-i}/(i!)$ and $P_1(i) \approx \text{Poisson}(i; 4^{-1}) = e^{-\frac{1}{4}}4^{-i}/(i!)$. We get

$$E(n) = \sum_{i_1=0}^{2^{n-1}}\sum_{i_2=0}^{2^{n-2}} (2i_1 + 4i_2)\frac{e^{-\frac{1}{2}}2^{-i_1}}{i_1!}\frac{e^{-\frac{1}{4}}4^{-i_2}}{i_2!}$$

$$= \sum_{i_1=1}^{2^{n-1}}\frac{e^{-\frac{1}{2}}(\frac{1}{2})^{i_1-1}}{(i_1-1)!}\sum_{i_2=0}^{2^{n-2}}\frac{e^{-\frac{1}{4}}(\frac{1}{4})^{i_2}}{i_2!} + \sum_{i_1=0}^{2^{n-1}}\frac{e^{-\frac{1}{2}}(\frac{1}{2})^{i_1}}{i_1!}\sum_{i_2=1}^{2^{n-2}}\frac{e^{-\frac{1}{4}}(\frac{1}{4})^{i_2-1}}{(i_2-1)!} .$$

As all sums converge towards 1 as n increases, the limit of $E(n)$ is 2. On the other hand, we remark that $E \leq E(n)$ because of Eq. (2), and that

$$E \geq \sum_{i_1=0}^{2^{n-2}}\sum_{i_2=0}^{2^{n-3}} (2i_1 + 4i_2)P_1(i_1)P_2(i_2)\underbrace{\sum_{c=0}^{2^n} [2i_1 + 4i_2 = c]}_{=1} = E(n-1) ,$$

so $E(n-1) \leq E \leq E(n)$. As $E(n)$ converges to 2 as n increases, so does E. $\square$

The expected probability of a boomerang characteristic $E_k^{-1}(E_k(x) \oplus b) \oplus E_k^{-1}(E_k(x \oplus a) \oplus b) = a$ is thus 2^{1-n} and not 2^{-n} as we might expect.

2.4 Experimental Results

Verification. To check the validity of our approach to estimate the statistical anomalies, we picked 2^{21} permutations from $\mathfrak{S}_{2^8}$ uniformly at random. We then counted the number N_t of permutations F such that $\lfloor A(F) \rfloor = t$, and we obtained the following results (only anomalies above 19 are listed):

$$A^\ell(F) : N_{19} = 1, N_{21} = 1 \qquad \overline{A}^\ell(F) : N_{19} = 1$$
$$A^d(F) : \text{See below} \qquad\qquad \overline{A}^d(F) : N_{20} = 1$$
$$A^b(F) : N_{19} = 3 \qquad\qquad\quad \overline{A}^b(F) : N_{20} = 2 \ .$$

We deduce that the anomalies other than $A^d(F)$ behave as we expect: in a set of size 2^t, we can expect to see about 1 permutation with an anomaly of t.

However, for $A^d(F)$, our results do not quite match the theory. Indeed, we have found too many permutations with a high differential anomaly for it to be a coincidence:

$$A^d(F) : \quad N_{19} = 7, N_{20} = 8, N_{21} = 2, N_{22} = 1, N_{23} = 2,$$
$$N_{24} = 1, N_{25} = 1, N_{26} = 1, N_{28} = 1 \ .$$

Recall that our estimates of the table-based anomalies rely on the assumption that the coefficients behave like independent random variables. While we experimentally found this assumption to yield accurate models in practice for all tables, it fails to accurately predict the behavior of the maximum value and its number of occurrences in the case of the DDT.

S-boxes from the Literature. We computed the statistical anomalies we defined above for several 8-bit S-boxes from the literature that we obtained from [36]. The results are given in Table 1. We also list the number N_V of vector spaces of dimension n contained in $\mathcal{Z}_s$; its importance will appear later in Sect. 3.

The statistical anomalies of the AES S-box, i.e. of the multiplicative inverse, are unsurprisingly very large. But they are *too* large: an anomaly cannot be higher than $\log_2(|\mathfrak{S}_{2^n}|)$. Our estimates do not hold for objects with properties as extreme as those of the inverse.

We can derive other results from this table. For example, 2-round SPNs have a high negative boomerang anomaly but 3-round ones loose this property. Classical 3-round Feistel networks, as used in ZUC_S0, have a boomerang uniformity which is maximum [12] so it is not surprising to see that they have a boomerang anomaly so high that we could not compute it. Even though the S-box of Zorro has a modified Feistel structure (it uses a sophisticated bit permutation rather than a branch swap), it still has a high negative boomerang anomaly.

Table 1. The statistical anomalies and number of vector spaces for some S-boxes from the literature.

Type	Cipher	$A^d(s)$	$\overline{A}^d(s)$	$A^\ell(s)$	$\overline{A}^\ell(s)$	$A^b(s)$	$\overline{A}^b(s)$	$N_V(s)$
Inverse	AES	7382.13	0.00	3329.43	0.00	9000.05	0.00	2
Logarithm	BelT	74.79	0.00	122.97	0.00	0.98	0.40	2
TKlog	Kuznyechik	80.63	0.00	34.35	0.00	14.18	0.00	3
SPN (2S)	CLEFIA_S0	2.56	0.19	25.62	0.00	0.00	15.60	6
	Enocoro	1.92	0.36	3.26	0.15	0.00	15.60	6
	Twofish_p0	1.36	0.70	3.16	0.17	0.00	33.84	6
	Twofish_p1	1.34	0.72	3.16	0.17	0.00	25.82	6
SPN (3S)	Iceberg	17.15	0.00	3.58	0.10	0.02	3.87	2
	Khazad	16.94	0.00	3.16	0.17	0.98	0.40	2
Feistel	Zorro	2.19	0.27	3.37	0.13	0.00	25.82	2
	ZUC_S0	16.15	0.00	3.16	0.17	0.00	NaN	368
Hill climbing	Kalyna_pi0	104.22	0.00	235.77	0.00	29.67	0.00	2
	Kalyna_pi1	122.64	0.00	268.07	0.00	29.67	0.00	2
	Kalyna_pi2	129.87	0.00	239.28	0.00	5.99	0.00	2
	Kalyna_pi3	122.64	0.00	242.92	0.00	26.44	0.00	2
Random	Turing	0.18	1.94	1.84	0.17	0.98	0.40	2
	MD2	1.36	0.70	0.10	2.41	0.98	0.40	2
	newDES	0.44	0.73	0.32	1.95	0.14	1.86	2
Unknown	Skipjack	0.18	1.94	54.38	0.00	0.98	0.40	2

As expected, the S-boxes that were generated using a random procedure have low positive and negative statistical anomalies. The S-box of MD2 was obtained using the digits of π, that of the newDES from the American declaration of independence, and that of Turing from the string "Alan Turing".

The correlation between the different statistical anomalies seems complex. On the one hand, there are S-boxes with very different linear and differential anomalies despite the fact that the square of the LAT coefficients corresponds to the Fourier transform of the DDT (see e.g. Skipjack). As evidenced by the anomalies of the S-boxes of Kalyna, which were obtained using a hill climbing method optimizing the differential and linear properties [25], these improvements lead to an observable increase of the boomerang anomaly but it can be marginal.

3 Identifying Structures

In this section, we go through the most common S-box structures, and present for each of them the density of the set of such S-boxes (up to affine-equivalence) and the methods that can be used to identify them. In practice, S-boxes operating on at least 6 bits usually fall into two categories: those that are based on the inverse in the finite field $\mathbb{F}_{2^n}$, and those using block cipher structures.

In both cases, the permutations are usually composed with affine permutations. In the context of white-box cryptography, it is common to compose functions with secret affine permutations so as to obfuscate the logic of the operations used. Hence, for both decomposing S-boxes and attacking white-box implementation, it is necessary to be able to remove these affine layers.

While recovering a monomial structure is simple even when it is masked by affine permutations (see Sect. 3.1 and our results on the S-box of Chiasmus), it is not the case with block cipher structures. In this section, we show how the the recovery of the pattern used in [7] to remove the affine layers of the Russian S-box can be efficiently automatized (Sect. 3.2), and applied to both SPNs (Sect. 3.3) and Feistel network (Sect. 3.4). The core algorithm needed for these attacks is one returning all the vector spaces contained in a set of elements of $\mathbb{F}_2^n$. We will present such an algorithm in Sect. 4.

These techniques allow us to identify the *structural anomalies* in S-boxes. In order to estimate the anomaly associated with each structure, we upper bound the number of permutation that can be built using each of those that we consider. The corresponding anomalies are summarized in Sect. 3.5.

3.1 Multiplicative Inverse

Such permutations have a very simple structure: there exists two affine permutations $A : \mathbb{F}_2^n \to \mathbb{F}_{2^n}$ and $B : \mathbb{F}_{2^n} \to \mathbb{F}_2^n$ such that the permutations F can be written $F = B \circ G \circ A$, where G is the permutation of $\mathbb{F}_{2^n}$ defined by $G(x) = x^{2^n-2}$. Their use was introduced in [31]; the AES [1] uses such an S-box.

In practice, the implementation of G requires the use of an encoding of the elements of $\mathbb{F}_{2^n}$ as elements of $\mathbb{F}_2^n$. Usually, it is achieved by mapping $x = (x_0, ..., x_{n-1}) \in \mathbb{F}_2^n$ to $\sum_{i=0}^{n-1} x_i \alpha^i$, where $\alpha \in \mathbb{F}_{2^n}$ is the root of an irreducible polynomial with coefficients in $\mathbb{F}_2$ of degree n. However, this encoding can be seen as being part of A and B.

Density of the set. There is only one function $x \mapsto x^{2^n-2}$. However, there are fewer than $(|\mathcal{L}_{2^n}|2^n)^2$ distinct permutations affine-equivalent to it. Indeed, $(x \times m)^{2^n-2} = x^{2^n-2} \times m^{2^n-2}$, meaning that for a given pair (A, B) of permutations of $\mathcal{L}_{2^n}$ we can define $2^n - 1$ pairs $(A_i, B_i) \in (\mathcal{L}_{2^n})^2$ such that $B_i \circ G \circ A_i = B_j \circ G \circ A_j$ for all i, j. The same reasoning applies to the Frobenius automorphisms because $(x^{2^i})^{2^n-2} = (x^{2^n-2})^{2^i}$. In the end, there are at most

$$\underbrace{|\mathcal{L}_{2^n}|^2}_{L_A \text{ and } L_B} \times \underbrace{2^{2n}}_{c_A \text{ and } c_B} \times \frac{1}{\underbrace{(2^n - 1)}_{\text{multiplication}} \times \underbrace{n}_{\text{Frobenius}}} = \frac{2^n}{n} \times (|\mathcal{L}_{2^n}|)^2$$

distinct permutations affine-equivalent to the multiplicative inverse.

How to recognize them? The Chinese cipher SMS4 [20] uses an 8-bit S-box whose structure was not explained. This prompted Liu et al. to try and recover said structure [27]. They successfully identified it as being affine equivalent to the multiplicative inverse using an *ad hoc* method.

There is a simple test that can be applied to check if a permutation is affine-equivalent to the multiplicative inverse when the input/output size is even.

Lemma 1. *Let $s : x \mapsto x^{2^n-2}$ be a permutation of $\mathbb{F}_{2^n}$ and $F \in \mathfrak{S}_{2^n}$ with n even be such that $F = B \circ s \circ A$ where $A : x \mapsto L_A(x) + c_A$ and $B : x \mapsto L_B(x) + c_B$ are affine permutations. Let $\{(a_i, b_i)\}$ be the set of all coordinates such that $\delta_F(a_i, b_i) = 4$. Then it holds that $b_i = L_B \left(L_A(a_i)^{2^n-2}\right)$ for all i, meaning that $a_i \mapsto b_i$ and s are identical up to translations.*

Proof. We have that $(x + a)^e + x^e = b$ has as many solutions as $(y + 1)^e + y^e = b/a^e$, meaning that all rows of its DDT contain the same coefficients: $\delta_s(a, b) = \delta_s(1, b/a^e)$. In the case of the inverse for n even, $\delta_s(1, c) \in \{0, 2\}$ for all $c \neq 1$ and $\delta_s(1, 1) = 4$. Such a function was called *locally-APN* in [9].

In our case, we have that $\delta_F(a, b) = \delta_s \left(L_A(a), L_B^{-1}(b)\right)$. Using the property we just established with $e = 2^n - 2$, we get $\delta_F(a, b) = \delta_s \left(1, L_B^{-1}(b)/(L_A(a))^{2^n-2}\right)$, where the second coordinate simplifies into $L_B^{-1}(b) \times L_A(a)$. As a consequence, $\delta_F(a, b) = 4$ if and only if $L_B^{-1}(b) = (L_A(a))^{2^n-2}$, which is equivalent to $b = L_B \left(L_A(a)^{2^n-2}\right)$.

In [38] and [37], two separate teams independently recovered the secret block cipher Chiasmus from an encryption tool called GSTOOL. Chiasmus is a German designed 64-bit block cipher which uses two S-boxes S and S^{-1}. Schuster had the intuition that it was built similarly to the AES S-box. He was right. Using Lemma 1 and the linear equivalence algorithm of [4], we found that the S-box of Chiasmus is also based on a finite field inversion. However, unlike in the AES, it uses *two* affine mappings with non-zero constants. A script generating the S-box of Chiasmus is provided in the appendix of the full version of this paper [10]. The S-box itself can be found in a SAGE [19] module [36].

We could also have recovered this structure using directly the algorithm of Biryukov et al. [4] or the more recent one of Dinur [21]. However, the above approach and these algorithms share the same shortcoming when it comes to identifying the structure in an unknown S-box $F \in \mathfrak{S}_{2^n}$: if we do not know the exact S-box to which F might be affine-equivalent then they cannot be applied. Even if we know that it might be affine-equivalent to an SPN or a Feistel network, we cannot find the corresponding affine masks.

To solve this problem, we identify patterns in the LAT of the permutations with specific structures that are present regardless of the subfunctions they contain. As a consequence, they can always be detected.

3.2   TU-Decomposition

The TU-decomposition is a general structure that was first introduced in [7] where it was shown that the S-box of the latest Russian standards has such a structure. Later, it was encountered again in the context of the *Big APN problem*, a long standing open question in discrete mathematics. Indeed, the only known solution to this problem is a sporadic 6-bit APN permutation that was found by Dillon et al. [13] and which was proved in [35] to yield a TU-decomposition. This structure was then further decomposed to obtain the so-called *open butterfly*. As we will show below, some Feistel and SPN structures also share this decomposition. Thus, the tools that can find TU-decomposition can also be used to identify these structures even in the presence of affine masks.

Definition 2 (TU$_t$-decomposition). *Let n and t be integers such that $0 < t < n$. We say that $F \in \mathfrak{S}_{2^n}$ has a TU$_t$-decomposition[4] if there exists:*

- *a family of 2^{n-t} permutations $T_y \in \mathfrak{S}_{2^t}$ indexed by $y \in \mathbb{F}_2^{n-t}$,*
- *a family of 2^t permutations $U_x \in \mathfrak{S}_{2^{n-t}}$ indexed by $x \in \mathbb{F}_2^t$, and*
- *two linear permutations $\mu : \mathbb{F}_2^n \to (\mathbb{F}_2^t \times \mathbb{F}_2^{n-t})$ and $\eta : (\mathbb{F}_2^t \times \mathbb{F}_2^{n-t}) \to \mathbb{F}_2^n$*

such that $F = \eta \circ G \circ \mu$, where G is the permutation of $\mathbb{F}_2^t \times \mathbb{F}_2^{n-t}$ such that $G(x,y) = \big(T_y(x), U_{T_y(x)}(y)\big)$. This structure is presented in Fig. 1a.

In other words, $F \in \mathfrak{S}_{2^n}$ has a TU$_t$-decomposition if and only if it is affine-equivalent to $G \in \mathfrak{S}_{2^n}$ with the following property: if $G_{\restriction t}$ is the restriction of G to its t bits of highest weight then $x \mapsto G_{\restriction t}(x \| a)$ is a permutation for all $a \in \mathbb{F}_2^{n-t}$.

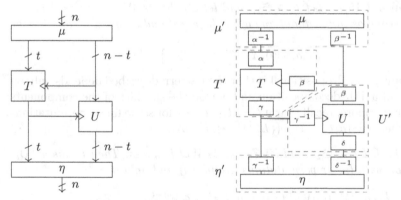

(a) TU$_t$-decomposition.   (b) Composing its components with linear permutations.

Fig. 1. Two functionally equivalent permutations.

---

[4] This is a simplified version of the TU$_t$-decomposition compared to [15]. Indeed, in that paper, the authors only impose that $T_y \in \mathfrak{S}_{2^{n-t}}$; U_x may have collisions. Since we are only considering bijective S-boxes here, we consider that $U_x \in \mathfrak{S}_{2^t}$.

Density of the Set. In order to define a permutation with a TU_t-decomposition, we need to choose 2^{n-t} permutations of $\mathfrak{S}_{2^t}$, 2^t permutations of $\mathfrak{S}_{2^{n-t}}$ and two linear permutations operating on n bits. However, several of the permutations generated in this way will be identical. Indeed, we can compose each T_y with a t-bit linear permutation $\alpha \in \mathcal{L}_{2^t}$ to obtain a permutation $T'_y = T_y \circ \alpha$. If we use T'_y and compose μ with α^{-1}, then we obtain the same overall permutation as when T_y and μ are used. More equivalent modifications can be made using linear permutations $\beta \in \mathcal{L}_{2^{n-t}}$, $\gamma \in \mathcal{L}_{2^t}$ and $\delta \in \mathcal{L}_{2^{n-t}}$, as summarized in Fig. 1b. Hence, the total number of n-bit permutations with TU_t-decompositions is at most

$$\#\mathsf{TU}_t \;\leq\; \underbrace{|\mathfrak{S}_{2^t}|^{2^{n-t}}}_{T_y} \times \underbrace{|\mathfrak{S}_{2^{n-t}}|^{2^t}}_{U_x} \underbrace{\left(\frac{|\mathcal{L}_{2^n}|}{|\mathcal{L}_{2^t}| \times |\mathcal{L}_{2^{n-t}}|} \right)^2}_{\mu \text{ and } \eta} .$$

This quantity is only a bound as permutations that are self affine-equivalent lead to identical permutations with different μ and η. We used this bound to compute the anomaly associated to the presence of a TU_t-decomposition in a permutation. It is given in Sect. 2.

How to recognize them? Let $F \in \mathfrak{S}_{2^n}$ be a permutation. As was established in Proposition 6 of [15], the presence of a TU_t-decomposition is equivalent to the presence of a specific vector space of zeroes of dimension n in $\mathcal{Z}_F$. Let us first recall the corresponding proposition in the particular case of permutations.

Proposition 4 ([15]). *Let $F \in \mathfrak{S}_{2^n}$ and let $\mathcal{Z}_F$ be its Walsh zeroes. Then F has a TU_t-decomposition without any affine layers if and only if $\mathcal{Z}_F$ contains the vector space*

$$\left\{ (0||a, b||0), a \in \mathbb{F}_2^t, b \in \mathbb{F}_2^{n-t} \right\} .$$

The advantage of Proposition 4 is that the pattern described depends only on the presence of a TU_t-decomposition and not on the specifics of the components T and U. Furthermore, recall that if $G = L_2 \circ F \circ L_1$ for some linear permutations L_1 and L_2 then $\mathcal{W}_G(a, b) = \mathcal{W}_F \left((L_1^{-1})^T(a), L_2^T(b) \right)$.

Corollary 1. *Let $F \in \mathfrak{S}_{2^n}$ and let $\mathcal{Z}_F$ be its Walsh zeroes. Then F has a TU_t-decomposition with linear permutations μ and η if and only if*

$$\left\{ \left((\mu^{-1})^T(0, a), \eta^T(b, 0) \right), a \in \mathbb{F}_2^t, b \in \mathbb{F}_2^{n-t} \right\} \subset \mathcal{Z}_F .$$

It is therefore sufficient to look for all the vector spaces of dimension n contained in $\mathcal{Z}_F$ to see if F has TU_t-decomposition. If we find a vector space that is not the Cartesian product of a subspace of $\{(x, 0), x \in \mathbb{F}_2^n\}$ with a subspace of $\{(0, y), y \in \mathbb{F}_2^n\}$ then F does not have a TU_t-decomposition but there exists a linear function L of $\mathbb{F}_2^n$ such that $F + L$ does [15]. Regardless, the key tool that allows the search for TU-decomposition is an efficient algorithm returning all the vector spaces of a given dimension that are contained in a set of elements of $\mathbb{F}_2^n$. Indeed, finding such vector spaces will allow us to recover all the values of $(\mu^{-1})^T(0, a)$ and $\eta^T(b, 0)$ for $(a, b) \in \mathbb{F}_2^t \times \mathbb{F}_2^{n-t}$, from which we will deduce information about μ and η. We present such an algorithm in Sect. 4 and we used it as a subroutine of program finding a TU_t-decomposition automatically (see the appendix of the full version [10]).

As observed in [15], the number of vector spaces of dimension n in $\mathcal{Z}_F$ is the same as the number of vector spaces of dimension n in the set of the coordinates of the zeroes in the DDT. Thus, we could equivalently present our results in terms of DDT.

3.3 Substitution-Permutation Networks

An n-bit SPN interleaves the parallel application of k possibly distinct m-bit S-boxes with n-bit linear permutations, where $k \times m = n$. We use the common [8] notation AS to denote a linear layer followed by an S-box layer. A SAS structure is depicted in Fig. 2a.

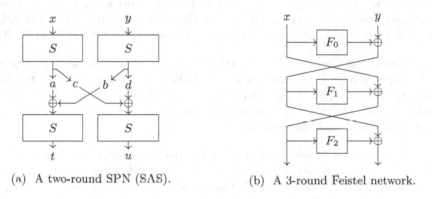

(a) A two-round SPN (SAS).   (b) A 3-round Feistel network.

Fig. 2. Two block-cipher-like S-box structures.

Let us estimate the number of r-round SPNs. As the S-box layers are interleaved with linear layers, we need to consider not the size of $\mathfrak{S}_{2^m}$ but instead the number of linear equivalence classes, which is at most $|\mathfrak{S}_{2^m}|/|\mathcal{L}_{2^m}|^2$. The number of permutations with a $A(SA)^r$ structure is then at most

$$\#A(SA)^r \;\leq\; \left(\frac{|\mathfrak{S}_{2^m}|}{|\mathcal{L}_{2^m}|^2}\right)^{rn/m} \times |\mathcal{L}_{2^n}|^{r+1} \;.$$

The corresponding anomalies for some values of n are given in Sect. 3.5.

How to recognize them? First of all, the algebraic degree of a 2-round SPN is at most equal to $n-2$ [11]. Hence, if a permutation is of degree $n-1$, it cannot have such a structure.

In Theorem 3, we will establish the existence of specific vector space of zeroes in the LAT of a 2-round SPN. However, in order to properly state this theorem, we first need to introduce the following notion.

Definition 3 (m-Valid minors). *Let k, m and n be integers such that $n = k \times m$. Let $L \in \mathcal{L}_{2^n}$ be a linear permutation. We define it using a k^2 block matrices $L_{i,j}$ of dimension $m \times m$:*

$$
L = \begin{bmatrix} L_{0,0} & \cdots & L_{0,k-1} \\ \cdots & & \cdots \\ L_{k-1,0} & \cdots & L_{k-1,k-1} \end{bmatrix}.
$$

We call a minor of the matrix L m-valid if there exists a pair I, J of subsets of $\{0, ..., k-1\}$ which are of the same size $0 < |I| = |J| < k$ and such that the rank of $L_{I,J} = [L_{i,j}]_{i \in I, j \in J}$ is equal to m.

In other words, an m-valid minor of L is a non-trivial minor of L that is obtained by taking complete m-bit chunks of this matrix, and which has maximum rank.

Theorem 3. *Let $F \in \mathfrak{S}_{2^n}$ be an ASASA structure built using L as its central linear layer and two layers of m-bit S-boxes. For each $I, J \subsetneq \{0, ..., k-1\}$ defining an m-valid minor of L, there exists a vector space of zeroes of dimension n in $\mathcal{Z}_F$.*

Proof. Because of Corollary 1, we restrict ourselves to the SAS structure. If we let the input blocks corresponding to the indices in I take all $2^{m|I|}$ possible values, then the output blocks with indices in J will also take all $2^{m|J|} = 2^{m|I|}$ possible values. There is thus a corresponding $\mathsf{TU}_{m|I|}$-decomposition and hence a corresponding vector space in $\mathcal{Z}_F$.

This verification is less efficient than the dedicated cryptanalysis methods presented in [30]. However, the aim here is not so much to recover the ASASA structure used, it is rather to identify the S-box as having such a structure in the first place. Using the following corollary, we can immediately understand why $N_V = \binom{2 \times 2}{2} = 6$ for several S-boxes in Table 1: it is a direct consequence of their 2-round SPN structure and of the strong diffusion of their inner linear layer.

Corollary 2. *Let $F \in \mathfrak{S}_{2^n}$ be the SAS structure built using L as its linear layer and two layers of m-bit S-boxes, where $n = k \times m$. If L is MDS over the alphabet of S-box words, then $\mathcal{Z}_F$ contains at least $\binom{2k}{k}$ vector spaces of dimension n.*

Proof. As L is MDS, all its minors and in particular those corresponding to the definition of m-minors have a maximum rank. There are $\sum_{i=1}^{k} \binom{k}{i} \times \binom{k}{i}$ such m-minors, to which we add the "free" vector space $\{(x, 0), x \in \mathbb{F}_2^n\}$ which is always present: there are at least $\sum_{i=0}^{k} \binom{k}{i}^2 = \binom{2k}{k}$ vector spaces in $\mathcal{Z}_F$.

3.4   Feistel Networks

The Feistel structure is a classical block cipher construction which is summarized in Fig. 2b. The number of permutations that are affine-equivalent to r-round Feistel networks that use permutations as the round functions is at most equal to

$$\underbrace{|\mathfrak{S}_{2^{n/2}}|^r}_{\text{round funcs.}} \times \underbrace{\frac{1}{(2^n)^{\lceil \frac{n}{2} \rceil}}}_{\text{constants}} \times \underbrace{|\mathcal{L}_{2^n}|^2}_{\text{outer layers}} \times \underbrace{\frac{1}{|\mathcal{L}_{2^{n/2}}|^2}}_{\text{branch transforms}} .$$

Indeed, we can apply $n/2$-bit linear permutations L and L' to each branch and, provided that the round functions are modified, we can cancel them out by applying L^{-1} and $(L')^{-1}$ on the output branches. We can also add constants freely to the output of the first $\lceil r/2 \rceil$ round functions, as explained in [5].

How to recognize them? There are efficient function-recovery techniques for up to 5-round Feistel networks [5]. However, as soon as affine masks are added, the corresponding techniques can no longer be applied. Still, as with the SPN structure, Feistel networks with few rounds exhibit specific vector spaces in their Walsh zeroes as was already observed for 4-round Feistel network in [7]. This means that it is possible to detect such structures using the vector spaces in their Walsh zeroes.

Theorem 4 ([7]). *Let F be a 4-round Feistel network such that round functions 2 and 3 are permutations. Then $\mathcal{W}_F(x||y, 0||y) = 0$ for all x, y in $\mathbb{F}_2^{n/2}$.*

This observation also holds for a 3-round Feistel. In fact, there are more vector spaces in such a structure.

Theorem 5. *Let F_0, F_1 and F_2 be functions of $\mathbb{F}_2^{n/2}$ such that $F_1 \in \mathfrak{S}_{2^{n/2}}$. Let $F \in \mathbb{F}_2^n$ be the 3-round Feistel network using F_0, F_1 and F_2 as its round functions. Then the set $\mathcal{Z}_F$ contains the following vector spaces of dimension n:*

1. $\{(x, 0), x \in \mathbb{F}_2^n\}, \{(0, y), y \in \mathbb{F}_2^n\}$,
2. $\{(x||0, y||0), (x, y) \in \mathbb{F}_2^{n/2} \times \mathbb{F}_2^{n/2}\}$,
3. $\{(x||y, x||0), (x, y) \in \mathbb{F}_2^{n/2} \times \mathbb{F}_2^{n/2}\}, \{(x||0, x||y), (x, y) \in \mathbb{F}_2^{n/2} \times \mathbb{F}_2^{n/2}\}$,
4. $\{(x||y, 0||y), (x, y) \in \mathbb{F}_2^{n/2} \times \mathbb{F}_2^{n/2}\}, \{(0||y, x||y), (x, y) \in \mathbb{F}_2^{n/2} \times \mathbb{F}_2^{n/2}\}$,

the fourth category being present if F_0 and F_2 are in $\in \mathfrak{S}_{2^{n/2}}$.

The proof of this theorem follows from direct applications of results in [15] and of these observations:

– if the 3-round Feistel network implies a specific vector space, it also implies the one with the coordinates swapped because its inverse is also a 3-round Feistel network,
– $(x, y) \mapsto F(x, y) \oplus (x, 0)$ is a permutation if $F_1 \in \mathfrak{S}_{2^{n/2}}$, and
– $(x, y) \mapsto F(x, y) \oplus (0, y)$ has a $\mathsf{TU}_{n/2}$-decomposition if $F_2 \in \mathfrak{S}_{2^{n/2}}$.

The details are provided in the appendix of the full version [10].

3.5   Structural Anomalies

In light of our results, we can quantify the anomaly associated to the presence of various structures. In this case, the mapping P considered maps $\mathfrak{S}_{2^n}$ to $\{0,1\}$: a permutation has a specific structure or it does not. The anomaly associated to a given structure is then

$$A_{\text{structure}} = -\log_2 \left(\frac{|\{G \in \mathfrak{S}_{2^n}, G \text{ has the structure}\}|}{|\mathfrak{S}_{2^n}|} \right),$$

meaning that the set sizes we extracted above allow us to quantify the anomalies associated to the TU_t-decomposition, the SPN structure, the Feistel network and the TKlog (see below for the latter). The corresponding anomalies are summarized in Table 2 for different values of n.

The existence of a TU-decomposition with $t = 1$ for $F \in \mathfrak{S}_{2^n}$ is equivalent to the presence of a component with a linear structure [15], i.e. to the existence of $a \in \mathbb{F}_2^n$ such that the Boolean function $x \mapsto a \cdot F(x)$ has a probability 1 differential. Thus, the corresponding row of Table 2 gives the anomaly corresponding to linear structures.

We can also compute the anomaly associated to the TKlog structure [34] used in the S-box of Streebog and Kuznyechik [22,23] called $\pi \in \mathfrak{S}_{2^8}$. A TKlog is a $2m$-bit permutation parametrized by an affine function $\kappa : \mathbb{F}_2^m \to \mathbb{F}_{2^{2m}}$ such that $\kappa(x) = \Lambda(x) \oplus \kappa(0)$ for some linear function Λ. This function must be such that $\text{Im}(\Lambda) \cup \mathbb{F}_{2^m}$ spans $\mathbb{F}_{2^{2m}}$. The TKlog also depends on a permutation s of $\mathfrak{S}_{2^m-1}$. It is defined as follows

$$\begin{cases} \pi(0) & = \kappa(0), \\ \pi\left(\alpha^{(2^m+1)j}\right) & = \kappa(2^m - j), \text{ for } 1 \le j < 2^m - 1, \\ \pi\left(\alpha^{i+(2^m+1)j}\right) & = \kappa(2^m - i) + \alpha^{(2^m+1)s(j)}, \text{ for } i < 2^m + 1, j < 2^m - 1, \end{cases}$$

(3)

where α is a root of a primitive polynomial p of degree $2m$, so that α^{2^m+1} is a multiplicative generator of $\mathbb{F}_{2^m}^*$. The number of TKlog, is then given by

$$\underbrace{\prod_{i=m}^{2m-1} (2^{2m} - 2^i)}_{\Lambda} \times \underbrace{|\mathfrak{S}_{2^m-1}|}_{s} \times \underbrace{\left(\phi(2^{2m} - 1)/(2m)\right)}_{\#\text{primitive polynomials}} \times \underbrace{2^{2m}}_{\kappa(0)}$$

where ϕ is Euler's totient function. As for the inverse function, the encoding of the elements of $\mathbb{F}_{2^{2m}}$ as binary strings can be considered to be part of the outer affine layers.

Table 2. Upper bounds on the anomalies of the affine-equivalence to some structures. For the TKlog, "AE" corresponds to permutations affine-equivalent to some TKlog and "pure" to TKLog themselves. S/r is the number of S-boxes used in each round, i.e. the number that are applied in parallel.

Structure	Parameters	$n = 6$	$n = 8$	$n = 12$	$n = 16$
$x \mapsto x^{2^n - 2}$	–	236.1	1570.6	42981.2	953548.5
TKlog	"pure"	258.7	1601.5	42870.7	952207.7
	AE	184.3	1469.0	42574.2	951683.2
TU-dec.	$t = 1$	8.8	95.7	1997.7	32699.7
	$t = n/2$	13.0	201.1	5215.3	91571.2
SPN	ASASA, $S/r = 2$	192.7	1435.4	41913.5	947036.0
	ASASASA, $S/r = 2$	158.2	1342.3	41316.3	943662.7
Feistel	3-round, $F_i \in \mathfrak{S}_{2^{n/2}}$	205.5	1443.3	41898.2	946980.9
	4-round, $F_i \in \mathfrak{S}_{2^{n/2}}$	220.8	1487.6	42194.2	948664.9

4   Vector Spaces Extraction Algorithms

Let S be a set of elements of $\mathbb{F}_2^n$. In this section, we describe an algorithm which extracts all the vector spaces of dimension at least d that are completely contained in S. As established in the previous section, the ability to solve this problem will allow us to identify TU-decompositions, some SPNs, and 3,4-round Feistel networks even in the presence of affine encodings. It can also test the CCZ-equivalence [16] of a function to a permutation, as was done by Dillon et al. [13] to find the first APN permutation operating on an even number of bits.

Our results can be interpreted using both the ordering relation over the integers and by reasoning over the respective position of the zeroes of the elements in $\mathbb{F}_2^n$. The following lemma links these two views.

Definition 4 (Most Significant Bit). *Let $x \in \mathbb{F}_2^n$ and let us write $x = (x[0], ..., x[n-1])$ where $x[0]$ is the least significant bit. We denote $MSB(x)$ the greatest index i such that $x[i] = 1$.*

Lemma 2. *For any $x \in \mathbb{F}_2^n$, it holds that*

$$x < x \oplus a \;\Leftrightarrow\; x[MSB(a)] = 0 \ ,$$

where the order relation is obtained by interpreting x and $x \oplus a$ as the binary representations of integers.

4.1   A Simple Approach and How Ours Improves It

Let us first present a naive approach to solving this problem. At its core, this approach is a tree search that builds the complete vector spaces iteratively.

Starting from a specific element $x \in S$ and vector space $V_x = \{0, x\}$, we loop over all the elements y such that $y > x$ and check whether $(x \oplus y) \in S$, in which case we build $V_{x,y} = V_x \cup \{y \oplus v, v \in V_x\}$. We then repeat this process by looking for $z > y$ such that $(z \oplus v) \in S$ for all $v \in V_{x,y}$. This process can then be iterated until complete bases $(x, y, z, ...)$ of vector spaces are found. Our approach is based on the same principles but it significantly outperforms this naive algorithm by solving its two main shortcomings.

First, the basis of a vector space is not unique. The condition that it be ordered, which is implied by the algorithm sketched above, is not sufficient to ensure uniqueness. This implies that the algorithm will be slowed down by the exploration of the branches that actually correspond to identical spaces, and that a post processing checking for duplicated spaces will be needed. Our algorithm will solve this problem and return exactly one basis for each vector space contained in S. These bases are called *Gauss-Jordan Bases (GJB)* and are introduced in Sect. 4.2.

Second, at each iteration, we need to consider all $z \in S$ such that z is strictly larger than the largest vector already in the basis being built. In our approach, we update at each iteration a set that contains all the elements z that could be used to construct a larger basis using a process which we call *vector extraction* (see Sect. 4.3). Like in the algorithm above, this set only contains elements that are strictly greater than the previous bases elements. However, it is also strictly larger than all the elements in the vector space spanned by this basis and its size is reduced by at least a factor 2 at each iteration. Using vector extractions, we can also skip the test that $(z \oplus v) \in S$ for all v in the current vector space which will increase the speed of our algorithm.

Besides, in each iteration, we use a heuristic method to consider only a subset of this set of z which is based on the number and positions of its zeroes, the *Bigger MSB Condition*.

In summary, we improve upon the algorithm above in the following ways:

- we construct exactly one basis per vector space contained in S (using GJB, see Sect. 4.2),
- we significantly reduce the number of vectors that can be considered in the next iterations (using vector extractions, see Sect. 4.3), and
- we further decrease the number of vectors that need to be explored at a given iteration using a specific filter (using the Bigger MSB condition, see Sect. 4.4).

Finally, the vector space extraction algorithm itself is presented in Sect. 4.5. An algorithm extracting affine spaces which uses the former as a subroutine is presented along with an actual implementation of the vector space algorithm in the appendix of the full version [10].

In [14], Canteaut et al. introduced an algorithm which, given an n-bit Boolean function f, lists all the affine spaces of dimension m such that f is constant (or affine) on them. Our algorithm can easily perform the same task. Indeed, f is affine on a subspace U if and only if $\{x || f(x), x \in U\}$ is an affine subspace, meaning that our affine space search algorithms can list all such spaces.

Using our implementation (see [10]), we only need about 12 min to reprove their Fact 22 which deals with a 14-bit Boolean function while they claim a runtime of 50 h in this case. Our machine is more recent and thus likely faster than theirs but not by a factor 250: our algorithm is inherently more efficient. It is also far more versatile, as we have established above.

4.2 Gauss-Jordan Bases

These objects are those which our vector space search will actually target. They were described in the context of Boolean functions in [14].

Definition 5 (GJB [14]). *For any vector space V of dimension d, the* Gauss-Jordan Basis (GJB) *of V is the set $\{v_0, ..., v_{d-1}\}$ such that $\langle v_0, ..., v_{d-1} \rangle = V$ which is the smallest such set when sorted in lexicographic order.*

For any space V there is *exactly one* GJB. Indeed, we can write down all of its bases, sort the elements in each of them in increasing order and then sort the reordered bases in lexicographic order. This implies that $v_i < v_{i+1}$ for all i. Some key properties of GJBs are given by the following lemma.

Lemma 3. *GJBs have the following properties.*

1. *If $\{v_0, ..., v_i\}$ is the GJB of $\langle v_0, ..., v_i \rangle$ then $\{v_0, ..., v_{i-1}\}$ is a GJB.*
2. *The basis $\{v_0, ..., v_{d-1}\}$ is a GJB if and only if*

$$\begin{cases} \forall j \in \{0, ..., d-2\}, \ MSB(v_j) < MSB(v_{j+1}) \\ \forall i \in \{1, ..., d-1\}, \forall j \in \{0, ..., i-1\}, v_i[MSB(v_j)] = 0 \ . \end{cases} \qquad (4)$$

3. *If $\{v_0, ..., v_{d-1}\}$ is a GJB then, for all $j \in \{0, ..., d-1\}$, $\langle v_0, ..., v_{d-1} \rangle$ contains exactly 2^j elements x such that $MSB(x) = MSB(v_j)$.*

Proof. We prove each point separately.

Point 1. A basis of $\langle v_0, ..., v_{i-1} \rangle$ lexicographically smaller than $\{v_0, ..., v_i\}$ could be used to build a basis of $\langle v_0, ..., v_i \rangle$, lexicographically smaller than its GJB, which is impossible.

Point 2. We prove each direction of the equivalence separately.

$\Rightarrow$ Suppose that $\{v_0, ..., v_{d-1}\}$ is indeed a GJB. Then $MSB(v_j) = MSB(v_{j+1})$ would imply that $MSB(v_j \oplus v_{j+1}) < MSB(v_j)$ which, in particular, would imply that $v_j \oplus v_{j+1} < v_j$. This would contradict that $\{v_0, ..., v_{d-1}\}$ is a GJB. Similarly, $MSB(v_j) > MSB(v_{j+1})$ would imply $v_j > v_{j+1}$ which is also a contradiction. We deduce that $MSB(v_j) < MSB(v_{j+1})$ for any $0 \le j < d-1$. Suppose now that $v_i[MSB(v_j)] = 1$ for some $j < i$. We deduce from Lemma 2 that $v_i \ge v_i \oplus v_j$, which is again a contradiction because $\{v_0, ..., v_{d-1}\}$ is minimal. We have thus established that if $\{v_0, ..., v_{d-1}\}$ is a GJB then it must satisfy the conditions in Eq. (4).

$\Leftarrow$ Let us now assume that these conditions hold. In this case, we have that $v_i < v_i \oplus \bigoplus_{j \in I} v_j$ for any subset I of $\{0, ..., i-1\}$ because the MSB of $\bigoplus_{j \in I} v_j$ is always strictly smaller than $\text{MSB}(v_i)$ and because of Lemma 2. Thus, adding v_i at the end of $\{v_0, ..., v_{i-1}\}$ yields a GJB of $\langle v_0, ..., v_i \rangle$. A simple induction then gives us the result.

Point 3. Using the first point of this lemma allows us to proceed via a simple induction over the size of the basis. If the basis is simply $\{v_0\}$ then the lemma obviously holds. Then, adding an element v_d to the end of a GJB of size d will add 2^d elements x such that $\text{MSB}(x) = \text{MSB}(v_d)$. $\square$

The last point of Lemma 3 allows a significant speed up of the search for such GJBs. To describe it, we introduce the following concept.

Definition 6 (MSB spectrum). *Let S be a set of elements in $\mathbb{F}_2^n$. The MSB spectrum of S is the sequence $\{N_i(S)\}_{0 \le i < n}$ such that*

$$N_i(S) = \#\{x \in S, MSB(x) = i\} .$$

Corollary 3 (MSB conditions). *If a set S of elements from $\mathbb{F}_2^n$ contains a vector space of dimension d, then there must exist a strictly increasing sequence $\{m_j\}_{0 \le j \le d-1}$ of length d such that*

$$N_{m_j}(S) \ge 2^j .$$

4.3   Vector Extractions

We now present a class of functions called *extractions* which will play a crucial role in our algorithms. We also prove their most crucial properties.

Definition 7 (Extraction). *Let $a \ne 0$ be some element of $\mathbb{F}_2^n$. The extraction of a, denoted $\mathcal{X}_a$, is a function mapping a subset S of $\mathbb{F}_2^n$ to $\mathcal{X}_a(S)$, where $x \in \mathcal{X}_a(S)$ if and only if all of the following conditions are satisfied:*

$$x \in S , \quad (x \oplus a) \in S , \quad a < x < (x \oplus a) .$$

In particular, $\mathcal{X}_a(S) \subseteq S$. Our algorithm will iterate such extractions to construct smaller and smaller sets without loosing any GJBs. This process is motivated by the following theorem.

Theorem 6. *Let $\{v_0, ..., v_{i-1}\}$ be elements of some subset S of $\mathbb{F}_2^n$ such that $0 \in S$ and such that $v_{j+1} \in (\mathcal{X}_{v_j} \circ ... \circ \mathcal{X}_{v_0})(S)$ for all $j < i$. Then it holds that $v_i \in (\mathcal{X}_{v_{i-1}} \circ ... \circ \mathcal{X}_{v_0})(S)$ if and only if $\langle v_0, ..., v_i \rangle \subseteq S$ and $\{v_0, ..., v_i\}$ is the GJB of this vector space.*

Proof. In order to prove the theorem, we proceed by induction over i using the validity of the theorem over bases of size i as our induction hypothesis. At step i, we assume that $v_0, ..., v_i$ are elements of S and that $v_{j+1} \in (\mathcal{X}_{v_j} \circ ... \circ \mathcal{X}_{v_0})(S)$ for all $j < i$.

Initialization i = 1. By definition of vector extraction, $v_1 \in \mathcal{X}_{v_0}(\mathcal{S})$ if and only if $v_1 \in \mathcal{S}$, and $v_0 \oplus v_1 \in \mathcal{S}$, $v_0 < v_1 < v_0 \oplus v_1$. As we assume $0, v_0 \in \mathcal{S}$, this is equivalent to $\{0, v_0, v_1, v_0 \oplus v_1\} = \langle v_0, v_1 \rangle$ being contained in $\mathcal{S}$ and to $\{v_0, v_1\}$ being a GJB.

Inductive Step i > 1 Let $v_i \in (\mathcal{X}_{v_{i-1}} \circ \dots \circ \mathcal{X}_{v_0})(\mathcal{S})$. From the induction hypothesis, we have that $\{v_0, \dots, v_{i-1}\}$ is a GJB. Using the second point of Lemma 3, we have that its extension $\{v_0, \dots, v_i\}$ is a GJB if and only if $v_i[\text{MSB}(v_j)] = 0$ (which is equivalent to $v_i < v_i \oplus v_j$) for all $0 \le j < i$ and $\text{MSB}(v_i) > \text{MSB}(v_{i-1})$.

By definition of $\mathcal{X}_{v_j}$, we have that $v_i < v_i \oplus v_j$ for all j such that $0 \le j < i$, so $\{v_0, \dots, v_i\}$ is a GJB if and only if $\text{MSB}(v_i) > \text{MSB}(v_{i-1})$. We have $v_{i-1} < v_i < v_i \oplus v_{i-1}$, which implies in particular $v_{i-1} < v_i \oplus v_{i-1}$, so that $v_i[\text{MSB}(v_{i-1})] = 0$. Thus, $v_i > v_{i-1}$ holds if and only if $\text{MSB}(v_i) > \text{MSB}(v_{i-1})$. □

Corollary 4. *If $\{e_0, \dots, e_{d-1}\}$ is the GJB of a vector space V such that $V \subseteq \mathcal{S} \subseteq \mathbb{F}_2^n$ then, for all $0 < j \le d-1$, we have*

$$\langle e_j, e_{j+1}, \dots, e_{d-1} \rangle \subseteq \left(\mathcal{X}_{e_{j-1}} \circ \dots \mathcal{X}_{e_1} \circ \mathcal{X}_{e_0} \right)(\mathcal{S}) .$$

Evaluating $\mathcal{X}_a$ imposes a priori to look whether $x \oplus a$ belongs in $\mathcal{S}$ for all $x \in \mathcal{S}$ such that $x < x \oplus a$. This verification can be implemented efficiently using a binary search when $\mathcal{S}$ is sorted. We can make it even more efficient using the following lemma.

Lemma 4. *Let $\mathcal{S}$ be a set of elements in $\mathbb{F}_2^n$ and let $a \in \mathcal{S}$. Then we have*

$$\mathcal{X}_a(\mathcal{S}) = \bigcup_{i=\text{MSB}(a)+1}^{n} \mathcal{X}_a \left(\{ x \in \mathcal{S}, \text{MSB}(x) = i \} \right)$$

4.4 Bigger MSB Condition

The following lemma provides a necessary condition for some $e_0 \in \mathcal{S}$ to be the first element of a GJB of size d.

Lemma 5 (Bigger MSB condition). *If e_0 is the first element in a GJB of size d of elements of a set $\mathcal{S}$ of elements in $\mathbb{F}_2^n$, then $\mathcal{S}'$ defined as*

$$\mathcal{S}' = \{ x \in \mathcal{S}, \text{MSB}(x) > \text{MSB}(e_0) \}$$

must satisfy the MSB condition of Corollary 3 for dimension $d-1$, i.e. there is a strictly increasing sequence $\{m_j\}$ of length $d-1$ such that

$$\# \{ x \in \mathcal{S}, \text{MSB}(x) = m_j \} > 2^j .$$

This lemma provides an efficient filter to know whether x can be the start of a GJB of size d which depends only on the MSB of x, so that it does not need to be evaluated for all $x \in \mathcal{S}$ but only once for each subset of $\mathcal{S}$ with a given MSB.

4.5 Vector Space Extraction Algorithm

Algorithm 1. GJBEXTRACTION algorithm.

1: **function** GJBEXTRACTION($\mathcal{S}$, d)
2:     $\mathcal{L} \leftarrow \{\}$
3:     **for all** $a \in \phi_d(\mathcal{S})$ **do**
4:         $s_a \leftarrow \mathcal{X}_a(\mathcal{S})$
5:         **if** $|s_a| \geq 2^{d-1} - 1$ **then**
6:             $\mathcal{L}' \leftarrow$ GJBEXTRACTION $(s_a, \max(d-1, 0))$
7:             **for all** $B \in \mathcal{L}'$ **do**
8:                 Add the GJB $(\{a\} \cup B)$ to $\mathcal{L}$
9:             **end for**
10:        **end if**
11:    **end for**
12:    **return** $\mathcal{L}$
13: **end function**

If we let ϕ_d be the identity then we can directly deduce from Theorem 6 and Corollary 4 that GJBEXTRACTION (as described in Algorithm 1) returns the unique GJBs of each and every vector space of dimension at least equal to d that is included in $\mathcal{S}$.

This algorithm can be seen as a tree search. The role of ϕ_d is then to cut branches as early as possible by allowing us to ignore elements that cannot possibly be the first element of a base of size d by implementing the Bigger MSB Condition of Lemma 5:

$$a \in \phi_d(\mathcal{S}) \quad \text{if and only if} \quad \exists \{m_j\}_{0 \leq j < d}, \begin{cases} m_{j+1} > m_j > \mathrm{MSB}(a) \ , \\ \# \left\{ x \in \mathcal{S}, \mathrm{MSB}(x) = m_j \right\} > 2^j \ . \end{cases}$$

Note that we only need to try and build such a sequence of increasing m_j once for each value of $\mathrm{MSB}(x)$ for $x \in \mathcal{S}$. It is possible to check for the existence of such a sequence in a time proportional to $|\mathcal{S}|$.

5 Conclusion

We have presented a comprehensive list of anomalies quantifying how unlikely the properties of a given S-box are. These can be of a statistical nature and we have pioneered the use of the BCT for this purpose. They can also correspond to the presence of a specific structure, many of which are particular cases of the TU-decomposition. To find TU-decompositions, we presented an efficient vector space algorithm which can be of independent interest. We have also showed how finding TU-decompositions can help bypass affine masks for several S-box structures.

We can apply our results to π, the 8-bit S-box used by both Streebog [22] and Kuznyechik [23]. It has very high anomalies (see Table 3) which means that the set of S-boxes with as strong a structure as the TKlog found in π is very small. This observation is coherent with the claim of [34] that the structure of π was deliberately inserted by its designers.

Table 3. Some of the anomalies of π.

	Statistical		Structural	
Differential	Linear	Boomerang	TU$_4$	TKlog
80.6[†]	34.4	14.2	201.1	1601.5

[†] This anomaly might be overestimated (Sect. 2.4).

We finally list some open problems that we have identified while working on this paper.

Open Problem 1. How can we better estimate the differential anomaly?

Open Problem 2. Why are there so many vector spaces in $\mathcal{Z}_F$ when F is a 3-round Feistel network of $\mathfrak{S}_{2^8}$?

Acknowledgement. We thank Jérémy Jean for shepherding this paper. We also thank Florian Wartelle for fruitful discussions about vector space search, and Anne Canteaut for proofreading a first draft of this paper. The work of Xavier Bonnetain receives funding from the European Research Council (ERC) under the European Union's Horizon 2020 research and innovation programme (grant agreement no. 714294 – acronym QUASYModo). The work of Shizhu Tian is supported by the National Science Foundation of China (No. 61772517, 61772516).

References

1. Advanced Encryption Standard (AES). National Institute of Standards and Technology (NIST), FIPS PUB 197, U.S. Department of Commerce, November 2001
2. Biham, E., Shamir, A.: Differential cryptanalysis of DES-like cryptosystems. In: Menezes, A.J., Vanstone, S.A. (eds.) CRYPTO 1990. LNCS, vol. 537, pp. 2–21. Springer, Heidelberg (1991). https://doi.org/10.1007/3-540-38424-3_1
3. Biham, E., Shamir, A.: Differential cryptanalysis of feal and N-hash. In: Davies, D.W. (ed.) EUROCRYPT 1991. LNCS, vol. 547, pp. 1–16. Springer, Heidelberg (1991). https://doi.org/10.1007/3-540-46416-6_1
4. Biryukov, A., De Cannière, C., Braeken, A., Preneel, B.: A toolbox for cryptanalysis: linear and affine equivalence algorithms. In: Biham, E. (ed.) EUROCRYPT 2003. LNCS, vol. 2656, pp. 33–50. Springer, Heidelberg (2003). https://doi.org/10.1007/3-540-39200-9_3
5. Biryukov, A., Leurent, G., Perrin, L.: Cryptanalysis of Feistel networks with secret round functions. In: Dunkelman, O., Keliher, L. (eds.) SAC 2015. LNCS, vol. 9566, pp. 102–121. Springer, Cham (2016). https://doi.org/10.1007/978-3-319-31301-6_6
6. Biryukov, A., Perrin, L.: On reverse-engineering S-boxes with hidden design criteria or structure. In: Gennaro, R., Robshaw, M. (eds.) CRYPTO 2015, Part I. LNCS, vol. 9215, pp. 116–140. Springer, Heidelberg (2015). https://doi.org/10.1007/978-3-662-47989-6_6

7. Biryukov, A., Perrin, L., Udovenko, A.: Reverse-engineering the S-box of Streebog, Kuznyechik and STRIBOBr1. In: Fischlin, M., Coron, J.-S. (eds.) EUROCRYPT 2016, Part I. LNCS, vol. 9665, pp. 372–402. Springer, Heidelberg (2016). https://doi.org/10.1007/978-3-662-49890-3_15

8. Biryukov, A., Shamir, A.: Structural cryptanalysis of SASAS. In: Pfitzmann, B. (ed.) EUROCRYPT 2001. LNCS, vol. 2045, pp. 395–405. Springer, Heidelberg (2001). https://doi.org/10.1007/3-540-44987-6_24

9. Blondeau, C., Canteaut, A., Charpin, P.: Differential properties of $x \mapsto x^{2^t-1}$. IEEE Trans. Inf. Theory **57**(12), 8127–8137 (2011)

10. Bonnetain, X., Perrin, L., Tian, S.: Anomalies and vector space search: tools for S-box analysis (full version). Cryptology ePrint Archive, Report 2019/528 (2019). https://eprint.iacr.org/2019/528

11. Boura, C., Canteaut, A.: On the influence of the algebraic degree of f^{-1} on the algebraic degree of $g \circ f$. IEEE Trans. Inf. Theory **59**(1), 691–702 (2013)

12. Boura, C., Perrin, L., Tian, S.: Boomerang uniformity of popular S-box constructions. In: WCC 2019: The Eleventh International Workshop on Coding and Cryptography (2019)

13. Browning, K.A., Dillon, J., McQuistan, M.T., Wolfe, A.J.: An APN permutation in dimension six. In: Post-proceedings of the 9th International Conference on Finite Fields and Their Applications, vol. 518, pp. 33–42. American Mathematical Society (2010)

14. Canteaut, A., Daum, M., Dobbertin, H., Leander, G.: Finding nonnormal bent functions. Discret. Appl. Math. **154**(2), 202–218 (2006). coding and Cryptography

15. Canteaut, A., Perrin, L.: On CCZ-equivalence, extended-affine equivalence, and function twisting. Finite Fields Appl. **56**, 209–246 (2019)

16. Carlet, C., Charpin, P., Zinoviev, V.: Codes, bent functions and permutations suitable for DES-like cryptosystems. Des. Codes Cryptogr. **15**(2), 125–156 (1998)

17. Cid, C., Huang, T., Peyrin, T., Sasaki, Y., Song, L.: Boomerang connectivity table: a new cryptanalysis tool. In: Nielsen, J.B., Rijmen, V. (eds.) EUROCRYPT 2018, Part II. LNCS, vol. 10821, pp. 683–714. Springer, Cham (2018). https://doi.org/10.1007/978-3-319-78375-8_22

18. Daemen, J., Rijmen, V.: Probability distributions of correlation and differentials in block ciphers. J. Math. Cryptol. **1**(3), 221–242 (2007)

19. Developers, T.S.: SageMath, the Sage Mathematics Software System (Version 7.5.1) (2017). http://www.sagemath.org

20. Diffie, W., (translators), G.L.: SMS4 encryption algorithm for wireless networks. Cryptology ePrint Archive, Report 2008/329 (2008). http://eprint.iacr.org/2008/329

21. Dinur, I.: An improved affine equivalence algorithm for random permutations. In: Nielsen, J.B., Rijmen, V. (eds.) EUROCRYPT 2018, Part I. LNCS, vol. 10820, pp. 413–442. Springer, Cham (2018). https://doi.org/10.1007/978-3-319-78381-9_16

22. Federal Agency on Technical Regulation and Metrology: Information technology – data security: Hash function (2012). English version available at http://wwwold.tc26.ru/en/standard/gost/GOST_R_34_11-2012_eng.pdf

23. Federal Agency on Technical Regulation and Metrology: Information technology – data security: Block ciphers (2015). English version available at http://wwwold.tc26.ru/en/standard/gost/GOST_R_34_12_2015_ENG.pdf

24. Helleseth, T. (ed.): EUROCRYPT 1993. LNCS, vol. 765. Springer, Heidelberg (1994). https://doi.org/10.1007/3-540-48285-7

25. Kazymyrov, O., Kazymyrova, V., Oliynykov, R.: A method for generation of high-nonlinear S-boxes based on gradient descent. Cryptology ePrint Archive, Report 2013/578 (2013). http://eprint.iacr.org/2013/578
26. Li, K., Qu, L., Sun, B., Li, C.: New results about the boomerang uniformity of permutation polynomials. CoRR abs/1901.10999 (2019). http://arxiv.org/abs/1901.10999
27. Liu, F., et al.: Analysis of the SMS4 block cipher. In: Pieprzyk, J., Ghodosi, H., Dawson, E. (eds.) ACISP 2007. LNCS, vol. 4586, pp. 158–170. Springer, Heidelberg (2007). https://doi.org/10.1007/978-3-540-73458-1_13
28. Lupanov, O.B.: On networks consisting of functional elements with delays. In: Lyapunov, A.A. (ed.) Systems Theory Research, pp. 43–83. Springer, New York (1973). https://doi.org/10.1007/978-1-4757-0079-4_3
29. Matsui, M.: Linear cryptanalysis method for DES cipher. In: Helleseth [24], pp. 386–397
30. Minaud, B., Derbez, P., Fouque, P.A., Karpman, P.: Key-recovery attacks on ASASA. J. Cryptol. 31(3), 845–884 (2018)
31. Nyberg, K.: Differentially uniform mappings for cryptography. In: Helleseth [24], pp. 55–64
32. O'Connor, L.: On the distribution of characteristics in bijective mappings. In: Helleseth [24], pp. 360–370
33. O'Connor, L.: Properties of linear approximation tables. In: Preneel, B. (ed.) FSE 1994. LNCS, vol. 1008, pp. 131–136. Springer, Heidelberg (1995). https://doi.org/10.1007/3-540-60590-8_10
34. Perrin, L.: Partitions in the S-box of Streebog and Kuznyechik. IACR Trans. Symm. Cryptol. 2019(1), 302–329 (2019)
35. Perrin, L., Udovenko, A., Biryukov, A.: Cryptanalysis of a theorem: decomposing the only known solution to the big APN problem. In: Robshaw, M., Katz, J. (eds.) CRYPTO 2016, Part II. LNCS, vol. 9815, pp. 93–122. Springer, Heidelberg (2016). https://doi.org/10.1007/978-3-662-53008-5_4
36. Perrin, L., Wiemer, F.: S-Boxes used in cryptographic schemes (2017). https://git.sagemath.org/sage.git/tree/src/sage/crypto/sboxes.py
37. Schejbal, J., Tews, E., Wälde, J.: Reverse engineering of CHIASMUS from GSTOOL. Presentation at the Chaos Computer Club (CCC) (2013)
38. Schuster, F.: Reverse engineering of CHIASMUS from GSTOOL. Presentation at the HGI-Kolloquium, January 2014. Slides available at https://prezi.com/ehrz4krw2z0d/hgi-chm/
39. Shannon, C.E.: The synthesis of two-terminal switching circuits. Bell Syst. Tech. J. 28(1), 59–98 (1949)
40. Tardy-Corfdir, A., Gilbert, H.: A known plaintext attack of FEAL-4 and FEAL-6. In: Feigenbaum, J. (ed.) CRYPTO 1991. LNCS, vol. 576, pp. 172–182. Springer, Heidelberg (1992). https://doi.org/10.1007/3-540-46766-1_12
41. Wagner, D.: The boomerang attack. In: Knudsen, L. (ed.) FSE 1999. LNCS, vol. 1636, pp. 156–170. Springer, Heidelberg (1999). https://doi.org/10.1007/3-540-48519-8_12

Isogenies (1)

CSI-FiSh: Efficient Isogeny Based Signatures Through Class Group Computations

Ward Beullens[1](✉), Thorsten Kleinjung[2], and Frederik Vercauteren[1]

[1] imec-COSIC, ESAT, KU Leuven, Leuven, Belgium
{ward.beullens,frederik.vercauteren}@esat.kuleuven.be
[2] EPFL IC LACAL, Station 14, 1015 Lausanne, Switzerland
thorsten.kleinjung@epfl.ch

Abstract. In this paper we report on a new record class group computation of an imaginary quadratic field having 154-digit discriminant, surpassing the previous record of 130 digits. This class group is central to the CSIDH-512 isogeny based cryptosystem, and knowing the class group structure and relation lattice implies efficient uniform sampling and a canonical representation of its elements. Both operations were impossible before and allow us to instantiate an isogeny based signature scheme first sketched by Stolbunov. We further optimize the scheme using multiple public keys and Merkle trees, following an idea by De Feo and Galbraith. We also show that including quadratic twists allows to cut the public key size in half for free. Optimizing for signature size, our implementation takes 390 ms to sign/verify and results in signatures of 263 bytes, at the expense of a large public key. This is 300 times faster and over 3 times smaller than an optimized version of SeaSign for the same parameter set. Optimizing for public key and signature size combined, results in a total size of 1468 bytes, which is smaller than any other post-quantum signature scheme at the 128-bit security level.

Keywords: Isogeny based cryptography · Digital signature · Class group · Group action · Fiat-Shamir

1 Introduction

Isogeny based cryptography was first proposed in 1997 by Couveignes [9] in a talk at the "séminaire de complexité et cryptographie" at the ENS, but his ideas on how class group actions could be used in cryptography were not published at that time. The same ideas were independently rediscovered in 2006 by Rostovtsev and Stolbunov [31]. Both Couveignes as well as Rostovtsev and Stolbunov

---

This work was supported in part by the Research Council KU Leuven grants C14/18/067 and STG/17/019. Ward Beullens is funded by an FWO fellowship. Date of this document: 2019.09.12.

© International Association for Cryptologic Research 2019
S. D. Galbraith and S. Moriai (Eds.): ASIACRYPT 2019, LNCS 11921, pp. 227–247, 2019.
https://doi.org/10.1007/978-3-030-34578-5_9

described a Diffie-Hellman like key agreement scheme (usually called CRS) using the class group of the endomorphism ring of ordinary elliptic curves. Rostovtsev and Stolbunov also describe an isogeny based identification scheme. However, none of these schemes can be considered practical.

A different approach was taken by Jao and De Feo who introduced SIDH (Supersingular Isogeny Diffie–Hellman) [22]. SIDH does not rely on class group actions as CRS, but exploits the simple fact that dividing out an elliptic curve by two (large) non-intersecting subgroups is commutative. SIDH uses supersingular curves, mainly for two reasons: firstly, constructing a supersingular elliptic curve with given group order is trivial, and secondly, their endomorphism ring is non-commutative which thwarts attacks by Kuperberg's algorithm [25]. SIDH forms the basis of a practical key-exchange protocol called SIKE [21], which is one of the main contenders in NIST's post-quantum standardization project [29].

A major improvement of CRS was made by Castryck et al. [6] by instantiating the scheme for supersingular curves over $\mathbb{F}_p$ and by restricting the endomorphism ring to $\mathbb{F}_p$-rational endomorphisms. This subring behaves very much like in the ordinary curve setting, so the CRS approach applies. The main advantage is that the class group action can be computed very efficiently since by construction, the supersingular curves have many small rational subgroups. The resulting cryptosystem is called CSIDH for Commutative Supersingular Isogeny Diffie-Hellman and is pronounced "sea-side".

Both SIDH and CSIDH result in efficient key-agreement schemes, but a practical isogeny based signature scheme is much harder to achieve. The first attempt was made by Stolbunov in his PhD thesis [35]; the signature scheme consists of the Fiat-Shamir transform applied to a standard three pass isogeny based identification scheme. The scheme can be securely instantiated under two assumptions: firstly, it should be possible to sample uniformly in the class group (this could be efficiently approximated) and secondly, each element in the class group has an efficiently computable canonical representation. Especially the second assumption is a major obstacle to instantiate Stolbunov's signature scheme.

This problem was partly remedied by De Feo and Galbraith in the signature scheme SeaSign [11] by employing "Fiat–Shamir with aborts". The main idea is, instead of using a canonical representation for each class group element, to use a majorly redundant representation and to apply rejection sampling to make the distribution of the class group elements, which are part of the signature, independent of the secret key. The drawback is that this redundant representation makes evaluating the class group action much less efficient. Several versions of SeaSign were presented offering trade-offs between signature size, public-key size, and secret-key size. Although signature sizes of less than one kilobyte at the 128-bit security level are possible, the scheme is again not practical taking several minutes to sign. Decru et al. [12] improved all variants of SeaSign, but the fastest parameter set still requires 2 min to sign a message.

A different approach was taken by Yoo et al. [38] who transform an SIDH-based zero-knowledge proof proposed by De Feo et al. [15] into a digital signature scheme. The resulting signatures however are rather large at $\sim$120 KB which is much larger than other post-quantum signature schemes. A similar approach was described by Galbraith et al. [17] who were able to compress the signatures down to roughly 10 KB. None of the above signature schemes is therefore practical, either due to lack of efficiency or due to the large signatures.

It is well known (see for instance Couveignes [9], Stolbunov's PhD [35] or Section 9.2 of [11]), that knowing the class group structure would resolve the two main problems with Stolbunov's signature scheme. Firstly, uniform sampling is now trivial, but more importantly, each element has an efficiently computable canonical representation. This immediately implies that rejection sampling is no longer necessary, thereby majorly speeding up the resulting signature scheme.

The computation of the class group of a quadratic imaginary number field is a classical problem in computational number theory, and the current best algorithms [4,20,23] are improvements of an algorithm due to Hafner and McCurley [18]. These algorithms have complexity $L_{1/2}(\Delta)$ with Δ the discriminant of the number field. The largest publicly known class group computation was for a 130-digit discriminant by Kleinjung [23].

The main contributions in this paper are as follows:

- We compute the class group structure and a relation lattice of the class group of the quadratic imaginary field corresponding to the CSIDH-512 parameter set having a 154-digit discriminant. This computation is described in Sect. 3.
- We present an efficient algorithm to compute the class group action of random class group elements by solving an approximate CVP-problem in the relation lattice. This strategy is described in Sect. 4 and is a combination of Babai nearest plane algorithm [1] and a random walk approach due to Doulgerakis, Laarhoven and de Weger [14]. Compared to native CSIDH which starts from an efficient representation, our algorithm is only 15% slower.
- In Sect. 5, we introduce CSI-FiSh (Commutative Supersingular Isogeny based Fiat-Shamir signatures, pronounce "sea-fish") which is based on Stolbunov's signature scheme [35] combined with optimisations similar to the ones described for SeaSign [11]. We also show that the public key size can be cut in half for free by including not only the curve, but also its quadratic twist. This implicitly doubles the number of curves in the public key for free, without affecting the security of the scheme. Finally, we prove that the resulting signature scheme is secure in the quantum random oracle model.
- We provide an efficient open-source implementation of CSI-FiSh and report on the implementation results in Sect. 6. As for SeaSign, CSI-FiSh allows for various trade-offs: the smallest signatures are 263 bytes and are also the fastest (~390 ms to sign/verify), but require a large public key of 2MB. Slightly larger signatures of 461 bytes require a public key of 16 KB which is comparable to multivariate schemes such as LUOV [3], but take ~670 ms to compute. Optimizing for public key and signature size combined, results in a total size of 1468 bytes which is smaller than any other post-quantum signature scheme at the 128-bit security level.

2   Preliminaries

We denote by $[a, b]$ with $a, b \in \mathbb{Z}, a \leq b$ the set $\{a, \ldots, b\}$. When considering reals instead of integers $[a, b]$ denotes the interval $a \leq r \leq b$ with $r \in \mathbb{R}$, whereas $[a, b[$ denotes $a \leq r < b$. The cardinality of a set S is denoted by $\#S$.

2.1   Elliptic Curves and Isogenies

The go-to general reference on elliptic curves is Silverman [33]. A good intro-duction to isogeny based cryptography can be found in the lecture notes by De Feo [10].

Let E be an elliptic curve over a finite field $\mathbb{F}_p$ with p a large prime, and let $\mathbf{0}_E$ denote the point at infinity on E. The curve E is called supersingular iff $\#E(\mathbb{F}_p) = p + 1$, and ordinary otherwise. Given two elliptic curves E and E', an isogeny ϕ is a morphism $\phi : E \to E'$ (i.e. can be expressed as fractions of polynomials) such that $\phi(\mathbf{0}_E) = \mathbf{0}_{E'}$. An isomorphism is an isogeny that has an inverse (which is also a morphism), and two elliptic curves are isomorphic iff they have the same j-invariant, which is a simple algebraic expression in the coefficients of the curve. Since an isogeny defines a group homomorphism from E to E', its kernel is a subgroup of E. Vice-versa, any subgroup $S \subset E(\mathbb{F}_{p^k})$ determines a (separable) isogeny $\phi : E \to E'$ with $\ker \phi = S$, i.e. $E' = E/S$. The equation for E' and the isogeny ϕ can be computed using Vélu's formulae [36] using $O(\#S(k \log p)^2)$ bit-operations. As such, it is only practical to handle fairly small subgroups S defined over small extensions of $\mathbb{F}_p$.

The ring of endomorphisms $\mathrm{End}(E)$ consists of all isogenies from E to itself, and $\mathrm{End}_{\mathbb{F}_p}(E)$ denotes the ring of endomorphisms defined over $\mathbb{F}_p$. For an ordi-nary curve $E/\mathbb{F}_p$ we have $\mathrm{End}(E) = \mathrm{End}_{\mathbb{F}_p}(E)$, but for a supersingular curve over $\mathbb{F}_p$ we have a strict inclusion $\mathrm{End}_{\mathbb{F}_p}(E) \subsetneq \mathrm{End}(E)$. In particular, it is known that for a supersingular curve over $\mathbb{F}_p$ its full endomorphism ring $\mathrm{End}(E)$ is an order in a quaternion algebra, whereas $\mathrm{End}_{\mathbb{F}_p}(E)$ is only an order in the imaginary quadratic field $\mathbb{Q}(\sqrt{-p})$. In the following we will denote this order $\mathcal{O} = \mathrm{End}_{\mathbb{F}_p}(E)$.

The ideal class group of $\mathcal{O}$ is the quotient of the group of fractional invert-ible ideals in $\mathcal{O}$ by the principal fractional invertible ideals, and will be denoted $\mathrm{Cl}(\mathcal{O})$. Given an $\mathcal{O}$-ideal $\mathfrak{a}$, we can consider the subgroup defined by the inter-section of the kernels of the endomorphisms in $\mathfrak{a}$, i.e. $S_{\mathfrak{a}} = \bigcap_{\alpha \in \mathfrak{a}} \ker \alpha$. Since this is a subgroup of E, we can divide out by $S_{\mathfrak{a}}$ and denote the isogenous curve $E/S_{\mathfrak{a}}$ by $\mathfrak{a} \star E$. This isogeny is well-defined and unique up to $\mathbb{F}_p$-isomorphism and the group $\mathrm{Cl}(\mathcal{O})$ acts via the operator $\star$ on the set $\mathcal{E}$ of $\mathbb{F}_p$-isomorphism classes of elliptic curves with $\mathbb{F}_p$-rational endomorphism ring $\mathcal{O}$. One can show that $\mathrm{Cl}(\mathcal{O})$ acts freely and transitively on $\mathcal{E}$, i.e. $\mathcal{E}$ is a principal homogeneous space for $\mathrm{Cl}(\mathcal{O})$.

In what follows we will assume that the class group $\mathrm{Cl}(\mathcal{O})$ is cyclic of order $N = \#\mathrm{Cl}(\mathcal{O})$ generated by the class of an ideal $\mathfrak{g}$. The more general case of non-cyclic class groups is a trivial extension and is not required in the application we consider.

2.2 CSIDH

Castryck et al. [6] proposed an efficient commutative group action $\star$ by crafting supersingular elliptic curves with many small $\mathbb{F}_p$-rational subgroups. Given that $\#E(\mathbb{F}_p) = p + 1$ for a supersingular curve, it is immediate that if p is chosen to be of the form $4 \cdot \ell_1 \cdots \ell_n - 1$, with ℓ_i small distinct odd primes, we have $\#E(\mathbb{F}_p) = 4 \cdot \ell_1 \cdots \ell_n$. Such curves therefore have, for each $i \in [1, n]$, an $\mathbb{F}_p$-rational subgroup of order ℓ_i. Since $p = -1 \bmod \ell_i$, we have that in $\mathbb{Q}(\sqrt{-p})$ the rational prime ℓ_i splits as $(\ell_i) = \langle \ell_i, \pi - 1 \rangle \langle \ell_i, \pi + 1 \rangle$, where $\pi = \sqrt{-p}$ represents the $\mathbb{F}_p$-Frobenius endomorphism. Note that the first ideal factor $\mathfrak{l}_i = \langle \ell_i, \pi - 1 \rangle$ corresponds to the subgroup of order ℓ_i defined over $\mathbb{F}_p$, and that the action of this ideal can be computed entirely over $\mathbb{F}_p$. Once this subgroup is determined, Vélu's formulae require $O(\ell_i(\log p)^2)$ bit operations. However, for small ℓ_i, finding a generator of this small subgroup requires (at least one) full-size scalar multiplication which dominates the cost of Vélu's formulae.

CSIDH considers the action of ideals of the form $\prod_{i=1}^n \mathfrak{l}_i^{e_i}$ where the exponents are chosen uniformly from some interval $[-B, B]$. This can be done by computing sequentially the action of $\mathfrak{l}_i$ exactly e_i times. Since the cost of each such action is dominated by the cost to determine the correct subgroup, we assume that the overall cost of computing such action is mostly determined by the ℓ_1-norm of its exponent vector, i.e. $|e_1| + \cdots + |e_n|$.

The base curve is taken to be $E_0 \colon y^2 = x^3 + x$ over $\mathbb{F}_p$ and instead of using the j-invariant, each isomorphism class of a curve with given endomorphism ring $\mathrm{End}_{\mathbb{F}_p}(E) = \mathcal{O} = \mathbb{Z}[\pi]$ is represented by a single coefficient $A \in \mathbb{F}_p$ defining the curve $E_A \colon y^2 = x^3 + Ax^2 + x$. Denote $\mathcal{A}$ the set of all such coefficients A, then we obtain a class group action $\star \colon \mathrm{Cl}(\mathcal{O}) \times \mathcal{A} \to \mathcal{A}$ or equivalently, assuming the class group is cyclic of order N, a group action $[] \colon \mathbb{Z}_N \times \mathcal{A} \to \mathcal{A}$. To simplify notation in the remainder of the paper, we will identify a curve E_A with its isomorphism class represented by the corresponding coefficient A.

Note however that in CSIDH, the order (and structure) of the class group are unknown, so only the action of ideals of the form $\prod_{i=1}^n \mathfrak{l}_i^{e_i}$ with e_i smallish are computable. This restriction brings up various questions: firstly, given the range of exponent vectors $[-B, B]^n$, do the ideals $\prod_{i=1}^n \mathfrak{l}_i^{e_i}$ cover the whole class group, and secondly, assuming the exponents are chosen uniformly in $[-B, B]$, is the resulting distribution of $\prod_{i=1}^n \mathfrak{l}_i^{e_i}$ uniform over $\mathrm{Cl}(\mathcal{O})$. It is clear that knowing the class group structure voids both questions as surjectivity and uniformity become trivial to attain. The only remaining problem then is to efficiently compute the action $[a]$ given a random exponent $a \in \mathbb{Z}_N$ (see Sect. 4 for an efficient solution).

2.3 Computational Problems

The main hardness assumption underlying group actions based on isogenies, is that it is hard to invert the group action:

Definition 1 (Group Action Inverse Problem (GAIP)). *Given a curve E, with $\mathrm{End}(E) = \mathcal{O}$, find an ideal $\mathfrak{a} \subset \mathcal{O}$ such that $E = \mathfrak{a} \star E_0$.*

Another advantage of knowing the class group structure and therefore uniform sampling, is that the GAIP is random self-reducible: given a problem instance E, we can shift this over a uniformly random $\mathfrak{b}$ to obtain $E' = \mathfrak{b} \star E$, which is uniformly distributed in $\mathcal{A}$. Given a solution $\mathfrak{c}$ for E', it is easy to see that $\mathfrak{c}\mathfrak{b}^{-1}$ is then a solution to the original problem.

The CSI-FiSh signature scheme relies on the hardness of random instances of a multi-target version of the inversion problem, which is shown to reduce tightly to the normal GAIP by [11] in the case that the class group structure is known.

Definition 2 (Multi-Target GAIP (MT-GAIP)). *Given k curves $E_1, \ldots, E_k$ with $\mathrm{End}(E_1) = \cdots = \mathrm{End}(E_k) = \mathcal{O}$, find an ideal $\mathfrak{a} \subset \mathcal{O}$ such that $E_i = \mathfrak{a} \star E_j$ for some $i, j \in \{0, \cdots, k\}$ with $i \neq j$.*

The best classical algorithm to solve the GAIP problem is a simple meet-in-the-middle approach, where one finds a collision between two breadth-first trees starting at E and E' respectively. The time complexity of this approach is $O(\sqrt{\#\mathrm{Cl}(\mathcal{O})})$. The best quantum algorithm for the GAIP problem reformulates it as a hidden shift problem [7] and then applies Kuperberg's algorithm [25, 26], which runs in time $2^{O(\sqrt{\log N})}$. Translating this subexponential complexity to concrete security estimates is a highly non-trivial endeavour and we refer to [5, 6, 30] for precise details.

In this paper we will only focus on the CSIDH-512 parameter set, which uses 74 small primes ℓ_i (so $n = 74$) and samples the exponents uniformly from the interval $[-5, 5]$ (so $B = 5$). The CSIDH authors assume that sampling exponent vectors in $[-5, 5]$ covers a subset of size $\sim 2^{256}$, which, as we will see, is a bit less than half of the total size of the class group. Class group elements (represented by their exponent vectors) require roughly 32 bytes, and each isomorphism class requires 64 bytes (one coefficient in $\mathbb{F}_p$). The average time taken to perform one such group action [6] is roughly 40 ms on a 3.5 GHz processor. This parameter set aimed to provide 128-bit classical security and to achieve NIST security level 1 quantumly [6]. However, recent works propose quantum attacks and claim that CSIDH-512 does not reach the NIST security level 1 [5, 30].

3 Class Group Computation

In order to uniformly sample and canonically represent class group elements, a class group computation of Hafner-McCurley type [18] was performed which, besides computing generators of the class group, also expresses the ideal classes of prime ideals with small norm in terms of these generators. This computation relied on the programs from [23], which work over the maximal order and thus we obtain generators for $\mathrm{Cl}(\mathcal{O}_{\mathbb{Q}(\sqrt{-p})})$, where p is the 512-bit prime used in CSIDH-512. This class group turns out to be cyclic and the class number is not divisible by 3. Since the conductor of the suborder $\mathcal{O}$ is (2) and 2 does not split in $\mathcal{O}_{\mathbb{Q}(\sqrt{-p})}$, we get $\#\mathrm{Cl}(\mathcal{O}) = 3\#\mathrm{Cl}(\mathcal{O}_{\mathbb{Q}(\sqrt{-p})})$ so that $\mathrm{Cl}(\mathcal{O})$ is also cyclic. Using the information from the computation over the maximal order, it is easy to find a generator of $\mathrm{Cl}(\mathcal{O})$ and to express the $\mathfrak{l}_i$ as powers of this generator. In total, the computation took an estimated effort of 52 core years on an inhomogenous cluster of number crunchers and desktop machines, consisting of around 800 cores with the "average" core running at around 3.3 GHz.

The class group computation consists of the following steps.

Relation Collection. Given a bound F (we chose $F = 7000000$), let $\mathcal{F}$ be the set of prime ideals of degree one with norm less than F and the prime ideal (2); the latter is only included for technical reasons. A relation is a decomposition $(a+\sqrt{-p}) = \prod_{\mathfrak{p} \in \mathcal{F}} \mathfrak{p}^{e_{a,\mathfrak{p}}}$ with $a, e_{a,\mathfrak{p}} \in \mathbb{Z}$. Such relations can be found by factoring the ideal $(a + \sqrt{-p})$ for random $a \in \mathbb{Z}$ which essentially amounts to factoring its norm $a^2 + p$. Since most a do not give rise to a relation, there exist many methods to speed up the search for relations. We used a sieving approach [23] and the large prime variation with up to three large primes; these details do not matter in the following and are suppressed.

The goal of this step is to generate sufficiently many relations such that the subsequent steps are able to determine the class group. In practice, this usually means that we can stop collecting relations when the number of relations slightly exceeds the number of prime ideals contained in their decompositions (which is at most $\#\mathcal{F}$). However, a bigger excess often reduces the running time of the subsequent steps significantly.

This step is one of the two main steps in terms of computational effort. Fortunately, it is trivially parallelized and has moderate memory requirements. In our computation it took an estimated time of 43 core years to collect 319.5 million relations over an extended factor base of size 32.7 million.

Building the Matrix. In this step the set of relations is converted into a matrix over $\mathbb{Z}$ with rows corresponding to prime ideals and columns corresponding to relations; the matrix entry belonging to the prime ideal $\mathfrak{p} \in \mathcal{F}$ and relation $(a + \sqrt{-p})$ is $e_{a,\mathfrak{p}}$. This matrix is overdetermined and very sparse. We now assume that the ideal classes of the prime ideals in $\mathcal{F}$ generate the class group. In practice, it is very likely that this assumption holds; moreover, it follows from GRH if F is chosen appropriately. Under the assumption above, one has a surjection $\mathbb{Z}^{\#\mathcal{F}}/\Lambda \to \mathrm{Cl}(\mathcal{O}_{\mathbb{Q}(\sqrt{-p})})$ where Λ is the lattice spanned by the columns. If the matrix has full rank, the covolume of Λ is a multiple of the class number. By performing elementary column operations as well as removing certain rows and columns one can reduce this matrix significantly while keeping it slightly overdetermined and sparse; this is done to reduce the complexity of the next steps.

In terms of running time this step is negligible but it has higher memory requirements and is not easily parallelisable. We reduced our set of 319.5 million relations over a factor base of size 32.7 million to a slightly overdetermined matrix with roughly 222 thousand rows.

Matrix Step. By dropping some columns from the matrix above one can obtain a square matrix and use the (block) Wiedemann algorithm modulo many small primes to compute its determinant over $\mathbb{Z}$ (cf. [8,37]). If the determinant is non-zero, it is a (usually) huge multiple of the class number. By repeating the determinant calculation for another square matrix obtained by dropping another set of columns one gets a second huge multiple of the class number. Their greatest common divisor is much smaller, thus can be factored, and for each of its prime factors one can check whether it is a divisor of the class number using quadratic forms.

This is the other main step, it is also easy to parallelize and has moderate memory requirements. For both determinant computations, we computed the determinant modulo roughly 7000 different 64-bit primes, which took roughly 4.3 core years per determinant. By taking the gcd of the determinants and removing an extra factor of 2, we obtained that

$$\#\mathrm{Cl}(\mathcal{O}_{\mathbb{Q}(\sqrt{-p})}) = 37 \times 1407181 \times 51593604295295867744293584889$$
$$\times 31599414504681995853008278745587832204909 \,.$$

The class group of the order $\mathcal{O}$ therefore has cardinality $3 \cdot \#\mathrm{Cl}(\mathcal{O}_{\mathbb{Q}(\sqrt{-p})})$ which is approximately equal to $2^{257.136}$.

Final Computations. In this step the r-Sylow group of $\mathrm{Cl}(\mathcal{O}_{\mathbb{Q}(\sqrt{-p})})$ is computed for each r dividing the class number together with the images of all involved prime ideals in this Sylow group. For small r this is easy and for large r the kernel of one of the square matrices from the previous step can be computed modulo r, e.g., using the Lanczos or Wiedemann algorithm. Finally, tying everything together a set of generators of the class group and for each involved prime ideal a representation in terms of these generators is obtained.

This step is negligible in terms of running time and has only moderate memory requirements. It turns out that the ideal $\mathfrak{l}_1 = \langle 3, \pi - 1 \rangle$ generates $\mathrm{Cl}(\mathcal{O})$, the discrete logs of the other $\mathfrak{l}_i$ are available in our GitHub repository [2].

Remark 3 Notice that all odd primes up to 373 split in $\mathbb{Q}(\sqrt{-p})$ thus improving the probablity that the ideal $(a + \sqrt{-p})$ gives rise to a relation. This facilitates the class group computation for our choice of p but the gain is much less than a factor of 2 compared to an average prime of the size of p.

4   Class Group Action

In this section we discuss how to compute the action of ideals represented as $\mathfrak{g}^a$, where $\mathfrak{g}$ is a generator of the class group. In practice, it will often be the case that one of the $\mathfrak{l}_i$ generates the class group already, and in fact, for the CSIDH-512 class group we can even take $\mathfrak{g} = \mathfrak{l}_1 = \langle 3, \pi - 1 \rangle$. Recall that for isogenies, there is no analogue of the standard square-and-multiply for exponentiation, so a different approach is required. Since we can only compute the group action efficiently for the prime ideals $\mathfrak{l}_i = \langle l_i, \pi - 1 \rangle$, our approach is to first use lattice reduction algorithms to rewrite $\mathfrak{g}^a$ as a product of the $\mathfrak{l}_i$ with small exponents. After this step, the action can be computed efficiently with Vélu's Formulae.

More concretely, the ideal $\mathfrak{l}_1^a$ corresponds to the exponent vector $\mathbf{e} = [a, 0, \cdots, 0]$, that needs to be reduced modulo the relation lattice:

$$L := \{\mathbf{z} = (z_1, \ldots, z_n) \in \mathbb{Z}^n : \prod_{i=1}^{n} \mathfrak{l}_i^{z_i} = (1)\}.$$

The lattice L has rank n and volume $N = \#\mathrm{Cl}(\mathcal{O})$ since by definition it is the kernel of the surjective group homomorphism that maps $\mathbb{Z}^n \rightarrow \mathrm{Cl}(\mathcal{O}) : \mathbf{z} = (z_1, \ldots, z_n) \mapsto \prod_{i=1}^{n} \mathfrak{l}_i^{z_i}$. Note that the relation lattice follows directly from the class group computation described in Sect. 3.

Since the complexity of a CSIDH action is mainly determined by the ℓ_1-norm of the exponent vector, we want to solve the Closest Vector Problem (CVP) in L for the ℓ_1-norm given the target vector $\mathbf{e}$. Indeed, any vector $\mathbf{z} \in L$ which is close to $\mathbf{e}$ for the ℓ_1 norm will result in an equivalent vector $\mathbf{e} - \mathbf{z}$ such that $\|\mathbf{e} - \mathbf{z}\|_1$ is small and thus efficiently computable.

A first approximation for solving the CVP for the ℓ_1-norm is to use either Babai's rounding or nearest plane algorithm [1]. Given a set of basis vectors $B := \{\mathbf{b}_1, \ldots, \mathbf{b}_n\}$, denote with $B^\star := \{\mathbf{b}_1^\star, \ldots, \mathbf{b}_n^\star\}$ the corresponding Gram-Schmidt orthogonalization vectors. Let $\mathcal{P}(B)$ denote the parallelepiped

$$\mathcal{P}(B) = \left\{ \sum_{i=1}^{n} \alpha_i \mathbf{b}_i \mid \alpha_i \in [-1/2, 1/2[\right\},$$

then Babai rounding returns a lattice vector in $\mathbf{e} + \mathcal{P}(B)$ and Babai's nearest plane in $\mathbf{e} + \mathcal{P}(B^\star)$. This shows that $\mathbf{e} - \mathbf{z}$ is either in $\mathcal{P}(B)$ or in $\mathcal{P}(B^\star)$ depending on the choice of algorithm. Given a basis B and corresponding Gram-Schmidt basis $B^\star$, it is therefore easy to bound $\|\mathbf{e} - \mathbf{z}\|_1$. This also shows that a basis with short and almost orthogonal vectors will give better results. In our experiments, we only used Babai's nearest plane algorithm since it is superior to Babai rounding.

Several notions of reductions and corresponding algorithms exist such as LLL [28], BKZ [32] or HKZ [24]. Since the lattice L is fixed for a given class group, a considerable effort can be spent in reducing the lattice basis during a precomputation. To analyze the impact of the quality of the basis, we computed three reductions: BKZ-40, BKZ-50 and HKZ. For each reduced basis, we then ran Babai nearest plane resulting in Table 1, where the average ℓ_1-norm and standard deviation are given for a sample size of 10^4 random exponents.

The above table should be compared with the expected ℓ_1-norm and standard deviation of vectors sampled according to the CSIDH distribution, i.e. uniform random in $[-B, B]^n$. For $B = 5$ and $n = 74$, we obtain $\mu = n2(5 + 4 + 3 + 2 + 1)/11 = 201.81$ and $\sigma = 13.76$, but note $(2B + 1)^{74} < N/2.2$ so less than half of the class group is covered by CSIDH.

To lower the ℓ_1-norm further, we can employ an algorithm due to Doulgerakis, Laarhoven and de Weger [14] (originally described in [27]). The idea of this

Table 1. ℓ_1-norm and ℓ_2-norm of Babai's nearest plane method and evaluation times of CSIDH-action on three different bases

	BKZ-40	BKZ-50	HKZ
ℓ_1-norm	$\mu = 240.67$	$\mu = 239.35$	$\mu = 237.50$
	$\sigma = 18.82$	$\sigma = 18.35$	$\sigma = 18.26$
ℓ_2-norm	$\mu = 35.13$	$\mu = 34.93$	$\mu = 34.67$
	$\sigma = 2.47$	$\sigma = 2.43$	$\sigma = 2.38$
Action evaluation time (10^6 cycles)	$\mu = 148.59$	$\mu = 148.41$	$\mu = 147.16$
	$\sigma = 12.91$	$\sigma = 12.57$	$\sigma = 12.46$

algorithm is pretty simple: given a list $\mathcal{S}$ of short vectors in the lattice L, it tries to construct a vector that is closer to $\mathbf{e}$ than the current vector $\mathbf{z}$ by considering $\mathbf{z} \pm \mathbf{s}$ for all $\mathbf{s} \in \mathcal{S}$. This procedure is then repeated on small random shifts of the target vector. The resulting DLW algorithm is described in Algorithm 1.

Algorithm 1 DLW algorithm - randomized slicer for solving CVP

Input: A list $\mathcal{S} \subset L$ of short vectors, target vector $\mathbf{e} \in \mathbb{Z}^n$, number of iterations M
Output: Approximate closest lattice vector $\mathbf{z}$ to $\mathbf{e}$
1: $\mathbf{z} \leftarrow \mathbf{0}$
2: **for** $i = 0, \ldots, M - 1$ **do**
3:     Randomize $\mathbf{e}$ with random small lattice vector to obtain $\mathbf{e}'$
4:     **for** $\mathbf{s} \in \mathcal{S}$ **do**
5:         **if** $\|\mathbf{e}' - \mathbf{s}\|_1 < \|\mathbf{e}'\|_1$ **then**
6:             $\mathbf{e}' \leftarrow \mathbf{e}' - \mathbf{s}$ and restart for loop in line (4)
7:         **end if**
8:     **end for**
9:     **if** $\|\mathbf{e}'\|_1 < \|\mathbf{e} - \mathbf{z}\|_1$ **then**
10:         $\mathbf{z} \leftarrow \mathbf{e} - \mathbf{e}'$
11:     **end if**
12: **end for**
13: **return** $\mathbf{z}$

We ran Algorithm 1 for varying sizes of lists of short vectors and varying number of iterations; the results can be found in Table 2.

Our experiments indicate that (on our setup) the fastest approach is to use the Babai nearest plane method with 2 iterations of the DLW algorithm, with a list of 10000 short vectors. In this case, the reduction takes $7.2 \cdot 10^6$ cycles on average, and evaluating the CSIDH action takes on average $128.1 \cdot 10^6$ cycles. In comparison, standard CSIDH-512 uses vectors sampled uniformly from $[-5, 5]^{74}$ (which does not sample uniformly from $\mathrm{Cl}(\mathcal{O})$) and takes on average $117.7 \cdot 10^6$ cycles. Hence, the additional cost of sampling uniformly is only 15%.

Table 2. ℓ_1-norm, ℓ_2-norm and evaluation time (reduction + action) of the DLW algorithm combined with Babai's nearest plane method on an HKZ basis

List size	Iterations	ℓ_1-norm	ℓ_2-norm	Time of reduction + action
1000	1	223.54 ± 13.29	34.07 ± 2.45	140.17 ± 10.32
1000	3	221.38 ± 11.82	33.79 ± 2.26	138.02 ± 10.24
1000	10	216.84 ± 10.14	33.21 ± 2.03	137.66 ± 9.82
3000	1	219.02 ± 12.02	33.65 ± 2.34	138.09 ± 10.25
3000	3	214.96 ± 10.33	33.03 ± 2.09	136.78 ± 9.46
3000	10	208.75 ± 8.55	32.12 ± 1.81	136.95 ± 8.73
10000	1	213.96 ± 10.92	33.09 ± 2.30	135.55 ± 9.53
10000	3	207.97 ± 9.10	32.08 ± 1.93	135.41 ± 8.82
10000	10	201.26 ± 7.47	31.05 ± 1.66	144.26 ± 7.94

5 The Signature Scheme

In this section we propose CSI-FiSh, an efficient isogeny based signature scheme. The basis of CSI-FiSh was already sketched by Stolbunov in his thesis [35, 2.B]. He applies the Fiat-Shamir transform [16] to an isogeny based identification scheme by Couveignes [9] and independently by Stolbunov [34].

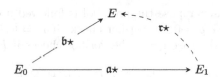

Fig. 1. The basic identification scheme for challenge $c = 1$.

5.1 The Basic Identification Scheme

The identification scheme is illustrated in Fig. 1 and works as follows: the public key of the prover consists of $E_1 = \mathfrak{a} \star E_0$ with $\mathfrak{a}$ a random element in $\mathrm{Cl}(\mathcal{O})$ and E_0 the base curve specified by the system parameters. Assuming that $\mathrm{Cl}(\mathcal{O})$ is cyclic with generator $\mathfrak{g}$, we can write $\mathfrak{a} = \mathfrak{g}^a$ with a random in $\mathbb{Z}_N$ and $N = \#\mathrm{Cl}(\mathcal{O})$. The prover samples a random element $\mathfrak{b} = \mathfrak{g}^b$ with $b \in_R \mathbb{Z}_N$ and commits to the (isomorphism class of the) curve $E = \mathfrak{g}^b \star E_0 = [b]E_0$. The verifier then chooses a random bit $c \in \{0, 1\}$ and sends this to the prover. If $c = 0$, the prover responds with $r = b$, and the verifier checks that $E = [r]E_0$, if $c = 1$, the prover responds with $r = b - a \bmod N$ and the verifier checks that $E = [r]E_1$. Note that reducing modulo N is required to avoid any leakage on a and that the check can be written as $E = [r]E_c$. A detailed description of the protocol is displayed in Fig. 2.

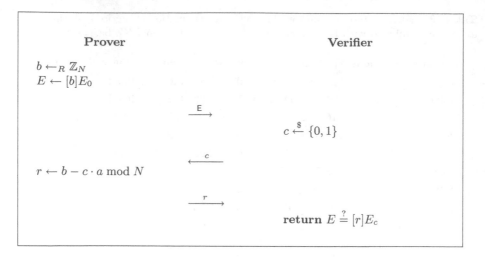

Fig. 2. The identification scheme of Couveignes and Stolbunov.

Theorem 4. *The Couveignes-Stolbunov protocol (Fig. 2) is a complete and secure Sigma protocol proving knowledge of a solution of a GAIP instance. That is, it enjoys completeness, special soundness and special Honest-Verifier Zero Knowledge.*

Proof. **Completeness.** Suppose the protocol is followed honestly, and suppose $E_1 = [a]E_0$. In the case $c = 0$ the verifier checks if $E = [b]E_0$, which is true by construction of E. In the case $c = 1$ the verifier checks if $E = [b - a]E_1$ which holds because

$$[b - a]E_1 = [b - a][a]E_0 = [b]E_0 = E.$$

Special Soundness. Suppose $(E, 0, r_0)$ and $(E, 1, r_1)$ are two transcripts that are accepted by the verifier. Then we have

$$E = [r_0]E_0 = [r_1]E_1,$$

from which it follows that $[r_0 - r_1]E_0 = E_1$. Hence, it is trivial to extract $r_0 - r_1$, which is a solution to the GAIP problem.

Special Honest-Verifier Zero Knowledge. Consider the simulator that, given a bit c picks a random $r \in \mathbb{Z}_N$, computes $E = [r]E_c$ and outputs the transcript (E, c, r). Then it is clear that the transcripts generated by the simulator are indistinguishable from transcripts of honest executions of the protocol with challenge equal to c: both the real transcripts and the simulated transcripts have uniformly random distributed values of r, and $E = [r]E_c$.   □

5.2   Optimizing the Sigma Protocol

Hashing. To reduce the communication cost (and hence the signature size after applying the Fiat-Shamir transform) it suffices for the Prover to send $\mathcal{H}(E)$

rather than E, for some collision resistant hash function $\mathcal{H}$. The verifier then computes $\mathcal{H}([r]E_c)$ and checks that it is equal to the hash value sent by the prover. If we are doing t rounds of the protocol in parallel to amplify soundness, it suffices to send a single hash of the concatenation of all the $E^{(i)}$ for i from 1 to t. Clearly the completeness and the Honest-Verifier Zero Knowledge properties of the scheme are not affected by this change. For special soundness, the collision resistance of $\mathcal{H}$ implies that if

$$\mathcal{H}([r_1^{(1)}]E_{c_1^{(1)}}|| \cdots ||[r_1^{(t)}]E_{c_1^{(t)}}) = \mathcal{H}([r_2^{(1)}]E_{c_2^{(1)}}|| \cdots ||[r_2^{(t)}]E_{c_2^{(t)}})$$

then $[r_1^{(i)}]E_{c_1^{(i)}} = [r_2^{(i)}]E_{c_2^{(i)}}$ for all i from 1 to t. Hence, if we model $\mathcal{H}$ as a random oracle it is sufficient for $\mathcal{H}$ to have output length 2λ, with λ the security level.

Larger Challenge Spaces. A well-known approach [11] to lower the soundness error is to increase the challenge space. To do this we move from the GAIP problem to the MT-GAIP problem. We now have $S - 1$ public keys instead of one, i.e. the public key now consists of the S-tuple $(E_0, E_1 = [a_1]E_0, \ldots, E_{S-1} = [a_{S-1}]E_0)$ (note that E_0 can be left out, it is just there to illustrate the notation) and the prover proves to the verifier that he knows an $s \in \mathbb{Z}_N$ such that $[s]E_i = E_j$ for some pair of curves in the public key (with $i \neq j$). The prover still chooses a random exponent $b \in_R \mathbb{Z}_N$ and computes $E^{(i)} = [b]E_0$. The verifier now sends a challenge $c \in [0, S[$, and the response consists of $r = b - a_c \bmod N$. The verifier then recomputes $[r]E_c$ and verifies that this is equal to $E^{(i)}$. Theorem 4 generalizes to the new identification scheme. In particular, since the challenge space now contains S elements the soundness error drops to $1/S$.

Theorem 5. *The adapted identification scheme is a complete and secure Sigma protocol proving knowledge of a solution of an MT-GAIP instance.*

Proof. The proof is completely analogous to the proof of Theorem 4. □

Doubling the Challenge Space with Twists. To increase the size of the challenge space even further, we exploit the fact that given a curve $E = [a]E_0$, its quadratic twist E^t (which can be computed very efficiently) is $\mathbb{F}_p$-isomorphic to $[-a]E_0$ [6]. Therefore, we can almost double the set of public key curves going from $E_0, E_1, \ldots, E_{S-1}$ to $E_{-S+1}, \cdots, E_0, \cdots, E_{S-1}$, where $E_{-i} = E_i^t$, without any increase in communication cost. Hence, the soundness error drops to $\frac{1}{2S-1}$. Theorem 5 still applies, but instead of a reduction from a random MT-GAIP instance, we now have a reduction from a random MT-GAIP instance subject to $E_{-i} = E_i^t$ (we call this twisted MT-GAIP). However, there is a simple reduction from this problem to MT-GAIP, which shows this optimization does not affect security.

Theorem 6. *Given an adversary $\mathcal{A}$ that solves a random instance of twisted MT-GAIP in time T and with probability ϵ, there exists an adversary $\mathcal{B}^{\mathcal{A}}$ that* solves a random instance of MT-GAIP in time $T + O(S)$ with probability at least $\epsilon/2$.

Proof. We describe the adversary $\mathcal{B}^{\mathcal{A}}$. Suppose $\mathcal{B}$ is given a random MT-GAIP instance $E_1, \cdots, E_k$, then he chooses k random bits $b_1, \cdots, b_k$ and defines curves

$$\tilde{E}_i = \begin{cases} E_i \text{ if } b_i = 0 \\ E_i^t \text{ if } b_i = 1 \end{cases},$$

then he sets $\tilde{E}_0 = E_0$ and $\tilde{E}_{-i} = \tilde{E}_i^t$ for all i in $\{1, \cdots, k\}$. This is a random twisted MT-GAIP instance that $\mathcal{B}$ then sends to $\mathcal{A}$. With probability ϵ, $\mathcal{A}$ responds with (a, i, j) such that $i \neq j$ and $\tilde{E}_i = [a]\tilde{E}_j$. Now we consider 2 cases:

- $i = -j$. In this case we have $\tilde{E}_i = [a]\tilde{E}_i^t$, which implies $\tilde{E}_i = [a/2]E_0$, so $\mathcal{B}$ outputs $((-1)^{b_{|i|}}a/2, |i|, 0)$, which is a valid solution to his MT-GAIP instance ($\#\mathrm{Cl}(\mathcal{O})$ is known to be odd, so the inverse of 2 always exists).
- $|i| \neq |j|$. In this case we have $\mathrm{sign}(i)(-1)^{b_{|i|}} = \mathrm{sign}(j)(-1)^{b_{|j|}}$ with probability $\frac{1}{2}$. In this case we have an equation of the form $E_i = [\pm a]E_j$ or $E_i^t = [\pm a]E_j^t$. Therefore B can output a valid solution to his MT-GAIP problem $(\pm a, |i|, |j|)$.

Shorter Public Keys. The previous section explains how one can improve the communication cost and the proving and verification time by considering multiple public key curves $E_i = [a_i]E_0$ for $i \in \{1, \cdots, S-1\}$. The drawback of this approach is that the public key now consists of $S - 1$ curves, so its size blows up as S increases. Note that at most t of these public key curves are used during each verification (where t is the number of parallel executions of the protocol to amplify soundness). Therefore, instead of including all the curves $E_1, \cdots, E_{S-1}$ in the public key, the public key can just be a commitment to those curves. The improvement in total communication cost comes from the fact that the response of the prover now only has to include the opening of at most t curves $E_{c_1}, \cdots, E_{c_t}$. If the commitment scheme is binding, then a cheating prover cannot open the commitment to an incorrect curve, so the security of the scheme is preserved. We use a Merkle tree construction to implement the binding commitments, because this allows for the efficient opening of a subset of the curves.

In particular, suppose for simplicity that $S - 1 = 2^d$ and let

$$h_{d,i} = \mathcal{H}(E_i || 2^d + i || \mathsf{MerkleKey}),$$

where $\mathsf{MerkleKey} \in \{0, 1\}^\lambda$ is a key which is chosen uniformly at random during key generation and included in both the secret and public keys. Then we define each internal node of the Merkle tree as the hash of its children, concatenated with its position in the tree and the $\mathsf{MerkleKey}$:

$$h_{k,i} = \mathcal{H}(h_{k+1,2i-1} || h_{k+1,2i} || 2^k + i || \mathsf{MerkleKey}).$$

It is an easy exercise to show that if we model $\mathcal{H}$ as a random oracle, the root of the Merkle tree is a binding commitment: An adversary making q queries to the random oracle has at most probability $\frac{q+1}{2^\lambda}$ of breaking the binding property. Note that the MerkleKey is not strictly required to prove soundness, but it prevents an adversary from attacking multiple public keys at the same time. A similar approach of reducing the public key size was proposed by [11]. They use the more complicated and slightly less efficient construction of [19], which is designed to be provably secure in the standard model. Since the Fiat-Shamir transform relies on the (Q)ROM anyway, there is no reason to use this approach.

5.3 Signatures

The above identification schemes can be turned into (non-interactive) signature schemes using the Fiat-Shamir transform [16], where the challenges $c_i \in \{-S + 1, \cdots, S - 1\}$ are simply obtained by hashing the ephemeral keys $E^{(i)}$ for $i = 1, \ldots, t$ together with the message m, i.e. $(c_1, \ldots, c_t) = \mathcal{H}(E^{(1)} || \ldots || E^{(t)} || m)$. The signature then consists of $(r_1, \ldots, r_t, c_1, \ldots, c_t)$, and the verifier recomputes the $E^{(i)} = [r_i]E_{c_i}$ and checks that indeed $(c_1, \ldots, c_t) = \mathcal{H}(E^{(1)} || \ldots || E^{(t)} || m)$. Figure 3 details the "simple" variant and corresponds to the identification scheme using multiple public keys. The "Merkle" variant reduces the size of the public key by using a Merkle tree as described above.

To achieve security level λ, we require $t = \lambda / \log_2 S$ and the resulting signature size is $t(\lceil \log_2 N \rceil + \lceil \log_2 S \rceil)$ bits for the simple variant. The "Merkle" variant needs to include the openings of Merkle paths in the signature, the total size of these openings depends on the leaves that are opened. For example, in the extremely unlikely case that all the t challenges are identical only one Merkle path needs to be opened. Both signing and verification require t CSIDH actions (including the time to construct a small representant of the ideal).

The results on Fiat-Shamir in the QROM of Don et al. [13] readily apply to our setting:

Theorem 7. *Assume the hash functions used are modeled as quantum random oracles, then CSI-FiSh is sEUF-CMA secure.*

Proof. The basic sigma protocol (without hashing) has special soundness and unique responses (for each i there exists only one value of $r_i \in \mathbb{Z}_N$ such that $[r_i]E_{c_i} = E^{(i)}$). Hence, Theorem 25 of [13] implies that the scheme also has the Quantum Proof of Knowledge property. The protocol also has more than λ bits of min entropy and perfect HVZK, so Theorem 22 of [13] implies that the Fiat-Shamir scheme is sEUF-CMA secure in the QROM.

For the variant with hashing, it is known that Quantum random oracles are collapsing, so it is immediate that the sigma protocol has quantum computationally unique responses. Hence, the claim again follows from Theorems 25 and 22 of [13].

Algorithm 2 KeyGen

Input: E_0, class number $N = \#\mathrm{Cl}(\mathcal{O})$
Output: sk, pk
 1: **for** $i \in \{1, \cdots, S-1\}$ **do**
 2:     $a_i \leftarrow_R \mathbb{Z}_N$
 3:     $E_i = [a_i]E_0$
 4: **end for**
 5: **pk** $= [E_i : i \in \{1, \cdots, S-1\}]$
 6: **return** $(\mathbf{sk} = \mathbf{a}, \mathbf{pk})$

Algorithm 3 Sign

Input: msg, sk $= \mathbf{a}$
Output: $\sigma = (r_1, \ldots, r_t, c_1, \ldots, c_t)$
 1: $a_0 \leftarrow 0$
 2: **for** $i = 1, \ldots, t$ **do**
 3:     $b_i \leftarrow_R \mathbb{Z}_N$, $E^{(i)} = [b_i]E_0$
 4: **end for**
 5: $(c_1, \ldots, c_t) = \mathcal{H}(E^{(1)}|| \ldots ||E^{(t)}||m)$
 6: **for** $i = 1, \ldots, t$ **do**
 7:     $r_i = b_i - \mathrm{sign}(c_i)a_{|c_i|} \bmod N$
 8: **end for**
 9: **return** $\sigma = (r_1, \ldots, r_t, c_1, \ldots, c_t)$

Algorithm 4 Verify

Input: msg, E_0, pk $= [E_i : i \in \{1, \cdots, S-1\}], \sigma$
Output: Valid / invalid
 1: Parse σ as $(r_1, \ldots, r_t, c_1, \ldots, c_t)$
 2: Define $E_{-i} = E_i^t$ for all $i \in \{1, \cdots, S-1\}$.
 3: **for** $i = 1, \ldots, t$ **do**
 4:     $E^{(i)} = [r_i]E_{c_i}$
 5: **end for**
 6: $(c'_1, \ldots, c'_t) = \mathcal{H}(E^{(1)}|| \ldots ||E^{(t)}||m)$
 7: **if** $(c_1, \ldots, c_t) == (c'_1, \ldots, c'_t)$ **then**
 8:     **return** Valid
 9: **else**
10:     **return** Invalid
11: **end if**

Fig. 3. The "simple" variant of the CSI-FiSh signature scheme.

6   Implementation Results

6.1   Parameter Choices

Slow Hash Functions. Because the QROM security proof is very non-tight it would not be practical to choose parameters in such a way that security is guaranteed by the proof. Instead, as is customary, we assume that the probablity of a successful attack is at most $Q \times E$, where Q is the number of hash function evaluations that an attacker makes, and E is the soundness error of the zero knowledge proof. So usually one would choose the parameters S and t such that $S^{-t} \leq 2^{-\lambda}$. In our implementation we choose a hash function that is a factor 2^k slower than a standard hash function (e.g. SHA-3), therefore it suffices to take our parameters such that $S^{-t} \leq 2^{-\lambda+k}$. We pick k in such a way that the time spent evaluating the slow hash function is small compared to the total signing and verification time. Since we can take smaller parameters this optimization slightly reduces both the signature size and the signing and verification time.

Proposed Parameter Sets. We have implemented several parameter sets for both the "simple" variant and the "Merkle" variant. For the simple variant the secret key is always small and the variable S controls a trade-off between on the one hand small public keys and fast key generation (when S is small), and on the other hand small signatures and fast signing and verification (when S is large). When we use the "Merkle" variant the public key is always small, but the secret key size increases with increasing value of S, because we store the entire Merkle tree to avoid having to recompute the public keys during signing.

Table 3. Parameter choices and benchmark results for the "simple" variant of CSI-FiSh .

S	t	k	$|\mathbf{sk}|$	$|\mathbf{pk}|$	$|\mathbf{sig}|$	KeyGen	Sign	Verify
2^1	56	16	16 B	128 B	1880 B	100 ms	2.92 s	2.92 s
2^2	38	14	16 B	256 B	1286 B	200 ms	1.98 s	1.97 s
2^3	28	16	16 B	512 B	956 B	400 ms	1.48 s	1.48 s
2^4	23	13	16 B	1 KB	791 B	810 ms	1.20 s	1.19 s
2^6	16	16	16 B	4 KB	560 B	3.3 s	862 ms	859 ms
2^8	13	11	16 B	16 KB	461 B	13 s	671 ms	670 ms
2^{10}	11	7	16 B	64 KB	395 B	52 s	569 ms	567 ms
2^{12}	9	11	16 B	256 KB	329 B	3.5 m	471 ms	469 ms
2^{15}	7	16	16 B	2 MB	263 B	28 m	395 ms	393 ms

6.2   Implementation Details and Benchmarking Results

Our proof-of-concept implementation is available on GitHub [2]. To evaluate the CSIDH action, we use the 20180826 version of the proof-of-concept implementation by Castryck et al. [6]. Our implementation depends on the eXtended Keccak Code Package for the implementation of SHAKE256, which we have used as hash function, commitment scheme and to expand randomness. The implementation of the Babai nearest plane step depends on the GMP library for its high precision arithmetic. Since we rely on the implementation of Castryck et al. [6], the implementation is not constant-time. Implementing an optimized constant-time implementation of CSI-FiSh is outside the scope of this paper and is left for future work.

Table 4. Parameter choices and benchmark results for the "Merkle" variant of CSI-FiSh .

S	t	k	$|\mathbf{sk}|$	$|\mathbf{pk}|$	$|\mathbf{sig}|$	KeyGen	Sign	Verify
2^8	13	11	8 KB	32 B	1995 B	13 s	671 ms	371 ms
2^{10}	11	7	32 KB	32 B	2086 B	52 s	567 ms	567 ms
2^{12}	9	11	128 KB	32 B	2022 B	3.5 m	467 ms	467 ms
2^{15}	7	16	1 MB	32 B	1953 B	28 m	399 ms	402 ms
2^{18}	6	14	8 MB	32 B	1990 B	3.8 h	335 ms	326 ms

All our benchmarking experiments are performed on a Dell OptiPlex 3050 machine with Intel Core i5-7500T CPU @ 2.70 GHz. The benchmarking results are displayed in Tables 3 and 4.

Remark 8. Like most discrete logarithm based signature schemes, it is possible to precompute the ephemeral keys in CSI-FiSh, i.e. all CSIDH actions can be computed offline, and the online phase then only consists of t modular subtractions, which are extremely fast.

7   Conclusions and Open Problems

We computed the class group of the imaginary quadratic field that is at the heart of the CSIDH-512 cryptosystem, and exploited the knowledge of the relation lattice to instantiate the first efficient isogeny based signature scheme called CSI-FiSh. The scheme is flexible in that it allows trade-offs between signature sizes, key sizes and the time to sign/verify. One parameter set of CSI-FiSh gives the smallest combined size of public key and signature, compared to any other existing post-quantum secure signature scheme at the 128-bit security level.

Should the CSIDH-512 parameters turn out to be insufficiently secure, then the class group computation in this paper can be repeated for a larger prime.

Even though the computation for the CSIDH-512 parameters already broke previous records, the effort of 52 core years is relatively small compared to other record computations such as for factoring and DLP, which often take thousands of core years. Our computation took less than a month with the resources available to us. Hence, there is still quite some room to compute class groups for increased parameters. Moreover, the class group can be computed in quantum polynomial time. Hence, it seems likely that quantum computers that can compute large class groups will be available well before there are quantum computers that can break CSIDH-512.

The main open problem, given that the class group is cyclic of order N, is to devise an identification scheme where the challenge is taken from $\mathbb{Z}_N$, instead of binary or from the small set $]-S, S[$. Note that the prover can simply mimick the discrete logarithm based constructions since he can now work in the *ring* $\mathbb{Z}_N$, and thus can create the typical response expressing a combination of the ephemeral key, secret key and challenge. The major problem however is how the verifier can verify this combination to be correct, since the group action still only allows to add a known constant in $\mathbb{Z}_N$. The impact of such an identification scheme would be major: the signature size could possibly be small as 64 bytes, the public key also 64 bytes and signing would require only one CSIDH action taking around 40 ms.

Acknowledgements. We would like to thank the department of Electrical Engineering at KU Leuven for providing the necessary computing power through the HTCondor framework. Many thanks also to Léo Ducas for computing the HKZ basis of the relation lattice and discussions on CVP solvers.

References

1. Babai, L.: On Lovász' lattice reduction and the nearest lattice point problem. Combinatorica **6**(1), 1–13 (1986)
2. Beullens, W.: CSI-FiSh: GitHub repository (2019). https://github.com/KULeuven-COSIC/CSI-FiSh
3. Beullens, W., Preneel, B.: Field lifting for smaller UOV public keys. In: Patra, A., Smart, N.P. (eds.) INDOCRYPT 2017. LNCS, vol. 10698, pp. 227–246. Springer, Cham (2017). https://doi.org/10.1007/978-3-319-71667-1_12
4. Biasse, J.-F.: Improvements in the computation of ideal class groups of imaginary quadratic number fields. Adv. Math. Commun. **4**(2), 141–154 (2010)
5. Bonnetain, X., Schrottenloher, A.: Submerging CSIDH. Cryptology ePrint Archive, Report 2018/537 (2018). https://eprint.iacr.org/2018/537
6. Castryck, W., Lange, T., Martindale, C., Panny, L., Renes, J.: CSIDH: an efficient post-quantum commutative group action. In: Peyrin, T., Galbraith, S. (eds.) ASIACRYPT 2018. LNCS, vol. 11274, pp. 395–427. Springer, Cham (2018). https://doi.org/10.1007/978-3-030-03332-3_15
7. Childs, A.M., Jao, D., Soukharev, V.: Constructing elliptic curve isogenies in quantum subexponential time. J. Math. Cryptol. **8**(1), 1–29 (2014)
8. Coppersmith, D.: Solving homogeneous linear equations over GF(2) via block Wiedemann algorithm. Math. Comput. **62**, 333–350 (1994)

9. Couveignes, J.M.: Hard Homogeneous Spaces. IACR Cryptology ePrint Archive 2006/291 (1997). https://ia.cr/2006/291
10. De Feo, L.: Mathematics of isogeny based cryptography (2017). https://defeo.lu/ema2017/poly.pdf
11. De Feo, L., Galbraith, S.D.: SeaSign: compact isogeny signatures from class group actions. In: Ishai, Y., Rijmen, V. (eds.) EUROCRYPT 2019. LNCS, vol. 11478, pp. 759–789. Springer, Cham (2019). https://doi.org/10.1007/978-3-030-17659-4_26
12. Decru, T., Panny, L., Vercauteren, F.: Faster SeaSign signatures through improved rejection sampling. In: Ding, J., Steinwandt, R. (eds.) PQCrypto 2019. LNCS, vol. 11505, pp. 271–285. Springer, Cham (2019). https://doi.org/10.1007/978-3-030-25510-7_15
13. Don, J., Fehr, S., Majenz, C., Schaffner, C.: Security of the Fiat-Shamir transformation in the quantum random-oracle model. arXiv preprint arXiv:1902.07556 (2019)
14. Doulgerakis, E., Laarhoven, T., de Weger, B.: Finding closest lattice vectors using approximate Voronoi cells. In: Ding, J., Steinwandt, R. (eds.) PQCrypto 2019. LNCS, vol. 11505, pp. 3–22. Springer, Cham (2019). https://doi.org/10.1007/978-3-030-25510-7_1
15. De Feo, L., Jao, D., Plût, J.: Towards quantum-resistant cryptosystems from supersingular elliptic curve isogenies. J. Math. Cryptol. 8(3), 209–247 (2014)
16. Fiat, A., Shamir, A.: How to prove yourself: practical solutions to identification and signature problems. In: Odlyzko, A.M. (ed.) CRYPTO 1986. LNCS, vol. 263, pp. 186–194. Springer, Heidelberg (1987). https://doi.org/10.1007/3-540-47721-7_12
17. Galbraith, S.D., Petit, C., Silva, J.: Identification protocols and signature schemes based on supersingular isogeny problems. In: Takagi, T., Peyrin, T. (eds.) ASIACRYPT 2017. LNCS, vol. 10624, pp. 3–33. Springer, Cham (2017). https://doi.org/10.1007/978-3-319-70694-8_1
18. Hafner, J.L., McCurley, K.S.: A rigorous subexponential algorithm for computation of class groups. J. Am. Math. Soc. 2, 837–850 (1989)
19. Hülsing, A., Rijneveld, J., Song, F.: Mitigating multi-target attacks in hash-based signatures. In: Cheng, C.-M., Chung, K.-M., Persiano, G., Yang, B.-Y. (eds.) PKC 2016. LNCS, vol. 9614, pp. 387–416. Springer, Heidelberg (2016). https://doi.org/10.1007/978-3-662-49384-7_15
20. Jacobson, M.J.: Applying sieving to the computation of quadratic class groups. Math. Comput. 68, 859–867 (1999)
21. Jao, D., et al.: SIKE. Submission to [29]. http://sike.org
22. Jao, D., De Feo, L.: Towards quantum-resistant cryptosystems from supersingular elliptic curve isogenies. In: Yang, B.-Y. (ed.) PQCrypto 2011. LNCS, vol. 7071, pp. 19–34. Springer, Heidelberg (2011). https://doi.org/10.1007/978-3-642-25405-5_2
23. Kleinjung, T.: Quadratic sieving. Math. Comput. 85(300), 1861–1873 (2016)
24. Korkine, A., Zolotareff, G.: Sur les formes quadratiques. Mathematische Annalen 6(3), 366–389 (1873)
25. Kuperberg, G.: A subexponential-time quantum algorithm for the dihedral hidden subgroup problem. SIAM J. Comput. 35(1), 170–188 (2005)
26. Kuperberg, G.: Another subexponential-time quantum algorithm for the dihedral hidden subgroup problem. In: TQC, LIPIcs, vol. 22, pp. 20–34. Schloss Dagstuhl - Leibniz-Zentrum fuer Informatik (2013)
27. Laarhoven, T.: Sieving for closest lattice vectors (with preprocessing). In: Avanzi, R., Heys, H. (eds.) SAC 2016. LNCS, vol. 10532, pp. 523–542. Springer, Cham (2017). https://doi.org/10.1007/978-3-319-69453-5_28

28. Lenstra, A.K., Lenstra, H.W., Lovász, L.: Factoring polynomials with rational coefficients. Mathematische Annalen **261**(4), 515–534 (1982)
29. National Institute of Standards and Technology. Post-Quantum Cryptography Standardization, December 2016. https://csrc.nist.gov/Projects/Post-Quantum-Cryptography/Post-Quantum-Cryptography-Standardization
30. Peikert, C.: He gives c-sieves on the CSIDH. Cryptology ePrint Archive, Report 2019/725 (2019). https://eprint.iacr.org/2019/725
31. Rostovtsev, A., Stolbunov, A.: Public-Key Cryptosystem Based on Isogenies. IACR Cryptology ePrint Archive 2006/145 (2006). https://ia.cr/2006/145
32. Schnorr, C.-P.: A hierarchy of polynomial time lattice basis reduction algorithms. Theor. Comput. Sci. **53**(2–3), 201–224 (1987)
33. Silverman, J.H.: The Arithmetic of Elliptic Curves. Graduate Texts in Mathematics. Springer, Dordrecht (2009). https://doi.org/10.1007/978-0-387-09494-6
34. Stolbunov, A.: Constructing public-key cryptographic schemes based on class group action on a set of isogenous elliptic curves. Adv. Math. Comm. **4**(2), 215–235 (2010)
35. Stolbunov, A.: Cryptographic schemes based on isogenies. Doctoral thesis, NTNU (2012)
36. Vélu, J.: Isogénies entre courbes elliptiques. CR Acad. Sci. Paris Ser. A. **273**, 305–347 (1971)
37. Wiedemann, D.H.: Solving sparse linear equations over finite fields. IEEE Trans. Inf. Theory **32**(1), 54–62 (1986)
38. Yoo, Y., Azarderakhsh, R., Jalali, A., Jao, D., Soukharev, V.: A post-quantum digital signature scheme based on supersingular isogenies. In: Kiayias, A. (ed.) FC 2017. LNCS, vol. 10322, pp. 163–181. Springer, Cham (2017). https://doi.org/10.1007/978-3-319-70972-7_9

Verifiable Delay Functions from Supersingular Isogenies and Pairings

Luca De Feo[1]($\boxtimes$) (ID), Simon Masson[2], Christophe Petit[3], and Antonio Sanso[4]

[1] Université Paris Saclay – UVSQ, LMV, CNRS UMR 8100, Versailles, France
luca.de-feo@uvsq.fr
[2] Thales and Université de Lorraine, Nancy, France
[3] University of Birmingham, Birmingham, UK
[4] Adobe Inc. and Ruhr Universität Bochum, Bochum, Germany

Abstract. We present two new Verifiable Delay Functions (VDF) based on assumptions from elliptic curve cryptography. We discuss both the advantages and drawbacks of our constructions, we study their security and we demonstrate their practicality with a proof-of-concept implementation.

1 Introduction

A Verifiable Delay Function (VDF), first formalized in 2018 by Boneh, Bonneau, Bünz and Fisch [10], is a function $f : X \to Y$ that takes a prescribed *wall-clock time* to evaluate, independently of the parallelism of the architecture employed, and such that its output can be verified efficiently. In a nutshell, it is required that anyone can evaluate f in T *sequential steps*, but no less, even with a large number of processors; on top of that, given an input x and an output y, anyone must be able to verify that $y = f(x)$ in a *short* amount of time, desirably in polylog(T).

An example of a *delay function* lacking efficient verification is a chained one-way function:

$$s \to H(s) \to H(H(s)) \to \cdots \to H^{(T)}(s) = a.$$

This clearly takes T *steps* to evaluate, even on a parallel computer, however the only feasible way to verify the output is to re-evaluate the function. Two related known crypto primitives are the time-lock puzzles defined by Rivest, Shamir, and Wagner in [65] and proofs of sequential work [20,53]. The problem with the former is that it is not publicly verifiable while the latter is not a function (i.e., it does not have a unique output).

A VDF based on univariate permutation polynomials over finite fields is presented in [10], along with other candidate constructions, none being entirely satisfactory (see next section). The same work listed as an open problem to find theoretically optimal VDFs based on simple assumptions closer to those typically found in other asymmetric protocols. Pietrzak [59] and Wesolowski [75] responded to the challenge by proposing two practical VDFs based on exponentiation in a group of unknown order. Both VDFs are surveyed in [11].

© International Association for Cryptologic Research 2019
S. D. Galbraith and S. Moriai (Eds.): ASIACRYPT 2019, LNCS 11921, pp. 248–277, 2019.
https://doi.org/10.1007/978-3-030-34578-5_10

Our Contribution. We present a new framework for VDFs, and two instantiations of this framework using isogenies of supersingular elliptic curves and bilinear pairings. Both our constructions are optimal and perfectly sound. We observe that the construction based on univariate permutation polynomials of Boneh et al. [10] also has both properties, but its security relies on an *ad hoc* limit assumption on the amount of parallelism available to the adversary. Moreover, unlike the VDF constructions of Pietrzak [59] and Wesolowski [75], ours are inherently non-interactive, the output being efficiently verifiable without attaching a proof. By using mathematical tools also used in other cryptographic contexts, our constructions benefit from pre-existing research in these areas both from an efficiency and security point of view. Finally, while the use of isogenies does not magically make our functions post-quantum (in fact they can be broken with a discrete logarithm computation), one of our two constructions still offers some partial resistance to quantum attacks; we call this property *quantum annoyance*.

The main drawback of our proposals is that, given current knowledge, the only secure way to instantiate our VDFs requires a *trusted setup*, or, said otherwise, that our VDFs can be easily backdoored. Indeed, both our setups require to start from a supersingular elliptic curve with unknown endomorphism ring. No general algorithm is known to compute the endomorphism ring of supersingular elliptic curves, however the only known ways to generate supersingular curves involve a random isogeny walk from a curve with small discriminant (e.g., $j = 0$ or $j = 1728$), and it has been shown that knowledge of the isogeny walk permits computing the endomorphism ring in polynomial time [30,46]. Hence, the only way to instantiate our VDFs involves a trusted setup that performs a random isogeny walk and then forgets it. We stress that trusted setups also appear in other constructions, and that does not rule them out for practical applications; in fact, the Ethereum cryptocurrency is currently considering standardization of a VDF based on a trusted RSA setup [28]. Furthermore, while it is clear that a trusted setup is necessary in the RSA setting, this looks much less like a fatality in our case: it is totally believable that in the near future a way is found to generate random supersingular curves with unknown endomorphism ring, thus bypassing the need for the trusted setup. Finally, a distributed trusted setup with $n - 1$ threshold security can be efficiently constructed in our case purely from isogeny assumptions, whereas the RSA setting requires heavy multi-party computation machinery and very large bandwidth.

Another limitation on the utility of our VDFs is that the time required to setup public parameters is of the same order of magnitude as that required to evaluate the function; furthermore, validating public parameters requires the same amount of time as evaluating the function, and the evaluator is required to use $O(T)$ storage for evaluating in optimal time. While these drawbacks are acceptable in applications that require delays in the order of minutes or hours (the majority of applications in blockchains), they prevent our VDFs from being used with very long delays. In our implementation, we propose some possible tradeoffs that mitigate these problems, however further research is needed to better address them.

Related Work. Isogenies and pairings were first used together for cryptographic purposes in several patents [14, 41, 42]. In particular, a patent by Broker, Charles and Lauter [14] describes a generalization of BLS signatures [12], where the secret scalar is replaced by a walk in an isogeny graph. We will construct our VDFs using a similar structure in Sect. 3.

More recently, Koshiba and Takashima [47, 48] have provided a framework and security definitions for some cryptographic protocols involving pairings and isogenies, called *isogenous pairing groups*. They also present key-policy attribute-based encryption schemes based on their framework.

Our new VDF construction does not fit within any of the previous frameworks: while the isogeny is secret there, here it is public. Moreover the isogeny involved in our construction has very large degrees to achieve the delay property; using isogenies of such degree would make any of the previous protocols unnecessarily slow. Security properties required for VDFs differ significantly in nature from traditional cryptographic protocols, and none of the computational assumptions previously used in isogeny-based cryptography, including those in [47], is relevant to our construction.

Outline. This paper is organized as follows. In Sect. 2 we formalize Verifiable Delay Functions and we go through some of the proposed solutions. Section 3 to Sect. 5 provide a description of our VDFs, together with a review of the basic theory of supersingular isogeny graphs. Section 6 gives security proofs and reviews the available attacks against our proposals. Finally Sect. 7 provides an optimized implementation of our VDFs, and related benchmarks.

2   Verifiable Delay Functions

In this section, we recall previous work on Verifiable Delay Functions (VDF).

2.1   Definition

We recall here the formal definition of a Verifiable Delay Function, following [10]. A VDF consists of three algorithms:

1. $\mathsf{Setup}(\lambda, T) \rightarrow (\mathsf{ek}, \mathsf{vk})$: is a procedure that takes a security parameter λ, a delay parameter T, and outputs public parameters consisting of an evaluation key ek and a verification key vk.
2. $\mathsf{Eval}(\mathsf{ek}, s) \rightarrow (a, \pi)$: is a procedure to evaluate the function on input s. It produces the output a from s, and a (possibly empty) proof π. This procedure is meant to be infeasible in time less than T.
3. $\mathsf{Verify}(\mathsf{vk}, s, a, \pi) \rightarrow \{\mathsf{true}, \mathsf{false}\}$: is a procedure to verify that a is indeed the correct output for s, with the help of the proof π.

A VDF shall satisfy three security properties: *Correctness*, stating that a honest evaluator always passes verification, *Soundness*, stating that a lying evaluator never passes verification, and *Sequentiality*, stating that it is impossible to correctly evaluate the VDF in time less than $T - o(T)$, even when using $\text{poly}(T)$ parallel processors. We will give formal security definitions in Sect. 6, but see also [10].

According to [10], the Setup routine should run in time $\text{poly}(\lambda)$; here we slightly relax this constraint and allow it to run in $\text{poly}(T, \lambda)$. Eval must be doable in time T; Verify in time $\text{poly}(\lambda)$. A VDF is said to be *optimal* when T is allowed to be in $o(2^\lambda)$ without harming security; note that it does not make sense to have $T \in O(2^\lambda)$, since in that case it is cheaper to break soundness than to run Eval.

2.2 Applications

We highlight a few applications of VDFs:

- Constructing a trustworthy **randomness beacon**, like the one introduced by Rabin in [62], where a public service produces a continuous stream of guaranteed unbiased randomness. The classic approach consisting in extracting randomness from entropy pool sources, such as stock prices or proof-of-work blockchains à la Bitcoin, has been shown to be manipulable by active attackers [58]. For example, while the price of a particular stock may seem unpredictable to a passive observer, a powerful trader can influence the market trend, making the random output biased. Here is where VDFs are useful: if the beacon is calculated by applying a VDF with a long enough delay to the entropy source, the malicious trader would not have the time to try to "adjust" the market at his own advantage.
  The other common solution based on the "commit-and-reveal" paradigm with **multiparty randomness** has also been shown to have flaws. Indeed a malicious party with the intention of manipulating the output might refuse to reveal his commitment after seeing the other opened commitments, forcing to restart the protocol. This can be mitigated by threshold techniques, as shown in [68], or by replacing commitments with VDFs, as shown by Lenstra and Wesolowski [51].
- VDFs may be used to reduce the energy consumption of blockchains based on proofs-of-work. An elegant idea by Cohen [19] combines proofs-of-resources with incremental VDFs in order to achieve **Consensus from Proof of Resources**. In particular, he describes a technique based on proof of space where the mining reward is roughly equal to the value of the space owned, without each miner running a large parallel computation. At high level this works as follows. Suppose a miner controls N out of S units of the total space and splits his proof π (proving control of the N units) into N pieces $\pi_1, \pi_2...\pi_N$. The miner then computes $H_i = \text{HASH}(\pi_i) \in [0, N]$ and $\tau = \min(H_1, ..., H_N)$. At this point the miner evaluates a VDF with time delay proportional to τ. The first miner that successfully computes the output is the "winner" and has the block assigned. For a miner that controls N units of the total space

this will happen with a probability that is about N/S. The Chia blockchain[1] has been designed to work with this model.

For a description of other applications of VDFs, such as **proof of replication** or **computational timestamping**, we refer to [10].

2.3   Existing Constructions

So far, few constructions meet the requirements of a VDF; we summarize them below.

Modular Square Roots. One of the earlier examples of a VDF can be found in the 1992 paper by Dwork and Naor [29]. The underlying idea is rather simple: given a prime number p such that $p = 3 \bmod 4$, a (canonical) square root $a = \sqrt{s} \bmod p$ can be computed using the formula $a = s^{\frac{p+1}{4}}$. This requires about $\log(p)$ sequential squaring operations. On the other hand, verifying correctness only requires to check that $a^2 = s$. While there is a gap between the evaluation and the verification operations, this simple approach has two issues: first, the gap is only polynomial in the delay parameter $T = \log(p)$, secondly, due to the possibility of parallelizing field multiplications, this gap vanishes asymptotically if the evaluator is provided with large amounts of parallelism (see also Table 1). Lenstra and Wesolowski introduced with Sloth [51] the possibility of chaining square root operations. The problem with this construction, though, is that it does not achieve asymptotically efficient verification.

Time-Lock Puzzles. Time-lock puzzles were introduced by Rivest, Shamir, and Wagner [65] to provide encryption that can only be decrypted at a set time in the future. They use a classical RSA modulus $N = pq$; the encryption key is then $a = s^{2^T} \bmod N$ for some starting value s. Now, it is clear that any party knowing $\varphi(N)$ can compute the value of a quickly (they can reduce the exponent $e = 2^T \bmod \varphi(N)$). But for everyone else the value of a is obtained by computing T sequential squaring operations.

The main reason why this construction cannot be classified as a VDF is that there is not an efficient way to perform public verification without giving away the factorization of N. This issue has recently been solved, independently, by Pietrzak and Wesolowski. We briefly present their constructions next; for a more in-depth survey, see [11].

Wesolowski's VDF. In 2018, Wesolowski presented a VDF based on groups of unknown order [75]. His work leverages the time lock puzzle described above, introducing a way to publicly verify the output $a = s^{2^T}$. He defines an interactive protocol where, after seeing the output a, the verifier sends to the prover a random prime $\ell < B$, where B is some small bound. The prover replies with the value $b = s^{\lfloor 2^T/\ell \rfloor}$; the verifier then checks that $a = b^\ell s^r$, where $r = 2^T \bmod \ell$.

---

[1] https://chia.net/.

Table 1. VDF comparison—Asymptotic VDF comparison: T represents the delay factor, λ the security parameter, s the number of processors. For simplicity, we assume that T is super-polynomial in λ. All times are to be understood up to a (global across a line) constant factor.

VDF	Sequential Eval	Parallel Eval	Verify	Setup	Proof size
Modular square root	T	$T^{2/3}$	$T^{2/3}$	T	—
Univariate permutation polynomials[a]	T^2	$> T - o(T)$	$\log(T)$	$\log(T)$	—
Wesolowski's VDF	$(1 + \frac{2}{\log(T)})T$	$(1 + \frac{2}{s\log(T)})T$	λ^4	λ^3	λ^3
Pietrzak's VDF	$(1 + \frac{2}{\sqrt{T}})T$	$(1 + \frac{2}{s\sqrt{T}})T$	$\log(T)$	λ^3	$\log(T)$
This work	T	T	λ^4	$T\lambda^3$	—
This work (optimized)	T	T	λ^4	$T\log(\lambda)$	—

[a]According to [10, § 5.1], one must limit the evaluator to $O(T^2)$ parallel processors for the bound on parallel Eval to hold. VDFs based on permutation polynomials can be evaluated in time $O(\log^2(T))$ using $O(T^{3.8})$ parallel processors.

Because the verifier only uses public randomness, this protocol can be made non-interactive using the Fiat–Shamir heuristic. Wesolowski's proposal shines for the shortness of the proof (only one group element) and the speed of the verification (only two group exponentiations).

Wesolowski suggests two ways of instantiating groups of unknown order. The first one is using RSA groups $(\mathbb{Z}/N\mathbb{Z})^*$, like in Rivest–Shamir–Wagner, and thus requires a trusted third party to produce the modulus N. The second is using class groups of imaginary quadratic number fields [15,52]. While the former instantiation is better studied in public key cryptography, the second has the advantage of not requiring a trusted setup.

Pietrzak's VDF. Concurrently with Wesolowski, Pietrzak [59] introduced another protocol to verify Rivest–Shamir–Wagner time-lock puzzles. Pietrzak's verification procedure is an interactive recursive protocol, where the prover outputs a proof π consisting of $O(\log(T))$ group elements, and the verifier needs about $O(\log(T))$ time to do the verification. The main advantage of his construction is that the prover only needs about $O(\sqrt{T})$ group multiplications to build π. Pietrzak presents his protocol using RSA groups, but class groups like in Wesolowski's VDF can also be used (although this affects slightly the computational assumptions needed for soundness).

Univariate Permutation Polynomials. Boneh, Bonneau, Bünz and Fisch explored in their seminal paper [10] an approach based on permutation polynomials over finite fields $\mathbb{F}_p$. In full generality, their proposal is a weaker form of VDF, where a certain amount of parallelism is needed to give an advantage to the evaluator (see [10, Definition 5]). The gist of their approach is that, given a permutation polynomial of degree T, inverting such polynomial implies computing polynomial GCDs. This operation takes $O(\log(p))$ multiplications of dense polynomials of degree $O(T)$, and it is conjectured that it cannot be done in less than T steps on at most $O(T^2)$ processors (see [10, Assumption 2]). On the other hand, any such polynomial can be evaluated, and thus verified, using $O(\log(T))$ operations on $O(T)$ processors, which is exponentially smaller. Moreover, there exists a family of permutation polynomials, due to Guralnick and Müller [37], that can be evaluated in $O(\log(T))$ operations without parallelism, and it is conjectured in [10] that the derived VDF is secure.

The drawbacks of this construction are that the parallelism of the evaluator needs to be polynomially bounded in T, and that it is based on assumptions that have been seldom studied in a cryptographic setting.

Incrementally Verifiable SNARK. For completeness we need to mention that a theoretical, albeit impractical, VDF can be constructed using Incrementally Verifiable SNARKs. Again, we refer to [10] for a deeper analysis of the topic.

We compare the asymptotic performance of the VDFs above and of our proposal in Table 1. Outside of modular square roots, all VDFs constructions meet the requirements of an optimal VDF, however each has its qualitative strengths and weaknesses: permutation polynomials require to bound the parallelism of the evaluator, and are based on little studied assumptions; VDFs derived from time-lock puzzles are interactive, have no perfect soundness, and may or may not require a trusted setup; ours need a trusted setup, and require an effort to validate public parameters comparable to evaluating the VDF.

3   A New VDF Construction Framework

We start by describing a framework for defining VDFs inspired by the BLS signature scheme based on pairing groups [12]. Recall that BLS uses a *pairing friendly* elliptic curve $E/\mathbb{F}_p$, with a non-degenerate bilinear pairing $e_N : X_1 \times X_2 \to \mathbb{F}_{p^k}$, where X_1, X_2 are subgroups of prime order N, and the extension degree k is called the *embedding degree*. The secret key in BLS is a scalar $s < N$, and the public key is a pair of points $P, sP \in X_1$. To sign a message m, the signer computes a hash $Q = H(m) \in X_2$, and gives back the signature sQ. The verifier then checks that $e_n(P, sQ) = e_n(sP, Q)$.

The BLS signature is also naturally a Verifiable Random Function $f_s : X_2 \to X_2$, where only the owner of the trapdoor s can evaluate f_s, while anyone can verify the result [56]; however, it is not a VDF, because both evaluation and verification are in polylog(N). Our generalization, instead, has efficient instantiations based on isogeny graphs of supersingular elliptic curves, where the evaluation can be made exponentially slower than the verification. If the trapdoor is kept secret, one obtains a signature/identification protocol based on walks in isogeny graphs; if the trapdoor is made public, one obtains a VDF.[2] We will present our instantiations in Sect. 5.

Let X_1, X_2, Y_1, Y_2, G be groups of prime order N, let $e_X : X_1 \times X_2 \to G$ and $e_Y : Y_1 \times Y_2 \to G$ be non degenerate bilinear pairings. Furthermore, assume that there is a pair of bijections $\phi : X_1 \to Y_1$ and $\hat{\phi} : Y_2 \to X_2$ that satisfy the following diagram,

$$
\begin{array}{ccc}
X_1 \times Y_2 & \xrightarrow{\phi \times 1} & Y_1 \times Y_2 \\
{\scriptstyle 1 \times \hat{\phi}} \downarrow & & \downarrow {\scriptstyle e_Y} \\
X_1 \times X_2 & \xrightarrow{e_X} & G
\end{array}
$$

Note that the diagram implies ϕ and $\hat{\phi}$ are group isomorphisms.

We shall assume that the pairings e_X, e_Y can be evaluated in time polylog(N), whereas both ϕ and $\hat{\phi}$ can be evaluated in sequential time T, where T is some parameter independent from N (but still in $o(N)$).

Let P be any generator of X_1, the public parameters of our system are going to be $(N, X_1, X_2, Y_1, Y_2, G, e_X, e_Y, P, \phi(P))$. From this setup, we derive two primitives:

An Identification Protocol. The maps ϕ and $\hat{\phi}$ are the trapdoor. The verifier gives an element $Q \in Y_2$ to the prover, the proof is the element $\hat{\phi}(Q)$. Then, the verifier checks that

$$e_X(P, \hat{\phi}(Q)) = e_Y(\psi(P), Q).$$

It should be apparent that BLS signatures correspond to the special case where $X_1 = Y_1$ and $X_2 = Y_2$ are orthogonal groups with respect to an elliptic pairing $e_X = e_Y$, and $\phi = \hat{\phi} = [s]$ is the multiplication endomorphism by a secret scalar s.

The same abstract scheme already appears in a patent by Broker, Charles and Lauter [14], although their implementation is different, and likely less efficient. We shall see in Sect. 6 that our instantiation presents the minor advantage over BLS signatures of being partially resistant to quantum attacks.

A VDF. The maps ϕ and $\hat{\phi}$ are also part of the public parameters. The VDF is the map $\hat{\phi}$, Eval simply amounts to evaluating it at points $Q \in Y_2$. To verify the output, one checks that

$$e_X(P, \hat{\phi}(Q)) = e_Y(\phi(P), Q).$$

It should be clear that, because the map $R \mapsto e_X(P, R)$ is an isomorphism, verification succeeds if and only if the output is correct; this will be used to prove

---

[2] Note that this is different from a *trapdoor VDF*, as defined by Wesolowski [75], where the trapdoor is used to efficiently compute the evaluation.

correctness and *soundness* in Sect. 6. By hypothesis, Eval takes T sequential steps, while the pairings can be evaluated in time polylog(N).

4   Preliminaries on Supersingular Curves

Before describing the instantiations, we review some basic facts on supersingular curves, pairings and isogenies. For details on elliptic curves over finite fields see [66,67,73], for their use in cryptography see [9,23,32], for ideal class groups of quadratic imaginary fields see [22], for maximal orders of quaternion algebras see [71,72].

Let E be an elliptic curve defined over a finite field $\mathbb{F}_q$ of characteristic p. Recall that the order of $E(\mathbb{F}_q)$ is $\#E(\mathbb{F}_q) = q + 1 - t$, where t is the *trace* of the *Frobenius endomorphism* π. Then, a curve is *supersingular* if and only if p divides t. Every supersingular curve is isomorphic to a curve defined over $\mathbb{F}_{p^2}$, so, for a fixed prime p, there is only a finite number of supersingular curves, up to isomorphism.

An *isogeny* of E is an algebraic group morphism from E to some other curve E'. For *separable* isogenies,[3] the *degree* is the size of their kernel; isogenies of degree ℓ are called ℓ-isogenies. A separable isogeny is said to be *cyclic* if its kernel is; we will mostly deal with cyclic isogenies in this work.

For any ℓ-isogeny $\phi : E \to E'$, there is a unique ℓ-isogeny $\hat{\phi} : E' \to E$, called the *dual* of ϕ, such that $\phi \circ \hat{\phi} = [\ell]$ on E' and $\hat{\phi} \circ \phi = [\ell]$ on E. This shows that being *ℓ-isogenous* is a symmetric relation, and that being isogenous is an equivalence relation. Further, a theorem of Tate states that two curves are isogenous over $\mathbb{F}_q$ if and only if they have the same number of points over $\mathbb{F}_q$, thus in particular a supersingular curve can only be isogenous to other supersingular curves.

One can define several bilinear pairings on supersingular curves. In this paper we will use the Weil pairing $e_N : E[N] \times E[N] \to \mu_N$ for describing the protocol, although the (reduced) Tate pairing is better suited for implementation purposes. The pairings will have embedding degree 2 or 1, depending on the VDF, construction. Most importantly, both pairings will satisfy the compatibility condition

$$e_N(\phi(P), Q) = e_N(P, \hat{\phi}(Q))$$

for any isogeny $\phi : E \to E'$ and points $P \in E[N]$, $Q \in E'[N]$. See [9, Chapters IX–X] for more details.

Graphs of supersingular isogenies have been studied by Mestre [55], Pizer [60, 61], Kohel [45], Delfs and Galbraith [26], among others. We distinguish two important families: graphs of ℓ-isogenies and curves *defined over a prime field* $\mathbb{F}_p$ (i.e., expressed by rational fractions with coefficients in $\mathbb{F}_p$), and graphs of ℓ-isogenies defined over the algebraic closure $\bar{\mathbb{F}}_p$ (or, equivalently, over $\mathbb{F}_{p^2}$). In the following, we shall assume that $p > 3$.

---

[3] An isogeny is separable if it induces a separable extension of function fields. We will only use separable isogenies in this work.

Graphs over $\mathbb{F}_p$. For the first case, Delfs and Galbraith showed that one obtains the same kinds of undirected graphs as for ordinary curves. In this case $t = 0$ and $\#E(\mathbb{F}_p) = p + 1$, thus there is a unique *isogeny class* containing all supersingular curves defined over $\mathbb{F}_p$. To give a more precise classification, following Kohel [45], we say that an isogeny $\phi : E \to E'$ is *horizontal* whenever $\mathrm{End}_{\mathbb{F}_p}(E) \simeq \mathrm{End}_{\mathbb{F}_p}(E')$; Delfs and Galbraith showed that there are one or two horizontal isogeny classes of supersingular curves over $\mathbb{F}_p$, according to whether $p = \pm 1 \bmod 4$. Precisely:

- If $p = 1 \bmod 4$, then $\mathrm{End}(E) \simeq \mathbb{Z}[\sqrt{-p}]$ for all curves, and the isogeny class contains h curves, up to $\mathbb{F}_p$-isomorphism, where h is the *class number* of the imaginary quadratic field $\mathbb{Q}(\sqrt{-p})$.
- If $p = -1 \bmod 4$, then $\mathrm{End}(E)$ is isomorphic to one of $\mathbb{Z}[\sqrt{-p}]$ or $\mathbb{Z}[(1 + \sqrt{-p})/2]$; the horizontal isogeny class associated to $\mathbb{Z}[(1 + \sqrt{-p})/2]$ is called the *surface* and contains h curves up to $\mathbb{F}_p$-isomorphism; the horizontal isogeny class associated to $\mathbb{Z}[\sqrt{-p}]$ is called the *floor*, and contains h or $3h$ curves, according to whether $p = 7 \bmod 8$ or $p = 3 \bmod 8$ respectively.

The connectivity of the ℓ-isogeny graphs will now depend on the chosen degree ℓ. Specifically:

- If ℓ is an odd prime and $\left(\frac{-p}{\ell}\right) = -1$ (i.e., $-p$ is not a square modulo ℓ), no ℓ-isogeny of supersingular curves is defined over $\mathbb{F}_p$, i.e., the ℓ-isogeny graph is made of isolated vertices.
- If ℓ is an odd prime and $\left(\frac{-p}{\ell}\right) = 1$, every curve has exactly two horizontal ℓ-isogenies, thus each horizontal isogeny class is partitioned into a finite number of cycles.
- If $\ell = 2$ and $p = 1 \bmod 4$, then every curve has exactly one horizontal ℓ-isogeny.
- If $\ell = 2$ and $p = -1 \bmod 4$, then every curve on the floor has exactly one non-horizontal ℓ-isogeny going to a curve on the surface, whereas for curves on the surface:
  - If $p = 7 \bmod 8$, they have exactly two horizontal ℓ-isogenies, plus one non-horizontal going to the floor, dual to the one coming from the floor;
  - If $p = 3 \bmod 8$, they have three non-horizontal isogenies going to three curves on the floor, dual to the ones coming from the floor.

In the rest of this work, we will only be interested in cycles of horizontal isogenies, thus either ℓ odd and $\left(\frac{-p}{\ell}\right) = 1$, or $\ell = 2$, $p = 7 \bmod 8$ and the curves on the surface.

Graphs over $\mathbb{F}_{p^2}$. Over $\mathbb{F}_{p^2}$ there is more than one isogeny class, indeed the trace t of a supersingular curve can take any of the values $0, \pm p, \pm 2p$. The values $t = 0$ and $t = \pm p$ produce exceptional classes made of only one element, and are thus not interesting for cryptography. The cases $t = \pm 2p$ produce two distinct classes, each with $\lfloor p/12 \rfloor + c_p$ elements, where $0 \le c_p \le 2$ is a constant depending only on $p \bmod 12$; these two classes are isomorphic in the sense that each curve in one is $\bar{\mathbb{F}}_p$-isomorphic to exactly one curve in the other, and thus we typically speak of supersingular graphs over $\bar{\mathbb{F}}_p$ and over $\mathbb{F}_{p^2}$ indistinctly.

For any prime $\ell \neq p$, the ℓ-isogeny graph of supersingular curves over $\mathbb{F}_{p^2}$ is an $(\ell+1)$-regular multi-graph, undirected outside of the two special vertices $j = 0, 1728$. In $\mathbb{F}_{p^2}$ we do not encounter the concept of horizontal isogenies anymore: every endomorphism ring is isomorphic to a maximal order in a quaternion algebra, and to every maximal order corresponds exactly a pair of ($\mathbb{F}_{p^2}/\mathbb{F}_p$-Galois conjugate) supersingular curves.

It is still true, however, that we may find inside the graph a sub-structure inherited from the graph of supersingular curves defined over $\mathbb{F}_p$. One may be tempted to think that the $\mathbb{F}_{p^2}$-graph contains the $\mathbb{F}_p$-graph as a subgraph, however the situation is slightly subtler: indeed, supersingular curves over $\mathbb{F}_p$ are isogenous to their quadratic twists, thus the $\mathbb{F}_p$-graph contains pairs of vertices that become isomorphic in $\mathbb{F}_{p^2}$. Hence, the ℓ-isogeny graph of curves and isogenies defined over $\mathbb{F}_p$ is a double cover (outside the ramification points at $j = 0, 1728$) of the $\mathbb{F}_p$-subgraph contained in the ℓ-isogeny graph over $\mathbb{F}_{p^2}$. Fear not: this technical detail will be completely irrelevant to us.

5   Two Instantiations with Supersingular Elliptic Curves

We now give two instantiations of the VDF described in Sect. 3, using supersingular elliptic curves for the pairing groups, and isogenies of prime power degree for the maps $\phi, \hat{\phi}$. We will see in Sect. 6 that the choice of the curves severely affects the security of the protocol, however we ignore this issue for the moment. In this section we will describe the VDFs using the Weil pairing, however for implementation purposes we will use the Tate pairing in Sect. 7.

5.1   VDF from Supersingular Curves over $\mathbb{F}_p$

Our first construction uses supersingular curves defined over a prime field $\mathbb{F}_p$. It shares similarities with the key exchange protocol CSIDH [16] and with the VDF based on class groups of imaginary quadratic fields by Wesolowski [75].

Let p be a prime such that $p + 1$ contains a large prime factor N. Let ℓ be one of:

- $\ell = 2$, only if $p = 7 \mod 8$, or
- a small prime such that $\left(\frac{-p}{\ell}\right) = 1$.

Let $E/\mathbb{F}_p$ be a supersingular elliptic curve, and denote by $e_N(\cdot, \cdot)$ the Weil pairing on $E[N]$. When $\ell = 2$ we shall add the requirement that $E[2] \subset E(\mathbb{F}_p)$, implying that E is on the surface. By construction $\#E(\mathbb{F}_p) = p + 1$, and $E(\mathbb{F}_p)$ contains exactly one cyclic subgroup of order N, that we shall use as $X_2 = E[N] \cap E(\mathbb{F}_p)$.

Let $u \in \mathbb{F}_p$ be any non quadratic residue. We define a map

$$v : E \to \tilde{E}$$
$$(x, y) \mapsto (u^2 x, u^3 y)$$

Setup(λ, T)
1. Choose primes N, p with the properties above, according to the security parameter λ;
2. Select a supersingular curve $E/\mathbb{F}_p$;
3. Choose a direction on the horizontal ℓ-isogeny graph, and compute a cyclic isogeny $\phi : E \to E'$ of degree ℓ^T, and its dual $\hat{\phi}$;
4. Choose a generator P of $X_1 = \upsilon^{-1}(\tilde{E}[N] \cap \tilde{E}(\mathbb{F}_p))$, and compute $\phi(P)$;
5. Output $(\mathsf{ek}, \mathsf{vk}) = (\hat{\phi}, (E, E', P, \phi(P)))$.

Eval($\hat{\phi}, Q \in Y_2$)
1. Compute and output $\hat{\phi}(Q)$.

Verify($E, E', P, Q, \phi(P), \hat{\phi}(Q)$)
1. Verify that $\hat{\phi}(Q) \in X_2 = E[N] \cap E(\mathbb{F}_p)$;
2. Verify that $e_N(P, \hat{\phi}(Q)) = e_N(\phi(P), Q)$.

Fig. 1. Instantiation of the Verifiable Delay Function over $\mathbb{F}_p$

to a *quadratic twist* $\tilde{E}$ of E, i.e., to a curve that is isomorphic to E over $\mathbb{F}_{p^2}$ but not over $\mathbb{F}_p$. By construction, $\tilde{E}$ has the same order $\#\tilde{E}(\mathbb{F}_p) = p + 1$, and it contains exactly one cyclic subgroup $\tilde{X}_1 = \tilde{E}[N] \cap \tilde{E}(\mathbb{F}_p)$; we shall then set X_1 to $\upsilon^{-1}(\tilde{X}_1)$. Finally, the restriction of the Weil pairing to $X_1 \times X_2$ is non-degenerate, as wanted.[4]

The map ϕ will be instantiated with an isogeny of degree ℓ^T, and the map $\hat{\phi}$ with its dual. In practice, we assume that these isogenies are stored as a sequence of T isogenies of degree ℓ (e.g., specified by their kernels), so that evaluating ϕ and $\hat{\phi}$ can be done in time polynomial in ℓ and linear in T. For a representation that is more compact by a (large) constant factor, see Sect. 7.

Because of the way we have chosen ℓ, the graph of (horizontal) ℓ-isogenies containing E is a cycle of length dividing the class number h, thus an isogeny of degree ℓ^T is obtained by choosing a *direction* on the cycle and composing T isogeny steps each of degree ℓ. The isogeny $\phi : E \to E'$ defines an image curve $E'/\mathbb{F}_p$ having the same group structure as E; in particular we define the cyclic groups $Y_1 = \upsilon^{-1}(\tilde{E}'[N] \cap \tilde{E}'(\mathbb{F}_p))$ and $Y_2 = E'[N] \cap E'(\mathbb{F}_p)$, where $\tilde{E}' = \upsilon(E')$ is a quadratic twist of E'.

Note that it is easy to sample uniformly from any of the groups X_1, X_2, Y_1, Y_2, in a way that does not reveal discrete logarithms:[5] one simply takes random points on the curves or on their twists and multiplies by the cofactor $(p + 1)/N$. The algorithms defining the VDF are described in Fig. 1.

The similarity with Wesolowski's VDF is evident here: all ℓ-isogenies with the same direction correspond to an ideal $\mathfrak{a}$ of norm ℓ inside the quadratic imaginary order $\mathcal{O} \simeq \mathrm{End}_{\mathbb{F}_p}(E)$, which is also a representative of an ideal class in $\mathrm{Cl}(\mathcal{O})$.

---

[4] We note that a distorsion map $X_1 \to X_2$ may be used to define a self-pairing on X_1, however efficient distorsion maps only exist for very few supersingular curves. Fortunately, we will not need distorsion maps.

[5] In the elliptic curve cryptography literature, this is typically called *hashing* into the groups.

Composing isogenies corresponds to multiplying ideals, thus ϕ corresponds to $\mathfrak{a}^T$ and $\hat{\phi}$ corresponds to $\mathfrak{a}^{-T}$ in $\mathrm{Cl}(\mathcal{O})$. While Wesolowski raises elements to the power 2^T, we only do the equivalent of raising to the power T, because no analogue of the square-and-multiply algorithm is known for composing isogenies. Of course, the fundamental difference is in the way we verify the computation.

5.2   VDF from Supersingular Curves over $\mathbb{F}_{p^2}$

Our second VDF is very similar to the previous one, but uses supersingular curves defined over $\mathbb{F}_{p^2}$, thus sharing some similarities with the Charles–Goren–Lauter hash function [17], and with SIDH [25,38]. It deviates slightly from the paradigm presented in Sect. 3 in that the inputs are not taken in a cyclic group, and evaluation is slower than the previous one by a factor of about 2 (see Sect. 7), but has some advantages over it that will be discussed in Sect. 6.

Like before, we choose a prime p such that $p+1$ contains a large prime factor N, and a small prime ℓ, e.g., $\ell = 2$.[6] We again choose a supersingular elliptic curve $E/\mathbb{F}_p$ (this will be necessary to define the orthogonal groups X_1, X_2), however we see it as a curve over $\mathbb{F}_{p^2}$, so that $t = -2p$ and $\#E(\mathbb{F}_{p^2}) = (p+1)^2$.

Like before, we define $X_1 = \upsilon^{-1}(\tilde{E}[N] \cap \tilde{E}(\mathbb{F}_p))$ and $X_2 = E[N] \cap E(\mathbb{F}_p)$, where $\tilde{E} = \upsilon(E)$ is a quadratic twist of E over $\mathbb{F}_p$. The maps $\phi, \hat{\phi}$ are again a cyclic isogeny of degree ℓ^T and its dual, however, over $\mathbb{F}_{p^2}$, there are $(\ell+1)\ell^{T-1}$ possible choices for them, instead of just two; we will select one of them by doing a non-backtracking[7] random walk in the full ℓ-isogeny graph.

On the image curve E', we define $Y_1 = \phi(X_1)$ and $Y_2 = \phi(X_2)$. However, we are now faced with a difficulty: there is no known efficient way to sample from Y_2 or Y_1, indeed E' is generally defined over $\mathbb{F}_{p^2}$ and it has therefore no $\mathbb{F}_p$-twists. To bypass this problem, we deviate from the abstract description of Sect. 3, obtaining an N-to-1 map instead of a bijection. Let π be the Frobenius endomorphism of $E/\mathbb{F}_p$, the *trace map* on $E/\mathbb{F}_{p^2}$ is the map

$$\mathrm{Tr} : E/\mathbb{F}_{p^2} \to E/\mathbb{F}_p,$$
$$P \mapsto P + \pi(P).$$

In particular, the trace map sends $E[N]$ to X_2, and satisfies

$$e_N(P, \mathrm{Tr}(R)) = e_N(P, (1+\pi)(R)) = e_N((1-\pi)(P), R) = e_N([2]P, R) = e_N(P, R)^2$$

for all $P \in X_1$ and $R \in E[N]$. We thus define our VDF as

$$f : E'[N] \to X_2,$$
$$Q \mapsto (\mathrm{Tr} \circ \hat{\phi})(Q);$$

verification is done by checking a pairing equation as before. The algorithms are described in Fig. 2.

---

[6] For this VDF, there is no practical reason to choose any other prime than $\ell = 2$.

[7] An isogeny walk is called *non-backtracking* if no isogeny step is followed by its dual, or, equivalently, if the full walk corresponds to a cyclic isogeny.

Setup(λ, T)
1. Choose primes N, p with the properties above, according to the security parameter λ;
2. Select a supersingular curve $E/\mathbb{F}_p$;
3. Perform a random non-backtracking walk of length T in the ℓ-isogeny $\mathbb{F}_{p^2}$-graph, defining a cyclic ℓ^T-isogeny $\phi : E \to E'$ and its dual $\hat{\phi}$;
4. Choose a generator P of $X_1 = v^{-1}(\tilde{E}[N] \cap \tilde{E}(\mathbb{F}_p))$, and compute $\phi(P)$;
5. Output $(\mathsf{ek}, \mathsf{vk}) = \big(\hat{\phi}, (E, E', P, \phi(P))\big)$.

Eval($\hat{\phi}, Q \in E'[N]$)
1. Compute and output $(\mathrm{Tr} \circ \hat{\phi})(Q)$.

Verify($E, E', P, Q, \phi(P), (\mathrm{Tr} \circ \hat{\phi})(Q)$)
1. Verify $(\mathrm{Tr} \circ \hat{\phi})(Q) \in X_2 = E[N] \cap E(\mathbb{F}_p)$;
2. Verify that $e_N(P, (\mathrm{Tr} \circ \hat{\phi})(Q)) = e_N(\phi(P), Q)^2$.

Fig. 2. Instantiation of the Verifiable Delay Function over $\mathbb{F}_{p^2}$

A bijective VDF over $\mathbb{F}_{p^2}$. If a bijection is wanted, an alternative VDF using the $\mathbb{F}_{p^2}$-graph would swap roles by having E' defined over $\mathbb{F}_p$, and E over $\mathbb{F}_{p^2}$. During the Setup phase, a basis (P, R) of $X_1 \times X_2$ is sampled by evaluating $\hat{\phi}/2^T$ on a basis of $Y_1 \times Y_2$, and it is added to the verification key vk. Then, sampling Q in Y_2 is easy, and verifying that $\hat{\phi}(Q) \in X_2$ can be done by checking that $e_N(R, \hat{\phi}(Q)) = 1$. However this protocol is less efficient, because verification requires two pairing computations instead of one.

5.3   Properties of the VDFs

In slight disagreement with the definitions of [10], the Setup routines presented here take $O(T)$ time to compute the isogenies $\phi, \hat{\phi}$, and produce evaluation keys of size $O(T)$. While the size of the evaluation key can be reduced by redoing parts of the computation in Eval (see Sect. 7), the only known way to verify the public parameters is to, essentially, rerun the Setup.

We also note that, although T can be arbitrary (we discuss bounds on T in the next section), neither of our VDFs is *incremental* in the sense of [10], meaning that a single parameter set produced by Setup shall support more than one delay T. A possible workaround is to have Setup include some intermediate curves in the verification key, so that a single Setup can be used for many delay parameters up to T, at the cost of increasing the size of the verification key.

Finally, the VDF over $\mathbb{F}_p$ is *decodable* in the sense of [10], meaning that given the output $\hat{\phi}(Q)$ one can compute the input Q (although not more efficiently than evaluating $\hat{\phi}$); the VDF over $\mathbb{F}_{p^2}$, on the other hand, is obviously not decodable because it is non-injective.

6   Security and Parameter Sizes

We now give formal security definitions and proofs, following [10]. A VDF must satisfy three security properties: *correctness*, *soundess*, and *sequentiality*, as defined below. In [10], soundness is a weaker property where the evaluator is allowed a negligible cheating probability; we introduce here the stronger notion of perfect soundness, which is achieved by our VDFs.

Definition 1 (Correctness, soundness). *The VDFs of Sect. 5 are correct if, for any λ, T, public parameters $(\mathsf{ek}, \mathsf{vk}) \leftarrow \mathsf{Setup}(\lambda, T)$, and all input Q, if $R \leftarrow \mathsf{Eval}(\mathsf{ek}, Q)$ then $\mathsf{Verify}(\mathsf{vk}, Q, R)$ outputs* true.

They are perfectly sound if for all λ, T, public parameters $(\mathsf{ek}, \mathsf{vk}) \leftarrow \mathsf{Setup}(\lambda, T)$, and all input Q, if $R \neq \mathsf{Eval}(\mathsf{ek}, Q)$ then $\mathsf{Verify}(\mathsf{vk}, Q, R)$ outputs false.

Theorem 1. *The VDFs of Sect. 5 are correct and perfectly sound.*

Proof. The map $R \mapsto e_N(P, R)$ is a group isomorphism between the output space $X_2 \subset E[N]$ and the multiplicative subgroup $\mu_N \subset \mathbb{F}_{p^2}$. Hence, verification succeeds if and only if the output is correct.

Sequentiality is the defining property of VDFs, and is much subtler to define. Intuitively, we want it to be impossible to evaluate the VDF *faster* than running Eval, even given an unbounded amount of parallel resources, and even if the adversary is allowed a *large* amount of precomputation after the public parameters are generated. We must of course exclude trivial cases where, for example, the adversary precomputes a list of input-output pairs, hence we model security as a game where the adversary is allowed a polynomial amount of precomputation, after which he receives a random input point Q and must produce the output $\hat{\phi}(Q)$ (or $\mathrm{Tr} \circ \hat{\phi}(Q)$) faster than Eval with non-negligible probability. We also introduce here a new definition: if the adversary cannot break sequentiality, even when he is allowed a quantum precomputation before seeing the point Q, we say that the VDF is quantum annoying.

Definition 2 (Sequentiality, quantum annoyance). *The VDFs of Sect. 5 are sequential if no pair of randomized algorithms $\mathcal{A}_0$, which runs in total time $\mathrm{poly}(T, \lambda)$, and $\mathcal{A}_1$, which runs in parallel time less than T, can win with non-negligible probability the following sequentiality game*

1. *$(\mathsf{ek}, \mathsf{vk}) \xleftarrow{\$} \mathsf{Setup}(\lambda, T)$, where the random input tape to Setup is filled with uniformly distributed bits,*
2. *$A \leftarrow \mathcal{A}_0(\lambda, \mathsf{ek}, \mathsf{vk}, T)$,*
3. *$Q \xleftarrow{\$} Y_2$, uniformly sampled,*
4. *$Q' \leftarrow \mathcal{A}_1(A, \mathsf{vk}, Q)$,*

where winning is defined as outputting $Q' = \hat{\phi}(Q)$ (or $Q' = \mathrm{Tr} \circ \hat{\phi}(Q)$).

Moreover, if $\mathcal{A}_0$ is allowed a quantum computation in $\mathrm{poly}(T, \lambda)$, we say that the VDFs are quantum annoying.

We leave aside the question of formally defining a computational model where "running in parallel time less than T" has a definite meaning; see [10,75] for details.

We shall see soon that Setup must use secret randomness to select the starting curve $E/\mathbb{F}_p$; after that, Setup is only left with choosing the isogeny $\phi : E \to E'$ and the generator $P \in E[N]$, and both choices can done using public randomness. Furthermore $\mathcal{A}_0$ is allowed poly(T) computation, so it can compute $\hat{\phi}$ and evaluate ϕ on P (and also evaluate $\hat{\phi}$ on polynomially many points of Y_2). Hence, choice of $E/\mathbb{F}_p$ aside, Setup can be absorbed into $\mathcal{A}_0$; this justifies defining the following problem, which is a simple rewording of the sequentiality hypothesis:

Definition 3. (Isogeny shortcut problem (over k)). *Let $E/\mathbb{F}_p$ be a curve uniformly sampled in the set of all supersingular curves defined over a finite field $\mathbb{F}_p$. Given an isogeny $\phi : E \to E'$ of degree ℓ^T to a curve E'/k, with $k = \mathbb{F}_p$ or $k = \mathbb{F}_{p^2}$; being allowed a precomputation taking total time poly(T, λ), evaluate $\hat{\phi}(Q)$ on a random point $Q \in E'[N] \cap E'(k)$ in parallel time less than T.*

6.1   Attacks

We now discuss three natural attack strategies on the isogeny shortcut problem, and we use them to set parameter sizes. We summarize their complexities in Table 2.

Pairing Inversion. The simplest attack exploits the same properties as the verification. It works both against the VDFs and the generalization of BLS signatures sketched in Sect. 3. Given $P, \phi(P), Q$, to compute $\hat{\phi}(Q)$ (or $(\mathrm{Tr} \circ \hat{\phi})(Q)$) it is enough to solve the *pairing inversion problem* $e_N(P, \cdot) = e_N(\phi(P), Q)$. Note that this attack must be repeated for each new input Q.

The hardness of the pairing inversion problem impacts the size of N and p. Given that our curves have embedding degrees 2 or 1, the best algorithm at our disposal is the Number Field Sieve for $\mathbb{F}_{p^2}$, with (heuristic) complexity $L_p(1/3)$. The current record for computing discrete logarithms in $\mathbb{F}_{p^2}$ is for a prime p of almost 300 bits [2], while for a security of 128 bits it is recommended to take p of around 1500 bits, and N of 256 bits. We will use the complexity of this attack to set parameter sizes in Sect. 7.3.

Computing Shortcuts. A different path to breaking our VDFs consists in finding a "simpler" isogeny from E to E', agreeing with ϕ on $E[N]$, but taking less parallel time to compute. This kind of attacks can be decomposed in two steps: first find a "simpler" isogeny $\psi : E \to E'$ (e.g., of lower degree), then find an endomorphism $\omega \in \mathrm{End}(E)$ such that $\omega \circ \hat{\psi}$ agrees with $\hat{\phi}$ on $E'[N]$.

Concerning the first step, when $\deg \phi$ is super-polynomial in p, a lower degree isogeny $\psi : E \to E'$ always exists; indeed Pizer [60,61] has shown that ℓ-isogeny graphs of supersingular curves over $\bar{\mathbb{F}}_p$ are optimal expanders for any prime ℓ, and thus have diameter in $O(\log(p))$, implying that there is an ℓ-isogeny walk connecting E to E' of degree polynomial in p. However, it may be difficult to compute such an isogeny in general: the best generic algorithm in the case of $\mathbb{F}_{p^2}$-graphs is a birthday paradox method [26,33], that finds a collision in $O(\sqrt{p})$ isogeny steps on average. Note that the only quantum speedup known for this problem is a generic Grover search, giving a square-root acceleration at best [8].

For curves over $\mathbb{F}_p$, computing the structure of the class group $\mathrm{Cl}(\mathrm{End}(E))$ allows an attacker to find an equivalent isogeny ψ, of (smooth) lower degree. A similar computation is at the hearth of the signature scheme CSI-FiSh [6], and has recently been demonstrated to be doable for primes of around 500 bits. Nevertheless, the asymptotically best algorithm, due to Jao and Soukharev [40], computes an equivalent isogeny of smooth subexponential degree using $L_p(1/2)$ operations, and is thus not better than the pairing inversion attack mentioned above. We will sketch later how a similar attack can be performed in polynomial time on a quantum computer.

After computing a "simpler" isogeny $\psi : E \to E'$, we are left with the problem of finding ω such that $\omega \circ \hat{\psi} = \hat{\phi}$ on $E'[N]$. This problem can be solved by computing discrete logarithms in $E[N]$, which is again not easier than the pairing inversion problem; however, this attack needs only be performed once on the public parameters, and can then be used to speed up any evaluation.

So far, we have only discussed the computation of *shortcuts* in the generic case; however, when E or E' are special curves, there are much better ways to solve this problem, that would lead to a complete break of our VDFs. We discuss this issue in Subsect. 6.2.

Parallel Isogeny Evaluation. Finally, the last attack path would be to find a better parallel algorithm for evaluating isogenies of degree ℓ^T. All known algorithms require to go through each of the T intermediate curves, one after the other. Barring shortcut techniques as described above, it seems unlikely that an algorithm "skipping" intermediate curves could exist. This is not dissimilar from the case of VDFs based on groups of unknown order, where one argues that in order to compute g^{2^T} all intermediate values g^{2^i} must be computed. After all, a 2-isogeny is only a simple generalization of the multiplication-by-2 map of an elliptic curve, it thus seems believable that a chain of 2-isogenies must be evaluated sequentially passing through all intermediate curves.

It is certainly possible to aggregate steps in blocks, e.g., replace two 2-isogenies with one 4-isogeny, as it is typically done in implementations of SIDH/SIKE [21]. This is analogous to replacing n squarings with a single power-of-2^n in group-based VDFs; previous work on parallel modular exponentiation suggests that, in some complexity models, there may be a small asymptotic gain in doing so [4], however the viability of these algorithms has never been validated in practice. At any rate, algorithms for parallel modular exponentiation would need to be adapted for isogeny evaluation, and we believe that, in this respect, isogeny-based VDFs can only be as weak as group-based VDFs, but no more. This is certainly the newest and most unusual problem in the area of elliptic curve cryptography, and the one that needs more investigation.

Bounds on T. None of the attacks so far has set an upper bound on T. By the birthday paradox, we shall take T smaller than the square root of the size of the isogeny graph, because a loop in the isogeny walk could be optimized away from Eval. Given that the size of the isogeny graphs is $O(\sqrt{p})$ and $O(p)$ respectively, we obtain bounds of $O(\sqrt[4]{p})$ for $\mathbb{F}_p$, and $O(\sqrt{p})$ for $\mathbb{F}_{p^2}$.

However, these bounds are much higher than the best attacks, that are subexponential in p. Thus T is effectively only bounded by the theoretical limit of being subexponential in λ.

On Future Attack Improvements. While the isogeny shortcut problem is new, we argue that improvements to any of the three attack strategies outlined above would have important consequences in cryptography, beyond our VDF constructions. Pairing inversion is a well-known problem in classical cryptography, and an attack on it will affect a large number of pairing-based protocols [34]. Shortening an isogeny walk from a curve leads to an endomorphism of this curve; this is believed to be hard computational task, which underlies the security of other cryptosystems [17,36]. Finally, faster parallel isogeny computations will benefit other isogeny-based cryptographic protocols, such as key exchange [1,16,38] and signatures [24,76].

Quantum Security. We briefly analyze our proposals in the post-quantum setting. Obviously, Shor's algorithm breaks the pairing inversion problems in polynomial time, thus our VDFs cannot be considered post-quantum. However, looking at Definition 2, we see that this attack can only be applied after the input point Q is given to $\mathcal{A}_1$; thus our VDFs have a chance of being *quantum annoying* as defined there. In a plausible future where quantum computers do exist, but are very expensive and slow, it may still be more interesting to evaluate the VDF in the legitimate way, rather than attack the pairing inversion problem with Shor's algorithm. We argue that, given current knowledge, our VDF over $\mathbb{F}_{p^2}$ is quantum annoying, whereas the one over $\mathbb{F}_p$ is not.

Indeed, as long as the input point Q is unknown, the only strategy currently available for $\mathcal{A}_0$ is to compute an isogeny shortcut, as described previously. In the $\mathbb{F}_{p^2}$ case, this would involve finding a cycle in the isogeny graph through $E/\mathbb{F}_p$ and $E'/\mathbb{F}_{p^2}$, a problem that is believed to be quantum-resistant when E and E' are generic supersingular curves [30,35].

For the $\mathbb{F}_p$ case, on the other hand, it is enough to compute the structure of $\mathrm{Cl}(\mathrm{End}(E))$, along with a basis of "short" generators, a task doable in polynomial time on a quantum computer using Kitaev's generalization of Shor's algorithm [44]. Then an isogeny $\psi : E \to E'$ of lower degree defined over $\mathbb{F}_p$ can be computed by solving a closest vector problem: although polynomial-time lattice reduction algorithms (both classical and quantum) can only reach isogeny degrees exponential in $\log(p)$, this may be enough to break some large delay parameters, and it can be very efficient in practice, as showcased by the signature scheme CSI-FiSh [6]. Finally, since ψ and ϕ are both defined over $\mathbb{F}_p$, the subgroup $X_2 = E[N] \cap E(\mathbb{F}_p)$ is an eigenspace for the endomorphism $\hat{\psi} \circ \phi$; then a discrete logarithm computation in X_2 finds a scalar s such that $[s] \circ \hat{\psi} = \hat{\phi}$ on Y_2.

Table 2. Complexity of the known attacks on the sequentiality of our VDFs, assuming the endomorphism rings of the supersingular curves are unknown (see Subsect. 6.2 for a polynomial time classical attack when the endomorphism rings are known). Computing shortcuts targets public parameters independently of the input to the VDFs, and can be thus be run as a pre-computation. Pairing inversion attacks a single input point, and must be re-run for every new input.

	Classical		Quantum	
	$\mathbb{F}_p$ graph	$\mathbb{F}_{p^2}$ graph	$\mathbb{F}_p$ graph	$\mathbb{F}_{p^2}$ graph
Computing shortcuts	$L_p(1/2)$	$O(\sqrt{p})$	$\text{polylog}(p)$	$O(\sqrt[4]{p})$
Pairing inversion	$L_p(1/3)$	$L_p(1/3)$	$\text{polylog}(p)$	$\text{polylog}(p)$

Security of the Identification Protocol. For completeness, we briefly come back to the security of the generalization of the BLS identification protocol sketched in Sect. 3.

We are not interested in sequentiality in this case, thus shortcut attacks are not relevant here. Instead, key recovery is equivalent to the problem of finding a secret isogeny $\phi : E \to E'$, given E, E', a basis (P, Q) of $E[N]$, and $\phi(P), \phi(Q)$. This problem is much more similar to classical problems in isogeny based cryptography, and is obviously harder than the isogeny shortcut problem.

The best known classical attacks, both for the $\mathbb{F}_p$ and the $\mathbb{F}_{p^2}$ case, are in the square root of the graph size (respectively, $O(\sqrt[4]{p})$ and $O(\sqrt{p})$). But key recovery is hard even for quantum computers: the best attack for the $\mathbb{F}_p$ case is Kuperberg's algorithm for the *Hidden Shift Problem* [5,7,13,18,39,49,50,63], which finds ϕ in $\exp(\sqrt{\log(p)})$ quantum operations; whereas in the $\mathbb{F}_{p^2}$ case quantum computers give a square-root speedup via Grover's algorithm at best [8].

Hence, both identification protocols have a security property similar to the *quantum annoyance* defined in Definition 2: any forgery requires running a new instance of Shor's algorithm, while key recovery is infeasible on quantum computers. This may be a useful replacement for basic BLS signatures in contexts where Shor's algorithm is slow and expensive, and signatures must be produced fast.

Finally, we remark that our protocol, unlike BLS, is *succinct*, in the sense that the secret isogeny is potentially sub-exponentially larger than the proof of knowledge. At present, this seems rather limited, since our protocol is not zero-knowledge, however we hope that further research may add more useful properties to it.

6.2   Shortcut Attacks on Special Curves

We now come back to the *shortcut* attacks analyzed previously. We saw that the best algorithms available in the general case have exponential or sub-exponential complexity, and are *in general* not better than a simple pairing inversion attack. However, when the endomorphism ring of the starting curve E is known, a much better algorithm exists, completely breaking sequentiality of our VDFs. We now present a sketch of the attack, and the only known solution to avoid it.

Attack Overview. We shall suppose that the delay parameter T is super-linear in $\log(p)$. To simplify our description we also assume that E is the curve defined by the equation $y^2 = x^3 + x$, with j-invariant $j = 1728$. However, the attack can be generalized to an arbitrary curve provided we know its endomorphism ring. It can also be applied to our VDF over $\mathbb{F}_p$, because an attacker is not bound to keep all computations in $\mathbb{F}_p$.

The attack has two main steps. First, we compute an alternative isogeny $\psi : E \to E'$ with a powersmooth and reasonably small degree (polynomial in p). This is achieved by adapting a strategy used in [30,57] to compute a collision to Charles–Goren–Lauter (CGL) hash function [17]. Second, we compute an endomorphism $\omega \in \text{End}(E)$ such that the actions of $\omega \circ \hat{\psi}$ and $\hat{\phi}$ are identical on $E[N]$. By expressing ω on a set of generators of $\text{End}(E)$, we are able to evaluate $\omega \circ \hat{\psi}$ efficiently on $E[N]$, and thus we can answer evaluation queries in a time much shorter than T.

Computing Shortcuts. Let $\phi : E = E_0 \to E_T = E'$ be given as a composition of degree ℓ isogenies. We now show how to compute an alternative isogeny $\psi : E \to E'$ with much shorter degree.

A natural idea to solve this problem is to translate this problem to an analogous problem in the quaternion algebra $B_{p,\infty}$ ramified at p and at infinity, solve the problem in the quaternion algebra, and translate the solution back to the geometric setting. Indeed $\text{End}(E_0)$ is isomorphic to a maximal order $\mathcal{O}_0$ of $B_{p,\infty}$, and by assumption on E this isomorphism is fully known. Translating the problem back and forth (from isogenies to their corresponding ideals and conversely) can be done using techniques dating back to Waterhouse [74], and the "quaternion isogeny" algorithm of Kohel, Lauter, Petit and Tignol (KLPT) [46] can be used to solve the problem in the quaternion algebra. Unfortunately, the translation algorithms require to compute torsion points of order $\deg \phi$, which have exponential size in general.

We adapt an idea used in the collision algorithm of [30,57] to avoid this problem. Let $\phi_i : E_0 \to E_i$ correspond to the first i steps of the isogeny. Let I_i be the corresponding ideal, and let $n(I_i) = \ell^i$ denote its norm. Assume we have already computed an ideal J_i in the class of I_i with powersmooth norm. We sketch how to compute an ideal in the class of I_{i+1} with powersmooth norm.

1. Compute the $\ell + 1$ ideals $K_{i+1,k}$, $k = 0, \ldots, \ell$ with norm $n(J_i)\ell$ such that $K_{i+1,k} \bmod n(J_i)\mathcal{O}_0 = J_i$ (algorithms for this task are provided in [43]).
2. Apply the powersmooth quaternion isogeny algorithm to each $K_{i+1,k}$ to obtain new ideals $J_{i+1,k}$ in the same classes respectively.
3. Translate each ideal $J_{i+1,k}$ to an isogeny $\psi_{i+1,k}$.
4. Identify the (usually unique) k such that the image of $\psi_{i+1,k}$ has j-invariant $j_{i+1} = j(E_{i+1})$.
5. Let $J_{i+1} = J_{i+1,k}$.

To obtain the desired isogeny ψ, we repeat those steps for $i = 1, \ldots, T-1$. When $i = T - 1$, we additionally set $\psi = \psi_{T,k}$.

The heuristic bounds and the experiments in [46] show that the degree of ψ_i is polynomial in p (more precisely $O(p^{7/2})$) and the computation can be completed in time $\mathrm{poly}(T, \log(p))$. The isogeny $\psi : E \to E'$ has powersmooth degree much smaller than that of ϕ, and can therefore be evaluated much faster.

Matching Image Points on the N-Torsion. Let $\iota : E \to E : (x,y) \to (-x, iy)$ where $i^2 = -1$, and let $\pi : E \to E : (x,y) \to (x^p, y^p)$. We have $\mathrm{End}(E) = \langle 1, \iota, \frac{1+\pi}{2}, \frac{\iota+\pi\iota}{2} \rangle$, so the endomorphism $\theta := \hat{\psi} \circ \phi$ can be written as $\theta = a_0 + a_1 \iota + a_2 \pi + a_3 \pi\iota$ with $a_0, a_1, a_2, a_3 \in \mathbb{Z}[1/2]$. Moreover we have

$$a_i = \langle \theta, \alpha_i \rangle := (\theta \circ \hat{\alpha}_i + \alpha_i \circ \hat{\theta})/2$$

for $\alpha_i = 1, \iota, \pi, \pi\iota$ respectively, and these coefficients can be computed using a variant of Schoof's algorithm [45, Theorem 81], by evaluating those maps on small torsion points and applying the Chinese remainder theorem. Note that $|a_i| \leq \deg \theta \deg \alpha_i$, so this computation can be performed in time $\mathrm{poly}(T, \log p)$.

If we now set $\omega = r\hat{\theta}$, where $r = \ell^T / (a_0^2 + a_1^2 + pa_2^2 + pa_3^2)$, then $\omega \circ \hat{\psi} = \hat{\phi}$. But ω can be evaluated at any point of E as

$$\omega(Q) = \sum [ra_i \bmod N]\, \hat{\alpha}_i(Q),$$

at a cost of only $O(\log(N))$ operations. Thus we can replace $\mathsf{Eval}(Q)$ with the evaluation of $\hat{\psi}$ followed by the evaluation of ω, for a total costs of only $\mathrm{polylog}(p)$, which is less than T by hypothesis.

Countering the Attack. The KLPT algorithm only works when the starting curve E has an endomorphism ring that is, in their words, *extremal* and *special*. *Extremal* means that E is defined over $\mathbb{F}_p$, a condition common to all instantiations of our VDF; however only few curves are also *special*, for example $j(E) = 1728$, or other curves with complex multiplication by an order with small discriminant.

The KPLT algorithm extends to a non-special curve E, when a path $E \to E_0$ to a special curve E_0 is known. Unfortunately, all known methods to select random supersingular curves do so by starting a random walk from some special curve; hence, there is no known way to produce a random supersingular curve $E/\mathbb{F}_p$ without producing a backdoor $E \to E_0$.

At present, the only way to counter the attack presented here is to use a trusted setup to produce a random curve $E/\mathbb{F}_p$, i.e., having a trusted authority (or many trusted authorities engaged in a multi-party protocol) compute a walk $E_0 \to E$ from a special curve E_0, and then throw the backdoor away.

A Note on Ordinary Curves. It is natural to ask whether it is possible to obtain VDFs from ordinary isogeny graphs. Although it is conceivable to have a variant of our VDF over $\mathbb{F}_p$ using ordinary curves, no secure instantiation is currently known. Indeed, all known ordinary pairing-friendly curves are obtained using variations of the CM method, and thus have small quadratic discriminant and small isogeny class. In this case it is possible to compute the structure of $\text{End}(E)$, and do a shortcut attack similar to the one above.

We proceed in two steps as before. We first find an isogeny $\psi : E \to E'$ of small powersmooth degree; since the isogeny class is small, this can even be done by exhaustive search.

Then, we are left with the problem of finding $\omega \in \text{End}(E)$ such that $\omega \circ \hat{\psi} = \hat{\phi}$ when restricted to $E[N]$. We proceed as before: using Schoof's algorithm we compute $\theta = \hat{\psi} \circ \phi = a + b\pi$ for some $a, b \in \mathbb{Q}$, then we set $\omega = \ell^T \hat{\theta}/(a^2 + pb^2)$, and we replace Eval by $\omega \circ \hat{\psi}$.

A family of ordinary pairing friendly elliptic curves with generic discriminant would provide the perfect instantiation for our VDFs, as it would not be vulnerable to any known shortcut attack, and thus would not need a trusted setup. Unfortunately, all known constructions of pairing-friendly elliptic curves use complex multiplication and hence produce curves with small discriminants [31].

7   Implementation

Our proposed VDFs can be easily implemented using the fundamental blocks already available for pairing-based and isogeny-based cryptography. A drawback of our method being the long setup time and the large evaluation key, we present here an implementation that improves both by orders of magnitude.

7.1   Eval

We focus on 2-isogenies, as they are the most obvious candidate for an implementation. There are two standard ways to compute a 2-isogeny walk from a curve $E : y^2 = f(x)$. The first is to factor the 2-division polynomial $f(x)$ to obtain all the points of order 2, then use Vélu's formulas [70] to test all directions and step in the wanted one. Since Vélu's formulas also produce the generator of the dual isogeny to the direction one is coming from, this root can be quotiented out from $f(x)$, and thus we are left with solving one square root per curve. The second way is to take a point at random on E and multiply it by the cofactor $\#E/2$. If we obtain a 2-torsion point defining the wanted direction, then we compute it and we move to the next curve; otherwise we try with a different point. Both ways require $O(\log(p))$ operations in the base field for one step, and thus $O(T\log(p))$ operations to compute the full isogeny walk. After the isogeny ϕ is computed, the list of the kernel points can be stored so to be able to evaluate ϕ in $O(T)$ operations. However, this implies storing T points and curves, which may require a large storage.

Fortunately, using isogeny evaluation techniques pioneered in SIDH [25], and applied in [27] to the CGL hash function [17], it is possible to absorb the $\log(p)$ factor and shorten the evaluation key size by the same amount. For this, we choose a prime of the form $p = 2^n f N - 1$, so that all curves in the isogeny graph have rational points of order 2^{n-1} or 2^n (depending on whether we use

$\mathbb{F}_p$-graphs or $\mathbb{F}_{p^2}$-graphs). This way, a single point P_i on E_i can be used to define n (or $n-1$) consecutive steps in the graph, and the corresponding isogeny can be evaluated in $n \log(n)$ operations using the *optimal strategy* techniques from [25].

More in detail, in the $\mathbb{F}_{p^2}$ case, the curve E_i has group structure $E(\mathbb{F}_{p^2}) \simeq (\mathbb{Z}/(p+1)\mathbb{Z})^2$, and is usually not defined over $\mathbb{F}_p$. We can compute a point P_i of order 2^n by taking a point at random and multiplying by fN, then verifying that P_i has the wanted order. We check that P_i does not start a backtracking isogeny and we use it to advance n steps in the graph, then we start again.

In the $\mathbb{F}_p$ case, because we chose a curve on the surface, the group structure is $E(\mathbb{F}_p) \simeq \mathbb{Z}/\frac{p+1}{2}\mathbb{Z} \times \mathbb{Z}/2\mathbb{Z}$ (see [54]), hence the highest order we can get for P_i is 2^{n-1}. Such point P_i will define 2^{n-2} horizontal isogeny steps in the "positive" direction determined by the ideal $(\pi - 1) \subset \text{End}(E)$, plus one last step that is either in the same direction, or going to the floor. To avoid "getting stuck" on the floor, we use P_i to advance $n-2$ steps, then start again.

Using these techniques, only $\approx T/n$ points need to be computed and the full walk is computed in $O(T \log n)$ operations. One has the choice between storing all the intermediate 2-torsion points, or storing only the higher order points P_i. In the first case, we use $O(T)$ storage and evaluation time; in the second case, we use $O(T/n)$ storage and $O(T \log n)$ evaluation time. Since $n \approx \log p$, the slowdown in the second case is likely to be negligible in front of other factors, such as data transfer delays, or speedups due to dedicated hardware.

In practice, we use a projective (x, z)-only Montgomery model for our curves, for which small degree isogeny formulas are the most efficient [21]. Points defined over $\mathbb{F}_{p^2}$ are then stored in $4 \log_2(p)$ bits, and a curve is represented by $y^2 = x^3 + ax^2 + x$ using $2 \log_2(p)$ bits. The isogeny $\hat{\phi}$ is decomposed in small degree isogenies, and each one is represented by its kernel and its image curve. If we choose to represent $\hat{\phi}$ as a composition of 2-isogenies, its representation is stored in $2T \log_2(p)$ bits. If we decide to represent it as a composition of 2^n-isogenies, storing kernels and curve coefficients requires $T/n(4 \log_2(p) + 2 \log_2(p)) = 6T \log_2(p)/n$ bits.

7.2   Verify

For verification, we apply standard optimization techniques for the pairing computation. We use Tate pairings instead of Weil pairings, thus the verification equation (e.g., in the $\mathbb{F}_p$-case)

$$f_{\hat{\phi}(Q)}(P)^{(p^2-1)/N} = f_Q(\phi(P))^{(p^2-1)/N}$$

can be checked by computing two Miller loops and one final exponentiation.

We stress that, while most of the implementation efforts on pairing have focused on ordinary elliptic curves with smaller field sizes, such as BN curves [3], our situation is somewhat different. In particular, our curves have large rho-value $\rho = \log(p)/\log(N)$, and thus the Tate pairing is to be preferred to the ate pairing, because it features a shorter Miller loop.

We use common optimizations for the Miller loop, such as quadratic twist tricks. In the final exponentiation, we benefit from the special form of the prime p, indeed

$$\frac{p^2 - 1}{N} = (p-1)\frac{p+1}{N} = (p-1)2^n f = (2^n f N - 2)2^n f = 2^{n+1} f (2^{n-1} f N - 1).$$

7.3 Benchmarks

To validate our proposals, we implemented a (non-optimized) proof of concept in SageMath [69]. For a 128-bit secure VDF, we choose a prime N of 256 bits, and set $n = 1244$, $f = 63$ to obtain a 1506-bit prime $p = 2^{1244} 63 N - 1$. To the present day, discrete logarithm computations in the subgroup of order N of $\mathbb{F}_{p^2}$, using the best available variants of NFS, are believed to require more than 2^{128} computations.

We ran benchmarks on an Intel Core i7-8700 processor clocked at 3.20 GHz. We measure the throughput of evaluation as a number of 2-isogeny steps per millisecond, testing for various delay parameters and averaging over them; this gives a rough idea of the degree of the isogeny needed to achieve the wanted delay. Since the duration of setup also depends on the degree of the isogeny, we use the same methodology to measure it. For verification, we simply give the (average) running time for a single verification, as this is the most pertinent measure. Currently, our pairing implementation is faster over $\mathbb{F}_p$ because these curves benefit of the distortion map to compute the pairing entirely over $\mathbb{F}_p$. Over $\mathbb{F}_{p^2}$, points are twice larger and many additional vertical lines and inversions are needed to compute the pairing. The results are given in Table 3.

Table 3. Benchmarks for our VDFs, on a Intel Core i7-8700 @ 3.20 GHz, with Sage-Math 8.5

Protocol	Step	ek size	Time	Throughput
$\mathbb{F}_p$ graph	Setup	238 kb	–	0.75 isog/ms
	Evaluation	–	–	0.75 isog/ms
	Verification	–	0.3 s	–
$\mathbb{F}_{p^2}$ graph	Setup	491 kb	–	0.35 isog/ms
	Evaluation	–	–	0.23 isog/ms
	Verification	–	4 s	–

We stress that these numbers only show that our VDFs are practical, however they do not say much on how they compare to other VDF proposals. Indeed, while setup and verification can be compared on the basis of their speed (in software), it is mostly meaningless to compare evaluation this way.

The meaningful comparison is on circuit surface and clock frequency for a single step of the evaluation loop. At this stage, it is impossible for us to give such numbers, however we can give some qualitative arguments to compare our VDFs to the competitors. At the 128 bits security level, the unit step in RSA-based VDFs is a squaring modulo an RSA modulus of more than 2000 bits. This unit step is roughly comparable to one multiplication in our field $\mathbb{F}_p$. In the simplest case, the unit step in our VDFs is the evaluation of a 2-isogeny over $\mathbb{F}_p$ (or $\mathbb{F}_{p^2}$); using the best formulas for Montgomery curves [64], this requires 2 parallel runs of 2 multiplications each. Thus we expect the circuit for one unit step of our VDF to have roughly double the surface and half the clock frequency. Similar considerations also apply to VDFs based on class groups.

8   Conclusion and Perspectives

We presented two new candidate Verifiable Delay Functions, based on assumptions from pairing-based and isogeny-based cryptography. Our VDFs are practical, and offer several advantages over previous proposals.

At present, our constructions require a trusted setup to generate initial parameters. It is an important open problem to find an algorithm to generate random supersingular curves in a way that does not reveal their endomorphism ring, and we encourage the community to work on it. As long as such an algorithm is missing, it is interesting to look for efficient multi-party algorithms for doing isogeny walks.

It would also be interesting to reduce the cost of validating public parameters, ideally to a time independent from the delay parameter T. Relatedly, our VDFs have large storage requirements for the evaluator; in our implementation we presented a way to mitigate this issue, however this creates a compromise between storage and evaluation time, that needs to be carefully considered by the evaluator, depending on the intended application. More research on practical ways to mitigate the price of the large storage is desirable.

Here we only sketched the shortcut attack against insecure instances using special curves. It would be interesting to do a more detailed analysis of its complexity, of its limitations, and of its possible generalizations; we leave this as future work. We also encourage research on alternative ways to break the Isogeny Shortcut Problem, for example finding ways to parallelize isogeny evaluation.

Finally, our VDFs can be seen as a generalization of BLS signatures: if the isogeny is kept secret, we obtain a proof of knowledge of an isogeny walk between two curves, that can be used for identification or signatures. At the moment, the only advantage over BLS signatures is a weak form of quantum resistance; we hope that further research would add useful properties to our protocol enabling more applications.

Acknowledgments. We would like to thank Bill Allombert, Razvan Barbulescu, Jeff Burdges, Wouter Castryck, Jeroen Demeyer, Andreas Enge, Steven Galbraith, Matthew Green, Philipp Jovanovic, Jean Kieffer, Enea Milio, Aurel Page, Lorenz Panny, Damien Robert, Barak Shani and Benjamin Wesolowski for fruitful discussions. We are grateful to the anonymous reviewers for their attentive reading and their helpful comments.

Luca De Feo was supported by the French *Programme d'Investissements d'Avenir* under the national project RISQ n° P141580-3069086/DOS0044212.

References

1. Azarderakhsh, R., et al.: Supersingular isogeny key encapsulation (2017). http://sike.org
2. Barbulescu, R., Gaudry, P., Guillevic, A., Morain, F.: Improving NFS for the discrete logarithm problem in non-prime finite fields. In: Oswald, E., Fischlin, M. (eds.) EUROCRYPT 2015. LNCS, vol. 9056, pp. 129–155. Springer, Heidelberg (2015). https://doi.org/10.1007/978-3-662-46800-5_6
3. Barreto, P.S.L.M., Naehrig, M.: Pairing-friendly elliptic curves of prime order. In: Preneel, B., Tavares, S. (eds.) SAC 2005. LNCS, vol. 3897, pp. 319–331. Springer, Heidelberg (2006). https://doi.org/10.1007/11693383_22
4. Bernstein, D., Sorenson, J.: Modular exponentiation via the explicit Chinese remainder theorem. Math. Comput. **76**(257), 443–454 (2007). https://doi.org/10.1090/S0025-5718-06-01849-7
5. Bernstein, D.J., Lange, T., Martindale, C., Panny, L.: Quantum circuits for the CSIDH: optimizing quantum evaluation of isogenies. In: Ishai, Y., Rijmen, V. (eds.) EUROCRYPT 2019. LNCS, vol. 11477, pp. 409–441. Springer, Cham (2019). https://doi.org/10.1007/978-3-030-17656-3_15
6. Beullens, W., Kleinjung, T., Vercauteren, F.: CSI-FiSh: efficient isogeny based signatures through class group computations. In: Galbraith, S.D., Moriai, S. (eds.) ASIACRYPT 2019. LNCS, vol. 11921, pp. 227–247. Springer, Heidelberg (2019)
7. Biasse, J.-F., Iezzi, A., Jacobson, M.J.: A note on the security of CSIDH. In: Chakraborty, D., Iwata, T. (eds.) INDOCRYPT 2018. LNCS, vol. 11356, pp. 153–168. Springer, Cham (2018). https://doi.org/10.1007/978-3-030-05378-9_9
8. Biasse, J.-F., Jao, D., Sankar, A.: A quantum algorithm for computing isogenies between supersingular elliptic curves. In: Meier, W., Mukhopadhyay, D. (eds.) INDOCRYPT 2014. LNCS, vol. 8885, pp. 428–442. Springer, Cham (2014). https://doi.org/10.1007/978-3-319-13039-2_25
9. Blake, I.F., Seroussi, G., Smart, N., et al.: Advances in Elliptic Curve Cryptography, London Mathematical Society Lecture Note Series, vol. 317. Cambridge University Press, New York (2005)
10. Boneh, D., Bonneau, J., Bünz, B., Fisch, B.: Verifiable delay functions. In: Shacham, H., Boldyreva, A. (eds.) CRYPTO 2018. LNCS, vol. 10991, pp. 757–788. Springer, Cham (2018). https://doi.org/10.1007/978-3-319-96884-1_25
11. Boneh, D., Bünz, B., Fisch, B.: A survey of two verifiable delay functions. Cryptology ePrint Archive, Report 2018/712 (2018). https://eprint.iacr.org/2018/712
12. Boneh, D., Lynn, B., Shacham, H.: Short signatures from the Weil pairing. J. Cryptol. **17**(4), 297–319 (2004). https://doi.org/10.1007/s00145-004-0314-9
13. Bonnetain, X., Schrottenloher, A.: Quantum security analysis of CSIDH and ordinary isogeny-based schemes. Cryptology ePrint Archive, Report 2018/537 (2018). https://eprint.iacr.org/2018/537
14. Broker, R.M., Charles, D.X., Lauter, K.E.: Cryptographic applications of efficiently evaluating large degree isogenies, US Patent 8,250,367, August 2012
15. Buchmann, J., Hamdy, S.: A survey on IQ cryptography. In: Proceedings of Public Key Cryptography and Computational Number Theory, pp. 1–15 (2001)

16. Castryck, W., Lange, T., Martindale, C., Panny, L., Renes, J.: CSIDH: an efficient post-quantum commutative group action. In: Peyrin, T., Galbraith, S. (eds.) ASIACRYPT 2018. LNCS, vol. 11274, pp. 395–427. Springer, Cham (2018). https://doi.org/10.1007/978-3-030-03332-3_15
17. Charles, D.X., Goren, E.Z., Lauter, K.E.: Cryptographic hash functions from expander graphs. J. Cryptol. **22**(1), 93–113 (2009). https://doi.org/10.1007/s00145-007-9002-x
18. Childs, A., Jao, D., Soukharev, V.: Constructing elliptic curve isogenies in quantum subexponential time. J. Math. Cryptol. **8**(1), 1–29 (2014)
19. Cohen, B.: Proofs of space and time. In: Blockchain Protocol Analysis and Security Engineering (2017). https://cyber.stanford.edu/sites/default/files/bramcohen.pdf
20. Cohen, B., Pietrzak, K.: Simple proofs of sequential work. In: Nielsen, J.B., Rijmen, V. (eds.) EUROCRYPT 2018. LNCS, vol. 10821, pp. 451–467. Springer, Cham (2018). https://doi.org/10.1007/978-3-319-78375-8_15
21. Costello, C., Longa, P., Naehrig, M.: Efficient algorithms for supersingular isogeny Diffie-Hellman. In: Robshaw, M., Katz, J. (eds.) CRYPTO 2016. LNCS, vol. 9814, pp. 572–601. Springer, Heidelberg (2016). https://doi.org/10.1007/978-3-662-53018-4_21
22. Cox, D.A.: Primes of the form $x^2 + ny^2$: Fermat, Class Field Theory, and Complex Multiplication. Wiley, New York (1997)
23. De Feo, L.: Mathematics of isogeny based cryptography (2017). http://arxiv.org/abs/1711.04062
24. De Feo, L., Galbraith, S.D.: SeaSign: compact isogeny signatures from class group actions. In: Ishai, Y., Rijmen, V. (eds.) EUROCRYPT 2019. LNCS, vol. 11478, pp. 759–789. Springer, Cham (2019). https://doi.org/10.1007/978-3-030-17659-4_26
25. De Feo, L., Jao, D., Plût, J.: Towards quantum-resistant cryptosystems from supersingular elliptic curve isogenies. J. Math. Cryptol. **8**(3), 209–247 (2014)
26. Delfs, C., Galbraith, S.D.: Computing isogenies between supersingular elliptic curves over $\mathbb{F}_p$. Des. Codes Crypt. **78**(2), 425–440 (2016). https://doi.org/10.1007/s10623-014-0010-1
27. Doliskani, J., Pereira, G.C.C.F., Barreto, P.S.L.M.: Faster cryptographic hash function from supersingular isogeny graphs. Cryptology ePrint Archive, Report 2017/1202 (2017). https://eprint.iacr.org/2017/1202
28. Drake, J.: Minimal VDF randomness beacon. Ethereum Res. (2018). https://ethresear.ch/t/minimal-vdf-randomness-beacon/3566
29. Dwork, C., Naor, M.: Pricing via processing or combatting junk mail. In: Brickell, E.F. (ed.) CRYPTO 1992. LNCS, vol. 740, pp. 139–147. Springer, Heidelberg (1993). https://doi.org/10.1007/3-540-48071-4_10
30. Eisenträger, K., Hallgren, S., Lauter, K., Morrison, T., Petit, C.: Supersingular isogeny graphs and endomorphism rings: reductions and solutions. In: Nielsen, J.B., Rijmen, V. (eds.) EUROCRYPT 2018. LNCS, vol. 10822, pp. 329–368. Springer, Cham (2018). https://doi.org/10.1007/978-3-319-78372-7_11
31. Freeman, D., Scott, M., Teske, E.: A taxonomy of pairing-friendly elliptic curves. J. Cryptol. **23**(2), 224–280 (2010). https://doi.org/10.1007/s00145-009-9048-z
32. Galbraith, S.D.: Mathematics of Public Key Cryptography. Cambridge University Press, New York (2012)
33. Galbraith, S.D., Hess, F., Smart, N.P.: Extending the GHS weil descent attack. In: Knudsen, L.R. (ed.) EUROCRYPT 2002. LNCS, vol. 2332, pp. 29–44. Springer, Heidelberg (2002). https://doi.org/10.1007/3-540-46035-7_3
34. Galbraith, S.D., Hess, F., Vercauteren, F.: Aspects of pairing inversion. IEEE Trans. Inf. Theor. **54**(12), 5719–5728 (2008). https://doi.org/10.1109/TIT.2008.2006431

35. Galbraith, S.D., Petit, C., Shani, B., Ti, Y.B.: On the security of supersingular isogeny cryptosystems. In: Cheon, J.H., Takagi, T. (eds.) ASIACRYPT 2016. LNCS, vol. 10031, pp. 63–91. Springer, Heidelberg (2016). https://doi.org/10.1007/978-3-662-53887-6_3

36. Galbraith, S.D., Petit, C., Silva, J.: Identification protocols and signature schemes based on supersingular isogeny problems. In: Takagi, T., Peyrin, T. (eds.) ASIACRYPT 2017. LNCS, vol. 10624, pp. 3–33. Springer, Cham (2017). https://doi.org/10.1007/978-3-319-70694-8_1

37. Guralnick, R.M., Müller, P.: Exceptional polynomials of affine type. J. Algebra **194**(2), 429–454 (1997). https://doi.org/10.1006/jabr.1997.7028

38. Jao, D., De Feo, L.: Towards quantum-resistant cryptosystems from supersingular elliptic curve isogenies. In: Yang, B.-Y. (ed.) PQCrypto 2011. LNCS, vol. 7071, pp. 19–34. Springer, Heidelberg (2011). https://doi.org/10.1007/978-3-642-25405-5_2

39. Jao, D., LeGrow, J., Leonardi, C., Ruiz-Lopez, L.: A polynomial quantum space attack on CRS and CSIDH. In: MathCrypt 2018 (2018)

40. Jao, D., Soukharev, V.: A subexponential algorithm for evaluating large degree isogenies. In: Hanrot, G., Morain, F., Thomé, E. (eds.) ANTS 2010. LNCS, vol. 6197, pp. 219–233. Springer, Heidelberg (2010). https://doi.org/10.1007/978-3-642-14518-6_19

41. Jao, D.Y., Montgomery, P.L., Venkatesan, R., Boyko, V.: Systems and methods for generation and validation of isogeny-based signatures, US Patent 7,617,397, November 2009

42. Jao, D.Y., Venkatesan, R.: Use of isogenies for design of cryptosystems, US Patent 7,499,544, March 2009

43. Kirschmer, M., Voight, J.: Algorithmic enumeration of ideal classes for quaternion orders. SIAM J. Comput. **39**(5), 1714–1747 (2010). https://doi.org/10.1137/080734467

44. Kitaev, A.Y.: Quantum measurements and the Abelian stabilizer problem. arXiv preprint quant-ph/9511026 (1995). https://arxiv.org/abs/quant-ph/9511026

45. Kohel, D.: Endomorphism rings of elliptic curves over finite fields. Ph.D. thesis, University of California at Berkley (1996)

46. Kohel, D.R., Lauter, K., Petit, C., Tignol, J.P.: On the quaternion-isogeny path problem. LMS J. Comput. Math. **17**(A), 418–432 (2014)

47. Koshiba, T., Takashima, K.: Pairing cryptography meets isogeny: a new framework of isogenous pairing groups. Cryptology ePrint Archive, Report 2016/1138 (2016). https://eprint.iacr.org/2016/1138

48. Koshiba, T., Takashima, K.: New assumptions on isogenous pairing groups with applications to attribute-based encryption. In: Lee, K. (ed.) ICISC 2018. LNCS, vol. 11396, pp. 3–19. Springer, Cham (2019). https://doi.org/10.1007/978-3-030-12146-4_1

49. Kuperberg, G.: A subexponential-time quantum algorithm for the dihedral hidden subgroup problem. SIAM J. Comput. **35**(1), 170–188 (2005)

50. Kuperberg, G.: Another subexponential-time quantum algorithm for the dihedral hidden subgroup problem. In: Severini, S., Brandao, F. (eds.) 8th Conference on the Theory of Quantum Computation, Communication and Cryptography (TQC 2013). Leibniz International Proceedings in Informatics (LIPIcs), vol. 22, pp. 20–34. Schloss Dagstuhl-Leibniz-Zentrum fuer Informatik, Dagstuhl (2013). https://doi.org/10.4230/LIPIcs.TQC.2013.20

51. Lenstra, A.K., Wesolowski, B.: A random zoo: sloth, unicorn, and trx. IACR Cryptology ePrint Archive 2015, 366 (2015). https://doi.org/cr.org/2015/366

52. Long, L.: Binary quadratic forms. Chia Network (2018). https://github.com/Chia-Network/vdf-competition/blob/master/classgroups.pdf
53. Mahmoody, M., Moran, T., Vadhan, S.: Publicly verifiable proofs of sequential work. In: Proceedings of the 4th Conference on Innovations in Theoretical Computer Science, pp. 373–388. ACM (2013)
54. Menezes, A., Vanstone, S., Okamoto, T.: Reducing elliptic curve logarithms to logarithms in a finite field. In: Proceedings of the Twenty-Third Annual ACM Symposium on Theory of Computing, STOC 1991, pp. 80–89. ACM, New York (1991). https://doi.org/10.1145/103418.103434
55. Mestre, J.F.: La méthode des graphes. Exemples et applications. In: Proceedings of the International Conference on Class Numbers and Fundamental Units of Algebraic Number Fields (Katata, 1986). Nagoya University, Nagoya (1986). http://boxen.math.washington.edu/msri06/refs/mestre-method-of-graphs/mestre-fr.pdf
56. Micali, S., Rabin, M., Vadhan, S.: Verifiable random functions. In: 40th Annual Symposium on Foundations of Computer Science (Cat. No. 99CB37039), pp. 120–130, October 1999. https://doi.org/10.1109/SFFCS.1999.814584
57. Petit, C., Lauter, K.: Hard and easy problems for supersingular isogeny graphs. Cryptology ePrint Archive, Report 2017/962 (2017). http://eprint.iacr.org/2017/962
58. Pierrot, C., Wesolowski, B.: Malleability of the Blockchain's entropy. Crypt. Commun. **10**(1), 211–233 (2018). https://doi.org/10.1007/s12095-017-0264-3
59. Pietrzak, K.: Simple verifiable delay functions. In: Blum, A. (ed.) 10th Innovations in Theoretical Computer Science Conference (ITCS 2019). Leibniz International Proceedings in Informatics (LIPIcs), vol. 124, pp. 60:1–60:15. Schloss Dagstuhl-Leibniz-Zentrum fuer Informatik, Dagstuhl (2018). https://doi.org/10.4230/LIPIcs.ITCS.2019.60
60. Pizer, A.K.: Ramanujan graphs and Hecke operators. Bull. Am. Math. Soc. (N.S.) **23**(1) (1990). https://doi.org/10.1090/S0273-0979-1990-15918-X
61. Pizer, A.K.: Ramanujan graphs. In: Computational Perspectives on Number Theory (Chicago, IL, 1995), AMS/IP Studies in Advanced Mathematics, vol. 7. American Mathematical Society, Providence (1998)
62. Rabin, M.O.: Transaction protection by beacons. J. Comput. Syst. Sci. **27**(2), 256–267 (1983). https://doi.org/10.1016/0022-0000(83)90042-9
63. Regev, O.: A subexponential time algorithm for the dihedral hidden subgroup problem with polynomial space. arXiv:quant-ph/0406151, June 2004. http://arxiv.org/abs/quant-ph/0406151
64. Renes, J.: Computing isogenies between montgomery curves using the action of (0, 0). In: Lange, T., Steinwandt, R. (eds.) PQCrypto 2018. LNCS, vol. 10786, pp. 229–247. Springer, Cham (2018). https://doi.org/10.1007/978-3-319-79063-3_11
65. Rivest, R.L., Shamir, A., Wagner, D.A.: Time-lock puzzles and timed-release crypto. Technical report, Cambridge, MA, USA (1996)
66. Silverman, J.H.: The Arithmetic of Elliptic Curves. GTM, vol. 106. Springer, New York (2009). https://doi.org/10.1007/978-0-387-09494-6
67. Sutherland, A.: Elliptic curves. Lecture Notes From a Course (18.783) at MIT (2017). http://math.mit.edu/classes/18.783/2017/lectures
68. Syta, E., et al.: Scalable bias-resistant distributed randomness. In: IEEE Symposium on Security and Privacy, pp. 444–460. IEEE Computer Society (2017)
69. The Sage Developers: SageMath, the Sage Mathematics Software System (Version 8.0) (2018). https://www.sagemath.org
70. Vélu, J.: Isogénies entre courbes elliptiques. Comptes Rendus de l'Académie des Sciences de Paris **273**, 238–241 (1971)

71. Vignéras, M.-F.: Arithmétique des Algèbres de Quaternions. LNM, vol. 800. Springer, Heidelberg (1980). https://doi.org/10.1007/BFb0091027
72. Voight, J.: Quaternion Algebras (2018). https://math.dartmouth.edu/~jvoight/quat-book.pdf
73. Washington, L.C.: Elliptic Curves: Number Theory and Cryptography, 2nd edn. CRC Press, New York (2008)
74. Waterhouse, W.C.: Abelian varieties over finite fields. Annales Scientifiques de l'École Normale Supérieure **2**(4), 521–560 (1969)
75. Wesolowski, B.: Efficient verifiable delay functions. In: Ishai, Y., Rijmen, V. (eds.) EUROCRYPT 2019. LNCS, vol. 11478, pp. 379–407. Springer, Cham (2019). https://doi.org/10.1007/978-3-030-17659-4_13
76. Yoo, Y., Azarderakhsh, R., Jalali, A., Jao, D., Soukharev, V.: A post-quantum digital signature scheme based on supersingular isogenies. In: Kiayias, A. (ed.) FC 2017. LNCS, vol. 10322, pp. 163–181. Springer, Cham (2017). https://doi.org/10.1007/978-3-319-70972-7_9

Strongly Secure Authenticated Key Exchange from Supersingular Isogenies

Xiu Xu[1,2,4], Haiyang Xue[1,2,3(✉)], Kunpeng Wang[1,2,4], Man Ho Au[3], and Song Tian[1,2]

[1] State Key Laboratory of Information Security, Institute of Information Engineering, Chinese Academy of Sciences, Beijing, China
haiyangxc@gmail.com
[2] Data Assurance and Communications Security Research Center, Beijing, China
[3] The Hong Kong Polytechnic University, Hung Hom, Hong Kong
[4] School of Cyber Security, University of Chinese Academy of Sciences, Beijing, China

Abstract. This paper aims to address the open problem, namely, to find new techniques to design and prove security of supersingular isogeny-based authenticated key exchange (AKE) protocols against the widest possible adversarial attacks, raised by Galbraith in 2018. Concretely, we present two AKEs based on a double-key PKE in the supersingular isogeny setting secure in the sense of CK^+, one of the strongest security models for AKE. Our contributions are summarised as follows. Firstly, we propose a strong OW-CPA secure PKE, $2PKE_{sidh}$, based on SI-DDH assumption. By applying modified Fujisaki-Okamoto transformation, we obtain a [OW-CCA, OW-CPA] secure KEM, $2KEM_{sidh}$. Secondly, we propose a two-pass AKE, $SIAKE_2$, based on SI-DDH assumption, using $2KEM_{sidh}$ as a building block. Thirdly, we present a modified version of $2KEM_{sidh}$ that is secure against leakage under the 1-Oracle SI-DH assumption. Using the modified $2KEM_{sidh}$ as a building block, we then propose a three-pass AKE, $SIAKE_3$, based on 1-Oracle SI-DH assumption. Finally, we prove that both $SIAKE_2$ and $SIAKE_3$ are CK^+ secure in the random oracle model and supports arbitrary registration. We also provide an implementation to illustrate the efficiency of our schemes. Our schemes compare favourably against existing isogeny-based AKEs. To the best of our knowledge, they are the first of its kind to offer security against arbitrary registration, wPFS, KCI, and MEX simultaneously. Regarding efficiency, our schemes outperform existing schemes in terms of bandwidth as well as CPU cycle count.

Keywords: Authenticated key exchange · Key encapsulation mechanism · Supersingular elliptic curve isogeny · Post quantum

1 Introduction

Authenticated Key Exchange. Allowing two parties to agree on a common shared key over a public but possibly insecure channel, key exchange (KE) is

© International Association for Cryptologic Research 2019
S. D. Galbraith and S. Moriai (Eds.): ASIACRYPT 2019, LNCS 11921, pp. 278–308, 2019.
https://doi.org/10.1007/978-3-030-34578-5_11

a fundamental cryptographic primitive. Many studies have investigated how to achieve KE protocols that provide authentication [4,6,12,27] and how to implement authenticated key exchange (AKE) with high efficiency [2,12,13,21,27–29] based on classical assumptions. Different of security models have been proposed, including BR model [4], CK model [6] and eCK model [27]. Introduced in [22] and reformulated by Fujioka et al. [12], currently, CK^+ security model is known as one of the 'strongest' and most 'desirable' security notions. The CK^+ model not only covers the security requirement in CK model, but also captures some advanced attacks such as the key compromise impersonation (KCI) attack, the maximal exposure (MEX) attack and the breaking of weak perfect forward secrecy (wPFS).

Supersingular Isogeny Diffie-Hellman Key Exchange (SIDH). Apart from lattice, code, hash and multivariate cryptography, supersingular elliptic curve isogeny is one of the most attractive candidates for post-quantum cryptography. The best-known protocol is Jao and De Feo's supersingular isogeny Diffie-Hellman key exchange (SIDH) [8] based on the hard problem of computing isogenies between supersingular elliptic curves. There are several interesting topics concerning SIDH in the literature. For example, computational efficiency [7,10,23], key compression [5], adaptive attacks on SIDH [17], relationship of the underlying complexity problems [9,19,32], signature schemes [16,31,35] and its standardization [20,24].

Recently, several work [14,15,26] have studied the important problem of designing AKE schemes from the basic SIDH primitive. As pointed out by Galbraith [15], there are several challenges in adapting the security proof of existing well-designed AKE schemes (most of them are based on discrete logarithm assumption) to the SIDH case:

- Many AKE schemes based on discrete logarithm assumption, such as MQV [28] and HMQV [22], require a richer algebraic structure the supersingular isogeny does not possess.
- The protocols involving long-term/static secret keys are vulnerable to the adaptive attack [17] aiming at the case where the static public key is used. More precisely, suppose that in a protocol Alice sets E_A as her static public key, and E_Y is an ephemeral public value sent by Bob. Galbraith et al. [17] showed that adversary Bob can send (E_Y, R', S') with maliciously-crafted points R' and S' to gradually learn Alice's static secret key.
- The gap assumption that holds in the discrete logarithm setting is crucial for security proof. However, the gap assumption does not hold in the SIDH setting when polynomial queries are submitted to an *unlimited* decisional solver.

The State of the Art of SIDH AKE. Recently, there are many exciting results on the generic and non-generic constructions of AKE over supersingular curves [14,15,26]. Galbraith [15] and Longa [26] showed how to adapt the generic constructions of secure AKE from basic primitives like IND-CCA encryption/KEMs, MACs, PRFs etc, including the schemes proposed by Boyd, Cliff,

Nieto and Paterson [2] (abbreviated as BCNP scheme), by Fujioka, Suzuki, Xagawa and Yoneyama [13] (abbreviated as FSXY scheme) and by Guilhem, Smart and Warinschi [18] (abbreviated as GSW scheme), to the SIDH setting by inserting an IND-CCA secure KEM based on SIDH. Particularly, Longa [26] showed how to use SIDH as basic building blocks to construct AKE schemes. However, these transformations lead either to more isogeny computations or increase in rounds of communication. The detailed analyses are examined and summarized in Table 1 of [15]. Here we make a more concrete comparison among these AKE schemes in the SIDH setting in Table 1.

With respect to non-generic constructions, Galbraith proposed two SIDH-AKE protocols [15], one of which is based on the Jeong-Katz-Lee [21] scheme TS2 (we call it Gal 1) and another is an SIDH variant of NAXOS scheme (we call it Gal 2). Very recently, Fujioka et al. [14] gave two Diffie-Hellman like isogeny-based AKEs, which we denote as FTTY 1 where the session key is extracted from the combination of two Diffie-Hellman values, and FTTY 2 where the session key is extracted from four Diffie-Hellman values, respectively. Unfortunately, all of these schemes only provide security against adversaries with limited capabilities, such as wPFS security (details are given in Sect. 1.3). Several known attacks are not taken into account, including arbitrary registrant for static public keys, the KCI attack, or the MEX attack. In an AKE system, the adversary-controlled parties may register arbitrary public keys and arbitrary registrant allows any party to register arbitrary public keys (even the same key with some other party) without any validity checks. In fact, neither Gal 1-2 nor FTTY 1-2 scheme allows the arbitrary registrant for the static public key. Otherwise, with malicious static public keys, a target secret key can be learned bit by bit, which implies that Gal 1-2 and FTTY 1-2 are not resistant to the adaptive attack. Moreover, Gal 1 is not resistant to the KCI attack and Gal 2 is not resistant to the MEX attack. Detailed analyses on those attacks against Gal 1-2 and FTTY 1-2 are given in the related works.

Thus, *"to find new techniques to design and prove security of AKE protocols in the SIDH setting, . . . give a full analysis of AKE that includes the widest possible adversarial goals."*, a quote from Galbraith [15], is the main problem to be addressed in the area of SIDH-based AKE. In this paper, we are motivated to address such an open problem.

1.1 Our Contributions

In this paper, we present two AKEs based on a double-key PKE in the SIDH setting and show that both of them allow arbitrary registrant and are CK^+ secure in the random oracle model. Our results are summarized as follows.

- We propose a strong OW-CPA secure PKE, $2PKE_{sidh}$, based on SI-DDH assumption. The strong OW-CPA security is exactly the [OW-CPA,·] security formalized in [34] which states that the PKE is still OW-CPA secure even if part of the public key is generated by the adversary. This construction may be of independent interest. Through the modified Fujisaki-Okamoto transformation [34], we obtain a [OW-CCA, OW-CPA] secure KEM, $2\mathsf{KEM}_{sidh}$, to be used as the building block of our AKE.

- With $2\mathsf{KEM}_{sidh}$ as the basic tool, we propose a two-pass AKE, SIAKE_2, based on SI-DDH assumption. SIAKE_2 is CK^+ secure in the random oracle model and supports arbitrary registration.
- We propose 1-Oracle SI-DH assumption, a strong version of the SI-DDH assumption. Contrary to its analogue, Oracle Diffie-Hellman problem [1] in the discrete logarithm setting, the 1-Oracle SI-DH problem only allows one query to the oracle. We revisit $2\mathsf{PKE}_{sidh}$ and provide a modified version of $2\mathsf{KEM}_{sidh}$, and show that under the 1-Oracle SI-DH assumption both of them are still secure against leakage.
- Using the modified $2\mathsf{KEM}_{sidh}$ as the basic tool, we propose a three-pass AKE, SIAKE_3, based on 1-Oracle SI-DH assumption. We prove that it supports arbitrary registration and is also CK^+ secure in the random oracle model.

From Table 1, we can observe that both SIAKE_2 and SIAKE_3 achieve the security against multiple possible adversaries, which to the best of our knowledge covers the most extensive adversarial goals, including arbitrary registrant, wPFS, KCI and MEX.

Table 1. Comparison of existing AKE protocols on supersingular isogeny. **Key Reg.** represents registering the static public key. "Arbi" means arbitrary registrant is allowed while "Honest" means only honest registrants is allowed. **Assump.** is the abbreviation of assumptions. "1-OSIDH" is the abbreviation of 1-Oracle SI-DH assumption. **Rd** denotes the number of protocol's communication round. **Init isog** and **Resp isog** represent the number of isogeny computation that the initiator and responder have to perform respectively. **Mess Size** denotes the total message size. "✓" indicates that the scheme can resist this kind of attack while "×" indicates it cannot. n is the security parameter.

Scheme	Key Reg.	Assum.	Model	wPFS	KCI	MEX	Rd	Init isog	Resp isog	Mess Size
Gal 1 [15]	Honest	SI-CDH	CK	✓	×	×	2	3	3	$108n$
Gal 2 [15]	Honest	SI-CDH	BR	✓	✓	×	2	4	4	$108n$
FTTY 1 [14]	Honest	SI-DDH	CK	✓	×	×	1	3	3	$72n$
FTTY 2 [14]	Honest	di-SI-DDH	CK^+	✓	✓	✓	1	5	5	$72n$
GSW [18]	Arbi.	SI-DDH	CK	✓	×	×	3	6	6	$186n$
BCNP [2,26]	Arbi.	SI-DDH	CK	✓	✓	×	2	6	6	$148n$
FSXY [13,26]	Arbi.	SI-DDH	CK^+	✓	✓	✓	2	6	6	$148n$
SIAKE_2	Arbi.	SI-DDH	CK^+	✓	✓	✓	2	6	5	$114n$
SIAKE_3	Arbi.	1-OSIDH	CK^+	✓	✓	✓	3	5	5	$80n$

1.2 Technique Overview

Our core ideas and techniques are illustrated in Fig. 1. Let E_0 be the starting curve, and $(P_1, Q_1), (P_2, Q_2)$ be the base points. E_{A_1}, E_{B_2}, E_X and E_Y are four intermediate curves which are part of static or ephemeral public keys. E_{A_1Y}, E_{XB_2} and E_{XY} are three final computing curves.

Let U_A, U_B be two parties in the AKEs. The SIDH works as follows: U_A chooses a secret, computes the isogeny $\phi_X : E_0 \to E_X$ with kernel G_X and publishes $X = (E_X, \phi_X(P_2), \phi_X(Q_2))$. U_B chooses a secret, computes the isogeny $\phi_Y : E_0 \to E_Y$ with kernel G_Y and publishes $Y = (E_Y, \phi_Y(P_1), \phi_Y(Q_1))$. They both can compute $E_{XY} \cong E_X/\phi_X(G_Y) \cong E_Y/\phi_Y(G_X)$. The strategy to provide authentication with the static and ephemeral components is that every user registers a static public key such that U_A's static public key is $pk_{A_1} = (E_{A_1}, \phi_{A_1}(P_2), \phi_{A_1}(Q_2))$ while U_B's static public key is $pk_{B_2} = (E_{B_2}, \phi_{B_2}(P_1), \phi_{B_2}(Q_1))$.

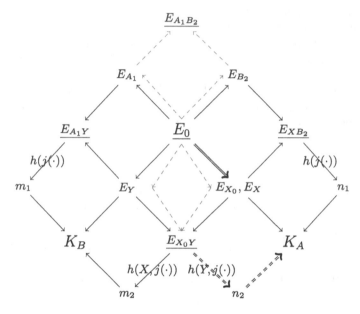

Fig. 1. Illustration of the core idea of SIAKE$_2$ and SIAKE$_3$. The red dashed lines illustrate the core ideas of Gal 1 scheme [15]. In SIAKE$_2$, E_X and E_{X_0} are two independent curves. In SIAKE$_3$, $E_X = E_{X_0}$ and the dashed double arrow is included. (Color figure online)

As shown in Fig. 1, there is a natural way to extract a session key from four Diffie-Hellman values $E_{A_1B_2}$, E_{A_1Y}, E_{XB_2} and E_{XY} (Actually, this is what FTTY2 scheme does). However, it is risky to take $E_{A_1B_2}$ into account. Let us recall the adaptive attack from Galbraith, Petit, Shani and Ti [17]. A malicious user U_B who registers his static public key E_{B_2} with specified points R', S', can learn one bit of the static secret key of U_A if he can also query the session key. As shown in Fig. 1 with dashed lines, Galbraith [15] involves $E_{A_1B_2}$ and E_{XY} for the session key. Under the adaptive attack [17], adversary could gradually learn the static secret key by malicious registrations. Thus, $E_{A_1B_2}$ could not be included in the session key when arbitrary registrant is allowed.

Although now only $E_{A_1 Y}$, $E_{X B_2}$, and E_{XY} are involved in the session key, the adaptive attack can still be launched if the CK$^+$ adversary (in case E_2 in Table 2) sends E_Y with specified points R', S' to U_A. With the ephemeral secret key for E_X and the session key, the adversary could still extract one bit of the static secret key. The problem can be tackled by a check of "validity" of $Y = (E_Y, R, S)$. Our solution is to employ the "re-encryption" technique used in Fujisaki-Okamoto (FO) transformation [11]. Precisely, $C = (Y, y_1, y_0)$ is the ciphertext under public key pk_{A_1} and X, where $Y = (E_0/\langle P_2 + [y]Q_2\rangle, \phi_Y(P_1)$, $\phi_Y(Q_1))$, $y_1 = h(j(E_{A_1 Y})) \oplus m_1$, $y_0 = h(j(E_{XY})) \oplus m_0$ and $y = G(m_1, m_0)$ for a hash function G, and the encapsulated key is $K_B = H(m_1, m_0, C)$. As a byproduct, we obtain the chosen ciphertext (CCA) secure KEM by the FO transformation and the "validity" of $Y = (E_Y, R, S)$ can be checked by U_A using $y = G(m_1, m_0)$ so that the adaptive attack fails to work.

Now the CCA secure KEM with "re-encryption" avoids the adaptive attack, but it is still not sufficient for CK$^+$ security. The CK$^+$ adversary has the capability to adaptively *send* messages and adaptively query the *session state* and *session key* of non-test sessions. The capability of adaptively *sending* messages in the test session means that the adversary is allowed to choose one-part of the challenge public key X^* for (Y^*, y_1^*, y_0^*), while the capability of querying the *session state* and *session key* of non-test sessions implies that the adversary is also allowed to query the decapsulation oracle which decapsulates the ciphertext under several other public keys X'. This feature has been analyzed by [34] and formalized as [OW-CCA, $\cdot$] security. The modified Fujisaki-Okamoto [34] states that putting the public key in the hashing step when generating the encapsulated key would be sufficient. Precisely, K_B encapsulated in (Y, y_1, y_0) is $H(X, m_1, m_2, C)$.

The last challenge that we are facing is the relationship between X and Y, which leads to the difficulty in simulating the CK$^+$ game. In the test session, on the one hand X is part of the public key (pk_{A_1}, X) under which the ciphertext (Y, y_1, y_0) is computed. On the other hand X is part of the ciphertext (X, x_1, x_0) in which K_A is encapsulated under public key (pk_{B_2}, Y). Precisely, in the test session $X = ((E_X, R_2, S_2), x_1, x_0)$ is sent by AKE adversary $\mathcal{A}$, and the simulator $\mathcal{S}$ obtains challenge ciphertext (Y^*, y_1^*, y_0^*) from the [OW-CCA, $\cdot$] challenger (which means the secret y in Y^* is unknown). But to simulate the CK$^+$ game, especially to maintain the consistency of hash lists, $\mathcal{S}$ should learn $h(j(E_X/\langle R_2 + [y]S_2\rangle))$ to extract K_A encapsulated in (X, x_1, x_0).

We propose two solutions for this problem. One method is to add an extra X_0 such that X_0 is part of the public key (pk_{A_1}, X_0) under which the ciphertext (Y, y_1, y_0) is computed, while X is part of the ciphertext (X, x_1) under public key E_{B_2} (we omit Y). The other solution is to strengthen the underlying assumption as 1-Oracle SI-DH assumption such that $h(j(E_X/\langle R_2 + [y]S_2\rangle))$ could be leaked.

In consequence, the two solutions lead to two AKEs, namely, SIAKE$_2$ and SIAKE$_3$.

- SOLUTION 1: We add an extra X_0 to take the position of X as part of the public key (pk_{A_1}, X_0) under which the ciphertext (Y, y_1, y_0) is computed, remove x_2 and set (X, x_1) as the ciphertext under public key E_{B_2} rather than (E_{B_2}, Y). Then the value of $h(j(E_X/\langle R_2 + [y]S_2\rangle))$ is not needed during the security proof. The drawback of this solution is that K_A' can not be included in the session state of U_B. Solution 1 leads to SIAKE$_2$.

- SOLUTION 2: We strengthen the underlying SI-DDH assumption to the 1-Oracle SI-DH assumption to allow the leakage of $h(j(E_X/\langle R_2 + [y]S_2\rangle))$. The 1-Oracle SI-DH assumption can be considered as a hashed SI-DDH assumption where a one-time hashed SI-CDH oracle is allowed. Note that considering $\langle R_2 + [y]S_2 \rangle = \langle [u]R_2 + [y][u]S_2 \rangle$ for any integer $1 \leq u \leq \ell_2^{e_2}$ and coprime to ℓ_2, we employ a simple trick of tailoring the hash function as $h(Y, j(E_{XY}))$ in x_2 and $h(X, j(E_{XY}))$ in y_2. This solution results in SIAKE$_3$.

1.3   Related Works and Their Analysis

Galbraith [15] proposed two SIDH variants of AKE, namely, Gal 1 from Jeong-Katz-Lee protocol [21] and Gal 2 from NAXOS protocol [27]. Considering the adaptive attack on static secret keys, Gal 1 protocol only allows honest registrants of static public keys and it is also vulnerable to the KCI attack. So far, neither has there been any concrete MEX attack on Gal 1, nor any formal proofs to show Gal 1 is resistant to the MEX attack. Gal 2 protocol is provably secure in BR model, which only allows honest registrants of static public keys (if the adversary gets the ephemeral secret key, like x, the adaptive attack still works), and can not resist the MEX attack.

Very recently, Fujioka et al. [14] gave two Diffie-Hellman like isogeny-based AKEs, namely, FTTY 1 and FTTY 2. FTTY 1 protocol, which is quite similar to Gal 1 scheme, is CK secure in the quantum random oracle model, but it only allows honest registrants and cannot resist the KCI attack. FTTY 2 is secure in CK$^+$ model, but it also only allows honest registrants.

Below we illustrate in detail the (in)capability of Gal 1-2 and FTTY 1-2 on resisting the adaptive attacks (if the arbitrary registrant is allowed), the KCI attack, and the MEX attack.

Adaptive Attacks If *Arbitrary* Registrant Is Allowed. Suppose that in a protocol Alice sets $E_{A_1}, \phi_{A_1}(P_2), \phi_{A_1}(Q_2)$ as her static public key. The goal of a malicious adversary is to compute Alice's static secret key. As illustrated in Fig. 1, the session key of Gal 1 is extracted from E_{XY} and $E_{A_1B_2}$. By applying the adaptive attacks [17], a malicious adversary can register (E_{B_2}, R', S') with specified points R' and S', rather than $\phi_{B_2}(P_1)$ and $\phi_{B_2}(Q_1)$, as the static public key for Bob. By checking whether the session key computed by Alice (which can be obtained from SessionKeyReveal query) is equal to that computed by Bob, one bit of Alice's static secret key is determined. The adversary gradually learns Alice's static secret key by registering several valid static public keys according to adaptive attacks. Such an attack can be applied to FTTY 1 directly and it also works for FTTY 2 if the adversary also has the ephemeral secret key x of Alice (which can be obtained by querying SessionStateReveal), which means that FTTY 2 also does not allow arbitrary registrant. Gal 2 does not allow arbitrary registrant either, since if the adversary has the ephemeral secret key x of Alice (which can be obtained from SessionStateReveal query), by honestly registering static public key for Bob, then sending (E_Y, R', S') with specified points R' and S', and checking whether the session key computed by Alice is equal to that computed by Bob, the adversary is able to learn one bit of Alice's static secret key.

KCI Attacks. KCI attacks state that if a static secret key is revealed, an adversary can try to impersonate any other honest parties in order to fool the owners of the exposed secret keys. Neither Gal 1 nor FTTY 1 are resistant to the KCI attack since each session key is extracted from E_{XY} and $E_{A_1B_2}$, and by generating $E_Y, \phi_Y(P_1), \phi_Y(Q_1)$ and sending it to Alice on behalf of Bob, with Alice's static secret key the adversary could compute the session key even if Bob's static secret key is unknown.

MEX Attacks. In MEX, an adversary aims to distinguish the session key from a random value under the disclosure of the ephemeral secret key of (at least) one party of the test session. Gal 2 is not resistant to the MEX attack since its session key is extracted from E_{XY}, E_{XB_2}, and E_{A_1Y}, thus it is easy for an adversary to compute those curves with the ephemeral secret key corresponding to E_X and E_Y.

2 Preliminaries

2.1 SIDH and Crypto-Friendly Description

We recall briefly the SIDH protocol using the same notation as [8,20]. Let p be a large prime of the form $p = \ell_1^{e_1} \ell_2^{e_2} \cdot f \pm 1$, where ℓ_1 and ℓ_2 are two small primes, and f is an integer cofactor. Then we can construct a supersingular elliptic curve E_0 defined over $\mathbb{F}_{p^2}$ with order $|E_0(\mathbb{F}_{p^2})| = (\ell_1^{e_1} \ell_2^{e_2} \cdot f)^2$. Let $\mathbb{Z}_m$ be the ring of residue classes modulo m. The subgroup $E_0[m]$ of m-torsion points is isomorphic to $\mathbb{Z}_m \times \mathbb{Z}_m$ for $m \in \{\ell_1^{e_1}, \ell_2^{e_2}\}$. Let P_1, Q_1 be two points that generate $E_0[\ell_1^{e_1}]$ and P_2, Q_2 be two points that generate $E_0[\ell_2^{e_2}]$. The public parameters are $(E_0; P_1, Q_1; P_2, Q_2; \ell_1, \ell_2, e_1, e_2)$.

The SIDH, as depicted in Fig. 2, works as follows. Alice chooses her secret key k_a from $\mathbb{Z}_{\ell_1^{e_1}}$ and computes the isogeny $\phi_A : E_0 \to E_A$ whose kernel is the subgroup $\langle R_A \rangle = \langle P_1 + [k_a]Q_1 \rangle$. She then sends to Bob her public key which

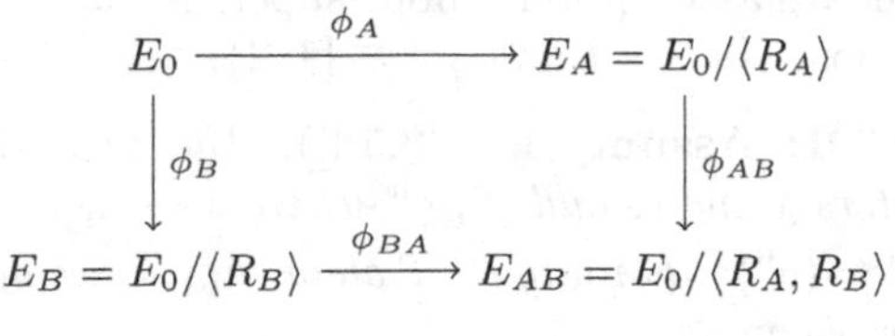

$$E_0 \xrightarrow{\phi_A} E_A = E_0/\langle R_A \rangle$$

$$\downarrow \phi_B \qquad\qquad\qquad \downarrow \phi_{AB}$$

$$E_B = E_0/\langle R_B \rangle \xrightarrow{\phi_{BA}} E_{AB} = E_0/\langle R_A, R_B \rangle$$

Fig. 2. SIDH

is E_A together with the two points $\phi_A(P_2), \phi_A(Q_2)$. Similarly, Bob chooses his secret key k_b from $\mathbb{Z}_{\ell_2^{e_2}}$ and computes the isogeny $\phi_B : E_0 \to E_B$ with kernel subgroup $\langle R_B \rangle = \langle P_2 + [k_b]Q_2 \rangle$. He sends to Alice his public key which is E_B together with the two points $\phi_B(P_1), \phi_B(Q_1)$. To get the shared secret, Alice computes the isogeny $\phi_{BA} : E_B \to E_{BA}$ with kernel subgroup generated by $\phi_B(P_1) + [k_a]\phi_B(Q_1)$. Similarly, Bob computes the isogeny $\phi_{AB} : E_A \to E_{AB}$ with kernel subgroup generated by $\phi_A(P_2) + [k_b]\phi_A(Q_2)$. Since the composed isogeny $\phi_{AB} \circ \phi_A$ has the same kernel $\langle R_A, R_B \rangle$ as $\phi_{BA} \circ \phi_B$, Alice and Bob can share the same j-invariant $j(E_{AB}) = j(E_{BA})$.

It will be helpful to have a crypto-friendly description of SIDH for the presentation of our AKEs. We follow the treatment of Fujioka et al. [14]. In what follows we assume $\{t, s\} = \{1, 2\}$, and denote the public parameters by $\mathfrak{g} = (E_0; P_1, Q_1, P_2, Q_2)$ and $\mathfrak{e} = (\ell_1, \ell_2, e_1, e_2)$. We define the sets of supersingular curves and those with an auxiliary basis as

$$\text{SSEC}_p = \{\text{supersingular elliptic curves } E \text{ over } \mathbb{F}_{p^2} \text{ with } E(\mathbb{F}_{p^2}) \simeq (\mathbb{Z}_{\ell_1^{e_1} \ell_2^{e_2} f})^2\};$$

$$\text{SSEC}_A = \{(E; P_t', Q_t') | E \in \text{SSEC}_p, (P_t', Q_t') \text{ is basis of } E[\ell_t^{e_t}]\};$$

$$\text{SSEC}_B = \{(E; P_s', Q_s') | E \in \text{SSEC}_p, (P_s', Q_s') \text{ is basis of } E[\ell_s^{e_s}]\}.$$

Let $\mathfrak{a} = k_a$ and $\mathfrak{b} = k_b$, then we define,

$$\mathfrak{g}^{\mathfrak{a}} = (E_A; \phi_A(P_t), \phi_A(Q_t)) \in \text{SSEC}_A,$$
$$\text{where } R_A = P_s + [k_a]Q_s, \phi_A : E_0 \to E_A = E_0/\langle R_A \rangle;$$

$$\mathfrak{g}^{\mathfrak{b}} = (E_B; \phi_B(P_s), \phi_B(Q_s)) \in \text{SSEC}_B,$$
$$\text{where } R_B = P_t + [k_b]Q_t, \phi_B : E_0 \to E_B = E_0/\langle R_B \rangle;$$

$$(\mathfrak{g}^{\mathfrak{b}})^{\mathfrak{a}} = j(E_{BA}), \text{where } R_{BA} = \phi_B(P_s) + [k_a]\phi_B(Q_s),$$
$$\phi_{BA} : E_B \to E_{BA} = E_B/\langle R_{BA} \rangle;$$

$$(\mathfrak{g}^{\mathfrak{a}})^{\mathfrak{b}} = j(E_{AB}), \text{ where } R_{AB} = \phi_A(P_t) + [k_b]\phi_A(Q_t),$$
$$\phi_{AB} : E_A \to E_{AB} = E_A/\langle R_{AB} \rangle.$$

Using this notation, the SIDH looks almost exactly like the classical Diffie-Hellman. That is, the public parameters are $\mathfrak{g}$ and $\mathfrak{e}$. Alice chooses a secret key $\mathfrak{a}$ and sends $\mathfrak{g}^{\mathfrak{a}}$ to Bob, while Bob chooses a secret key $\mathfrak{b}$ and sends $\mathfrak{g}^{\mathfrak{b}}$ to Alice. The shared key is, as we expect, $j = (\mathfrak{g}^{\mathfrak{b}})^{\mathfrak{a}} = (\mathfrak{g}^{\mathfrak{a}})^{\mathfrak{b}}$.

2.2   Standard SIDH Assumptions

We describe two standard assumptions about supersingular isogeny based on the crypto-friendly notation. Let $s \neq t$ and $s, t \in \{1, 2\}$.

Definition 1 (SI-CDH Assumption [8,14]). *The SI-CDH problem is that, given public parameters $\mathfrak{g}$ and $\mathfrak{e}$, and $\mathfrak{g}^{\mathfrak{a}}$, $\mathfrak{g}^{\mathfrak{b}}$ where $\mathfrak{a} \leftarrow \mathbb{Z}_{\ell_s^{e_s}}$, $\mathfrak{b} \leftarrow \mathbb{Z}_{\ell_t^{e_t}}$, compute the j-invariant $(\mathfrak{g}^{\mathfrak{a}})^{\mathfrak{b}} = (\mathfrak{g}^{\mathfrak{b}})^{\mathfrak{a}}$. For any PPT algorithm $\mathcal{A}$, we define the advantage of solving SI-CDH problem as*

$$Adv_{\mathcal{A}}^{sicdh} = Pr[j' = (\mathfrak{g}^{\mathfrak{a}})^{\mathfrak{b}} | j' \leftarrow \mathcal{A}(\mathfrak{g}, \mathfrak{e}, \mathfrak{g}^{\mathfrak{a}}, \mathfrak{g}^{\mathfrak{b}})].$$

The SI-CDH assumption states: for any PPT algorithm $\mathcal{A}$, the advantage of solving SI-CDH problem is negligible.

Definition 2 (SI-DDH Assumption [8,14]). *Let $\mathfrak{g}$ and $\mathfrak{e}$ be that defined in SI-CDH assumption. Let D_0 and D_1 be two distributions defined as:*

$$D_1 := \{\mathfrak{e}, \mathfrak{g}, \mathfrak{g}^a, \mathfrak{g}^b, (\mathfrak{g}^a)^b \mid a \leftarrow \mathbb{Z}_{\ell_s^{e_s}}, b \leftarrow \mathbb{Z}_{\ell_t^{e_t}}\}$$

$$D_0 := \{\mathfrak{e}, \mathfrak{g}, \mathfrak{g}^a, \mathfrak{g}^b, (\mathfrak{g}^s)^t \mid a, s \leftarrow \mathbb{Z}_{\ell_s^{e_s}}, b, t \leftarrow \mathbb{Z}_{\ell_t^{e_t}}\}$$

The SI-DDH problem is that given a random sample from D_b depending on $b \leftarrow \{0,1\}$, guess b. The advantage of solving SI-DDH problem for any PPT algorithm $\mathcal{A}$ is

$$Adv_{\mathcal{A}}^{siddh} = Pr[b' = b \mid b' \leftarrow \mathcal{A}(\mathfrak{d}_b \leftarrow D_b), b \leftarrow \{0,1\}] - 1/2.$$

The SI-DDH assumption states: for any PPT algorithm $\mathcal{A}$, the advantage of solving SI-DDH problem is negligible.

2.3 CK$^+$ Security Model

We recall the CK$^+$ model introduced by [22] and later refined by [12], which is a CK model [6] integrated with the weak PFS, resistance to KCI and MEX properties. We focus on 3-pass and 2-pass protocols in this paper. For simplicity, we only show the model specified to 2-pass protocols. As for 3-pass protocol, we can extend it by adding an extra message in the matching session identifier and Send definitions.

In an AKE protocol, U_i denotes a party indexed by i, who is modeled as a probabilistic polynomial time (PPT) interactive Turing machine. We assume that each party U_i owns a static pair of secret-public key (sk_i, pk_i), where the static public key is related to U_i's identity by a certification authority (CA). No other actions by the CA are required or assumed. In particular, we make no assumption on whether the CA requires a proof-of possession of the private key from a registrant of a public key, and we do not assume any specific checks on the value of a public key.

Session. Each party can be activated to run an instance called a *session*. A party can be activated to initiate the session by an incoming message of the form $(\Pi, \mathcal{I}, U_A, U_B)$ or respond to an incoming message of the form $(\Pi, \mathcal{R}, U_B, U_A, X_A)$, where Π is a protocol identifier, $\mathcal{I}$ and $\mathcal{R}$ are role identifiers corresponding to *initiator* and *responder*. Activated with $(\Pi, \mathcal{I}, U_A, U_B)$, U_A is called the session *initiator*. Activated with $(\Pi, \mathcal{R}, U_B, U_A, X_A)$, U_B is called the session *responder*.

According to the specification of AKE, the party creates randomness which is generally called *ephemeral secret key*, computes and maintains a *session state*, generates outgoing messages, and completes the session by outputting a session key and erasing the session state. Note that Canetti-Krawczyk [6] defines session state as session-specific secret information, but leaves it up to a protocol to specify which information is included in a session state. LaMacchia et al. [27] explicitly set all random coins used by a party in a session as session-specific secret information and call it *ephemeral secret key*. Here we require that the session state at least contains the ephemeral secret key.

A session may also be aborted without generating a session key. The initiator U_A creates a session state and outputs X_A, then may receive an incoming message of the forms $(\Pi, \mathcal{I}, U_A, U_B, X_A, X_B)$ from the responder U_B, and may compute the session key SK. On the contrary, the responder U_B outputs X_B, and may compute the session key SK. We say that a session is *completed* if its owner computes the session key.

A session is associated with its owner, a peer, and a session identifier. If U_A is the initiator, the session identifier is sid $= (\Pi, \mathcal{I}, U_A, U_B, X_A)$ or sid $= (\Pi, \mathcal{I}, U_A, U_B, X_A, X_B)$, which denotes U_A as an owner and U_B as a peer. If U_B is the responder, the session is identified by sid $= (\Pi, \mathcal{R}, U_B, U_A, X_A, X_B)$, which denotes U_B as an owner and U_A as a peer. The *matching session* of $(\Pi, \mathcal{I}, U_A, U_B, X_A, X_B)$ is $(\Pi, \mathcal{R}, U_B, U_A, X_A, X_B)$ and vice versa.

Adversary. Adversary $\mathcal{A}$ is modeled as follows to capture real attacks in open networks, including the control of communication and the access to some of the secret information.

- Send(message): $\mathcal{A}$ sends messages in one of the forms: $(\Pi, \mathcal{I}, U_A, U_B)$, $(\Pi, \mathcal{R}, U_B, U_A, X_A)$, or $(\Pi, \mathcal{I}, U_A, U_B, X_A, X_B)$, and obtains the response.
- SessionKeyReveal(sid): if the session sid is completed, $\mathcal{A}$ obtains the session key SK for sid.
- SessionStateReveal(sid): $\mathcal{A}$ obtains the session state of the owner of sid if the session is not completed. The session state includes all ephemeral secret keys and intermediate computation results except for immediately erased information, but does not include the static secret key.
- Corrupt(U_i): By this query, $\mathcal{A}$ learns all information of U_A (including the static secret, session states and session keys stored at U_A). In addition, from the moment that U_A is corrupted, all its actions may be controlled by $\mathcal{A}$.

Freshness. Let sid* $= (\Pi, \mathcal{I}, U_A, U_B, X_A, X_B)$ or $(\Pi, \mathcal{I}, U_A, U_B, X_A, X_B)$ be a completed session between honest users U_A and U_B. If the matching session of sid* exists, denote it by $\overline{\text{sid}}^*$. We say session sid* is fresh if $\mathcal{A}$ does not query: (1) SessionStateReveal(sid*), SessionKeyReveal(sid*), and SessionStateReveal($\overline{\text{sid}}^*$), SessionKeyReveal($\overline{\text{sid}}^*$) if $\overline{\text{sid}}^*$ exists; (2) SessionStateReveal(sid*) and SessionKeyReveal(sid*) if $\overline{\text{sid}}^*$ does not exist.

Security Experiment. The adversary $\mathcal{A}$ could make a sequence of the queries described above. During the experiment, $\mathcal{A}$ makes the query of Test(sid*), where sid* must be a fresh session. Test(sid*) select random bit $b \in \{0, 1\}$, and return the session key held by sid* if $b = 0$; and return a random key if $b = 1$. The experiment continues until $\mathcal{A}$ returns b' as a guess of b. The adversary $\mathcal{A}$ wins the game if the test session sid* is still fresh and $b' = b$. The advantage of the adversary $\mathcal{A}$ is defined as $\text{Adv}_{\Pi}^{ck+}(\mathcal{A}) = \Pr[\mathcal{A} \text{ wins}] - \frac{1}{2}$.

Definition 3. *We say that a AKE protocol* Π *is secure in the* CK^+ *model if the following conditions hold:*
Correctness: *If two honest parties complete matching sessions, then they both compute the same session key except with negligible probability.*
Soundness: *For any PPT adversary* $\mathcal{A}$, $\mathrm{Adv}_{\Pi}^{\mathrm{CK}+}(\mathcal{A})$ *is negligible for the test session* sid^*,

1. *the static secret key of the owner of* sid^* *is given to* $\mathcal{A}$, *if* $\overline{\mathsf{sid}}^*$ *does not exist.*
2. *the ephemeral secret key of the owner of* sid^* *is given to* $\mathcal{A}$, *if* $\overline{\mathsf{sid}}^*$ *does not exist.*
3. *the static secret key of the owner of* sid^* *and the ephemeral secret key of* $\overline{\mathsf{sid}}^*$ *are given to* $\mathcal{A}$, *if* $\overline{\mathsf{sid}}^*$ *exists.*
4. *the ephemeral secret key of* sid^* *and the ephemeral secret key of* $\overline{\mathsf{sid}}^*$ *are given to* $\mathcal{A}$, *if* $\overline{\mathsf{sid}}^*$ *exists.*
5. *the static secret key of the owner of* sid^* *and the static secret key of the peer of* sid^* *are given to* $\mathcal{A}$, *if* $\overline{\mathsf{sid}}^*$ *exists.*
6. *the ephemeral secret key of* sid^* *and the static secret key of the peer of* sid^* *are given to* $\mathcal{A}$, *if* $\overline{\mathsf{sid}}^*$ *exists.*

As indicated in Table 2, the CK^+ model captures all non-trivial patterns of exposure of static and ephemeral secret keys listed in Definition 3, and these ten cases cover wPFS, resistance to KCI, and MEX attacks.

Table 2. The behavior of AKE adversary in CK^+ model. $\overline{\mathsf{sid}}^*$ is the matching session of sid^*, if it exists. "Yes" means that there exists $\overline{\mathsf{sid}}^*$ and "No" means not. sk_A (resp. sk_B) means the static secret key of A (resp. B). ek_A (resp. ek_D) is the ephemeral secret key of A (resp. B) in sid^* or $\overline{\mathsf{sid}}^*$ if there exists. "$\checkmark$" means the secret key may be revealed to adversary, "$\times$" means the secret key is not revealed. "-" means the secret key does not exist.

Event	Case	sid^*	$\overline{\mathsf{sid}}^*$	sk_A	ek_A	ek_B	sk_B	Security
E_1	1	A	No	$\checkmark$	$\times$	-	$\times$	KCI
E_2	2	A	No	$\times$	$\checkmark$	-	$\times$	MEX
E_3	2	B	No	$\times$	-	$\checkmark$	$\times$	MEX
E_4	1	B	No	$\times$	-	$\times$	$\checkmark$	KCI
E_5	5	A or B	Yes	$\checkmark$	$\times$	$\times$	$\checkmark$	wPFS
E_6	4	A or B	Yes	$\times$	$\checkmark$	$\checkmark$	$\times$	MEX
$E_{7\text{-}1}$	3	A	Yes	$\checkmark$	$\times$	$\checkmark$	$\times$	KCI
$E_{7\text{-}2}$	3	B	Yes	$\times$	$\checkmark$	$\times$	$\checkmark$	KCI
$E_{8\text{-}1}$	6	A	Yes	$\times$	$\checkmark$	$\times$	$\checkmark$	KCI
$E_{8\text{-}2}$	6	B	Yes	$\checkmark$	$\times$	$\checkmark$	$\times$	KCI

2.4 2-Key PKE and KEM

In this section, we provide the definitions of 2-key PKE and 2-key KEM, as well as the modified Fujisaki-Okamoto transformation proposed by Xue et al. [34].

A 2-key PKE with a plaintext space $\mathcal{M}$ and a ciphertext space $\mathcal{C}$ consists of a quadruple of PPT algorithms 2PKE=(KeyG1, KeyG0, Enc, Dec) described as follows:

- KeyG1(n, pp): on input a security parameter n and public parameter pp, output a pair of public and secret keys (pk_1, sk_1).
- KeyG0(n, pp): on input a security parameter n and public parameter pp, output a pair of public and secret keys (pk_0, sk_0).
- Enc$(pk_1, pk_0, m; r)$: on input public keys pk_1, pk_0 and a plaintext $m \in \mathcal{M}$, output a ciphertext $C \in \mathcal{C}$.
- Dec(sk_1, sk_0, C): on input secret keys sk_1, sk_0 and a cipheretext $C \in \mathcal{C}$, output a plaintext m.

CORRECTNESS. For $(pk_1, sk_1) \leftarrow$ KeyG1(n, pp), $(pk_0, sk_0) \leftarrow$ KeyG0(n, pp) and $C \leftarrow$ Enc$(pk_1, pk_0, m; r)$, then we have Dec$(sk_1, sk_0, C) = m$.

Game [**OW-CPA**, ·] on pk_1	Game [·, **OW-CPA**] on pk_0
01 $(pk_1, sk_1) \leftarrow$ KeyG1(n, pp);	07 $(pk_0, sk_0) \leftarrow$ KeyG0(n, pp);
02 $(state, pk_0^*) \leftarrow \mathcal{A}_1(pk_1)$;	08 $(state, pk_1^*) \leftarrow \mathcal{B}_1(pk_0)$;
03 $m \leftarrow \mathcal{M}$;	09 $m \leftarrow \mathcal{M}$;
04 $c^* \leftarrow$ Enc(pk_1, pk_0^*, m);	10 $c^* \leftarrow$ Enc(pk_1^*, pk_0, m);
05 $m' \leftarrow \mathcal{A}_2(state, c^*)$;	11 $m' \leftarrow \mathcal{B}_2(state, c^*)$;
06 return $m' \overset{?}{=} m$	12 return $m' \overset{?}{=} m$

Fig. 3. The [OW-CPA, ·] (resp. [·, OW-CPA]) game of 2PKE for adversaries $\mathcal{A}$ (resp. $\mathcal{B}$).

The security games of 2PKE are formalized in Fig. 3. We define the advantage of $\mathcal{A}$ winning in the game [OW-CPA, ·] as $\mathrm{Adv}_{2\mathsf{PKE}}^{[\mathsf{OW\text{-}CPA},\cdot]}(\mathcal{A}) = \Pr[[\mathsf{OW\text{-}CPA}, \cdot]^{\mathcal{A}} \Rightarrow 1]$, and the advantage of $\mathcal{B}$ in the game [·, OW-CPA] as $\mathrm{Adv}_{2\mathsf{PKE}}^{[\cdot,\mathsf{OW\text{-}CPA}]}(\mathcal{B}) = \Pr[[\cdot, \mathsf{OW\text{-}CPA}]^{\mathcal{B}} \Rightarrow 1]$, respectively.

The 2-key key encapsulation (2-key KEM) 2KEM is defined similarly.

- KeyGen1(n, pp): on input a security parameter n and public parameter pp, output a pair of public-secret keys (pk_1, sk_1). In order to show the randomness that is used, we denote key generation algorithm as KeyGen1(n, r).
- KeyGen0(n, pp): on input a security parameter n and public parameter pp, output a pair of public and secret keys (pk_0, sk_0).
- Encaps(pk_1, pk_0): on input public keys pk_1, pk_0, output a ciphertext c and encapsulated key k in key space $\mathcal{K}$. Sometimes, we explicitly add the randomness r and denote it as Encaps$(pk_1, pk_0; r)$.
- Decaps(sk_1, sk_0, c): on input secret keys sk_1, sk_0 and a ciphertext c, output a key k.

CORRECTNESS. For $(pk_1, sk_1) \leftarrow \mathsf{KeyGen1}(n, pp)$, $(pk_0, sk_0) \leftarrow \mathsf{KeyGen0}(n, pp)$ and $(c, k) \leftarrow \mathsf{Encaps}(pk_1, pk_0)$, it holds that $\mathsf{Decaps}(sk_1, sk_0, c) = k$.

Game [OW-CCA, ·] on pk_1	Game [·, OW-CPA] on pk_0
01 $(pk_1, sk_1) \leftarrow \mathsf{KeyGen1}(n, pp)$;	07 $(pk_0, sk_0) \leftarrow \mathsf{KeyGen0}(n, pp)$;
02 $L_0 = \{(-, -, -)\}$;	08 $(state, pk_1^*) \leftarrow \mathcal{B}_1(pk_0)$;
03 $(state, pk_0^*) \leftarrow \mathcal{A}_1^{\mathcal{O}_{cca}, \mathcal{O}_{leak0}}(pk_1)$;	09 $(c^*, k^*) \leftarrow \mathsf{Encaps}(pk_1^*, pk_0)$;
04 $(c^*, k^*) \leftarrow \mathsf{Encaps}(pk_1, pk_0^*)$;	10 $k' \leftarrow \mathcal{B}_2(state, c^*)$;
05 $k' \leftarrow \mathcal{A}_2^{\mathcal{O}_{cca}, \mathcal{O}_{leak0}}(state, c^*)$;	11 return $k' \stackrel{?}{=} k^*$
06 return $k' \stackrel{?}{=} k^*$	

Fig. 4. The [OW-CCA, ·] (resp. [·, OW-CPA]) game of 2KEM for adversaries $\mathcal{A}$ (resp. $\mathcal{B}$). The oracles $\mathcal{O}_{leak0}$ and $\mathcal{O}_{cca}$ are defined in the following.

The security games of 2KEM are formalized in Fig. 4. On the i-th query of $\mathcal{O}_{leak0}$, the challenger generates $(pk_0^i, sk_0^i) \leftarrow \mathsf{KeyGen0}(r_0^i)$, sets $L_0 = L_0 \cup \{(pk_0^i, sk_0^i)\}$ and returns (pk_0^i, sk_0^i) to adversary $\mathcal{A}$. $\mathcal{O}_{cca}(pk_0', c')$ works as follows: If $pk_0' \in [L_0]_1$ and $(c', pk_0') \neq (c^*, pk_0^*)$, compute and return the corresponding $k' \leftarrow \mathsf{Decaps}(sk_1, sk_0', c')$, otherwise return $\perp$.

We define the advantage of $\mathcal{A}$ winning in the game [OW-CCA,·] as

$$\mathsf{Adv}_{2KEM}^{[OW-CCA,\cdot]}(\mathcal{A}) = \Pr[[OW\text{-}CCA, \cdot]^{\mathcal{A}} \Rightarrow 1],$$

and the advantage of $\mathcal{B}$ winning in the game [·, OW-CPA] as:

$$\mathsf{Adv}_{2KEM}^{[\cdot, OW-CPA]}(\mathcal{B}) = \Pr[[\cdot, OW\text{-}CPA]^{\mathcal{B}} \Rightarrow 1].$$

According to [34], the modified Fujisaki-Okamoto transformation in Fig. 5 builds a [OW-CCA, OW-CPA] secure 2-Key KEM from any [OW-CPA, OW-CPA] secure 2-key PKE. Note that in [34] they consider the decryption failure, but we do not take the decryption failure into account here since the encryption scheme based on SI-DDH is perfectly correct.

Lemma 1 (Theorem 7 [34]). *For any [OW-CCA, ·] adversary $\mathcal{C}$, or [·, OW-CPA] adversary $\mathcal{D}$ against 2KEM with at most q_H queries to random oracle H, there are [OW-CPA, ·] adversary $\mathcal{A}$, or [·, OW-CPA] adversary $\mathcal{B}$ against 2PKE, that make at most q_H (resp. q_G) queries to random oracle H (resp. G) s.t.*

$$\mathsf{Adv}_{2KEM}^{[OW-CCA,\cdot]}(\mathcal{C}) \leq \frac{q_H}{2^n} + q_H \cdot \mathsf{Adv}_{2PKE}^{[OW-CPA,\cdot]}(\mathcal{A}),$$

$$\mathsf{Adv}_{2KEM}^{[\cdot, OW-CPA]}(\mathcal{D}) \leq \mathsf{Adv}_{2PKE}^{[\cdot, OW-CPA]}(\mathcal{B}).$$

KeyGen1(n)	KeyGen0(n)
$(pk_1', sk_1') \leftarrow \mathsf{KeyG1}$	$(pk_0', sk_0') \leftarrow \mathsf{KeyG0}$
$s_1 \leftarrow \{0,1\}^n$	$sk_0 = sk_0'$
$sk_1 = (sk_1', s_1)$	$pk_0 = pk_0'$
$pk_1 = pk_1'$	return (K, c)
Encaps(pk_1, pk_0);	Decaps(sk_1, sk_0, c)
$m \leftarrow \mathcal{M}$	$m' = \mathsf{Dec}(sk_1', sk_0', c)$
$c \leftarrow \mathsf{Enc}(pk_1, pk_0, m; G(m))$	$c' = \mathsf{Enc}(pk_1, pk_0, m'; G(m'))$
$K = H(pk_0, m, c)$	if $c \neq c'$, let $m' = s_1$
return (K, c)	return $K = H(pk_0, m', c)$

Fig. 5. The modified Fujisaki-Okamoto from [OW-CPA, OW-CPA] secure 2-key PKE to [OW-CCA, OW-CPA] secure 2-key KEM 2KEM.

3   [OW-CCA, OW-CPA] Secure KEM from SIDH

We now propose a [OW-CCA, OW-CPA] secure 2-key KEM from supersingular isogeny. It is the core building block for our AKEs. At first, we propose a [OW-CPA, OW-CPA] 2-key PKE from supersingular isogeny, and then apply the modified Fujisaki-Okamoto transformation to obtain a 2-key KEM.

Choose $p = \ell_1^{e_1} \ell_2^{e_2} \cdot f \pm 1, E_0, \{P_1, Q_1\}, \{P_2, Q_2\}$ as above. Let $h : \{0,1\}^* \rightarrow \{0,1\}^n$ be a random hash function from pair-wise independent hash function families $\mathcal{H}$. Let $\mathfrak{g} = (E_0; P_1, Q_1, P_2, Q_2)$ and $\mathfrak{e} = (\ell_1, \ell_2, e_1, e_2)$ be public parameters. Let $\{s, t\} = \{1, 2\}$. The [OW-CPA, OW-CPA] 2-key PKE 2PKE$_{sidh}$ is built as follows.

- KeyG1(n,pp): on input security parameter and public parameter, randomly choose a secret $\mathfrak{a}_1 \leftarrow \mathbb{Z}_{\ell_s^{e_s}}$ and compute $\mathfrak{g}^{\mathfrak{a}_1}$. Then output

$$sk_1 := \mathfrak{a}_1, pk_1 := \mathfrak{g}^{\mathfrak{a}_1}.$$

- KeyG0(n,pp): on input security parameter and public parameter, randomly choose a secret $\mathfrak{a}_0 \leftarrow \mathbb{Z}_{\ell_s^{e_s}}$ and compute $\mathfrak{g}^{\mathfrak{a}_0}$. Then output

$$sk_0 := \mathfrak{a}_0, pk_0 := \mathfrak{g}^{\mathfrak{a}_0}.$$

- Enc(pk_1, pk_0, m): on input public keys and a message $m = m_1 \| m_0 \in \{0,1\}^{2n}$, randomly choose $\mathfrak{b} \leftarrow \mathbb{Z}_{\ell_t^{e_t}}$ and compute $\mathfrak{g}^{\mathfrak{b}}, h((\mathfrak{g}^{\mathfrak{a}_1})^{\mathfrak{b}}) \oplus m_1$ and $h((\mathfrak{g}^{\mathfrak{a}_0})^{\mathfrak{b}}) \oplus m_0$. The ciphertext is

$$c := \left(\mathfrak{g}^{\mathfrak{b}}, h\left((\mathfrak{g}^{\mathfrak{a}_1})^{\mathfrak{b}}\right) \oplus m_1, h\left((\mathfrak{g}^{\mathfrak{a}_0})^{\mathfrak{b}}\right) \oplus m_0\right).$$

- Dec(sk_1, sk_0, c): on input secret keys $sk_1 = \mathfrak{a}_1$, $sk_0 = \mathfrak{a}_0$ and ciphertext $c = (\mathfrak{c}_1, c_2, c_3)$, compute $m_1 := c_2 \oplus h(\mathfrak{c}_1^{\mathfrak{a}_1})$ and $m_0 := c_3 \oplus h(\mathfrak{c}_1^{\mathfrak{a}_0})$. The plaintext is $m = m_1 \| m_0$.

The correctness of 2PKE$_{sidh}$ is straightforward due to the correctness of SIDH.

Lemma 2. *Under the SI-DDH assumption, $2PKE_{sidh}$ is [OW-CPA, OW-CPA] secure. Precisely, for any PPT [OW-CPA, ·] (resp. [·, OW-CPA]) adversary $\mathcal{A}$ (resp. $\mathcal{C}$), there exists algorithm $\mathcal{B}$ (resp. $\mathcal{D}$) such that*

$$Adv_{2PKE_{sidh}}^{[OW\text{-}CPA,\cdot]}(\mathcal{A}) \leq 2Adv_{\mathcal{B}}^{siddh} + 1/2^n + negl,$$

$$(resp.\ \ Adv_{2PKE_{sidh}}^{[\cdot,OW\text{-}CPA]}(\mathcal{C}) \leq 2Adv_{\mathcal{D}}^{siddh} + 1/2^n + negl).$$

Proof. We reduce the [OW-CPA, ·] security to the underlying SI-DDH assumption. It is analogous for the [·, OW-CPA] security. We prove the [OW-CPA, ·] security via a sequence of games.

Game 0: This is the original [OW-CPA, ·] challenge game in Fig. 3. We denote the event that the adversary wins the games as Succ_0.

Game 1: In this game we modify [OW-CPA, ·] challenge game by requiring that the adversary wins the game if $m'_1 = m_1$. We denote this event as Succ_1 (In Game i ($i \geq 1$), we denote this event as Succ_i). Note that in Game 0, the adversary wins only if both $m'_1 = m_1$ and $m'_0 = m_0$. Thus, we have $\Pr[\mathsf{Succ}_0] \leq \Pr[\mathsf{Succ}_1]$.

Game 2: In this game, we modify the computation of challenge ciphertext. Specifically, $(\mathfrak{g}^b)^{\mathfrak{a}_1}$ is replaced by a random j-invariant j^*. We construct an algorithm $\mathcal{B}$ to solve the SI-DDH problem given an instance $(\mathfrak{g}, \mathfrak{g}_1, \mathfrak{g}_2, j)$, if there exists an algorithm $\mathcal{A}$ to distinguish Game 1 and Game 2.

$\mathcal{B}(\mathfrak{e}, \mathfrak{g}, \mathfrak{g}_1, \mathfrak{g}_2, j)$

01 $pk_1 \leftarrow \mathfrak{g}_1$
02 $pk_0^*, \text{state} \leftarrow \mathcal{A}(pk_1)$
03 $m_1 \leftarrow \{0,1\}^n$
04 $\mathfrak{c}_1^* = \mathfrak{g}_2,\ c_2^* = h(j) \oplus m_1,\ c_3^* \leftarrow \{0,1\}^n$
05 $c^* = (\mathfrak{c}_1^*, c_2^*, c_3^*)$
06 $m'_1 || m'_0 \leftarrow \mathcal{A}(\text{state}, c^*)$
07 If $m'_1 = m_1$, $b' = 1$, else $b' \leftarrow \{0,1\}$.

If $(\mathfrak{g}, \mathfrak{g}_1, \mathfrak{g}_2, j)$ is an SI-DDH tuple, $\mathcal{B}$ perfectly simulates Game 1, else $\mathcal{B}$ perfectly simulates Game 2. In the SI-DDH challenge, we have

$$\begin{aligned}
\mathrm{Adv}_{\mathcal{B}}^{siddh} &= \Pr[b = b'] - 1/2 \\
&= 1/2(\Pr[b' = 1|b = 1] - \Pr[b' = 1|b = 0]) \\
&= 1/2(\Pr[b' = 1|\text{Game 1}] - \Pr[b' = 1|\text{Game 2}]) \\
&= 1/2(\Pr[\mathsf{Succ}_1] - \Pr[\mathsf{Succ}_2]).
\end{aligned}$$

Game 3: In this game, we modify the computation of the challenge ciphertext. Specifically, $h(j^*)$ is replaced by a random string h^*. Now c_2^* is a completely random string. Thus, the advantage to compute m_1 is $\Pr[\mathsf{Succ}_3] = 1/2^n$. Note that, since h is a pairwise independent hash function, by the leftover hash lemma, $|\Pr[\mathsf{Succ}_2] - \Pr[\mathsf{Succ}_3]|$ is negligible.

To sum them up, we have that $\Pr[\mathsf{Succ}_0] \leq 2\mathrm{Adv}_{\mathcal{B}}^{siddh} + 1/2^n + negl$.   □

Remark 1: By setting pk_0 and sk_0 to be empty and the ciphertext to be c_1, c_2, the scheme is exactly the ElGamal scheme and is OW-CPA secure under the SI-DDH assumption.

Applying the modified Fujisaki-Okamoto in Fig. 5, we get a [OW-CCA, OW-CPA] secure 2-key KEM $2KEM_{sidh}$ in Fig. 6. Let $G : \{0,1\}^{2n} \to \{0,1\}^*$ and $H : \{0,1\}^* \to \{0,1\}^{2n}$ be hash functions. Note that there is a subtle difference between the Fig. 6 and the modified Fujisaki-Okamoto in Fig. 5 that the "re-encryption" only needs to check the correctness of c_1.

KeyGen1	KeyGen0
$a_1 \leftarrow \mathbb{Z}_{\ell_s^{e_s}}$, $s_1 \leftarrow \{0,1\}^{2n}$	$a_0 \leftarrow \mathbb{Z}_{\ell_s^{e_s}}$
$pk_1 := g^{a_1}$, $sk_1 := (a_1, s_1)$	$pk_0 := g^{a_0}$, $sk_0 := a_0$

Encaps(pk_1, pk_0)	**Decaps**(sk_1, sk_0)
$m_1, m_0 \leftarrow \{0,1\}^n$, $b := G(m_1, m_0)$	$m_1' := c_2 \oplus h(c_1^{a_1})$
$c_1 = g^b$, $c_2 = h((g^{a_1})^b) \oplus m_1$	$m_0' := c_3 \oplus h(c_1^{a_0})$
$c_3 = h((g^{a_0})^b) \oplus m_0$	$b := G(m_1', m_0')$
$c := (c_1, c_2, c_3)$	If $c_1 \neq g^b$, $m_1 \| m_0 = s_1$
$K := H(pk_0, m_1 \| m_0, c)$	$K := H(pk_0, m_1 \| m_0, c)$

Fig. 6. The [OW-CCA, OW-CPA] secure $2KEM_{sidh}$.

Theorem 1. *Under the SI-DDH assumption, $2KEM_{sidh}$ is [OW-CCA, OW-CPA] secure in the random oracle model. Precisely, for any PPT [OW-CCA, ·] (resp. [·, OW-CPA]) adversary $\mathcal{A}$ (resp. $\mathcal{C}$) with at most q_H queries to H oracle, there exists algorithm $\mathcal{B}$ (resp. $\mathcal{D}$) solving SI-DDH problem such that*

$$Adv_{2KEM_{sidh}}^{[OW\text{-}CCA,\cdot]}(\mathcal{A}) \leq \frac{q_H}{2^{2n}} + q_H \cdot \left(2Adv_{\mathcal{B}}^{siddh} + 1/2^n + negl\right),$$

$$(resp. \quad Adv_{2KEM_{sidh}}^{[\cdot, OW\text{-}CPA]}(\mathcal{C}) \leq 2Adv_{\mathcal{D}}^{siddh} + 1/2^n + negl).$$

Proof. According to Lemma 1, the [OW-CCA, OW-CPA] security of $2KEM_{sidh}$ is guaranteed by the [OW-CPA, OW-CPA] security of $2PKE_{sidh}$. By applying Lemma 2, the [OW-CCA, OW-CPA] security is finally reduced to the underlying SI-DDH assumption.   □

Remark 2: By setting pk_0 and sk_0 to be empty, the message space to be $\{0,1\}^n$, the input of G to be $(m_1, -)$ and the ciphertext to be c_1, c_2, the scheme is exactly the FO transformed ElGamal scheme and is OW-CCA secure under the SI-DDH assumption.

4   Two-Pass SIAKE

In this section, we propose a two-pass AKE based on SI-DDH assumption. The two-pass AKE $SIAKE_2$ is shown in Fig. 7.

U_A	U_B
$sk_{A_1} := (\mathfrak{a}_1 \in \mathbb{Z}_{\ell_1^{e_1}}, s_{A1} \leftarrow \{0,1\}^{2n})$	$sk_{B_2} := (\mathfrak{b}_2 \in \mathbb{Z}_{\ell_2^{e_2}}, s_{B2} \leftarrow \{0,1\}^{2n})$
$pk_{A_1} := \mathfrak{g}^{\mathfrak{a}_1}$	$pk_{B_2} := \mathfrak{g}^{\mathfrak{b}_2}$
$sk_{A_2} := (\mathfrak{a}_2 \in \mathbb{Z}_{\ell_2^{e_2}}, s_{A2} \leftarrow \{0,1\}^{2n})$	$sk_{B_1} := (\mathfrak{b}_1 \in \mathbb{Z}_{\ell_1^{e_1}}, s_{B1} \leftarrow \{0,1\}^{2n})$
$pk_{A_2} := \mathfrak{g}^{\mathfrak{a}_2}$	$pk_{B_1} := \mathfrak{g}^{\mathfrak{b}_1}$

U_A		U_B
$r_A \leftarrow \mathbb{Z}_{\ell_1^{e_1}}, n_1 \leftarrow g(r_A, \mathfrak{a}_1)$		
$\mathfrak{x} \leftarrow G(n_1), \mathfrak{x}_0 \leftarrow \mathbb{Z}_{\ell_1^{e_1}}.$		$r_B \leftarrow \mathbb{Z}_{\ell_2^{e_2}}, m_1 \| m_0 \leftarrow g(r_B, \mathfrak{b}_2)$
$X_0 := \mathfrak{g}^{\mathfrak{x}_0}$		$\mathfrak{y} \leftarrow G(m_1, m_0)$
$X := \mathfrak{g}^{\mathfrak{x}}, x_1 := h((\mathfrak{g}^{\mathfrak{b}_2})^{\mathfrak{x}}) \oplus n_1$	$\xrightarrow{X, x_1, X_0}$	$Y := \mathfrak{g}^{\mathfrak{y}}, y_1 := h((\mathfrak{g}^{\mathfrak{a}_1})^{\mathfrak{y}}) \oplus m_1$
$K_A := H(n_1, X, x_1)$		$y_0 := h((\mathfrak{g}^{\mathfrak{x}_0})^{\mathfrak{y}}) \oplus m_0$
$m_1' := y_1 \oplus h((\mathfrak{g}^{\mathfrak{y}})^{\mathfrak{a}_1})$	$\xleftarrow{Y, y_1, y_0}$	$K_B := H(X_0, m_1, m_0, Y, y_1, y_0)$
$m_0' := y_0 \oplus h((\mathfrak{g}^{\mathfrak{y}})^{\mathfrak{x}_0})$		
$\mathfrak{y}' \leftarrow G(m_1', m_0')$		$n_1' := x_1 \oplus h((\mathfrak{g}^{\mathfrak{x}})^{\mathfrak{b}_2}), \mathfrak{x}' \leftarrow G(n_1')$
If $Y \neq \mathfrak{g}^{\mathfrak{y}'}, m_1' \| m_0' := s_{A1}$		If $X \neq \mathfrak{g}^{\mathfrak{x}'}, n_1' := s_{B2}$
$K_B' := H(X_0, m_1', m_2', Y, y_1, y_0)$		$K_A' := H(n_1', X, x_1)$
$SK := \hat{H}(sid, K_A, K_B')$		$SK := \hat{H}(sid, K_A', K_B)$

Fig. 7. A Compact 2-pass AKE SIAKE_2 Based on SI-DDH. Here sid is $\big(U_A, U_B, pk_{A_1}, pk_{B_2}, X, x_1, X_0, Y, y_1, y_0\big)$.

Public Parameters: Let $\mathfrak{e} = (\ell_1, \ell_2, e_1, e_2)$ and $\mathfrak{g} = (E_0; P_1, Q_1, P_2, Q_2)$. Let $g : \{0,1\}^* \rightarrow \{0,1\}^{2n}$, $h : \{0,1\}^n \rightarrow \{0,1\}^n$, $G : \{0,1\}^{2n} \rightarrow \{0,1\}^*$, $H : \{0,1\}^* \rightarrow \{0,1\}^{2n}$, $\hat{H} : \{0,1\}^* \rightarrow \{0,1\}^n$ be hash functions.

Register: Any user registers two sets of public-secret keys. One set of keys is assigned by the user as initiator, and another set is assigned as responder. For user U_A, it first chooses $sk_{A_1} := (\mathfrak{a}_1 \in \mathbb{Z}_{\ell_1^{e_1}}, s_{A1} \leftarrow \{0,1\}^{2n})$ and computes $pk_{A_1} := \mathfrak{g}^{\mathfrak{a}_1}$, then chooses $sk_{A_2} := (\mathfrak{a}_2 \in \mathbb{Z}_{\ell_2^{e_2}}, s_{A2} \leftarrow \{0,1\}^{2n})$ and computes $pk_{A_2} := \mathfrak{g}^{\mathfrak{a}_2}$.

Phase 1: User U_A randomly chooses $r_A, \mathfrak{x}_0 \leftarrow \mathbb{Z}_{\ell_1^{e_1}}$ as two ephemeral randomness. Let $n_1 \leftarrow g(r_A, \mathfrak{a}_1)$, $\mathfrak{x} := G(g(r_A, \mathfrak{a}_1))$. Then U_A computes $X_0 := \mathfrak{g}^{\mathfrak{x}_0}$, $X := \mathfrak{g}^{\mathfrak{x}}$, $x_1 := h((\mathfrak{g}^{\mathfrak{b}_2})^{\mathfrak{x}}) \oplus n_1$, and sends X_0, X, x_1 to U_B. U_A computes $K_A := H(n_1, X, x_1)$.

Phase 2: User U_B randomly chooses $r_B \leftarrow \mathbb{Z}_{\ell_2^{e_2}}$ as the ephemeral randomness and computes $m_1 \| m_0 \leftarrow g(r_B, s_b)$, $\mathfrak{y} \leftarrow G(m_1, m_0)$, and $Y := \mathfrak{g}^{\mathfrak{y}}$. On receiving (X_0, X, x_1) from U_A, U_B computes $y_1 := h((\mathfrak{g}^{\mathfrak{a}_1})^{\mathfrak{y}}) \oplus m_1$, $y_0 := h((\mathfrak{g}^{\mathfrak{x}_0})^{\mathfrak{y}}) \oplus m_0$, $K_B := H(X, m_1, m_0, Y, y_1, y_0)$, and sends (Y, y_1, y_0) to U_A. U_B decrypts X, x_1 to extract n_1' and $\mathfrak{x}' \leftarrow G(n_1')$. If $X \neq \mathfrak{g}^{\mathfrak{x}}$, set $n_1' := s_{B2}$. Let $K_A' := H(n_1', X, x_1)$. The session key is $SK := \hat{H}(sid, K_A', K_B)$ where sid is $\big(U_A, U_B, pk_{A_1}, pk_{B_2}, X, x_1, X_0, Y, y_1, y_0\big)$.

Phase 3: On receiving (Y, y_1, y_0) from U_B, U_A computes $m_1' := y_1 \oplus h((\mathfrak{g}^{\mathfrak{y}})^{\mathfrak{a}_1})$, $m_0' := y_0 \oplus h((\mathfrak{g}^{\mathfrak{y}})^{\mathfrak{r}_0})$ to extract $\mathfrak{y}' \leftarrow G(m_1', m_0')$. If $Y \neq \mathfrak{g}^{\mathfrak{y}}$, set $m_1'\|m_0' := s_{A1}$. Let $K_B' := H(X_0, m_1', m_0', Y, y_1, y_0)$. The session key is $SK := \hat{H}(sid, K_A, K_B')$ where sid is $(U_A, U_B, pk_{A_1}, pk_{B_2}, X, x_1, X_0, Y, y_1, y_0)$.

The session state owned by U_A consists of the ephemeral secret key $r_A, \mathfrak{r}_0$, the decapsulated key K_B' and the encapsulated key K_A. The session state owned by U_B consists of the ephemeral secrete key r_B and the encapsulated key K_B, but not the decapsulated key K_A'.

Theorem 2. *Under the SI-DDH assumption, SIAKE_2 is CK^+ secure in the random oracle model. Precisely, if the number of users is N and there are at most l sessions between any two users, for any PPT adversary $\mathcal{A}$ against SIAKE_2 with q times of hash oracle queries, there exists $\mathcal{B}$ s.t.*

$$Adv_{\mathsf{SIAKE}_2}^{CK^+}(\mathcal{A}) \leq 1/2 + N^2 \cdot l \cdot q \cdot \left(4Adv_{\mathcal{B}}^{siddh} + \frac{q+1}{2^n} + negl\right).$$

Proof sketch: Obviously, U_A sends X_0 and a OW-CCA secure ciphertext X, x_1 under public key pk_{B_2} to U_B. U_B responds with a [OW-CCA, OW-CPA] secure ciphertext Y, y_1, y_0 under public keys pk_{A_1} and X_0 to U_A. We first assume that the AKE adversary only has the capability to Send message and does not query SessionKeyReveal and SessionStateReveal on non-test sessions. Then under the assumption of [OW-CPA, OW-CPA] security, SIAKE_2 is secure. Take the event E_3 (one of the behaviors presented in Appendix A Table 6) as an example, where the adversary may send X_0 in the test session and he/she knows $\mathfrak{b}_2$ but not $\mathfrak{a}_1$ or r_B. Since the adversary does not know $\mathfrak{a}_1$ and $\mathfrak{y}$, the [OW-CPA, OW-CPA] security guarantees that K_B encapsulated in (Y, y_1, y_0) is secure (thus SK is random assuming $\hat{H}$ is a random oracle) even the adversary chooses part of the public key X_0. Note that to simulate the CK^+ game and reduce the advantage of the AKE adversary to the advantage of solving underlying [OW-CPA, $\cdot$] game, the simulator does not hold the static secret key $\mathfrak{a}_1$ of U_A. It is safe if the adversary does not make SessionKeyReveal and SessionStateReveal queries. However if the adversary makes SessionKeyReveal queries that involves U_A, the simulator fails to compute the encapsulated key and session key. Nevertheless, when the underlying KEM is [OW-CCA, OW-CPA] secure, the simulator could query the strong decapsulation oracle to get the encapsulated key and session key, so the reduction works. In other events, the proof proceeds similarly.

Proof. We give representative security proof in two cases E_5 and E_3 in Table 2, where one is wPFS and the other is the MEX attack. The other cases can be easily extended or modified from the proof of E_3, so they are omitted here. Table 3 presents the outline of reduction.

wPFS E_5. The proof of this case proceeds via a sequence of games, i.e. Game 0 to 2. In this case, the test session sid^* (with owner as responder or initiator) has a matching session $\overline{\mathsf{sid}}^*$. Both static secret keys of the initiator and the responder are leaked to $\mathcal{A}$. We denote the event that the AKE adversary $\mathcal{A}$ outputs b' such that $b = b'$ as Succ_i in Game i.

Table 3. The outline of security reduction for SIAKE_2.

Assumption	2-Key PKE	2-Key KEM	Cases in Table 2
SI-DDH	$[\cdot, \text{OW-CPA}], pk_0 = \mathfrak{g}^{\mathfrak{r}_0}$	$[\cdot, \text{OW-CPA}], pk_0 = \mathfrak{g}^{\mathfrak{r}_0}$	E_5
SI-DDH	$[\text{OW-CPA}, \cdot], pk_1 = \mathfrak{g}^{\mathfrak{a}_1}$	$[\text{OW-CCA}, \cdot], pk_1 = \mathfrak{g}^{\mathfrak{a}_1}$	$E_3, E_4, E_6, E_{7\text{-}2}, E_{8\text{-}1}$
SI-DDH	OW-CPA	OW-CCA, $pk_1 = \mathfrak{g}^{\mathfrak{b}_2}$	$E_1, E_2, E_{7\text{-}1}, E_{8\text{-}2}$

Game 0: This is the original CK^+ game in case E_5. In the test session, the adversary owns all the static secret keys, i.e. $\mathfrak{a}_1, \mathfrak{a}_2, \mathfrak{b}_1, \mathfrak{b}_2$ asssuming the test session is between U_A and U_B.

Game 1: In this game, we change the way to generate $m_1 \| m_0$ in the test session by replacing $m_1 \| m_0 \leftarrow g(r_B, \mathfrak{b}_2)$ with $m_1 \| m_0 \leftarrow \{0,1\}^{2n}$. Since g is a random oracle, $\Pr[\mathsf{Succ}_0] - \Pr[\mathsf{Succ}_1] \leq N^2 \cdot l \cdot \frac{q}{2^n}$.

Game 2: In this game, we change the session key in the test session by replacing $\hat{H}(sid, K'_A, K_B)$ with a random bit-string in $\{0,1\}^n$. Obviously, $\Pr[\mathsf{Succ}_2] = 1/2$.

We construct an algorithm $\mathcal{B}$ to solve the $[\cdot, \text{OW-CPA}]$ security of $2\mathsf{KEM}_{sidh}$, if there exists an algorithm $\mathcal{A}$ to distinguish Game 1 and Game 2.

On receiving the public key pk_0 from the $[\cdot, \text{OW-CPA}]$ challenger, to simulate the CK^+ game, $\mathcal{B}$ randomly chooses two parties U_A, U_B and the i-th session as a guess of the test session with success probability $1/N^2 l$. $\mathcal{B}$ computes and sets all the static secrets and public key pairs by himself for all N users U_P as both responder and initiator. Particularly, $\mathcal{B}$ sets the static secret and public key pair (pk_{B_2}, sk_{B_2}) for U_B as responder, and sets pk_{A_1} for U_A as initiator. $\mathcal{B}$ sends pk_{A_1} to $[\cdot, \text{OW-CPA}]$ challenger and receives the challenge ciphertext C^*. Then $\mathcal{B}$ simulates all the communications and SessionStateReveal and SessionKeyReveal as those in Game 1 except the test session. In the test session, $\mathcal{B}$ sets $X_0 = pk_0$ and responds $(Y, y_1, y_0) = C^*$.

Finally, $\mathcal{B}$ checks the hash list queried by $\mathcal{A}$. If there exists some $(U_A, U_B, pk_{A_1}, pk_{B_2}, X, x_1, X_0, C^*, K_A, K_B)$ in the list such that K_A is the key encapsulated in (X, x_1) (since (X, x_1) is honestly generated by $\mathcal{B}$, it can compute K_A), $\mathcal{B}$ chooses a random one and outputs K_B, otherwise $\perp$. Denote flag as the event that $\mathcal{A}$ explicitly queries $(U_A, U_B, pk_{A_1}, pk_{B_2}, X, x_1, X_0, C^*, K_A, K_B)$ to the oracle $\hat{H}$ such that K_A is the key encapsulated in (X, x_1) and K_B is the key encapsulated in C^*. If flag does not happen, $\mathcal{B}$ perfectly simulates both Game 1 and Game 2. Thus,

$$\Pr[\mathsf{Succ}_1] - \Pr[\mathsf{Succ}_2] \leq \Pr[\mathsf{flag}] \leq N^2 \cdot l \cdot \mathsf{Adv}_{2\mathsf{PKE}_{sidh}}^{[\cdot, \text{OW-CPA}]}(\mathcal{C}).$$

By Lemma 2, $\Pr[\mathsf{Succ}_0] \leq 1/2 + N^2 \cdot l \cdot \left(\frac{q}{2^n} + 2\mathsf{Adv}_{\mathcal{B}}^{siddh} + 1/2^n + negl \right)$.

MEX E_3. In this case, the test session sid^* with its owner as responder does not have a matching session which means that X, x_1, X_0 is sent by adversary. And the randomness r_B are leaked to $\mathcal{A}$. It is more complicated than E_5. At first, (X, x_1, X_0) in the test session is generated by $\mathcal{A}$ rather than $\mathcal{B}$. However, (X, x_1) is the ciphertext under public key pk_{B_2}, and the encapsulated key K_A can be extracted with sk_{B_2}. Furthermore, the challenge public key that the security relies upon is the static public key, and this will affect the simulation of answering SessionStateReveal and SessionKeyReveal queries. Fortunately, $2PKE_{sidh}$ provides a strong decapsulation oracle to answer those queries.

The proof also proceeds via a sequence of games, i.e., Game 0 to 2. We denote the event that $\mathcal{A}$ outputs b' such that $b = b'$ as $Succ_i$ in Game i.

Game 0: This is the original CK^+ game in case E_3. In the test session, r_B is leaked to the adversary assuming the test session is between U_A and U_B.

Game 1: In this game, we change the way to generate $m_1 \| m_0$ in the test session by replacing $m_1 \| m_0 \leftarrow g(r_B, \mathfrak{b}_2)$ with $m_1 \| m_0 \leftarrow \{0,1\}^{2n}$. Although r_B is leaked to $\mathcal{A}$, since g is a random oracle, $\mathcal{A}$ will not find this change without querying g with $r_B, \mathfrak{b}_2$. We denote Askg as the event $\mathcal{A}$ queries g with $r_B, \mathfrak{b}_2$. If event Askg happens, we can extract $\mathfrak{b}_2$ and utilize it to solve the underlying SI-DDH problem. Precisely, given $(\mathfrak{g}, \mathfrak{g}_1, \mathfrak{g}_2, j)$, $\mathcal{B}$ randomly chooses U_B as a guess of the responder in the test session with success probability $\frac{1}{2N}$. $\mathcal{B}$ sets $pk_{B_2} := \mathfrak{g}_2$. When event Askg happens, $\mathcal{B}$ uses $\mathfrak{b}_2$ to output $j \overset{?}{=} \mathfrak{g}_1^{\mathfrak{b}_2}$.

$$\Pr[Succ_0] - \Pr[Succ_1] \leq 2N \cdot Adv_{\mathcal{B}}^{siddh}.$$

Game 2: In this game, we change the session key in the test session by replacing $\hat{H}(sid, K'_A, K_B)$ with a random bit-string in $\{0,1\}^n$. Obviously, $\Pr[Succ_2] = 1/2$.

We construct an algorithm $\mathcal{B}$ to solve the $[OW\text{-}CCA, \cdot]$ security of $2KEM_{sidh}$, if there exists an algorithm $\mathcal{A}$ to distinguish Game 1 and Game 2.

On receiving the public key pk_1 from the $[OW\text{-}CPA, \cdot]$ challenger, to simulate the CK^+ game, $\mathcal{B}$ randomly chooses two parties U_A, U_B and the i-th session as a guess of the test session with success probability $1/N^2 l$. $\mathcal{B}$ computes and sets all the static secret and public key pairs on his own for all N users U_P as both responder and initiator except the static public key for U_A as initiator.

- Specifically, $\mathcal{B}$ sets the static secret and public key pair (pk_{A_2}, sk_{A_2}) that invloves U_A as responder, and sets pk_1 (receiving from the $[OW\text{-}CPA, \cdot]$ challenger) for U_A as initiator.
- In the test session, on receiving (X, x_1, X_0) from $\mathcal{A}$, $\mathcal{B}$ sends $pk_0^* = X_0$ to the $[OW\text{-}CCA, \cdot]$ challenger and receives the challenge ciphertext C^*. Then $\mathcal{B}$ returns C^* to $\mathcal{A}$ as response.
- $\mathcal{B}$ simulates all the communications and SessionStateReveal and SessionKeyReveal queries as those in Game 1 except that involves U_A as initiator (since $\mathcal{B}$ does not know sk_{A_1}).
- For those SessionStateReveal and SessionKeyReveal queries involves U_A as initiator (for example, U_A honestly sends out X', x'_1, X'_0 and receives (Y', y'_1, y'_0)), $\mathcal{B}$ queries the $\mathcal{O}$ oracle with $(X'_0; Y', y'_1, y'_0)$ provided by the $[OW\text{-}CCA, \cdot]$ challenger to extract the encapsulated key and maintains the consistency of the $\hat{H}$ list with SessionStateReveal and SessionKeyReveal queries.

Finally, $\mathcal{B}$ checks the hash list queried by $\mathcal{A}$. If there exists some $(U_A, U_B, pk_{A_1}, pk_{B_2}, X, x_1, X_0, C^*, K_A, K_B)$ in the list such that K_A is the key encapsulated in (X, x_1) (since (X, x_1) is honestly generated by $\mathcal{B}$, it can compute

K_A), $\mathcal{B}$ chooses a random one and outputs K_B, otherwise $\perp$. Denote flag as the event that $\mathcal{A}$ explicitly queries $(U_A, U_B, pk_{A_1}, pk_{B_2}, X, x_1, X_0, C^*, K_A, K_B)$ to the oracle $\hat{H}$ such that K_A is the key encapsulated in (X, x_1) and K_B is the key encapsulated in C^*. If flag does not happen, $\mathcal{B}$ perfectly simulates both Game 1 and Game 2. Thus,

$$\Pr[\mathsf{Succ}_1] - \Pr[\mathsf{Succ}_2] \leq \Pr[\mathsf{flag}] \leq N^2 \cdot l \cdot \mathrm{Adv}_{2\mathsf{KEM}_{sidh}}^{[\mathrm{OW\text{-}CCA},\cdot]}(\mathcal{C}).$$

By Theorem 1, to sum up,

$$\Pr[\mathsf{Succ}_0] \leq 1/2 + N^2 \cdot l \cdot q \cdot \left(4\mathrm{Adv}_{\mathcal{B}}^{\mathsf{siddh}} + 1/2^n + negl\right). \qquad \square$$

5   Three-Pass SIAKE

We first enhance the SI-DDH assumption to 1-Oracle SI-DH assumption, and analyze its reliability. Based on this assumption, we propose the three-pass SIAKE$_3$.

5.1   1-Oracle SI-DH and Implied 2-Key KEM

The 1-Oracle SI-DH assumption is inspired by the Oracle Diffie-Hellman assumption over classical group given by Abdalla, Bellare and Rogaway [1] for analyzing DHIES. Let $G := <g>$ and $|G| = p$ be a prime. The Oracle Diffie-Hellman assumption states that, given (g, g^a, g^b, h), it is difficult to decide whether $h = H(g^{ab})$ or not (where H is a hash function), even the solver could make polynomial queries to an oracle $H_B(\cdot)$ which will return $H(v^b)$ with $v \in G$ satisfying $v \neq g^a$. Under the Oracle Diffie-Hellman assumption, the DHIES scheme is chosen ciphertext secure [1].

However, the Oracle Diffie-Hellman assumption can not be directly extended in the supersingular isogeny setting. As we have presented several times before, the adaptive attack [17] would allow extraction of every bit of b with polynomial queries to $H_B(\cdot)$ with specified points, implying the analogue of Oracle Diffie-Hellman problem in the supersingular isogeny setting could be solved. Moreover, in the classical group, if $v \neq g^a$, then $v^b \neq (g^a)^b$. However, in the supersingular isogeny setting, even if $v \neq g^a \in \mathrm{SSEC}_A$, it is possible that v^b is equal to $(g^a)^b$.

Fortunately, only one query to $H_B(\cdot)$ with $v \neq g^a$ is needed for our purpose and the adaptive attack does not work. Furthermore, when $H_B(v) = H(v, v^b)$, even if $v \neq g^a$, the case $H(v, v^b) = H(g^a, (g^a)^b)$ occurs with negligible probability.

Definition 4 (1-Oracle SI-DH Assumption). *Let* $H : \{0,1\}^* \to \{0,1\}^n$ *be a hash function. Let* $\mathfrak{e}$ *and* $\mathfrak{g}$ *be public parameters as defined in SI-DDH assumption. Let* D_0 *and* D_1 *be two distributions:*

$$D_1 := \{\mathfrak{e}, \mathfrak{g}, \mathfrak{g}^\mathfrak{a}, \mathfrak{g}^\mathfrak{b}, H(\mathfrak{g}^\mathfrak{a}, (\mathfrak{g}^\mathfrak{a})^\mathfrak{b}) | \mathfrak{a} \leftarrow \mathbb{Z}_{\ell_s^{e_s}}, \mathfrak{b} \leftarrow \mathbb{Z}_{\ell_t^{e_t}}\}$$
$$D_0 := \{\mathfrak{e}, \mathfrak{g}, \mathfrak{g}^\mathfrak{a}, \mathfrak{g}^\mathfrak{b}, h | \mathfrak{a} \leftarrow \mathbb{Z}_{\ell_s^{e_s}}, \mathfrak{b} \leftarrow \mathbb{Z}_{\ell_t^{e_t}}, h \leftarrow \{0,1\}^n\}$$

The 1-Oracle SI-DH problem is, given a random sample from D_b depending on $b \leftarrow \{0,1\}$, and a one-time oracle H_B, guessing b. The one-time oracle H_B can be queried only one time with $\mathfrak{y} \in SSEC_A$ and $\mathfrak{y} \neq \mathfrak{g}^\mathfrak{a}$, and it will return $H(\mathfrak{y}, \mathfrak{y}^\mathfrak{b})$. The advantage of $\mathcal{A}$ to solve the 1-Oracle SI-DH problem is

$$Adv_{\mathcal{A}}^{1osidh} = Pr[b' = b | \mathcal{A}^{H_B(\cdot)}(\mathfrak{d}_b \leftarrow D_b) = b', b \leftarrow \{0,1\}] - 1/2.$$

The 1-Oracle SI-DH assumption states that for any PPT algorithm $\mathcal{A}$, $Adv_{\mathcal{A}}^{1osidh}$ is negligible.

We emphasize that the adversary is allowed to query the hashed SIDH oracle H_B only once with $\mathfrak{y} \neq \mathfrak{g}^\mathfrak{a}$. If there are polynomial queries, the 1-Oracle SI-DH problem can be solved by the adaptive attack in [17]. Please also notice that the hash function involves $\mathfrak{g}^\mathfrak{a}$ or $\mathfrak{y}$ as input besides the j-invariant. Otherwise the 1-Oracle SI-DH problem is easy. Let $\mathfrak{g}^\mathfrak{a} = (E_A, \phi_A(P_t), \phi_A(Q_t))$. Since $\langle \phi_A(P_s) + [y]\phi_A(Q_s) \rangle = \langle [u]\phi_A(P_s) + [y][u]\phi_A(Q_s) \rangle$ for any integer $1 \leq u \leq \ell_s^{e_s}$ and coprime to ℓ_s, the attacker sets $E_Y = E_A$, $R = [u]\phi_A(P_s)$, $S = [u]\phi_A(Q_s)$ and $\mathfrak{y} = (Y, R, S)$. Then $(\mathfrak{g}^\mathfrak{a})^\mathfrak{b}$ and $\mathfrak{y}^\mathfrak{b}$ will produce the same j-invariant. However, when taking $\mathfrak{g}^\mathfrak{a}$ or $\mathfrak{y}$ as input of H, any query with $\mathfrak{y} \neq \mathfrak{g}^\mathfrak{a}$ to H_B will get a completely different value.

1-Gap SI-DH problem is similar to the SI-CDH problem but the adversary is given access to a highly restricted SI-DDH oracle.

Definition 5 (1-Gap SI-DH Assumption). *Let $\mathfrak{e}$ and $\mathfrak{g}$ be public parameters. The 1-Gap SI-DH problem is that, given $\mathfrak{g}^\mathfrak{a}$, $\mathfrak{g}^\mathfrak{b}$ (where $\mathfrak{a} \leftarrow \mathbb{Z}_{\ell_s^{e_s}}$, $\mathfrak{b} \leftarrow \mathbb{Z}_{\ell_t^{e_t}}$), and an oracle $\mathcal{O}_{siddh}(\mathfrak{y}, \cdot)$, compute the j-invariant $(\mathfrak{g}^\mathfrak{a})^\mathfrak{b} = (\mathfrak{g}^\mathfrak{b})^\mathfrak{a}$. Here, $\mathfrak{y} \in SSEC_A$ is chosen by the adversary $\mathcal{A}$ at any time before its first queries to $\mathcal{O}_{siddh}(\mathfrak{y}, \cdot)$. $\mathcal{O}_{siddh}(\mathfrak{y}, j)$ will return 1 if $j = \mathfrak{y}^\mathfrak{b}$, and 0 otherwise. For any PPT algorithm $\mathcal{A}$, we define the advantage of solving 1-Gap SI-DH problem as*

$$Adv_{\mathcal{A}}^{1gsidh} = Pr[j' = (\mathfrak{g}^\mathfrak{a})^\mathfrak{b} | \mathcal{A}^{\mathcal{O}_{siddh}(\mathfrak{y}, \cdot)}(\mathfrak{g}, \mathfrak{e}, \mathfrak{g}^\mathfrak{a}, \mathfrak{g}^\mathfrak{b}) \rightarrow (\mathfrak{y}, j')].$$

The 1-Gap SI-DH assumption states: for any PPT algorithm $\mathcal{A}$, the advantage of solving 1-Gap SI-DH problem is negligible.

We emphasize that if the adversary is allowed to query $\mathcal{O}_{siddh}(\cdot, \cdot)$ with unlimited numbers of $\mathfrak{y}$, 1-Gap SI-DH problem can be solved using the adaptive attack in [17]. However, here $\mathcal{O}_{siddh}(\cdot, \cdot)$ oracle only allows to be queried once with $\mathfrak{y}$ of adversary's choice.

Discussion. These two assumptions are "non-standard" for supersingular isogeny. The adaptive attack [17] and its extension can not easily break these new assumptions. We encourage more works on the analysis of the hardness of these two problems.

The following theorem shows that the 1-Gap SI-DH assumption implies the 1-Oracle SI-DH assumption when the hash function H is modeled as a random oracle.

Theorem 3. *For any algorithm $\mathcal{A}$ against the 1-Oracle SI-DH problem there exists an algorithm $\mathcal{B}$ against the 1-Gap SI-DH problem such that*

$$Adv_{\mathcal{A},H}^{1osidh}(n) \leq q_H \cdot Adv_{\mathcal{B}}^{1gsidh}(n),$$

where q_H is the number of times to query $\mathcal{O}_{\mathsf{siddh}}(\mathfrak{y},\cdot)$.

Proof. Let $\mathcal{A}$ be any algorithm solving the 1-Oracle SI-DH problem. We construct an algorithms $\mathcal{B}$ to solve the 1-Gap SI-DH problem using $\mathcal{A}$ as a subroutine in Fig. 8. The challenge is how to maintain the hash list so as to keep the consistency with the one-time Oracle H_B. Actually, the limited oracle $\mathcal{O}_{\mathsf{siddh}}(\cdot,\cdot)$ would help $\mathcal{B}$ to fix it.

Algorithm $\mathcal{B}^{\mathcal{O}_{\mathsf{siddh}}(\cdot,\cdot)}\left(\mathfrak{e},\mathfrak{g},\mathfrak{g}^a,\mathfrak{g}^b\right)$

01 $h_0, h_1 \leftarrow \{0,1\}^n$	One time $H_B(\mathfrak{y})$
02 $b \leftarrow \{0,1\}$	01 Choose $\mathfrak{y}$ as the base of $\mathcal{O}_{\mathsf{siddh}}$
03 Run $\mathcal{A}^{H_B(\cdot),H}(\mathfrak{g},\mathfrak{g}^a,\mathfrak{g}^b,h_b)$	02 if $\exists (\mathfrak{y},j',h') \in L_H \wedge \mathcal{O}_{\mathsf{siddh}}(\mathfrak{y},j')=1$
04 a. For one-time query H_B	03 return h'
05 do as one-time H_B	04 else $h'' \leftarrow \{0,1\}^n$, $L_H = L_H \cup \{\mathfrak{y},j',h''\}$
06 b. For the H-query	05 return h''
07 do as $H(\mathfrak{x},j')$	$H(\mathfrak{x},j')$
08 c. Let b' be the output of $\mathcal{A}$	01 if $\exists(\mathfrak{x},j',h') \in L_H$ return h'
09 return $(\cdot,j,\cdot) \leftarrow L_H$	02 otherwise $h \leftarrow \{0,1\}^n$, $L_H = L_H \cup \{(\mathfrak{x},j',h)\}$
10 return j	03 return h

Fig. 8. Algorithm $\mathcal{B}$ for attacking the 1-Gap SI-DH problem.

Note that in Fig. 8, if $H_B(\mathfrak{y})$ is asked at first and returns a random h, then when $(\mathfrak{y},j')$ is queried to H such that $\mathcal{O}_{\mathsf{siddh}}(\mathfrak{y},j')=1$, it will return h. If $H(\mathfrak{y},j')$ is asked at first and returns a random h, then when $\mathfrak{y}$ is asked to H_B such that $\mathcal{O}_{\mathsf{siddh}}(\mathfrak{y},j')=1$, it will return that h.

Let Ask be the event that $(\mathfrak{g}^a,(\mathfrak{g}^a)^b)$ is queried to H and $\overline{\mathsf{Ask}}$ be the complement of Ask. If Ask does not happen, there is no way to tell whether h_b is equal to $H(\mathfrak{g}^a,(\mathfrak{g}^a)^b)$ or not. Thus we have that

$$
\begin{aligned}
Adv_{\mathcal{A},H}^{1osidh} &= \Pr[\mathcal{A}^{H_B(\cdot)}(\mathfrak{b} \leftarrow D_b) = b] - 1/2 \\
&= \Pr[\mathcal{A}^{H_B(\cdot)}(\mathfrak{b} \leftarrow D_b) = b \wedge \mathsf{Ask}] + \Pr[\mathcal{A}^{H_B(\cdot)}(\mathfrak{b} \leftarrow D_b) = b \wedge \overline{\mathsf{Ask}}] - 1/2 \\
&= \Pr[\mathcal{A}^{H_B(\cdot)}(\mathfrak{b} \leftarrow D_b) = b \wedge \mathsf{Ask}] \\
&\leq \Pr[\mathsf{Ask}] \leq q_H \cdot Adv_{\mathcal{B}}^{1gsidh}.
\end{aligned}
$$

$\square$

We now modify the $2\mathsf{PKE}_{sidh}$ and denote the new scheme as $2\mathsf{PKE}_{1osidh}$. The key generation algorithms are the same. In the encryption algorithm, $h\left((\mathfrak{g}^b)^{a_1}\right)$ is replaced by $h\left(\mathfrak{g}^b,(\mathfrak{g}^b)^{a_1}\right)$ and $h\left(((\mathfrak{g}^b)^{a_0})\right)$ is replaced by $h\left(\mathfrak{g}^b,(\mathfrak{g}^b)^{a_0}\right)$. Thus the ciphertext is $c := \left(\mathfrak{g}^b, h\left(\mathfrak{g}^b,(\mathfrak{g}^b)^{a_1}\right) \oplus m_1, h\left(\mathfrak{g}^b,(\mathfrak{g}^b)^{a_0}\right) \oplus m_0\right)$.

Lemma 3. *The following holds.*

- *Under the 1-Oracle SI-DH assumption, the scheme* $2PKE_{1osidh}$ *is [OW-CPA, ·] secure even* $H(pk_0^*, pk_0^{*b})$ *is given to the adversary besides the challenge ciphertext* $c^* = (\mathfrak{c}_1^* = \mathfrak{g}^b, c_1, c_2)$.
- *If the [OW-CPA, ·] game is changed as that* pk_0^* *is generated by the challenger and the corresponding* sk_0^* *is leaked to the adversary, then under the SI-DDH assumption,* $2PKE_{1osidh}$ *satisfies this [OW-CPA, ·] security even* $H(pk_0^*, pk_0^{*b})$ *is given to the adversary besides the challenge ciphertext* $c^* = (\mathfrak{c}_1^* = \mathfrak{g}^b, c_1, c_2)$.
- *Under the SI-DDH assumption, the scheme* $2PKE_{1osidh}$ *is [·, OW-CPA] secure.*

Proof. The [·, OW-CPA] security is the same with that in Lemma 2. We reduce the [OW-CPA, ·] security with leakage to the underlying 1-Oracle SI-DH assumption.
Game 0: This is the original [OW-CPA, ·] challenge game in Fig. 3. We denote the event that the adversary wins the games as Succ_0.
Game 1: In this game, we modify the computation of challenge ciphertext. Specifically, $h(\mathfrak{g}^b, (\mathfrak{g}^b)^{a_1}$ is replaced by a random bit $h \leftarrow \{0,1\}^n$. We construct an algorithm $\mathcal{B}$ to solve the 1-Oracle SI-DH problem given an instance $(\mathfrak{g}, \mathfrak{g}_1, \mathfrak{g}_2, h)$, and a one-time oacle $\mathcal{H}_B(\cdot)$, if there exists an algorithm $\mathcal{A}$ to distinguish Game 0 and Game 1.

$$\underline{\mathcal{B}^{\mathcal{H}_B(\cdot)}(\mathfrak{e}, \mathfrak{g}, \mathfrak{g}_1, \mathfrak{g}_2 = \mathfrak{g}^b, h)}$$

01 $pk_1 \leftarrow \mathfrak{g}_1$
02 $pk_0^*, state \leftarrow \mathcal{A}(pk_1)$
03 $m_1 \leftarrow \{0,1\}^n, m_0 \leftarrow \{0,1\}^n$
04 Query $\mathcal{H}_B$ with pk_0^* and get pk_0^{*b}
04 $\mathfrak{c}_1^* = \mathfrak{g}_2, c_2^* = h \oplus m_1, c_3^* = h(pk_0^*, pk_0^{*b}) \oplus m_0$
05 $c^* = (\mathfrak{c}_1^*, c_2^*, c_3^*)$
06 $m_1' || m_0' \leftarrow \mathcal{A}(state, C^*)$
07 If $m_1' = m_1, b' = 1$, else $b' \leftarrow \{0,1\}$.

If $(\mathfrak{g}, \mathfrak{g}_1, \mathfrak{g}_2, h)$ is a 1-Oracle SI-DH tuple, $\mathcal{B}$ perfectly simulates Game 0, else $\mathcal{B}$ perfectly simulates Game 1. In the 1-Oracle SI-DH challenge, we have

$$\begin{aligned}
\mathrm{Adv}_{\mathcal{B}}^{1osidh} &= \Pr[b = b'] - 1/2 \\
&= 1/2(\Pr[b' = 1 | b = 1] - \Pr[b' = 1 | b = 0]) \\
&= 1/2(\Pr[b' = 1 | \text{Game 0}] - \Pr[b' = 1 | \text{Game 1}]) \\
&= 1/2(\Pr[\mathsf{Succ}_0] - \Pr[\mathsf{Succ}_1]).
\end{aligned}$$

Note that in this game, the [OW-CPA, ·] advantage is less than $1/2^n$. To Sum up, we have that, $\Pr[\mathsf{Succ}_0] \leq 2\mathrm{Adv}_{\mathcal{B}}^{siddh} + 1/2^n$. □

Similarly, we make the same modification to the $2KEM_{sidh}$ and denote the new scheme as $2KEM_{1osidh}$.

Theorem 4. *The following holds in the random oracle model.*

- *Under the 1-Oracle SI-DH assumption, the scheme $2KEM_{1osidh}$ is $[OW\text{-}CCA,$ $\cdot]$ secure in the random oracle model, even $h(pk_0^*, pk_0^{*b})$ is given to the adversary besides the challenge ciphertext $c^* = (\mathfrak{c}_1^* = \mathfrak{g}^{\mathfrak{b}}, c_1, c_2)$.*
- *If the $[OW\text{-}CCA, \cdot]$ game is changed as that pk_0^* is generated by challenger and the corresponding sk_0^* is leaked to the adversary, then under the SI-DDH assumption, $2KEM_{1osidh}$ satisfies this $[OW\text{-}CPA, \cdot]$ security even $H(pk_0^*, pk_0^{*b})$ is given to the adversary besides the challenge ciphertext $c^* = (\mathfrak{c}_1^* = \mathfrak{g}^{\mathfrak{b}}, c_1, c_2)$.*
- *Under the SI-DDH assumption, the scheme $2KEM_{1osidh}$ is $[\cdot, OW\text{-}CPA]$ secure.*

5.2   A Three-Pass AKE Based on 1-Oracle SI-DH Assumption

The three-pass AKE SIAKE_3 is shown in Fig. 9. The public parameters and register are the same with those for SIAKE_2.

Phase 1: User U_A chooses ephemeral randomness r_A. Let $n_1 \| n_0 \leftarrow g(r_A, \mathfrak{a}_1)$ and $\mathfrak{x} \leftarrow G(n_1, n_0)$. Then U_A computes $X := \mathfrak{g}^{\mathfrak{x}}$, $x_1 := h(g^{b_2}, (\mathfrak{g}^{b_2})^{\mathfrak{x}}) \oplus n_1$, and sends X, x_1 to U_B.

Phase 2: User U_B chooses ephemeral randomness $r_B \leftarrow \mathbb{Z}_{\ell_2^{e_2}}$, computes $m_1 \| m_0 \leftarrow g(r_B, \mathfrak{b}_2)$, $\mathfrak{y} \leftarrow G(m_1, m_0)$, and $Y := \mathfrak{g}^{\mathfrak{y}}$. On receiving (X, x_1, X_0) from U_A, if $X := pk_{B_2}$, aborts, else U_B computes $y_1 := h(g^{\mathfrak{a}_1}, (\mathfrak{g}^{\mathfrak{a}_1})^{\mathfrak{y}}) \oplus m_1$, $y_0 := h(X, (\mathfrak{g}^{\mathfrak{x}})^{\mathfrak{y}}) \oplus m_0$, $K_B := H(X, m_1, m_0, Y, y_1, y_0)$, and sends (Y, y_1, y_0) to U_A.

Phase 3: On receiving (Y, y_1, y_0) from U_B, if $Y := pk_{A_1}$, aborts, else U_A decrypts Y, y_1, y_0 to extract $m_1' \| m_0'$ and $\mathfrak{y}' \leftarrow G(m_1', m_0')$. If $Y \neq \mathfrak{g}^{\mathfrak{y}'}$, then $m_1' \| m_0' := s_{A1}$. U_A computes $K_B' := H(X, m_1', m_0', Y, y_1, y_0)$ and the session key as $SK := \hat{H}(sid, K_A, K_B')$, where sid is $(U_A, U_B, pk_{A_1}, pk_{B_2}, X, x_1, x_0, Y, y_1, y_0)$.

Phase 4: If $X := pk_{B_2}$, then aborts, else U_B decrypts X, x_1, x_0 to extract n_1', n_0' and $\mathfrak{x}' \leftarrow G(n_1', n_0')$. If $X \neq \mathfrak{g}^{\mathfrak{x}'}$, then $n_1' \| n_0' := s_{B2}$. Let $K_A' := H(Y, n_1', n_0', X, x_1, x_0)$. The session key is computed as $SK := \hat{H}(sid, K_A', K_B)$ where sid is $(U_A, U_B, pk_{A_1}, pk_{B_2}, X, x_1, Y, y_1, y_0, x_0)$.

The session state of U_A consists of r_A, K_B' and K_A. The session state of U_B consists of r_B, K_B and K_A'.

Theorem 5. *Under the 1-Oracle SI-DH assumption, SIAKE_3 is CK^+ secure in the random oracle model. Precisely, if the number of users is N and there are at most l sessions between any two users, for any PPT adversary $\mathcal{A}$ against SIAKE_3 with q times of hash oracle queries, there exists $\mathcal{B}$ s.t.*

$$Adv_{\mathsf{SIAKE}_3}^{CK^+}(\mathcal{A}) \leq 1/2 + N^2 \cdot l \cdot q \cdot \left(4Adv_{\mathcal{B}}^{1osidh} + \frac{q+1}{2^n} + negl \right).$$

Please refer full paper [33] for the concrete proof. We only give the proof sketch here: Obviously, U_A sends $[OW\text{-}CCA, OW\text{-}CPA]$ secure X, x_1, x_0 under public keys pk_{B_2} and Y to U_B. U_B responds with $[OW\text{-}CCA, OW\text{-}CPA]$ secure ciphertexts Y, y_1, y_0 under public keys pk_{A_1} and X_0 to U_A. The proof of wPFS security is

U_A	U_B
$sk_{A_1} := (\mathfrak{a}_1 \in \mathbb{Z}_{\ell_1^{e_1}}, s_{A1} \leftarrow \{0,1\}^{2n})$	$sk_{B_2} := (\mathfrak{b}_2 \in \mathbb{Z}_{\ell_2^{e_2}}, s_{B2} \leftarrow \{0,1\}^{2n})$
$pk_{A_1} := \mathfrak{g}^{\mathfrak{a}_1}$	$pk_{B_2} := \mathfrak{g}^{\mathfrak{b}_2}$
$sk_{A_2} := (\mathfrak{a}_2 \in \mathbb{Z}_{\ell_2^{e_2}}, s_{A2} \leftarrow \{0,1\}^{2n})$	$sk_{B_1} := (\mathfrak{b}_1 \in \mathbb{Z}_{\ell_1^{e_1}}, s_{B1} \leftarrow \{0,1\}^{2n})$
$pk_{A_2} := \mathfrak{g}^{\mathfrak{a}_2}$	$pk_{B_1} := \mathfrak{g}^{\mathfrak{b}_1}$

$$r_A \leftarrow \mathbb{Z}_{\ell_1^{e_1}}, \; n_1\|n_0 \leftarrow g(r_A, \mathfrak{a}_1) \qquad r_B \leftarrow \mathbb{Z}_{\ell_2^{e_2}}, \; m_1\|m_0 \leftarrow g(r_B, \mathfrak{b}_2)$$

$$\mathfrak{x} \leftarrow G(n_1, n_0) \qquad\qquad \mathfrak{y} \leftarrow G(m_1, m_0)$$

$$X := \mathfrak{g}^{\mathfrak{x}}, \; x_1 := h(\mathfrak{g}^{\mathfrak{b}_2}, (\mathfrak{g}^{\mathfrak{b}_2})^{\mathfrak{x}}) \oplus n_1 \quad \xrightarrow{\;X,\,x_1\;} \quad Y := \mathfrak{g}^{\mathfrak{y}}, \; y_1 := h(\mathfrak{g}^{\mathfrak{a}_1}, (\mathfrak{g}^{\mathfrak{a}_1})^{\mathfrak{y}}) \oplus m_1$$

$$\boxed{\text{If } X := pk_{A_1}, \bot}$$

$$\boxed{\text{If } Y := pk_{B_2}, \bot} \quad \xleftarrow{\;Y,\,y_1,\,y_0\;} \quad y_0 := h(X, (\mathfrak{g}^{\mathfrak{x}})^{\mathfrak{y}}) \oplus m_0$$

$$\boxed{x_0 := h(Y, (\mathfrak{g}^{\mathfrak{y}})^{\mathfrak{x}}) \oplus n_0} \qquad K_B := H(X, m_1, m_0, Y, y_1, y_0)$$

$$K_A := H(Y, n_1, n_0, X, x_1, x_0) \quad \boxed{x_0} \quad \longrightarrow$$

$$m_1' := y_1 \oplus h((\mathfrak{g}^{\mathfrak{y}})^{\mathfrak{a}_1}) \qquad n_1' := x_1 \oplus h((\mathfrak{g}^{\mathfrak{x}})^{\mathfrak{b}_2}$$

$$m_0' := y_0 \oplus h(X, (\mathfrak{g}^{\mathfrak{y}})^{\mathfrak{x}}) \qquad n_0' := x_0 \oplus h(X, (\mathfrak{g}^{\mathfrak{x}})^{\mathfrak{y}})$$

$$\mathfrak{y}' := G(m_1', m_0') \qquad\qquad \mathfrak{r}' :\leftarrow G(n_1', n_0')$$

$$\text{If } Y \neq \mathfrak{g}^{\mathfrak{y}'}, \; m_1'\|m_0' := s_{A1} \qquad \text{If } X \neq \mathfrak{g}^{\mathfrak{r}'}, \; n_1'\|n_0' := s_{B2}$$

$$K_B' := H(X, m_1', m_2', Y, y_1, y_0) \qquad K_A' := H(Y, n_1', n_0', X, x_1, x_0)$$

$$SK := \hat{H}(sid, K_A, K_B') \qquad\qquad SK := \hat{H}(sid, K_A', K_B)$$

Fig. 9. A Compact 3-pass AKE SIAKE_3 based on SIDH. Here sid is $(U_A, U_B, pk_{A_1}, pk_{B_2}, X, x_1, x_0, Y, y_1, y_0)$. The boxed arguments are the main differences with SIAKE_2. Besides, the input of h includes the first part of the public key.

exactly the same as that of SIAKE_2, but different for other security cases. The main observation is the same: since the underlying KEM is [OW-CCA, ·] secure, the simulator could query the strong decapsulation oracle to get the encapsulated key and session key and simulate the SessionKeyReveal and SessionStateReveal. However, this is not sufficient. Take E_3 for example, given Y^*, y_1^*, y_0^* as the challenge ciphertext, the simulator obviously does not know the randomness of Y^*, but in the test session Y^* is the public key of (X, x_1, x_0). Fortunately, the underlying 1-Oracle SI-DH assumption provides this capability to encapsulate one ciphertext.

6   Implementation and Comparison

We implement SIAKE_2 and SIAKE_3, and compare their performance with [13], [2,26] and the lattice-based Kyber-AKE [3].

We adopt the curve SIKEp751 in SIKE [20] that is proceeding the second round of NIST's post-quantum standardization. The performance is benchmarked on an Intel(R) Core i7-6567U CPU @3.30 GHz processor supporting the

Skylake micro-architecture. Kyer-AKE is an AKE based on lattice and others are all considered in the SIDH setting. The comparison of bandwidth is shown in Table 4. The comparison of efficiency is shown in Table 5.

Table 4. Comparison of message sizes. "-" stands for no messages to be transmitted. The message sizes are counted in byte.

Scheme	$A \to B$	$B \to A$	$A \to B$	total(byte)
Kyber-AKE [3]	2272	2368		4640
FSXY [13]	1160	1160	–	2320
BCNP [2,26]	1160	1160	–	2320
SIAKE₂	1160	628	–	1788
SIAKE₃	596	628	32	1176

Table 5. Comparison of cycle counts. Cycle counts are rounded to 10^6 cycles by taking the average of 1,000 trials.

Scheme	A(initial)	B	A(end)	B(end)	total
FSXY [13]	6,238	14,779	10,124		31,141
BCNP-Lon [2]	11,146	20,092	9,563		40,801
SIAKE₂	6,828	13,917	6,641		27,386
SIAKE₃	5,966	4,429	4,922	9,575	24,892

7 Conclusion and Open Problem

We propose two AKEs based on supersingular isogeny assumptions. Both of them achieve CK$^+$ security and support arbitrary registration in the classical random oracle model. However, to fully explain their quantum-resistance, their security in the quantum random oracle model should be analyzed. We leave it as an open problem and future work.

Acknowledgements. Haiyang Xue is supported by the National Natural Science Foundation of China (No. 61602473, No. 61672019), and the National Cryptography Development Fund MMJJ20170116. Xiu Xu is supported by the National Natural Science Foundation of China (No.61872442). Man Ho Au is supported by the Research Grant Council of Hong Kong (Grant No. 25206317). Song Tian is supported by the National Natural Science Foundation of China (No. 61802401).

References

1. Abdalla, M., Bellare, M., Rogaway, P.: The oracle Diffie-Hellman assumptions and an analysis of DHIES. In: Naccache, D. (ed.) CT-RSA 2001. LNCS, vol. 2020, pp. 143–158. Springer, Heidelberg (2001). https://doi.org/10.1007/3-540-45353-9_12
2. Boyd, C., Cliff, Y., Gonzalez Nieto, J., Paterson, K.G.: Efficient one-round key exchange in the standard model. In: Mu, Y., Susilo, W., Seberry, J. (eds.) ACISP 2008. LNCS, vol. 5107, pp. 69–83. Springer, Heidelberg (2008). https://doi.org/10.1007/978-3-540-70500-0_6
3. Bos, J., et al.: CRYSTALS - Kyber: a CCA-secure module-lattice-based KEM. In: 2018 IEEE Symposium on Security and Privacy, pp. 353–367 (2018)
4. Bellare, M., Rogaway, P.: Entity authentication and key distribution. In: Stinson, D.R. (ed.) CRYPTO 1993. LNCS, vol. 773, pp. 232–249. Springer, Heidelberg (1994). https://doi.org/10.1007/3-540-48329-2_21
5. Costello, C., Jao, D., Longa, P., Naehrig, M., Renes, J., Urbanik, D.: Efficient compression of SIDH public keys. In: Coron, J.-S., Nielsen, J.B. (eds.) EUROCRYPT 2017. LNCS, vol. 10210, pp. 679–706. Springer, Cham (2017). https://doi.org/10.1007/978-3-319-56620-7_24
6. Canetti, R., Krawczyk, H.: Analysis of key-exchange protocols and their use for building secure channels. In: Pfitzmann, B. (ed.) EUROCRYPT 2001. LNCS, vol. 2045, pp. 453–474. Springer, Heidelberg (2001). https://doi.org/10.1007/3-540-44987-6_28
7. Costello, C., Longa, P., Naehrig, M.: Efficient algorithms for supersingular isogeny Diffie-Hellman. In: Robshaw, M., Katz, J. (eds.) CRYPTO 2016. LNCS, vol. 9814, pp. 572–601. Springer, Heidelberg (2016). https://doi.org/10.1007/978-3-662-53018-4_21
8. De Feo, L., Jao, D., Plût, J.: Towards quantum-resistant cryptosystems from supersingular elliptic curve isogenies. J. Math. Cryptology 8(3), 209–247 (2014)
9. Eisenträger, K., Hallgren, S., Lauter, K., Morrison, T., Petit, C.: Supersingular isogeny graphs and endomorphism rings: reductions and solutions. In: Nielsen, J.B., Rijmen, V. (eds.) EUROCRYPT 2018. LNCS, vol. 10822, pp. 329–368. Springer, Cham (2018). https://doi.org/10.1007/978-3-319-78372-7_11
10. Faz-Hernádnez, A., López, J., Ochoa-Jimenez, E., Rodríguez-Henríquez, F.: A faster software implementation of the supersingular isogeny Diffie-Hellman key exchange protocol. IEEE Trans. Comput. 67(11), 1622–1636 (2018)
11. Fujisaki, E., Okamoto, T.: Secure integration of asymmetric and symmetric encryption schemes. In: Wiener, M. (ed.) CRYPTO 1999. LNCS, vol. 1666, pp. 537–554. Springer, Heidelberg (1999). https://doi.org/10.1007/3-540-48405-1_34
12. Fujioka, A., Suzuki, K., Xagawa, K., Yoneyama, K.: Strongly secure authenticated key exchange from factoring, codes, and lattices. In: Fischlin, M., Buchmann, J., Manulis, M. (eds.) PKC 2012. LNCS, vol. 7293, pp. 467–484. Springer, Heidelberg (2012). https://doi.org/10.1007/978-3-642-30057-8_28
13. Fujioka, A., Suzuki, K., Xagawa, K., Yoneyama, K.: Practical and post-quantum authenticated key exchange from one-way secure key encapsulation mechanism. In: AsiaCCS 2013, pp. 83–94 (2013)
14. Fujioka, A., Takashima, K., Terada, S., Yoneyama, K.: Supersingular isogeny Diffie–Hellman authenticated key exchange. In: Lee, K. (ed.) ICISC 2018. LNCS, vol. 11396, pp. 177–195. Springer, Cham (2019). https://doi.org/10.1007/978-3-030-12146-4_12

15. Galbraith, S.D.: Authenticated key exchange for SIDH. IACR Cryptology ePrint Archive 2018/266
16. Galbraith, S.D., Petit, C., Silva, J.: Identification protocols and signature schemes based on supersingular isogeny problems. In: Takagi, T., Peyrin, T. (eds.) ASIACRYPT 2017. LNCS, vol. 10624, pp. 3–33. Springer, Cham (2017). https://doi.org/10.1007/978-3-319-70694-8_1
17. Galbraith, S.D., Petit, C., Shani, B., Ti, Y.B.: On the security of supersingular isogeny cryptosystems. In: Cheon, J.H., Takagi, T. (eds.) ASIACRYPT 2016. LNCS, vol. 10031, pp. 63–91. Springer, Heidelberg (2016). https://doi.org/10.1007/978-3-662-53887-6_3
18. Guilhem, C.D.S., Smart, N.P., Warinschi, B.: Generic forward-secure key agreement without signatures. In: Nguyen, P., Zhou, J. (eds.) ISC 2017. LNCS, vol. 10599, pp. 114–133. Springer, Cham (2017). https://doi.org/10.1007/978-3-319-69659-1_7
19. Galbraith, S.D., Vercauteren, F.: Computational problems in supersingular elliptic curve isogenies. IACR Cryptology ePrint Archive 2017/774
20. Jao, D., Azarderakhsh, R., Campagna, M., et al.: Supersingular Isogeny Key Encapsulation. https://csrc.nist.gov/Projects/Post-Quantum-Cryptography/Round-1-Submissions
21. Jeong, I.R., Katz, J., Lee, D.H.: One-round protocols for two-party authenticated key exchange. In: Jakobsson, M., Yung, M., Zhou, J. (eds.) ACNS 2004. LNCS, vol. 3089, pp. 220–232. Springer, Heidelberg (2004). https://doi.org/10.1007/978-3-540-24852-1_16
22. Krawczyk, H.: HMQV: a high-performance secure Diffie-Hellman protocol. In: Shoup, V. (ed.) CRYPTO 2005. LNCS, vol. 3621, pp. 546–566. Springer, Heidelberg (2005). https://doi.org/10.1007/11535218_33
23. Koziel, B., Azarderakhsh, R., Mozaffari-Kermani, M.: A high-performance and scalable hardware architecture for isogeny-based cryptography. IEEE Trans. Comput. **67**, 1594–1609 (2018)
24. Kirkwood, D., Lackey, B.C., McVey, J., Motley, M., Solinas, J.A., Tuller, D.: Failure is not an option: standardization issues for post-quantum key agreement. In: Workshop on Cybersecurity in a Post-Quantum World (2015)
25. LeGrow, J.: Post-quantum security of authenticated key establishment protocols. Master's thesis, University of Waterloo (2016)
26. Longa, P.: A note on post-quantum authenticated key exchange from supersingular isogenies. IACR Cryptology ePrint Archive 2018/267
27. LaMacchia, B., Lauter, K., Mityagin, A.: Stronger security of authenticated key exchange. In: Susilo, W., Liu, J.K., Mu, Y. (eds.) ProvSec 2007. LNCS, vol. 4784, pp. 1–16. Springer, Heidelberg (2007). https://doi.org/10.1007/978-3-540-75670-5_1
28. Menezes, A., Qu, M., Vanstone, S.: Some new key agreement protocols providing mutual implicit authentication. In: Selected Areas in Cryptography (1995)
29. Matsumoto, T., Takashima, Y., Imai, H.: On seeking smart public-key-distribution systems. IEICE Trans. (1976–1990) **69**(2), 99–106 (1986)
30. Okamoto, T.: Authenticated key exchange and key encapsulation in the standard model. In: Kurosawa, K. (ed.) ASIACRYPT 2007. LNCS, vol. 4833, pp. 474–484. Springer, Heidelberg (2007). https://doi.org/10.1007/978-3-540-76900-2_29
31. Sun, X., Tian, H., Wang, Y.: Toward quantum-resistant strong designated verifier signature from isogenies. In: INCoS 2012, pp. 292–296 (2012)
32. Urbanik, D., Jao, D.: SoK: the problem landscape of SIDH. IACR Cryptology ePrint Archive 2018/336

33. Xu, X., Xue, H., Wang, K., Liang, B., Au, H., Tian, S.: Strongly secure authenticated key exchange from supersingular isogenies, IACR Cryptology ePrint Archive 2018/760
34. Xue, H., Lu, X., Li, B., Liang, B., He, J.: Understanding and constructing AKE via double-key key encapsulation mechanism. In: Peyrin, T., Galbraith, S. (eds.) ASIACRYPT 2018. LNCS, vol. 11273, pp. 158–189. Springer, Cham (2018). https:// doi.org/10.1007/978-3-030-03329-3_6
35. Yoo, Y., Azarderakhsh, R., Jalali, A., Jao, D., Soukharev, V.: A post-quantum digital signature scheme based on supersingular isogenies. In: Kiayias, A. (ed.) FC 2017. LNCS, vol. 10322, pp. 163–181. Springer, Cham (2017). https://doi.org/10.1007/978-3-319-70972-7_9

Obfuscation

Dual-Mode NIZKs from Obfuscation

Dennis Hofheinz[✉] and Bogdan Ursu

Karlsruhe Institute of Technology, Karlsruhe, Germany
{dennis.hofheinz,bogdan.ursu}@kit.edu

Abstract. Two standard security properties of a non-interactive zero-knowledge (NIZK) scheme are soundness and zero-knowledge. But while standard NIZK systems can only provide one of those properties against unbounded adversaries, *dual-mode NIZK systems* allow to choose dynamically and adaptively which of these properties holds unconditionally. The only known dual-mode NIZK schemes are Groth-Sahai proofs (which have proved extremely useful in a variety of applications), and the FHE-based NIZK constructions of Canetti et al. and Peikert et al, which are concurrent and independent to this work. However, all these constructions rely on specific algebraic settings.

Here, we provide a generic construction of dual-mode NIZK systems for all of NP. The public parameters of our scheme can be set up in one of two indistinguishable ways. One way provides unconditional soundness, while the other provides unconditional zero-knowledge. Our scheme relies on subexponentially secure indistinguishability obfuscation and subexponentially secure one-way functions, but otherwise only on comparatively mild and generic computational assumptions. These generic assumptions can be instantiated under any one of the DDH, k-LIN, DCR, or QR assumptions.

As an application, we reduce the required assumptions necessary for several recent obfuscation-based constructions of multilinear maps. Combined with previous work, our scheme can be used to construct multilinear maps from obfuscation and a group in which the strong Diffie-Hellman assumption holds. We also believe that our work adds to the understanding of the construction of NIZK systems, as it provides a conceptually new way to achieve dual-mode properties.

Keywords: Non-interactive zero-knowledge · Dual-mode proof systems · Indistinguishability obfuscation

1 Introduction

Obfuscation and Structured Assumptions. Indistinguishability obfuscation (iO) is a powerful cryptographic object, and along with one-way functions, it implies almost every cryptographic primitive, from deniable encryption [42] to functional encryption [26] and fully-homomorphic encryption [18]. However, it is not currently known whether iO gives rise to structures in which algebraic assumptions hold (such as DDH, DCR, LWE etc.). In this work, we are motivated by the following open problem:

© International Association for Cryptologic Research 2019
S. D. Galbraith and S. Moriai (Eds.): ASIACRYPT 2019, LNCS 11921, pp. 311–341, 2019.
https://doi.org/10.1007/978-3-030-34578-5_12

Can structured objects (such as DDH groups) be bootstrapped from unstructured objects (like generic one-way functions and iO)?

We make progress in this direction by developing the first construction of dual-mode non-interactive zero-knowledge (NIZK) proof systems from unstructured assumptions (iO, one-way functions and lossy trapdoor functions). This dual-mode NIZK can be used in the constructions from [1,2,21], allowing us to answer this question in the affirmative.

Zero-Knowledge Proof Systems. Zero-knowledge (ZK) proof systems [28,29] are (implicitly or explicitly) at the heart of countless cryptographic constructions. In a ZK proof system, a prover P tries to convince a verifier V of the validity of a statement x. "Validity" usually means that $x \in L$ for some language $L \in$ NP. In this case, P obtains a witness w to $x \in L$. For security, we require *soundness*, which means that no dishonest prover can convince V of a false statement $x \notin L$. Additionally, we may want to protect P (and in particular the used witness w) in several ways. For instance, the protocol is *zero-knowledge* if it is possible to efficiently simulate (transcripts of) protocol runs even without w. Alternatively, we can require the protocol to be *witness-hiding* or *witness-indistinguishable* [23].

ZK proof systems can be interactive or non-interactive (the latter of which means that the prover sends only one message to the verifier). In this work, we are interested in non-interactive ZK (NIZK) proof systems [10]. There exist already various NIZK proof systems, ranging from generic [22,24,42] to highly efficient constructions based on concrete number-theoretic assumptions [24,32,44]. Some of these systems only allow to prove $x \in L$ for specific languages L, while others can be used to prove statements from arbitrary languages $L \in$ NP.

Dual-Mode Proof Systems. Some NIZK systems enjoy statistical security, i.e., information-theoretic soundness or zero-knowledge guarantees. However, interestingly, no NIZK system can be statistically sound *and* statistically zero-knowledge simultaneously. Hence, a NIZK system can be secure only *either* against unbounded malicious provers *or* against unbounded malicious verifiers.

Fortunately, there is a compromise that combines the best of both worlds: Groth-Sahai proofs [32] are statistically sound or statistically zero-knowledge depending on the choice of public parameters crs. Furthermore, both choices of parameters are computationally indistinguishable. This "dual-mode" property leads to comparatively simple proofs for complex protocols (e.g., for anonymous credentials [4] or payment systems [33]). In the case of [2,21], a proof without using dual-mode properties in fact does not seem obvious at all.[1]

---

[1] A bit more technically, dual-mode NIZK proofs allow to use both witness extraction or simulation trapdoors in different stages of the proof, depending on the chosen mode. (This is helpful in case of [4,33] and crucial in [2,21].) Furthermore, in complex settings with mutually dependent statements and witnesses, statistical properties are easier seen to compose.

Until recently, only Groth-Sahai proofs [32] (and their variants, e.g., [9, 20, 35]) were known to possess this dual-mode property.[2] These proof systems all rely on a very specific and structured algebraic setting (pairing-friendly cyclic groups). In contrast, we rely on generic rather than algebraic techniques, resulting in a fundamentally new way of obtaining dual-mode proof systems.

Concurrent Work. Concurrently and independently to this work, [19, 39] have put forward breakthrough approaches to obtain dual-mode NIZKs from the LWE assumption. These constructions rely on rich algebraic structures and are non-blackbox. In contrast, our techniques are generic and our perspective is closer to computational complexity, in that we investigate whether the existence of a powerful non-algebraic object (iO) can lead to algebraic ones.

Our Contribution. In this paper, we give the first generic construction of dual-mode NIZK proofs from (the combination of) the following ingredients:

- subexponentially secure indistinguishability obfuscation (iO, [3, 26]),
- subexponentially secure one-way functions,
- a (selectively) subexponentially secure functional encryption scheme,
- lossy encryption [5, 40], and
- lossy functions (LFs), a relaxation of lossy trapdoor functions [41] which we introduce in this paper.

We stress that some of our ingredients are implied by (a combination of) others: Functional encryption can be constructed from iO and one-way functions [26]. Conversely, subexponentially secure functional encryption implies subexponentially secure iO and one-way functions (e.g., [8] and the references therein). Furthermore, both LFs and lossy encryption are implied by lossy trapdoor functions [41].

As a side note, we remark that thus, a subexponential variant of any of the DDH, k-LIN, QR, DCR, or LWE assumptions, along with subexponential iO implies all of our ingredients.[3]

Of course, since we assume iO, our construction is far from practical. Still, it has interesting theoretical applications. For instance, it allows to instantiate dual-mode NIZK proofs in the recent works [1, 2, 21] without any additional assumptions, and in particular without pairing-friendly groups. (Incidentally, these works already assume what we need for our construction.)

In particular, combining our results with the scheme from [1], shows that it is possible to obtain a very structured object (namely, a cyclic group in which Diffie-Hellman and similar assumptions hold) solely from an unstructured and generic object (iO), and a mildly structured object (a lossy trapdoor function).[4]

---

[2] We do not consider NIZK proofs in the random oracle model (such as [37]) here.

[3] See [11, 25, 41] for the corresponding instantiations of lossy trapdoor functions from these concrete assumptions.

[4] Indeed, except for a dual-mode NIZK proof system, all assumptions in [1] can be instantiated from subexponentially secure iO and a subexponentially secure lossy trapdoor function. We note, however, that [1] construct a group in which elements have only a non-unique representation and no canonical form. Hence, their group might not be considered a "standard group", but still has a rich algebraic structure.

Similarly, implementing [2,21] with our system (instead of with Groth-Sahai proofs) yields a pairing-friendly group (with non-unique representation) from iO and a DDH group (both subexponentially secure). Therefore, we also give an answer to the following open problem (Fig. 1):

Can bilinear groups be bootstrapped from DDH groups and iO?

Previous work	This work + [1,2,21]
[2] iO + Pairings + SDDH ⇒ Multilinear Maps	iO + SDDH ⇒ Multilinear Maps
[21] iO + Pairings + SDDH ⇒ Graded Encoding Schemes	iO + SDDH ⇒ Graded Encoding Schemes
[1] iO + Pairings ⇒ Interactively Secure Groups	iO + LTDF ⇒ Interactively Secure Groups

Fig. 1. Some implications on previous results. "iO", "LTDF" and "SDDH" denote subexponential versions of indistinguishability obfuscation, lossy trapdoor functions and the "Strong DDH" (a q-type variant of the Diffie-Hellman assumption).

Open Problems. We note that the groups from [1,2,21] all enjoy non-unique representations of group elements. That is, equality of group elements can be tested, but there does not exist a canonical form. Removing this limitation remains an open problem.

Our Techniques

Existing Generic Approaches. Before explaining our main ideas, we first mention that generic constructions of NIZKs from iO already exist. Namely, [42] present a NIZK construction that only assumes iO and one-way functions. Their construction is (even perfectly) zero-knowledge. However, proofs are in their case simply signatures of the corresponding statement x. Thus, their construction is inherently limited to computational soundness, in the sense that it is not clear how to tweak this construction to obtain statistical soundness.

Secondly, it is possible to construct a notion of trapdoor permutations from iO that is in turn sufficient to construct statistically sound NIZK proofs [17] (cf. [6,7,22,30]). However, it is not clear how to tweak this NIZK construction to obtain statistical zero-knowledge.

The Hidden Bits Model. Similarly to [17], our starting point is also the generic NIZK construction from [22]. This work presents a statistically sound and perfectly zero-knowledge NIZK protocol in an ideal model of computation called the "hidden bits model" (HBM).[5] It will be helpful to first recall the HBM

---

[5] Since their protocol is formulated in an ideal model of computation, it does not contradict our remark above about the impossibility of simultaneously achieving statistical soundness and statistical zero-knowledge. One of the two statistical properties will be lost when implementing this ideal model.

before going further. In a nutshell, the HBM gives the prover P access to an ideal random bitstring $\mathsf{hrs} = (\mathsf{hrs}_1, \ldots, \mathsf{hrs}_t) \in \{0,1\}^t$. Next, P selects a subset $\mathcal{I} \subseteq [t]$ and a proof π. Then, the verifier V is activated with $\mathcal{I}, \pi$, the subset $(\mathsf{hrs}_i)_{i \in \mathcal{I}}$ of hrs that is selected by $\mathcal{I}$, and of course the instance x. Finally, V is supposed to output a verdict $b \in \{0,1\}$.

Two Ways to Implement the HBM. Note that the power of the HBM stems from the fact that hrs is ideally random (and cannot be tampered with by P), but only revealed in part to V. When implementing the HBM, we will necessarily have to compromise on some of these properties. However, it will be interesting to see what the consequences of such compromises are. Specifically, when implementing the HBM in the HBM-based NIZK protocol of [22], we can observe the following:

(a) if we implement the HBM such that hrs is truly random (or selected from a small set of possible hrs values, each of which is individually truly random), then the resulting NIZK protocol is statistically sound and computationally zero-knowledge,

(b) if we implement the HBM such that the unopened bits $(\mathsf{hrs}_i)_{i \notin \mathcal{I}}$ are statistically hidden from V, then the resulting NIZK protocol is statistically zero-knowledge and computationally sound.

Known implementations of the HBM (e.g., [22,30,31]) follow (a), and thus enjoy statistical soundness guarantees. Our main strategy will be to build a dual-mode NIZK proof system by implementing the HBM in a way that allows to switch (by switching public parameters) between (a) and (b).

A First Approach. Our first step will be to set up the hidden string hrs as

$$\mathsf{hrs} = \mathsf{H}(X) \oplus \mathsf{crs}$$

for a value X chosen freely by P, a yet-to-be-defined function H, and a truly random "randomizing string" crs fixed in the public parameters. If H is a pseudorandom generator (that admits a suitable partial opening process, see [31] for an explicit formulation), this yields the core of existing HBM implementations. In particular, if H has a small image, then we are in case (a) above, and the resulting NIZK is statistically sound.

However, suppose we can switch (in a computationally indistinguishable way) $\mathsf{H}(X)$ to have a large image, such that in fact $\mathsf{H}(X) \in \{0,1\}^t$ is close to uniformly distributed for random X. We call such a "switchable" object a lossy function (LF). An LF can be easily constructed, e.g., by universally hashing the output of a lossy trapdoor function F. For suitable choices of parameters, $\mathsf{H}(X) := h(F(X))$ is close to uniform if F is injective (and X random), and has a small range if F does.

With $\mathsf{H}(X)$ close to uniform, we are in case (b) above, assuming that the process itself of revealing $\mathsf{hrs}_\mathcal{I}$ does not reveal additional information about other bit positions. Hence, we obtain a statistically zero-knowledge NIZK protocol, and in summary even a dual-mode NIZK that can be switched between statistically sound and statistically zero-knowledge modes of operation.

Managing the Opening Process. The main problem with our first approach is that it is not clear how to *partially* open a subset $\mathsf{hrs}_{\mathcal{I}}$ of hrs to a verifier V. Previous HBM implementations (e.g., [22,31]) devised elaborate ways to partially open suitably designed pseudorandom generators (in the role of H above). We cannot use those techniques for two reasons. First, their opening process might reveal statistical information about the unopened parts of hrs. Second, these techniques require specific H functions, and do not appear to work with "switchable" functions H as we need. Hence, we use the strong ingredients mentioned above to design our own opening process.

We will use a functional encryption scheme FE. We will publicize a truly random crs, a statement Z from a language L' that is hard to decide, along with an FE public key fmpk, and a corresponding secret key sk_f for the following function f:

$$\mathsf{f}(X, \mathcal{I}, z, T) := \begin{cases} (T, \mathcal{I}) & \text{if } z \text{ is a witness to} Z \in L' \\ (\mathsf{H}(X)_{\mathcal{I}}, \mathcal{I}) & \text{else.} \end{cases}$$

An opening consists of an encryption

$$C = \mathsf{FE.Enc}(\mathsf{fmpk}, (X, \mathcal{I}, 0, 0))$$

that will decrypt to $\mathsf{f}(X, \mathcal{I}, 0, 0) = \mathsf{H}(X)_{\mathcal{I}}$ under sk_f. The verifier will receive this opening, retrieve $\mathsf{H}(X)_{\mathcal{I}}$ with sk_f, and compute $\mathsf{hrs}_{\mathcal{I}} = \mathsf{H}(X)_{\mathcal{I}} \oplus \mathsf{crs}_{\mathcal{I}}$.

Observe that this process has the following properties:

- If $Z \notin L'$, then $\mathsf{sk}_f(C) = (\mathsf{H}(X)_{\mathcal{I}}, \mathcal{I})$ always. Hence, if additionally H has a small range, we are in case (a) above, and the corresponding NIZK protocol is statistically sound.
- If $Z \in L'$ with witness z, then any prover who knows z can efficiently open $\mathsf{hrs}_{\mathcal{I}}$ arbitrarily, by encrypting $(0, \mathcal{I}, z, T)$ for $T = \mathsf{crs}_{\mathcal{I}} \oplus \mathsf{hrs}_{\mathcal{I}}$ and the desired $\mathsf{hrs}_{\mathcal{I}}$. Furthermore, such openings obviously do not contain any information about potential other positions of hrs. This means we are in case (b) above, and the corresponding NIZK protocol is statistically zero-knowledge.

By using FE's security, it is possible to show that these two types of openings are indistinguishable to a verifier. However, as formulated, they are of course not indistinguishable to a prover yet. Hence, we will additionally publicize an obfuscated algorithm PC that will get as input a statement x with witness w, and random coins r. Depending on the mode (sound or zero-knowledge), $\mathsf{PC}(x, w, r)$ will then either encrypt $(X, \mathcal{I}, 0, 0)$ or $(0, \mathcal{I}, z, T)$, for pseudorandom X and T derived from r.

A Taste of the Security Proof. For security, we will show that the public parameters in both modes are computationally indistinguishable. The security proof is somewhat technical, and we would like to highlight only one interesting theme here. Namely, observe that the prover algorithm PC is inherently probabilistic. In the proof, we need to modify PC's behavior, and in particular decouple its output distribution from its input w. Specifically, when aiming at statistical soundness, the output of PC will encrypt, and thus depend on w. But when trying to achieve zero-knowledge, PC's output should not reveal (in a statistical sense) which witness w has been used.[6]

This decoupling process is particularly cumbersome to go through because PC itself is public and can be run on arbitrary inputs. Any change that essentially makes PC ignore its w input will be easily detectable. Hence, we add an indirection that helps to remove dependencies on w. Specifically, we let PC first compute $a = \mathsf{LE.Enc}(\mathsf{lpk}, (x, w); r)$ using a lossy encryption scheme LE. If the corresponding public key lpk is injective (i.e., leads to decryptable ciphertexts), then a determines w. Hence, any case distinction (or hybrid argument) we make for different values of w can alternatively be made for different values of a. On the other hand, if lpk is lossy, then a will be statistically independent of the plaintext (x, w).

Hence, a can be used as a single value that (a) can serve as a "fingerprint" of (or in some sense even as a substitute for) w in the proof, but (b) can be easily made independent of w by switching lpk into lossy mode. Equipped with this gadget, we will structure the proof as a large hybrid argument over all values of a (encrypted at this point with an injective lpk). In each step, we modify PC's behavior for one particular value of (x, w), and change the corresponding FE ciphertext C from an encryption of $(X, \mathcal{I}, 0, 0)$ to $(0, \mathcal{I}, z, T)$ for a pseudorandom value T derived from a.

Roadmap. After recalling some preliminaries in Sect. 2, we present our proof system in Sect. 3, followed by its analysis in Sect. 4. In the full version, we provide a schematic overview over our main proof, a proof of a technical lemma, a recap of the HBM-based NIZK from [22], and an analysis of the (statistical) extractability of our scheme.

2   Preliminaries

Notation. Throughout this paper, λ denotes the security parameter. For a natural number $n \in \mathbb{N}$, $[n]$ denotes the set $\{1, \ldots, n\}$. A probabilistic polynomial time algorithm (PPT, also denoted *efficient* algorithm) runs in time polynomial in the (implicit) security parameter λ. A positive function f is *negligible* if for any polynomial p there exists a bound $B > 0$ such that, for any integer $k \geq B$, $f(k) \leq 1/|p(k)|$. An event depending on λ occurs with *overwhelming probability* when its probability is at least $1 - \mathsf{negl}(\lambda)$ for a negligible function negl. Given a finite set S, the notation $x \leftarrow_\mathrm{R} S$ means a uniformly random assignment of an element of S to the variable x. If A is a probabilistic algorithm, $y \leftarrow_\mathrm{R} A(\cdot)$ denotes the process of running A on some appropriate input and assigning its output to y. The notation $\mathcal{A}^{\mathcal{O}}$ indicates that the algorithm $\mathcal{A}$ is given oracle access to $\mathcal{O}$. We denote $a \leftarrow A; b \leftarrow B(a); \ldots$ for running the experiment where a is chosen from A, after which b is chosen from B, which might depend on a and so on. This determines a probability distribution over the outputs and we

---

[6] Formally, to achieve zero-knowledge, we must achieve witness-indistinguishability.

write $\Pr[a \leftarrow A; b \leftarrow B(a); \ldots : C(a, b, \ldots)]$ for the probability of the condition $C(a, b, \ldots)$ being satisfied after running the experiment. For two distributions D_1, D_2, we denote by $\Delta(D_1, D_2)$ the statistical distance. We also write $D_1 \equiv D_2$ when the distributions are identical, $D_1 \approx_c D_2$ when the distributions are computationally indistinguishable and $D_1 \approx_\epsilon D_2$ when $\Delta(D_1, D_2) \leq \epsilon$.

2.1   Puncturable Pseudorandom Function

A pseudorandom function (PRF) originally introduced in [27], is a tuple of PPT algorithms PRF = (PRF.KeyGen, PRF.Eval). Let $\mathcal{K}$ denote the key space, $\mathcal{X}$ denote the domain, and $\mathcal{Y}$ denote the range. The key generation algorithm PRF.KeyGen on input of 1^λ, outputs a random key from $\mathcal{K}$ and the evaluation algorithm PRF.Eval on input of a key K and $x \in \mathcal{X}$, evaluates the function $F \colon \mathcal{K} \times \mathcal{X} \mapsto \mathcal{Y}$. The core property of PRFs is that, on a random choice of key K, no probabilistic polynomial-time adversary should be able to distinguish $F(K, \cdot)$ from a truly random function, when given black-box access to it. Puncturable PRFs (pPRFs) have the additional property that some keys can be generated *punctured* at some point, so that they allow to evaluate the PRF at all points except for the punctured point. As observed in [13,14,36], it is possible to construct such punctured keys for the original construction from [27], which can be based on any one-way functions [34].

Definition 1 (Puncturable Pseudorandom Function [13,14,36]**).** *A puncturable pseudorandom function (pPRF) is with punctured key space $\mathcal{K}_p$ is a triple of PPT algorithms* (PRF.KeyGen, PRF.Puncture, PRF.Eval) *such that:*

- PRF.KeyGen(1^λ) *outputs a random key $K \in \mathcal{K}$,*
- PRF.Puncture(K, x), *on input $K \in \mathcal{K}$, $x \in \mathcal{X}$, outputs a punctured key $K\{x\} \in \mathcal{K}_p$,*
- PRF.Eval(K', x'), *on input a key K' (punctured or not), and a point x', outputs an evaluation of the PRF.*

We require PRF *to meet the following conditions:*

Functionality preserved under puncturing. *For all $\lambda \in \mathbb{N}$, for all $x \in \mathcal{X}$,*

$$\Pr[K \leftarrow_{\mathrm{R}} \mathsf{PRF.KeyGen}(1^\lambda), K\{x\} \leftarrow_{\mathrm{R}} \mathsf{PRF.Puncture}(K, x):$$
$$\forall x' \in \mathcal{X} \setminus \{x\}: \mathsf{PRF.Eval}(K, x') = \mathsf{PRF.Eval}(K\{x\}, x')] = 1.$$

Pseudorandom at punctured points. *For every stateful* PPT *adversary $\mathcal{A}$ and every security parameter $\lambda \in \mathbb{N}$, the advantage of $\mathcal{A}$ in* Exp-s-pPRF *(described in Fig. 2) is negligible, namely:*

$$\mathsf{Adv}_{\mathsf{s\text{-}cPRF}}(\lambda, \mathcal{A}) := \left| \Pr[\mathsf{Exp\text{-}s\text{-}pPRF}(1^\lambda, \mathcal{A}) = 1] - \frac{1}{2} \right| \leq \mathsf{negl}(\lambda).$$

Sub-exponential Security. We say that PRF is sub-exponentially secure when it satisfies Definition 1 and in addition it satisfies: for every PPT adversary $\mathcal{A}$, the advantage $\mathsf{Adv}_{\mathsf{s\text{-}cPRF}}(\lambda, \mathcal{A}) \leq \frac{1}{2^{\lambda^\epsilon}}$, for some positive constant $0 < \epsilon < 1$.

Definition 1 corresponds to a selective security notion for puncturable pseudorandom functions; adaptive security could be considered, but will not be required in our work. For ease of notation we often write $F(\cdot, \cdot)$ instead of $\mathsf{PRF.Eval}(\cdot, \cdot)$.

Experiment $\mathsf{Exp\text{-}s\text{-}pPRF}(1^\lambda, \mathcal{A})$

Experiment $\mathsf{Exp\text{-}s\text{-}pPRF}_{\mathcal{A}}(\lambda)$

$x^* \leftarrow_{\mathrm{R}} \mathcal{A}(1^\lambda)$, $b \leftarrow_{\mathrm{R}} \{0, 1\}$,
$K \leftarrow_{\mathrm{R}} \mathsf{PRF.KeyGen}(1^\lambda)$,
$K\{x^*\} \leftarrow_{\mathrm{R}} \mathsf{PRF.Puncture}(K, x^*)$,
$y_0 \leftarrow \mathsf{PRF.Eval}(K, x^*)$, $y_1 \leftarrow_{\mathrm{R}} \mathcal{Y}$
$b' \leftarrow_{\mathrm{R}} \mathcal{A}(K\{x^*\}, y_b)$
Return $b = b'$

Fig. 2. Experiment $\mathsf{Exp\text{-}s\text{-}pPRF}_{\mathcal{A}}(\lambda)$ for the pseudo-randomness at punctured points.

2.2 Lossy Functions

We generalize the notion of LTDF (lossy trapdoor function) due to [41] and introduce lossy functions. LTDFs (Lossy trapdoor functions) can be sampled in two indistinguishable modes: an injective and a lossy mode. When sampling injective functions, the setup also provides a trapdoor which can be used to invert the function. Unlike LTDFs, for lossy functions we require that functions can be sampled in two modes, but in which one mode is "more lossy" than the other. Thus, instead of an injective and a lossy mode, we have a "less lossy" and a "more lossy" mode, which we denote as "dense" and "lossy" modes. Since we do not necessarily have injectivity in the dense setting, we also do not have trapdoors as in LTDFs.

Definition 2 (Lossy Functions). *A tuple* $\mathsf{LF} = (\mathsf{Setup}, \mathsf{Eval})$ *of* PPT *algorithms is a family of* (n, k, m, i)-*lossy functions if the following properties hold:*

- *Sampling functions: Both* $\mathsf{Setup}(1^\lambda, \mathsf{dense})$ *of dense functions and* $\mathsf{Setup}(1^\lambda, \mathsf{lossy})$ *of lossy functions output a function index* s. *We require that* $\mathsf{Eval}(s, \cdot)$ *is a deterministic function on* $\{0,1\}^n \to \{0,1\}^m$ *in both cases. In the following, we use the shorthand notation* $s(\cdot) := \mathsf{Eval}(s, \cdot)$.
- *Dense functions have images statistically close to uniformly random: for all* $s \leftarrow_{\mathrm{R}} \mathsf{LF}(1^\lambda, \mathsf{dense})$, *we have that:*

$$\Delta((s(U_n), s), (U_m, s)) \leq \frac{1}{2^i}.$$

- *Lossy functions have small image size: The image size of lossy functions is bounded by* 2^k. *In particular, for all* $s \leftarrow_{\mathrm{R}} \mathsf{Setup}(1^\lambda, \mathrm{lossy})$,

$$|\{\mathsf{Eval}(s,x) : x \in \{0,1\}^n\}| \leq 2^k.$$

- *Indistinguishability: The outputs of* $\mathsf{Setup}(1^\lambda, \mathrm{lossy})$ *and* $\mathsf{Setup}(1^\lambda, \mathit{dense})$ *are computationally indistinguishable, i.e.* $\{\mathsf{Setup}(1^\lambda, \mathrm{lossy})\} \approx_{\mathrm{c}} \{\mathsf{Setup}(1^\lambda, \mathit{dense})\}$

We can generalise Definition 2 even further. Instead of asking that in dense mode the evaluation of the function is statistically close to a uniformly random, we may instead define the dense mode as having $H_\infty(\mathsf{Eval}(s, U_n)) \geq m+2\log\left(\frac{1}{\epsilon}\right)$. Then, by the leftover hash lemma, we can combine LF with a 2-universal hash function to ensure that the output is statistically close to uniformly random as in Definition 2. For clarity, we do not use this generalization in our proofs.

Concrete Instantiations: The lossy trapdoor functions from [41] are also lossy functions in the sense of Definition 2. Moreover, composed with 2-universal hash functions, they satisfy the necessary parameters in our construction (see Sect. 3). This would yield suitable lossy functions based on DDH and LWE.

2.3   Lossy Encryption

Definition 3. *[5,40]: A lossy public-key encryption scheme is a tuple* $\mathsf{LE} = (\mathsf{Gen}, \mathsf{Enc}, \mathsf{Dec})$ *of polynomial-time algorithms such that*

- $\mathsf{Gen}(1^\lambda, \mathrm{inj})$ *outputs keys* $(\mathsf{pk}, \mathsf{sk})$, *keys generated by* $\mathsf{Gen}(1^\lambda, \mathrm{inj})$ *are called injective keys.*
- $\mathsf{Gen}(1^\lambda, \mathrm{lossy})$ *outputs keys* $(\mathsf{pk}_{\mathrm{lossy}}, \perp)$, *keys generated by* $\mathsf{Gen}(1^\lambda, \mathrm{lossy})$ *are called lossy keys.*
- $\mathsf{Enc}(\mathsf{pk}, \cdot, \cdot) : M \times R \to C$.

Additionally, the algorithms must satisfy the following properties:

1. *Correctness on injective keys. For all plaintexts* $x \in X$,

$$\Pr[(\mathsf{pk}, \mathsf{sk}) \leftarrow_{\mathrm{R}} \mathsf{Gen}(1^\lambda, \mathrm{inj}); r \leftarrow R : \mathsf{Dec}(\mathsf{sk}, \mathsf{Enc}(\mathsf{pk}, x, r)) = x] = 1.$$

2. *Indistinguishability of keys. Public keys* pk *are computationally indistinguishable in lossy and injective modes. Specifically, if* $\mathrm{proj} : (\mathsf{pk}, \mathsf{sk}) \to \mathsf{pk}$ *is the projection map, then:*

$$\{\mathrm{proj}(\mathsf{Gen}(1^\lambda, \mathrm{inj}))\} \approx_{\mathrm{c}} \{\mathrm{proj}(\mathsf{Gen}(1^\lambda, \mathrm{lossy}))\}.$$

3. *Lossiness of lossy keys. For all* $(\mathsf{pk}_{\mathrm{lossy}}, \perp) \leftarrow_{\mathrm{R}} \mathsf{Gen}(1^\lambda, \mathrm{lossy})$, *and all* $x_0, x_1 \in M$, *the two distributions* $\{r \leftarrow_{\mathrm{R}} R : (\mathsf{pk}_{\mathrm{lossy}}, \mathsf{Enc}(\mathsf{pk}_{\mathrm{lossy}}, x_0, r))\}$ *and* $\{r \leftarrow_{\mathrm{R}} R : (\mathsf{pk}_{\mathrm{lossy}}, \mathsf{Enc}(pk_{\mathrm{lossy}}, x_1, r))\}$ *are statistically close, i.e. the statistical distance is negligible in* λ.

We define a lossy encryption scheme LE *to be* μ-*lossy if for all* $(\mathsf{pk}_{\text{lossy}}, \perp) \leftarrow_R$ $\mathsf{Gen}(1^\lambda, \text{lossy})$ *and for all* x_0, x_1, *we have that:*

$$\{r \leftarrow_R R : (\mathsf{pk}_{\text{lossy}}, \mathsf{Enc}(\mathsf{pk}_{\text{lossy}}, x_0, r))\} \approx_\mu \{r \leftarrow_R R : (\mathsf{pk}_{\text{lossy}}, Enc(pk_{\text{lossy}}, x_1, r))\}$$

2.4 Functional Encryption

Definition 4. *[12,38,43] A functional encryption scheme for a class of functions* $\mathcal{F} = \mathcal{F}(1^\lambda)$ *over message space* $\mathcal{M} = \mathcal{M}_\lambda$ *consists of four polynomial time algorithms* $\mathsf{FE} = (\mathsf{Setup}, \mathsf{KeyGen}, \mathsf{Enc}, \mathsf{Dec})$:

1. $\mathsf{Setup}(1^\lambda)$ – *on input the security parameter* λ *outputs master public key* mpk *and master secret key* msk.
2. $\mathsf{KeyGen}(\mathsf{msk}, f)$ – *on input the master secret key* msk *and a description of function* $f \in \mathcal{F}$ *and outputs a corresponding secret key* sk_f.
3. $\mathsf{Enc}(\mathsf{mpk}, x)$ – *on input the master public key* mpk *and a string* x, *outputs a ciphertext* ct.
4. $\mathsf{Dec}(\mathsf{sk}_f, \mathsf{ct})$ – *on inputs the secret key* sk_f *and a ciphertext encrypting message* $m \in M$, *outputs* $f(m)$.

A functional encryption scheme is perfectly correct for $\mathcal{F}$ *if for all* $f \in \mathcal{F}$ *and all messages* $m \in \mathcal{M}$:

$$\Pr[(\mathsf{mpk}, \mathsf{msk}) \leftarrow_R \mathsf{Setup}(1^\lambda) : \mathsf{Dec}(\mathsf{KeyGen}(\mathsf{msk}, f), \mathsf{Enc}(\mathsf{mpk}, m)) = f(m)] = 1$$

In addition, for the proof of Theorem 14, we need a stronger property from the functional encryption schemes we use in our construction, which we call special correctness of decryption keys. Special correctness requires that decrypting any (potentially maliciously generated) ciphertext under the decryption key sk_f yields a result which lies in the range of the function f. The functional encryption scheme based on iO and one-way functions from [26] satisfies this property.

Definition 5 (Special correctness of decryption keys). *A functional encryption scheme satisfies special correctness if for all* $\lambda \in \mathbb{N}$, *for all* ct, *for all* $f \in \mathcal{F}$, *it holds that:*

$$\Pr\left[\begin{array}{l} (\mathsf{mpk}, \mathsf{msk}) \leftarrow_R \mathsf{Setup}(1^\lambda), \\ \mathsf{sk}_f \leftarrow_R \mathsf{KeyGen}(\mathsf{msk}, f) \end{array} : \mathsf{Dec}(\mathsf{sk}_f, \mathsf{ct}) \in \mathsf{Im}(f) \cup \{\perp\} \right] \geq 1 - \mathsf{negl}(\lambda),$$

where $\mathsf{Im}(f) = \{f(m) : m \in \mathcal{M}\}$ *denotes the image of the function* f.

Definition 6 (Selectively Indistinguishable Security). *A functional encryption scheme* FE *is selectively indistinguishable secure (SEL-IND-FE-CPA) if for all stateful* PPT *adversaries* $\mathcal{A}$, *the advantage of* $\mathcal{A}$ *in the experiment* Exp-s-IND-FE-CPA *described in Fig. 3 is negligible, namely:*

$$\mathsf{Adv}^{\mathsf{FE}}_{\mathsf{Exp}\text{-}s\text{-}\mathsf{IND}\text{-}\mathsf{FE}\text{-}\mathsf{CPA}}(\lambda, \mathcal{A}) := \left| \Pr[\mathsf{Exp}\text{-}s\text{-}\mathsf{IND}\text{-}\mathsf{FE}\text{-}\mathsf{CPA}^{\mathsf{FE}}(1^\lambda, \mathcal{A}) = 1] - \frac{1}{2} \right| \leq \mathsf{negl}(\lambda)$$

$$
\begin{array}{|l|}
\hline
\textbf{Experiment Exp-}s\textbf{-IND-FE-CPA}^{\mathsf{FE}}(1^\lambda, \mathcal{A}) \\
\hline
(m_0, m_1) \leftarrow_{\mathrm{R}} \mathcal{A}(1^\lambda); \\
(\mathsf{mpk}, \mathsf{msk}) \leftarrow_{\mathrm{R}} \mathsf{FE.Setup}(1^\lambda) \\
b \leftarrow_{\mathrm{R}} \{0,1\} \\
\mathsf{ct} \leftarrow_{\mathrm{R}} \mathsf{FE.Enc}(\mathsf{mpk}, m_b) \\
b' \leftarrow_{\mathrm{R}} \mathcal{A}^{\mathsf{FE.KeyGen}(\mathsf{msk},\cdot)}(\mathsf{mpk}, \mathsf{ct}) \\
\text{Return } b = b' \\
\hline
\end{array}
$$

Fig. 3. Experiment Exp-s-IND-FE-CPA for the selective indistinguishable security of FE. The queries of $\mathcal{A}$ to oracle FE.KeyGen(msk, $\cdot$) are restricted to functions f such that $f(m_0) = f(m_1)$.

Definition 7 (Sub-exponential Selectively Indistinguishability Security). *A functional encryption scheme* FE *is sub-exponentially selectively indistinguishability secure if it satisfies Definition 6 and in addition: for all PPT adversaries $\mathcal{A}$:*

$$
\mathsf{Adv}^{\mathsf{FE}}_{\mathsf{Exp}\text{-}s\text{-IND-FE-CPA}}(\lambda, \mathcal{A}) \leq \frac{1}{2^{\lambda^\epsilon}}, \text{ for some positive constant } 0 < \epsilon < 1.
$$

2.5 Indistinguishability Obfuscation

Definition 8 (Indistinguishability Obfuscator[3,26]). *A uniform PPT machine* iO *is called an indistinguishability obfuscator for a circuit class $\mathcal{C}_\lambda$ if the following conditions are satisfied:*

– *For all security parameters $\lambda \in \mathbb{N}$, for all $C \in \mathcal{C}_\lambda$, for all inputs x, we have:*

$$
Pr[C'(x) = C(x) : C' \leftarrow_{\mathrm{R}} \mathsf{iO}(\lambda, C)] = 1
$$

– *For any (not necessarily uniform) PPT distinguisher $\mathcal{A}$, for all security parameters $\lambda \in \mathbb{N}$, for all pairs of circuits $C_0, C_1 \in \mathcal{C}_\lambda$, we have that if $C_0(x) = C_1(x)$ for all inputs x, then:*

$$
\mathsf{Adv}^{\mathsf{iO}}(\lambda, \mathcal{A}) := |\Pr[\mathcal{A}(\mathsf{iO}(\lambda, C_0)) = 1] - \Pr[\mathcal{A}(\mathsf{iO}(\lambda, C_1)) = 1]| \leq \mathsf{negl}(\lambda)
$$

Sub-exponential Security. We say that iO is sub-exponentially secure when it satisfies Definition 8 and also it satisfies that: for every (not necessary uniform) PPT distinguisher $\mathcal{A}$, the advantage $\mathsf{Adv}^{\mathsf{iO}}(\lambda, \mathcal{A})$ is bounded by $\frac{1}{2^{\lambda^\epsilon}}$, for some positive constant $0 < \epsilon < 1$.

2.6 Dual-Mode NIWI Proof Systems

A dual-mode non-interactive witness indistinguishable (DM-NIWI) proof system [32] is a special type of non-interactive witness indistinguishable (NIWI) proof system, in which the common reference string (CRS) generation is dual-mode. The dual-mode property means that these systems have common reference string algorithms which generate indistinguishable CRS in "binding" or "hiding" modes. The system satisfies statistical soundness and extractability in binding mode and statistical witness indistinguishability in hiding mode.

Definition 9. *A binary relation R is polynomially bounded if it is decidable in polynomial time and there is a polynomial p such that $|w| \leq p(|x|)$, for all $(x, w) \in R$. For any such relation and any x we set $L_R = \{x|\ \exists w\ s.t.\ (x, w) \in R\}$.*

Definition 10 (Dual-mode non-interactive witness indistinguishable proof systems[32]). *Let R be a polynomially-bounded binary relation R. A dual-mode non-interactive witness indistinguishable (DM-NIWI) proof system for language $\mathcal{L}_R \in$ NP is a tuple of PPT algorithms* DM-NIWI = (Setup, Prove, Verify, Extract).

Setup$(1^\lambda, \text{binding})$ *on input the security parameter, outputs a common reference string* crs *which we call binding. It also outputs the corresponding extraction trapdoor* td_{ext}.

Setup$(1^\lambda, \text{hiding})$ *on input the security parameter, outputs a common reference string* crs, *which we call a hiding* crs.

Prove(crs, x, w), *on input* crs, *a statement x and a witness w, outputs a proof π.*

Verify(crs, x, π), *on input* crs, *a statement x and a proof π, outputs either 1 or 0.*

Extract$(\text{td}_{\text{ext}}, x, \pi)$ *on input the extraction trapdoor* td_{ext}, *a statement x and a proof π, it outputs a witness w.*

We require the DM-NIWI *to meet the following properties:*

CRS indistinguishability. *Common reference strings generated via* Setup$(1^\lambda, \text{binding})$ *and* Setup$(1^\lambda, \text{hiding})$ *are computationally indistinguishable. More formally, for all non-uniform PPT adversaries $\mathcal{A}$, the advantage of $\mathcal{A}$ in the experiment* Exp-CRS-IND *described in Fig. 4 is negligible, namely:*

$$\text{Adv}^{\text{DM-NIWI}}_{\text{Exp-CRS-IND}}(\lambda, \mathcal{A}) := \big|\ \Pr[\text{Exp-CRS-IND}^{\text{DM-NIWI}}_0(1^\lambda, \mathcal{A}) = 1] -$$

$$\Pr[\text{Exp-CRS-IND}^{\text{DM-NIWI}}_1(1^\lambda, \mathcal{A}) = 1]\big| \leq \text{negl}(\lambda)$$

Experiment Exp-CRS-IND$^{\text{DM-NIWI}}_b(1^\lambda, \mathcal{A})$
if $b = 0$ then
$\quad$ (crs, td_{ext}) $\leftarrow_\text{R}$ Setup$(1^\lambda, \text{binding})$
else
$\quad$ (crs) $\leftarrow_\text{R}$ Setup$(1^\lambda, \text{hiding})$
$b' \leftarrow_\text{R} \mathcal{A}(\text{crs})$
Return $b = b'$

Fig. 4. Experiment Exp-CRS-IND$^{\text{DM-NIWI}}_b$ for CRS indistinguishability.

Perfect completeness in both modes. *For every* $(x, w) \in R$, *we have that:*

$$\Pr\left[\begin{array}{l} \text{crs} \leftarrow_R \text{Setup}(1^\lambda, \text{binding}), \\ \pi \leftarrow_R \text{Prove}(\text{crs}, x, w) \end{array} : \text{Verify}(\text{crs}, x, \pi) = 1\right] = 1.$$

The same holds when instead of $\text{crs} \leftarrow_R \text{Setup}(1^\lambda, \text{binding})$, *we have* $\text{crs} \leftarrow_R \text{Setup}(1^\lambda, \text{hiding})$.

Statistical soundness in binding mode. *The system is statistically sound if for every (possibly unbounded) adversary* $\mathcal{A}$, *we have that*

$$\Pr\left[\begin{array}{l} (\text{crs}, \text{td}_{\text{ext}}) \leftarrow_R \text{Setup}(1^\lambda, \text{binding}), \\ (x, \pi) \leftarrow_R \mathcal{A}(\text{crs}) \end{array} : \text{Verify}(\text{crs}, x, \pi) = 1 \land x \notin \mathcal{L}_R\right] = \text{negl}(\lambda).$$

Statistical extractability in binding mode. *For any* (x, π), *it holds that:*

$$\Pr\left[\begin{array}{l} (\text{crs}, \text{td}_{\text{ext}}) \leftarrow_R \text{Setup}(1^\lambda, \text{binding}), \\ w \leftarrow_R \text{Extract}(\text{crs}, \text{td}_{\text{ext}}, x, \pi) \end{array} : \left(\begin{array}{c} \text{Verify}(\text{crs}, x, \pi) = 1 \\ \implies (x, w) \in R \end{array}\right)\right] = 1 - \text{negl}(\lambda).$$

Note: In binding mode, statistical extractability implies statistical soundness.

Statistical witness-indistinguishability in hiding mode. *We say that the DM-NIWI system is statistically witness-indistinguishable if for every* x, w_0, w_1 *with both* $(x, w_0) \in R$ *and* $(x, w_1) \in R$, *proofs of* x *with witness* w_0 *are indistinguishable from proofs of* x *with witness* w_1. *More formally, for every interactive (potentially unbounded) adversary* $\mathcal{A}$:

$$\left| \Pr\left[\begin{array}{l} \text{crs} \leftarrow_R \text{Setup}(1^\lambda, \text{hiding}), \\ (x, w_0, w_1) \leftarrow_R \mathcal{A}(\text{crs}), \\ b \leftarrow_R \{0, 1\}, \\ \pi \leftarrow_R \text{Prove}(\text{crs}, x, w_b) \end{array} : \mathcal{A}(\text{crs}, \pi) = b\right] - \frac{1}{2} \right| \leq \text{negl}(\lambda),$$

where $\mathcal{A}$ *is restricted to choosing* (x, w_0, w_1), *such that both* $(x, w_0) \in R$ *and* $(x, w_1) \in R$.

Remark. Like with the original presentation of Groth and Sahai [32], we focus our presentation on *witness-indistinguishable* (and not zero-knowledge) proof systems. Unlike zero-knowledge, witness-indistinguishability has useful compositional properties (see [23]). If zero-knowledge is desired, however, a simple transformation is possible: instead of proving $x \in L$, prove $x \in L \lor \hat{x} \in \hat{L}$ with our system, where $\hat{L}$ is any fixed hard-to-decide language, and $\hat{x}$ is a fixed instance determined in crs. In binding mode, set up $\hat{x} \notin \hat{L}$, so that $x \in L \lor \hat{x} \in \hat{L}$ implies $x \in L$. In hiding mode, set up $\hat{x} \in \hat{L}$, in which case a witness to this fact can be used as a simulation trapdoor to efficiently simulated proofs that achieve statistical zero-knowledge.

2.7   Hidden Bits Non-interactive Zero-Knowledge

In our construction, we rely on a NIZK protocol in the hidden bits model. The hidden-bits model was introduced by [22] and is an idealized setting in which the bits of the common reference string are hidden from the verifier (but not from the prover). We call this the hidden reference string hrs.

When the prover computes a proof, it can choose which bits of hrs to reveal to the verifier. Denote the revealed bit set by $\mathcal{I}$, then by $\text{hrs}_{\mathcal{I}}$ we will refer to the corresponding revealed bits of the hrs. Our construction can be based on the hidden-bits NIZK from [22], which proves graph Hamiltonicity and therefore covers any NP statement. Nevertheless, our construction is generic enough to be based on any hidden-bits NIZK with statistical soundness and perfect zero-knowledge (if we only had statistical ZK, then we would only get statistical correctness of DM-NIWI). The hidden-bits NIZK from [22] satisfies both statistical soundness and perfect ZK.

Definition 11. [22] *A pair of* PPT *algorithms* $\text{NIZK}_H = (\text{P}_H, \text{V}_H)$ *is a NIZK proof system in the hidden-bits model if it satisfies the following properties:*

1. *Completeness: there exists a polynomial r denoting the length of the hidden random string, such that for every $(x, w) \in \mathcal{R}$ we have that:*

$$\Pr_{\text{P}_H, \text{hrs} \leftarrow \{0,1\}^{t(|x|,\lambda)}} [(\pi, \mathcal{I}) \leftarrow \text{P}_H(x, w, \text{hrs}) : \text{V}_H(x, \text{hrs}_{\mathcal{I}}, \mathcal{I}, \pi) = 1] = 1$$

   where $\mathcal{I} \subseteq [t(|x|, \lambda)]$ and $\text{hrs}_{\mathcal{I}} = \{\text{hrs}[i] : i \in \mathcal{I}\}$.
2. *Statistical Soundness: for every $x \notin \mathcal{L}$ we have that:*

$$\Pr_{\text{hrs} \leftarrow \{0,1\}^{t(|x|,\lambda)}} [\exists \pi, \mathcal{I} : \text{V}_H(x, \text{hrs}_{\mathcal{I}}, \mathcal{I}, \pi) = 1] < \frac{1}{2^{\lambda+|x|}}.$$

3. *Perfect Zero-Knowledge: there exists a PPT algorithm S_H such that:*

$$D_0 := \{(\text{hrs}_{\mathcal{I}}, \pi, \mathcal{I}) : \text{hrs} \leftarrow \{0,1\}^{t(|x|,\lambda)}, (\pi, \mathcal{I}) \leftarrow \text{P}_H(x, w, \text{hrs})\}_{(x,w)\in\mathcal{R}} \equiv$$
$$\equiv \{\text{S}_H(x)\}_{(x,w)\in\mathcal{R}} =: D_1$$

   For ease of notation, we denote by $\Delta_{\text{ZeroKnowledge}}^{\text{NIZK}_H}(\lambda) := \Delta(D_0, D_1)$ the statistical distance between distributions D_0 and D_1. In the case of perfect ZK, $\Delta_{\text{ZeroKnowledge}}^{\text{NIZK}_H}(\lambda) := \Delta(D_0, D_1) = 0$.

3   Construction

In Fig. 5, we describe our DM-NIWI candidate. Our scheme uses a hidden-bits NIZK proof system $\text{NIZK}_H = (\text{P}_H, \text{V}_H)$ as a building block. To distinguish common reference strings and proofs between the two proof systems, we denote by lowercase (π, hrs) the proofs and hidden reference strings for NIZK_H. In contrast, the common reference string and proofs of DM-NIWI are denoted as CRS and Π, respectively.

The CRS of DM-NIWI contains the public key lpk of a lossy encryption scheme LE, a lossy function H, uniformly random Z and crs, a functional decryption function sk_f and an obfuscated program PC. Prover program $\text{PC}(x, w, r)$ first encrypts (x, w) using randomness r to obtain $a = \mathsf{LE.Enc}(\mathsf{lpk}, (x, w); r)$. Then it computes either a HidingProof or a BindingProof depending on the mode and outputs as proof a FE ciphertext C and a hidden-bits proof π. The verifier decrypts C using sk_f and then uses the hidden-bits verifier to check proof π.

Notation and Parameters. For security parameter λ, we denote by $p(|x| + \lambda)$ the ciphertext size of LE. By $p_2(|x|, \lambda)$, we denote the size of the randomness needed to compute FE ciphertexts, while $p_3(|x|, \lambda)$ denotes the size of the random tape needed by the hidden-bits simulator S_H. Recall that $t(|x|, \lambda)$ is the polynomial from Definition 11. Then LF must be a $(p_1(|x|, \lambda), \lambda, t(|x|, 2\lambda + |x|), p(|x| + \lambda) + \lambda)$-lossy function. Consider the subexponential security level of iO, FE and PRF to be $\frac{1}{2^{\kappa^\epsilon}}$, for some constant $0 < \epsilon < 1$. Then κ must be chosen as $(p(|x| + \lambda) + \lambda)^{(1/\epsilon)}$.

4 Security Proof

Theorem 12. *Let* PRF *be a subexponentially-secure puncturable pseudo-random function,* iO *be a subexponentially-secure obfuscator,* PRG *a secure pseudo-random generator,* LE *a secure lossy encryption scheme and* FE *a subexponentially-secure selectively-*IND-CPA *functional encryption scheme, then the scheme* DM-NIWI $=$ (DM-NIWI.Setup, DM-NIWI.Prover, DM-NIWI.Verifier) *described in Fig. 5 is a secure dual-mode non-interactive witness-indistinguishable system.*

4.1 Completeness

Lemma 13. *The* DM-NIWI *system in Fig. 5 is perfectly complete.*

Proof. Completeness follows from the completeness of the hidden-bits NIZK_H, the perfect ZK of NIZK_H, the perfect correctness of FE and the functionality of iO (the fact that for all programs C, we have that $\mathsf{iO}(C)$ is functionally equivalent to C). Consider any $(x, w) \in R$ and $(C, \pi) = \mathsf{DM\text{-}NIWI.Prover}(\mathsf{CRS}, x, w, r)$. We want to show that $\mathsf{DM\text{-}NIWI.Verifier}(C, \pi, \mathsf{CRS}) = 1$ with probability 1.

Case 1: CRS $\leftarrow_{\mathrm{R}}$ DM-NIWI.Setup$(1^\lambda, \text{binding})$ Since (C, Π) is a proof computed by the honest prover, we know that $(\pi, \mathcal{I}) \leftarrow \mathsf{P}_H(x, w, \mathsf{hrs})$, where hrs is derived from a, the lossy encryption of (x, w). From the perfect correctness of FE, we have that indeed $(T \oplus \mathsf{crs})_\mathcal{I} = \mathsf{hrs}_I$. Therefore, from the perfect correctness of NIZK_H, it follows that $\mathsf{V}_H(\mathcal{I}, (T \oplus \mathsf{crs})_\mathcal{I}, x, \pi)$ accepts with probability 1.

Case 2: CRS $\leftarrow_{\mathrm{R}}$ DM-NIWI.Setup$(1^\lambda, \text{hiding})$ Since (C, Π) is a proof computed by the honest prover, we know that $(\mathsf{hrs}_\mathcal{I}, \pi, \mathcal{I}) \leftarrow \mathsf{S}_H(x; r_3)$, where r_3 is the random tape used by the hidden-bits simulator S_H. By the perfect correctness of FE, decrypting C yields indeed $\mathsf{hrs}_\mathcal{I} \oplus \mathsf{crs}_\mathcal{I}$, therefore we can recover $\mathsf{hrs}_\mathcal{I}$. Now, since NIZK_H has perfect zero-knowledge, it follows that $\mathsf{V}_H(\mathcal{I}, (T \oplus \mathsf{crs})_\mathcal{I}, x, \pi)$ accepts with probability 1 (or otherwise simulated proofs would not be identically distributed to real ones).

Setup(1^λ, mode)
———————————————
  PRG $\leftarrow_R$ PRG.Setup(1^λ)
  if mode = binding then
    H $\leftarrow_R$ LF.Setup(1^λ, lossy)
  else
    H $\leftarrow_R$ LF.Setup(1^λ, dense)
  (lpk, lsk) $\leftarrow_R$ LE.Setup(1^λ, lossy)
  $K_1, K_2, K_3 \leftarrow_R$ PRF.KeyGen(1^κ)
  (fmpk, fmsk) $\leftarrow_R$ FE.Setup(1^κ)
  $\mathsf{sk_f} \leftarrow_R$ FE.KeyGen(fmsk, f)
  crs $\leftarrow_R \{0,1\}^{t(|x|, 2\lambda + |x|)}$
  $z \leftarrow_R \{0,1\}^\lambda$
  if mode = binding then
    $Z \leftarrow_R \{0,1\}^{2\lambda + |x|}$
  else
    $Z \leftarrow$ PRG(z)
  PC = iO(ProgProv$_{\text{mode,crs}}$)
  CRS := (H, fmpk, lpk, $\mathsf{sk_f}$, crs, Z, PC)
  if mode = binding then
    Return (CRS, td$_{\text{ext}}$:= fmsk)
  Return CRS

Prover(PC, x, w, r)
———————————————
  Return Π := PC(x, w, r)

Verifier(CRS, $x, \Pi := (C, \pi)$)
———————————————
  $(T, \mathcal{I}) \leftarrow$ FE.Dec($\mathsf{sk_f}, C$)
  hrs$_\mathcal{I} \leftarrow T \oplus$ crs$_\mathcal{I}$
  return $V_H(x, \text{hrs}_\mathcal{I}, \mathcal{I}, \pi)$

ProgProv$_{\text{mode,crs}}(x, w, r)$
———————————————
  Hardcoded: Keys K_1, K_2, K_3, z
  if $(x, w) \notin R$
    Return $\bot$
  $a \leftarrow_R$ LE.Enc(lpk, $(x, w); r$)
  if mode = binding then
    $(C, \pi) =$ BindingProof$_{\text{crs}}(x, w, a)$
  else
    $(C, \pi) =$ HidingProof$_{\text{crs}}(x, a)$
  Return $\Pi := (C, \pi)$

BindingProof$_{\text{crs}}(x, w, a)$
———————————————
  Hardcoded : Keys K_1, K_2
  $X \leftarrow$ PRF(K_1, a)
  hrs $\leftarrow$ H(X) $\oplus$ crs
  $(\pi, \mathcal{I}) \leftarrow P_H(x, w, \text{hrs})$
  $r_2 \leftarrow$ PRF(K_2, a)
  $C =$ FE.Enc(fmpk, $(X, \mathcal{I}, 0, 0); r_2$)
  Return $\Pi := (C, \pi)$

HidingProof$_{\text{crs}}(x, a)$
———————————————
  Hardcoded : Keys K_2, K_3
  $r_3 \leftarrow$ PRF(K_3, a)
  $(\text{hrs}_\mathcal{I}, \pi, \mathcal{I}) \leftarrow S_H(x; r_3)$
  $T \leftarrow$ hrs$_\mathcal{I} \oplus$ crs$_\mathcal{I}$
  $r_2 \leftarrow$ PRF(K_2, a)
  $C =$ FE.Enc(fmpk, $(0, \mathcal{I}, z, T); r_2$)
  Return $\Pi := (C, \pi)$

f($C =$ FE.Enc(fmpk, $(X, \mathcal{I}, z, T))$)
———————————————
  Hardcoded : Parameters Z, H
  if PRG(z) = Z then return $(T, \mathcal{I})$.
  else return (H(X)$_\mathcal{I}, \mathcal{I}$)

Fig. 5. Dual-mode NIWI scheme DM-NIWI = (Setup, Prover, Verifier). LF is a class of lossy functions, PRG.Setup outputs pseudo-random generators from $\{0.1\}^\lambda$ to $\{0,1\}^{2\lambda + |x|}$, FE is a functional encryption scheme, LE is a lossy encryption scheme, iO is an indistinguishability obfuscator and (P_H, V_H) is the hidden-bits model NIZK from [22]. Parameter κ is chosen so that the sub-exponential security level is sufficient.

4.2 Soundness

Theorem 14. *When in binding mode, the DM-NIWI system in Fig. 5 is statistically sound.*

Proof. Here we use the soundness of the hidden-bits scheme, coupled with the lossiness of function H.

Since crs is uniformly random, computing hrs := $H(PRF(K_1, a)) \oplus$ crs will yield another uniformly random string and will allow us to use the soundness of the hidden-bits system. Moreover, we leverage the lossiness of H to ensure that an adversary cannot influence the hrs sufficiently enough as to be able to cheat. This is because the honest verifier applies H automatically when it functionally decrypts ciphertext C.

More formally, fix some $x \in \{0,1\}^n \setminus \mathcal{L}$. We prove that with overwhelming probability over the common reference string, there is no proof Π which will be accepted by the verifier. This is a selective notion which we later amplify to obtain the security notion from Definition 10.

We want to bound $\Pr_{(CRS,td_{ext}) \leftarrow_R Setup(1^\lambda, binding)}[\exists \Pi : Verifier(\Pi, CRS) = 1]$. We can rewrite this probability as:

$$\Pr_{\substack{Z \leftarrow_R \{0,1\}^{2\lambda+|x|} \\ crs \leftarrow_R \{0,1\}^{t(|x|,2\lambda+|x|)} \\ H, PC, fmpk, fmsk, sk_f}}[\exists(\pi, C) : Verifier((\pi, C), (H, fmpk, lpk, sk_f, crs, Z, PC)) = 1]$$

Now, we condition on the event E that Z does not have a PRG preimage, which happens with probability $1 - \frac{1}{2^{\lambda+|x|}}$. From the functionality of iO and the special correctness of the FE scheme (see Definition 5), the adversary must produce a ciphertext which decrypts to a value in the range of the function f. If Z has no preimage, then being in the range of the function f is equivalent to being of the form $H(X)_{\mathcal{I}}$, for some X (recall that $H(X)_{\mathcal{I}}$ denotes the subset $\mathcal{I}$ of the bits of $H(X)$). Note that both the functional equivalence of iO and the special correctness of the functional encryption scheme are statistical properties. Therefore, the probability above is less or equal than:

$$\Pr_{crs \leftarrow_R \{0,1\}^{t(|x|,2\lambda+|x|)}}[\exists(\pi, X, \mathcal{I}) : V_H(x, (crs \oplus H(X))_{\mathcal{I}}, \mathcal{I}, \pi) = 1]$$

The next step is to bound the number of possible values of hrs. Recall that hrs := $H(PRF(K_1, a)) \oplus$ crs. From the lossiness of H, we know that there are at most 2^k images of H, where k is the second parameter of H (see Definition 2). Thus, we can compute an union bound over all these images $H(X)$, bounding the above probability by:

$$2^k \times \Pr_{crs \leftarrow_R \{0,1\}^{t(|x|,2\lambda+|x|)}}[\exists(\pi, \mathcal{I}) : V_H(x, (crs \oplus H(X))_{\mathcal{I}}, \mathcal{I}, \pi) = 1]$$

Now, recall that we denote crs $\oplus H(X)$ as hrs. Since crs is uniformly randomly distributed, so is hrs, and we can rewrite the probability above as:

$$2^k \times \Pr_{hrs \leftarrow_R \{0,1\}^{t(|x|,2\lambda+|x|)}}[\exists(\pi, \mathcal{I}) : V_H(x, hrs_{\mathcal{I}}, \mathcal{I}, \pi) = 1]$$

Finally, by using the soundness of the hidden-bits NIZK, we know that:

$$\Pr_{hrs \leftarrow_R \{0,1\}^{t(|x|,2\lambda+|x|)}}[\exists(\pi, \mathcal{I}) : V_H(x, hrs_{\mathcal{I}}, \mathcal{I}, \pi) = 1] \le \frac{1}{2^{2\lambda+|x|}}$$

Therefore, we can conclude that:

$$\Pr_{(\mathsf{CRS},\mathsf{td_{ext}}) \leftarrow_{\mathrm{R}} \mathsf{Setup}(1^\lambda, \mathrm{binding})}[\exists \Pi : \mathsf{Verifier}(\Pi, \mathsf{CRS}) = 1] \leq \frac{1}{2^{2\lambda+|x|-k}}.$$

The only remaining step is to amplify the security from the selective variant we have just proven to the adaptive one from Definition 10. We eliminate the restriction that x is fixed by computing a union bound over all possible values of x. In particular, for H parameter $k = \lambda$, we conclude that for every unbounded adversary $\mathcal{A}$:

$$\Pr\left[\begin{array}{l} (\mathsf{CRS},\mathsf{td_{ext}}) \leftarrow_{\mathrm{R}} \mathsf{Setup}(1^\lambda, \mathrm{binding}), \\ (x, \Pi) \leftarrow_{\mathrm{R}} \mathcal{A}(\mathsf{CRS}) \end{array} : \mathsf{Verifier}(\mathsf{CRS}, x, \Pi) = 1 \wedge x \notin \mathcal{L}_R\right] = \frac{1}{2^\lambda}.$$

As a last check, we must ensure that event $\neg E$ still happens with negligible probability. If we compute the same union bound as above, the probability of $\neg E$ is now bounded by $\frac{1}{2^\lambda}$. Therefore, the system is statistically sound.

4.3 Witness Indistinguishability

Theorem 15. *In hiding mode, the* DM-NIWI *system from Fig. 5 is statistically witness-indistinguishable.*

Proof. By using the statistical lossiness of LE, we show that no (potentially unbounded) adversary $\mathcal{A}$ can break the witness-indistinguishability of DM-NIWI. Recall that the lossiness of LE implies that for all $(\mathsf{lpk}, \bot) \leftarrow \mathsf{LE.Gen}(1^\lambda, \mathrm{lossy})$, and for all x, w_0, w_1, encryptions of (x, w_0) are statistically indistinguishable from encryptions of (x, w_1). More formally:

$$D_0 := \{r \leftarrow R : (\mathsf{lpk}, \mathsf{LE.Enc}(\mathsf{lpk}, (x, w_0), r))\} \approx_{\frac{1}{2^\lambda}}$$

$$\approx_{\frac{1}{2^\lambda}} \{r \leftarrow R : (\mathsf{lpk}, \mathsf{LE.Enc}(\mathsf{lpk}, (x, w_1), r))\} =: D_1.$$

The goal is to show that for every hiding CRS and for every (x, w_0, w_1), with both $(x, w_0) \in R$ and $(x, w_1) \in R$, proofs for (x, w_0) are statistically indistinguishable from proofs for (x, w_1). Fix (x, w_0, w_1) and let D_b' be the following distribution:

$$D_b' := \{\mathsf{CRS} \leftarrow_{\mathrm{R}} \mathsf{DM\text{-}NIWI.Setup}(1^\lambda, \mathrm{hiding}) : \pi \leftarrow_{\mathrm{R}} \mathsf{DM\text{-}NIWI.Prove}(\mathsf{CRS}, x, w_b)\} \quad (1)$$

We want to prove that we have that $D_0' \approx_{\frac{1}{2^\lambda}} D_1'$. To achieve this, we exhibit a probabilistic function F which on input D_b outputs D_b', i.e. $F(D_b) = D_b'$, without needing to know bit b. If such an F exists, then $D_0 \approx_{\frac{1}{2^\lambda}} D_1$ implies that $F(D_0) \approx_{\frac{1}{2^\lambda}} F(D_1)$. Function F works as follows:

1. F obtains public key lpk from D_b. Then F esentially computes DM-NIWI. $\mathsf{Setup}(1^\lambda)$ and chooses all the parameters itself, except for lpk which comes from D_b.

In more detail, F chooses the PRG, a dense function H, keys K_1, K_2, K_3, master keys (fmpk, fmsk) and functional key $\mathsf{sk_f}$ just as in DM-NIWI.Setup(1^λ). It also draws uniformly random strings z and crs. It then sets $Z = \mathsf{PRG}(z)$ and uses all these parameters to construct program $\mathsf{ProgProv}_{\mathrm{hiding,crs}}$, which it obfuscates obtaining PC.

2. For hiding CRS, we have that PC obfuscates $\mathsf{ProgProv}_{\mathrm{hiding,crs}}$. Therefore, F can compute the output of DM-NIWI.Prove(CRS, x, w_b) even without knowing bit b: F has access to ciphertext ct from distribution D_b. Ciphertext ct can originate from either (x, w_0) or (x, w_1). F simply computes $(C, \pi) \leftarrow_{\mathrm{R}} \mathsf{HidingProof}_{\mathrm{crs}}(x, \mathsf{ct})$ and uses (C, π) to construct distribution D'_b. Observe that this is only possible because $\mathsf{HidingProof}_{\mathrm{crs}}(x, \mathsf{ct})$ crucially only has x and ct as inputs and does not directly depend on witnesses w_0, w_1 themselves.

We have shown that $F(D_0) \approx_{\frac{1}{2^\lambda}} F(D_1)$, for every (x, w_0, w_1) and for all hiding CRS $\leftarrow_{\mathrm{R}}$ DM-NIWI.Setup(1^λ, hiding). This concludes witness-indistinguishability as defined in Definition 10. (In Definition 10, the adversary can choose (x, w_0, w_1) after seeing the CRS, but since $F(D_0) \approx_{\frac{1}{2^\lambda}} F(D_1)$ for every (x, w_0, w_1) and for every hiding CRS, the adversary will not have advantage greater that $\frac{1}{2^\lambda}$).

4.4 CRS Indistinguishability

Theorem 16. *The* DM-NIWI *system from Fig. 5 satisfies computational indistinguishability between common reference strings generated in binding mode and common reference strings generated in hiding mode.*

Proof. The proof proceeds by a sequence of games where G_0 is defined exactly as Exp-CRS-IND$_0$($1^\lambda, \mathcal{A}$) (see Fig. 4). G_0 corresponds to the experiment in which adversary $\mathcal{A}$ against crs indistinguishability receives common reference strings in binding mode. A high-level summary is provided in Fig. 6. For any game G_i, we denote by $\mathsf{Adv}_i(\mathcal{A})$ the advantage of $\mathcal{A}$ in G_i, that is, $\Pr[G_i(1^\lambda, \mathcal{A}) = 1]$, where the probability is taken over the random coins of G_i and $\mathcal{A}$. At a high level, we use four hybrid games G_0, G_1, G_2 and G_3. The proof is in three phases:

1. In the first phase, we transition from G_0 to G_1. Game G_1 is defined to be the same as G_0, except for the following two changes: First, we switch the mode of the lossy function H from lossy to dense. This is done with the end goal of ensuring that the output of H is uniformly distributed at specific values of a. Secondly, we use the security of the PRG to change Z from being uniformly random to being in the image of the PRG. This is done by setting $Z = \mathsf{PRG}(z)$. To anticipate, this will provide us with a trapdoor for replacing functional ciphertext encoding X with ciphertexts encoding hrs_I. The fact that $G_0 \approx_{\mathrm{c}} G_1$ is proven in Lemma 17.

2. In the second phase, we transition from G_1 to G_2. Game G_2 is defined to be precisely the same as G_1, except that DM-NIWI.Setup(1^λ) computes PC = iO($\mathsf{ProgProv}_{\mathrm{hiding,crs}}$). This transition only makes changes in the program

ProgProv. By iterating over all values of a, for each a we replace real proofs by simulated proofs from the hidden-bits simulator S_H.

We carefully leverage PRF security, the injective mode of LE and the density of H to ensure that for a specific a^*, its corresponding hrs^* is of the form $\beta \oplus crs$, for uniformly random β. Then we use functional encryption security to replace the functional ciphertext corresponding to a^* to one which only leaks $hrs_{\mathcal{I}}$. But at this stage, since only $hrs_{\mathcal{I}}$ is encoded in the ciphertext, we can use the zero knowledge of the hidden-bits NIZK to replace real proofs by simulated ones. We formally prove that $G_1 \approx_c G_2$ in Theorem 19.

3. In the third stage, we define G_3 to be the same as $\mathsf{Exp\text{-}CRS\text{-}IND}_1(1^\lambda, \mathcal{A})$. The only difference between G_2 and G_3 is that in the later, the public key of the lossy encryption scheme LE is switched from injective to lossy mode. We prove that $G_2 \approx_c G_3$ in Lemma 18.

Lemma 17 (From G_0 to G_1). *For every PPT adversary $\mathcal{A}$, it holds that* $|\mathsf{Adv}_0(\mathcal{A}) - \mathsf{Adv}_1(\mathcal{A})| \leq \mathsf{negl}(\lambda)$.

Proof. The only differences between G_0 and G_1 are the fact that Z is changed from $Z \leftarrow_R \{0,1\}^{2\lambda + |x|}$ to $Z \leftarrow \mathsf{PRG}(z)$ and function H is changed from $H \leftarrow \mathsf{LF.Setup}(1^\lambda, \mathsf{lossy})$ to $H \leftarrow \mathsf{LF.Setup}(1^\lambda, \mathsf{dense})$. The lemma follows from the security of the PRG and from the computational indistinguishability of the modes of the lossy function LF. Namely, if $\mathcal{A}$ can distinguish between G_0 and G_1, there exists either a PPT adversary $\mathcal{B}_1$ that can break the security of the PRG or a PPT adversary $\mathcal{B}_2$ that can distinguish with non-negligible advantage between the lossy and dense modes of LF.

Game	(lpk, lsk)	H	Z	PC	Mode or Remark
G_0	$\mathsf{LE.Setup}(1^\lambda, \mathsf{inj})$	$\mathsf{LF.Setup}(1^\lambda, \mathsf{lossy})$	$Z \leftarrow_R \{0,1\}^{2\lambda+|x|}$	$\mathrm{iO}(\mathsf{ProgProv}_{\mathsf{binding}})$	Binding
G_1	$\mathsf{LE.Setup}(1^\lambda, \mathsf{inj})$	$\mathsf{LF.Setup}(1^\lambda, \mathsf{dense})$	$Z \leftarrow \mathsf{PRG}(z)$	$\mathrm{iO}(\mathsf{ProgProv}_{\mathsf{binding}})$	Lemma 17
G_2	$\mathsf{LE.Setup}(1^\lambda, \mathsf{inj})$	$\mathsf{LF.Setup}(1^\lambda, \mathsf{dense})$	$Z \leftarrow \mathsf{PRG}(z)$	$\mathrm{iO}(\mathsf{ProgProv}_{\mathsf{hiding}})$	Theorem 19
G_3	$\mathsf{LE.Setup}(1^\lambda, \mathsf{lossy})$	$\mathsf{LF.Setup}(1^\lambda, \mathsf{dense})$	$Z \leftarrow \mathsf{PRG}(z)$	$\mathrm{iO}(\mathsf{ProgProv}_{\mathsf{hiding}})$	Lemma 18 Hiding

Fig. 6. An overview of the games used in the proof of Theorem 16, changes between consecutive games are highlighted with gray boxes.

Lemma 18 (From G_2 to G_3). *For every PPT adversary $\mathcal{A}$, it holds that* $|\mathsf{Adv}_2(\mathcal{A}) - \mathsf{Adv}_3(\mathcal{A})| \leq \mathsf{negl}(\lambda)$.

Proof. The only change between G_2 and G_3 is that the (lpk, lsk) keys of LE are changed from injective to lossy. The lemma follows directly from the fact that $\{\mathsf{proj}(\mathsf{LE.Gen}(1^\lambda, \mathsf{inj}))\} \approx_c \{\mathsf{proj}(\mathsf{LE.Gen}(1^\lambda, \mathsf{lossy}))\}$, where $\mathsf{proj} : (lpk, lsk) \rightarrow lpk$ and from the fact that lsk is not used anywhere in the construction.

Theorem 19 (From G_1 to G_2). *For every* PPT *adversary* $\mathcal{A}$, *there exist* PPT *adversaries* $\mathcal{B}_1, \mathcal{B}_2, \mathcal{B}_3$, *such that:*

$$|\mathsf{Adv}_0(\mathcal{A}) - \mathsf{Adv}_1(\mathcal{A})| \leq 2^{p(|x|+\lambda)} \left(8 \cdot \mathsf{Adv}^{\mathsf{iO}}(\kappa, \mathcal{B}_1) + 4 \cdot \mathsf{Adv}_{\mathsf{s\text{-}cPRF}}(\kappa, \mathcal{B}_2) + \right.$$

$$\left. \mathsf{Adv}^{\mathsf{FE}}_{\mathsf{Exp\text{-}s\text{-}IND\text{-}FE\text{-}CPA}}(\kappa, \mathcal{B}_3) + \Delta^{\mathsf{NIZK}_H}_{\mathsf{ZeroKnowledge}}(\lambda) + \frac{1}{2^{p(|x|+\lambda)+\lambda}} \right).$$

Proof. The proof strategy is to iterate over all values of $a = \mathsf{LE.Enc}(\mathsf{lpk}, (x, w), r)$ and make changes to the obfuscation of the program $\mathsf{ProgProv}$. We define a series of hybrids H_{1,a^*}, for all $a^* \in \{0,1\}^{p(|x|+\lambda)}$ in Fig. 7. Briefly, hybrid H_{1,a^*} is defined as follows:

Hybrid H_{1,a^*} is defined in the same way as game G_1, except that:

1. $\mathsf{DM\text{-}NIWI.Setup}$ is changed such that the computation of the public parameter $\mathsf{PC} = \mathsf{iO}(\mathsf{ProgProv}_{\mathsf{binding,crs}})$ is replaced by $\mathsf{PC} = \mathsf{iO}(\mathsf{ProgProv}_{1,a^*})$.
2. Program $\mathsf{ProgProv}_{1,a^*}$ on inputs x, w, r is the program which first computes $a = \mathsf{LE.Enc}(\mathsf{lpk}, (x, w), r)$. Then it compares a with hardcoded value a^* and for $a < a^*$, it computes $(C, \pi) = \mathsf{HidingProof}_{\mathsf{crs}}(x, a)$, while for $a \geq a^*$ it computes $(C, \pi) = \mathsf{BindingProof}_{\mathsf{crs}}(x, w, a)$. It then returns proof (C, π).

Note that hybrid $\mathsf{H}_{1,0^{p(|x|+\lambda)}}$ is the same as game G_1, while hybrid $\mathsf{H}_{1,1^{p(|x|+\lambda)}}$ is the same as game $G_2 = \mathsf{Exp\text{-}CRS\text{-}IND}_1(1^\lambda, \mathcal{A})$. Just as before, for every hybrid H_i, we denote by $\mathsf{Adv}_i(\mathcal{A})$ the advantage of $\mathcal{A}$ in H_i, that is, $\Pr[\mathsf{G}_i(1^\lambda, \mathcal{A}) = 1]$. In Theorem 20, we formally prove that every two consecutive hybrids $\mathsf{H}(1, a^*)$ and $\mathsf{H}(1, a^* + 1)$ are computationally indistinguishable, i.e. $\mathsf{H}_{(1,a^*-1)} \approx_c \mathsf{H}_{(1,a^*)}$, for every $a^* \in [2^{p(|x|+\lambda)}]$.

Hybrid H_{1,a^*}	
$\mathsf{Setup}(1^\lambda, \mathsf{mode})$	$\mathsf{ProgProv}_{1,a^*}(x, w, r)$
$\quad \mathsf{PRG} \leftarrow_R \mathsf{PRG.Setup}(1^\lambda)$	$\quad$ if $(x, w) \notin R$
$\quad \mathsf{H} \leftarrow_R \mathsf{LF.Setup}(1^\lambda, \mathsf{dense})$	$\quad\quad$ Return $\perp$
$\quad (\mathsf{lpk}, \mathsf{lsk}) \leftarrow_R \mathsf{LE.Setup}(1^\lambda, \mathsf{inj})$	$\quad$ Hardcoded: Keys K_1, K_2, K_3, z
$\quad K_1, K_2, K_3 \leftarrow_R \mathsf{PRF.KeyGen}(1^\lambda)$	$\quad a \leftarrow_R \mathsf{LE.Enc}(\mathsf{lpk}, (x, w); r)$
$\quad (\mathsf{fmpk}, \mathsf{fmsk}) \leftarrow_R \mathsf{FE.Setup}(1^\lambda)$	$\quad$ if $a < a^*$ then
$\quad \mathsf{sk_f} \leftarrow_R \mathsf{FE.KeyGen}(\mathsf{fmsk}, f)$	$\quad\quad (C, \pi) = \mathsf{HidingProof}_{\mathsf{crs}}(x, w, a)$
$\quad \mathsf{crs} \leftarrow_R \{0,1\}^{t(|x|, 2\lambda+|x|)}$	$\quad$ if $a \geq a^*$
$\quad z \leftarrow_R \{0,1\}^\lambda$	$\quad\quad (C, \pi) = \mathsf{BindingProof}_{\mathsf{crs}}(x, a)$
$\quad Z \leftarrow \mathsf{PRG}(z)$	$\quad$ Return $\Pi := (C, \pi)$
$\quad \mathsf{PC} = \mathsf{iO}(\mathsf{ProgProv}_{1,a^*})$	
$\quad \mathsf{CRS} := (\mathsf{H}, \mathsf{fmpk}, \mathsf{lpk}, \mathsf{sk_f}, \mathsf{crs}, Z, \mathsf{PC})$	
$\quad$ Return CRS	

Fig. 7. Hybrid $\mathsf{H}_{(1,a^*)}$ for the proofs of Theorems 19 and 20. Note that the Prover, Verifier, BindingProof, HidingProof and function f are the same as defined in Fig. 5 and are not represented again for succinctness. Changes between hybrids $\mathsf{H}(1, a^*)$ and game G_1 are highlighted in light gray.

Theorem 20 (From $H_{(1,a^*)}$ to $H_{(1,(a^*+1))}$). *For every PPT adversary $\mathcal{A}$, there exist PPT adversaries $\mathcal{B}_1, \mathcal{B}_2, \mathcal{B}_3$, such that:*

$$|\mathsf{Adv}_{(1,a^*)}(\mathcal{A}) - \mathsf{Adv}_{(1,(a^*+1))}(\mathcal{A})| \leq 8 \cdot \mathsf{Adv}^{\mathsf{iO}}(\kappa, \mathcal{B}_1) + 4 \cdot \mathsf{Adv}_{\mathsf{s\text{-}cPRF}}(\kappa, \mathcal{B}_2) +$$

$$\mathsf{Adv}^{\mathsf{FE}}_{\mathsf{Exp\text{-}s\text{-}IND\text{-}FE\text{-}CPA}}(\kappa, \mathcal{B}_3) + \Delta^{\mathsf{NIZK}_H}_{\mathsf{ZeroKnowledge}}(\lambda) + \frac{1}{2^{p(|x|+\lambda)+\lambda}}.$$

Proof. We prove this through a sequence of hybrids $H_{(1,a^*)}$ up to $H_{(15,a^*)}$, where hybrid $H_{(15,a^*)}$ is identical to hybrid $H_{(1,(a^*+1))}$. In terms of notation, hybrid $H_{(i,a^*)}$ will have $\mathsf{PC} = \mathsf{iO}(\mathsf{ProgProv}_{i,a^*,\mathsf{crs}})$. The proof strategy is to leverage the properties of $\mathsf{iO}, \mathsf{FE}, \mathsf{PRF}s, \mathsf{LE}$ and H in order to replace actual proofs computed by the hidden-bits prover P_H to simulated proofs computed by S_H. Notice that in $H_{(1,a^*)}$, proofs corresponding to a are computed by subprogram $\mathsf{BindingProof}_{\mathsf{crs}}(x,w,a)$, while in $H_{(15,a^*)}$ they are computed by subprogram $\mathsf{HidingProof}_{\mathsf{crs}}(x,w)$. This is the only difference between the two hybrids. In order to replace subprogram $\mathsf{BindingProof}_{\mathsf{crs}}()$ by $\mathsf{HidingProof}_{\mathsf{crs}}()$ we define a series of subprograms $\mathsf{HybridProof}_{i,a^*,\mathsf{crs}}$, for $i \in [15]$. As expected, every hybrid $H_{(i,a^*)}$ will be defined to be identical to H_{1,a^*}, except that for $a = a^*$, $(C,\pi) = \mathsf{HybridProof}_{i,a^*,\mathsf{crs}}(x,w,a)$. The hybrids are described in Fig. 7. For a detailed decription of subprograms $\mathsf{HybridProof}_{i,a^*,\mathsf{crs}}$, see Fig. 9. More figures are provided in the full version (Fig. 8).

Hybrid $H_{(2,a^*)}$. In this hybrid, the subprogram $\mathsf{HybridProof}_{2,a^*,\mathsf{crs}}$ is changed so that key K_1 is punctured at point a^*. This is a standard punctured programming technique. Once we puncture the key, only $K_1\{a^*\}$ is hardcoded in the program, along with the evaluation of $r_1^* \leftarrow \mathsf{PRF}(K_1, a^*)$, but not K_1

Hybrid $H_{1,a^*}, \ldots, H_{15,a^*}$	
Setup(1^λ, mode)	$\mathsf{ProgProv}_{i,a^*,\mathsf{crs}}(x,w,r)$
$\quad \mathsf{PRG} \leftarrow_R \mathsf{PRG.Setup}(1^\lambda)$	$\quad$ if $(x,w) \notin R$
$\quad \mathsf{H} \leftarrow_R \mathsf{LF.Setup}(1^\lambda, \mathsf{dense})$	$\quad\quad$ Return $\bot$
$\quad (\mathsf{lpk}, \mathsf{lsk}) \leftarrow_R \mathsf{LE.Setup}(1^\lambda, \mathsf{inj})$	$\quad a \leftarrow_R \mathsf{LE.Enc}(\mathsf{lpk}, (x,w); r)$
$\quad K_1, K_2, K_3 \leftarrow_R \mathsf{PRF.KeyGen}(1^\kappa)$	$\quad$ if $a < a^*$ then
$\quad (\mathsf{fmpk}, \mathsf{fmsk}) \leftarrow_R \mathsf{FE.Setup}(1^\kappa)$	$\quad\quad (C,\pi) = \mathsf{HidingProof}_{\mathsf{crs}}(x,w,a)$
$\quad \mathsf{sk_f} \leftarrow_R \mathsf{FE.KeyGen}(\mathsf{fmsk}, \mathsf{f})$	$\quad$ if $a = a^*$
$\quad \mathsf{crs} \leftarrow_R \{0,1\}^{t(|x|,2\lambda+|x|)}$	$\quad\quad (C,\pi) = \mathsf{HybridProof}_{i,a^*,\mathsf{crs}}(x,w,a)$
$\quad z \leftarrow_R \{0,1\}^\lambda$	$\quad$ if $a > a^*$
$\quad Z \leftarrow \mathsf{PRG}(z)$	$\quad\quad (C,\pi) = \mathsf{BindingProof}_{\mathsf{crs}}(x,a)$
$\quad \mathsf{PC} = \mathsf{iO}(\mathsf{ProgProv}_{i,a^*,\mathsf{crs}})$	$\quad$ Return $\Pi := (C,\pi)$
$\quad \mathsf{CRS} := (\mathsf{H}, \mathsf{fmpk}, \mathsf{lpk}, \mathsf{sk_f}, \mathsf{crs}, Z, \mathsf{PC})$	
$\quad$ Return CRS	

Fig. 8. Hybrids $H_{(i,a^*)}$ for the proofs of Theorems 19 and 20. Note that the Prover, Verifier, BindingProof, HidingProof and function f are the same as defined in Fig. 5 and are not represented again for succinctness. For $i = 1$, subprogram $\mathsf{HybridProof}_{1,a^*,\mathsf{crs}} = \mathsf{BindingProof}_{\mathsf{crs}}$ and for $i = 15$, $\mathsf{HybridProof}_{15,a^*,\mathsf{crs}} = \mathsf{HidingProof}_{\mathsf{crs}}$. All $\mathsf{ProgProv}_{i,a^*,\mathsf{crs}}(x,w,r)$ are padded so that they have equal sizes.

itself. Observe that key K_1 is punctured in $\mathsf{ProgProv}_{2,a^*,\mathsf{crs}}$ and all its sub-programs as well. In $\mathsf{H}_{(i,a^*)}, i \in [15]$ subprograms $\mathsf{BindingProof}_{\mathsf{crs}}(x,w,a)$ and $\mathsf{HidingProof}_{\mathsf{crs}}(x,w,a)$ are never called on inputs $a \neq a^*$, so they never need the evaluation of $\mathsf{PRF}(K_1, a^*)$.

This puncturing can be done since a^* is a parameter of the hybrid (we are enumerating over all values of a). Since the programs are functionally equivalent, this change is computationally indistinguishable by the security of iO. Observe that when we hardcode a value in a subprogram $\mathsf{HybridProof}_{i,a^*,\mathsf{crs}}$, it is understood that this value is also hardcoded in $\mathsf{ProgProv}_{i,a^*,\mathsf{crs}}$. A full description of $\mathsf{HybridProof}_{2,a^*,\mathsf{crs}}$ can be found in Fig. 9. This shows the following lemma:

Lemma 21 (From $\mathsf{H}_{(1,a^*)}$ to $\mathsf{H}_{(2,a^*)}$). *For every PPT adversary $\mathcal{A}$, there exists a PPT adversary $\mathcal{B}$, such that:* $|\mathsf{Adv}_{(1,a^*)}(\mathcal{A}) - \mathsf{Adv}_{(2,a^*)}(\mathcal{A})| \leq \mathsf{Adv}^{\mathsf{iO}}(\kappa, \mathcal{B})$.

Hybrid $\mathsf{H}_{(3,a^*)}$. Here subprogram $\mathsf{HybridProof}_{3,a^*,\mathsf{crs}}$ is changed so that r_1^* is now a uniformly random value hardcoded inside our program. This change is computationally indistinguishable by the pseudorandomness at punctured points of PRF (we are replacing the evaluation at $K_1\{a^*\}$ by a uniformly random). A full description of subprogram $\mathsf{HybridProof}_{3,a^*,\mathsf{crs}}$ can be found in Fig. 9. This shows the following lemma:

Lemma 22 (From $\mathsf{H}_{(2,a^*)}$ to $\mathsf{H}_{(3,a^*)}$). *For every PPT adversary $\mathcal{A}$, there exists a PPT adversary $\mathcal{B}$, such that:* $|\mathsf{Adv}_{(2,a^*)}(\mathcal{A}) - \mathsf{Adv}_{(3,a^*)}(\mathcal{A})| \leq \mathsf{Adv}_{\mathsf{s\text{-}cPRF}}(\kappa, \mathcal{B})$.

Hybrid $\mathsf{H}_{(4,a^*)}$. Subprogram $\mathsf{HybridProof}_{2,a^*,\mathsf{crs}}$ is changed so that key K_2 is punctured at point a^*. This is by the same argument as in Lemma 21 and uses the security of iO. Once we puncture the key, only $K_2\{a^*\}$ is hardcoded in all subroutines of $\mathsf{ProgProv}_{4,a^*,\mathsf{crs}}$, along with the evaluation of $r_2^* \leftarrow \mathsf{PRF}(K_2, a^*)$, but not K_2 itself. This shows the following lemma:

Lemma 23 (From $\mathsf{H}_{(3,a^*)}$ to $\mathsf{H}_{(4,a^*)}$). *For every PPT adversary $\mathcal{A}$, there exists a PPT adversary $\mathcal{B}$, such that:* $|\mathsf{Adv}_{(3,a^*)}(\mathcal{A}) - \mathsf{Adv}_{(4,a^*)}(\mathcal{A})| \leq \mathsf{Adv}^{\mathsf{iO}}(\kappa, \mathcal{B})$.

Hybrid $\mathsf{H}_{(5,a^*)}$. Here subprogram $\mathsf{HybridProof}_{5,a^*,\mathsf{crs}}$ is changed so that r_2^* is now a uniformly random value hardcoded inside our program. This change is computationally indistinguishable by the pseudorandomness at punctured points of PRF (we are replacing the evaluation at $K_2\{a^*\}$ by a uniformly random). The full description of $\mathsf{HybridProof}_{5,a^*,\mathsf{crs}}$ can be found in the full version. This shows the following lemma:

Lemma 24 (From $\mathsf{H}_{(4,a^*)}$ to $\mathsf{H}_{(5,a^*)}$). *For every PPT adversary $\mathcal{A}$, there exists a PPT adversary $\mathcal{B}$, such that:* $|\mathsf{Adv}_{(4,a^*)}(\mathcal{A}) - \mathsf{Adv}_{(5,a^*)}(\mathcal{A})| \leq \mathsf{Adv}_{\mathsf{s\text{-}cPRF}}(\kappa, \mathcal{B})$.

Hybrid $\mathsf{H}_{(6,a^*)}$. Subprogram $\mathsf{HybridProof}_{6,a^*,\mathsf{crs}}$ precomputes and hardcodes the (C^*, π^*) corresponding to a^*. For this we make the crucial observation that for every a, there exists only one corresponding (x, w). This follows from the perfect correctness of the lossy encryption scheme LE, because LE is in injective mode

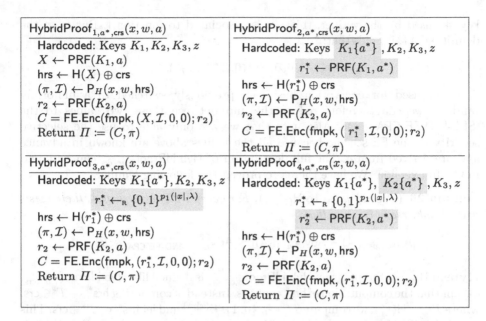

Fig. 9. Descriptions of HybridProof$_{i,a^*,\text{crs}}$, for $i = 1 \ldots 4$. In each subprogram, the changes relative to the previous subprogram are highlighted in gray. When we hardcode a value in a subprogram HybridProof$_{i,a^*,\text{crs}}$, it is understood that this value is also hardcoded in ProgProv$_{i,a^*,\text{crs}}$. If a key K is punctured in HybridProof$_{i,a^*,\text{crs}}$, we understand that it is punctured in ProgProv$_{i,a^*,\text{crs}}$ and all its subprograms as well. Note that HybridProof$_{1,a^*,\text{crs}}$ is the same as BindingProof$_{\text{crs}}$.

and because $a = \text{LE.Enc}(\text{lpk}, (x, w); r)$. To compute this hybrid, we use lsk to decrypt a^* and obtain the corresponding (x^*, w^*). Thus, if a^* is known in advance this means (x^*, w^*) is also known in advance. Since crs is a parameter of the circuit and also known in advance, we can compute hrs$^* \leftarrow \text{H}(r_1^*) \oplus \text{crs}$, $(\pi^*, \mathcal{I}^*) \leftarrow P_H(x^*, w^*, \text{hrs}^*)$ and $C^* = \text{FE.Enc}(\text{fmpk}, (r_1^*, \mathcal{I}^*, 0, 0); r_2^*)$. We hardcode (C^*, π^*) and these are also the returned values when HybridProof$_{6,a^*,\text{crs}}$ is invoked on (x^*, w^*, a^*). Since ProgProv$_{6,a^*,\text{crs}}$ is functionally equivalent to ProgProv$_{5,a^*,\text{crs}}$, this step is justified by iO security. The full description of HybridProof$_{6,a^*,\text{crs}}$ can be found in the full version. From all the above, we have the following lemma:

Lemma 25 (From $H_{(5,a^*)}$ to $H_{(6,a^*)}$). *For every PPT adversary $\mathcal{A}$, there exists a PPT adversary $\mathcal{B}$, such that:* $|\text{Adv}_{(5,a^*)}(\mathcal{A}) - \text{Adv}_{(6,a^*)}(\mathcal{A})| \leq \text{Adv}^{\text{iO}}(\kappa, \mathcal{B})$.

Hybrid $H_{(7,a^*)}$. To obtain subprogram HybridProof$_{7,a^*,\text{crs}}$, we use the selective security of the functional encryption scheme FE to switch ciphertext $C^* = \text{FE.Enc}(\text{fmpk}, (r_1^*, \mathcal{I}^*, 0, 0); r_2^*)$ to ciphertext $C^* = \text{FE.Enc}(\text{fmpk}, (0, \mathcal{I}^*, z, T_{\mathcal{I}^*}^*); r_2^*)$. We argue that these two ciphertexts are indistinguishable. Consider decryption key sk_f used by the verifier, this key is associated to function f. But from the definition of f, it holds that:

$$f(r_1^*, \mathcal{I}^*, 0, 0) = f(0, \mathcal{I}^*, z, T_{\mathcal{I}^*}^*).$$

Since r_2^* used for encryption has been previously switched to a uniformly random, we can therefore reduce the gap between these two games to the SEL-IND-FE-CPA game. Also note that we are only able to use the selective security of the FE scheme because all the values above are known in advance and are derived from a. The full description of $\mathsf{HybridProof}_{7,a^*,\mathsf{crs}}$ can be found in the full version. We have therefore proven the following lemma:

Lemma 26 (From $H_{(6,a^*)}$ to $H_{(7,a^*)}$). *For every PPT adversary $\mathcal{A}$, there exists a PPT adversary $\mathcal{B}$, such that:*

$$|\mathsf{Adv}_{(6,a^*)}(\mathcal{A}) - \mathsf{Adv}_{(7,a^*)}(\mathcal{A})| \leq \mathsf{Adv}_{\mathsf{Exp}\text{-}s\text{-}\mathsf{IND}\text{-}\mathsf{FE}\text{-}\mathsf{CPA}}^{\mathsf{FE}}(\kappa, \mathcal{B}).$$

Hybrid $H_{(8,a^*)}$. Subprogram $\mathsf{HybridProof}_{8,a^*,\mathsf{crs}}$ is defined like $\mathsf{HybridProof}_{7,a^*,\mathsf{crs}}$, except that the computation of hrs^* changes. Instead of computing $\mathsf{hrs}^* \leftarrow T^* \oplus \mathsf{crs}$, where $T^* \leftarrow H(r_1^*)$, we compute $T^* \leftarrow_R \{0,1\}^{p_1(|x|,\lambda)}$ and let $\mathsf{hrs}^* \leftarrow T^* \oplus \mathsf{crs}$. This step is justified by the dense mode of H. From Definition 2, we know that for uniformly random r_1^*, we have $H(r_1^*)$ statistically indistinguishable from a uniformly random. Moreover, by choosing the security parameter in $\mathsf{LF}.\mathsf{Setup}$ $(1^\lambda, \mathsf{dense})$ to be large enough, we can offset the $2^{p(|x|+\lambda)}$ factor coming from enumerating over all values of a. The full description of $\mathsf{HybridProof}_{8,a^*,\mathsf{crs}}$ can be found in the full version. We have therefore proven the following lemma:

Lemma 27 (From $H_{(7,a^*)}$ to $H_{(8,a^*)}$). *For every (potentially unbounded) adversary $\mathcal{A}$, it holds that:*

$$|\mathsf{Adv}_{(7,a^*)}(\mathcal{A}) - \mathsf{Adv}_{(8,a^*)}(\mathcal{A})| \leq \frac{1}{2^{p(|x|+\lambda)+\lambda}}.$$

Hybrid $H_{(9,a^*)}$. In this hybrid, we use the zero-knowledge property of the hidden-bits NIZK system to replace real proofs by simulated ones. Subprogram $\mathsf{HybridProof}_{9,a^*,\mathsf{crs}}$ is defined like $\mathsf{HybridProof}_{8,a^*,\mathsf{crs}}$, but now the precomputation of the program involves choosing a uniformly random $r_3^* \leftarrow_R \{0,1\}^{p_3(|x|,\lambda)}$. Polynomial $p_3(|x|, \lambda)$ represents the size of the random tape needed by the hidden-bits simulator S_H. Proofs are now simulated, i.e. $(\mathsf{hrs}_{I^*}^*, \pi^*, \mathcal{I}^*) \leftarrow S_H(x^*; r_3^*)$

We now argue that this hybrid is statistically indistinguishable from the previous one. The reason this works is that we already used FE security to ensure that only the revealed bits of the $\mathsf{hrs}_{I^*}^*$ are encoded in ciphertext C^* and also that hrs^* is uniformly random. This, coupled with the fact that in $H_{(9,a^*)}$ only the value of the real proof (C^*, π^*) is hardcoded means we can use the ZK property of NIZK_H. In $\mathsf{HybridProof}_{9,a^*,\mathsf{crs}}$ we can hardcode only the simulated proof, and there is no need to include the simulator code in $\mathsf{ProgProv}_{9,a^*,\mathsf{crs}}$.

The full description of $\mathsf{HybridProof}_{9,a^*,\mathsf{crs}}$ can be found in the full version, along with the proof of the following lemma:

Lemma 28 (From $H_{(8,a^*)}$ to $H_{(9,a^*)}$). *Let $a^* = \mathsf{LE.Enc}(\mathsf{lpk}, (x^*, w^*); r)$. Then it holds that either:*

1. *if $(x^*, w^*) \in R$, then $H_{(8,a^*)}$ and $H_{(9,a^*)}$ are statistically close. Namely, for every (potentially unbounded) adversary $\mathcal{A}$,*

$$|\mathsf{Adv}_{(8,a^*)}(\mathcal{A}) - \mathsf{Adv}_{(9,a^*)}(\mathcal{A})| \leq \Delta^{\mathsf{NIZK}_H}_{\mathsf{ZeroKnowledge}}(\lambda).$$

2. *if $(x^*, w^*) \notin R$, then $H_{(8,a^*)}$ and $H_{(9,a^*)}$ are computationally indistinguishable. Namely, for every PPT adversary $\mathcal{A}$, there exists PPT adversary $\mathcal{B}$, such that:*

$$|\mathsf{Adv}_{(8,a^*)}(\mathcal{A}) - \mathsf{Adv}_{(9,a^*)}(\mathcal{A})| \leq \mathsf{Adv}^{\mathsf{iO}}(\kappa, \mathcal{B}).$$

Hybrid $H_{(10,a^*)}$. In subprogram $\mathsf{HybridProof}_{10,a^*,\mathsf{crs}}$, the only change made is that r_2^* is changed from a uniformly random value (as in hybrid $H_{(9,a^*)}$) to $r_2^* \leftarrow \mathsf{PRF}(K_2, a^*)$. This change is justified by the pseudo-randomness of $\mathsf{PRF}(K_2, \cdot)$ at punctured point a^*. The full description of $\mathsf{HybridProof}_{10,a^*,\mathsf{crs}}$ can be found in the full version. We have the following lemma:

Lemma 29 (From $H_{(9,a^*)}$ to $H_{(10,a^*)}$). *For every PPT adversary $\mathcal{A}$, there exists a PPT adversary $\mathcal{B}$, such that:*

$$|\mathsf{Adv}_{(9,a^*)}(\mathcal{A}) - \mathsf{Adv}_{(10,a^*)}(\mathcal{A})| \leq \mathsf{Adv}_{\mathsf{s\text{-}cPRF}}(\kappa, \mathcal{B}).$$

Hybrid $H_{(11,a^*)}$. In subprogram $\mathsf{HybridProof}_{11,a^*,\mathsf{crs}}$, the only change made is that r_2 is not precomputed anymore (as in hybrid $H_{(10,a^*)}$).

Value $r_2 \leftarrow \mathsf{PRF}(K_2, a^*)$ is now compted on the fly. This means C must also be computed on the fly in this hybrid. These changes are justified by the fact that the two programs are functionally equivalent and thus their obfuscations computationally indistinguishable. The full description of $\mathsf{HybridProof}_{11,a^*,\mathsf{crs}}$ can be found in the full version. This shows the following lemma:

Lemma 30 (From $H_{(10,a^*)}$ to $H_{(11,a^*)}$). *For every PPT adversary $\mathcal{A}$, there exists a PPT adversary $\mathcal{B}$, such that:*

$$|\mathsf{Adv}_{(10,a^*)}(\mathcal{A}) - \mathsf{Adv}_{(11,a^*)}(\mathcal{A})| \leq \mathsf{Adv}^{\mathsf{iO}}(\kappa, \mathcal{B}).$$

Hybrid $H_{(12,a^*)}$. In subprogram $\mathsf{HybridProof}_{12,a^*,\mathsf{crs}}$, we puncture key K_3 at $K_3\{a^*\}$ and only hardcode this punctured key in our programs. This change is justified by the fact that the two programs are functionally equivalent and thus their obfuscations computationally indistinguishable. The full description of $\mathsf{HybridProof}_{12,a^*,\mathsf{crs}}$ can be found in the full version. This shows the following:

Lemma 31 (From $H_{(11,a^*)}$ to $H_{(12,a^*)}$). *For every PPT adversary $\mathcal{A}$, there exists a PPT adversary $\mathcal{B}$, such that:*

$$|\mathsf{Adv}_{(10,a^*)}(\mathcal{A}) - \mathsf{Adv}_{(11,a^*)}(\mathcal{A})| \leq \mathsf{Adv}^{\mathsf{iO}}(\kappa, \mathcal{B}).$$

Hybrid $H_{(13,a^*)}$**.** Subprogram $\mathsf{HybridProof}_{13,a^*,\mathsf{crs}}$ is changed so that r_3^* is not a hard-wired uniformly random value anymore, but is chosen as $r_3^* \leftarrow \mathsf{PRF}(K_3, a^*)$. This change is justified by the pseudo-randomness of $\mathsf{PRF}(K_3, \cdot)$ at punctured point a^*. The full description of $\mathsf{HybridProof}_{13,a^*,\mathsf{crs}}$ can be found in the full version. From the above, we have:

Lemma 32 (From $H_{(12,a^*)}$ **to** $H_{(13,a^*)}$**).** *For every PPT adversary* $\mathcal{A}$*, there exists a PPT adversary* $\mathcal{B}$*, such that:*

$$|\mathsf{Adv}_{(12,a^*)}(\mathcal{A}) - \mathsf{Adv}_{(13,a^*)}(\mathcal{A})| \leq \mathsf{Adv}_{\mathsf{s\text{-}cPRF}}(\kappa, \mathcal{B}).$$

Hybrid $H_{(14,a^*)}$**.** In subprogram $\mathsf{HybridProof}_{14,a^*,\mathsf{crs}}$ the key K_3 is not punctured anymore at a^*. This means that $r_3 \leftarrow \mathsf{PRF}(K_3, a)$ is not hardwired anymore. As a consequence, the simulated proofs are also not hardcoded. Since this program is functionally equivalent to $\mathsf{HybridProof}_{14,a^*,\mathsf{crs}}$, we justify this change by the security of iO. The full description of $\mathsf{HybridProof}_{14,a^*,\mathsf{crs}}$ can be found in the full version. From the above, we have:

Lemma 33 (From $H_{(13,a^*)}$ **to** $H_{(14,a^*)}$**).** *For every PPT adversary* $\mathcal{A}$*, there exists a PPT adversary* $\mathcal{B}$*, such that:*

$$|\mathsf{Adv}_{(13,a^*)}(\mathcal{A}) - \mathsf{Adv}_{(14,a^*)}(\mathcal{A})| \leq \mathsf{Adv}^{\mathsf{iO}}(\kappa, \mathcal{B}).$$

Hybrid $H_{(15,a^*)}$**.** In subprogram $\mathsf{HybridProof}_{15,a^*,\mathsf{crs}}$ the key K_1 is not punctured anymore at a^*. Key K_1 is not even used anymore in this subprogram, therefore this program is functionally equivalent to $\mathsf{HybridProof}_{14,a^*,\mathsf{crs}}$. We thus justify this change by the security of iO. The full description of $\mathsf{HybridProof}_{15,a^*,\mathsf{crs}}$ can be found in the full version. From all the above, we have:

Lemma 34 (From $H_{(14,a^*)}$ **to** $H_{(15,a^*)}$**).** *For every PPT adversary* $\mathcal{A}$*, there exists a PPT adversary* $\mathcal{B}$*, such that:*

$$|\mathsf{Adv}_{(14,a^*)}(\mathcal{A}) - \mathsf{Adv}_{(15,a^*)}(\mathcal{A})| \leq \mathsf{Adv}^{\mathsf{iO}}(\kappa, \mathcal{B}).$$

References

1. Agrikola, T., Hofheinz, D.: Interactively Secure Groups from Obfuscation. In: Abdalla, M., Dahab, R. (eds.) PKC 2018, Part II. LNCS, vol. 10770, pp. 341–370. Springer, Cham (2018). https://doi.org/10.1007/978-3-319-76581-5_12
2. Albrecht, M.R., Farshim, P., Hofheinz, D., Larraia, E., Paterson, K.G.: Multilinear maps from obfuscation. In: Kushilevitz, E., Malkin, T. (eds.) TCC 2016, Part I. LNCS, vol. 9562, pp. 446–473. Springer, Heidelberg (2016). https://doi.org/10.1007/978-3-662-49096-9_19
3. Barak, B., et al.: On the (im)possibility of obfuscating programs. In: Kilian, J. (ed.) CRYPTO 2001. LNCS, vol. 2139, pp. 1–18. Springer, Heidelberg (2001). https://doi.org/10.1007/3-540-44647-8_1

4. Belenkiy, M., Camenisch, J., Chase, M., Kohlweiss, M., Lysyanskaya, A., Shacham, H.: Randomizable proofs and delegatable anonymous credentials. In: Halevi, S. (ed.) CRYPTO 2009. LNCS, vol. 5677, pp. 108–125. Springer, Heidelberg (2009). https://doi.org/10.1007/978-3-642-03356-8_7

5. Bellare, M., Hofheinz, D., Yilek, S.: Possibility and impossibility results for encryption and commitment secure under selective opening. In: Joux, A. (ed.) EUROCRYPT 2009. LNCS, vol. 5479, pp. 1–35. Springer, Heidelberg (2009). https://doi.org/10.1007/978-3-642-01001-9_1

6. Bitansky, N., Paneth, O.: ZAPs and Non-Interactive Witness Indistinguishability from Indistinguishability Obfuscation. In: Dodis, Y., Nielsen, J.B. (eds.) TCC 2015, Part II. LNCS, vol. 9015, pp. 401–427. Springer, Heidelberg (2015). https://doi.org/10.1007/978-3-662-46497-7_16

7. Bitansky, N., Paneth, O., Wichs, D.: Perfect Structure on the Edge of Chaos. In: Kushilevitz, E., Malkin, T. (eds.) TCC 2016, Part I. LNCS, vol. 9562, pp. 474–502. Springer, Heidelberg (2016). https://doi.org/10.1007/978-3-662-49096-9_20

8. Bitansky, N., Vaikuntanathan, V.: Indistinguishability obfuscation from functional encryption. In: Guruswami, V (ed.) 56th FOCS, pp. 171–190. IEEE Computer Society Press, October 2015

9. Blazy, O., Fuchsbauer, G., Izabachène, M., Jambert, A., Sibert, H., Vergnaud, D.: Batch groth–sahai. In: Zhou, J., Yung, M. (eds.) ACNS 2010. LNCS, vol. 6123, pp. 218–235. Springer, Heidelberg (2010). https://doi.org/10.1007/978-3-642-13708-2_14

10. Blum, M., Feldman, P., Micali, S.: Non-interactive zero-knowledge and its applications (extended abstract). In: 20th ACM STOC, pp. 103–112. ACM Press, May 1988

11. Boldyreva, A., Fehr, S., O'Neill, A.: On notions of security for deterministic encryption, and efficient constructions without random oracles. In: Wagner, D. (ed.) CRYPTO 2008. LNCS, vol. 5157, pp. 335 359. Springer, Heidelberg (2008). https://doi.org/10.1007/978-3-540-85174-5_19

12. Boneh, D., Sahai, A., Waters, B.: Functional encryption: definitions and challenges. In: Ishai, Y. (ed.) TCC 2011. LNCS, vol. 6597, pp. 253–273. Springer, Heidelberg (2011). https://doi.org/10.1007/978-3-642-19571-6_16

13. Boneh, D., Waters, B.: Constrained pseudorandom functions and their applications. In: Sako, K., Sarkar, P. (eds.) ASIACRYPT 2013, Part II. LNCS, vol. 8270, pp. 280–300. Springer, Heidelberg (2013). https://doi.org/10.1007/978-3-642-42045-0_15

14. Boyle, E., Goldwasser, S., Ivan, I.: Functional signatures and pseudorandom functions. In: Krawczyk, H. (ed.) PKC 2014. LNCS, vol. 8383, pp. 501–519. Springer, Heidelberg (2014). https://doi.org/10.1007/978-3-642-54631-0_29

15. Canetti, R., Chen, Y., Holmgren, J., Lombardi, A., Rothblum, G.N., Rothblum, R.: Fiat-shamir from simpler assumptions. IACR Cryptology ePrint Archive 2018:1004 (2018)

16. Canetti, R., Chen, Y., Reyzin, L.: On the correlation intractability of obfuscated pseudorandom functions. In: Kushilevitz, E., Malkin, T. (eds.) TCC 2016, Part I. LNCS, vol. 9562, pp. 389–415. Springer, Heidelberg (2016). https://doi.org/10.1007/978-3-662-49096-9_17

17. Canetti, R., Lichtenberg, A.: Certifying trapdoor permutations, revisited. In: TCC 2018 (2018). http://eprint.iacr.org/2017/631

18. Canetti, R., Lin, H., Tessaro, S., Vaikuntanathan, V.: Obfuscation of probabilistic circuits and applications. In: Dodis, Y., Nielsen, J.B. (eds.) TCC 2015, Part II. LNCS, vol. 9015, pp. 468–497. Springer, Heidelberg (2015). https://doi.org/10.1007/978-3-662-46497-7_19
19. Canetti, R., Lombardi, A., Wichs, D.: Non-interactive zero knowledge and correlation intractability from circular-secure FHE. Cryptology ePrint Archive, Report 2018/1248 (2018). http://eprint.iacr.org/
20. Escala, A., Groth, J.: Fine-tuning groth-sahai proofs. In: Krawczyk, H. (ed.) PKC 2014. LNCS, vol. 8383, pp. 630–649. Springer, Heidelberg (2014). https://doi.org/10.1007/978-3-642-54631-0_36
21. Farshim, P., Hesse, J., Hofheinz, D., Larraia, E.: Graded encoding schemes from obfuscation. In: Abdalla, M., Dahab, R. (eds.) PKC 2018, Part II. LNCS, vol. 10770, pp. 371–400. Springer, Cham (2018). https://doi.org/10.1007/978-3-319-76581-5_13
22. Feige, U., Lapidot, D., Shamir, A.: Multiple noninteractive zero knowledge proofs under general assumptions. SIAM J. Comput. 29(1), 1–28 (1999)
23. Feige, U., Shamir, A.: Witness indistinguishable and witness hiding protocols. In: 22nd ACM STOC, pp. 416–426. ACM Press, May 1990
24. Fiat, A., Shamir, A.: How to prove yourself: practical solutions to identification and signature problems. In: Odlyzko, A.M. (ed.) CRYPTO 1986. LNCS, vol. 263, pp. 186–194. Springer, Heidelberg (1987). https://doi.org/10.1007/3-540-47721-7_12
25. Freeman, D.M., Goldreich, O., Kiltz, E., Rosen, A., Segev, G.: More constructions of lossy and correlation-secure trapdoor functions. J. Cryptol. 26(1), 39–74 (2013)
26. Garg, S., Gentry, C., Halevi, S., Raykova, M., Sahai, A., Waters, B.: Candidate indistinguishability obfuscation and functional encryption for all circuits. In: 54th FOCS, pp. 40–49. IEEE Computer Society Press, October 2013
27. Goldreich, O., Goldwasser, S., Micali, S.: How to construct random functions (extended abstract). In: 25th FOCS, pp. 464–479. IEEE Computer Society Press, October 1984
28. Goldreich, O., Micali, S., Wigderson, A.: Proofs that yield nothing but their validity or all languages in NP have zero-knowledge proof systems. J. ACM 38(3), 691–729 (1991)
29. Goldwasser, S., Micali, S., Rackoff, C.: The knowledge complexity of interactive proof-systems (extended abstract). In: 17th ACM STOC, pp. 291–304. ACM Press, May 1985
30. Goldwasser, S., Ostrovsky, R.: Invariant signatures and non-interactive zero-knowledge proofs are equivalent. In: Brickell, E.F. (ed.) CRYPTO 1992. LNCS, vol. 740, pp. 228–245. Springer, Heidelberg (1993). https://doi.org/10.1007/3-540-48071-4_16
31. Groth, J., Ostrovsky, R., Sahai, A.: Non-interactive zaps and new techniques for NIZK. In: Dwork, C. (ed.) CRYPTO 2006. LNCS, vol. 4117, pp. 97–111. Springer, Heidelberg (2006). https://doi.org/10.1007/11818175_6
32. Groth, J., Sahai, A.: Efficient non-interactive proof systems for bilinear groups. In: Smart, N. (ed.) EUROCRYPT 2008. LNCS, vol. 4965, pp. 415–432. Springer, Heidelberg (2008). https://doi.org/10.1007/978-3-540-78967-3_24
33. Hartung, G., Hoffmann, M., Nagel, M., Rupp, A.: BBA+: improving the security and applicability of privacy-preserving point collection. In: Thuraisingham, B.M., Evans, D., Malkin, T., Xu, D. (eds.) ACM CCS 2017, pp. 1925–1942. ACM Press, October/November 2017
34. Håstad, J., Impagliazzo, R., Levin, L.A., Luby, M.: A pseudorandom generator from any one-way function. SIAM J. Comput. 28(4), 1364–1396 (1999)

35. Herold, G., Hesse, J., Hofheinz, D., Ràfols, C., Rupp, A.: Polynomial spaces: a new framework for composite-to-prime-order transformations. In: Garay, J.A., Gennaro, R. (eds.) CRYPTO 2014, Part I. LNCS, vol. 8616, pp. 261–279. Springer, Heidelberg (2014). https://doi.org/10.1007/978-3-662-44371-2_15

36. Kiayias, A., Papadopoulos, S., Triandopoulos, N., Zacharias, T.: Delegatable pseudorandom functions and applications. In: Sadeghi, A.-R., Gligor, V.D., Yung, M. (eds.) ACM CCS 2013, pp. 669–684. ACM Press, November 2013

37. Lindell, Y.: An efficient transform from sigma protocols to NIZK with a CRS and non-programmable random oracle. In: Dodis, Y., Nielsen, J.B. (eds.) TCC 2015, Part I. LNCS, vol. 9014, pp. 93–109. Springer, Heidelberg (2015). https://doi.org/10.1007/978-3-662-46494-6_5

38. O'Neill, A.: Definitional issues in functional encryption. Cryptology ePrint Archive, Report 2010/556 (2010). http://eprint.iacr.org/2010/556

39. Peikert, C., Shiehian, S.: Noninteractive zero knowledge for NP from (plain) learning with errors. IACR Cryptology ePrint Archive 2019:158 (2019)

40. Peikert, C., Vaikuntanathan, V., Waters, B.: A framework for efficient and composable oblivious transfer. In: Wagner, D. (ed.) CRYPTO 2008. LNCS, vol. 5157, pp. 554–571. Springer, Heidelberg (2008). https://doi.org/10.1007/978-3-540-85174-5_31

41. Peikert, C., Waters, B.: Lossy trapdoor functions and their applications. In: Ladner, R.E., Dwork, C. (eds.) 40th ACM STOC, pp. 187–196. ACM Press, May 2008

42. Sahai, A., Waters, B.: How to use indistinguishability obfuscation: deniable encryption, and more. In: Shmoys, D.B. (ed.) 46th ACM STOC, pp. 475–484. ACM Press, May/June 2014

43. Sahai, A., Waters, B.: Fuzzy identity-based encryption. In: Cramer, R. (ed.) EUROCRYPT 2005. LNCS, vol. 3494, pp. 457–473. Springer, Heidelberg (2005). https://doi.org/10.1007/11426639_27

44. Schnorr, C.P.: Efficient identification and signatures for smart cards. In: Brassard, G. (ed.) CRYPTO 1989. LNCS, vol. 435, pp. 239–252. Springer, New York (1990). https://doi.org/10.1007/0-387-34805-0_22

Output Compression, MPC, and iO for Turing Machines

Saikrishna Badrinarayanan[1](✉), Rex Fernando[1], Venkata Koppula[2], Amit Sahai[1], and Brent Waters[3]

[1] UCLA, Los Angeles, USA
{saikrishna,rex,sahai}@cs.ucla.edu
[2] Weizmann Institute of Science, Rehovot, Israel
venkata.koppula@weizmann.ac.il
[3] UT Austin and NTT Research, Austin, USA
bwaters@cs.utexas.edu

Abstract. In this work, we study the fascinating notion of output-compressing randomized encodings for Turing Machines, in a *shared randomness model*. In this model, the encoder and decoder have access to a shared random string, and the efficiency requirement is, the size of the encoding must be independent of the running time and output length of the Turing Machine on the given input, while the length of the shared random string is allowed to grow with the length of the output. We show how to construct output-compressing randomized encodings for Turing machines in the shared randomness model, assuming iO for circuits and any assumption in the set {LWE, DDH, N^{th} Residuosity}.

We then show interesting implications of the above result to basic feasibility questions in the areas of secure multiparty computation (MPC) and indistinguishability obfuscation (iO):

1. **Compact MPC for Turing Machines in the Random Oracle Model.** In the context of MPC, we consider the following basic feasibility question: does there exist a malicious-secure MPC protocol for Turing Machines whose communication complexity is independent of the running time and output length of the Turing Machine when executed on the combined inputs of all parties? We call such a protocol as a *compact* MPC protocol. Hubáček and Wichs [HW15] showed via an incompressibility argument, that, even for the restricted setting of circuits, it is impossible to construct a malicious secure two party computation protocol in the plain model where the communication complexity is independent of the output length. In this work, we show how to evade this impossibility by compiling any (non-compact) MPC protocol in the plain model to a *compact* MPC protocol for Turing Machines in the Random Oracle Model, assuming output-compressing randomized encodings in the shared randomness model.

2. **Succinct iO for Turing Machines in the Shared Randomness Model.** In all existing constructions of iO for Turing Machines, the size of the obfuscated program grows with a bound on the input length. In this work, we show how to construct an iO scheme for

© International Association for Cryptologic Research 2019
S. D. Galbraith and S. Moriai (Eds.): ASIACRYPT 2019, LNCS 11921, pp. 342–370, 2019.
https://doi.org/10.1007/978-3-030-34578-5_13

Turing Machines in the shared randomness model where the size of the obfuscated program is independent of a bound on the input length, assuming iO for circuits and any assumption in the set {LWE, DDH, N^{th} Residuosity}.

1 Introduction

In this work, we study the fascinating notion of output-compressing randomized encodings for Turing machines. We explore the implication of such encodings to a natural and surprisingly unexplored form of secure multiparty computation for Turing Machines, and also to indistinguishability obfuscation for Turing Machines.

Output-compressing randomized encodings were introduced in the works of Ananth and Jain [AJ15] and Lin, Pass, Seth and Telang [LPST16] as a generalization of randomized encodings [IK00] and succinct randomized encodings [KLW15, BGL+15, CHJV15]. Recall that in an output-compressing randomized encoding scheme for Turing machines, there exists an encode algorithm that takes as input a Turing machine M and an input x. It outputs an encoding $\widetilde{M_x}$ such that the decode algorithm, given this encoding $\widetilde{M_x}$, can compute the output $M(x)$. The efficiency requirement is that for any machine M and input x, the size of the encoding is $\mathsf{poly}(|M|, |x|, \lambda)$, for some fixed polynomial poly, where λ is the security parameter. In particular, the size of the encoding should be *independent of the output length* and the running time of the machine M on input x.[1] In those papers, the authors defined both indistinguishability based and simulation based security notions. In this work, we will focus on the stronger notion of simulation based security. This notion requires an output-compressing randomized encoding scheme to have a corresponding simulator Sim, that, for any Turing machine M and input x, given just the output $M(x)$, along with the size of the machine $|M|$ and the input length $|x|$, outputs a simulated encoding $\widetilde{M_x}$ that is indistinguishable from a real encoding of the machine M and input x.[2] As stated here, this goal is impossible in the standard model due to an "incompressibility" argument as shown by Lin et al. [LPST16]. Such incompressibility arguments have been a source of impossibility proofs in many areas of cryptography such as functional encryption, garbled circuits and secure multiparty computation [BSW11, AIKW13, CIJ+13, AGVW13, HW15] and this is perhaps the reason why simulation secure output compressing randomized encodings have not been well-studied so far.

Our starting observation is that the above impossibility fails to hold in a *shared randomness model*, where the size of the randomness can grow with

---

[1] The size can depend logarithmically on the output length and running time.

[2] We actually consider a stronger notion where part of the input need not be hidden, and we require that the size of the encoding should not grow with this revealed part. This is a generalization of the notion of partial garbling schemes introduced by Ishai and Wee [IW14].

the output length. More formally, both the encoder and decoder share a random string (whose size can grow with the output length) and we require two properties: (1) For any machine M and input x, the size of the encoding is $\mathsf{poly}(|M|, |x|, \lambda)$, for some fixed polynomial poly. (2) There exists a simulator Sim, that, for any Turing machine M and input x, given just the output $M(x)$, along with the length of the machine $|M|$ and the input length $|x|$, outputs a pair of a simulated encoding $\widetilde{M_x}$ and a shared random string that is indistinguishable from the pair of a real encoding and a uniformly random string.

Our first main result is that we can, in fact, construct output-compressing randomized encodings for Turing machines in the shared randomness model, assuming indistinguishability obfuscation (iO) for circuits along with any assumption in {Decisional Diffie Hellman (DDH), Learning With Errors (LWE), N^{th} Residuosity} where the size of the shared randomness equals the output length. Recall that iO is necessary because output-compressing randomized encodings for Turing machines implies iO for circuits as shown by Lin et al. [LPST16] (it is easy to see that this implication to iO remains true even in the shared randomness model). We describe the techniques used in our construction in Sect. 2.1. We then use this new tool to tackle basic feasibility questions in the context of two fundamental areas in Cryptography: secure multiparty computation (MPC) and indistinguishability obfuscation (iO).

Compact MPC for Turing Machines with Unbounded Output in the Random Oracle model. The first basic feasibility question we address is the following: Consider a set of n mutually distrusting parties with inputs $x_1, \ldots, x_n$ respectively that agree on a Turing machine M. Their goal is to securely compute the output $M(x_1, \ldots, x_n)$ without leaking any information about their respective inputs, where we stress that the output can be of any unbounded polynomial size. Crucially, we require that the communication complexity of the protocol (the sum of the length of the messages exchanged by all the parties) is $\mathsf{poly}(|M|, |x_1|, \ldots, |x_n|, \lambda)$ for some fixed polynomial poly where λ is the security parameter. In particular, the communication complexity should be independent of the output length and the running time of the machine M on input $(x_1, \ldots, x_n)$. We call such an MPC protocol to be *compact*. Indeed, this communication efficiency requirement is the most natural efficiency requirement in the context of MPC for Turing machines.

Remarkably, this extremely basic question, in the context of Turing machines, has never been considered before to the best of our knowledge (see related work below for comparison with previous work). At first glance, one may think that Fully Homomorphic Encryption (FHE), one of the most powerful primitives in Cryptography, should help solve this problem. The reason being that, at least in the two party setting, FHE allows one party to encrypt its input and send it to the other party, who can then homomorphically evaluate the function to be computed "under the hood" and compute an encryption of the final output. However, its then not clear how this evaluator would learn the output since he does not have the decryption key. Sending the encryption of the final output to the other party would also blow up the communication complexity. This is related to the question posed by Hubáček and Wichs [HW15], where they consider a circuit based model, a special case of our notion. That is, they consider n parties who wish to securely evaluate a circuit on their joint inputs such that the communication complexity of the protocol is independent of the output length of the circuit. They show how to achieve semi-honest secure two party computation with this efficiency requirement assuming iO for circuits and a somewhere statistically binding (SSB) hash function. Further, they showed that in the context of malicious adversaries,[3] in the standard model, it is impossible to construct a secure computation protocol with such efficiency requirement even for just two party computation.

Our approach to this problem is motivated by an unwillingness to give up on malicious secure compact MPC. To that end we must find a way to evade the impossibility result, and we do so by considering the well-studied programmable random oracle (RO) model [BR93, Nie02, DSW08, Wee09, CJS14, CDG+18]. We stress that the RO model is typically exploited in pursuit of efficiency improvements, but here we are seeking to use it to establish basic feasibility results. Indeed, the RO model has enabled important feasibility results in the past which were impossible in the plain model, for example unconditional non-interactive zero-knowledge arguments for NP with sub-linear communication [IMS12] and Universal Samplers [HJK+16]. In addition, a straightforward modification of the impossibility argument in [HW15] shows the programmable RO model is the weakest model in which we can hope to obtain simulation-secure compact MPC. In the programmable RO model, the simulator is allowed to choose the RO's responses to the adversary *adaptively*, based on the adversary's previous messages. If we restrict the simulator to choosing the RO's responses *selectively*, before any interaction with the adversary, then this model is not sufficient to achieve compact MPC. This also rules out the possibility of compact MPC in the CRS model.[4] Aside from its theoretical interest in terms of basic feasibility, our work motivates the following question: is there a weaker notion of security for MPC for which compact MPC is realizable in the plain model? A full answer to this question is outside the scope of this paper, but we believe that this is an excellent topic for future work. As a starting point, in the full version of our paper we sketch a simple example where the techniques in our paper can still yield meaningful security guarantees in the plain model.

More specifically, we show how to construct a *compact* constant round MPC protocol for Turing machines in the RO model secure against malicious adversaries, assuming iO for circuits and any assumption in {DDH, LWE, N^{th} Residuosity}. Recall that by *compact*, we mean that the communication complexity of the protocol is independent of the output length and running time of the Turing machine being evaluated on the joint inputs of the parties. We obtain this result by using output-compressing randomized encodings in the shared randomness

---

[3] Their impossibility in fact even ruled out the simpler setting of honest but deterministic adversaries - such an adversary behaves honestly in the protocol execution but fixes its random tape to some deterministic value.

[4] See the full version of the paper for a full presentation of this argument, based on Theorem 4.3 in [HW15].

model to compile any non-compact malicious secure constant round MPC protocol (even just for circuits) in the plain model into a *compact* constant round MPC protocol for Turing machines in the RO model while preserving the round complexity. We again stress that to the best of our knowledge, this is the first MPC protocol for Turing machines where the communication complexity is bounded by a polynomial in the description length of the machine and the input lengths of all the parties. We also observe that as a corollary of our work, we obtain the first malicious secure compact MPC protocol in the circuit based model of Hubáček and Wichs [HW15], in the RO model. We describe the techniques used in our construction in Sect. 2.2.

Succinct iO for Turing Machines for Bounded Inputs in the Shared Randomness Model. The problem of bootstrapping from iO for circuits to iO for Turing machines has been the subject of intense study over the last few years. In 2015, in three concurrent works [KLW15, BGL+15, CHJV15][5] showed how to construct iO for Turing machines where the size of the obfuscation grows with a bound on the input length to the Turing machine. In this work, we ask the following question: can we construct iO for Turing machines in the shared randomness model where the obfuscator and evaluator have a shared random string that grows with the input bound but the size of the obfuscation does not?

Lin et al. [LPST16] showed that output-compressing randomized encodings are closely related to iO for Turing machines. That is, they showed that simulation secure output-compressing randomized encodings in the plain model implies iO for Turing machines with unbounded inputs.[6] In particular, this implies iO for Turing machines with bounded inputs where the size of the obfuscation does not grow with the input bound. As we know, simulation secure output-compressing randomized encodings are impossible in the plain model. However, in turns out that this implication does not carry over in the shared randomness model. That is, if we start with output-compressing randomized encodings in the shared randomness model and apply the transformation in [LPST16], in the resulting iO scheme, the size of the obfuscation does in fact grow with the input bound. The key obstacle is that in the transformation, the obfuscation consists of an output-compressing randomized encoding that is the root of a GGM-like tree [GGM86]. This encoding, on evaluation, outputs another output-compressing randomized encoding corresponding to its child node and the process is repeated. In order to evaluate the obfuscated program on an input of length n, the evaluator has to traverse the obfuscated program up to a depth of length n. As a result, the machine being encoded in the root needs the shared randomness for each layer, up to a depth of length n. Hence, the size of the machine encoded in the root

---

[5] Recently, concurrent to our work, [AL18, AM18, GS18] also showed how to construct iO for Turing machines where, similar to [KLW15, BGL+15, CHJV15], the size of the obfuscation grows with a bound on the input length to the Turing machine.

[6] Lin et al. [LPST16] in fact showed that a weaker notion of distributional indistinguishability based secure output-compressing randomized encodings suffices to imply iO for Turing machines with unbounded inputs. However, they also supplement this by showing that it is impossible, in general, to construct such encodings.

grows with the input bound and so does the size of the obfuscated program. Note that this approach fails even if the size of the shared randomness for the encoding is just 1 bit (independent of the length of the output).

We show how to overcome this obstacle by taking a completely different approach. In our solution, the obfuscated program consists of an output-compressing randomized encoding in which, crucially, neither the machine being encoded nor the input to the machine, depends on the input bound of the obfuscation scheme. Hence, the size of the encoding, and therefore, also the size of the obfuscation, does not grow with the input bound. We elaborate more about the techniques used in our construction in Sect. 2.3. Concretely, letting n denote the input bound, we obtain iO for Turing machines M in the shared randomness model where the size of the obfuscation is $\mathsf{poly}_1(|M|, \lambda)$ for some fixed polynomial poly_1, and where the obfuscator and evaluator have a shared random string of length $\mathsf{poly}(n, \lambda)$ for some fixed polynomial poly. Our assumptions are again iO for circuits and any assumption in $\{\text{DDH}, \text{LWE}, N^{th} \text{ Residuosity}\}$.

On Reuse of the Shared Randomness. We note that it is possible for multiple output-compressing randomized encodings to reuse the shared randomness in a limited way. Namely, if we have several output-compressing randomized encodings, and we can construct hybrids such that only one randomized encoding needs to be simulated at a time, then all of the encodings can share the same CRS. This applies to the succinct iO construction: multiple circuits can be obfuscated using a single shared random string. Moreover, modulo a preprocessing phase which can be shared among all obfuscations, the time to obfuscate M is independent of the output length or running time of M.

1.1 Our Results

In this paper, we achieve the following results.

(1) Output-compressing randomized encodings.
We prove the following theorem:

Theorem 1 (Informal). *There exists an output-compressing randomized encoding scheme for Turing machines in the shared randomness model assuming the existence of:*

- *iO for circuits (AND)*
- *$A \in \{DDH, LWE, N^{th} \text{ Residuosity}\}$.*

Further, the length of the shared randomness is equal to the output length.

(2) Compact MPC for Turing machines with unbounded output in the RO model.
We prove the following theorem:

Theorem 2 (Informal). *For any n, $t > 0$, there exists a constant round compact MPC protocol amongst n parties for Turing machines in the Programmable Random Oracle model that is malicious secure against up to t corruptions assuming the existence of:*

- *Output-compressing randomized encodings in the shared randomness model (AND)*
- *Constant round MPC protocol amongst n parties in the plain model that is malicious secure against up to t corruptions.*

Once again, recall that by *compact*, we mean that the communication complexity of the protocol is independent of the output length and running time of the Turing machine being evaluated on the joint inputs of the parties. Here, we note that the above compiler even works if the underlying MPC protocol is for circuits. That is, we can convert any constant round protocol for circuits into a constant round protocol for Turing machines (with an input bound) by first converting the Turing machine into a (potentially large) circuit.

Also, we can instantiate the underlying MPC protocol in the following manner to get a round optimal compact MPC: append a non-interactive zero knowledge argument based on DLIN in the common random string model [GOS06] to either the two round semi-malicious MPC protocol of [MW16] that is based on LWE in the common random string model or the ones of [GS18, BL18] that are based on DDH/N^{th} residuosity in the plain model, to get two round malicious secure MPC protocols in the common random string model. We can then implement the common random string required for the underlying protocol via the RO. We thus achieve the following corollary:

Corollary 1. *Assuming the existence of:*

- *iO for circuits (AND)*
- *DDH, or LWE, or N^{th} Residuosity (AND)*
- *DLIN,*

there exists a compact, round optimal *(two round) MPC protocol π for Turing machines in the Programmable Random Oracle model that is malicious secure against a dishonest majority.*

Our result also gives a malicious secure *compact* MPC protocol in the circuit-based setting of [HW15] in the RO model. We also achieve other interesting corollaries by instantiating the underlying MPC protocol in the setting of super-polynomial simulation or in the setting of concurrent executions. We elaborate on both the above points in Sect. 6.

(3) Succinct iO for Turing machines for bounded inputs in the shared randomness model.
We prove the following theorem:

Theorem 3 (Informal). *There exists an iO scheme for Turing machines in the shared randomness model where the size of the obfuscated program is independent of the input bound assuming the existence of:*

- *iO for circuits,*
- *DDH, or LWE, or N^{th} Residuosity.*

1.2 Related Work

Lin, Pass, Seth and Telang [LPST16] construct OCREs from compact functional encryption (which is implied by iO), in the common *reference* string model. This is different from the shared randomness model in that the CRS which is shared among all parties must be generated in a specific fashion: in particular, [LPST16] require that the CRS be a specific function secret key. This model requires more trust be placed in the trusted setup phase. We note that our construction of compact MPC requires strong OCREs in the shared randomness model; [LPST16] does not consider strong OCREs, but even if a construction did exist in the common reference string model, to the best of our knowledge, it would not be sufficient to construct compact MPC.

A series of works [OS97, GHL+14, GGMP16, Mia16, HY16, LO17] consider MPC for RAM programs. However, in all of them, the communication complexity of the protocol grows with the running time of the RAM program. As a result, the communication complexity of the protocol in the Turing machine model would also grow with the output length. We stress that in our work, we require that the communication complexity can grow with neither output length nor running time of the Turing machine.

Ananth et al. [AJS17] construct an iO scheme for Turing machines in which, for any machine M and input bound L, the size of the obfuscation is $|M| + \mathsf{poly}(L, \lambda)$. However, in our setting, we require that the size be independent of this bound L.

2 Technical Overview

2.1 Output Compressing Randomized Encodings

We will now discuss a high-level overview of our output-compressing randomized encoding (OcRE) scheme in the *shared randomness model*. Let $\mathcal{M}$ be a family of Turing machines with output size bounded by o-len. An OcRE scheme for $\mathcal{M}$ in the shared randomness model consists of a setup algorithm, an encoding algorithm and a decoding algorithm. The setup algorithm takes as input security parameter λ together with a string rnd of length o-len, and outputs a succinct encoding key ek of size $\mathsf{poly}(\lambda)$.[7] This encoding key is used by the encoding algorithm, which takes as input a machine $M \in \mathcal{M}$, an input $x \in \{0,1\}^*$, and outputs an encoding $\widetilde{M_x}$. Finally, the decoding algorithm can use $\widetilde{M_x}$ and rnd to recover $M(x)$. For efficiency, we require that the encoding time depends only on $|M|$, $|x|$ and security parameter λ. In particular, the size of the encoding should not grow with the output length o-len or the running time of M on x.[8]

---

[7] We will assume o-len is at most 2^λ.

[8] Strictly speaking, it is allowed to depend polylogarithmically on the running time of M on input x; for this overview, we will ignore this polylogarithmic dependence on the running time.

The starting point of our construction is the succinct randomized encoding scheme of [KLW15], which is an encoding scheme for *boolean* Turing machines, and the size of the encoding depends only on $|M|, |x|$ and security parameter λ. We want to use this tool as a building block to build an encoding scheme for *general* Turing machines (i.e. with multi-bit output) where the size of the encoding still only depends on $|M|, |x|$ and λ. As a first step, let us consider the following approach. The encoding algorithm outputs an obfuscated program $\mathsf{Prog}[M, x]$, which has M and x hardwired, takes input $j \in$ [o-len], and outputs a KLW encoding of M_j, x (the randomness for computing the encoding is obtained by applying a PRF on j). Here, M_j is a boolean Turing machine which, on input x, outputs the jth bit of $M(x)$. The decoding algorithm runs Prog for each $j \in$ [o-len], obtains o-len different encodings, and then decodes each of them to obtain the entire output bit by bit. Clearly, this construction satisfies the efficiency requirement. This is because the size of the program Prog depends only on $|M|, |x|$, and hence the size of the encoding only depends on $|M|, |x|, \lambda$. As far as security is concerned, it is easy to show that this scheme satisfies indistinguishability-based security; that is, if (M_0, x_0) and (M_1, x_1) are two pairs such that $M_0(x_0) = M_1(x_1)$, $|M_0| = |M_1|$, $|x_0| = |x_1|$, then the obfuscation of $\mathsf{Prog}[M_0, x_0]$ is computationally indistinguishable from the obfuscation of $\mathsf{Prog}[M_1, x_1]$. Unfortunately, recall that our goal is simulation security, and it is not possible to simulate an obfuscation of $\mathsf{Prog}[M, x]$, given only $M(x)$ as input. In particular, if $y = M(x)$ is a long pseudorandom string (whose length can be much longer than the size of $\mathsf{Prog}[M,]$), then should be hard to compress y to a short encoding (as shown by Lin et al. [LPST16]).

As noted in the previous section, we will evade the "incompressibility" argument by allowing the shared randomness to have size that grows with the output length. Our goal will be to allow the simulator to embed the output of the machine M in this randomness. Our second attempt is as follows. The setup algorithm computes a short commitment ek to the shared randomness (say with a Merkle tree), and outputs ek as the encoding key. The encoding algorithm computes an obfuscation of $\mathsf{Prog}[M, x, \mathsf{ek}]$, which has M, x, ek hardwired, takes as input an index j, a bit b (which is supposed to be the jth bit of the shared randomness), and an opening π that the bit b is indeed the jth bit of the shared random string. The program checks the proof π, and then computes a KLW encoding of (M_j, x).

While the bit b is essentially ignored in the real-world encoding, it is used by the simulator in the ideal world. In the ideal world, the simulator, on receiving $M(x)$, masks it with a pseudorandomly generated one-time pad and outputs the resultant string as the shared randomness, and the short commitment ek is computed as in real world. For the encoding, it outputs an obfuscation of $\mathsf{Prog\text{-}sim}[\mathsf{ek}]$, which takes as input (j, b, π), checks the proof π, unmasks the bit b to obtain $M(x)_j$ and simulates the KLW randomized encoding using $M(x)_j$. This program has behavior identical to $\mathsf{Prog}[M, x, \mathsf{ek}]$ as long as the adversary only gives openings to the original bits of the shared randomness.

There is a simple problem with this idea: obfuscation only guarantees indistinguishability of programs that are functionally equivalent, and although the security of a Merkle tree would make it computationally infeasible for an adversary to come up with an opening to a wrong value, these inputs do in fact exist. To fix this problem, we use a special iO-compatible family of hash functions called 'somewhere-statistically binding (SSB) hash', introduced by [HW15]. Intuitively, this primitive is similar to a merkle tree except for two additional features. First, it allows a given position to be statistically "bound", where for that index it is only possible to give an opening for the correct bit. So there are three algorithms, Setup, Open, and Verify, as in the case of a Merkle tree, but Setup additionally takes as input a position to bind. If j is the bound position for H then there is no opening π for a bit $b \neq x_j$ such that $\mathsf{Verify}(\pi, b, j, H(x))$ accepts. Second, this bound position is hidden, so we can change it without being detected. Using this new hash allows us to make a series of hybrids where we change the shared randomness one bit at a time without giving up indistinguishability.

2.2 Compact MPC for Turing Machines in the Random Oracle Model

We now describe the techniques used in our round preserving compiler from any non-compact constant round malicious secure MPC protocol in the plain model to a *compact* constant round malicious secure MPC protocol in the RO model, using output-compressing randomized encodings in the shared randomness model.

To begin with, consider any constant round MPC protocol π in the plain model. For simplicity, lets assume that every party broadcasts a message in each round. In order to make it compact, our main idea is a very simple one: use output-compressing randomized encodings to compress the messages sent by every party in each round so that they are independent of the output length and running time of the machine. That is, instead of sending the actual message of protocol π, each party just sends an output-compressing randomized encoding of a machine and its private input that generates the actual message.

More precisely, consider a party P with input x that intends to send a message msg_1 in the first round as part of executing protocol π. Let's denote M to be the Turing machine that all the parties wish to evaluate. Let M_1 denote the algorithm used by the first party to generate this message msg_1 in the first round. Now, instead of sending msg_1, P sends an encoding of machine M_1 and input (x, r) where r is the randomness used by party P in protocol π. The recipient first decodes this encoding to receive P's first round message of protocol π - msg_1. Without loss of generality, let's assume that the length of randomness r is only proportional to the input length (else, internally, M_1 can apply a pseudorandom generator). In terms of efficiency, the description of the machine M_1 only depends on M, and so it is easy to see that the size of the encoding does not depend on the non-compact message msg_1. A natural initial observation is that in order to construct a simulator for the protocol, we need to generate simulated encodings. However, as we know that simulation secure output-compressing randomized encodings are impossible, we will resort to using our new encodings constructed in the shared randomness model.

Need for Random Oracle. Recall that in the introduction we ruled out the possibility of malicious-secure compact MPC in the CRS model. As a result, it must be the case that our protocol is not a compact and secure MPC protocol in the CRS model. We illustrate what goes wrong with a naive use of our output-compressing randomized encodings. After receiving a message in the first round from every other party, P first decodes all these messages to compute a transcript trans for protocol π. P then computes an encoding of machine M_2 and input (x, r, trans) where M_2 is the machine used to generate the next message msg_2 and sends this in round 2. Looking ahead to the security proof, the simulator will have to generate a simulated encoding of this message and also simulate the shared randomness. To do that, the simulated shared randomness will have to depend on $M_2(x, r, \text{trans})$. Notice that the simulator will have to decide the simulated CRS *before* beginning the protocol execution. This is not possible, however, because the value trans depends on the adversary's input and randomness, both of which are not even picked before the adversary receives the CRS.

We use the programmable RO model to circumvent this. Now, in each round, along with its encoding, P also sends a short index. The recipient first queries the RO on this index to compute the shared randomness that is then used to decode. Looking ahead to the proof, the simulator can pick a random index that the RO has not been queried on so far and "program" the RO's output to be the simulated shared randomness. This can be executed after receiving the transcript of the previous round and before sending the pair of index and simulated encoding in any round.

Strong Output-Compressing Randomized Encodings. Next, it turns out that, in fact, just standard output-compressing randomized encodings do not suffice for the above transformation. To see why, consider any round j. Let trans denote the transcript of the underlying protocol π at the end of round $(j - 1)$. Now, in round j, party P sends an encoding of machine M_j and input (x, r, trans), where M_j is the machine used to generate the jth round message. However, the size of trans could depend on the output length of the protocol because trans denotes the transcript of the underlying non-compact protocol π. A natural attempt to solve would be to let trans be the transcript of the new compact protocol up to this point instead of the underlying protocol, and to let M_j decode the transcript when forming the next message. This also turns out to be problematic, though, since we now need a randomized encoding of a machine M_j which accesses the RO. As a result, since the size of the encoding in each round grows with the input to the machine being encoded, the size of the messages in each round also does depend on the output length. Thus we are seemingly back to square one, since our transformation still yields a non-compact protocol.

In order to solve this issue, we make the crucial observation that the part of the input to the machine being encoded that actually grows with the output length of the protocol is actually public information. That is, we do not care about any privacy for this part of the input and only require that the size of the encoding does not grow with this public input. Corresponding to this, we define a new stronger version of output-compressing randomized encodings in the shared randomness model, which we call *strong* output-compressing randomized encodings. In more detail, the encoding algorithm takes as input a machine M, a private input x_1 and a public input x_2 and outputs an encoding. Informally, the efficiency requirement is that the size of the encoding is $\mathsf{poly}(|M|, |x_1|)$ for a fixed polynomial poly and does not depend on x_2, in addition to being independent of the output length and running time. Further, security requires that, in addition to the output $M(x_1, x_2)$, the simulator is also given the public input x_2 and the tuple of honest encoding and honest shared randomness should be indistinguishable from the tuple of simulated encoding and simulated shared randomness. Thus, if we use strong output-compressing randomized encodings, we overcome the issue. Our construction of strong output-compressing randomized encodings is very similar to the construction in Sect. 2.1 except that we replace the succinct notion called succinct partial randomized encodings. More details can be found in Sect. 5.

Another subtle detail is that, while proving security, in the sequence of hybrids, it is essential that we first switch the encodings to be simulated before switching the messages of the protocol π from real to simulated. This is because we can not afford to send honest encodings of simulated messages of protocol π as the description of the simulator's machine to generate these messages could grow with the output bound. One interesting consequence of the above point is that our transformation is oblivious to whether the underlying simulator rewinds or runs in super-polynomial time. As a result, our construction naturally extends even to the setting of concurrent security if the underlying protocol is concurrently secure.

Notice that our compiler to solve this very basic feasibility question is in fact, remarkably simple, which further highlights the power of simulation secure output-compressing randomized encodings in the shared randomness model. We refer the reader to Sect. 6 for more details about our compact MPC protocol and proof.

Implication in the Circuit Model of [HW15]. First, recall that in the setting of Hubácek and Wichs [HW15], the goal is to construct an MPC protocol for circuits where the communication complexity is independent of the output length of the circuit. At first glance, it might seem that our construction trivially implies a result in the circuit setting as well. However, this is not quite directly true. Observe that in our protocol, the communication complexity grows with the description of the Turing machine and so, when we convert the circuit to the Turing machine model, the communication complexity grows with the size of the circuit. In the case of a circuit, the output length can in fact be proportional to the size of the circuit. To circumvent this, we will consider a Turing machine representation of a Universal circuit, that takes as input a circuit C and an input x and evaluates $C(x)$. Now, notice that the size of this universal circuit, and by extension, the size of the Turing machine evaluated, is independent of the circuit being evaluated. Further, we will set the circuit being computed - C, to be part of the "public" input to each strong output-compressing randomized encoding that is computed in each round of the protocol. Since all parties have knowledge of C, we don't need to hide this input. As a result, neither the machine being encoded nor the private input depend on the circuit being evaluated and this solves the problem. That is, the communication complexity of the resulting compiled protocol is independent of the output length of the circuit.

2.3   Succinct iO for Turing Machines in the Shared Randomness Model

We now describe the techniques used in our construction of iO for Turing machines in the shared randomness model where the size of the obfuscated program does not grow with a bound on the input length. We will denote such obfuscation schemes as *succinct* iO schemes in this section. First, we recall from the introduction that the transformation of Lin et al. [LPST16] to go from output-compressing randomized encodings to succinct iO does not work in the shared randomness model. Briefly, the reason was that if we want to support Turing machines with input length n, then there must be n chunks of the shared randomness, and the 'top-level' encoding in the LPST scheme must contain a commitment to each of the n chunks, and as a result, the size grows with n.

Therefore, our obfuscation scheme will have a completely different structure. Recall that [KLW15] showed an obfuscation scheme where the size of obfuscation of M with input bound n grows with the security parameter, input bound and machine size (but does not depend on the running time of M on any input). We will use such *weakly-succinct* obfuscation scheme to obtain succinct $i\mathcal{O}$.

Consider a program P that takes as input a Turing machine M, input bound n, and outputs a weakly-succinct obfuscation of M with input bound n (the randomness for obfuscation can be generated using a pseudorandom generator). The size of the output grows with n, size of M and security parameter λ. But the important thing to note here is that the size of program P does not grow with input bound n. Therefore, we can use output-compressing randomized encodings to construct succinct iO. The obfuscation algorithm simply outputs an encoding of program P with inputs (M, n). Clearly, the size of this encoding does not grow with n (using the efficiency property of ocre). The proof of security follows from the security of the obfuscation scheme and the output-compressing randomized encoding scheme.

Finally, an informed reader might recall that the LPST construction required the security parameter to grow at each level, while in our case, we can work with a single security parameter. The reason for this is because their security reduction loses a factor of 2 for each level, and therefore the security parameter must grow at each level. In our case, we have a different proof structure, and the switch from encoding of P, M_0 to P, M_1 in the security proof is a single-step jump.

Organization. We first describe some preliminaries in Sects. 3 and 4. In Sect. 5, we describe the construction of strong output-compressing randomized encodings for Turing machines in the shared randomness model. Then, in Sect. 6, we construct compact MPC protocols in the random oracle model. Finally, we defer to the full version of the paper our construction of succinct iO for Turing machines and succinct partial randomized encodings.

3   Preliminaries

We will use λ to denote the security parameter throughout the rest of the paper. For any string s of length n, let $s[i]$ denote the ith bit of s. Without loss of generality, we assume all Turing machines are oblivious.

We defer to the full version of our paper for some additional preliminaries, including the definition of secure multiparty computation in the random oracle model.

4   Randomized Encodings: Definitions

4.1   Succinct Partial Randomized Encodings

In this section, we introduce the notion of succinct partial randomized encodings (spRE). This is similar to the notion of succinct randomized encodings, except that the adversary is allowed to learn part of the input. For efficiency, we require that if the machine has size m, and ℓ bits of input are hidden, then the size of randomized encoding should be polynomial in the security parameter λ, ℓ and m. In particular, the size of the encoding does not depend on the entire input's length (this is possible only because we want to hide ℓ bits of the input; the adversary can learn the remaining bits of the input). This notion is the Turing Machine analogue of *partial garbling* of arithmetic branching programs, studied by Ishai and Wee [IW14].

A succinct partial randomized encoding scheme SPRE for a class of boolean Turing machines $\mathcal{M}$ consists of a preprocessing algorithm Preprocess, encoding algorithm Encode, and a decoding algorithm Decode with the following syntax.

Preprocess($1^\lambda, x_2 \in \{0,1\}^*$): The preprocessing algorithm takes as input security
    parameter λ (in unary), string $y \in \{0,1\}^*$ and outputs a string hk.
Encode($M \in \mathcal{M}, T \in \mathbb{N}, x_1 \in \{0,1\}^*, \text{hk} \in \{0,1\}^{p(\lambda)}$): The encoding algorithm
    takes as input a Turing machine $M \in \mathcal{M}$, time bound $T \in \mathbb{N}$, partial input
    $x_1 \in \{0,1\}^*$, string hk $\in \{0,1\}^{p(\lambda)}$, and outputs an encoding $\widehat{M}$.
Decode($\widehat{M}, x_2, \text{hk}$): The decoding algorithm takes as input an encoding $\widetilde{M}$, a
    string $x_2 \in \{0,1\}^*$, string hk and outputs $y \in \{0,1,\perp\}$.

Definition 1. *Let $\mathcal{M}$ be a family of Turing machines. A randomized encoding scheme* SPRE = (Preprocess, Encode, Decode) *is said to be a succinct partial randomized encoding scheme if it satisfies the following correctness, efficiency and security properties.*

- *Correctness: For every machine $M \in \mathcal{M}$, string $x = (x_1, x_2) \in \{0,1\}^*$, security parameter λ and $T \in \mathbb{N}$, if* hk $\leftarrow$ Preprocess$(1^\lambda, x_2)$, *then* Decode(Encode$(M, T, x_1, \mathsf{hk}), x_2$) = TM$(M, x, T)$.
- *Efficiency: There exist polynomials $p_{\mathsf{prep}}, p_{\mathsf{enc}}$ and p_{dec} such that for every machine $M \in \mathcal{M}$, $x = (x_1, x_2) \in \{0,1\}^*$, $T \in \mathbb{N}$ and $\lambda \in \mathbb{N}$, if* hk $\leftarrow$ Preprocess$(1^\lambda, x_2)$, *then* $|\mathsf{hk}| = p_{\mathsf{prep}}(\lambda)$, *the time to encode $\widetilde{M} \leftarrow$* Encode(M, T, x_1, hk) *is bounded by $p_{\mathsf{enc}}(|M|, |x_1|, \log T, \lambda)$, and the time to decode $\widetilde{M}$ is bounded by* min(Time$(M, x, T) \cdot p_{\mathsf{dec}}(\lambda, \log T)$.
- *Security: For every PPT adversary $\mathcal{A} = (\mathcal{A}_1, \mathcal{A}_2)$, there exists a PPT simulator $\mathcal{S}$ such that for all PPT distinguishers $\mathcal{D}$, there exists a negligible function negl$(\cdot)$ such that for all $\lambda \in \mathbb{N}$,* $\Pr[1 \leftarrow \mathcal{D}(\mathsf{Expt\text{-}SPRE\text{-}Real}_{\mathsf{SPRE}, \mathcal{A}}(\lambda))] - \Pr[1 \leftarrow \mathcal{D}(\mathsf{Expt\text{-}SPRE\text{-}Ideal}_{\mathsf{SRE}, \mathcal{A}, \mathcal{S}}(\lambda))] \leq$ negl(λ), *where* Expt-SPRE-Real *and* Expt-SPRE-Ideal *are defined in Fig. 1. Moreover, the running time of $\mathcal{S}$ is bounded by some polynomial $p_{\mathcal{S}}(|M|, |x_1|, \log T, \lambda)$.*

Experiments Expt-SPRE-Real$_{\mathsf{SPRE}, \mathcal{A}}(\lambda)$ **and** Expt-SPRE-Ideal$_{\mathsf{SPRE}, \mathcal{A}, \mathcal{S}}(\lambda)$

Expt-SPRE-Real$_{\mathsf{SPRE}, \mathcal{A}}(\lambda)$:   Expt-SPRE-Ideal$_{\mathsf{SPRE}, \mathcal{A}, \mathcal{S}}(\lambda)$:

- $(M, x = (x_1, x_2), T, \sigma) \leftarrow$ - $(M, x = (x_1, x_2), T, \sigma) \leftarrow \mathcal{A}_1(1^\lambda)$,
  $\mathcal{A}_1(1^\lambda)$. $t^* = $ min $(T, $ Time $(M, x))$, out $=$
- hk $\leftarrow$ Preprocess$(x_2, 1^\lambda)$.   TM (M, x, T).
- $\widetilde{M}$ $\leftarrow$ - hk $\leftarrow$ Preprocess$(1^\lambda, x_2)$.
  Encode(M, T, x_1, hk).   - $\widetilde{M} \leftarrow \mathcal{S}\left(1^{|M|}, 1^{|x_1|}, \mathsf{hk}, 1^\lambda, \mathsf{out}, t^*\right)$.
- Experiment   outputs   - Experiment outputs $\mathcal{A}_2(\widetilde{M}, \sigma)$.
  $\mathcal{A}_2(\widetilde{M}, \sigma)$.

Fig. 1. Simulation Security Experiments for partial randomized encodings

Our construction of succinct partial randomized encodings is closely related to the succinct randomized encodings scheme by [KLW15] and we defer the details to the full version of our paper.

4.2 Strong Output-Compressing Randomized Encodings in the Shared Randomess Model

The notion of succinct randomized encodings (defined in the full version of our paper) was originally defined for boolean Turing machines. We can also consider randomized encodings for Turing machines with long outputs. Using (standard) succinct randomized encodings, one can construct randomized encodings for Turing machines with multi-bit outputs, where the size of encodings grows linearly with the output size. In a recent work, Lin et al. [LPST16] introduced a stronger notion called *output-compressing randomized encodings*, where the size of the encoding only depends sublinearly on the output length. Lin et al. also showed that simulation based security notions of output-compressing randomized encodings are impossible to achieve. In this work, we consider a stronger notion of output-compressing randomized encodings in the shared randomness model where the encoder and decoder have access to a shared random string (denoted by crs). Here, the machine also takes another public input x_2 along with a private input x_1 with the requirement that the size of the encoding should only grow polynomially in the size of the machine and the private input x_1. In particular, it does not grow with x_2 or the running time of the machine or its output length. We define it formally below.

A strong output-compressing randomized encoding scheme S.OcRE = (Setup, Encode, Decode) in the shared randomness model consists of three algorithms with the following syntax.

Setup($1^\lambda, 1^{\text{o-len}}, \text{crs} \in \{0,1\}^{\text{o-len}}$): The setup algorithm takes as input security parameter λ, output-bound o-len and a shared random string crs of length o-len. It outputs an encoding key ek.

Encode($(M, \text{tmf}(\cdot)), x = (x_1, x_2), T, \text{ek}$): The encoding algorithm takes as input an oblivious Turing Machine M with tape movement function $\text{tmf}(\cdot)$, input x consisting of a private part x_1 and a public part x_2, time bound $T \leq 2^\lambda$ (in binary) and an encoding key ek, and outputs an encoding $\widetilde{M_x}$.

Decode($\widetilde{M_x}, x_2, \text{crs}$): The decoding algorithm takes as input an encoding $\widetilde{M_x}$, a public input x_2, the shared random string crs and outputs $y \in \{0,1\}^* \cup \{\bot\}$.

Definition 2. *A strong output-compressing randomized encoding scheme S.OcRE = (Setup, Encode, Decode) in the shared randomness model is said to be secure if it satisfies the following correctness, efficiency and security requirements.*

- *Correctness: For all security parameters $\lambda \in \mathbb{N}$, output-length bound o-len $\in \mathbb{N}$, crs $\in \{0,1\}^{\text{o-len}}$, machine M with tape movement function $\text{tmf}(\cdot)$, input $x = (x_1, x_2)$, time bound T such that $|M(x)| \leq$ o-len, if ek $\leftarrow$ Setup($1^\lambda, 1^{\text{o-len}}, \text{crs}$), $\widetilde{M_x} \leftarrow$ Encode($(M, \text{tmf}(\cdot)), x, T\text{ek}$), then Decode($\widetilde{M_x}, x_2, \text{crs}$) = TM($M, x, T$).*
- *Efficiency: There exist polynomials p_1, p_2, p_3 such that for all $\lambda \in \mathbb{N}$, o-len $\in \mathbb{N}$, crs $\in \{0,1\}^{\text{o-len}}$:*
  1. *If ek $\leftarrow$ Setup($1^\lambda, 1^o, \text{crs}$), $|\text{ek}| \leq p_1(\lambda, \log o)$.*
  2. *For every Turing machine M, time bound T, input $x = (x_1, x_2) \in \{0,1\}^*$, if $\widetilde{M_x} \leftarrow$ Encode(M, x, T, ek), then $|\widetilde{M_x}| \leq p_2(|M|, |x_1|, \log|x_2|, \log T, \log o, \lambda)$.*
  3. *The running time of Decode($\widetilde{M_x}, x_2, \text{crs}$) is at most $\min(T, \text{Time}(M, x)) \cdot p_3(\lambda, \log T)$.*
- *Security: For every PPT adversary $\mathcal{A} = (\mathcal{A}_1, \mathcal{A}_2)$, there exists a simulator $\mathcal{S}$ such that for all PPT distinguishers $\mathcal{D}$, there exists a negligible function $negl(\cdot)$ such that for all $\lambda \in \mathbb{N}$,*

$$\Pr[1 \leftarrow \mathcal{D}(\text{Expt-S.OcRE-Real}_{\text{S.OcRE}, \mathcal{A}}(\lambda))]$$
$$- \Pr[1 \leftarrow \mathcal{D}(\text{Expt-S.OcRE-Ideal}_{\text{S.OcRE}, \mathcal{A}, \mathcal{S}}(\lambda))] \leq negl(\lambda),$$

where Expt-S.OcRE-Real and Expt-S.OcRE-Ideal are defined in Fig. 2.

Experiments Expt-S.OcRE-Real$_{\text{S.OcRE},\mathcal{A}}(\lambda)$ **and**
Expt-S.OcRE-Ideal$_{\text{S.OcRE},\mathcal{A},\mathcal{S}}(\lambda)$

Expt-S.OcRE-Real$_{\text{S.OcRE},\mathcal{A}}(\lambda)$:

- $(1^{\text{o-len}}, (M, \text{tmf}(\cdot)), x = (x_1, x_2), T, \sigma) \leftarrow$
  $\mathcal{A}_1(1^{\lambda})$.
- $\text{crs} \leftarrow \{0,1\}^{\text{o-len}}$,
  $\text{ek} \leftarrow \text{Setup}(1^{\lambda}, 1^{\text{o-len}}, \text{crs})$.
- $\widetilde{M} \leftarrow \text{Encode}((M, \text{tmf}(\cdot)), x, T, \text{ek})$.
- Experiment outputs $\mathcal{A}_2(\text{crs}, \text{ek}, \widetilde{M}, \sigma)$.

Expt-S.OcRE-Ideal$_{\text{S.OcRE},\mathcal{A}}(\lambda)$:

- $(1^{\text{o-len}}, (M, \text{tmf}(\cdot)), x = (x_1, x_2), T, \sigma) \leftarrow$
  $\mathcal{A}_1(1^{\lambda})$.
- Let $t^* = \min(T, \text{Time}(M, x))$ and $b^* =$
  $\text{TM}(M, x, T)$.
- $s \leftarrow \mathcal{S}(1^{|M|}, 1^{|x_1|}, \text{tmf}(\cdot), x_2, t^*, b^*, 1^{\lambda})$.
- Let $s = (\text{crs}, \widetilde{M})$.
- $\text{ek} \leftarrow \text{Setup}(1^{\lambda}, 1^{\text{o-len}}, \text{crs})$.
- Experiment outputs $\mathcal{A}_2(\text{crs}, \text{ek}, \widetilde{M}, \sigma)$.

Fig. 2. Simulation Security Experiments for strong output-compressing randomized encodings in the shared randomness model

Remark: In particular, note that strong output-compressing randomized encodings (S.OcRE) implies output-compressing randomized encodings (OcRE) by setting the public input x_2 to be $\bot$.

5 Strong Output-Compressing Randomized Encodings in the CRS Model

In this section, we show a construction of strong output-compressing randomized encodings in the common random string (CRS) model. Formally, we show the following theorem:

Theorem 4. *Assuming the existence of iO for circuits and somewhere statistically binding (SSB) hash and Puncturable PRFs and Succinct partial randomized encodings for single-bit output Turing machines, There exists a strong output-compressing randomized encoding scheme for Turing machines in the shared randomness model.*

Instantiating the SSB hash and the succinct partial randomized encodings, we get the following corollary:

Corollary 2. *Assuming the existence of iO for circuits and any $A \in \{DDH, LWE, N^{th}$ Residuosity$\}$, There exists a strong output-compressing randomized encoding scheme for Turing machines in the shared randomness model.*

Notation and Primitives Used: We will be using the following cryptographic primitives for our construction:

- Indistinguishability obfuscation for circuits (Ckt.Obf, Ckt.Eval).
- Succinct partial randomized encodings for single-bit output Turing machines (SPRE.Preprocess, SPRE.Encode, SPRE.Decode). Without loss of generality, we assume that the algorithm SPRE.Encode uses λ bits of randomness - it can internally apply a PRG on this randomness if a larger amount is required.

- Somewhere statistically binding hash(SSB.Gen, SSB.Open, SSB.Verify).
- A Puncturable PRF $(F_1, \text{PPRF.Puncture}_1)$ that takes inputs of size λ and outputs 1 bit.
- A Puncturable PRF $(F_2, \text{PPRF.Puncture}_2)$ that takes inputs of size λ and outputs λ bits.

5.1   Construction

S.OcRE.Setup$(1^\lambda, 1^o, \text{crs} \in \{0,1\}^o)$: The setup algorithm does the following:
  1. Choose hash function $H \leftarrow \text{SSB.Gen}(1^\lambda, o, 0).$[9]
  2. Compute $h = H(\text{crs})$ and set $\text{ek} = (h, H)$.

S.OcRE.Encode$(M, x = (x_1, x_2), T, \text{ek} = (h, H))$: The encoding algorithm does the following:
  1. Compute $\text{hk} = \text{SPRE.Preprocess}(1^\lambda, x_2)$.
  2. Choose a key K_{SPRE} for the puncturable PRF F_2.
  3. Let M_i denote the turing machine that, on input x, runs the machine M on input x and outputs the ith bit of $M(x)$. Let t denote $|\text{SPRE.Encode}(M_i, T, x_1, \text{hk}; r)|$ using any random string r.
  4. Compute $\widetilde{\text{Prog}} \leftarrow \text{Ckt.Obf}(\text{Prog}, 1^\lambda)$ where the program Prog is defined in Fig. 3. Note that the size of the program Prog is padded appropriately so that it is equal to the size of the program Prog-sim defined later in Fig. 4.
  5. Output $\widetilde{M_x} = (\widetilde{\text{Prog}}, t, H)$.

S.OcRE.Decode$(\widetilde{M_x} = (\widetilde{\text{Prog}}, t, H), x_2, \text{crs})$: For each $i \in [o]$, the decoding algorithm computes bit out_i as follows:

Prog

Inputs : Index $i \in [o]$, bit $\text{str} \in \{0,1\}$, proof π, index $j \in [t]$.
Hardwired : Hash value $h \in \{0,1\}^\lambda$, machine M, input x_1, PRF key K_{SPRE}, bound T, preprocessed value hk.

  1. Verify proof π : Check if $\text{SSB.Verify}(H, h, i, \text{str}, \pi) = 1$. If not, output $\perp$.
  2. Recall that M_i denotes the turing machine that, on input x, runs the machine M on input x and outputs the ith bit of $M(x)$. Compute $\text{out} = \text{SPRE.Encode}(M_i, T, x_1, \text{hk}; F_2(K_{\text{SPRE}}, i))$ and output the jth bit of out.

Fig. 3. Circuit Prog

---

[9] We modify the syntax of the SSB hash system slightly to allow the binding index to range from $0, \ldots, o$ and without loss of generality, just set $\text{SSB.Gen}(1^\lambda, o, 0) = \text{SSB.Gen}(1^\lambda, o, 1)$. That is, when the binding index is set as 0, we actually don't care at what index the hash system is bound at and will not actually use the statistically binding property. This is just to be consistent with the definition of the SSB hash system.

1. Parse $\mathsf{crs} = (\mathsf{crs}[1], \mathsf{crs}[2], \ldots, \mathsf{crs}[o])$, where each $\mathsf{crs}[j]$ is a bit.
2. Compute SSB proof for each $\mathsf{crs}[j]$; that is, compute $\pi[j] = \mathsf{SSB.Open}(H, \mathsf{crs}, j)$.
3. For $j = 1$ to t, do:
   (a) Compute $\widetilde{M_i}[j] = \mathsf{Ckt.Eval}(\widetilde{\mathsf{Prog}}, (i, \mathsf{crs}[i], \pi[i], j))$.
4. Let $\widetilde{M_i} = (\widetilde{M_i}[1]\ \widetilde{M_i}[2]\ \ldots\ \widetilde{M_i}[t])$. Compute $\mathsf{out}_i = \mathsf{SPRE.Decode}(\widetilde{M_i}, x_2)$.

Finally, it outputs $(\mathsf{out}_1\ \mathsf{out}_2\ \ldots\ \mathsf{out}_o)$.

Correctness and Succinctness. Correctness follows from the correctness of $(\mathsf{SPRE.Encode}, \mathsf{SPRE.Decode})$ and $(\mathsf{Ckt.Obf}, \mathsf{Ckt.Eval})$.

Below we show the three efficiency properties required by the definition.

1. If $\mathsf{ek} \leftarrow \mathsf{Setup}(1^\lambda, 1^o, \mathsf{crs})$, $|\mathsf{ek}| = \ell_{\mathsf{hash}}(\lambda) + \ell_{\mathsf{fn}}(\lambda)$, where ℓ_{hash} and ℓ_{fn} are from SSB.
2. For every Turing machine M, time bound T, input $x = (x_1, x_2) \in \{0,1\}^*$, if $\widetilde{M_x} \leftarrow \mathsf{Encode}(M, x, T, \mathsf{ek})$, then $|\widetilde{M_x}| = (|prog| + |t|) \le |\mathsf{Prog}| + \mathsf{poly}(\lambda)$. Prog is padded to be the same length as the programs used in the hybrids and Prog-sim, so $|\mathsf{Prog}|$ is the maximum of the length of these programs. By inspecting the values hardwired in each of these programs we get $|\mathsf{Prog}| \le p(|h|, |M|, |x_1|, |hk|, k, \log o, t)$, where k is the maximum size of the keys of F_1 and F_2. By the efficiency of SPRE, the definition of SSB hashes and the definition of puncturable PRFs we get that $|\mathsf{Prog}| \le p_2(\lambda, |M|, |x_1|, \log o)$ and thus $|\widetilde{M_x}| \le p_2(\lambda, |M|, |x_1|, \log |x_2|, \log o)$ for some fixed polynomial p_2.
3. The running time of $\mathsf{Decode}(\widetilde{M_x}, x_2, \mathsf{crs})$ is at most $O(o \times t_1 + o \times t \times t_2)$ where t_1 is the running time of $\mathsf{SPRE.Decode}(\widetilde{M_i}, x_2)$ and t_2 is the running time of $\mathsf{Ckt.Eval}(\widetilde{\mathsf{Prog}}, (i, \mathsf{crs}[i], \pi[i], j))$. By the efficiency of the SPRE scheme and the iO scheme we have $\mathsf{Decode}(\widetilde{M_x}, x_2, \mathsf{crs}) \le \min(T, \mathsf{Time}(M, x)) \cdot p_3(\lambda, \log T)$.

5.2   Proof of Security

Description of Simulator. The simulator S.OcRE.Sim gets as input the value $M(x)$ (which is the output of the machine M on input x) and the public part of the input x_2, and it must simulate the shared random string crs and an encoding $\widetilde{M_x}$ of the machine M and x. We now describe the simulator.

S.OcRE.Sim$(1^{|M|}, 1^{|x_1|}, x_2, 1^\lambda, M(x), T)$:
The simulator does the following:

1. Compute $\mathsf{hk} = \mathsf{SPRE.Preprocess}(1^\lambda, x_2)$.
2. Choose a key K_{crs} for the puncturable PRF F_1 and a key K_{sim} for the puncturable PRF F_2.
3. Then, for each i, compute $\mathsf{crs}[i] = M(x)_i \oplus w^i$ where $w^i = F(K_{\mathsf{crs}}, i)$ and $M(x)_i$ denotes the ith bit of $M(x)$. The shared random string is set to be $(\mathsf{crs}[1]\ \mathsf{crs}[2]\ \ldots\ \mathsf{crs}[o])$.
4. Choose a hash function $H \leftarrow \mathsf{SSB.Gen}(1^\lambda, o, 0)$ and compute $h = H(\mathsf{crs})$.

5. Compute $\widetilde{\mathsf{Prog\text{-}sim}} \leftarrow \mathsf{Ckt.Obf}(\mathsf{Prog\text{-}sim}, 1^\lambda)$, where $\mathsf{Prog\text{-}sim}$ is defined in Fig. 4.
6. Let M_i denote the turing machine that, on input x, runs the machine M on input x and outputs the ith bit of $M(x)$. Let t denote $|\mathsf{SPRE.Encode}(M_i, T, z, \mathsf{hk}; r)|$ using any random string r and any input z such that $|z| = |x_1|$.
7. Set $\widetilde{M_x} = (\widetilde{\mathsf{Prog\text{-}sim}}, t)$.

Prog-sim

Inputs : Index $i \in [o]$, bit $\mathsf{str} \in \{0,1\}$, proof π, index $j \in [t]$
Hardwired : Hash $h \in \{0,1\}^\lambda$, machine M, PRF keys $K_{\mathsf{sim}}, K_{\mathsf{crs}}$, preprocessed value hk.

1. Verify proof π : Check if $\mathsf{SSB.Verify}(H, h, i, \mathsf{str}, \pi) = 1$. If not, output $\perp$.
2. Do the following:
   (a) Let $w = F_1(K_{\mathsf{crs}}, i)$ and $y = w \oplus \mathsf{str}$.
   (b) Compute $\mathsf{out} = \mathsf{SPRE.Sim}(1^{|M_i|}, 1^{|x_1|}, \mathsf{hk}, 1^\lambda, y, T; r)$ where $r = F_2(K_{\mathsf{sim}}, i)$.
   (c) Output j^{th} bit of out.

Fig. 4. Simulated program Prog-sim

Hybrids. We will show that the real and ideal worlds are indistinguishable via a sequence of $(o+2)$ hybrid experiments Hyb_0 to Hyb_{o+1} where Hyb_0 corresponds to the real world and Hyb_{o+1} corresponds to the ideal world. For each $i \in [o]$, in hybrid Hyb_{i^*}, the first i^* bits of the CRS are computed as encryptions of output bits (with the w's as one time pads). The encoding of M, x does not compute the SRE for $i \le i^*$. More formally:

Hybrid Hyb_{i^*}:
The challenger does the following:

1. Compute $\mathsf{hk} = \mathsf{SPRE.Preprocess}(1^\lambda, x_2)$.
2. Choose a key K_{crs} for the puncturable PRF F_1 and two keys $K_{\mathsf{sim}}, K_{\mathsf{SPRE}}$ for the puncturable PRF F_2.
3. Then, for each $i \le i^*$, compute $\mathsf{crs}[i] = M(x)_i \oplus w^i$ where $w^i = F_1(K_{\mathsf{crs}}, i)$ and $M(x)_i$ denotes the ith bit of $M(x)$.
4. For each $i > i^*$, pick $\mathsf{crs}[i]$ uniformly at random.
5. The shared random string is set to be $(\mathsf{crs}[1]\ \mathsf{crs}[2]\ \dots\ \mathsf{crs}[o])$.
6. Choose a hash function $H \leftarrow \mathsf{SSB.Gen}(1^\lambda, o, i^*)$ and compute $h = H(\mathsf{crs})$. Set $\mathsf{ek} = h$.
7. Compute $\widetilde{\mathsf{Prog\text{-}}i^*} \leftarrow \mathsf{Ckt.Obf}(\mathsf{Prog\text{-}}i^*, 1^\lambda)$, where $\mathsf{Prog\text{-}}i^*$ is defined in Fig. 5.
8. Let M_i denote the turing machine that, on input x, runs the machine M on input x and outputs the ith bit of $M(x)$. Let t denote $|\mathsf{SPRE.Encode}(M_i, T, x_1, \mathsf{hk}; r)|$ using any random string r.
9. Set $\widetilde{M_x} = (\widetilde{\mathsf{Prog\text{-}}i^*}, t)$.

Prog-i^*

Inputs : Index $i \in [o]$, bit str $\in \{0,1\}$, proof π, index $j \in [t]$
Hardwired : Index i^*, Hash $h \in \{0,1\}^\lambda$, machine M, input x_1, PRF keys $K_{\text{crs}}, K_{\text{sim}}, K_{\text{SPRE}}$, bound T, preprocessed value hk.

1. Verify proof π : Check if SSB.Verify$(H, h, i, \text{str}, \pi) = 1$. If not, output $\bot$.
2. If $i \leq i^*$, do the following:
   (a) Let $w = F_1(K_{\text{crs}}, i)$ and $y = w \oplus \text{str}$.
   (b) Compute out $=$ SPRE.Sim$(1^{|M_i|}, 1^{|x_1|}, \text{hk}, 1^\lambda, y, T; r)$ where $r = F_2(K_{\text{sim}}, i)$.
   (c) Output j^{th} bit of out.
3. Else, if $i > i^*$: Recall that M_i denotes the turing machine that, on input x, runs the machine M on input x and outputs the ith bit of $M(x)$. Compute out $=$ SPRE.Encode$(M_i, T, x_1, \text{hk}; F_2(K_{\text{SPRE}}, i))$ and output the jth bit of out.

Fig. 5. Hybrid program Prog-i^*

Hybrid Hyb_{o+1}:
Identical to Hyb_o except that the value x_1 is not hardwired into Prog-i^*.

We include the proof of hybrid indistinguishability in the full version of the paper.

6   Compact MPC

We consider the problem of constructing a malicious secure compact MPC protocol for Turing machines. Consider a set of n mutually distrusting parties with inputs $x_1, \ldots, x_n$ respectively that agree on a TM M. Their goal is to securely compute the output $M(x_1, \ldots, x_n)$ without leaking any information about their respective inputs where the output can be of any unbounded polynomial size. We first define the notion of a *compact* MPC protocol. Let λ denote the security parameter and let Comm.Compl(π) denote the communication complexity (sum of the lengths of all messages exchanged by all parties) of any protocol π. Let Time$(\mathcal{M}, \text{x})$ denote the running time of turing machine $\mathcal{M}$ on input x.

Definition 3. *An MPC protocol π is said to be* compact *if there exists a fixed polynomial* poly *such that for all machines M and inputs $(x_1, \ldots, x_n)$,* Comm.Compl(π) $=$ poly$(|M|, |x_1|, \ldots, |x_n|, \lambda, \log(\text{Time}(\mathcal{M}, \text{x})))$. *In particular, the communication complexity is independent of the output length and the running time of the machine on the inputs of all the parties.*

In this section, we give a round preserving compiler from any constant round (non-compact) malicious secure MPC protocol in the plain model to a malicious secure *compact* MPC protocol for Turing machines in the random oracle (RO) model.

Formally, we prove the following theorem:

Theorem 5. *For all $n, t > 0$, assuming the existence of:*

- *A (constant) k round[10] MPC protocol amongst n parties in the plain model that is malicious secure against up to t corruptions (AND)*
- *Strong OCRE in the shared randomness model,*

there exists a k round compact MPC protocol π amongst n parties for Turing machines in the Programmable Random Oracle model that is malicious secure against up to t corruptions.

Here, we note that the above compiler even works if the underlying MPC protocol is for circuits. That is, we can convert any constant round protocol for circuits into a constant round protocol for Turing machines (with an input bound) by first converting the Turing machine into a (potentially large) circuit.

Corollaries:

We can instantiate the strong OCRE from our construction in Sect. 5. We now discuss several corollaries on instantiating the underlying MPC protocol with various protocols in literature based on different models.

1. Instantiating the MPC protocol with the round optimal[11] plain model construction of [BGJ+18] that is secure against a dishonest majority based on DDH/N^{th} Residuosity, we get a four round *compact* MPC protocol π for Turing machines in the RO model that is secure against a dishonest majority assuming iO for circuits and DDH/N^{th} Residuosity.
2. We can also instantiate the underlying MPC protocol with protocols that are secure in the Common Random String model by using the RO's output on some fixed string to implement the common random string. In particular, combining the two round semi-malicious MPC protocol of [MW16] that is based on LWE in the common random string model or the ones of [GS18, BL18] that are based on DDH/N^{th} residuosity in the plain model, with a noninteractive zero knowledge argument based on DLIN in the common random string model [GOS06], we get two round malicious secure MPC protocols in the common random string model. As a result, we have the following corollary:

Corollary 3. *Assuming the existence of iO for circuits and A where $A \in \{LWE, DDH, N^{th}\ Residuosity\}$ and DLIN, there exists a round optimal (two round) compact MPC protocol π for Turing machines in the Programmable Random Oracle model that is malicious secure against a dishonest majority.*

3. We note that our transformation works even on instantiating the underlying constant round MPC protocol with ones that are secure in the setting of super-polynomial simulation [Pas03, BGI+17] or in the concurrent (self-composable) setting [GGJS12, BGI+17] to yield *compact* versions of the same in the RO model.

---

[10] Observe that our round preserving compiler in fact works for any MPC protocol where the number of rounds is independent of the machine being evaluated.

[11] Recall that in the plain model, the optimal round complexity is 4.

Implication to [HW15] Model. Finally, we observe that our transformation also has an implication to the circuit-based model of Hubácek and Wichs [HW15] as elaborated in Sect. 2.2. Thus, we get the following corollary:

Theorem 6. *For all $n, t > 0$, assuming the existence of a constant round MPC protocol amongst n parties in the plain model that is malicious secure against up to t corruptions, and strong OCRE in the shared randomness model, there exists a constant round MPC protocol π amongst n parties for all polynomial sized circuits in the RO model that is malicious secure against up to t corruptions where the communication complexity of the protocol is independent of the output length of the circuit. That is, there exists a fixed polynomial* poly *such that, for all circuits* C *and all inputs* $(x_1, \ldots, x_n) \in$ Domain(C), Comm.Compl$(\pi) =$ poly$(|x_1|, \ldots, |x_n|, \lambda)$.

6.1   Construction

Notation and Primitives Used:

- Let λ denote the security parameter and RO be a random oracle that takes as input a tuple $(r, 1^{\text{len}})$ where $|r| = \lambda$ and outputs a string of length len.
- Consider n parties $P_1, \ldots, P_n$ with inputs $x_1, \ldots, x_n$ respectively (with $|x_i| = \lambda$ for each $i \in [n]$) who wish to evaluate any turing machine $\mathcal{M}$ on their joint inputs.
- Let S.OcRE $=$ (S.OcRE.Setup, S.OcRE.Encode, S.OcRE.Decode) be a strong OCRE scheme in the shared randomness model.
- Let π^{plain} be a t round MPC protocol for turing machines in the plain model that is malicious secure against a dishonest majority. For simplicity, we assume that the protocol works using a broadcast channel - that is, in each round, every party broadcasts a message to all other parties.
- Let NextMsg$_k(\cdot)$ denote the algorithm used by any party to compute the kth round of protocol π^{plain} and let Out$(\cdot)$ denote the algorithm used by any party to compute the final output. Also, without loss of generality, assume that in protocol π^{plain}, each party uses randomness rand$_i$ of length λ.[12]

Remark: To ease the exposition, we assume that the Random Oracle can output arbitrarily long strings by also taking the desired output length as input to the oracle. In reality, let's say it outputs strings of length $p(\lambda)$ where p is a polynomial. Then, in the protocol below, each party can output a starting query index $r_{i,j}$ and an offset $o_{i,j}$ to indicate that the shared random string is actually the concatenation of RO$(r_{i,j}), \ldots,$ RO$(r_{i,j} + o_{i,j})$. Note that $|o_{i,j}| \leq \lambda$.

---

[12] Internally, we can apply a PRG to expand this to any length of randomness we require. Here, we are implicitly assuming that the protocol requires each party to use uniformly random strings. This is true of almost every constant round MPC protocol.

Protocol: The protocol is described below.

1. **Round 1:**
   Each party P_i does the following:
   - Pick a random string $r_{i,1} \in \{0,1\}^\lambda$. Let $\mathsf{len}_{i,1} = |\mathsf{NextMsg}_1(x_i; \mathsf{rand}_i)|$.
   - Compute $\mathsf{crs}_{i,1} = \mathsf{RO}(r_{i,1}, 1^{\mathsf{len}_{i,1}})$.
   - Compute $\mathsf{ek}_{i,1} = \mathsf{S.OcRE.Setup}(1^\lambda, 1^{\mathsf{len}_{i,1}}, \mathsf{crs}_{i,1})$.
   - Compute $\mathsf{msg}_{i,1} = \mathsf{S.OcRE.Encode}(\mathsf{NextMsg}_1, ((x_i, \mathsf{rand}_i), \bot), 2^\lambda, \mathsf{ek}_{i,1})$.
   - Output $(\mathsf{msg}_{i,1}, r_{i,1}, \mathsf{len}_{i,1})$.

2. **Round 2 ... t:**
   For each subsequent round k, each party P_i does the following:
   - Let τ_{k-2} denote the transcript of the underlying protocol π^{plain} after round $(k-2)$. $\tau_0 = \bot$.
   - Set $\tau_{k-1} = \tau_{k-2}$.
   - For each party P_j, $(j \neq i)$ do the following:
     - Parse its previous round message as $(\mathsf{msg}_{j,k-1}, r_{j,k-1}, \mathsf{len}_{j,k-1})$.
     - Compute $\mathsf{crs}_{j,k-1} = \mathsf{RO}(r_{j,k-1}, 1^{\mathsf{len}_{j,k-1}})$.
     - Compute $\mathsf{msg}^{\mathsf{plain}}_{j,k-1} = \mathsf{S.OcRE.Decode}(\mathsf{msg}_{j,k-1}, \tau_{k-2}, \mathsf{crs}_{j,k-1})$.
     - Append $\mathsf{msg}^{\mathsf{plain}}_{j,k-1}$ to τ_{k-1}.
   - Pick a random string $r_{i,k} \in \{0,1\}^\lambda$. Let $\mathsf{len}_{i,k} = |\mathsf{NextMsg}_k(x_i; \mathsf{rand}_i, \tau_{k-1})|$.
   - Compute $\mathsf{crs}_{i,k} = \mathsf{RO}(r_{i,k}, 1^{\mathsf{len}_{i,k}})$.
   - Compute $\mathsf{ek}_{i,k} = \mathsf{S.OcRE.Setup}(1^\lambda, 1^{\mathsf{len}_{i,k}}, \mathsf{crs}_{i,k})$.
   - Compute $\mathsf{msg}_{i,k} = \mathsf{S.OcRE.Encode}(\mathsf{NextMsg}_k, ((x_i, \mathsf{rand}_i), \tau_{k-1}), 2^\lambda, \mathsf{ek}_{i,k})$.
   - Output[13] $(\mathsf{msg}_{i,k}, r_{i,k}, \mathsf{len}_{i,k})$.

3. **Output Computation:**
   Each party P_i does the following:
   - Let τ_{t-1} denote the transcript of the underlying protocol π^{plain} after round $(t-1)$.
   - Set $\tau_t = \tau_{t-1}$.
   - For each party P_j, $(j \neq i)$ do the following:
     - Parse its previous round message as $(\mathsf{msg}_{j,t}, r_{j,t}, \mathsf{len}_{j,t})$.
     - Compute $\mathsf{crs}_{j,t} = \mathsf{RO}(r_{j,t}, 1^{\mathsf{len}_{j,t}})$.
     - Compute $\mathsf{msg}^{\mathsf{plain}}_{j,t} = \mathsf{S.OcRE.Decode}(\mathsf{msg}_{j,t}, \tau_{t-1}, \mathsf{crs}_{j,t})$.
     - Append $\mathsf{msg}^{\mathsf{plain}}_{j,t}$ to τ_t.
   - Output $\mathsf{Out}(x_i, \mathsf{rand}_i, \tau_t)$.

Efficiency of the Protocol:
The size of the messages sent in round k by each party P_i is $3 \cdot \max\{|(\mathsf{msg}_{i,k}, r_{i,k}, \mathsf{len}_{i,k})|\}_{i,k}$. By the definition of strong output-compressing randomized encodings, $|\mathsf{msg}_{i,k}| \leq \mathsf{p}_2(|\mathsf{NextMsg}_k|, |(x_i, \mathsf{rand}_i)|, \log T, \lambda)$ where p_2 is a polynomial. $|\mathsf{rand}_i| = \lambda$, $|\mathsf{NextMsg}_k| = \mathsf{p}_3(|M|)$ where M is the original functionality and p_3 is a polynomial. Also, we know T is at most 2^λ. So $|\mathsf{msg}_{i,k}| \leq \mathsf{p}_3(|M|, |x_i|, \lambda)$ for some polynomial p_3. We know that $|r_{i,k}| = \lambda$ and

---

[13] Note that to send $\mathsf{len}_{i,k}$, the length of the message is $\log \mathsf{len}_{i,k}$ and so at most λ.

$\|\mathsf{len}_{i,k}\| \leq \lambda$. Therefore, the size of the messages sent in round k by each party P_i is at most $\mathsf{p}_3(|M|, |x_i|, \lambda)$.

Since π^{plain} is a constant-round protocol, the total communication complexity of our protocol π is at most $\mathsf{p}(n, |M|, |x_1|, \ldots, |x_n|, \lambda)$ for a fixed polynomial p.

6.2 Security Proof

In this section, we formally prove Theorem 6.

Consider an adversary $\mathcal{A}$ who corrupts t parties where $t < n$. Let's say the simulator $\mathsf{Sim}^{\mathsf{plain}}$ for protocol π^{plain} consists of 4 algorithms $(\mathsf{Sim}_1^{\mathsf{plain}}, \mathsf{Sim}_2^{\mathsf{plain}}, \mathsf{Sim}_3^{\mathsf{plain}}, \mathsf{Sim}_{\mathsf{Out}}^{\mathsf{plain}})$ where: $\mathsf{Sim}_1^{\mathsf{plain}}(j, \cdot)$ outputs the adversary's view for the jth of the first t_1 rounds, $\mathsf{Sim}_2^{\mathsf{plain}}$ queries the ideal functionality to receive the output, $\mathsf{Sim}_3^{\mathsf{plain}}(j, \cdot)$ outputs the adversary's view for the jth round of the last $(t - t_1)$ rounds and $\mathsf{Sim}_{\mathsf{Out}}^{\mathsf{plain}}(i, \cdot)$ computes the output of honest party P_i.[14] Also, let's denote the size of $\mathsf{Sim}^{\mathsf{plain}}(\cdot)$ by $s(\lambda)$.

Description of Simulator. The strategy of the simulator Sim for our protocol π against a malicious adversary $\mathcal{A}$ is described below.

1. **Round 1 ... t_1:**
   For each round k and each honest party P_i, Sim does the following:
   - Let τ_{k-2} denote the transcript of the underlying protocol π^{plain} after round $(k-2)$. $\tau_0 = \bot$.
   - Set $\tau_{k-1} = \tau_{k-2}$.
   - For each party P_j, $(j \neq i)$, if $k > 1$, do the following:
     • Parse its previous round message as $(\mathsf{msg}_{j,k-1}, r_{j,k-1}, \mathsf{len}_{j,k-1})$.
     • Compute $\mathsf{crs}_{j,k-1} = \mathsf{RO}(r_{j,k-1}, 1^{\mathsf{len}_{j,k-1}})$.
     • Compute $\mathsf{msg}_{j,k-1}^{\mathsf{plain}} = \mathsf{S.OcRE.Decode}(\mathsf{msg}_{j,k-1}, \tau_{k-2}, \mathsf{crs}_{j,k-1})$.
     • Append $\mathsf{msg}_{j,k-1}^{\mathsf{plain}}$ to τ_{k-1}.
   - Compute $\mathsf{msg}_{i,k}^{\mathsf{plain}} = \mathsf{Sim}_1^{\mathsf{plain}}(k, \tau_{k-1}, \mathsf{st})$ where st denotes the state of $\mathsf{Sim}^{\mathsf{plain}}$.
   - Pick a random string $r_{i,k} \in \{0,1\}^\lambda$.
   - Compute $(\mathsf{msg}_{i,k}, \mathsf{crs}_{i,k}) \leftarrow \mathsf{S.OcRE.Sim}(1^{|s(\lambda)|}, 1^{(2 \cdot \lambda + |\tau_{k-1}|)}, 1^\lambda, \mathsf{msg}_{i,k}^{\mathsf{plain}}, 1^\lambda)$.
   - Set $\mathsf{RO}(r_{i,k}, 1^{|\mathsf{crs}_{i,k}|}) = \mathsf{crs}_{i,k}$.
   - Output[15] $(\mathsf{msg}_{i,k}, r_{i,k}, |\mathsf{crs}_{i,k}|)$.
2. **Query to Ideal Functionality:**
   Sim queries $\mathsf{Sim}_2^{\mathsf{plain}}(\tau_{k_1}, \mathsf{st})$ and receives an output y in return.
3. **Round $(t_1 + 1)$ ... t:**
   For each round k and each honest party P_i, Sim does the following:
   - Let τ_{k-2} denote the transcript of the underlying protocol π^{plain} after round $(k-2)$. $\tau_0 = \bot$.

---

[14] $\mathsf{Sim}_1^{\mathsf{plain}}$ also outputs some state that is fed as input to the subsequent algorithms and similarly for $\mathsf{Sim}_2^{\mathsf{plain}}, \mathsf{Sim}_3^{\mathsf{plain}}$.

[15] As before, note that to send the message $|\mathsf{crs}_{i,k}|$, the length of the string is $\log |\mathsf{crs}_{i,k}|$.

- Set $\tau_{k-1} = \tau_{k-2}$.
- For each party P_j, $(j \neq i)$, if $k > 1$, do the following:
  - Parse its previous round message as $(\mathsf{msg}_{j,k-1}, r_{j,k-1}, \mathsf{len}_{j,k-1})$.
  - Compute $\mathsf{crs}_{j,k-1} = \mathsf{RO}(r_{j,k-1}, 1^{\mathsf{len}_{j,k-1}})$.
  - Compute $\mathsf{msg}_{j,k-1}^{\mathsf{plain}} = \mathsf{S.OcRE.Decode}(\mathsf{msg}_{j,k-1}, \tau_{k-2}, \mathsf{crs}_{j,k-1})$.
  - Append $\mathsf{msg}_{j,k-1}^{\mathsf{plain}}$ to τ_{k-1}.
- Compute $\mathsf{msg}_{i,k}^{\mathsf{plain}} = \mathsf{Sim}_3^{\mathsf{plain}}(k, y, \tau_{k-1}, \mathsf{st})$ where st denotes the state of $\mathsf{Sim}^{\mathsf{plain}}$.
- Pick a random string $r_{i,k} \in \{0, 1\}^\lambda$.
- Compute
  $(\mathsf{msg}_{i,k}, \mathsf{crs}_{i,k}) \leftarrow \mathsf{S.OcRE.Sim}(1^{|s(\lambda)|}, 1^{(2 \cdot \lambda + |\tau_{k-1}|)}, 1^\lambda, \mathsf{msg}_{i,k}^{\mathsf{plain}}, 1^\lambda)$.
- Set $\mathsf{RO}(r_{i,k}, 1^{|\mathsf{crs}_{i,k}|}) = \mathsf{crs}_{i,k}$.
- Output $(\mathsf{msg}_{i,k}, r_{i,k}, |\mathsf{crs}_{i,k}|)$.

4. **Output Computation:**
Sim does the following:
- For each honest party P_i, do:
  - Let τ_{t-1} denote the transcript of the underlying protocol π^{plain} after round $(t-1)$.
  - Set $\tau_t = \tau_{t-1}$.
  - For each party P_j, $(j \neq i)$ do the following:
    * Parse its previous round message as $(\mathsf{msg}_{j,k-1}, r_{j,k-1}, \mathsf{len}_{j,k-1})$.
    * Compute $\mathsf{crs}_{j,k-1} = \mathsf{RO}(r_{j,k-1}, 1^{\mathsf{len}_{j,k-1}})$.
    * Compute $\mathsf{msg}_{j,t}^{\mathsf{plain}} = \mathsf{S.OcRE.Decode}(\mathsf{msg}_{j,t}, \tau_{t-1}, \mathsf{crs}_{j,t})$.
    * Append $\mathsf{msg}_{j,t}^{\mathsf{plain}}$ to τ_t.
  - If $\mathsf{Sim}_{\mathsf{Out}}^{\mathsf{plain}}(i, y, \tau_t, \mathsf{st}) = \bot$, send $\bot$ to the ideal functionality and stop.
- Instruct the ideal functionality to deliver output to the honest parties.

Remarks: Note that if $\mathsf{Sim}^{\mathsf{plain}}$ is a rewinding simulator, our simulator Sim will also be a rewinding simulator.

We include the full proof of indistinguishability in the full version of the paper.

Acknowledgements. The first, second and fourth author's research is supported in part from a DARPA/ARL SAFEWARE award, NSF Frontier Award 1413955, and NSF grant 1619348, BSF grant 2012378, a Xerox Faculty Research Award, a Google Faculty Research Award, an equipment grant from Intel, and an Okawa Foundation Research Grant. This material is based upon work supported by the Defense Advanced Research Projects Agency through the ARL under Contract W911NF-15-C- 0205. The views expressed are those of the authors and do not reflect the official policy or position of the Department of Defense, the National Science Foundation, or the U.S. Government. The first author's research is also supported in part by the IBM PhD Fellowship. The third author's research is supported by the Israel Science Foundation (Grant No. 468/14), Binational Science Foundation (Grants No. 2016726, 2014276), and by the European Union Horizon 2020 Research and Innovation Program via ERC Project REACT (Grant No. 756482) and via Project PROMETHEUS (Grant 780701). The fifth author's research is supported by NSF CNS-1908611, CNS-1414082 and Packard Foundation Fellowship.

368   S. Badrinarayanan et al.

References

[AGVW13] Agrawal, S., Gorbunov, S., Vaikuntanathan, V., Wee, H.: Functional encryption: new perspectives and lower bounds. In: Canetti, R., Garay, J.A. (eds.) CRYPTO 2013, Part II. LNCS, vol. 8043, pp. 500–518. Springer, Heidelberg (2013). https://doi.org/10.1007/978-3-642-40084-1_28

[AIKW13] Applebaum, B., Ishai, Y., Kushilevitz, E., Waters, B.: Encoding functions with constant online rate or how to compress garbled circuits keys. In: Canetti, R., Garay, J.A. (eds.) CRYPTO 2013. LNCS, vol. 8043, pp. 166–184. Springer, Heidelberg (2013). https://doi.org/10.1007/978-3-642-40084-1_10

[AJ15] Ananth, P., Jain, A.: Indistinguishability obfuscation from compact functional encryption. In: Gennaro, R., Robshaw, M. (eds.) CRYPTO 2015. LNCS, vol. 9215, pp. 308–326. Springer, Heidelberg (2015). https://doi.org/10.1007/978-3-662-47989-6_15

[AJS17] Ananth, P., Jain, A., Sahai, A.: Indistinguishability obfuscation for turing machines: constant overhead and amortization. In: Katz, J., Shacham, H. (eds.) CRYPTO 2017. LNCS, vol. 10402, pp. 252–279. Springer, Cham (2017). https://doi.org/10.1007/978-3-319-63715-0_9

[AL18] Ananth, P., Lombardi, A.: Succinct garbling schemes from functional encryption through a local simulation paradigm. Cryptology ePrint Archive, Report 2018/759 (2018). https://eprint.iacr.org/2018/759

[AM18] Agrawal, S., Maitra, M.: Functional encryption and indistinguishability obfuscation for turing machines from minimal assumptions. In: TCC (2018)

[BGI+17] Badrinarayanan, S., Garg, S., Ishai, Y., Sahai, A., Wadia, A.: Two-message witness indistinguishability and secure computation in the plain model from new assumptions. In: Takagi, T., Peyrin, T. (eds.) ASIACRYPT 2017. LNCS, vol. 10626, pp. 275–303. Springer, Cham (2017). https://doi.org/10.1007/978-3-319-70700-6_10

[BGJ+17] Badrinarayanan, S., Goyal, V., Jain, A., Khurana, D., Sahai, A.: Round optimal concurrent MPC via strong simulation. In: Kalai, Y., Reyzin, L. (eds.) TCC 2017. LNCS, vol. 10677, pp. 743–775. Springer, Cham (2017). https://doi.org/10.1007/978-3-319-70500-2_25

[BGJ+18] Badrinarayanan, S., Goyal, V., Jain, A., Kalai, Y.T., Khurana, D., Sahai, A.: Promise zero knowledge and its applications to round optimal MPC. In: Shacham, H., Boldyreva, A. (eds.) CRYPTO 2018. LNCS, vol. 10992, pp. 459–487. Springer, Cham (2018). https://doi.org/10.1007/978-3-319-96881-0_16

[BGL+15] Bitansky, N., Garg, S., Lin, H., Pass, R., Telang, S.: Succinct randomized encodings and their applications. In: Proceedings of the Forty-Seventh Annual ACM on Symposium on Theory of Computing, STOC 2015, Portland, OR, USA, 14–17 June, pp. 439–448 (2015)

[BL18] Benhamouda, F., Lin, H.: k-round multiparty computation from k-round oblivious transfer via garbled interactive circuits. In: Nielsen, J.B., Rijmen, V. (eds.) EUROCRYPT 2018. LNCS, vol. 10821, pp. 500–532. Springer, Cham (2018). https://doi.org/10.1007/978-3-319-78375-8_17

[BR93] Bellare, M., Rogaway, P.: Random Oracles are practical: a paradigm for designing efficient protocols. In: Proceedings of the 1st ACM Conference on Computer and Communications Security, CCS 1993, Fairfax, Virginia, USA, 3–5 November, pp. 62–73 (1993)

[BSW11] Boneh, D., Sahai, A., Waters, B.: Functional encryption: definitions and challenges. In: Ishai, Y. (ed.) TCC 2011. LNCS, vol. 6597, pp. 253–273. Springer, Heidelberg (2011). https://doi.org/10.1007/978-3-642-19571-6_16

[CDG+18] Camenisch, J., Drijvers, M., Gagliardoni, T., Lehmann, A., Neven, G.: The wonderful world of global random Oracles. In: Nielsen, J.B., Rijmen, V. (eds.) EUROCRYPT 2018. LNCS, vol. 10820, pp. 280–312. Springer, Cham (2018). https://doi.org/10.1007/978-3-319-78381-9_11

[CHJV15] Canetti, R., Holmgren, J., Jain, A., Vaikuntanathan, V.: Succinct garbling and indistinguishability obfuscation for RAM programs. In: Proceedings of the Forty-Seventh Annual ACM on Symposium on Theory of Computing, STOC 2015, Portland, OR, USA, 14–17 June, pp. 429–437 (2015)

[CIJ+13] De Caro, A., Iovino, V., Jain, A., O'Neill, A., Paneth, O., Persiano, G.: On the achievability of simulation-based security for functional encryption. In: Canetti, R., Garay, J.A. (eds.) CRYPTO 2013, Part II. LNCS, vol. 8043, pp. 519–535. Springer, Heidelberg (2013). https://doi.org/10.1007/978-3-642-40084-1_29

[CJS14] Canetti, R., Jain, A., Scafuro, A.: Practical UC security with a global random Oracle. In: Proceedings of the 2014 ACM SIGSAC Conference on Computer and Communications Security, Scottsdale, AZ, USA, 3–7 November, pp. 597–608 (2014)

[DSW08] Dodis, Y., Shoup, V., Walfish, S.: Efficient constructions of composable commitments and zero-knowledge proofs. In: Wagner, D. (ed.) CRYPTO 2008. LNCS, vol. 5157, pp. 515–535. Springer, Heidelberg (2008). https://doi.org/10.1007/978-3-540-85174-5_29

[GGJS12] Garg, S., Goyal, V., Jain, A., Sahai, A.: Concurrently secure computation in constant rounds. In: Pointcheval, D., Johansson, T. (eds.) EUROCRYPT 2012. LNCS, vol. 7237, pp. 99–116. Springer, Heidelberg (2012). https://doi.org/10.1007/978-3-642-29011-4_8

[GGM86] Goldreich, O., Goldwasser, S., Micali, S.: How to construct random functions. J. ACM 33(4), 792–807 (1986)

[GGMP16] Garg, S., Gupta, D., Miao, P., Pandey, O.: Secure multiparty RAM computation in constant rounds. In: Hirt, M., Smith, A. (eds.) TCC 2016, Part I. LNCS, vol. 9985, pp. 491–520. Springer, Heidelberg (2016). https://doi.org/10.1007/978-3-662-53641-4_19

[GHL+14] Gentry, C., Halevi, S., Lu, S., Ostrovsky, R., Raykova, M., Wichs, D.: Garbled RAM revisited. In: Nguyen, P.Q., Oswald, E. (eds.) EUROCRYPT 2014. LNCS, vol. 8441, pp. 405–422. Springer, Heidelberg (2014). https://doi.org/10.1007/978-3-642-55220-5_23

[GOS06] Groth, J., Ostrovsky, R., Sahai, A.: Non-interactive zaps and new techniques for NIZK. In: Dwork, C. (ed.) CRYPTO 2006. LNCS, vol. 4117, pp. 97–111. Springer, Heidelberg (2006). https://doi.org/10.1007/11818175_6

[GS18] Garg, S., Srinivasan, A.: A simple construction of iO for turing machines. Cryptology ePrint Archive, Report 2018/771 (2018). https://eprint.iacr.org/2018/771

[HJK+16] Hofheinz, D., Jager, T., Khurana, D., Sahai, A., Waters, B., Zhandry, M.: How to generate and use universal samplers. In: Cheon, J.H., Takagi, T. (eds.) ASIACRYPT 2016. LNCS, vol. 10032, pp. 715–744. Springer, Heidelberg (2016). https://doi.org/10.1007/978-3-662-53890-6_24

[HW15] Hubácek, P., Wichs, D.: On the communication complexity of secure function evaluation with long output. In: Proceedings of the 2015 Conference on Innovations in Theoretical Computer Science, ITCS 2015, Rehovot, Israel, 11–13 January, pp. 163–172 (2015)

[HY16] Hazay, C., Yanai, A.: Constant-round maliciously secure two-party computation in the RAM Model. In: Hirt, M., Smith, A. (eds.) TCC 2016, Part I. LNCS, vol. 9985, pp. 521–553. Springer, Heidelberg (2016). https://doi.org/10.1007/978-3-662-53641-4_20

[IK00] Ishai, Y., Kushilevitz, E.: Randomizing polynomials: a new representation with applications to round-efficient secure computation. In: 41st Annual Symposium on Foundations of Computer Science, FOCS 2000, Redondo Beach, California, USA, 12–14 November, pp. 294–304 (2000)

[IMS12] Ishai, Y., Mahmoody, M., Sahai, A.: On efficient zero-knowledge PCPs. In: Cramer, R. (ed.) TCC 2012. LNCS, vol. 7194, pp. 151–168. Springer, Heidelberg (2012). https://doi.org/10.1007/978-3-642-28914-9_9

[IW14] Ishai, Y., Wee, H.: Partial garbling schemes and their applications. In: Esparza, J., Fraigniaud, P., Husfeldt, T., Koutsoupias, E. (eds.) ICALP 2014, Part I. LNCS, vol. 8572, pp. 650–662. Springer, Heidelberg (2014). https://doi.org/10.1007/978-3-662-43948-7_54

[KLW15] Koppula, V., Lewko, A.B., Waters, B.: Indistinguishability obfuscation for turing machines with unbounded memory. In: Proceedings of the Forty-Seventh Annual ACM on Symposium on Theory of Computing, STOC 2015, Portland, OR, USA, 14–17 June, pp. 419–428 (2015)

[LO17] Lu, S., Ostrovsky, R.: Black-box parallel garbled RAM. In: Katz, J., Shacham, H. (eds.) CRYPTO 2017, Part II. LNCS, vol. 10402, pp. 66–92. Springer, Cham (2017). https://doi.org/10.1007/978-3-319-63715-0_3

[LPST16] Lin, H., Pass, R., Seth, K., Telang, S.: Output-compressing randomized encodings and applications. In: Kushilevitz, E., Malkin, T. (eds.) TCC 2016, Part I. LNCS, vol. 9562, pp. 96–124. Springer, Heidelberg (2016). https://doi.org/10.1007/978-3-662-49096-9_5

[Mia16] Miao, P.: Cut-and-choose for garbled RAM. IACR Cryptology ePrint Archive 2016:907 (2016)

[MW16] Mukherjee, P., Wichs, D.: Two round multiparty computation via multi-key FHE. In: Fischlin, M., Coron, J.-S. (eds.) EUROCRYPT 2016, Part II. LNCS, vol. 9666, pp. 735–763. Springer, Heidelberg (2016). https://doi.org/10.1007/978-3-662-49896-5_26

[Nie02] Nielsen, J.B.: Separating random Oracle proofs from complexity theoretic proofs: the non-committing encryption case. In: Yung, M. (ed.) CRYPTO 2002. LNCS, vol. 2442, pp. 111–126. Springer, Heidelberg (2002). https://doi.org/10.1007/3-540-45708-9_8

[OS97] Ostrovsky, R., Shoup, V.: Private information storage (extended abstract). In: Proceedings of the Twenty-Ninth Annual ACM Symposium on the Theory of Computing, El Paso, Texas, USA, 4–6 May, pp. 294–303 (1997)

[Pas03] Pass, R.: Simulation in quasi-polynomial time, and its application to protocol composition. In: Biham, E. (ed.) EUROCRYPT 2003. LNCS, vol. 2656, pp. 160–176. Springer, Heidelberg (2003). https://doi.org/10.1007/3-540-39200-9_10

[Wee09] Wee, H.: Zero knowledge in the random Oracle model, revisited. In: Matsui, M. (ed.) ASIACRYPT 2009. LNCS, vol. 5912, pp. 417–434. Springer, Heidelberg (2009). https://doi.org/10.1007/978-3-642-10366-7_25

Collusion Resistant Watermarking Schemes for Cryptographic Functionalities

Rupeng Yang[1,2], Man Ho Au[2(✉)], Junzuo Lai[3(✉)], Qiuliang Xu[4(✉)],
and Zuoxia Yu[2]

[1] School of Computer Science and Technology, Shandong University,
Jinan 250101, China
orbbyrp@gmail.com
[2] Department of Computing, The Hong Kong Polytechnic University,
Hung Hom, Hong Kong, China
csallen@comp.polyu.edu.hk, zuoxia.yu@gmail.com
[3] College of Information Science and Technology, Jinan University,
Guangzhou 510632, China
laijunzuo@gmail.com
[4] School of Software, Shandong University,
Jinan 250101, China
xql@sdu.edu.cn

Abstract. A cryptographic watermarking scheme embeds a message into a program while preserving its functionality. Recently, a number of watermarking schemes have been proposed, which are proven secure in the sense that given *one* marked program, any attempt to remove the embedded message will substantially change its functionality.

In this paper, we formally initiate the study of collusion attacks for watermarking schemes, where the attacker's goal is to remove the embedded messages given *multiple* copies of the same program, each with a different embedded message. This is motivated by practical scenarios, where a program may be marked multiple times with different messages.

The results of this work are twofold. First, we examine existing cryptographic watermarking schemes and observe that all of them are vulnerable to collusion attacks. Second, we construct collusion resistant watermarking schemes for various cryptographic functionalities (e.g., pseudorandom function evaluation, decryption, etc.). To achieve our second result, we present a new primitive called puncturable functional encryption scheme, which may be of independent interest.

Keywords: Watermarking · Watermarkable PRF · Collusion resistance · Public extraction

© International Association for Cryptologic Research 2019
S. D. Galbraith and S. Moriai (Eds.): ASIACRYPT 2019, LNCS 11921, pp. 371–398, 2019.
https://doi.org/10.1007/978-3-030-34578-5_14

1   Introduction

A watermarking scheme allows one to embed some information into a program[1] without significantly changing its functionality. It has many natural applications, including ownership protection, information leaker tracing, etc.

The formal definition of watermarking schemes for programs is first presented by Barak et al. in [BGI+01]. Subsequently, new properties of watermarking schemes are presented in [HMW07, NW15, CHV15]. They are briefly summarized below.

- **Unremovability:** This is the essential security property for watermarking schemes, which requires that it should be hard to *remove* or *modify* the embedded information in a marked program without destroying it.
- **Public Extraction:** Anyone should be able to extract the embedded information in a marked program. In other words, the extraction key will be made public.
- **Public Marking:** Anyone should be able to embed information into a program. In other words, the marking key will be made public.
- **Unforgeability:** Only the authorized entity who holds the marking key should be able to embed information into a program. Obviously, it requires keeping the marking key secret and is not compatible with the "public marking" property.
- **Message-Embedding:** This property allows one to embed a given string (instead of merely a mark symbol) into the watermarked program.

Despite being a natural concept and perceived to have a wide range of applications, watermarking schemes provably secure against arbitrary removal strategies were not presented until 2015. In [CHN+16] (which is a merged version of [NW15] and [CHV15]), Cohen et al. construct a publicly extractable watermarking scheme for the evaluation algorithm of pseudorandom functions (PRFs) from indistinguishability obfuscators. Based on the watermarkable PRF families, they also construct watermarkable public key encryption (PKE) schemes and watermarkable signature schemes. However, Cohen et al.'s schemes do not achieve standard unforgeability. Subsequently, Yang et al. [YAL+18] improve the watermarkable PRF in [CHN+16] to achieve both standard unforgeability and public extraction simultaneously.

In another line of research, initiated by Boneh et al. in [BLW17], watermarkable PRFs are constructed from variants of constraint-hiding constrained PRFs (e.g., privately programmable PRF and translucent puncturable PRF). Boneh et al.'s scheme is constructed from privately programmable PRF, which is instantiated from indistinguishability obfuscator in [BLW17]. Subsequently, based on a translucent puncturable PRF, Kim and Wu [KW17] present the first construction of watermarkable PRF from standard lattice assumptions. Then,

---

[1] In this paper, we focus on watermarking schemes for programs and only consider those with provable security against arbitrary removal strategies. We refer readers to Sect. 1.2 for an extended introduction to the area.

Peikert and Shiehian [PS18] construct privately programmable PRF from LWE, which provides another way to instantiate watermarkable PRF from standard assumptions. Recently, in [QWZ18] and [KW19], watermarkable PRFs with public marking are constructed from constraint-hiding constrained PRF and puncturable extractable PRF respectively, both of which can be instantiated from standard lattice assumptions.

Besides, a very simple yet elegant construction of watermarking scheme for any PKE scheme is presented by Baldimtsi et al. [BKS17]. However, their scheme does not support multi-message-embedding inherently. That is, each program can only be marked with at most one message during the life-time of the scheme.

Collusion Resistance of Watermarking Schemes. In practical applications, it is usually required that unremovability of watermarking schemes should hold under "collusion attacks", where the attacker can access several copies of the same program embedded with different information. As a concrete example, consider the following scenario. A software development company developed a program and would like to outsource its testing to several organizations. To prevent these organizations from leaking the program, the company will employ a watermarking scheme to embed the name of the target organization into the copy being sent. Here, the watermarking scheme should enable the company to trace program leakers even when a few target organizations collude.

However, for all previous watermarking schemes [CHN+16, BLW17, KW17, BKS17, PS18, YAL+18, QWZ18, KW19], the unremovability is only proved against an adversary who attempts to remove or modify the embedded message given a *single* marked program[2], and it is unknown whether they are secure against collusion attacks. Thus, the following question arises naturally:

Can we build collusion resistant watermarking scheme?

1.1   Our Results

In this paper, we explore the existence of watermarking schemes secure against collusion attacks. First, we observe that unfortunately, all existing watermarking schemes are *vulnerable* to collusion attacks (we elaborate this in Sect. 2). Then, we consider how to develop watermarkable cryptographic primitives secure against the collusion attacks. Specifically, our contributions are as follows.

- We present the notion of *collusion resistant watermarking scheme* to capture collusion attacks. It requires a stronger unremovability (namely, collusion resistant unremovability) that allows the adversary to obtain watermarked circuits embedded with different messages for the same functionality.

---

[2] In a concurrent work [GKM+19], collusion resistant watermarking schemes for public-key cryptographic primitives are presented. However, their constructions are under a relaxed notion of functionality-preserving. In this work, we achieve collusion resistance while preserving the original "statistical functionality-preserving" proposed in [CHN+16].

- We give a construction of *collusion resistant watermarkable PRF*, which is the first watermarkable cryptographic primitive provably secure against the collusion attacks. To achieve this, we introduce a new message-embedding technique in the watermarking setting and propose a new primitive, namely, *puncturable functional encryption scheme*, which we believe will find additional applications in constructing advanced cryptographic primitives.
- Based on our construction of collusion resistant watermarkable PRF, we also construct watermarkable PKE schemes and watermarkable signature schemes, both of which have collusion resistant unremovability.

We compare the main features achieved by current watermarking schemes and our watermarking schemes in Table 1. We remark that in addition to collusion resistance, our schemes can achieve many desirable features, including public extraction, unforgeability, and message-embedding.

Table 1. The comparison.

		Unforgeability	Public extraction	Public marking	Message embedding	Collusion resistance
[CHN+16]	PRF	✗	✓	✗	✓	✗
	PKE	✗	✓	✗	✓	✗
	Signature	✗	✓	✗	✓	✗
[YAL+18]	PRF	✓	✓	✗	✓	✗
[BLW17]	PRF	✓	✗	✗	✓	✗
[KW17]	PRF	✓	✗	✗	✓	✗
[QWZ18]	PRF	✗	✗	✓	✓	✗
[KW19]	PRF	✓	✗	✗	✓	✗
	PRF	✓†	✗	✓	✓	✗
[BKS17]	PKE	✓	✗	✗	✗	-
	PKE	✓	✓	✗	✗	-
This work	PRF	✓	✓	✗	✓	✓
	PKE	✓	✓	✗	✓	✓
	Signature	✓	✓	✗	✓	✓

†: Weaker versions of unforgeability are achieved for this scheme.

The presented collusion resistant watermarking schemes are built on several cryptographic primitives, which can be constructed from indistinguishability obfuscator and standard lattice assumptions.

Theorem 1.1 (Informal). *Assuming the worst-case hardness of appropriately parameterized GapSVP and SIVP problems and the existence of indistinguishability obfuscator, there exist collusion resistant watermarkable PRF/PKE/signature schemes.*

Remark 1.1. It is worth noting that our constructions of collusion resistant watermarking schemes rely on the existence of indistinguishability obfuscator.

However, this seems essential, at least for collusion resistant watermarkable PRF. To see this, recall that as proved in [BGI+01], watermarking scheme perfectly preserving the functionality of the watermarked program does not exist. Thus, a marked key of PRF must evaluate differently with the original key on some inputs, i.e., the marked key can be viewed as a constrained key of the original key. Besides, the marked key should hide its constrained inputs, since otherwise, the attacker is likely to remove the embedded messages via resetting outputs on constrained inputs. Therefore, we can approximately view a collusion resistant watermarkable PRF as a collusion resistant constraint-hiding constrained PRF, which, as shown in [CC17], can imply indistinguishability obfuscator. Nonetheless, we are not able to formalize this intuition. It is an interesting open problem to give a formal construction of indistinguishability obfuscator from collusion resistant watermarkable PRF.

1.2 Related Works

Additional Related Works on Watermarking Schemes. In this paper, we concentrate on watermarking schemes provably secure against arbitrary removal strategies. There are also numerous works (see [CMB+07] and references therein) attempting to use ad hoc techniques to watermark a wide class of digital objects, such as images, audios, videos, etc. However, these constructions lack rigorous security analysis and are (potentially) vulnerable to some attacks.

In another line of research [NSS99, YF11, Nis13], watermarking schemes for cryptographic objects (e.g., the key, the signature, etc.) are constructed and rigorously analyzed. However, their security definition considers a restricted adversary that will not change the format of the watermarked objects.

Puncturable Symmetric Key Functional Encryption. One byproduct of this work is a new primitive called puncturable functional encryption. A similar primitive, which is called puncturable symmetric key functional encryption, is also studied in previous works [BV15, KNT18]. In particular, it is used to construct the indistinguishability obfuscator in these works.

We stress that these two types of primitives are incomparable. First, while succinctness is the key property for a puncturable symmetric key functional encryption scheme, it is not required in our puncturable functional encryption scheme. Thus, our scheme cannot be used in constructions of indistinguishability obfuscators. On the other hand, our puncturable functional encryption scheme will puncture a secret key on a ciphertext, but in a puncturable symmetric key functional encryption scheme, secret keys are punctured on a message or on a tag. Thus, their schemes are also inapplicable to our setting.

Traitor Tracing Scheme. The notion of collusion resistant watermarking scheme is somewhat similar to the notion of traitor tracing scheme, which aims at tracing secret key leakers among a set of users holding functionally equivalent secret keys in a broadcast encryption setting. Since first presented in [CFN94], traitor tracing has been formally studied for a long time (see e.g.,

[BSW06, BN08, BZ14, NWZ16, GKW18, CVW+18] and references therein for an overview of previous works).

Generally, in a traitor tracing scheme, there is a common public key pk and each user holds a different secret key. Data encrypted under the common public key can be decrypted by all users in the system. Moreover, there exists a tracing algorithm, which outputs a set of users on input a "pirate decoder" that can decrypt ciphertexts under pk. It is guaranteed that the tracing algorithm can identify at least one of the users in the coalition that produces the pirate decoder.

Comparing Watermarking and Traitor Tracing. Both (collusion resistant) watermarking and traitor tracing will issue copies of a program (or a key), which are embedded with some information, to users and aim at recovering the embedded information from a functionally-similar program/key generated by them. However, solutions to the traitor tracing problem do not yield watermarking schemes directly, since these two notions also have several inherent differences.

First, in a traitor tracing scheme, secret keys of users are issued by a center, while in a watermarking scheme, user can choose their watermarked programs themselves. Another difference is that in a traitor tracing scheme, secret keys of all users are functionally equivalent, while in a watermarking scheme, programs with different functionalities can be watermarked in the same watermarking scheme. Besides, traitor tracing schemes focus on tracing secret key leakers in an encryption scheme, while watermarking schemes aim at marking general purpose programs (although we only know how to watermark some specific cryptographic functionalities currently).

A Closer Look at How to Construct Traitor Tracing Schemes. In [BSW06], Boneh et al. present a classic paradigm to construct traitor tracing schemes, which is also used or adapted in many subsequent works [BZ14, NWZ16, GKW18]. The construction proceeds in two steps.

First, a private linear broadcast encryption (PLBE) scheme is constructed. Recall that a PLBE scheme has a sequence $(sk_1, \ldots, sk_N)$ of N secret keys for a public key and each ciphertext is labeled with an integer in $[0, N]$. A secret key sk_i is only able to decrypt a ciphertext with label j when $j < i$. Thus, a ciphertext with label 0 can be decrypted by all secret keys, while a ciphertext with label N can not be decrypted by any secret key. Also, it is required that it is computationally infeasible to distinguish a ciphertext with label j and that with label $j - 1$ if sk_j is not given.

A PLBE scheme implies a traitor tracing scheme [BSW06, GKW18]. More concretely, the traitor tracing scheme supports a user set of size N and the ith user in that set is given secret key sk_i. Broadcast messages will be encrypted with label 0. When tracing colluders from a pirate decoder, the tracing algorithm feeds the decoder with ciphertexts labeled with 0 to N sequentially and outputs i if there exists a "large gap" in decryption success probability between ciphertexts labeled with $i - 1$ and those labeled with i. Note that the decoder can decrypt with a high success probability on ciphertext labeled with 0 (due to the usefulness of the decoder) and can decrypt with a negligible success probability on ciphertext labeled with N (due to the security of PLBE), thus, there must exists a large gap in decryption success probability between $i-1$ and i for some $i \in [N]$. Also, as no one could distinguish ciphertexts labeled with $i-1$ and that labeled with i without sk_i, the large gap must occur between $i-1$ and i such that the colluders possess sk_i. Therefore, the tracing algorithm can recover at least one of the colluders.

1.3 Roadmap

The rest of the paper is organized as follows. We give an overview of our construction in Sect. 2. Then in Sect. 3, we review notations used in this work. We present the formal definition of collusion resistant watermarkable PRF in Sect. 4. Then in Sect. 5, we define and construct puncturable functional encryption, which is employed to construct collusion resistant watermarkable PRF. We show our main construction of collusion resistant watermarkable PRF in Sect. 6 and present constructions of collusion resistant watermarking schemes for public key primitives in Sect. 7. Finally, in Sect. 8, we conclude our work with a few possible future works.

2 Technical Overview

In this section, we provide an overview of our construction of collusion resistant watermarkable PRF. Our starting point is the watermarking scheme WM_0 presented in [CHN+16] (or more accurately, its variant in [YAL+18]). We first explain why WM_0 (and all previous watermarking schemes) are not collusion resistant and describe the main challenges in achieving collusion resistance. Then we give a high-level idea on how to address these challenges.

A Brief Overview of WM_0. Roughly speaking, WM_0 works as follows. The extraction key/marking key pair of WM_0 is a public key/secret key pair (pk, sk) of a PKE scheme. To embed a message msg into a PRF key k, the marking algorithm outputs an obfuscation of the following circuit, which evaluates the function $\mathsf{PRF}(k, \cdot)$ correctly at all points, except for some "punctured points".

$$\mathsf{C}(x) = \begin{cases} f(\mu) \oplus msg & \text{if } \mu = \mathsf{Dec}(sk, x) \in \mathcal{V} \\ \mathsf{PRF}(k, x) & \text{otherwise.} \end{cases}$$

Here, Dec is the decryption algorithm of the underlying PKE scheme, $\mathcal{V}$ is a set defined by the PRF key k and f is a suitable function.

When extracting the embedded message from a watermarked circuit, the extraction algorithm first samples a string $\mu \in \mathcal{V}$ and encrypts it with the public key pk. Next, it evaluates the circuit on the ciphertext and obtains an output z. Finally, it computes $msg = z \oplus f(\mu)$. The above extraction procedure will be repeated multiple times and the extraction algorithm will output the majority result or an "UNMARKED" symbol if no majority is found.

Security of the scheme relies on the fact that punctured points (i.e. those decrypted to a string in $\mathcal{V}$) are hidden[3]. As a result, the adversary, who is only allowed to alter the marked circuit slightly, is not able to change the output values on a large enough fraction of punctured points, and thus the extraction algorithm can still extract the correct message.

Why WM_0 is Not Collusion Resistant? However, if watermarked circuits embedded with different messages for the same PRF key k are given, one can easily locate all punctured points via comparing the outputs of the circuits. In addition, it is easy to modify or remove the embedded messages via resetting outputs on all punctured points.

In more detail, given two circuits C_1 and C_2 that are generated by embedding different messages, say msg_1 and msg_2, into the same PRF key k, an attacker can output a circuit C^* embedded with a new message msg^* as follow:

$$C^*(x) = \begin{cases} C_1(x) \oplus msg_1 \oplus msg^* & \text{if } C_1(x) \neq C_2(x). \\ C_1(x) & \text{otherwise.} \end{cases}$$

It is not hard to see that C^* will compute the PRF with key k correctly on almost all inputs except that it will output $f(\mu) \oplus msg^*$ on an input whose decryption μ is in $\mathcal{V}$. Therefore, the attacker can compromise the unremovability of WM_0 via a collusion attack[4].

Since nearly all[5] previous watermarking schemes are constructed following the blueprint proposed in [CHN+16], we can use a similar strategy to show that they are not collusion resistant. We stress that all collusion attacks are based on the fragility of the way messages are embedded and do not take advantage of the concrete instantiations of the schemes.

The Challenge in Achieving Collusion Resistance. To better explain why WM_0 is not able to achieve collusion resistance, we describe WM_0 in a modular manner.

In a high level, on input a PRF key k and a message msg, the marking algorithm of WM_0 works as follows:

1. Generates two sequences $\mathcal{X} = (x_1, \ldots, x_l)$ and $\mathcal{Y} = (y_1, \ldots, y_l)$, where x_i and y_i are in the input space and the output space of the watermarked PRF respectively. More concretely, in WM_0, for each pair (x_i, y_i), $x_i = \texttt{Enc}(pk, \mu)$ and $y_i = f(\mu)$ for some $\mu \in \mathcal{V}$.

---

[3] One could find some punctured points via generating them from public information, but cannot distinguish a random punctured point from a random point in the input space.

[4] We remark that this will not affect the claimed security of WM_0. The attacks only show that WM_0 is not applicable in scenarios where collusion attacks are a legit threat.

[5] The watermarking scheme proposed in [BKS17] is constructed in a different approach, however, it cannot embed different messages into the same program.

2. Encodes the message msg into a sequence $\mathcal{Z} = (z_1, \ldots, z_l) = \texttt{encode}(\mathcal{X}, \mathcal{Y}, msg)$, where z_i is also in the output space of the watermarked PRF. In more detail, messages are encoded into $\mathcal{Z}$ via a simple "exclusive or" operation in WM_0, i.e., $z_i = y_i \oplus msg$ for $i \in [1, l]$.
3. Outputs a circuit that computes the PRF with k correctly on inputs outside $\mathcal{X}$ and outputs z_i on input x_i (here, x_i is called a punctured point).

Correspondingly, we can abstract the extraction algorithm of WM_0, which takes as input a watermarked circuit C, as follows:

1. Samples a set of pairs $\{x_i, y_i\}$ in $\mathcal{X} \times \mathcal{Y}$.
2. Evaluates $z_i = \mathsf{C}(x_i)$ for each x_i.
3. Recovers the message $msg = \texttt{decode}(\{x_i, y_i, z_i\})$. Here, the decoding algorithm outputs the majority of $y_i \oplus z_i$.

The key observation underlying our collusion attack is that the simple "xor" encoding scheme is fragile in the collusion setting. First, for two different messages msg and msg', let $(z_1, \ldots, z_l) = \texttt{encode}(\mathcal{X}, \mathcal{Y}, msg)$ and $(z_1', \ldots, z_l') = \texttt{encode}(\mathcal{X}, \mathcal{Y}, msg')$, then we have $z_i \neq z_i'$ for $i \in [1, l]$. This makes it easy to locate all punctured points in $\mathcal{X}$ by comparing outputs of circuits embedded with different messages. In addition, it is easy to overwrite the encoded message in a codeword $\mathcal{Z} = (z_1, \ldots, z_l)$. For example, one can reset $z_i = z_i \oplus \Delta$ for $i \in [1, l]$ to xor the encoded message with Δ.

In [KW17, QWZ18, KW19], different message encoding schemes are applied. However, all of them inherit the aforementioned weakness to some extent, and thus are not robust against collusion attacks.

To solve this problem, we need to develop a robust message encoding scheme, where $\texttt{decode}$ can recover the original embedded messages even if a collusion attacker can locate some punctured points[6] and will reset outputs on its located punctured points. Next, we explore how to develop a robust message encoding scheme and integrate it with the other part of WM_0.

Addressing the Challenge: A Robust Message Encoding Scheme. We design our encoding scheme via using ideas from the realm of traitor tracing. In particular, our scheme is inspired by the well-known framework presented in [BSW06] (we recall this framework in Sect. 1.2).

The message space of our encoding scheme is $[1, N]$[7]. The input of the encoding algorithm is two sequences $\mathcal{X} = (x_1, \ldots, x_l)$, $\mathcal{Y} = (y_1, \ldots, y_l)$ and a message $msg \in [1, N]$. Here, we divide the whole sequence $\mathcal{X}$ into N parts, namely, $\mathcal{X}_1, \ldots, \mathcal{X}_N$, each of which is labeled with an index in $[1, N]$ (we elaborate how to define $\mathcal{X}_i$ later). To encode a message msg, the encoding algorithm sets $z_i = y_i$ if $x_i \in \mathcal{X}_1 \cup \mathcal{X}_2 \cup \ldots \mathcal{X}_{msg}$ and sets z_i to be the correct PRF output otherwise. The output of the encoding algorithm is the sequence $(z_1, \ldots, z_l)$.

---

[6] This seems unavoidable since circuits embedded with different messages should be run differently on some points to enable message extraction.

[7] Here, we assume that N is polynomial in the security parameter and will show how to remove this restriction later.

We also modify the decoding algorithm. It takes as input a set of tuples (x_i, y_i, z_i), where (x_i, y_i) is sampled from $\mathcal{X} \times \mathcal{Y}$ and z_i is the output of the tested circuit on input x_i, and works as follows:

1. Set $p_0 = 1$ and $p_{N+1} = 0$.
2. For $ind \in [1, N]$, estimate the fraction p_{ind} of "correctly reprogrammed" points in set $\mathcal{X}_{ind}$, where a point x_i is "correctly reprogrammed" if $y_i = z_i$. This can be accomplished via testing polynomially-many points in $\mathcal{X}_{ind}$.
3. If there exists $ind \in [0, N]$ such that $|p_{ind} - p_{ind+1}|$ is noticeable (i.e., a "large gap" at ind is found), output the message $msg = ind$. Here, $msg = 0$ denotes the code is not decodable (i.e., the circuit is unmarked).

Next, we argue why our new message encoding scheme is robust under collusion attacks. Observe that, given a few (say 2) circuits C_1 and C_2 embedded with messages msg_1 and msg_2 respectively (w.l.o.g. assuming $msg_1 < msg_2$), the attacker can locate punctured points in $\mathcal{X}_{ind}$ for $ind \in (msg_1, msg_2]$ by comparing outputs of C_1 and C_2. However, we note that

- If the attacker cannot distinguish punctured points in $\mathcal{X}_{ind_1}$ and $\mathcal{X}_{ind_2}$ for $ind_1, ind_2 \in (msg_1, msg_2]$, it cannot make $|p_{ind_1} - p_{ind_2}|$ noticeable via resetting outputs on located punctured points.
- If the attacker cannot distinguish a punctured point $x_i \in \mathcal{X}_{ind}$ from a random point for $ind \notin (msg_1, msg_2]$, it will not be able to reset the output on such x_i. Thus, we have $p_{ind} = 1$ for $ind \in [1, msg_1]$ and $p_{ind} = 0$ for $ind \in (msg_2, N]$.

Consequently, if the aforementioned indistinguishability properties are guaranteed, the large gap(s) must occur at either msg_1 or msg_2 (or at both points), i.e., the decoding algorithm could output the embedded message(s).

One problem of the above solution is that the message space is restricted to be a polynomial-size set. This is because the decoding algorithm needs to scan all indices linearly to find a large gap. Addressing this problem, we employ the refined binary search presented in [BCP14,NWZ16] to search the "large gap". The search algorithm can find all (polynomially-many) large gap points from an *exponentially large* interval in a pre-defined polynomial time, as long as $|p_{ind_1} - p_{ind_2}|$ is negligible for all (adaptively chosen) interval $[ind_1, ind_2] \subseteq [0, N + 1]$ not containing a large gap point. In this way, we can set the message space to be $[1, N]$ for an exponentially large N.

Towards Integrating Our New Encoding Scheme with $\mathsf{WM_0}$. Next, we integrate our encoding scheme with the remaining part of $\mathsf{WM_0}$. First, we will specify how to label punctured points with indices. Then, we will show how to achieve indistinguishability properties required by our robust message encoding scheme. More precisely, we will argue that for a collusion attacker, who can locate some punctured points via comparing outputs of watermarked circuits embedded with different messages, both the unlocated punctured points and labels of the located punctured points are hidden.

Labeling Punctured Points with Indices. Recall that in $\mathsf{WM_0}$, the domain of the PRF is the ciphertext space of a PKE scheme and punctured points are encryptions of plaintexts in a set $\mathcal{V}$. To label a punctured point with an index ind, we append ind to the underlying plaintext, i.e., we define $\mathcal{X}_{ind} = \{\text{Enc}(pk, \mu \| ind)\}_{\mu \in \mathcal{V}}$, where pk is the public key of the underlying PKE scheme and serves as WM_0's extraction key.

Hiding Punctured Points and Labels. Next, we explore how to hide unlocated punctured points and labels of located punctured points. For simplicity, we consider an adversary who gets two watermarked circuits C_1 and C_2 for the same PRF key k, which are embedded with messages msg_1 and msg_2 respectively, where $msg_1 < msg_2$. Recall that our message encoding scheme is able to recover the embedded messages if the following two properties are guaranteed:

- Pseudorandomness of punctured points in $\mathcal{X}_{ind}$ for an adaptively chosen $ind \notin (msg_1, msg_2]$.
- Indistinguishability between punctured points in $\mathcal{X}_{ind_1}$ and $\mathcal{X}_{ind_2}$ for adaptively chosen $ind_1, ind_2 \in (msg_1, msg_2]$.

Unfortunately, the PKE scheme employed in WM_0, which is a puncturable encryption scheme, does not provide the desired properties. To see this, consider an input x from $\mathcal{X}_{ind}$, where $ind \in (msg_1, msg_2]$. Since $C_1(x) \neq C_2(x)$, a secret key that can decrypt x must be included in both C_1 and C_2 (otherwise, the circuit cannot recognize it and deal with it properly). However, the puncturable encryption scheme cannot guarantee indistinguishability on ciphertexts that are decryptable.

To bridge the gap, we present a new cryptographic primitive that we call *puncturable functional encryption* and replace puncturable encryption used in WM_0 with it. Roughly speaking, a puncturable functional encryption scheme enhances a functional encryption scheme with the puncturing capability and enjoys both security of functional encryption schemes and that of puncturable encryption schemes. Especially, similar to a functional encryption, it has the *"adaptive indistinguishability"* property, which could ensure indistinguishability of ciphertexts as long as no secret key distinguishing them is provided. Also, similar to a puncturable encryption, it has the *"ciphertext pseudorandomness"* property, which could ensure pseudorandomness of a ciphertext given a secret key punctured on it.

Now, for two punctured points x_1 and x_2 in $\mathcal{X}_{ind_1}$ and $\mathcal{X}_{ind_2}$ respectively, where $ind_1, ind_2 \in (msg_1, msg_2]$, since none of them will be reprogrammed in C_1 while both of them will be reprogrammed in C_2, secret keys hardwired in C_1 and C_2 do not need to distinguish them. Thus, their indistinguishability comes from the adaptive indistinguishability of the puncturable functional encryption scheme directly. Meanwhile, for a punctured points x in $\mathcal{X}_{ind}$ for $ind \notin (msg_1, msg_2]$, since $C_1(x) = C_2(x)$, we can regard C_1 and C_2 as the same circuit when considering pseudorandomness of x. Thus, the pseudorandomness of x can be reduced to the ciphertext pseudorandomness of the puncturable functional encryption scheme, just as what has been argued in the original security proof (in the non-collusion setting) for WM_0.

Constructing Puncturable Functional Encryption. To construct a puncturable functional encryption scheme, we employ a functional encryption scheme,
a puncturable encryption scheme, and a statistical sound non-interactive zero-
knowledge (NIZK) proof. We integrate them via a "two-layer encryption" approach.

More precisely, a plaintext is first encrypted into an inner ciphertext using the
functional encryption scheme. Then the NIZK proof is employed to prove that
the inner ciphertext is properly encrypted. Finally, both the inner ciphertext and
the proof is encrypted into an outer ciphertext under the puncturable encryption
scheme. When decrypting a ciphertext, the decryption algorithm first decrypts the
outer ciphertext. It aborts if the proof is invalid and outputs the decryption of
the inner ciphertext otherwise. Main security properties of the constructed puncturable functional encryption (namely, adaptively indistinguishability and ciphertext pseudorandomness) reduce to corresponding security properties of underlying
functional encryption and puncturable encryption respectively.

3   Notations

Let a be a string, we use $\|a\|$ to denote the length of a. Let $\mathcal{S}$ be a finite set, we
use $\|\mathcal{S}\|$ to denote the size of $\mathcal{S}$, and use $s \xleftarrow{\$} \mathcal{S}$ to denote sampling an element s
uniformly from set $\mathcal{S}$. For a string a and a set $\mathcal{S}$ of strings, we use $a\|\mathcal{S}$ to denote the
set $\{x : \exists s \in \mathcal{S}, x = a\|s\}$. For n elements $e_1, \ldots, e_n$, we use $\{e_1, \ldots, e_n\}$ to denote
a set containing these elements and use $(e_1, \ldots, e_n)$ to denote an ordered list of
these elements. We write $negl(\cdot)$ to denote a negligible function, and write $poly(\cdot)$
to denote a polynomial. For integers $a \le b$, we write $[a, b]$ to denote all integers from
a to b. For two circuits C_1 and C_2, we write $\mathsf{C}_1 \equiv \mathsf{C}_2$ to denote that for any input x,
$\mathsf{C}_1(x) = \mathsf{C}_2(x)$. Following the syntax in [BLW17], for a circuit family C indexed by
a few, say m, constants, we write $C[c_1, \ldots, c_m]$ to denote a circuit with constants
$c_1, \ldots, c_m$.

Chernoff Bound. We make use of the Chernoff bound in our security proof. There
are various forms of the Chernoff bound, here we use the one from [Goe15].

Lemma 3.1 (Chernoff Bounds). *Let* $X = \sum_{i=1}^{n} X_i$, *where* $X_i = 1$ *with probability* p_i *and* $X_i = 0$ *with probability* $1 - p_i$, *and all* X_i *are independent. Let*
$\mu = \mathbb{E}(X) = \sum_{i=1}^{n} p_i$. *Then*

$$\Pr[X \ge (1+\delta)\mu] \le e^{-\frac{\delta^2}{2+\delta}\mu} \text{ for all } \delta > 0;$$

$$\Pr[X \le (1-\delta)\mu] \le e^{-\frac{\delta^2}{2}\mu} \text{ for all } 0 < \delta < 1.$$

Besides, we also employ some cryptographic primitives and their definitions are
recalled in the full version of this paper.

4   Definition of Collusion Resistant Watermarkable PRF

In this section, we give the formal definition of the collusion resistant watermarkable PRF, which is adapted from definitions of watermarkable PRF in previous works [CHN+16, BLW17, KW17]. The main difference between our definition and previous ones is that the unremovability holds against an adversary that can obtain polynomially-many (instead of one) watermarked circuits for the same PRF key from the challenge oracle. Besides, the extraction algorithm takes an additional parameter q, which can be roughly viewed as the number of colluders, as input. The correctness and the unforgeability hold for arbitrary positive integer q; for the unremovability, a large enough q is needed. In particular, if q is larger than the number of colluders, the extraction algorithm can extract a non-empty subset of the coalition, while using a smaller q may lead to an error symbol.

Remark 4.1. Our definition of collusion resistant unremovability implicitly requires that the adversary is only allowed to obtain a bounded number (i.e., q) of watermarked circuits from the challenge oracle. Thus, it falls into the category of "bounded collusion resistance". Nonetheless, in our definition, the bound q does not need to be fixed in the setup phase and may be varied in different extraction procedures. In fact, if the extractor has a way to know the number of colluders in advance, the scheme remains secure against an arbitrary number of colluders. Besides, since the extraction algorithm is able to detect if a smaller q is used, in practice, the extractor can re-execute the extraction algorithm with a larger q after receiving an error message from the extraction algorithm.

Definition 4.1 (Watermarkable PRFs [CHN+16, BLW17, KW17, adapted]). *Let* PRF $=$ (PRF.KeyGen, PRF.Eval) *be a PRF family with key space* $\mathcal{K}$, *input space* $\{0,1\}^n$ *and output space* $\{0,1\}^m$. *The watermarking scheme with message space* $\mathcal{M}$ *for* PRF *(more accurately, the evaluation algorithm of* PRF*) consists of three algorithms:*

- **Setup.** *On input the security parameter* λ, *the setup algorithm outputs the mark key* MK *and the extraction key* EK.
- **Mark.** *On input the mark key* MK, *a secret key* $k \in \mathcal{K}$ *of* PRF, *and a message* $msg \in \mathcal{M}$, *the marking algorithm outputs a marked circuit* C.
- **Extract.** *On input the extraction key* EK, *a circuit* C, *and a parameter* q, *the extraction algorithm outputs either a set* $\mathcal{L} \subseteq \mathcal{M}$ *or a symbol* UNMARKED *or an error symbol* $\perp$.

Definition 4.2 (Watermarking Correctness). *Correctness of the watermarking scheme requires that for any* $k \in \mathcal{K}$, $msg \in \mathcal{M}$, *and any polynomial* $q \geq 1$, *let* $(MK, EK) \leftarrow \texttt{Setup}(1^\lambda)$, C $\leftarrow \texttt{Mark}(MK, k, msg)$, *we have:*

- **Functionality Preserving.** C$(\cdot)$ *and* PRF.Eval$(k, \cdot)$ *compute identically on all but a negligible fraction of inputs.*
- **Extraction Correctness.** $\Pr[\texttt{Extract}(EK, \texttt{C}, q) \neq \{msg\}] \leq negl(\lambda)$.

Before presenting the security definition of collusion resistant watermarkable PRF, we first introduce oracles the adversaries can query during the security experiments. Here, the marking oracle is identical to the one defined in previous works, while we redefine the challenge oracle to capture the scenario that the adversary can obtain multiple circuits embedded with different messages for the same secret key.

- **Marking Oracle** $\mathcal{O}_{MK}^M(\cdot, \cdot)$. On input a message $msg \in \mathcal{M}$ and a PRF key $k \in \mathcal{K}$, the oracle returns a circuit $C \leftarrow \text{Mark}(MK, k, msg)$.
- **Challenge Oracle** $\mathcal{O}_{MK}^C(\cdot)$. On input a polynomial-size set M of messages from $\mathcal{M}$, the oracle first samples a key $k^* \leftarrow \text{PRF.KeyGen}(1^\lambda)$. Then, for each $msg_i^* \in$ M, it computes $C_i^* \leftarrow \text{Mark}(MK, k^*, msg_i^*)$. Finally, it returns the set $\{C_1^*, \ldots, C_Q^*\}$, where $Q = \|M\|$.

Definition 4.3 (Collusion Resistant Unremovability). *The watermarking scheme for a PRF is collusion resistant unremovable if for any polynomial q, for all polynomial-time (PPT) and unremoving-admissible adversaries $\mathcal{A}$, we have* $\Pr[\text{ExptUR}_{\mathcal{A},q}(\lambda) = 1] \leq negl(\lambda)$, *where we define the experiment ExptUR and unremoving-admissibility as follows:*

1. *The challenger samples $(MK, EK) \leftarrow \text{Setup}(1^\lambda)$ and returns EK to $\mathcal{A}$.*
2. *Then, $\mathcal{A}$ is allowed to make multiple queries to the marking oracle.*
3. *Next, $\mathcal{A}$ submits a set M* of Q messages in $\mathcal{M}$ to the challenge oracle and gets a set C* of circuits back.*
4. *Then, $\mathcal{A}$ is further allowed to make multiple queries to the marking oracle.*
5. *Finally $\mathcal{A}$ submits a circuit $\tilde{C}$. The experiment outputs 0 if*
   (a) $q < Q$ and either $\text{Extract}(EK, \tilde{C}, q)$ is a non-empty subset of M* or it equals to the error symbol $\perp$.
   (b) $q \geq Q$ and $\text{Extract}(EK, \tilde{C}, q)$ is a non-empty subset of M*.
   Otherwise, the experiment outputs 1.

Here, an adversary $\mathcal{A}$ is unremoving-admissible if there exists circuit $C_i^* \in C^*$ that C_i^* and $\tilde{C}$ compute identically on all but a negligible fraction of inputs.

Definition 4.4 (δ-Unforgeability). *The watermarking scheme for a PRF is δ-unforgeable if for any polynomial $q \geq 1$ and for all PPT and δ-unforging-admissible adversaries $\mathcal{A}$, we have $\Pr[\text{ExptUF}_{\mathcal{A},q}(\lambda) = 1] \leq negl(\lambda)$, where we define the experiment ExptUF and unforging-admissiability as follows:*

1. *The challenger samples $(MK, EK) \leftarrow \text{Setup}(1^\lambda)$ and returns EK to $\mathcal{A}$.*
2. *Then, $\mathcal{A}$ is allowed to make multiple queries to the marking oracle.*
3. *Finally, $\mathcal{A}$ submits a circuit $\tilde{C}$. The experiment outputs 0 if $\text{Extract}(EK, \tilde{C}, q) =$ UNMARKED; otherwise, the experiment output 1.*

Here, let Q' be the number of queries $\mathcal{A}$ made to the marking oracle, then an adversary $\mathcal{A}$ is δ-unforging-admissible if for all $i \in [1, Q']$, its submitted circuit $\tilde{C}$ and the circuit C_i compute differently on at least a δ fraction of inputs, where C_i is the output of the marking oracle on the ith query.

5   Puncturable Functional Encryption

In this section, we define puncturable functional encryption and give a concrete construction. A puncturable functional encryption scheme can achieve functionalities and security of both puncturable encryption schemes and functional encryption schemes. Besides, as we will use the puncturable functional encryption scheme together with an indistinguishability obfuscator, we also require it to have an "iO-compatible correctness", which demands a decryption consistency for different secret keys. More precisely, when using two secret keys sk_1, sk_2 for functions f_1, f_2 respectively, for any string ct in the ciphertext space, either both secret keys will fail in decrypting it or there exists a plaintext μ in the plaintext space that decrypting ct under sk_1 and sk_2 will lead to $f_1(\mu)$ and $f_2(\mu)$ respectively.

5.1   Definition of Puncturable Functional Encryption

Definition 5.1 (Puncturable Functional Encryption). *A puncturable functional encryption scheme for a family of function $\mathcal{F}$[8] with plaintext space $\{0,1\}^m$ and ciphertext space $\{0,1\}^n$ consists of five algorithms:*

- **Setup.** *On input the security parameter λ, the setup algorithm outputs the master public key/master secret key pair (mpk, msk).*
- **KeyGen.** *On input the master secret key msk and a function $f \in \mathcal{F}$, the key generation algorithm outputs a secret key sk for f.*
- **Enc.** *On input the master public key mpk and a message $msg \in \{0,1\}^m$, the encryption algorithm outputs the ciphertext ct.*
- **Dec.** *On input a secret key sk and a ciphertext $ct \in \{0,1\}^n$, the decryption algorithm outputs a string msg or a decryption failure symbol $\bot$.*
- **Puncture.** *On input a secret key sk and two ciphertexts ct_1, ct_2, the puncture algorithm outputs a punctured secret key sk'.*

Next, we describe properties of puncturable functional encryption schemes.

Definition 5.2 (Properties of Puncturable Functional Encryption). *A puncturable functional encryption scheme $\mathsf{PFE} = (\mathsf{Setup}, \mathsf{KeyGen}, \mathsf{Enc}, \mathsf{Dec}, \mathsf{Puncture})$ with plaintext space $\{0,1\}^m$, ciphertext space $\{0,1\}^n$ and supported function family $\mathcal{F}$ is required to have the following properties.*

- **Correctness.** *For any message $msg \in \{0,1\}^m$ and any $f \in \mathcal{F}$, let $(mpk, msk) \leftarrow \mathsf{Setup}(1^\lambda)$, $sk \leftarrow \mathsf{KeyGen}(msk, f)$, and $ct \leftarrow \mathsf{Enc}(mpk, msg)$, then we have $\Pr[\mathsf{Dec}(sk, ct) = f(msg)] = 1$.*
- **Sparseness.** *For any $f \in \mathcal{F}$, let $(mpk, msk) \leftarrow \mathsf{Setup}(1^\lambda)$, $sk \leftarrow \mathsf{KeyGen}(msk, f)$, and $ct \xleftarrow{\$} \{0,1\}^n$, then we have $\Pr[\mathsf{Dec}(sk, ct) \neq \bot] \leq negl(\lambda)$.*

---

[8] In this work, we concentrate on schemes supporting function family $\mathcal{F}$ of polynomial-size circuit with output space $\{0,1\}^m$.

- **Punctured Correctness.** For any $f \in \mathcal{F}$, any strings $ct_0, ct_1 \in \{0,1\}^n$ and any unbounded adversary $\mathcal{A}$, we have

$$\Pr\left[\begin{array}{l} (mpk, msk) \leftarrow \texttt{Setup}(1^\lambda); \\ sk \leftarrow \texttt{KeyGen}(msk, f); \\ sk' \leftarrow \texttt{Puncture}(sk, \{ct_0, ct_1\}); \\ ct \leftarrow \mathcal{A}(mpk, msk, sk, sk'); \end{array} : \begin{array}{l} ct \notin \{ct_0, ct_1\} \wedge \\ \texttt{Dec}(sk, ct) \neq \texttt{Dec}(sk', ct) \end{array}\right] \leq negl(\lambda)$$

- **iO-Compatible Correctness.** For each master public key/master secret key pair (mpk, msk), the ciphertext space can be divided into two disjoint parts, namely, the valid ciphertext set $\mathcal{V}_{(mpk,msk)}$ and the invalid ciphertext set $\mathcal{I}_{(mpk,msk)}$, which satisfy $\mathcal{V}_{(mpk,msk)} \cup \mathcal{I}_{(mpk,msk)} = \{0,1\}^n$ and $\mathcal{V}_{(mpk,msk)} \cap \mathcal{I}_{(mpk,msk)} = \emptyset$. The iO-compatible correctness requires that:
  1. For any $f \in \mathcal{F}$ and any unbounded adversary $\mathcal{A}$, we have:

$$\Pr\left[\begin{array}{l} (mpk, msk) \leftarrow \texttt{Setup}(1^\lambda); \\ sk \leftarrow \texttt{KeyGen}(msk, f); \\ ct \leftarrow \mathcal{A}(mpk, msk, sk); \end{array} : \begin{array}{l} ct \in \mathcal{I}_{(mpk,msk)} \wedge \\ \texttt{Dec}(sk, ct) \neq \perp \end{array}\right] \leq negl(\lambda)$$

  2. For any $f_1, f_2 \in \mathcal{F}$ and any unbounded adversary $\mathcal{A}$, we have:

$$\Pr\left[\begin{array}{l} (mpk, msk) \leftarrow \texttt{Setup}(1^\lambda); \\ sk_1 \leftarrow \texttt{KeyGen}(msk, f_1); \\ sk_2 \leftarrow \texttt{KeyGen}(msk, f_2); \\ ct \leftarrow \mathcal{A}(mpk, msk, sk_1, sk_2); \end{array} : \begin{array}{l} ct \in \mathcal{V}_{(mpk,msk)} \wedge \\ (\forall msg \in \{0,1\}^m, \\ \texttt{Dec}(sk_1, ct) \neq f_1(msg) \vee \\ \texttt{Dec}(sk_2, ct) \neq f_2(msg)) \end{array}\right] \leq negl(\lambda)$$

- **Adaptive Indistinguishability.** For any PPT adversary $\mathcal{A}_1, \mathcal{A}_2$, we have:

$$\Pr\left[\begin{array}{l} (mpk, msk) \leftarrow \texttt{Setup}(1^\lambda); \\ (st, msg_0, msg_1) \leftarrow \mathcal{A}_1^{\mathcal{O}_{msk}(\cdot)}(mpk); \\ b \leftarrow \{0,1\}; \\ ct \leftarrow \texttt{Enc}(mpk, msg_b); \\ b' \leftarrow \mathcal{A}_2(st, ct); \end{array} : b = b'\right] \leq 1/2 + negl(\lambda)$$

where $\mathcal{O}_{msk}$ takes as input a function $f \in \mathcal{F}$ and outputs a secret key $sk \leftarrow \texttt{KeyGen}(msk, f)$; for all f submitted to the oracle $\mathcal{O}_{msk}$, $f(msg_0) = f(msg_1)$; and the $\mathcal{O}_{msk}$ can only be queried two times. Note that in our security proof for collusion resistant watermarkable PRF, we only require a two-key security, thus we just define this type of adaptive indistinguishability here.

- **Ciphertext Pseudorandomness.** *For any PPT adversary* $\mathcal{A}_1$, $\mathcal{A}_2$, *we have:*

$$\Pr\left[\begin{array}{l} (st, msg, f) \leftarrow \mathcal{A}_1(1^\lambda); \\ (mpk, msk) \leftarrow \texttt{Setup}(1^\lambda); \\ sk \leftarrow \texttt{KeyGen}(msk, f); \\ ct_0 \leftarrow \texttt{Enc}(mpk, msg); \\ ct_1 \xleftarrow{\$} \{0,1\}^n; \\ sk' \leftarrow \texttt{Puncture}(sk, \{ct_0, ct_1\}); \\ b \leftarrow \{0,1\}; \\ b' \leftarrow \mathcal{A}_2(st, mpk, sk', ct_b, ct_{1-b}); \end{array} : b = b'\right] \leq 1/2 + negl(\lambda)$$

5.2   Construction of Puncturable Functional Encryption

In this section, we present our construction of puncturable functional encryption.

Let λ be the security parameter. Let n, m, l, n' be positive integers that are polynomial in λ. Our construction is based on the following three building blocks:

- A functional encryption scheme FE = (FE.Setup, FE.KeyGen, FE.Enc, FE.Dec) with plaintext space $\{0,1\}^m$, ciphertext space $\{0,1\}^n$ and encryption randomness space $\mathcal{R}$. Also, we require that it supports a family $\mathcal{F}$ of polynomial-size circuit with output space $\{0,1\}^m$.
- A statistically sound NIZK proof system NIZK = (NIZK.KeyGen, NIZK.Prove, NIZK.Verify) for $\mathcal{L}$, where

$$\mathcal{L} = \{(mpk, ct) : \exists (msg, r), ct = \texttt{FE.Enc}(mpk, msg; r)\}.$$

  and require that the proof size is n' when proving a statement in $\mathcal{L}$.
- A puncturable encryption scheme PE = (PE.KeyGen, PE.Puncture, PE.Enc, PE.Dec) with plaintext space $\{0,1\}^{n+n'}$ and ciphertext space $\{0,1\}^l$.

We construct PFE = (PFE.Setup, PFE.KeyGen, PFE.Puncture, PFE.Enc, PFE.Dec) for $\mathcal{F}$, which has a plaintext space $\{0,1\}^m$ and a ciphertext space $\{0,1\}^l$, as follows:

- **Setup.** On input a security parameter λ, the setup algorithm generates $(mpk, msk) \leftarrow$ FE.Setup(1^λ), $crs \leftarrow$ NIZK.KeyGen(1^λ), and $(pk, sk) \leftarrow$ PE.KeyGen(1^λ). Then it outputs the master public key $MPK = (mpk, crs, pk)$ and the master secret key $MSK = (msk, sk, mpk, crs)$ of PFE.
- **KeyGen.** On input a master secret key $MSK = (msk, sk, mpk, crs)$ of PFE and a function $f \in \mathcal{F}$, the key generation algorithm generates $fsk \leftarrow$ FE.KeyGen(msk, f) and outputs a secret key $SK = (fsk, sk, mpk, crs)$ of PFE.
- **Enc.** On input a master public key $MPK = (mpk, crs, pk)$ of PFE and a message $msg \in \{0,1\}^m$, the encryption algorithm first samples $r \in \mathcal{R}$. Then, it computes $ct =$ FE.Enc$(mpk, msg; r)$, and $\pi \leftarrow$ NIZK.Prove$(crs, (mpk, ct), (msg, r))$. Finally, it outputs $CT \leftarrow$ PE.Enc$(pk, ct\|\pi)$.

- **Dec.** On input a secret key $SK = (fsk, sk, mpk, crs)$ of PFE and a ciphertext $CT \in \{0,1\}^l$, the decryption algorithm first decrypts CT with the secret key of PE and gets $ct\|\pi \leftarrow$ PE.Dec(sk, CT). It aborts and outputs $\perp$ if $ct\|\pi =\perp$ or NIZK.Verify$(crs, (mpk, ct), \pi) = 0$. Otherwise, it outputs FE.Dec(fsk, ct).
- **Puncture.** On input a secret key $SK = (fsk, sk, mpk, crs)$ of PFE and two ciphertexts $CT_1, CT_2 \in \{0,1\}^l$, the puncture algorithm generates $sk' \leftarrow$ PE.Puncture$(sk, \{CT_1, CT_2\})$ and outputs $SK' = (fsk, sk', mpk, crs)$.

Theorem 5.1. *If* FE *is a secure functional encryption for* $\mathcal{F}$ *with perfect correctness and (two-key) adaptive security,* NIZK *is a NIZK proof system with adaptively statistical soundness and adaptive zero-knowledge for language* $\mathcal{L}$, *and* PE *is a secure puncturable encryption scheme, then* PFE *is a secure puncturable functional encryption as defined in Sect. 5.1.*

We give proof of Theorem 5.1 in the full version of this paper.

6   Construction of Collusion Resistant Watermarkable PRF

In this section, we show how to obtain collusion resistant watermarkable PRF families. In particular, we construct a collusion resistant watermarking scheme for any puncturable PRF with weak key-injectivity and constrained one-wayness.

Let λ be the security parameter. Let δ be a positive real value and $d = \lambda/\delta = poly(\lambda)$. Let n, m, l, κ be positive integers that are polynomial in λ and $n = l + poly(\lambda)$. Let

$$\mathsf{PRF} = (\mathsf{PRF.KeyGen}, \mathsf{PRF.Eval}, \mathsf{PRF.Constrain}, \mathsf{PRF.ConstrainEval})$$

be a family of puncturable PRF with key space $\mathcal{K}$, input space $\{0,1\}^n$, and output space $\{0,1\}^m$. Our watermarking scheme for PRF is built on the following building blocks.

- A puncturable functional encryption scheme PFE = (PFE.Setup, PFE.KeyGen, PFE.Puncture, PFE.Enc, PFE.Dec) with plaintext space $\{0,1\}^{(d+1)\cdot l+\kappa}$, ciphertext space $\{0,1\}^n$ and encryption randomness space $\mathcal{R}$. Also, we require that it supports a family $\mathcal{F}$ of polynomial-size circuits with output space $\{0,1\}^{(d+1)\cdot l+\kappa}$.
- A family of prefix puncturable PRF F = (F.KeyGen, F.Eval, F.Constrain, F.ConstrainEval) with input space $\{0,1\}^{(d+1)\cdot l}$ and output space $\mathcal{K}$.
- An indistinguishability obfuscator iO for all polynomial-size circuits.
- Two pseudorandom generators $\mathsf{G} : \{0,1\}^l \rightarrow \{0,1\}^n$ and $\mathsf{G}' : \{0,1\}^{\frac{l}{2}} \rightarrow \{0,1\}^l$.
- A family of collision-resistant hash function $\mathcal{H}$ with input space $\{0,1\}^{d\cdot m}$ and output space $\{0,1\}^l$.

We construct WM = (WM.Setup, WM.Mark, WM.Extract), which has a message space $\{0,1\}^\kappa \backslash \{0^\kappa\} = [1, 2^\kappa - 1]$, as follows:

- **Setup.** On input a security parameter λ, the setup algorithm first samples $H \xleftarrow{\$} \mathcal{H}$ and generates $K \leftarrow \mathsf{F.KeyGen}(1^\lambda)$. Then it generates $(mpk, msk) \leftarrow \mathsf{PFE.Setup}(1^\lambda)$ and $sk \leftarrow \mathsf{PFE.KeyGen}(msk, \mathtt{ID})$, where $\mathtt{ID} : \{0,1\}^{(d+1)\cdot l+\kappa} \to \{0,1\}^{(d+1)\cdot l+\kappa}$ is the identity function, i.e., for any $x \in \{0,1\}^{(d+1)\cdot l+\kappa}$, $ID(x) = x$. Next, it computes $\mathtt{E} \leftarrow \mathsf{iO}(\mathtt{Ext}[mpk, K])$, where $\mathtt{Ext}$ is defined in Fig. 1[9]. Finally, the output of the setup algorithm is (MK, EK) where $MK = (sk, K, H)$ and $EK = (H, \mathtt{E})$.
- **Mark.** On input a mark key $MK = (sk, K, H)$, a secret key $k \in \mathcal{K}$ for PRF and a message msg, the marking algorithm outputs a circuit $\mathtt{C} \leftarrow \mathsf{iO}(\mathtt{M}[sk, K, H, k, msg])$, where $\mathtt{M}$ is defined in Fig. 1[10].
- **Extract.** On input an extraction key $EK = (H, \mathtt{E})$, a circuit $\mathtt{C}$, and a parameter q, the extraction algorithm first computes $\epsilon = 1/((\kappa + 1) \cdot q + 1)$, $T = \lambda/\epsilon^2$, and $S = q \cdot (\kappa + 1)$ and sets a variable $counter = 0$. Then it computes $\mathcal{L} = \mathtt{Trace}(0, 2^\kappa, 1, 0, \epsilon, T, \mathtt{E}, H, \mathtt{C})$, where $\mathtt{Trace}(\cdot)$ is defined in Fig. 1.

  In this procedure, the algorithm also maintains the variable $counter$ and increase it by 1 each time the function $\mathtt{Test}(\cdot)$ defined in Fig. 1 is invoked. The algorithm aborts and outputs $\perp$ once $counter > S$. In case the algorithm does not abort, it checks the set $\mathcal{L}$ returned by $\mathtt{Trace}$. It outputs $\perp$ if $\mathcal{L} = \emptyset$ and outputs UNMARKED if $\mathcal{L} = \{0\}$. Otherwise, it outputs $\mathcal{L}$.

Theorem 6.1. *If* PRF *is a secure puncturable PRF with weak key-injectivity and constrained one-wayness,* PFE *is a secure puncturable functional encryption scheme as defined in Sect. 5.1,* F *is a secure prefix puncturable PRF,* G *and* G′ *are pseudorandom generators,* $\mathcal{H}$ *is a family of collision-resistant hash function, and* iO *is a secure indistinguishability obfuscator, then* WM *is a secure watermarking scheme with collusion resistant unremovability and δ-unforgeability, as defined in Sect. 4, for* PRF.

We present the proof of Theorem 6.1 in the full version of this paper.

Here, we provide a brief overview on how to prove the collusion resistant unremovability of WM. For simplicity, we consider an adversary who only gets two circuits $\mathtt{C}_1$ and $\mathtt{C}_2$ for the same secret key k embedded with messages msg_1 and msg_2 respectively, where $msg_1 < msg_2$, and omit its advantage in viewing the public key and querying the marking oracle.

Following the syntax used in Sect. 2, we denote an input encrypted from $t_1 \| \ldots \| t_d \| b \| ind$ satisfying $b = H(\mathsf{PRF.Eval}(k, \mathsf{G}(t_1)), \ldots, \mathsf{PRF.Eval}(k, \mathsf{G}(t_d)))$ as a punctured point labeled with an index ind. Also, we use $\mathcal{X}_{ind}$ to denote the set of all punctured points labeled with the index ind.

First, as shown in [BCP14, NWZ16], the $\mathtt{Trace}$ algorithm can output a nonempty subset of $\{msg_1, msg_2\}$ if the adversary cannot distinguish (1) two punctured points labeled with different indices adaptively chosen from $(msg_1, msg_2]$ and

---

[9] The circuit $\mathtt{Ext}$, as well as all circuits $\mathtt{Ext}^{(\cdot)}$ appeared in the security proofs for WM will be padded to the same size.

[10] The circuit $\mathtt{M}$, as well as all circuits $\mathtt{M}^{(\cdot)}$ appeared in the security proof for WM will be padded to the same size.

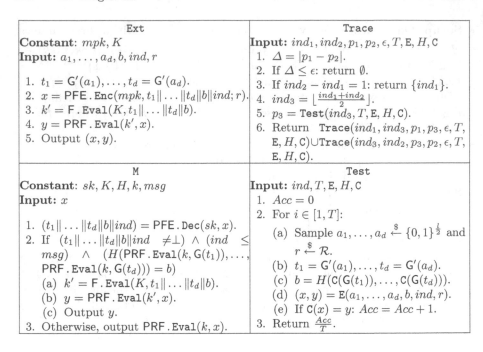

Fig. 1. The circuit Ext, the circuit M, the function Trace, and the function Test

(2) a punctured point labeled with an index adaptively chosen outside $(msg_1, msg_2]$ and a random point.

For two punctured points in $\mathcal{X}_{ind_1}$ and $\mathcal{X}_{ind_2}$ respectively, where $ind_1, ind_2 \in (msg_1, msg_2]$, both of them are properly punctured and reprogrammed in C_2 while none of them are punctured in C_1, thus the decryption (in both C_1 and C_2) do not need to distinguish them. So, their indistinguishability comes from the adaptive indistinguishability of PFE.

The adaptive indistinguishability of PFE also implies indistinguishability of two punctured points in $\mathcal{X}_{ind_1}$ and $\mathcal{X}_{ind_2}$ when both ind_1 and ind_2 are in $[1, msg_1]$ or both of them are in $(msg_2, 2^\kappa - 1]$. This could reduce the problem of claiming the pseudorandomness of a punctured point labeled with an index adaptively chosen from $[1, msg_1]$ (or $(msg_2, 2^\kappa - 1]$) to the problem of claiming the pseudorandomness of a punctured points from $\mathcal{X}_1$ (resp. $\mathcal{X}_{2^\kappa-1}$), where the latter claim can be implied by the ciphertext pseudorandomness of PFE. In this way, pseudorandomness of punctured points in $\mathcal{X}_{ind}$ for $ind \notin (msg_1, msg_2]$ is proved.

It is worth noting that when arguing indistinguishability between a punctured point from $\mathcal{X}_1$ and a random input, we also need to show that the marked circuits are able to hide punctured points that are punctured and identically reprogrammed in all circuits. This indicates that our construction of watermarkable PRF involves a collusion resistant constraint-hiding constrained PRF implicitly.

7 Collusion Resistant Watermarking Schemes for Other Cryptographic Functionalities

In this section, we show how to construct watermarking schemes for advanced cryptographic functionalities, including the decryption algorithm of a PKE scheme and the signing algorithm of a signature scheme. The constructions are based on the observation that the PKE scheme (and the signature scheme) constructed in [SW14] has a decryption algorithm (resp. signing algorithm) that is nothing more than a puncturable PRF evaluation. The observation was initially presented in [NW15, CHN+16] and was used to construct the watermarkable PKE scheme and the watermarkable signature scheme therein.

Here, as an example, we give a detailed description for how to construct collusion resistant watermarkable PKE schemes and omit the construction for collusion resistant watermarkable signature schemes. We start by presenting the formal definition of watermarkable PKE scheme. Then we give our construction based on a puncturable PRF, an indistinguishability obfuscator, a puncturable functional encryption scheme, and some standard cryptographic primitives.

7.1 The Definition

The collusion resistant watermarkable PKE scheme can be defined similarly as collusion resistant watermarkable PRF, with the main difference being that in the challenge oracle, the adversary is further given the public key corresponding to the watermarked secret key.

Definition 7.1 (Watermarkable PKEs [CHN+16, adapted]**).** *Let* $\mathsf{PKE} = (\mathsf{PKE.KeyGen}, \mathsf{PKE.Enc}, \mathsf{PKE.Dec})$ *be a PKE scheme with secret key space $\mathcal{SK}$. The watermarking scheme with message space $\mathcal{M}$ for* PKE *(more accurately, the decryption algorithm of* PKE*) consists of three algorithms:*

- **Setup.** *On input the security parameter λ, the setup algorithm outputs the mark key MK and the extraction key EK.*
- **Mark.** *On input the mark key MK, a secret key $sk \in \mathcal{SK}$ of* PKE*, and a message $msg \in \mathcal{M}$, the marking algorithm outputs a marked circuit C.*
- **Extract.** *On input the extraction key EK, a circuit C, and a parameter q, the extraction algorithm outputs either a set $\mathcal{L} \subseteq \mathcal{M}$ or a symbol* $\mathsf{UNMARKED}$ *or an error symbol $\perp$.*

Definition 7.2 (Watermarking Correctness). *Correctness of the watermarking scheme requires that for any $sk \in \mathcal{SK}$, $msg \in \mathcal{M}$, and any polynomial $q \geq 1$, let $(MK, EK) \leftarrow \mathsf{Setup}(1^\lambda)$, $\mathsf{C} \leftarrow \mathsf{Mark}(MK, sk, msg)$, we have:*

- **Functionality Preserving.** $\mathsf{C}(\cdot)$ *and* $\mathsf{PKE.Dec}(sk, \cdot)$ *compute identically on all but a negligible fraction of inputs.*
- **Extraction Correctness.** $\Pr[\mathsf{Extract}(EK, \mathsf{C}, q) \neq \{msg\}] \leq negl(\lambda)$.

Before presenting the security definition of the collusion resistant watermarkable PKE, we first introduce oracles the adversaries can query during the security experiments. Note that in the challenge oracle, the adversary is further given the challenge public key.

- **Marking Oracle** $\mathcal{O}_{MK}^M(\cdot, \cdot)$. On input a message $msg \in \mathcal{M}$ and a secret key key $sk \in \mathcal{SK}$, the oracle returns a circuit $\mathsf{C} \leftarrow \mathsf{Mark}(MK, sk, msg)$.
- **Challenge Oracle** $\mathcal{O}_{MK}^C(\cdot)$. On input a polynomial-size set M of messages from $\mathcal{M}$, the oracle first generates a key pair $(sk^*, pk^*) \leftarrow \mathsf{PKE.KeyGen}(1^\lambda)$. Then, for each $msg_i^* \in$ M, it computes $\mathsf{C}_i^* \leftarrow \mathsf{Mark}(MK, sk^*, msg_i^*)$. Finally, it returns the set $\{\mathsf{C}_1^*, \ldots, \mathsf{C}_Q^*\}$, where $Q = \|\mathsf{M}\|$, and the public key pk^*.

Definition 7.3 (Collusion Resistant Unremovability). *The watermarking scheme for a PKE is collusion resistant unremovable if for any polynomial q, for all PPT and unremoving-admissible adversaries $\mathcal{A}$, we have $\Pr[\mathsf{ExptUR}_{\mathcal{A},q}(\lambda) = 1] \leq negl(\lambda)$, where we define the experiment ExptUR and unremoving-admissibility as follows:*

1. *The challenger samples $(MK, EK) \leftarrow \mathsf{Setup}(1^\lambda)$ and returns EK to $\mathcal{A}$.*
2. *Then, $\mathcal{A}$ is allowed to make multiple queries to the marking oracle.*
3. *Next, $\mathcal{A}$ submits a set M^* of Q messages in $\mathcal{M}$ to the challenge oracle and gets a set C^* of circuits as well as a public key pk^* back.*
4. *Then, $\mathcal{A}$ is further allowed to make multiple queries to the marking oracle.*
5. *Finally $\mathcal{A}$ submits a circuit $\tilde{\mathsf{C}}$. The experiment outputs 0 if*
   (a) *$q < Q$ and either $\mathsf{Extract}(EK, \tilde{\mathsf{C}}, q)$ is a non-empty subset of M^* or it equals to the error symbol $\bot$.*
   (b) *$q \geq Q$ and $\mathsf{Extract}(EK, \tilde{\mathsf{C}}, q)$ is a non-empty subset of M^*.*
   Otherwise, the experiment outputs 1.

Here, an adversary $\mathcal{A}$ is unremoving-admissible if there exists circuit $\mathsf{C}_i^* \in \mathsf{C}^*$ that C_i^* and $\tilde{\mathsf{C}}$ compute identically on all but a negligible fraction of inputs.

Definition 7.4 (δ-Unforgeability). *The watermarking scheme for a PKE is δ-unforgeable if for any polynomial $q \geq 1$ and for all PPT and δ-unforging-admissible adversaries $\mathcal{A}$, we have $\Pr[\mathsf{ExptUF}_{\mathcal{A},q}(\lambda) = 1] \leq negl(\lambda)$, where we define the experiment ExptUF and unforging-admissiability as follows:*

1. *The challenger samples $(MK, EK) \leftarrow \mathsf{Setup}(1^\lambda)$ and returns EK to $\mathcal{A}$.*
2. *Then, $\mathcal{A}$ is allowed to make multiple queries to the marking oracle.*
3. *Finally, $\mathcal{A}$ submits a circuit $\tilde{\mathsf{C}}$. The experiment outputs 0 if $\mathsf{Extract}(EK, \tilde{\mathsf{C}}, q) = \mathsf{UNMARKED}$; otherwise, the experiment output 1.*

Here, let Q' be the number of queries $\mathcal{A}$ made to the marking oracle, then an adversary $\mathcal{A}$ is δ-unforging-admissible if for all $i \in [1, Q']$, its submitted circuit $\tilde{\mathsf{C}}$ and the circuit C_i compute differently on at least a δ fraction of inputs, where C_i is the output of the marking oracle on the ith query.

7.2   The Construction

Let λ be the security parameter. Let δ be a positive real value and $d = \lambda/\delta = poly(\lambda)$. Let n, m, l, κ be positive integers that are polynomial in λ and $n = l + poly(\lambda)$. Our watermarkable PKE scheme is built from the following building blocks:

- A family of puncturable PRF PRF = (PRF.KeyGen, PRF.Eval, PRF.Constrain, PRF.ConstrainEval) with key space $\mathcal{K}$, input space $\{0,1\}^n$, and output space $\{0,1\}^m$.
- A puncturable functional encryption scheme PFE = (PFE.Setup, PFE.KeyGen, PFE.Puncture, PFE.Enc, PFE.Dec) with plaintext space $\{0,1\}^{(d+1)\cdot l+\kappa}$, ciphertext space $\{0,1\}^n$ and encryption randomness space $\mathcal{R}$. Also, we require that it supports a family $\mathcal{F}$ of polynomial-size circuit with output space $\{0,1\}^{(d+1)\cdot l+\kappa}$.
- A family of prefix puncturable PRF F = (F.KeyGen, F.Eval, F.Constrain, F.ConstrainEval) with input space $\{0,1\}^{(d+1)\cdot l}$ and output space $\mathcal{K}$.
- An indistinguishability obfuscator iO for all polynomial-size circuits.
- Three pseudorandom generators $G : \{0,1\}^l \to \{0,1\}^n$, $G' : \{0,1\}^{\frac{l}{2}} \to \{0,1\}^l$, and $\tilde{G} : \{0,1\}^\lambda \to \{0,1\}^n$.
- A family of collision-resistant hash function $\mathcal{H}$ with input space $\{0,1\}^{d\cdot m}$ and output space $\{0,1\}^l$.

For completeness, we first recall how PKE scheme PKE is constructed in [SW14].

- **KeyGen.** On input a security parameter λ, the key generation algorithm first samples $k \xleftarrow{\$} \mathcal{K}$. Then, it computes $P \leftarrow iO(\texttt{Encrypt}[k])$, where Encrypt is defined in Fig. 2 and is properly padded. Finally, the output of the key generation algorithm is (pk, sk) where $pk = P$ and $sk = k$.
- **Enc.** On input a public key $pk = P$ and a message $msg \in \{0,1\}^m$, the encryption algorithm samples $r \xleftarrow{\$} \{0,1\}^\lambda$ and outputs $P(msg, r)$.
- **Dec.** On input a secret key $sk = k$ and a ciphertext $ct = (x, z)$, the decryption algorithm outputs $msg = \texttt{PRF.Eval}(k, x) \oplus z$.

Encrypt

Constant: k
Input: msg, r

1. $x = \tilde{G}(r)$.
2. $z = \texttt{PRF.Eval}(k, x) \oplus msg$.
3. Output $ct = (x, z)$.

Fig. 2. The circuit Encrypt.

Next, we construct the watermarking scheme WM = (WM.Setup, WM.Mark, WM.Extract) for the above constructed PKE scheme, which has a message space $\{0,1\}^\kappa \backslash \{0^\kappa\} = [1, 2^\kappa - 1]$, as follows:

- **Setup.** On input a security parameter λ, the setup algorithm first samples $H \xleftarrow{\$} \mathcal{H}$ and generates $K \leftarrow$ F.KeyGen(1^λ). Then it generates $(mpk, msk) \leftarrow$ PFE.Setup(1^λ) and $sk \leftarrow$ PFE.KeyGen(msk, ID), where ID : $\{0,1\}^{(d+1)\cdot l+\kappa} \rightarrow \{0,1\}^{(d+1)\cdot l+\kappa}$ is the identity function, i.e., for any $x \in \{0,1\}^{(d+1)\cdot l+\kappa}$, $ID(x) = x$. Next, it computes $\mathbf{E} \leftarrow$ iO(Ext$[mpk, K]$), where Ext is defined in Fig. 3 and is properly padded. Finally, the output of the setup algorithm is (MK, EK) where $MK = (sk, K, H)$ and $EK = (H, \mathbf{E})$.
- **Mark.** On input a mark key $MK = (sk, K, H)$, a secret key $k \in \mathcal{K}$ for PKE and a message msg, the marking algorithm outputs a circuit $\mathbf{C} \leftarrow$ iO(M$[sk, K, H, k, msg]$), where M is defined in Fig. 3 and is properly padded.
- **Extract.** On input an extraction key $EK = (H, \mathbf{E})$, a circuit $\mathbf{C}$, and a parameter q, the extraction algorithm first computes $\epsilon = 1/((\kappa + 1) \cdot q + 1)$, $T = \lambda/\epsilon^2$, and $S = q \cdot (\kappa + 1)$ and sets a variable $counter = 0$. Then it computes $\mathcal{L} = \text{Trace}(0, 2^\kappa, 1, 0, \epsilon, T, \mathbf{E}, H, \mathbf{C})$, where $\text{Trace}(\cdot)$ is defined in Fig. 3.
  In this procedure, the algorithm also maintains the variable $counter$ and increase it by 1 each time the function $\text{Test}(\cdot)$ defined in Fig. 3 is invoked. The algorithm aborts and outputs $\perp$ once $counter$ exceeds S. In case the algorithm does not abort, it checks the set $\mathcal{L}$ returned by Trace. It outputs $\perp$ if $\mathcal{L} = \emptyset$ and outputs UNMARKED if $\mathcal{L} = \{0\}$. Otherwise, it outputs $\mathcal{L}$.

Theorem 7.1. *If* PRF *is a secure puncturable PRF with weak key-injectivity and constrained one-wayness,* PFE *is a secure puncturable functional encryption scheme as defined in Sect. 5.1,* F *is a secure prefix puncturable PRF,* G, G' *and* $\tilde{\mathsf{G}}$ *are pseudorandom generators,* $\mathcal{H}$ *is a family of collision-resistant hash function, and* iO *is a secure indistinguishability obfuscator, then* WM *is a secure watermarking scheme with collusion resistant unremovability and* δ-unforgeability for PKE.

Proof. Proof of Theorem 7.1 can be proceeded similiarly as the proof of Theorem 6.1, so we omit its details here.

One subtle issue in the proof is that the adversary can additionally obtain a public key from the challenge oracle, which is an obfuscated circuit containing the challenge key k^*. So, we need to further argue that the public key will not leak additional information of k^*. Recall that through the whole security proof, either k^* or its equivalent version or its contrained version punctured on a random point will appear in the view of the adversary. In the first case, the public key will not provide additional information about k^*. In the second case, k^* can be replaced with its equivalent version in the public key and due to the indistinguishability of iO, this cannot be detected by the adversary. In the third case, k^* can be replaced with its contrained version in the public key. Since the probability that the random punctrued point falls in the range of $\tilde{\mathsf{G}}$ is negligible, by the indistinguishability of iO, this will also not affect the adversary's advantage.

Remark 7.1. We remark that the above strategy is not fully applicable in the watermarkable signature setting. This is because in the verification key of the signature scheme constructed in [SW14], the pseudorandom random function will compute

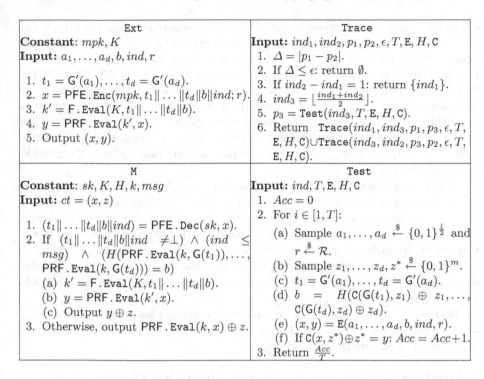

Ext	Trace
Constant: mpk, K	**Input:** $ind_1, ind_2, p_1, p_2, \epsilon, T, \mathsf{E}, H, \mathsf{C}$
Input: $a_1, \dots, a_d, b, ind, r$	1. $\Delta = \lvert p_1 - p_2 \rvert$.
	2. If $\Delta \leq \epsilon$: return $\emptyset$.
1. $t_1 = \mathsf{G}'(a_1), \dots, t_d = \mathsf{G}'(a_d)$.	3. If $ind_2 - ind_1 = 1$: return $\{ind_1\}$.
2. $x = \mathsf{PFE.Enc}(mpk, t_1 \Vert \dots \Vert t_d \Vert b \Vert ind; r)$.	4. $ind_3 = \lfloor \frac{ind_1 + ind_2}{2} \rfloor$.
3. $k' = \mathsf{F.Eval}(K, t_1 \Vert \dots \Vert t_d \Vert b)$.	5. $p_3 = \mathsf{Test}(ind_3, T, \mathsf{E}, H, \mathsf{C})$.
4. $y = \mathsf{PRF.Eval}(k', x)$.	6. Return $\mathsf{Trace}(ind_1, ind_3, p_1, p_3, \epsilon, T,$
5. Output (x, y).	$\mathsf{E}, H, \mathsf{C}) \cup \mathsf{Trace}(ind_3, ind_2, p_3, p_2, \epsilon, T,$
	$\mathsf{E}, H, \mathsf{C})$.
M	**Test**
Constant: sk, K, H, k, msg	**Input:** $ind, T, \mathsf{E}, H, \mathsf{C}$
Input: $ct = (x, z)$	1. $Acc = 0$
	2. For $i \in [1, T]$:
1. $(t_1 \Vert \dots \Vert t_d \Vert b \Vert ind) = \mathsf{PFE.Dec}(sk, x)$.	(a) Sample $a_1, \dots, a_d \xleftarrow{\$} \{0,1\}^{\frac{l}{2}}$ and
2. If $(t_1 \Vert \dots \Vert t_d \Vert b \Vert ind \neq \bot) \wedge (ind \leq$	$r \xleftarrow{\$} \mathcal{R}$.
$msg) \wedge (H(\mathsf{PRF.Eval}(k, \mathsf{G}(t_1))), \dots,$	(b) Sample $z_1, \dots, z_d, z^* \xleftarrow{\$} \{0,1\}^m$.
$\mathsf{PRF.Eval}(k, \mathsf{G}(t_d))) = b)$.	(c) $t_1 = \mathsf{G}'(a_1), \dots, t_d = \mathsf{G}'(a_d)$.
(a) $k' = \mathsf{F.Eval}(K, t_1 \Vert \dots \Vert t_d \Vert b)$.	(d) $b = H(\mathsf{C}(\mathsf{G}(t_1), z_1) \oplus z_1, \dots,$
(b) $y = \mathsf{PRF.Eval}(k', x)$.	$\mathsf{C}(\mathsf{G}(t_d), z_d) \oplus z_d)$.
(c) Output $y \oplus z$.	(e) $(x, y) = \mathsf{E}(a_1, \dots, a_d, b, ind, r)$.
3. Otherwise, output $\mathsf{PRF.Eval}(k, x) \oplus z$.	(f) If $\mathsf{C}(x, z^*) \oplus z^* = y$: $Acc = Acc + 1$.
	3. Return $\frac{Acc}{T}$.

Fig. 3. The circuit Ext, the circuit M, the function Trace, and the function Test for the watermarkable PKE scheme.

on all points in its domain (rather than points in the range of a pseudorandom generator), thus, we cannot argue indistinguishability between a verification key generated from a normal key and that generated from a constrained key. To circumvent this problem, we modify the construction of signature scheme slightly and use a watermarked PRF key in the obfuscated circuit of the verification key. But this will lead to a weaker watermarkable signature scheme, which needs the marking key of the watermarking scheme when generating a signing key/verification key pair of the signature scheme.

8 Conclusion and Future Works

In this work, we initiate the study of collusion resistant watermarking by defining and constructing collusion resistant watermarking schemes for common cryptographic functionalities, including PRF, PKE, and signature.

One may note that watermarking schemes constructed in this work only achieve a $negl(\cdot)$-unremovability, which guarantees that no attacker can remove or modify the embedded message in a watermarked program via altering the program on a *negligible* fraction of inputs. A stronger form of unremovability, which is called ϵ-unremovability, considers attackers that can alter the watermarked program on a

ϵ fraction of inputs for some non-negligible ϵ. In this setting, since the attacker is able to reset the outputs on a non-negligible fraction of inputs, internal variables generated during the extraction procedure may significantly depart from what is expected. In previous works with ϵ-unremovability (e.g., [CHN+16, QWZ18, KW19]), this issue is tackled by repeating some sub-procedure multiple times and deciding based on majority. Unfortunately, in our construction, as the extraction algorithm needs to analyze the fraction of reprogrammed points in a set, it seems implausible to use the "repeating-and-choosing-majority" trick. How to construct collusion resistant watermarking schemes with ϵ-unremovability for non-negligible ϵ is an interesting open problem.

Another interesting direction is to explore the possibility of instantiating a collusion resistant watermarkable PRF from standard assumptions. As discussed in Sect. 1.1, a collusion resistant watermarkable PRF can be approximately viewed as a collusion resistant constraint-hiding constrained PRF, which can imply indistinguishability obfuscator. However, we have not provided a formal reduction. It is interesting to formally construct an indistinguishability obfuscator from a collusion resistant watermarkable PRF or construct a collusion resistant watermarkable PRF from standard assumptions.

Besides, it is also interesting to construct collusion resistant watermarking schemes with other desirable features, e.g., constructing collusion resistant watermarking schemes with public marking.

Acknowledgement. We appreciate the anonymous reviewers for their valuable suggestions. Part of this work was supported by the National Natural Science Foundation of China (Grant No. 61572294, 61602396, 61632020, U1636205), Early Career Scheme research grant (ECS Grant No. 25206317) from the Research Grant Council of Hong Kong, the Innovation and Technology Support Programme of Innovation and Technology Fund of Hong Kong (Grant No. ITS/356/17), and the MonashU-PolyU-Collinstar Capital Joint Lab on Blockchain. Junzuo Lai was supported by National Natural Science Foundation of China (Grant No. 61922036, 61572235), and Guangdong Natural Science Funds for Distinguished Young Scholar (No. 2015A030306045).

References

[BCP14] Boyle, E., Chung, K.-M., Pass, R.: On extractability obfuscation. In: Lindell, Y. (ed.) TCC 2014. LNCS, vol. 8349, pp. 52–73. Springer, Heidelberg (2014). https://doi.org/10.1007/978-3-642-54242-8_3

[BGI+01] Barak, B., et al.: On the (im)possibility of obfuscating programs. In: Kilian, J. (ed.) CRYPTO 2001. LNCS, vol. 2139, pp. 1–18. Springer, Heidelberg (2001). https://doi.org/10.1007/3-540-44647-8_1

[BKS17] Baldimtsi, F., Kiayias, A., Samari, K.: Watermarking public-key cryptographic functionalities and implementations. In: Nguyen, P., Zhou, J. (eds.) ISC 2017. LNCS, vol. 10599, pp. 173–191. Springer, Cham (2017). https://doi.org/10.1007/978-3-319-69659-1_10

[BLW17] Boneh, D., Lewi, K., Wu, D.J.: Constraining pseudorandom functions privately. In: Fehr, S. (ed.) PKC 2017. LNCS, vol. 10175, pp. 494–524. Springer, Heidelberg (2017). https://doi.org/10.1007/978-3-662-54388-7_17

[BN08]   Boneh, D., Naor, M.: Traitor tracing with constant size ciphertext. In: CCS, pp. 501–510. ACM (2008)

[BSW06]   Boneh, D., Sahai, A., Waters, B.: Fully collusion resistant traitor tracing with short ciphertexts and private keys. In: Vaudenay, S. (ed.) EUROCRYPT 2006. LNCS, vol. 4004, pp. 573–592. Springer, Heidelberg (2006). https://doi.org/10.1007/11761679_34

[BV15]   Bitansky, N., Vaikuntanathan, V.: Indistinguishability obfuscation from functional encryption. In: FOCS, pp. 171–190. IEEE (2015)

[BZ14]   Boneh, D., Zhandry, M.: Multiparty key exchange, efficient traitor tracing, and more from indistinguishability obfuscation. In: Garay, J.A., Gennaro, R. (eds.) CRYPTO 2014. LNCS, vol. 8616, pp. 480–499. Springer, Heidelberg (2014). https://doi.org/10.1007/978-3-662-44371-2_27

[CC17]   Canetti, R., Chen, Y.: Constraint-hiding constrained PRFs for NC^1 from LWE. In: Coron, J.-S., Nielsen, J.B. (eds.) EUROCRYPT 2017. LNCS, vol. 10210, pp. 446–476. Springer, Cham (2017). https://doi.org/10.1007/978-3-319-56620-7_16

[CFN94]   Chor, B., Fiat, A., Naor, M.: Tracing traitors. In: Desmedt, Y.G. (ed.) CRYPTO 1994. LNCS, vol. 839, pp. 257–270. Springer, Heidelberg (1994). https://doi.org/10.1007/3-540-48658-5_25

[CHN+16] Cohen, A., Holmgren, J., Nishimaki, R., Vaikuntanathan, V., Wichs, D.: Watermarking cryptographic capabilities. In: STOC, pp. 1115–1127 (2016)

[CHV15]   Cohen, A., Holmgren, J., Vaikuntanathan, V.: Publicly verifiable software watermarking. Cryptology ePrint Archive, Report 2015/373 (2015). https://eprint.iacr.org/2015/373

[CMB+07] Cox, I., Miller, M., Bloom, J., Fridrich, J., Kalker, T.: Digital Watermarking and Steganography. Morgan Kaufmann, Burlington (2007)

[CVW+18] Chen, Y., Vaikuntanathan, V., Waters, B., Wee, H., Wichs, D.: Traitor-tracing from LWE made simple and attribute-based. In: Beimel, A., Dziembowski, S. (eds.) TCC 2018. LNCS, vol. 11240, pp. 341–369. Springer, Cham (2018). https://doi.org/10.1007/978-3-030-03810-6_13

[GKM+19] Goyal, R., Kim, S., Manohar, N., Waters, B., Wu, D.J.: Watermarking public-key cryptographic primitives. In: Boldyreva, A., Micciancio, D. (eds.) CRYPTO 2019. LNCS, vol. 11694, pp. 367–398. Springer, Cham (2019). https://doi.org/10.1007/978-3-030-26954-8_12

[GKW18]   Goyal, R., Koppula, V., Waters, B.: Collusion resistant traitor tracing from learning with errors. In: STOC (2018)

[Goe15]   Goemans, M.: Lecture notes on Chernoff bounds, February 2015. http://math.mit.edu/~goemans/18310S15/chernoff-notes.pdf

[HMW07]   Hopper, N., Molnar, D., Wagner, D.: From weak to strong watermarking. In: Vadhan, S.P. (ed.) TCC 2007. LNCS, vol. 4392, pp. 362–382. Springer, Heidelberg (2007). https://doi.org/10.1007/978-3-540-70936-7_20

[KNT18]   Kitagawa, F., Nishimaki, R., Tanaka, K.: Obfustopia built on secret-key functional encryption. In: Nielsen, J.B., Rijmen, V. (eds.) EUROCRYPT 2018. LNCS, vol. 10821, pp. 603–648. Springer, Cham (2018). https://doi.org/10.1007/978-3-319-78375-8_20

[KW17]   Kim, S., Wu, D.J.: Watermarking cryptographic functionalities from standard lattice assumptions. In: Katz, J., Shacham, H. (eds.) CRYPTO 2017. LNCS, vol. 10401, pp. 503–536. Springer, Cham (2017). https://doi.org/10.1007/978-3-319-63688-7_17

[KW19] Kim, S., Wu, D.J.: Watermarking PRFs from lattices: stronger security via extractable PRFs. In: Boldyreva, A., Micciancio, D. (eds.) CRYPTO 2019. LNCS, vol. 11694, pp. 335–366. Springer, Cham (2019). https://doi.org/10.1007/978-3-030-26954-8_11

[Nis13] Nishimaki, R.: How to watermark cryptographic functions. In: Johansson, T., Nguyen, P.Q. (eds.) EUROCRYPT 2013. LNCS, vol. 7881, pp. 111–125. Springer, Heidelberg (2013). https://doi.org/10.1007/978-3-642-38348-9_7

[NSS99] Naccache, D., Shamir, A., Stern, J.P.: How to copyright a function? In: Imai, H., Zheng, Y. (eds.) PKC 1999. LNCS, vol. 1560, pp. 188–196. Springer, Heidelberg (1999). https://doi.org/10.1007/3-540-49162-7_14

[NW15] Nishimaki, R., Wichs, D.: Watermarking cryptographic programs against arbitrary removal strategies. Cryptology ePrint Archive, Report 2015/344 (2015). https://eprint.iacr.org/2015/344

[NWZ16] Nishimaki, R., Wichs, D., Zhandry, M.: Anonymous traitor tracing: how to embed arbitrary information in a key. In: Fischlin, M., Coron, J.-S. (eds.) EUROCRYPT 2016. LNCS, vol. 9666, pp. 388–419. Springer, Heidelberg (2016). https://doi.org/10.1007/978-3-662-49896-5_14

[PS18] Peikert, C., Shiehian, S.: Privately constraining and programming PRFs, the LWE way. In: Abdalla, M., Dahab, R. (eds.) PKC 2018. LNCS, vol. 10770, pp. 675–701. Springer, Cham (2018). https://doi.org/10.1007/978-3-319-76581-5_23

[QWZ18] Quach, W., Wichs, D., Zirdelis, G.: Watermarking PRFs under standard assumptions: public marking and security with extraction queries. In: Beimel, A., Dziembowski, S. (eds.) TCC 2018. LNCS, vol. 11240, pp. 669–698. Springer, Cham (2018). https://doi.org/10.1007/978-3-030-03810-6_24

[SW14] Sahai, A., Waters, B.: How to use indistinguishability obfuscation: deniable encryption, and more. In: STOC, pp. 475–484. ACM (2014)

[YAL+18] Yang, R., Au, M.H., Lai, J., Xu, Q., Yu, Z.: Unforgeable watermarking schemes with public extraction. In: Catalano, D., De Prisco, R. (eds.) SCN 2018. LNCS, vol. 11035, pp. 63–80. Springer, Cham (2018). https://doi.org/10.1007/978-3-319-98113-0_4

[YF11] Yoshida, M., Fujiwara, T.: Toward digital watermarking for cryptographic data. IEICE Trans. Fundam. Electron. Commun. Comput. Sci. 94(1), 270–272 (2011)

Multiparty Computation (1)

Valiant's Universal Circuits Revisited: An Overall Improvement and a Lower Bound

Shuoyao Zhao[1,3], Yu Yu[1,2(✉)], Jiang Zhang[2], and Hanlin Liu[1]

[1] Department of Computer Science and Engineering, Shanghai Jiao Tong University,
Shanghai 200240, China
zsyintl@126.com, yuyuathk@gmail.com
[2] State Key Laboratory of Cryptology, P.O. Box 5159, Beijing 100878, China
jiangzhang09@gmail.com
[3] PlatON co., Limited, Hong Kong SAR, China

Abstract. A universal circuit (UC) is a general-purpose circuit that can simulate arbitrary circuits (up to a certain size n). At STOC 1976 Valiant presented a graph theoretic approach to the construction of UCs, where a UC is represented by an edge universal graph (EUG) and is recursively constructed using a dedicated graph object (referred to as supernode). As a main end result, Valiant constructed a 4-way supernode of size 19 and an EUG of size $4.75n \log n$ (omitting smaller terms), which remained the most size-efficient even to this day (after more than 4 decades).

Motivated by the emerging applications of UCs in various privacy preserving computation scenarios, we revisit Valiant's universal circuits, and propose a 4-way supernode of size 18, and an EUG of size $4.5n \log n$. As confirmed by our implementations, we reduce the size of universal circuits (and the number of AND gates) by more than 5% in general, and thus improve upon the efficiency of UC-based cryptographic applications accordingly. Our approach to the design of optimal supernodes is computer aided (rather than by hand as in previous works), which might be of independent interest. As a complement, we give lower bounds on the size of EUGs and UCs in Valiant's framework, which significantly improves upon the generic lower bound on UC size and therefore reduces the gap between theory and practice of universal circuits.

1 Introduction

A universal circuit (UC)[1] refers to a circuit that can be programmed to simulate any Boolean circuit C up to a given size. That is, a UC takes as input program bits p_C (that encodes C) in addition to an input x, and produces as output $UC(x, p_C) = C(x)$. This is analogous to a central processing unit (CPU) that carries out the computations specified by the instructions of a computer program.

---

[1] As a slight abuse of abbreviation, we use UC as the shorthand for universal circuit, and the readers should not confuse it with universal composability.

© International Association for Cryptologic Research 2019
S. D. Galbraith and S. Moriai (Eds.): ASIACRYPT 2019, LNCS 11921, pp. 401–425, 2019.
https://doi.org/10.1007/978-3-030-34578-5_15

1.1   Applications of Universal Circuits

Universal circuits have received sustained research interests and have been found useful in various privacy-preserving computation applications. We recall a few below, whose efficiency would benefit from the improvement of universal circuits.

Program Obfuscation. Garg et al. [11] used UCs to construct universal branching programs which was in turn used to build a candidate indistinguishability obfuscation (iO). More recently Zimmerman [36] proposed an approach to obfuscation by viewing UC as a keyed program for circuit families.

Private Function Evaluation. Universal circuits are an essential tool to transform a multi-party computation (MPC) protocol into one for private function evaluation (PFE). UC-based PFE was studied in [21] and was later improved and extended in [6,23]. A general framework for PFE protocols that allows for instantiations from various concrete protocols in different settings was proposed in [26] and was then extended to malicious adversary setting in [27]. Furthermore, the actively secure non-interactive secure computation (NISC) technique [1] can be applied to UC to realize actively secure non-interactive PFE, which is beyond the reach of the framework of [26,27].

Batched Execution of 2PC. Another interesting application of UC is efficient batch execution for secure two-party computation (2PC). The batch execution techniques [18,22] were originally intended for amortizing the cost of maliciously secure garbled circuits for the same function, and UCs can now enable batched execution for circuits of different functions (realized by the same UC).

Universal Models of Computation. Valiant's UCs motivated the design of universal parallel computers [10,25]. Both depth-optimized [7] and size-optimized [31] approaches to UCs were adapted in [5] to universal quantum circuits.

Other Applications. UCs were used to hide the functions in verifiable computation [8] and multi-hop homomorphic encryption [15], to hide queries in database management systems (DBMSs) [9,28] and to reduce verifier's preprocessing costs in NIZK argument [14]. Attrapadung [4] used UCs to transform the attribute-based encryption (ABE) schemes for any polynomial-size circuits [12,16] into ciphertext-policy ABE. UCs were also used to build the ABE scheme in [13].

1.2   Related Works

Valiant viewed a Boolean circuit as a directed acyclic graph (DAG) and introduced an edge-universal graph (EUG) that edge embeds arbitrary DAGs (of a certain size) in a way that is analogous (and can be translated) to a universal circuit and its simulation of arbitrary circuits. Following Valiant and his follow-up works [17,19,23,31], we assume WLOG that the circuit has s inputs, t outputs, g gates of fan-in and fan-out 2, and let $n = s + g$ be the main parameter. Valiant gave a recursive construction of EUGs (and UCs) based on a k-way supernode (a graph object based on EUG, abbreviated as SN) parameterized by some constant k. As the main results, Valiant constructed a 2-way supernode of size 5 and a 4-way supernode of size 19, which gives rise to EUGs of size $5n \log n$ and $4.75n \log n$ respectively (and UCs of size approximately four times that of the corresponding EUGs, all omitting non-dominant terms). Later Cook and Hoover [7] gave a depth-preserving construction of UC with optimal depth $O(d)$ but larger size $O(n^3 d / \log n)$, where d is the depth of circuit simulated. More recently, there have been ongoing efforts of implementations and optimizations of UC under Valiant's framework. Kolesnikov and Schneider [21] proposed a practical UC with size-complexity roughly $0.25n \log^2 n$ and gave a first implementation of UC-based PFE under the Fairplay 2PC framework [24]. Despite not being asymptotically optimal their construction [21] outperforms Valiant's UC for small scale circuits. Lipmaa et al. [23,29] further brought down the size of Valiant 4-way UC from $19n \log n$ to $18 \log n$ by reducing the number of XOR gates (while keeping the same number of AND gates). Moreover, Lipmaa et al. gave a general construction of k-way supernode and showed that their design has smallest size when $k = 3.147$. Independent of Lipmaa et al.'s work [23], Kiss and Schneider [19] mainly focused on PFE, a prominent application of UC, for which the size of UC (and especially the number of AND gates) is significantly optimized. Further, they [19] borrowed building blocks from [21] and proposed hybrid constructions of UCs for circuits with long inputs and outputs. Günther et al. [17] implemented Valiant's 4-way UC and then provided a hybrid UC construction with further improved practical efficiency by combining Valiant's 2-way and 4-way UCs.

Table 1. A comparison of previous results and ours in terms of the sizes of 4-way supernodes, EUGs, UCs and the number of AND gates, omitting non-dominant terms.

	$|\mathsf{SN}(4)|$	$|\mathsf{EUG}_2(n)|$	$|\mathsf{UC}^g_{s,t}|$	#(AND gates)
Valiant's UC [31]	19	$4.75n \log n$	$19n \log n$	$4.75n \log n$
Kolesnikov et al. [21]	N/A	$0.25n \log^2 n$	$n \log^2 n$	$0.25n \log^2 n$
Lipmaa et al. [23]	19	$4.75n \log n$	$18n \log n$	$4.75n \log n$
Our result	18	$4.5n \log n$	$17.75n \log n$	$4.5n \log n$

Valiant's 4-way universal circuits remained to date the most efficient construction (i.e., $4.75n \log n$). Motivated by aforementioned UC-based cryptographic applications, the efficiency improvement efforts towards making them practical and the trend of circuit size towards 10-million-gate or even billion-gate scale (e.g., [3,35]), it is natural to raise the following question:

Can we build more efficient UCs with better constant factors (i.e., smaller than 4.75) and is there a tighter bound on the size of EUG in Valiant's framework?

1.3   Our Contributions

We propose an algorithm that automates the search for optimal k-way supernodes (practical for $k \leq 4$), which yields a 4-way supernode of size 18 and depth 13 (as shown in Fig. 1), improving upon the counterpart by Valiant [31] of size 19 and depth 14. Plugging it into Valiant's framework immediately brings down the size complexity of Valiant's UC (resp., EUG) from $19n \log n$ (resp., $4.75n \log n$) to $18n \log n$ (resp., $4.5n \log n$), where the size of UC $18n \log n$ can be further reduced to $17.75n \log n$ using the techniques from [23]. In general, our 4-way supernode achieves an overall improvement of more than 5% in graph (circuit) size, along with a reduction of over 6% in graph (circuit) depth as a by-product. We refer to Table 1 for a detailed comparison with related works. As far as secure computation scenarios such as MPC and PFE are concerned, a practical efficiency indicator would be the number of AND gates (i.e., excluding XOR gates) and in this respect our work is also currently the best (more than 5% improvement over previous works). We implement our UC [33], evaluate its performance with a comparison to existing implementations (see Table 3) based on circuits of basic functions suitable for MPC and FHE, suggested by Tillich and Smart [30].

Furthermore, our supernode can be plugged into Valiant's 4-way UC or any applications that use the 4-way supernode as a blackbox to achieve improvements accordingly. For example, our 4-way supernode was used in the recent hybrid UC [2], which was based on the hybrid UC from [17] by replacing Valiant's 4-way counterpart. The engineering efforts of adapting the existing implementations to ours are affordable by replacing the supernode components, thanks to the modularity of Valiant's framework.

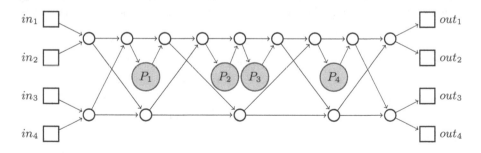

Fig. 1. A 4-way supernode that consists of 18 nodes (excluding inputs and outputs).

Our approach to the design of supernodes is computer aided (rather than by hand as in previous works), which could be of independent interest. Although not specific to 4-way supernodes, the time complexity of our algorithm when used in search of optimal k-way supernodes for $k \geq 5$ becomes impractically large. We stress that the implementations of k-way UC for $k \geq 5$, even if they exist with smaller size, are less desirable in practice. This is because the complexity of the conversion from an arbitrary circuit to the corresponding UC (which includes EUG generation, edge embedding, etc.) blows up dramatically with respect to k. This justifies why Valiant's 2-way UCs were implemented in [19] earlier than its 4-way counterpart in [17] despite that the latter has slightly smaller circuit size. Still, for theoretical interests, we give a lower bound on the size of k-way supernodes (over all k's) as a complement, which in turn implies a lower bound on the size of universal circuit in Valiant's framework. That is, the size of an $\mathsf{EUG}_2(n)$ (resp., UC) is lower bounded by $3.644n \log n$ (resp., $14.576n \log n$). We note that a generic lower bound on UC size $\Omega(n \log n)$ was folklore, where the hidden constant (implicit in [32, Theorem 8.1]) is quite small (about 1 as sketched in Sect. 4.1). We attribute this gap (14.576 vs. 1) to that either the generic bound is not tight or Valiant's approach to UC construction, despite its generality and modularity, might be only asymptotically optimal (i.e., not having a good constant factor). Given that most existing UC constructions were built upon Valiant's framework, we believe that our lower bound can be of practical relevance. Finally, it is left as an interesting open problem whether the gap between our construction and proved lower bound, $4.5n \log n$ vs. $3.644n \log n$, can be further reduced.

2   Preliminaries and Valiant's UC Construction

In this section, we give basic notations and definitions about universal circuits and explain Valiant's construction of universal circuits for completeness and accessibility. We refer to [23] for an excellent exposition on Valiant's framework.

2.1   Notations and Definitions

Notations. $|G|$ (resp., $|C|$) refers to the size of a graph G (resp., circuit C), namely, the number of nodes (resp., gates) in G (resp., C). In this paper, we stick to the graph theoretical (rather than the standard electronics) terminology, where a circuit is represented by a Directed Acyclic Graph (DAG), inputs, outputs and gates are considered as nodes and wires are seen as edges of the DAG. $C_{s,t}^g$ denotes a circuit with s inputs, t outputs and size up to g, and $\mathsf{UC}_{s,t}^g$ denotes a universal circuit which simulates arbitrary $C_{s,t}^g$. $\mathsf{DAG}_d(n)$ is a DAG of size n and fan-in (and fan-out) d. Valiant [31] introduced Edge-Universal Graph (EUG) as defined in Definition 2 below. Loosely speaking, Universal Circuits to circuits are like Edge-Universal Graphs to Directed Acyclic Graphs. We use $\mathsf{EUG}_d(n)$ to denote an edge-universal graph that edge-embeds arbitrary $\mathsf{DAG}_d(n)$. Note that we have $|\mathsf{UC}_{s,t}^g| > g$ (resp., $|\mathsf{EUG}_d(n)| > n$) because $\mathsf{UC}_{s,t}^g$ (resp., $\mathsf{EUG}_d(n)$) simulates (resp., edge-embeds) any $C_{s,t}^g$ (resp., $\mathsf{DAG}_d(n)$). We refer to the nodes of $\mathsf{EUG}_d(n)$ which are mapped from the corresponding vertices in $\mathsf{DAG}_d(n)$ as "poles" and other nodes which are used to simulate the structure of $\mathsf{DAG}_d(n)$ as common nodes.

Definition 1 (Universal Circuit). *A circuit* $\mathsf{UC}_{s,t}^g$ *is called a universal circuit, if for any circuit with s inputs, t outputs, size up to g (denoted by* $\mathsf{C}_{s,t}^g$*), there exists a set of program bits* $p \in \{0,1\}^m$ *such that* $\mathsf{UC}_{s,t}^g$ *can be programmed to realize* $\mathsf{C}_{s,t}^g$*, i.e.,* $\forall x \in \{0,1\}^s, \mathsf{UC}_{s,t}^g(x,p) = \mathsf{C}_{s,t}^g(x)$*.*

Definition 2 (Edge-Universal Graphs). *An edge-embedding* ϱ *of* $G = (V,E)$ *into* $G^* = (V^*, E^*)$ *is a mapping that maps* V *into* V^* *one to one, and* E *into directed paths in* G^* *(i.e.,* $(i,j) \in E$ *maps to a path from* $\varrho(i)$ *to* $\varrho(j)$*) that are pairwise edge-disjoint. A graph* G^* *is an edge-universal graph for* $\mathsf{DAG}_d(n)$ *if it has distinguished poles* $P_1, \ldots, P_n$ *such that every* $G \in \mathsf{DAG}_{d_0}(n_0)$*, with* $d_0 \leq d$ *and* $n_0 \leq n$*, can be edge-embedded into* G^* *by a mapping* ϱ *such that* $\varrho(i) = P_i$ *for each* $i \in V$*. This should hold for any labeling of* G*.*

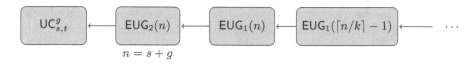

$$n = s + g$$

Fig. 2. A high-level view of Valiant universal circuit construction [23].

2.2 From Edge-Universal Graphs to Universal Circuits

As depicted in Fig. 2, Valiant's UC construction consists of the following steps:

1. Construct a $\mathsf{UC}_{s,t}^g$ from an $\mathsf{EUG}_2(n)$, where $n = g + s$;
2. Construct an $\mathsf{EUG}_2(n)$ from an $\mathsf{EUG}_1(n)$;
3. Construct an $\mathsf{EUG}_1(n)$ given an $\mathsf{EUG}_1(\lceil n/k \rceil - 1)$ for some constant k;
4. Repeat Step 3 recursively until reaching an EUG of some small size that can be trivially constructed.

Construct $\mathsf{UC}_{s,t}^g$ **from** $\mathsf{EUG}_2(n)$**.** To build a universal circuit $\mathsf{UC}_{s,t}^g$ from a $\mathsf{EUG}_2(n)^2$, each node in $\mathsf{EUG}_2(n)$ should be implemented by Boolean gates and each edge is a wire of $\mathsf{UC}_{s,t}^g$. The details are as follows.

– Each pole is implemented by a universal gate (UG). A 2-input UG supports any of the 16 possible gate types represented by the 4 control bits of the gate table (c_1, c_2, c_3, c_4). It computes function $ug: \{0,1\}^2 \times \{0,1\}^4 \to \{0,1\}$ as follows:

$$ug(x_1, x_2, c_1, c_2, c_3, c_4) = \overline{x_1 x_2} c_1 + \overline{x_1} x_2 c_2 + x_1 \overline{x_2} c_3 + x_1 x_2 c_4 \qquad (1)$$

A UG can be implemented with 3 AND and 6 XOR gates [23]. The control bits c_1, c_2, c_3, c_4 are part of the program bits of the universal circuit.

---

[2] Definition 2 puts no limits on the fan-in/fan-out of EUG, but Valiant's UC construction requires the underlying EUG to be a DAG_2.

- Each common node with indegree and outdegree both 2 can be implemented by an X-switching gate [20], that computes $f_X : \{0,1\}^2 \times \{0,1\} \to \{0,1\}^2$ (Fig. 3a). The inputs of an X-switching gate are forwarded to its outputs, switched or not switched, depending on control bit c. This block can be implemented with 1 AND gate and 3 XOR gates (Fig. 3c).
- Each common node with indegree 2 and outdegree 1 can be implemented by a Y-switching gate [20], that computes $f_Y : \{0,1\}^2 \times \{0,1\} \to \{0,1\}$ (Fig. 3b). A Y-switching gate takes as input two bits and produces one of them as output, depending on control bit c. This block can be implemented with 1 AND gate and 2 XOR gates (Fig. 3d).
- Each common node with indegree 1 and outdegree 2 (i.e., splitter gate) is replaced by two outgoing wires to copy its input to the two outputs.
- Each common node with indegree 1 and outdegree 1 is replaced by a wire.

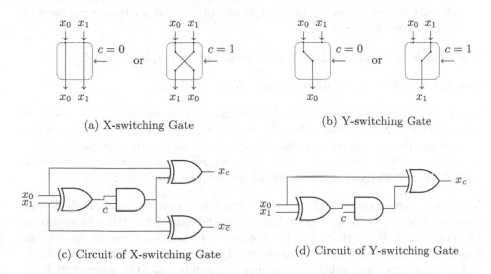

(a) X-switching Gate

(b) Y-switching Gate

(c) Circuit of X-switching Gate

(d) Circuit of Y-switching Gate

Fig. 3. Switching gates and their circuit implementations.

This completes the construction of $\mathsf{UC}^g_{s,t}$ from $\mathsf{EUG}_2(n)$. It remains to show how $\mathsf{UC}^g_{s,t}$ simulates a given circuit $\mathsf{C}^g_{s,t}$ (as intended for a universal circuit), where simulation is essentially setting the input wires and the program (and control) bits for all universal gates and switching gates.

Simulate $\mathbf{C}^g_{s,t}$ Using $\mathbf{UC}^g_{s,t}$. Following [17,23,31], we assume WLOG that the circuits have fan-in/fan-out bounded by two, and it is well-known that any circuit of unbounded fan-in/fan-out can be transformed into a functionally equivalent one by paying reasonable prices in size ($\mathsf{C}^g_{s,t} \subset \mathsf{C}^{2g+t,2}_{s,t}$). [31, Cor 3.1].

We model the circuit $\mathsf{C}^g_{s,t}$ as a graph $G_C = (V_C, E_C)$ where each input wire and each gate are represented as a node and each wire is represented by an edge in the graph. The derived graph is a $\mathsf{DAG}_2(n)$ with $n = s + g$. By Definition 2, it is possible to embed G_C into an $\mathsf{EUG}_2(n)$, such that for every edge $(v_i, v_j) \in E_C$, there is a path from v_i to v_j that is edge-disjoint to other paths. These paths constitute set $Q = \{Q_1, Q_2, \ldots, Q_{|E_C|}\}$, which will be used to determine the control bits of the switching gates in $\mathsf{UC}_{s,t}^g$, the universal circuit corresponding to the $\mathsf{EUG}_2(n)$ above. We set the control bits and input wires as follow.

- **Control bits of switching gates.** For an X-(/Y-)switching gate G_S of $\mathsf{UC}_{s,t}^g$, we denote by N_S the corresponding node in $\mathsf{EUG}_2(n)$. If a path $Q_i \in Q$ passes through N_S, we set the control bit of G_S to satisfy the direction of Q_i through N_S.[3] If no paths go through N_S, we can set arbitrary binary value for the control bit of G_S.
- **Control bits of universal gates and input wires of universal circuit.** For a universal gate G_U of $\mathsf{UC}_{s,t}^g$, we denote by N_U the corresponding pole in $\mathsf{EUG}_2(n)$. If N_U represents a gate of the given circuit $C_{s,t}^g$, we set the control bits of G_U to realize the gate. If N_U represents an input of $C_{s,t}^g$, we can set arbitrary binary values for the control bits of G_U and set the output wire of G_U as an input wire of $\mathsf{UC}_{s,t}^g$.

This completes the simulation. Now we analyze the complexity of $\mathsf{UC}_{s,t}^g$.

Lemma 1. $|\mathsf{UC}_{s,t}^g| \leq 4|\mathsf{EUG}_2(n)| + 5n$, where $n = s + g$

Proof. From the construction of $\mathsf{UC}_{s,t}^g$, we know that the size of $\mathsf{UC}_{s,t}^g$ is related to the numbers of X-switching gates (denoted by n_X), Y-switching gates (denoted by n_Y) and the universal gates (exactly n), which can be expressed as: $|\mathsf{UC}_{s,t}^g| = 4n_X + 3n_Y + 9n \leq 4(n_X + n_Y + n) + 5n \leq 4|\mathsf{EUG}_2(n)| + 5n$, as switching gates (which amount to $n_X + n_Y$) are part of the common nodes in $\mathsf{EUG}_2(n)$.

In Valiant's supernode design, the fan-in/fan-out of every common node is two, meaning that there are no Y-switching gates and splitters in the corresponding UC (i.e., $n_Y = 0$). In that case, the inequality in Lemma 1 can be used as an equality. Later, the supernode designed by Lipmaa et al. [23] additionally utilized Y-switching gates and splitters to reduce the number of XOR gates, which we will elaborate in the next section. In summary, we reduce the construction of UC to that of $\mathsf{EUG}_2(n)$, which will be our focus for the remainder of this section.

2.3   Edge-Universal Graphs: From $\mathsf{EUG}_1(n)$ to $\mathsf{EUG}_2(n)$

Next we show how to construct from $\mathsf{EUG}_1(n)$ to $\mathsf{EUG}_2(n)$.

Lemma 2 (Lemma 2.1 from [31]). *For any* $\mathsf{DAG}_d(n) = (V, E)$, E *can be regarded as the union of d disjoint set E_i, i.e., $E = \cup_{i=1}^d E_i$, such that each (V, E_i) is a* $\mathsf{DAG}_1(n)$.

---

[3] Since N_S is a common node, it cannot be an endpoint of a path. For a X-switching gate G_S, there may be two paths passing through N_S, for which only a single control bit is needed as paths in Q are edge-disjoint by definition.

Lemma 3 ([23]). *An $\mathsf{EUG}_2(n)$ can be constructed from two instances of $\mathsf{EUG}_1(n)$.*

Proof. An $\mathsf{EUG}_2(n)$ is constructed from two $\mathsf{EUG}_1(n)$, which can be achieved by merging every two poles in the same positions of the two $\mathsf{EUG}_1(n)$. Then we prove that any $\mathsf{DAG}_2(n) = (V, E)$ can be edge-embedded into the $\mathsf{EUG}_2(n)$. By Lemma 2 we can divide E into two sets E_1 and E_2 such that each (V, E_i) is a $\mathsf{DAG}_1(n)$, and therefore we can embed each in a separate $\mathsf{EUG}_1(n)$. The edge-embedding from (V, E) to $\mathsf{EUG}_2(n)$ is the combination of two edge-embeddings from (V, E_i) to the respective $\mathsf{EUG}_1(n)$. This completes the $\mathsf{EUG}_2(n)$ construction.

As we mentioned before, when constructing a $\mathsf{UC}_g^{s,t}$ we need the $\mathsf{EUG}_2(n)$ to be a DAG_2. So the $\mathsf{EUG}_1(n)$ used to construct this $\mathsf{EUG}_2(n)$ also needs to be a DAG_2 and the indegree (outdegree) of poles of $\mathsf{EUG}_1(n)$ should be 1. Therefore, when we talk about Valiant's construction, the edge-universal graphs $\mathsf{EUG}_1(n)$ and $\mathsf{EUG}_2(n)$ should meet the requirements above.

2.4   Edge-Universal Graphs: From $\mathsf{EUG}_1(\lceil n/k \rceil - 1)$ to $\mathsf{EUG}_1(n)$

Now that we reduce the construction of $\mathsf{UC}_{s,t}^g$ to the design of $\mathsf{EUG}_1(n)$. What we will show next is a reduction of $\mathsf{EUG}_1(n)$ to itself of smaller sizes (which can be done recursively until reaching an EUG_1 of trivial size we have on hand). The recursion relies on an essential building block called supernode (see Definition 3) and we use it to reduce $\mathsf{EUG}_1(n)$ to $\mathsf{EUG}_1(n/k)$ in each step.

Definition 3 (Supernode). *A k-way supernode $\mathsf{SN}(k)$ is an edge-universal-graph with k inputs $\{in_1, \ldots, in_k\}$, k outputs $\{out_1, \ldots, out_k\}$, k poles $P = \{P_1, \ldots, P_k\}$ and m other nodes (called common nodes), such that any graph $G = (V, E) \in \mathsf{DAG}_1(3k)$, where $V = \{in_1, \ldots, in_k\} \cup \{P_1, \ldots, P_k\} \cup \{out_1, \ldots, out_k\}$, and every edge $e = (v_1, v_2) \in E$ satisfies the conditions below:*

1. If $v_1 \in \{in_1, \ldots, in_k\}$ then $v_2 \in P$.
2. If $v_2 \in \{out_1, \ldots, out_k\}$ then $v_1 \in P$.
3. $v_1 \notin \{out_1, \ldots, out_k\}$.
4. $v_2 \notin \{in_1, \ldots, in_k\}$.

can be edge embedded into $\mathsf{SN}(k)$. The size[4] of $\mathsf{SN}(k)$ is the defined as $m + k$.

As an example, Fig. 1 is a 4-way supernode. Given a k-way supernode, we can reduce the problem of EUG construction to itself (of smaller sizes) in a recursive way. This is stated as the theorem below and for self-containedness we sketch its main idea (visualized in Fig. 4) and refer to the appendix for a full proof. That is, given an $\mathsf{EUG}_1(\lceil \frac{n}{k} \rceil - 1)$ and $\mathsf{SN}(k)$, we construct a $\mathsf{EUG}_1(n)$ as follows. We connect $\lceil \frac{n}{k} \rceil$ k-way supernodes together by merging the inputs and outputs

---

[4] As a slight abuse of definition, the size of a supernode is different from that of a graph by excluding input and output nodes. As we will see, it comes in handy when composing the components to build a large EUG and calculating its size.

of two adjacent supernodes one by one (e.g. merge out_1^1 and in_1^2 into one[5]). We divide those merged nodes into k groups and invoke $\mathsf{EUG}_1(\lceil \frac{n}{k} \rceil - 1)$ for each group (see Fig. 4).

Theorem 1 ([23,31]). *Given an* $\mathsf{EUG}_1(\lceil \frac{n}{k} \rceil - 1)$ *and a k-way supernode* $\mathsf{SN}(k)$, *there exists an explicit construction of* $\mathsf{EUG}_1(n)$ *of size*

$$k \cdot |\mathsf{EUG}_1(\lceil \frac{n}{k} \rceil - 1)| + \lceil \frac{n}{k} \rceil \cdot |\mathsf{SN}(k)|.$$

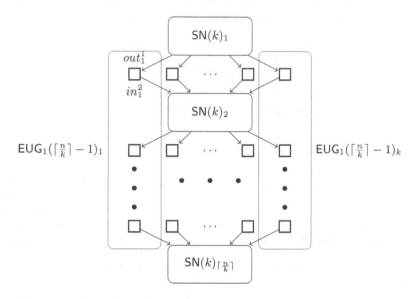

Fig. 4. Valiant's construction of $\mathsf{EUG}_1(n)$ based on $\mathsf{EUG}_1(\lceil \frac{n}{k} \rceil - 1)$ and $\mathsf{SN}(k)$.

With $\mathsf{SN}(k)$ we recursively reduce the problem to itself of smaller sizes, and we just need an EUG_1 of small size, say $\mathsf{EUG}_1(k)$, at initialization. Note that $\mathsf{EUG}_1(k)$ is already implied by and can be extracted from $\mathsf{SN}(k)$. In summary, $\mathsf{SN}(k)$ can be used to build EUGs of arbitrary size. We refer to this approach to UC construction (from supernodes) as Valiant's construction (or Valiant's framework) and see Fig. 4 for the high-level overview. Clearly, the complexity of Valiant's framework is related to the size of the supernode used, which will be analyzed in the next subsection.

2.5 Circuit Complexity in Valiant's Framework

Valiant's approach to universal circuits remains the most efficient to date, and thus we consider the complexity of UC and EUG constructed in Valiant's framework. The following equations are from Theorem 1 and Lemma 3:

$$|\mathsf{EUG}_2(n)| = 2|\mathsf{EUG}_1(n)| - n, \tag{2}$$

---

[5] in_j^i (out_j^i) denotes the j-th input (output) of the i-th supernode (denoted by $\mathsf{SN}(k)_i$).

$$|\mathsf{EUG}_1(n)| = k|\mathsf{EUG}_1(\lceil\frac{n}{k}\rceil - 1)| + \lceil\frac{n}{k}\rceil|\mathsf{SN}(k)|. \tag{3}$$

By using recurrence relation above, we get

$$|\mathsf{EUG}_2(n)| = \frac{2|\mathsf{SN}(k)|}{k\log k}n\log n - O(n), \tag{4}$$

$$|\mathsf{CircuitEUG}_2(n)| = \frac{2|\mathsf{CircuitSN}(k)|}{k\log k}n\log n - O(n), \tag{5}$$

where $\mathsf{CircuitEUG}_d(n)$ denotes the circuit counterpart of $\mathsf{EUG}_2(n)$ in Eq. 4. The size of UC can be estimated by combining Eq. 4 with Lemma 1 [31]:

$$|\mathsf{UC}^g_{s,t}| = \frac{8|\mathsf{SN}(k)|}{k\log k}n\log n - O(n), \text{where } n = s + t + 2g. \tag{6}$$

Next, we consider depth and from Fig. 4 we know:

$$\mathsf{depth}(\mathsf{EUG}_1(n)) = \lceil\frac{n}{k}\rceil\mathsf{depth}(\mathsf{SN}(k)) + (\lceil\frac{n}{k}\rceil - 1)$$

$$= \frac{n}{k}(\mathsf{depth}(\mathsf{SN}(k)) + 1) + O(1). \tag{7}$$

Combining with Lemma 3, we have:

$$\mathsf{depth}(\mathsf{UC}^g_{s,t}) = \mathsf{depth}(\mathsf{CircuitEUG}_1(n))$$

$$= \lceil\frac{n}{k}\rceil\mathsf{depth}(\mathsf{CircuitSN}(k)) + (\lceil\frac{n}{k}\rceil - 1)\mathsf{depth}(\mathsf{X\text{-}switching}). \tag{8}$$

The depth of the circuit of $\mathsf{SN}(k)$ is $3 \times \mathsf{depth}(\mathsf{SN}(k))$[6] as the X- and Y-switching gates are both of depth 3 (see Fig. 3). Thus, its depth complexity is:

$$\mathsf{depth}(\mathsf{UC}^g_{s,t}) = \frac{3 \times \mathsf{depth}(\mathsf{SN}(k)) + 3}{k}n + O(1). \tag{9}$$

Table 2. The known results of UC size and depth.

k	Supernode size	Supernode depth	$|\mathsf{UC}^g_{s,t}|$	$\mathsf{depth}(\mathsf{UC}^g_{s,t})$
2-way	5	5	$20n\log n$ [31]	$9n$
3-way	12	7	$20.19n\log n$ [17]	$8n$
Valiant's 4-way	19	14	$19n\log n$ [17,31]	$11.25n$
Our 4-way	18	13	$18n\log n$	$10.5n$

We summarize in Table 2 known results about the size and depth of supernode and corresponding UCs. As we can see, the size and depth of Valiant's universal circuits crucially depend on the respective size and depth of the underlying k-way supernode. This motivates our search for a smaller supernode for some practical value of k.

---

[6] Similar to the size of supernode, we define the depth of $\mathsf{SN}(k)$ as the length of the longest path minus 2 (i.e., excluding inputs and outputs), denoted by $\mathsf{depth}(\mathsf{SN}(k))$.

3   A New Design of Supernode via Automated Search

In this section, we introduce an automated approach to the design of supernodes. As a main end result, we get a better 4-way supernode with an overall improvement of more than 5% on the efficiency of UC constructions and their applications, stated as the theorem below. We refer to the external link [34] for a lengthy (computer generated) proof that Fig. 1 gives a 4-way supernode, where all effective DAGs are exhausted and their edge-embeddings into the supernode are provided. As we will show, it is already size optimal (as a 4-way supernode) as 4-way supernodes of size 17 do not exist.

Theorem 2 (4-way SN and EUG, revisited). *The graph in Fig. 1 is a 4-way supernode with 18 nodes (excluding inputs and outputs), which implies an* $\mathsf{EUG}_2(n)$ *of size* $4.5n \log n - O(n)$ *and depth* $3.5n + O(1)$.

3.1   Construction of Supernodes

While giving constructions of 2-way and 4-way supernodes in his work [31], Valiant gave no details on how the constructions were obtained. Lipmaa et al. [23] formalized and explained the k-way supernode construction methodology in a modular and intuitive way. As depicted in the right-hand of Fig. 5, a general design of k-way supernode consists of two layers of permutation-networks (PNs) at both ends and an EUG augmented with $k - 1$ additional nodes in between. For $k = 4$, the size of $\mathsf{SN}(4)$ following the general design is

$$2|\mathsf{PN}| + |\mathsf{EUG}_1(k)| + k - 1 = 10 + 7 + 3 = 20.$$

Looking back, Valiant's 4-way supernode can be regarded as an optimized version of the general design by saving a node from one of the permutation networks (see the comparison in Fig. 5). One might think that by exploiting the symmetry it is possible to save two nodes (one from each permutation network) to get a 4-way supernode of smaller size (i.e., 18). Unfortunately, this intuition does not work because the resulting graph would not be a supernode any more, which was refuted by our supernode testing algorithm (presented in the next subsection). It remained open if one can construct more size-efficient supernodes. Next we will present an algorithm for testing whether a graph is supernode or not, and an automated searching algorithm for more size-efficient supernodes.

3.2   Supernode Test for Graphs

As the first step, we propose a method to check whether a graph (with k inputs, k outputs, k poles and m common nodes) is a k-way supernode or not. A k-way supernode is an edge-universal-graph that edge embeds any graph $G \in \mathsf{DAG}_1(3k)$ (see Definition 3) and thus it seems necessary to enumerate all $G \in \mathsf{DAG}_1(3k)$. For efficiency, we observe that it suffices to enumerate over a special type of graph called pole-complete graphs, and the remaining graphs can be omitted as they are already implied. As we will see in the next section, the notion of pole-complete graphs will also be useful for proving the lower bound.

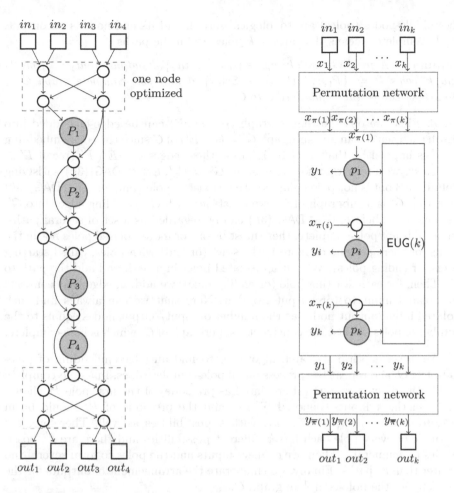

Fig. 5. A comparison of Valiant's $\mathsf{SN}(4)$ and the general design of $\mathsf{SN}(k)$ from [23].

Definition 4 (Pole-complete Graph). *For $G = (V, E) \in \mathsf{DAG}_1(3k)$ with k inputs, k outputs, and k poles $P_1, \ldots, P_k$ that are topologically ordered, we say that G is pole-complete if*

1. *Every edge of G satisfies the four properties stated in Definition 3;*
2. *For any pole $p \in \{P_1, \ldots, P_k\}$, there exist $e_1 = (v_1, v_2), e_2 = (v_3, v_4) \in E$ such that $v_2 = p$ and $v_3 = p$.*

We denote by F_k the number of all the k-way pole-complete graphs $G \in \mathsf{DAG}_1(3k)$.

Informally, for any $G = (V, E) \in \mathsf{DAG}_1(3k)$ to be edge-embedded into the candidate supernode (Definition 3), we can see G as a set of paths. We call G pole-complete if for each path its start-node is an input (from $\{in_1, \ldots, in_k\}$), the middle-nodes (poles) are topological sorted, and its end-node is an output. "Pole-complete" means that all the k poles are in the paths.

Lemma 4. *A graph G_0 with k inputs $\{in_1, \ldots, in_k\}$, k outputs $\{out_1, \ldots, out_k\}$, and k poles $P = \{P_1, \ldots, P_k\}$ is a $\mathsf{SN}(k)$ if any pole-complete graph $G \in \mathsf{DAG}_1(3k)$ can be edge-embedded into G_0.*

Proof. First, we observe that if graph $G = (V, E)$ can be edge-embedded into graph G_0, then so can any subgraph $G' = (V', E')$ of G since the edge-embedding of G' is implied by that of G by ignoring those edges $e \in E \setminus E'$ (recall $E' \subset E$). Next, we prove that for any graph $G' = (V', E') \in \mathsf{DAG}_1(3k)$ satisfying Definition 3 but is not pole-complete, there exists a pole-complete $G \in \mathsf{DAG}_1(3k)$ such that G' is a subgraph of G. We construct such G by adding edges into G'. As mentioned before, $G' \in \mathsf{DAG}_1(3k)$ can be regarded as a set of several paths. Since G' is not pole-complete, there must be one or more isolated poles not in the paths, or there are one or more paths start (or end) with poles, called starting poles (or ending poles). We put all isolated poles in a path and add the path to G'. Then, for each starting pole (or ending pole), we add an edge that connects an isolated input to (or output from) it. Note that we can always find such isolated input/output nodes as the number of input/output nodes equals to the number of poles. At last, we construct a supergraph of G' which is pole-complete.

We use a depth-first-search algorithm to find an edge-embedding of pole-complete G, and repeat the process on all pole-complete ones. In a pole-complete graph, the precursor-node (abbreviated as pre-node) of the first pole P_1 should reside in the k inputs, denoted by in_i, and the pre-node of P_2 should be in $\{P_1, in_1, \ldots, in_{i-1}, in_{i+1}, \ldots, in_k\}$, with k possibilities as well. Therefore, the pre-node of every pole each has k different possibilities and there are k^k possibilities to enumerate. Then, we connect inputs and the poles to form several (no greater than k) paths. Finally, we enumerate the arrangement of outputs for the paths to get the pole-complete graph G.

3.3 Search for More Size-Efficient k-way Supernodes

As given in Definition 3, we define the size of a supernode $\mathsf{SN}(k)$ as the sum of the numbers of poles and common nodes and we find it convenient to compute the size of EUG in Valiant's framework (see Footnote 4). Thus, the supernode of size n has $n + 2k$ nodes (k inputs, k outputs, k poles and $n - k$ common nodes). To search for $\mathsf{SN}(k)$ of size n, we number the nodes in $\mathsf{SN}(k)$ as $N_1, N_2, \ldots, N_{n+2k}$ with $N_1, N_2, \ldots, N_k$ as inputs, $N_{n+k+1}, N_{n+k+2}, \ldots, N_{n+2k}$ as outputs and $N_{k+1}, N_{k+2}, \ldots, N_{n+k}$ as poles and common nodes (collectively referred to as middle nodes). The idea of searching for a $SN(k)$ of size n is to enumerate the pre-nodes of each node in the graph, and output if it is a supernode (using the supernode test method from the last subsection). For example, if the inputs have no pre-nodes, we can just set the k inputs as isolated nodes at initialization. For a middle node N_i ($k < i < n + k + 1$), the number of its pre-nodes can be one (if N_i is a pole) or two (otherwise), so we must consider both possibilities. Upon the enumeration of N_j as N_i's pre-node candidate, we should check whether N_j is legal or not, in particular, if N_j's out-degree is 2 or N_j is an input or pole and its out-degree is 1, then N_j is not a pre-node of N_i (because the $\mathsf{SN}(k)$'s fan-out is 2 and the out-degree of an input or pole must be 1). This condition for N_j is described as "N_j's out-degree is not full" in line 8 and line 18 of Algorithm 3.3. At last, we add the k outputs as the successor nodes of the nodes whose out-degree is not full. The steps above allow for an automated search over all candidates. However, the above search is not efficient as it enumerates all candidates, many of which could have been ruled out from supernode tests. So we add the pruning method to improve efficiency. After choosing a middle node as the j-th pole, we check whether graph G we construct can be a part of $\mathsf{SN}(k)$ or not, for which we need to enumerate all the $\mathsf{DAG}_1(k+j)$ (with k inputs and j poles, see Definition 3) and check whether those $\mathsf{DAG}_1(k+j)$s can be edge-embedded into G or not. We refer to Algorithm 3.3 for the pseudocode of search for supernode $\mathsf{SN}(k)$ of size n, where the pruning method is invoked in line 10.

3.4   New Constructions

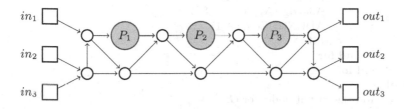

Fig. 6. A 3-way supernode that consists of 12 nodes.

We run the automated tool on a PC to search for k-way supernodes. We start with 3-way supernodes (the case of $k = 2$ is trivial). The search for $\mathsf{SN}(3)$ of size 11 failed, and an outcome of $\mathsf{SN}(3)$ of size 12 is illustrated in Fig. 6, which is already known in literature [17].

We proceed to the case $k = 4$. For the 4-way supernode of size 17, the search exits in a couple of minutes without any outcome, meaning that no such exist. For the 4-way supernode of size 18, the search runs in a number of minutes and returns the outcomes[7], which are depicted in the Fig. 1. This beats the best previously known result by Valiant [31] of size 19. As a result, we improve the size of $\mathsf{EUG}_2(n)$ from $4.75n \log n$ to $4.5n \log n$ (omitting smaller terms).

Moving from $k = 4$ to $k = 5$ seems a tiny step. However, for $k = 5$ the search algorithm is not terminating due to the substantially higher time complexity. For the 4-way supernode of size 18, we search for 6859734 candidate graphs (already

---

[7] The search algorithm outputs a few hundred of outcomes many of which are isomorphic to each other, but our verification is by hand and is certainly not exhaustive.

S. Zhao et al.

Algorithm 1. The search algorithm for $\mathsf{SN}(k)$ of size n

---
Require: k, n
Ensure: All k-way supernodes of size n (if exists)
1: Initialize the graph G
2: ADDNODE($G,k+1$)
3:
4: **function** ADDNODE(G, i)
5:     **if** $i \geq k + n$ **then**
6:         **if** #(G's pole)$< k$ **then**
7:             **for** $j = 1 \rightarrow i - 1$ **do**
8:                 **if** N_j's outdegree is not full **then**
9:                     Addedge(N_j, N_i) to G
10:                     **if** G passes the pruning method test **then**
11:                         ADDNODE($G,i+1$)
12:                     **end if**
13:                 **end if**
14:             **end for**
15:         **end if**
16:         **for** $j = 1 \rightarrow i - 1$ **do**
17:             **for** $k = 1 \rightarrow j - 1$ **do**
18:                 **if** (N_j's outdegree is not full) and (N_k's outdgree is not full) **then**
19:                     Addedge(N_j, N_i) to G
20:                     Addedge(N_k, N_i) to G
21:                     ADDNODE($G, i + 1$)
22:                 **end if**
23:             **end for**
24:         **end for**
25:     **else**
26:         Add the output nodes for G;
27:         **if** G is a Supernode **then**
28:             output G;
29:         **end if**
30:     **end if**
31: **end function**

---

after pruning) and for each candidate we should enumerate 5056 $\mathsf{DAG}_1(3 \times 4)$s to decide whether it is a supernode or not. That justifies why it takes several minutes to get the results. Nevertheless, for $k = 5$ we target at supernodes of size 26 (any 5-way supernode with size 27 or more yields an $\mathsf{EUG}_2(n)$ of size greater than $4.5n \log n$), then the number of candidate graphs grows rapidly to almost 2^{47}, and for each candidate we need to enumerate about 2^{18} $\mathsf{DAG}_1(3 \times 5)$s, where the product 2^{65} is beyond the reach of a PC. We did try other methods (e.g. SAT solvers) to improve the efficiency for $k = 5$. But the attempt failed due to the difficulty of finding out the SAT formula determining whether a DAG can be embedded into a supernode candidate or not.

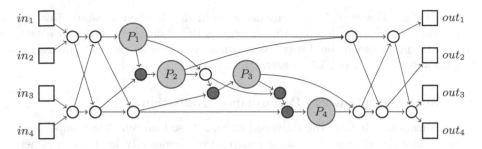

Fig. 7. The 4-way split supernode construction from [23], where each green node can be implemented by a Y-switching gate.

By replacing each common node with an X-switching gate and each pole with a universal gate, we immediately convert the $\mathsf{EUG}_2(n)$ to a universal circuit of size $18n \log n + O(n)$ and thus improve upon the Valiant's UC of size $19n \log n$. However, while our UC size seems the same as $18n \log n$ achieved by Lipmaa et al. [23], their UC construction was based on Valiant's supernode and decreased its total number of gates by replacing 4 X-switching gates with 4 Y-switching gates (see Fig. 7). In other words, their construction reduces only the number of XOR gates (and that of AND gates remain the same as [31]) and thus the improvement may not be appreciated by applications such as MPC and PFE with UC, where XOR gates can be evaluated for free [21]. Further, we can use the same idea from [23] to save some XOR gates. For example, based on our supernode we change an X-switching gate to Y-switching gate (the black node in Fig. 8), and the size of universal circuit now becomes $17.75n \log n + O(n)$, which is better than [23].

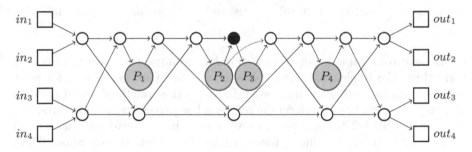

Fig. 8. Our 4-way supernode can be improved (in the sense of circuit size) by replacing an X-switching gate with a Y-Switching gate at the black node.

At last, our 4-way UCs are also shallower than the counterparts in literature [23,31]. The depth of Valiant's $\mathsf{SN}(4)$ is 14 but ours is 13. From Eqs. 7 and 9, we know that the depth of the EUG (resp. UC) based on our 4-way supernode is $3.5n$ (resp. $10.5n$), which is better than (and improves by 6.67%) Valiant's $3.75n$

(resp. $11.25n$). However, if one only cares about depth, then he would just use 3-way supernode of depth 7 (see Fig. 6) to get a UC of depth $8n$. Otherwise said, the depth improvement on 4-way UC is considered as a by-product (instead of a main advantage) of our UC construction.

3.5   Implementation and Performance Evaluation

As we mentioned before, the universal circuits based on our 4-way supernode have smaller circuit size than other constructions especially for large n (when emulating large-size circuits). We implement our 4-way construction [33] and compare it with the implementations of Valiant's 2-way [19], 4-way and their hybrid [17]. Table 3 evaluates the performances based on circuits of basic functions suitable for MPC and FHE, provided by Tillich and Smart [30]. In particular, Table 3 compares the number of AND gates in our universal circuits with other works[8], where our work is tabulated in the last column of Table 3 and the statistics of other works are picked from [17, Table 5].

Table 3. A comparison (in terms of the number of AND gates) of the (Kiss et al.'s 2-way, Günther et al.'s 4-way and hybrid, and our 4-way) UC implementations to simulate sample circuits from [30].

Circuit	$n = g + s$	2-way UC [19]	4-way UC [17]	Hybrid UC [17]	Our 4-way UC
Credit Checking	82	$1.50 \cdot 10^3$	$1.51 \cdot 10^3$	$1.49 \cdot 10^3$	$1.50 \cdot 10^3$
Mobile Code	160	$3.65 \cdot 10^3$	$3.88 \cdot 10^3$	$3.61 \cdot 10^3$	$3.82 \cdot 10^3$
ADD-32	342	$9.58 \cdot 10^3$	$9.55 \cdot 10^3$	$9.44 \cdot 10^3$	$9.30 \cdot 10^3$
MULT-32X32	12202	$6.54 \cdot 10^5$	$6.50 \cdot 10^5$	$6.35 \cdot 10^5$	$6.24 \cdot 10^5$
AES-exp	38518	$2.39 \cdot 10^6$	$2.38 \cdot 10^6$	$2.31 \cdot 10^6$	$2.27 \cdot 10^6$
DES-exp	32207	$1.98 \cdot 10^6$	$1.94 \cdot 10^6$	$1.90 \cdot 10^6$	$1.87 \cdot 10^6$
SHA-256	201206	$1.49 \cdot 10^7$	$1.46 \cdot 10^7$	$1.44 \cdot 10^7$	$1.39 \cdot 10^7$

As seen from Table 3, our construction has no advantage over (and is even worse than) the implementations of Kiss et al.s and Günther et al.'s for small circuits (n up to up to a few hundreds). But with the growth of circuit size, our construction starts to outperform the rest by a few percentage points. Curiously, in the case of SHA-256, the number of AND gates in our 4-way universal circuit is about $1.39 \cdot 10^7$ and Valiant' 4-way is $1.46 \cdot 10^7$. Their ratio is about 0.952, which is very close to $18/19$ and therefore confirms our analysis that the constant factor (in the of number of AND gates, as well as the size of the EUG) has been improved from 4.75 to 4.5. Even taking into consideration the optimization (e.g., using the hybrid of 2-way and 4-way) [17], our construction still has its advantage [2].

---

[8] Recall that the number of AND gates of Lipmaa et al.'s circuits (Fig. 7) remains the same with Valiant's 4-way construction since it saves only XOR gates, so the comparison does not include the Lipmaa et al.'s work.

4 A Lower Bound on Circuit Size in Valiant's Framework

Our search algorithm is intended for arbitrary k-way supernodes, but the time complexity is too large to be practical for $k \geq 5$. In this section, we aim to find a lower bound (for all k's) on the size of Valiant's EUG (and UC), which is in turn based on that of the supernode.

4.1 A Generic Lower Bound on Circuit Size

Valiant showed a generic bound $\Omega(n \log n)$ to argue the asymptotic optimality of his construction [31], where constant behind Ω could be extracted from Wegener's book [32, Theorem 8.1] by carefully checking its (somewhat nested) proof. We mention that this could be seen directly from a counting argument which we informally sketch below (and stress that it is not a proof and refer to [32] for formal details). That is, consider an arbitrary $C_{s,t}^g$ with inputs and gates topologically sorted (inputs followed by gates), i.e., $in_1, \cdots, in_n, g_{s+1}, \cdots, g_{n=s+g}$, and assume that they are c different symmetric gates (e.g., XOR and AND) of fan-in 2. Then, for each g_i $(i > s)$ there are $\binom{i-1}{2}$ choices of inputs and therefore the logarithm of the cardinality:

$$\log |C_{s,t}^g| \geq \log \left(\frac{(n!)^2 \cdot (\frac{c}{2})^{n-s}}{n!} \right) = n \log n - O(n),$$

where the $n!$ in the denominator accounts for that the topological sorting of inputs and gates are not unique (but up to the permutation of the nodes). Finally, the input length of the universal circuit is lower bounded by $\log |C_{s,t}^g|$ and so is the size of UC. Apparently, there are some loose steps, such as the order of gates cannot be arbitrarily permuted but this does not affect the lower bound by a factor of more than 2. A major lossy step is that we only require the size of the UC (of fan-in 2) to be at least the same as that of the input (in order for every input to contribute to the output the UC must be a connected DAG). In fact, a UC would need much more gates than its inputs to accomplish the simulation, and therefore additional knowledge about a specific UC framework could be helpful to improve this generic bound.

There remains a substantial gap between the constant factor in the generic (not specific to Valiant's UC framework) lower bound (i.e., 1) and that of known constructions (19 for Valiant's UC [31] and reduced to 18 in this work). Further, the generic bound sheds no light on the lower bound on the size of Valiant's EUG. Motivated by that most existing UCs are constructed under Valiant's framework, we aim to find a better (much lifted) lower bound on the size of EUG (and UC) in Valiant's framework.

4.2 Size of k-way Supernode

Recall that sizes of EUG and UC can both be based on that of the supernode (see Eqs. 4 and 6 reproduced below):

$$|\mathsf{EUG}_2(n)| = \frac{2|\mathsf{SN}(k)|}{k \log k} n \log n - O(n),$$

$$|\mathsf{UC}^g_{s,t}| = \frac{8|\mathsf{SN}(k)|}{k \log k} n \log n - O(n),$$

where the smaller term $O(n)$ is often omitted. Thus, our task is to lower bound $\frac{2|\mathsf{SN}(k)|}{k \log k}$ by some constant. Recall that F_k denotes the number of all the k-way pole-complete graphs (Definition 4). We use the following lemma to reduce our task to the approximation of F_k.

Lemma 5. $|\mathsf{SN}(k)| \geq \lceil \log(F_k) + k \rceil$.

Proof. Every pole-complete graph G can be configured (by setting the control bits) to be edge-embedded into $\mathsf{SN}(k)$, and the common nodes should be switching gates. Therefore, for an $\mathsf{SN}(k)$ we need set the control bits of its $|\mathsf{SN}(k)| - k$ common nodes to cater for all pole-complete graphs (amount to F_k), i.e., $2^{|\mathsf{SN}(k)|-k} \geq F_k$, where $|\mathsf{SN}(k)|$ is an integer. This completes the proof.

$$|\mathsf{EUG}_2(n)| = \frac{2|\mathsf{SN}(k)|}{k \log k} n \log n - O(n) \geq \frac{2\lceil\log(F_k)+k\rceil}{k \log k} n \log n - O(n)$$

Our next job is to lower bound $g(k) \overset{\text{def}}{=} \frac{2\lceil\log(F_k)+k\rceil}{k \log k}$ as a function of $k \in N^+$.

4.3   A Guess for the Constant Factor

In order to lower bound $g(k)$, it would be ideal to give an approximation of F_k and then take the minimum over all k's. However, a general closed-form expression for F_k seems difficult. We further define $A_{i,k}$ in Definition 5 and give the relation between F_k and $A_{i,k}$ in Lemma 6. We also provide a recursion formula for $A_{i,k}$ in Lemma 7, which facilitates the computation of $A_{i,k}$ (by dynamic programming) for small values of i and k. With the above, we are able to compute $g(k)$ for k up to a few thousand (see Table 4 for values when $k < 100$). Based on the values computed, we have the guess that $g(k) > 3.644$, where $g(k)$ is monotonically decreasing for $k \leq 69$ and monotonically increasing for $k \geq 69$ with minimum $g(k) \approx 3.6442$ achieved at $k = 69$. The former (monotonic decreasing) statement is verified by computing all $g(k)$ for all $k \leq 69$ and a proof of the latter (monotonic increasing) is deferred to the next subsection.

Definition 5. *Let $A_{i,k}$ denote the number of ways to spread k different balls into i $(i \leq k)$ identical boxes with the condition that no boxes are empty.*

Lemma 6. $F_k = \sum_{i=1}^{k} \left(\frac{k!}{(k-i)!}\right)^2 A_{i,k}$.

Proof. If $G = (V, E) \in \mathsf{DAG}_1(3k)$ is a k-way pole-complete graph, by Definition 4, we know that G can be regarded as a set of paths. It remains to sum up the numbers of pole-complete graphs for $1 \leq i \leq k$ paths: the number of ways to "put" k poles into i paths is $A_{i,k}$ by Definition 5, and there are $\frac{k!}{(k-i)!}$ ways to link i start-nodes (resp., end-nodes) to k inputs (resp., outputs) for these paths. Thus, $\left(\frac{k!}{(k-i)!}\right)^2 A_{i,k}$ different pole-complete graphs for each value of i and we sum up (for $i = 1$ to $i = k$) to get the final result.

Lemma 7. *1.* $A_{1,k} = 1, \forall k \in \mathbb{N}^+$;

2. $A_{i,k} = \sum_{j=0}^{k-i} \binom{k-1}{j} A_{i-1,k-j-1}.$

Proof. The first statement is trivial and we just need to prove the second one. Recall that in Definition 5 balls are all distinct while boxes are identical. We assume WLOG that ball #1 is in box #1, and let j be the number of other balls (in addition to ball #1) in box #1, where $j \le k - i$ is required to make sure that no boxes are empty. After choosing these j balls ($\binom{k-1}{j}$ different choices), it remains to put the rest $k - j - 1$ balls into the remaining $i - 1$ boxes, which can be done in $A_{i-1,k-j-1}$ different ways by definition.

We compute the values of $g(k)$ and other functions of k for k up to a few thousand, and list only partial results (up to $k = 99$) in Table 4 due to lack of space, from which we guess $g(k) > 3.644$ (recall that $g(69)$ is actually greater than 3.644). Note that it is tight at $k = 2$ ($g(2) = 5$) but not tight at $k = 4$ as $g(4) = 4.25$ but the constant factor of our size optimal UC is 4.5.

Table 4. The values of $\lceil \log(F_k) + k \rceil$ and $g(k)$ for $k < 100$.

k	2	3	4	5	...	68	69	70	...	98	99
$\lceil \log(F_k) + k \rceil$	5	11	17	23	...	755	768	782	...	1182	1197
$g(k) = \frac{2\lceil \log(F_k)+k \rceil}{k \log k}$	5	4.63	4.25	3.96	...	3.6478	3.6442	3.6453	...	3.6468	3.6477

4.4   The Lower Bound

We proceed to the proof of $g(k) = \frac{2\lceil \log(F_k)+k \rceil}{k \log k} > 3.644$ for $k \ge 69$. We give its proof in Lemma 8 but only for $k \ge 1478$, and gap (values of $g(k)$ for $70 \le k \le 1477$) is verified by computer. Note that there is nothing special with 1478, which is attributed to the loss of tightness by some inequality applied in its proof (such that 3.644 can only be obtained when $k = 1478$ in the right-hand of the inequality).

Lemma 8. $g(k) = \frac{2\lceil \log(F_k)+k \rceil}{k \log k} > 3.644$ *for all* $k \ge 1478$.

Proof. From Lemma 6, we have

$$F_k = \sum_{i=1}^{k} \left(\frac{k!}{(k-i)!}\right)^2 A_{i,k} \ge \sum_{i=k-1}^{k} \left(\frac{k!}{(k-i)!}\right)^2 A_{i,k} = (A_{k-1,k} + A_{k,k})(k!)^2,$$

and $A_{k,k} = 1, A_{k-1,k} = \binom{k}{2} = \frac{(k-1)k}{2}$ (Definition 5). Thus, $F_k \ge (\frac{(k-1)k}{2}+1)(k!)^2$. It follows from Stirling's formula $k! \ge \sqrt{2\pi k}(\frac{k}{e})^k$ that

$$F_k \ge (2\pi k)\left(\frac{(k-1)k}{2} + 1\right)\left(\frac{k}{e}\right)^{2k},$$

and therefore

$$g(k) \geq \frac{2\log(F_k) + k}{k \log k} \geq \frac{2\log(\pi k((k-1)k + 2)(\frac{k}{e})^{2k}) + k}{k \log k}$$

$$= 4 - \frac{(4\log e - 1)k - \log(\pi k((k-1)k + 2))}{k \log k} \overset{\text{def}}{=} h(k),$$

where by taking the derivative we know that $h(k)$ in the right-hand is monotonically increasing for $k \geq 2$, as also visualized in Fig. 9, and the conclusion follows by finding the threshold T such that $h(k) \geq h(T) \approx 3.644$ for all $k \geq T$. By enumeration we find out $T = 1478$. Recall that values of $g(k)$ for $70 \leq k \leq 1477$ have been verified by computer.

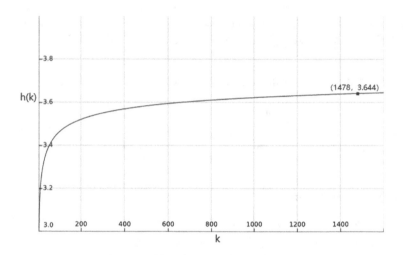

Fig. 9. The graph of $h(k)$ as a function of k.

Combining Eq. 4, Lemmas 5 and 8, we have the following theorem:

Theorem 3. *We have the following lower bound on the size of* $\mathsf{EUG}_2(n)$:

$$|\mathsf{EUG}_2(n)| > 3.644n \log n,$$

for all sufficiently large n.

5   Concluding Remarks

We revisit Valiant's graph theoretic approach to the construction of universal circuits, and show that its supernode can be improved in both size and depth, which yields more efficient universal circuits (with a more than 5% improvement). We give a lower bound on the size of UC to complement our explicit constructions, which reduces the gap between theory and practice of UCs.

Acknowledgments. Yu Yu was supported by the National Natural Science Foundation of China (Grant Nos. 61872236 and 61572192) and the National Cryptography Development Fund (Grant number MMJJ20170209). Jiang Zhang is supported by the National Key Research and Development Program of China (Grant No. 2017YFB0802005, 2018YFB0804105), the National Natural Science Foundation of China (Grant Nos. 6160204661932019), and the Young Elite Scientists Sponsorship Program by CAST (2016QNRC001). Yu Yu was also funded in part by the Anhui Initiative in Quantum Information Technologies (Grant number AHY150100). Shuoyao Zhao is funded by the privacy-preserving computation project from PlatON Network. We thank the anonymous reviewers of ASIACRYPT 2019 for their helpful comments.

A   Proofs Omitted in the Main Body

A.1   Proof of Theorem 1

To prove the graph in Fig. 4 is an $\mathsf{EUG}_1(n)$, we need to prove that any $\mathsf{DAG}_1(n) = (V, E)$ can be edge-embedded into it. At first, we sort the nodes of a given $\mathsf{DAG}_1(n)$ in their topological order: $V_1, V_2, \ldots, V_n$. And the edge-embed mapping ϱ can be defined as: $\varrho(V_i)$ is the i-th pole of the supernodes from top to bottom, or formally, the $(i \bmod k)$-th pole of $\mathsf{SN}(k)_{\lceil \frac{i}{k} \rceil}$. For each node V_i in the $\mathsf{DAG}_1(n)$, it may have a precursor-node (denote by V_i^{pre}) and a successor-node (denote by V_i^{suc}). Then we assign the $[V_i]_{in}$-th input and the $[V_i]_{out}$-th output of $\mathsf{SN}(k)_{\lceil \frac{i}{k} \rceil}$ $(in_{[V_i]_{in}}^{\lceil \frac{i}{k} \rceil}$ and $out_{[V_i]_{out}}^{\lceil \frac{i}{k} \rceil})$ to V_i to make sure that $[V_i]_{in} = [V_i^{pre}]_{out}, [V_i]_{out} = [V_i^{suc}]_{in}$ and no inputs and outputs of supernodes are reused. The method for assignment can be find in [17]. At last, for every edge $(V_i, V_j) \in E$ ($i < j$ due to the topological sorting), we give an edge-disjoint path from $\varrho(V_i)$ to $\varrho(V_j)$ as follow. Due to $V_i^{suc} = V_j$ and $V_j^{pre} = V_i$, we know that $[V_i]_{out} = [V_j]_{in}$, which means $out_{[V_i]_{out}}^{\lceil \frac{i}{k} \rceil}$ and $in_{[V_j]_{in}}^{\lceil \frac{j}{k} \rceil}$ are both in the edge-universal graph: $\mathsf{EUG}_1(\lceil \frac{n}{k} \rceil - 1)_{[V_i]_{out}}$, so there is an edge-disjoint path from $out_{[V_i]_{out}}^{\lceil \frac{i}{k} \rceil}$ to $in_{[V_j]_{in}}^{\lceil \frac{j}{k} \rceil}$. As $\mathsf{SN}(k)_{\lceil \frac{i}{k} \rceil}$ is a supernode, there must be a edge-disjoint path from $\varrho(V_i)$ to $out_{[V_i]_{out}}^{\lceil \frac{i}{k} \rceil}$. Similarly, the edge-disjoint path from $in_{[V_j]_{in}}^{\lceil \frac{j}{k} \rceil}$ to $\varrho(V_i)$ can also be found. We connect these three paths to complete edge-embedding.

References

1. Afshar, A., Mohassel, P., Pinkas, B., Riva, B.: Non-interactive secure computation based on cut-and-choose. In: Nguyen, P.Q., Oswald, E. (eds.) EUROCRYPT 2014. LNCS, vol. 8441, pp. 387–404. Springer, Heidelberg (2014). https://doi.org/10.1007/978-3-642-55220-5_22
2. Alhassan, M.Y., Günther, D., Kiss, Á., Schneider, T.: Efficient and scalable universal circuits. Cryptology ePrint Archive, Report 2019/348 (2019). https://eprint.iacr.org/2019/348
3. Araki, T., et al.: Optimized honest-majority MPC for malicious adversaries - breaking the 1 billion-gate per second barrier. In: 2017 IEEE Symposium on Security and Privacy (SP 2017), pp. 843–862 (2017)

4. Attrapadung, N.: Fully secure and succinct attribute based encryption for circuits from multi-linear maps. Cryptology ePrint Archive, Report 2014/772 (2014). https://eprint.iacr.org/2014/772

5. Bera, D., Fenner, S.A., Green, F., Homer, S.: Efficient universal quantum circuits. Quantum Inf. Comput. **10**(1&2), 16–27 (2010). http://www.rintonpress.com/xxqic10/qic-10-12/0016-0027.pdf

6. Bicer, O., Bingol, M.A., Kiraz, M.S., Levi, A.: Towards practical PFE: an efficient 2-party private function evaluation protocol based on half gates. Cryptology ePrint Archive, Report 2017/415 (2017). https://eprint.iacr.org/2017/415

7. Cook, S.A., Hoover, H.J.: A depth-universal circuit. SIAM J. Comput. **14**(4), 833–839 (1985)

8. Fiore, D., Gennaro, R., Pastro, V.: Efficiently verifiable computation on encrypted data. In: Proceedings of the 2014 ACM SIGSAC Conference on Computer and Communications Security (CCS 2014), pp. 844–855 (2014)

9. Fisch, B.A., et al.: Malicious-client security in blind seer: a scalable private DBMS. In: 2015 IEEE Symposium on Security and Privacy (SP 2015), pp. 395–410 (2015)

10. Galil, Z., Paul, W.J.: An efficient general purpose parallel computer. In: Proceedings of the 13th Annual ACM Symposium on Theory of Computing (STOC 1981), pp. 247–262 (1981)

11. Garg, S., Gentry, C., Halevi, S., Raykova, M., Sahai, A., Waters, B.: Candidate indistinguishability obfuscation and functional encryption for all circuits. SIAM J. Comput. **45**(3), 882–929 (2016)

12. Garg, S., Gentry, C., Halevi, S., Sahai, A., Waters, B.: Attribute-based encryption for circuits from multilinear maps. In: Canetti, R., Garay, J.A. (eds.) CRYPTO 2013. LNCS, vol. 8043, pp. 479–499. Springer, Heidelberg (2013). https://doi.org/10.1007/978-3-642-40084-1_27

13. Garg, S., Gentry, C., Halevi, S., Zhandry, M.: Fully secure attribute based encryption from multilinear maps. IACR Cryptology ePrint Archive 2014, 622 (2014). http://eprint.iacr.org/2014/622

14. Gennaro, R., Gentry, C., Parno, B., Raykova, M.: Quadratic span programs and succinct NIZKs without PCPs. In: Johansson, T., Nguyen, P.Q. (eds.) EUROCRYPT 2013. LNCS, vol. 7881, pp. 626–645. Springer, Heidelberg (2013). https://doi.org/10.1007/978-3-642-38348-9_37

15. Gentry, C., Halevi, S., Vaikuntanathan, V.: i-hop homomorphic encryption and rerandomizable yao circuits. In: Rabin, T. (ed.) CRYPTO 2010. LNCS, vol. 6223, pp. 155–172. Springer, Heidelberg (2010). https://doi.org/10.1007/978-3-642-14623-7_9

16. Gorbunov, S., Vaikuntanathan, V., Wee, H.: Attribute-based encryption for circuits. J. ACM **62**(6), 45:1–45:33 (2015)

17. Günther, D., Kiss, Á., Schneider, T.: More efficient universal circuit constructions. In: Takagi, T., Peyrin, T. (eds.) ASIACRYPT 2017. LNCS, vol. 10625, pp. 443–470. Springer, Cham (2017). https://doi.org/10.1007/978-3-319-70697-9_16

18. Huang, Y., Katz, J., Kolesnikov, V., Kumaresan, R., Malozemoff, A.J.: Amortizing garbled circuits. In: Garay, J.A., Gennaro, R. (eds.) CRYPTO 2014. LNCS, vol. 8617, pp. 458–475. Springer, Heidelberg (2014). https://doi.org/10.1007/978-3-662-44381-1_26

19. Kiss, Á., Schneider, T.: Valiant's universal circuit is practical. In: Fischlin, M., Coron, J.-S. (eds.) EUROCRYPT 2016. LNCS, vol. 9665, pp. 699–728. Springer, Heidelberg (2016). https://doi.org/10.1007/978-3-662-49890-3_27

20. Kolesnikov, V., Schneider, T.: Improved garbled circuit: free XOR gates and applications. In: Aceto, L., Damgård, I., Goldberg, L.A., Halldórsson, M.M., Ingólfsdóttir, A., Walukiewicz, I. (eds.) ICALP 2008. LNCS, vol. 5126, pp. 486–498. Springer, Heidelberg (2008). https://doi.org/10.1007/978-3-540-70583-3_40
21. Kolesnikov, V., Schneider, T.: A practical universal circuit construction and secure evaluation of private functions. In: Tsudik, G. (ed.) FC 2008. LNCS, vol. 5143, pp. 83–97. Springer, Heidelberg (2008). https://doi.org/10.1007/978-3-540-85230-8_7
22. Lindell, Y., Riva, B.: Blazing fast 2PC in the offline/online setting with security for malicious adversaries. In: Proceedings of the 22nd ACM SIGSAC Conference on Computer and Communications Security (CCS 2015), pp. 579–590 (2015)
23. Lipmaa, H., Mohassel, P., Sadeghian, S.: Valiant's universal circuit: Improvements, implementation, and applications. Cryptology ePrint Archive, Report 2016/017 (2016). https://eprint.iacr.org/2016/017
24. Malkhi, D., Nisan, N., Pinkas, B., Sella, Y.: Fairplay - secure two-party computation system. In: Proceedings of the 13th USENIX Security Symposium, pp. 287–302 (2004)
25. Meyer auf der Heide, F.: Efficiency of universal parallel computers. In: Theoretical Computer Science, pp. 221–241 (1983)
26. Mohassel, P., Sadeghian, S.: How to hide circuits in MPC an efficient framework for private function evaluation. In: Johansson, T., Nguyen, P.Q. (eds.) EUROCRYPT 2013. LNCS, vol. 7881, pp. 557–574. Springer, Heidelberg (2013). https://doi.org/10.1007/978-3-642-38348-9_33
27. Mohassel, P., Sadeghian, S., Smart, N.P.: Actively secure private function evaluation. In: Sarkar, P., Iwata, T. (eds.) ASIACRYPT 2014. LNCS, vol. 8874, pp. 486–505. Springer, Heidelberg (2014). https://doi.org/10.1007/978-3-662-45608-8_26
28. Pappas, V., et al.: Blind seer: a scalable private DBMS. In: 2014 IEEE Symposium on Security and Privacy (SP 2014), pp. 359–374 (2014)
29. Sadeghian, S.S.: New Techniques for Private Function Evaluation. Ph.D. thesis, University of Calgary (2015)
30. Tillich, S., Smart, N.: Circuits of basic functions suitable for MPC and FHE (2015). https://homes.esat.kuleuven.be/%7Ensmart/MPC/
31. Valiant, L.G.: Universal circuits (preliminary report). In: Proceedings of the 8th Annual ACM Symposium on Theory of Computing (STOC 1976), pp. 196–203 (1976)
32. Wegener, I.: The complexity of boolean functions. ECCC books, lectures and surveys (1987). https://bit.ly/2I7MGJi
33. Zhao, S.: The c++ source code of our 4-way uc implementation (2018). https://github.com/Anonymous8012/UC
34. Zhao, S.: A proof for that the graph in Figure 1 is a 4-way supernode. shared in a double-blind way (registration/log-in not required for upload and download) (2018). https://www.filedropper.com/sn-proof
35. Zhu, R., Cassel, D., Sabry, A., Huang, Y.: nanoPI: extreme-scale actively-secure multi-party computation. In: Proceedings of the 2018 ACM SIGSAC Conference on Computer and Communications Security (CCS 2018), pp. 862–879 (2018)
36. Zimmerman, J.: How to obfuscate programs directly. In: Oswald, E., Fischlin, M. (eds.) EUROCRYPT 2015, Part II. LNCS, vol. 9057, pp. 439–467. Springer, Heidelberg (2015). https://doi.org/10.1007/978-3-662-46803-6_15

The Broadcast Message Complexity of Secure Multiparty Computation

Sanjam Garg[1(✉)], Aarushi Goel[2], and Abhishek Jain[2]

[1] University of California, Berkeley, USA
`sanjamg@berkeley.edu`
[2] Johns Hopkins University, Baltimore, USA
{`aarushig,abhishek`}`@cs.jhu.edu`

Abstract. We study the *broadcast message complexity* of secure multiparty computation (MPC), namely, the total number of messages that are required for securely computing any functionality in the broadcast model of communication.

MPC protocols are traditionally designed in the simultaneous broadcast model, where each round consists of *every* party broadcasting a message to the other parties. We show that this method of communication is sub-optimal; specifically, by eliminating simultaneity, it is, in fact, possible to reduce the broadcast message complexity of MPC.

More specifically, we establish tight lower and upper bounds on the broadcast message complexity of n-party MPC for every $t < n$ corruption threshold, both in the plain model as well as common setup models. For example, our results show that the optimal broadcast message complexity of semi-honest MPC can be much lower than $2n$, but necessarily requires at least three rounds of communication. We also extend our results to the malicious setting in setup models.

1 Introduction

The ability to securely compute on private datasets of individuals has wide applications of tremendous benefits to society. Secure multiparty computation (MPC) [2,8,19,25] provides a solution to the problem of computing on private data by allowing a group of mutually distrusting parties to jointly evaluate any function over their private inputs in a manner that reveals nothing beyond the output of the function.

Broadcast Message Complexity. Traditionally, the most popular communication model for the design of MPC protocols is the *broadcast* model, where parties communicate with each other by sending messages over an authenticated broadcast channel. Indeed, starting from [19], most computationally secure protocols in the literature are designed in the broadcast model.

Viewing a broadcast channel as a resource, in this work, we initiate the study of the *broadcast message complexity* of MPC, namely, the number of messages that are required for securely computing any functionality in the broadcast model. Specifically, we ask the following basic question:

ⓒ International Association for Cryptologic Research 2019
S. D. Galbraith and S. Moriai (Eds.): ASIACRYPT 2019, LNCS 11921, pp. 426–455, 2019.
https://doi.org/10.1007/978-3-030-34578-5_16

What is the broadcast message complexity of n-party MPC w.r.t. $t < n$
corruptions (for every t)?

At first, it may seem that the above question can be easily resolved by appealing to the known bounds on the round complexity of MPC. For example, in the case of semi-honest corruptions (for any $t \geqslant 1$), *two* rounds are known to be necessary [21]. Then, it may seem that the broadcast message complexity in this case must be at least $2n$ since each of the n parties must presumably send a message in each of the two rounds. In this work, we show that the above intuition is *incorrect*.

Simultaneity is Wasteful. MPC protocols are traditionally designed in the simultaneous broadcast model, where in each round, *every* party sends a message. We show that this model is wasteful, and that by eliminating simultaneity, it is possible to reduce the number of required messages.

Specifically, we consider the general setting where in each round, any subset of parties may send a message. In this setting, we show that the broadcast message complexity of MPC can be much lower than in the simultaneous broadcast model.

1.1 Our Results

We study the broadcast message complexity of MPC in the plain model, as well as common setup models, including the public-key infrastructure (PKI) model and the common reference string (CRS) model. We provide a tight characterization of broadcast message complexity as well as the number of rounds necessary for achieving optimal number of broadcasts. In particular, our results show that two rounds are insufficient for achieving optimal broadcasts; instead, at least three rounds are necessary. We elaborate on our results below.

I. Broadcast Message Complexity. We first investigate the broadcast message complexity of semi-honest MPC in the plain model. We provide a tight characterization that varies with the number of corrupted parties t and the number of output parties $|\mathcal{O}|$, where $\mathcal{O}$ denotes the set of parties who can learn the output.

Theorem 1 (Informal). *For any $t < n - 1$ semi-honest, static corruptions and $|\mathcal{O}| > 1$ (resp., $|\mathcal{O}| = 1|$) output parties, $n + t + 1$ (resp., $n + t$) broadcasts are necessary and sufficient for MPC in the plain model. For $t = n - 1$ corruptions, the broadcast message complexity is $n + t$ (resp., $n + t - 1$) when $|\mathcal{O}| > 1$ (resp., $|\mathcal{O}| = 1|$).*

A few remarks about the above theorem are in order: (1) Our lower bound also holds in the CRS model. (2) Our positive result is based on any two-round semi-honest oblivious transfer (OT), which is the *optimal* assumption for $t \geqslant n/2$. In the CRS model, it can be extended to achieve UC security against malicious corruptions based on two-round malicious-secure OT.

We next show that the broadcast message complexity of MPC is lower in the PKI model, where the parties first post their respective public keys on a bulletin board.

Theorem 2 (Informal). *For any $t \leqslant n - 1$ semi-honest, static corruptions and $|\mathcal{O}| > n - t$ (resp., $|\mathcal{O}| \leqslant n - t$) output parties, $n + t$ (resp., $n + t - 1$) broadcasts are necessary and sufficient for MPC in the bare PKI model.*

We, in fact, provide two different positive results in this model:

- Our first construction works in the honest majority setting (i.e., $t < n/2$) and achieves security even against *malicious* adversaries. It does not require any additional assumptions beyond public-key encryption, and is therefore *optimal* in that sense. Interestingly, we achieve this result by drawing a connection to the security notion of guaranteed output delivery.
- Our second construction works for any $t < n$ corruptions and achieves security against semi-honest adversaries based on any two-round semi-honest OT. In the CRS model, this construction can be extended using standard techniques to achieve UC security against malicious adversaries.

II. Round Complexity. While two rounds are known to be necessary and sufficient for semi-honest MPC, we show that they are insufficient for achieving optimal broadcast message complexity. In particular, we show that *three* rounds are necessary and sufficient. This result holds both in the plain model as well as the PKI and CRS models.

Theorem 3. *Three rounds are necessary and sufficient for semi-honest MPC with optimal broadcast message complexity.*

We, in fact, prove two strengthenings of the above theorem:

- We show that three rounds are also sufficient for achieving security against malicious adversaries, either in the PKI model for $t < n/2$ corruptions or in the CRS model for $t < n$ corruptions.
- We show that in the plain model, any three round protocol that achieves optimal broadcast message complexity must necessarily utilize a *unique communication pattern*, where a communication pattern specifies which parties speak in which round(s). We also prove an analogous result in the PKI model.

The table below provides a summary of our lower bounds for broadcast message complexity and round complexity.

Model	Corruptions	Rounds	Output parties	Broadcasts
Plain	$1 \leqslant t < n - 1$	3	$\|\mathcal{O}\| > 1$	$n + t + 1$
			$\|\mathcal{O}\| = 1$	$n + t$
Plain	$t = n - 1$	3	$\|\mathcal{O}\| > 1$	$2n - 1$
			$\|\mathcal{O}\| = 1$	$2n - 2$
PKI	$1 \leqslant t \leqslant n - 1$	3	$\|\mathcal{O}\| > n - t$	$n + t$
			$\|\mathcal{O}\| \leqslant n - t$	$n + t - 1$

III. Application to P2P Model. While we focus on broadcast message complexity in this work, our positive results can also be used to obtain MPC protocols in the point-to-point (P2P) communication model with *optimal* P2P message complexity for *any* corruption threshold.

The P2P message complexity of (computationally secure) MPC was recently studied by Ishai et al. [22] who established lower and upper bounds for $t = n - 1$. Subsequently, [23] extended their lower bound to any $t < n$, but left open the problem of obtaining a matching upper bound for general t. We show that our construction from Theorem 2 for general $t < n$ can be used to resolve this open problem.

Theorem 4 (Informal). *Assuming the existence of two-round semi-honest OT, for any $t < n$ semi-honest, static corruptions and $|\mathcal{O}|$ output parties, $(n+t+|\mathcal{O}|-2)$ messages are sufficient for MPC in the P2P communication model.*

1.2 Technical Overview

Starting Ideas. Recall that two rounds are known to be necessary for MPC, even for achieving security against semi-honest adversaries [21]. Further, in all known two-round MPC protocols in the broadcast model [3,5,6,14,16–18,24], each party broadcasts a message in each round, resulting in a total of $2n$ messages.

At first, it may seem that this is inherent. Indeed, consider the scenario where one of the n parties, say P_i, does not send any message in the first round, and instead only sends a message in the second round. Can we construct a secure protocol in the plain model with this communication pattern? The answer is no, and to see this, recall that the security guarantee of semi-honest MPC stipulates that an adversary can only learn a *single* function output corresponding to a fixed set of inputs. To achieve this guarantee, a protocol transcript must somehow "fix" an input of each party. In the above scenario, since P_i only sends a message in the second round, its input cannot be fixed.[1] Therefore, an adversarial P_i can launch the following *residual function attack*: it first completes an execution of the protocol to obtain a transcript, and then replaces its message in the transcript with a freshly computed message w.r.t. a different input. It now computes its output function to learn a new output, w.r.t. the same set of inputs of the other parties, thereby violating MPC security.

The above still leaves open the possibility of designing a protocol where P_i only sends a message in the first round. In this case, P_i's input can indeed be fixed by the honest party messages sent in the second round. Unfortunately, it turns out that this is still not sufficient, even against the minimal corruption threshold of $t = 1$. The reason is that an adversary can simply "spoof" all the other parties P_j (where $j \neq i$). That is, after obtaining a protocol transcript, the adversary can simply replace the messages of all the other parties P_j with freshly computed messages w.r.t. different inputs, while keeping P_i's message intact. Now, the adversary is able to learn multiple outputs w.r.t. a fixed input of P_i, thereby violating MPC security.

---

[1] Recall that the messages sent by honest parties in any round are independent of each other.

Towards a Template. Our main insight is that *by increasing the round complexity, we can decrease the broadcast message complexity*. To explain the basic idea, let us consider a toy scenario with $n = 5$ and $t = 2$. Our goal here is to obtain a template that requires $n + t + 1 = 8$ messages, as per Theorem 1. Clearly, to achieve this broadcast message complexity, two parties must send only one message each. Now, consider the following communication pattern:

R1. In the first round, P_4 and P_5 send a message.
R2. In the second round, P_1, P_2 and P_3 send a message.
R3. In the third round, P_1, P_2 and P_3 send a message.

Since $t = 2$, at least one of P_1, P_2, P_3 must be honest. Let P_i be that party. Then, P_i's message in the third round must fix the inputs of *all* the other parties. Therefore, it would seem that this template should already work. Unfortunately, this is not the case as the spoofing attack we discussed earlier is also applicable here. Indeed, an adversary can simply spoof P_1, P_2, P_3 and launch a residual function attack on the inputs of P_4 or P_5 in a similar manner as above.

Upon closer inspection, we find that the reason for the spoofing attack in the above template is that while P_i can fix the input of all the parties, P_i's *input itself is not fixed by any other party*. Indeed, this is why the spoofing attack includes spoofing of P_i as well.

To address this issue, we modify the above template by exchanging rounds one and two. That is, we consider the following template:

R1. In the first round, P_1, P_2 and P_3 send a message.
R2. In the second round, P_4 and P_5 send a message.
R3. In the third round, P_1, P_2 and P_3 send a message.

In the technical sections, we show that the above template indeed works. The key point is that now, not only can P_i fix the inputs of all the other adversarial and honest parties, but crucially, the other honest parties, *who send messages in round two*, can also fix P_i's input (which must be used to compute its first round message). This raises several questions:

- Does the above idea generalize to any n and t?
- How can we prove a lower bound on the broadcast message complexity?
- Does the lower bound stay intact in the public-key model, or does it change?
- Are three rounds really necessary?
- Is the above communication pattern necessary, or can we also achieve security with other communication patterns?
- How can we construct protocols with optimal broadcast message complexity?

In the technical sections, we show that the above idea indeed generalizes to any n and t; the specific details vary depending upon the number of output parties and the number of corruptions, as well as whether we are working in the plain model or the public-key model.

We now proceed to address the remaining questions.

Lower Bounds on Broadcast Message Complexity. Our proof for lower bound on broadcast message complexity in Sect. 3 is simple and relies on establishing the minimum number of parties who must send *two* messages in the protocol.

We start by proving that in the plain model, for $t < n - 1$ and $|\mathcal{O}| > 1$ output parties, the number of parties that broadcast more than one message in the protocol must be strictly greater than the number of corrupted parties. Let us consider a toy example with $n = 5$ and $t = 2$, where all parties receive the output. Let us assume for contradiction that the number of parties that broadcast more than one message is equal to the number of corrupted parties. For example, suppose that P_1, P_2, P_3 broadcast a single message, while P_4 and P_5 broadcast more than one messages. Now, consider an adversary that corrupts both P_4 and P_5. Let P_1 be the first party to broadcast its message amongst P_1, P_2, P_3. Note that in this case, the message of P_1 does not depend on the messages (or inputs) of P_2 and P_3. The adversary can simply spoof P_2 and P_3 and launch a residual function attack on the inputs of P_1 as discussed before. Therefore, in order to prevent such attacks at least three parties must broadcast at least two messages each.

As we show in the technical section, the above idea generalizes to any n and $t < n - 1$ and any $|\mathcal{O}| > 1$ output parties. Now, in an n-party protocol, each party must broadcast at least one message for its input to be included in the computation. Thus, the total broadcast message complexity in this setting must be at least $2(t + 1) + 1(n - (t + 1)) = n + t + 1$. We use this result to establish lower bounds for $|\mathcal{O}| = 1$ output party when $t < n - 1$ parties are corrupted.

We prove our lower bound for $t = n - 1$ in the plain model and for any $t < n$ in the PKI model using a similar approach as above. However the optimal lower bound in this case is lower than in the plain model; intuitively, this is because in this case, spoofing attacks are not possible. Specifically, we establish that the number of parties that broadcast more than one messages in this case must be greater than or equal to the number of corrupted parties. This means that the total broadcast message complexity in this case must be at least $2(t) + 1(n - t) = n + t$.

Lower Bounds on Round Complexity. In Sect. 4, we prove that at least three rounds are necessary for achieving optimal broadcast message complexity. Our proof generalizes the intuition discussed earlier for the toy example:

- We first show that any party that broadcasts a single message must not do so in the last round of the protocol. Roughly, this is because in this case, there is no opportunity for the input of this party to be "fixed" by messages of the other parties. Indeed, an adversary can otherwise simply corrupt this party and launch a residual function attack on the inputs of all the other honest parties in the manner as discussed earlier in the toy example.
- Given the observation, we show that two round MPC with optimal message complexity is impossible. Roughly, this is because, in any such two round protocol, all the parties that send a single message must necessarily do so in the first round. However, in this case, the adversary can launch a residual function attack on the inputs of any one of the honest parties that broadcast their only message in the first round, as discussed earlier in the toy example.

Interestingly, this lower bound also holds in the public-key model, regardless of the number of corruptions.

In Sect. 4.3, we also prove that in the plain model, there is a *unique* communication pattern that must be used to achieve optimal broadcast message complexity. This communication pattern is a generalization of the one discussed above; roughly, we prove that the parties who send one message must speak in the second round, while the parties who send two messages must speak in the first and the third rounds! In the public-key model, we do not establish uniqueness of communication pattern; instead, we show that there is a specific class of communication patterns that must be used to achieve optimal broadcast message complexity.

Upper Bounds. To establish positive results on optimal broadcast message complexity, we provide multiple transformations.

Let us first focus on $t < n/2$ corruptions. In this setting, we establish our positive result in the PKI model by drawing a connection with the notion of *guaranteed output delivery*, which, roughly speaking, concerns with ensuring that the honest parties are able to compute the output even if the corrupted parties abort the computation prematurely. More Specifically,

- We show a general compiler from any two round MPC protocol with *"strong"* guaranteed output delivery (namely, where in the second round, for any $t < n/2$, only $t + 1$ honest parties are required to send a message in order for all the honest parties to compute output[2]) against fail-stop adversaries into a three round *semi-honest* protocol with optimal broadcast message complexity.
- Further, we show that if the underlying two round protocol additionally achieves security with abort against malicious adversaries, then our resulting three round protocol also achieves security against *malicious* adversaries security.

Instantiating our compiler with the recent protocol of Ananth et al. [1] (which satisfies both of the aforementioned properties) yields a malicious-secure MPC protocol with optimal broadcast message complexity based on public-key encryption. Finally, we remark that this transformation inherently fails in the plain model since two round MPC over broadcast channels with guaranteed output delivery is impossible in the plain model, even in the semi-honest setting [20].

Let us now consider the case where $t < n$. We show a general transformation from any two round MPC that achieves security against *dishonest majority* into a three round MPC with optimal broadcast message complexity. The transformation is simple and works by having a subset of parties (say S_1) send out encrypted secret shares of their private states to the other parties (say S_2), who can compute upon these states to generate messages on behalf of the parties in S_1. In order for this approach to work, it is crucial that at least one party in S_2 is honest, and indeed, this is why we require that the underlying two-round protocol achieves security against dishonest majority. This transformation works both in the plain model as well as the public-key model. Instantiating it with

---

[2] When $n = 2t + 1$, this is the same as guaranteed output delivery. However, for $n > 2t + 1$, this is a strengthening of guaranteed output delivery.

the two-round protocols of [3,18], we obtain a protocol with optimal broadcast message complexity based on OT.

Finally, we also show that our positive results in the PKI model can be used to obtain tight upper bounds on P2P message complexity (for any corruption threshold), resolving an open question from [22,23]. We note that if we use a naive transformation from a broadcast model protocol to a P2P model protocol (as discussed above), the resulting protocol would also require the public-key infrastructure used by the underlying protocol. To overcome this, we show alternative, direct transformations from our specific broadcast model protocols to obtain P2P model protocols with optimal P2P message complexity. We refer the reader to Sect. 7.2 for more details.

1.3 Related Work

To the best of our knowledge, no prior work has studied the broadcast message complexity of MPC.

P2P Message Complexity. The most closely related work to ours is the recent work of Ishai et al. [22] who study the message complexity of computationally-secure MPC in the P2P model (i.e., where the parties only rely on P2P channels). For $t = n - 1$ corruptions and $|\mathcal{O}|$ output parties, they show that $2n + |\mathcal{O}| - 3$ P2P messages are necessary and sufficient for semi-honest MPC, even in the correlated randomness setup model. Mittal [23] extended their lower bound to any $t < n$ corruptions and showed that at least $(n + t + |\mathcal{O}| - 2)$ P2P messages are necessary for $|\mathcal{O}|$ output parties. However, they left open the problem of obtaining a matching upper bound, which we resolve in this work.

We note that the lower bounds on P2P message complexity can be used to derive some lower bounds on broadcast message complexity. The basic idea is simple and works by transforming any broadcast model protocol Π into a P2P model protocol Π' executed over a "chain" communication pattern, where the parties are arranged as per their speaking order in Π.[3] At each step, each party computes its new message and sends it together with the aggregated transcript it received from the previous party to the next party on the chain. The last party on the chain computes the output. We give a formal description of this transformation in the full version our paper.

However, this approach has two important shortcomings. First, it does *not* give optimal lower bounds in the plain model. Second, it only works in extremal cases where the number of output parties $|\mathcal{O}|$ in Π are either $|\mathcal{O}| = 1$ or $|\mathcal{O}| = n$.[4] In particular, it is unclear how to obtain P2P message complexity $k - 1$ if the

---

[3] If multiple parties speak in the same round in Π, they can be arranged in any order.

[4] In the case of $|\mathcal{O}| = 1$, we simply add the output party as the last node on the chain. With this approach, we obtain a protocol with P2P message complexity k, starting from a protocol with broadcast message complexity k. For the case of $|\mathcal{O}| = n$, we can actually do better, and simply delete the last message (since the last node on the chain can compute it on its own), resulting in a protocol with P2P message complexity $k - 1$.

number of output parties is $1 < |\mathcal{O}| < n$. This is because, in this case, the underlying protocol Π in the broadcast model may not contain an output party in the last round.

To obtain a full picture with optimal lower bounds, our work instead provides a *direct* approach to proving lower bounds on broadcast message complexity. Previously, the P2P message complexity of MPC in the information-theoretic setting with a bounded fraction of corrupted parties was studied in [9,12,13], in different models.

Other Works. We also mention the works of [4,7,11,15] who consider MPC protocols that achieve sublinear communication complexity by assigning the computation to a small random subset of parties in the honest majority setting. They do not give any specific bounds on the P2P or broadcast message complexity of MPC.

2 Preliminaries

2.1 Secure Multi-party Computation

A secure multi-party computation protocol is a protocol executed by n parties $P_1, \cdots, P_n$ for a n-party functionality $\mathcal{F}$.

Communication Model. We consider two kinds of protocols: (1) ones that only rely upon an authenticated broadcast channel, (2) and ones that only rely upon private point-to-point channels. We discuss each case separately:

- *Broadcast model:* In almost all prior work in the broadcast model of communication, in each round of the protocol, *all* parties broadcast a message. We consider a generalization of this setting, where in any round, any subset of parties may broadcast a message. We define the broadcast message complexity as follows:

Definition 1 (Broadcast Message Complexity). *The broadcast message complexity of a protocol is the total number of broadcast messages sent by all the parties in the protocol. The broadcast message complexity of MPC for a functionality f is the minimum number of broadcast messages required for securely computing f.*

- *Point-to-point model:* While our focus is on the broadcast message complexity, we also consider protocols in the point-to-point (P2P) communication model (i.e., where the parties only use private point-to-point channels, and no broadcasts). We define the P2P message complexity as follows:

Definition 2 (P2P Message Complexity). *The P2P message complexity of a protocol is the total number of private messages sent by all the parties in the protocol. The P2P message complexity of MPC is the minimum number of P2P messages required for securely computing any functionality.*

Security. One of the primary goals in secure computation is to protect the honest parties against dishonest behavior from the corrupted parties. This is usually modeled using a central adversarial entity, that controls the set of corrupted parties and instructs them on how to operate. That is, the adversary obtains the views of the corrupted parties, consisting of their inputs, random tapes and incoming messages, and provides them with the messages that they are to send in the execution of the protocol. In our protocols we only consider static adversaries, meaning that the adversary selects the set of parties that it wants to corrupt at the start of the protocol. We discuss the following security models in this work:

- **Security against Semi-honest Adversaries:** A semi-honest adversary always follows the instructions of the protocol. This is an "honest but curious" adversarial model, where the adversary might try to learn extra information by analyzing the transcript of the protocol later.

Definition 3. *Let f be an n-party functionality. We say that a protocol Π t-securely computes $\mathcal{F}$ in the presence of a semi-honest, non-uniform PPT adversary $\mathcal{A}$ that corrupts a subset A of t parties, if there exists a PPT simulator algorithm $\mathcal{S}$ such that for every security parameter λ, and all input vectors $\mathbf{x} \in \{0,1\}^{\lambda \times n} = \{x_1, \ldots, x_n\}$, it holds that:*

$$\{\mathcal{S}(1^\lambda, \{x_i\}_{i \in \mathsf{A}}, f(\mathbf{x})), f(\mathbf{x})\} \approx_c \{\text{view}_{\mathcal{A}}^{\Pi}(1^\lambda, \mathbf{x}), \text{out}_{\mathcal{A}}^{\Pi}(1^\lambda, \mathbf{x})\}$$

- **Security Against Fail-Stop Adversaries:** A fail-stop adversary instructs the corrupted parties to follow the protocol as a semi-honest adversary, but it may also instruct a corrupted party to halt early (only sending some of its messages in a round). The decision to abort or not may depend on its view. Fail-stop adversaries may be rushing or non-rushing. We consider the following security notions against fail-stop adversaries:

Guaranteed Output Delivery: Secure computation against fail-stop adversaries with guaranteed output delivery ensures that the honest parties always learn the function output (computed over the inputs of "active" parties) even if some parties prematurely abort the protocol. It is well known that guaranteed output delivery is impossible to realize for general functions in the dishonest majority setting [10].

Strong Guaranteed Output Delivery: Note that guaranteed output delivery ensures that the honest parties can always reconstruct the output as long as *all* the honest parties send messages in the last round. We require a stronger variant of this notion, where it suffices for any $t + 1$ honest parties to broadcast messages in the last round. Observe that if $n = 2t + 1$ (i.e., if there are exactly $t + 1$ honest parties in the system), then this notion is equivalent to the standard notion of guaranteed output delivery. However for $n > 2t + 1$, this notion is strictly stronger than standard guaranteed output delivery.

2.2 MPC with Strong Guaranteed Output Delivery

For our semi-honest construction in the honest majority setting (i.e., for $t < n/2$) with optimal message complexity, we make use of a two round MPC protocol that achieves *strong guaranteed output* delivery against fail-stop adversaries. As defined above, in a protocol that achieves strong guaranteed output delivery, it suffices for any $t + 1$ honest parties to broadcast a message in the last round. Thus, the message complexity of such a two round protocol is $n+t+1$. Although note that with $n+t+1$ messages, this protocol only achieves security with abort, since the adversary can always corrupt the parties that send messages in the last round. However, this weakened security is sufficient for us. We show how to reduce the message complexity of this protocol to $n + t$ by adding an additional round.

Interestingly, we observe that if such a two round protocol also achieves security with abort against malicious adversaries, then our resulting protocols with optimal message complexity in the PKI model for $t < n/2$ can also be proved maliciously secure, without requiring any additional assumptions. We observe that the two round MPC protocol from Corollary 7 of Ananth et al. [1] satisfies both these properties that we require. We give a sketch of the proof for the following theorem in the full version our paper.

Theorem 5 (Implicit from [1]). *Assuming the existence of public-key encryption, there exists a two-round secure MPC protocol that achieves strong guaranteed output against $t < n/2$ fail-stop corruptions and achieves security with abort against $t < n/2$ malicious corruptions in the PKI model.*

2.3 Functionalities of Interest

Our lower bounds rely on residual function attacks (as described earlier), where only one honest party's input is fixed, and the adversary can evaluate the function on multiple different inputs (by changing the inputs of other parties). For most functionalities, this is a *non-trivial* information that cannot be simulated. In fact, it usually leads to a complete break in the privacy of the honest party whose input is fixed. For concreteness, we present our lower-bounds using one such functionality called the *multi-party OT functionality* defined in [22]. This functionality is a variant of oblivious transfer where each party has three-input bits. At the end, based on the first input bits of all parties, the output parties only learn one of the input bits of all parties.

Definition 4 (*MOT* Functionality). *For $n > 2$ and nonempty $\mathcal{O} \subseteq [n]$, let $MOT : X^n \to Y^n$ be the $n-$party functionality defined as follows:*

- *The input domain of each party is $X = \{0,1\}^3$ and the output domain is $Y = \{0,1\}^{n+1}$.*
- *Given input (c_i, x_i^0, x_i^1) from each party P_i, the functionality lets $c = c_1 \oplus \ldots \oplus c_n$ and outputs $(c, x_1^c, \ldots, x_n^c)$ to all parties $P_j, j \in \mathcal{O}$ (the output of party P_j for $j \notin \mathcal{O}$ is the fixed string 0^{n+1}).*

For simplicity, the proofs of all the lower bounds in this work are described with respect to the MOT functionality. However, it should be easy to see that all our proofs extend to any such non-trivial functionality.

3   Lower Bounds on Broadcast Message Complexity

In this section, we provide lower bounds on the broadcast message complexity of MPC in the plain model and the bare public-key model. We show that the broadcast message complexity is different in the two models, and further depends on the number of corruptions t and the number of output parties $|\mathcal{O}|$, where $\mathcal{O}$ is the set of parties who learn the output.

3.1   Plain Model

We first investigate the lower bounds on broadcast message complexity of semi-honest MPC protocols in the plain model. We start by proving our lower bound for $t < n - 1$ corruptions and $|\mathcal{O}| > 1$ output parties. In this case, we first show that for a secure MPC protocol, at least $t + 1$ parties must broadcast more one messages in Lemma 1. Using this result, it is easy to see that even if these $t + 1$ parties send two messages each, the total number of messages required are $2(t+1) + 1(n - (t+1)) = n + t + 1$, since each party in an n-party protocol must broadcast at least one message. Finally we show how this result can be used to get a lower bound for $|\mathcal{O}| = 1$ output party.

We now formally state the following two theorems, for $1 \leqslant t < (n-1)$, and $t = n - 1$, respectively. In this subsection, we only give a proof for Theorem 6. The proof of Theorem 7, which follows similarly to Theorem 6, except that it does not rely on spoofing attacks, is deferred to the full version our paper.

Theorem 6. *In the plain model, the broadcast message complexity of n-party MPC for non-trivial functionalities secure against $1 \leqslant t < (n-1)$ semi-honest, static corruptions is $n + t + 1$ if the number of output parties is $|\mathcal{O}| > 1$, and $n + t$ if $|\mathcal{O}| = 1$.*

Theorem 7. *In the plain model, the broadcast message complexity of n-party MPC for non-trivial functionalities secure against $t = n - 1$ semi-honest, static corruptions is $2n - 1$ if the number of output parties is $|\mathcal{O}| > 1$, and $2n - 2$ if $|\mathcal{O}| = 1$.*

Proof of Theorem 6. We divide the proof into two cases, depending upon the number of output parties.

Case 1 : $|\mathcal{O}| > 1$. Let Π be a secure n-party broadcast channel MPC protocol for the MOT functionality in the plain model with $|\mathcal{O}| > 1$, that is secure against a semi-honest adversary that corrupts $1 \leqslant t < (n-1)$ parties. Let $\mathcal{S}_1$ be the set of parties that broadcast a single message in Π and $\mathcal{S}_{>1}$ be the set of parties that broadcast more than one messages. We start by proving the following lemma.

Lemma 1. *There must be at least $t + 1$ parties in Π that broadcast more that 1 message, i.e., $|\mathcal{S}_{>1}| \geqslant t + 1$*

Proof. Let us assume for the sake of contradiction that $|\mathcal{S}_{>1}| \leqslant t$. Let $\mathcal{A}$ be an adversary who corrupts all the parties in $\mathcal{S}_{>1}$ and no other party, i.e., all parties in $\mathcal{S}_1$ are honest. Since $|\mathcal{S}_{>1}| \leqslant t$, this is a valid adversary.

Let $P^* \in \mathcal{S}_1$ be the first party to broadcast a message amongst all parties in $\mathcal{S}_1$. We note that there might be more than one such party in $\mathcal{S}_1$ that broadcast their messages simultaneously in a round. In that case, w.l.o.g. we let P^* be the lexicographically first party amongst those. Let $\mathcal{S}_1^* = \mathcal{S}_1 \setminus \{P^*\}$ be the set of all other parties in $\mathcal{S}_1$. Let $\mathcal{P}$ denote the set of all parties in Π and let (x_i, r_i) denote the input and randomness of party $P_i \in \mathcal{P}$. We now describe the strategy of $\mathcal{A}$.

- $\mathcal{A}$ runs an honest execution of Π where it sets $x_j = 000$ for every corrupted party $P_j \in \mathcal{S}_{>1}$. Let trans_Π be the transcript of this execution.
- Let P_k be any party in $\mathcal{S}_1^*$. $\mathcal{A}$ then runs two mental experiments where in the first experiment it sets $x_j = 000$ for every $P_j \in \mathcal{S}_1^*$ and in the second experiment it sets $x_k = 100$ and $x_j = 000$ for every $P_j \in \mathcal{S}_1^* \setminus \{P_k\}$. Let P^* broadcast its message in round ℓ and let $\mathrm{trans}_\Pi^{<\ell}$ be the transcript of honest execution up to round ℓ. Given $\mathrm{trans}_\Pi^{<\ell}$, the message sent by P^* in the honest execution and the new set of inputs, $\mathcal{A}$ uses the next message function of the remaining parties $P_j \in \mathcal{P} \setminus \{P^*\}$ to compute their messages from round ℓ onwards. Let $\mathrm{trans}_{\Pi 1}$ and $\mathrm{trans}_{\Pi 2}$ denote the transcripts of the two mental experiments. Note that since $|\mathcal{O}| > 1$, there is at least one output party in the set $\mathcal{P} \setminus \{P^*\}$. It uses the output function of any output party $P_i \in \mathcal{O} \cap (\mathcal{S}_{>1} \cup \mathcal{S}_1^*)$ to compute outputs $y_1 = \mathrm{Out}_\Pi(i, x_i, r_i, \mathrm{trans}_{\Pi 1})$ and $y_2 = \mathrm{Out}_\Pi(i, x_i, r_i, \mathrm{trans}_{\Pi 2})$.

Claim. $y_1 = (c^*, x_1^{c^*}, \ldots, x_n^{c^*})$, where $x_i = 000$ for each $P_i \in \mathcal{P} \setminus \{P^*\}$ and c^* is the first input bit of party P^*.

Proof. Since P^* is the first party to broadcast a message amongst all parties in $\mathcal{S}_1$, its message does not depend on messages from any other party in $\mathcal{S}_1$. Thus $\mathrm{trans}_{\Pi 1}$ represents honestly computed transcript of Π where the inputs of all parties in $\mathcal{S}_1^*$ have been replaced with 000. Therefore, from the correctness of Π, we get $y_1 = (c^*, x_1^{c^*}, \ldots, x_n^{c^*})$. $\qquad\square$

Claim. $y_2 = ((1 - c^*), x_1^{(1-c^*)}, \ldots, x_n^{(1-c^*)})$ where $x_k = 100$ for any one party $P_k \in \mathcal{S}_1^*$ and $x_i = 000$ for each $P_i \in \mathcal{P} \setminus \{P^*, P_k\}$.

The proof of this claim is similar to the proof of the previous claim.

From the above claims, we can see that the two outputs y_1 and y_2 reveal both the input bits of the honest party P^*. Such a protocol is clearly not secure. Therefore our assumption is wrong and there must be at least $t + 1$ parties in Π that broadcast more that 1 messages. This concludes the proof of Lemma 1. We now use this lemma to prove the first part of Theorem 6. $\qquad\square$

Let us assume for the sake of contradiction that there exists a semi-honest secure MPC protocol Π in the plain model, that has a broadcast message complexity of $n + t$ for $|\mathcal{O}| > 1$ output parties. From Lemma 1, we know that at least $t + 1$ parties must broadcast at least 2 messages. This means that there is at least one party out of the remaining $n - (t + 1)$ parties, that doesn't send a message, i.e., the output of the protocol is independent of this party's input. But we know that for correctness of output of the MOT functionality, every party's input is necessary for computation. Therefore the output computed by this protocol is incorrect. Thus, our assumption is wrong and such a protocol with broadcast complexity $n + t$ cannot exist.

Case2 : $|\mathcal{O}| = 1$. We now prove the second part of Theorem 6. Let us assume for the sake of contradiction that there exists an n-party broadcast channel MPC protocol for any non-trivial functionality in the plain model with $|\mathcal{O}| = 1$, that is secure against a semi-honest adversary that corrupts $1 \leqslant t < (n - 1)$ parties and has a broadcast message complexity of $n + t - 1$. This protocol can be easily transformed into another protocol Π' with the same corruption threshold, where $|\mathcal{O}| = n$. This can be obtained by adding a round at the end of Π where the output party broadcasts the output. Clearly, every party learns the output in Π' and it only has a broadcast message complexity of $n + t$. But from the first part of Theorem 6, we know that such a protocol with a broadcast message complexity of $n + t$ cannot exist. Therefore, our assumption is wrong and the minimum broadcast message complexity for such a protocol with one output party is $n + t$. This completes the proof of Theorem 6.   □

3.2   PKI Model

We now investigate the lower bounds on broadcast message complexity of semi-honest MPC protocols against $1 \leqslant t \leqslant (n - 1)$ corruptions in the PKI model. We observe that the lower bound for $|\mathcal{O}| \leqslant n - t$ output parties follows similar to the proof of Theorem 7 using the lower bounds of Mittal in [23] on the P2P message complexity.

For $|\mathcal{O}| > n - t$ parties, we start by showing that in a secure MPC protocol in the PKI model, at least t parties must broadcast more than one message each in Lemma 2. The proof of this lemma is very similar to the proof of Lemma 1, except that now it is not possible for the adversary to spoof other parties in the PKI model. Using this result, as before it is easy to see that even if these t parties send two messages each, the total number of messages required are $2(t) + 1(n - t) = n + t$, since each party must broadcast a message in an n-party protocol. We now formally prove the following theorem.

Theorem 8. *In the PKI model, the broadcast message complexity of n-party MPC for non-trivial functionalities secure against $1 \leqslant t \leqslant (n - 1)$ semi-honest, static corruptions is $n + t$ if the number of output parties is $|\mathcal{O}| > n - t$, and $n + t - 1$ if $|\mathcal{O}| \leqslant n - t$.*

Proof. The lower bound for $|\mathcal{O}| \leqslant n - t$ and $|\mathcal{O}| = n$ output parties can be derived from the lower bound given in [23]. Intuitively, it can be shown that, if there exists a broadcast protocol in this setting with $n + t - 2$ broadcast message complexity, and $|\mathcal{O}| \leqslant n - t$ output parties, then the lower bound given in [23] on the P2P message complexity will be violated. Similarly the bound of $n + t$ messages for $|\mathcal{O}| = n$ output parties also holds. We defer the full proof for this setting to the full version of our paper.

But this still leaves open the question about broadcast message complexity of MPC with $1 \leqslant t \leqslant n - 1$ semi-honest corruptions and $n - t < |\mathcal{O}| < n$ output parties in th PKI model. We know prove the lower bound of $n + t$ messages for $n - t < |\mathcal{O}| < n$ output parties. The following proof also works for $|\mathcal{O}| = n$ output parties. We prove this bound for the *MOT* functionality, but this proof can be easily extended for any non-trivial functionality. Let Π be an secure n-party broadcast channel MPC protocol for the *MOT* functionality in the PKI model with $|\mathcal{O}| > t + 1$, that is secure against a semi-honest adversary that corrupts $1 \leqslant t \leqslant (n-1)$ parties. Let $\mathcal{S}_1$ be the set of parties that broadcast a single message in Π and $\mathcal{S}_{>1}$ be the set of parties that broadcast more than one messages. We start by proving the following lemma.

Lemma 2. *There must be at least t parties in Π that broadcast more that 1 message, i.e., $|\mathcal{S}_{>1}| \geqslant t$.*

Proof. Let us assume for the sake of contradiction that $|\mathcal{S}_{>1}| = (t-1)$. Let $P_{\mathsf{last}} \in \mathcal{S}_1$ be the last party to broadcast a message amongst all parties in $\mathcal{S}_1$. Note that there might be more than one such parties in $\mathcal{S}_1$ that broadcast their messages simultaneously in a round. In that case we let P_{last} be the lexicographically last party amongst those. Let $\mathcal{A}$ be an adversary who corrupts P_{last} and all the parties in $\mathcal{S}_{>1}$. Since $|\mathcal{S}_{>1}| = (t - 1)$, this is a valid adversary. Let P^* be any honest party. From the above definition of $\mathcal{A}$, we know that $P^* \in \mathcal{S}_1$. Let $\mathcal{P}$ denote the set of all parties in Π and let (x_i, r_i) denote the input and randomness of party $P_i \in \mathcal{P}$. We now describe the strategy of $\mathcal{A}$.

- $\mathcal{A}$ runs an honest execution of Π where it sets $x_j = 000$ for every corrupted party $P_j \in \mathcal{S}_{>1} \cup \{P_{\mathsf{last}}\}$. Let trans_Π be the transcript of this execution. It uses the output function of any corrupted output party $P_o \in \mathcal{O} \cap (\mathcal{S}_{>1} \cup \{P_{\mathsf{last}}\})$ to compute the output $(c, x_1^c, \ldots, x_n^c) = \mathsf{Out}_\Pi(o, x_o, r_o, \mathsf{trans}_\Pi)$. Since $|\mathcal{O}| > n - t$, there is at least one corrupt output party.
- $\mathcal{A}$ then runs a mental experiment where it sets $x_{\mathsf{last}} = 100$. Let P_{last} broadcast its message in round ℓ and let $\mathsf{trans}_\Pi^{\leqslant \ell}$ be the transcript of honest execution up to round ℓ. Given $\mathsf{trans}_\Pi^{\leqslant \ell}$ and the new sets of inputs, $\mathcal{A}$ uses the next message function of all the corrupted parties to compute their messages from round ℓ onwards. Let trans_Π' denote the transcript of the mental experiment. It uses the output function of the output party P_o to compute the output $y' = \mathsf{Out}_\Pi(o, x_o, r_o, \mathsf{trans}_\Pi')$.

Claim. $y' = ((1 - c), x_1^{1-c}, \ldots, x_n^{1-c})$, where $x_{\mathsf{last}} = 100$.

Proof. Since P_{last} is the last party to broadcast a message amongst all parties in S_1, messages of other parties (honest parties) in S_1 do not depend on P_{last}'s message. Thus trans'_Π represents an honestly computed transcript of Π where only the input of P_{last} has been replaced with 100. Therefore, from the correctness of Π, $y' = ((1-c), x_1^{1-c}, \ldots, x_n^{1-c})$. $\qquad\square$

From the above claim, we see that the output of the honest execution and y' reveal both the input bits of the honest party P^*. Such a protocol is clearly not secure. Therefore our assumption is wrong and there must be at least t parties in Π that broadcast more that 1 messages. $\qquad\square$

We now use this lemma to prove Theorem 8. Let us assume for the sake of contradiction that there exists a semi-honest secure MPC protocol Π in the PKI model for $1 \leqslant t \leqslant n-1$, that has a broadcast message complexity of $n+t-1$. From Lemma 2, we know that at least t parties must broadcast at least 2 messages. Since $2 \times (t) = 2t$ and $(n+t-1)-(2t) = n-t-1$, there is at least one party that doesn't send a message, i.e., the output of the protocol is independent of this party's input. But we know that for correctness of output of the MOT functionality, every party's input is necessary for computation. Therefore the output computed by this protocol is incorrect. Thus, our assumption is wrong and such a protocol with broadcast complexity $n+t-1$ cannot exist. This completes the proof of Theorem 8. $\qquad\square$

4 Lower Bounds on Round Complexity

In this section, we investigate the minimal round complexity of semi-honest MPC with optimal broadcast message complexity. The following theorem summarizes our results.

Theorem 9. *Three-rounds are necessary for semi-honest MPC with optimal broadcast message complexity. This result holds regardless of the model (plain or bare public key), the number of corruptions or the number of output parties.*

We divide this proof into two parts. In Sect. 4.1, we consider MPC protocols in the plain model with $1 \leqslant t < (n-1)$ corruptions. Later in Sect. 4.2, we consider MPC protocols in the plain model with $t = n-1$ corruptions and in the PKI model with $1 \leqslant t < n$ corruptions.

4.1 Plain Model : $1 \leqslant t < (n-1)$

We start by proving in Lemma 3, that the last round in a secure MPC protocol in the plain model with $t < n-1$ semi-honest corruptions cannot consist of messages from parties that broadcast a single message in the protocol.

Next we use this result to show that at least three rounds are necessary for optimal message complexity in the plain model with $t < n-1$ semi-honest corruptions. Intuitively, assuming for contradiction that there exists such a two-round protocol with optimal message complexity, from Lemma 3 we know that

all the parties that send a single message in the protocol must broadcast their
message in the first round, and all the other parties broadcast their messages
in both the first and second rounds. The adversary can now launch a residual
function attack on the inputs of any one party that sends a single message by
spoofing all other honest parties. This is possible because the message of this
honest party that sends its only message in the first round, does not depend
on the messages (or the inputs) of any other party. The adversary can keep
recomputing the remaining transcript using different inputs of other parties to
compute different outputs of the function.

We now give a formal proof for the MOT functionality, but it is easy to
see that this proof can be extended to any non-trivial functionality. Let Π be
a secure n-party broadcast channel MPC protocol for the MOT functionality
in the plain model with minimum broadcast message complexity, that is secure
against a semi-honest adversary who may corrupt up to $1 \leqslant t < (n-1)$ parties.
Let $\mathcal{S}_1$ be the set of parties that broadcast a single message in Π and $\mathcal{S}_2$ be the
set of parties that broadcast two messages. We start by proving the following
lemma.

Lemma 3. *The last round in Π does not consist of messages from parties that
broadcast a single message in the protocol.*

Proof. Let us assume for the sake of contradiction that there is a party $P_{\mathsf{last}} \in \mathcal{S}_1$
that broadcasts its message in the last round ℓ. Let $\mathcal{A}$ be an adversary who
corrupts any output party $P_o \in \mathcal{O}$. Let $\mathcal{P}$ denote the set of all parties in Π and
let (x_i, r_i) denote the input and randomness of party $P_i \in \mathcal{P}$. We now describe
the strategy of $\mathcal{A}$.

- $\mathcal{A}$ runs an honest execution of Π where it sets $x_o = 000$ for the corrupt output
  party P_o. Let trans_Π be the transcript of this execution.
- $\mathcal{A}$ then runs two mental experiments where in the first experiment it sets
  the input of party P_{last}, $x_{\mathsf{last}} = 000$ and in the second experiment it sets
  $x_{\mathsf{last}} = 100$. Let $\mathsf{trans}_\Pi^{\leqslant \ell}$ denote the transcript of the honest execution of Π,
  up to round ℓ. Given $\mathsf{trans}_\Pi^{\leqslant \ell}$ and the new inputs, $\mathcal{A}$ computes P_{last}'s new
  messages in the two mental experiments. Let $\mathsf{trans}_{\Pi 1}$ and $\mathsf{trans}_{\Pi 2}$ denote the
  final transcripts of the two mental experiments. It uses the output function
  of the output party P_o to compute outputs $y_1 = \mathsf{Out}_\Pi(o, x_o, r_o, \mathsf{trans}_{\Pi 1})$ and
  $y_2 = \mathsf{Out}_\Pi(o, x_o, r_o, \mathsf{trans}_{\Pi 2})$.

Claim. $y_1 = (c, x_1^c, \ldots, x_n^c)$, where $x_{\mathsf{last}} = 000$ and c is the xor of the first input
bits of all other parties in $\mathcal{P}$.

Proof. Since P_{last} broadcasts its message only in the last round, the messages of
all other parties in the protocol are independent of its message. Thus $\mathsf{trans}_{\Pi 1}$ represents an honestly computed transcript of Π where the input of P_{last} is replaced
with 000. Therefore, from the correctness of Π, we get that $y_1 = (c, x_1^c, \ldots, x_n^c)$. $\qquad \square$

Claim. $y_2 = ((1 - c), x_1^{(1-c)}, \ldots, x_n^{(1-c)})$ where $x_{\mathsf{last}} = 100$ and $1 - c$ is the xor of the first input bits of all other parties in $\mathcal{P}$.

The proof of this claim is similar to the proof of the previous claim.

From the above claims, we can see that the two outputs y_1 and y_2 reveal both the input bits of all the honest parties $P_i \in \mathcal{P} \setminus \{P_{\mathsf{last}}, P_o\}$. Such a protocol is clearly not secure. Therefore our assumption is wrong and there must be at least $t + 1$ parties in Π that broadcast more that 1 messages. $\square$

We now use this lemma to prove the first part of Theorem 9.
We prove this theorem separately for the following cases:

Case 1: $|\mathcal{O}| = 1$. From Theorem 6, we know that the broadcast message complexity of Π is $n + t$, i.e., $|\mathcal{S}_1| = n - t$ and $|\mathcal{S}_2| = t$. Let us assume for the sake of contradiction that there are only 2 rounds in Π. From Lemma 3, we know that in a 2 round protocol, all the parties in $\mathcal{S}_1$ must broadcast their messages in the first round. Let P_o be the output party.

Let $\mathcal{A}$ be an adversary who corrupts all parties in $\mathcal{S}_2$. Since $|\mathcal{S}_2| = t$, this is a valid adversary. Let $\mathcal{P}$ denote the set of all parties in Π and let (x_i, r_i) denote the input and randomness of party $P_i \in \mathcal{P}$. We now describe the strategy of $\mathcal{A}$. $\mathcal{A}$ runs an honest execution of Π where it sets $x_i = 000$ for every corrupted party $P_i \in \mathcal{S}_2$. Let trans_Π be the transcript of this execution. We now have the following cases:

$\mathbf{P_o \in \mathcal{S}_2}$: The adversary computes the output of the honest execution $y = (c, x_1^c, \ldots, x_n^c) = \mathsf{Out}_\Pi(o, x_o, r_o, \mathsf{trans}_\Pi)$.

It then runs a mental experiment where it sets the input of P_o, $x_o = 100$. Given the first round messages of all other parties from the honest execution, it computes the new first round message of P_o and the second round messages of all parties in $\mathcal{S}_2$. Let trans'_Π denote the transcript of the mental experiment. It uses the output function of the output party P_o to compute the new output $y' = \mathsf{Out}_\Pi(o, x_o, r_o, \mathsf{trans}'_\Pi)$.

$\mathbf{P_o \in \mathcal{S}_1}$: $\mathcal{A}$ runs two mental experiments, where it sets $x_o = 000$ and $x_o = 100$ respectively. It computes P_o's messages in the two mental experiments using these new inputs. It also computes the second round messages of all corrupted parties given P_o's new message and the remaining first round messages from honest execution. Let $\mathsf{trans}_{\Pi 1}$ and $\mathsf{trans}_{\Pi 2}$ denote the transcripts in the two mental experiments. It then uses the output function of P_o to compute outputs $y_1 = \mathsf{Out}_\Pi(o, x_o, r_o, \mathsf{trans}_{\Pi 1})$ and $y_2 = \mathsf{Out}_\Pi(o, x_o, r_o, \mathsf{trans}_{\Pi 2})$.

We now analyze these two cases separately:

Analysis for $\mathbf{P_o \in \mathcal{S}_2}$.

Claim. $y' = ((1 - c), x_1^{(1-c)}, \ldots, x_n^{(1-c)})$.

Proof. Since all honest parties only broadcast a message in the first round, their messages are independent of the messages from any other party. Thus trans'_Π represents an honestly computed transcript of Π where the input of x_o has been replaced with 100. Therefore, from the correctness of Π, $y' = ((1 - c), x_1^{(1-c)}, \ldots, x_n^{(1-c)})$ $\square$

From the above claim, we can see that y and y' reveal both the input bits of all the honest parties. Such a protocol is clearly insecure. Therefore our assumption is wrong there must be at least 3 rounds in Π in this case.

Analysis for $P_o \in S_1$.

Claim. $y_1 = (c, x_1^c, \ldots, x_n^c)$, where $x_o = 000$ and c is the xor of the first input bits of all other parties in $\mathcal{P}$.

Proof. Since all parties in S_1 broadcast their message in the first round, their messages are independent of the messages from any other party. Thus $\text{trans}_{\Pi1}$ represents an honestly computed transcript of Π where the input of P_o is replaced with 000. Therefore, from the correctness of Π, we get that $y_1 = (c, x_1^c, \ldots, x_n^c)$.   □

Claim. $y_2 = ((1-c), x_1^{(1-c)}, \ldots, x_n^{(1-c)})$ where $x_o = 100$ and c is the xor of the first input bits of all other parties in $\mathcal{P}$.

The proof of this claim is similar to the proof of the previous claim.

From the above claims, we can see that y_1 and y_2 reveal both the input bits of all the honest parties. Such a protocol is clearly insecure. Therefore our assumption is wrong there must be at least 3 rounds in Π in this case.

Case 2: $|\mathcal{O}| > 1$. From Theorem 6, we know that the broadcast message complexity of Π is $n + t + 1$, i.e., $|S_1| = n - t - 1$ and $|S_2| = t + 1$. Let us assume for the sake of contradiction that there are only 2 rounds in Π. From Lemma 3, we know that in a 2 round protocol, all the parties in S_1 must broadcast their messages in the first round.

Let $\mathcal{A}$ be an adversary who corrupts all but one party in S_2. Let P_{remain} be the remaining honest party in S_2. Since $|S_2| = t + 1$, this is a valid adversary. Let $\mathcal{P}$ denote the set of all parties in Π and let (x_i, r_i) denote the input and randomness of party $P_i \in \mathcal{P}$. We now describe the strategy of $\mathcal{A}$. $\mathcal{A}$ runs an honest execution of Π where it sets $x_i = 000$ for every corrupted party $P_i \in S_2 \setminus \{P_{\text{remain}}\}$. Let trans_Π be the transcript of this execution. We can have the following cases:

One of the Parties in S_2 Is an Output Party: It then runs two mental experiments where in the first experiment, it sets the input $x_{\text{remain}} = 000$ and in the second experiment it sets $x_{\text{remain}} = 100$. Given the new input and first round messages of all other parties from the honest execution, it computes the new first and second round messages of P_{remain} and the second round messages of all other parties in S_2. Let $\text{trans}_{\Pi1}$ and $\text{trans}_{\Pi2}$ denote the transcripts of the two mental experiments. It uses the output function of the output party $P_o \in S_2$ to compute outputs $y_1 = \text{Out}_\Pi(o, x_o, r_o, \text{trans}_{\Pi1})$ and $y_2 = \text{Out}_\Pi(o, x_o, r_o, \text{trans}_{\Pi2})$.

None of the Parties in S_2 Is an Output Party: Let $P_o \in S_1$ be an output party. $\mathcal{A}$ runs two mental experiments where in the first experiment, it sets $x_o = 000$ and $x_{\text{remain}} = 000$ and in the second experiment it sets $x_o = 100$ and $x_{\text{remain}} = 000$. Given the new sets of inputs and the first round messages of all other parties from the honest execution, it computes the new first round messages of P_o and P_{remain}. It also computes the new second round messages of all parties in S_2. Let $\text{trans}_{\Pi 1}$ and $\text{trans}_{\Pi 2}$ denote the transcripts in the two mental experiments. It then uses the output function of P_o to compute outputs $y_1 = \text{Out}_\Pi(o, x_o, r_o, \text{trans}_{\Pi 1})$ and $y_2 = \text{Out}_\Pi(o, x_o, r_o, \text{trans}_{\Pi 2})$.

Remark. Note that if $t = n - 2$, since $|\mathcal{O}| > 1$, at least one of the parties in S_2 will always be an output party. The second case can only occur if there are at least 3 honest parties. Therefore, if the adversary spoofs two honest parties P_o and P_{remain}, it can still compromise the privacy of at least one honest party. We analyze the two cases separately:

Analysis for the case when one of the parties in S_2 is an output party:

Claim. $y_1 = (c, x_1^c, \ldots, x_n^c)$, where $x_{\text{remain}} = 000$ and c is the xor of first input bits of all parties other than P_{remain} in the honest execution.

Proof. Since all parties in S_1 broadcast their messages in the first round, their messages are independent of the messages from any other party. Thus $\text{trans}_{\Pi 1}$ represents an honestly computed transcript of Π where the input of P_{remain} has been changed is replaced with 000. Therefore, from the correctness of Π, we get that $y_1 = (c, x_1^c, \ldots, x_n^c)$. □

Claim. $y_2 = ((1 - c), x_1^{(1-c)}, \ldots, x_n^{(1-c)})$, where c is the xor of first input bits of all parties other than P_{remain} in the honest execution.

The proof of this claim is similar to the proof of the previous claim.
From the above claims, we can see that y_1 and y_2 reveal both the input bits of all the honest parties. Such a protocol is clearly insecure. Therefore our assumption is wrong there must be at least 3 rounds in Π in this case.

Analysis for the case when none of the parties in S_2 is an output party:

Claim. $y_1 = (c, x_1^c, \ldots, x_n^c)$, where $x_o = 000$, $x_{\text{remain}} = 000$ and c is the xor of first input bits of all parties other than P_{remain} and P_o in the honest execution.

Claim. $y_2 = ((1 - c), x_1^{(1-c)}, \ldots, x_n^{(1-c)})$, where $x_o = 100$, $x_{\text{remain}} = 000$ and c is the xor of first input bits of all parties other than P_{remain} and P_o in the honest execution.

The proofs of these claims are similar to the proofs of the two claims in the previous case. From the above claims, we can see that y_1 and y_2 reveal both the input bits of all the other honest parties. Such a protocol is clearly insecure. Therefore our assumption is wrong there must be at least 3 rounds in Π in this case. This completes the proof for the first part of Theorem 9.

4.2   Plain Model : $t = n - 1$ and PKI Model : $1 \leqslant t \leqslant n - 1$

Similar to the previous subsection, we start by proving that even in this setting, the last round round of a secure MPC protocol cannot consist of messages from parties that broadcast a single message in the protocol. The rest of the proof also works very similar to the one in the previous subsection. We now give a formal proof for the lower bound on number of rounds in the plain model with $t = n - 1$ corruptions. The proof for PKI model with $1 \leqslant t \leqslant n - 1$ corruptions follows similarly.

Let Π be any n-party broadcast channel MPC protocol for any non-trivial functionality in the plain model with minimum broadcast message complexity, that is secure against a semi-honest adversary who may corrupt up to $t = (n-1)$ parties. Let S_1 be the set of parties that broadcast a single message in Π and S_2 be the set of parties that broadcast two messages. Let $\mathcal{O}$ be the set of output parties. We start with the following lemma.

Lemma 4. *The last round in Π does not consist of messages from parties that broadcast a single message in the protocol.*

The proof of this lemma is similar to the proof of Lemma 3. Now we prove Theorem 9. Let us assume for the sake of contradiction that there are only 2 rounds in Π. From Lemma 4, we know that in a 2 round protocol, all the parties in S_1 must broadcast their messages in the first round. We have the following cases:

Case 1: $|\mathcal{O}| = 1$. From Theorem 7, we know that the broadcast message complexity of Π is $2n - 2$, i.e., $|S_1| = 2$ and $|S_2| = n - 2$. Let $P_o \in \mathcal{O}$ be the only output party.

Claim. In this case $P_o \in S_1$.

Proof. If we have protocol with broadcast message complexity $2n - 2$, where the output party sends a message in the last round, we can always get a protocol with broadcast message complexity $2n - 3$ where the output party does not send a message in the last round. Instead it computes the last round message offline and learns the output. But this clearly violates the lower bound of $2n - 2$ on the broadcast message complexity of such protocols. Therefore P_o does not send a message in the last round and hence $P_o \in S_1$.   □

Now let $\mathcal{A}$ be an adversary who corrupts all parties in S_2 and the output party P_o. Note that since $\mathcal{A}$ only corrupts t parties, this is a valid adversary. Clearly in this case, the message of the honest party does not depend on the messages of any of the corrupted parties. After running an honest execution of Π, the adversary can simply change the inputs of the corrupted parties while keeping the message of the honest party same and learn multiple different outputs. Thus, Π is clearly insecure and it must have at least three-rounds.

Case 2: $|\mathcal{O}| > 1$. From Theorem 7, we know that the broadcast message complexity of Π is $2n - 1$, i.e., $|S_1| = 1$ and $|S_2| = n - 1$. Since there are at least 2 output parties, one of them is definitely in S_2. Let $\mathcal{A}$ be an adversary that chooses to corrupt all the parties in S_2. Clearly in this case, the honest party sends its message in the first round and therefore its message is not dependent on the messages from any of the corrupted parties. After running an honest execution of Π, the adversary can simply change the inputs of the corrupted parties while keeping the message of the honest party same and learn multiple different outputs. Thus, Π is clearly insecure and there must be at least three-rounds in Π.

4.3   Communication Pattern

Since our broadcast model of communication allows for only a subset of parties to send a message in each broadcast round, there are a number of possible communication patterns in which parties may broadcast their messages. However, not all these combinations are viable for obtaining a secure MPC protocol. In the previous section, we already established that all protocols with minimum broadcast message complexity must comprise of at least three-rounds. We inspect the exact communication patterns for secure MPC protocols with optimal broadcast message complexity.

Plain Model: $1 \leqslant t \leqslant n - 1$ We show that any MPC protocol with optimal broadcast message complexity in the plain model must follow a unique communication pattern. We state the formal result and give a proof in the full version our paper.

PKI Model: $1 \leqslant t \leqslant n - 1$ We show that any MPC protocol with optimal broadcast message complexity in the PKI model must use a communication pattern from a specific class of communication patterns (which is a strict subset of all possible communication patterns). We call it a class of communication patterns because there are more than one communication patterns that fall into the same category of communication patterns that can be use to obtain a secure MPC protocol. We state the formal result and give a proof in the full version our paper.

5   Positive Result in the PKI Model : $t < \frac{n}{2}$

In this section we describe a general compiler to get a three-round semi-honest MPC protocol secure against $t < \frac{n}{2}$ corruptions with optimal broadcast message complexity in the PKI model from any two round MPC protocol with strong guaranteed output delivery against $t < \frac{n}{2}$ fail-stop corruptions in the PKI model. Using the two-round protocol from Theorem 5, that also achieves security with abort against $t < \frac{n}{2}$ malicious adversaries, our resulting three round protocol with optimal broadcast message complexity is also secure against malicious corruptions.

5.1   Overview

To enable the honest output parties to learn the output in an MPC protocol that satisfies strong guaranteed output delivery against $t < \frac{n}{2}$ fail-stop corruptions and security with abort against $t < \frac{n}{2}$ malicious corruptions, only $t + 1$ honest parties are required to participate in the last round. It is easy to observe that such a protocol would provide security with abort against $t < \frac{n}{2}$ malicious corruptions if any $t + 1$ parties participate in the last round. This already gives us a maliciously secure MPC protocol with broadcast message complexity of $n+t+1$. To further reduce the broadcast message complexity, we add an extra round in the middle where one of the parties sends it first and second message at the same time. This gives us a three-round maliciously secure MPC protocol against $t < \frac{n}{2}$ corruptions and minimal broadcast message complexity for $|\mathcal{O}| > n - t$ output parties. This protocol can also be transformed into a protocol for $|\mathcal{O}| \leqslant n - t$ output parties. Her we describe a compiler for $|\mathcal{O}| > n - t$ output parties. In the full version of our paper we discuss how this can be extended to $|\mathcal{O}| \leqslant n - t$ output parties in this setting. Let Φ be a two-round protocol that achieves strong guaranteed output delivery against $t < \frac{n}{2}$ fail-stop corruptions and security with abort against $t < \frac{n}{2}$ malicious corruptions, then the transformed three-round protocol has the following template:

R1: Parties $P_1, \ldots, P_{n-1}$ send their first round messages of Φ in the first round.
R2: Party P_n sends its first and second round messages of Φ in the second round.
R3: Parties $P_1, \ldots, P_t$ send their second round messages of Φ in the third round.

This gives us the following theorem statement.

Theorem 10. *Let Φ be a two-round MPC protocol with strong guaranteed output delivery against $t < \frac{n}{2}$ fail-stop corruptions and security with abort against $t < \frac{n}{2}$ malicious corruption with $|\mathcal{O}| = n$ output parties in the PKI model. Then there exists a general compiler that transforms Φ into a three-round maliciously secure MPC protocol with minimum broadcast message complexity in the PKI model that tolerates $t < \frac{n}{2}$ corruptions.*

Applying Theorem 10 to the protocol from Theorem 5, we get the following.

Corollary 1. *Assuming public-key encryption, there exists a three-round maliciously secure MPC protocol with minimum broadcast complexity in the PKI model that tolerates up to $t < \frac{n}{2}$ corruptions.*

5.2   Our Compiler for $|\mathcal{O}| > n - T$

Let $\mathcal{P} = \{P_1, \ldots, P_n\}$ be the set of parties in the protocol and let $\{x_1, \ldots, x_n\}$, $\{r_1, \ldots, r_n\}$, $\{\mathsf{pk}_1, \ldots, \mathsf{pk}_n\}$ and $\{\mathsf{sk}_1, \ldots, \mathsf{sk}_n\}$ be their respective inputs, randomness, public keys and secret keys. Let λ be the security parameter.

Round 1. Each party P_i for $i \in [n-1]$ does the following:
It computes the first round message Φ_i^1 using its input x_i, randomness r_i, secret key sk_i and public keys of all parties: $\Phi_i^1 \leftarrow \mathsf{NextMsg}_\Phi^1(1^\lambda, i, x_i, \mathsf{sk}_i, \{\mathsf{pk}_1, \ldots, \mathsf{pk}_n\}, \bot; r_i)$ and broadcasts $M_i^1 := \Phi_i^1$ to all other parties.

Round 2. Party P_n does the following:

1. Computes the first round message Φ_n^1 using its input x_n and randomness r_n:
   $\Phi_n^1 \leftarrow \mathsf{NextMsg}_\Phi^1(1^\lambda, n, x_n, \mathsf{sk}_i, \{\mathsf{pk}_1, \ldots, \mathsf{pk}_n\}, \bot; r_n)$
2. For $i \in [n-1]$, it parses M_i^1 as Φ_i^1 and sets $\mathsf{trans}_\Phi^1 := \{\Phi_i^1\}_{i \in [n]}$.
3. Computes the second round message Φ_n^2 using its input x_n, randomness r_n and previous round transcript trans_Φ^1:
   $\Phi_n^2 \leftarrow \mathsf{NextMsg}_\Phi^2(1^\lambda, n, x_n, \mathsf{sk}_i, \{\mathsf{pk}_1, \ldots, \mathsf{pk}_n\}, \mathsf{trans}_\Phi^1; r_n)$
4. Broadcasts $M_n^2 := (\Phi_n^1, \Phi_n^2)$

At the end of Round 2. Each party P_i for $i \in [n-1]$ does the following:
For j from 1 to $n-1$, parses M_j^1 as Φ_j^1. It parses M_n^2 as (Φ_n^1, Φ_n^2). Finally it sets $\mathsf{trans}_\Phi^1 := \{\Phi_j^1\}_{j \in [n]}$.

Round 3. Each party P_i for $i \in [t]$ does the following:
It computes the second round message $\Phi_i^2 \leftarrow \mathsf{NextMsg}_\Phi^2(1^\lambda, i, x_i, \mathsf{sk}_i, \{\mathsf{pk}_1, \ldots, \mathsf{pk}_n\}, \mathsf{trans}_\Phi^1; r_i)$ using its input x_i, randomness r_i and previous round transcript trans_Φ^1 and broadcasts $M_i^3 := (\Phi_i^2)$ to all other parties.

Output Phase. Each party P_i for $i \in [n]$ does the following:
For $j \in [t]$, it parses M_j^3 as (Φ_j^2). Then it sets $\mathsf{trans}_\Phi^2 := \{\{\Phi_j^2\}_{j \in [t]}, \Phi_n^2\}$. Finally it runs the output phase of Φ, $\mathsf{Out}_\Phi(i, x_i, r_i, \mathsf{sk}_i, \{\mathsf{pk}_1, \ldots, \mathsf{pk}_n\}, \mathsf{trans}_\Phi^1, \mathsf{trans}_\Phi^2)$ to learn the output.

This completes the description of our compiler. We provide a proof of security in the full version our paper.

6 Positive Result in the PKI Model : $t < n$

In this section we describe a general compiler to get a three-round semi-honest MPC protocol against $t < n$ corruptions with optimal broadcast message complexity in the PKI model from any two-round semi-honest MPC with dishonest majority in the plain model.

6.1 Overview

We start with any two round N-party semi-honest MPC protocol Φ, secure against $N-1$ corruptions, where $N = (n-t+2) \times (t+1)$. Let $\mathcal{P} = \{P_1, \ldots, P_n\}$ be the set of parties in our protocol Π and $\{x_1, \ldots, x_n\}$ be their respective inputs. Let the n-party functionality that they compute on these inputs be $f(x_1, \ldots, x_n)$. We consider an N-party functionality F such that

$$F(x_1, \ldots, x_t, x_{(t+1)_1}, \ldots, x_{(t+1)_{(t+1)}}, \ldots, x_{(n-1)_1}, \ldots, x_{(n-1)_{(t+1)}}, x_n)$$
$$:= f(x_1, \ldots, x_t, x_{(t+1)_1} \oplus \cdots \oplus x_{(t+1)_{(t+1)}}, \ldots, x_{(n-1)_1} \oplus \cdots \oplus x_{(n-1)_{(t+1)}}, x_n)$$

The main idea behind this compiler is to first let $n - t - 1$ parties in Π split their inputs into $t + 1$ additive shares each. Then the n parties together compute the N-input function F using Φ. Here we describe a compiler for $|\mathcal{O}| > n - t$ output parties. In the full version we show how this can be extended to the case where the number of output parties are $|\mathcal{O}| \leqslant n - t$. In the full version our paper, we also show how to extend these protocols to the malicious setting. The transformed three-round protocol for $|\mathcal{O}| > n - t$ output parties has the following template:

R1: Parties $P_1, \ldots, P_{n-1}$ participate in the first round.
R2: Only Party P_n participates in the second round.
R3: Parties $P_1, \ldots, P_t$ participate in the third round.

This gives us the following theorem statement.

Theorem 11. *Let Φ be a two-round semi-honest MPC protocol with dishonest majority and $|\mathcal{O}| = n$ output parties in the plain model. Then there exists a general compiler that transforms Φ into a three-round MPC protocol with minimum broadcast message complexity in the PKI model that tolerates up to $t < n$ semi-honest corruptions.*

Applying Theorem 11 to the protocol from Theorem 5.1 from [18], we get the following Corollary.

Corollary 2. *Assuming the existence of two-message semi-honest OT, there exists a three-round semi-honest MPC protocol with minimum broadcast complexity in the PKI model that tolerates up to $t < n$ corruptions.*

6.2   Our Compiler

Next, we describe the compiler for $|\mathcal{O}| > n - t$ output parties in detail.

Building Blocks. The main primitives required in this construction are: (1) A two-round semi-honest MPC protocol Φ for N parties in the plain/CRS model that only uses broadcast channels. (2) An additive secret sharing scheme. We denote this by $\mathsf{SS} := (\mathsf{Share}, \mathsf{Reconstruct})$. (3) A public-key encryption scheme $\mathcal{E} := (\mathsf{Gen}, \mathsf{Enc}, \mathsf{Dec})$.

Protocol. Let $\mathcal{P} = \{P_1, \ldots, P_n\}$ be the set of parties in the protocol and let $\{x_1, \ldots, x_n\}$, $\{r_1, \ldots, r_n\}$, $\{\mathsf{pk}_1, \ldots, \mathsf{pk}_n\}$ and $\{\mathsf{sk}_1, \ldots, \mathsf{sk}_n\}$ be their respective inputs, randomness, public keys and secret keys. Let λ be the security parameter.

Round 1. Each party P_i for $i \in [t]$ does the following:

It computes the first round message $\Phi_i^1 \leftarrow \mathsf{NextMsg}_\Phi^1(1^\lambda, i, x_i, \perp; r_i)$ using its input x_i and randomness r_i and broadcasts $M_i^1 := (\Phi_i^1)$ to all other parties. Each party P_i for $i \in \{t+1, \ldots, n-1\}$ does the following:

1. Uses an additive secret sharing scheme SS to compute $t + 1$ shares of its input x_i and randomness r_i using some random string s_i as follows:
   $\{x_{i_1}, \ldots, x_{i_t}, x_{i_n}\} \leftarrow \mathsf{Share}(1^\lambda, x_i; s_i)$ and $\{r_{i_1}, \ldots, r_{i_t}, x_{i_n}\} \leftarrow \mathsf{Share}(1^\lambda, r_i; s_i)$

2. Encrypts each input and randomness share x_{i_j} and r_{i_j} under public key pk_j for $j \in \{1, \ldots, t, n\}$: $c_{i_j} \leftarrow \mathsf{Enc}(\mathsf{pk}_j, (x_{i,j}, r_{i,j}); s_i)$
3. Computes the first round message $\varPhi_{i_j}^1$ using each of its input and randomness share x_{i_j} and r_{i_j} for $j \in \{1, \ldots, t, n\}$: $\varPhi_{i_j}^1 \leftarrow \mathsf{NextMsg}_{\varPhi}^1(1^\lambda, i_j, x_{i_j}, \bot; r_{i_j})$
4. Broadcasts $M_i^2 := (\{c_{i_j}, \varPhi_{i_j}^1\}_{j \in \{1,\ldots,t,n\}})$ to all other parties.

Round 2. Party P_n does the following:

1. Computes the first round message $\varPhi_n^1$ using its input x_n and randomness r_n. $\varPhi_n^1 \leftarrow \mathsf{NextMsg}_{\varPhi}^1(1^\lambda, n, x_n, \bot; r_n)$
2. **For** j from $t+1$ to $n-1$:
   (a) Parses M_j^2 as $\{c_{j_k}, \varPhi_{j_k}^1\}_{k \in [t+1]}$.
   (b) Decrypts c_{j_n} to obtain x_{j_n} and r_{j_n}: $(x_{j_n}, r_{j_n}) := \mathsf{Dec}(\mathsf{sk}_i, c_{j_n})$
3. Sets $\mathsf{trans}_{\varPhi}^1 := \{\{\varPhi_j^1\}_{j \in \{1,\ldots,t,n\}}, \{\varPhi_{j_k}^1\}_{j \in \{t+1,\ldots,n-1\}, k \in [t+1]}\}$
4. Computes the second round message $\varPhi_n^2$ using its input x_n, randomness r_n and previous round transcript $\mathsf{trans}_{\varPhi}^1$: $\varPhi_n^2 \leftarrow \mathsf{NextMsg}_{\varPhi}^2(1^\lambda, n, x_n, \mathsf{trans}_{\varPhi}^1; r_n)$
5. For each $j \in \{t+1, \ldots, n-1\}$, it computes the second round message $\varPhi_{j_n}^2$ using input and randomness share x_{j_n} and r_{j_n} and previous round transcript $\mathsf{trans}_{\varPhi}^1$: $\varPhi_{j_n}^2 \leftarrow \mathsf{NextMsg}_{\varPhi}^2(1^\lambda, j_n, x_{j_n}, \mathsf{trans}_{\varPhi}^1; r_{j_n})$
6. Broadcasts $M_n^2 := (\varPhi_n^1, \varPhi_n^2, \{\varPhi_{j_n}^2\}_{j \in \{t+1,\ldots,n-1\}})$

At the end of Round 2. Each party P_i for $i \in [t]$ does the following:

1. **For** j from $t+1$ to $n-1$, it parses M_j^2 as $\{c_{j_k}, \varPhi_{j_k}^1\}_{k \in \{1,\ldots,t,n\}}$ and decrypts c_{j_i} to obtain x_{j_i} and r_{j_i}: $(x_{j_i}, r_{j_i}) := \mathsf{Dec}(\mathsf{sk}_i, c_{j_i})$
2. **For** j from 1 to t, it parses M_j^1 as $(\varPhi_j^1)$.
3. Parses M_n^2 as $(\varPhi_n^1, \varPhi_n^2, \{\varPhi_{j_n}^2\}_{j \in \{t+1,\ldots,n-1\}})$
4. Sets $\mathsf{trans}_{\varPhi}^1 := \{\{\varPhi_j^1\}_{j \in \{1,\ldots,t,n\}}, \{\varPhi_{j_k}^1\}_{j \in \{t+1,\ldots,n-1\}, k \in \{1,\ldots,t,n\}}\}$

Round 3. Each party P_i for $i \in [t]$ does the following:

1. Computes the second round message $\varPhi_i^2$ using its own input x_i, randomness r_i and previous round transcript $\mathsf{trans}_{\varPhi}^1$: $\varPhi_i^2 \leftarrow \mathsf{NextMsg}_{\varPhi}^2(1^\lambda, i, x_i, \mathsf{trans}_{\varPhi}^1; r_i)$
2. For each $j \in \{t+1, \ldots, n-1\}$, it computes the second round message $\varPhi_{j_i}^2$ using input and randomness share x_{j_i} and r_{j_i} and previous round transcript $\mathsf{trans}_{\varPhi}^1$. For each $j \in \{t+1, \ldots, n\}$: $\varPhi_{j_i}^2 \leftarrow \mathsf{NextMsg}_{\varPhi}^2(1^\lambda, j_i, x_{j_i}, \mathsf{trans}_{\varPhi}^1; r_{j_i})$
3. Broadcasts $M_i^3 := (\varPhi_i^2, \{\varPhi_{j_i}^2\}_{j \in \{t+1,\ldots,n\}})$

Output Phase. Each party P_i for $i \in [n]$ does the following: For j from 1 to t, it parses M_j^3 as $(\varPhi_j^2, \{\varPhi_{j_k}^2\}_{k \in \{t+1,\ldots,n-1\}})$. Then it sets $\mathsf{trans}_{\varPhi}^2 := \{\{\varPhi_j^2\}_{j \in \{1,\ldots,t,n\}}, \{\varPhi_{j_k}^2\}_{j \in \{t+1,\ldots,n-1\}, k \in \{1,\ldots,t,n\}}\}$. Finally, it runs the output phase of $\varPhi$, $\mathsf{Out}_{\varPhi}(i, x_i, r_i, \mathsf{trans}_{\varPhi}^1, \mathsf{trans}_{\varPhi}^2)$ to learn the output.

This completes the description of the compiler. We prove its security in the full version our paper.

7   Extensions

The protocols presented in the previous sections can be extended in various ways to obtain different protocols with additional properties.

7.1   Protocol in the Plain Model for $1 \leqslant t < n - 1$:

Such a three-round protocol can be obtained by slightly modifying the compiler from Sect. 6.2. In the first round, parties $P_1, \ldots, P_t$ behave exactly as they do in the previous compiler, additionally they also send their public keys. P_n also sends its first message of the underlying protocol in the first round along with its public key. Parties $P_{t+1}, \ldots, P_{n-1}$ compute their messages exactly as do are doing in the previous compiler. The only difference is that now they send these messages in the second round. Then in the third round, parties $P_1, \ldots, P_t$ behave exactly as they do in the previous compiler. Additionally P_n also sends its remaining message in the third round. This compiler can also be instantiated using two-round protocols from [3,18]. The resulting protocol has a broadcast message complexity of $n + t + 1$ messages which is optimal for $|\mathcal{O}| > 1$ output parties. The broadcast message complexity of this protocol can be reduced by one if there is a *single* output party. If one less party broadcasts a message in the third round and instead computes this message and output offline, we get a protocol with broadcast message complexity of $n + t$, which is also optimal for $|\mathcal{O}| = 1$ output party. Similar to the previous one, this result can also be extended to achieve malicious security in the CRS model while preserving the optimal broadcast message complexity. This can be done by instantiating the above compiler using the two-round maliciously secure protocol from the work of Garg et al. in [18] based on two-round OT in the CRS model with simulation-based security against malicious receivers and semi-honest senders along with an equivocation property. We give a similar to extension to obtain a protocol for $t = n - 1$ in the plain model with optimal message complexity in the full version our paper.

7.2   P2P Message Complexity

In [22,23], Ishai et al. and Mittal give a lower bound of $n + t - 1$ messages on the P2P message complexity of MPC for $|\mathcal{O}| = 1$ output party with $t < n$ corruptions. While Ishai et al. do give a construction for $t = n - 1$, the work of Mittal in [23] does not give a positive result for this lower bound for $t < n - 1$. In this section we give a protocol with optimal P2P message complexity. At first, it might seem that the positive results discussed in our work in broadcast setting would directly give a protocol with optimal P2P message complexity by applying a simple. But this is in fact not true. If we apply this transformation to our protocol in the plain model, we only get a protocol with P2P message complexity of $n + t$ for $|\mathcal{O}| = 1$, which is not optimal. If we instead apply this transformation to our protocols from the PKI model, we do get a protocol with optimal P2P message complexity, but the resulting protocol is also in the PKI model, which is not optimal in the assumptions. Below we describe an extension to our protocols from the PKI model to obtain protocols that are optimal in the assumptions as well as the P2P message complexity. The protocol given in Sect. 6.2 can transformed as follows:

- P_1 computes its first round message as described in that protocol and forwards it to party P_2 along with the public key.
- For $i \in \{2, \ldots, t\}$, Party P_i computes its first round message as described in that protocol and forwards it to party P_{i+1} along with its public key and all the messages received from P_{i-1}.
- Now that party P_{t+1} has access to the public keys of the first t parties, it computes its first round message as described in that protocol except that it does not encrypt the shares for party P_n, instead the shares for P_n are kept in the clear. It forwards its message along with all the messages received from P_t to P_{t+2}.
- For $i \in \{t+2, \ldots, n-1\}$, party P_i computes its message exactly as P_t does above and forwards it along with all the messages received from P_{i-1} to P_{i+1}.
- Party P_n computes its message exactly as it does in the described protocol, except that it does not need to decrypt the shares, instead it receives all the shares in the clear from P_{n-1}. It forwards its message along with all the other messages (except the secret shares intended for P_n) received from P_{n-1} to P_1.
- For $i \in \{1, \ldots, t-1\}$, Party P_i computes its second message as described in that protocol and forwards it to party P_{i+1} along with all the messages received from P_{i-1}.
- At the end Party P_t can compute the output.

This gives us an $n+t-1$ message P2P protocol without any setup assumptions. This protocol can be trivially extended to obtain a protocol with $|\mathcal{O}|$ output parties that has $n+t+|\mathcal{O}|-2$ messages. This can be done by having P_t forward the output of the protocol to all the other output parties, using $|\mathcal{O}|-1$ additional messages.

Acknowledgments. The first author is supported in part from DARPA/ARL SAFE-WARE Award W911NF15C0210, AFOSR Award FA9550-15-1-0274, AFOSR Award FA9550-19-1-0200, AFOSR YIP Award, NSF CNS Award 1936826, DARPA and SPAWAR under contract N66001-15-C-4065, a Hellman Award and research grants by the Okawa Foundation, Visa Inc., and Center for Long-Term Cybersecurity (CLTC, UC Berkeley). The second and third authors are supported in part by NSF SaTC grant 1814919 and Darpa Safeware grant W911NF-15-C-0213. The views expressed are those of the authors and do not reflect the official policy or position of the funding agencies.

References

1. Ananth, P., Choudhuri, A.R., Goel, A., Jain, A.: Round-optimal secure multiparty computation with honest majority. In: Shacham, H., Boldyreva, A. (eds.) CRYPTO 2018. LNCS, vol. 10992, pp. 395–424. Springer, Cham (2018). https://doi.org/10.1007/978-3-319-96881-0_14

2. Ben-Or, M., Goldwasser, S., Wigderson, A.: Completeness theorems for non-cryptographic fault-tolerant distributed computation (extended abstract). In: 20th Annual ACM Symposium on Theory of Computing, pp. 1–10. ACM Press, Chicago, 2–4 May 1988

3. Benhamouda, F., Lin, H.: k-round multiparty computation from k-round oblivious transfer via garbled interactive circuits. In: Nielsen, J.B., Rijmen, V. (eds.) EURO-CRYPT 2018. LNCS, vol. 10821, pp. 500–532. Springer, Cham (2018). https://doi.org/10.1007/978-3-319-78375-8_17

4. Boyle, E., Chung, K.-M., Pass, R.: Large-scale secure computation: multi-party computation for (Parallel) RAM programs. In: Gennaro, R., Robshaw, M. (eds.) CRYPTO 2015. LNCS, vol. 9216, pp. 742–762. Springer, Heidelberg (2015). https://doi.org/10.1007/978-3-662-48000-7_36

5. Boyle, E., Gilboa, N., Ishai, Y.: Group-based secure computation: optimizing rounds, communication, and computation. In: Coron, J.-S., Nielsen, J.B. (eds.) EUROCRYPT 2017. LNCS, vol. 10211, pp. 163–193. Springer, Cham (2017). https://doi.org/10.1007/978-3-319-56614-6_6

6. Boyle, E., Gilboa, N., Ishai, Y., Lin, H., Tessaro, S.: Foundations of homomorphic secret sharing. In: Karlin, A.R. (ed.) ITCS 2018: 9th Innovations in Theoretical Computer Science Conference, vol. 94, pp. 21:1–21:21. LIPIcs, Cambridge, 11–14 January 2018

7. Boyle, E., Goldwasser, S., Tessaro, S.: Communication locality in secure multi-party computation. In: Sahai, A. (ed.) TCC 2013. LNCS, vol. 7785, pp. 356–376. Springer, Heidelberg (2013). https://doi.org/10.1007/978-3-642-36594-2_21

8. Chaum, D., Crépeau, C., Damgård, I.: Multiparty unconditionally secure protocols (extended abstract). In: 20th Annual ACM Symposium on Theory of Computing, pp. 11–19. ACM Press, Chicago, 2–4 May 1988

9. Chor, B., Kushilevitz, E.: A communication-privacy tradeoff for modular addition. Inf. Process. Lett. **45**(4), 205–210 (1993). https://doi.org/10.1016/0020-0190(93)90120-X

10. Cleve, R.: Limits on the security of coin flips when half the processors are faulty (extended abstract). In: 18th Annual ACM Symposium on Theory of Computing, pp. 364–369. ACM Press, Berkeley, 28–30 May 1986

11. Cramer, R., Damgård, I., Nielsen, J.B.: Multiparty computation from threshold homomorphic encryption. In: Pfitzmann, B. (ed.) EUROCRYPT 2001. LNCS, vol. 2045, pp. 280–300. Springer, Heidelberg (2001). https://doi.org/10.1007/3-540-44987-6_18

12. Damgård, I., Nielsen, J.B., Ostrovsky, R., Rosén, A.: Unconditionally secure computation with reduced interaction. In: Fischlin, M., Coron, J.-S. (eds.) EUROCRYPT 2016. LNCS, vol. 9666, pp. 420–447. Springer, Heidelberg (2016). https://doi.org/10.1007/978-3-662-49896-5_15

13. Damgård, I., Nielsen, J.B., Polychroniadou, A., Raskin, M.: On the communication required for unconditionally secure multiplication. In: Robshaw, M., Katz, J. (eds.) CRYPTO 2016. LNCS, vol. 9815, pp. 459–488. Springer, Heidelberg (2016). https://doi.org/10.1007/978-3-662-53008-5_16

14. Dodis, Y., Halevi, S., Rothblum, R.D., Wichs, D.: Spooky encryption and its applications. In: Robshaw, M., Katz, J. (eds.) CRYPTO 2016. LNCS, vol. 9816, pp. 93–122. Springer, Heidelberg (2016). https://doi.org/10.1007/978-3-662-53015-3_4

15. Garay, J., Ishai, Y., Ostrovsky, R., Zikas, V.: The price of low communication in secure multi-party computation. In: Katz, J., Shacham, H. (eds.) CRYPTO 2017. LNCS, vol. 10401, pp. 420–446. Springer, Cham (2017). https://doi.org/10.1007/978-3-319-63688-7_14

16. Garg, S., Gentry, C., Halevi, S., Raykova, M.: Two-round secure MPC from indistinguishability obfuscation. In: Lindell, Y. (ed.) TCC 2014. LNCS, vol. 8349, pp. 74–94. Springer, Heidelberg (2014). https://doi.org/10.1007/978-3-642-54242-8_4
17. Garg, S., Srinivasan, A.: Garbled protocols and two-round MPC from bilinear maps. In: 58th Annual Symposium on Foundations of Computer Science, pp. 588–599. IEEE Computer Society Press (2017)
18. Garg, S., Srinivasan, A.: Two-round multiparty secure computation from minimal assumptions. In: Nielsen, J.B., Rijmen, V. (eds.) EUROCRYPT 2018. LNCS, vol. 10821, pp. 468–499. Springer, Cham (2018). https://doi.org/10.1007/978-3-319-78375-8_16
19. Goldreich, O., Micali, S., Wigderson, A.: How to play any mental game or a completeness theorem for protocols with honest majority. In: Aho, A. (ed.) 19th Annual ACM Symposium on Theory of Computing, pp. 218–229. ACM Press, New York City, 25–27 May 1987
20. Dov Gordon, S., Liu, F.-H., Shi, E.: Constant-round MPC with fairness and guarantee of output delivery. In: Gennaro, R., Robshaw, M. (eds.) CRYPTO 2015. LNCS, vol. 9216, pp. 63–82. Springer, Heidelberg (2015). https://doi.org/10.1007/978-3-662-48000-7_4
21. Halevi, S., Lindell, Y., Pinkas, B.: Secure computation on the web: computing without simultaneous interaction. In: Rogaway, P. (ed.) CRYPTO 2011. LNCS, vol. 6841, pp. 132–150. Springer, Heidelberg (2011). https://doi.org/10.1007/978-3-642-22792-9_8
22. Ishai, Y., Mittal, M., Ostrovsky, R.: On the message complexity of secure multiparty computation. In: Abdalla, M., Dahab, R. (eds.) PKC 2018. LNCS, vol. 10769, pp. 698–711. Springer, Cham (2018). https://doi.org/10.1007/978-3-319-76578-5_24
23. Mittal, M.: Necessary and sufficient conditions for general interaction patterns for MPC. UCLA thesis for Master of Science in Computer Science (2017)
24. Mukherjee, P., Wichs, D.: Two round multiparty computation via multi-key FHE. In: Fischlin, M., Coron, J.-S. (eds.) EUROCRYPT 2016. LNCS, vol. 9666, pp. 735–763. Springer, Heidelberg (2016). https://doi.org/10.1007/978-3-662-49896-5_26
25. Yao, A.C.C.: How to generate and exchange secrets (extended abstract). In: 27th Annual Symposium on Foundations of Computer Science, pp. 162–167. IEEE Computer Society Press, Toronto, 27–29 October 1986

Beyond Honest Majority: The Round Complexity of Fair and Robust Multi-party Computation

Arpita Patra[✉] and Divya Ravi

Indian Institute of Science, Bengaluru, India
{arpita,divyar}@iisc.ac.in

Abstract. Two of the most sought-after properties of Multi-party Computation (MPC) protocols are fairness and guaranteed output delivery (GOD), the latter also referred to as robustness. Achieving both, however, brings in the necessary requirement of malicious-minority. In a generalised adversarial setting where the adversary is allowed to corrupt both actively and passively, the necessary bound for a n-party fair or robust protocol turns out to be $t_a+t_p < n$, where t_a, t_p denote the threshold for active and passive corruption with the latter subsuming the former. Subsuming the malicious-minority as a boundary special case, this setting, denoted as dynamic corruption, opens up a range of possible corruption scenarios for the adversary. While dynamic corruption includes the entire range of thresholds for (t_a, t_p) starting from $(\lceil \frac{n}{2} \rceil - 1, \lfloor n/2 \rfloor)$ to $(0, n-1)$, the boundary corruption restricts the adversary only to the boundary cases of $(\lceil \frac{n}{2} \rceil - 1, \lfloor n/2 \rfloor)$ and $(0, n-1)$. Notably, both corruption settings empower an adversary to control majority of the parties, yet ensuring the count on active corruption never goes beyond $\lceil \frac{n}{2} \rceil - 1$. We target the round complexity of fair and robust MPC tolerating dynamic and boundary adversaries. As it turns out, $\lceil n/2 \rceil + 1$ rounds are necessary and sufficient for fair as well as robust MPC tolerating dynamic corruption. The non-constant barrier raised by dynamic corruption can be sailed through for a boundary adversary. The round complexity of 3 and 4 is necessary and sufficient for fair and GOD protocols respectively, with the latter having an exception of allowing 3 round protocols in the presence of a single active corruption. While all our lower bounds assume pair-wise private and broadcast channels and are resilient to the presence of both public (CRS) and private (PKI) setup, our upper bounds are broadcast-only and assume only public setup. The traditional and popular setting of malicious-minority, being restricted compared to both dynamic and boundary setting, requires 3 and 2 rounds in the presence of public and private setup respectively for both fair as well as GOD protocols.

Keywords: Fairness · Guaranteed output delivery · MPC · Round complexity · Dynamic · Boundary

A. Patra—Supported by SERB Women Excellence Award 2017 (DSTO 1706). Divya Ravi would like to acknowledge financial support by Tata Trusts Travel Grant 2019.

S. D. Galbraith and S. Moriai (Eds.): ASIACRYPT 2019, LNCS 11921, pp. 456–487, 2019.
https://doi.org/10.1007/978-3-030-34578-5_17

1   Introduction

Secure multi-party computation (MPC) [1–3], which is arguably the most general problem in cryptography, allows a group of mutually distrustful parties to compute a joint function on their inputs without revealing any information beyond the result of the computation. While the distrust amongst the parties is modelled by a centralized adversary $\mathcal{A}$ who can corrupt a subset of the parties, the security of an MPC protocol is captured by a real-world versus ideal-world paradigm. According to this paradigm, adversarial attacks in a real execution of the MPC protocol can be translated to adversarial attacks in the ideal-world where the parties interact directly with a trusted-third party who accepts private inputs, computes the desired function and returns the output to the parties; thereby trivially achieving *correctness* (function output is correctly computed on parties' inputs) and *privacy* ($\mathcal{A}$ learns nothing about the private inputs of honest parties, beyond what is revealed by the output).

Two of the most sought-after properties of MPC protocols are fairness and robustness (alternately, guaranteed output delivery a.k.a. GOD). The former ensures that adversary obtains the output if and only if honest parties do, while the latter guarantees that the adversary cannot prevent honest parties from obtaining the output. Both these properties are trivially attainable in the presence of any number of *passive* (semi-honest) corruption where the corrupt parties follow the protocol specifications but the adversary learns the internal state of the corrupt parties. However, in the face of stringent *active* (malicious) corruption where the parties controlled by the adversary deviate arbitrarily from the protocol; fairness and GOD can be achieved only if the adversary corrupts atmost minority of the parties (referred to as malicious minority) [4]. Opening up the possibility of corrupting parties in both passive and active style, the generalized feasibility condition for a n-party fair or robust protocol turns out to be $t_a + t_p < n$, where t_a, t_p denote the threshold for active and passive corruption, with the latter subsuming the former [5]. We emphasize that t_p is a measure of the *total* number of passive corruptions that includes the actively corrupt parties; therefore the feasibility condition $t_a + t_p < n$ implies $t_a \leq \lceil n/2 \rceil - 1$. In its most intense and diverse avatar, referred as *dynamic-admissible*, the adversary can take control of the parties in one of the ways drawn from the entire range of admissible possibilities of (t_a, t_p) starting from $(\lceil \frac{n}{2} \rceil - 1, \lfloor n/2 \rfloor)$ to $(0, n-1)$. In a milder setting, referred as *boundary-admissible*, the adversary is restricted only to the boundary cases, namely $(\lceil n/2 \rceil - 1, \lfloor n/2 \rfloor)$ and $(0, n-1)$. Subsuming the traditional malicious-minority and passive-majority (majority of the parties controlled by passive adversary) setting for achieving fairness and GOD as special cases, both dynamic as well as boundary setting give the adversary more freedom and consequently more strength to the protocols. Notably, both empower an adversary to control majority of the parties, yet ensuring the count on active corruption never goes beyond $\lceil \frac{n}{2} \rceil - 1$.

The study of protocols in dynamic and boundary setting is well motivated and driven by theoretical and practical reasons. Theoretically, the study of generalized adversarial corruptions gives deeper insight into how passive and active strategies combine to influence complexity parameters of MPC such as efficiency, security notion achieved and round complexity. Practically, the protocols in dynamic and boundary setting offer strong defence and are more tolerant and better-fit in practical scenarios where the attack can come in many unforeseen ways. Indeed, deploying such protocols in practice is far more safe than traditional malicious-minority and passive-majority protocols that completely break down in the face of boundary adversaries, let alone dynamic adversaries. For instance, consider MPC in server-aided setting where instead of assuming only actively corrupt clients and honest servers, the collusion of client-server is permitted where some of the servers can be passively monitored. This model is quite realistic as it does not contradict the reputation of the system (since the passive servers follow protocol specifications and can thereby never be exposed/caught). The option of allowing corruption in both passive and active styles is quite relevant in such scenarios. Driven by the above credible reasons and extending the study of exact round complexity of fair and robust protocols beyond the traditional malicious-minority setting [6–8], in this work, we aim to settle the same for the regime of dynamic and boundary corruption.

Related Work. We begin with outlining the most relevant literature of round complexity of fair and robust MPC protocols in the traditional adversarial settings involving only single type of adversary (either passive or active). To begin with, 2 rounds are known to be necessary to realize any MPC protocol, regardless of the type of adversary, no matter whether a setup is assumed or not as long as the setup (when assumed) is independent of the inputs of the involved parties [9]. A 1-round protocol is susceptible to "residual function attack" where an adversary can evaluate the function on multiple inputs by running the computation with different values for his inputs with fixed inputs for the honest parties. The result of [6] shows necessity of 3 rounds for fairness in the plain and CRS setting, when the number of malicious corruptions is at least 2 (i.e. $t \geq 2$), irrespective of the number of parties, assuming the parties are connected by pairwise-private and broadcast channels. Complementing this result, the lower bound of [8] extends the necessity of 3 rounds for any t (including $t = 1$) as long as $n/3 < t < n/2$. The work of [7] shows 3 to be the lower bound for fairness in the presence of CRS, assuming broadcast-only channels (no private channels).

In terms of the upper bounds, the works of [10,11] showed that 2-rounds are sufficient to achieve robustness in the passive-majority setting. In accordance with the impossibility of [4] and sufficiency of honest-majority shown by classical result of [12], the upper bounds in the malicious setting involve $t < n/2$ parties. These include the 3-round constructions of [7,13,14] based on tools such as Zaps, multi-key FHE, dense crypto-systems. The protocol of [7] can be collapsed to two rounds given access to a PKI. In the information-theoretic setting involving $t < n/4$ malicious corruptions, the work of [15] presents a 3-round perfectly-secure robust protocol. In the domain of small-number of parties, round optimal protocols achieving fairness and robustness appear in [8,16].

Moving on to the setting of generalized adversary, there are primarily two adversarial models that are most relevant to us. The first model initiated by

[17] consider a mixed adversary (referred to as graceful degradation of *corruptions*) that can *simultaneously* perform different types of corruptions. Feasibility results in this model appeared in the works of [18–21]. The dynamic-admissible adversary considered in our work is consistent with this model since it involves simultaneous active and passive corruptions. The second model proposed by [22] concerns protocols that are secure against an adversary that can either choose to corrupt a subset of parties with particular corruption type (say, passively) or alternately a different subset (typically smaller) of parties with a second corruption type (say, actively), but only *single* type of corruption occurs at a time. Referred to as graceful degradation of *security* [22–28], such protocols achieve different security guarantees based on the set of corrupted parties; for instance robustness/information-theoretic security against the smaller corruption set and abort/computational security against the larger corruption set. We note that the boundary-admissible adversary when n is odd, involves either purely active (since $t_a = t_p$ holds when $(t_a, t_p) = (\lceil n/2 \rceil - 1, \lfloor n/2 \rfloor)$) corruptions or purely passive corruptions (where $(t_a, t_p) = (0, n-1)$); thereby fitting in the second model (Infact, boundary-admissible adversary for odd n degenerates to the adversarial model studied in "best-of-both-worlds" MPC [28]). However, in case of even n, the boundary-admissible adversary with $(t_a, t_p) = (\lceil n/2 \rceil - 1, \lfloor n/2 \rfloor)$ would involve simultaneous passive and active corruption as $t_p = t_a + 1$ and fit in the prior model. Lastly, both graceful degradation of security and corruptions were generalized in the works of [5, 29]. To the best of our knowledge, the interesting and natural question of round complexity has not been studied in these stronger adversarial models.

1.1 Our Results

In this work, we target and resolve the exact round complexity of fair and robust MPC protocols in both dynamic and boundary setting. This is achieved via 3 lower bounds that hold assuming *both* CRS and PKI setup and 5 upper bounds that assumes CRS *alone*. In terms of network setting, while our lower bounds hold assuming *both* pairwise-private and broadcast channels, all our upper bounds use broadcast channel *alone*. All our upper bounds are generic compilers that transform a 2-round protocol achieving unanimous abort (either all honest parties obtain output or none of them do) or identifiable abort (corrupt parties are identified in case honest parties do not obtain the output) against malicious majority to a protocol achieving the stronger guarantees of fairness/robustness against stronger adversaries (namely, dynamic and boundary adversaries). The need for CRS in our constructions stems from the underlying 2-round protocol achieving unanimous or identifiable abort. We leave open the question of constructing tight upper bounds or coming up with new lower bounds in the plain model. We elaborate on the results below.

Dynamic Adversary. We recall that in this challenging setting, the adversary has the freedom to choose from the entire range of corruption thresholds for (t_a, t_p) starting from $(\lceil n/2 \rceil - 1, \lfloor n/2 \rfloor)$ to $(0, n-1)$. Our first lower bound establishes that $\lceil n/2 \rceil + 1$ rounds are necessary to achieve fairness against dynamic adversary. Since robustness is a stronger security notion, the same lower bound holds for GOD as well. This result not only rules out the possibility of constant-round fair protocols but also gives the *exact* lower bound. We give two matching upper bounds, one for fairness and the other for robustness, where the former is subsumed by and acts as a stepping stone to the latter. These results completely settle the round complexity of this setting in the CRS model.

Boundary Adversary. The leap in round complexity ebb in the milder boundary adversarial setting where adversary is restricted to the boundary cases of $(\lceil n/2 \rceil - 1, \lfloor n/2 \rfloor)$ and $(0, n-1)$. Our two lower bounds of this setting show that 4 and 3 rounds are necessary to achieve robustness and fairness respectively against the boundary adversary. Our first 4-round lower bound is particularly interesting, primarily due to two reasons. (1) As mentioned earlier, when n is odd, the boundary cases reduce to pure active ($t_a = t_p$ when $(t_a, t_p) = (\lceil n/2 \rceil - 1, \lfloor n/2 \rfloor)$) and pure passive ($(t_a, t_p) = (0, n-1)$) corruptions. We note that security against malicious-minority and passive-majority are known to be attainable independently in just 2 rounds assuming access to CRS and PKI [7,10,11]. Hence, our 4-round lower bound encapsulates the difficulty in designing protocols tolerant against an adversary who can choose among his two boundary corruption types arbitrarily. (2) This lower bound can be circumvented in case of single malicious corruption i.e. against a special-case boundary adversary restricted to corruption scenarios $(t_a, t_p) = (1, \lfloor n/2 \rfloor)$ and $(t_a, t_p) = (0, n-1)$. (We refer to such an adversary as special-case boundary adversary with $t_a \leq 1$). This observation augments the rich evidence in literature [16,30,31] which show the impact of single corruption on feasibility results. With respect to our second lower bound for fairness against boundary adversary, we first note that the 3-round lower bound for fairness in the presence of CRS is trivial given the feasibility results of [6–8]. However, they break down assuming access to PKI. Thus, the contribution of our second lower bound is to show that the 3-round lower bound holds for boundary adversary even in the presence of PKI. We complement these two lower bounds by three tight upper bounds. The upper bounds achieving robustness include a 4-round protocol for the general case and a 3-round protocol for the special-case of one malicious corruption that demonstrates the circumvention of our first lower bound. Lastly, our third upper bound is a 3-round construction achieving fairness, demonstrating the tightness of our second lower bound.

Our results appear in the table below with comparison to the round complexity in the traditional settings of achieving fairness and robustness. Since PKI (private) setup subsumes CRS (public) setup which further subsumes plain model (no setup), the lower and upper bounds are specified with their maximum tolerance and minimum need respectively amongst these setup assumptions. The results provide us further insights regarding how disparity in adversarial setting affects round complexity. Note that the round complexity of fair protocols in the CRS model against an adversary corrupting minority of parties maliciously, remains unaffected in the setting of boundary adversary; which is a stronger variant of the former. On the other hand, this switch of adversarial setting causes the lower bound of robust protocols in the model assuming both CRS and PKI to jump from 2 to 4. Lastly, the gravity of dynamic corruption on round complexity is evident in the leap from constant-rounds of $3, 4$ in the boundary corruption case to $\lceil n/2 \rceil + 1$.

Adversary	Security	Rounds	Lower bound	Upper Bound
Passive-majority	Fair, GOD	2	[9] (private)	[10,11] (plain)
Malicious-minority	Fair, GOD	3	[7,8] (public)	[13,14] (plain)
	Fair, GOD	2	[9] (private)	[7] (private)
Boundary	Fair	**3**	**[This]** (private)	**[This]** (public)
	GOD	**4 (3 when $t_a \leq 1$)**	**[This]** (private)	**[This]** (public)
Dynamic	Fair, GOD	$\lceil \frac{n}{2} \rceil + 1$	**[This]** (private)	**[This]** (public)

1.2 Techniques

In this section, we give a glimpse into the techniques used in our lower bounds and matching upper bound constructions.

Lower Bounds. We present 3 lower bounds, all of which hold assuming access to *both* CRS and PKI– **(a)** $\lceil n/2 \rceil + 1$ rounds are necessary to achieve fairness against dynamic adversary. **(b)** 4 rounds are necessary to achieve robustness against a boundary adversary. **(c)** 3 rounds are necessary to achieve fairness against a boundary adversary.

The first lower bound **(a)** effectively captures the power of dynamic corruption stemming from the ambiguity caused by the total range of thresholds (t_a, t_p) starting from $(\lceil n/2 \rceil - 1, \lfloor n/2 \rfloor)$ to $(0, n - 1)$. The proof navigates through this sequence starting with maximal active corruption and proceeds to scenarios of lesser active corruptions one at a time. An inductive argument neatly captures how the value of t_p growing alongside decreasing values of t_a can be exploited by adversarial strategies violating fairness, eventually dragging the round complexity all the way upto $\lceil n/2 \rceil + 1$. The lower bounds **(b)** and **(c)** are shown by considering a specific set of small number of parties and assume the existence of a 3 (2) round robust (fair) protocol for contradiction respectively. Subsequently, inferences are drawn based on cleverly-designed strategies exploiting the properties of GOD and fairness. These inferences and strategies are interconnected in a manner that builds up to a strategy violating privacy, thereby leading to a final contradiction.

Upper Bounds. We present 5 upper bounds, in the broadcast-only setting comprising of two upper bounds each for fairness and GOD against dynamic and boundary adversary respectively and lastly, an additional 3-round upper bound for GOD against the special case of single malicious corruption by boundary adversary in order to demonstrate the circumvention of lower bound (**b**). Tightness of this upper bound follows from lower bound (**c**) (that holds for single malicious corruption) as GOD implies fairness. Our upper bounds can be viewed as "compiled" protocols obtained upon plugging in any 2-round broadcast-only protocols [10,11] achieving unanimous abort against malicious majority. While the fair upper-bounds do not require any additional property from the underlying 2-round protocol, our robust protocols demand the property of *identifiable abort* and *function-delayed* property i.e. the first round of the protocol is independent of the function to be computed and the number of parties. Looking ahead, this enables us to run many parallel instances of the round 1 in the beginning and run the second round sequentially as and when failure happens to compute a new function (that gets determined based on the identities of the corrupt parties). Assumption wise, all our upper bound constructions rely on 2-round maliciously-secure oblivious transfer (OT) in common random/reference string models. We now give a high-level overview of the specific challenges we encounter in each of our upper bounds and the techniques we use to tackle them.

Dynamic Adversary: The two upper bounds against dynamic adversary show sufficiency of $\lceil n/2 \rceil + 1$ rounds to achieve fairness and robustness against dynamic admissible adversary. The upper bound for fairness is built upon the protocol of [5] that introduces a special-kind of sharing, which we refer to as levelled-sharing where a value is divided into summands (adding upto the value) and each summand is shared with varying degrees. The heart of the protocol of [5] lies in its gradual reconstruction of the levelled-shared output (obtained by running an MPC protocol with unanimous abort), starting with the summand corresponding to the highest degree down to the lowest. The argument for fairness banks on the fact that the more the adversary raises its disruptive power in an attempt to control reconstruction of more number of summands, the more it looses its eavesdropping capability and consequently learns fewer number of summands by itself and vice versa. This discourages an adversary from misbehaving as using maximal disruptive power reduces its eavesdropping capability such that he falls short of learning the next summand in sequence without the help of honest parties. The innovation of our fair protocol lies in delicately fixing the parameters of levelled-sharing in a manner that optimal round complexity can be attained whilst maintaining fairness.

Next, we point that since the fair protocol consumes the optimal round complexity of $\lceil n/2 \rceil + 1$ even in the case of honest execution, the primary hurdle in our second upper bound is to be able to carry out re-runs when an adversary disrupts computation to achieve robustness without consuming extra rounds. Banking on the player-elimination technique, we use identifiability to bar the corrupt parties disrupting computation from participating thereafter. Having parallel execution of Round 1 of all the required re-reruns helps us get closer to the optimal bound. While these approaches aid to a great extent, the final saviour comes in the form of a delicate and crucial observation regarding how the thresholds of the levelled-sharing can be manipulated carefully, accounting for the cheaters identified so far. This trick exploits the pattern of reduced corruption scenarios obtained upon cheater identification and helps to compensate for the rounds consumed in subprotocols that were eventually disrupted by the adversary. The analysis of the round complexity of the protocol being subtle, we use an intricate recursive argument to capture all scenarios and show that the optimal lower bound is never exceeded. Lastly, we point that both upper bound constructions against dynamic adversary assume equivocal non-interactive commitment (such as Pedersen commitment [32]). The GOD upper bound additionally assumes the existence of Non-Interactive Zero-Knowledge (NIZK) in the common random/reference string model.

Boundary Adversary: The three upper bounds against boundary-admissible adversary restricted to corruption scenarios either $(t_a, t_p) = (\lceil n/2 \rceil - 1, \lfloor n/2 \rfloor)$ or $(t_a, t_p) = (0, n - 1)$ show that **(a)** 4 rounds are sufficient to achieve robustness against boundary-admissible adversary **(b)** 3 rounds are sufficient to achieve robustness against special-case boundary-admissible adversary when $t_a \leq 1$ i.e. adversary corrupts with parameters either $(t_a, t_p) = (1, \lfloor n/2 \rfloor)$ or $(t_a, t_p) = (0, n - 1)$ **(c)** 3 rounds are sufficient to achieve fairness against boundary-admissible adversary. At a high-level, all the three upper bounds begin with a 2-round protocol secure against malicious majority that computes threshold sharing of the output. Intuitively, this seems to serve as the only available option as protocols customized for malicious minority typically breach privacy when views of majority of the parties are combined (thereby will break down against $t_p < n$ semi-honest corruptions). On the flip side, protocols customized for exclusively passive majority may violate correctness/privacy in the presence of even single malicious corruption. Subsequently, this natural route bifurcates into two scenarios based on whether the adversary allows the computation of the threshold sharing of output to succeed or not. In case of success, all the three upper bounds proceed via the common route of reconstruction which is guaranteed to be robust by the property of threshold sharing. The distinctness of the 3 settings (accordingly the upper bounds) crops up in the alternate scenario i.e. when the computation of threshold sharing of output aborts. While in upper bound **(c)**, parties simply terminate with $\perp$ maintaining fairness enabled by privacy of the threshold sharing; the upper bounds **(a)** and **(b)** demanding stronger guarantee of robustness cannot afford to do so. These two upper bounds exploit the fact that the corruption scenario has now been identified to be the boundary case having active corruptions, thereby protocols tolerating malicious minority can now be executed. While the above outline is inspired by the work of [28], we point that we need to tackle the exact corruption scenarios as that of the protocols of [28] only when n is odd. On the other hand when n is even, the extreme case for active corruption accommodates an additional passive corruption ($t_p = t_a + 1$). Apart from hitting the optimal round complexity, tackling the distinct boundary cases for odd and even n in a unified way brings challenge for our protocol. To overcome these challenges, in addition to techniques of identification and elimination of corrupt parties who disrupt computation, we employ tricks such as parallelizing without compromising on security to achieve the optimum round complexity. Assumption wise, while both the robust constructions (a) and (b) rely on NIZKs, the former additionally assumes Zaps (2-round, public-coin witness-indistinguishable protocols) and public-key encryption.

2 Preliminaries

We consider a set of parties $\mathcal{P} = \{P_1, \ldots P_n\}$. Our upper bounds assume the parties connected by a broadcast channel and a setup where parties have access to common reference string (CRS). Our lower bounds hold even when the parties are additionally connected by pairwise-secure and authentic channels and for a stronger setup, namely assuming access to CRS as well as public-key infrastructure (PKI). Each party is modelled as a probabilistic polynomial time Turing (PPT) machine. We assume that there exists a PPT adversary $\mathcal{A}$, who can corrupt a subset of these parties.

We consider two kinds of adversarial settings in this work. In both settings, the $\mathcal{A}$ is characterised by two thresholds (t_a, t_p), where he may corrupt upto t_p parties passively, and upto t_a of these parties even actively. Note that t_p is the total number of passive corruptions that includes the active corruptions and additional parties that are exclusively passively corrupt. We now define dynamic and boundary admissible adversaries.

Definition 1 (Dynamic-admissible Adversary). *An adversary attacking an n-party MPC protocol with threshold (t_a, t_p) is called dynamic-admissible as long as $t_a + t_p < n$ and $t_a \leq t_p$.*

Definition 2 (Boundary-admissible Adversary). *An adversary attacking an n-party MPC protocol with threshold (t_a, t_p) is called boundary-admissible as long as he corrupts either with parameters (a) $(t_a, t_p) = (\lceil \frac{n}{2} \rceil - 1, \lfloor n/2 \rfloor)$ or (b) $(t_a, t_p) = (0, n - 1)$.*

In our work, we also consider a special-case of boundary adversary with $t_a \leq 1$ where the adversary corrupts either with parameters $(t_a, t_p) = (1, \lfloor n/2 \rfloor)$ or $(t_a, t_p) = (0, n - 1)$.

Notation. We denote the cryptographic security parameter by κ. A negligible function in κ is denoted by $\texttt{negl}(\kappa)$. A function $\texttt{negl}(\cdot)$ is negligible if for every polynomial $p(\cdot)$ there exists a value N such that for all $m > N$ it holds that $\texttt{negl}(m) < \frac{1}{p(m)}$. Composition of two functions, f and g (say, $h(x) = g(f(x))$) is denoted as $g \diamond f$. We use $[n]$ to denote the set $\{1, \ldots n\}$ and $[a, b]$ to denote the set $\{a, a + 1 \ldots b\}$ when $a \leq b$ or the set $\{a, a - 1, \ldots b\}$ when $a > b$. Lastly, for dynamic-admissible adversary, we denote the set of active and passively corrupt parties by $\mathcal{D}$ and $\mathcal{E}$ respectively, where $|\mathcal{D}| = t_a$ and $|\mathcal{E}| = t_p$.

Roadmap. Our lower and upper bounds for dynamic and boundary corruption appear in Sects. 3–4 and in Sects. 5–6 respectively. The security definitions and proofs appear in the full version [33].

3   Lower Bounds for Dynamic Corruption

In this section, we show that $\lceil \frac{n}{2} \rceil + 1$ rounds are necessary to achieve MPC with fairness against a dynamic-admissible $\mathcal{A}$ with threshold (t_a, t_p). This result shows impossibility of constant-round fair and robust protocols in the setting of dynamic corruption.

Theorem 1. *No $\lceil \frac{n}{2} \rceil$-round n-party MPC protocol can achieve fairness tolerating a dynamic-admissible adversary $\mathcal{A}$ with threshold (t_a, t_p) in a setting with pairwise-private and broadcast channels, and a setup that includes* CRS *and* PKI.

Proof. We prove the theorem by contradiction. Suppose there exists a $\lceil \frac{n}{2} \rceil$-round n-party MPC protocol π computing any function $f(x_1 \ldots x_n)$ (where x_i denotes the input of party P_i) that achieves fairness against a dynamic-admissible $\mathcal{A}$ with corruption threshold (t_a, t_p) and in the presence of a setup with CRS and PKI. At a high-level, our proof argument defines a sequence of hybrid executions of π, navigating through all the possible admissible corruption scenarios assuming $t_a + t_p = n - 1$ and starting with the maximum admissible value of $t_a = \lceil n/2 \rceil - 1$. Our first hybrid under the spell of a dynamic-admissible adversary, corrupting $\lceil n/2 \rceil - 1$ parties actively and stopping their communication in the last round, lets us conclude that the joint view of the honest and passively-corrupted parties by the end of penultimate round must hold the output in order for π to satisfy fairness. If not, while ceasing communication in the last round does not prevent $\mathcal{A}$ from getting all the messages in the last round and thereby the output, the honest parties do fail to compute the output due to the non-cooperation of t_a parties, violating fairness. The views of the passively corrupt parties need to be taken into account as they follow protocol steps correctly and assist in output computation. Leveraging the fact that drop of t_a leads to rise of t_p, we then propose a new hybrid where t_a is demoted by 1 and consequently t_p grows big enough to subsume the list of honest and passive-corruption from the previous hybrid. As the view of the adversary in this hybrid holds the output by the end of penultimate round itself, its actively-corrupt parties need not speak in the penultimate round. Now fairness in the face of current strategy of the actively-corrupted parties needs the joint view of the honest and passively-corrupted parties by the end of $\lceil n/2 \rceil - 2$ round to hold the output. This continues with the set of honest and passively-corrupted parties growing by size one between every two hybrids. Propagating this pattern to the earlier rounds eventually lets us conclude that an adversary with threshold $(t_a, t_p) = (0, n - 1)$ (no active corruption case) can obtain the output at the end of Round 1 itself. This leads us to a final strategy that violates privacy of π via residual attack. This completes the proof sketch. We now prove the sequence of lemmas to complete the proof.

Lemma 1. *In an execution of π where all parties behave honestly upto (and including) Round $(\lceil \frac{n}{2} \rceil - i)$ for $i \in [\lceil \frac{n}{2} \rceil - 1]$, there exists a set of parties S^i with size $(\lfloor \frac{n}{2} \rfloor + i)$ whose combined view at the end of Round $\lceil \frac{n}{2} \rceil - i$ suffices to compute the output.*

Proof. We prove the lemma by induction. Let $\mathcal{P} = \{P_1, P_2, ..., P_n\}$ denote the set of parties and $\mathcal{D}(\mathcal{E})$ denote the set of actively (passively) corrupt parties where $\mathcal{D} \subseteq \mathcal{E}$. Here $|\mathcal{D}| = t_a$ and $|\mathcal{E}| = t_p$.

Base Case ($i = 1$): We consider an execution of the protocol π with a dynamic-admissible adversary $\mathcal{A}$ corrupting parties with threshold $(t_a, t_p) = (\lceil \frac{n}{2} \rceil - 1, \lfloor n/2 \rfloor)$ and an adversarial strategy $\mathcal{A}_1$ as follows. The set of actively corrupt parties $\mathcal{D}$ behave honestly upto (and including) Round $\lceil \frac{n}{2} \rceil - 1$ and simply remain silent in the last round i.e. the $\lceil \frac{n}{2} \rceil$th round. Since $\mathcal{A}$ receives all the desired communication throughout the protocol, it follows directly from the correctness of π that $\mathcal{A}$ must be able to compute the output. Since π is assumed to be fair, the honest parties must also be able to compute the output even without the $\lceil \frac{n}{2} \rceil$th round communication from parties in $\mathcal{D}$. We can now conclude that the combined view of parties in $\mathcal{P} \setminus \mathcal{D}$ at the end of Round $\lceil \frac{n}{2} \rceil - 1$ must suffice to compute the output. Thus, the set $S^1 = \mathcal{P} \setminus \mathcal{D}$ of parties with size $n - t_a = n - (\lceil \frac{n}{2} \rceil - 1) = \lfloor \frac{n}{2} \rfloor + 1$ hold a combined view at the end of Round $\lceil \frac{n}{2} \rceil - 1$ that suffices to compute the output. This completes the base case.

Induction Hypothesis ($i = \ell$). Suppose the statement is true for $i = \ell$ i.e. if all parties behave honestly upto (and including) Round $(\lceil \frac{n}{2} \rceil - \ell)$, then there exists a set of parties, say S^ℓ, with $|S^\ell| = (\lfloor \frac{n}{2} \rfloor + \ell)$ whose combined view at the end of $(\lceil \frac{n}{2} \rceil - \ell)$th round, suffices to compute the output.

Induction Step ($i = \ell + 1$). We consider an execution of the protocol π with a dynamic-admissible adversary $\mathcal{A}$ corrupting parties with threshold $(t_a, t_p) = (\lceil \frac{n}{2} \rceil - \ell - 1, \lfloor \frac{n}{2} \rfloor + \ell)$ and $\mathcal{E} = S^\ell$ as defined in the induction hypothesis and an adversarial strategy $\mathcal{A}_{\ell+1}$ as follows. The set of actively corrupt parties $\mathcal{D}$ behave honestly upto (and including) Round $(\lceil \frac{n}{2} \rceil - \ell - 1)$ and simply remain silent from Round $(\lceil \frac{n}{2} \rceil - \ell)$ onwards. Since $\mathcal{A}$ receives all the desired communication upto (and including) Round $(\lceil \frac{n}{2} \rceil - \ell)$ of π (as per an honest execution) on behalf of parties in $\mathcal{E}$, it follows directly from the induction hypothesis that the combined view of the parties in $\mathcal{E}$ where $|\mathcal{E}| = \lfloor \frac{n}{2} \rfloor + \ell$ must suffice to compute the output. Since π is assumed to be fair, the honest parties must also be able to compute the output even though the parties in $\mathcal{D}$ stop communicating from Round $(\lceil \frac{n}{2} \rceil - \ell)$ onwards. We can now conclude that the combined view of parties in $\mathcal{P} \setminus \mathcal{D}$ at the end of Round $(\lceil \frac{n}{2} \rceil - \ell - 1)$ must suffice to compute the output. Thus, the set $S^{\ell+1} = \mathcal{P} \setminus \mathcal{D}$ of parties with size $n - t_a = n - (\lceil \frac{n}{2} \rceil - \ell - 1) = \lfloor \frac{n}{2} \rfloor + \ell + 1$ hold a combined view at the end of Round $(\lceil \frac{n}{2} \rceil - \ell - 1)$ that suffices to compute the output. This completes the induction hypothesis and the proof of Lemma 1. □

Lemma 2. *There exists an adversary $\mathcal{A}$ that is able to compute the output at the end of Round 1 of π.*

Proof. When $i = \lceil \frac{n}{2} \rceil - 1$, Lemma 1 implies that if all parties behave honestly in Round 1, then there exists a set $S^{\lceil \frac{n}{2} \rceil - 1}$ of $(\lfloor \frac{n}{2} \rfloor + \lceil \frac{n}{2} \rceil - 1) = n - 1$ parties whose combined view suffices to compute the output at the end of Round 1.

Consequently, a dynamic-admissible adversary $\mathcal{A}$ corrupting the parties with threshold $(t_a, t_p) = (0, n-1)$ and $(\mathcal{D} = \emptyset, \mathcal{E} = S^{\lceil \frac{n}{2} \rceil - 1})$ must be able to compute the output at the end of Round 1 itself.   □

Lemma 3. *Protocol π does not achieve privacy.*

Proof. It follows directly from Lemma 2 that there exists an adversary $\mathcal{A}$ with threshold $(t_a, t_p) = (0, n-1)$ corrupting a set of $(n-1)$ parties passively, say $\mathcal{E} = \{P_1, \ldots P_{n-1}\}$, that is able to compute the output at the end of Round 1 itself. Thus, $\mathcal{A}$ can obtain multiple evaluations of the function f by locally plugging in different values for $\{x_1, \ldots, x_{n-1}\}$ while honest P_n's input x_n remains fixed. This residual function attack violates privacy of P_n. As a concrete example, let f be a common output function computing $x_1 \wedge x_n$, where x_i $(i \in \{1, n\})$ denotes a single bit. During the execution of π, $\mathcal{A}$ behaves honestly with input $x_1 = 0$ on behalf of P_1. However, the passively-corrupt P_1 can locally plug-in $x_1 = 1$ and learn x_n (via the output $x_1 \wedge x_n$). This is a clear breach of privacy, as in the ideal world, $\mathcal{A}$ participating honestly with input $x_1 = 0$ on behalf of P_1 would learn nothing about x_n; in contrast to the execution of π where $\mathcal{A}$ learns x_n regardless of his input. This completes the proof.   □

We have thus arrived at a contradiction to our assumption that π securely computes f and achieves fairness. This completes the proof of Theorem 1.   □

4   Upper Bounds for Dynamic Corruption

In this section, we describe two n-party upper bounds tolerating a dynamic-admissible adversary $\mathcal{A}$ with threshold (t_a, t_p). The first upper bound achieves fairness and is a stepping stone to the construction of the second upper bound that achieves guaranteed output delivery. Both the upper bounds comprise of $\lceil n/2 \rceil + 1$ rounds in the presence of CRS, tightly matching our lower bound result of Sect. 3. We start with an important building block needed for both the fair and GOD protocols.

4.1   Levelled-Sharing of a Secret

Our protocols in the dynamic corruption setting involve a special kind of sharing referred as levelled sharing, which is inspired by and a generalized variant of the sharing defined in [5]. The sharing is parameterized with two thresholds, α and β with $\alpha \geq \beta$, that dictate the number of levels as $\alpha - \beta + 1$. To share a secret in (α, β)-levelled-shared fashion, $\alpha - \beta + 1$ additive shares (levels) of the secret, indexed from α to β are created and each additive share is then Shamir-shared [34] using polynomial of degree that is same as its assigned index. Further each Shamir-sharing is authenticated using a non-interactive commitment scheme, to ensure detectably correct reconstruction. For technical reasons in the simulation-based security proof, we need an instantiation of commitment scheme that allows equivocation of commitment to any message with the help of trapdoor and provides statistical hiding and computational binding. Denoting such a commitment scheme by eNICOM (Equivocal Non-Interactive Commitment), we present both the formal definition and an instantiation based on Pedersen's commitment scheme [32] in the full version [33]. While the sharing will involve the entire population $\mathcal{P}$ in our fair protocol, it may be restricted to many different subsets of $\mathcal{P}$, each time after curtailing identified actively corrupt parties. The definition therefore is formalized with respect to a set $\mathcal{Q} \subseteq \mathcal{P}$.

Definition 3 ((α, β)-levelled sharing). *A value v is said to be (α, β)-levelled-shared with $\alpha \geq \beta$ amongst a set of parties $\mathcal{Q} \subseteq \mathcal{P}$ if every honest or passively corrupt party P_i in $\mathcal{Q}$ holds L_i as produced by $f_{\mathsf{LSh}}^{\alpha,\beta}(v)$ given in Fig. 1.*

Function $f_{\mathsf{LSh}}^{\alpha,\beta}(v)$

1. Choose uniformly random summands $s_\alpha, s_{\alpha-1}, \ldots s_\beta$ with $\sum_{i=\beta}^{\alpha} s_j = v$
2. For $j \in [\alpha, \beta]$, do the following:
   - Choose a random polynomial $g_j(x)$ of degree j with $g_j(0) = s_j$.
   - Sample the public parameter for eNICOM as $(\mathsf{epp}, t) \leftarrow \mathsf{eGen}(1^\kappa)$. For each share $s_{jk} = g_j(k)$, run $(c_{jk}, o_{jk}) \leftarrow \mathsf{eCom}(\mathsf{epp}, s_{jk}; r_{jk})$ $(P_k \in \mathcal{Q})$ where r_{jk} denotes randomness.
3. Set $L_i = (\{s_{ji}, o_{ji}\}_{j \in [\alpha,\beta]}, \{c_{jk}\}_{j \in [\alpha,\beta], P_k \in \mathcal{Q}})$ for $P_i \in \mathcal{Q}$.

Fig. 1. Function $f_{\mathsf{LSh}}^{\alpha,\beta}$ for computing (α, β)-levelled sharing

In our protocols the function $f_{\mathsf{LSh}}^{\alpha,\beta}$ will be realized via an MPC protocol, whereas, given the (α, β)-levelled-sharing, we will use a levelled-reconstruction protocol $\mathsf{LRec}^{\alpha,\beta}()$ that enforce reconstruction of the summands one at a time starting with s_α. This levelled reconstruction ensures a remarkable property tolerating any dynamic-admissible adversary– if the adversary can disrupt reconstruction of s_i, then it cannot learn s_{i-1} using its eavesdropping power. This property is instrumental in achieving fairness against the strong dynamic-admissible adversary. The protocol is presented in Fig. 2. Its properties and round complexity are stated below. Note that starting with the feasibility condition $t_a + t_p < n = |\mathcal{P}|$, expelling a set of actively corrupt parties, say $\mathcal{B}$, makes the following impact on t_a, t_p and $\mathcal{P}$: $t_a = t_a - |\mathcal{B}|$, $t_p = t_p - |\mathcal{B}|$ and $\mathcal{P} = \mathcal{P} \setminus \mathcal{B}$. Consequently, the updated t_a, t_p and $\mathcal{P}$ continue to satisfy $t_a + t_p < |\mathcal{P}|$. Below, we will therefore use the fact that $t_a + t_p < |\mathcal{Q}|$, where $\mathcal{Q}$ denotes the relevant set of parties (i.e. the set of parties remaining after possibly expelling a set of identified actively corrupt parties).

Lemma 4. $\mathsf{LRec}^{\alpha,\beta}$ *satisfies the following properties–*

i. Correctness. *Each honest P_i participating in $\mathsf{LRec}^{\alpha,\beta}$ with input L_i as generated by $f_{\mathsf{LSh}}^{\alpha,\beta}(v)$, outputs either v or $\perp$ except with negligible probability.*

Protocol LRec$^{\alpha,\beta}$

Inputs: Each P_i ($P_i \in \mathcal{Q}$) has input $L_i = (\{s_{ji}, o_{ji}\}_{j \in [\alpha,\beta]}, \{c_{jk}\}_{j \in [\alpha,\beta], P_k \in \mathcal{Q}})$.
Output: Secret v or $\perp$ with set $\mathcal{B}$ constituting indices of the identified actively corrupt parties.

- For $j = \alpha$ down to β, P_i does the following round-by-round:
    - Broadcasts (s_{ji}, o_{ji}) and receive (s_{jk}, o_{jk}) from all $P_k \in \mathcal{Q}$ where $k \neq i$.
    - Initialize $\mathsf{Z}_j = i$ and populate Z_j in order to compute s_j as follows:
        - For each $k \neq i$, if commitment c_{jk} opens to s_{jk} via opening o_{jk}, then add k to Z_j.
        - If $|\mathsf{Z}_j| \geq j+1$, interpolate a j-degree polynomial $g_j(x)$ satisfying $g_j(k) = s_{jk}$ for $k \in \mathsf{Z}_j$ and compute $s_j = g_j(0)$. Else output $\perp$, set $\mathcal{B} = \mathcal{Q} \setminus \mathsf{Z}_j$ and terminate.
- Output $v = s_\alpha + \ldots s_\beta$.

Fig. 2. Protocol LRec$^{\alpha,\beta}$

ii. Fault-Identification. *If an adversary disrupts the reconstruction of s_j, then* $|\mathcal{B}| \geq |\mathcal{Q}| - j$.

iii. Fairness. *If an adversary disrupts the reconstruction of s_j, then it does not learn s_{j-1}.*

iv. Round Complexity. *It terminates within $\alpha - \beta + 1$ rounds.*

Proof. **i.** Consider an honest P_i participating with input $L_i = (\{s_{ji}, o_{ji}\}_{j \in [\alpha,\beta]}, \{c_{jk}\}_{j \in [\alpha,\beta], P_k \in \mathcal{Q}})$. We observe P_i outputs $v' \neq \{v, \perp\}$ only if at least one of the summands, say s_j ($j \in [\alpha, \beta]$) is incorrectly set. This can happen only if P_i adds at least one index k to Z_j such that P_k sends an incorrect share $s'_{jk} \neq s_{jk}$. This occurs when (s'_{jk}, o'_{jk}) received from P_k is such that c_{jk} opens to s'_{jk} via o'_{jk} but $s'_{jk} \neq s_{jk}$. It now follows directly from the binding of eNICOM that this violation occurs with negligible probability. This completes the proof.

ii. Firstly, it follows from the property of Shamir-secret sharing and binding property of eNICOM that reconstruction of s_j would fail only if $|\mathsf{Z}_j| \leq j$. Next, note that as per the steps in Fig. 2, each honest P_i would output $\mathcal{B} = \mathcal{Q} \setminus \mathsf{Z}_j$ if reconstruction of s_j fails. We can thus conclude that $|\mathcal{B}| = |\mathcal{Q}| - |\mathsf{Z}_j| \geq |\mathcal{Q}| - j$.

iii. To prove fairness, we first prove that if an adversary can disrupt the reconstruction of s_j, then it cannot learn s_{j-1} using its eavesdropping power. Since as per the protocol, the honest parties do not participate in the reconstruction of s_{j-1} when they fail to reconstruct s_j, the security of s_{j-1} follows from the information-theoretic security of Shamir-sharing and the statistical security (hiding) of eNICOM.

An adversary can disrupt reconstruction of s_j only if $|\mathsf{Z}_j| \leq j$. It is easy to check that Z_j would constitute the non-actively corrupt parties (honest and purely passive parties) i.e. $\mathcal{Q} \setminus \mathcal{D} \subseteq \mathsf{Z}_j$. Thus, $|\mathcal{Q} \setminus \mathcal{D}| = |\mathcal{Q}| - t_a \leq |\mathsf{Z}_j| \leq j$. Lastly, to maintain $t_a + t_p < |\mathcal{Q}|$, it must hold that $t_p \leq |\mathcal{Q}| - t_a - 1 \leq j - 1$.

Thus, the adversary corrupting $t_p \le j - 1$ parties cannot learn s_{j-1} using its eavesdropping power.

iv. $\mathsf{LRec}^{\alpha,\beta}$ involves reconstruction of summands s_α down to s_β, each of which consumes one round; totalling upto $\alpha - \beta + 1$.   □

4.2   Upper Bound for Fair MPC

The key insight for this protocol comes from [5] that builds on an MPC protocol with abort security to compute the function output in $(n-1,1)$-levelled-sharing form, followed by levelled-reconstruction to tackle dynamic corruption. Fairness is brought to the system by relying on the fairness of the levelled-reconstruction. In particular, the adversary is disabled to reconstruct $(i-1)$th summand, as a punitive action, when it disrupts reconstruction of the ith summand for the honest parties. In the marginal case, if the adversary disrupts the MPC protocol for computing the levelled-sharing and does not let the honest parties get their output, we disable it to reconstruct the $(n-1)$th summand itself.

In a (α, β)-levelled-reconstruction, the parameters α and β dictate the round complexity. The closer they are the better round complexity we obtain. The α and β in [5] are $n-2$ apart, shooting the round complexity of reconstruction to $n-1$. We depart from the construction of [5] in two ways to build a $(\lceil \frac{n}{2} \rceil + 1)$-round fair protocol. Firstly and prominently, we bring α and β much closer, cutting down $\lfloor \frac{n}{2} \rfloor$ summands from the levelled-secret sharing and bringing down the number of levels to just $n-1-\lfloor \frac{n}{2} \rfloor$ from $n-1$ of [5]. Second, we plug in the round-optimal (2-round) MPC protocol of [10,11] achieving unanimous abort against malicious majority in the CRS model for computing the levelled-sharing of the output, making overall a $(\lceil \frac{n}{2} \rceil + 1)$-round fair protocol. We discuss the first departure in detail below.

Our innovation lies in fixing the best values of α and β without flouting fairness. The value of α and β, in essence determines the indispensable summands that we cannot do without. Every possible *non-zero* threshold for active corruption maps to a crucial summand that the adversary using its corresponding admissible passive threshold cannot learn by itself, whilst the pool of non-disruptive set of parties, i.e. the set of honest and purely passive parties, can. This unique summand, being the 'soft spot' for the adversary, forces him to cooperate until the reconstruction of the immediate previous summand. As soon as the adversary does so, the honest parties turn self-reliant to compute the output, upholding fairness. We care only about the non-zero possibilities for the threshold of active corruption, as an all-passive adversary holds no power at its disposal to disrupt, leading to robust output reconstruction by all. For the minimum non-zero value of 1 active corruption, the unique summand is s_{n-2} that the adversary cannot learn using its admissible eavesdropping capacity of $n-2$, yet the set of non-disruptive parties, which is of size $n-1$, can. On the other extreme, for the maximum value of $\lceil \frac{n}{2} \rceil - 1$, the unique summand is $s_{\lfloor \frac{n}{2} \rfloor}$ that the adversary cannot learn using its admissible eavesdropping capacity of $\lfloor \frac{n}{2} \rfloor$, yet the set of non-disruptive parties, which is of size $\lfloor \frac{n}{2} \rfloor + 1$, can. This sets the values of α and β as $n-2$ and $\lfloor \frac{n}{2} \rfloor$ respectively, making the number of crucial summands only $\lceil \frac{n}{2} \rceil - 1$. The distance between these two parameters captures the number of possible corruption scenarios with non-zero active corruption.

In the table below (Table 1), we display for each admissible adversarial corruption (this set subsumes the crucial summands that we retain), whether the adversary and the set of non-disruptive parties respectively by themselves, can learn the summand, using its maximum eavesdropping capability and putting together their shares respectively. The pattern clearly displays the following feature: irrespective of the corruption scenario that the adversary follows, its maximum power to disrupt and eavesdrop remains one summand apart i.e. if it can disrupt ith summand with its maximum disruptive capability (and fall short of its power for failing the $(i-1)$th one), then its maximum eavesdropping capability does not allow it to learn $(i-1)$th summand by itself. Our fair protocol $\pi_{\mathsf{fair}}^{\mathsf{dyn}}$ tolerating dynamic corruption appears in Fig. 3. Assumption wise, $\pi_{\mathsf{fair}}^{\mathsf{dyn}}$ relies on 2-round maliciously-secure OT in the common random/reference string model (when π_{ua} is instantiated with protocols of [10,11]) and eNICOM (used in $\mathsf{LRec}^{\alpha,\beta}()$ and instantiated using Pedersen's commitment scheme).

Table 1. Levelled-reconstruction where $(a = \mathtt{Y/N}, b = \mathtt{Y/N})$ under s_i indicates if $\mathcal{A}$ and non-active parties respectively can reconstruct s_i or not ($\mathtt{Y}$ = Yes, $\mathtt{N}$ = No)

$(t_a = |\mathcal{D}|, t_p = |\mathcal{E}|)$	$|\mathcal{P} \setminus \mathcal{D}|$	s_{n-2}	s_{n-3}	s_{n-4}		s_{n-i-1}		$s_{\lfloor n/2 \rfloor +1}$	$s_{\lfloor n/2 \rfloor}$
$(0, n-1)$	n	(Y, Y)	(Y, Y)	(Y, Y)	... ...		...	(Y, Y)	(Y, Y)
$(1, n-2)$	$n-1$	(N, Y)	(Y, Y)	(Y, Y)	... ...		...	(Y, Y)	(Y, Y)
$(2, n-3)$	$n-2$	(N, N)	(N, Y)	(Y, Y)	... ...		...	(Y, Y)	(Y, Y)
...	...	...	...	...	... ...		...	...	...
$(i, n-i-1)$	$n-i$	(N, N)	(N, N)	(N, N)	...	(N, Y)	...	(Y, Y)	(Y, Y)
...	...	...	...	...	... ...		...	...	...
$(\lceil n/2 \rceil - 1, \lfloor n/2 \rfloor)$	$\lfloor n/2 \rfloor + 1$	(N, N)	(N, N)	(N, N)	... ...		...	(N, N)	(N, Y)

Protocol $\pi_{\mathsf{fair}}^{\mathsf{dyn}}$

Inputs: Party P_j has x_j for $j \in [n]$

Building blocks: (a) Protocol π_{ua} achieving security with unanimous abort against malicious majority (b) Protocol $\mathsf{LRec}^{\alpha,\beta}$ for reconstructing a (α, β)-levelled-shared value (Fig. 2); (c) Function $f_{\mathsf{LSh}}^{n-2, \lfloor \frac{n}{2} \rfloor}$ (Fig 1).

Output: $y = f(x_1 \ldots x_n)$ or $\perp$

Round 1 – 2: Every P_j runs protocol π_{ua} to compute the function $f_{\mathsf{LSh}}^{n-2, \lfloor \frac{n}{2} \rfloor} \diamond f$ with input x_j to obtain L_j as the output. If $L_j = \perp$, it outputs $\perp$ and halts.

Round 3 – $(\lceil n/2 \rceil + 1)$: Each P_j participates in $\mathsf{LRec}^{n-2, \lfloor \frac{n}{2} \rfloor}$ with input L_j and outputs the outcome of $\mathsf{LRec}^{n-2, \lfloor \frac{n}{2} \rfloor}$.

Fig. 3. Fair MPC against dynamic-admissible adversary

We state the formal theorem below.

Theorem 2. *Assuming the presence of a 2-round MPC protocol π_{ua} achieving unanimous abort against malicious majority, protocol π_{fair}^{dyn} with n parties satisfies correctness, achieves fairness and has a round complexity of $\lceil n/2 \rceil + 1$ rounds.*

Proof. Correctness of π_{fair}^{dyn} follows directly from correctness of π_{ua} and $\mathsf{LRec}^{n-2,\lfloor \frac{n}{2} \rfloor}$ (Lemma 4). The security proof appears in the full version [33]. Round complexity of π_{fair}^{dyn} includes 2 rounds of π_{ua} and the round complexity of $\mathsf{LRec}^{n-2,\lfloor \frac{n}{2} \rfloor}$ which is $\left(n - 2 - \lfloor \frac{n}{2} \rfloor + 1\right) = \lceil n/2 \rceil - 1$ (Lemma 4); totalling upto $\lceil n/2 \rceil + 1$ rounds.   □

4.3   Upper Bound for GOD MPC

At a broad level, robustness is achieved by rerunning our fair protocol as soon as failure occurs which can surface either in the underlying MPC or during reconstruction of any of the summands of the output. Taking inspiration from the player-elimination framework [35,36], we maintain a history of deviating/disruptive behaviour across the runs and bar the identified parties from further participating. Such a paradigm calls for sequential runs and brings great challenge when round complexity is the concern. We hit the optimal round complexity banking on several ideas and interesting observations. First, we turn the underlying MPC protocol for computing (α, β)-levelled-sharing of the output to achieve *identifiability* so that any disruptive behaviour can be brought to notice. Slapping NIZK on the 2-round broadcast-only construction of [10] readily equips it with identifiability, without inflating the round complexity. Second, we leverage the *function-delayed* property of a modified variant of the protocol of [10] (proposed by [13]) where the first round messages are made independent of the function to be computed and the number of parties. This enables us to run many parallel instances (specifically $\lceil n/2 \rceil$) of the round 1 in the beginning and run the second round sequentially as and when failure happens to compute a new function each time as follows– (a) it hard-cores default input for the parties detected to be disruptive so far and (b) the output now is levelled-shared with new thresholds α and β each of which are smaller than the previous run by a function of the number of fresh catch, say δ. The latter brings the most crucial impact on the round complexity. Recall that the distance between α and β that impacts the round complexity, is directly coupled with the number of possible corruption scenarios with non-zero active corruption. Starting with the initial value of $\lceil \frac{n}{2} \rceil - 1$, each catch by δ reduces number of possible corruption scenarios (with non-zero active corruption) and the distance between α and β by δ.

In the protocol, we maintain a number of dynamic variables which are updated during the run– (a) $\mathcal{L}$: the set of parties not identified to be actively corrupt and thus referred as alive; this set is initialized to $\mathcal{P}$; (b) $\mathcal{C}$: the set of parties identified as actively corrupt; this set initialized to $\emptyset$; (c) $\mathfrak{n}$: the parameter that dictates the number of corruption scenarios as $\lceil \frac{\mathfrak{n}}{2} \rceil$ and the possible corruption cases as $\{(0, \mathfrak{n} - 1), \ldots, (\lceil \mathfrak{n}/2 \rceil - 1, \lfloor \mathfrak{n}/2 \rfloor)\}$; this is initialized to n that dictates the initial number of corruption cases as $\lceil \frac{n}{2} \rceil$ and the possible corruption cases as $\{(0, n-1), \ldots, (\lceil n/2 \rceil - 1, \lfloor n/2 \rfloor)\}$. After every failure and a fresh catch of a set $\mathcal{B}$ of active corruptions, the sets $\mathcal{L}, \mathcal{C}$ and $\mathfrak{n}$ are updated as $\mathcal{L} = \mathcal{L} \setminus \mathcal{B}, \mathcal{C} = \mathcal{C} \cup \mathcal{B}$ and $\mathfrak{n} = \mathfrak{n} - 2|\mathcal{B}|$. The reduction of $\mathfrak{n}$ by $2|\mathcal{B}|$ denotes counting the reduction for active as well as passive corruptions. For every value of $\mathfrak{n}$, the formula for the total number of corruption scenarios, the values for (α, β) (that speaks about the indispensable summands as discussed in the fair protocol) and the number of corruption scenarios with non-zero active corruption (which denotes the distance between (α, β)) remain the same– namely $\lceil \frac{\mathfrak{n}}{2} \rceil$, $(\mathfrak{n} - 2, \lfloor \mathfrak{n}/2 \rfloor)$ and $\lceil \frac{\mathfrak{n}}{2} \rceil - 1$. In the marginal case, $\mathfrak{n}$ becomes either 1 or 2, the former when n is odd and all active corruptions are exposed making $(t_a, t_p) = (0, 0)$ and the latter when n is even and $(t_a, t_p) = (0, 1)$. With no active corruption in $\mathcal{L}$, the Round 2 of the MPC can be run to compute the output itself (instead of its levelled-sharing) robustly in both the marginal cases.

As the protocol follows an inductive behaviour based on $\mathfrak{n}$, to enable better understanding, we present below a snapshot of how the corruption scenarios shrinks after every catch of δ active corruptions. The first column indicates a set of possible corruption scenarios, with (t_a, t_p) varying from $(0, \mathfrak{n} - 1)$ to $(\lceil \mathfrak{n}/2 \rceil - 1, \lfloor \mathfrak{n}/2 \rfloor)$. If δ cheaters are identified, the first δ rows can simply be discarded as it is established that $t_a \geq \delta$. The number of feasible corruptions is thus slashed by δ. Next, these δ identified cheaters are eliminated, which reduces each (t_a, t_p) of the rows that sustained ($t_a = \delta$ onwards) by δ as shown by column 2. Finally, the column 3 displays column 2 with $\mathfrak{n}$ updated as $\mathfrak{n} - 2\delta$. The formal description of the protocol $\pi_{\text{god}}^{\text{dyn}}$ appears in Fig. 4. Assumption wise, $\pi_{\text{god}}^{\text{dyn}}$ relies on 2-round maliciously-secure OT in the common random/reference string model, NIZK (when π_{idua} is instantiated with function-delayed variant of the protocol of [10] satisfying identifiability) and eNICOM (instantiated using Pedersen's commitment scheme).

(t_a, t_p)	(t_a, t_p) after δ cheater identification	(t_a, t_p) after updating $\mathfrak{n} = \mathfrak{n} - 2\delta$
$(0, \mathfrak{n} - 1)$	–	–
$(1, \mathfrak{n} - 2)$	–	–
$\ldots$	$\ldots$	$\ldots$
$(\delta, \mathfrak{n} - \delta - 1)$	$(0, \mathfrak{n} - 2\delta - 1)$	$(0, \mathfrak{n} - 1)$
$(\delta + 1, \mathfrak{n} - \delta - 2)$	$(1, \mathfrak{n} - 2\delta - 2)$	$(1, \mathfrak{n} - 2)$
$\ldots$	$\ldots$	$\ldots$
$(\lceil \mathfrak{n}/2 \rceil - 1, \lfloor \mathfrak{n}/2 \rfloor)$	$(\lceil \mathfrak{n}/2 \rceil - 1 - \delta, \lfloor \mathfrak{n}/2 \rfloor - \delta)$	$(\lceil \mathfrak{n}/2 \rceil - 1, \lfloor \mathfrak{n}/2 \rfloor)$

We now analyze the round-complexity and correctness of $\pi_{\text{god}}^{\text{dyn}}$ below.

Lemma 5. $\pi_{\text{god}}^{\text{dyn}}$ *terminates in* $\lceil n/2 \rceil + 1$ *rounds.*

Proof. Consider an execution of $\pi_{\mathrm{god}}^{\mathrm{dyn}}$ (initialized with $\mathfrak{n} = n$). The outline of the proof is as follows: We give an inductive argument to prove the following - 'If Step 2 is executed with parameter $\mathfrak{n}$, then Step 2 terminates within $\lceil \frac{\mathfrak{n}}{2} \rceil$ rounds'. Assuming this claim holds, it follows directly that during the execution with $\mathfrak{n} = n$, Step 2 would terminate within $\lceil \frac{n}{2} \rceil$ rounds; thereby implying that the round complexity of $\pi_{\mathrm{god}}^{\mathrm{dyn}}$ is atmost $\lceil \frac{n}{2} \rceil + 1$ (adding the round for Step 1). We now prove the above claim by strong induction on $\mathfrak{n} \geq 1$.

Base Case ($\mathfrak{n} = 1, 2$*):* It follows directly from description in Fig. 4 that Step 2 terminates in $\lceil \mathfrak{n}/2 \rceil = 1$ round when $\mathfrak{n} = 1, 2$.

Induction Hypothesis ($\mathfrak{n} \leq \ell$*):* Assume Step 2 terminates in $\lceil \mathfrak{n}/2 \rceil$ rounds for $\mathfrak{n} \leq \ell$.

Protocol $\pi_{\mathrm{god}}^{\mathrm{dyn}}$

Inputs: Party P_i has x_i for $i \in [n]$

Building blocks: (a) Protocol π_{idua} achieving identifiable abort against malicious majority and having function-delayed property; (b) Protocol $\mathrm{LRec}^{\alpha, \beta}$ for reconstructing a (α, β)-levelled-shared value (Fig. 2); (c) Function $f_{\mathrm{LSh}}^{\alpha, \beta}$ (Fig 1).

Output: $y = f(x_1 \ldots x_n)$

Step 1: P_i runs $\lceil n/2 \rceil$ parallel instances of Round 1 of π_{idua}, each using input x_i and independent randomness. Note that this round is independent of the function to be computed and number of parties. Initialize $k = 1$.

Step 2: Initialize, $\mathcal{L} = \mathcal{P}$, $\mathcal{C} = \emptyset$, $\mathfrak{n} = n$. Let $f^{\mathcal{C}}$ denote the function that is same as f except that the inputs of parties in $\mathcal{C}$ are hardcoded with default inputs. P_i executes the following steps:

    2.1 If $\mathfrak{n} = 1, 2$, then run Round 2 of π_{idua} (considering kth instance of Round 1) among parties in $\mathcal{L}$ using input x_i to compute $f^{\mathcal{C}}$ and output the output of π_{idua} and terminate. (This corresponds to the case of no active corruptions.)

    2.2 Run Round 2 of π_{idua} (considering kth instance of Round 1) among parties in $\mathcal{L}$ using input x_i to compute $f_{\mathrm{LSh}}^{\mathfrak{n}-2, \lfloor \frac{\mathfrak{n}}{2} \rfloor} \diamond f^{\mathcal{C}}$ and obtain L_i. If $L_i = \perp$ and $\mathcal{B}$ is set of parties identified to be corrupt, update $\mathcal{C} = \mathcal{C} \cup \mathcal{B}$, $\mathcal{L} = \mathcal{L} \setminus \mathcal{B}$, $\mathfrak{n} = \mathfrak{n} - 2|\mathcal{B}|$, $k = k + 1$ and repeat this step using updated value of $\mathfrak{n}$. Otherwise, participate in $\mathrm{LRec}^{\mathfrak{n}-2, \lfloor \frac{\mathfrak{n}}{2} \rfloor}$ with input L_i. If $(\perp, \mathcal{B})$ is the output, then update $\mathcal{L}, \mathcal{C}, \mathfrak{n}, k$ as above and repeat this step using updated value of $\mathfrak{n}$. Otherwise, output the output of $\mathrm{LRec}^{\mathfrak{n}-2, \lfloor \frac{\mathfrak{n}}{2} \rfloor}$ and terminate.

Fig. 4. Robust MPC against dynamic-admissible adversary

Induction step ($\mathfrak{n} = \ell + 1$*):* Consider an execution of Step 2 with parameter $\mathfrak{n} = \ell + 1$. We analyze the following 3 exhaustive scenarios - (1) Suppose neither

π_{idua} nor $\text{LRec}^{n-2,\lfloor\frac{n}{2}\rfloor}$ fails. (2) Suppose π_{idua} aborts. (3) Suppose π_{idua} does not abort but $\text{LRec}^{n-2,\lfloor\frac{n}{2}\rfloor}$ fails. We show that in each of them, Step 2 terminates within $\lceil n/2 \rceil = \lceil \frac{\ell+1}{2} \rceil$ rounds; thereby completing the induction step.

Suppose neither π_{idua} nor $\text{LRec}^{n-2,\lfloor\frac{n}{2}\rfloor}$ fails. Then Step 2 involves following number of rounds– 1 (for Round 2 of π_{idua}) + number of rounds in $\text{LRec}^{n-2,\lfloor\frac{n}{2}\rfloor}$ i.e. $(n - 2 - \lfloor\frac{n}{2}\rfloor + 1) = \lceil\frac{n}{2}\rceil = \lceil(\ell+1)/2\rceil$ in total.

Suppose π_{idua} aborts. Then $\mathcal{B}$ must comprise of at least one active party, implying that $\delta \geq 1$, where $\delta = |\mathcal{B}|$ and subsequently n is updated to $n = (n - 2\delta) \leq (\ell+1-2) = (\ell-1)$. Note that Step 2 now involves following number of rounds– 1 (for Round 2 of π_{idua}) + number of rounds in which Step 2 terminates when re-run with updated parameter n i.e. $\lceil n/2 \rceil$ by induction hypothesis. Thus, the total number of rounds in Step 2 is $(1 + \lceil n/2 \rceil) \leq (1 + \lceil\frac{\ell-1}{2}\rceil) = \lceil\frac{\ell+1}{2}\rceil$.

Suppose π_{idua} does not abort but reconstruction $\text{LRec}^{n-2,\lfloor\frac{n}{2}\rfloor}$ fails. Say adversary disrupts reconstruction of summand s_{n-r} in Round r of Step 2 (Round $r - 1$ of $\text{LRec}^{n-2,\lfloor n/2 \rfloor}$), where $r \in [2, \lceil n/2 \rceil]$. It follows from fault identification property of Lemma 4 that $|\mathcal{B}| \geq |\mathcal{L}| - (n-r) \geq r$ (since $|\mathcal{L}| \geq n$ always holds). Consequently, $\delta = |\mathcal{B}| \geq r$ and updated parameter $n = n - 2\delta \leq \ell + 1 - 2r$. We now analyze the round complexity. Note that Step 2 involves following number of rounds– r (Reconstruction failed in Round $r \geq 2$ of Step 2 run with $n = \ell + 1$) + number of rounds in which Step 2 terminates when re-run with updated parameter n i.e. $\lceil n/2 \rceil$ by induction hypothesis. Thus total number of rounds in Step 2 is $(r + \lceil n/2 \rceil) \leq (r + \lceil\frac{\ell+1-2r}{2}\rceil) = \lceil\frac{\ell+1}{2}\rceil$.

We point that induction hypothesis for $n = n - 2\delta$ with $\delta \geq 1$ can be applied as $n \geq 1$ holds always in $\pi_{\text{god}}^{\text{dyn}}$ due to the following: the maximal value of δ is $\lceil n/2 \rceil - 1$ i.e. the maximum possible number of actively corrupt parties. This completes the proof. $\quad\square$

Theorem 3. *Assuming the presence of a 2-round protocol π_{idua} achieving identifiable abort against malicious majority and having function-delayed property; protocol $\pi_{\text{god}}^{\text{dyn}}$ with n parties satisfies correctness, achieves guaranteed output delivery and has a round-complexity of $\lceil n/2 \rceil + 1$ rounds.*

Proof. Correctness of $\pi_{\text{god}}^{\text{dyn}}$ follows directly from correctness of π_{idua} and correctness of $\text{LRec}^{n-2,\lfloor\frac{n}{2}\rfloor}$ (Lemma 4). The formal security proof appears in the full version [33]. Round complexity follows from Lemma 5. $\quad\square$

5   Lower Bounds for Boundary Corruption

In this section, we present two lower bounds for MPC protocol tolerating boundary-admissible adversaries and in the presence of CRS and PKI setup. Recall that such an adversary is restricted to corruption scenarios either $(t_a, t_p) = (\lceil n/2 \rceil - 1, \lfloor n/2 \rfloor)$ or $(t_a, t_p) = (0, n - 1)$. We show that *three* and *four* rounds are necessary to achieve fairness and GOD respectively against a boundary-admissible adversary. It is to be noted that GOD is the de facto notion achieved in the pure passive corruption setting of $(t_a, t_p) = (0, n - 1)$.

5.1   Impossibility of 3-Round Robust MPC

In this section, we show that it is impossible to design a 3-round robust MPC protocol against boundary-admissible adversary with threshold (t_a, t_p) assuming both CRS and PKI. Notably, this lower bound is indeed surprising as the individual security guarantees translate to GOD against malicious-minority [7] and passive-majority [10,11] for odd n (as $t_a = t_p$ wrt $(t_a, t_p) = (\lceil n/2 \rceil - 1, \lfloor n/2 \rfloor))$, both of which are known to be attainable in just 2 rounds in the presence of CRS and PKI. Furthermore, it turns out interestingly that this lower bound does not hold against a boundary-admissble adversary with $t_a \leq 1$ (i.e. boundary adversary corrupting with either $(t_a, t_p) = (1, \lfloor n/2 \rfloor)$ or $(t_a, t_p) = (0, n - 1))$, and can be circumvented for this special case. In fact, we demonstrate a 3-round robust protocol in Sect. 6.3, against this special-case boundary-admissible adversary.

Theorem 4. *Assume parties have access to pairwise-private and broadcast channels, and a setup that includes* CRS *and* PKI*. Then, there exist functions f for which there is no 3-round protocol computing f that achieves guaranteed output delivery against boundary-admissible adversary.*

Proof. We prove the theorem for $n = 5$ parties. Let $\mathcal{P} = \{P_1, \ldots P_5\}$ denote the set of parties, where the adversary $\mathcal{A}$ may corrupt either with parametes $(t_a, t_p) = (2, 2)$ or $(t_a, t_p) = (0, 4)$. Here, the corruption scenarios translate to upto 2 active corruptions or upto 4 pure passive corruptions. We prove the theorem by contradiction. Suppose there exists a 3-round protocol π computing a common output function f that achieves GOD against such a boundary-admissible adversary.

At a high level, we discuss three adversarial strategies $\mathcal{A}_1, \mathcal{A}_2$ and $\mathcal{A}_3$, where $\mathcal{A}_i$ is launched in an execution Σ_i of protocol π. While $\mathcal{A}_1, \mathcal{A}_2$ involve the case of active corruption of $\{P_1\}$ and $\{P_1, P_2\}$ respectively, $\mathcal{A}_3$ deals with the strategy of pure passive corruption of $\{P_1, P_3, P_4, P_5\}$. The executions are assumed to be run for the same input tuple $(x_1, x_2, x_3, x_4, x_5)$ and the same random inputs $(r_1, r_2, r_3, r_4, r_5)$ of the parties. Let $\widetilde{x}_i$ denote the default input of P_i. (Same random inputs are considered for simplicity and without loss of generality. The same arguments hold for distribution ensembles as well.) First, when $\mathcal{A}_1$ is launched in Σ_1 we conclude that the output $\widetilde{y}$ at the end of the execution should be based on default input of P_1 and actual inputs of the remaining parties i.e. $\widetilde{y} = f(\widetilde{x_1}, x_2, x_3, x_4, x_5)$. Next, strategy Σ_2 involving actively corrupt $\{P_1, P_2\}$ is designed such that corrupt P_2 obtains the same view in Σ_2 as an honest P_2 in Σ_1 and therefore computes the output $\widetilde{y}$ at the end of Σ_2. (Here, view of P_i includes x_i, r_i, the messages received during π and the knowledge related to CRS and PKI setup.) Lastly, a carefully designed strategy $\mathcal{A}_3$ by semi-honest parties $\{P_1, P_3, P_4, P_5\}$ allows $\mathcal{A}$ to obtain $\widetilde{y} = f(\widetilde{x_1}, x_2, x_3, x_4, x_5)$, in addition to the correct output i.e. $y = f(x_1, x_2, x_3, x_4, x_5)$ at the end of execution Σ_3. This is a contradiction as it violates the security of π and can explicitly breach the privacy of honest P_2. This completes the proof overview.

We assume that the communication done in Round 2 and Round 3 of π is via broadcast alone. This holds without loss of generality since the parties can engage in point-to-point communication by exchanging random pads in the first round and then use these random pads to unmask later broadcasts. We use the following notation: Let $\mathsf{p}_{i \to j}^1$ denote the pairwise communication from P_i to P_j in round 1 and b_i^r denotes the broadcast by P_i in round r, where $r \in [3], \{i, j\} \in [5]$. These values may be function of CRS and the PKI setup as per the protocol specifications. Let V_i^ℓ denotes the view of party P_i at the end of execution Σ_ℓ ($\ell \in [3]$) of π. Below we describe the strategies $\mathcal{A}_1, \mathcal{A}_2$ and $\mathcal{A}_3$.

$\mathcal{A}_1$: $\mathcal{A}$ corrupts $\{P_1\}$ actively here. P_1 behaves honestly in Round 1 and simply remains silent in Round 2 and Round 3.

$\mathcal{A}_2$: $\mathcal{A}$ corrupts $\{P_1, P_2\}$ actively here. The active misbehavior of P_1 is same as in $\mathcal{A}_1$ i.e. P_1 behaves honestly in Round 1 and stops communicating thereafter. On the other hand, P_2 participates honestly upto Round 2 and remains silent in Round 3.

$\mathcal{A}_3$: $\mathcal{A}$ corrupts $\{P_1, P_3, P_4, P_5\}$ passively here. The semi-honest parties behave as per protocol specification throughout the execution Σ_3 to obtain the correct output. The passive strategy of $\{P_1, P_3, P_4, P_5\}$ is to ignore the Round 3 message from honest P_2 and locally compute the output based on the scenario of execution Σ_2 i.e. imagining that P_1 stopped after Round 1 and P_2 stopped after Round 2.

We now present a sequence of lemmas to complete the proof.

Lemma 6. *At the end of Σ_1, parties compute output $\widetilde{y} = f(\widetilde{x_1}, x_2, x_3, x_4, x_5)$, where $\widetilde{x_1}$ denotes the default input of P_1.*

Proof. Firstly, since Σ_1 involves active behavior only by P_1, it follows directly from correctness and robustness of π that the output computed at the end of Σ_1, say y' should be based on actual inputs x_i for $i \in \{2, 3, 4, 5\}$. Now, there are two possibilities with respect to input of P_1 i.e. y' is based on either x_1 (i.e. the input used by P_1 in Round 1 of Σ_1) or $\widetilde{x_1}$ (default input). In case of the latter, the lemma holds directly. We now assume the former for contradiction.

Suppose the output y' is based on x_1 rather than $\widetilde{x_1}$. Since P_1 stops communicating after Round 1, we can conclude that the combined views of $\{P_2, P_3, P_4, P_5\}$ must suffice to compute the output $y' = f(x_1, \ldots, x_5)$ at the end of Round 1 itself. If this holds, we argue that π cannot be secure as follows: Suppose π is such that when all parties participate honestly in Round 1, the combined view of $\{P_2, P_3, P_4, P_5\}$ suffices to compute the output at the end of Round 1 itself. Then, in an execution of π, an adversary corrupting $\{P_2, P_3, P_4, P_5\}$ purely passively (corresponding to $(t_a, t_p) = (0, 4)$) can learn the output on various inputs of its choice, keeping x_1 fixed. This residual attack breaches privacy of honest P_1 (A concrete example of such an f appears in the full version [33]). We have thus arrived at a contradiction. This completes the proof that y' must be based on $\widetilde{x_1}$, rather than x_1 and consequently $y' = \widetilde{y} = f(\widetilde{x_1}, x_2, x_3, x_4, x_5)$ must be the output computed at the end of Σ_1. $\square$

Lemma 7. *At the end of Σ_2, parties compute output $\widetilde{y} = f(\widetilde{x_1}, x_2, x_3, x_4, x_5)$, where $\widetilde{x_1}$ denotes the default input of P_1.*

Proof. Recall that $\mathcal{A}_2$ is similar to $\mathcal{A}_1$ involving active P_1, except that P_2 is active as well with the strategy of behaving honestly upto Round 2 and remaining silent in Round 3. Since executions Σ_1 and Σ_2 proceed identically upto Round 2, it is easy to check that the view of corrupt P_2 in Σ_2 is same as honest P_2 in Σ_1. It now follows directly from Lemma 6 that P_2 computes the output $\widetilde{y} = f(\widetilde{x_1}, x_2, x_3, x_4, x_5)$. By correctness and robustness of π computing the common output function f, it must hold that all parties output $\widetilde{y}$ at the end of Σ_2. □

Lemma 8. *The combined view of parties $\{P_3, P_4, P_5\}$ at the end of Round 2 of Σ_2 suffices to compute the output of Σ_2 i.e. $\widetilde{y}$.*

Proof. We note that as per $\mathcal{A}_2$, both $\{P_1, P_2\}$ do not communicate in Round 3; implying that the combined view of honest parties $\{P_3, P_4, P_5\}$ at the end of Round 2 of Σ_2 must suffice to compute the output of Σ_2 i.e. $\widetilde{y}$ (Lemma 7). □

Lemma 9. *An adversary executing strategy $\mathcal{A}_3$ obtains the value $\widetilde{y} = f(\widetilde{x_1}, x_2, x_3, x_4, x_5)$, in addition to the correct output $y = f(x_1, x_2, x_3, x_4, x_5)$ at the end of Σ_3.*

Proof. Firstly, Σ_3 must lead to computation of correct output i.e. $y = f(x_1, x_2, x_3, x_4, x_5)$ by all parties since $\mathcal{A}_3$ involves only semi-honest corruptions. Next, it is easy to check that the combined view of adversary corrupting $\{P_1, P_3, P_4, P_5\}$ passively at the end of Round 2 of Σ_3 subsumes the combined view of honest parties $\{P_3, P_4, P_5\}$ at the end of Round 2 of Σ_2. It now follows directly from Lemma 8 that the adversary can obtain the output $\widetilde{y}$ as well.

In more detail, $\mathcal{A}$ launching $\mathcal{A}_3$ in Σ_3 can compute the output as per the scenario of Σ_2 as follows- Let $\overline{b}_i^3$ for $i \subset \{2, 3, 4, 5\}$ denotes the message broadcast by honest P_i (as per its next-message function) in Round 3 in case P_1 behaves honestly in Round 1 but is silent in Round 2. Locally compute $\{\overline{b}_3^3, \overline{b}_4^3, \overline{b}_5^3\}$ ($\overline{b}_i^3$ is a function of P_i's ($i \in \{3, 4, 5\}$) view at the end of Round 2) by imagining that P_1 did not send Round 2 message and compute $\widetilde{y}$ by ignoring the message sent by honest P_2 in Round 3. Thus, by following strategy $\mathcal{A}_3$, $\mathcal{A}$ obtains multiple evaluations of f i.e. both y and $\widetilde{y}$ which violates the security of π. (We give a concrete example of such an f that breaches privacy of honest P_2 in the full version.) This completes the proof of the lemma. □

Thus, we have arrived at a contradiction to our assumption that π is secure; completing the proof of Theorem 4. □

We present a natural extension of the above proof for $n > 5$, a concrete example of f and a brief intuition of why the above lower bound argument does not hold when malicious corruption $t_a \leq 1$ in the full version [33].

5.2   Impossibility of 2-Round Fair MPC

We begin with the observation that the existing 3-round lower bounds of [6–8] for fair malicious-minority MPC do not carry over in our setting. The lower bound of both [6,7] break down when the parties have access to a PKI (as acknowledged/demonstrated in their work). The result of [8], assuming access to pairwise-private and broadcast channels, also breaks down when parties have access to a PKI (elaborated in the full version [33]). The proof, originally given without the mention of CRS, seems to withstand a CRS.

We now present our lower bound formally.

Theorem 5. *There exist functions f for which there is no 2-round n-party MPC protocol that achieves fairness against boundary-admissible adversary, in a setting with pairwise-private and broadcast channels, and a setup that includes CRS and PKI.*

Proof. We prove the theorem for $n = 3$ parties, where boundary-admissible adversary $\mathcal{A}$ chooses corruption parameters either $(t_a, t_p) = (1, 1)$ or $(t_a, t_p) = (0, 2)$. Here, the corruption scenarios translate to either upto 1 active corruption or upto 2 purely passive corruptions. Let $\{P_1, P_2, P_3\}$ denote the set of parties with P_i having input x_i. Suppose by contradiction, π is a 2-round MPC protocol computing f that achieves fairness against $\mathcal{A}$. To be more specific, π is fair if $(t_a, t_p) = (1, 1)$ and achieves GOD otherwise (as GOD is the de-facto security guarantee incase of no active corruptions i.e. $(t_a, t_p) = (0, 2)$). On a high-level, we first exploit fairness of π to conclude that the combined view of a set of 2 parties suffices for output computation at the end of Round 1. (Here, view of P_i includes x_i, its randomness r_i, the messages received during π and the knowledge related to CRS and PKI setup.) Next, considering a strategy where the adversary $\mathcal{A}$ corrupts this set of 2 parties purely passively leads us to conclude that $\mathcal{A}$ can compute the output at the end of Round 1 itself; leading upto a final contradiction. We now present a sequence of claims to complete the formal proof.

Lemma 10. *Protocol π must be such that the combined view of $\{P_2, P_3\}$ at the end of Round 1 suffices for output computation.*

Proof. The proof of the lemma is straightforward. Assume $\mathcal{A}$ corrupting P_1 actively (with $(t_a, t_p) = (1, 1)$) with the following strategy: P_1 behaves honestly in Round 1 and simply remains silent in Round 2. It is easy to check that P_1 would obtain the output due to correctness of π, as he receives the entire protocol communication as per honest execution. Since π is fair, the honest parties $\{P_2, P_3\}$ must also obtain the output at the end of π; even without P_1's communication in Round 2. Thus, we conclude that the combined view of $\{P_2, P_3\}$ at the end of Round 1 suffices for output computation.   □

Lemma 11. *There exists an adversarial strategy such that the adversary obtains the output at the end of Round 1.*

Proof. The proof follows directly from Lemma 10 – $\mathcal{A}$ corrupting $\{P_2, P_3\}$ purely passively $((t_a, t_p) = (0, 2))$ would obtain the output at the end of Round 1.   □

Lemma 12. *Protocol π does not achieve privacy.*

Proof. It is implied from Lemma 11 that $\mathcal{A}$ corrupting $\{P_2, P_3\}$ purely passively can obtain multiple evaluations of the function f by locally plugging in different values for $\{x_2, x_3\}$ while honest P_1's input x_1 remains fixed. This 'residual function attack' violates privacy of P_1. We refer to the argument in Lemma 3 for a concrete example.   □

We have arrived at a contradiction, concluding the proof of Theorem 5. It is easy to check that this argument can be extended for higher values of n.   □

6   Upper Bounds for Boundary Corruption

In this section, we describe three upper bounds with respect to the boundary-admissible adversary $\mathcal{A}$ with threshold (t_a, t_p). We first present a robust upper bound in 4 rounds for the general case. Next, we present a 3-round robust protocol for the special case of single active corruption, which circumvents our lower bound of Sect. 5.1. Our fair 3-round upper bound can be arrived at by simplifying the robust general-case construction and appears in full version [33]. Note that even the fair construction is robust in the corruption scenario of no active corruptions i.e. $(t_a, t_p) = (0, n-1)$. The security guarantees differ only in case of corruption scenario involving malicious corruptions. All the above three constructions are round-optimal, following our lower bound results of Sects. 5.1 and 5.2. We start with a building block commonly used across all our constructs.

6.1   Authenticated Secret Sharing

We introduce the primitive of Authenticated Secret Sharing [28,37] used in our upper bounds against the boundary-admissible $\mathcal{A}$.

Definition 4 (α-authenticated sharing). *A value v is said to be α-authenticated-shared amongst a set of parties $\mathcal{P}$ if every honest or passively corrupt party P_i in $\mathcal{P}$ holds S_i as produced by $f_{\mathsf{ASh}}^\alpha(v)$ given in Fig. 5.*

Function $f_{\mathsf{ASh}}^\alpha(v)$

1. α *shamir-sharing of secret v:* Choose random $a_1, a_2 \ldots a_\alpha \in \mathbb{F}$, where $\mathbb{F}$ denotes a finite field. Build the α-degree polynomial $A(x) = a_0 + a_1 x + a_2 x^2 + a_3 x^3 + \cdots + a_{\alpha-1} x^{\alpha-1} + a_\alpha x^\alpha$, where $a_0 = v$. Let $\mathsf{sh}_i = A(i)$ for $i \in [n]$.
2. *Authentication of shares:* For all $i, j \in [n]$, choose random one-time message-authentication codes (MAC) [38] keys $k_{ij} \in \{0,1\}^\kappa$ and compute $\mathsf{tag}_{ij} = \mathsf{Mac}_{k_{ij}}(\mathsf{sh}_i)$.
3. Output $S_i = \left(\mathsf{sh}_i, \{k_{ji}\}_{j \in [n]}, \{\mathsf{tag}_{ij}\}_{j \in [n]}\right)$ for $i \in [n]$.

Fig. 5. Authenticated secret-sharing

In our upper bounds, the function f^α_{ASh} is realized via MPC protocols. The reconstruction will be done via protocol ARec^α (Fig. 6) amongst the parties. We state the relevant properties below (proof appears in the full version [33]):

Protocol ARec^α

Inputs: P_i participates with $S_i = (\mathsf{sh}_i, \{k_{ji}\}_{j\in[n]}, \{\mathsf{tag}_{ij}\}_{j\in[n]})$
Output: Secret v'

Each P_i does the following:

1. Broadcast $(\mathsf{sh}_i, \{\mathsf{tag}_{ij}\}_{j\in[n]})$ and receive $(\mathsf{sh}'_j, \mathsf{tag}'_{ji})$ from $j \neq i$.
2. Each P_i outputs v' as follows:.
   - Initialize Val to $\{i\}$. For $j \neq i$, if $\mathsf{Mac}_{k_{ji}}(\mathsf{sh}'_j) = \mathsf{tag}'_{ji}$, set $\mathsf{sh}_j = \mathsf{sh}'_j$ and add j to Val; else set $\mathsf{sh}_j = \perp$.
   - If $|\mathsf{Val}| \geq \alpha+1$, interpolate a α degree polynomial $A'(x)$ satisfying $A'(\gamma) = \mathsf{sh}_\gamma$ for $\gamma \in \mathsf{Val}$. Output $\perp$ if the above fails, else output $v' = A'(0)$.

Fig. 6. Protocol for reconstruction of an authenticated-secret

Lemma 13. *The pair $(f^\alpha_{\mathsf{ASh}}, \mathsf{ARec}^\alpha)$ satisfies the following:*

i. Privacy. *For all $v \in \mathbb{F}$, the output $(S_1, \ldots, S_n) \leftarrow f^\alpha_{\mathsf{ASh}}(v)$ satisfies the following– $\forall \{i_1, \ldots i_{\alpha'}\} \subset [n]$ with $\alpha' \leq \alpha$, the distribution of $\{S_{i_1}, \ldots, S_{i_{\alpha'}}\}$ is statistically independent of v.*

ii. Correctness. *For all $v \in \mathbb{F}$, the value v' output by all honest parties at the end of $\mathsf{ARec}^\alpha(S'_1, \ldots S'_n)$ satisfies the following– For all $(S_1, \ldots, S_n) \leftarrow f^\alpha_{\mathsf{ASh}}(v)$ and $(S'_1, \ldots, S'_n)$ such that $S'_i = S_i$ corresponding to atleast $\alpha + 1$ parties P_i, it holds that $\Pr[v' \neq v] \leq \mathsf{negl}(\kappa)$ for a computational security parameter κ.*

iii. Round complexity. *ARec^α terminates in one round.*

6.2 Upper Bound for Robust MPC: The General Case

In a setting where either at most $n - 1$ passive corruption or at most $(\lceil \frac{n}{2} \rceil - 1)$ active corruption takes place, [28] presents a protocol relying on two types of MPC protocol. An actively-secure protocol against malicious majority is used to compute an authenticated-sharing of the output with threshold $(\lceil \frac{n}{2} \rceil - 1)$. When this protocol succeeds, the output is computed via reconstruction of the authenticated-sharing. On the other hand, a failure is tackled via running a honest-majority (malicious minority) actively-secure protocol, relying on the conclusion that the protocol is facing a malicious-minority. When n is odd, we need to tackle the exact corruption scenarios as that of the protocols of [28]. On the other hand when n is even, the extreme case for active corruption accommodates an additional passive corruption. Apart from hitting optimal round complexity, tackling the distinct boundary cases for odd and even n in a unified way brings challenge for our protocol.

We make the following effective changes to the approach of [28]. First, we invoke a 2-round actively-secure protocol π_{idua} with identifiable abort against malicious majority (can be instantiated with protocols of [10,11] augmented with NIZKs) to compute $\lfloor \frac{n}{2} \rfloor$-authenticated-sharing of the output. When we expel the identified corrupt parties in case of failure (which may occur in corruption scenario $(t_a, t_p) = (\lceil n/2 \rceil - 1, \lfloor n/2 \rfloor)$), the remaining population always displays honest-majority, no matter whether n is odd or even. (For instance, elimination of 1 corrupt party results in $t' \leq (t_p - 1) = \lfloor n/2 \rfloor - 1$ total corruptions among $n' = (n-1)$ remaining parties which satisfies $n' \geq 2t' + 1$.) The honest-majority protocol π_{god} is then invoked to compute the function f where the inputs of the identified parties are hard-coded to default values. The change in the degree of authenticated sharing ensures that an adversary choosing to corrupt in the boundary case of $\lceil \frac{n}{2} \rceil - 1$ active corruption and zero (when n is odd) or one (when n is even) additional purely passive corruption, cannot learn the output by itself collating the information it gathers during π_{idua}. Without the change, the adversary could ensure that π_{idua} leads to a failure for the honest parties and yet could learn outputs from both π_{idua} and π_{god} with different set of adversarial-inputs. Lastly, the function and input independence property of Round 1 of the 3-round honest-majority protocol of [7,13] allows us to superimpose this round with the run of π_{idua}. Both these instantiations of π_{god} are also equipped to tackle the probable change in population for the remaining two rounds (when identified corrupt parties are expelled) and the change in the function to be computed

---

Protocol $\pi_{\mathsf{god}}^{\mathsf{bou}}$

Inputs: Party P_i has x_i for $i \in [n]$
Building Blocks: (a) 2-round protocol π_{idua} achieving identifiable abort against malicious majority; (b) 3-round honest-majority actively-secure robust protocol π_{god} with additional property of Round 1 being function and input independent; (c) Protocol $\mathsf{ARec}^{\lfloor n/2 \rfloor}$ for reconstructing an $\lfloor n/2 \rfloor$-authenticated-shared secret (Fig. 6); (d) Function $f_{\mathsf{ASh}}^{\lfloor n/2 \rfloor}$ (Fig. 5).
Output: $y = f(x_1 \ldots x_n)$

Round 1–2: The parties run π_{idua} computing the function $f_{\mathsf{ASh}}^{\lfloor n/2 \rfloor} \diamond f$ with input x_i to obtain output $(S_i = (\mathsf{sh}_i, \{k_{ji}\}_{j \in [n]}, \{\mathsf{tag}_{ij}\}_{j \in [n]}), \mathcal{B})$, where $\mathcal{B}$ denotes the set of identified cheaters. Additionally, the parties run (input-independent and function-independent) Round 1 of π_{god}.
Round 3–4: If $S_i = \bot$, the parties in $\mathcal{P} \setminus \mathcal{B}$ run Round 2 and 3 of π_{god} computing $f^{\mathcal{B}}$ (f with the inputs of parties in $\mathcal{B}$ are hardcoded to default values) and output y as the outcome of π_{god}. Else, participate in $\mathsf{ARec}^{\lfloor n/2 \rfloor}$ with input S_i and output the outcome of $\mathsf{ARec}^{\lfloor n/2 \rfloor}$.

Fig. 7. Robust MPC against boundary-admissible adversary (with hard-coded default inputs for the identified corrupt parties). Our protocol appears in Fig. 7. Assumption wise, π_{god}^{bou} relies on 2-round maliciously-secure OT in the common random/reference string model, NIZK (when π_{idua} is instantiated with function-delayed variant of the protocol of [10] satisfying identifiability), Zaps and public-key encryption (when π_{god} is instantiated with protocol of [13]). We state the formal theorem below.

Theorem 6. *Assuming the presence of a 2-round protocol π_{idua} achieving identifiable abort against malicious majority and a 3-round robust protocol π_{god} against malicious minority (with special property of Round 1 being function and input-independent), the 4-round MPC protocol π_{god}^{bou} (Fig. 7) satisfies correctness and achieves guaranteed output delivery against boundary-admissible $\mathcal{A}$.*

Proof. Correctness of π_{god}^{bou} follows directly from that of π_{idua}, π_{god} and $\mathsf{ARec}^{\lfloor n/2 \rfloor}$ (Lemma 13). We prove its security in the full version [33]. □

We conclude this section with a simplification to π_{god}^{bou} that can be adopted if additional access to PKI is assumed. In such a case, parallelizing Round 1 of π_{god} with Round 1 of π_{idua} can be avoided and the 2-round robust protocol of [7] against malicious minority assuming CRS and PKI setup can be used to instantiate π_{god} (which would be run in Rounds 3-4 of π_{god}^{bou}). Both our 4-round constructions with CRS (Fig. 7) and its simplified variant with CRS and PKI are tight upper bounds, in light of the impossibility of Sect. 5.1 that holds in the presence of CRS and PKI.

6.3 Upper Bound for Robust MPC: The Single Corruption Case

Building upon the ideas of Sects. 6.2 and 4.3, a 3-round robust MPC $\pi_{god}^{bou,1}$ against the special-case boundary-admissible adversary can be constructed as follows. Similar to π_{god}^{bou}, Round 1 and 2 involve running protocol π_{idua} realizing $\lfloor n/2 \rfloor$-authenticated secret-sharing of the function output. When π_{idua} does not result in abort, $\pi_{god}^{bou,1}$ proceeds to reconstruction of output; identical to π_{god}^{bou} and thereby terminating in 3 rounds. However, when π_{idua} results in output $\bot$, we exploit the advantage of atmost one malicious corruption by noting that once the single actively-corrupt party is expelled, the parties involved thereafter comprise only of the honest and purely passive parties. We adopt the idea of Sect. 4.3 and re-run Round 2 of π_{idua} among the remaining parties to compute the function output directly, with input of the expelled party substituted with default input. This step demands the function-delayed property of π_{idua} i.e. Round 1 is independent of the function to be computed and the number of parties. In order to accommodate this re-run, two instances of Round 1 of π_{idua} are run in Round 1 of $\pi_{god}^{bou,1}$. It is easy to see that robustness is ensured as π_{idua} is robust in the absence of actively-corrupt parties. Lastly, we point that similar to Sect. 4.3, we use the modified variant of the 2-round protocol of [10] to instantiate π_{idua} that is function-delayed and achieves identifiability. The formal description of $\pi_{god}^{bou,1}$ appears in Fig. 8. This upper bound is tight, following the impossibility of 2-round fair MPC (that holds for single malicious corruption) proven in Sect. 5.2

as GOD implies fairness. Assumption wise, $\pi_{god}^{bou,1}$ relies on 2-round maliciously-secure OT in the common random/reference string model and NIZK (when π_{idua} is instantiated with above mentioned variant of the protocol of [10]).

Protocol $\pi_{god}^{bou,1}$

Inputs: Party P_i has x_i for $i \in [n]$

Building Blocks: (a) 2-round protocol π_{idua} achieving identifiable abort against malicious majority and having function-delayed property; (b) Protocol $ARec^{\lfloor n/2 \rfloor}$ for reconstructing an $\lfloor n/2 \rfloor$-authenticated-shared secret (Fig. 6); (c) Function $f_{ASh}^{\lfloor n/2 \rfloor}$ (Fig. 5).

Output: $y = f(x_1 \ldots x_n)$

Round 1: P_i does the following: Run 2 instances of Round 1 of π_{idua}, each using input x_i and independent randomness. Note that this round is independent of the function to be computed and the number of parties.

Round 2: P_i does the following: Run Round 2 of π_{idua} (based on first instance of Round 1 of π_{idua}) among $\mathcal{P}$ computing the function $f_{ASh}^{\lfloor n/2 \rfloor} \diamond f$ using input x_i to obtain output $(S_i = (\mathsf{sh}_i, \{k_{ji}\}_{j \in [n]}, \{\mathsf{tag}_{ij}\}_{j \in [n]}), \mathcal{B})$, where $\mathcal{B}$ denotes the set of identified cheaters.

Round 3: If $S_i = \bot$, the parties in $\mathcal{P} \setminus \mathcal{B}$ run Round 2 of π_{idua} (based on second instance of Round 1 of π_{idua}) computing $f^{\mathcal{B}}$ (where the inputs of the party in $\mathcal{B}$ is hardcoded to default value) and output y as the outcome of this (second) instance of π_{idua}. Else, participate in $ARec^{\lfloor n/2 \rfloor}$ with input S_i and output the outcome of $ARec^{\lfloor n/2 \rfloor}$.

Fig. 8. Robust MPC against special-case boundary-admissible adversary

We state the formal theorem below.

Theorem 7. *Assuming the presence of a 2-round protocol π_{idua} achieving identifiable abort against malicious majority and having function-delayed property, the 3-round MPC protocol $\pi_{god}^{bou,1}$ (Fig. 8) satisfies correctness and achieves guaranteed output delivery against special-case boundary-admissible $\mathcal{A}$ with corruption parameters either $(t_a, t_p) = (1, \lfloor n/2 \rfloor)$ or $(t_a, t_p) = (0, n - 1)$.*

Proof. Correctness of $\pi_{god}^{bou,1}$ follows directly from correctness of π_{idua}, and correctness of $ARec^{\lfloor n/2 \rfloor}$ (Lemma 13). We prove its security in full version [33]. □

References

1. Goldreich, O., Micali, O., Wigderson, O.: How to play any mental game or a completeness theorem for protocols with honest majority. In: ACM STOC (1987)
2. Chaum, D., Damgård, I.B., van de Graaf, J.: Multiparty computations ensuring privacy of each party's input and correctness of the result. In: Pomerance, C. (ed.) CRYPTO 1987. LNCS, vol. 293, pp. 87–119. Springer, Heidelberg (1988). https://doi.org/10.1007/3-540-48184-2_7

3. Yao, A.C.: Protocols for secure computations (extended abstract). In: FOCS (1982)
4. Cleve, R.: Limits on the security of coin flips when half the processors are faulty (extended abstract). In: ACM STOC (1986)
5. Hirt, M., Maurer, U., Lucas, C.: A dynamic tradeoff between active and passive corruptions in secure multi-party computation. In: Canetti, R., Garay, J.A. (eds.) CRYPTO 2013. LNCS, vol. 8043, pp. 203–219. Springer, Heidelberg (2013). https://doi.org/10.1007/978-3-642-40084-1_12
6. Gennaro, R., Ishai, Y., Kushilevitz, E., Rabin, T.: On 2-round secure multiparty computation. In: Yung, M. (ed.) CRYPTO 2002. LNCS, vol. 2442, pp. 178–193. Springer, Heidelberg (2002). https://doi.org/10.1007/3-540-45708-9_12
7. Dov Gordon, S., Liu, F.-H., Shi, E.: Constant-round MPC with fairness and guarantee of output delivery. In: Gennaro, R., Robshaw, M. (eds.) CRYPTO 2015. LNCS, vol. 9216, pp. 63–82. Springer, Heidelberg (2015). https://doi.org/10.1007/978-3-662-48000-7_4
8. Patra, A., Ravi, D.: On the exact round complexity of secure three-party computation. In: Shacham, H., Boldyreva, A. (eds.) CRYPTO 2018. LNCS, vol. 10992, pp. 425–458. Springer, Cham (2018). https://doi.org/10.1007/978-3-319-96881-0_15
9. Halevi, S., Lindell, Y., Pinkas, B.: Secure computation on the web: computing without simultaneous interaction. In: Rogaway, P. (ed.) CRYPTO 2011. LNCS, vol. 6841, pp. 132–150. Springer, Heidelberg (2011). https://doi.org/10.1007/978-3-642-22792-9_8
10. Garg, S., Srinivasan, A.: Two-round multiparty secure computation from minimal assumptions. In: Nielsen, J.B., Rijmen, V. (eds.) EUROCRYPT 2018. LNCS, vol. 10821, pp. 468–499. Springer, Cham (2018). https://doi.org/10.1007/978-3-319-78375-8_16
11. Benhamouda, F., Lin, H.: k-round multiparty computation from k-round oblivious transfer via garbled interactive circuits. In: Nielsen, J.B., Rijmen, V. (eds.) EUROCRYPT 2018. LNCS, vol. 10821, pp. 500–532. Springer, Cham (2018). https://doi.org/10.1007/978-3-319-78375-8_17
12. Rabin, T., Ben-Or, M.: Verifiable secret sharing and multiparty protocols with honest majority (extended abstract). In: STOC (1989)
13. Ananth, P., Choudhuri, A.R., Goel, A., Jain, A.: Round-optimal secure multiparty computation with honest majority. In: Shacham, H., Boldyreva, A. (eds.) CRYPTO 2018. LNCS, vol. 10992, pp. 395–424. Springer, Cham (2018). https://doi.org/10.1007/978-3-319-96881-0_14
14. Badrinarayanan, S., Jain, A., Manohar, N., Sahai, A.: Secure MPC: laziness leads to GOD. IACR Cryptology ePrint Archive 2018, p. 580 (2018)
15. Applebaum, B., Brakerski, Z., Tsabary, R.: Degree 2 is complete for the round-complexity of malicious MPC. In: EUROCRYPT (2019)
16. Ishai, Y., Kumaresan, R., Kushilevitz, E., Paskin-Cherniavsky, A.: Secure computation with minimal interaction, revisited. In: Gennaro, R., Robshaw, M. (eds.) CRYPTO 2015. LNCS, vol. 9216, pp. 359–378. Springer, Heidelberg (2015). https://doi.org/10.1007/978-3-662-48000-7_18
17. Dolev, D., Dwork, C., Waarts, O., Yung, M.: Perfectly secure message transmission. J. ACM 40(1), 17–47 (1993)
18. Fitzi, M., Hirt, M., Maurer, U.: Trading correctness for privacy in unconditional multi-party computation (extended abstract). In: Krawczyk, H. (ed.) CRYPTO 1998. LNCS, vol. 1462, pp. 121–136. Springer, Heidelberg (1998). https://doi.org/10.1007/BFb0055724

19. Fitzi, M., Hirt, M., Maurer, U.: General adversaries in unconditional multi-party computation. In: Lam, K.-Y., Okamoto, E., Xing, C. (eds.) ASIACRYPT 1999. LNCS, vol. 1716, pp. 232–246. Springer, Heidelberg (1999). https://doi.org/10.1007/978-3-540-48000-6_19

20. Hirt, M., Maurer, U., Zikas, V.: MPC vs. SFE: unconditional and computational security. In: Pieprzyk, J. (ed.) ASIACRYPT 2008. LNCS, vol. 5350, pp. 1–18. Springer, Heidelberg (2008). https://doi.org/10.1007/978-3-540-89255-7_1

21. Beerliová-Trubíniová, Z., Fitzi, M., Hirt, M., Maurer, U., Zikas, V.: MPC vs. SFE: perfect security in a unified corruption model. In: Canetti, R. (ed.) TCC 2008. LNCS, vol. 4948, pp. 231–250. Springer, Heidelberg (2008). https://doi.org/10.1007/978-3-540-78524-8_14

22. Chaum, D.: The spymasters double-agent problem: multiparty computations secure unconditionally from minorities and cryptographically from majorities. In: Brassard, G. (ed.) CRYPTO 1989. LNCS, vol. 435, pp. 591–602. Springer, New York (1990). https://doi.org/10.1007/0-387-34805-0_52

23. Lucas, C., Raub, D., Maurer, U.M.: Hybrid-secure MPC: trading information-theoretic robustness for computational privacy. In: ACM PODC (2010)

24. Fitzi, M., Hirt, M., Holenstein, T., Wullschleger, J.: Two-threshold broadcast and detectable multi-party computation. In: Biham, E. (ed.) EUROCRYPT 2003. LNCS, vol. 2656, pp. 51–67. Springer, Heidelberg (2003). https://doi.org/10.1007/3-540-39200-9_4

25. Fitzi, M., Holenstein, T., Wullschleger, J.: Multi-party computation with hybrid security. In: Cachin, C., Camenisch, J.L. (eds.) EUROCRYPT 2004. LNCS, vol. 3027, pp. 419–438. Springer, Heidelberg (2004). https://doi.org/10.1007/978-3-540-24676-3_25

26. Ishai, Y., Kushilevitz, E., Lindell, Y., Petrank, E.: On combining privacy with guaranteed output delivery in secure multiparty computation. In: Dwork, C. (ed.) CRYPTO 2006. LNCS, vol. 4117, pp. 483–500. Springer, Heidelberg (2006). https://doi.org/10.1007/11818175_29

27. Katz, J.: On achieving the "best of both worlds" in secure multiparty computation. In: ACM STOC (2007)

28. Ishai, Y., Katz, J., Kushilevitz, E., Lindell, Y., Petrank, E.: On achieving the "best of both worlds" in secure multiparty computation. SIAM J. Comput. **40**(1), 122–141 (2011)

29. Hirt, M., Lucas, C., Maurer, U., Raub, D.: Graceful degradation in multi-party computation (extended abstract). In: ICITS (2011)

30. Patra, A., Choudhary, A., Rabin, T., Rangan, C.P.: The round complexity of verifiable secret sharing revisited. In: Halevi, S. (ed.) CRYPTO 2009. LNCS, vol. 5677, pp. 487–504. Springer, Heidelberg (2009). https://doi.org/10.1007/978-3-642-03356-8_29

31. Backes, M., Kate, A., Patra, A.: Computational verifiable secret sharing revisited. In: Lee, D.H., Wang, X. (eds.) ASIACRYPT 2011. LNCS, vol. 7073, pp. 590–609. Springer, Heidelberg (2011). https://doi.org/10.1007/978-3-642-25385-0_32

32. Pedersen, T.P.: Non-interactive and information-theoretic secure verifiable secret sharing. In: Feigenbaum, J. (ed.) CRYPTO 1991. LNCS, vol. 576, pp. 129–140. Springer, Heidelberg (1992). https://doi.org/10.1007/3-540-46766-1_9

33. Patra, A., Ravi, A.: Beyond honest majority: the round complexity of fair and robust multi-party computation. Cryptology ePrint Archive, Report 2019/998 (2019). https://eprint.iacr.org/2019/998

34. Shamir, A.: How to share a secret. Commun. ACM **22**(11), 612–613 (1979)

35. Hirt, M., Maurer, U., Przydatek, B.: Efficient secure multi-party computation. In: Okamoto, T. (ed.) ASIACRYPT 2000. LNCS, vol. 1976, pp. 143–161. Springer, Heidelberg (2000). https://doi.org/10.1007/3-540-44448-3_12

36. Hirt, M., Maurer, U.: Robustness for free in unconditional multi-party computation. In: Kilian, J. (ed.) CRYPTO 2001. LNCS, vol. 2139, pp. 101–118. Springer, Heidelberg (2001). https://doi.org/10.1007/3-540-44647-8_6

37. Ishai, Y., Kushilevitz, E., Prabhakaran, M., Sahai, A., Yu, C.-H.: Secure protocol transformations. In: Robshaw, M., Katz, J. (eds.) CRYPTO 2016. LNCS, vol. 9815, pp. 430–458. Springer, Heidelberg (2016). https://doi.org/10.1007/978-3-662-53008-5_15

38. Goldreich, O.: The Foundations of Cryptography - volume 2, Basic Applications. Cambridge University Press, Cambridge (2004)

Card-Based Cryptography Meets Formal Verification

Alexander Koch$^{(\boxtimes)}$, Michael Schrempp, and Michael Kirsten

Karlsruhe Institute of Technology (KIT), Karlsruhe, Germany
{alexander.koch,kirsten}@kit.edu, michi.schrempp@freenet.de

Abstract. Card-based cryptography provides simple and practicable protocols for performing secure multi-party computation (MPC) with just a deck of cards. For the sake of simplicity, this is often done using cards with only two symbols, e.g., ♣ and ♡. Within this paper, we target the setting where all cards carry distinct symbols, catering for use-cases with commonly available standard decks and a weaker indistinguishability assumption. As of yet, the literature provides for only three protocols and no proofs for non-trivial lower bounds on the number of cards. As such complex proofs (handling very large combinatorial state spaces) tend to be involved and error-prone, we propose using formal verification for finding protocols and proving lower bounds. In this paper, we employ the technique of software bounded model checking (SBMC), which reduces the problem to a bounded state space, which is automatically searched exhaustively using a SAT solver as a backend.

Our contribution is twofold: (a) We identify two protocols for converting between different bit encodings with overlapping bases, and then show them to be card-minimal. This completes the picture of tight lower bounds on the number of cards with respect to runtime behavior and shuffle properties of conversion protocols. For computing AND, we show that there is no protocol with finite runtime using four cards with distinguishable symbols and fixed output encoding, and give a four-card protocol with an expected finite runtime using only random cuts. (b) We provide a general translation of proofs for lower bounds to a bounded model checking framework for automatically finding card- and length-minimal protocols and to give additional confidence in lower bounds. We apply this to validate our method and, as an example, confirm our new AND protocol to have a shortest run for protocols using this number of cards.

Keywords: Secure multiparty computation · Card-based cryptography · Formal verification · Bounded model checking · Standard decks

1 Introduction

Card-based cryptographic protocols allow to perform secure multi-party computation (MPC), i.e., jointly computing a function while not revealing more

© International Association for Cryptologic Research 2019
S. D. Galbraith and S. Moriai (Eds.): ASIACRYPT 2019, LNCS 11921, pp. 488–517, 2019.
https://doi.org/10.1007/978-3-030-34578-5_18

information about each individual input than absolutely necessary, with just a (regular) deck of playing cards, as long as they have indistinguishable backs. Let us start with an example. Assume that Alice and Bob meet in a bar and spend the evening together. After quite some chat, they would like to find out whether to have a second date. They are faced with the following problem: In case only one of them likes to meet again, this would cause an uncomfortable embarrassment, if he or she is the first to come out.[1] Fortunately, Alice is a notable cryptographer and likes card games, so she has with her a standard deck of cards. She remembers the protocol by Niemi and Renvall [NR99] for computing the AND function of two bits, here for outputting "yes", if both players share this mutual interest, and "no" otherwise. Doing so using an MPC protocol hides the input of the respective other player, unless it is obvious from their own input and output, hence hiding a "yes"-choice given of only one player, from the other.

In order to get a feeling for how such card-based protocols work, let us introduce the said protocol by Niemi and Renvall. It uses five cards with distinguishable symbols, which we denote – for simplicity[2] – as $\boxed{1}\,\boxed{2}\,\boxed{3}\,\boxed{4}$ and $\boxed{5}$. It is essential that the cards' backs are indistinguishable, such that when they are put face-down on the table, the only thing observable is $\boxed{?}\boxed{?}\boxed{?}\boxed{?}\boxed{?}$. With these cards, the two players can encode a commitment to a bit (yes or no) by the order of two cards $\boxed{i}\,\boxed{j}$, $i,j \in \{1,\dots,5\}$ (with $i \neq j$) via the encoding

$$\boxed{i}\boxed{j} \;\hat{=}\; \begin{cases} 0, & \text{if } i < j, \\ 1, & \text{if } i > j. \end{cases}$$

Alice inputs her bit by putting the cards $\boxed{1}\,\boxed{2}$ face-down and in the respective order on the table (she puts $\boxed{1}\,\boxed{2}$ for input 0, and $\boxed{2}\,\boxed{1}$ for input 1), while Bob does the same using his cards $\boxed{3}\,\boxed{4}$. We need an additional helper-card, here a $\boxed{5}$, which is put to the left of the players' cards.

The protocol starts by swapping Alice's second card with Bob's first card in the card sequence (pile) on the table. The resulting card configuration has an interesting property, namely that the order of the cards $\boxed{1}$ and $\boxed{4}$ in this sequence already encodes the output of the protocol, i.e., it reads $\boxed{4}\,\boxed{1}$ if the output is 1, and $\boxed{1}\,\boxed{4}$ otherwise. Hence, by securely removing the cards $\boxed{2}$ and $\boxed{3}$ (which is explained below), one directly obtains the output. We see this by inspecting all possible cases:

Bits	Input sequence	After swap	Removing $\boxed{2}+\boxed{3}$
$(0,0)$	$\boxed{5}\,\boxed{1}\,\boxed{2}\,\boxed{3}\,\boxed{4}$	$\boxed{5}\,\boxed{1}\,\boxed{3}\,\boxed{2}\,\boxed{4}$	$\boxed{5}\,\boxed{1}\,\boxed{x}\,\boxed{x}\,\boxed{4}$
$(0,1)$	$\boxed{5}\,\boxed{1}\,\boxed{2}\,\boxed{4}\,\boxed{3}$	$\boxed{5}\,\boxed{1}\,\boxed{4}\,\boxed{2}\,\boxed{3}$	$\boxed{5}\,\boxed{1}\,\boxed{4}\,\boxed{x}\,\boxed{x}$
$(1,0)$	$\boxed{5}\,\boxed{2}\,\boxed{1}\,\boxed{3}\,\boxed{4}$	$\boxed{5}\,\boxed{2}\,\boxed{3}\,\boxed{1}\,\boxed{4}$	$\boxed{5}\,\boxed{x}\,\boxed{x}\,\boxed{1}\,\boxed{4}$
$(1,1)$	$\boxed{5}\,\boxed{2}\,\boxed{1}\,\boxed{4}\,\boxed{3}$	$\boxed{5}\,\boxed{2}\,\boxed{4}\,\boxed{1}\,\boxed{3}$	$\boxed{5}\,\boxed{x}\,\boxed{4}\,\boxed{1}\,\boxed{x}$

---

[1] This is known as the "dating problem".
[2] Alice and Bob in the story might, e.g., use 7, 8, 9, 10 and a queen with any symbol.

We can remove the cards $\boxed{2}$ and $\boxed{3}$, while keeping the relative order of all cards in the sequence intact, by cutting the cards, i.e., rotating the sequence by a random offset which is unknown to the players. We can then securely turn the first card and remove it in case it is $\boxed{2}$ or $\boxed{3}$. Due to the cut, the turned card is random, and hence it does not reveal anything about the inputs. When both cards are removed, we reach a configuration where $\boxed{5}$ is the first card by the same procedure where the two remaining cards encode the AND result. Here, the $\boxed{5}$ played the crucial role of a separator that keeps the relative order of the remaining cards, starting from the separator, intact when doing a random cut. (A formal version of this protocol is given in Protocol 2 and Fig. 7.)

In this paper, we are interested in whether we can do away with the helping card $\boxed{5}$, and whether there are simpler protocols. Moreover, in order to handle the increasing combinatorial state space (relative to protocols on decks of just ♣ and ♡), we introduce formal verification to the field of card-based cryptography.

1.1 Secure Multiparty Computation with Cards

In combining different protocols, one can do much more than just computing the AND function. For example, it is possible to compute arbitrary Boolean circuits by combining the well-known fact that any circuit can be expressed using only NOT and AND gates, with a method to duplicate the physically encoded bit in case of forking wires, which we make explicit by a COPY gate. In the encoding above, NOT simply inverts the order of the two cards, and a COPY-protocol is given, e.g., in [M16]. Using this setup, we can do general MPC for any function *without needing to trust a possibly corrupted computer*.

A particular advantage of protocols using physical assumptions is that they can provide a *bridge to reality*. Examples of this are given in [GBG14,FFN14], where the authors give a protocol for proving in zero-knowledge that a nuclear warhead (to be disarmed due to an international treaty) conforms to a prescribed template, without giving away anything about its internal design. In our setting of cryptography with cards, this bridge is used if the cryptographic protocol is embedded in a real card game, e.g., to prevent cheating[3]. Here, using computers is not only cumbersome, but there is no guarantee that the card sequence on my hand is the one I input into the software, hence no bridge to the physical world.

Another application of such protocols is to explain MPC in an interesting and motivating way to students in cryptography lectures. Card-based cryptography tries to find protocols for the above-mentioned AND and COPY functionalities which are card-minimal, simple and practicable. For simplicity, many protocols in card-based cryptography work with specially constructed decks, e.g., of only two symbols, ♣ and ♡. This is easy for explanation, and there are nice and easily describable protocols, such as the five-card trick by den Boer [dB89] and the six-card AND protocol by Mizuki and Sone [MS09].

---

[3] As an example, in a Duplicate Bridge tournament, one might prove that all sessions are handed the same cards, eliminating the need of a trusted dealer (no pun intended).

However, the setting where all cards are distinguishable, as described above, has several advantages. Firstly, we assume little about the indistinguishability of cards, which leads to stronger security guarantees. (This is more similar to the indistinguishable version of tamper-evident seals, such as scratch-off cards, by Moran and Naor [MN10].) We only need the backs (or envelopes wrapping the cards, if one wishes) to be indistinguishable. Secondly, these standard decks are more commonly available, in contrast to constructed decks. If one were to use standard decks for the protocols above, they would need multiple copies of the same card. Thirdly, considering this setting may lead to protocols using less cards than the optimal ones in the two-symbol deck setting. In fact, as our paper shows, one may use less cards than in the two-symbol deck setting. For example, our new four-card Las Vegas AND protocol presented in Sect. 5 uses only a very basic, practicable shuffling mechanism, namely random cuts, and uses one card less than the provably card-minimal Las Vegas AND protocol (restricted to certain types of practical shuffles) in the two-symbol deck setting. As of yet, there has only been little research in this direction, with [NR99,M16] being the only works that consider the setting where all cards have distinguishable symbols, called "standard deck" setting. Nothing is known about non-trivial lower bounds on the number of cards. This is likely due to the large state space, as there are many more distinguishable card re-orderings compared to the two-symbol case.

Within this paper, our interest is to find an automatic way of constructing compact card-based protocols which are secure and correct, based on only the two standard operations *turn* and *shuffle*, given the desired number of cards. We exploit the observation that, to the best of our knowledge, all findings in the literature employ only protocols of comparatively small length using only a small number of cards. Based on the hypothesis that we may always find some number n which is greater than or equal to any length-minimal card-protocol, we apply the automatic off-the-shelf formal program-verification technique *software bounded model checking (SBMC)* [BCC+99]. This technique allows, given such a bound n, to encode a program verification task into a decidable set of logical equations, which can then be solved by a SAT or an SMT solver. In this work, we propose an automatic method based on SBMC that, given the desired numbers of cards and protocol length, either constructs such a protocol if and only if one exists, or proves the underlying SAT formula to be unsatisfiable, i.e., shows that no such protocol exists. Based thereon, we propose that the cumbersome and error-prone task of finding such protocols or proving their non-existence by hand may be supported or complemented by such an automatic approach which is flexibly adaptable to a variety of card-based protocols and desired restrictions.

Prior to our work, it was not yet clear which role the input encoding plays when devising new protocols. This is the question on whether it can make a difference regarding the possibility of a protocol if we provide, e.g., $\boxed{1}\boxed{2}$ to Alice and $\boxed{3}\boxed{4}$ to Bob, or $\boxed{1}\boxed{3}$ to Alice and $\boxed{2}\boxed{4}$ to Bob. We provide an analysis of this question, showing that with certain restrictions, there is a relatively large freedom in choosing the input (and/or output) bases. This is a useful prerequisite in proving the impossibility of a protocol with a given number of cards.

1.2 Contribution

Our contribution consists in providing interesting new protocols and impossibility results, as well as a fully automatic method based on formal verification to support such findings. The specific advances therein are the following (cf. also Table 1 for a comparison to the literature):

(1) A four-card AND protocol in the standard deck setting, improving upon [NR99] by one card, and reaching the theoretical minimum on the number of cards. W.r.t. shuffling, this protocol only uses an expected number of 6 random cuts, compared to 7.5 random cuts in a (shortened) variant of [NR99]. Additionally, it has a natural interpretation and using only random cuts makes it easy to implement in an actively secure way, cf. [KW17].

(2) We show that under certain conditions the cards for encoding input or output can be chosen freely. For one-bit output protocols and if five or more cards are available, we can freely choose both input and output bases by only extending the protocol by expected three shuffle and three turn steps. For this matter, we identify two protocols for converting a bit encoding if the new encoding shares one card with the old one.

(3) We show that there is no finite-runtime protocol for converting between bases with non-empty intersection using four cards. Moreover, there cannot be a finite-runtime AND protocol with four cards if we fix the basis in advance.

(4) We introduce formal verification to card-based cryptography by providing a technique which automatically finds new protocols using as few as possible operations and searches for lowest bounds on card-minimal protocols.

Table 1. Minimum number of cards required by AND and basis conversion protocols, subject to the running time and shuffle restrictions specified in the first two columns. Note that random cuts are a subclass of uniform closed shuffles.

Running time	Shuffle Restr.	#Cards	Protocol	Lower bound
AND PROTOCOLS:				
Las vegas	Random cuts	4	Theorem 3	– (trivial)
Finite	–	$\Big\} \geq 5^{\text{a}}, \leq 8$	[M16, Sect. 3.4]	Theorem 2
Finite	Uniform closed			
DISJOINT BASIS CONVERT PROTOCOLS:				
Finite	Uniform closed	4	[M16, Sect. 3.2]	– (trivial)
OVERLAPPING BASIS CONVERT PROTOCOLS:				
Las Vegas	Random cuts	3	Theorem 4	– (trivial)
Finite	–	$\Big\} \ 5$	Theorem 5	Theorem 1
Finite	Uniform closed			

[a] Lower bound result only holds for fixed output basis, flexible case is still open.

1.3   Related Work

The feasibility of card-based cryptographic MPC is due to [dB89, CK93, NR98], with a formal model given by [MS14]. The only two papers looking at standard deck solutions are [NR99, M16]. Lower bounds on card-based cryptographic protocols are given by [KWH15, KKW+17, K18] for the two-symbol deck setting. The card-minimal protocol for this setting, using only practicable (i.e., uniform closed) shuffles, is given by [AHM+18] and uses five cards. The state trees used for protocols in this paper are devised by [KWH15, KKW+17].

To the best of our knowledge, this is the first work which applies formal methods to the field of card-based cryptography. However, a large range of research has been done using formal methods in the more general field of secure two-party and multiparty computations. This can be clustered into either analyzing security protocols given as high-level, abstract (and usually idealized) models, or program-based approaches targeting real(istic) protocol (software) implementations. Avalle, Pironti, and Sisto [APS14] further structure this into the two main approaches of automated model extraction and automated code generation. We refer the interested reader to overviews as given by Blanchet [B12] or Avalle, Pironti, and Sisto, and only go into a few selected works for which we identified closer links to our approach, e.g., using software bounded model checking (SBMC), SAT solvers on real(istic) protocol implementations, or relating in the analyzed security model. Standard cryptographic assumptions using lower-level computational models are – albeit more realistic – usually harder to formalize and automate. One notable line of research is CBMC-GC [FHK+14] which builds on top of the tool CBMC [CKL04]. It uses SBMC in a compiler framework translating secure computations of ANSI C programs into an optimized Boolean circuit which can subsequently be implemented securely utilizing the garbled circuit approach. Another similar setting to ours is analyzed in [RSH19], where also an "honest-but-curious" attacker model is assumed. Therein, a domain-specific language is built on top of the F* language, a full-featured, verification-oriented, effectful programming language [SHK+16]. Swamy et al. then implement MPC programs with enabled formal verification provided by the semantics of the language.

1.4   Outline

We give the computational model of card-based protocols, security definitions, etc. and the necessary preliminaries as well as a basic setup for software bounded model checking in Sect. 2. Section 3 discusses which freedom one has when choosing the specific cards for encoding inputs and outputs to card-based protocols and introduces a formal relabeling operation. We give lower bounds on the number of cards for AND and basis-conversion protocols in Sect. 4. A four-card Las Vegas AND protocol and two basis-conversion protocols are presented in Sect. 5 and Sect. 6, respectively. Section 7 gives results from applying our formal verification setup based on SBMC to our new AND protocol.

2 Preliminaries

In this section, we first formally introduce card-based protocols with their computational model (including some basic required notions), a convenient formal protocol representation, a suitable security notion, and the formal requirements for proving lower bounds. Secondly, we introduce our applied formal technique called software bounded model checking, on which, thirdly, we establish our general technique for automatically finding card- and length-minimal protocols.

2.1 Card-Based Protocols

Formally, a *deck* $\mathcal{D}$ of cards is a multiset over a *(deck) alphabet* or symbol set Σ. We denote multisets by $[\![\cdot]\!]$, e.g., $[\![\heartsuit, \heartsuit, \clubsuit, \clubsuit]\!]$ is a deck over $\{\heartsuit, \clubsuit\}$. In this paper, we focus mainly on decks $\mathcal{D} = [\![1, \ldots, n]\!]$, $n \in \mathbb{N}$, where each symbol occurs exactly once. Following [M16], we call these decks *standard decks*, because decks of common card games are a good representation of such formal decks.

For encoding a bit, we additionally assume a linear order on the card symbols in Σ, which is the usual order on $\mathbb{N}$ for standard decks, and $\clubsuit < \heartsuit$ for simple two-element decks. Two face-down cards with distinct symbols $s_1, s_2 \in \Sigma$ then *encode a bit* via the following encoding rule introduced in [NR99]:

$$s_1\, s_2 \,\hat{=}\, \begin{cases} 0, & \text{if } s_1 < s_2, \\ 1, & \text{if } s_1 > s_2. \end{cases}$$

Card-based protocols proceed by mainly two actions on the sequence or pile of cards: We can introduce uncertainty (about which card is which) by shuffling them in arbitrary or in certain controlled ways, e.g., by cutting the cards in quick succession, so that players do not know which card ended up where in the card sequence (or pile). Slightly more formal, a (uniform) shuffle is specified by a permutation set, from which one element is drawn uniformly at random and applied to the cards, without the players learning which one it was. Secondly, we may turn over cards and publicly learn their symbol, and act on the basis of this information. Moreover, we may deterministically permute the cards.

Permutations and Groups. Let S_n denote the *symmetric group* on $\{1, \ldots, n\}$. For elements $x_1, \ldots, x_k \in \{1, \ldots, n\}$ the *cycle* $(x_1\ x_2\ \ldots\ x_k)$ is the *cyclic* permutation π with $\pi(x_i) = x_{i+1}$ for $1 \le i < k$, $\pi(x_k) = x_1$ and $\pi(x) = x$ for all x not occurring in the cycle. Every permutation can be written as a composition of pairwise disjoint cycles. For example, $(1\ 3\ 2)(4\ 5)$ maps $1 \mapsto 3, 3 \mapsto 2, 2 \mapsto 1, 4 \mapsto 5$, and $5 \mapsto 4$. The identity permutation is denoted as id.

Given permutations $\pi_1, \ldots, \pi_k \in S_n$, $\langle \pi_1, \ldots, \pi_k \rangle$ denotes the group generated by $\pi_1, \ldots, \pi_k$. A shuffle is a *random cut* if its permutation set is the group $\langle \pi \rangle = \{\pi^0, \ldots, \pi^{l-1}\}$ generated by a single element π *which is a cycle* $(x_1\ x_2\ \ldots\ x_l)$. A shuffle is called a *random bisection cut* if its permutation set is generated by a π which is the composition of pairwise disjoint cycles of length 2. Finally, an S_k-*shuffle* is a shuffle with permutation set S_k.

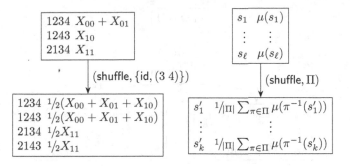

Fig. 1. A shuffle operation, given by example (left), and via the general rule (right).

Computational Model and Protocol Tree Representation. For our formal descriptions, we make heavy use of the KWH trees introduced in [KWH15] and shown to be equivalent to the computational model of [MS14, MS17] in [KKW+17]. We start by the start node

$$
\begin{array}{ll}
12\,34 & X_{00} \\
12\,43 & X_{01} \\
21\,34 & X_{10} \\
21\,43 & X_{11}
\end{array}
$$

and add eventually needed further cards ($\boxed{5}$, $\boxed{6}$, ...) to the right of the players bits. The state (or KWH) tree is directed, with annotations at the outgoing edges of the state, specifying the action that is performed next. Let μ be the state with the outgoing annotation, then the actions are defined as:

1. (shuffle, Π) leads to a μ' as in Fig. 1, where $\Pi \subseteq S_{|\mathcal{D}|}$ is a permutation set.
2. (turn, T) branches the tree into states μ_v for each observation v possible by revealing the cards at positions from the set $T \subseteq \{1, \ldots, |\mathcal{D}|\}$, as in Fig. 2. μ_v contains the sequences from μ which are compatible with the observation v. For each sequence s compatible with v, we have $\mu_v(s) := \mu(s)/\Pr[v]$, where $\Pr[v] \in (0, 1]$ is the probability of observing v.
3. (perm, π) permutes the sequences of μ according to π.
4. (result, p_1, p_2) stops the computation and returns the cards at p_1, p_2 as output.

We start by a state that encodes the input sequences attached to their respective symbolic input probabilities, see [KKW+17] for a thorough explanation:

$$
\begin{array}{ll}
12\,34 & X_{00} \\
12\,43 & X_{01} \\
21\,34 & X_{10} \\
21\,43 & X_{11}
\end{array}
$$

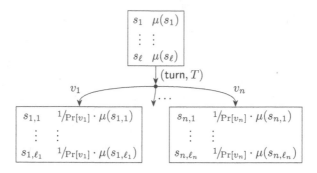

Fig. 2. A turn operation. Here, $v_1, \ldots, v_n$, are the possible observation by turning the cards at positions in T. For each $i \in \{1, \ldots, n\}$ the $s_{i,1}, \ldots, s_{i,\ell_i}$ are the sequences from $s_1, \ldots, s_\ell$ which are compatible with v_i. Note that in secure protocols, the probability of observing v_i, denoted as $\Pr[v_i]$, is constant.

A protocol computes a Boolean function $f \colon \{0,1\}^2 \to \{0,1\}$ if the start state (tree root) encodes each $b \in \{0,1\}^2$ in the first four cards (the remaining cards being at fixed positions), and in the leaf nodes of the protocol's state tree, it holds for the positions given by the result operation that the cards at these positions encode a value $o \in \{0,1\}$ if all X_i occurring in $\mu(s)$ for sequence s satisfy $f(i) = o$ *(Correctness)*. We say that a protocol has *finite runtime* if its tree is finite. It is a *Las Vegas* protocol, if it is not finite runtime, but the expected length of any path in its tree is finite. Note that while we consider looping protocols, we do not consider the case where a complete restart is necessary. For self-similar infinite trees, we simplify by drawing edges to earlier states.

Security of Card-Based Protocols. We slightly adjust the security notion from the literature to standard decks. For more details, we refer to [K19]. Since different encodings for the same bit are possible, we want the encoding basis of the output bit to not give away anything about the inputs. We say that a protocol is *secure* if at any turn operation the probability for each observation v is a constant $\rho \in [0,1]$ (using $\sum_{i \in \{0,1\}^2} X_i = 1$), *and additionally* if at any result operation the probability of each output basis is constant in the same sense.

As in [KKW+17], for our impossibility proofs and formalizations with bounded model checkers, it is useful to consider a weaker form of security, which is a necessary criterion for security as defined above: A protocol is *possibilistically output-secure*, if at any state of the protocol, every output can still be possible. This weakens the normal security guarantee, as the probability for a given input sequence could be higher in this state. One could even be able to exclude a specific input sequence, if the corresponding output can still be possible through another input sequence. Together with possibilistic input-security, this discussion leads to the following formal definition:

Definition 1 (cf. [KKW+17]). *A protocol* $\mathcal{P} = (\mathcal{D}, U, Q, A)$ *computing a function* $f : \{0,1\}^2 \rightarrow \{0,1\}$ *has* possibilistic input security *(*possibilistic output security*) if it is correct, i.e., output* $O = f(I)$ *almost surely and for uniformly[4] random input* I *and any visible sequence trace* v *with* $\Pr[v] > 0$ *as well as any input* $i \in \{0,1\}^2$ *(any output* $o \in \{0,1\}$*) we have* $\Pr[v \mid I = i] > 0$ *(*$\Pr[v \mid f(I) = o]$*).*

Proving Lower Bounds. We call two states, μ and μ', similar, if μ is equal to μ' up to row or column permutation. This is an interesting equivalence relation for reducing the state space and we make use of it in our impossibility results.

As in [KKW+17, Definition 3], we define reduced states, where states are not annotated by their symbolic probabilities, but by the result that is specified by their inputs. This simplifies impossibility proofs by reducing information and the state space. Any such reduced tree captures only a weak form of security, possibilistic security, as discussed above where each output (reachable in principle) needs to be still possible. Showing that a protocol is impossible even in this weak setting implies its general impossibility.

To obtain a reduced state tree, we project all the symbolic probabilities of the sequences in a state tree to a *type* (representing the possible future output associated with the sequence in a correct protocol, see below), which can be any $o \in \{0,1\}$. For this, let $\mathcal{P}$ be a protocol computing a function $f : \{0,1\}^2 \rightarrow \{0,1\}$ and μ be a state in the state tree. For any sequence s with $\mu(s)$ being a polynomial with positive coefficients for the variables $X_{b_1}, \ldots, X_{b_i}$ ($i \geq 1$), set $\hat{\mu}(s) := o \in \{0,1\}$ if $o = f(b_1) = f(b_2) = \ldots = f(b_i)$ in the resulting *reduced state* $\hat{\mu}$. We call sequences in $\hat{\mu}$ according to their type o-*sequences*.

For proving impossibility results, we make use of the backwards calculus as given in [K18]. We highlight the main ideas here, but refer to it for reference. Denote by $\mathsf{shuf}^{-1}(\mathcal{G})$, for a set of states $\mathcal{G}$, the *set of states that are transformed into a state in* $\mathcal{G}$ *by a shuffle*. The trivial shuffle is allowed, i.e., $\mathcal{G} \subseteq \mathsf{shuf}^{-1}(\mathcal{G})$. Moreover, $\mathsf{turn}_f^{-1}(\mathcal{G})$ is the set of states being in $\mathcal{G}$ or having a turnable position i such that all immediate successor states from a turn at i are in $\mathcal{G}$. Define by $\mathsf{cl}_f(\mathcal{G})$ *the closure* of $\mathsf{turn}_f^{-1}(\cdot)$ and $\mathsf{shuf}^{-1}(\cdot)$ operations on $\mathcal{G}$. Hence, it holds that if the start state is not in $\mathsf{cl}_f(\mathcal{G})$, then no finite-runtime protocol can exist.

2.2 Automatic Formal Verification Using SBMC

In the following, we introduce an automatic technique from formal program verification, namely software bounded model checking (SBMC), to the field of card-based cryptography. We first describe the general technique of using SBMC to check for software properties, before we explain how we apply it to search for cryptographically secure card-based protocols. In a nutshell, we translate the task to a reachability problem in software programs (which will later-on be a program encoding operations on an abstract state tree as described above), which the SBMC tool encodes into an instance of the SAT problem.

---

[4] Actually, the distribution does not matter, as long as $\Pr[I = i] > 0$ for all $i \in \{0,1\}^k$.

We assume we are given an imperatively defined function f under the form of an imperative program (for example, written in the C language), that uses some parameter values taken among a set of possible start values I. An entry $i \in I$ is a list of values, one value for each such parameter: it gives a value to everything that a run of f depends on, such as its input variables, or anything that is considered non-deterministic (i.e., of arbitrary, but fixed, value for any concrete evaluation of f) from the point of view of f. For this reason, those parameters are qualified as "non-deterministic", to distinguish them from normal parameters used in a programming language to pass information around. Moreover, some values can be "derived", thus, computed in f from the non-deterministic parameter values, or declared as constants in f, and both values of non-deterministic parameters or derived values can then be used as normal parameters in the program. We are also given a software property to be checked about f, in the form $C^{\mathrm{ant}} \Rightarrow C^{\mathrm{cons}}$, where ant and $cons$ stand for antecedent and consequence respectively. Both C^{ant} and C^{cons} are sets of Boolean statements. A Boolean statement is a statement of f that evaluates to a Boolean value, for example, a simple statement checking that some computed intermediate value is positive. An entry i is said to satisfy a set of Boolean statements if and only if all Boolean statements in the set evaluate to true during the execution of f using the non-deterministic parameter values i, and is said to fail the set of Boolean statements otherwise. The property $C^{\mathrm{ant}} \Rightarrow C^{\mathrm{cons}}$ requires that for all possible entries $i \in I$, if i satisfies C^{ant}, then i satisfies C^{cons}. As an example, assume f computes, given i, two intermediate integer values v_1 and v_2, and then returns a third value v_3. The property to be checked could, e.g., be: if v_1 is negative, then v_2 is positive and v_3 is odd. A solver that is asked to check a software property $C^{\mathrm{ant}} \Rightarrow C^{\mathrm{cons}}$ thus exhaustively searches for an entry i that satisfies C^{ant} but fails C^{cons}. The property is valid if and only if there does not exist any such entry i, i.e., it is impossible to find.

SBMC is a fully-automatic static program analysis technique used to verify whether such a software property is valid, given a function and a property to be checked. It covers all possible inputs within a specified bound. It is static in the sense that programs are analyzed without executing them on concrete values or considering any side channels. Instead, programs are symbolically executed and exhaustively checked for errors up to a certain bound, restricting the number of loop iterations to limit runs through the program to a bounded length. This is done by unrolling the control flow graph of the program and translating it into a formula in a decidable logic that is satisfiable if and only if a program run exists which satisfies C^{ant} and fails C^{cons}. The variables in the formula are the non-deterministic parameters of f, and their possible values are taken from I.

This reduces the problem to a decidable satisfiability problem. Modern SAT-solving technology can then be used to verify whether such a program run exists, in which case an erroneous input has been found, and the run is presented to the user. If the solver cannot find such a program run, it may be either because the property is valid, or because it is invalid only for some run which exceeds the bound. In some cases, SBMC is also able to infer statically which bound is sufficient to bring a definitive conclusion.

2.3   Automatic Formal Verification for Card-Based Protocols

Our approach employs a standardized program representation of the KWH trees introduced in [KWH15] (and described in the beginning of this section). This allows a general programmatic encoding of both shuffle and turn operations, as well as of the fixed input state (indicated by the input card sequences from the table in the very beginning of this paper), the non-deterministic reachable states, and the logical function to be computed securely.

The input state is trivially derived from the specified numbers of cards as the size and order of the players' commitments is fixed and the (without loss of generality) consecutively ordered card sequence of (distinguishable) helper-cards is simply prepended to the input card sequence, annotated with their respective input probabilities. Any input state thus consists of exactly four distinguishable card sequences. Based on this input state, the program performs a loop, which successively performs turn or shuffle operations based on the input state and computes the resulting states from which it continues performing turn or shuffle operations. The loop ends when the specified bound (representing the length of the protocol to be found) is reached, checks whether the final state is indeed a valid computation of the secure function, and (if and only if the check is successful) the found protocol is then presented to the user.

However, this task involves multiple computational complexities, most notably both the number of (possibly) reachable states, and the choice of the next operation, i.e., either choosing the card(s) to be turned or which shuffle to perform. We partially overcome the first computational complexity by not considering Las Vegas protocols as this relieves us from checking every reachable sequence of states to be finite. In fact, we compute all reachable states after every protocol operation, but only check each of them to be valid, and then proceed our operations on only one of them, which is non-deterministically chosen among them. The second computational complexity consists in first non-deterministically choosing whether to shuffle or to turn, and then to perform the respective operation. The turn operation is less interesting as it is mostly the obvious implementation for updating the computed state and its probabilities using mostly standard imperative program operations, except that the turn observations are again non-deterministically chosen, hence making the SBMC tool consider any of them to be possible. The more interesting operation is the shuffle operation, as it must randomly draw a set of permutations on which the thereby reachable states are computed. We implement this by non-deterministically choosing a set of permutations from a precomputed set of all generally possible permutations. Both the amount[5] and the choices of the respective permutations are chosen non-deterministically. Moreover, we restrict our experiments to only closed shuffles and proceed by restricting the computed set of permutations to be either closed or of size one (i.e., a simple permutation).

Finally, after iterating the afore-mentioned loop for the specified bound number with the described operations and restricting that final state indeed computes

---

[5] In order to keep the execution times still manageable for our experiments, we bound this amount by the (arguably quite reasonable) number 8.

the secure function, we specify the software property C^{cons} to be checked simply as the Boolean value `false`. This trivially unsatisfiable property implies that the verification task always fails once there exist input and non-deterministic parameters such that the respective program run reaches the statement in the program which checks this property. The SBMC tool exhaustively searches for a run of the specified length through the program which leads from the starting state to a correct and secure state which satisfies the given security notion, i.e., reaches the above-mentioned statement. Hence, if there exists any protocol of the specified length which computes the secure function and for which the specified operations and valid intermediate states (representing KWH-trees) exist, such a protocol is presented by our method. If no such protocol can be found, we know there is no card-based protocol of the specified length satisfying all our restrictions on permitted turn and shuffle operations, as well as intermediate and final states. This means there exists no model for the SAT formula which encodes the set of all permitted program runs given our specified requirements.

Hence, assuming our translation of KWH trees and respective protocol operations into a simple imperative program are correct, this method can then be used in an iterative manner to strengthen the bounds from the literature. Note that this is largely based on the so-called "small-scope hypothesis", i.e., a large number of bugs are already exposed for small program runs. We apply this hypothesis to the setting of card-based security protocols as all protocols in the literature only use a small number of turn and shuffle operations and the length of any found protocol is below ten operations.

This approach can be generalized to search for card-based protocols using a pre-defined number of actions and adhering to a given formal security notion. We have written a general program[6] to search for such situations parameterized in the desired restrictions on actions and security notions. Note that, in order to cope with the still considerable state space size, we use the refined security notion of output-possibilistic security.

3   On the Choice of Cards for Input and Output

We essentially show that the choice of input basis (or output basis, but not necessarily both) is irrelevant for the functioning of the protocol. In rare cases, one has to append two operations to existing protocols to make them fully basis flexible. In the Niemi–Renvall protocol shown above, the protocol description specifies Alice's cards to be of symbols $1, 2$, and Bob's to be of symbols $3, 4$ and the helping card to be a 5. To simplify later proofs and to demonstrate an interesting symmetry in card-based protocols, we show that this choice is irrelevant for the functioning of the protocol.

---

[6] The program is available under https://github.com/mi-ki/cardCryptoVerification.

For this, we define a *relabeling* from deck alphabet Σ to a deck alphabet Σ', i.e., a bijective function $\lambda \colon \Sigma \to \Sigma'$.[7] A relabeling of a sequence $s = (s_1, \ldots, s_n)$ is a relabeling of each of its symbols, i.e., $\lambda(s) := (\lambda(s_1), \ldots, \lambda(s_n))$. A relabeling of a state is given by the relabeling of all its sequences, a relabeling of a protocol/state (sub)tree is the relabeling of all its states as in Figs. 3 and 5.

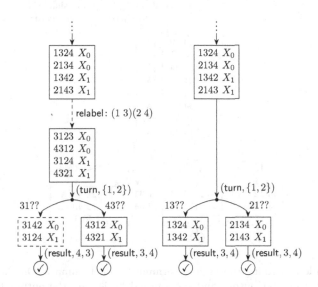

Fig. 3. Example of the relabel action, swapping the card symbols of 1 and 3, and of 2 and 4, respectively. This action is for abbreviated writing only, it does not actually relabel the physical cards, which seems impossible without learning their symbols. Hence, the tree on the left is virtually translated to the right. Note that the relabeling only affects the sequences, the observations at edges belonging to turn actions and may swap the order of the indices in result operations.

Lemma 1. *If $\mathcal{P}$ is a protocol with deterministic output basis, one can relabel the cards without affecting the functioning.*

Note that the deterministic output basis restriction is important, because if we have a randomized output encoding such as in Fig. 4 on the left, a relabeling might affect the monotonicity of the encoding of only one of the possible output bases. In this case, we make use of the following lemma, as illustrated Fig. 4.

Lemma 2. *Every protocol with one-bit output and a randomized output basis can be transformed into a protocol with deterministic output basis, by inserting a shuffle and a turn before any result operation with randomized output basis.*

---

[7] In case of the decks being a subset of $\mathbb{N}$, we may use usual permutation notation. We require that if λ maps x to y, the cardinalities of x and y are equal in the deck.

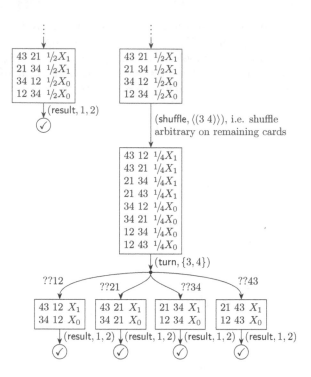

Fig. 4. Example of making the basis deterministic, cf. Lemma 2. On the left you see a tree part with one-bit output and randomized basis, i.e., the output basis may be $\{1,2\}$ or $\{3,4\}$, each with a probability of $1/2$. We can make it known to the players, i.e., deterministic, by splitting up the state via an S_k-shuffle (here: $k = 2$) on the remaining cards (so that they no longer contain any information), turning these and then doing the result operation. By what is visible in the turn, one can derive the output basis.

4   Impossibility of Finite-Runtime Four-Card AND and Basis Conversion with Overlapping Bases

In this section we give our main impossibility results.

Theorem 1. *There is no four-card finite-runtime basis conversion protocol for overlapping bases with deck $\mathcal{D} = [\![1,2,3,4]\!]$.*

Proof Sketch. We proceed by using the backwards calculus technique from [K18], as described in Sect. 2.1. That is, we show that if we start with the set of (highly-structured) final states $\mathcal{G}_0$ of basis conversion protocols and enlarge this set iteratively by states which reach the given states by a shuffle or a turn, we obtain the closure $\mathsf{cl}_\mathsf{f}(\mathcal{G}_0)$. If we consider only reduced states, the set of possible states is finite, so applying $\mathsf{turn}_\mathsf{f}^{-1}(\cdot)$ and $\mathsf{shuf}^{-1}(\cdot)$ operations to the growing set of states, starting from $\mathcal{G}_0$, will become stationary. It remains to show that the start state is not contained in the closure. We assume w.l.o.g. the input basis

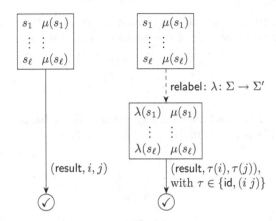

Fig. 5. The formal rule for relabeling leaf nodes of one-bit output protocols. Let $r_1 = s_k[i], r_2 = s_k[j] \in \mathcal{D}$ be the output symbols (before relabeling) of some arbitrary sequence s_k of μ. Then, $\tau = \mathrm{id}$, if $r_1 < r_2$ implies $\lambda(r_1) < \lambda(r_2)$ (λ is monotone on r_1, r_2) and $\tau = (i\ j)$ otherwise.

$\{1, 2\}$ with helping cards 3 and 4, and the output basis $\{o_1 < o_2\}$ such that $|\{1, 2\} \cap \{o_1, o_2\}| = 1$. For simplicity, we want the output basis $\{1, 3\}$ and argue later why this choice did not affect the proof statement. Hence, the final state is any choice of at least one 1-sequence and one 0-sequence of the state on the left:

13 24 0	
13 42 0	
31 24 1	12 34 0
31 42 1	21 34 1

The state on the right is the start state of a basis-conversion protocol. Both states are considered up to similarity.

We have $\mathrm{shuf}^{-1}(\mathcal{G}_0) = \mathcal{G}_0$, i.e., shuffling steps do not help in the last step of a output-possibilistically secure protocol, because any subset of a final state which contains at least one 1-sequence and one 0-sequence (required as 1-/0-sequences cannot be generated out of thin air by a shuffle), is already final. Hence, we consider $\mathcal{G}_1 := \mathrm{turn}_f^{-1}(\mathcal{G}_0)$, i.e., the states turnable at a position i, where all immediate child nodes when turning at i are in $\mathcal{G}_0$. W.l.o.g. we assume the turn to be at position 4. By [K18, Lemma 3], we use that $\mathcal{G}_1 = \mathrm{turn}_f^{-1}(\mathcal{G}_0) = \mathcal{G}_0 \cup \mathrm{turn}_f^{-1}(\mathrm{cc}(\mathcal{G}_0))$, where $\mathrm{cc}(\mathcal{G}_0)$ is the subset of $\mathcal{G}_0$ with states that have a constant column:

13 24 0	13 42 0
31 24 1	31 42 1

However, we aim to enlarge this set (which we can do since our claim is only made stronger by monotonicity of the backwards operations) by the states

24 13	0
42 13	1

24 31	0
42 31	1

,

because they would be reachable anyway via a disjoint basis conversion due to [M16, Sect. 3.2]. The states from $\mathcal{G}_1 \setminus \mathcal{G}_0$ look as follows:

$\dots a$	0
$\dots a$	1
$\dots b$	0
$\dots b$	1
$\dots c$	0
$\dots c$	1
$\dots d$	0
$\dots d$	1

where at least two of the blocks are present, and $a, b, c, d \in \mathcal{D}$ are pairwise distinct. Note that the start state cannot be of this form, as it contains only two sequences. To show that another backwards turn step does not enlarge the set by showing that $\mathsf{cc}(\mathcal{G}_1) = \mathsf{cc}(\mathcal{G}_0)$. For this, note that the states from $\mathsf{cc}(\mathcal{G}_0)$ have two constant columns, but with the specific pairing that if one is 1, the other is 3 and vice versa, or if one is 2, the other is 4 and vice versa. Hence, having another constant column in the state from $\mathcal{G}_1 \setminus \mathcal{G}_0$ above, say at position 3, would need the same symbol (given by the pairing) in the fourth column. Hence, it can only have two sequences, i.e., it is already in $\mathcal{G}_0$. This shows that $\mathsf{turn}_\mathsf{f}^{-1}(\mathcal{G}_1) = \mathcal{G}_1$.

Now, for the main step of the proof, set $\mathcal{G}_2 := \mathsf{shuf}^{-1}(\mathcal{G}_1)$ and $\mathcal{G}_3 := \mathsf{turn}_\mathsf{f}^{-1}(\mathcal{G}_2)$. Because the shuffling is unrestricted, applying another backwards shuffle to $\mathcal{G}_2$ cannot give a larger set, as we can always combine two shuffles into one. The remaining proof will show that $\mathcal{G}_3 = \mathcal{G}_2$ in which case no further enlargement is possible. Afterwards, showing that the start state is not in $\mathcal{G}_2$ finishes the proof.

As $\mathcal{G}_2$'s states are subsets of $\mathcal{G}_1$'s states, $\mathsf{cc}(\mathcal{G}_2)$'s general form is on the left:

$\dots da$	0
$\dots da$	1
$\dots db$	?
$\dots dc$	?

$\dots da$	0
$\dots da$	1
$\dots db$	?
$(\dots ab$	?)
$\dots dc$	?
$(\dots ac$	?)
$(\dots xd$	?)
$(\dots yd$	?)

where ? can be either 0 or 1 and x, y are either both a, or one is b and the other c. To see this, observe that it is a subset of the state on the right where we leave out at least all sequences interfering with our wish of a constant column in this position (in parentheses on the right). Our aim is to show that these states are more specifically the states of $\mathsf{cc}(\mathcal{G}_0)$ again, i.e., it is impossible to reach any state of form in $\mathcal{G}_1$ via a shuffle from these states. Due to the complexity of the situation, we do a case distinction on the number of sequences of $\mu \in \mathsf{cc}(\mathcal{G}_2)$.

Let us consider only the first case, the other cases are analogously and are to be found in a full version of the paper. Let μ contain *two sequences*. If they were both from the first block, the state would trivially be in $\mathsf{cc}(\mathcal{G}_0)$. This leaves us with two choices, either include a sequence ending with da or exclude it. For concreteness, we choose w.l.o.g. $a = 2$, $d = 4$, $b = 1$ and $c = 3$, and have this:

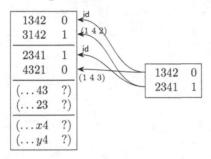

Reaching this state on the left by a shuffle should contain at least $\{\mathsf{id}, (1\ 4\ 3), (1\ 4\ 2)\}$. But if we apply $(1\ 4\ 2)$ to the first sequence gives a sequence 3241 which is not possible on the left side due to its trailing 1. The other cases are similar.

Theorem 2. *There is no four-card finite-runtime AND protocol with deck $\mathcal{D} = [\![1, 2, 3, 4]\!]$ with fixed-in-advance output basis.*

Proof Sketch. If the output basis is not given using only Alice's or only Bob's cards, this follows from Theorem 1, because if there would be such an AND protocol, by fixing the second bit to 1 one could easily generate a basis-convert protocol, which is impossible. In the remaining case, e.g., of the output basis being Alice's cards, say 1, 2, this would not be a basis-convert, as the bit remains unchanged. In this case, a close analysis of the proof of Theorem 1 above yields that the theorem also holds in this case. We omit the details, and refer to the full version.

5   Card-Minimal Protocols for AND

Theorem 3. *There is a four-card Las Vegas AND protocol with deck $\mathcal{D} = [\![1, 2, 3, 4]\!]$ using only random cuts.*

Proof. See Fig. 6 and Protocol 1.

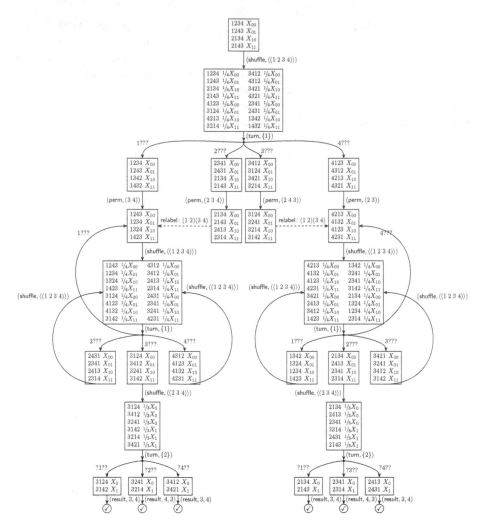

Fig. 6. Four-card Las Vegas AND protocol using random cuts, cf. Protocol 1. Here, $X_0 := X_{00} + X_{01} + X_{10}$ and $X_1 := X_{11}$. The relabel operations are not actual actions to be performed but help abbreviate the write-up of the protocol, see Sect. 3.

Table 2. The different states of Protocol 1 after ① was revealed in the first turn. The permutation to be applied is (3 4). The situation is similar in all other cases.

Bits	Sequence	After permutation	Removing ③
$(0,0)$	① ② ③ ④	① ② ④ ③	① ② ④ x
$(0,1)$	① ② ④ ③	① ② ③ ④	① ② x ④
$(1,0)$	① ③ ④ ②	① ③ ② ④	① x ② ④
$(1,1)$	① ④ ③ ②	① ④ ② ③	① ④ ② x

To get a better understanding of why the protocol works and how it is related to the protocol of [NR99], let us consider exemplarily the case that the first card to be revealed is a 1, the other cases are analogous. In this situation, let us look at the different cases, given in Table 2. Using the method as before, we can remove ③ by performing a random cut while leaving the relative order intact (① here is assigned the role of the ⑤ in Niemi and Renvall's protocol) and waiting until it appears when turning. Later we can remove the ① from the remaining cards, to get the output encoded using the cards ② and ④. A closer analysis of the situation after removing ③ shows that one can take a shortcut when one is not bound to the output being cards ②④ (which is not our goal, because in the other cases besides the first turn being 1 it is different anyway, and one would have to add conversion protocols to ensure this). The situation is as follows: The remaining three cards are either a cyclic rotation (cut) of the sequence ①②④, if the output is 0, or a cyclic rotation of the sequence ①④②, otherwise. A cut cannot rotate a sequence of the former type to become the other, or vice versa. After the cut we can safely turn any card and, from the resulting symbol, deduce in which order the other cards must be output to encode the protocol result.

Protocol 1. Our four-card AND protocol. The first bit is in basis $\{1,2\}$, the second in $\{3,4\}$, and the output in $\{1,2,3,4\} \setminus \{v_2, v_3\}$, where v_2, v_3 are the last two revealed symbols. See Fig. 3 for a KWH tree representation.

$(\mathsf{shuffle}, \langle (1\ 2\ 3\ 4) \rangle)$
$v_1 := (\mathsf{turn}, \{1\})$
if $v_1 = 1$ **then** $(\mathsf{perm}, (3\ 4))$
else if $v_1 = 2$ **then** $(\mathsf{perm}, (2\ 3\ 4))$
else if $v_1 = 3$ **then** $(\mathsf{perm}, (2\ 4\ 3))$
else if $v_1 = 4$ **then** $(\mathsf{perm}, (2\ 3))$

Let $\pi := (1\ 3)(2\ 4)$
repeat
$\quad\big|\quad (\mathsf{shuffle}, \langle (1\ 2\ 3\ 4) \rangle)$
$\quad\big|\quad v_2 := (\mathsf{turn}, \{1\})$
until $v_2 = \pi(v_1)$

$(\mathsf{shuffle}, \langle (2\ 3\ 4) \rangle)$
$v_3 := (\mathsf{turn}, \{2\})$
Let $\sigma := (1\ 4)(2\ 3)$
if $v_3 = \sigma(v_2)$ **then** $(\mathsf{result}, 4, 3)$
else $(\mathsf{result}, 3, 4)$

For an analysis of the number of shuffle steps in the protocol, observe that we have performed two shuffles until we reach the loop condition, which holds with probability $1/4$. After the loop, we have one additional shuffle step. Hence, the expected number of shuffles is $3 + \sum_{n=1}^{\infty} \left(1 - \frac{1}{4}\right)^n = 6$.

Comparison to [NR99]. The previous protocol, using five cards, was described in the introduction. For a pseudo-code description, see Protocol 2.

Protocol 2. Five-card AND protocol by Niemi and Renvall [NR99]. The first bit is in basis $\{1, 2\}$, the second in basis $\{3, 4\}$. The output basis is $\{1, 4\}$. See also Fig. 7 for a KWH tree representation.

$(\mathsf{perm}, (3\ 4))$
repeat
$\quad | \quad (\mathsf{shuffle}, \langle (1\ 2\ 3\ 4\ 5) \rangle)$
$\quad | \quad v := (\mathsf{turn}, \{1\})$
until $v = 2\ or\ v = 3$
repeat
$\quad | \quad (\mathsf{shuffle}, \langle (2\ 3\ 4\ 5) \rangle)$
$\quad | \quad v := (\mathsf{turn}, \{2\})$
until $v = 2\ or\ v = 3$
repeat
$\quad | \quad (\mathsf{shuffle}, \langle (3\ 4\ 5) \rangle)$
$\quad | \quad v := (\mathsf{turn}, \{3\})$
until $v = 5$
$(\mathsf{result}, 4, 5)$

As Niemi and Renvall state, their running time in the number of shuffle steps is calculated as follows: Their protocol starts with a shuffle and repeats this with probability $3/5$. The second loop contains a shuffle and has a repeating probability of $3/4$. The shuffle in the final loop is repeated with probability $2/3$. In total, the expected running time is $3 + \sum_{n=1}^{\infty} \left(\frac{3}{5}\right)^n + \sum_{n=1}^{\infty} \left(\frac{3}{4}\right)^n + \sum_{n=1}^{\infty} \left(\frac{2}{3}\right)^n = 3 + 1.5 + 3 + 2 = 9.5$. However, for a fair comparison to our protocol, we eliminate the last loop from their protocol, as its only function is to ensure that the output is in basis $\{1, 4\}$, which our protocol does not guarantee. In this case, the modified Niemi–Renvall protocol has an expected number of $3 + 1.5 + 3 = 7.5$ shuffle steps. Hence, our four-card AND protocol needs one card less and outperforms the Niemi–Renvall protocol by an expected number of 1.5 shuffle steps.

6   Card-Minimal Protocols for Basis Conversion with Overlapping Bases

In this section, we give two protocols for converting a basis encoding in the case where the old and the new encoding share a card. The first protocol has an expected (finite) running time of three shuffle and turn operations. While it has not been explicit in the literature, it is in a way implicit in the protocol by Niemi and Renvall [NR99], as the authors aimed to get a fixed-in-advance output basis.

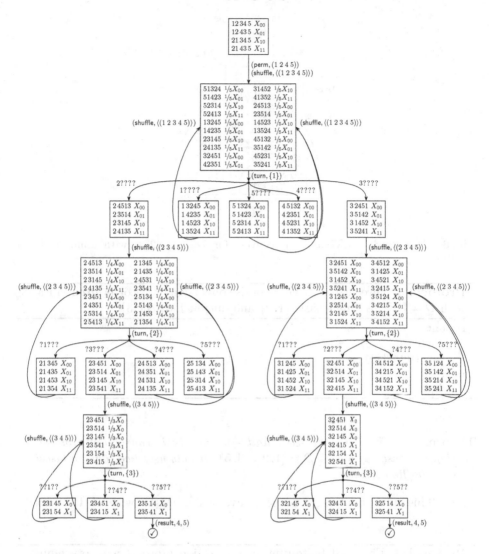

Fig. 7. KWH tree of the five-card AND protocol of [NR99] with $\mathcal{D} = [\![1, 2, 3, 4, 5]\!]$ using only random cuts, cf. Protocol 2. Note that $X_0 := X_{00} + X_{01} + X_{10}$ and $X_1 := X_{11}$. The output is in basis $\{1, 4\}$.

Theorem 4. *There is a three-card Las Vegas basis-conversion protocol for overlapping bases with deck $\mathcal{D} = [\![1, 2, 3]\!]$ and uniform closed shuffles.*

Proof. See Fig. 8 and Protocol 3.

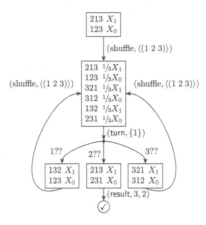

Fig. 8. Three-card Las Vegas basis convert for $\mathcal{D} = [\![1,2,3]\!]$ with uniform closed shuffles.

Protocol 3. Three-card Las Vegas basis conversion protocol as given in Fig. 8 with $\mathcal{D} = [\![1,2,3]\!]$, input basis $\{1,2\}$ and output basis $\{1,3\}$

---

repeat
  | (shuffle, $\langle (1\ 2\ 3) \rangle$)
  | $v := (\text{turn}, \{1\})$
until $v = 2$
(result, 3, 2)

Theorem 5. *There is a five-card finite-runtime basis conversion protocol for overlapping bases with deck $\mathcal{D} = [\![1,2,3,4,5]\!]$. It only uses two random bisection cuts as shuffle operations.*

Proof. This is just applying the basis conversion of [M16] twice, cf. Protocol 4. □

Protocol 4. Five-card finite-runtime conversion protocol with overlapping bases for $\mathcal{D} = [\![1,2,3,4,5]\!]$, input basis $\{1,2\}$ and output basis $\{1,3\}$

(shuffle, $\langle (1\ 2)(4\ 5) \rangle$)
$v := (\text{turn}, \{1\})$
if $v = 2$ **then** (perm, $(1\ 2)(4\ 5)$)

(shuffle, $\langle (1\ 3)(4\ 5) \rangle$)
$v := (\text{turn}, \{4\})$
if $v = 4$ **then** (result, 1, 3)
else (result, 3, 1)

```
1 struct sequence {
2   uint val[numberOfCards];
3   struct fractions probs;
4 };
```

Listing 1. C struct holding the state trees.

7   An Illustration of Our Verification Methodology

In the following, we exemplify our translation of card-based cryptographic protocols using standard decks to a specific the bounded model checker CBMC which takes programs in the C language, and compute a secure AND function. For our experiments, we used CBMC 5.11 [CKL04] with the built-in solver based on the SAT-solver MiniSat 2.2.0 [ES03]. All experiments are performed on an AMD Opteron(tm) 2431 CPU at 2.40 GHz with 6 cores and 32 GB of RAM.

We translate KWH trees in the C language using a simple encoding into a bounded C program with only static structures and no pointers, e.g., we employ C structs (see Listing 1) holding an array of card sequences for the sequence s, attached with their respective values for each probability (for the probabilistic security notion) or dependency (for output-possibilistic security) X_i occurring in $\mu(s)$, which is simply encoded by another C struct `fractions`. The sequences are constructed using non-deterministic values restricted by respective software conditions to enforce a lexicographic ordering. Moreover, we assign the starting values in $\mu(s)$ with fixed (i.e., deterministic) values based on the constructed sequences. Subsequently, an array of (consecutively) reachable states is constructed non-deterministically using simple implementations of the turn and the shuffle operation as explained in Sect. 2. We then repeatedly (after each turn/shuffle) check whether all possible resulting (non-deterministic) states correctly and securely compute the specified function, e.g., here a secure AND.

An example shuffle operation is shown in Listing 2 for the case of output-possibilistic security. Therein, the keyword `__CPROVER_assume` is used by the bounded model checker to restrict all program runs passing this statement to satisfy the specified (Boolean) condition. By assigning values using the special function `nondet_uint()`, we assign a non-deterministic non-negative integer number, which is restricted to values greater than zero and at most of value `NUM_POSS_SEQ` (which is a variable computed by the pre-processor and is the maximum number of sequences possible with the given deck) in the following program statement. In the shown example, the non-determinism is used to construct a set of permitted permutation sets (to be used by the shuffle operation), which makes the SBMC tool inspect the following program code for all possible assignments of this value. If necessary, this may result in a fully exhaustive search, however, the prover is often able to restrict the domain based on further program statements and dependencies seen in the rest of the program. A similar trick is used when computing the concrete permutations using the non-deterministic value of `permIndex` in order to check all possible permutations which possibly

```
1  uint permSetSize = nondet_uint();
2  __CPROVER_assume (0 < permSetSize);
3  __CPROVER_assume (permSetSize <= NUM_POSS_SEQ);
4  uint permutationSet[permSetSize][numberOfCards];
5  uint takenPermutations[NUM_POSS_SEQ] = { 0 };
6
7  for (uint i = 0; i < permSetSize; i++) {
8    uint permIndex = nondet_uint();
9    __CPROVER_assume (permIndex < NUM_POSS_SEQ);
10   __CPROVER_assume (!takenPermutations[permIndex]);
11
12   takenPermutations[permIndex] = 1;
13   for (uint j = 0; j < numberOfCards; j++) {
14     permutationSet[i][j] =
15       startState.seq[permIndex][j] - 1;
16   }
17 }
18 struct state result =
19   doShuffle(startState, permutationSet, permSetSize);
20 __CPROVER_assume (isBottomFree(result));
```

Listing 2. Simplified shuffle operation for CBMC.

move the values, but preserve all existing numbers in the sequence itself. This is done using the int-array takenPermutations, which is first initialized to zero and, when choosing a concrete permutation, assumed to be zero at position permIndex, however set to the number one right afterwards (such that it is not permitted to be chosen again). In the subsequent inner loop, the permutations are assigned choosing the according cards from the sequences in the start state using the non-deterministic value permIndex. Finally, the shuffle is applied, resulting in the state variable result, which is then checked using a further method isBottomFree to not contain any sequences with impermissible values for X_i, which would result in incorrect computations of the AND function.

We applied our approach to the computation of a secure AND protocol using four cards in order to, firstly, substantiate our proof that no protocol of a length below six can be found, and, secondly, automatically find a permitted protocol using six operations. Using our approach, we were able to show that no four-card protocol exists using five operations within 57 h and constructed an output-possibilistic protocol using six operations within 31 h. The sizes of the constructed formulas consisted of between 150 and 180 million SAT clauses.

8   Conclusion

In this paper, we proposed a new method to search card-based protocols for any secure computation, by giving a general formal translation applicable to be used by the formal technique of software bounded model checking (SBMC). This method allows us to find new protocols automatically, and prove lower bounds on required shuffle and turn operations for any protocol, and provide an example for the computation of a minimal AND protocol. We also found a new protocol that only uses the theoretical minimum of four distinguishable cards for an AND computation. Moreover, we supported this finding by our automatic method in showing the impossibility of any protocol using less shuffle and turn operations using only practicable shuffles (random cuts). The protocol is hence optimal w.r.t. the running time restriction "restart-free Las-Vegas". For the four-card standard deck setting, we showed that there is no finite runtime protocol, regardless of the shuffle operations used. This result completes the picture of tight lower bounds for four cards. Finally, we showed tight lower bounds on basis conversions for single bits and proposed the missing protocols, and establish the theorem that using a minimum of five cards, both input- and output-bases can be chosen freely, which fosters our impossibility result for four cards.

Open Problems. Let us point out some open problems in the card-based security area that could be approached based on the findings in this paper: (1) For finite-runtime protocols, there exist no proven tight lower bounds on the required number of cards (five to eight cards). We recommend more research applying computer-aided formal methods at this point, as the state space for five or more cards is very large. (2) Our verification approach is fast for finding protocols and/or lower bounds on the operations needed in a protocol for given shuffle-restrictions. However, this is based on the assumption that protocols exist already for a given predefined length to find or confirm impossibility results. Investigating computer-aided formal methods for universal impossibility results might be worthwhile. (3) The two most common settings in card-based cryptography are the standard deck setting with only distinguishable cards and the two-color decks using ♣ and ♡. However, it may be possible that by mixing these settings (e.g., only distinguishable cards with one pair of identical cards), we might find more efficient protocols (especially in the finite runtime setting). For such a mixed setting, [SM19] provide nice results to use in further research.

Appendix: Further Protocols

This appendix contains the 8-card AND protocol of [M16] (Fig. 9) and a second four-card protocol which uses a number of 4.5 shuffles in expectation, which are, however, non-closed and hence, more impractical to implement, cf. Fig. 10.

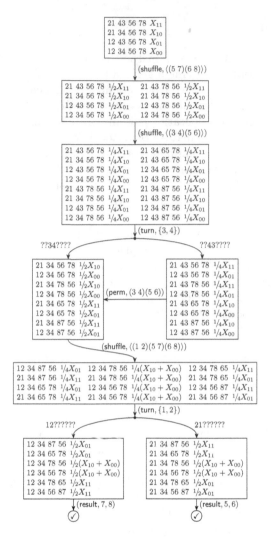

Fig. 9. The eight-card finite-runtime AND protocol of [M16], with $\mathcal{D} = [\![1, \ldots, 8]\!]$ and uniform-closed shuffles. Output is in basis $\{5, 6\}$ or $\{7, 8\}$, each with probability $1/2$.

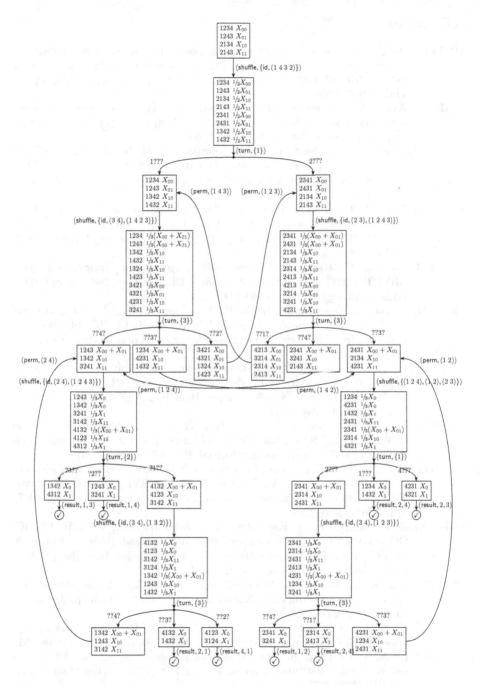

Fig. 10. A four-card Las Vegas AND protocol with deck $\mathcal{D} = [\![1, 2, 3, 4]\!]$ and uniform shuffles. Note that $X_0 := X_{00} + X_{01} + X_{10}$ and $X_1 := X_{11}$. The output is in one of the bases $\{1, 3\}, \{1, 4\}, \{2, 3\}, \{3, 4\}$, determined by the position of the final state in the tree, and can be converted as needed.

References

[AHM+18] Abe, Y., Hayashi, Y.-I., Mizuki, T., Sone, H.: Five-card AND protocol in committed format using only practical shuffles. In: Emura, K., et al. (ed.) APKC@AsiaCCS 2018 ACM, pp. 3–8 (2018). https://doi.org/10. 1145/3197507.3197510

[APS14] Avalle, M., Pironti, A., Sisto, R.: Formal verification of security protocol implementations: a survey. Formal Asp. Comput. 26(1), 99–123 (2014). https://doi.org/10.1007/s00165-012-0269-9

[B12] Blanchet, B.: Security protocol verification: symbolic and computational models. In: Degano, P., Guttman, J.D. (eds.) POST 2012. LNCS, vol. 7215, pp. 3–29. Springer, Heidelberg (2012). https://doi.org/10.1007/978-3-642-28641-4_2

[BCC+99] Biere, A., Cimatti, A., Clarke, E., Zhu, Y.: Symbolic model checking without BDDs. In: Cleaveland, W.R. (ed.) TACAS 1999. LNCS, vol. 1579, pp. 193–207. Springer, Heidelberg (1999). https://doi.org/10.1007/3-540-49059-0_14

[CK93] Crépeau, C., Kilian, J.: Discreet solitary games. In: Stinson, D.R. (ed.) CRYPTO 1993. LNCS, vol. 773, pp. 319–330. Springer, Heidelberg (1994). https://doi.org/10.1007/3-540-48329-2_27

[CKL04] Clarke, E., Kroening, D., Lerda, F.: A tool for checking ANSI-C programs. In: Jensen, K., Podelski, A. (eds.) TACAS 2004. LNCS, vol. 2988, pp. 168–176. Springer, Heidelberg (2004). https://doi.org/10.1007/978-3-540-24730-2_15

[dB89] Boer, B.: More efficient match-making and satisfiability The Five Card Trick. In: Quisquater, J.-J., Vandewalle, J. (eds.) EUROCRYPT 1989. LNCS, vol. 434, pp. 208–217. Springer, Heidelberg (1990). https://doi.org/ 10.1007/3-540-46885-4_23

[ES03] Eén, N., Sörensson, N.: An extensible SAT-solver. In: Giunchiglia, E., Tacchella, A. (eds.) SAT 2003. LNCS, vol. 2919, pp. 502–518. Springer, Heidelberg (2004). https://doi.org/10.1007/978-3-540-24605-3_37

[FFN14] Fisch, B., Freund, D., Naor, M.: Physical zero-knowledge proofs of physical properties. In: Garay, J.A., Gennaro, R. (eds.) CRYPTO 2014. LNCS, vol. 8617, pp. 313–336. Springer, Heidelberg (2014). https://doi.org/10.1007/ 978-3-662-44381-1_18

[FHK+14] Franz, M., Holzer, A., Katzenbeisser, S., Schallhart, C., Veith, H.: CBMC-GC: an ANSI C compiler for secure two-party computations. In: Cohen, A. (ed.) CC 2014. LNCS, vol. 8409, pp. 244–249. Springer, Heidelberg (2014). https://doi.org/10.1007/978-3-642-54807-9_15

[GBG14] Glaser, A., Barak, B., Goldston, R.J.: A zero-knowledge protocol for nuclear warhead verification. Nature 510, 497–502 (2014). https://doi.org/ 10.1038/nature13457

[K18] Koch, A.: The Landscape of Optimal Card-based Protocols (2018). Cryptology ePrint Archive, Report 2018/951 https://eprint.iacr.org/2018/951

[K19] Koch, A.: Cryptographic protocols from physical assumptions. Ph.D. thesis, Karlsruhe Institute of Technology (KIT) (2019). https://doi.org/10. 5445/IR/1000097756

[KKW+17] Kastner, J., et al.: The minimum number of cards in practical card-based protocols. In: Takagi, T., Peyrin, T. (eds.) ASIACRYPT 2017. LNCS, vol. 10626, pp. 126–155. Springer, Cham (2017). https://doi.org/10.1007/978-3-319-70700-6_5

[KW17]   Koch, A., Walzer, S.: Foundations for Actively Secure Card-based Cryptography (2017). Cryptology ePrint Archive, Report 2017/423 https://eprint.iacr.org/2017/423

[KWH15] Koch, A., Walzer, S., Härtel, K.: Card-based cryptographic protocols using a minimal number of cards. In: Iwata, T., Cheon, J.H. (eds.) ASIACRYPT 2015. LNCS, vol. 9452, pp. 783–807. Springer, Heidelberg (2015). https://doi.org/10.1007/978-3-662-48797-6_32

[M16]   Mizuki, T.: Efficient and secure multiparty computations using a standard deck of playing cards. In: Foresti, S., Persiano, G. (eds.) CANS 2016. LNCS, vol. 10052, pp. 484–499. Springer, Cham (2016). https://doi.org/10.1007/978-3-319-48965-0_29

[MN10]   Moran, T., Naor, M.: Basing cryptographic protocols on tamper-evident seals. Theor. Comput. Sci. **411**(10), 1283–1310 (2010). https://doi.org/10.1016/j.tcs.2009.10.023

[MS09]   Mizuki, T., Sone, H.: Six-card secure AND and four-card secure XOR. In: Deng, X., Hopcroft, J.E., Xue, J. (eds.) FAW 2009. LNCS, vol. 5598, pp. 358–369. Springer, Heidelberg (2009). https://doi.org/10.1007/978-3-642-02270-8_36

[MS14]   Mizuki, T., Shizuya, H.: A formalization of card-based cryptographic protocols via abstract machine. Int. J. Inf. Sec. **13**(1), 15–23 (2014). https://doi.org/10.1007/s10207-013-0219-4

[MS17]   Mizuki, T., Shizuya, H.: Computational model of card-based cryptographic protocols and its applications. IEICE Trans. **100**(A.1), 3–11 (2017). https://doi.org/10.1587/transfun.E100.A.3

[NR98]   Niemi, V., Renvall, A.: Secure multiparty computations without computers. Theor. Comput. Sci. **191**(1–2), 173–183 (1998). https://doi.org/10.1016/S0304-3975(97)00107-2

[NR99]   Niemi, V., Renvall, A.: Solitaire zero-knowledge. Fundam Inform. **38**(1–2), 181–188 (1999). https://doi.org/10.3233/FI-1999-381214

[RSH19] Rastogi, A., Swamy, N., Hicks, M.: Wys^*: a DSL for verified secure multiparty computations. In: Nielson, F., Sands, D. (eds.) POST 2019. LNCS, vol. 11426, pp. 99–122. Springer, Cham (2019). https://doi.org/10.1007/978-3-030-17138-4_5

[SHK+16] Swamy, N., et al.: Dependent types and multimonadic effects in F. In: Bodik, R., Majumdar, R. (eds.) POPL 2016, pp. 256–270. ACM (2016). https://doi.org/10.1145/2837614.2837655

[SM19]   Shinagawa, K., Mizuki, T.: Secure computation of any boolean function based on any deck of cards. In: Chen, Y., Deng, X., Lu, M. (eds.) FAW 2019. LNCS, vol. 11458, pp. 63–75. Springer, Cham (2019). https://doi.org/10.1007/978-3-030-18126-0_6

Quantum

Quantum Algorithms for the Approximate k-List Problem and Their Application to Lattice Sieving

Elena Kirshanova[1]($\boxtimes$), Erik Mårtensson[2], Eamonn W. Postlethwaite[3], and Subhayan Roy Moulik[4]

[1] I. Kant Baltic Federal University, Kaliningrad, Russia
elenakirshanova@gmail.com
[2] Department of Electrical and Information Technology, Lund University, Lund, Sweden
erik.martensson@eit.lth.se
[3] Information Security Group, Royal Holloway, University of London, Egham, UK
eamonn.postlethwaite.2016@rhul.ac.uk
[4] Department of Computer Science, University of Oxford, Oxford, UK
subhayan.roy.moulik@cs.ox.ac.uk

Abstract. The Shortest Vector Problem (SVP) is one of the mathematical foundations of lattice based cryptography. Lattice sieve algorithms are amongst the foremost methods of solving SVP. The asymptotically fastest known classical and quantum sieves solve SVP in a d-dimensional lattice in $2^{cd+o(d)}$ time steps with $2^{c'd+o(d)}$ memory for constants c, c'. In this work, we give various quantum sieving algorithms that trade computational steps for memory.

We first give a quantum analogue of the classical k-Sieve algorithm [Herold–Kirshanova–Laarhoven, PKC'18] in the Quantum Random Access Memory (QRAM) model, achieving an algorithm that heuristically solves SVP in $2^{0.2989d+o(d)}$ time steps using $2^{0.1395d+o(d)}$ memory. This should be compared to the state-of-the-art algorithm [Laarhoven, Ph.D Thesis, 2015] which, in the same model, solves SVP in $2^{0.2653d+o(d)}$ time steps and memory. In the QRAM model these algorithms can be implemented using poly(d) width quantum circuits.

Secondly, we frame the k-Sieve as the problem of k-clique listing in a graph and apply quantum k-clique finding techniques to the k-Sieve.

Finally, we explore the large quantum memory regime by adapting parallel quantum search [Beals et al., Proc. Roy. Soc. A'13] to the 2-Sieve, and give an analysis in the quantum circuit model. We show how to solve SVP in $2^{0.1037d+o(d)}$ time steps using $2^{0.2075d+o(d)}$ quantum memory.

1 Introduction

The Shortest Vector Problem (SVP) is one of the central problems in the theory of lattices. For a given d-dimensional Euclidean lattice, usually described by a

---

The full version of this article can be found at https://eprint.iacr.org/2019/1016.

S. D. Galbraith and S. Moriai (Eds.): ASIACRYPT 2019, LNCS 11921, pp. 521–551, 2019.
https://doi.org/10.1007/978-3-030-34578-5_19

basis, to solve SVP one must find a shortest non zero vector in the lattice. This problem gives rise to a variety of efficient, versatile, and (believed to be) quantum resistant cryptographic constructions [AD97, Reg05]. To obtain an estimate for the security of these constructions it is important to understand the complexities of the fastest known algorithms for SVP.

There are two main families of algorithms for SVP, (1) algorithms that require $2^{\omega(d)}$ time and $\mathrm{poly}(d)$ memory; and (2) algorithms that require $2^{\Theta(d)}$ time and memory. The first family includes lattice enumeration algorithms [Kan83, GNR10]. The second contains sieving algorithms [AKS01, NV08, MV10], Voronoi cell based approaches [MV10] and others [ADRSD15, BGJ14]. In practice, it is only enumeration and sieving algorithms that are currently competitive in large dimensions [ADH+19, TKH18]. Practical variants of these algorithms rely on *heuristic* assumptions. For example we may not have a guarantee that the returned vector will solve SVP exactly (e.g. pruning techniques for enumeration [GNR10], lifting techniques for sieving [Duc18]), or that our algorithm will work as expected on arbitrary lattices (e.g. sieving algorithms may fail on orthogonal lattices). Yet these heuristics are natural for lattices often used in cryptographic constructions, and one does not require an exact solution to SVP to progress with cryptanalysis [ADH+19]. Therefore, one usually relies on heuristic variants of SVP solvers for security estimates.

Among the various attractive features of lattice based cryptography is its potential resistance to attacks by quantum computers. In particular, there is no known quantum algorithm that solves SVP on an arbitrary lattice significantly faster than existing classical algorithms.[1] However, some quantum speed-ups for SVP algorithms are possible in general.

It was shown by Aono–Nguyen–Shen [ANS18] that enumeration algorithms for SVP can be sped up using the *quantum backtracking* algorithm of Montanaro [Mon18]. More precisely, with quantum enumeration one solves SVP on a d-dimensional lattice in time $2^{\frac{1}{4e}d \log d + o(d \log d)}$, a square root improvement over classical enumeration. This algorithm requires $\mathrm{poly}(d)$ classical and quantum memory. This bound holds for both provable and heuristic versions of enumeration. Quantum speed-ups for sieving algorithms have been considered by Laarhoven–Mosca–van de Pol [LMvdP15] and later by Laarhoven [Laa15]. The latter result presents various quantum sieving algorithms for SVP. One of them achieves time and classical memory of order $2^{0.2653d + o(d)}$ and requires $\mathrm{poly}(d)$ quantum memory. This is the best known quantum time complexity for heuristic sieving algorithms. Provable single exponential SVP solvers were considered in the quantum setting by Chen–Chang–Lai [CCL17]. Based on [ADRSD15, DRS14], the authors describe a $2^{1.255d + o(d)}$ time, $2^{0.5d + o(d)}$ classical and $\mathrm{poly}(d)$ quantum memory algorithm for SVP. All heuristic and provable results rely on the classical memory being quantumly addressable.

---

[1] For some families of lattices, like ideal lattices, there exist quantum algorithms that solve a variant of SVP faster than classical algorithms, see [CDW17, PMHS19]. In this work, we consider arbitrary lattices.

A drawback of sieving algorithms is their large memory requirements. Initiated by Bai–Laarhoven–Stehlé, a line of work [BLS16, HK17, HKL18] gave a family of heuristic sieving algorithms, called tuple lattice sieves, or k-Sieves for some fixed constant k, that offer time-memory trade-offs. Such trade-offs have proven important in the current fastest SVP solvers, as the ideas of tuple sieving offer significant speed-ups in practice, [ADH+19]. In this work, we explore various directions for *asymptotic* quantum accelerations of tuple sieves.

Our Results.

1. In Sect. 4 we show how to use a quantum computer to speed up the k-Sieve of Bai–Laarhoven–Stehlé [BLS16] and its improvement due to Herold–Kirshanova–Laarhoven [HKL18] (Algorithms 4.1, 4.2). One data point achieves a time complexity of $2^{0.2989d+o(d)}$, while requiring $2^{0.1395d+o(d)}$ classical memory and poly(d) width quantum circuits. In the **Area** × **Time** model this beats the previously best known algorithm [Laa15] of time and memory complexities $2^{0.2653d+o(d)}$; we almost halve the constant in the exponent for memory at the cost of a small increase in the respective constant for time.
2. Borrowing ideas from [Laa15] in the full version [KMPR19, App. B] we give a quantum k-Sieve that exploits nearest neighbour techniques. For $k = 2$, we recover Laarhoven's $2^{0.2653d+o(d)}$ time and memory quantum algorithm.
3. In Sect. 5 the k-Sieve is reduced to listing k-cliques in a graph. By generalising the triangle finding algorithm of [BdWD+01] this approach leads to an algorithm that matches the performance of Algorithm 4.1, when optimised for memory, for all k.
4. In Sect. 6 we specialise to listing 3-cliques (triangles) in a graph. Using the quantum triangle finding algorithm of [LGN17] allows us, in the *query model*,[2] to perform the 3-Sieve using $2^{0.3264d+o(d)}$ *queries*.
5. In Sect. 7 we describe a quantum circuit consisting only of gates from a universal gate set (e.g. CNOT and single qubit rotations) of depth $2^{0.1038d+o(d)}$ and width $2^{0.2075d+o(d)}$ that implements the 2-Sieve as proposed classically in [NV08]. In particular we consider exponential *quantum* memory to make significant improvements to the number of time steps. Our construction adapts the parallel search procedure of [BBG+13].

All the results presented in this work are asymptotic in nature: our algorithms have time, classical memory, quantum memory complexities of orders $2^{cd+o(d)}$, $2^{c'd+o(d)}$, poly(d) or $2^{c''d+o(d)}$ respectively, for $c, c', c'' \in \Theta(1)$, which we aim to minimise. We do not attempt to specify the $o(d)$ or poly(d) terms.

---

[2] This means that the complexity of the algorithm is measured by the number of oracle calls to the adjacency matrix of a graph.

Our Techniques. We now briefly describe the main ingredients of our results.

1. A useful abstraction of the k-Sieve is the *configuration problem*, first described in [HK17]. It consists of finding k elements that satisfy certain pairwise inner product constraints from k exponentially large lists of vectors. Assuming $(\mathbf{x}_1, \ldots, \mathbf{x}_k)$ is a solution tuple, the ith element $\mathbf{x}_i$ can be obtained via a brute force search either over the ith input list [BLS16], or over a certain sublist of the ith list [HK17], see Fig. 1b. We replace the brute force searches with calls to Grover's algorithm and reanalyse the configuration problem. The search for $\mathbf{x}_i$ within such a data structure can itself be sped up by Grover's algorithm.

2. The configuration problem can be reduced to the k-clique problem in a graph with vertices representing elements from the lists given by the configuration problem. Vertices are connected by an edge if and only if the corresponding list elements satisfy some inner product constraint. Classically, this interpretation yields no improvements to configuration problem algorithms. However we achieve quantum speed-ups by generalising the triangle finding algorithm of Buhrman et al. [BdWD+01] and applying it to k-cliques.

3. We apply the triangle finding algorithm of Le Gall–Nakajima [LGN17] and exploit the structure of our graph instance. In particular we form many graphs from unions of sublists of our lists, allowing us to alter the sparsity of said graphs.

4. To make use of more quantum memory we run Grover searches in parallel. The idea is to allow simultaneous queries by several processors to a large, shared, quantum memory. Instead of looking for a "good" $\mathbf{x}_i$ for one *fixed* tuple $(\mathbf{x}_1, \ldots, \mathbf{x}_{i-1})$, one could think of parallel searches aiming to find a "good" $\mathbf{x}_i$ for several tuples $(\mathbf{x}_1, \ldots, \mathbf{x}_{i-1})$. The possibility of running several Grover's algorithms concurrently was shown in the work of Beals et al. [BBG+13]. Based on this result we specify all the subroutines needed to solve the shortest vector problem using large quantum memory.

2 Preliminaries

We denote by $\mathsf{S}^d \subset \mathbb{R}^{d+1}$ the d-dimensional unit sphere. We use soft-$\mathcal{O}$ notation to denote running times, that is $T = \widetilde{\mathcal{O}}(2^{cd})$ suppresses subexponential factors in d. By $[n]$ we denote the set $\{1, \ldots, n\}$. The norm considered in this work is Euclidean and is denoted by $\| \cdot \|$.

For any set $\mathbf{x}_1, \ldots, \mathbf{x}_k$ of vectors in $\mathbb{R}^d$, the *Gram matrix* $C \in \mathbb{R}^{k \times k}$ is given by $C_{i,j} = \langle \mathbf{x}_i, \mathbf{x}_j \rangle$, the set of pairwise scalar products. For $I \subset [k]$, we denote by $C[I]$ the $|I| \times |I|$ submatrix of C obtained by restricting C to the rows and columns indexed by I. For a vector $\mathbf{x}$ and $i \in [k]$, $\mathbf{x}[i]$ denotes the ith entry. For a function f, by O_f we denote a unitary matrix that implements f.

Lattices. Given a basis $B = \{\mathbf{b}_1, \ldots, \mathbf{b}_m\} \subset \mathbb{R}^d$ of linearly independent vectors $\mathbf{b}_i$, the lattice generated by B is defined as $\mathcal{L}(B) = \{\sum_{i=1}^m z_i \mathbf{b}_i : z_i \in \mathbb{Z}\}$. For simplicity we work with lattices of full rank ($d = m$). The Shortest Vector

Problem (SVP) is to find, for a given B, a shortest non zero vector of $\mathcal{L}(B)$. Minkowski's theorem for the Euclidean norm states that a shortest vector of $\mathcal{L}(B)$ is bounded from above by $\sqrt{d} \cdot \det(B)^{1/d}$.

Quantum Search. Our results rely on Grover's quantum search algorithm [Gro96] which finds "good" elements in a (large) list. The analysis of the success probability of this algorithm can be found in [BBHT98]. We also rely on the generalisation of Grover's algorithm, called Amplitude Amplification, due to Brassard–Høyer–Mosca–Tapp [BHMT02] and a result on parallel quantum search [BBG+13].

Theorem 1 (Grover's algorithm [Gro96, BBHT98]). *Given quantum access to a list L that contains t "good" elements (the value t is not necessarily known) and a function $f\colon L \to \{0,1\}$, described by a unitary O_f, which determines whether an element is "good" or not, we wish to find a solution $i \in [|L|]$, such that for $f(x_i) = 1, x_i \in L$. There exists a quantum algorithm, called Grover's algorithm, that with probability greater than $1-t/|L|$ outputs one "good" element using $\mathcal{O}(\sqrt{|L|/t})$ calls to O_f.*

Theorem 2 (Amplitude Amplification [BHMT02, Theorem 2]). *Let $\mathcal{A}$ be any quantum algorithm that makes no measurements and let $\mathcal{A}\,|0\rangle = |\Psi_0\rangle + |\Psi_1\rangle$, where $|\Psi_0\rangle$ and $|\Psi_1\rangle$ are spanned by "bad" and "good" states respectively. Let further $a = \langle \Psi_1|\Psi_1\rangle$ be the success probability of $\mathcal{A}$. Given access to a function f that flips the sign of the amplitudes of good states, i.e. $f\colon |x\rangle \mapsto -|x\rangle$ for "good" $|x\rangle$ and leaves the amplitudes of "bad" $|x\rangle$ unchanged, the amplitude amplification algorithm constructs the unitary $Q = -\mathcal{A}R\mathcal{A}^{-1}O_f$, where R is the reflection about $|0\rangle$, and applies Q^m to the state $\mathcal{A}\,|0\rangle$, where $m = \lfloor \frac{\pi}{4} \arcsin(\sqrt{a}) \rfloor$. Upon measurement of the system, a "good" state is obtained with probability at least $\max\{a, 1-a\}$.*

Theorem 3 (Quantum Parallel Search [BBG+13]). *Given a list L, with each element of bit length d, and $|L|$ functions that take list elements as input $f_i\colon L \to \{0,1\}$ for $i \in [|L|]$, we wish to find solution vectors $\mathbf{s} \in [|L|]^{|L|}$. A solution has $f_i(\mathbf{x}_{\mathbf{s}[i]}) = 1$ for all $i \in [|L|]$. Given unitaries $U_{f_i}\colon |\mathbf{x}\rangle\,|b\rangle \to |\mathbf{x}\rangle\,|b \oplus f_i(\mathbf{x})\rangle$ there exists a quantum algorithm that, for each $i \in [|L|]$, either returns a solution $\mathbf{s}[i]$ or if there is no such solution, returns no solution. The algorithm succeeds with probability $\Theta(1)$ and, given that each U_{f_i} has depth and width $\operatorname{poly}\log(|L|, d)$, can be implemented using a quantum circuit of width $\widetilde{\mathcal{O}}(|L|)$ and depth $\widetilde{\mathcal{O}}(\sqrt{|L|})$.*

Computational Models. Our algorithms are analysed in the quantum circuit model [KLM07]. We set each wire to represent a qubit, i.e. a vector in a two dimensional complex Hilbert space, and assert that we have a set of universal gates. We work in the noiseless quantum theory, i.e. we assume there is no (or negligible) decoherence or other sources of noise in the computational procedures.

The algorithms given in Sects. 4 and 5 are in the QRAM model and assume quantumly accessible classical memory [GLM08]. More concretely in this model we store all data, e.g. the list of vectors, in classical memory and only demand that this memory is quantumly accessible, i.e. elements in the list can be efficiently accessed in coherent superposition. This enables us to design algorithms that, in principle, do not require large quantum memories and can be implemented with only poly(d) qubits and with the $2^{\Theta(d)}$ sized list stored in classical memory. Several works [BHT97, Kup13] suggest that this memory model is potentially easier to achieve than a full quantum memory.

In Sect. 6 we study the algorithms in the query model, which is the typical model for quantum triangle or k-clique finding algorithms. Namely, the complexity of our algorithm is measured in the number of oracle calls to the adjacency matrix of a graph associated to a list of vectors.

Acknowledging the arguments against the feasibility of QRAM and whether it can be meaningfully cheaper than quantum memory [AGJO+15] we also consider, Sect. 7, algorithms that use exponential quantum memory in the quantum circuit model without assuming QRAM.

3   Sieving as Configuration Search

In this section we describe previously known *classical* sieving algorithms. We will not go into detail or give proofs, which can be found in the relevant references.

Sieving algorithms receive on input a basis $B \in \mathbb{R}^{d \times d}$ and start by sampling an exponentially large list L of (long) lattice vectors from $\mathcal{L}(B)$. There are efficient algorithms for sampling lattice vectors, e.g. [Kle00]. The elements of L are then iteratively combined to form shorter lattice vectors, $\mathbf{x}_{\text{new}} = \mathbf{x}_1 \pm \mathbf{x}_2 \pm \ldots \pm \mathbf{x}_k$ such that $\|\mathbf{x}_{\text{new}}\| \leq \max_{i \leq k}\{\|\mathbf{x}_i\|\}$, for some $k \geq 2$. Newly obtained vectors $\mathbf{x}_{\text{new}}$ are stored in a new list and the process is repeated with this new list of shorter vectors. It can be shown [NV08, Reg09] that after poly(d) such iterations we obtain a list that contains a shortest vector. Therefore, the asymptotic complexity of sieving is determined by the cost of finding k-tuples whose combination produces shorter vectors. Under certain heuristics, specified below, finding such k-tuples can be formulated as the approximate k-List problem.

Definition 1 (Approximate k-List problem). *Assume we are given k lists $L_1, \ldots, L_k$ of equal exponential (in d) size $|L|$ and whose elements are i.i.d. uniformly chosen vectors from S^{d-1}. The approximate k-List problem is to find $|L|$ solutions, where a solution is a k-tuple $(x_1, \ldots, x_k) \in L_1 \times \ldots \times L_k$ satisfying $\|\mathbf{x}_1 + \ldots + \mathbf{x}_k\| \leq 1$.*

The assumption made in analyses of heuristic sieving algorithms [NV08] is that the lattice vectors in the new list after an iteration are thought of as i.i.d. uniform vectors on a thin spherical shell (essentially, a sphere), and, once normalised, on S^{d-1}. Hence sieves do not "see" the discrete structure of the lattice from the vectors operated on. The heuristic becomes invalid when the vectors become short. In this case we assume we have solved SVP. Thus, we may not find a *shortest* vector, but an approximation to it, which is enough for most cryptanalytic purposes.

We consider k to be constant. The lists $L_1, \ldots, L_k$ in Definition 1 may be identical. The algorithms described below are applicable to this case as well. Furthermore, the approximate k-List problem only looks for solutions with $+$ signs, i.e. $\|\mathbf{x}_1 + \ldots + \mathbf{x}_k\| \leq 1$, while sieving looks for arbitrary signs. This is not an issue, as we may repeat an algorithm for the approximate k-List problem $2^k = \mathcal{O}(1)$ times in order to obtain all solutions.

Configuration Search. Using a concentration result on the distribution of scalar products of $\mathbf{x}_1, \ldots, \mathbf{x}_k \in \mathsf{S}^{d-1}$ shown in [HK17], the approximate k-List problem can be reduced to the configuration problem. In order to state this problem, we need a notion of configurations.

Definition 2 (Configuration). *The configuration $C = \mathrm{Conf}(\mathbf{x}_1, \ldots, \mathbf{x}_k)$ of k points $\mathbf{x}_1, \ldots, \mathbf{x}_k \in \mathsf{S}^{d-1}$ is the Gram matrix of the $\mathbf{x}_i$, i.e. $C_{i,j} = \langle \mathbf{x}_i, \mathbf{x}_j \rangle$.*

A configuration $C \in \mathbb{R}^{k \times k}$ is a positive semidefinite matrix. Rewriting the solution condition $\|\mathbf{x}_1 + \ldots + \mathbf{x}_k\|^2 \leq 1$, one can check that a configuration C for a solution tuple satisfies $\mathbf{1}^{\mathrm{t}} C \mathbf{1} \leq 1$. We denote the set of such "good" configurations by

$$\mathscr{C} = \{C \in \mathbb{R}^{k \times k} : C \text{ is positive semidefinite and } \mathbf{1}^{\mathrm{t}} C \mathbf{1} \leq 1\}.$$

It has been shown [HK17] that rather than looking for k-tuples that form a solution for the approximate k-List problem, we may look for k-tuples that satisfy a constraint on their configuration. It gives rise to the following problem.

Definition 3 (Configuration problem). *Let $k \in \mathbb{N}$ and $\varepsilon > 0$. Suppose we are given a target configuration $C \in \mathscr{C}$. Given k lists $L_1, \ldots, L_k$ all of exponential (in d) size $|L|$, whose elements are i.i.d. uniform from S^{d-1}, the configuration problem consists of finding a $1 - o(1)$ fraction of all solutions, where a solution is a k-tuple $(\mathbf{x}_1, \ldots, \mathbf{x}_k)$ with $\mathbf{x}_i \in L_i$ such that $|\langle \mathbf{x}_i, \mathbf{x}_j \rangle - C_{i,j}| \leq \varepsilon$ for all i, j.*

Solving the configuration problem for a $C \in \mathscr{C}$ gives solutions to the approximate k-List problem. For a given $C \in \mathbb{R}^{k \times k}$ the number of expected solutions to the configuration problem is given by $\det(C)$ as the following theorem shows.

Theorem 4 (Distribution of configurations [HK17, Theorem 1]). *If $\mathbf{x}_1, \ldots, \mathbf{x}_k$ are i.i.d. from S^{d-1}, $d > k$, then their configuration $C = \mathrm{Conf}(\mathbf{x}_1, \ldots, \mathbf{x}_k)$ follows a distribution with density function*

$$\mu = W_{d,k} \cdot \det(C)^{\frac{1}{2}(d-k)} \mathrm{d}C_{1,2} \ldots \mathrm{d}C_{d-1,d}, \tag{1}$$

where $W_{d,k} = \mathcal{O}_k(d^{\frac{1}{4}(k^2-k)})$ is an explicitly known normalisation constant that only depends on d and k.

This theorem tells us that the expected number of solutions to the configuration problem for C is given by $\prod_i |L_i| \cdot (\det C)^{d/2}$. If we want to apply an algorithm for the configuration problem to the approximate k-List problem (and to sieving), we require that the expected number of output solutions to the configuration problem is equal to the size of the input lists. Namely, C and the input lists L_i of size $|L|$ should (up to polynomial factors) satisfy $|L|^k \cdot (\det C)^{d/2} = |L|$. This condition gives a lower bound on the size of the input lists. Using Chernoff bounds, one can show (see [HKL18, Lemma 2]) that increasing this bound by a poly(d) factor gives a sufficient condition for the size of input lists, namely

$$|L| = \tilde{\mathcal{O}}\left(\left(\frac{1}{\det(C)}\right)^{\frac{d}{2(k-1)}}\right). \tag{2}$$

Classical Algorithms for the Configuration Problem. The first classical algorithm for the configuration problem for $k \geq 2$ was given by Bai–Laarhoven–Stehlé [BLS16]. It was later improved by Herold–Kirshanova [HK17] and by Herold–Kirshanova–Laarhoven [HKL18] (Fig. 1b). These results present a family of algorithms for the configuration problem that offer time-memory trade-offs. In Sect. 4 we present quantum versions of these algorithms.

Both algorithms [BLS16, HKL18] process the lists from left to right but in a different manner. For each $\mathbf{x}_1 \in L_1$ the algorithm from [BLS16] applies a filtering procedure to L_2 and creates the "filtered" list $L_2(\mathbf{x}_1)$. This filtering procedure takes as input an element $\mathbf{x}_2 \in L_2$ and adds it to $L_2(\mathbf{x}_1)$ iff $|\langle \mathbf{x}_1, \mathbf{x}_2 \rangle - C_{1,2}| \leq \varepsilon$. Having constructed the list $L_2(\mathbf{x}_1)$, the algorithm then iterates over it: for each $\mathbf{x}_2 \in L_2(\mathbf{x}_1)$ it applies the filtering procedure to L_3 with respect to $C_{2,3}$ and obtains $L_3(\mathbf{x}_1, \mathbf{x}_2)$. Throughout, vectors in brackets indicate fixed elements with respect to which the list has been filtered. Filtering of the top level lists $(L_1, \dots, L_k)$ continues in this fashion until we have constructed $L_k(\mathbf{x}_1, \dots, \mathbf{x}_{k-1})$ for fixed values $\mathbf{x}_1, \dots, \mathbf{x}_{k-1}$. The tuples of the form $(\mathbf{x}_1, \dots, \mathbf{x}_{k-1}, \mathbf{x}_k)$ for all $\mathbf{x}_k \in L_k(\mathbf{x}_1, \dots, \mathbf{x}_{k-1})$ form solutions to the configuration problem.

The algorithms from [HK17, HKL18] apply more filtering steps. For a fixed $\mathbf{x}_1 \in L_1$, they not only create $L_2(\mathbf{x}_1)$, but also $L_3(\mathbf{x}_1), \dots, L_k(\mathbf{x}_1)$. This speeds up the next iteration over all $\mathbf{x}_2 \in L_2(\mathbf{x}_1)$, where now the filtering step with respect to $C_{2,3}$ is applied not to L_3, but to $L_3(\mathbf{x}_1)$, as well as to $L_4(\mathbf{x}_1), \dots, L_k(\mathbf{x}_1)$, each of which is smaller than L_i. This speeds up the construction of $L_3(\mathbf{x}_1, \mathbf{x}_2)$. The algorithm continues with this filtering process until the last inner product check with respect to $C_{k-1,k}$ is applied to all the elements from $L_k(\mathbf{x}_1, \dots, \mathbf{x}_{k-2})$ and the list $L_k(\mathbf{x}_1, \dots, \mathbf{x}_{k-1})$ is constructed. This gives solutions of the form $(\mathbf{x}_1, \dots, \mathbf{x}_{k-1}, \mathbf{x}_k)$ for all $\mathbf{x}_k \in L_k(\mathbf{x}_1, \dots, \mathbf{x}_{k-1})$. The concentration result, Theorem 4, implies the outputs of algorithms from [BLS16] and [HK17, HKL18] are (up to a subexponential fraction) the same. Pseudocode for [HK17] can be found in the full version [KMPR19, App. A].

Important for our analysis in Sect. 4 will be the the result of [HKL18] that describes the sizes of all the intermediate lists that appear during the configuration search algorithms via the determinants of submatrices of the target configuration C. The next theorem gives the expected sizes of these lists and the time complexity of the algorithm from [HKL18].

Theorem 5 (Intermediate list sizes [HKL18, Lemma 1] and time complexity of configuration search algorithm). *During a run of the configuration search algorithms described in Figs. 1a and b, given an input configuration $C \in \mathbb{R}^{k \times k}$ and lists $L_1, \ldots, L_k \subset S^{d-1}$ each of size $|L|$, the intermediate lists for $1 \le i < j \le k$ are of expected sizes*

$$\mathbb{E}[|L_j(\mathbf{x}_1, \ldots, \mathbf{x}_i)|] = |L| \cdot \left(\frac{\det(C[1, \ldots, i, j])}{\det(C[1 \ldots i])} \right)^{d/2}. \tag{3}$$

The expected running time of the algorithm described in Fig. 1b is

$$T_{\text{k-Conf}}^{C} = \max_{1 \le i \le k} \left[\prod_{r=1}^{i} |L_r(\mathbf{x}_1, \ldots, \mathbf{x}_{r-1})| \cdot \max_{i+1 \le j \le k} |L_j(\mathbf{x}_1, \ldots, \mathbf{x}_{i-1})| \right]. \tag{4}$$

Finding a Configuration for Optimal Runtime. For a given i the square bracketed term in Eq. (4) represents the expected time required to create all filtered lists on a given "level". Here "level" refers to all lists filtered with respect to the same fixed $\mathbf{x}_1, \ldots, \mathbf{x}_{i-1}$, i.e. a row of lists in Fig. 1b. In order to find an optimal configuration C that minimises Eq. (4), we perform numerical optimisations using the Maple™ package [Map].[3] In particular, we search for $C \in \mathscr{C}$ that minimises Eq. (4) under the condition that Eq. (2) is satisfied (so that we actually obtain enough solutions for the k-List problem). Figures for the optimal runtime and the corresponding memory are given in Table 1. The memory is determined by the size of the input lists computed from the optimal C using Eq. (2). Since the k-List routine determines the asymptotic cost of k-Sieve, the figures in Table 1 are also the constants in the exponents for complexities of k-Sieves.

Table 1. Asymptotic complexity exponents for the approximate k-List problem, base 2. The table gives optimised runtime and the corresponding memory exponents for the classical algorithm from [HKL18], see Fig. 1b.

k	2	3	4	5	6	...	16	17	18
Time	0.4150	0.3789	0.3702	0.3707	0.3716		0.3728	0.37281	0.37281
Space	0.2075	0.1895	0.1851	0.1853	0.1858		0.1864	0.18640	0.18640

Interestingly, the optimal runtime constant turns out to be equal for large enough k. This can be explained as follows. The optimal C achieves the situation where all the expressions in the outer max in Eq. (4) are equal. This implies that creating all the filtered lists on level i asymptotically costs the same as creating all the filtered lists on level $i + 1$ for $2 \le i \le k - 1$. The cost of creating filtered lists $L_i(\mathbf{x}_1)$ on the second level (assuming that the first level consists of the input lists) is of order $|L|^2$. This value, $|L|^2$, becomes (up to poly(d) factors) the

---

[3] The code is available at https://github.com/ElenaKirshanova/QuantumSieve.

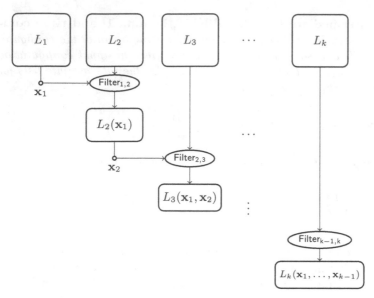

(a) The algorithm of Bai et al. [BLS16] for the configuration problem.

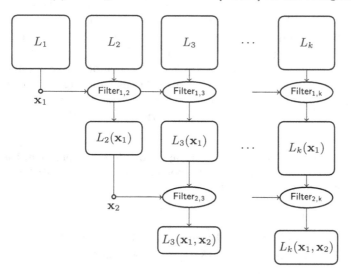

(b) The algorithm of Herold et al. [HKL18] for the configuration problem.

Fig. 1. Algorithms for the configuration problem. Procedures $\mathsf{Filter}_{i,j}$ receive as input a vector (e.g. $\mathbf{x}_1$), a list of vectors (e.g. L_2), and a real number $C_{i,j}$, the target inner product. It creates another shorter list (e.g. $L_2(\mathbf{x}_1)$) that contains all vectors from the input list whose inner product with the input vector is within some small ε from the target inner product.

running time of the whole algorithm (compare the Time and Space constants for $k = 16, 17, 18$ in Table 1). The precise shape of $C \in \mathscr{C}$ that makes the costs per level equal can be obtained by equating all the terms in the max of Eq. (4) and minimising the value $|L|^2$ under these constraints. Even for small k these computations become rather tedious and we do not attempt to express $C_{i,j}$ as a function of k, which is, in principal, possible.

Finding a Configuration for Optimal Memory. If we want to optimise for memory, the optimal configuration C has all its off diagonal elements $C_{i,j} = -1/k$. We call such a configuration *balanced*. It is shown in [HK17] that such C maximises $\det(C)$ among all $C \in \mathscr{C}$, which, in turn, minimises the sizes of the input lists (but does not lead to optimal running time as the costs per level are not equal).

4 Quantum Configuration Search

In this section we present several quantum algorithms for the configuration problem (Definition 3). As explained in Sect. 3, this directly translates to quantum sieving algorithms for SVP. We start with a quantum version of the BLS style configuration search [BLS16], then we show how to improve this algorithm by constructing intermediate lists. In the full version [KMPR19, App. B] we show how nearest neighbour methods in the quantum setting speed up the latter algorithm.

Recall the configuration problem: as input we receive k lists $L_i, i \in [k]$ each of size a power of two,[4] a configuration matrix $C \in \mathbb{R}^{k \times k}$ and $\varepsilon \geq 0$. To describe our first algorithm we denote by $f_{[i],j}$ a function that takes as input $(i+1)$ many d-dimensional vectors and is defined as

$$f_{[i],j}(\mathbf{x}_1, \ldots, \mathbf{x}_i, \mathbf{x}) = \begin{cases} 1, & |\langle \mathbf{x}_\ell, \mathbf{x} \rangle - C_{\ell,j}| \leq \varepsilon, \quad \ell \in [i] \\ 0, & \text{else.} \end{cases}$$

A reversible embedding of $f_{[i],j}$ is denoted by $O_{f_{[i],j}}$. Using these functions we perform a check for "good" elements and construct the lists $L_j(\mathbf{x}_1, \mathbf{x}_2, \ldots, \mathbf{x}_i)$. Furthermore, we assume that any vector encountered by the algorithm fits into $\bar{d}$ qubits. We denote by $|\mathbf{0}\rangle$ the $\bar{d}$-tensor of 0 qubits, i.e. $|\mathbf{0}\rangle = |0^{\otimes \bar{d}}\rangle$.

The input lists, $L_i, i \in [k]$, are stored classically and are assumed to be quantumly accessible. In particular, we assume that we can efficiently construct a uniform superposition over all elements from a given list by first applying Hadamards to $|\mathbf{0}\rangle$ to create a superposition over all indices, and then by querying $L[i]$ for each i in the superposition. That is, we assume an efficient circuit for $\frac{1}{\sqrt{|L|}} \sum_i |i\rangle |\mathbf{0}\rangle \rightarrow \frac{1}{\sqrt{|L|}} \sum_i |i\rangle |L[i]\rangle$. For simplicity, we ignore the first qubit that

---

[4] This is not necessary but it enables us to efficiently create superpositions $|\Psi_{L_i}\rangle$ using Hadamard gates. Since our lists L_i are of sizes $2^{cd+o(d)}$ for a large d and a constant $c < 1$, this condition is easy to satisfy by rounding cd.

stores indices and we denote by $|\Psi_L\rangle$ a uniform superposition over all the elements in L, i.e. $|\Psi_L\rangle = \frac{1}{\sqrt{|L|}}\sum_{\mathbf{x}\in L}|\mathbf{x}\rangle$.

The idea of our algorithm for the configuration problem is the following. We have a global *classical* loop over $\mathbf{x}_1 \in L_1$ inside which we run our quantum algorithm to find a $(k-1)$ tuple $(\mathbf{x}_2,\ldots,\mathbf{x}_k)$ that together with $\mathbf{x}_1$ gives a solution to the configuration problem. We expect to have $\mathcal{O}(1)$ such $(k-1)$ tuples per $\mathbf{x}_1$.[5] At the end of the algorithm we expect to obtain such a solution by means of amplitude amplification (Theorem 2). In Theorem 6 we argue that this procedure succeeds in finding a solution with probability at least $1 - 2^{-\Omega(d)}$.

Inside the classical loop over $\mathbf{x}_1$ we prepare $(k-1)\bar{d}$ qubits, which we arrange into $k-1$ registers, so that each register will store (a superposition of) input vectors, see Fig. 2. Each such register is set in uniform superposition over the elements of the input lists: $|\Psi_{L_2}\rangle \otimes |\Psi_{L_3}\rangle \otimes \cdots \otimes |\Psi_{L_k}\rangle$. We apply Grover's algorithm on $|\Psi_{L_2}\rangle$. Each Grover's iteration is defined by the unitary $Q_{1,2} = -H^{\otimes\bar{d}}RH^{\otimes\bar{d}}O_{f_{[1],2}}$. Here H is the Hadamard gate and R is the rotation around $|0\rangle$. We have $|L_2(\mathbf{x}_1)|$ "good" states out of $|L_2|$ possible states in $|\Psi_{L_2}\rangle$, so after $\mathcal{O}\left(\sqrt{\frac{|L_2|}{|L_2(\mathbf{x}_1)|}}\right)$ applications of $Q_{1,2}$ we obtain the state

$$|\Psi_{L_2(\mathbf{x}_1)}\rangle = \frac{1}{\sqrt{|L_2(\mathbf{x}_1)|}} \sum_{\mathbf{x}_2\in L_2(\mathbf{x}_1)} |\mathbf{x}_2\rangle. \tag{5}$$

In fact, what we create is a state close to Eq. (5) as we do not perform any measurement. For now, we drop the expression "close to" for all the states in this description, and argue about the failure probability in Theorem 6.

Now consider the state $|\Psi_{L_2(\mathbf{x}_1)}\rangle \otimes |\Psi_{L_3}\rangle$ and the function $f_{[2],3}$ that uses the first and second registers and a fixed $\mathbf{x}_1$ as inputs. We apply the unitary $Q_{2,3}$ to $|\Psi_{L_3}\rangle$, where $Q_{2,3} = -H^{\otimes\bar{d}}RH^{\otimes\bar{d}}O_{f_{[2],3}}$. In other words, for all vectors from L_3, we check if they satisfy the inner product constraints with respect to $\mathbf{x}_1$ and $\mathbf{x}_2$. In this setting there are $|L_3(\mathbf{x}_1,\mathbf{x}_2)|$ "good" states in $|\Psi_{L_3}\rangle$ whose amplitudes we aim to amplify. Applying Grover's iteration unitary $Q_{2,3}$ the order of $\mathcal{O}\left(\sqrt{\frac{|L_3|}{|L_3(\mathbf{x}_1,\mathbf{x}_2)|}}\right)$ times, we obtain the state

$$|\Psi_{L_2(\mathbf{x}_1)}\rangle |\Psi_{L_3(\mathbf{x}_1,\mathbf{x}_2)}\rangle = \frac{1}{\sqrt{|L_2(\mathbf{x}_1)|}} \sum_{\mathbf{x}_2\in L_2(\mathbf{x}_1)} |\mathbf{x}_2\rangle \left(\frac{1}{\sqrt{|L_3(\mathbf{x}_1,\mathbf{x}_2)|}} \sum_{\mathbf{x}_3\in L_3(\mathbf{x}_1,\mathbf{x}_2)} |\mathbf{x}_3\rangle\right).$$

We continue creating the lists $L_{i+1}(\mathbf{x}_1,\mathbf{x}_2,\ldots,\mathbf{x}_i)$ by filtering the *initial* list L_{i+1} with respect to $\mathbf{x}_1$ (fixed by the outer classical loop), and with respect to $\mathbf{x}_2,\ldots,\mathbf{x}_i$ (given in a superposition) using the function $f_{[i],i+1}$. At level $k-1$ we obtain the state $|\Psi_{L_2(\mathbf{x}_1)}\rangle \otimes |\Psi_{L_3(\mathbf{x}_1,\mathbf{x}_2)}\rangle \otimes \cdots \otimes |\Psi_{L_{k-1}(\mathbf{x}_1,\ldots,\mathbf{x}_{k-2})}\rangle$. For the last

---

[5] This follows by multiplying the sizes of the lists $L_i(\mathbf{x}_1,\ldots\mathbf{x}_{i-1})$ for all $2 \leq i \leq k$.

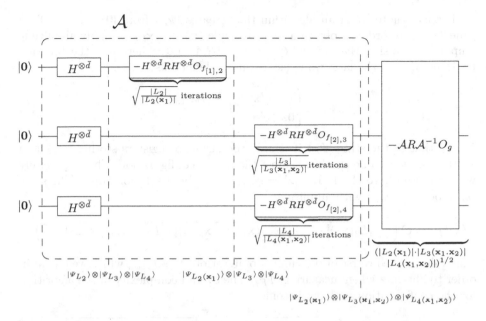

Fig. 2. Quantum circuit representing the quantum part of Algorithm 4.1 with $k = 4$, i.e. this circuit is executed inside the loop over $\mathbf{x}_1 \in L_1$. The Hadamard gates create the superposition $|\Psi_{L_2}\rangle \otimes |\Psi_{L_3}\rangle \otimes |\Psi_{L_4}\rangle$. We apply $\sqrt{\frac{|L_2|}{|L_2(\mathbf{x}_1)|}}$ Grover iterations to $|\Psi_{L_2}\rangle$ to obtain the state $|\Psi_{L_2(\mathbf{x}_2)}(\mathbf{x}_1)\rangle \otimes |\Psi_{L_3}\rangle \otimes |\Psi_{L_4}\rangle$. We then apply (sequentially) $\mathcal{O}\left(\sqrt{\frac{|L_3|}{|L_3(\mathbf{x}_1,\mathbf{x}_2)|}}\right)$ *resp.* $\mathcal{O}\left(\sqrt{\frac{|L_4|}{|L_4(\mathbf{x}_1,\mathbf{x}_2)|}}\right)$ Grover iterations to the second *resp.* third registers, where the checking function takes as input the first and second *resp.* the first and third registers. This whole process is $\mathcal{A}$ and is repeated $\mathcal{O}(\sqrt{|L_2(\mathbf{x}_1)| \cdot |L_3(\mathbf{x}_1,\mathbf{x}_2)| \, |L_4(\mathbf{x}_1,\mathbf{x}_2)|})$ times inside the amplitude amplification. Final measurement gives a triple $(\mathbf{x}_2, \mathbf{x}_3, \mathbf{x}_4)$ which, together with a fixed $\mathbf{x}_1$, forms a solution to the configuration problem.

list L_k we filter with respect to $\mathbf{x}_1, \ldots, \mathbf{x}_{k-2}$ as for the list L_{k-1}. Finally, for a fixed $\mathbf{x}_1$, the "filtered" state we obtained is of the form

$$|\Psi_F\rangle = |\Psi_{L_2(\mathbf{x}_1)}\rangle \otimes |\Psi_{L_3(\mathbf{x}_1,\mathbf{x}_2)}\rangle \otimes \ldots \otimes |\Psi_{L_{k-1}(\mathbf{x}_1,\ldots,\mathbf{x}_{k-2})}\rangle \otimes |\Psi_{L_k(\mathbf{x}_1,\ldots,\mathbf{x}_{k-2})}\rangle .$$
(6)

The state is expected to contain $\mathcal{O}(1)$ many $(k-1)$-tuples $(\mathbf{x}_2, \ldots, \mathbf{x}_k)$ which together with $\mathbf{x}_1$ give a solution to the configuration problem. To prepare the state $|\Psi_F\rangle$ for a fixed $\mathbf{x}_1$, we need

$$T_{\text{InGrover}} = \mathcal{O}\left(\sqrt{\left(\frac{|L_2|}{|L_2(\mathbf{x}_1)|}\right)} + \ldots + \sqrt{\left(\frac{|L_k|}{|L_k(\mathbf{x}_1, \ldots, \mathbf{x}_{k-2})|}\right)}\right)$$
(7)

unitary operations of the form $(-H^{\otimes \bar{d}})RH^{\otimes \bar{d}}O_{f_{[i],j}}$. This is what we call the "inner" Grover procedure.

Let us denote by $\mathcal{A}$ an algorithm that creates $|\Psi_F\rangle$ from $|0\rangle \otimes \ldots \otimes |0\rangle$ in time T_{InGrover}. In order to obtain a solution tuple $(\mathbf{x}_2, \ldots, \mathbf{x}_k)$ we apply amplitude amplification using the unitary $Q_{\text{Outer}} = -\mathcal{A}R\mathcal{A}^{-1}O_g$, where g is the function that operates on the last two registers and is defined as

$$g(\mathbf{x}, \mathbf{x}') = \begin{cases} 1, & |\langle \mathbf{x}, \mathbf{x}' \rangle - C_{k-1,k}| \leq \varepsilon \\ 0, & \text{else.} \end{cases} \tag{8}$$

Notice that in the state $|\Psi_F\rangle$ it is only the last two registers storing $\mathbf{x}_{k-1}$ and $\mathbf{x}_k$ that are left to be checked against the target configuration. This is precisely what we use O_g to check. Let $|\mathbf{z}\rangle = |\mathbf{x}_2, \ldots, \mathbf{x}_k\rangle$ be a solution tuple. The state $|\mathbf{z}\rangle$ appears in $|\Psi_F\rangle$ with amplitude

$$\langle \mathbf{z}|\Psi_F\rangle = \mathcal{O}\left(\left(\sqrt{|L_2(\mathbf{x}_1)|} \cdot \ldots \cdot |L_{k-1}(\mathbf{x}_1, \ldots, \mathbf{x}_{k-2})| \cdot |L_k(\mathbf{x}_1, \ldots, \mathbf{x}_{k-2})| \right)^{-1} \right).$$

This value is the inverse of the number of iteration steps Q_{Outer} which we repeat in order to obtain $\mathbf{z}$ when measuring $|\Psi_F\rangle$. The overall complexity of the algorithm for the configuration problem becomes

$$T_{\text{BLS}}^{\text{Q}} = \mathcal{O}\left(|L_1| \left(\sqrt{\left(\frac{|L_2|}{|L_2(\mathbf{x}_1)|} \right)} + \ldots + \sqrt{\left(\frac{|L_k|}{|L_k(\mathbf{x}_1, \ldots, \mathbf{x}_{k-2})|} \right)} \right) \right.$$
$$\left. \cdot \sqrt{|L_2(\mathbf{x}_1)| \cdot |L_3(\mathbf{x}_1, \mathbf{x}_2)| \cdot \ldots \cdot |L_k(\mathbf{x}_1, \ldots, \mathbf{x}_{k-2})|} \right), \tag{9}$$

where all the filtered lists in the above expression are assumed to be of expected size greater than or equal to 1. For certain target configurations intermediate lists are of sizes less than 1 in expectation (see Eq. (1)), which should be understood as the expected number of times we need to construct these lists to obtain 1 element in them. So there will exist elements in the superposition for which a solution does not exist. Still, for the elements, for which a solution does exist (we expect $\mathcal{O}(1)$ of these), we perform $\mathcal{O}(\sqrt{|L|})$ Grover iterations during the "inner" Grover procedure, and during the "outer" procedure these "good" elements contribute a $\mathcal{O}(1)$ factor to the running time. Therefore formally, each $|L_i(\mathbf{x}_1, \ldots, \mathbf{x}_{i-1})|$ in Eq. (9) should be changed to $\max\{1, |L_i(\mathbf{x}_1, \ldots, \mathbf{x}_{i-1})|\}$. Alternatively, one can enforce that intermediate lists are of size greater than 1 by choosing the target configuration appropriately.

The procedure we have just described is summarised in Algorithm 4.1. If we want to use this algorithm to solve the Approximate k-List problem (Definition 1), we additionally require that the number of output solutions is equal to the size of the input lists. Using the results of Theorem 4, we can express the complexity of Algorithm 4.1 for the Approximate k-List problem via the determinant of the target configuration C and its minors.

Algorithm 4.1. Quantum algorithm for the Configuration Problem

---

Input: $L_1, \ldots, L_k-$ lists of vectors from S^{d-1}, target configuration $C_{i,j} = \langle \mathbf{x}_i , \mathbf{x}_j \rangle \in \mathbb{R}^{k \times k}-$ a Gram matrix, $\varepsilon > 0$.
Output: $L_{\text{out}}-$ list of k-tuples $(\mathbf{x}_1, \ldots, \mathbf{x}_k) \in L_1 \times \cdots \times L_k$, s.t. $|\langle \mathbf{x}_i , \mathbf{x}_j \rangle - C_{ij}| \leq \varepsilon$ for all i, j.

1:   $L_{\text{out}} \leftarrow \emptyset$
2:   **for all** $\mathbf{x}_1 \in L_1$ **do**
3:      Prepare the state $|\Psi_{L_2}\rangle \otimes \ldots \otimes |\Psi_{L_k}\rangle$
4:      **for all** $i = 2 \ldots k-1$ **do**
5:         Run Grover's on the ith register with the checking function $f_{[i-1],i}$ to transform the state $|\Psi_{L_i}\rangle$ to the state $|\Psi_{L_i(\mathbf{x}_1,\ldots,\mathbf{x}_{i-1})}\rangle$.
6:      Run Grover's on the kth register with the checking function $f_{[k-2],k}$ to transform the state $|\Psi_{L_k}\rangle$ to the state $|\Psi_{L_k(\mathbf{x}_1,\ldots,\mathbf{x}_{k-2})}\rangle$.
7:      Let $\mathcal{A}$ be unitary that implements steps 3–6, i.e.

$$\mathcal{A} |0^{\otimes k}\rangle \rightarrow |\Psi_F\rangle .$$

8:      Run amplitude amplification using the unitary $-\mathcal{A}R\mathcal{A}^{-1}O_g$, where g is defined in Eq. (8).
9:      Measure all the registers, obtain a tuple $(\mathbf{x}_2, \ldots, \mathbf{x}_k)$.
10:     **if** $(\mathbf{x}_1, \ldots, \mathbf{x}_k)$ satisfies C **then**
11:        $L_{\text{out}} \leftarrow L_{\text{out}} \cup \{(\mathbf{x}_1, \ldots, \mathbf{x}_k)\}$.

Theorem 6. *Given input $L_1, \ldots, L_k \subset \mathsf{S}^{d-1}$ and a configuration $C \in \mathscr{C}$, such that Eq. (2) holds, Algorithm 4.1 solves the Approximate k-List problem in time*

$$T_{\text{k-List}} = \widetilde{\mathcal{O}} \left(\left(\left(\frac{1}{\det(C)} \right)^{\frac{k+1}{2(k-1)}} \cdot \sqrt{\det(C[1 \ldots k-1])} \right)^{d/2} \right) \tag{10}$$

using $M_{\text{k-List}} = \widetilde{\mathcal{O}} \left(\left(\frac{1}{\det(C)} \right)^{\frac{d}{2(k-1)}} \right)$ classical memory and $\text{poly}(d)$ quantum memory with success probability at least $1 - 2^{-\Omega(d)}$.

Proof. From Theorem 4, the input lists $L_1, \ldots, L_k$ should be of sizes $|L| = \widetilde{\mathcal{O}} \left(\left(\frac{1}{\det(C)} \right)^{\frac{d}{2(k-1)}} \right)$ to guarantee a sufficient number of solutions. This determines the requirement for classical memory. Furthermore, since all intermediate lists are stored in the superposition, we require quantum registers of size $\text{poly}(d)$.

Next, we can simplify the expression for T_{BLS}^Q given in Eq. (9) by noting that $|L_2(\mathbf{x}_1)| \geq |L_3(\mathbf{x}_1, \mathbf{x}_2)| \geq \ldots \geq |L_{k-1}(\mathbf{x}_1, \ldots, \mathbf{x}_{k-2})| = |L_k(\mathbf{x}_1, \ldots, \mathbf{x}_{k-2})|$. The dominant term in the sum appearing in Eq. (9) is $\sqrt{\left(\frac{|L_k|}{|L_k(\mathbf{x}_1,\ldots,\mathbf{x}_{k-2})|} \right)}$.

From Theorem 5, the product $\sqrt{|L_2(\mathbf{x}_1)| \cdot \ldots \cdot |L_{k-1}(\mathbf{x}_1, \ldots, \mathbf{x}_{k-2})|}$ in Eq. (9) can be simplified to $|L|^{\frac{k-2}{2}} \left(\sqrt{\det(C[1 \ldots k-1])} \right)^{d/2}$, from where we arrive at the expression for $T_{\text{k-List}}$ as in the statement.

The success probability of Algorithm 4.1 is determined by the success probability of the amplitude amplification run in Step 8. For this we consider the precise form of the state $|\Psi_F\rangle$ given in Eq. (6). This state is obtained by running $k-1$ (sequential) Grover algorithms. Each tensor $|\Psi_{L_i(\mathbf{x}_1,\ldots,\mathbf{x}_{i-1})}\rangle$ in this state is a superposition

$$|\Psi_{L_i(\mathbf{x}_1,\ldots,\mathbf{x}_{i-1})}\rangle = \sqrt{\frac{1-\epsilon_i}{|L_i(\mathbf{x}_1,\ldots,\mathbf{x}_{i-1})|}} \sum_{\mathbf{x}\in L_i(\mathbf{x}_1,\ldots,\mathbf{x}_{i-1})} |\mathbf{x}\rangle$$
$$+ \sqrt{\frac{\epsilon_i}{|L_i \setminus L_i(\mathbf{x}_1,\ldots,\mathbf{x}_{i-1})|}} \sum_{\mathbf{x}\in L_i\setminus L_i(\mathbf{x}_1,\ldots,\mathbf{x}_{i-1})} |\mathbf{x}\rangle,$$

where $\epsilon_i < \frac{|L_i(\mathbf{x}_1,\ldots,\mathbf{x}_i)|}{|L_i|} \leq 2^{-\Omega(d)}$. The first inequality comes from the success probability of Grover's algorithm, Theorem 1, the second inequality is due to the fact that all lists on a "lower" level are exponentially smaller than lists on a "higher" level, see Theorem 5. Therefore, the success probability of the amplitude amplification is given by $\prod_{i=2}^{k-1} \frac{1-\epsilon_i}{|L_i(\mathbf{x}_1,\ldots,\mathbf{x}_{i-1})|} \cdot \frac{1-\epsilon_k}{|L_k(\mathbf{x}_1,\ldots,\mathbf{x}_{k-2})|} \geq (1-2^{-\Omega(d)}) \prod_{i=2}^{k-1} |L_i(\mathbf{x}_1,\ldots,\mathbf{x}_{i-1})|^{-1}$. According to Theorem 2, after performing $\mathcal{O}\left(\prod_{i=2}^{k} |L_i(\mathbf{x}_1,\ldots,\mathbf{x}_i)| |L_k(\mathbf{x}_1,\ldots,\mathbf{x}_{k-2})|\right)$ amplitude amplification iterations, in Step 9 we measure a "good" $(\mathbf{x}_2,\ldots,\mathbf{x}_k)$ with probability at least $1-2^{-\Omega(d)}$.   □

4.1 Quantum Version of the Configuration Search Algorithm From [HKL18]

The main difference between the two algorithms for the configuration problem – the algorithm due to Bai–Laarhoven–Stehlé [BLS16] and due to Herold–Kirshanova–Laarhoven [HKL18] – is that the latter constructs intermediate filtered lists, Fig. 1. We use quantum enumeration to construct and classically store these lists.

For a fixed $\mathbf{x}$, quantum enumeration repeatedly applies Grover's algorithm to an input list L_i, where each application returns a random vector from the filtered list $L_i(\mathbf{x})$ with probability greater than $1-2^{-\Omega(d)}$. The quantum complexity of obtaining one vector from $L_i(\mathbf{x})$ is $\mathcal{O}\left(\sqrt{\frac{|L_i|}{|L_i(\mathbf{x})|}}\right)$. We can also check that the returned vector belongs to $L_i(\mathbf{x})$ by checking its inner product with $\mathbf{x}$. Repeating this process $\widetilde{\mathcal{O}}(|L_i(\mathbf{x})|)$ times, we obtain the list $L_i(\mathbf{x})$ stored classically in time $\widetilde{\mathcal{O}}(\sqrt{|L_i| \cdot |L_i(\mathbf{x})|})$. The advantage of constructing the lists $L_i(\mathbf{x})$ is that we can now efficiently prepare the state $|\Psi_{L_2(\mathbf{x})}\rangle \otimes \ldots \otimes |\Psi_{L_k(\mathbf{x})}\rangle$ (cf. Line 3 in Algorithm 4.1) and run amplitude amplification on the states $|\Psi_{L_i(\mathbf{x})}\rangle$ rather than on $|\Psi_{L_i}\rangle$. This may give a speed up if the complexity of the Steps 3–11 of Algorithm 4.1, which is of order $\widetilde{\mathcal{O}}(T_{\text{BLS}}^{\text{Q}}/|L_1|)$, dominates the cost of quantum enumeration, which is of order $\widetilde{\mathcal{O}}(\sqrt{|L_i| \cdot |L_i(\mathbf{x})|})$. In general, we can continue creating the "levels" as in [HKL18] (see Fig. 1b) using quantum enumeration and at some level switch to the quantum BLS style algorithm. For example, for some level $1 < j \leq k-1$, we apply quantum enumeration to obtain $L_i(\mathbf{x}_1, \ldots, \mathbf{x}_{j-1})$ for all $i > j$. Then for all $(j-1)$-tuples $(\mathbf{x}_1, \ldots, \mathbf{x}_{j-1}) \in L_1 \times \ldots \times L_{j-1}(\mathbf{x}_1, \ldots, \mathbf{x}_{j-2})$, apply Grover's algorithm as in steps 3–11 of Algorithm 4.1 but now to the states $|\Psi_{L_j(\mathbf{x}_1, \ldots, \mathbf{x}_{j-1})}\rangle \otimes \cdots \otimes |\Psi_{L_k(\mathbf{x}_1, \ldots, \mathbf{x}_{j-1})}\rangle$. Note that since we have these lists stored in memory, we can efficiently create this superposition. In this way we obtain a quantum "hybrid" between the HKL and the BLS algorithms: until some level j, we construct the intermediate lists using quantum enumeration, create superpositions over all the filtered lists at level j for some fixed values $\mathbf{x}_1, \ldots, \mathbf{x}_{j-1}$, and apply Grover's algorothm to find (if it exists) the $(k - j + 1)$ tuple $(\mathbf{x}_j, \ldots, \mathbf{x}_k)$. Pseudocode for this approach is given in Algorithm 4.2.

Algorithm 4.2. Hybrid quantum algorithm for the Configuration Problem

---

Input: $L_1, \ldots, L_k$, lists of vectors from S^{d-1}, target configuration $C_{i,j} = \langle \mathbf{x}_i, \mathbf{x}_j \rangle \in \mathbb{R}^{k \times k}$, $\varepsilon > 0$, $2 \leq j \leq k - 1$, level we construct the intermediate filtered lists until.
Output: L_{out} − list of k-tuples $(\mathbf{x}_1, \ldots, \mathbf{x}_k) \in L_1 \times \cdots \times L_k$, s.t. $|\langle \mathbf{x}_i, \mathbf{x}_j \rangle - C_{ij}| \leq \varepsilon$ for all i, j.

1:   $L_{\text{out}} \leftarrow \emptyset$
2:   **for all** $\mathbf{x}_1 \in L_1$ **do**
3:      Use quantum enumeration to construct $L_i(\mathbf{x}_1)$ for $\forall i \geq 2$
4:      **for all** $\mathbf{x}_2 \in L_2(\mathbf{x}_1)$ **do**
5:        Use quantum enumeration to construct $L_i(\mathbf{x}_1, \mathbf{x}_2)$, $\forall i \geq 3$

6:          $\ddots$
7:            **for all** $\mathbf{x}_{j-1} \in L_{j-1}(\mathbf{x}_1, \ldots, \mathbf{x}_{j-2})$ **do**
8:              Use quantum enumeration to construct $L_i(\mathbf{x}_1, \ldots, \mathbf{x}_{j-1})$, $\forall i \geq j$
9:              Prepare the state $|\Psi_{L_j(\mathbf{x}_1, \ldots, \mathbf{x}_{j-1})}\rangle \otimes \cdots \otimes |\Psi_{L_k(\mathbf{x}_1, \ldots, \mathbf{x}_{j-1})}\rangle$
10:             **for all** $i = j + 1 \ldots k - 1$ **do**
11:               Run Grover's on the ith register with the checking function $f_{[i-1],i}$ to transform the state $|\Psi_{L_i(\mathbf{x}_1, \ldots, \mathbf{x}_{j-1})}\rangle$ to the state $|\Psi_{L_i(\mathbf{x}_1, \ldots, \mathbf{x}_{i-1})}\rangle$.
12:               Run Grover's on the kth register with the checking function $f_{[k-2],k}$ to transform the state $|\Psi_{L_k(\mathbf{x}_1, \ldots, \mathbf{x}_{j-1})}\rangle$ to the state $|\Psi_{L_k(\mathbf{x}_1, \ldots, \mathbf{x}_{k-2})}\rangle$.
13:               Let $\mathcal{A}$ be unitary that implements Steps 9–12, i.e.

$$\mathcal{A}|0^{\otimes(k-j+1)}\rangle \rightarrow |\Psi_{L_j(\mathbf{x}_1, \ldots, \mathbf{x}_{j-1})}\rangle \otimes |\Psi_{L_k(\mathbf{x}_1, \ldots, \mathbf{x}_{k-2})}\rangle$$

14:               Run amplitude amplification using the unitary $-\mathcal{A}R\mathcal{A}^{-1}O_g$, where g is defined in Eq. (8).
15:               Measure all the registers, obtain a tuple $(\mathbf{x}_j, \ldots, \mathbf{x}_k)$.
16:               **if** $(\mathbf{x}_1, \ldots, \mathbf{x}_k)$ satisfies C **then**
17:                 $L_{\text{out}} \leftarrow L_{\text{out}} \cup \{(\mathbf{x}_1, \ldots, \mathbf{x}_k)\}$.

Let us now analyse Algorithm 4.2. To simplify notation, we denote $L_i^{(j)} = L_i(\mathbf{x}_1, \ldots, \mathbf{x}_{j-1})$ for all $i \geq j$, letting $L_i^{(1)}$ be the input lists L_i (so the upper index denotes the level of the list).

All $\mathcal{O}$ notations are omitted. Each quantum enumeration of $L_i^{(j)}$ from $L_i^{(j-1)}$ costs $\sqrt{\left|L_i^{(j-1)}\right|\left|L_i^{(j)}\right|}$. On level $1 \le \ell \le j-1$, we repeat such an enumeration $\prod_{r=1}^{\ell-1}\left|L_r^{(r)}\right|$ times to create the intermediate lists, once for each $(\mathbf{x}_1, \ldots, \mathbf{x}_{\ell-1})$. Once the lists $L_i^{(j)}$, $i \ge j$, are constructed, Grover's algorithm gives the state $\left|\Psi_{L_j^{(j)}}\right\rangle \ldots \left|\Psi_{L_{k-1}^{(k-1)}}\right\rangle \left|\Psi_{L_k^{(k-1)}}\right\rangle$ in time $\left(\sqrt{\frac{\left|L_{j+1}^{(j)}\right|}{\left|L_{j+1}^{(j+1)}\right|}} + \ldots + \sqrt{\frac{\left|L_{k-1}^{(j)}\right|}{\left|L_{k-1}^{(k-1)}\right|}} + \sqrt{\frac{\left|L_k^{(j)}\right|}{\left|L_k^{(k-1)}\right|}}\right)$ (Steps 11–12 in Algorithm 4.2). On Step 14 the unitary $\mathcal{A}$ must be executed $\sqrt{\left|L_j^{(j)}\right| \cdot \ldots \cdot \left|L_{k-1}^{(k-1)}\right| \cdot \left|L_k^{(k-1)}\right|}$ times to ensure that the measurement of the system gives the "good" tuple $(\mathbf{x}_j, \ldots, \mathbf{x}_k)$.

Such tuples may not exist: for $j \ge 3$, i.e. for *fixed* $\mathbf{x}_1, \mathbf{x}_2$, we expect to have less than 1 such tuples. So most of the time, the measurement will return a random $(k - j + 1)$-tuple, which we classically check against the target configuration C. Overall, given on input a level j, the runtime of Algorithm 4.2 is

$$
\begin{aligned}
T_{\text{Hybrid}}^{\text{Q}}(j) = \max_{1 \le \ell \le j-1}\left\{ \prod_{r=1}^{\ell-1}\left|L_r^{(r)}\right| \cdot \max_{\ell \le i \le k}\left\{ \sqrt{\left|L_i^{(\ell)}\right|\left|L_i^{(\ell+1)}\right|}\right\}\right\}, \\
\prod_{r=1}^{j-1}\left|L_r^{(r)}\right| \left(\sqrt{\frac{\left|L_{j+1}^{(j)}\right|}{\left|L_{j+1}^{(j+1)}\right|}} + \ldots + \sqrt{\frac{\left|L_{k-1}^{(j)}\right|}{\left|L_{k-1}^{(k-1)}\right|}} + \sqrt{\frac{\left|L_k^{(j)}\right|}{\left|L_k^{(k-1)}\right|}}\right) \\
\cdot \sqrt{\left|L_j^{(j)}\right| \cdot \ldots \cdot \left|L_{k-1}^{(k-1)}\right| \cdot \left|L_k^{(k-1)}\right|}\Bigg\}.
\end{aligned}
\tag{11}
$$

Similar to Eq. (9), all the list sizes in the above formula are assumed to be greater than or equal to 1. If, for a certain configuration it happens that the expected size of a list is less than 1, it should be replaced with 1 in this expression. The above complexity can be expressed via the subdeterminants of the target configuration C using Theorem 5. An optimal value of level j for a given C can be found via numerical optimisations that searches for j that minimises Eq. (11).

Speed-Ups With Nearest Neighbour Techniques. We can further speed up the creation of filtered lists in both Algorithms 4.1 and 4.2 with a quantum version of nearest neighbour search. In the full version [KMPR19, App. B] we describe a locality sensitive filtering (LSF) technique (first introduced in [BDGL16]) in the quantum setting, extending the idea of Laarhoven [Laa15] to $k > 2$.

Numerical Optimisations. We performed numerical optimisations for the target configuration C which minimises the runtime of the two algorithms for the configuration problem given in this section. The upper part of Table 2 gives time optimal c for Eq. (10) and the c' of the corresponding memory requirements for various k. These constants decrease with k and, eventually, those for time become close to the value 0.2989. The explanation for this behaviour is the following: looking at Eq. (9) the expression decreases when the lists $L_i(\mathbf{x}_1, \dots, \mathbf{x}_{i-1})$ under the square root become smaller. When k is large enough, in particular, once $k \geq 6$, there is a target configuration that ensures that $|L_i(\mathbf{x}_1, \dots, \mathbf{x}_{i-1})|$ are of expected size 1 for levels $i \geq 4$. So for $k \geq 6$, under the observation that the maximal value in the sum appearing in Eq. (9) is attained by the last summand, the runtime of Algorithm 4.1 becomes $T_{\mathrm{BLS}}^{\mathrm{Q}} = |L_1|^{3/2} \cdot \sqrt{|L_2(\mathbf{x}_1)| \, |L_3(\mathbf{x}_1, \mathbf{x}_2)|}$. The list sizes can be made explicit using Eq. (3) when a configuration C is such that $|L_i(\mathbf{x}_1, \dots, \mathbf{x}_{i-1})|$ are of expected size 1. Namely, for $k \geq 6$ and for configuration C that minimises the runtime exponent, Eq. (9) with the help of Eq. (3) simplifies to $\left(\left(\frac{1}{\det C} \right)^{\frac{5}{2(k-1)}} \sqrt{\det C[1,2,3]} \right)^{d/2}$.

Table 2. Asymptotic complexity exponents for the approximate k-List problem, base 2. The top part gives optimised runtime exponents and the corresponding memory exponents for Algorithm 4.1. These are the results of the optimisation (minimisation) of the runtime expression given in Eq. (10). The middle part gives the runtime and memory exponents for Algorithm 4.2, again optimising for time, with $j = 2$, i.e. when we use quantum enumeration to create the second level lists $L_i(\mathbf{x}_1)$, $i \geq 2$. The bottom part gives the exponents for Algorithm 4.2 with $j = 2$ in the memory optimal setting.

k	2	3	4	5	6	...	28	29	30
				Quantum version of [BLS16] Algorithm 4.1					
Time	0.3112	0.3306	0.3289	0.3219	0.3147	...	0.29893	0.29893	0.29893
Space	0.2075	0.1907	0.1796	0.1685	0.1596	...	0.1395	0.1395	0.1395
			Quantum Hybrid version of [BLS16, HKL18] Algorithm 4.2						
Time	0.3112	0.3306	0.3197	0.3088	0.3059	...	0.29893	0.29893	0.29893
Space	0.2075	0.1907	0.1731	0.1638	0.1595	...	0.1395	0.1395	0.1395
		Low memory Quantum Hybrid version of [BLS16, HKL18] Algorithm 4.2							
Time	0.3112	0.3349	0.3215	0.3305	0.3655	...	0.6352	0.6423	0.6490
Space	0.2075	0.1887	0.1724	0.1587	0.1473	...	0.0637	0.0623	0.0609

The optimal runtime exponents for the hybrid, Algorithm 4.2, with $j = 2$ are given in the middle part of Table 2. Experimentally, we establish that $j = 2$ is optimal for small values of k and that this algorithm has the same behaviour for large values of k as Algorithm 4.1. The reason is the following: for the runtime optimal configuration C the intermediate lists on the same level increase in size "from left to right", i.e. $|L_2(\mathbf{x}_1)| \leq |L_3(\mathbf{x}_1)| \leq \dots, \leq |L_k(\mathbf{x}_1)|$. It turns out that $|L_k(\mathbf{x}_1)|$ becomes almost $|L_k|$ (i.e. the target inner product is very close to 0), so quantumly enumerating this list brings no advantage over Algorithm 4.1 where we use the initial list L_k, of essentially the same size, in Grover's algorithm.

5   Quantum Configuration Search via k-Clique Listing

In this section we introduce a distinct approach to finding solutions of the configuration problem, Definition 3, via k-clique listing in graphs. We achieve this by repeatedly applying k-clique finding algorithms to the graphs. Throughout this section we assume that $L_1 = \cdots = L_k = L$. We first solve the configuration problem with $k = 3$, C the balanced configuration with all off diagonals equal to $-1/3$ and the size of L determined by Eq. (2). We then adapt the idea to the case for general k. In the full version [KMPR19, App. C] we give the $k = 4$ balanced case and consider unbalanced configurations.

Let $G = (V, E)$ be an undirected graph with known vertices and an oracle $O_G \colon V^2 \to \{\texttt{True}, \texttt{False}\}$. On input $(\mathbf{x}_1, \mathbf{x}_2) \in V^2$, O_G returns $\texttt{True}$ if $(\mathbf{x}_1, \mathbf{x}_2) \in E$ and $\texttt{False}$ otherwise. A k-clique is $\{\mathbf{x}_1, \ldots, \mathbf{x}_k\}$ such that $O_G(\mathbf{x}_i, \mathbf{x}_j) = \texttt{True}$ for $i \neq j$. Given k, $(\mathbf{x}_i, \mathbf{x}_j) \in E \iff |\langle \mathbf{x}_i, \mathbf{x}_j \rangle + 1/k| \leq \varepsilon$ for some $\varepsilon > 0$. In both cases, the oracle computes a d dimensional inner product and compares the result against the target configuration. Throughout we let $|V| = n$ and $|E| = m$.

5.1   The Triangle Case

We start with the simple triangle finding algorithm of [BdWD+01]. A triangle is a 3-clique. Given the balanced configuration and $k = 3$ on S^{d-1}, we have

$$n = |L| = \tilde{\mathcal{O}}\left((3\sqrt{3}/4)^{d/2} \right), \quad m = |L|\,|L(\mathbf{x}_1)| = \tilde{\mathcal{O}}\left(n^2 (8/9)^{d/2} \right) \qquad (12)$$

by Eq. (2) and Theorem 5 respectively,[6] We expect $\Theta(n)$ triangles to be found [HKL18]. The algorithm of [BdWD+01] consists of three steps:

1. Use Grover's algorithm to find any edge $(\mathbf{x}_1, \mathbf{x}_2) \in E$ among all potential $\mathcal{O}(n^2)$ edges.
2. Given an edge $(\mathbf{x}_1, \mathbf{x}_2)$ from Step 1, use Grover's algorithm to find a vertex $\mathbf{x}_3 \in V$, such that $(\mathbf{x}_1, \mathbf{x}_2, \mathbf{x}_3)$ is a triangle.
3. Apply amplitude amplification on Steps 1–2.

Note that the algorithm searches for any triangle in the graph, not a fixed one. To be more explicit about the use of the oracle O_G, below we describe a circuit that returns a triangle. Step 1 takes the state $\dfrac{1}{n} \displaystyle\sum_{(\mathbf{x}_1, \mathbf{x}_2) \in V^2} |\mathbf{x}_1\rangle \otimes |\mathbf{x}_2\rangle$ and applies $\mathcal{O}(\sqrt{n^2/m})$ times the Grover iteration given by $-H^{\otimes 2\bar{d}} R H^{\otimes 2\bar{d}} O_G$. The output is the state $\sqrt{\dfrac{\epsilon}{n^2 - m}} \displaystyle\sum_{(\mathbf{x}_1, \mathbf{x}_2) \notin E} |\mathbf{x}_1\rangle \otimes |\mathbf{x}_2\rangle + \sqrt{\dfrac{1-\epsilon}{m}} \displaystyle\sum_{(\mathbf{x}_1, \mathbf{x}_2) \in E} |\mathbf{x}_1\rangle \otimes |\mathbf{x}_2\rangle$, where ϵ represents the probability of failure. We disregard this as in the proof of Theorem 6. We then join with a uniform superposition over the vertices to create

---

[6] As we are in the balanced configuration case, and our input lists are identical, Theorem 5 has no dependence on j.

the state $\frac{1}{\sqrt{m}} \sum\limits_{(\mathbf{x}_1, \mathbf{x}_2) \in E} |\mathbf{x}_1\rangle \otimes |\mathbf{x}_2\rangle \otimes \frac{1}{\sqrt{n}} \sum\limits_{\mathbf{x}_3 \in V} |\mathbf{x}_3\rangle$ and apply $-H^{\otimes 3d} R H^{\otimes 3d} O_G^{\mathcal{A}}$

$\mathcal{O}(\sqrt{n})$ times. This oracle $O_G^{\mathcal{A}}$ outputs True on a triple from V^3 if each pair of vertices has an edge. We call the final state $|\Psi_F\rangle$. Let $\mathcal{A}|0^{\otimes 3}\rangle \to |\Psi_F\rangle$, then we apply amplitude amplification with $\mathcal{A}$ repeated some number of times determined by the success probability of $\mathcal{A}$ calculated below.

Given that oracle queries O_G or $O_G^{\mathcal{A}}$ have some poly(d) cost, we may calculate the time complexity of this method directly from the query complexity. The cost of the first step is $\mathcal{O}(\sqrt{n^2/m})$ and the second step $\mathcal{O}(\sqrt{n})$. From Eq. (12), and that the costs of Step 1 and Step 2 are additive, we see that $\mathcal{O}(\sqrt{n})$ dominates, therefore Steps 1–2 cost $\mathcal{O}(\sqrt{n})$. The probability that Step 2 finds a triangle is the probability that Step 1 finds an edge of a triangle. Given that there are $\Theta(n)$ triangles, this probability is $\Theta(n/m)$, therefore by applying the amplitude amplification in Step 3, the cost of finding a triangle is $\mathcal{O}(\sqrt{m})$.[7]

The algorithm finds one of the n triangles uniformly at random. By the coupon collector's problem we must repeat the algorithm $\tilde{\mathcal{O}}(n)$ times to find all the triangles. Therefore the total cost of finding all triangles is $\tilde{\mathcal{O}}(n\sqrt{m}) = \tilde{\mathcal{O}}(|L|^{3/2}|L(\mathbf{x}_1)|^{1/2}) \approx 2^{0.3349d + o(d)}$ using $2^{0.1887d + o(d)}$ memory. This matches the complexity of Algorithm 4.1 for $k = 3$ in the balanced case.

5.2   The General k-Clique Case

The algorithm generalises to arbitrary constant k. We have a graph with $|L|$ vertices, $|L||L(\mathbf{x}_1)|$ edges, ..., $|L||L(\mathbf{x}_1)| \ldots |L(\mathbf{x}_1, \ldots, \mathbf{x}_{i-1})|$ i-cliques for $i \in \{3, \ldots, k-1\}$, and $\Theta(|L|)$ k-cliques. The following algorithm finds a k-clique, with $2 \leq i \leq k-1$

1. Use Grover's algorithm to find an edge $(\mathbf{x}_1, \mathbf{x}_2) \in E$ among all potential $\mathcal{O}(|L|^2)$ edges.

$$\vdots$$

i. Given an i-clique $(\mathbf{x}_1, \ldots, \mathbf{x}_i)$ from step $i - 1$, use Grover's algorithm to find a vertex $\mathbf{x}_{i+1} \in V$, such that $(\mathbf{x}_1, \ldots, \mathbf{x}_{i+1})$ is an $(i+1)$-clique.

$$\vdots$$

k. Apply amplitude amplification on Steps 1–$(k-1)$.

The costs of Steps 1–$(k-1)$ are additive. The dominant term is from Step $k-1$, a Grover search over $|L|$, equal to $\mathcal{O}(\sqrt{|L|})$. To determine the cost of finding one k-clique, we need the probability that Steps 1–$(k-1)$ find a k-clique. We calculate the following probabilities, with $2 \leq i \leq k-2$

---

[7] Note that this differs from [BdWD+01] as in general either of Step 1 or 2 may dominate and we also make use of the existence of $\Theta(n)$ triangles.

1. The probability that Step 1 finds a good edge, that is, an edge belonging to a k-clique.
i. The probability that Step i finds a good $(i+1)$-clique given that Step $i-1$ finds a good i-clique.

In Step 1 there are $\mathcal{O}(|L||L(\mathbf{x}_1)|)$ edges to choose from, $\Theta(|L|)$ of which belong to a k-clique. Thus the success probability of this Step is $\Theta(1/|L(\mathbf{x}_1)|)$. Thereafter, in Step i, given an i-clique $(\mathbf{x}_1,\ldots,\mathbf{x}_i)$ there are $\mathcal{O}(\max\{|L(\mathbf{x}_1,\ldots,\mathbf{x}_i)|,1\})$ $(i+1)$-cliques on the form $(\mathbf{x}_1,\ldots,\mathbf{x}_i,\mathbf{x}_{i+1})$, $\Theta(1)$ of which are good. The success probability of Steps 1–$(k-1)$ is equal to $\Theta\left(\prod_{i=1}^{k-2}\max\{|L(\mathbf{x}_1,\ldots,\mathbf{x}_i)|,1\}^{-1}\right)$. By applying amplitude amplification at Step k, we get the cost

$$
\mathcal{O}\left(\sqrt{|L|}\sqrt{\prod_{i=1}^{k-2}\max\{|L(\mathbf{x}_1,\ldots,\mathbf{x}_i)|,1\}}\right),
$$

for finding one k-clique. Multiplying the above expression by $\widetilde{\mathcal{O}}(|L|)$ gives the total complexity for finding $\Theta(|L|)$ k-cliques. This matches the complexity of Algorithm 4.1, Eq. (9), for balanced configurations for all k.

In the full version [KMPR19, App. C] we show how to adapt the above to unbalanced configurations and achieve the same complexity as Algorithm 4.1.

6   Quantum Configuration Search via Triangle Listing

Given the phrasing of the configuration problem as a clique listing problem in graphs, we restrict our attention to the balanced $k = 3$ case and appeal to recent work on triangle finding in graphs. Let the notation be as in Sect. 5, and in particular recall Eq. (12) then a triangle represents a solution to the configuration problem.

The operations counted in the works discussed here are queries to an oracle that returns whether an edge exists between two vertices in our graph. While, in the case of [BdWD+01], it is simple to translate this cost into a time complexity, for the algorithms which use more complex quantum data structures [Gal14, LGN17] it is not. In particular, the costs of computing various auxiliary databases from certain sets is not captured in the total query cost.

The quantum triangle finding works we consider are [BdWD+01, Gal14, LGN17]. In [BdWD+01] a simple algorithm based on nested Grover search and amplitude amplification is given which finds a triangle in $\mathcal{O}(n+\sqrt{nm})$ queries to O_G. For sufficiently sparse graphs G, with sparsity measured as $m = \mathcal{O}(n^c)$ and G becoming more sparse as c decreases, this complexity attains the optimal $\Omega(n)$. This is the algorithm extended in Sect. 5. In [Gal14] an algorithm is given that finds a triangle in $\widetilde{\mathcal{O}}(n^{5/4})$ queries to O_G. This complexity has no dependence on sparsity and is the currently best known result for generic graphs. Finally in [LGN17] an interpolation between the two previous results is given as the sparsity of the graph increases.

Theorem 7 ([LGN17, **Theorem 1**]). *There exists a quantum algorithm that solves, with high probability, the triangle finding problem over graphs of n vertices and m edges with query complexity*

$$
\begin{cases}
\mathcal{O}(n + \sqrt{nm}) & \text{if } 0 \le m \le n^{7/6} \\
\widetilde{\mathcal{O}}(nm^{1/14}) & \text{if } n^{7/6} \le m \le n^{7/5} \\
\widetilde{\mathcal{O}}(n^{1/6}m^{1/3}) & \text{if } n^{7/5} \le m \le n^{3/2} \\
\widetilde{\mathcal{O}}(n^{23/30}m^{4/15}) & \text{if } n^{3/2} \le m \le n^{13/8} \\
\widetilde{\mathcal{O}}(n^{59/60}m^{2/15}) & \text{if } n^{13/8} \le m \le n^{2}.
\end{cases}
$$

More specifically it is shown that for $c \in (7/6, 2)$ a better complexity can be achieved than shown in [BdWD+01, Gal14]. Moreover at the end points the two previous algorithms are recovered; [BdWD+01] for $c \le 7/6$ and [Gal14] for $c = 2$. We recall that these costs are in the query model, and that for $c > 7/6$, where we do not recover [BdWD+01], we do not convert them into time complexity.

We explore two directions that follow from the above embedding of the configuration problem into a graph. The first is the most naïve, we simply calculate the sparsity regime (as per [LGN17]) that the graph, constructed as in Sect. 5.1, lies in.

The second splits our list into triples of distinct sublists and considers graphs formed from the union of said triples of sublists. The sublists are parameterised such that the sparsity and the expected number of triangles in these new graphs can be altered.

6.1 Naïve Triangle Finding

With $G = (V, E)$ and n, m as in (12), we expect to have

$$
m = \mathcal{O}\left(n^{2+\delta}\right) = \mathcal{O}\left(n^{1.5500}\right), \quad \delta = \log(8/9)/\log(3\sqrt{3}/4).
$$

Therefore finding a single triangle takes $\widetilde{\mathcal{O}}(n^{23/30}m^{4/15}) = \widetilde{\mathcal{O}}\left(n^{1.1799}\right)$ queries to O_G [LGN17]. If, to list the expected $\Theta(n)$ triangles, we have to repeat this algorithm $\widetilde{\mathcal{O}}(n)$ times this leads to a total O_G query complexity of $\widetilde{\mathcal{O}}(n^{2.1799}) = 2^{0.4114d+o(d)}$ which is not competitive with classical algorithms [HK17] or the approach of Sect. 5.

6.2 Altering the Sparsity

Let n remain as in Eq. (12) and $\gamma \in (0,1)$ be such that we consider $\Gamma = n^{1-\gamma}$ disjoint sublists of L, $\ell_1, \ldots, \ell_\Gamma$, each with $n' = n^\gamma$ elements. There are $\mathcal{O}(n^{3(1-\gamma)})$ triples of such sublists, (ℓ_i, ℓ_j, ℓ_k), with i, j, k pairwise not equal and the union of the sublists within one triple, $\ell_{ijk} = \ell_i \cup \ell_j \cup \ell_k$, has size $\mathcal{O}(n')$. Let $G_{ijk} = (\ell_{ijk}, E_{ijk})$ with $(\mathbf{x}_1, \mathbf{x}_2)$ in $\ell_{ijk} \times \ell_{ijk}$, $(\mathbf{x}_1, \mathbf{x}_2) \in E_{ijk} \iff |\langle \mathbf{x}_1, \mathbf{x}_2 \rangle + 1/3| \le \varepsilon$. Using Theorem 5, each G_{ijk} is expected to have

$$
m' = \mathcal{O}\left(|\ell_{ijk}| |\ell_{ijk}(x_1)|\right) = \mathcal{O}\left((n')^2(8/9)^{d/2}\right) = \mathcal{O}\left(n^{2\gamma}(8/9)^{d/2}\right)
$$

edges. By listing all triangles in all G_{ijk} we list all triangles in G, and as n is chosen to expect $\Theta(n)$ triangles in G, we have sufficiently many solutions for the underlying k-List problem. We expect, by Theorem 5

$$|\ell_{ijk}||\ell_{ijk}(\mathbf{x}_1)||\ell_{ijk}(\mathbf{x}_1,\mathbf{x}_2)| = |\ell_{ijk}| \left(|\ell_{ijk}|(8/9)^{d/2}\right)\left(|\ell_{ijk}|(2/3)^{d/2}\right)$$
$$= \mathcal{O}(n^{3\gamma})(16/27)^{d/2} = \mathcal{O}(n^{3\gamma-2})$$

triangles per ℓ_{ijk}. We must at least test each ℓ_{ijk} once, even if $\mathcal{O}(n^{3\gamma-2})$ is subconstant. The sparsity of ℓ_{ijk} given γ is calculated as

$$m' = \mathcal{O}\left((n')^{2+\beta(\gamma)}\right), \ \beta(\gamma) = \frac{\log(8/9)}{\gamma\log(3\sqrt{3}/4)}.$$

For given γ the number of ℓ_{ijk} to test is $\mathcal{O}(n^{3(1-\gamma)})$, the number of triangles to list per ℓ_{ijk} is $\mathcal{O}(n^{3\gamma-2})$ – we always perform at least one triangle finding attempt and assume listing them all takes $\widetilde{\mathcal{O}}(n^{3\gamma-2})$ repeats – and we are in the sparsity regime $c(\gamma) = 2 + \beta(\gamma)$ [LGN17]. Let a,b represent the exponents of n', m' respectively[8] in Theorem 7 given by $m' = (n')^{c(\gamma)}$. We therefore minimise, for $\gamma \in (0,1)$, the exponent of n in $\mathcal{O}(n^{3(1-\gamma)}) \cdot \widetilde{\mathcal{O}}(n^{3\gamma-2}) \cdot \widetilde{\mathcal{O}}((n')^a (m')^b)$,

$$3(1-\gamma) + \max\{0, 3\gamma-2\} + a\gamma + \left(2\gamma + \frac{\log(8/9)}{\log(3\sqrt{3}/4)}\right)b.$$

The minimal query complexity of $n^{1.7298+o(d)} = 2^{0.326d+o(d)}$ is achieved at $\gamma = \frac{2}{3}$.

The above method leaves open the possibility of finding the same triangle multiple times. In particular if a triangle exists in $G_{ij} = (\ell_{ij}, E_{ij})$, with ℓ_{ij} and E_{ij} defined analogously to ℓ_{ijk} and E_{ijk}, then it will be found in G_{ijk} for all k, that is $\mathcal{O}(n^{1-\gamma})$ many times. Worse yet is the case where a triangle exists in $G_i = (\ell_i, E_i)$ where it will be found $\mathcal{O}(n^{2(1-\gamma)})$ times. However, in both cases the total number of rediscoveries of the same triangle does not affect the asymptotic complexity of this approach. Indeed in the ℓ_{ij} case this number is the product $\mathcal{O}(n^{2(1-\gamma)}) \cdot \mathcal{O}(n^{3\gamma} \cdot (8/9)^{d/2}) \cdot \mathcal{O}(n^{1-\gamma}) = \mathcal{O}(n)$, the product of the number of ℓ_{ij}, the number of triangles[9] per ℓ_{ij} and the number of rediscoveries per triangle in ℓ_{ij} respectively. Similarly, this value is $\mathcal{O}(n)$ in the ℓ_i case and as we are required to list $\mathcal{O}(n)$ triangles the asymptotic complexity remains the same.

7   Parallelising Quantum Configuration Search

In this section we deviate slightly from the k-List problem and the configuration framework and target SVP directly. On input we receive $\{\mathbf{b}_1,\ldots,\mathbf{b}_d\} \subset \mathbb{R}^d$, a basis of $\mathcal{L}(B)$. Our algorithm finds and outputs a short vector from $\mathcal{L}(B)$. As in all the algorithms described above, we will be satisfied with an approximation to the shortest vector and with heuristic analysis.

---

[8] Note that we are considering G_{ijk} rather than G here, hence the $n \leftrightarrow n', m \leftrightarrow m'$ notation change.

[9] Given that $|\ell_i| = n^\gamma, |\ell_{ij}| = 2n^\gamma, |\ell_{ijk}| = 3n^\gamma$ the expected numbers of triangles differ only by a constant.

We describe an algorithm that can be implemented using a quantum circuit of width $\widetilde{\mathcal{O}}(N)$ and depth $\widetilde{\mathcal{O}}(\sqrt{N})$, where $N = 2^{0.2075d+o(d)}$. We therefore require our input and output to be less than $\widetilde{\mathcal{O}}(\sqrt{N})$, and if we were to phrase the 2-Sieve algorithm as a 2-List problem we would not be able to read in and write out the data. Our algorithm uses $\text{poly}(d)$ classical memory. For the analysis, we make the same heuristic assumptions as in the original 2-Sieve work of Nguyen–Vidick [NV08].

All the vectors encountered by the algorithm (except for the final measurement) are kept in quantum memory. Recall that for a pair of normalised vectors $\mathbf{x}_1, \mathbf{x}_2$ to form a "good" pair, i.e. to satisfy $\|\mathbf{x}_1 \pm \mathbf{x}_2\| \leq 1$, it must hold that $|\langle \mathbf{x}_1, \mathbf{x}_2 \rangle| \geq \frac{1}{2}$. The algorithm described below is the quantum parallel version of 2-Sieve. Each step is analysed in the subsequent lemmas.

Algorithm 7.1. A parallel quantum algorithm for 2-Sieve

Input: $\{\mathbf{b}_1, \ldots, \mathbf{b}_d\} \subset \mathbb{R}^d$ a lattice basis
Output: $\mathbf{v} \in \mathcal{L}(B)$, a short vector from $\mathcal{L}(B)$

1: Set $N \leftarrow 2^{0.2075d+o(d)}$ and set $\lambda = \Theta(\sqrt{d} \cdot \det(B)^{1/d})$ the target length.
2: Generate a list $L_1 \leftarrow \{\mathbf{x}_1, \ldots, \mathbf{x}_N\}$ of lattice vectors using an efficient lattice sampling procedure, e.g. [Kle00].
3: Construct a list $L_2 \leftarrow \{\mathbf{x}'_1, \ldots, \mathbf{x}'_N\}$ such that $|\langle \mathbf{x}_i, \mathbf{x}'_i \rangle| \geq 1/2$ for $\mathbf{x}'_i \in L_1$. If no such $\mathbf{x}'_i \in L_1$ exists, set $\mathbf{x}'_i \leftarrow \mathbf{0}$.
4: Construct a list $L_3 \leftarrow \{\mathbf{y}_i : \mathbf{y}_i \leftarrow \min\{\|\mathbf{x}_i \pm \mathbf{x}'_i\|\}\}$ for all $i \leq N\}$
5: Swap the labels L_1, L_3. Reinitialise L_2 and L_3 to the zero state by transferring their contents to auxiliary memory.
6: Repeat Steps 3–5 $\text{poly}(d)$ times.
7: Output a vector from L_1 of Euclidean norm less than λ.

Several remarks about Algorithm 7.1.

1. The bound on the repetition factor on Step 6 is, as in classical 2-Sieve algorithms, appropriately set to achieve the desired norm of the returned vectors. In particular, it suffices to repeat Steps 2–5 $\text{poly}(d)$ times [NV08].
2. In classical 2-Sieve algorithms, if $\mathbf{x}_i$ does not have a match $\mathbf{x}'_i$, it is simply discarded. Quantumly we cannot just discard an element from the system, so we keep it as the zero vector. This is why, as opposed to the classical setting, we keep our lists of exactly the same size throughout all the iterations.
3. The target norm λ is appropriately set to the desired length. The algorithm can be easily adapted to output several, say T, short vectors of $\mathcal{L}(B)$ by repeating Step 7 T times.

Theorem 8. *Given on input a lattice basis $\mathcal{L}(B) = \{\mathbf{b}_1, \ldots, \mathbf{b}_d\} \subset \mathbb{R}^d$, Algorithm 7.1 heuristically solves the shortest vector problem on $\mathcal{L}(B)$ with constant success probability. The algorithm can be implemented using a uniform family of quantum circuits of width $\widetilde{\mathcal{O}}(N)$ and depth $\widetilde{\mathcal{O}}(\sqrt{N})$, where $N = 2^{0.2075d+o(d)}$.*

We prove the above theorem in several lemmas. Here we only give proof sketches and defer more detailed proofs to the full version [KMPR19, App. D]. In the first lemma we explain the process of generating a database of vectors of size N having N processors. The main routines, Steps 3–5, are analysed in Lemma 2. Finally, in Step 7 we use Grover's algorithm to amplify the amplitudes of small norm vectors.

Lemma 1. *Step (2) of Algorithm 7.1 can be implemented using a uniform family of quantum circuits of width $\widetilde{\mathcal{O}}(N)$ and depth $\operatorname{poly} \log(N)$.*

Lemma 2. *Steps (3–5) of Algorithm 7.1 can be implemented using a uniform family of quantum circuits of width $\widetilde{\mathcal{O}}(N)$ and depth $\widetilde{\mathcal{O}}(\sqrt{N})$.*

Lemma 3. *Step (7) of the Algorithm 7.1 can be implemented using a uniform family of quantum circuits of width $\widetilde{\mathcal{O}}(N)$ and depth $\widetilde{\mathcal{O}}(\sqrt{N})$.*

Before we present our proofs for the above lemmas, we briefly explain our computational model. We assume that each input vector $\mathbf{b}_i$ is encoded in $\bar{d} = poly(d)$ qubits and we say that it is stored in a single register. We also consider the circuit model and assume we have at our disposal a set of elementary gates – Toffoli, and all 1-qubit unitary gates (including the Hadamard and Pauli X), i.e. a universal gate set that can be implemented efficiently. We further assume that any parallel composition of unitaries can be implemented simultaneously. For brevity, we will often want to interpret (computations consisting of) parallel processes to be running on parallel processors. We emphasise that this is inconsequential to the computation and our analysis. However, thinking this way greatly helps to understand the physical motivation and convey the intuition behind the computation.

Proof sketch of Lemma 1. The idea is to copy the *cell* of *registers*, $|B\rangle$, encoding the basis $B = \{\mathbf{b}_1, \ldots, \mathbf{b}_d\}$ to N processors, where each processor is equipped with $\operatorname{poly} \log(N)$ qubits. The state $|B\rangle$ itself is a classical (diagonal) state made of $\bar{d}^2 = \mathcal{O}(\log^2(N))$ qubits. To copy B to all N processors, it takes $\lceil \log(N) \rceil$ steps each consisting of a cascade of CNOT operations.

Each of the processors samples a single $\mathbf{x}_i$ using a randomised sampling algorithm, e.g. [Kle00]. This is an efficient classical procedure that can be implemented by a reversible circuit of $poly(d)$ depth and width. The exact same circuit can be used to realise the sampling on a quantum processor.

Each processor i, having computed the $\mathbf{x}_i$, now keeps $\mathbf{x}_i$ locally and also copies it to a distinguished cell L1. The state of the system can be described as

$$|\mathbf{x}_1\rangle_{\mathrm{P}_1} |\mathbf{x}_2\rangle_{\mathrm{P}_2} \ldots |\mathbf{x}_N\rangle_{\mathrm{P}_N} |\mathbf{x}_1, \mathbf{x}_2 \ldots \mathbf{x}_N\rangle_{\mathrm{L}1} |\text{ancilla}\rangle$$

where P_i is the register in possession of processor i. The total depth of the circuit is $\mathcal{O}(\log(N))$ to copy plus $\operatorname{poly} \log(N)$ to sample plus $\mathcal{O}(1)$ to copy to the list L_1. Each operation is carried out by N processors and uses $\operatorname{poly} \log(N)$ qubits. Thus the total depth of a quantum circuit implementing Step (2) is $\operatorname{poly} \log(N)$ and its width is $\widetilde{\mathcal{O}}(N)$. $\qquad\square$

Proof sketch of Lemma 2. The key idea to construct the list L_2 is to let each processor P_i, which already has a copy of $|\mathbf{x}_i\rangle$, $\mathbf{x}_i \in L_1$, search through L_1 (now stored in the distinguished cell L1) to find a vector $\mathbf{x}_i'$ such that $|\langle \mathbf{x}_i, \mathbf{x}_i' \rangle| \geq 1/2$ (if no such $\mathbf{x}_i' \in L_1$, set $\mathbf{x}_i' = 0$). The key ingredient is to parallelise this search, i.e. let all processors do the search at the same time. The notion of parallelisation is however only a (correct) interpretation of the operational meaning of the unitary transformations. It is important to stress that we make no assumptions about how data structures are stored, accessed and processed, beyond what is allowed by the axioms of quantum theory and the framework of the circuit model.

For each processor i, we define a function $f_i(\mathbf{y}) = 1$ if $|\langle \mathbf{x}_i, \mathbf{y}\rangle| \geq 1/2$ and 0 otherwise; and let W_f and D_f be the maximal width and depth of a unitary implementing any f_i. It is possible to implement a quantum circuit of $\widetilde{\mathcal{O}}(N \cdot W_f)$ width and $\widetilde{\mathcal{O}}(\sqrt{N} D_f)$ depth that can in parallel find solutions to all $f_i, 1 \leq i \leq N$ [BBG+13]. This quantum circuit searches through the list in parallel, i.e. each processor can simultaneously access the memory and search. Note, f_i is really a reduced transformation. The "purification" of f_i is a two parameter function $f \colon L_1 \times L_1 \to \{0,1\}$. However, in each processor i, one of the inputs is "fixed and hardcoded" to be $\mathbf{x}_i$. The function f itself admits an efficient implementation in the size of the inputs, since this is the inner product function and also has a classical reversible circuit consisting of Toffoli and NOT gates. Once the search is done, it is expected with probability greater than $1 - 2^{-\Omega(d)}$ that each processor i will have found an index j_i, s.t. $|\langle \mathbf{x}_i, \mathbf{x}_{j_i}\rangle| \geq 1/2$, $\mathbf{x}_i, \mathbf{x}_{j_i} \in L_1$. One can always check if the processor found a solution, otherwise the search can be repeated a constant number of times. If none of the searches found a "good" j_i, we set $\mathbf{x}_{j_i} = \mathbf{0}$. Else, if any of the searches succeed, we keep that index j_i.

At this point we have a virtual list L_2, which consists of all indices j_i. We create a list L_3 in another distinguished cell, by asking each processor to compute $\mathbf{y}_i^+ = \mathbf{x}_i + \mathbf{x}_{j_i}$ and $\mathbf{y}_i^- = \mathbf{x}_i - \mathbf{x}_{j_i}$ and copy into the ith register the shorter of $\mathbf{y}_i^+$ and $\mathbf{y}_i^-$, in the Euclidean length. The state of the system now is,

$$|\mathbf{x}_1\rangle_{P1} \cdots |\mathbf{x}_N\rangle_{PN} |\mathbf{y}_1\rangle_{P1} \cdots |\mathbf{y}_L\rangle_{PN} |\mathbf{x}_1 \ldots \mathbf{x}_N\rangle_{L1} |\mathbf{y}_1 \ldots \mathbf{y}_N\rangle_{L3} |\text{ancilla}\rangle.$$

A swap between qubits say, S and R, is just $CNOT_{SR} \circ CNOT_{RS} \circ CNOT_{SR}$, and thus the Swap in Step 5 between L_1 and L_2 can be done with a depth 3 circuit. Finally reinitialise the lists L_2 and L_3 by swapping them with two registers of equal size that are all initialised to zero. This unloads the data from the main memories (L2, L3) and enables processors to reuse them for the next iteration.

The total depth of the circuit is $\widetilde{\mathcal{O}}(\sqrt{N})$ (to perform the parallel search for "good" indices j_i), $\operatorname{poly}\log N$ (to compute the elements of the new list L_3 and copy them), and $\mathcal{O}(1)$ (to swap the content in memory registers). Thus, in total we have constructed a circuit of $\widetilde{\mathcal{O}}(\sqrt{N})$ depth and $\widetilde{\mathcal{O}}(N)$ width. $\square$

Proof sketch of Lemma 3. Given a database of vectors of size N and a norm threshold λ, finding a vector from the database of Euclidean norm less than λ amounts to Grover's search over the database. It can be done with a quantum circuit of depth $\widetilde{\mathcal{O}}(\sqrt{N})$. It could happen that the threshold λ is set to be too small, in which case Grover's search returns a random element form the database. In that case, we repeat the whole algorithm with an increased value for λ. After $\Theta(1)$ repetitions, we heuristically obtain a short vector from $\mathcal{L}(B)$.   □

Proof sketch of Theorem 8. As established from the lemmas above, each of Step 2, Steps 3–5 and Step 7 can be realised using a family of quantum circuits of depth and width (at most) $\widetilde{\mathcal{O}}(\sqrt{N})$ and $\widetilde{\mathcal{O}}(N)$ respectively. However, Steps 3–5 run $\mathcal{O}(\mathrm{poly}(d))$ times, thus the total depth of the circuit now goes up by at most a multiplicative factor of $\mathcal{O}(\mathrm{poly}(d)) = \mathcal{O}(\mathrm{poly}\log(N))$. The total depth and width of a circuit implementing Algorithm 7.1 remains as $\widetilde{\mathcal{O}}(\sqrt{N})$ and $\widetilde{\mathcal{O}}(N)$ respectively as $\widetilde{\mathcal{O}}$ notation suppresses subexponential factors.   □

7.1   Distributed Configuration Search: Classical Analogue

Algorithm 7.1 should be compared with a classical model where there are $N = 2^{0.2075d+o(d)}$ computing nodes, each equipped with $\mathrm{poly}(d)$ memory. It suffices for these nodes to have a nearest neighbour architecture, where node i is connected to nodes $i-1$ and $i+1$, and arranged like beads in a necklace. We cost one time unit for $\mathrm{poly}(d)$ bits sent from any node to an adjacent node. A comparable distributed classical algorithm would be where each node, i, receives the basis B and samples a vector $\mathbf{v}_i$. In any given round, node i sends $\tilde{\mathbf{v}}_i$ to node $i+1$ and receives $\tilde{\mathbf{v}}_{i-1}$ from node $i-1$ (in the first round $\tilde{\mathbf{v}}_i := \mathbf{v}_i$). Then each node checks if the vector pair $(\mathbf{v}_i, \tilde{\mathbf{v}}_{i-1})$ gives a shorter sum or difference. If yes, it computes $\mathbf{v}_i^{(2)} = \min\{\mathbf{v}_i \pm \tilde{\mathbf{v}}_{i-1}\}$ and sets $\tilde{\mathbf{v}}_i := \mathbf{v}_{i-1}$. After N rounds every node i has compared their vector $\mathbf{v}_i$ with all N vectors sampled. The vectors $\mathbf{v}_i$ can be discarded and the new round begins with $\mathbf{v}_i^{(2)}$ being the new vector. The process is repeated $\mathrm{poly}(d)$ many times leading to $\mathcal{O}(N) \cdot \mathrm{poly}(d)$ time steps. Thus this distributed algorithm needs $\widetilde{\mathcal{O}}(N) = 2^{0.2075d+o(d)}$ time.

Acknowledgements. Most of this work was done while EK was at ENS de Lyon, supported by ERC Starting Grant ERC-2013-StG-335086-LATTAC and by the European Union PROMETHEUS project (Horizon 2020 Research and Innovation Program, grant 780701). EM is supported by the Swedish Research Counsel (grant 2015-04528) and the Swedish Foundation for Strategic Research (grant RIT17-0005). EWP is supported by the EPSRC and the UK government (grant EP/P009301/1). SRM is supported by the Clarendon Scholarship, Google-DeepMind Scholarship and Keble Sloane Robinson Award.

We are grateful to the organisers of the Oxford Post-Quantum Cryptography Workshop held at the Mathematical Institute, University of Oxford, March 18–22, 2019, for arranging the session on Quantum Cryptanalysis, where this work began. We would like to acknowledge the fruitful discussions we had with Gottfried Herold during this session.

Finally, we would like to thank the AsiaCrypt'19 reviewers, whose constructive comments helped to improve the quality of this paper.

References

[AD97] Ajtai, M., Dwork, C.: A public-key cryptosystem with worst-case/average-case equivalence. In: STOC 1997, pp. 284–293 (1997)

[ADH+19] Albrecht, M.R., Ducas, L., Herold, G., Kirshanova, E., Postlethwaite, E.W., Stevens, M.: The general sieve kernel and new records in lattice reduction. In: Ishai, Y., Rijmen, V. (eds.) EUROCRYPT 2019. LNCS, vol. 11477, pp. 717–746. Springer, Cham (2019). https://doi.org/10.1007/978-3-030-17656-3_25

[ADRSD15] Aggarwal, D., Dadush, D., Regev, O., Stephens-Davidowitz, N.: Solving the shortest vector problem in 2^n time using discrete Gaussian sampling: extended abstract. In: STOC 2015, pp. 733–742 (2015)

[AGJO+15] Arunachalam, S., Gheorghiu, V., Jochym-O'Connor, T., Mosca, M., Srinivasan, P.V.: On the robustness of bucket brigade quantum RAM. New J. Phys. **17**(12), 123010 (2015)

[AKS01] Ajtai, M., Kumar, R., Sivakumar, D.: A sieve algorithm for the shortest lattice vector problem. In: Proceedings of the 33rd Annual ACM Symposium on Theory of Computing, STOC 2001, pp. 601–610 (2001)

[ANS18] Aono, Y., Nguyen, P.Q., Shen, Y.: Quantum lattice enumeration and tweaking discrete pruning. In: Peyrin, T., Galbraith, S. (eds.) ASIACRYPT 2018. LNCS, vol. 11272, pp. 405–434. Springer, Cham (2018). https://doi.org/10.1007/978-3-030-03326-2_14

[BBG+13] Beals, R., et al.: Efficient distributed quantum computing. Proc. R. Soc. A **469**(2153), 20120686 (2013)

[BBHT98] Boyer, M., Brassard, G., Høyer, P., Tapp, A.: Tight bounds on quantum searching. Fortschritte der Physik **46**(4–5), 493–505 (1998)

[BDGL16] Becker, A., Ducas, L., Gama, N., Laarhoven, T.: New directions in nearest neighbor searching with applications to lattice sieving. In: Proceedings of the Twenty-Seventh Annual ACM-SIAM Symposium on Discrete Algorithms, SODA 2016, pp. 10–24 (2016)

[BdWD+01] Buhrman, H., et al.: Quantum algorithms for element distinctness. In: Proceedings of the 16th Annual Conference on Computational Complexity, CCC 2001, Washington, DC, USA, pp. 131–137. IEEE Computer Society (2001)

[BGJ14] Becker, A., Gama, N., Joux, A.: A sieve algorithm based on overlattices. LMS J. Comput. Math. **17**(A), 49–70 (2014)

[BHMT02] Brassard, G., Høyer, P., Mosca, M., Tapp, A.: Quantum amplitude amplification and estimation. In: Quantum Computation and Quantum Information: A Millennium Volume, vol. 305, pp. 53–74 (2002). Earlier version in arxiv:quant-ph/0005055

[BHT97] Brassard, G., Høyer, P., Tapp, A.: Quantum algorithm for the collision problem. ACM SIGACT News (Cryptology Column) **28**, 14–19 (1997)

[BLS16] Bai, S., Laarhoven, T., Stehlé, D.: Tuple lattice sieving. LMS J. Comput. Math. **19**, 146–162 (2016)

[CCL17] Chen, Y., Chung, K.-M., Lai, C.-Y.: Space-efficient classical and quantum algorithms for the shortest vector problem. arXiv e-prints, August 2017

[CDW17] Cramer, R., Ducas, L., Wesolowski, B.: Short Stickelberger class relations and application to Ideal-SVP. In: Coron, J.-S., Nielsen, J.B. (eds.) EUROCRYPT 2017. LNCS, vol. 10210, pp. 324–348. Springer, Cham (2017). https://doi.org/10.1007/978-3-319-56620-7_12

[DRS14] Dadush, D., Regev, O., Stephens-Davidowitz, N.: On the closest vector problem with a distance guarantee. In: 2014 IEEE 29th Conference on Computational Complexity (CCC), pp. 98–109, June 2014

[Duc18] Ducas, L.: Shortest vector from lattice sieving: a few dimensions for free. In: Nielsen, J.B., Rijmen, V. (eds.) EUROCRYPT 2018. LNCS, vol. 10820, pp. 125–145. Springer, Cham (2018). https://doi.org/10.1007/978-3-319-78381-9_5

[Gal14] Gall, F.L.: Improved quantum algorithm for triangle finding via combinatorial arguments. In: 2014 IEEE 55th Annual Symposium on Foundations of Computer Science, pp. 216–225, October 2014

[GLM08] Giovannetti, V., Lloyd, S., Maccone, L.: Quantum random access memory. Phys. Rev. Lett. **100**, 160501 (2008)

[GNR10] Gama, N., Nguyen, P.Q., Regev, O.: Lattice enumeration using extreme pruning. In: Gilbert, H. (ed.) EUROCRYPT 2010. LNCS, vol. 6110, pp. 257–278. Springer, Heidelberg (2010). https://doi.org/10.1007/978-3-642-13190-5_13

[Gro96] Grover, L.K.: A fast quantum mechanical algorithm for database search. In: Proceedings of the Twenty-eighth Annual ACM Symposium on Theory of Computing, STOC 1996, pp. 212–219 (1996)

[HK17] Herold, G., Kirshanova, E.: Improved algorithms for the approximate k-list problem in Euclidean norm. In: PKC 2017, pp. 16–40 (2017)

[HKL18] Herold, G., Kirshanova, E., Laarhoven, T.: Speed-ups and time-memory trade-offs for tuple lattice sieving. In: Public-Key Cryptography - PKC 2018, pp. 407–436 (2018)

[Kan83] Kannan, R.: Improved algorithms for integer programming and related lattice problems. In: Proceedings of the Fifteenth Annual ACM Symposium on Theory of Computing, STOC 1983, pp. 193–206 (1983)

[Kle00] Klein, P.N.: Finding the closest lattice vector when it's unusually close. In: SODA, pp. 937–941 (2000)

[KLM07] Kaye, P., Laflamme, R., Mosca, M.: An Introduction to Quantum Computing. Oxford University Press, Oxford (2007)

[KMPR19] Kirshanova, E., Mårtensson, E., Postlethwaite, E.W., Moulik, S.R.: Quantum algorithms for the approximate k-list problem and their application to lattice sieving. Cryptology ePrint Archive, Report 2019/1016 (2019). https://eprint.iacr.org/2019/1016

[Kup13] Kuperberg, G.: Another subexponential-time quantum algorithm for the dihedral hidden subgroup problem. In: TQC-2013, pp. 20–34 (2013)

[Laa15] Laarhoven, T.: Search problems in cryptography. PhD thesis, Eindhoven University of Technology (2015)

[LGN17] Le Gall, F., Nakajima, S.: Quantum algorithm for triangle finding in sparse graphs. Algorithmica **79**(3), 941–959 (2017)

[LMvdP15] Laarhoven, T., Mosca, M., van de Pol, J.: Finding shortest lattice vectors faster using quantum search. Designs, Codes and Cryptography **77**(2), 375–400 (2015)

[Map] Maplesoft, a division of Waterloo Maple Inc., Waterloo, Ontario. Standard worksheet interface, Maple 2016.0, feb. frm[o]-7 2016

[Mon18] Montanaro, A.: Quantum-walk speedup of backtracking algorithms. Theory Comput. **14**(15), 1–24 (2018)

[MV10]   Micciancio, D., Voulgaris, P.: Faster exponential time algorithms for the shortest vector problem. In: Proceedings of the Twenty-First Annual ACM-SIAM Symposium on Discrete Algorithms, SODA 2010, pp. 1468–1480 (2010)

[NV08]   Nguyen, P.Q., Vidick, T.: Sieve algorithms for the shortest vector problem are practical. J. Math. Cryptology **2**(2), 181–207 (2008)

[PMHS19] Pellet-Mary, A., Hanrot, G., Stehlé, D.: Approx-SVP in ideal lattices with pre-processing. In: Ishai, Y., Rijmen, V. (eds.) EUROCRYPT 2019. LNCS, vol. 11477, pp. 685–716. Springer, Cham (2019). https://doi.org/10.1007/978-3-030-17656-3_24

[Reg05] Regev, O.: On lattices, learning with errors, random linear codes, and cryptography. In: Proceedings of the Thirty-Seventh Annual ACM Symposium on Theory of Computing, STOC 2005, pp. 84–93 (2005)

[Reg09] Regev, O.: Lecture notes: lattices in computer science (2009). http://www.cims.nyu.edu/~regev/teaching/lattices_fall_2009/index.html. Accessed 30 Apr 2019

[TKH18] Teruya, T., Kashiwabara, K., Hanaoka, G.: Fast lattice basis reduction suitable for massive parallelization and its application to the shortest vector problem. In: PKC 2018, pp. 437–460 (2018)

Quantum Attacks Without Superposition Queries: The Offline Simon's Algorithm

Xavier Bonnetain[1,3]([✉]), Akinori Hosoyamada[2,4], María Naya-Plasencia[1],
Yu Sasaki[2], and André Schrottenloher[1]

[1] Inria, Paris, France
{xavier.bonnetain,maria.naya_plasencia,andre.schrottenloher}@inria.fr
[2] NTT Secure Platform Laboratories, Tokyo, Japan
{hosoyamada.akinori,sasaki.yu}@lab.ntt.co.jp
[3] Collège Doctoral, Sorbonne Université, 75005 Paris, France
[4] Nagoya University, Nagoya, Japan

Abstract. In symmetric cryptanalysis, the model of superposition queries has led to surprising results, with many constructions being broken in polynomial time thanks to Simon's period-finding algorithm. But the practical implications of these attacks remain blurry. In contrast, the results obtained so far for a quantum adversary making classical queries only are less impressive.

In this paper, we introduce a new quantum algorithm which uses Simon's subroutines in a novel way. We manage to leverage the algebraic structure of cryptosystems in the context of a quantum attacker limited to classical queries and offline quantum computations. We obtain improved quantum-time/classical-data tradeoffs with respect to the current literature, while using only as much hardware requirements (quantum and classical) as a standard exhaustive search with Grover's algorithm. In particular, we are able to break the Even-Mansour construction in quantum time $\tilde{O}(2^{n/3})$, with $O(2^{n/3})$ classical queries and $O(n^2)$ qubits only. In addition, we improve some previous superposition attacks by reducing the data complexity from exponential to polynomial, with the same time complexity.

Our approach can be seen in two complementary ways: *reusing* superposition queries during the iteration of a search using Grover's algorithm, or alternatively, removing the memory requirement in some quantum attacks based on a collision search, thanks to their algebraic structure.

We provide a list of cryptographic applications, including the Even-Mansour construction, the FX construction, some Sponge authenticated modes of encryption, and many more.

Keywords: Simon's algorithm · Classical queries · Symmetric cryptography · Quantum cryptanalysis · Even-Mansour construction · FX construction

© International Association for Cryptologic Research 2019
S. D. Galbraith and S. Moriai (Eds.): ASIACRYPT 2019, LNCS 11921, pp. 552–583, 2019.
https://doi.org/10.1007/978-3-030-34578-5_20

1 Introduction

Ever since Shor [39] introduced his celebrated quantum polynomial-time algorithm for solving factorization and Discrete Logarithms, both problems believed to be classically intractable, post-quantum cryptography has become a subject of wide interest. Indeed, the security of classical cryptosystems relies on computational assumptions, which until recently, were made with respect to classical adversaries; if quantum adversaries are to be taken into account, the landscape of security is bound to change dramatically.

While it is difficult to assert the precise power of quantum computers, which are yet to come, it is still possible to study quantum algorithms for cryptographic problems, and to estimate the computational cost of solving these problems for a quantum adversary. The ongoing project by NIST [35] for post-quantum *asymmetric* schemes aims to replace the current mostly used ones by new standards.

In *symmetric* cryptography, the impact of quantum computing seems, at first sight, much more limited. This is because the security of most of symmetric-key schemes is not predicated on structured problems. Symmetric-key schemes are required to be computed extremely efficiently, and designers must avoid such computationally expensive operations. Grover's quantum search algorithm [22], another cornerstone of quantum computing, speeds up by a quadratic factor exhaustive search procedures. This has led to the common saying that "doubling the key sizes" should ensure a similar level of post-quantum security.

However, the actual post-quantum security of symmetric-key schemes requires more delicate treatment. Recovering the secret key via exhaustive search is only one of all the possible approaches. The report of the National Academy of Sciences on the advent of quantum computing [34] also states that "it is possible that there is some currently unknown clever quantum attack" that would perform much better than Grover's algorithm. Indeed, cryptographers are making significant progress on quantum attackers with *superposition queries*, which break many symmetric-key schemes in polynomial time.

Quantum Generic Attacks in Q1 and Q2 Models. Quantum attacks can be mainly classified into two types [20,23,25], Q1 model and Q2 model, assuming different abilities for the attacker. In the Q1 model, attackers have an access to a quantum computer to perform any offline computation, while they are only allowed to make online queries in a classical manner. In the Q2 model, besides the offline quantum computation, attackers are allowed to make superposition queries to a quantum cryptographic oracle. Here, we briefly review previous results in these models to introduce the context of our results.

The Q2 model is particularly interesting as it yields some attacks with a very low cost. Kuwakado and Morii [29,30] showed that the Even-Mansour cipher and the three-round Feistel networks, classically proven secure if their underlying building blocks are ideal, were broken in polynomial time. This exponential speedup, the first concerning symmetric cryptography, was obtained thanks to Simon's algorithm [40] for recovering a Boolean hidden shift. Later on, more results have been obtained in this setting, with more generic constructions broken [24,31], and an exponential acceleration of *slide attacks*, which target ciphers with a self-similar structure. Versions of these attacks [6] for constructions with modular additions use Kuperberg's algorithm [27], allowing a better than quadratic speed-up. All these attacks, however, run in the model of *superposition queries*, which models a quantum adversary having some inherently quantum access to the primitives attacked. As such, they do not give any improvement when the adversary only has classical access.

Stated differently, the attacks in the Q1 model are particularly relevant due to their impact on current data communication technology. However, the quantum algorithms that have been exploited for building attacks in the Q1 model are very limited and have not allowed more than a quadratic speed-up. The most used algorithm is the simple quantum exhaustive search with Grover's algorithm. A possible direction is the collision finding algorithm that is often said to achieve "$2^{n/3}$ complexity" versus $2^{n/2}$ classically. However, even in this direction, there are several debatable points; basic quantum algorithms for finding collisions have massive quantum hardware requirements [9]. There is a quantum-hardware-friendly variant [12], but then the time complexity becomes suboptimal.

In summary, attacks using Simon's algorithm could achieve a very low complexity but could only be applied in the Q2 model, a very strong model. In contrast, attacks in the Q1 model are practically more relevant, but for now the obtained speed-ups were not surprising.

Another model to consider when designing quantum attacks is whether the attacker has or not a big amount of quantum memory available. Small quantum computers seem like the most plausible scenario, and therefore attacks needing a polynomial amount of qubits are more practically relevant. Therefore, the most *realistic* scenario is Q1 with small quantum memory.

Our Main Contribution. The breakthrough we present in this paper is the first application of Simon's algorithm [40] in the Q1 model, which requires significantly less than $\mathcal{O}\left(2^{n/2}\right)$ classical queries and offline quantum computations, only with $\mathsf{poly}(n)$ qubits, and no qRAM access (where n is the size of the secret). Namely, we remove the superposition queries in previous attacks. The new idea can be applied to a long list of ciphers and modes of operation. Let us illustrate the impact of our attacks by focusing on two applications:

The first application is the key recovery on the Even-Mansour construction, which is one of the simplest attacks using Simon's algorithm. Besides the polynomial time attacks in the Q2 model, Kuwakado and Morii also developed an attack in the Q1 model with $\mathcal{O}\left(2^{n/3}\right)$ classical queries, quantum computations, qubits, and classical memory [30]. The extension of this Q1 attack by Hosoyamada and Sasaki [23] recovers the key with $\mathcal{O}\left(2^{3n/7}\right)$ classical queries, $\mathcal{O}\left(2^{3n/7}\right)$ quantum computations, polynomially many qubits and $\mathcal{O}\left(2^{n/7}\right)$ classical memory (to balance classical queries and quantum computations). Our attack in the Q1 model only uses polynomially many qubits, yet only requires $\mathcal{O}\left(2^{n/3}\right)$ classical queries, $\mathcal{O}\left(n^3 2^{n/3}\right)$ quantum computations and $\mathsf{poly}(n)$ classical memory.

The second application is the key recovery on the FX-construction $FX_{k,k_{in},k_{out}}$, which computes a ciphertext c from a plaintext p by $c \leftarrow E_k(p \oplus k_{in}) \oplus k_{out}$, where E is a block cipher, k is an m-bit key and k_{in}, k_{out} are two n-bit keys. Leander and May proposed an attack in the Q2 model with $\mathcal{O}\left(n2^{m/2}\right)$ superposition queries, $\mathcal{O}\left(n^3 2^{m/2}\right)$ quantum computations, $\mathsf{poly}(n)$ qubits and $\mathsf{poly}(n)$ classical memory [31].[1] They combined Simon's algorithm and Grover's algorithm in a clever way, while it became inevitable to make queries in an adaptive manner. For the Q1 model, the meet-in-the-middle attack [23] can recover the key with $\mathcal{O}\left(2^{3(m+n)/7}\right)$ complexities. Our results can improve the previous attacks in two directions. One is to reduce the amount of superposition queries in the Q2 model to the polynomial order and convert the adaptive attack to a non-adaptive one. The other is to completely remove the superposition queries. The comparison of previous quantum attacks and our attacks on Even-Mansour and the FX construction is shown in Table 1. Other interesting complexity trade-offs are possible, as shown in detail in Sects. 4 and 5.

Table 1. Previous and new quantum attacks on Even-Mansour and FX, assuming that $m = \mathcal{O}(n)$.

Target	Model	Queries	Time	Q-memory	C-memory	Reference
EM	Q2	$\mathcal{O}(n)$	$\mathcal{O}(n^3)$	$\mathcal{O}(n)$	$\mathcal{O}(n^2)$	[30]
	Q1	$\mathcal{O}(2^{n/3})$	$\mathcal{O}(2^{n/3})$	$\mathcal{O}(2^{n/3})$	$\mathcal{O}(2^{n/3})$	[30]
	Q1	$\mathcal{O}(2^{3n/7})$	$\mathcal{O}(2^{3n/7})$	$\mathcal{O}(n)$	$\mathcal{O}(2^{n/7})$	[23]
	Q1	$\mathcal{O}(2^{n/3})$	$\mathcal{O}(n^3 2^{n/3})$	$\mathcal{O}(n^2)$	$\mathcal{O}(n)$	Section 5
FX	Q2	$\mathcal{O}(n2^{m/2})$	$\mathcal{O}(n^3 2^{m/2})$	$\mathcal{O}(n^2)$	0	[31]
	Q2	$\mathcal{O}(n)$	$\mathcal{O}(n^3 2^{m/2})$	$\mathcal{O}(n^2)$	$\mathcal{O}(n)$	Section 4
	Q1	$\mathcal{O}(2^{3(m+n)/7})$	$\mathcal{O}(2^{3(m+n)/7})$	$\mathcal{O}(n)$	$\mathcal{O}(2^{(m+n)/7})$	[23]
	Q1	$\mathcal{O}(2^{(m+n)/3})$	$\mathcal{O}(n^3 2^{(m+n)/3})$	$\mathcal{O}(n^2)$	$\mathcal{O}(n)$	Section 5

Our New Observation. Here we describe our new algorithm used in the Q1 model with the Even-Mansour construction as an example. Recall that the encryption E_{k_1,k_2} of the Even-Mansour construction is defined as $E_{k_1,k_2}(x) = P(x \oplus k_1) \oplus k_2$, where P is a public permutation and $k_1, k_2 \in \{0,1\}^n$ are the secret keys. Roughly speaking, our attack guesses $(2n/3)$-bit of k_1 (denoted by $k_1^{(2)}$ in Fig. 1) by using the Grover search, and checks if the guess is correct by applying Simon's algorithm to the remaining $(n/3)$-bit of k_1 (denoted by $k_1^{(1)}$ in Fig. 1). If we were in the Q2 model, we could recover k_1 using the technique by Leander and May [31] in time $\tilde{\mathcal{O}}(2^{n/3})$. However, their technique is not applicable in the Q1 setting since quantum queries are required.

Our core observation that realizes the above idea in the Q1 model is that, we can judge whether a function $f \oplus g$ has a period (i.e., we can apply Simon's algorithm) without any quantum query to g, if we have the quantum state

---

[1] Here we are assuming that m is in $\mathcal{O}(n)$, which is the case for usual block ciphers.

$|\psi_g\rangle := (\sum_x |x\rangle|g(x)\rangle)^{\otimes cn}$ (c is a small constant): If we have the quantum state $|\psi_g\rangle$, then we can make the quantum state $|\psi_{f \oplus g}\rangle := (\sum_x |x\rangle|(f \oplus g)(x)\rangle)^{\otimes cn}$ by making $\mathcal{O}(n)$ quantum queries to f. Once we obtain $|\psi_{f \oplus g}\rangle$, by applying the Hadamard operation $H^{\otimes n}$ to each $|x\rangle$ register, we obtain the quantum state

$$\left(\sum_{x_1, u_1} (-1)^{u_1 \cdot x_1} |u_1\rangle|(f \oplus g)(x_1)\rangle\right) \otimes \cdots \otimes \left(\sum_{x_{cn}, u_{cn}} (-1)^{u_{cn} \cdot x_{cn}} |u_{cn}\rangle|(f \oplus g)(x_{cn})\rangle\right)$$

Then, roughly speaking, $\dim(\mathrm{Span}(u_1, \ldots, u_{cn})) < n$ always holds if $f \oplus g$ has a secret period s, while $\dim(\mathrm{Span}(u_1, \ldots, u_{cn})) = n$ holds with a high probability if $f \oplus g$ does not have any period. Since the dimension of the vector space can be computed in time $\mathcal{O}(n^3)$, we can judge if $f \oplus g$ has a period in time $\mathcal{O}(n^3)$. Note that we can reconstruct the quantum data $|\psi_g\rangle$ after judging whether $(f \oplus g)$ has a period (with some errors) by appropriately performing uncomputations, which help us use these procedures as a subroutine without measurement in other quantum algorithms.

For the Even-Mansour construction, we set $g : \{0, 1\}^{n/3} \rightarrow \{0, 1\}^n$ by $g(x) := E_{k_1, k_2}(x\|0^{2n/3})$. Then we can make the quantum state $|\psi_g\rangle$ by classically querying x to g for *all* $x \in \{0, 1\}^{n/3}$, which requires $2^{n/3}$ classical queries. After obtaining the state $|\psi_g\rangle$, we guess $k_1^{(2)}$. Suppose that here our guess is $k' \in \{0, 1\}^{2n/3}$. We define $f_{k'} : \{0, 1\}^{n/3} \rightarrow \{0, 1\}^n$ by $f_{k'}(x) := P(x\|k')$. Then, roughly speaking, our guess is correct if and only if the function $f_{k'} \oplus g$ has a period $k_1^{(1)}$. Thus we can judge whether the guess is correct without quantum queries to g, by using our technique described above. Since $k_1^{(2)}$ can be guessed in time $\tilde{\mathcal{O}}(2^{n/3})$ by using the Grover search, we can recover the keys by making $\mathcal{O}(2^{n/3})$ classical queries and $\tilde{\mathcal{O}}(2^{n/3})$ offline quantum computations.

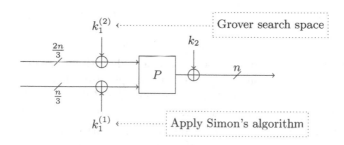

Fig. 1. Idea of our Q1 attack on the Even-Mansour construction.

We will show how we can similarly attack the FX construction in the Q1 model, by guessing additional key bits (see Fig. 2).

Moreover, our attack idea in the Q1 model can also be used to reduce the number of quantum queries of attacks in the Q2 model. The Leander and May's attack on the FX construction in the Q2 model [31] guesses the m-bit key k of the FX construction $\mathrm{FX}_{k, k_{in}, k_{out}}$ and checks whether the guess is correct by

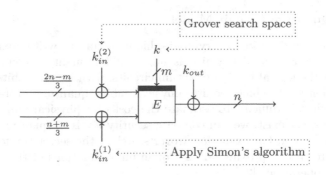

Fig. 2. Idea of our Q1 attack on the FX construction.

using Simon's algorithm, which requires $\mathcal{O}(2^{m/2})$ online quantum queries and $\tilde{\mathcal{O}}(2^{m/2})$ offline quantum computations. Roughly speaking, the guess k' for the key k is correct if and only if $(f_{k'} \oplus g)(x)$ has the secret period k_{in}, where $f_{k'}(x) = E_{k'}(x)$ and $g(x) = \mathrm{FX}_{k,k_{in},k_{out}}(x)$. In the Q2 model, we can make the quantum state $|\psi_g\rangle = (\sum_x |x\rangle|g(x)\rangle)^{\otimes cn}$ by making $\mathcal{O}(n)$ quantum queries to g. Thus, by our new attack idea described above, we can break the FX construction with $\mathcal{O}(n)$ online quantum queries and $\tilde{\mathcal{O}}(2^{m/2})$ offline quantum computations, which exponentially improves the attack by Leander and May from the viewpoint of *quantum query* complexity.

This exponential improvement on the quantum query complexity is due to the separation of offline queries and online computations: In the previous attack on the FX construction in the Q2 model by Leander and May, we have to do online queries and offline computations alternately in each iteration of the Grover search. Thus the number of online quantum queries becomes exponential in the previous attack. On the other hand, in our new attack, the online queries (i.e., the procedures to make the quantum state $|\psi_g\rangle$) are completely separated from offline computations. This enables us to decrease the number of quantum queries exponentially, while we still need exponentially many offline computations.

Paper Organization. Section 2 gives preliminaries. Section 3 describes our main algorithms. Section 4 shows applications of our algorithms in the Q2 model. Section 5 shows applications of our algorithms in the Q1 model. Section 6 discusses further applications of our algorithm. Section 7 concludes the paper.

2   Preliminaries

In this section, we introduce some quantum computing notions and review Simon's and Grover's algorithms. We refer to [36] for a broader presentation.

2.1   The Quantum Circuit Model

It has become standard in the cryptographic literature to write quantum algorithms in the circuit model, which is universal for quantum computing. We only consider the logical level of quantum circuits, with logical qubits, not their implementation level (which requires physical qubits, quantum error-correction, *etc*). Although it is difficult to estimate the cost of a physical implementation which does not yet exist, we can compare security levels as quantum operation counts in this model. For example, Grover search of the secret key for AES-128 is known to require approximately 2^{64} quantum evaluations of the cipher, and 2^{84} quantum operations [21].

Qubits and Operations. A quantum circuit represents a sequence of quantum operations, denoted as *quantum gates*, applied to a set of *qubits*. An individual qubit is a quantum object whose state is an element of a two-dimensional Hilbert space, with basis $|0\rangle, |1\rangle$ (analogs of the classical logical 0 and 1). Hence, the state is described as a linear combination of $|0\rangle, |1\rangle$ with complex coefficients (a *superposition*). We add to this a normalization condition: $\alpha|0\rangle + \beta|1\rangle$ is such that $|\alpha|^2 + |\beta|^2 = 1$. When it is clear from context, we dismiss common normalization factors.

When n qubits are given, the computational basis has 2^n vectors, which are all n-bit strings. The qubits start in a state $|0\rangle$, for example a fixed spin or polarization. The sequence of quantum gates that is applied modifies the superposition, thanks to constructive and destructive interferences. In the end, we measure the system, and obtain some n-bit vector in the computational basis, which we expect to hold a meaningful result.

All computations are (linear) unitary operators of the Hilbert space, and as such, are reversible (this holds for the individual gates, but also for the whole circuit). In general, any classical computation can be made reversible (and so, implemented as a quantum circuit) provided that one uses sufficiently many *ancilla qubits* (which start in the state $|0\rangle$ and are brought back to $|0\rangle$ after the computation). Generally, on input $|x\rangle$, we can perform some computation, copy the result to an output register using CNOT gates, and uncompute (perform backwards the same operations) to restore the initial state of the ancilla qubits. Uncomputing a unitary U corresponds to applying its adjoint operator U^*.

By the principle of *deferred measurements*, any measure that occurs inside the quantum circuit can be deferred to the end of the computation.

Quantum Oracles. Many quantum algorithms require an oracle access. The difference they make with classical algorithms with this respect is that classical oracles (*e.g.* cryptographic oracles such as a cipher with unknown key) are queried "classically", with a single value, while quantum oracles are unitary operators. We consider oracle calls of the type:

which XOR their output value to an output register (ensuring reversibility). If we consider that $|y\rangle$ starts in the state $|0\rangle$, then $f(x)$ is simply written here. If the function f can be accessed through O_f, we say it has superposition oracle access.

Quantum RAM. Additionally to the use of "plain" quantum circuits with universal quantum computation, many algorithms require quantum random-access, or being able to access at runtime a *superposition* of memory cells. This is a strong requirement, since this requires an extensive quantum hardware (the qRAM) and a huge architecture that is harder to build than a quantum circuit with a limited number of qubits. Shor's algorithm, Simon's algorithm, Grover's algorithm do not require qRAM, if their oracle calls do not either, contrary to, *e.g.*, the algorithm for quantum collision search of [9], whose optimal speedup can be realized only by using massive qRAM.

Our algorithm has no such requirement, which puts it on the same level of practicality as Grover's algorithm for attacking symmetric primitives.

2.2 Simon's Algorithm

Simon's algorithm [40] gives an exponential speedup on the following problem.

Problem 1 (Simon's problem). Suppose given access to a function $f : \{0,1\}^n \rightarrow \{0,1\}^n$ that is either injective, or such that there exists $s \in \{0,1\}^n$ with:

$$\forall x, f(x) = f(y) \iff y = x \text{ or } y = x \oplus s,$$

then find α.

In other words, the function f has a hidden Boolean period. It is also easy to extend this algorithm to a hidden Boolean shift, when we want to decide whether two functions f and g are such that $g(x) = f(x \oplus s)$ for all x. In practice, f can fall in any set X provided that it can be represented efficiently, but in our examples, we will consider functions producing bit strings.

Solving this problem with classical oracle access to f requires $\Omega\left(2^{n/2}\right)$ queries, as we need to find a collision of f (or none, if there is no hidden period). Simon [40] gives an algorithm which only requires $\mathcal{O}(n)$ superposition queries. We fix $c \geq 1$ a small constant to ensure a good success probability and repeat cn times Algorithm 1.

We obtain either:

- a list of cn random values of y;
- a list of cn random values of y in the hyperplane $y \cdot s = 0$.

It becomes now easy to test whether s exists or not. If it doesn't, the system of equations obtained has full rank. If it does exist, we can find it by solving the system. Judging whether there exists such an s and actually finding it (if it exists) can be done in time $\mathcal{O}\left(n^3\right)$ by Gaussian elimination.

Algorithm 1. Quantum subroutine of Simon's algorithm.

1: Start in the all-zero state $|0\rangle|0\rangle$ where the first register contains n qubits and the second represents elements of X.

2: Apply Hadamard gates to obtain:

$$\sum_{x \in \{0,1\}^n} |x\rangle|0\rangle$$

3: Query O_f to obtain:

$$\sum_{x \in \{0,1\}^n} |x\rangle|f(x)\rangle = \sum_{a \in X} \left(\sum_{x \in \{0,1\}^n | f(x)=a} |x\rangle \right) |a\rangle$$

4: Measure a (alternatively, we can defer this measurement), get a random value $a \in X$ and:

$$\sum_{x \in \{0,1\}^n | f(x)=a} |x\rangle$$

5: Apply Hadamard gates:

$$\sum_{y \in \{0,1\}^n} \left(\sum_{x \in \{0,1\}^n | f(x)=a} (-1)^{x \cdot y} \right) |y\rangle$$

6: Now measure the y register. There are two cases.
   - Either f hides no period s, in which case we get a random y.
   - Either f hides a period s, in which case the amplitude of $|y\rangle$ is:

$$\sum_{x \in \{0,1\}^n | f(x)=a} (-1)^{x \cdot y} = (-1)^{x_0 \cdot y} + (-1)^{(x_0 \oplus s) \cdot y}$$

   which is zero if $y \cdot s = 1$ and non-zero otherwise.
   - In that case, measuring gives a random y such that $y \cdot s = 0$.

Simon's Algorithm in Cryptography. This algorithm has been used in many attacks on modes of operation and constructions where recovering a secret requires to find a hidden shift between two functions having bit-string inputs. Generally, the functions to which Simon's algorithm is applied are not injective, and random collisions can occur. But a quick analysis (as done *e.g.* in [24]) shows that even in this case, a mild increase of the constant c will increase the success probability to a sufficient level. To be precise, the following proposition holds.

Proposition 1 (Theorem 2 in [24]). *Suppose that $f : \{0,1\}^n \to X$ has a period $s \neq 0^n$, i.e., $f(x \oplus s) = f(x)$ for all $x \in \{0,1\}^n$, and satisfies*

$$\max_{t \neq \{s,0^n\}} \Pr_x \left[f(x \oplus t) = f(x) \right] \leq \frac{1}{2}. \tag{1}$$

When we apply Simon's algorithm to f, it returns s with a probability at least $1 - 2^n \cdot (3/4)^{cn}$.

2.3 Grover's Algorithm

Grover's algorithm [22] allows a quadratic speedup on classical exhaustive search. Precisely, it solves the following problem:

Problem 2 (Grover's problem). Consider a set X (the "search space") whose elements are represented on $\lceil \log_2(|X|) \rceil$ qubits, such that the uniform superposition $\sum_{x \in X} |x\rangle$ is computable in $\mathcal{O}(1)$ time. Given oracle access to a function $f : X \to \{0,1\}$ (the "test"), find $x \in X$ such that $f(x) = 1$.

Classically, if there are 2^t preimages of 1, we expect one to be found in time (and oracle accesses to f) $\mathcal{O}(|X|/2^t)$. Quantumly, Grover's algorithm finds one in time (and oracle accesses to O_f) $\tilde{\mathcal{O}}\left(\sqrt{|X|/2^t}\right)$. In particular, if there is one preimage of 1, the running time is $\tilde{\mathcal{O}}\left(\sqrt{|X|}\right)$. If the superposition oracle for f uses a ancilla qubits, then Grover's algorithm requires $a + \lceil \log_2(|X|) \rceil$ qubits only.

Grover's algorithm works first by producing the superposition $\sum_{x \in |X|} |x\rangle$. It applies $\tilde{\mathcal{O}}\left(\sqrt{|X|/2^t}\right)$ times an operator which, by querying O_f "moves" some amplitude towards the preimages of 1.

3 Simon's Algorithm with Asymmetric Queries

In this section, we introduce a problem that can be seen as a general combination of Simon's and Grover's problems, and that will be solved by an according combination of algorithmic ideas. The problem has many cryptographic applications, and it will be at the core of our improved Q2 and Q1 time-memory-data tradeoffs.

Problem 3 (Asymmetric Search of a Period). Let $F : \{0,1\}^m \times \{0,1\}^n \to \{0,1\}^\ell$ and $g : \{0,1\}^n \to \{0,1\}^\ell$ be two functions. We consider F as a family of functions indexed by $\{0,1\}^m$ and write $F(i, \cdot) = f_i(\cdot)$. Assume that we are given quantum oracle access to F, and classical or quantum oracle access to g. (In the Q1 setting, g will be a classical oracle. In the Q2 setting, g will be a quantum oracle.)

Assume that there exists exactly one $i \in \{0,1\}^m$ such that $f_i \oplus g$ has a hidden period, *i.e.*: $\forall x \in \{0,1\}^n, f_{i_0}(x) \oplus g(x) = f_{i_0}(x \oplus s) \oplus g(x \oplus s)$ for some s. Furthermore, assume that:

$$\max_{\substack{i \in \{0,1\}^m \setminus \{i_0\} \\ t \in \{0,1\}^n \setminus \{0^n\}}} \Pr_{x \leftarrow \{0,1\}^n} \left[(f_i \oplus g)(x \oplus t) = (f_i \oplus g)(x) \right] \leq \frac{1}{2} \qquad (2)$$

Then find i_0 and s.

In our cryptographic applications, g will be a keyed function such that adversaries have to make online queries to evaluate it, while F will be a function such that adversaries can evaluate it offline. For example, the problem of recovering keys of the FX construction $\mathrm{FX}_{k,k_{in},k_{out}}(x) = E_k(x \oplus k_{in}) \oplus k_{out}$ can be regarded as a simple cryptographic instantiation of Problem 3: Set $g(x) := \mathrm{FX}_{k,k_{in},k_{out}}(x)$ and $F(i,x) := E_i(x)$. Then, roughly speaking, the function $f_i \oplus g$ has a period k_{in} if $k = i$, whereas it does not have any period if $i \neq k$ and Condition (2) holds. Thus we can know whether $i = k$ by checking whether $f_i \oplus g$ has a period.

Justification of Condition (2). We added Condition (2) in Problem 3 because the problem would be much harder to solve if we do not suppose any condition on f_i. Such assumptions are standard in the litterature of quantum attacks using Simon's algorithm (see for example [24, Sections 2.2 and 4] or [4, Section 3]). This is reasonable for cryptographic applications, as a block cipher is expected to behave like a random permutation, which makes the functions we construct in our applications behave like random functions. This assumption is made in [24, 31], and such functions satisfy Condition (2) with an overwhelming probability. Moreover, as remarked in [24], a cryptographic construction that fails to satisfy Condition (2) would exhibit some poor differential properties which could be used for cryptanalysis.

3.1   Existing Techniques to Solve the Problem

Here we explain existing algorithms to solve Problem 3 in both the Q1 model and the Q2 model, with the algorithms to recover keys of the FX construction as an example. Note that we consider the situation in which exponentially many qubits are *not* available.

The Model Q1. In the Q1 model, when we are allowed to make only classical queries to $y := \mathrm{FX}_{k,k_{in},k_{out}}$, there exists a Q1 algorithm to attack the FX construction that uses a kind of meet-in-the-middle technique [23]. However, it does not make use of the exponential speed-up of Simon's algorithm, and its time complexity and query complexity is $\mathcal{O}\left(2^{3(n+m)/7}\right)$ (for $m \leq 4n/3$).

The Model Q2. Problem 3 can be solved with $\mathcal{O}\left(n2^{m/2}\right)$ superposition queries to $F(i,x) = E_i(x)$ and $g(x) = \mathrm{FX}_{k,k_{in},k_{out}}(x)$, and in time $\mathcal{O}\left(n^3 2^{m/2}\right)$, using the Grover-meet-Simon algorithm of [31]. Indeed, we make a Grover search on index $i \in \{0,1\}^m$. When testing whether a guess i for the key k is correct, we perform $\mathcal{O}(n)$ queries to F and $\mathcal{O}(n)$ queries to g, to check whether $f_i \oplus g$ has a hidden period, hence whether the guess i is correct. Moreover, since superposition access to F and g is allowed, we can test i in superposition as well.

3.2   An Algorithm for Asymmetric Search of a Shift

Here we describe our new algorithms to solve Problem 3. We begin with explaining two observations on the Grover-meets-Simon algorithm in the Q2 model described in Sect. 3.1, and how to improve it. Then we describe how to use the idea to make a good algorithm to solve Problem 3 in the Q1 model.

Two Observations. Our first observation is that, when doing the Grover search over i for Problem 3, each time a new i is tested, a new function f_i is queried. But, in contrast, the function g is always the same. We would like to take this asymmetry into account, namely, to make less queries to g since it does not change. This in turn has many advantages: queries to g can become more costly than queries to f_i.

Our second observation is that, for each $i \in I$, once we have a superposition $|\psi_g\rangle = \bigotimes^{cn} \left(\sum_{x \in \{0,1\}^n} |x\rangle|g(x)\rangle \right)$ and given a quantum oracle access to f_i, we can obtain the information if $f_i \oplus g$ has a period or not without making queries to g.

From $|\psi_g\rangle$, we can make the state $|\psi_{f_i \oplus g}\rangle = \bigotimes^{cn} \left(\sum_{x \in \{0,1\}^n} |x\rangle \right.$ $\left. |f_i(x) \oplus g(x)\rangle \right)$ by making queries to f_i. By applying usual Simon's procedures on $|\psi_{f_i \oplus g}\rangle$, we can judge if $f_i \oplus g$ has a period. Moreover, by appropriately performing uncomputations, we can recover $|\psi_g\rangle$ (with some errors) and reuse it in other procedures.

With these observations in mind, below we give an intuitive description of our algorithm Alg-PolyQ2 to solve Problem 3 in the Q2 model (we name our algorithm Alg-PolyQ2 because it will be applied to make Q2 attacks with *polynomially* many online queries in later sections). The main ideas of Alg-PolyQ2 are separating an online phase and offline computations, and iteratively reusing the quantum data $|\psi_g\rangle$ obtained by the online phase.

Algorithm Alg-PolyQ2(informal)

1. Online phase: Make cn quantum queries to g to prepare $|\psi_g\rangle$.
2. Offline computations: Run the Grover search over $i \in \{0,1\}^m$. For each fixed i, run a testing procedure test such that: (a) test checks if i is a good element (i.e., $f_i \oplus g$ has a period) by using $|\psi_g\rangle$ and making queries to f_i, and (b) after checking if i is good, appropriately performs uncomputations to recover the quantum data $|\psi_g\rangle$.

A formal description of Alg-PolyQ2 is given in Algorithm 2. We fix a constant $c \geq 1$, to be set later depending on the probability of error wanted.

We show how to implement the testing procedure test in Algorithm 3 without any new query to g, using only exactly $2cn$ superposition queries to F. To write this procedure clearly, we consider a single function f in input, but remark that it works as well if f is a superposition of f_i (as will be the case when test is called as the oracle of a Grover search).

In practice, Algorithm 3 works up to some error (see Remark 1), which is amplified at each iteration of Algorithm 2. The complexity and success probability (including the errors) of Alg-PolyQ2 can be analyzed as below.

Proposition 2. *Suppose that m is in $\mathcal{O}(n)$. Let c be a sufficiently large constant.[2] Consider the setting of Problem 3: let $i_0 \in \{0,1\}^m$ be the good element such that $g \oplus f_{i_0}$ is periodic and assume that (2) holds. Then Alg-PolyQ2*

---

[2] See Proposition 5 for a concrete estimate.

Algorithm 2. Alg-PolyQ2.

1: Start in the all-zero state.
2: Using cn queries to g, create the state:

$$|\psi_g\rangle = \bigotimes^{cn} \left(\sum_{x \in \{0,1\}^n} |x\rangle|g(x)\rangle \right)$$

The circuit now contains $|\psi_g\rangle$, the "g-database", and additional registers on which we can perform Grover search. Notice that $|\psi_g\rangle$ contains cn independent (and disentangled) registers.

3: Create the uniform superposition over indices $i \in \{0,1\}^m$:

$$|\psi_g\rangle \otimes \sum_{i \in \{0,1\}^m} |i\rangle$$

4: Apply Grover iterations. The testing oracle is a unitary operator **test** that takes in input a register for $|i\rangle$ and the "g-database", and tests in superposition whether $f_i \oplus g$ has a hidden period. If this is the case, it returns $|b \oplus 1\rangle$ on input $|b\rangle$. Otherwise it returns $|b\rangle$. (Algorithm 3 gives the details for **test** in the case that i is fixed.)

The most important feature of **test** is that it does not change the g-database (up to some errors). The registers holding $|\psi_g\rangle$ are disentangled before and after the application of **test**.

5: After $\mathcal{O}\left(2^{m/2}\right)$ Grover iterations, measure the index i.
6: If the hidden shift is also wanted, apply a single instance of Simon's algorithm (or re-use the database and perform a slightly extended computation of **test** to retrieve the result).

---

finds i_0 with a probability in $\Theta(1)$ by making $\mathcal{O}(n)$ quantum queries to g and $\mathcal{O}(n2^{m/2})$ quantum queries to F.[3] The offline computation (the procedures excluding the ones to prepare the state $|\psi_g\rangle$) of Alg-PolyQ2 is done in time $\mathcal{O}\left((n^3 + nT_F)2^{m/2}\right)$, where T_F is the time required to evaluate F once.

See Section A in the full version of the paper [5] for a proof.

Remark 1. Intuitively, the error produced in each iteration of Algorithm 3 is bounded by the maximum, on i, of: $p^{(i)} := \Pr\left[\dim(\text{Span}(u_1, \ldots, u_{cn})) < n\right]$, when $u_1, \ldots, u_{cn}$ are produced with Simon's algorithm, *i.e.* the probability that

---

[3] In later applications, F will be instantiated with unkeyed primitives, and quantum queries to F are emulated with offline computations of primitives such as block ciphers.

Algorithm 3. The procedure test that checks if a function $f \oplus g$ has a period against the g-database, without any new query to g.

1: We start with the g-database:

$$|\psi_g\rangle = \bigotimes^{cn} \left(\sum_{x \in \{0,1\}^n} |x\rangle |g(x)\rangle \right)$$

2: Using cn superposition queries to f, build the state:

$$|\psi_{f \oplus g}\rangle = \bigotimes^{cn} \left(\sum_{x \in \{0,1\}^n} |x\rangle |g(x) \oplus f(x)\rangle \right)$$

We will now perform, in a reversible way, the exact computations of Simon's algorithm to find if $g \oplus f$ has a hidden period or not (in which case f and g have a hidden shift).

3: Apply $\left(H^{\otimes n} \otimes I_m \right)^{cn} \otimes I_1$ to $|\psi_{f \oplus g}\rangle \otimes |b\rangle$, to obtain

$$\left(\sum_{u_1, x_1 \in \{0,1\}^n} (-1)^{u_1 \cdot x_1} |u_1\rangle |(f \oplus g)(x_1)\rangle \right) \otimes \cdots \qquad (3)$$

$$\cdots \otimes \left(\sum_{u_{cn}, x_{cn} \in \{0,1\}^n} (-1)^{u_{cn} \cdot x_{cn}} |u_{cn}\rangle |(f \oplus g)(x_{cn})\rangle \right) \otimes |b\rangle.$$

4: Compute $d := \dim(\mathrm{Span}(u_1, \ldots, u_{cn}))$, set $r := 0$ if $d = n$ and $r := 1$ if $d < n$, and add r to b. Then uncompute d and r, and obtain

$$\sum_{\substack{u_1, \ldots, u_{cn} \\ x_1, \ldots, x_{cn}}} (-1)^{u_1 \cdot x_1} |u_1\rangle |(f \oplus g)(x_1)\rangle \otimes \cdots \qquad (4)$$

$$\cdots \otimes (-1)^{u_{cn} \cdot x_{cn}} |u_{cn}\rangle |(f \oplus g)(x_{cn})\rangle \otimes |b \oplus r\rangle.$$

Note that r in (4) depends on $u_1, \ldots, u_{cn}$ and now the last register may be entangled with the registers of $u_1, \ldots, u_{cn}$.

5: Uncompute $\left(H^{\otimes n} \otimes I_m \right)^{cn} \otimes I_1$.

6: Using cn new superposition queries to f, revert $|\psi_{f \oplus g}\rangle$ to $|\psi_g\rangle$.
   There are two cases:
   - If $f \oplus g$ has a hidden period, then $r = 1$ always holds. Hence, in the output register, we always write 1.
   - If $f \oplus g$ does not have a hidden period, then with high probability, $r = 0$. Hence, in the output register, we write 0.

Simon's algorithm returns the incorrect answer "$f_i \oplus g$ is periodic" even though $f_i \oplus g$ is not periodic. From condition (2), we can show that $p^{(i)} \leq 2^{(n+1)/2}((1 + \frac{1}{2})/2)^{cn/2}$ holds (see Lemma 1 in the full version of the paper [5]).

Remark 2. Alg-PolyQ2 finds the index i such that $f_i \oplus g$ has a period, but does not return the actual period of $f_i \oplus g$. However, we can find the actual period of $f_i \oplus g$ (after finding i with Alg-PolyQ2) by applying Simon's algorithm to $f_i \oplus g$.

Summary. With Alg-PolyQ2, we realize an "asymmetric" variant of Simon's algorithm, in which we store a "compressed" database for a single function g, which is not modified (up to some errors) while we test whether another function f has a hidden shift with g, or not. An immediate application of this algorithm will be to achieve an exponential improvement of the query complexity of some Q2 attacks on symmetric schemes. Indeed, in the context where Simon's algorithm and Grover's algorithm are combined, it may be possible to perform the queries to the secret-key cryptographic oracle only once, and so, to lower the query complexity to $\mathcal{O}(n)$.

3.3   Asymmetric Search with Q1 Queries

In Alg-PolyQ2, (online) queries to g and (offline) queries to F are separated, and only cn superposition queries to g are made. Hence another tradeoff is at our reach, which was not possible when g was queried in each Grover iteration: removing superposition queries to g completely.

Algorithm 4. Producing the g-database $|\psi_g\rangle$.

> **Input:** Classical query access to g
> **Output:** The g-database:
>
> $$|\psi_g\rangle = \bigotimes^{cn} \left(\sum_{x \in \{0,1\}^n} |x\rangle |g(x)\rangle \right)$$
>
> 1: Start with the all-zero state
> $$\bigotimes^{cn} |0\rangle |0\rangle$$
> 2: Apply Hadamard gates:
> $$\bigotimes^{cn} \sum_{x \in \{0,1\}^n} |x\rangle |0\rangle$$
> 3: For each $y \in \{0,1\}^n$, query (classically) $g(y)$, then apply a unitary which writes $g(y)$ in the second register if the first contains the value y.

This requires now to query *the whole codebook* for g to prepare the quantum state $|\psi_g\rangle$. Once $|\psi_g\rangle$ is built, the second offline phase runs in exactly the same way. Building $|\psi_g\rangle$ costs roughly 2^n time (and classical queries), while going through the search space for f takes $2^{m/2}$ iterations (and quantum queries to F). We call our new algorithm in the Q1 model Alg-ExpQ1 because it will be applied to make Q1 attacks with *exponentially* many online queries in later sections. The optimal point arrives when $m = 2n$.

Below we give an intuitive description of our algorithm Alg-ExpQ1 to solve Problem 3 in the Q1 model. As described above, the difference between Alg-ExpQ1 and Alg-PolyQ2 is the online phase to prepare $|\psi_g\rangle$.

Algorithm Alg-ExpQ1(informal)

1. Online phase: Make 2^n classical queries to g and prepare the state $|\psi_g\rangle$.
2. Offline computations: Run the Grover search over $i \in \{0,1\}^m$. For each fixed i, run a testing procedure test such that: (a) test checks if i is a good element (i.e., $f_i \oplus g$ has a period) by using $|\psi_g\rangle$ and making queries f_i, and (b) after checking if i is good, appropriately perform uncomputations to recover the quantum data $|\psi_g\rangle$.

A formal description of Alg-ExpQ1 is the same as that of Alg-PolyQ2 (Algorithm 2) except that we make 2^n classical queries to g to prepare the quantum state $|\psi_g\rangle$. See Algorithm 4 for formal description of the online phase.

The complexity and success probability (including the errors) of Alg-ExpQ1 can be analyzed as below.

Proposition 3. *Suppose that m is in $\mathcal{O}(n)$. Let c be a sufficiently large constant.[4] Consider the setting of Problem 3: let $i_0 \in \{0,1\}^m$ be the good element such that $g \oplus f_{i_0}$ is periodic and assume that (2) holds. Then Alg-ExpQ1 finds i_0 with a probability in $\Theta(1)$ by making $\mathcal{O}(2^n)$ classical queries to g and $\mathcal{O}(n2^{m/2})$ quantum queries to F.[5] The offline computation (the procedures excluding the ones to prepare the state $|\psi_g\rangle$) of Alg-ExpQ1 is done in time $\mathcal{O}((n^3 + nT_F)2^{m/2})$, where T_F is the time required to evaluate F once.*

A proof is given in Section A in the full version of the paper [5].

Finding Actual Periods. The above algorithm Alg-ExpQ1 returns the index i_0 such that $f_{i_0} \oplus g$ has a period, but does not return the actual period. Therefore, if we want to find the actual period of $f_{i_0} \oplus g$ after finding i_0, we have to apply Simon's algorithm to $f_{i_0} \oplus g$ again. Now we can make only classical queries to g, though, we can use the same idea with Alg-ExpQ1 to make an algorithm SimQ1 that finds the period of $f_{i_0} \oplus g$. Again, let c be a positive integer constant.

Algorithm SimQ1

1. Make 2^n classical queries to g and prepare the quantum state $|\psi_g\rangle$.
2. Make cn quantum queries to f_{i_0} to obtain the quantum state $\left|\psi_{f_{i_0} \oplus g}\right\rangle = \bigotimes^{cn} \left(\sum_x |x\rangle |f_{i_0}(x) \oplus g(x)\rangle\right)$.
3. Apply $H^{\otimes n}$ to each $|x\rangle$ register to obtain the state

$$\bigotimes^{cn} \left(\sum_{x,u} (-1)^{x \cdot u} |u\rangle |f_{i_0}(x) \oplus g(x)\rangle\right) .$$

---

[4] See Proposition 5 for a concrete estimate.
[5] Again, in later applications, F will be instantiated with unkeyed primitives, and quantum queries to F are emulated with offline computations of primitives such as block ciphers.

4. Measure all $|u\rangle$ registers to obtain cn vectors $u_1, \ldots, u_{cn}$.
5. Compute the dimension d of the vector space V spanned by $u_1, \ldots, u_{cn}$. If $d \neq n-1$, return $\perp$. If $d = n-1$, compute the vector $v \neq 0^n \in \{0,1\}^n$ that is orthogonal to V.

Obviously the probability that the above algorithm SimQ1 returns the period of $f_{i_0} \oplus g$ is the same as the probability that the original Simon's algorithm returns the period, under the condition that cn quantum queries can be made to the function $f_{i_0} \oplus g$. Thus, from Proposition 1, the following proposition holds.

Proposition 4. *Suppose that $f_{i_0} \oplus g$ has a period $s \neq 0^n$ and satisfies*

$$\max_{t \neq \{s, 0^n\}} \Pr_x \left[(f_{i_0} \oplus g)(x \oplus t) = (f_{i_0} \oplus g)(x) \right] \leq \frac{1}{2}. \tag{5}$$

Then SimQ1 returns s with a probability at least $1 - 2^n \cdot (3/4)^{cn}$ by making $\mathcal{O}\left(2^n\right)$ classical queries to g and cn quantum queries to f_{i_0}. The offline computation of SimQ1 (the procedures excluding the ones to prepare the state $|\psi_g\rangle$) runs in time $\mathcal{O}\left(n^3 + nT_f\right)$, where T_f is the time required to evaluate f_{i_0} once.

Proposition 5 (Concrete cost estimates). *In practice, for Propositions 2 and 3, $c \simeq m/\left(n \log_2(4/3)\right)$ is sufficient.*

Proof. We need to have $4\lfloor \pi / \left(4 \arcsin\left(2^{-m/2}\right)\right)\rfloor 2^{(n+1)/2}(3/4)^{cn/2} < 1/2$.

In practice, $\arcsin(x) \simeq x$ and the rounding has a negligible impact. Hence, we need that $m/2 + (n+1)/2 + \log_2(\pi) + \log_2(3/4)cn/2 < -1$.

This reduces to $c > \log_2(4/3)^{-1} \left(m + 3 + 2\log_2(\pi)\right)/n \simeq m/\left(n \log_2(4/3)n\right)$.

Remark 3. If $m = n$, this means $c \simeq 2.5$, and if $m = 2n$, $c \simeq 5$.

4   Q2 Attacks on Symmetric Schemes with Reduced Query Complexity

This section shows that our new algorithm Alg-PolyQ2 can be used to construct Q2 attacks on various symmetric schemes. By using Alg-PolyQ2 we can exponentially reduce the number of quantum queries to the keyed oracle compared to previous Q2 attacks, with the same time cost.

In each application, we consider that one evaluation of each primitive (e.g., a block cipher) can be done in time $\mathcal{O}(1)$, for simplicity. For our practical estimates, we use the cost of the primitive as our unit, and consider that it is greater than the cost of solving the linear equation system. In addition, we assume that key lengths of n-bit block ciphers are in $\mathcal{O}(n)$, which is the case for usual block ciphers.

4.1   An Attack on the FX Construction

Here we show a Q2 attack on the FX construction. As described in Sect. 3, the FX construction builds an n-bit block cipher $FX_{k,k_{in},k_{out}}$ with $(2n+m)$-bit keys $(k_{in}, k_{out} \in \{0,1\}^n$ and $k \in \{0,1\}^m)$ from another n-bit block cipher E_k with m-bit keys as

$$FX_{k,k_{in},k_{out}}(x) := E_k(x \oplus k_{in}) \oplus k_{out}. \tag{6}$$

This construction is used to obtain a block cipher with long $((2n + m)$-bit) keys from another block cipher with short (m-bit) keys. Roughly speaking, in the classical setting, the construction is proven to be secure up to $\mathcal{O}\left(2^{(n+m)/2}\right)$ queries and computations if the underlying block cipher is secure [26].

Concrete block ciphers such as DESX, proposed by Rivest in 1984 and analyzed in [26], PRINCE [8], and PRIDE [1] are designed based on the FX construction. To estimate security of these block ciphers against quantum computers, it is important to study quantum attacks on the FX construction.

As briefly explained in Sect. 3, the previous Q2 attack by Leander and May [31] breaks the FX construction by making $\mathcal{O}\left(n2^{m/2}\right)$ quantum queries, and its time complexity is $\mathcal{O}\left(n^3 2^{m/2}\right)$.

Application of Our Algorithm Alg-PolyQ2. Below we show that, by applying our algorithm Alg-PolyQ2, we can recover keys of the FX construction with only $\mathcal{O}\left(n\right)$ quantum queries. The time complexity of our attack remains $\mathcal{O}\left(n^3 2^{m/2}\right)$, which is the same as Leander and May's.

Attack Idea. As explained in Sect. 3, the problem of recovering the keys k and k_{in} of the FX construction $F_{k,k_{in},k_{out}}$ can be reduced to Problem 3: Define F : $\{0,1\}^m \times \{0,1\}^n \rightarrow \{0,1\}^n$ and $g : \{0,1\}^n \rightarrow \{0,1\}^n$ by

$$F(i,x) = E_i(x) \oplus E_i(x \oplus 1)$$
$$g(x) = FX_{k,k_{in},k_{out}}(x) \oplus FX_{k,k_{in},k_{out}}(x \oplus 1).$$

Then

$$f_k(x) \oplus g(x) = f_k(x \oplus k_{in}) \oplus g(x \oplus k_{in}) \tag{7}$$

holds, i.e., $f_k \oplus g(x)$ has a period k_{in} (note that $f_k(x) = F(k,x)$). If E is a secure block cipher and E_i is a random permutation for each i, intuitively, $f_i \oplus g$ does not have any period for $i \neq k$. Thus the problem of recovering k and k_{in} is reduced to Problem 3 and we can apply our algorithm Alg-PolyQ2. Formally, the attack procedure is as follows.

Attack Description

1. Run Alg-PolyQ2 for the above F and g to recover k.
2. Apply Simon's algorithm to $f_k \oplus g$ to recover k_{in}.
3. Compute $k_{out} = E_k(0^n) \oplus FX_{k,k_{in},k_{out}}(0^n)$.

Next we give a complexity analysis of the above attack.

Analysis. We assume that $m = \mathcal{O}(n)$, which is the case for usual block ciphers. If E is a secure block cipher and E_i is a random permutation for each $i \in \{0,1\}^m$, we can assume that $f_k \oplus g = E_k \oplus E_k(\cdot \oplus 1) \oplus \mathrm{FX}_{k,k_{in},k_{out}} \oplus \mathrm{FX}_{k,k_{in},k_{out}}(\cdot \oplus 1)$ is far from periodic for all $i \neq k$, and that assumption (2) in Problem 3 holds.

Hence, by Proposition 2, Alg-PolyQ2 recovers k with a high probability by making $\mathcal{O}(n)$ quantum queries to g and $\mathcal{O}(n2^{m/2})$ quantum queries to F, which implies that k is recovered only with $\mathcal{O}(n)$ quantum queries made to $\mathrm{FX}_{k,k_{in},k_{out}}$, and in time $\mathcal{O}(n^3 2^{m/2})$. (Note that one evaluation of g (resp., F) can be done by $\mathcal{O}(1)$ evaluations of $\mathrm{FX}_{k,k_{in},k_{out}}$ (resp., E).)

From Proposition 1, the second step can be done with $\mathcal{O}(n)$ quantum queries in time $\mathcal{O}(n^3)$. It is obvious that the third step can be done efficiently.

In summary, our attack recovers the keys of the FX construction with a high probability by making $\mathcal{O}(n)$ quantum queries to the (keyed) online oracle, and it runs in time $\mathcal{O}(n^3 2^{m/2})$.

Applications to DESX, PRINCE and PRIDE. DESX [26] has a 64-bit state, two 64-bit whitening key and one 56-bit inner key. From Propositions 2 and 5, we can estimate that our attack needs roughly 135 quantum queries and 2^{29} quantum computations of the cipher circuit.

PRINCE [8], and PRIDE [1] are two ciphers using the FX construction with a 64-bit state, a 64-bit inner key and two 64-bit whitening keys. Hence, from Propositions 2 and 5, we can estimate that our attack needs roughly 155 quantum queries and 2^{33} quantum computations of the cipher circuit.

5   Q1 Attacks on Symmetric Schemes

This section shows that our new algorithm Alg-ExpQ1 can be used to construct Q1 attacks on various symmetric schemes, with a tradeoff between online classical queries, denoted below by D, and offline quantum computations, denoted below by T.

All the algorithms that we consider run with a single processor, but they can use quantum or classical memories, whose amount is respectively denoted by Q (number of qubits) and M. Again, we consider that one evaluation of each primitive (*e.g.* a block cipher) can be done in time $\mathcal{O}(1)$, for simplicity, and we assume that key lengths of n-bit block ciphers are in $\mathcal{O}(n)$.

5.1   Tradeoffs for the Even-Mansour Construction

The Even-Mansour construction [19] is a simple construction to make an n-bit block cipher E_{k_1,k_2} from an n-bit public permutation P and two n-bit keys k_1, k_2 (see Fig. 3). The encryption E_{k_1,k_2} is defined as $E_{k_1,k_2}(x) := P(x \oplus k_1) \oplus k_2$, and the decryption is defined accordingly.

In the classical setting, roughly speaking, the Even-Mansour construction is proven secure up to $\mathcal{O}(2^{n/2})$ online queries and offline computations [19]. In fact there exists a classical attack with tradeoff $TD = 2^n$, which balances at $T = D = 2^{n/2}$ [15].

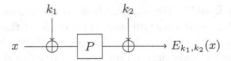

Fig. 3. The Even-Mansour construction.

Previous Q1 Attacks on the Even-Mansour Construction. Kuwakado and Morii gave a Q1 attack that recovers keys of the Even-Mansour construction with $\mathcal{O}\left(2^{n/3}\right)$ classical queries and qubits, and $\mathcal{O}\left(2^{n/3}\right)$ offline quantum computations [30]. Their attack is based on a claw-finding algorithm by Brassard *et al.* [9], and gives the tradeoff $T^2 D = 2^n$, with additional $Q = D$ qubits. The balanced point $2^{n/3}$ is significantly smaller than the classical balanced point $2^{n/2}$. However, if we want to recover keys with this attack in time $T \ll 2^{n/2}$, we need an exponential amount of qubits.

Main Previous Attacks with Polynomial Qubits. The best classical attacks allow a trade-off of $D \cdot T = 2^n$ (see [18] for other trade-offs involving memory). With Grover we could recover the keys with a complexity of $2^{n/2}$ and 2 plaintexts-ciphertext pairs, (P_1, C_1) and (P_2, C_2), by performing an exhaustive search over the value of k_1 that would verify $P(P_1 \oplus k_1) \oplus P(P_2 \oplus k_1) = C_1 \oplus C_2$. In [23], Hosoyamada and Sasaki also gave a tradeoff $D \cdot T^6 = 2^{3n}$ for $D \leq 2^{3n/7}$ under the condition that only polynomially many qubits are available, by using the multi-target preimage search by Chailloux et al. [12]. D and T are balanced at $D = T = 2^{3n/7}$, which is smaller than the classical balanced point $2^{n/2}$. The attack uses only polynomially many qubits, but requires $M = D^{1/3} = 2^{n/7}$ classical memory. At the balanced point, this still represents an exponentially large storage. Note that this is the only previous work that recover keys in time $T \ll 2^{n/2}$ with polynomially many qubits.

Table 2. Tradeoffs for Q1 attacks on the Even-Mansour construction. In this table we omit to write order notations, and ignore polynomial factors in the first and last rows.

Reference	Classical attack	Grover	[23]	[30]	[Ours]
Tradeoff of D and T	$D \cdot T = 2^n$	$T = 2^{n/2}$, $D = $ constant	$D \cdot T^6 = 2^{3n}$ $(D \leq 2^{3n/7})$	$D = 2^{n/3}$, $T = 2^{n/3}$	$D \cdot T^2 = 2^n$
Num. of qubits	–	poly(n)	poly(n)	$2^{n/3}$	poly(n)
Classical memory	D	poly(n)	$D^{1/3}$	poly(n)	poly(n)
Balanced point of D and T	$2^{n/2}$	–	$2^{3n/7}$	–	$2^{n/3}$

Application of Alg-ExpQ1. We explain how to use our algorithm Alg-ExpQ1 to attack the Even-Mansour construction. The tradeoff that we obtain is $T^2 \cdot D = 2^n$, the same as the attack by Kuwakado and Morii above. It balances at $T = D = 2^{n/3}$, but we use only $\mathsf{poly}(n)$ qubits and $\mathsf{poly}(n)$ classical memory. See Table 2 for comparison of attack complexities under the condition that $\mathsf{poly}(n)$ many qubits are available.

Attack Idea. The core observation of Kuwakado and Morii's polynomial-time attack in the Q2 model [30] is that the n-bit secret key k_1 is the period of the function $E_{k_1,k_2}(x) \oplus P(x)$, and thus Simon's algorithm can be applied if quantum queries to E_{k_1,k_2} are allowed. The key to this exponential speed up (compared to the classical attack) is to exploit the algebraic structure of E_{k_1,k_2} (the hidden period of the function) with Simon's algorithm.

On the other hand, the previous Q1 (classical query) attacks described above use only generic multi-target preimage search algorithms that do not exploit any algebraic structures. Hence being able to exploit the algebraic structure in the Q1 model should give us some advantage.

Our algorithm Alg-ExpQ1 realizes this idea. It first makes classical online queries to emulate the quantum queries required by Simon's algorithm (the g-database above) and then runs a combination of Simon's and Grover's algorithms offline (Grover search is used to find the additional m-bit secret information). A naive way to attack in the Q1 model would be to immediately combine Kuwakado and Morii's Q2 attack with Alg-ExpQ1. However, we would have to query the whole classical codebook to emulate quantum queries, which is too costly (and there is no Grover search step).

Our new attack is as follows: We divide the n-bit key k_1 in $k_1^{(1)}$ of u bits and $k_1^{(2)}$ of $n - u$ bits and apply Simon's algorithm to recover $k_1^{(1)}$, while we guess $k_1^{(2)}$ by the Grover search (see Fig. 4). Then, roughly speaking, Alg-ExpQ1 recovers the key by making $D = 2^u$ classical queries and $T = 2^{(n-u)/2}$ offline Grover search iterations (note that the offline computation cost for Simon's algorithm is $\mathsf{poly}(n)$ and we ignore polynomial factors here for simplicity), which yields the tradeoff $D \cdot T^2 = 2^n$, only with $\mathsf{poly}(n)$ qubits and $\mathsf{poly}(n)$ classical space.

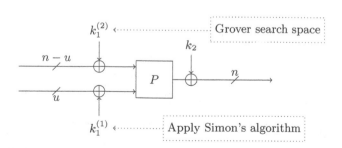

Fig. 4. Idea of our Q1 attack on the Even-Mansour construction.

Attack Description. Here we give the description of our Q1 attack. Let u be an integer such that $0 \le u \le n$. Define $F : \{0,1\}^{n-u} \times \{0,1\}^u \to \{0,1\}^n$ by

$$F(i,x) = P(x\|i), \tag{8}$$

and define $g : \{0,1\}^u \to \{0,1\}^n$ by $g(x) = E_{k_1,k_2}(x\|0^{n-u})$.

Note that $F(k_1^{(2)},x) \oplus g(x)$ has the period $k_1^{(1)}$ since $F(k_1^{(2)},x) \oplus g(x) = P(x\|k_1^{(2)}) \oplus P((x \oplus k_1^{(1)})\|k_1^{(2)}) \oplus k_2$. Our attack is described as the following procedure:

1. Run Alg-ExpQ1 for the above F and g to recover $k_1^{(2)}$.
2. Recover $k_1^{(1)}$ by applying SimQ1 to $f_{k_1^{(2)}}$ and g.
3. Compute $k_2 = E_{k_1,k_2}(0^n) \oplus P(k_1)$.

Analysis. Below we assume that u is not too small, e.g., $u \ge n/\log_2 n$. This assumption is not an essential restriction since, if u is too small, then the complexity of the first step becomes almost the same as the Grover search on k_1, which is not of interest.

If P is a random permutation, we can assume that $f_i \oplus g = P(\cdot\|i) \oplus E_{k_1,k_2}(\cdot\|0^{n-u})$ is far from periodic for all $i \ne k_1^{(2)}$, and that assumption (2) in Problem 3 holds.

Hence, by Proposition 3, Alg-ExpQ1 in Step 1 recovers $k_1^{(2)}$ with a high probability by making $\mathcal{O}(2^u)$ classical queries to g and the offline computation of Alg-ExpQ1 runs in time $\mathcal{O}(n^3 2^{(n-u)/2})$. Here, notice that one evaluation of g (resp. F) can be done in $\mathcal{O}(1)$ evaluations of E_{k_1,k_2} (resp. P). In addition, from Proposition 4, SimQ1 in Step 2 recovers $k_1^{(1)}$ with a high probability by making $\mathcal{O}(2^u)$ classical queries to g and the offline computation of Alg-ExpQ1 runs in time $\mathcal{O}(n^3)$. Step 3 requires $\mathcal{O}(1)$ queries to E_{k_1,k_2} and $\mathcal{O}(1)$ offline computations.

In summary, our attack recovers keys of the Even-Mansour construction with a high probability by making $D = \mathcal{O}(2^u)$ classical queries to E_{k_1,k_2} and doing $T = \mathcal{O}(n^3 2^{(n-u)/2})$ offline computations, which balances at $T = D = \tilde{\mathcal{O}}(2^{n/3})$. By construction of Alg-ExpQ1 and SimQ1, our attack uses poly(n) qubits and poly(n) classical memory.

Applications to Concrete Instances. The Even-Mansour construction is a commonly used cryptographic construction. The masks used in Even-Mansour are often derived from a smaller key, which can make a direct key-recovery using Grover's algorithm more efficient. This is for example the case in the CAESAR candidate Minalpher [38]. In general, we need to have a secret key of at least two thirds of the state size for our attack to beat the exhaustive search.

The Farfalle construction [2] degenerates to an Even-Mansour construction if the input message is only 1 block long (Fig. 5). Instances of this construction use variable states and key sizes. The Kravatte instance [2] has a state size of 1600 bits, and a key size between 256 and 320 bits, which leads to an attack at a whopping cost of 2^{533} data and time, while the direct key exhaustive seach would cost at most 2^{160}. Xoofff [16] has a state size of 384 bits and a key size between 192 and 384 bits. Our attack needs 2^{128} data, which is exactly the data limit of Xoofff. Hence, it is relevant if the key size is greater than 256.

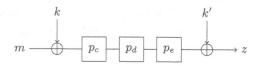

Fig. 5. One-block Farfalle.

5.2 Tradeoffs for the FX Construction

The FX construction [26] $\mathrm{FX}_{k,k_{in},k_{out}}$, computes a ciphertext c from a plaintext p by $c \leftarrow E_k(p \oplus k_{in}) \oplus k_{out}$, where E is a block cipher, k is an m-bit key and k_{in}, k_{out} are two n-bit keys. In the classical setting, there exists a classical attack with tradeoff $TD = 2^{n+m}$, which balances at $T = D = 2^{(n+m)/2}$ (see, for example, [17] for more details and memory trade-offs).

Previous Q1 Attacks on the FX Construction. Applying Grover as we did before on Even-Mansour on the keys k_{in} and k, we can recover the keys with only two pairs of plaintext-ciphertext and a time complexity of $2^{(n+m)/2}$, while only needing a polynomial number of qubits.

In [23], Hosoyamada and Sasaki proposed a tradeoff $D \cdot T^6 = 2^{3(n+m)}$ for $D \leq \min\{2^n, 2^{3(n+m)/7}\}$ with a polynomial amount of qubits, by using the multi-target preimage search by Chailloux et al. [12]. The balance occurs at $D = T = 2^{3(n+m)/7}$ (if $m \leq 4n/3$), which is smaller than the classical balanced point $2^{(n+m)/2}$. The attack requires $M = D^{1/3}$ classical memory, thus the attack still requires exponentially large space at the balanced point. This was the only Q1 attack with time $T \ll 2^{(n+m)/2}$ and a polynomial amount of qubits.

Application of Alg-ExpQ1. We explain how to apply our algorithm Alg-ExpQ1 to the FX construction. Our new tradoff is $T^2 \cdot D = 2^{n+m}$ for $D \leq 2^n$, which balances at $T = D = 2^{(n+m)/3}$ (for $m \leq 2n$), using only $\mathrm{poly}(n)$ qubits and $\mathrm{poly}(n)$ classical memory. See Table 3 for comparison of attack complexities under the condition that only $\mathrm{poly}(n)$ qubits are available.

Attack Idea. Recall that, in the Q1 attack on the Even-Mansour construction in Sect. 5.1, we divided the first key k_1 to two parts $k_1^{(1)}$ and $k_1^{(2)}$ and applied Simon's algorithm to $k_1^{(1)}$ while we performed Grover search on $k_1^{(2)}$.

In a similar manner, for the FX construction $\mathrm{FX}_{k,k_{in},k_{out}}$ we divide the n-bit key k_{in} in $k_{in}^{(1)}$ of u bits and $k_{in}^{(2)}$ of $(n-u)$ bits. We apply Simon's algorithm to recover $k_{in}^{(1)}$ while we perform Grover search on k in addition to $k_{in}^{(2)}$ (see Fig. 6).

Table 3. Tradeoffs for Q1 attacks on the FX construction. In this table we omit to write order notations, and ignore polynomial factors in the first and last rows.

Reference	Classical attack	Grover	[23]	[Ours]
Tradeoff of D and T	$D \cdot T = 2^{n+m}$ $(D \leq 2^n)$	$T = 2^{(n+m)/2}$ $D = $ constant	$D \cdot T^6 = 2^{3(n+m)}$ $(D \leq \min\{2^n, 2^{3n/7}\})$	$D \cdot T^2 = 2^{n+m}$ $(D \leq 2^n)$
Num. of qubits	–	poly(n)	poly(n)	poly(n)
Class. memory	D	poly(n)	$D^{1/3}$	poly(n)
Balanced point of D and T	$2^{(n+m)/2}$ $(m \leq n)$	–	$2^{3(n+m)/7}$ $(m \leq 4n/3)$	$2^{(n+m)/3}$ $(m \leq 2n)$

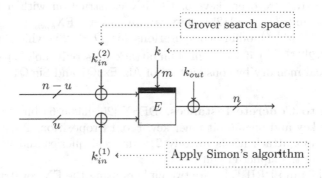

Fig. 6. Idea of our Q1 attack on the FX construction.

Then, roughly speaking, by applying Alg-ExpQ1 we can recover the key by making $D = 2^u$ classical queries and $T = 2^{(n-u)/2}$ offline Grover iterations (note that the offline computation cost for the Simon's algorithm is poly(n) and we ignore polynomial factors here for simplicity), which yields the tradeoff $D \cdot T^2 = 2^{(n+m)}$ for $D \leq 2^n$, with only poly(n) qubits and poly(n) classical memories.

Attack Description. Here we give the description of our Q1 attack. Let u be an integer such that $0 \leq u \leq n$. Define $F : \{0,1\}^{m+(n-u)} \times \{0,1\}^u \rightarrow \{0,1\}^n$ by

$$F(i\|j, x) = E_i(x\|j)(i \in \{0,1\}^m, j \in \{0,1\}^{n-u}), \tag{9}$$

and define $g : \{0,1\}^u \rightarrow \{0,1\}^n$ by $g(x) = \text{FX}_{k,k_{in},k_{out}}(x\|0^{n-u})$.

Note that $F(k\|k_{in}^{(2)}, x) \oplus g(x)$ has the period $k_{in}^{(1)}$ since $F(k\|k_{in}^{(2)}, x) \oplus g(x) = E_k(x\|k_{in}^{(2)}) \oplus E_k((x \oplus k_{in}^{(1)})\|k_{in}^{(2)}) \oplus k_{out}$. Our attack procedure runs as follows:

1. Run Alg-ExpQ1 for the above F and g to recover k and $k_{in}^{(2)}$.
2. Recover $k_{in}^{(1)}$ by applying SimQ1 to $f_{k\|k_{in}^{(2)}}$ and g.
3. Compute $k_{out} = \text{FX}_{k,k_{in},k_{out}}(0^n) \oplus E_k(k_{in})$.

Analysis. We assume that $m = \mathcal{O}(n)$, which is the case for usual block ciphers. In the same way as in the analysis for the attack on the Even-Mansour construction in Sect. 5.1, if E is a (pseudo) random permutation family and u is not too small (*e.g.* $u \geq n/\log_2 n$), we observe that the assumption (2), rephrased as:

$$\max_{t\in\{0,1\}^n\setminus\{0^n\}} \Pr_{x\in\{0,1\}^n} \left[E_i\left(x||j\right) \oplus E_i\left(x\oplus t||j\right) \oplus E_k\left(x\oplus k_{in}^{(1)}||k_{in}^{(2)}\right)\right.$$

$$\left. \oplus E_k\left(x \oplus t \oplus k_{in}^{(1)}||k_{in}^{(2)}\right) = 0\right] \leq 1/2 \qquad (10)$$

holds for all $(i, j) \neq (k, k_1^{(2)})$ with overwhelming probability.

This again implies that the claims of Propositions 3 and 4 hold for Alg-ExpQ1 in Step 1 and SimQ1 in Step 2, respectively.

Thus our attack recovers keys of the FX construction with a high probability by making $D = \mathcal{O}(2^u)$ classical queries to $\text{FX}_{k,k_{in},k_{out}}$ and doing $T = \mathcal{O}\left(n^3 2^{(m+n-u)/2}\right)$ offline computations for $D \leq 2^n$, which balances at $T = D = \tilde{\mathcal{O}}(2^{(n+m)/3})$ if $m \leq 2n$. Our attack uses only $\text{poly}(n)$ qubits and $\text{poly}(n)$ classical memory by construction of Alg-ExpQ1 and SimQ1.

Application to Concrete Instances. DESX [26] has a 64-bit state, two 64-bit whitening key and one 56-bit inner key. From Propositions 2 and 5, we can estimate that our attack needs roughly 2^{42} classical queries and 2^{40} quantum computations of the cipher circuit.

PRINCE [8], and PRIDE [1] are two ciphers using the FX construction with a 64-bit state, a 64-bit inner key and two 64-bit whitening keys. Hence, from Propositions 2 and 5, we can estimate that our attack needs roughly 2^{45} quantum queries and 2^{43} quantum computations of the cipher circuit.

We can also see some encryption modes as an instance of the FX construction. This is for example the case of the XTS mode [32], popular for disk encryption. It is generally used with AES-256 and two whitening keys that depend on the block number and another 256-bit key. Hence, with the full codebook of one block, we can obtain the first key and the value of the whitening keys of the corresponding block. Once the first key is known, the second can easily be brute-forced from a few known plaintext-ciphertext couples in other blocks.

Adiantum [14] is another mode for disk encryption that uses a variant of the FX construction with AES-256 and Chacha. There is however one slight difference: the FX masking keys are added with a modular addition instead of a xor. The FX construction is still vulnerable [6], but we will need to use Kuperberg's algorithm [28] instead of Simon's algorthm. As before, with the full codebook on one block, we can recover the AES and Chacha keys in a time slightly larger than 2^{256}.

5.3   Other Applications

Chaskey. The lightweight MAC Chaskey [33] is very close to an Even-Mansour construction (see Fig. 7). Since the last message block (m_2 in Fig. 7) is XORed to the key K_1, we can immediately apply our Q1 attack and recover K_1 and the value of the state before the xoring of the last message block. As π is a permutation easy to invert, this allows to retrieve K. The Chaskey round function applies on 128 bits. It contains 16 rounds with 4 modular additions on 32 bits, 4 XORs on 32 bits and some rotations. With a data limit of 2^{48}, as advocated in the specification, our attack would require roughly $2^{(128-48)/2} \times 2^{19} = 2^{59}$ quantum gates, where the dominant cost is solving the 80-dimensional linear system inside each iteration of Grover's algorithm.

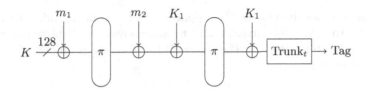

Fig. 7. Two-block Chaskey example.

Sponges. Our attack can be used on sponges if there is an input injected on a fixed state. In general, it has two drawbacks: the nonce has to be fixed, and the cost of the attack is at least $2^{c/2}$ with c the capacity of the sponge, which is often the classical security parameter. However, there are some cases where our attack is of interest.

In particular, our attack needs a set of values that contains an affine space. If a nonce was injected the same way the messages are, then we only need to know the encryptions of identical messages, with a set of nonces that fills an affine space. Nonce-respecting adversaries are generally allowed to choose the nonce, but here, the mere assumption that the nonce is incremented for each message (which is the standard way nonces are processed in practice) is sufficient: A set of 2^k consecutive values contains an affine space of $(\mathbb{Z}/(2))^{k-1}$.

This is the case in the Beetle mode of lightweight authenticated encryption [13], whose initialization phase is described as $(K_1 \oplus N)\|K_2 \mapsto f((K_1 \oplus N)\|K_2)$, where $K_1, N \in \{0,1\}^r$, $K_2 \in \{0,1\}^c$, and f is a $(r+c)$-bit permutation (Fig. 8).

Here, the nonce is directly added to the key K_1, but as the key has the same length as the state, the attack would still work if the nonce was added after the first permutation. In Beetle[Light+], the rate is $r = 64$ bits and the capacity $c = 80$ bits. The rate is sufficiently large to embed 48 varying bits for the nonce; in that case, by making 2^{48} classical queries and 2^{48} Grover iterations, we can recover the secret $K_1\|K_2$. In Beetle[Secure+], $r = c = 128$ bits. We can recover $K_1\|K_2$ with 2^{85} messages and Grover iterations.

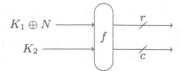

Fig. 8. Beetle state initialization.

6 Discussion

In this section, we discuss on the application of our attack idea to related-key attacks, to some slide attacks, and to an extension of Problem 3. See also Section B in the full version of the paper [5] for discussions on adaptive attacks and non-adaptive attacks.

6.1 Related Keys

Consider a block cipher E_k with a key and block size of n bits. In the related-key setting, as introduced in [41], we are not only allowed to make chosen plaintext or ciphertext queries to a secret-key oracle hiding k, but also to query $E_{k \oplus \ell}(m)$ for any n-bit difference ℓ and message m. Classically, this is a very powerful model, but it becomes especially meaningful when the block cipher is used inside a mode of operation (*e.g.* a hash function) in which key differences can be controlled by the attacker. It is shown in [41] that a secret key recovery in this model can be performed in $2^{n/2}$ operations, as it amounts to find a collision between some query $E_{k \oplus \ell}(m)$ and some offline computation $E_{\ell'}(m)$ (we can use more than a single plaintext m to ensure an overwhelming success probability).

Rötteler and Steinwandt [37] noticed that, if a quantum adversary has *superposition* access to the oracle that maps ℓ to $E_{k \oplus \ell}(m)$, it can mount a key-recovery in polynomial time using Simon's algorithm. Indeed, one can define a function:

$$f(x) = E_{k \oplus x}(m) \oplus E_x(m)$$

which has k as hidden period, apply Simon's algorithm and recover k. This attack works for any block cipher, even ideal. In contrast, in the Q2 quantum attacker model, we know that some constructions are broken, but it does not seem to be the case for all of them.

With our algorithm Alg-ExpQ1, we are able to translate this related-key superposition attack into an attack where the related-key oracle is queried only classically, but the attacker has quantum computing power. We write $k = k_1 || k_2$ where k_1 has $n/3$ bits and k_2 has $2n/3$ bits. We query $E_{(k_1 || k_2) \oplus (\ell_1 || 0)}(m)$ for a fixed m and all $n/3$-bit differences ℓ_1. Then we perform a Grover search on k_2. The classical security level in presence of a related-key oracle of this form, which is $2^{n/2}$, is reduced quantumly to $2^{n/3}$. This shows that the transition to a quantum setting has an impact on the related-key security even if the oracle remains classical.

As a consequence, we could complete the security claims of the 16-round version of the block cipher SATURNIN [10], a submission to the ongoing NIST lightweight cryptography competition[6]. The authors of SATURNIN gave security claims against quantum attackers meeting the best generic attacks. No claims were given regarding the Q_1 model for related-key attacks. Our result gives the best generic quantum related-key attack on ideal block ciphers without superposition queries, and sets the level of security that should be expected from a block cipher in this setting: the key can be recovered in quantum time $\tilde{\mathcal{O}}\left(2^{n/3}\right)$ for a block cipher of n bits (and using $2^{n/3}$ classical related-key queries). The corresponding security level for SATURNIN$_{16}$, which has blocks of 256 bits, lies at $2^{256/3} = 2^{85}$: we can say that in the Q_1 related-key setting, SATURNIN$_{16}$ should have no attack with time complexity lower than 2^{85}.

6.2 Slide Attacks

Quantum slide attacks are a very efficient quantum counterpart of the classical slide attacks [3]. They have been introduced in [24], with a polynomial-time attack on 1-round self-similar ciphers. In many cases, our algorithm does not improve these attacks, because they are already too efficient and do not rely on a partial exhaustive search. Still, some of them use a partial exhaustive search. This is the case of the slide attack against 2 round self-similar ciphers of [31] and the slide attacks against whitened Feistels of [7].

For example, we can see a 2 round self-similar cipher as an example of iterated FX cipher, as in Fig. 9. Define functions p_i, F_i, and g as

$$p_i((b,x)) = \begin{cases} (0, E_i(x)) & \text{if } b = 0 \\ (1, x) & \text{if } b = 1 \end{cases}, \quad F_i((b,x),y) = \begin{cases} y \oplus x & \text{if } b = 0 \\ E_i(y) \oplus x & \text{if } b = 1 \end{cases},$$

and $g((b,x)) = \text{iFX}(x)$. We have the property that $\text{iFX}(E_{k_2}(x \oplus k_1)) \oplus (x \oplus k_1) = E_{k_2}(\text{iFX}(x)) \oplus x$. Hence, we have the hidden period $(1, k_1)$ in the function $f_{k_2}((b,x)) = F_{k_2}((b,x), g(p_{k_2}(b,x)))$. To apply our attack, we need to compute $\sum_{x,b} |x\rangle|b\rangle|f_i((b,x))\rangle$ from the state $\sum_x |x\rangle|\text{iFX}(x)\rangle$. We first need to add one qubit to obtain $\sum_x |x\rangle(|0\rangle + |1\rangle)|\text{iFX}(x)\rangle$. Then, conditioned on the second register to be 0, we transform x into $E_i^{-1}(x)$. Next, conditioned on the second register to be 1, we transform $\text{iFX}(x)$ into $E_i(\text{iFX}(x))$. Finally, we add the first register to the third. Hence, we can apply our attack, and retrieve k_1 and k_2 using $\mathcal{O}\left(|k_1|\right)$ queries and $\mathcal{O}\left(|k_1|^3 2^{|k_2|/2}\right)$ time, assuming $|k_1| = \Omega(|k_2|)$.

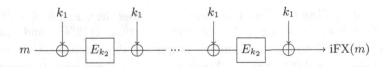

Fig. 9. Iterated-FX cipher.

[6] https://csrc.nist.gov/Projects/Lightweight-Cryptography.

The above problem of recovering keys can be generalized as the following problem, which can be solved by the same strategy as above.

Problem 4 (Constructing and Finding a Hidden Period). Let g : $\{0,1\}^n \to \{0,1\}^\ell$ be a function, $i \in I$, $p_i : \{0,1\}^n \to \{0,1\}^n$ be a permutation and F_i : $\{0,1\}^n \times \{0,1\}^\ell \to \{0,1\}^\ell$ be a function such that $F_i(x,\cdot)$ is a permutation. Assume that there exists $i_0 \in I$ such that $f_{i_0}(x) = F_{i_0}(x, g(p_{i_0}(x)))$ has a period, *i.e.*: $\forall x \in \{0,1\}^n$, $f_{i_0}(x) = f_{i_0}(x \oplus s)$ for some s. Assume that we are given quantum oracle access to F_i and p_i and classical or quantum oracle access to g. (In the Q1 setting, g will be a classical oracle. In the Q2 setting, g will be a quantum oracle.) Then find i_0 and s.

This problem assumes that g is a keyed function, and that we can reversibly transform $(x, g(x))$ into a couple $(y, f_i(y))$, with f_i a periodic function if $i = i_0$. We can see this transformation as a generalization of the CCZ equivalence [11], where the function mapping the graph of g and the graph of f_i do not need to be an affine function. There may also be more than one solution (in which case we just want to find one), or there may be none, just as Grover's algorithm can handle cases with many expected solutions, or distinguish whether there is a solution or not. Note that Problem 3 is a special case of the above problem, in the case where p_i is the identity, and F_i is only the xoring of g and another function.

7   Conclusion

In this paper, we have introduced a new quantum algorithm, in which we make use of Simon's algorithm in an *offline* way. The idea of making $\mathsf{poly}(n)$ superposition queries to the oracle (with, as input, a uniform superposition), storing them as some compressed database on n^2 qubits, and reusing them during the iterations of a Grover search, yielded surprising results. This idea, initially targeting the query complexity of some Q2 attacks on cryptographic schemes, enabled us to find new quantum-time/classical-data tradeoffs. Our result has three consequences, each of which answers a long-standing question in post-quantum cryptography.

Simon's Algorithm Can Be Used in an Offline Setting. We provided the first example of use of Simon's algorithm (or more precisely, its core idea) in an offline setting, without quantum oracle queries.

Improving More Than the Time Complexity. Consider the example of our attack on the Even-Mansour construction in quantum time $\widetilde{\mathcal{O}}\left(2^{n/3}\right)$ and classical queries $\mathcal{O}\left(2^{n/3}\right)$. With the same number of queries, the classical attack requires $\mathcal{O}\left(2^{2n/3}\right)$ time *and* $\mathcal{O}\left(2^{n/3}\right)$ classical memory to store the queries. In our attack, we do not need this storage. To the best of our knowledge, this is the first time that a quantum Q1 attack provides a quadratic speedup while the needs of hardware are also reduced.

Q2 Attacks Make a Difference. Schemes which do not have an attack in the superposition model cannot be attacked by our algorithm. We showed that their algebraic structure, which makes the superposition attack possible, indeed made a practical difference when it came to Q1 attacks. We believe that this question needs further investigation.

Acknowledgements. The authors thank Léo Perrin for proofreading this article and Elena Kirshanova for helpful remarks. This project has received funding from the European Research Council (ERC) under the European Union's Horizon 2020 research and innovation programme (grant agreement n° 714294 - acronym QUASYModo).

References

1. Albrecht, M.R., Driessen, B., Kavun, E.B., Leander, G., Paar, C., Yalçın, T.: Block ciphers – focus on the linear layer (feat. PRIDE). In: Garay, J.A., Gennaro, R. (eds.) CRYPTO 2014. LNCS, vol. 8616, pp. 57–76. Springer, Heidelberg (2014). https://doi.org/10.1007/978-3-662-44371-2_4
2. Bertoni, G., Daemen, J., Hoffert, S., Peeters, M., Assche, G.V., Keer, R.V.: Farfalle: parallel permutation-based cryptography. IACR Trans. Symmetric Cryptol. **2017**(4), 1–38 (2017). https://tosc.iacr.org/index.php/ToSC/article/view/801
3. Biryukov, A., Wagner, D.: Slide attacks. In: Knudsen, L. (ed.) FSE 1999. LNCS, vol. 1636, pp. 245–259. Springer, Heidelberg (1999). https://doi.org/10.1007/3-540-48519-8_18
4. Bonnetain, X.: Quantum key-recovery on full AEZ. In: Adams, C., Camenisch, J. (eds.) SAC 2017. LNCS, vol. 10719, pp. 394–406. Springer, Cham (2018). https://doi.org/10.1007/978-3-319-72565-9_20
5. Bonnetain, X., Hosoyamada, A., Naya-Plasencia, M., Sasaki, Y., Schrottenloher, A.: Quantum attacks without superposition queries: the offline simon algorithm. IACR Cryptology ePrint Archive 2019, 614 (2019). https://eprint.iacr.org/2019/614
6. Bonnetain, X., Naya-Plasencia, M.: Hidden shift quantum cryptanalysis and implications. In: Peyrin, T., Galbraith, S. (eds.) ASIACRYPT 2018. LNCS, vol. 11272, pp. 560–592. Springer, Cham (2018). https://doi.org/10.1007/978-3-030-03326-2_19
7. Bonnetain, X., Naya-Plasencia, M., Schrottenloher, A.: On quantum slide attacks. In: Selected Areas in Cryptography - SAC 2019. Lecture Notes in Computer Science, Springer (2020)
8. Borghoff, J., et al.: PRINCE – a low-latency block cipher for pervasive computing applications. In: Wang, X., Sako, K. (eds.) ASIACRYPT 2012. LNCS, vol. 7658, pp. 208–225. Springer, Heidelberg (2012). https://doi.org/10.1007/978-3-642-34961-4_14
9. Brassard, G., HØyer, P., Tapp, A.: Quantum cryptanalysis of hash and claw-free functions. In: Lucchesi, C.L., Moura, A.V. (eds.) LATIN 1998. LNCS, vol. 1380, pp. 163–169. Springer, Heidelberg (1998). https://doi.org/10.1007/BFb0054319
10. Canteaut, A., et al.: Saturnin: a suite of lightweight symmetric algorithms for post-quantum security (2019). https://project.inria.fr/saturnin/files/2019/05/SATURNIN-spec.pdf
11. Carlet, C., Charpin, P., Zinoviev, V.: Codes, bent functions and permutations suitable for DES-like cryptosystems. Designs Codes Crypt. **15**(2), 125–156 (1998)

12. Chailloux, A., Naya-Plasencia, M., Schrottenloher, A.: An efficient quantum collision search algorithm and implications on symmetric cryptography. In: Takagi, T., Peyrin, T. (eds.) ASIACRYPT 2017. LNCS, vol. 10625, pp. 211–240. Springer, Cham (2017). https://doi.org/10.1007/978-3-319-70697-9_8

13. Chakraborti, A., Datta, N., Nandi, M., Yasuda, K.: Beetle family of lightweight and secure authenticated encryption ciphers. IACR Trans. Crypt. Hardw. Embed. Syst. **2018**(2), 218–241 (2018). https://doi.org/10.13154/tches.v2018.i2.218-241

14. Crowley, P., Biggers, E.: Adiantum: length-preserving encryption for entry-level processors. IACR Trans. Symmetric Cryptol. **2018**(4), 39–61 (2018). https://doi.org/10.13154/tosc.v2018.i4.39-61

15. Daemen, J.: Limitations of the Even-Mansour construction. In: Imai, H., Rivest, R.L., Matsumoto, T. (eds.) ASIACRYPT 1991. LNCS, vol. 739, pp. 495–498. Springer, Heidelberg (1993). https://doi.org/10.1007/3-540-57332-1_46

16. Daemen, J., Hoffert, S., Assche, G.V., Keer, R.V.: The design of xoodoo and xoofff. IACR Trans. Symmetric Cryptol. **2018**(4), 1–38 (2018). https://doi.org/10.13154/tosc.v2018.i4.1-38

17. Dinur, I.: Cryptanalytic time-memory-data tradeoffs for FX-constructions with applications to PRINCE and PRIDE. In: Oswald, E., Fischlin, M. (eds.) EUROCRYPT 2015. LNCS, vol. 9056, pp. 231–253. Springer, Heidelberg (2015). https://doi.org/10.1007/978-3-662-46800-5_10

18. Dinur, I., Dunkelman, O., Keller, N., Shamir, A.: Cryptanalysis of Iterated Even-Mansour schemes with two keys. In: Sarkar, P., Iwata, T. (eds.) ASIACRYPT 2014. LNCS, vol. 8873, pp. 439–457. Springer, Heidelberg (2014). https://doi.org/10.1007/978-3-662-45611-8_23

19. Even, S., Mansour, Y.: A construction of a cipher from a single pseudorandom permutation. J. Cryptol. **10**(3), 151–162 (1997). https://doi.org/10.1007/s001459900025

20. Gagliardoni, T.: Quantum Security of Cryptographic Primitives. Ph.D. thesis, Darmstadt University of Technology, Germany (2017). http://tuprints.ulb.tu-darmstadt.de/6019/

21. Grassl, M., Langenberg, B., Roetteler, M., Steinwandt, R.: Applying Grover's algorithm to AES: quantum resource estimates. In: Takagi, T. (ed.) PQCrypto 2016. LNCS, vol. 9606, pp. 29–43. Springer, Cham (2016). https://doi.org/10.1007/978-3-319-29360-8_3

22. Grover, L.K.: A fast quantum mechanical algorithm for database search. In: Miller, G.L. (ed.) Proceedings of the Twenty-Eighth Annual ACM Symposium on the Theory of Computing, Philadelphia, Pennsylvania, USA, 22–24 May 1996, pp. 212–219. ACM (1996). http://doi.acm.org/10.1145/237814.237866

23. Hosoyamada, A., Sasaki, Y.: Cryptanalysis against symmetric-key schemes with online classical queries and offline quantum computations. In: Smart, N.P. (ed.) CT-RSA 2018. LNCS, vol. 10808, pp. 198–218. Springer, Cham (2018). https://doi.org/10.1007/978-3-319-76953-0_11

24. Kaplan, M., Leurent, G., Leverrier, A., Naya-Plasencia, M.: Breaking symmetric cryptosystems using quantum period finding. In: Robshaw, M., Katz, J. (eds.) CRYPTO 2016. LNCS, vol. 9815, pp. 207–237. Springer, Heidelberg (2016). https://doi.org/10.1007/978-3-662-53008-5_8

25. Kaplan, M., Leurent, G., Leverrier, A., Naya-Plasencia, M.: Quantum differential and linear cryptanalysis. IACR Trans. Symmetric Cryptol. **2016**(1), 71–94 (2016). http://tosc.iacr.org/index.php/ToSC/article/view/536

26. Kilian, J., Rogaway, P.: How to protect DES against exhaustive key search. In: Koblitz, N. (ed.) CRYPTO 1996. LNCS, vol. 1109, pp. 252–267. Springer, Heidelberg (1996). https://doi.org/10.1007/3-540-68697-5_20
27. Kuperberg, G.: A subexponential-time quantum algorithm for the dihedral hidden subgroup problem. SIAM J. Comput. **35**(1), 170–188 (2005). https://doi.org/10.1137/S0097539703436345
28. Kuperberg, G.: Another subexponential-time quantum algorithm for the dihedral hidden subgroup problem. In: TQC 2013, LIPIcs, vol. 22, pp. 20–34. Schloss Dagstuhl - Leibniz-Zentrum fuer Informatik (2013)
29. Kuwakado, H., Morii, M.: Quantum distinguisher between the 3-round feistel cipher and the random permutation. In: IEEE International Symposium on Information Theory, ISIT 2010, Proceedings, pp. 2682–2685. IEEE (2010)
30. Kuwakado, H., Morii, M.: Security on the quantum-type Even-Mansour cipher. In: Proceedings of the International Symposium on Information Theory and Its Applications, ISITA 2012, pp. 312–316. IEEE (2012)
31. Leander, G., May, A.: Grover meets Simon – quantumly attacking the FX-construction. In: Takagi, T., Peyrin, T. (eds.) ASIACRYPT 2017. LNCS, vol. 10625, pp. 161–178. Springer, Cham (2017). https://doi.org/10.1007/978-3-319-70697-9_6
32. Martin, L.: XTS: a mode of AES for encrypting hard disks. IEEE Secur. Privacy **8**(3), 68–69 (2010). https://doi.org/10.1109/MSP.2010.111
33. Mouha, N., Mennink, B., Van Herrewege, A., Watanabe, D., Preneel, B., Verbauwhede, I.: Chaskey: an efficient MAC algorithm for 32-bit microcontrollers. In: Joux, A., Youssef, A. (eds.) SAC 2014. LNCS, vol. 8781, pp. 306–323. Springer, Cham (2014). https://doi.org/10.1007/978-3-319-13051-4_19
34. National Academies of Sciences, Engineering, and Medicine: Quantum Computing: Progress and Prospects. The National Academies Press, Washington, DC (2018). https://www.nap.edu/catalog/25196/quantum-computing-progress-and-prospects
35. National Institute of Standards and Technlology: Submission requirements and evaluation criteria for the post-quantum cryptography standardization process (2016). https://csrc.nist.gov/CSRC/media/Projects/Post-Quantum-Cryptography/documents/call-for-proposals-final-dec-2016.pdf
36. Nielsen, M.A., Chuang, I.: Quantum Computation and Quantum Information. AAPT (2002)
37. Rötteler, M., Steinwandt, R.: A note on quantum related-key attacks. Inf. Process. Lett. **115**(1), 40–44 (2015). https://doi.org/10.1016/j.ipl.2014.08.009
38. Sasaki, Y., et al.: Minalpher v1.1. CAESAR competition (2015). https://competitions.cr.yp.to/round2/minalpherv11.pdf
39. Shor, P.W.: Algorithms for quantum computation: discrete logarithms and factoring. In: 35th Annual Symposium on Foundations of Computer Science, pp. 124–134. IEEE Computer Society (1994)
40. Simon, D.R.: On the power of quantum computation. In: 35th Annual Symposium on Foundations of Computer Science, pp. 116–123 (1994)
41. Winternitz, R.S., Hellman, M.E.: Chosen-key attacks on a block cipher. Cryptologia **11**(1), 16–20 (1987). https://doi.org/10.1080/0161-118791861749

Quantum Random Oracle Model
with Auxiliary Input

Minki Hhan[1]([✉]), Keita Xagawa[2], and Takashi Yamakawa[2]

[1] Seoul National University, Seoul, Republic of Korea
hhan_@snu.ac.kr
[2] NTT Secure Platform Laboratories,
3-9-11, Midori-cho Musashino-shi, Tokyo 180-8585, Japan
{keita.xagawa.zv,takashi.yamakawa.ga}@hco.ntt.co.jp

Abstract. The random oracle model (ROM) is an idealized model where hash functions are modeled as random functions that are only accessible as oracles. Although the ROM has been used for proving many cryptographic schemes, it has (at least) two problems. First, the ROM does not capture quantum adversaries. Second, it does not capture non-uniform adversaries that perform preprocessings. To deal with these problems, Boneh et al. (Asiacrypt'11) proposed using the quantum ROM (QROM) to argue post-quantum security, and Unruh (CRYPTO'07) proposed the ROM with auxiliary input (ROM-AI) to argue security against preprocessing attacks. However, to the best of our knowledge, no work has dealt with the above two problems simultaneously.

In this paper, we consider a model that we call the QROM with (classical) auxiliary input (QROM-AI) that deals with the above two problems simultaneously and study security of cryptographic primitives in the model. That is, we give security bounds for one-way functions, pseudorandom generators, (post-quantum) pseudorandom functions, and (post-quantum) message authentication codes in the QROM-AI.

We also study security bounds in the presence of quantum auxiliary inputs. In other words, we show a security bound for one-wayness of random permutations (instead of random functions) in the presence of quantum auxiliary inputs. This resolves an open problem posed by Nayebi et al. (QIC'15). In a context of complexity theory, this implies $\mathsf{NP} \cap \mathsf{coNP} \not\subseteq \mathsf{BQP/qpoly}$ relative to a random permutation oracle, which also answers an open problem posed by Aaronson (ToC'05).

1 Introduction

1.1 Background

Random Oracle Model with Auxiliary Input. The random oracle model (ROM) introduced by Bellare and Rogaway [BR93] is a remarkably useful tool for analyzing security of practical cryptographic schemes. In the ROM, we model a

---

This work was done in part while the first author was conducting an internship program in NTT Secure Platform Laboratories, Japan.

S. D. Galbraith and S. Moriai (Eds.): ASIACRYPT 2019, LNCS 11921, pp. 584–614, 2019.
https://doi.org/10.1007/978-3-030-34578-5_21

hash function as a truly random function that is only accessible as an oracle and assume that an adversary has no a priori knowledge about the function. This means that the traditional definition of the ROM does not capture *non-uniform* adversaries who perform heavy offline preprocessings to generate auxiliary information (also called advice) of the random function. Indeed, a non-uniform attack is effective in some cases [Hel80, FN99, DTT10]. For example, Hellman [Hel80] showed that one can speed up an inversion of a permutation by using the power of preprocessing. Bernstein and Lange [BL13] pointed out that non-uniform attacks are a potential threat in the real world by exhibiting some examples of (unrealistic) non-uniform attacks. To deal with such non-uniform attacks, Unruh [Unr07] introduced the *random oracle model with auxiliary input* (ROM-AI) where an adversary can perform arbitrarily heavy preprocessing to generate auxiliary information of the random function. He gave a generic tool for analyzing security in the ROM-AI by introducing another model called the bit-fixing ROM and showed that a random oracle is one-way and that RSA-OAEP [BR95] remains secure in the ROM-AI. Subsequently, Dodis, Guo, and Katz [DGK17], and Coretti, Dodis, Guo, and Steinberger [CDGS18] further studied the ROM-AI to show (tighter) security bounds for several natural applications including one-way functions (OWFs), collision resistant hash functions (CRHFs), pseudo-random generators (PRGs), pseudorandom functions (PRFs), message authentication codes (MACs), and more.

Quantum Random Oracle Model. The ROM has been strengthened in another direction called the *quantum ROM* (QROM) [BDF+11], where an adversary can access the random oracle quantumly. This is a natural model when considering post-quantum security since a random oracle is an idealization of a hash function that can be quantumly evaluated by an adversary once quantum computers are available. Since many proof techniques in the ROM cannot be directly translated into ones in the QROM, many studies have given security proofs in the QROM for schemes that are originally proven secure in the ROM (e.g., [Zha12b, Unr15, ES15, TU16, HRS16, CBH+18, KLS18, SXY18, JZC+18, KYY18, AHU19, DFMS19, LZ19]).

Quantum Random Oracle Model with (Quantum) Auxiliary Input. Although both the ROM-AI and QROM have been studied thoroughly, to the best of our knowledge, no work has considered both these extensions simultaneously. In this work, we consider a mix of them and initiate the study of the *QROM with auxiliary input*. In particular, we consider both the QROM with *classical* auxiliary input (QROM-AI) and the QROM with *quantum* auxiliary input (QROM-QAI). Both these models reasonably extend the QROM to capture adversaries with preprocessing in some sense. The QROM-AI captures an adversary that performs a long classical preprocessing to prepare classical auxiliary information that will be used in the future when quantum computers become available. This model is reasonable in the current situation in which quantum computers are not available yet and in a future situation in which quantum computers are available, but are far less efficient than classical computers. On the other hand, the QROM-QAI would be more reasonable in the situation where a highly efficient quantum computer is available at the time of preprocessing. The motivation of this work is to study security of natural applications of random oracles in these models.

The work most relevant to the above problem is that of Nayebi, Aaronson, Belovs, and Trevisan [NABT15], which showed a lower bound for the number of queries to invert a random permutation with classical auxiliary input. However, their result is not sufficient for our purpose in several aspects. First, they only considered a random *permutation* whereas we consider a random *function*. Since a hash function in the real world is not a permutation, we need to consider a random function instead of a random permutation to derive implications in the real world. Second, they only considered a lower bound for one-wayness whereas we are also interested in other applications such as CRHFs, PRGs, PRFs, and MACs. Third, they did not consider the effect of *salting*, which is a technique to use a random string that is chosen after the preprocessing as a public parameter. Salting is widely deployed in the real world, and sufficiently long salt defeats non-uniform attacks in the ROM-AI [DGK17, CDGS18]. Finally, they only considered settings where auxiliary inputs are classical, and their result seems difficult to directly extend to the setting where auxiliary inputs are quantum. Indeed, they left it extending their result to the quantum auxiliary input setting as an open problem. Thus it remains unknown if we can obtain security bounds for the security of OWFs, CRHFs, PRGs, PRFs, and MACs and if salting is effective in the QROM-AI and QROM-QAI.

1.2   Our Results

In this work, we initiate the study of the QROM-AI and the QROM-QAI, and give security bounds for several cryptographic applications in the QROM-AI. However, we do not know if we can extend them to ones in the QROM-QAI. Nonetheless, we make a step toward the goal by proving that a random permutation (instead of a random function) is hard to invert even with a quantum auxiliary input. This answers the open problem raised by Nayebi et al. [NABT15]. We describe more details of our results below.

Security Bounds in QROM-AI. We prove security bounds for natural "salted" constructions of OWFs, PRGs, PRFs, and MACs in the QROM-AI. A caveat of our results for PRFs and MACs is that we only consider *classical queries* for PRF and MAC oracles whereas queries to the random oracle can be quantum. To clarify this limitation, we denote them as pqPRFs and pqMACs.[1] On the other hand, we denote quantum-accessible PRFs and MACs as qPRFs and qMACs. We note that the attack models of pqPRFs and pqMACs make sense as post-quantum security models a setting where honest parties are all classical and only adversaries are quantum.

---

[1] "pq" stands for "post-quantum".

Table 1. Security bounds and best known attacks using an S-bit auxiliary input and T queries to the random oracle for "salted" constructions of primitives in the QROM-AI. The first two primitives (unkeyed primitives) are constructed from a random oracle $\mathcal{O} : [K] \times [N] \to [M]$ where $[K]$ is the domain of the salt, $[N]$ is the domain of the input (or the seed for PRGs), $[M]$ is the domain of the outputs, and we let $\alpha := \min(N, M)$. The latter two primitives (keyed primitives) are constructed from a random oracle $\mathcal{O} : [K] \times [N] \times [L] \to [M]$ where $[K]$ is the domain of the salt, $[N]$ is the domain of the key, $[L]$ is the domain of the inputs, and $[M]$ is the domain of the outputs (or authenticators for MACs). Q_{prf} denotes the number of queries to the PRF oracle in the security bound for pqPRFs. We omit constant factors and logarithmic terms for simplicity.

	Security bounds in QROM-AI (Ours)	Best known attacks in QROM-AI
OWFs	$\left(\frac{ST^2}{K\alpha} + \frac{T^2 N}{\alpha^2}\right)^{1/2}$	$\min\left\{\frac{ST}{K\alpha}, \left(\frac{S^2 T}{K^2 \alpha^2}\right)^{1/3}\right\} + \frac{T^2}{\alpha}$
PRGs	$\left(\frac{ST^4}{KN} + \frac{T^4}{N}\right)^{1/6}$	$\left(\frac{ST}{KN}\right)^{1/2} + \frac{T^2}{N}$
pqPRFs	$\left(\frac{ST^4}{KN} + \frac{T^4}{N}\right)^{1/4} + Q_{\text{prf}}\left(\frac{ST^2}{KN}\right)^{1/6}$	$\left(\frac{ST}{KN}\right)^{1/2} + \frac{T^2}{N}$
pqMACs	$\left(\frac{ST^4}{KN} + \frac{T^4}{N} + \frac{1}{M}\right)^{1/3}$	$\min\left\{\frac{ST}{KN}, \left(\frac{S^2 T}{K^2 N^2}\right)^{1/3}\right\} + \frac{T^2}{N} + \frac{1}{M}$

Our results are summarized in Table 1. (An extended table that includes security bounds and attacks in the ROM-AI can be found in the full version.) The notations used in the table are the same as those used in [DGK17]. The "Security bounds in QROM-AI" column indicates upper bounds of advantages to break these primitives by an adversary that makes T quantum queries to the random oracle and is given a classical auxiliary input of size at most S bits. The "Best known attacks in QROM-AI" column indicates advantages that are achieved by the best known attacks. (the full version briefly explains how we filled this column.) Though our bounds in the QROM-AI are much less tight than those in the ROM-AI and far from matching the best known attacks, we can derive some meaningful implications from them. For example, our bounds imply the computational hardness of these primitives if the size of domain and ranges are sufficiently large[2]. Moreover, our bounds imply that if we use a large enough salt, these primitives remain secure even if an adversary prepares a very long auxiliary input. That is, if the size K of the domain of the salt is exponentially larger than the auxiliary input size S, then terms that depend on S are negligible. This extends similar results in the ROM-AI [DGK17,CDGS18] to the QROM-AI.

On Quantum Auxiliary Input. Unfortunately, we could not obtain any meaningful security bound in the QROM-QAI where quantum auxiliary inputs are available. Nonetheless, we give a security bound for a closely related problem:

---

[2] More precisely, if both S and T are polynomial in the security parameter and (appropriate parts of) domains and ranges of the random oracle are exponentially large then our bounds become negligibly small.

one-wayness of a random permutation (instead of a random function) with *quantum auxiliary input*. That is, we show that the probability of inverting a random function $\mathcal{O} : [K] \times [N] \rightarrow [N]$ such that $\mathcal{O}(a, \cdot)$ is a permutation over $[N]$ for all $a \in [K]$ with an S-qubit quantum auxiliary input and T quantum queries is $\widetilde{O}\left(\left(\frac{ST^2}{KN} + \frac{T^2}{N} \right)^{1/3} \right)$. This answers the open problem raised by Nayebi et al. [NABT15]. Before our work, such a result was known in the setting where an auxiliary input is classical and $K = 1$ [NABT15], which gave a security bound $\widetilde{O}(\sqrt{ST^2/N})$.[3]

Our result also has an implication in complexity theory. Specifically, it implies an oracle separation of $\mathsf{NP} \cap \mathsf{coNP}$ and $\mathsf{BQP}/\mathsf{qpoly}$ which is the class of problems solvable by a polynomial-size quantum algorithm with a polynomial-size quantum advice [NY04, Aar05]. That is, we have $\mathsf{NP} \cap \mathsf{coNP} \not\subseteq \mathsf{BQP}/\mathsf{qpoly}$ relative to a random permutation oracle. This affirmatively answers the open problem left by Aaronson [Aar05], who showed the existence of an oracle relative to which $\mathsf{NP} \not\subseteq \mathsf{BQP}/\mathsf{qpoly}$ and left it open to show the existence of an oracle relative to which $\mathsf{NP} \cap \mathsf{coNP} \not\subseteq \mathsf{BQP}/\mathsf{qpoly}$.

1.3   Technical Overview

Our main tool is the *compression technique* developed by Genarro, Gertner, Katz, and Trevisan [GT00, GGKT05]. The basic idea behind the technique is a very simple information theoretic argument: For sets $\mathcal{M}, \mathcal{C}$, if there exist an encoding algorithm $E : \mathcal{M} \rightarrow \mathcal{C}$ and a decoding algorithm $D : \mathcal{C} \rightarrow \mathcal{M}$ such that $D(E(m)) = m$ holds with high probability (over the uniformly random choice of m), then the cardinality of $\mathcal{C}$ cannot be much smaller than that of $\mathcal{M}$. More precisely, if the decoding succeeds with probability δ, then we must have $|\mathcal{C}| \geq \delta |\mathcal{M}|$. This holds even if the encoder and the decoder share a randomness of any length [DTT10]. We call this information theoretical bound the *compression lemma*. In the following, we explain how to apply this to derive security bounds in the QROM-AI. We omit salting for simplicity since similar methods still work with salting.

OWFs in QROM-AI. Here, we explain how to obtain a security bound for OWFs in the QROM-AI. First, we review the case of random permutations, which is shown by Nayebi et al. [NABT15] because this is much simpler. Suppose that we have a random permutation $f : [N] \rightarrow [N]$ and an adversary $\mathcal{A}$ that succeeds in inverting f with high probability, say $2/3$, for ε-fraction of $x \in [N]$ by using S-bit classical auxiliary information of f and T quantum queries to f. We want to give an upper bound for ε.

The idea is to construct an encoder that compresses the truth table of the random oracle by using the power of the adversary $\mathcal{A}$ and then invoke the compression lemma. Specifically, we choose a random subset $R \subset [N]$ by putting

---

[3] They claim that their security bound is $\widetilde{O}(ST^2/N)$. However, their definition of one-wayness is weaker than ours, and if we use our definition, then the quadratic security loss naturally occurs. See the full version for more detailed discussion.

each element $x \in [N]$ into R with a certain probability, which will be used as the shared randomness between the encoder and the decoder. Then we define the set $G \subset R$ of good elements where we say that $x \in R$ is good if $\mathcal{A}$ succeeds in inverting $f(x)$ with high probability and $\mathcal{A}$'s total query magnitude on any $x' \in R \setminus \{x\}$ is "small" when it runs on the input $f(x)$. By appropriately setting parameters, we can show that G is "not too small" with high probability. Then the encoder generates an encoding that consists of a "partial truth table" of f on $[N] \setminus G$, the description of the set $f(G)$ and the auxiliary input that is used by $\mathcal{A}$. The decoder recovers the whole truth table of f by inverting f on each element of $f(G)$ by running $\mathcal{A}$. Here, we have to be careful about the fact that the decoder is not given the whole truth table of f and cannot correctly simulate the oracle f for $\mathcal{A}$. Thus, when the decoder tries to invert $y \in f(G)$ in f, it defines a function g_y by

$$g_y(x) := \begin{cases} f(x) & \text{if } x \notin R \\ y & \text{if } x \in R, \end{cases}$$

and uses g_y instead of f. Though f and g_y do not match on $R \setminus \{x\}$, by the definition of the good elements, $\mathcal{A}$'s query magnitude on $R \setminus \{x\}$ is "small," and thus $\mathcal{A}$ still succeeds in inverting y with high probability with the oracle access to g_y instead of f. Then the decoder can recover $x = f^{-1}(y)$ by computing the output distribution of $\mathcal{A}$ and taking the value that is output with the highest probability.[4] By repeating this for every $y \in f(G)$, the decoder can recover the whole truth table of f. On the other hand, the encoding is smaller than the original truth table of f since it "forgets" the truth table on the subset G that is "not too small." By setting parameters appropriately, we can derive the security bound.

For random functions instead of random permutations, the difference is that a preimage of y may not be unique, and we have to bound the probability that an adversary finds any of them. In that case, even if an adversary succeeds in inverting the random function with high probability, there may not be any particular value that is output with constant probability. Thus the decoder has to use a value that is output by the adversary with sub-constant probability for recovering the truth table. This only gives a somewhat bad bound related to this probability, even if we resolve other technical difficulties.

To deal with this problem, we include a randomness used in the measurement of the final state of $\mathcal{A}$ as a part of the shared randomness between the encoder and decoder. With a fixed randomness for the measurement, the decoder can *deterministically simulate* $\mathcal{A}$[5] and decide the value that is supposed to be used for recovering the table. With this idea (among others), we extend the above result to the case of random functions.

---

[4] Since the compression lemma works for unbounded-time encoders and decoders, we can assume that the decoder has an unbounded computational power to simulate quantum computations.

[5] Since the decoder has unbounded computational power, it can control the randomness for measurements in executions of the quantum algorithm $\mathcal{A}$.

PRGs in QROM-AI. For obtaining security bounds for PRGs, we first consider (an average case version of) Yao's box problem [Yao90] similarly to the classical case [DTT10, DGK17]. In Yao's box problem, we consider a random oracle $\mathcal{O}$: $[N] \rightarrow \{0, 1\}$ and an adversary that tries to compute $\mathcal{O}(x)$ for uniform $x \in [N]$ by using an S-bit classical auxiliary input and T quantum queries to $\mathcal{O}$ *without querying x itself* (i.e., $\mathcal{A}$'s query magnitude on x is 0 in the quantum case). If we obtain a proper bound for Yao's box problem, then a bound for PRGs follows as discussed below. To construct PRGs, we consider a random oracle $\mathcal{O} : [N] \rightarrow [M]$ and want to bound the advantage of $\mathcal{A}$ to distinguish $\mathcal{O}(x)$ for $x \leftarrow [N]$ from a truly random string $y \leftarrow [M]$ by using an S-bit classical auxiliary input and T quantum queries to $\mathcal{O}$.

First, we argue that $\mathcal{A}$'s total query magnitude on x is "small." This holds because if it is "not small," then we can use $\mathcal{A}$ to invert $\mathcal{O}$ with "non-small" probability by measuring one of its queries, which contradicts the bound for the one-wayness of $\mathcal{O}$. Then we can convert $\mathcal{A}$ to an algorithm $\mathcal{A}'$ whose query magnitude on x is 0 while only slightly degrading its distinguishing advantage.[6] Now, $\mathcal{A}'$ distinguishes $\mathcal{O}(x)$ from a random string without querying x at all. By Yao's equivalence of distinguishability and predictability [Yao82], there exists an algorithm $\mathcal{B}$ such that for some $i \in [\log M]$, it predicts the i-th bit of $\mathcal{O}(x)$ given an advice $\mathsf{st}_{\mathcal{O}}$ of S-bit, x, and the first $i - 1$ bits of $\mathcal{O}(x)$ making T quantum queries to $\mathcal{O}$ without querying x to $\mathcal{O}$. This is exactly an algorithm that solves Yao's box problem by also considering the first $i - 1$ bits of $\mathcal{O}(x)$ as a part of the auxiliary input.[7] Therefore we can apply the bound for Yao's box problem to derive a security bound for PRGs in the QROM-AI.

What is left is how to derive a security bound for Yao's box problem.[8] Basically, we follow the classical counterpart that was shown by De et al. [DTT10], which is roughly described as follows. First, we choose a random subset $R \subset [N]$ by putting each element of $x \in [N]$ into R with a certain probability, which will be used as the shared randomness between the encoder and the decoder. Then we define the set G of good elements where we say that $x \in [N]$ is good if (A): $x \in R$, and (B): for any query x' made by $\mathcal{A}$ with input x, we have $x' \notin R$.[9] Then we partition G into two subsets G_0 that consists of all $x \in G$ such that $\mathcal{A}$ correctly guesses $\mathcal{O}(x)$ on input x, and $G_1 := G \setminus G_0$. By some analyses of probabilities, they showed that $|G|$ is "not too small" and $|G_0| - |G_1| = \Omega(\varepsilon|G|)$ with "non-small" probability where ε is $\mathcal{A}$'s advantage (i.e., $\mathcal{A}$ returns the correct answer with probability $1/2 + \varepsilon$). Then they construct an encoder that outputs the partial truth table of $\mathcal{O}$ on $[N] \setminus G$, the description of the set G_0, and the

---

[6] In the actual proof, we rely on the *semi-classical one-way to hiding theorem* recently given by Ambainis, Hamburg, and Unruh [AHU19].

[7] More precisely, since an auxiliary input cannot depend on x, we consider the partial truth table of $\mathcal{O}$ that gives the first $i - 1$ bits of $\mathcal{O}(x)$ for all x as a part of the auxiliary input.

[8] Nayebi et al. [NABT15] also studied Yao's box problem. However, they only considered the worst case, so their result is not applicable for our purpose.

[9] Recall that this is a review of the classical case, and thus this condition is well-defined.

Quantum Random Oracle Model with Auxiliary Input

auxiliary input used by $\mathcal{A}$. The decoder can recover the whole truth table of $\mathcal{O}$ by running $\mathcal{A}$ on each $x \in G$ and negating it if $x \in G_1$.[10] We note that the decoder never gets stuck in simulating the oracle since all of $\mathcal{A}$'s queries are outside R where the decoder knows the value of $\mathcal{O}$. They showed that the encoding size is much smaller than the whole truth table when $|G_0| - |G_1|$ is "large". (Note that the needed number of bits to represent the set G_0 is smaller when $|G_0| - |G_1|$ is larger since the number of possible choices of G_0 and G_1 is smaller when $|G_0| - |G_1|$ is larger assuming $|G_0| > |G_1|$.) More specifically, they showed that we can obtain a meaningful bound when $|G|$ is "not too small" and we have $|G_0| - |G_1| = \Omega(\varepsilon|G|)$, which occurs with "non-small" probability.

When generalizing this strategy to the quantum setting, there are several obstacles.

First, the condition (B) is not well-defined in the quantum setting. This can be easily adapted by requiring that $\mathcal{A}$'s query magnitudes on elements of R are "small" instead of requiring $\mathcal{A}$ to not query any of them.

Second, the sets G_0 and G_1 are not well-defined in the quantum setting since we cannot assume $\mathcal{A}$ is deterministic in the quantum setting. This can be resolved by including the randomness for measurements in the shared randomness between the encoder and decoder similarly to the case of OWFs.

Third, in the classical setting, for proving that $|G|$ is "not too small" and we have $|G_0| - |G_1| = \Omega(\varepsilon|G|)$ with "non-small" probability, we use the fact that the probability that x is good (i.e., $\Pr[x \in G]$) is constant for all $x \in [N]$. In the classical setting, this can be assumed without loss of generality since we can force an adversary to not make the same queries twice. On the other hand, this cannot be assumed in the quantum setting, and $\Pr[x \in G]$ may depend on x. Fortunately, we can still show that if we choose parameters appropriately, then $\Pr[x \in G]$ are well-balanced, i.e., maximal and minimal values of $\Pr[x \in G]$ are very close. By using this, we can still prove that $|G|$ is "not too small" and we have $|G_0| - |G_1| = \Omega(\varepsilon|G|)$ with "non-small" probability though the proof becomes more involved.

With these ideas, we obtain a security bound for Yao's box problem in the quantum setting.

pqPRFs and pqMACs in QROM-AI. With ideas used for OWFs and PRGs as explained above, the results for pqPRFs and pqMACs in the ROM-AI in [DGK17] can be naturally translated into ones in the QROM-AI. Since the original bounds in [DGK17] only considered classical accesses to PRF/MAC oracles, our results inherit this. One thing we have to care about here is that classical PRF and MAC oracles are not unitary, and we cannot assume that measurements are deferred to the end of the computation by the adversary. Thus for applying our technique of deterministic simulation of quantum computations, we include randomness for all measurements that are possibly done in the middle of the computation by the adversary in the shared randomness between the

---

[10] Though the encoding does not contain the description of G, the decoder can recover it from R.

encoder and decoder. We note that the size of shared randomness does not affect the limitation of a compression, and this does not make our bounds worse.

Bound for Inverting Permutations with Quantum Advice. Next, we move on to discussing quantum auxiliary inputs. Our strategy is to use the compression technique similarly to the case of the classical auxiliary inputs. However, if we consider quantum auxiliary inputs, we first have to extend the compression lemma to the setting where encodings are quantum. Fortunately, such an extension is already known [Nay99, NS06], and both papers showed that the bound is almost the same as the classical case.

Given this, one may think that security bounds in the QROM-AI are quite easy to extend to ones in the QROM-QAI. However, this is not the case. Recall that decoders in these proofs run an adversary $\mathcal{A}$ many times. On the other hand, we cannot reuse a quantum auxiliary input since it may be broken in each running of $\mathcal{A}$. Thus, an encoding has to contain as many copies of the auxiliary input as the number of executions of $\mathcal{A}$ by the decoder, in which case the encoding is no longer small. Indeed, Nayebi et al. [NABT15] mentioned that their result is difficult to extend to the quantum auxiliary input setting for this reason.

We overcome this issue by using a general principle of quantum information, often called the *gentle measurement lemma* [Win99, AR19], which states that if we can predict the outcome of a measurement with probability almost 1, then the measurement barely damages the quantum state. To apply the lemma, we amplify the success probability of an adversary $\mathcal{A}$ to almost 1 by running it many times.[11] Especially, if the correct solution of a problem in question is unique (as in the inversion problem of a permutation), then $\mathcal{A}$ outputs a certain value with probability almost 1. In this case, the quantum auxiliary input is not damaged much in each running of $\mathcal{A}$ due to the gentle measurement lemma and can be reused many times in the decoding procedure. We note that the decoder still needs a certain number of copies of the auxiliary input since it has to run the adversary many times to amplify the success probability. However, the number of copies needed is not too large since the adversary's error probability decreases exponentially in the number of repetitions. Thus, the encoding does not become too large, and we can obtain a meaningful bound. This is how we obtain a security bound for inverting a random permutation with quantum advice.

We note that the above method crucially relies on the solution of the problem being unique. Otherwise, even if an adversary's success probability is almost 1, its output may still have high entropy, in which case the gentle measurement lemma is not applicable. This is why we limit our attention to random *permutations* instead of random *functions*.

---

[11] A similar idea was used by Aaronson [Aar05] to show limitations of quantum one-way communication and algorithms with quantum advice.

1.4 Limitations and Open Problems

Though we made progress in understanding the power of non-uniform attacks in the quantum setting, our results contain many limitations.

1. We do not have any result for CRHFs in the QROM-AI/QROM-QAI.
2. Our results on PRFs and MACs in the QROM-AI are limited to pqMACs and pqPRFs where oracles (except for the random oracle) are classical.
3. All security bounds shown in this paper are much less tight than the counterparts in the classical setting, and far from matching the best known attacks. We note that known security bounds of many primitives including OWFs, PRGs, PRFs, and MACs in the ROM-AI do not match the best known attacks even in the classical setting [DGK17,CDGS18].
4. Our techniques cannot be used for analyzing schemes on the basis of computational assumptions since it would be difficult to capture these assumptions with the compression technique. We note that this limitation is overcome by using another technique called the *pre-sampling technique* instead of a compression technique in the classical setting [Unr07,CDGS18].
5. We have no security bound in the QROM-QAI. A possible approach toward that is to extend our result on one-wayness of a random permutation with quantum auxiliary input.

We leave the above limitations as open problems to be overcome.

Also, we are not aware of any non-trivial attack in the QROM-AI or QROM-QAI that outperforms ones in the ROM-AI except for attacks that just ignore auxiliary inputs (e.g., Grover's algorithm [Gro96] and BHT [BHT97] algorithm). We leave it as an interesting open problem to give a non-trivial attack that utilizes auxiliary inputs against any primitive in the QROM-AI or QROM-QAI.

1.5 Related Work

Security Bounds against Non-uniform Attacks in Other Models. Corrigan-Gibbs and Kogan [CK18] studied non-uniform attacks in the generic group model (GGM), showed security bounds for several problems including the discrete logarithm problem that matches the best known attack. Their results are based on the compression technique. Coretti, Dodis, and Guo [CDG18] studied non-uniform attacks in the random permutation model (RPM), ideal-cipher model (IPM), and GGM, and showed security bounds for many applications in these models by developing a general tool to analyze them. Their results are based on the pre-sampling technique. We note that both above works only consider classical attacks.

Quantum-Accessible PRFs and MACs. Zhandry [Zha12a] gave the first constructions of qPRFs from OWFs or learning with errors (LWE) assumption in the standard model as well as a separation between pqPRFs and qPRFs.

Boneh and Zhandry [BZ13] formally defined qMACs and showed that qPRFs are sufficient to construct them. A stronger and the best current security notion for qMACs was proposed by Garg, Yuen, and Zhandry [GYZ17].

We note that these works focus on constructions in the standard model, whereas this work focuses on hash-based constructions in the QROM-AI or QROM-QAI that are much more efficient.

Compression Technique in Quantum Setting. Besides Nayebi et al. [NABT15], Hosoyamada and Yamakawa [HY18] also used the compression technique in the quantum setting to show a black-box separation of CRHFs from one-way permutations. Their technique is incomparable with ours as they showed bounds for inverting random permutations in the presence of a specific quantum oracle that finds collisions whereas we show bounds for several applications of a random oracle in the presence of any bounded-length auxiliary inputs.

2   Preliminaries

Notations. We say a function $\varepsilon(n)$ is negligible if $\varepsilon(n) < 1/|p(n)|$ for any polynomial p for sufficiently large n. For a positive integer n, we write $[n] = \{1, \ldots, n\}$ to denote the set of positive integers less than or equal to n. In tilde notations $\widetilde{O}(f(A, B, \cdots))$ or $\widetilde{\Omega}(f(A, B, \cdots))$, we ignore non-negative degree polylogarithmic factors with respect to all capital variables which appear in the context. For example, we write $(T^2/N) \cdot \log M = \widetilde{O}(T^2/N)$. To denote the event that a probabilistic or quantum algorithm $\mathcal{A}$ with input z outputs x, we write $\mathcal{A}(z) \to x$.

Quantum algorithms have intrinsic randomness when they perform measurements. The probability that a quantum algorithm $\mathcal{A}$ outputs x on an input z is denoted by $\Pr_{\mathcal{A}}[\mathcal{A}(z) \to x]$. To denote quantum objects such as quantum states or a quantum-accessible oracle, we use the ket notation $|\cdot\rangle$. For example, $|\phi\rangle$ denotes a quantum state, while x is a classical string. For basics of quantum computing, we refer readers to [NC00].

2.1   Oracle-Aided Quantum Algorithm

An oracle-aided quantum algorithm is a quantum algorithm that can perform quantum computations and can access oracles. In this paper, we consider three types of oracles: quantum-accessible oracle, classical-accessible oracle, and semi-classical oracle [AHU19], which is explained in the next subsection. A quantum-accessible oracle that computes a function $f : X \to Y$ applies a unitary that transforms a query $|x, y\rangle$ to $|x, y \oplus f(x)\rangle$, and returns the resulting state. A classical-accessible oracle that computes a function $f : X \to Y$, given a query $|x, y\rangle$, first measures the input register $|x\rangle$, and then returns $|x, y \oplus f(x)\rangle$. Note that a classical-accessible oracle is not unitary. We often use $\mathcal{A}^{|f\rangle}$ to mean that $\mathcal{A}$ accesses a quantum-accessible oracle that computes f and $\mathcal{A}^f$ to mean that $\mathcal{A}$ accesses classical-accessible oracle that computes f. We allow an oracle-aided quantum algorithm to make queries in parallel. Its query depth d is defined to be the number of oracle calls counting parallel queries as one query.

2.2 Semi-classical Oracle

In this section, we review *semi-classical oracles* introduced in [AHU19]. Here, we only define a semi-classical oracle for the indicator function of a set S since we only need it in this paper. A semi-classical oracle $\mathcal{O}_S^{SC}$ for a set $S \subseteq X$ is queried with two registers, an input register Q with $\mathbb{C}^X$ and an output register R with space $\mathbb{C}^2$. When queried with a value $|x\rangle$ in Q, the oracle returns whether $x \in S$ in the output register R. More formally, it performs a measurement with projectors M_0 and M_1, where $M_0 := \sum_{x \in X \setminus S} |x\rangle \langle x|$ and $M_1 := \sum_{x \in S} |x\rangle \langle x|$, and initializes R to $|0\rangle$ or $|1\rangle$ corresponding to the measurement result.

In the execution of a quantum algorithm $\mathcal{A}^{\mathcal{O}_S^{SC}}$, Find denotes the event that $\mathcal{O}_S^{SC}$ returns $|1\rangle$. This event is well-defined, since $\mathcal{O}_S^{SC}$ measures its outputs.

Punctured Oracle. If H is an oracle with domain X and codomain Y, we define $|H\rangle \setminus S$ as an oracle which, on input x, first queries $\mathcal{O}_S^{SC}(x)$ and then queries $H(x)$. The lemma ([AHU19, Lemma 1]) states that the outcome of $\mathcal{A}^{|H\rangle \setminus S}$ is independent of $H(x)$ for all $x \in S$ when Find does not occur. We review the semi-classical oneway-to-hiding lemma (the SC-O2H lemma in short):

Lemma 1 (The SC-O2H lemma [AHU19, Theorem 1]). *Let $S \subseteq X$ be random. Let $G, H \colon X \to Y$ be random functions satisfying $\forall x \notin S\ [G(x) = H(x)]$. Let z be a random bit string. (S, G, H, z may have an arbitrary joint distribution.)*

Let $\mathcal{A}$ be an oracle-aided quantum algorithm of query depth d (not necessarily unitary). Let

$$P_{\text{left}} := \Pr[b = 1 : b \leftarrow \mathcal{A}^{|H\rangle}(z)],$$
$$P_{\text{right}} := \Pr[b = 1 : b \leftarrow \mathcal{A}^{|G\rangle}(z)],$$
$$P_{\text{find}} := \Pr[\text{Find} : A^{|G\rangle \setminus S}(z)] = \Pr[\text{Find} : A^{|H\rangle \setminus S}(z)].$$

Then we have

$$|P_{\text{left}} - P_{\text{right}}| \le 2\sqrt{(d+1) \cdot P_{\text{find}}} \ \text{and} \ |\sqrt{P_{\text{left}}} - \sqrt{P_{\text{right}}}| \le 2\sqrt{(d+1) \cdot P_{\text{find}}}.$$

The lemma also holds with bound $\sqrt{(d+1) \cdot P_{\text{find}}}$ for the following alternative definition of P_{right}:

$$P_{\text{right}} := \Pr[b = 1 \wedge \neg \text{Find} : b \leftarrow A^{|G\rangle \setminus S}(z)].$$

We often denote the above probability by $\Pr[\neg \text{Find} : A^{|G\rangle \setminus S}(z) \to 1]$ for notational simplicity.

Lemma 2 (Search in semi-classical oracle [AHU19, Theorem 2 and Corollary 1]). *Let $\mathcal{A}$ be any oracle-aided quantum algorithm making at most q queries (depth d) to a semi-classical oracle with domain X. Let $S \subseteq X$ and $z \in \{0,1\}^*$. (S, z may have an arbitrary joint distribution.)*

Let $\mathcal{B}$ be an algorithm that on input z chooses $i \leftarrow \{1, \ldots, d\}$; runs $\mathcal{A}^{\mathcal{O}_{\emptyset}^{SC}}(z)$ until (just before) the i-th query; then measures all query input registers in the computational basis and outputs the set T of measurement outcomes.

Then we have

$$\Pr[\text{Find} : \mathcal{A}^{\mathcal{O}_{S}^{SC}}(z)] \leq 4d \cdot \Pr[S \cap T \neq \emptyset : T \leftarrow \mathcal{B}(z)].$$

In particular, if S and z are independent, $\mathcal{A}$ makes at most q queries, and we let $P_{\max} := \max_{x \in X} \Pr[x \in S]$, then we have

$$d \cdot \Pr[S \cap T \neq \emptyset : T \leftarrow \mathcal{B}(z)] \leq q \cdot P_{\max}.$$

Remark 1. In the above lemmas, the input z is assumed to be a classical string. However, we can obtain exactly the same bound even if z is a quantum state. This is because any quantum state can be described by a classical string with an exponential blowup of the size, and the above lemmas are only about query-complexities and the size of z does not matter.

3   Quantum ROM with Classical AI

In this section, we show security bounds for primitives in the QROM-AI.

3.1   Preparations

First, we prepare some lemmas and notations that are used in our proofs.

Compression Lemma. The following lemma states that there exists an information-theoretic lower bound for a compression algorithm.

Lemma 3 ([DTT10, Fact 8.1]). *Let M, C, R be sets. Let $E : M \times R \to C$ and $D : C \times R \to M$ be deterministic algorithms. For $\delta \in [0, 1]$, if we have*

$$\Pr_{r \leftarrow R}[D(E(m, r), r) = m] \geq \delta$$

for all $m \in M$, then we have $|C| \geq \delta|M|$, which can be rephrased as $\log|C| \geq \log|M| - \log 1/\delta$.

We use the above lemma (which we call the *compression lemma*) to derive security bounds for various primitives in the QROM-AI by constructing a pair of encoding and decoding algorithms that compress the truth table of a random function by using the power of an adversary against the primitive. Note that we encode a function into a classical bit string while we use a quantum adversary.

Simulating Measurement. Quantum algorithms are inherently randomized due to the intrinsic randomness of measurements. However, if we do not care about the running-time, we can fix the randomness in the measurement by classically simulating the execution of the algorithm.

More precisely, we can classically simulate an execution of any quantum algorithm $\mathcal{A}(z)$ with a randomness $r \in [0, 1]^{12}$ by first computing the final state, which is known to be possible in classical exponential time, and then choosing a measurement result in accordance with the randomness r, where we assume that $\mathcal{A}$ performs only one measurement at the end of its execution without loss of generality. We denote this procedure by $\mathsf{Sim}_r(\mathcal{A}(z))$. If we consider many inputs $z \in Z$ and a corresponding random coin $R = \{r_z\} \in [0, 1]^{|Z|}$, we just denote $\mathsf{Sim}_{r_z}(\mathcal{A}(z))$ by $\mathsf{Sim}_R(\mathcal{A}(z))$ for notational simplicity. We note that exactly the same procedure is possible for an oracle-aided quantum algorithm $\mathcal{A}^{|f\rangle}$ that accesses a quantum oracle $|f\rangle$ that computes a function f *if the simulator knows the whole truth table of f* since we can think of the combination of $\mathcal{A}$ and $|f\rangle$ as a single quantum algorithm. We also note that almost the same procedure is possible for an oracle-aided quantum algorithm $\mathcal{A}^{|f\rangle,g}$ that accesses both a quantum oracle $|f\rangle$ and a classical oracle g if the simulator knows the whole truth table of f and g with the following modification. The difference from the case of a quantum oracle is that the oracle may not be unitary and we are no longer able to assume that the algorithm performs a measurement once, and it may perform a measurement in the middle of the computation. This can be dealt with by augmenting the amount of randomness used by the simulator so that fresh randomness is available in the simulation of each measurement.

Since the compression lemma (Lemma 3) holds even for an unbounded-time encoder and decoder that may share unbounded-size randomness, we can allow them to simulate a (oracle-aided) quantum algorithm classically in the above way.

Notations. In this section, we consider a random oracle with the domain $[K] \times [N]$ (or $[K] \times [N] \times [L]$ for the case of pqPRFs and pqMACs) and the codomain $[M]$. We omit to state a distribution of a random oracle $\mathcal{O}$ if that is uniformly chosen from the set of functions with the corresponding domain and codomain. We use a and x (or k for the case of pqPRFs and pqMACs) to represent elements of $[K]$ and $[N]$ respectively throughout the section, and often omit to state distributions when they are uniform. For example, we write $\Pr_{a,x}[f(a, x) = y]$ instead of $\Pr_{a \leftarrow [K], x \leftarrow [N]}[f(a, x) = y]$.

3.2   Function Inversion

The following theorem is the main result of this section.

---

[12] In an actual simulation, the randomness should be approximated by a rational number up to a sufficient precision. We just think of the randomness as a real number for simplicity.

Theorem 1. *Let $\mathcal{O} \in \mathsf{Func}([K] \times [N], [M])$ be a random oracle. Suppose that $\mathcal{A}$ is an oracle-aided quantum algorithm that takes an S-bit classical advice $\mathsf{st}_\mathcal{O}$ (that may depend on $\mathcal{O}$) as input, makes at most T oracle queries, and satisfies*

$$\Pr_{\mathcal{A},\mathcal{O},a,x}\left[\mathcal{O}(a,x) = \mathcal{O}(a,x') : \mathcal{A}^{|\mathcal{O}\rangle}(\mathsf{st}_\mathcal{O}, a, \mathcal{O}(a,x)) \to x'\right] = \varepsilon.$$

Then it holds that

$$\varepsilon^2 = \tilde{O}\left(\frac{ST^2}{K\min(M,N)} + \frac{T^2N}{\min(M,N)^2}\right).$$

The main idea of the proof of this theorem is to compress the truth table of the random function into a smaller encoding by using an algorithm that inverts the function. Then by applying Lemma 3, we obtain a bound for the advantage to invert the function. Specifically, we encode a function into an encoding that consists of a partial truth table and information to recover the remaining part of the truth table similarly to [DGK17].

We also introduce another lemma, which can be seen as a variant of the above theorem. This lemma is used for proving lower bounds for other problems in the next sections. In this lemma, we give an upper bound for the probability that the event Find occurs when an adversary is given a punctured oracle on the correct answer. (See Sect. 2.2 for the definitions of Find and the punctured oracle.) This corresponds to [DGK17, Corollary 1], which gives a bound for the probability that an adversary *ever queries* the correct answer to the oracle in the classical case.

Lemma 4. *Let $\mathcal{O} \in \mathsf{Func}([K] \times [N], [M])$ be a random oracle. Suppose that $\mathcal{A}$ is an oracle-aided quantum algorithm that takes an S-bit classical advice $\mathsf{st}_\mathcal{O}$ (that may depend on $\mathcal{O}$) as input, and makes at most T oracle queries. Then it holds that*

$$\Pr_{\mathcal{A},\mathcal{O},a,x}\left[\mathsf{Find} : \mathcal{A}^{|\mathcal{O}\rangle \setminus \{(a,x)\}}(\mathsf{st}_\mathcal{O}, a, \mathcal{O}(a,x))\right] = O\left(\frac{ST^2}{KN} + \frac{T^2\log N}{N}\right).$$

Proof of Theorem 1. First, we consider an adversary $\mathcal{A}$ (which we call a *biased adversary*) that breaks the one-wayness in a slightly stronger sense. Namely, we assume that we have

$$\Pr_{\mathcal{O},a,x}\left[\Pr_{\mathcal{A}}[\mathcal{A}^{|\mathcal{O}\rangle}(\mathsf{st}_\mathcal{O}, a, \mathcal{O}(a,x)) \to x' \wedge \mathcal{O}(a,x) = \mathcal{O}(a,x')] \geq c\right] \geq \varepsilon$$

for a fixed constant c. We will later show that we have

$$\varepsilon = \tilde{O}\left(\frac{ST^2}{K\min(M,N)} + \frac{T^2N}{\min(M,N)^2}\right)$$

in this setting. For the time being, we assume that the above statement is true and prove the theorem. Suppose that there exists an algorithm $\mathcal{A}$ such that

$$\Pr_{\mathcal{A},\mathcal{O},a,x}\left[\mathcal{O}(a,x) = \mathcal{O}(a,x') : \mathcal{A}^{|\mathcal{O}\rangle}(\mathsf{st}_\mathcal{O}, a, \mathcal{O}(a,x)) \to x'\right] = \varepsilon'.$$

By an averaging argument, at least an $(\varepsilon'/2)$-fraction of $(\mathcal{O}, a, x)$ satisfies

$$\Pr_{\mathcal{A}}\left[\mathcal{O}(a, x) = \mathcal{O}(a, x') : \mathcal{A}^{|\mathcal{O}\rangle}(\mathsf{st}_{\mathcal{O}}, a, \mathcal{O}(a, x)) \to x'\right] \geq \varepsilon'/2.$$

Applying the amplitude amplification [BHMT02], we obtain another algorithm $\mathcal{A}'$ that uses $\mathcal{A}$, $\mathcal{A}^{-1}$ and $\mathcal{O}$ as sub-routines $O(\varepsilon'^{-1/2})$ times and satisfies

$$\Pr_{\mathcal{A}'}\left[\mathcal{O}(a, x) = \mathcal{O}(a, x') : \mathcal{A}'^{|\mathcal{O}\rangle}(\mathsf{st}_{\mathcal{O}}, a, \mathcal{O}(a, x)) \to x'\right] = \Omega(1),$$

where we abuse the notation to use $\mathcal{A}$ and $\mathcal{A}^{-1}$ to mean the unitary part of $\mathcal{A}$ and its inverse, respectively. By the bound for the biased adversary, we have $\varepsilon' = \widetilde{O}\left(\frac{ST^2/\varepsilon'}{K\min(M,N)} + \frac{T^2 N/\varepsilon'}{\min(M,N)^2}\right)$, which implies

$$\varepsilon'^2 = \widetilde{O}\left(\frac{ST^2}{K\min(M, N)} + \frac{T^2 N}{\min(M, N)^2}\right)$$

as desired.

Now it suffices to prove the bound for the biased adversary. For the sake of contradiction, we assume that we have

$$\varepsilon = \widetilde{\Omega}(ST^2/K\min(M, N) + T^2 N/\min(M, N)^2). \tag{1}$$

Note that it particularly implies $CT^2 \leq \varepsilon KN$ for a sufficiently large C since the tilde notation hides a non-negative degree polylogarithmic factor and $T^2/KN = O(ST^2/K\min(M, N))$ holds.[13] Here, to apply Lemma 1, we consider another adversary $\mathcal{B}$ that takes a list L of classical strings as an additional input and works as follows:

$\mathcal{B}^{|f\rangle}(\mathsf{st}_{\mathcal{O}}, a, y, L)$: It runs $\mathcal{A}^{|f\rangle}(\mathsf{st}_{\mathcal{O}}, a, y)$. Then $\mathcal{B}$ outputs 1 if the answer z of the algorithm $\mathcal{A}$ satisfies $(a, z) \in L$, and outputs 0 otherwise.

Note that the assumption on the biased adversary $\mathcal{A}$ can be rephrased as

$$\Pr_{\mathcal{O}, a, x}\left[\Pr_{\mathcal{B}}[\mathcal{B}^{|\mathcal{O}\rangle}(\mathsf{st}_{\mathcal{O}}, a, \mathcal{O}(a, x), \mathcal{O}_a^{-1}(\mathcal{O}(a, x))) \to 1] \geq c\right] \geq \varepsilon$$

where $\mathcal{O}_a(x) := \mathcal{O}(a, x)$ and $\mathcal{O}_a^{-1}(y) := \{(a, x) : \mathcal{O}(a, x) = y\}$. Here, we state a claim about the size of $\mathcal{O}_a^{-1}(y)$ whose proof can be found in the full version.

Claim 1. *Except for an $(\varepsilon/4)$-fraction of $\mathcal{O} \in \mathsf{Func}([K] \times [N], [M])$, we have*

$$|\mathcal{O}_a^{-1}(y)| = |\{x : \mathcal{O}_a(x) = y\}| = \widetilde{O}(N/\min(N, M))$$

for all $(a, y) \in [K] \times [M]$.

---

[13] Looking ahead, this is used in the proof of Claim 2.

By an averaging argument, at least an $(\varepsilon/2)$-fraction of $f \in \mathsf{Func}([K] \times [N], [M])$ satisfies

$$\Pr_{a,x}\left[\Pr_{\mathcal{B}}[\mathcal{B}^{|f\rangle}(\mathsf{st}_f, a, f(a,x), f_a^{-1}(f(a,x))) \to 1] \geq c\right] \geq \varepsilon/2.$$

Combining this with Claim 1, at least an $(\varepsilon/4)$-fraction of $\mathsf{Func}([K] \times [N], [M])$, denoted by $\mathcal{F}$, simultaneously satisfies $\Pr_{\mathcal{B}}[\mathcal{B}^{|f\rangle}(\mathsf{st}_f, a, f(a,x), f_a^{-1}(f(a,x))) \to 1] \geq c$ and $|f_a^{-1}(y)| = \tilde{O}(N/\min(N,M))$ for all $(a,y) \in [K] \times [M]$. We define $\beta = \tilde{O}(N/\min(M,N))$ so that we have $|f_a^{-1}(y)| \leq \beta$ for all (a,y).

We fix an arbitrary function $f \in \mathcal{F}$ and write L to denote the set $f_a^{-1}(f(a,x))$. We will describe an encoder that compresses the truth table of f to generate an encoding that consists of a partial truth table of f and other information to recover the remaining part of the truth table by using the algorithm $\mathcal{A}$. What is non-trivial is that the decoder has to simulate the algorithm $\mathcal{A}$ that makes queries to f though it is given only a partial truth table of f as a part of the encoding. We will show that this is actually possible by using the SC-O2H lemma (Lemma 1) below.

A public randomness r shared by the encoder and decoder (in Lemma 3) specifies R_1 and R_2 as explained below. A set $R_1 \subset [K] \times [M]$ is chosen so that each $(a,y) \in [K] \times [M]$ is included in R_1 with probability $d/T(T+1)$ for a fixed constant $d \leq c^2/1280$. Let $R_{(a,x)} := R_1 \setminus \{(a, f(a,x))\}$. For a set $S \subset [K] \times [M]$, we define $S_a := \{y \in [M] : (a,y) \in S\}$ and $f^{-1}(S) := \cup_{a \in [K]} f_a^{-1}(S_a)$.

We say that $(a,x) \in I$ is good if both

(A) $(a, f(a,x)) \in R_1$,

(B) $\Pr[\mathsf{Find} : \mathcal{B}^{|f\rangle \setminus f^{-1}(R_{(a,x)})}(\mathsf{st}_f, a, f(a,x), L)] \leq \dfrac{c^2}{16(T+1)}$

hold. We denote the set of good elements by G. Note that if we have $f(a,x) = f(a,x')$, then we have $(a,x) \in G$ if and only if $(a,x') \in G$.

Here, we state a claim that states that G is "not too small" with high probability whose proof is given in the full version.

Claim 2. $\Pr_{R_1}[|G| \geq \delta \varepsilon KN/T^2] \geq 0.8$ *for some constant* $\delta > 0$.

For $y \in [M]$, we define a function $g_y : [K] \times [N] \to [M]$ by

$$g_y(z) = \begin{cases} f(z), & \text{if } z \in ([K] \times [N]) \setminus f^{-1}(R_1), \\ y, & \text{otherwise.} \end{cases}$$

By the SC-O2H lemma (Lemma 1), for any $(a,x) \in G$, it holds that

$$\left|\Pr_{\mathcal{B}}[\mathcal{B}^{|f\rangle}(\mathsf{st}_f, a, f(a,x), L) \to 1] - \Pr_{\mathcal{B}}[\mathcal{B}^{|g_{f(a,x)}\rangle}(\mathsf{st}_f, a, f(a,x), L) \to 1]\right|$$

$$\leq 2\sqrt{(T+1) \cdot \Pr[\mathsf{Find} : \mathcal{B}^{|f\rangle \setminus f^{-1}(R_{(a,x)})}(\mathsf{st}_f, a, f(a,x), L)]} \leq c/2,$$

where we used the condition (B) for deriving the last inequality. Since we have $\Pr_{\mathcal{B}}[\mathcal{B}^{|f\rangle}(\mathsf{st}_f, a, f(a,x), L) \to 1] \geq c$, we have

$$\Pr_{\mathcal{B}}[\mathcal{B}^{|g_{f(a,x)}\rangle}(\mathsf{st}_f, a, f(a,x), L) \to 1] \geq \frac{c}{2}$$

for any $(a,x) \in G$. It is easy to see that this can be rephrased as

$$\Pr_{\mathcal{A}}[\mathcal{A}^{|g_{f(a,x)}\rangle}(\mathsf{st}_f, a, f(a,x)) \to x' \wedge f(a,x) = f(a,x')] \geq c/2.$$

The randomness R_2, which is another random coin specified by r, is used for the simulation

$$\mathsf{Sim}_{R_2}\left(\mathcal{A}^{|g_{f(a,x)}\rangle}(\mathsf{st}_f, a, f(a,x))\right)$$

of $\mathcal{A}^{|g_{f(a,x)}\rangle}(\mathsf{st}_f, a, f(a,x))$.[14] It outputs x' such that $f(a,x) = f(a,x')$ with probability at least $c/2$ over the choice of R_2. Then for at least a $(c/4)$-fraction of R_2, the simulation of $\mathcal{A}$ with oracle access to $|g_{f(a,x)}\rangle$ instead of $|f\rangle$ outputs a correct preimage for at least a $(c/4)$-fraction of (a,x). More precisely, for at least a $(c/4)$-fraction of R_2, the following condition is satisfied:

(∗) There exists at least a $(c/4)$-fraction of good elements (a,x), which we denote by X, such that we have

$$\mathsf{Sim}_{R_2}\left(\mathcal{A}^{|g_{f(a,x)}\rangle}(\mathsf{st}_f, a, f(a,x))\right) \to x' \text{ such that } f(a,x) = f(a,x')$$

for all $(a,x) \in X$.

We again remark that $(a,x) \in X$ and $(a,x') \in X$ are equivalent if $f(a,x) = f(a,x')$. We say that (R_1, R_2) is good if the following three conditions all hold:

1) $|G| \geq \delta\varepsilon KN/T^2$,   2) the condition (∗),   3) $|R_1| = \Theta(\varepsilon KM/T^2)$.

By Claim 2, the first statement holds with probability at least 0.8 (over the choice of R_1), and the second holds with probability at least $c/4$ (over the choice of R_2 for any fixed R_1) as discussed above, and the last holds with probability $1 - o(1)$ by the Chernoff bound. Therefore, the probability that (R_1, R_2) is good is $\Omega(1)$. When (R_1, R_2) is good, we clearly have $|X| = \Omega(\varepsilon KN/T^2)$ by definition.

Now we are ready to explicitly describe the encoder and decoder for f. Note that the decoder will correctly recover f as long as (R_1, R_2) is good. The encoder induces R_1, R_2 from the given public randomness. The encoder computes $X_a := \{x : (a,x) \in X\}$, $Y_a := \{y : y = f(a,x) \text{ for } x \in X_a\}$, $Y := \cup_{a \in [K]}\{(a,y) : y \in Y_a\}$, and $R_a = R_1 \cap (\{a\} \times [M])$ for all $a \in [K]$. Then, $|Y| \geq |X|/\beta$ holds by the definition of β.

For each $a \in [K]$, the encoder computes a set $Z_a \subset [N]$ as the set consisting of outputs of simulations $\mathsf{Sim}_{R_2}\left(\mathcal{A}^{|g_y\rangle}(\mathsf{st}_f, a, y)\right)$ for all $y \in Y_a$. We note that Z_a is well-defined since the simulation is deterministic once R_2 is fixed. Let $Z := \cup_{a \in [K]}\{(a,z) : z \in Z_a\}$. Clearly, we have $|Z_a| = |Y_a|$ and $|Z| = |Y|$. Now the function $f \in \mathcal{F}$ is encoded as follows, given the public randomness R_1, R_2.

---

[14] Specifically, R_2 consists of independent random coins $r_2(a,y)$ for each $(a,y) \in [K] \times [M]$ to simulate $\mathcal{A}^{|g_y\rangle}(\mathsf{st}_f, a, y)$.

- The advice string st_f: S bits.
- The description of Z_a with its size for each $a \in [K]$: $\log N + \log \binom{N}{|Z_a|}$ bits.
- The description of Y_a with its size for each $a \in [K]$: $\log M + \log \binom{|R_a|}{|Y_a|}$ bits.
- The values of f on $([K] \times [N]) \setminus Z$: $(KN - |Z|) \log M$ bits.

The values are encoded in the lexicographic order of their inputs. The size of the third component is derived by observing $Y_a \subset R_a$. Given this encoding and random sets R_1, R_2, the decoder fills the truth table of f as follows:

1. Reconstruct st_f, Y_a, Z_a, Y, and Z.
2. Fill the truth table of f on $([K] \times [N]) \setminus Z$.
3. Recover the set $f^{-1}(R_1) \subset [K] \times [N]$: this is done by 1) including all elements of Z (which are definitely in $f^{-1}(R_1)$ since they are good) and 2) including all $(a, x) \notin Z$ such that $f(a, x) \in R_1$, which can be checked by using the partial truth table on $([K] \times [N]) \setminus Z$.
4. Recover the function values on Z. This step is done by simulating the algorithm $\mathcal{A}$. More precisely, for each $(a, y) \in Y_a$, the decoder executes the simulation $\mathsf{Sim}_{R_2}\left(\mathcal{A}^{|g_y\rangle}(\mathsf{st}_f, a, y)\right)$ to obtain an output z and set the value of f on (a, z) to be y. By the definition of Z, this simulation correctly recovers the function values if the randomness (R_1, R_2) is good. Note that since the decoder has already recovered $f^{-1}(R_1)$, the decoder can simulate the function g_y.

The decoder successfully recovers f as long as (R_1, R_2) is good, which happens with probability $\Omega(1)$. The overall encoding size is

$$S + K \log N + K \log M + \sum_{a \in [K]} \left(\log \binom{N}{|Z_a|} + \log \binom{|R_a|}{|Y_a|} \right) + (KN - |Z|) \log M$$
$$\geq \log(\varepsilon M^{KN}) + O(1) = KN \log M + \log \varepsilon + O(1),$$
(2)

by the compression lemma (Lemma 3). Since we have $\log \binom{a}{b} \leq b \log(ea/b)$, $|Z_a| = |Y_a|$, and $|Z| = |Y|$, we obtain

$$\sum_{a \in [K]} \log \binom{N}{|Y_a|} + \sum_{a \in [K]} \log \binom{|R_a|}{|Y_a|} - |Y| \log M$$
$$\leq \sum_{a \in [K]} |Y_a| \log \left(\frac{eN}{|Y_a|} \right) + \sum_{a \in [K]} |Y_a| \log \left(\frac{e|R_a|}{|Y_a|} \right) - |Y| \log M$$
$$\leq |Y| \log \left(\frac{eKN}{|Y|} \right) + |Y| \log \left(\frac{e|R_1|}{|Y|} \right) - |Y| \log M$$
$$= |Y| \log \left(\frac{e^2 KN |R_1|}{M|Y|^2} \right),$$

where the second inequality is obtained by using log-concavity (or Jensen's inequality for log with weights $|Y_a|$ and $|R_a|$.) Combining this bound with the inequality (2), we obtain

$$S + K \log(MN) \geq |Y| \log \left(\frac{M|Y|^2}{e^2 K N |R_1|} \right) + \widetilde{O}(1), \tag{3}$$

where we used (1) to remove the $\log \varepsilon$ term in the right-hand side. Using $|X| = \Omega(\varepsilon K N / T^2)$, $|Y| \geq |X|/\beta$, and $|R_1| = \Theta(\varepsilon K M / T^2)$, we obtain $|Y|^2/|R_1| = \Omega(\varepsilon K N^2 / M T^2 \beta^2)$. This implies $|Y|^2/|R_1| \geq D \varepsilon K N^2 / M T^2 \beta^2$ for some constant D. If $D \varepsilon N / T^2 \beta^2 \leq e^3$ holds, then we have $\varepsilon \leq (e^3 T^2 N / D) \cdot (\beta/N)^2 = \widetilde{O}(T^2 N / \min(M, N)^2)$ since $\beta/N = \widetilde{O}(1/\min(M, N))$. Otherwise, we have $\frac{M|Y|^2}{e^2 K N |R_1|} \geq \frac{M}{e^2 K N} \cdot \frac{D \varepsilon K N^2}{M T^2 \beta^2} \geq e$. Putting this bound and the bound $|Y| \geq |X|/\beta = \Omega(\varepsilon K N / T^2 \beta)$ into (3), we obtain

$$O\left(S + K \log \max(M, N)\right) \geq |Y| + \widetilde{O}(1) = \Omega\left(\frac{\varepsilon K N}{\beta T^2} \right),$$

which implies $\varepsilon = \widetilde{O}\left(\frac{ST^2}{K \min(M,N)} + \frac{T^2}{\min(M,N)} \right)$. Combining the two cases, we obtain

$$\varepsilon = \widetilde{O}\left(\frac{ST^2}{K \min(M, N)} + \frac{T^2 N}{\min(M, N)^2} \right).$$

□

Proof sketch of Lemma 4. The proof is very similar to the proof of Theorem 1 except some parts. The main differences are

1. the algorithm does not output an element in $[N]$, and
2. we cannot apply the amplitude amplification since it uses a semi-classical oracle that is not unitary.

The first problem is resolved by considering another algorithm $\mathcal{B}$ that outputs the query register of the semi-classical oracle whenever Find occurs, and the second problem is circumvented by amplifying the success probability just by a parallel repetition. We note that there are two technical differences that make the proof easier: we choose the random coin R as a subset of $[K] \times [N]$ instead of $[K] \times [M]$ and need not consider a counterpart of Claim 1. The detailed proof can be found in the full version.

□

3.3 Pseudorandom Generators

In this section, we prove that a random function is a secure PRG even if we allow an adversary to make quantum queries to the function and to obtain a classical advice string. Our result is stated as follows.

Theorem 2. *Let $\mathcal{O} \in \mathsf{Func}([K] \times [N], [M])$ be a random oracle. Suppose that $\mathcal{A}$ is an oracle-aided quantum algorithm that takes an S-bit classical advice $\mathsf{st}_{\mathcal{O}}$ (that may depend on $\mathcal{O}$) as input, and makes at most T oracle queries. Then it holds that*

$$\left| \Pr_{\mathcal{A},\mathcal{O},a,x} \left[\mathcal{A}^{|\mathcal{O}\rangle}(\mathsf{st}_{\mathcal{O}}, a, \mathcal{O}(a,x)) \to 1 \right] \right| - \left| \Pr_{\mathcal{A},\mathcal{O},a,y} \left[\mathcal{A}^{|\mathcal{O}\rangle}(\mathsf{st}_{\mathcal{O}}, a, y) \to 1 \right] \right|$$

$$= \widetilde{O} \left(\sqrt[6]{\frac{ST^4}{KN} + \frac{T^4}{N}} \right),$$

where y is uniform in $[M]$.

For proving Theorem 2, we need the following lemma, which can be seen as a security bound for a quantum average case version of Yao's box problem [Yao90]. We note that the classical average case version was proven in [DTT10, Lemma 8.4] and quantum worst-case version was proven in [NABT15, Theorem 1], neither of which suffices for our purpose.

Lemma 5. *Let $\mathcal{F} \subset \mathsf{Func}([N], \{0,1\})$ be a set of functions. Suppose that $\mathcal{A}$ is an oracle-aided quantum algorithm that takes an S-bit classical advice st_f (that may depend on $f \in \mathcal{F}$) as input, makes at most T oracle queries, has query magnitudes 0 on its second input (i.e. x) for all queries, and satisfies*

$$\Pr_{\mathcal{A},x}[\mathcal{A}^{|f\rangle}(\mathsf{st}_f, x) \to f(x)] \geq \frac{1}{2} + \varepsilon$$

for all $f \in \mathcal{F}$. Then there is a pair of an encoder and decoder for the truth tables of functions in $\mathcal{F}$ with recovery probability $\Omega(\varepsilon^5/T^2)$ and encoding length at most $S + N - \Omega(\varepsilon^6 N/T^2)$. In particular, this implies $\varepsilon^6 = O(ST^2/N)$ for $\mathcal{F} = \mathsf{Func}([N], \{0,1\})$.

This lemma can be proven similarly to its classical counterpart in [DTT10, Lemma 8.4] except for some technical issues as discussed in Sect. 1.3. The proof of this lemma can be found in the full version. Now, we are ready to prove Theorem 2.

Proof of Theorem 2. We first sketch the outline of the proof by the following diagram:

$$p_0 := \Pr_{\mathcal{A},\mathcal{O},a,x}[\mathcal{A}^{|\mathcal{O}\rangle}(\mathsf{st}_{\mathcal{O}}, a, \mathcal{O}(a,x)) \to 1]$$

$$\overset{\text{O2H+Lemma 4}}{\approx} \quad p_1 := \Pr_{\mathcal{A},\mathcal{O},a,x}[\neg\mathsf{Find}: \mathcal{A}^{|\mathcal{O}\rangle\setminus\{(a,x)\}}(\mathsf{st}_{\mathcal{O}}, a, \mathcal{O}(a,x)) \to 1]$$

$$\overset{\text{Lemma 5}}{\approx} \quad p_2 := \Pr_{\mathcal{A},\mathcal{O},a,x}[\neg\mathsf{Find}: \mathcal{A}^{|\mathcal{O}\rangle\setminus\{(a,x)\}}(\mathsf{st}_{\mathcal{O}}, a, y) \to 1]$$

$$\overset{\text{O2H+Lemma 4}}{\approx} \quad p_3 := \Pr_{\mathcal{A},\mathcal{O},a,x}[\mathcal{A}^{|\mathcal{O}\rangle}(\mathsf{st}_{\mathcal{O}}, a, y) \to 1].$$

We assume that M is a power of 2 for simplicity.

Step 1. $|p_0 - p_1| = \tilde{O}\left(\sqrt[4]{\frac{ST^4}{KN}} + \frac{T^4}{N}\right)$

This is simply proven by using the SC-O2H lemma. More precisely, by Lemma 1,

$$|p_0 - p_1| \leq \sqrt{(T+1)\Pr_{\mathcal{A},\mathcal{O},a,x}\left[\mathsf{Find} : \mathcal{A}^{|\mathcal{O}\rangle\backslash\{(a,x)\}}(\mathsf{st}_{\mathcal{O}}, a, \mathcal{O}(a,x))\right]}$$

holds, which is bounded by $\tilde{O}\left(\sqrt[4]{\frac{ST^4}{KN}} + \frac{T^4}{N}\right)$ by Lemma 4.

Step 2. $|p_2 - p_3| = \tilde{O}\left(\sqrt[4]{\frac{ST^4}{KN}} + \frac{T^4}{N}\right)$

This is exactly the same as Step 1.

Step 3. $|p_1 - p_2| = \tilde{O}\left(\sqrt[6]{\frac{ST^2}{KN}}\right)$

First, we consider an oracle-aided quantum algorithm $\mathcal{B}$ that uses $\mathcal{A}$ as a sub-routine as follows.

$\mathcal{B}^{|\mathcal{O}\rangle}(\mathsf{st}_{\mathcal{O}}, a, x, y)$: It runs $\mathcal{A}^{|\mathcal{O}\rangle\backslash\{(a,x)\}}(\mathsf{st}_{\mathcal{O}}, a, y)$. If the event Find occurs w.r.t. the running of $\mathcal{A}$, $\mathcal{B}$ immediately halts and returns 0. Otherwise, $\mathcal{B}$ returns what $\mathcal{A}$ outputs.

We note that $\mathcal{B}$ can simulate the oracle $|\mathcal{O}\rangle \backslash \{(a,x)\}$ for $\mathcal{A}$ since it knows the punctured point (a,x). Moreover, $\mathcal{B}$'s query magnitude on (a,x) is 0 since before making a query to $\mathcal{O}$, it performs a partial measurement to check if the query is equal to (a,x) and immediately aborts if so by the definition of the punctured oracle. By the construction of $\mathcal{B}$, it is easy to see that

$$p_1 = \Pr_{\mathcal{B},\mathcal{O},a,x}[\mathcal{B}^{|\mathcal{O}\rangle}(\mathsf{st}_{\mathcal{O}}, a, x, \mathcal{O}(a,x)) \to 1],$$

$$p_2 = \Pr_{\mathcal{B},\mathcal{O},a,x}[\mathcal{B}^{|\mathcal{O}\rangle}(\mathsf{st}_{\mathcal{O}}, a, x, y) \to 1].$$

Let $|p_1 - p_2| = \varepsilon$. By Yao's equivalence of pseudorandomness to unpredictability [Yao82], there exists an $i \in [\log M]$, an oracle-aided quantum algorithm $\mathcal{C}$ whose query magnitude at (a,x) is 0, and an advice string $\tilde{\mathsf{st}}_{\mathcal{O}}$ that have at most $S + 1$ bits such that

$$\Pr_{\mathcal{C},\mathcal{O},a,x}[\mathcal{C}^{|\mathcal{O}\rangle}(\tilde{\mathsf{st}}_{\mathcal{O}}, a, x, \mathcal{O}_1(a,x), \cdots, \mathcal{O}_{i-1}(a,x)) \to \mathcal{O}_i(a,x)] \geq \frac{1}{2} + \frac{\varepsilon}{\log M},$$

where $\mathcal{O}_i(a,x)$ denotes the i-th bit of $\mathcal{O}(a,x)$.

If we define $T_{\mathcal{O}}$ as a partial truth table of $\mathcal{O}$ that specifies the first $i-1$ bits of $\mathcal{O}(a,x)$ for all $(a,x) \in [K] \times [N]$, then there is another algorithm $\mathcal{D}$ (that just runs $\mathcal{C}$ once) whose query magnitude on (a,x) is 0 that satisfies

$$\Pr_{\mathcal{D},\mathcal{O},a,x}[\mathcal{D}^{|\mathcal{O}\rangle}(\tilde{\mathsf{st}}_{\mathcal{O}}, T_{\mathcal{O}}, a, x) \to \mathcal{O}_i(a,x)] \geq \frac{1}{2} + \frac{\varepsilon}{\log M}.$$

Then at least an $(\varepsilon/\log M)$-fraction of $\mathcal{O}$ satisfies

$$\Pr_{\mathcal{D},a,x}[\mathcal{D}^{|\mathcal{O}\rangle}(\widetilde{\mathrm{st}}_\mathcal{O}, T_\mathcal{O}, a, x) \to \mathcal{O}_i(a, x)] \geq \frac{1}{2} + \frac{\varepsilon}{2\log M}.$$

By Lemma 5, there exists a pair of an encoder and decoder for this fraction of functions with the success probability $\Omega(\varepsilon^5/T^2 \log^5 M)$ and encoding size

$$KN + KN \cdot (\log M - 1) + S + O(1) - \Omega\left(\frac{\varepsilon^5 KN}{T^2 \log^6 M}\right).$$

By Lemma 3, it holds that

$$KN \log M + S + O(1) - \Omega\left(\frac{\varepsilon^6 KN}{T^2 \log^6 M}\right) \geq \log\left(\frac{\varepsilon M^{KN}}{\log M}\right) + \log(\varepsilon^5/T^2 \log^5 M)$$

or $O\left(S + \log\left(\frac{T^2 \log^6 M}{\varepsilon^6}\right)\right) \geq \Omega\left(\frac{\varepsilon^6 KN}{T^2 \log^6 M}\right)$, which implies $\varepsilon = \tilde{O}\left(\sqrt[6]{\frac{ST^2}{KN}}\right)$ as desired.[15]

Overall, we obtain $|p_0 - p_3| = \tilde{O}\left(\sqrt[6]{\frac{ST^4}{KN}} + \frac{T^4}{N}\right)$. $\qquad\square$

3.4   Post-quantum Pseudorandom Functions

The main theorem of this subsection is that random oracles are secure pqPRFs in the QROM-AI, which is formally stated as follows.

Theorem 3. *Let $\mathcal{O} \in \mathsf{Func}([K] \times [N] \times [L], \{0,1\})$ be a random oracle. Suppose that $\mathcal{A}$ is an oracle-aided quantum algorithm that takes an S-bit classical advice $\mathrm{st}_\mathcal{O}$ (that may depend on $\mathcal{O}$) as input, and makes at most T (quantum) queries to the oracle $\mathcal{O}$ and at most Q classical queries to the other oracle. Then it holds that*

$$\left|\Pr_{\mathcal{A},\mathcal{O},a,k}\left[\mathcal{A}^{|\mathcal{O}\rangle, \mathcal{O}(a,k,\cdot)}(\mathrm{st}_\mathcal{O}, a) \to 1\right] - \Pr_{\mathcal{A},\mathcal{O},a,F}\left[\mathcal{A}^{|\mathcal{O}\rangle, F}(\mathrm{st}_\mathcal{O}, a) \to 1\right]\right|$$
$$= \tilde{O}\left(\sqrt[4]{\frac{ST^4}{KN}} + \frac{T^4}{N} + Q\sqrt[6]{\frac{ST^2}{KN}}\right),$$

where F is uniform in $\mathsf{Func}([L], \{0,1\})$.

The proof can be done similarly to Theorem 2 except that we need an extended variant of Lemma 5. The proof of Theorem 3 can be found in the full version.

---

[15] More concretely, $\varepsilon^6 > CST^2 \log^6 M(1 + \log KN)/KN$ for sufficiently large C implies contradiction.

3.5   Post-quantum MACs

The main theorem of this subsection is that random oracles are secure pqMACs in the QROM-AI, which is formally stated as follows.

Theorem 4. *Let $\mathcal{O} \in \mathsf{Func}([K] \times [N] \times [L], [M])$ be a random oracle. Suppose that $\mathcal{A}$ is an oracle-aided quantum algorithm that takes an S-bit classical advice $\mathsf{st}_{\mathcal{O}}$ (that may depend on $\mathcal{O}$) as input, and makes at most T oracle queries to the oracle $\mathcal{O}$. Then it holds that*

$$\Pr_{\mathcal{A},\mathcal{O},a,k} \left[\mathcal{A}^{|\mathcal{O}\rangle, \mathcal{O}(a,k,\cdot)}(\mathsf{st}_{\mathcal{O}}, a) \to (m,t) \wedge \mathcal{O}(a,k,m) = t \right] = \tilde{O}\left(\sqrt[3]{\frac{ST^4}{KN}} + \frac{T^4}{N} + \frac{1}{M} \right)$$

where $\mathcal{A}$ never queries m to its second oracle.

The proof can be found in the full version.

4   Random Permutation with Quantum AI

In this section, we give a security bound for inverting random permutations with *quantum auxiliary input.*

4.1   Preparations

First, we prepare some lemmas that are needed for proving our results.

Quantum Compression Lemma. Nayak [Nay99] generalized the seminal result of Holevo [Hol73] to relate the number of qubits that is needed to transmit n-bit classical information and the success probability of it.

Theorem 5. *[Nay99, NS06, adapted] Suppose that Alice holds an n-bit string x and wants to convey it to Bob via a (noiseless) quantum channel. If, for any x, the probability that Bob successfully recovers x is $p \in (0, 1]$, then the number of qubits m transmitted by Alice is at least $n - \log 1/p$.*

Note that the above statement is very similar to the compression argument in the classical setting. Using this Theorem 5, we can obtain the following quantum compression lemma. The proof is postponed to the full version.

Lemma 6 (Quantum compression lemma). *Let M, R be a set. Let E be a procedure that takes $(x, r) \in M \times R$ and outputs a m-qubit quantum state and D a procedure that takes a quantum state along with string $r \in R$. If we have*

$$\Pr_r[D(E(x,r), r) = x] \geq p$$

for all $x \in M$, then it holds that $m \geq \log|M| - 2\log 1/p + 1$.

Rewinding Quantum Advice. Here, we describe a way to reuse a quantum advice for quantum algorithms when the outputs of the algorithms are fixed values with very high probability. We note that a similar idea has been used in several works [Aar05, AR19].

Specifically, Aaronson [Aar05] implicitly proved the following lemma by using the *gentle measurement lemma* [Win99], whose proof can be found in the full version for completeness.

Lemma 7 (Implicit in [Aar05]). *Let ρ be any (mixed) quantum state, n be any positive integer, and for $i \in [n]$, let $\mathcal{A}_i$ be a unitary quantum algorithm (i.e., $\mathcal{A}_i$ is unitary except for the final measurement) such that $\Pr[\mathcal{A}_i(\rho) = x_i] > 1 - \frac{1}{9n^4}$ for some classical string x_i. Then there exists an algorithm $\mathcal{B}$ such that $\Pr[\mathcal{B}(\rho) = \{x_i\}_{i \in [n]}] > 2/3$.*

4.2   Bound for Inverting Random Permutations

Theorem 6. *Let $\mathcal{O} \in \mathsf{Func}([K] \times [N], [N])$ be a random permutation with salt (i.e., $\mathcal{O}(a, \cdot)$ is a random permutation). Suppose that $\mathcal{A}$ is an oracle-aided quantum algorithm that takes an S-bit quantum advice $|\mathsf{st}_{\mathcal{O}}\rangle$ (that may depend on $\mathcal{O}$) as input, makes at most T oracle queries, and satisfies*

$$\Pr_{\mathcal{A}, \mathcal{O}, a, x}\left[\mathcal{A}^{|\mathcal{O}\rangle}(|\mathsf{st}_{\mathcal{O}}\rangle, a, \mathcal{O}(a, x)) \to x\right] = \varepsilon,$$

Then it holds that $\varepsilon^3 = \widetilde{O}\left(\frac{ST^2}{KN} + \frac{T^2}{N}\right)$.

Remark 2. In the above, we assumed the advice $|\mathsf{st}_{\mathcal{O}}\rangle$ is a pure state. This does not lose generality since any S-qubit mixed state can be realized as half of a $2S$-qubit pure state by purification.

Proof of Theorem 6. By an averaging argument, there exists a set of functions $\mathcal{F}$ that is an $\varepsilon/2$-fraction of random oracles such that

$$\Pr_{\mathcal{A}, a, x}[\mathcal{A}^{|f\rangle}(|\mathsf{st}_f\rangle, a, f(a, x)) \to x] \geq \varepsilon/2$$

for all $f \in \mathcal{F}$. Fix $f \in \mathcal{F}$. Again, by an averaging argument, there are at least $\varepsilon/4 \cdot KN$ elements (a, x) satisfying

$$\Pr_{\mathcal{A}}[\mathcal{A}^{|f\rangle}(|\mathsf{st}_f\rangle, a, f(a, x)) \to x] \geq \varepsilon/4.$$

We denote the set of such (a, x) by I and call it *semi-good*.

Now we consider an algorithm $\mathcal{B}$ that is an "amplified version" of $\mathcal{A}$ that satisfies

$$\Pr_{\mathcal{B}}[\mathcal{B}^{|f\rangle}(|\widetilde{\mathsf{st}}_f\rangle, a, f(a, x)) \to x] \geq 3/4$$

for all $(a, x) \in I$. More precisely, $\mathcal{B}$ runs $\Theta(1/\varepsilon)$ copies of $\mathcal{A}$ in parallel except measurements, checks the correctness of outputs of $\mathcal{A}$ (before measurements) by querying them to f, and then outputs x if any of them is the correct answer x and $\perp$ otherwise. The number and depth of queries of $\mathcal{B}$ are $T' = \Theta(T/\varepsilon)$ and $D' = T + 1$, respectively, and the quantum advice $|\widetilde{\mathsf{st}}_f\rangle$ is $\Theta(S/\varepsilon)$-qubit.

Then a random set $R \subset [K] \times [N]$ is chosen that will serve as a random public coin for encoding, so that $(a, x) \in R$ with probability $p = d/T'(T + 2)$ (independently for each (a, x)) for some constant d ($d < 1/46080$ suffices). Here, we may assume that $p|I| \geq C$ for a sufficiently large constant C ($C \geq 16 \ln 10$ suffices) since otherwise we have $\varepsilon^2 KN/T^2 = O(1)$ in which case the statement of Theorem 6 trivially holds.[16]

We say that $(a, x) \in I$ is good if both

$$(A) \ (a, x) \in R, \quad (B) \ \Pr_{\mathcal{B}}[\mathsf{Find} : \mathcal{B}^{|f\rangle \backslash (R \backslash \{(a,x)\})}(|\widetilde{\mathsf{st}}_f\rangle, a, f(a, x))] \leq \frac{1}{576(T + 2)}$$

hold. A set of good elements is denoted by G.

Then the following claim can be proven similarly to Claim 2. The proof can be found in the full version.

Claim 3. $\Pr_R[|G| \geq \delta\varepsilon^2 KN/T^2] > 0.8$ *for some constant* δ.

We say that R is good if $|G| \geq \delta\varepsilon^2 KN/T^2$. We now fix a good R. For $y \in [N]$, we define a function $g_y : [K] \times [N] \to [N]$ by

$$g_y(a, z) = \begin{cases} f(a, z) & \text{if } (a, z) \notin R, \\ y & \text{otherwise.} \end{cases}$$

We note that g_y agrees with f on $R \setminus \{(a, x)\}$ where (a, x) is any preimage of y in f (i.e., $f(a, x) = y$). Here, we consider an algorithm $\mathcal{C}$ that works similarly to $\mathcal{B}$ except that it takes x as an additional input and returns 1 if $\mathcal{B}$'s output is x and 0 otherwise. By Lemma 1 and Remark 1, for any $(a, x) \in G$, we have

$$\left| \Pr_{\mathcal{C}}[\mathcal{C}^{|g_{f(a,x)}\rangle}(|\widetilde{\mathsf{st}}_f\rangle, a, x, f(a, x)) \to 1] - \Pr_{\mathcal{C}}[\mathcal{C}^{|f\rangle}(|\widetilde{\mathsf{st}}_f\rangle, a, x, f(a, x)) \to 1] \right|$$
$$\leq 2\sqrt{(T + 2) \Pr_{\mathcal{C}}[\mathsf{Find} : \mathcal{C}^{|f\rangle \backslash (R \backslash \{(a,x)\})}(|\widetilde{\mathsf{st}}_f\rangle, a, x, f(a, x))]}$$

which is clearly equivalent to

$$\left| \Pr_{\mathcal{B}}[\mathcal{B}^{|g_{f(a,x)}\rangle}(|\widetilde{\mathsf{st}}_f\rangle, a, f(a, x)) \to x] - \Pr_{\mathcal{B}}[\mathcal{B}^{|f\rangle}(|\widetilde{\mathsf{st}}_f\rangle, a, f(a, x)) \to x] \right|$$
$$\leq 2\sqrt{(T + 2) \Pr_{\mathcal{B}}[\mathsf{Find} : \mathcal{B}^{|f\rangle \backslash (R \backslash \{(a,x)\})}(|\widetilde{\mathsf{st}}_f\rangle, a, f(a, x))]} \leq \frac{1}{12}.$$

Thus we have

$$\Pr_{\mathcal{B}}[\mathcal{B}^{|g_{f(a,x)}\rangle}(|\widetilde{\mathsf{st}}_f\rangle, a, f(a, x)) \to x] \geq \frac{3}{4} - \frac{1}{12} = \frac{2}{3}.$$

---

[16] Looking ahead, this is used in the proof of Claim 3.

Note that the algorithm $\mathcal{B}$ outputs one particular answer x or $\perp$, so we can amplify the success probability by running $O(\log(KN))$ copies of $\mathcal{B}$ in parallel and taking an output of any execution of $\mathcal{B}$ that is not $\perp$ as its final output if any (before the measurement). We call this algorithm $\widetilde{\mathcal{B}}$, which satisfies

$$\Pr_{\widetilde{\mathcal{B}}}[\widetilde{\mathcal{B}}^{|g_{f(a,x)}\rangle}(|\overline{\mathsf{st}}_f\rangle, a, f(a, x)) \to x] \geq 1 - \frac{1}{9(KN)^4},$$

where $|\overline{\mathsf{st}}_f\rangle$ is $O(S\log(KN)/\varepsilon)$ qubits.

Now we are ready to encode the function f for good R. Let $R_a := R \cap (\{a\} \times [N])$ and $G_a = G \cap (\{a\} \times [N])$. The encoding of f includes the following information:

- The advice string $|\overline{\mathsf{st}}_f\rangle$: $O(S\log(KN)/\varepsilon)$ qubits.
- The set $f(R_a)$ for each $a \in [K]$: $\sum_a \log\binom{N}{|R_a|}$ bits.
- The values of f on $(\{a\} \times [N]) \setminus R_a$ for each $a \in [K]$: $\sum_a \log(N - |R_a|)!$ bits.
- The cardinality of G_a for each $a \in [K]$: $K \log N$ bits.
- The set $f(G_a)$ for each $a \in [K]$: $\sum_a \log\binom{|R_a|}{|G_a|}$ bits.
- The values of f on $R_a \setminus G_a$: $\sum_a \log(|R_a| - |G_a|)!$ bits.

The decoding procedure initializes an empty table to store the values of f and then fills the table as follows:

1. Recover $|\overline{\mathsf{st}}_f\rangle$, G_a, and G.
2. Fill the values of f on inputs in $([K] \times [N]) \setminus R$. This can be done since the decoder knows R as a shared random string.
3. Fill the table of f for G by the following procedures. For each $(a, y) \in f(G_a)$, let $x \in [N]$ be the inversion of y at a, i.e., $y = f(a, x)$ (which is unknown to the decoder so far). Note that the function g_y can be evaluated by the decoder since it only needs values of f on $([K] \times [N]) \setminus R$ which is already recovered. As discussed above, we have

$$\Pr_{\widetilde{\mathcal{B}}}[\widetilde{\mathcal{B}}^{|g_{f(a,x)}\rangle}(|\overline{\mathsf{st}}_f\rangle, a, f(a, x)) \to x] \geq 1 - \frac{1}{9(KN)^4}.$$

Then the decoder uses the procedure in Lemma 7 to recover x for all $(a, y) \in f(G)$. Noting that $|f(G)| \leq KN$, by Lemma 7, the decoder succeeds in correctly recovering x for all $(a, y) \in f(G)$ with probability at least $2/3$. We note that the set G is also recovered at this point.
4. The decoder fills the values of f on inputs in $R \setminus G$ by using the partial truth table and the description of G that is recovered in the previous step.

The decoding procedure succeeds with a constant probability (over the choice of R and the randomness of measurements) since a constant fraction of R is good and the decoding succeeds with a constant probability for good R.

The overall encoding size except the size of advice string and the size of G_a is

$$\sum_{a \in [K]} \left(\log \binom{N}{|R_a|} + \log(N - |R_a|)! + \log \binom{|R_a|}{|G_a|} + \log(|R_a| - |G_a|)! \right)$$

$$= \sum_{a \in [K]} \log \left(\frac{N!}{(N - |R_a|)!|R_a|!} \cdot (N - |R_a|)! \cdot \frac{|R_a|!}{(|R_a| - |G_a|)!|G_a|!} \cdot (|R_a| - |G_a|)! \right)$$

$$= K \log N! - \sum_{a \in [K]} \log |G_a|!$$

$$\leq K \log N! - \sum_{a \in [K]} |G_a| \log(|G_a|/e) \leq K \log N! - |G| \log \left(\frac{|G|}{eK} \right),$$

where we used the fact that $n! \geq (n/e)^n$ and $x \log x$ is convex in the last two inequalities. Then by Lemma 6, we obtain the inequality

$$O \left(\frac{S \log(KN)}{\varepsilon} + K \log N \right) \geq |G| \log \left(\frac{|G|}{eK} \right) + \Theta(1).$$

Then we have either $|G|/eK < 2$, which implies $\varepsilon^2 = O(T^2/N)$, or

$$O \left(\frac{S \log(KN)}{\varepsilon} + K \log N \right) \geq |G| \geq \delta \varepsilon^2 KN/T^2.$$

Combining them, we obtain $\varepsilon^3 = \tilde{O} \left(\frac{ST^2}{KN} + \frac{T^2}{N} \right)$. $\square$

4.3   Implication in Complexity Theory

Here, we discuss an implication of the result of the previous section in complexity theory. We denote by BQP/qpoly the class of languages that can be decided in quantum polynomial time with a polynomial-size quantum advice.[17] Then the following theorem follows from Theorem 6. The proof is postponed to the full version.

Theorem 7. NP $\cap$ coNP $\not\subseteq$ BQP/qpoly *relative to a random permutation oracle with probability* 1.

Acknowledgment. We thank anonymous reviewers of Asiacrypt 2019 and Andreas Hülsing for their helpful comments. Minki Hhan was partially supported by the Institute for Information & Communications Technology Promotion (IITP) Grant through the Korean Government (MSIT), (Development of lattice-based post-quantum public-key cryptographic schemes), under Grant 2017-0-00616 and by the Samsung Research Funding Center of Samsung Electronics under Project SRFC-TB1403-52.

---

[17] This class was originally introduced by Nishimura and Yamakami [NY04] with the name BQP/*Qpoly, and renamed to BQP/qpoly by Aaronson [Aar05]. See these papers for the detailed definition.

References

[Aar05] Aaronson, S.: Limitations of quantum advice and one-way communication. Theory Comput. **1**(1), 1–28 (2005)

[AHU19] Ambainis, A., Hamburg, M., Unruh, D.: Quantum security proofs using semi-classical oracles. In: Boldyreva, A., Micciancio, D. (eds.) CRYPTO 2019, Part II. LNCS, vol. 11693, pp. 269–295. Springer, Cham (2019). https://doi.org/10.1007/978-3-030-26951-7_10

[AR19] Aaronson, S., Rothblum, G.: Gentle measurement of quantum states and differential privacy. In: STOC 2019, pp. 322–333 (2019)

[BDF+11] Boneh, D., Dagdelen, Ö., Fischlin, M., Lehmann, A., Schaffner, C., Zhandry, M.: Random oracles in a quantum world. In: Lee, D.H., Wang, X. (eds.) ASIACRYPT 2011. LNCS, vol. 7073, pp. 41–69. Springer, Heidelberg (2011). https://doi.org/10.1007/978-3-642-25385-0_3

[BHMT02] Brassard, G., Hoyer, P., Mosca, M., Tapp, A.: Quantum amplitude amplification and estimation. Quantum Comput. Quantum Inf. **305**, 53–74 (2002)

[BHT97] Brassard, G., Høyer, P., Tapp, A.: Quantum cryptanalysis of hash and claw-free functions. SIGACT News **28**(2), 14–19 (1997)

[BL13] Bernstein, D.J., Lange, T.: Non-uniform cracks in the concrete: the power of free precomputation. In: Sako, K., Sarkar, P. (eds.) ASIACRYPT 2013, Part II. LNCS, vol. 8270, pp. 321–340. Springer, Heidelberg (2013). https://doi.org/10.1007/978-3-642-42045-0_17

[BR93] Bellare, M., Rogaway, P.: Random oracles are practical: a paradigm for designing efficient protocols. In: ACM CCS 1993, pp. 62–73 (1993)

[BR95] Bellare, M., Rogaway, P.: Optimal asymmetric encryption. In: De Santis, A. (ed.) EUROCRYPT 1994. LNCS, vol. 950, pp. 92–111. Springer, Heidelberg (1995). https://doi.org/10.1007/BFb0053428

[BZ13] Boneh, D., Zhandry, M.: Quantum-secure message authentication codes. In: Johansson, T., Nguyen, P.Q. (eds.) EUROCRYPT 2013. LNCS, vol. 7881, pp. 592–608. Springer, Heidelberg (2013). https://doi.org/10.1007/978-3-642-38348-9_35

[CBH+18] Czajkowski, J., Groot Bruinderink, L., Hülsing, A., Schaffner, C., Unruh, D.: Post-quantum security of the sponge construction. In: Lange, T., Steinwandt, R. (eds.) PQCrypto 2018. LNCS, vol. 10786, pp. 185–204. Springer, Cham (2018). https://doi.org/10.1007/978-3-319-79063-3_9

[CDG18] Coretti, S., Dodis, Y., Guo, S.: Non-uniform bounds in the random-permutation, ideal-cipher, and generic-group models. In: Shacham, H., Boldyreva, A. (eds.) CRYPTO 2018, Part I. LNCS, vol. 10991, pp. 693–721. Springer, Cham (2018). https://doi.org/10.1007/978-3-319-96884-1_23

[CDGS18] Coretti, S., Dodis, Y., Guo, S., Steinberger, J.: Random oracles and non-uniformity. In: Nielsen, J.B., Rijmen, V. (eds.) EUROCRYPT 2018, Part I. LNCS, vol. 10820, pp. 227–258. Springer, Cham (2018). https://doi.org/10.1007/978-3-319-78381-9_9

[CK18] Corrigan-Gibbs, H., Kogan, D.: The discrete-logarithm problem with preprocessing. In: Nielsen, J.B., Rijmen, V. (eds.) EUROCRYPT 2018, Part II. LNCS, vol. 10821, pp. 415–447. Springer, Cham (2018). https://doi.org/10.1007/978-3-319-78375-8_14

[DFMS19] Don, J., Fehr, S., Majenz, C., Schaffner, C.: Security of the fiat-shamir transformation in the quantum random-oracle model. In: Boldyreva, A., Micciancio, D. (eds.) CRYPTO 2019, Part II. LNCS, vol. 11693, pp. 356–383. Springer, Cham (2019). https://doi.org/10.1007/978-3-030-26951-7_13

[DGK17] Dodis, Y., Guo, S., Katz, J.: Fixing cracks in the concrete: random oracles with auxiliary input, revisited. In: Coron, J.-S., Nielsen, J.B. (eds.) EUROCRYPT 2017, Part II. LNCS, vol. 10211, pp. 473–495. Springer, Cham (2017). https://doi.org/10.1007/978-3-319-56614-6_16

[DTT10] De, A., Trevisan, L., Tulsiani, M.: Time space tradeoffs for attacks against one-way functions and PRGs. In: Rabin, T. (ed.) CRYPTO 2010. LNCS, vol. 6223, pp. 649–665. Springer, Heidelberg (2010). https://doi.org/10.1007/978-3-642-14623-7_35

[ES15] Eaton, E., Song, F.: Making existential-unforgeable signatures strongly unforgeable in the quantum random-oracle model. In: TQC 2015, pp. 147–162 (2015). https://eprint.iacr.org/2015/878

[FN99] Fiat, A., Naor, M.: Rigorous time/space trade-offs for inverting functions. SIAM J. Comput. 29(3), 790–803 (1999)

[GGKT05] Gennaro, R., Gertner, Y., Katz, J., Trevisan, L.: Bounds on the efficiency of generic cryptographic constructions. SIAM J. Comput. 35(1), 217–246 (2005)

[Gro96] Grover, L.K.: A fast quantum mechanical algorithm for database search. In: STOC 1996, pp. 212–219 (1996)

[GT00] Gennaro, R., Trevisan, L.: Lower bounds on the efficiency of generic cryptographic constructions. In: FOCS 2000, pp. 305–313 (2000)

[GYZ17] Garg, S., Yuen, H., Zhandry, M.: New security notions and feasibility results for authentication of quantum data. In: Katz, J., Shacham, H. (eds.) CRYPTO 2017, Part II. LNCS, vol. 10402, pp. 342–371. Springer, Cham (2017). https://doi.org/10.1007/978-3-319-63715-0_12

[Hel80] Hellman, M.E.: A cryptanalytic time-memory trade-off. IEEE Trans. Inf. Theory 26(4), 401–406 (1980)

[Hol73] Holevo, A.S.: Bounds for the quantity of information transmitted by a quantum communication channel. Probl. Peredachi Informatsii 9(3), 3–11 (1973)

[HY18] Hosoyamada, A., Yamakawa, T.: Finding collisions in a quantum world: quantum black-box separation of collision-resistance and one-wayness. Cryptology ePrint Archive, Report 2018/1066 (2018)

[HRS16] Hülsing, A., Rijneveld, J., Song, F.: Mitigating multi-target attacks in hash-based signatures. In: Cheng, C.-M., Chung, K.-M., Persiano, G., Yang, B.-Y. (eds.) PKC 2016, Part I. LNCS, vol. 9614, pp. 387–416. Springer, Heidelberg (2016). https://doi.org/10.1007/978-3-662-49384-7_15

[JZC+18] Jiang, H., Zhang, Z., Chen, L., Wang, H., Ma, Z.: IND-CCA-secure key encapsulation mechanism in the quantum random oracle model, revisited. In: Shacham, H., Boldyreva, A. (eds.) CRYPTO 2018, Part III. LNCS, vol. 10993, pp. 96–125. Springer, Cham (2018). https://doi.org/10.1007/978-3-319-96878-0_4

[KLS18] Kiltz, E., Lyubashevsky, V., Schaffner, C.: A concrete treatment of fiat-shamir signatures in the quantum random-oracle model. In: Nielsen, J.B., Rijmen, V. (eds.) EUROCRYPT 2018, Part III. LNCS, vol. 10822, pp. 552–586. Springer, Cham (2018). https://doi.org/10.1007/978-3-319-78372-7_18

[KYY18] Katsumata, S., Yamada, S., Yamakawa, T.: Tighter security proofs for GPV-IBE in the quantum random oracle model. In: Peyrin, T., Galbraith, S. (eds.) ASIACRYPT 2018, Part II. LNCS, vol. 11273, pp. 253–282. Springer, Cham (2018). https://doi.org/10.1007/978-3-030-03329-3_9

[LZ19] Liu, Q., Zhandry, M.: Revisiting post-quantum fiat-shamir. In: Boldyreva, A., Micciancio, D. (eds.) CRYPTO 2019, Part II. LNCS, vol. 11693, pp. 326–355. Springer, Cham (2019). https://doi.org/10.1007/978-3-030-26951-7_12

[NABT15] Nayebi, A., Aaronson, S., Belovs, A., Trevisan, L.: Quantum lower bound for inverting a permutation with advice. Quantum Inf. Comput. 15(11–12), 901–913 (2015)

[Nay99] Nayak, A.: Optimal lower bounds for quantum automata and random access codes. In: FOCS 1999, pp. 369–376 (1999)

[NC00] Nielsen, M.A., Chuang, I.L.: Quantum Computation and Quantum Information, vol. 2. Cambridge University Press, Cambridge (2000)

[NS06] Nayak, A., Salzman, J.: Limits on the ability of quantum states to convey classical messages. J. ACM 53(1), 184–206 (2006)

[NY04] Nishimura, H., Yamakami, T.: Polynomial time quantum computation with advice. Inf. Process. Lett. 90(4), 195–204 (2004)

[SXY18] Saito, T., Xagawa, K., Yamakawa, T.: Tightly-secure key-encapsulation mechanism in the quantum random oracle model. In: Nielsen, J.B., Rijmen, V. (eds.) EUROCRYPT 2018, Part III. LNCS, vol. 10822, pp. 520–551. Springer, Cham (2018). https://doi.org/10.1007/978-3-319-78372-7_17

[TU16] Targhi, E.E., Unruh, D.: Post-quantum security of the fujisaki-okamoto and OAEP transforms. In: Hirt, M., Smith, A. (eds.) TCC 2016, Part II. LNCS, vol. 9986, pp. 192–216. Springer, Heidelberg (2016). https://doi.org/10.1007/978-3-662-53644-5_8

[Unr07] Unruh, D.: Random oracles and auxiliary input. In: Menezes, A. (ed.) CRYPTO 2007. LNCS, vol. 4622, pp. 205–223. Springer, Heidelberg (2007). https://doi.org/10.1007/978-3-540-74143-5_12

[Unr15] Unruh, D.: Non-interactive zero-knowledge proofs in the quantum random oracle model. In: Oswald, E., Fischlin, M. (eds.) EUROCRYPT 2015, Part II. LNCS, vol. 9057, pp. 755–784. Springer, Heidelberg (2015). https://doi.org/10.1007/978-3-662-46803-6_25

[Win99] Winter, A.: Coding theorem and strong converse for quantum channels. IEEE Trans. Inf. Theory 45(7), 2481–2485 (1999)

[Yao82] Yao, A.C.-C.: Theory and applications of trapdoor functions. In: FOCS 1982, pp. 80–91 (1982)

[Yao90] Yao, A.C.-C.: Coherent functions and program checkers. In: STOC 1990, pp. 84–94 (1990)

[Zha12a] Zhandry, M.: How to construct quantum random functions. In: FOCS 2012, pp. 679–687 (2012)

[Zha12b] Zhandry, M.: Secure identity-based encryption in the quantum random oracle model. In: Safavi-Naini, R., Canetti, R. (eds.) CRYPTO 2012. LNCS, vol. 7417, pp. 758–775. Springer, Heidelberg (2012). https://doi.org/10.1007/978-3-642-32009-5_44

QFactory: Classically-Instructed Remote Secret Qubits Preparation

Alexandru Cojocaru[1]($\boxtimes$), Léo Colisson[2], Elham Kashefi[1,2],
and Petros Wallden[1]

[1] School of Informatics, University of Edinburgh,
10 Crichton Street, Edinburgh EH8 9AB, UK
`a.d.cojocaru@sms.ed.ac.uk`
[2] Laboratoire d'Informatique de Paris 6 (LIP6), Sorbonne Université,
4 Place Jussieu, 75252 Paris CEDEX 05, France

Abstract. The functionality of classically-instructed remotely prepared random secret qubits was introduced in (Cojocaru et al. 2018) as a way to enable classical parties to participate in secure quantum computation and communications protocols. The idea is that a classical party (client) instructs a quantum party (server) to generate a qubit to the server's side that is random, unknown to the server but known to the client. Such task is only possible under computational assumptions. In this contribution we define a simpler (basic) primitive consisting of only BB84 states, and give a protocol that realizes this primitive and that is secure against the strongest possible adversary (an arbitrarily deviating malicious server). The specific functions used, were constructed based on known trapdoor one-way functions, resulting to the security of our basic primitive being reduced to the hardness of the Learning With Errors problem. We then give a number of extensions, building on this basic module: extension to larger set of states (that includes non-Clifford states); proper consideration of the abort case; and verifiablity on the module level. The latter is based on *"blind self-testing"*, a notion we introduced, proved in a limited setting and conjectured its validity for the most general case.

Keywords: Classical delegated quantum computation · Learning With Errors · Provable security

1 Introduction

In the coming decades, advances in quantum technologies may cause major shifts in the mainstream computing landscape. In the meantime, we can expect to see quantum devices with high variability in terms of architectures and capacities, the so-called noisy, intermediate-scale quantum (NISQ) devices [46] (such as those being developed by IBM, Rigetti, Google, IonQ) that are currently available to users via classical cloud platforms. In order to be able to proceed to the next milestone for the utility of these devices in a wider industrial base, the issues of privacy and integrity of the data manipulation must be addressed.

© International Association for Cryptologic Research 2019
S. D. Galbraith and S. Moriai (Eds.): ASIACRYPT 2019, LNCS 11921, pp. 615–645, 2019.
https://doi.org/10.1007/978-3-030-34578-5_22

Early proposals for secure and verifiable delegated quantum computing based on simple obfuscation of data already exist [2,5,10,14,20,22,24,34,40,41]. However, these schemes require a reliable long-distance quantum communication network, connecting all the interested parties, which remains a challenging task.

For these reasons, there has recently been extensive research focusing on the practicality aspect of secure and verifiable delegated quantum computation. One direction is to reduce the required communications by exploiting classical fully-homomorphic-encryption schemes [3,11,18], or by defining their direct quantum analogues [29,30,44,50]. Different encodings, on the client side, could also reduce the quantum communication [24,34]. However, in all these approaches, the client still requires some quantum capabilities. While no-go results indicate restrictions on which of the above properties are jointly achievable for classical clients [1,4,42,54], recent breakthroughs based on post-quantum secure trapdoor one-way functions, paved the way for developing entirely new approaches towards fully-classical client protocols for emerging quantum servers. The first such procedures were proposed in [32] allowing a classical client to securely delegate a universal quantum computation to a remote untrusted server. The key technical idea was the ability to perform a CNOT quantum gate that is controlled by an encrypted classical bit. To achieve this a classical primitive of trapdoor claw-free functions pair was used. It was later followed by the work of [7], where the construction achieved stronger security guarantee and based on more standard cryptographic assumptions. Building on this, a single device certifiable randomness was achieved in [8], where the randomness is information theoretical, but the certification is based on the computational limitations of quantum devices. Finally, using post-hoc verification of quantum computations [21], and the above ideas to generate a single qubit "blind measurement device", [33] gave the first protocol achieving classical client verification of universal quantum computation.

All these constructions, while they used similar techniques, proved the desired properties in a monolithic way. An alternative approach was taken in [15] where the idea was to replace the quantum channel (that is used in many different protocol implementing blind and/or verifiable quantum computation) with a module running between a classical client and a quantum server. It was shown then how a classical client could use this module (referred to as QFactory) to achieve secure delegated universal quantum computing, but potentially also, other functionalities such as multi-party quantum computation. However, the security proof was made in a weak "honest-but-curious" model, and the full proof of security was left as an open question. In this paper, we extend the security proof to a fully malicious adversary. All our proofs are made using reductions to hardness assumptions (namely LWE), and the simplicity of the main protocol suggests that an extention to a composable model such as Universal Composability [12] or Abstract Cryptography (AC) [35] should be possible (but left as a future work).

Concurrently with our work, [23] also took this modular approach. Technically they followed closely the ideas from [8,32,33], but the basic primitive they derive (in a verifiable version) is the one we introduced in [15]. They gave protocols for a *verifiable* version of the secret single qubit generation, while they also gave a proof in the AC model. Their AC proof relies on a strong hypothesis that they call "measurement buffer" that forces the adversary to give the state that he is supposed to measure to the simulator, enforcing (essentially) a trusted measurement. They also state that the stand-alone proof does not require this assumption. To our view, this assumption is very high price for moving to the AC framework, which is why in our current work we do not focus on composability while we work towards resolving this issue as part of the future work we mentioned. Moreover, in [23] they do not investigate a crucial "abort" case of the protocol, which is related to the properties of the functions required for the protocol implementation. Specifically, properties such as two-regularity can only be achieved probabilistically, causing the security of the protocol to fail whenever the function property is not satisfied. This means that they need to use a family of functions that is secure only under the assumption that $SIVP_\gamma$ is hard for a superpolynomial γ, while the standard assumption is that $SIVP_\gamma$ is secure only for a polynomial γ [7].

Following the modularity of [15], we present a universal yet minimal functionality module that is fully secure and verifiable at the module level and could be used as a black box in other client-server applications to replace the need for a reliable long-distance quantum communication network. The price one has to pay is a reduction from information-theoretic security (achievable using quantum communication) to post-quantum computational security via our modules. The ultimate vision would be to develop a hybrid network of classical and quantum communication channels, depending on the desired security level and the technology development of NISQ devices allowing classical or quantum links [53].

1.1 Our Contributions

In [15] was defined a classical client - quantum server functionality of delegated pseudo-secret random qubit generator (PSRQG) that can replace the need for quantum channel between parties in certain quantum communication protocols, with the only trade-off being that the protocols would become computationally secure (against *quantum* adversaries). However, the proof of security was done in a weak model called "honest-but-curious". In this paper (full version at [16]):

1. We present a new protocol called Malicious 4-states QFactory in Sect. 3 that achieves the functionality of classically instructed remote secret generation of the states $\{|0\rangle, |1\rangle, |+\rangle, |-\rangle\}$ (known as the BB84 states), given 2 cryptographic functions: (1) a trapdoor one-way function that is quantum-safe, two-regular and collision resistant and (2) a homomorphic, hardcore predicate. The novelty of this new protocol reflects in both simplicity of construction and proof, as well as enhanced security, namely the protocol is secure against any arbitrarily deviating adversary. The target output qubit set is one of the four BB84 states, states that form the core requirement of any quantum communication protocol.

   Then, in Subsect. 3.3, we present the security of the Malicious 4-states QFactory against any fully malicious server, by proving that the basis of the generated qubits are completely hidden from any adversary, using the properties of the two functions, the security being based on the hardness of the Learning with Errors problem.

2. While the above-mentioned results do not depend on the specific function used, the existence of such functions (with all desired properties) makes the functionality a practical primitive that can be employed as described in this paper. In Sect. 4, we describe how to construct the two-regular, collision resistant, trapdoor one-way family of functions and the homomorphic, hardcore predicate. Furthermore, we prove using reductions in Subsect. 4.2 that the resulting functions maintain all the required properties.

3. In order to demonstrate the modular construction of the basic Malicious 4-states QFactory, we also present in Sect. 5, a secure and efficient extension to the functionality of generating 8 states, called the Malicious 8-states QFactory protocol (where the security refers to the fact that the basis of the new state is completely hidden). The set of output states $\{|+_\theta\rangle \mid \theta \in \{0, \frac{\pi}{4}, ..., \frac{7\pi}{4}\}\}$ (no longer within the Clifford group) are used in various protocols, including protocols for verifiable blind quantum computation.

4. While the protocol introduced in Sect. 3 requires (for the security proof) a family of functions having 2 preimages with probability super-polynomially close to 1, we also define in Sect. 7 a protocol named Malicious-Abort 4-states QFactory, that is secure when the functions have 2 preimages with only a constant (greater than 1/2) probability. Indeed, even if the parameters used for the first category of functions are implicitly used in some protocols [32], the second category of functions is strictly more secure and more standard in the cryptographic literature [7]. The Malicious-Abort 4-states QFactory protocol is proven secure also for this second category of functions, assuming that the classical Yao's XOR lemma also applies for one-round protocols (with classical messages) with quantum adversaries.

5. With a simple construction in Sect. 6, we extend our basic module, in a "blind-measurement" device, where the server performs a single qubit measurement in either the Z or X basis, but he is ignorant of the measurement basis (while the client knows). This type of blind measurement was the basis for the paper of [33], where a classical-client verification of quantum computation protocol was first given. Here we see how our module can also offer this type of functionality.

6. The Malicious 8-states QFactory can be further extended in order to offer a notion of verification for QFactory in Sect. 8, the new protocol being called Verifiable QFactory. We demonstrate that this notion of verifiability of QFactory is suitable, by showing that it is sufficient to obtain *verifiable blind quantum computation*. Such protocol would be the first classical client, verifiable and *blind* quantum computation protocol.

   We introduce in Subsect. 8.2 a novel framework called *blind self-testing*, which differs from the standard self-testing by replacing the non-locality assumptions for such tests with blindness conditions. We describe how this technique can be used to prove the verifiability of QFactory. Note however, that the security of the Verifiable QFactory Protocol 8.2 is conjectured, while we expect that the full proof would follow using the most general case of the novel notion of *blind self-testing* that we introduced. Finally, we prove how a (much simpler) i.i.d. blind self-testing is achievable.

1.2   Overview of the Protocols and Proofs

The Protocol. The general idea is that a classical client communicates with a quantum server instructing him to perform certain actions. By the end of the interaction, the client obtains a random value $B = B_1 B_2 \in \{00, 01, 10, 11\}$, while the server (if he followed the protocol) ends up with the state $H^{B_1} X^{B_2} |0\rangle$, i.e. with one of the BB84 states. Moreover, the server, irrespective of whether he followed the protocol or how he deviated, cannot guess the value of the (basis) bit B_1 any better than making a random guess (more details in Subsect. 3.3).

This module is sufficient to perform (either directly or with simple extensions) multiple secure computation protocols including blind quantum computation.

To achieve such a task, we require three central elements. Firstly, the quantum operations performed by the server should not be repeatable, in order to avoid letting the (adversarial) server run multiple times these operations and obtain multiple copies of the same output state. That would (obviously) compromise the security since direct tomography of a single qubit is straightforward. This can be achieved if the protocol includes a measurement of many qubits, where the probability of getting twice the same outcome would be exponentially small. The second element is that the server should not be able to efficiently classically simulate the quantum computation that he needs to perform. This is to stop the server from running everything classically and obtaining the explicit classical description of the output state. This is achieved using techniques from post-quantum cryptography and specifically the Learning-With-Errors problem. Lastly, the computation has to be easy to perform for the client, since she needs to know the output state. This asymmetry (easy for client/hard for server) can be achieved only in the computational setting, where the client has some extra trapdoor information. The protocol requires the following cryptographic primities defined formally in Definition 8:

- $\mathcal{F}$: a family of 2-regular, collision resistant, trapdoor one-way functions (that can be constructed from a family of injective, homomorphic, trapdoor one-way functions $\mathcal{G}$);
- $d_0(t_k)$: a hardcore predicate of the index of the functions in $\mathcal{F}$. More precisely, every function $f_k \in \mathcal{F}$ has an associated hardcore bit d_0 that is hard to guess given only k, but easy to compute given the trapdoor t_k;
- h: a predicate such that $h(x) \oplus h(x') = d_0$ for any x, x' with $f_k(x) = f_k(x')$

Given these functions, the protocol steps are: The client sends the descriptions of the functions f_k (from the family $\mathcal{F}$) and h. The server's actions are described by the circuit given in Fig. 1 (see Sect. 3), classically instructed by the client: prepares one register at $\otimes^n H |0\rangle$ and second register at $|0\rangle^m$; then applies U_{f_k} using the first register as control and the second as target; measures the second register in the computational basis, obtains the outcome y. Through these steps server produces a superposition of the 2 preimages x and x' of y for the function f_k, i.e. $|x\rangle + |x'\rangle$. Next, server is instructed to apply the unitary corresponding to function h (targeting a new qubit $|0\rangle$) and to measure all but this new qubit in the Hadamard basis (the measurement outcomes will be denoted as b), which will be the output of the protocol. This last step intuitively magnifies the randomness of all the qubits to this final output qubit.

Then, it can be proven that, in an honest run, this output state is:

$$|\text{out}\rangle = H^{B_1} X^{B_2} |0\rangle, \text{ where}$$
$$B_1 = h(x) \oplus h(x') = d_0(t_k) =: d_0$$
$$B_2 = (d_0 \times (b \cdot (x \oplus x'))) \oplus h(x)h(x')$$

Therefore, the client can efficiently obtain the description of the output state, namely B_1 and B_2 by inverting y, to obtain the 2 preimages x and x' using his secret trapdoor information t_k.

Security. Informally speaking the desired security property of the module is to prove that the server cannot guess better than randomly the basis bit B_1 of what the client has, no matter how the server deviates or what answers he returns. In other words, we prove that given that the client chooses k randomly, then no matter which messages y and b the server returns, he cannot determine B_1.

Specifically, using the properties of the 2 cryptographic functions, we show that the basis of the output state is independent of the messages sent by server and essentially, the basis is fixed by the client at the beginning of the protocol.

Here it is important to emphasize that the simplicity of our modular construction allow us to make a direct reduction from the above security property to the cryptographic assumptions of our primitives functions $\mathcal{F}$, d_0 and h. Indeed, from the expression above, we can see that at the end of the interaction the client has recorded as the basis bit the expression $B_1 = h(x) \oplus h(x') = d_0(t_k)$, which is a hardcore bit and is therefore hard to guess given only k.

The Primitive Construction. In order to use this module in practise, it is crucial to have functions that satisfy our cryptographic requirements, and explore the choices of parameters that ensure that all these properties are jointly satisfied. Building on the function construction of [15] we gave specific choices that achieve these properties. The starting point is the injective, trapdoor one-way family of functions $\bar{\mathcal{G}}$ from [39], where the hardness of the function is derived from the Learning With Errors problem.

More precisely, to sample a function f_k, we first sample a matrix $K \in \mathbb{Z}_q^{m \times n}$ using the construction of [39] (that provides an injective and trapdoor function), a uniform vector $s_0 \in \mathbb{Z}_q^n$, an error $e_0 \in \mathbb{Z}_q^m$ according to a small Gaussian[1] and a random bit d_0, and we compute

$$y_0 = K s_0 + e_0 + d_0 \times \left(\tfrac{q}{2} 0 \ldots 0\right)^T \tag{1.1}$$

The hardcore property of d_0 will directly come from the fact that under LWE assumption, no adversary can distinguish a LWE instance $K s_0 + e_0$ from a random vector, so it is not possible to know if we added or not a constant vector. The function f_{K,y_0} will then be defined as follow:

$$f_{K,y_0}(s, e, c, d) = K s + e + c \times y_0 + d \times \left(\tfrac{q}{2} 0 \ldots 0\right)^T \tag{1.2}$$

---

[1] But big enough to make sure the function is secure.

Note that c and d are bits, and the error e is chosen in a bigger space[2] than e_0 to ensure that the function f_{K,y_0} has two preimages with good probability. Moreover, if we define $h(s, e, c, d) = d$, it is easy to see that for all preimages x, x' with $f(x) = f(x')$, we have:

$$h(x) \oplus h(x') = d_0$$

The Extended Protocol. In order to use the above protocol for applications such as blind quantum computing [10], we need to be able to produce states taken from the (extended) set of eight states $\{|+_\theta\rangle, \theta \in \{0, \frac{\pi}{4}, ..., \frac{7\pi}{4}\}\}$. Importantly, we still need to ensure that the bits corresponding to the basis of each qubits produced, remain hidden. Here we prove how given two states produced by the basic protocol described previously, which we denote as $|in_1\rangle$ and $|in_2\rangle$, we can obtain a single state from the 8-states set, denoted $|out\rangle$, ensuring that no information about the bits of the basis of $|out\rangle$ is leaked[3].

To achieve this, we need to find an operation (see Fig. 2 in Sect. 5.1), that in the honest case maps the indices of the inputs to those of the output using a map that satisfies certain conditions. This relation (inputs/output) should be such that learning anything about the basis of the output state implies learning non-negligible information for the basis of (one) input. This directly means, that any computationally bounded adversary that can break the basis blindness of the output, can use this to construct an attack that would also break the basis blindness of at least one of the inputs, i.e. he would break the security guarantees of the basic module that was proven earlier.

Other Properties. To further demonstrate the utility of our core module, as a building block for other client-server protocols, one might wish to expand further the desired properties of the basic functionality. First we give a direct use of our gadget, to construct a "blind-measurement" device. Such device is essential for (non-blind) verification schemes based on post-hoc verification method [21] and directly relates our work with that of [33]. Next, to obtain the verifiability of the module (i.e. imposing an honest behaviour on the server) we propose a generalization of the self-testing, where the non-locality condition is replaced by the blindness property and the analysis is done in the computational setting. Finally, to further improve the practicality of the black box call of the QFactory we also present the security against abort scenario that could be achieved based on a quantum version of Yao's XOR Lemma. However, these additional properties require stronger basic assumptions that we leave as an open question to be removed or proven correct separately.

---

[2] But small enough to make sure the partial functions $f(\cdot, \cdot, c, \cdot)$ are still injective.

[3] Note that one of the input states is exactly the output of the basic module, while the second comes from a slightly modified version (essentially rotated in the XY-plane of the Bloch sphere).

2   Preliminaries

We assume basic familiarity with quantum notions, a good reference is [43].

For a state $|+_\theta\rangle = \frac{1}{\sqrt{2}}(|0\rangle + e^{i\theta}|1\rangle)$, where $\theta \in \{0, \frac{\pi}{4}, ..., \frac{7\pi}{4}\}$, we use the notation:

$$\theta = \frac{\pi}{4}L$$

Additionally, as L is a 3-bit string, we write it as $L = L_1 L_2 L_3$, where L_1, L_2, L_3 represent the bits of L.

As a result when we refer to the basis of the $|+_\theta\rangle$ state, it is equivalent to referring to the last 2 bits of L, thus saying that nothing is leaked about the basis of this state, is equivalent to saying nothing is leaked about the bits L_2 and L_3.

For a set of 4 quantum states $\{|0\rangle, |1\rangle, |+\rangle, |-\rangle\}$, we denote the index of each state using 2 bits: B_1, B_2, with $B_1 = 0$ if and only if the state is $|0\rangle$ or $|1\rangle$, and $B_2 = 0$ if and only if the state is $|0\rangle$ or $|+\rangle$, i.e. $H^{B_1} X^{B_2}|0\rangle$. We will use interchangeably the Dirac notation and the basis/value notation.

In the following sections, we will consider polynomially bounded malicious adversaries, usually denoted by $\mathcal{A}$. The honest clients will be denoted with the π letter, and both honest parties and adversaries can output some values, that could eventually be used in other protocols. To denote that two parties π_A and $\mathcal{A}$ interact in a protocol, and that π_A outputs a while $\mathcal{A}$ outputs b, we write $(a, b) \leftarrow (\pi_A \| \pi_B)$ (we may forget the left hand side, or replace variables with underscores "_" if it is not relevant). We can also refer to the values of the classical messages send between the two parties using something like $\Pr[a = \texttt{accept} \mid (\pi_A \| \mathcal{A})]$, and this probability is implicitly over the internal randomness of π_A and $\mathcal{A}$. To specify a two-party protocol, it is enough to specify the two honest parties (π_A, π_B). Moreover, if the protocol is just made of one round of communication, we can just write $y \leftarrow \mathcal{A}(x)$ with x the first message sent to $\mathcal{A}$, and y the messages sent from $\mathcal{A}$. Finally, a value with a tilde, such as $\tilde{d}$, represents a guess from an adversary.

We are considering protocols secure against quantum adversaries, so we assume that all the properties of our functions hold for a general Quantum Polynomial Time (QPT) adversary, rather than the usual Probabilistic Polynomial Time (PPT) one. We will denote $\mathcal{D}$ the domain of the functions, while $\mathcal{D}(n)$ is the subset of strings of length n. The following definitions are for PPT adversaries, however in this paper we will generally use quantum-safe versions of those definitions and thus security is guaranteed against QPT adversaries.

Definition 1 (One-way). *A function family* $\{f_k : \mathcal{D} \to \mathcal{R}\}_{k \in \mathcal{K}}$ *is **one-way** if:*

- *There exists a PPT algorithm that can compute $f_k(x)$ for any index k, outcome of the PPT parameter-generation algorithm Gen and any input $x \in \mathcal{D}$;*
- *Any QPT algorithm $\mathcal{A}$ can invert f_k with at most negligible probability over the choice of k:*

$$\Pr_{\substack{k \leftarrow Gen(1^n) \\ x \leftarrow \mathcal{D} \\ rc \leftarrow \{0,1\}^*}} [f(\mathcal{A}(k, f_k(x)) = f(x)] \leq \mathsf{negl}(n)$$

where rc represents the randomness used by $\mathcal{A}$.

Definition 2 (Collision resistant). *A family of functions* $\{f_k : \mathcal{D} \to \mathcal{R}\}_{k \in \mathcal{K}}$ *is collision resistant if:*

- *There exists a PPT algorithm that can compute $f_k(x)$ for any index k, outcome of the PPT parameter-generation algorithm Gen and any input $x \in \mathcal{D}$;*
- *Any QPT algorithm $\mathcal{A}$ can find two inputs $x \neq x'$ such that $f_k(x) = f_k(x')$ with at most negligible probability over the choice of k:*

$$\Pr_{\substack{k \leftarrow Gen(1^n) \\ rc \leftarrow \{0,1\}^*}} [\mathcal{A}(k) = (x, x') \text{ such that } x \neq x' \text{ and } f_k(x) = f_k(x')] \leq \mathsf{negl}(n)$$

where rc is the randomness of $\mathcal{A}$ (rc will be omitted from now).

Definition 3 (k-regular). *A deterministic function $f: \mathcal{D} \to \mathcal{R}$ is **k-regular** if $\forall y \in \mathrm{Im}\, f$, we have $|f^{-1}(y)| = k$.*

Definition 4 (Trapdoor Function). *A family of functions $\{f_k : \mathcal{D} \to \mathcal{R}\}$ is a **trapdoor function** if:*

- *There exists a PPT algorithm Gen which on input 1^n outputs (k, t_k), where k represents the index of the function. We also suppose that it is possible to derive the index k from the trapdoor t_k using a function Pub, i.e. $k = \mathsf{Pub}(t_k)$*
- *$\{f_k : \mathcal{D} \to \mathcal{R}\}_{k \in \mathcal{K}}$ is a family of one-way functions;*
- *There exists a PPT algorithm Inv, which on input t_k (which is called the trapdoor information) output by $\mathsf{Gen}(1^n)$ and $y = f_k(x)$ can invert y (by returning all preimages of y[4]) with non-negligible probability over the choice of (k, t_k) and uniform choice of x.*

Definition 5 (Hardcore Predicate). *A function $hc: \mathcal{D} \to \{0,1\}$ is a **hardcore predicate** for a function f if:*

- *There exists a PPT algorithm that, for any input x, can compute $hc(x)$;*
- *Any QPT algorithm $\mathcal{A}$ when given $f(x)$, can compute $hc(x)$ with negligible better than $1/2$ probability:*
  $\Pr_{\substack{x \leftarrow \mathcal{D}(n) \\ rc \leftarrow \{0,1\}^*}} [\mathcal{A}(f(x), 1^n) = hc(x)] \leq \frac{1}{2} + \mathsf{negl}(n)$, *where rc is the randomness used by $\mathcal{A}$;*

The Learning with Errors problem (LWE) is described in the following way:

Definition 6 (LWE problem (informal)). *Given s, an n dimensional vector with elements in $\mathbb{Z}_q$, for some modulus q, the task is to distinguish between a set of polynomially many noisy random linear combinations of the elements of s and a set of polynomially many random numbers from $\mathbb{Z}_q$.*

---

[4] While in the standard definition of trapdoor functions it suffices for the inversion algorithm Inv to return one of the preimages of any output of the function, in our case we require a two-regular tradpdoor function where the inversion procedure returns both preimages for any function output.

Regev [47] and Peikert [45] have given quantum and classical reductions from the average case of LWE to problems such as approximating the length of the shortest vector or the shortest independent vectors problem in the worst case, which are conjectured to be hard even for quantum computers.

Theorem 1 (Reduction LWE, [47, Theorem 1.1]). *Let n, q be integers and $\alpha \in (0, 1)$ be such that $\alpha q > 2\sqrt{n}$. If there exists an efficient algorithm that solves* $\mathrm{LWE}_{q, \bar{\Psi}_\alpha}$*, then there exists an efficient quantum algorithm that approximates the decision version of the shortest vector problem* GAPSVP *and the shortest independent vectors problem* SIVP *to within* $\tilde{O}(n/\alpha)$ *in the worst case.*

Definition 7 (Function Unitary). *For any function $f : A \to B$ that can be described by a polynomially-sized classical circuit, we define the controlled-unitary U_f, as acting in the following way:*

$$U_f \ket{x} \ket{y} = \ket{x} \ket{y \oplus f(x)} \quad \forall x \in A \ \forall y \in B, \tag{2.1}$$

where we name the first register $\ket{x}$ control and the second register $\ket{y}$ target. Given the classical description of this function f, we can always define a QPT algorithm that efficiently implements U_f.

3   The Malicious 4-States QFactory Protocol

3.1   Requirements and Protocol

The Malicious 4-states QFactory Protocol described Protocol 3.1 uses a family of cryptographic functions $\mathcal{F}$ and a function h having the following properties (see Sect. 4 to see how this family of functions can be constructed from a family of injective, trapdoor and (pseudo) homomorphic functions):

Definition 8 (2-regular homomorphic-hardcore family). *A family $\mathcal{F} = \{f_k : \mathcal{D}' \to \mathcal{R}\}_{k \in \mathcal{K}}$ is said to be a 2-regular homomorphic-hardcore family with respect to $h_k : \mathcal{D}' \to \{0, 1\}$ and $d_0 : \mathcal{T} \to \{0, 1\}$ ($\mathcal{T}$ is the set of trapdoors t_k) if:*

- *it is 2-regular, collision resistant and trapdoor*
- *for all k, h_k can be described by a polynomial classical circuit*
- *d_0 is a hardcore predicate for* Pub*, i.e. given a random index $k = \mathrm{Pub}_{\mathcal{F}}(t_k)$, it should be impossible to get $d_0 := d_0(t_k)$ with probability better than $1/2 + \mathsf{negl}(n)$, i.e. for any QPT adversary $\mathcal{A}$:*

$$\Pr\left[\mathcal{A}(k) = d_0(t_k) \mid (k, t_k) \leftarrow \mathsf{Gen}_{\mathcal{F}}\right] \leq \frac{1}{2} + \mathsf{negl}(n) \tag{3.1}$$

- *for all $k \in \mathcal{K}$ and $x, x' \in \mathcal{D}'$ such that $f_k(x) = f_k(x')$, we have:*

$$h_k(x) \oplus h_k(x') = d_0 \tag{3.2}$$

We also extend this definition to δ-2-regular homomorphic-hardcore family, when the function is δ-2-regular, i.e. 2-regular with probability δ (see the full paper [16] for a formal definition).

Protocol 3.1 Malicious 4-states QFactory Protocol: classical delegation of the BB84 states

Requirements:

Public: A δ-2-regular homomorphic-hardcore family $\mathcal{F}$ with respect to $\{h_k\}$ and d_0, as described above. For simplicity, we will represent the sets $\mathcal{D}'$ (respectively $\mathcal{R}$) using n (respectively m) bits strings: $\mathcal{D}' = \{0,1\}^n$, $\mathcal{R} = \{0,1\}^m$. In this protocol, we require δ to be negligibly close to 1, see Section 7 for an extensions to a constant δ.

Stage 1: Preimages superposition

– Client: runs the algorithm $(k, t_k) \leftarrow \text{Gen}_{\mathcal{F}}(1^n)$.

– Client: instructs Server to prepare one register at $\otimes^n H \lvert 0 \rangle$ and second register initiated at $\lvert 0 \rangle^m$.

– Client: sends k to Server and the Server applies U_{f_k} using the first register as control and the second as target.

– Server: measures the second register in the computational basis, obtains the outcome y. Here, in an honest run, the Server would have a state $(\lvert x \rangle + \lvert x' \rangle) \otimes \lvert y \rangle$ with $f_k(x) = f_k(x') = y$ and $y \in \text{Im } f_k$.

Stage 2: Output preparation

– Server: applies U_{h_k} on the preimage register $\lvert x \rangle + \lvert x' \rangle$ as control and another qubit initiated at $\lvert 0 \rangle$ as target. Then, measures all the qubits, but the target in the $\{\frac{1}{\sqrt{2}}(\lvert 0 \rangle \pm \lvert 1 \rangle)\}$ basis, obtaining the outcome $b = (b_1, ..., b_n)$. Now, the Server returns both y and b to the Client.

– Client: using the trapdoor t_k computes the preimages of y:

– if y does not have exactly two preimages x, x' (the server is cheating with overwhelming probability), defines $B_1 = d_0(t_k)$, and chooses $B_2 \in \{0, 1\}$ uniformly at random

– if y has exactly two preimages x, x', defines $B_1 = h_k(x) \oplus h_k(x') = d_0(t_k)$, and B_2 as defined in Theorem 2.

Output: If the protocol is run honestly, the state that the Server has produced is (with overwhelming probability) the BB84 state $\lvert \text{out} \rangle = H^{B_1} X^{B_2} \lvert 0 \rangle$, having the basis $B_1 = h_k(x) \oplus h_k(x') = d_0$ (see Theorem 2 for the exact value of B_2). The output of the Server is $\lvert \text{out} \rangle$, and the output of the Client is (B_1, B_2).

3.2   Correctness of Malicious 4-States QFactory

In an honest run, the description of the output state of the protocol depends on measurement results $y \in \text{Im } f_k$ and b, but also on the 2 preimages x and x' of y.

The output state of Malicious 4-states QFactory belongs to the set of states $\{\lvert 0 \rangle, \lvert 1 \rangle, \lvert + \rangle, \lvert - \rangle\}$ and its exact description is the following:

Theorem 2. *In an honest run, with overwhelming probability the output state $\lvert \text{out} \rangle$ of the Malicious 4-states QFactory Protocol (Protocol 3.1) is a BB84 state whose basis is $B_1 = h_k(x) \oplus h_k(x') = d_0$, and:*

– *if $d_0 = 0$, then the state is $\lvert h_k(x) \rangle$ (computational basis, also equal to $\lvert h_k(x') \rangle$)*
– *if $d_0 = 1$, then if $\sum_i b_i \cdot (x_i \oplus x_i') = 0 \mod 2$, the state is $\lvert + \rangle$, otherwise the state is $\lvert - \rangle$ (Hadamard basis).*

i.e.

$$|\text{out}\rangle = H^{B_1} X^{B_2} |0\rangle \tag{3.3}$$

with

$$B_1 = h_k(x) \oplus h_k(x') = d_0 \tag{3.4}$$

$$B_2 = (d_0 \times (b \cdot (x \oplus x'))) \oplus h(x)h(x') \tag{3.5}$$

(the inner product is taken modulo 2, and $x \oplus x'$ is a bitwise xor)

Proof. The operations performed by the quantum server, can be described as:

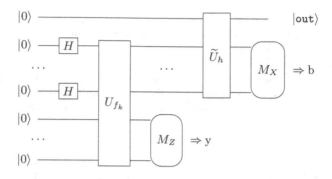

Fig. 1. The circuit computed by the Server

$$|0\rangle \otimes |0^n\rangle \otimes |0^m\rangle \xrightarrow{I_2 \otimes H^{\otimes n} \otimes I_2^{\otimes m}} |0\rangle \otimes \sum_{x \in \mathcal{D}} |x\rangle \otimes |0^m\rangle \xrightarrow{I_2 \otimes U_{f_k}}$$

$$|0\rangle \otimes \sum_{x \in \mathcal{D}} |x\rangle \otimes |f_k(x)\rangle \xrightarrow{f_k \, 2\text{-regular}} |0\rangle \otimes \sum_{y \in \text{Im}(f_k)} (|x\rangle + |x'\rangle) \otimes |y\rangle \xrightarrow{I_2 \otimes I_2^{\otimes n} \otimes M_Z^{\otimes m}}$$

$$|0\rangle \otimes (|x\rangle + |x'\rangle) \otimes |y\rangle \xrightarrow{\tilde{U}_h \otimes I_2^{\otimes m}} (|h(x)\rangle \otimes |x\rangle + |h(x')\rangle \otimes |x'\rangle) \otimes |y\rangle \xrightarrow{I_2 \otimes M_X^{\otimes n} \otimes I_2^{\otimes m}}$$

$$|\text{out}\rangle \otimes |b_1\rangle ... \otimes |b_n\rangle \otimes |y\rangle \Rightarrow |\text{out}\rangle = H^{d_0} X^{d_0(b \cdot (x \oplus x')) \oplus h(x)h(x')} |0\rangle$$

where $\tilde{U}_h$ is a "swapped" U_h, acting on the first register as target and input register as control: $|0\rangle |x\rangle \xrightarrow{\tilde{U}_h} |h(x)\rangle |x\rangle$. For more detailed computations, see the full paper.   □

It can be noticed that, in an honest run of the protocol, using y and the trapdoor information of the function f_k, the Client obtains x and x' and thus can efficiently determine what is the output state that the Server has prepared. In the next section, we prove that no malicious adversary can distinguish between the 2 possible bases $\{|0\rangle, |1\rangle\}$ and $\{|+\rangle, |-\rangle\}$ of the output qubit, or equivalently distinguish whether B_1 is 0 or 1.

3.3   Security Against Malicious Adversaries of Malicious 4-States QFactory

In any run of the protocol, honest or malicious, the state that the client believes that the server has is given by Theorem 2. Therefore, the task that a malicious server wants to achieve, is to be able to guess, as good as he can, the description of the output state that the client (based on the public communication) thinks the server has produced. In particular, in our case, the server needs to guess the bit B_1 (corresponding to the basis) of the (honest) output state.

Note that we want to make sure that the server cannot guess the basis bit B_1 (for most applications [10,22] basis blindness is sufficient as indicated in [19]), and we do not care about the value bit B_2 simply because it is not possible to say that B_2 cannot be guessed with probability better than random. Indeed, even in the honest case, or in the "perfect" case with a quantum channel, the server can always measure the qubit $|out\rangle$ he has to extract the value bit (for example by measuring it in a random basis (computational or Hadamard) and outputting the outcome of the measurement, he will succeed with probability $\frac{1}{2} \times \frac{1}{2} + \frac{1}{2} \times 1 = \frac{3}{4} > 1/2$). Additionally, partial blindness of B_2 is implicit in our work, since learning B_2 leads to leaking partial information about B_1, in the case that the server possesses the honest output state $H^{B_1} X^{B_2} |0\rangle$. Optimal bounds for B_2's leakage are not known if the server is malicious and without verification, is non-trivial and will be studied as a future work.

Definition 9 (4 states basis blindness). *We say that a protocol (π_A, π_B) achieves **basis-blindness** with respect to an ideal list of 4 states $S = \{S_{B_1, B_2}\}_{(B_1, B_2) \in \{0,1\}^2}$ if:*

- *S is the set of states that the protocol outputs, i.e.:*

$$\Pr\left[|\phi\rangle = S_{B_1 B_2} \in S \mid ((B_1, B_2), |\phi\rangle) \leftarrow (\pi_A \| \pi_B) \right] \geq 1 - \mathsf{negl}(n)$$

- *and no information is leaked about the index bit B_1 of the output state of the protocol, i.e for all QPT adversary $\mathcal{A}$:*

$$\Pr\left[B_1 = \tilde{B}_1 \mid ((B_1, B_2), \tilde{B}_1) \leftarrow (\pi_A \| \mathcal{A}) \right] \leq 1/2 + \mathsf{negl}(n)$$

Theorem 3 (Malicious 4-states QFactory is secure). *Protocol 3.1 satisfies 4-states basis blindness with respect to the ideal list of states $S = \{H^{B_1} X^{B_2} |0\rangle\}_{B_1, B_2} = \{|0\rangle, |1\rangle, |+\rangle, |-\rangle\}$.*

Proof. The advantage of our construction is that this theorem is now a direct application of the definition of the family $\mathcal{F}$ (Definition 8). Indeed, let us suppose that there exists a QPT adversary $\mathcal{A}$ such that:

$$\Pr\left[B_1 = \tilde{B}_1 \mid ((B_1, B_2), \tilde{B}_1) \leftarrow (\pi_A \| \mathcal{A}) \right] \geq 1/2 + \frac{1}{\mathsf{poly}(n)}$$

where π_A (respectively π_B) is the honest Client (respectively Server) of Protocol 3.1. From Theorem 2, we notice that the value of B_1 is always equal to $d_0(t_k)$.

Moreover, our adversary is just a one-round adversary, so we can rewrite the previous equation as:

$$\Pr\left[d_0(t_k) = \mathcal{A}(k) \mid (k, t_k) \leftarrow \mathsf{Gen}_{\mathcal{F}}\right] \geq 1/2 + \frac{1}{\mathsf{poly}(n)}$$

But d_0 is a hardcore predicate, so this contradicts Eq. 3.1. So no QPT adversary $\mathcal{A}$ can guess the basis B_1 with probability better than $1/2 + \mathsf{negl}(n)$.   □

Remark 1. In the run of the Malicious 4-states QFactory protocol, the adversary/server has no access to the abort/accept bit, specifying whether the Client wants to abort the protocol after receiving the image y from the server (the abort occurs when y does not have exactly two preimages). So that's why this first protocol is correct with overwhelming probability only when $\delta > 1 - \mathsf{negl}(n)$. See Sect. 7 to see how we address this issue for constant δ.

4   Function Implementation

4.1   General Construction of 2-Regular Homomorphic-Hardcore Family

To complete the construction of Malicious 4-states QFactory, we must find functions $\mathcal{F}$, h, and d_0 satisfying the properties described in Definition 8. We first explain a general method to construct a 2-regular function from an injective homomorphic function (the generalisation to δ-2-regularity from pseudo-homomorphic functions is treated in the full paper), and we give in the next section a candidate that achieves the two other properties required in our definition (homomorphic-hardcore predicate) whose security is based on the cryptographic problem LWE.

Lemma 1. *It is possible to construct a family of functions $\mathcal{F} : \{f_{k'} : \mathcal{D} \times \{0,1\} \to \mathcal{R}\}$, $h_{k'}$ and d_0 that are a 2-regular homomorphic-hardcore family (Definition 8) from a family of functions $\mathcal{G} = \{g_k : \mathcal{D} \to \mathcal{R}\}_k$ that is injective, trapdoor, homomorphic and such that there exists a homomorphic hardcore predicate $h_k : \mathcal{D} \to \{0,1\}$ for all $g_k \in \mathcal{G}$.*

Proof. Because $\mathcal{G}$ and $\mathcal{D}$ are homomorphic, there exist 2 operations "$+_{\mathcal{D}}$" acting on $\mathcal{D}$ and "$+_{\mathcal{R}}$" acting on $\mathcal{R}$ such that $\forall k, \forall z_1, z_2 \in \mathcal{D}$, $g_k(z_1 +_{\mathcal{D}} z_2) = g_k(z_1) +_{\mathcal{R}} g_k(z_2)$ and $h(z_1) \oplus h(z_2) = h(z_2 +_{\mathcal{D}} z_1) = h(z_2 -_{\mathcal{D}} z_1)$. Then, the functions $\mathcal{F}$, h'_k, d_0 are constructed as follow. First, to generate a private key, we generate a private key of $\mathcal{G}$, and we pick a random element z_0 (see $\mathsf{Gen}_{\mathcal{F}}(1^n)$ on the right). And then we define $f_{k'} : \mathcal{D} \times \{0,1\} \to \mathcal{R}$ as $f_{k'}(z, c) = g_k(z) +_{\mathcal{R}} c \cdot y_0$, we also define $h'_{k'} : \mathcal{D} \times \{0,1\} \to \mathcal{R}$

$\mathsf{Gen}_{\mathcal{F}}(1^n)$
1 : $(k, t_k) \leftarrow_{\$} \mathsf{Gen}_{\mathcal{G}}(1^n)$
2 : $z_0 \leftarrow_{\$} \mathcal{D}$
3 : $y_0 = g_k(z_0)$
4 : $t'_{k'} = (t_k, z_0)$
5 : $k' = (k, y_0)$
6 :   **return** $(k', t'_{k'})$

as $h'_{k'}(z, c) = h_k(z)$ and $d_0 : \mathcal{T}' \to \{0,1\}$ (where $\mathcal{T}'$ is the sets of trapdoors $t'_{k'}$) as $d_0(t_k, z_0) = h_k(z_0)$. Now, it is easy to see that this family is 2-regular homomorphic-hardcore family, as proven in the full paper.   □

4.2   Construction of δ-2-regular Homomorphic-Hardcore Family $\mathcal{F}$

We will now give an explicit implementation of a family $\mathcal{G}$ that is injective, trapdoor, (pseudo) homomorphic with a homomorphic-hardcore predicate d_0, and then we will rely on a construction similar to Lemma 1 to produce a family $\mathcal{F}$, h, and d_0 with the properties described in Definition 8 needed by Protocols 3.1 and 7.1. Note that we defined in a previous work [15] a similar construction, but without the additional homomorphic-hardcore property.

The starting point is the injective, trapdoor one-way family of functions $\bar{\mathcal{G}} = \{\bar{g}_K : \mathbb{Z}_q^n \times E^m \to \mathbb{Z}_q^m\}_K$[5] from [39] (where E defines the set of integers bounded in absolute value by some "big-enough" value μ which will be defined later, and additions are matrix additions modulo q, where q is an even integer).

$$\bar{g}_K(s,e) = Ks + e$$

Then, to sample a function from the family $\mathcal{F} = \{f_k : \mathbb{Z}_q^n \times E^m \times \{0,1\} \times \{0,1\} \to \mathbb{Z}_q^m\}$, we will first sample a random matrix $K \in \mathbb{Z}_q^{m \times n}$ with the trapdoor matrix R using the construction from [39], as well as a uniform random vector $s_0 \in \mathbb{Z}_q^n$, a random small error vector $e_0 \in \mathbb{Z}_q^m$ sampled according to a "small-enough" Gaussian distribution $\mathcal{D}_{\alpha' q}^m$ on integers and a (uniform) random bit $d_0 \in \{0,1\}$. Now, after defining the constant vector $v = \left(\frac{q}{2}\, 0 \dots 0\right)^T$, and

$$y_0 := Ks_0 + e_0 + d_0 \times v$$

the trapdoor is set to $t_k := (R, s_0, e_0, d_0)$, and the public index is $k = (K, y_0)$. We can already note at that step that d_0 is a hardcore-predicate:

Lemma 2. The function $d_0(t_k) := d_0$ is a hardcore predicate of k, i.e. for all QPT adversaries $\mathcal{A}$,

$$\Pr[\mathcal{A}(k) = d_0(t_k)] \leq \frac{1}{2} + \mathsf{negl}(n)$$

Now, we can define $f_k : \mathbb{Z}_q^n \times E^m \times \{0,1\} \times \{0,1\} \to \mathbb{Z}_q^m$ as follow:

$$f_k(s,e,c,d) = Ks + e + c \times y_0 + d \times v$$

and $h : \mathbb{Z}_q^n \times E^m \times \{0,1\} \times \{0,1\} \to \{0,1\}$ as:

$$h(s,e,c,d) = d$$

The intuition behind this construction is more or less the same as the general construction presented in Subsect. 4.1. Moreover, the first two terms $As + e$ are useful for the security, the $c \times y_0$ term is needed to ensure the 2-regularity (the two images will differ by $(s_0, e_0, 1, d_0)$), and the last term $d \times v$ is mostly useful to provide the hardcore property. More precisely:

---

[5] The bar on top of $\bar{\mathcal{G}}$ denotes the version where there is not yet the hardcore bit d_0.

- This function cannot have more than 2 preimages because the partial functions $f(\cdot, \cdot, c, \cdot)$ are injective (because $\bar{g}_K$ is injective)
- h is the homomorphic-hardcore predicate required by Definition 8. Indeed, if there is a collision, i.e. if $f_k(s, e, 0, d) = f_k(s', e', 1, d')$, it is easy to see that $d \oplus d' = d_0$ (q is even, and operations are modulo q), i.e. that $h(x) \oplus h(x') = d_0$
- finally, for an appropriate choice of parameters (see Lemma 3), this function is 2-regular with good probability. Indeed, if for a random element $(s, e, 0, d)$ there exists $(s', e', 1, d')$ with $f_k(s, e, 0, d) = f_k(s', e', 1, d')$, then $e = e' + e_0$. But e_0 is sampled from a set significantly smaller than E, so with good probability $e' = e - e_0$ will belong to E.

Note on the Parameters: α' is chosen to make sure that the sampled elements are small compared to μ (the upper bound on E), but such that the noise is still big enough for security. On the contrary, μ must stay small enough to ensure that the function does not have more than two preimages. Our previous work provides a set of parameters having all the required constraints:

Lemma 3 (from [15]). *The family of functions $\mathcal{F}$ is δ-2-regular with good (constant greater than 1/2) probability, trapdoor, one-way and collision resistant (all these properties are true even against a quantum attacker), assuming that there is no quantum algorithm that can efficiently solve SIVP_γ for $\gamma = \mathsf{poly}(n)$, for the following choices of parameters:*

$$q = 2^{5\lceil log(n)\rceil + 21}$$
$$m = 23n + 5n \lceil log(n)\rceil$$
$$\mu = 2mn\sqrt{23 + 5log(n)}$$
$$\alpha' = \frac{\mu}{m\sqrt{mq}} \tag{4.1}$$

Moreover, we can find another set of parameters such that this probability δ is negligibly close to one assuming that SIVP_γ is secure for a superpolynomial γ (depending on the value of δ, you may choose Protocol 3.1 ($\delta \sim 1$) or Protocol 7.1 ($\delta > 1/2$)).

We can now formalize the above intuitions:

Theorem 4. *The family $\mathcal{F}$ defined above with appropriate parameters such as the one defined in Lemma 3 is a δ-2-regular homomorphic-hardcore family.*

Proof. The proofs that $h_k(x) \oplus h_k(x') = d_0$, and that g_K is injective and one-way can be found in the full paper, the Lemma 3 ensures that the family is δ-2-regular, the hardcore property comes from Lemma 2, and the other properties are trivial to check. $\quad\square$

5 The Malicious 8-States QFactory Protocol

In order to use the Malicious 4-states QFactory functionality for applications such as blind quantum computing [10], we need to be able to produce states from the set $\{|+_\theta\rangle, \theta \in \{0, \frac{\pi}{4}, ..., \frac{7\pi}{4}\}\}$, always ensuring that the bases of these qubits remain hidden. Here we prove how by obtaining two states of Malicious 4-states QFactory Protocol, we can obtain a single state from the 8-states set, while no information about the bases of the new output state is leaked.

To achieve this, we need to find an operation, that in the honest case maps the correct inputs to the outputs, in such a way, that the index of the output state corresponding to the basis, is directly related with the bases bits of the input states. This relation should be such that learning anything about the basis of the output state implies learning non-negligible information about the input. This directly means, that any computationally bounded adversary that breaks the 8-states basis blindness of the output, also breaks the 4-states basis blindness of at least one of the inputs.[6]

Protocol 5.1 Malicious 8-states QFactory

Requirements: Same as in Protocol Protocol 3.1
Input: Client runs twice the algorithm $Gen_\mathcal{F}(1^n)$, obtaining $(k^1, t_k^1), (k^2, t_k^2)$. Client keeps t_k^1, t_k^2 private.
Protocol:
– Client: runs Malicious 4-states QFactory algorithm to obtain a state $|\text{in}_1\rangle$ and a "rotated" Malicious 4-states QFactory to obtain a state $|\text{in}_2\rangle$ (by rotated Malicious 4-states QFactory we mean a Malicious 4-states QFactory, but where the last set of measurements in the $|\pm\rangle$ basis (Fig. 1) is replaced by measurements in the $\left|\pm\frac{\pi}{2}\right\rangle$ basis).
– Client: records measurement outcomes $(y^1, b^1), (y^2, b^2)$ and computes and stores the corresponding indices of the output states of the 2 Malicious 4-states QFactory runs: (B_1, B_2) for $|\text{in}_1\rangle$ and (B'_1, B'_2) for $|\text{in}_2\rangle$.
– Client: instructs Server to apply the Merge Gadget (Fig. 2) on the states $|\text{in}_1\rangle, |\text{in}_2\rangle$.
– Server: returns the 2 measurement results s_1, s_2.
– Client: using $(B_1, B_2), (B'_1, B'_2), s_1, s_2$ computes the index $L = L_1 L_2 L_3 \in \{0,1\}^3$ of the output state.
Output: If the protocol is run honestly, the state that the Server has produced is:

$$|\text{out}\rangle = X^{(s_2+B_2)\cdot B_1} Z^{B'_2 + B_2(1-B_1) + B_1[s_1 + (s_2+B_2)B'_1]} R(\frac{\pi}{2})^{B_1} R(\frac{\pi}{4})^{B'_1} |+\rangle \qquad (5.1)$$

5.1 Correctness of Malicious 8-States QFactory

We prove the existence of a mapping $\mathcal{M}$ (which we will call Merge Gadget), from 2 states $|\text{in}_1\rangle$ and $|\text{in}_2\rangle$, where $|\text{in}_1\rangle \in \{|0\rangle, |1\rangle, |+\rangle, |-\rangle\}$ and $|\text{in}_2\rangle \in \{|+\rangle, |-\rangle, |+_y\rangle, |-_y\rangle\}$ to a state $|\text{out}\rangle = |+_{L \cdot \frac{\pi}{4}}\rangle$, where $L = L_1 L_2 L_3 \in \{0,1\}^3$. Namely, as defined in Protocol 5.1, $\mathcal{M}$ is acting in the following way:

---

[6] Here it is worth pointing out that a similar result (in a more complicated method) was achieved in [19]. That technique however, is applied in the information theoretic setting.

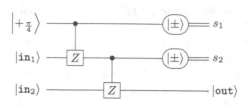

Fig. 2. Merge gadget

$$\mathcal{M}(|\mathrm{in}_1\rangle, |\mathrm{in}_2\rangle) = M_{X,2} M_{X,1\wedge Z_{2,3}\wedge Z_{1,2}} \left[|+\tfrac{\pi}{4}\rangle \otimes |\mathrm{in}_1\rangle \otimes |\mathrm{in}_2\rangle \right] \qquad (5.2)$$

Theorem 5. *In an honest run, the Output state of the Malicious 8-states QFactory Protocol is of the form* $|+_{L \cdot \frac{\pi}{4}}\rangle$, *where* $L = L_1 L_2 L_3 \in \{0,1\}^3$.

It can also be noticed that, in an honest run of Malicious 8-states QFactory, the client can efficiently determine L: using b^1, b^2, y^1, y^2 and the trapdoors t_k^1, t_k^2, he first obtains (B_1, B_2) and (B_1', B_2'), and after receiving s_1, s_2, he determines the description of the state prepared by the server.

5.2 Security Against Malicious Adversaries of Malicious 8-States QFactory

In any run of the protocol, honest or malicious, the state that the client believes that the server has, is given by Theorem 5.

Therefore, as in the case of Malicious 4-states QFactory, the task that a malicious server wants to achieve, is to be able to guess, as good as he can, the index of the output state that the client thinks the server has produced. In particular, in our case, the server needs to guess the bits L_2 and L_3 (corresponding to the basis) of the (honest) output state.

Definition 10 (8 states basis blindness). *Similarly, we say that a protocol* (π_A, π_B) *achieves* **basis-blindness** *with respect to an ideal list of 8 states* $S = \{S_{L_1,L_2,L_3}\}_{(L_1,L_2,L_3)\in\{0,1\}^3}$ *if:*

- *S is the set of states that the protocol outputs, i.e.:*

$$\Pr\left[|\phi\rangle = S_{L_1,L_2,L_3} \in S \mid ((L_1, L_2, L_3), |\phi\rangle) \leftarrow (\pi_A \| \pi_B) \right] = 1$$

- *and if no information is leaked about the "basis" bits* (L_2, L_3) *of the output state of the protocol, i.e for all QPT adversary* $\mathcal{A}$:

$$\Pr\left[L_2 = \tilde{L}_2 \text{ and } L_3 = \tilde{L}_3 \mid ((L_1, L_2, L_3), (\tilde{L}_2, \tilde{L}_3)) \leftarrow (\pi_A \| \mathcal{A}) \right] \leq 1/4 + \mathsf{negl}(n)$$

Theorem 6. *Malicious 8-states QFactory satisfies 8-state basis blindness with respect to the ideal set of states* $S = \{|+_{\pi L/4}\rangle\}_{L\in\{0,...,7\}} = \{|+\rangle, |+_{\frac{\pi}{4}}\rangle, .., |+_{\frac{7\pi}{4}}\rangle\}$.

Sketch Proof (The full proof can be found in the full paper). We prove this result by reduction showing that, if there exists a QPT adversary $\mathcal{A}$ that is able to break the 8-states basis blindness property of Malicious 8-states QFactory (determine the indices L_2 and L_3 with probability $\frac{1}{4} + \frac{1}{poly_1(n)}$ for some polynomial function $poly_1$), then we can construct a QPT adversary $\mathcal{A}'$ that can break the 4-states basis blindness of the Malicious 4-states QFactory protocol (determine the basis bit with probability $\frac{1}{2} + \frac{1}{poly_2(n)}$, for some polynomial $poly_2(\cdot)$).   □

6 Blind Measurement Gadget

In this section we show how our basic module can be used to achieve another task, that of blind-measurement. The task is the following: we want a classical client to instruct a quantum server to measure one of his qubits in either the Pauli X or Z basis, in a way that the server is not aware of which of the two bases was actually used. We give below a gadget that achieves this task using a single output of the Malicious QFactory 4-states. We note also, that other blind-measurements, between different sets of bases, are also possible using our module, but we focus on this one since it is this type of measurement needed for post-hoc verification [21] and thus is the basis for classical verification protocols such as that of [33].

The following gadget Fig. 3 achieves the desired task. Note, that we consider a general state $|\psi\rangle$ where the measurement is performed on the first of its qubits (thus the second wire in the figure represents all the non-measured qubits). Depending on the value of B_1, the actual outcome is Z or X and the measurement outcome is obtained from either s_1 or s_2 (see details in the full paper).

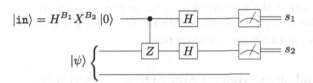

Fig. 3. Blind measurement gadget

7 Malicious-Abort 4-States QFactory: Treating Abort Case

In this section, we will discuss an extension of Malicious 4-states QFactory, whose aim is to achieve basis blindness even against adversaries that try to exploit the fact that Malicious 4-states QFactory can abort when there is only one preimage associated to the y returned by the server. One may think that we could just send back this `accept/abort` bit to the server, but unfortunately it could leak additional information on the hardcore bit d_0 (which corresponds to the basis B_1 of the produced qubit) to the server, and from an information theory point of view, as soon as the probability of acceptance is small enough, we cannot guarantee that this bit remains secret. On the other hand, for honest servers, the probability of aborting is usually non-negligible, so we cannot neglect this case.

We stress out that it is also possible to guarantee that for honest servers this probability goes negligibly close to 1 by making an appropriate choice of parameters for the function. In that case the initial protocol of Malicious QFactory defined Sect. 3 is secure, but this comes (as far as we know), at the cost of using a function with is "less" secure. More specifically, instead of having a reduction to GapSVP with a polynomial γ, the reduction usually goes to GapSVP with a super-polynomial γ. Such function parameters have been used implicitly in other works [32] ([7] later removed this assumption), and for now they are believed to be secure (the best known polynomial algorithm cannot break GapSVP with a γ smaller than exponential), but these assumptions are usually not widely accepted in the cryptography community, and that's why we aim to remove this non-standard assumption.

The solution we propose in this section uses the assumption that the classical Yao's XOR Lemma also applies for one-round protocols (with classical messages) against quantum adversary. This lemma roughly states that if you cannot guess the output bit of one round with probability better than η, then it's hard to guess the output bit of t independents rounds with probability much better than $1/2 + \eta^t$. As far as we know, this lemma has been proven only in the classical case (see [25] for a review of this theorem as well as the main proof methods), and other works [52] even extend this lemma to protocols, and also to quantum setting [28,49]. Unfortunately, these works focus on communication and query complexity and are not really usable in our case.

In the following, we will call "accepted run" a run of Malicious 4-states QFactory such that the y received from the server has 2 preimages ("probability of success" also refers to the probability of this event when the server is honest), and otherwise we call it an "aborted run".

7.1   The Malicious-Abort 4-State QFactory Protocol

In a nutshell, the solution we propose is to run several instances of Malicious 4-states QFactory, by remarking that we do not need to discard the aborted runs. Indeed, it is easy to see that in these cases, the produced qubits will always be in the same basis (denoted by 0). The idea is then to implement on the server side a circuit that will output a qubit having as basis the XOR of all the basis of the accepted runs (without even leaking which runs are accepted or not), and check on client's side that the number of accepted runs is high enough (this will happen with probability exponentially close to 1 for honest servers). If it is the case, the client will just output the XOR of the basis of the accepted run, and otherwise (i.e. if the server is malicious), he will just pick a random bit value.

Unfortunately, in practice things are a bit more complicated, and in order to be able to write the proof of security we need to divide all the t runs into n_c "chunks" of size t_c, and test them individually. Here is a more precise (but still high level) description of the protocol and proof's ideas, the full proofs being in the full paper:

- firstly, we run $t = n_c \times t_c$ parallel instances of Malicious 4-states QFactory, without revealing the abort bit for any of these instances;
- then the key point to note is that for honest servers, if y_i has only one preimage then the output qubit produced by the server at the end of the protocol will be either $|0\rangle$ or $|1\rangle$, but cannot be $|+\rangle$ or $|-\rangle$ (with one preimage we do not have a superposition). In other words, the basis is always the $\{|0\rangle, |1\rangle\}$ basis (denoted as 0) so we do not really need to abort. Therefore, at the end, (for honest runs) the basis of the output qubits will be equal for all $i \in [\![0, t]\!]$ to $\beta_i = d_{0,i} \cdot a_i$, where $a_i = 1$ iff y_i has two preimages, and $a_i = 0$ otherwise. Of course, this distribution will be biased against 0, but it is not a problem. See Lemma 4 for proof.
- then, it also appears that from t qubits in the basis $\beta_1, \ldots, \beta_t$, we have a way to produce a single qubit belonging to the set $\{|0\rangle, |1\rangle, |+\rangle, |-\rangle\}$ whose basis B_1 is the XOR of the basis of the t qubits, i.e. $B_1 = \oplus_{i=1}^t \beta_i$ (see Lemma 5).
- Then, the client will test every chunk, by checking if the proportion of accepted runs in every chunk is greater than a given value p_c. If all chunks have enough accepted runs, then the client just computes and outputs the good value for the basis (which is the XOR of the hardcore bit of all the accepted runs) and value bits. However, if at least one chunk doesn't have enough accepted runs (which shouldn't happen if the server is honest), then the client just outputs random values for the basis and value bit, not correlated with server's qubit (equivalent to saying that a malicious server can always throw the qubit and pick a new qubit, not correlated with client's one).
- Correctness: if the probability to have two preimages for an honest server is at least a constant p_a greater than $1/2$ (the parameters we proposed in [15] have this property), and if t is chosen high enough, the fraction of accepted runs will be close to p_a, and we can show that the probability to have a fraction of accepted runs smaller than a given constant $p_b < p_a$ is exponentially (in t) close to 0. So with overwhelming probability, all the chunks will have enough accepted runs, i.e. honest servers will have a qubit corresponding to the output of the client.
- Soundness: to prove the security of this scheme, we first prove that it is impossible for any adversary to guess the output of one chunk with a probability bigger than a constant $\eta < 1$ (otherwise we have a direct reduction that breaks the hardcore bit property of g_K). Now, using the quantum version of Yao's XOR Lemma that we conjecture at Conjecture 1, we can deduce that no malicious server is able to guess the XOR of the t_c chunks/instances with probability better than $1/2 + \eta^{t_c} + \mathsf{negl}(n)$, which goes negligibly close to $1/2$ when $t_c = \Omega(n)$.

Putting everything together, the parties will just run $t = n_c \cdot t_c$ Malicious 4-states QFactory in parallel, the client will then check if $\sum_i a_i$ is higher than $p_c \cdot t_c$ for all the n_c chunks, and if so he will set $B_1 = \oplus_{i=1}^{t} d_i \cdot a_i$ (server has a circuit to produce a qubit in this basis as well). Otherwise B_1 will be set to a uniformly chosen random bit (it is equivalent to say that a malicious server can destroy the qubit, and this is also unavoidable even with a real quantum communication), and we still have correctness with overwhelming probability for honest clients.

The exact algorithm is described in Protocol 7.1, while the security result is shown in Theorem 7 (and the proofs can be found in the full paper).

7.2   Correctness and Security of Malicious-Abort 4-State QFactory

Now, we will formalize the previous statements, the proofs are in the full paper.

Conjecture 1 (Yao's XOR Lemma for one-round protocols (classical messages) against quantum adversary).
Let n be the security parameter, $f_n : \mathcal{X}_n \times \mathcal{Y}_n \to \{0,1\}$ be a (possibly non-deterministic) function family (usually not computable in polynomial time), and χ_n be a distribution on $\mathcal{X}_n$ efficiently samplable. If there exists $\delta(n)$ such that $|\delta(n)| \geq \frac{1}{\text{poly}(n)}$ and such that for all QPT (in n) adversary $\mathcal{A}_n : \mathcal{X}_n \to \mathcal{Y}_n \times \{0,1\}$:

$$\Pr\left[\tilde{\beta} = f_n(x,y) \mid (y, \tilde{\beta}) \leftarrow \mathcal{A}_n(x), x \leftarrow \chi_n\right] \leq 1 - \delta(n)$$

then, for all $t \in \mathbb{N}^*$, there is no QPT adversary $\mathcal{A}'_n : \mathcal{X}_n^t \to \mathcal{Y}_n^t \times \{0,1\}$ such that:

$$\Pr\left[\tilde{\beta} = \bigoplus_{i=1}^{t} f_n(x_i, y_i) \mid (y_1, \ldots, y_t, \tilde{\beta}) \leftarrow \mathcal{A}'_n(x_1, \ldots, x_t), \forall i, x_i \leftarrow \chi_n\right]$$
$$\geq \frac{1}{2} + (1 - \delta(n))^t + \text{negl}(n)$$

Lemma 4 (Aborted runs are useful). *If π_{A_4} and π_{B_4} are following the Malicious 4-states QFactory protocol honestly, and if y has not 2 preimages, then the output qubit produced by π_{B_4} is in the basis $\{|0\rangle, |1\rangle\}$.*

Lemma 5 (Gadget circuit $\text{Gad}_\oplus$ computes XOR). *If we denote by b_i the basis of $|\text{in}_i\rangle$ (equal to 0 if the basis is 0/1, and 1 if the basis is +/−), and if we run the circuit $\text{Gad}_\oplus$ (inspired by measurement based quantum computing) represented Fig. 4 on these inputs, then basis of $|\text{out}\rangle$ is equal to $\oplus_{i=1}^{t} b_i$.*

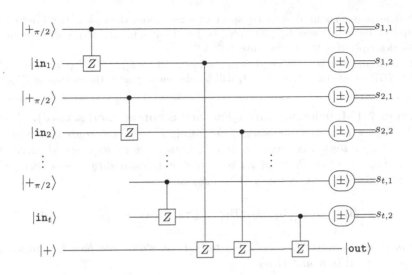

Fig. 4. The XOR gadget circuit $\mathtt{Gad}_\oplus$ (run on server side)

We will now describe here the protocol of Malicious-Abort 4-states QFactory:

Protocol 7.1 Malicious-Abort 4-states QFactory Protocol

Requirements:

Public: The family of functions $\mathcal{F}$ and h described above, such that the probability of having two pre-images for a random image is greater than a constant $p_a > 1/2$.

This protocol is based on the constants $t_c \in \mathbb{N}$ (number of repetitions per chunk), $n_c \in \mathbb{N}$ (number of chunks), $p_a \in (1/2, 1]$ (lower bound on probability of accepted run in the honest protocol), $p_c \in (1/2, 1] < p_a$ (fraction of the runs per chunk that must be accepted). These constants can be chosen to have overwhelming probability of success for honest players, and negligible advantage for an adversary trying to guess the basis.

Stage 1: Run multiple QFactories

– Client: prepares $t = n_c \times t_c$ public keys/trapdoors:

$$(k^{(i,j)}, t_{k^{(i,j)}}) \leftarrow \mathrm{Gen}_{\mathcal{F}}(1^n), \text{ where } i \in [\![1, n_c]\!], j \in [\![1, t_c]\!]$$

The Client then sends the public keys $k^{(i,j)}$ to the Server, together with h.

– Server and Client: follow Protocol 3.1 t times, with the keys sent at the step before. Client receives $((y^{(i,j)}, b^{(i,j)}))_{i,j}$, and sets for all i, j: $a^{(i,j)} = 1$ iff $|f^{-1}(y^{(i,j)})| = 2$, otherwise $a^{(i,j)} = 0$, and $B_1^{(i,j)}$ and $B_2^{(i,j)}$ like in Protocol 3.1 when $a^{(i,j)} = 1$ (otherwise $B_1^{(i,j)} = 0$ and $B_2^{(i,j)} = h(f^{-1}(y))$). Server will get t outputs $|\mathbf{in}_{(i,j)}\rangle$.

Stage 2: Combine runs and output

– Server: applies circuit Figure 4 on the t outputs $|\mathbf{in}_t\rangle$, and outputs $|\mathbf{out}\rangle$.

– Client: checks that for all chunks $i \in [\![1, n_c]\!]$ the number of accepted runs is high enough, i.e. $\sum_j a^{(i,j)} \geq p_c t_c$.

- If at least one chunk does not respect this condition, then picks two random bits B_1 (the basis bit) and B_2 (the value bit) and outputs (B_1, B_2), corresponding to the description of the BB84 state $H^{B_1} X^{B_2} |0\rangle$.
- If all chunks respect this condition, then sets $B_1 := \bigoplus_{i,j} B_1^{(i,j)}$ (the final basis is the XOR of all the basis), and B_2 will be chosen to match the output of Figure 4.

Theorem 7 (Malicious-Abort QFactory is correct and secure). *Assuming Conjecture 1, if the probability of the family $\mathcal{F}$ to have two preimages for any image is bigger than a constant $p_a > 1/2$, then there exists a set of parameters p_c, t_c and n_c such that Protocol 7.1 is correct with probability exponentially close to 1 and basis-blind, i.e. for any QPT adversary $\mathcal{A}$:*

$$\Pr\left[\tilde{B}_1 = B_1 \mid ((B_1, B_2), \tilde{B}_1) \leftarrow (\pi_{A_4 \oplus} \| \mathcal{A})\right] \leq 1/2 + \mathsf{negl}(n)$$

More precisely, we need $t_c \in (1/2, p_c)$ to be a constant, and both t_c and n_c need to be polynomial in n and $\Omega(n)$.

8   Verifiable QFactory

In the previous protocols, Malicious 4-states QFactory and Malicious 8-states QFactory, the produced qubits came with the guarantee of *basis-blindness* (Definitions 9 and 10). While the property refers to the ability of a malicious adversary to guess the honest basis bit(s), it tells nothing about the actual state that a deviating server might produce. For a number of applications and most notably for *verifiable blind quantum computation* [22], the basis-blindness property is not sufficient. What is needed is a stronger property, *verification*, that ensures that the produced state was prepared correctly even in a malicious run.

8.1   Verifiable QFactory Functionality

There are two issues with trying to define a verification property for QFactory. The first is that the adversarial server can always abort, therefore the verification property can only ensure that the probability of non-aborting *and* cheat is negligible. The second issue is that, since the final state is in the hands of the server, the server can always apply a final deviation on the state[7]. This is not different from what happens in protocols that do have quantum communication. In that case, the adversarial receiver (server) can also apply a deviation on the state received before using the state in any subsequent protocol. This deviation could even be the server replacing the received state with a totally different state.

Here, we define the strongest notion of verifiable QFactory possible, which exactly captures the idea of being able to recover the ideal state from the real state without any knowledge of the (secret) index of the ideal state. This notion is

---

[7] However that deviation needs to be independent of anything that is secret.

sufficient for any protocol that includes communication of random secret qubits of the form $|+_{L\pi/4}\rangle$ which includes a verifiable quantum computation protocol and furthermore, it is also possible to relax slightly the definition of verifiable QFactory, as it is proven in the full paper.

Definition 11 (Verifiable QFactory). *Consider a party that is given a state uniformly chosen from a set of eight states* $S = \{\rho_L \,|\, L \in \{0, 1, ..., 7\}\}$ *or an abort bit, where S is basis-blind i.e. given a state sampled uniformly at random from S, it is impossible to guess the last two bits of the index L of the state within the set S with non-negligible advantage. We say that this party has a Verifiable QFactory if, it aborts with small probability and when he does not abort, there exists an isometry Φ, that is independent of the index L, such that:*

$$\Phi(\rho_L) \stackrel{\epsilon}{\approx} |+_{L\pi/4}\rangle \langle +_{L\pi/4}| \otimes \sigma_{junk} \tag{8.1}$$

where the state σ_{junk} is independent of the index L.

It is worth stressing, that if the security setting is computational (as in this work), the basis-blindness and the approximate equality above involve a QPT distinguisher, while the isometry Φ needs to be computable in polynomial time.

8.2 Blind Self-testing

Before giving a verifiable QFactory protocol, we define a new concept of blind self-testing, that will be essential in proving the security of the former. Self-testing is a technique developed [31, 36–38, 51] that ensures that given some measurement statistics, classical parties can be certain that some untrusted quantum state (and operations), that two or more quantum parties share, is essentially (up to some isometry) the state that the parties believe they have. In high-level, we are going to use a test of this kind in order to certify that the output of Verifiable QFactory is indeed the desired one.

Existing results, that we will call *non-local self-testing*, only deal with how to exploit the non-locality (the fact that the quantum state tested is shared between non-communicating parties) to test the state and operations. Naturally, the correctness is up to a local isometry (something that the servers can apply, while preserving the non-communication condition).

Here, instead of testing a single non-local state, we test a family of states, where the *non-locality* property is replaced by the *blindness* property - the fact that server is not aware (is blind) of which state from the possibly known family of states he is actually given in each run of the protocol. To see how this is closely related, one can imagine the usual non-local self-testing of the singlet state, where one quantum side (Alice) actually performs a measurement (as instructed). From the point of view of the other quantum side (Bob), he has a single state that, in the honest run, is one of the BB84 states, while he is totally oblivious about the basis of this state (if that was not the case, it would lead to signalling the basis choice of Alice's measurement). However, this is, by no means the most general case. Here we introduce the concept of *blind self-testing* formalising the above intuition.

We give here the most general case of blind self-testing and we conjecture that it holds. In the full paper we also list three simpler scenarios (of increasing complication) that lead to the most general case given here, following similar steps with the extension of simple i.i.d. self-testing to fully robust and rigid self-testing in existing literature [17,26,31,38,48]. The security proof of the first case can be found in the full paper, while complete analysis of the most general blind self-testing goes beyond the scope of this work.

Protocol 8.1 Blind self-testing: The general case

– Server prepares a single state ρ_{tot} (consisting of N qubits in the honest run). This state has a corresponding index consisting of N 3-bit indices L_i ($L_i \in \{0,...,7\}\ \forall i \in \{1,...,N\}$), and the server is basis blind with respect to each of these N indices, i.e. (being computationally bounded) he cannot determine with non-negligible advantage the two basis bits of any index L_i. On the other hand, client knows the indices L_i's.
– The client, randomly chooses a fraction f of the qubits to be used as tests and announces the set of corresponding indices $T = \{i_1, \cdots, i_{fN}\} \subset \{1, 2, ..., N\}$ to the server.
– For each test qubit $i_j \in T$, the client chooses a random measurement index $M_{i_j} \in \{000, \cdots, 111\}$ and instructs the server to measure the corresponding qubit in the $\left\{|+_{M_{i_j}\pi/4}\rangle, |-_{M_{i_j}\pi/4}\rangle\right\}$ basis.
– The server returns the test measurement results $\{c_{(i_j)}\}$.
— For each fixed pair (L, M), the client gathers all the test positions that correspond to that pair and from the relative frequencies, the client obtains an estimate for the probability $p_{L,M}$ (where by convention we have that $p_{L,M}$ corresponds to the +1 outcome, while $1 - p_{L,M}$ to the −1).
– If $|p_{L,M} - \cos^2((L-M)\pi/8)| \geq \epsilon_2$ for any pair (L, M) the client aborts.
Output: If the client does not abort (and this happens with non-negligible probability), then there exists an index-independent polynomial isometry $\Phi = \Phi_{k_1} \otimes \cdots \Phi_{k_l}$, given by products of the isometries in Fig. 5, that is applied to a random subset of non-tested qubits i, such that:

$$\Phi(Tr_{\text{all but } k_1, \cdots, k_l \text{ qubits}} \rho_{tot}) \overset{\epsilon(\epsilon_1, \epsilon_2)}{\approx} \left(|+_{L_{k_1}\pi/4}\rangle_{k_1} \otimes \cdots \otimes |+_{L_{k_l}\pi/4}\rangle_{k_l}\right) \otimes \sigma_{\text{junk}} \quad (8.2)$$

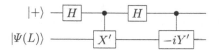

Fig. 5. The isometry of the blind self-testing. Note that the controlled gates are controlled in the X-basis, i.e. $\wedge U_{12}(a|+\rangle + b|-\rangle)_1 \otimes (|\psi\rangle)_2 = a|+\rangle_1 \otimes |\psi\rangle_2 + b|-\rangle_1 \otimes U|\psi\rangle_2$.

In this most general setting, we make no assumption on the state ρ_{tot} produced by server and want to recover the full tensor product structure of the resulting states given by Eq. (8.2). In the self-testing literature, Azuma-Hoeffding, quantum de-Finetti theorems and rigidity results [6,9,13,27] were used to uplift the simple i.i.d. case and prove security in the general setting.

8.3   The Verifiable QFactory Protocol

In this section we introduce a protocol for the final version of our functionality, Verifiable QFactory. Here, we give the protocol, show the correctness and the security, namely that the protocol achieves the verification property from Definition 11, based on the conjectured security of the most general *blind self-testing* given in Protocol 8.1. The basic idea is the following: repeat the Malicious 8-states QFactory multiple times, then the client chooses a random fraction of the output qubits and uses them for a test and next instructs the server to measure the test qubits in random angles and, finally, the client checks their statistics. Since the server does not know the states (or to be more precise, the basis bits), he is unlikely to succeed in guessing the correct statistics unless he is honest. (up to some trivial relabelling). The output qubits and the measurement angles, need to be from the set of 8-states, which is one of the reasons we wanted to give the 8-states extension of our Malicious 4-states QFactory.

Protocol 8.2 Verifiable QFactory

Requirements: Same as in Protocol Protocol 3.1
Input: Client runs N times the algorithm $(k^{(i)}, t_k^{(i)}) \leftarrow \text{Gen}_{\mathcal{F}}(1^n)$, where $i \in \{1, \cdots, N\}$ denotes the ith run. He keeps the $t_k^{(i)}$'s private.
Protocol:
– Client: runs N times the Malicious 8-states QFactory Protocol 5.1.
   – Client: records measurement outcomes $y^{(i)}, b^{(i)}$ and computes and stores the corresponding index of the output state $L^{(i)}$.
   – Client: instructs the server to measure a random fraction rf of the output states, each in a randomly chosen basis of the form $\{|+_{M^{(i)}\pi/4}\rangle, |-_{M^{(i)}\pi/4}\rangle\}$. Here $M^{(i)}$ is the index of the measurement instructed.
   – Server: returns the measurement outcomes $c^{(i)}$.
   – Client: for each pair (L, M) collects the results $c^{(j)}$ for all j's that have the specific pair and with the relative frequency obtains an estimate for the probability $p(L, M)$.
   – Client: aborts unless all the estimates of the probabilities $p(L, M)$ are ϵ-close to the ideal one i.e. $p(L, M) \stackrel{\epsilon}{\approx} |\langle +_{M\pi/4} |+_{L\pi/4}\rangle|^2$.
Output: Probability of non-abort and being far from the ideal state[8] is negligible ϵ':

$$p(\text{non-abort} \wedge \Delta(\rho_{L^{(i_1)}...L^{(i_{N(1-f)})}}, \rho_{\text{ideal}}) \geq t(n)) \leq \epsilon' \tag{8.3}$$

where $i_1, ..., i_{N(1-f)}$ refer to the unmeasured qubits and where

$$\Phi(\rho_{\text{ideal}}) = \otimes_{k=1}^{N(1-f)} |+_{L^{(i_k)}\pi/4}\rangle \langle +_{L^{(i_k)}\pi/4}| \otimes \sigma_{\text{junk}} \tag{8.4}$$

σ_{junk} is a constant density matrix, ϵ, ϵ' are negligible and $t(\cdot)$ is non-negligible function.
   Moreover, in an honest run, the probability of aborting is negligible and the output is:

$$\rho_{\text{honest}} = \otimes_{k=1}^{N(1-f)} |+_{L^{(i_k)}\pi/4}\rangle \langle +_{L^{(i_k)}\pi/4}| \tag{8.5}$$

---

[8] The distance Δ used here depends on the setting. In our case it is understood as a QPT distinguisher.

Theorem 8 (correctness). *If Protocol 8.2 is run honestly, it aborts with negligible probability and the output (non-measured) qubits are exactly in a product state of the form $|+_{L^{(i_k)}\pi/4}\rangle\langle+_{L^{(i_k)}\pi/4}|$. Thus, the trivial isometry (the identity) suffices to recover the state of Eq. (8.1), and where there is no junk state.*

Proof. In an honest run, each of the outputs of different Malicious 8-states QFactory runs, are of the correct form, therefore measuring any of those outputs in the $\{|\pm_{M\pi/4}\rangle\}$ basis returns the correct statistics with high probability. Hence, the protocol does not abort, while the remaining states are prepared correctly.

$\square$

Theorem 9 (security). *Protocol 8.2 is a Verifiable QFactory (Definition 11), i.e. the probability of accepting the tests and having a state far from the ideal is negligible irrespective of the deviation of the adversary, assuming that the self-testing Protocol 8.1 is correct.*

In the full paper we also explain how this task is very similar with self-testing results, and provide the first step for our self-testing result.

Acknowledgements. LC is very grateful to Céline Chevalier for all the discussions he had with her, and to Antoine Joux for the very pertinent comments. He would also like to give a special thanks to Geoffroy Couteau, Omar Fawzi and Alain Passelègue who gave him great advices concerning security proof methods. AC and PW are very grateful to Atul Mantri, Thomas Zacharias, Yiannis Tselekounis and Vedran Dunjko for very helpful and interesting discussions. The work was supported by the following grants FA9550-17-1-0055, EPSRC grants: EP/N003829/1 and EP/M013243/1, and by the French ANR Project ANR-18-CE39-0015 CryptiQ.

References

1. Aaronson, S., Cojocaru, A., Gheorghiu, A., Kashefi, E.: On the implausibility of classical client blind quantum computing. arXiv preprint arXiv:1704.08482 (2017)
2. Aharonov, D., Ben-Or, M., Eban, E., Mahadev, U.: Interactive Proofs for Quantum Computations. arXiv e-prints, page arXiv:1704.04487, April 2017
3. Alagic, G., Dulek, Y., Schaffner, C., Speelman, F.: Quantum fully homomorphic encryption with verification. In: Takagi, T., Peyrin, T. (eds.) ASIACRYPT 2017. LNCS, vol. 10624, pp. 438–467. Springer, Cham (2017). https://doi.org/10.1007/978-3-319-70694-8_16
4. Armknecht, F., Gagliardoni, T., Katzenbeisser, S., Peter, A.: General impossibility of group homomorphic encryption in the quantum world. In: Krawczyk, H. (ed.) PKC 2014. LNCS, vol. 8383, pp. 556–573. Springer, Heidelberg (2014). https://doi.org/10.1007/978-3-642-54631-0_32
5. Arrighi, P., Salvail, L.: Blind quantum computation. Int. J. Quantum Inf. **04**, 10 (2003)
6. Azuma, K.: Weighted sums of certain dependent random variables. Tohoku Math. J. Second Ser. **19**(3), 357–367 (1967)
7. Brakerski, Z.: Quantum FHE (Almost) as secure as classical. In: Shacham, H., Boldyreva, A. (eds.) CRYPTO 2018. LNCS, vol. 10993, pp. 67–95. Springer, Cham (2018). https://doi.org/10.1007/978-3-319-96878-0_3

8. Brakerski, Z., Christiano, P., Mahadev, U., Vazirani, U.V., Vidick, T.: A cryptographic test of quantumness and certifiable randomness from a single quantum device. In: 2018 IEEE 59th Annual Symposium on Foundations of Computer Science (FOCS), pp. 320–331 (2018)

9. Brandao, F.G., Harrow, A.W.: Quantum de Finetti theorems under local measurements with applications. In: Proceedings of the Forty-Fifth Annual ACM Symposium on Theory of Computing, STOC 2013, pp. 861–870. ACM, New York (2013)

10. Broadbent, A., Fitzsimons, J., Kashefi., J.: Universal blind quantum computation. In: Proceedings of the 2009 50th Annual IEEE Symposium on Foundations of Computer Science, FOCS 2009, pp. 517–526. IEEE Computer Society, Washington, DC (2009)

11. Broadbent, A., Jeffery, S.: Quantum homomorphic encryption for circuits of low T-gate complexity. In: Gennaro, R., Robshaw, M. (eds.) CRYPTO 2015. LNCS, vol. 9216, pp. 609–629. Springer, Heidelberg (2015). https://doi.org/10.1007/978-3-662-48000-7_30

12. Canetti, R.: Universally composable security: a new paradigm for cryptographic protocols. Cryptology ePrint Archive, Report 2000/067 (2000). https://eprint.iacr.org/2000/067

13. Caves, C.M., Fuchs, C.A., Schack, R.: Unknown quantum states: the quantum de finetti representation. J. Math. Phys. 43(9), 4537–4559 (2002)

14. Childs, A.M.: Secure assisted quantum computation. Quantum Info. Comput. 5(6), 456–466 (2005)

15. Cojocaru, A., Colisson, L., Kashefi, E., Wallden, P.: On the possibility of classical client blind quantum computing. CoRR, abs/1802.08759 (2018)

16. Cojocaru, A., Colisson, L., Kashefi, E., Wallden, P.: QFactory: classically-instructed remote secret qubits preparation. arXiv e-prints arXiv:1904.06303, April 2019

17. Coladangelo, A., Grilo, A., Jeffery, S., Vidick, S.: Verifier-on-a-leash: new schemes for verifiable delegated quantum computation, with quasilinear resources. arXiv preprint arXiv:1708.07359 (2017)

18. Dulek, Y., Schaffner, C., Speelman, F.: Quantum homomorphic encryption for polynomial-sized circuits. In: Robshaw, M., Katz, J. (eds.) CRYPTO 2016. LNCS, vol. 9816, pp. 3–32. Springer, Heidelberg (2016). https://doi.org/10.1007/978-3-662-53015-3_1

19. Dunjko, V., Kashefi, V.: Blind quantum computing with two almost identical states. arXiv e-prints arXiv:1604.01586, April 2016

20. Dunjko, V., Kashefi, E., Leverrier, A.: Blind quantum computing with weak coherent pulses. Phys. Rev. Lett. 108, 200502 (2011)

21. Fitzsimons, J.F., Hajdusek, M., Morimae, T.: Post hoc verification of quantum computation. Phys. Rev. Lett. 120, 040501 (2018)

22. Fitzsimons, J.F., Kashefi, E.: Unconditionally verifiable blind quantum computation. Phys. Rev. A 96, 012303 (2017)

23. Gheorghiu, A., Vidick, T.: Computationally-secure and composable remote state preparation. arXiv e-prints arXiv:1904.06320, April 2019

24. Giovannetti, V., Maccone, L., Morimae, T., Rudolph, T.G.: Efficient universal blind quantum computation. Phys. Rev. Lett. 111, 230501 (2013)

25. Goldreich, O., Nisan, N., Wigderson, A.: On Yao's XOR-Lemma. In: Goldreich, O. (ed.) Studies in Complexity and Cryptography. Miscellanea on the Interplay between Randomness and Computation. LNCS, vol. 6650, pp. 273–301. Springer, Heidelberg (2011). https://doi.org/10.1007/978-3-642-22670-0_23

26. Haur Yang, T., Navascués, M.: Robust self testing of unknown quantum systems into any entangled two-qubit states. Phys. Rev. A **87**, 10 (2012).
27. Hoeffding, W.: Probability inequalities for sums of bounded random variables. J. Am. Stat. Assoc. **58**(301), 13–30 (1963)
28. Klauck, H., Spalek, R., de Wolf, R.: Quantum and Classical Strong Direct Product Theorems and Optimal Time-Space Tradeoffs. arXiv e-prints, pages quant-ph/0402123, February 2004
29. Lai, C.-Y., Chung, K.-M.: On statistically-secure quantum homomorphic encryption. arXiv preprint arXiv:1705.00139 (2017)
30. Liang, M.: Quantum fully homomorphic encryption scheme based on universal quantum circuit. Quantum Inf. Process. **14**(8), 2749–2759 (2015)
31. Magniez, F., Mayers, D., Mosca, M., Ollivier, H.: Self-testing of quantum circuits, January 2006
32. Mahadev, U.: Classical homomorphic encryption for quantum circuits. In: FOCS, pp. 332–338. IEEE Computer Society (2018)
33. Mahadev, U.: Classical verification of quantum computations. In: FOCS, pp. 259–267. IEEE Computer Society (2018)
34. Mantri, A., Pérez-Delgado, C.A., Fitzsimons, J.F.: Optimal blind quantum computation. Phys. Rev. Lett. **111**(23), 230502 (2013)
35. Maurer, U., Renner, R.: Abstract cryptography. In: In Innovations in Computer Science, Tsinghua University Press (2011)
36. Mayers, D., Yao, A.: Self testing quantum apparatus. Quantum Inf. Comput. **4**, 273 (2003)
37. McKague, M.: Self-testing graph states. In: Bacon, D., Martin-Delgado, M., Roetteler, M. (eds.) TQC 2011. LNCS, vol. 6745, pp. 104–120. Springer, Heidelberg (2014). https://doi.org/10.1007/978-3-642-54429-3_7
38. Mckague, M., Haur Yang, T., Scarani, V.: Robust self testing of the singlet. J. Phys. A Math. Theoretical **45**, 045013 (2012)
39. Micciancio, D., Peikert, C.: Trapdoors for lattices: simpler, tighter, faster, smaller. In: Pointcheval, D., Johansson, T. (eds.) EUROCRYPT 2012. LNCS, vol. 7237, pp. 700–718. Springer, Heidelberg (2012). https://doi.org/10.1007/978-3-642-29011-4_41
40. Morimae, T., Dunjko, V., Kashefi, E.: Ground state blind quantum computation on aklt state. Quantum Info. Comput. **15**(3–4), 200–234 (2015)
41. Morimae, T., Fujii, K.: Blind topological measurement-based quantum computation. Nature Commun. **3**, 1036 (2012)
42. Newman, M., Shi, Y.: Limitations on transversal computation through quantum homomorphic encryption. arXiv preprint arXiv:1704.07798 (2017)
43. Nielsen, M.A., Chuang, I.L.: Quantum Computation and Quantum Information: 10th Anniversary Edition. Cambridge University Press, Cambridge (2010)
44. Ouyang, Y., Tan, S.-H., Fitzsimons, J.: Quantum homomorphic encryption from quantum codes. arXiv preprint arXiv:1508.00938 (2015)
45. Peikert, C.: Public-key cryptosystems from the worst-case shortest vector problem: extended abstract. In: Proceedings of the Forty-First Annual ACM Symposium on Theory of Computing, STOC 2009, pp. 333–342. ACM, New York (2009)
46. Preskill, J.: Quantum computing in the NISQ era and beyond. Quantum **2**, 79 (2018)
47. Regev, O.: On lattices, learning with errors, random linear codes, and cryptography. In: Proceedings of the Thirty-Seventh Annual ACM Symposium on Theory of Computing, STOC 2005, pp. 84–93. ACM, New York (2005)

48. Reichardt, B.W., Unger, F., Vazirani, U.: A classical leash for a quantum system: command of quantum systems via rigidity of CHSH games. In: Proceedings of the 4th Conference on Innovations in Theoretical Computer Science, ITCS 2013, pp. 321–322. ACM, New York (2013)
49. Sherstov, A.A.: Strong direct product theorems for quantum communication and query complexity. arXiv e-prints arXiv:1011.4935, November 2010
50. Tan, S.-H., Kettlewell, J.A., Ouyang, Y., Chen, L., Fitzsimons, J.F.: A quantum approach to homomorphic encryption. Sci. Rep. **6**, 33467 (2016)
51. van Dam, W., Magniez, F., Mosca, M., Santha, M.: Self-testing of universal and fault-tolerant sets of quantum gates. SIAM J. Comput. **37**(2), 611–629 (2007)
52. Viola, E., Wigderson, A.: Norms, XOR lemmas, and lower bounds for polynomials and protocols. Theory Comput. **4**(7), 137–168 (2008)
53. Wehner, S., Elkouss, D., Hanson, R.: Quantum internet: a vision for the road ahead. Science **362**(6412), 303 (2018)
54. Yu, L., Pérez-Delgado, C.A., Fitzsimons, J.F.: Limitations on information-theoretically-secure quantum homomorphic encryption. Phys. Rev. A **90**(5), 050303 (2014)

E-cash and Blockchain

Quisquis: A New Design for Anonymous Cryptocurrencies

Prastudy Fauzi[1]($\boxtimes$), Sarah Meiklejohn[2], Rebekah Mercer[3],
and Claudio Orlandi[4]

[1] Simula UiB, Bergen, Norway
prastudy.fauzi@gmail.com
[2] University College London, London, UK
[3] O(1) Labs, San Francisco, USA
[4] Department of Computer Science, DIGIT, Aarhus University, Aarhus, Denmark

Abstract. Despite their usage of pseudonyms rather than persistent identifiers, most existing cryptocurrencies do not provide users with any meaningful levels of privacy. This has prompted the creation of privacy-enhanced cryptocurrencies such as Monero and Zcash, which are specifically designed to counteract the tracking analysis possible in currencies like Bitcoin. These cryptocurrencies, however, also suffer from some drawbacks: in both Monero and Zcash, the set of potential unspent coins is always growing, which means users cannot store a concise representation of the blockchain. Additionally, Zcash requires a common reference string and the fact that addresses are reused multiple times in Monero has led to attacks to its anonymity.

In this paper we propose a new design for anonymous cryptocurrencies, Quisquis, that achieves provably secure notions of anonymity. Quisquis stores a relatively small amount of data, does not require trusted setup, and in Quisquis each address appears on the blockchain at most twice: once when it is generated as output of a transaction, and once when it is spent as input to a transaction. Our result is achieved by combining a DDH-based tool (that we call updatable keys) with efficient zero-knowledge arguments.

1 Introduction

Bitcoin was introduced in 2008 [30], and at a high level it relies on the use of *addresses*, associated with a public and private key pair, to keep track of who owns which coins. Users of the system can efficiently create and operate many different addresses, which gives rise to a form of pseudo-anonymity. As is now well known, however, Bitcoin and other cryptocurrencies relying on this level of pseudo-anonymity can, in practice, have these addresses linked together and even linked back to their real-world identities with little effort [3,26,28,33,34,37].

Due to this, there has now been an extensive body of work aiming to provide privacy-enhanced solutions for cryptocurrencies, although even some of these new solutions have also been subjected to empirical analyses pointing out the

© International Association for Cryptologic Research 2019
S. D. Galbraith and S. Moriai (Eds.): ASIACRYPT 2019, LNCS 11921, pp. 649–678, 2019.
https://doi.org/10.1007/978-3-030-34578-5_23

extent to which they can be de-anonymized as well [18–20, 25, 27, 29, 40]. These solutions typically fall into two main categories.

First, *tumblers* (also known as mixers or mixing services) act as opt-in overlays to existing cryptocurrencies such as Bitcoin [16, 23, 36] and Ethereum [24], and achieve enhanced privacy by allowing senders to mix their coins with those of other senders. While these are effective and arguably have a high chance of adoption due to their integration with existing cryptocurrencies, they also have some limitations. In particular, they are generally either dependent on trusting a central mixer, which leaves users vulnerable to attacks on availability, or they require significant coordination amongst the parties wishing to mix, which leads to higher latency as users must wait for other people to mix with them.

Second, there are cryptocurrencies with privacy features built in at the protocol level. Of these, the ones that have arguably achieved the most success are Dash [1], Monero [31], and Zcash [6]. Dash is derived from a tumbler solution, Coinjoin [23], and thus inherits the properties discussed there. In Monero, senders specify some number of addresses to "mix in" to their own transaction, and then use this list of public keys to form a ring signature and hide which specific address was theirs. Observers of the blockchain thus learn only that some unknown number of coins have moved from one of these input public keys. In Zcash, users can put coins into a "shielded pool." When they wish to spend these coins, they prove in zero-knowledge that they have the right to spend some specific coins in the pool, without revealing which ones.

Between Monero and Zcash, there are already several differences. For example, because users in Monero specify rings themselves, they achieve a form of *plausible deniability*: no one can tell if a user meant to be involved in a given transaction, or if their address was simply used in a ring without their consent. In Zcash, in contrast, every other user in a user's anonymity set has no such deniability, as they at one point intentionally put coins into the shielded pool.

One limitation central to both cryptocurrencies, however, is the information that peers in the network are required to keep. In Bitcoin, the list of all addresses with a positive balance can be thought of as a set of *unspent transaction outputs* (UTXOs). When a sender spends coins, their address ceases to be a UTXO, so is replaced in the set with the address of their recipient. Full nodes can thus collapse the blockchain into this UTXO set, and check for double spending simply by checking if a given input address is in the set or not. In other words, it acts as a concise representation of the entire history of the blockchain. In October 2017, for example, there had been over 23 million Bitcoin transactions and the total size of the blockchain was over 130 GB, but the size of the UTXO set was only 3 GB [12].

In Monero and Zcash, however, addresses can (essentially) never be removed from the UTXO set, as it is never clear if an address has spent its contents or was simply used as part of the anonymity set in the transaction of a different sender. The size of the UTXO set is thus monotonically increasing: with every transaction, it can only grow and never shrink. This has a significant impact on full nodes, as they must effectively store the entire blockchain without the option of the concise representation possible in Bitcoin.

Our Contributions. We present Quisquis, a new design for anonymous cryptocurrencies that resolves the limitations outlined above for existing solutions. In particular, users are able to form transactions on their own, so do not need to wait for other interested users and incur the associated latency. They can also involve the keys of other users without their permission, which gives the same degree of plausible deniability as Monero. Finally, each transaction acts to replace all the input public keys in the UTXO set with all the output public keys, thus allowing the UTXO set to behave in the same manner as in Bitcoin. Furthermore, our transactions are relatively inexpensive to compute and verify, taking around 471 ms to compute and 71 ms to verify for an anonymity set of size 16, with proofs of size approximately 13 kB.

As a brief technical overview, Quisquis achieves anonymity using a primitive that we formalize in Sect. 3 called *updatable* public keys, which allows users to create updated public keys, indistinguishable from ones that are freshly generated, without changing the underlying secret key. After formally defining our threat model in Sect. 4, we present our full construction of Quisquis in Sect. 5. Roughly, senders take the keys of other users, including their intended recipients, to form a list of public keys that act as the input to a transaction. A sender can now "re-distribute their wealth" among these input keys, acting to move some of their own coins to the recipient and keeping the (hidden) balances of the other members of the anonymity set the same. To ensure anonymity, the output public keys are all updated, and all balances and amounts are given only in committed form. Thus, by design, in Quisquis every address can only ever appear at most twice on the blockchain: once when it is generated in the output of the transaction, and once when it is spent as input to a different transaction. This greatly reduces (compared, e.g., to Monero) the ability of an attacker to perform de-anonymization attacks based on how often a certain address participates in transactions.

To ensure integrity, the sender proves in zero-knowledge that they have correctly updated the keys and have not taken money away from anyone except themselves. Crucially, because the witness for the zero-knowledge proof is limited to this single transaction (as opposed to encompassing other parts of the blockchain), we can use standard discrete-log-based techniques as opposed to the heavyweight zk-SNARKs required in Zcash. This means that security can depend entirely on DDH, and no trusted setup is required (as we use the random oracle model to make the proofs non-interactive and to generate other system parameters and random values using "nothing up my sleeves" methods). As the design of Quisquis is modular, other tradeoffs could be achieved as well: for instance, it could be possible to instantiate Quisquis with zk-SNARKs as well, thus achieving even smaller transactions and faster verification at the cost of much slower transaction generation and the stronger assumptions underlying zk-SNARKs.

To demonstrate the efficiency of Quisquis, we implement it and present performance benchmarks in Sect. 7. We then provide a thorough comparison with existing solutions in Sect. 8 before concluding in Sect. 9.

2   Cryptographic Primitives

2.1   Notation

Let $\log_g h$ be the discrete log of h with respect to g. Define $(a,b)^c := (a^c, b^c)$ and $(a,b) \cdot (c,d) := (ac, bd)$. For vectors a and b, let $a \circ b$ be the Hadamard product of a and b; i.e., the vector c such that $c_i = a_i b_i$. We use $y \leftarrow A(x)$ to denote assigning to y the output of a deterministic algorithm A on input x, and $y \xleftarrow{\$} A(x)$ if A is randomized; i.e., we sample a random r and then run $y \leftarrow A(x; r)$. We use $[A(x)]$ to denote the set of values that have non-zero probability of being output by A on inputs x. We use $r \xleftarrow{\$} R$ for sampling an element r uniformly at random from a set R. If $y = (y_1, \ldots, y_n) \xleftarrow{\$} A(x)$ then we often denote y_i by $\boldsymbol{y}_i$.

2.2   Zero-Knowledge Arguments of Knowledge

Let R be a binary relation for instances x and witnesses w, and let L be its corresponding language; i.e., $L = \{x \mid \exists w \colon (x,w) \in R\}$. An interactive proof is a protocol where a prover P tries to convince a verifier V, by an exchange of messages, that an instance x is in the language L. The set of messages exchanged is known as a *transcript*, from which a verifier can either accept or reject the proof. The proof is *public-coin* if an honest verifier generates his responses to P uniformly at random. An interactive proof is a special honest-verifier zero-knowledge argument of knowledge if it satisfies the following properties:

- Perfect completeness: if $x \in L$, an honest P always convinces an honest V.
- Special honest-verifier zero-knowledge (SHVZK): there exists a simulator S that, given $x \in L$ and an honestly generated verifier's challenge c, produces an accepting transcript which has the same (or indistinguishably different) distribution as a transcript between honest P, V on input x.
- Argument of knowledge: if P convinces V of an instance x, there exists an extractor with oracle access to P that runs in expected polynomial-time to extract the witness w.

A public-coin SHVZK argument of knowledge can be turned into a non-interactive zero knowledge (NIZK) argument of knowledge using the Fiat-Shamir heuristic. Essentially, non-interactivity is achieved by replacing the verifier's random challenge with the output of a hash function, which in the security proof is modeled as a random oracle.

2.3 Commitments

We use a commitment scheme Commit relative to a public key pk that, given a message $m \in \mathcal{M}$ and randomness $r \in \mathcal{R}$, computes com $\leftarrow$ Commit$_{pk}(m; r)$. Our commitments must satisfy two properties: first, they are computationally hiding, meaning for any two messages m_0, m_1, an adversary has negligible advantage in distinguishing between Commit$_{pk}(m_0; U_{\mathcal{R}})$ and Commit$_{pk}(m_1; U_{\mathcal{R}})$, where $U_{\mathcal{R}}$ is the uniform distribution over the randomness space. Second, they are unconditionally binding, meaning even given the sk relative to pk, a commitment cannot be opened to two different messages.

Beyond these two basic properties, we require two extra properties from our commitments. First, they must be homomorphic in the sense that for some operation $\odot$ it holds that Commit$_{pk}(m) \odot$ Commit$_{pk}(m') =$ Commit$_{pk}(m + m')$ (for appropriate randomness). Second, they must be *key-anonymous*, meaning that for any honestly generated keys pk_0, pk_1 and adversarially chosen m, the tuple $(m, pk_0, pk_1,$ Commit$_{pk_0}(m))$ is indistinguishable from $(m, pk_0, pk_1,$ Commit$_{pk_1}(m))$.

We can construct such commitments in a group $(\mathbb{G}, g, p)$ where the DDH problem is hard, by essentially performing an ElGamal encryption in the exponent relative to public keys of the form pk $= (g_i, h_i)$ (which are what we use in our later constructions). In particular, Commit$_{pk}(v; r)$ returns com $= (c, d)$ where $c = g_i{}^r$ and $d = g^v h_i{}^r$. It is easy to verify that this commitment scheme is unconditionally binding, computationally hiding, key-anonymous, and additively homomorphic.

Finally, we also use *extended Pedersen commitments* in the constructions of our zero-knowledge (ZK) arguments; i.e., schemes that commit to a vector of values using a single group element.

3 Updatable Public Keys

This section introduces the notion of an updatable public key (UPK), in which public keys can be updated in a public fashion, and such that they are indistinguishable from freshly generated keys. This idea has been considered before in the context of several cryptographic primitives, such as signatures [4,14] and public-key encryption [39], but we wish to define it solely for keys, regardless of the primitive they are used to support.

We begin by defining security for UPKs. Our definitions of indistinguishability and unforgeability resemble those that have already been used for Bitcoin *stealth keys* [24] and in the context of other cryptographic primitives [4,22,39].

Indeed, we could continue to be inspired by stealth keys in our construction of a UPK scheme, but given their reliance on hash functions this would render us unable to prove statements about the keys using discrete log-based techniques, as we would like to do in our construction of Quisquis in Sect. 5. We thus present instead a purely algebraic UPK scheme based on DDH, inspired by "incomparable public keys" [39].

3.1   Security Definitions

An *updatable public key system* (UPK) is described by the following algorithms:

- params $\xleftarrow{\$}$ Setup(1^κ) outputs the parameters of the scheme, including the public and secret key spaces $\mathcal{PK}, \mathcal{SK}$. These are given implicitly as input to all other algorithms.
- (pk, sk) $\xleftarrow{\$}$ Gen(1^κ) takes as input a security parameter κ and outputs a public key pk $\in \mathcal{PK}$ and a secret key sk $\in \mathcal{SK}$.
- ($\{\mathsf{pk}'_i\}_{i=1}^n$) $\xleftarrow{\$}$ Update($\{\mathsf{pk}_i\}_{i=1}^n$) takes as input public keys (pk$_1, \ldots$, pk$_n$) and outputs a new set of public keys (pk$'_1, \ldots$, pk$'_n$).
- $0/1 \leftarrow$ VerifyKP(pk, sk) takes as input pk $\in \mathcal{PK}$ and sk $\in \mathcal{SK}$ and checks whether or not (pk, sk) is a valid key pair.
- $0/1 \leftarrow$ VerifyUpdate(pk', pk, r) takes as input public keys pk', pk, and randomness r and checks if pk' was output by Update(pk; r).

We require a UPK to satisfy the following properties.

Definition 1 (Correctness). *A UPK satisfies perfect* correctness *if the following three properties hold for all* (pk, sk) $\in$ [Gen(1^κ)]: *(1) the keys verify, meaning* VerifyKP(pk, sk) $= 1$; *(2) the update process can be verified, meaning* VerifyUpdate(Update(pk; r), pk, r) $= 1$ *for all* $r \in \mathcal{R}$; *and (3) the updated keys verify, meaning* VerifyKP(pk', sk) $= 1$ *for all* pk' $\in$ [Update(pk)].

We next define indistinguishability, which says that an adversary cannot distinguish between a freshly generated public key and an updated version of a public key it already knows.

Definition 2 (Indistinguishability). *Consider the following experiment:*

1. (pk*, sk*) $\xleftarrow{\$}$ Gen(1^κ);
2. pk$_0$ $\xleftarrow{\$}$ Update(pk*);
3. (pk$_1$, sk$_1$) $\xleftarrow{\$}$ Gen(1^κ).

A UPK satisfies indistinguishability *if for any PPT adversary $\mathcal{A}$:*

$$| \Pr[\mathcal{A}(\mathsf{pk}^*, \mathsf{pk}_0) = 1] - \Pr[\mathcal{A}(\mathsf{pk}^*, \mathsf{pk}_1) = 1]| \leq \mathsf{negl}(\kappa).$$

Finally, we require that an adversary should not be able to learn the secret key of an updated public key (unless it already knew the secret key for the original public key). This is formalized by saying that the adversary cannot produce a public key for which it knows both the secret key and the randomness needed to explain this public key as an update of an honestly generated public key.

Definition 3 (Unforgeability). *A UPK satisfies* unforgeability *if for any PPT adversary $\mathcal{A}$:*

$$\Pr[\mathsf{VerifyKP}(\mathsf{pk}', \mathsf{sk}') = 1 \wedge \mathsf{VerifyUpdate}(\mathsf{pk}', \mathsf{pk}, r) = 1$$
$$| (\mathsf{pk}, \mathsf{sk}) \xleftarrow{\$} \mathsf{Gen}(1^\kappa); (\mathsf{sk}', \mathsf{pk}', r) \xleftarrow{\$} \mathcal{A}(\mathsf{pk})] \leq \mathsf{negl}(\kappa).$$

3.2   UPKs from DDH

We present a construction of UPK based over a prime-order group $(\mathbb{G}, g, p)$ where the DDH assumption is believed to hold. Thus, our Setup outputs only publicly verifiable parameters, and does not need to be run by a trusted party. The rest of the algorithms are as follows:

- Gen(1^{κ}): Sample $r, \mathsf{sk} \xleftarrow{\$} \mathbb{F}_p$ and output $\mathsf{pk} = (g^r, g^{r \cdot \mathsf{sk}})$.
- Update($\{\mathsf{pk}_i\}_{i=1}^n$): Parse $\mathsf{pk}_i = (g_i, h_i)$. Sample $r \xleftarrow{\$} \mathbb{F}_p$ and compute $\mathsf{pk}_i' = \mathsf{pk}_i^r = (g_i^r, h_i^r)$ for all i.
- VerifyKP(pk, sk): Parse $\mathsf{pk} = (g', h')$ and output $(g')^{\mathsf{sk}} \overset{?}{=} h'$.
- VerifyUpdate($\mathsf{pk}', \mathsf{pk}, r$): Output Update($\mathsf{pk}; r) \overset{?}{=} \mathsf{pk}'$.

Lemma 1. *The scheme above is a UPK satisfying Definitions 1–3 if the DDH assumption holds in $(\mathbb{G}, g, p)$.*

Proof. Correctness is straightforward to verify. To prove indistinguishability, our reduction receives a DDH challenge $\mathsf{chl} = (g, g^x, g^y, g^z)$, samples a value $r \xleftarrow{\$} \mathbb{F}_p$, and defines $\mathsf{pk}^* = (g^r, g^{xr})$ and $\mathsf{pk}' = (g^{yr}, g^{zr})$. It then invokes the indistinguishability adversary $\mathcal{A}$ on input $(\mathsf{pk}^*, \mathsf{pk}')$. If chl is a DDH tuple then pk' is distributed identically to pk_0, and if chl is not a DDH tuple then pk' is distributed identically to pk_1. Therefore, our reduction has the same (non-negligible) advantage in the DDH game as the $\mathcal{A}$ has in the indistinguishability game.

To prove unforgeability, our reduction receives a DL challenge $\mathsf{chl} = (g, h)$, picks a random $t \xleftarrow{\$} \mathbb{F}_p$, and sets $(g_0, h_0) = (g^t, h^t)$. The reduction now runs $(s, (g_1, h_1), r) \xleftarrow{\$} A(g_0, h_0)$, and outputs s. The input to the adversary in the reduction is distributed identically as in the definition of security. The winning condition of the security definition requires that $h_1 = g_1^s$ and $(g_1, h_1) = (g_0^r, h_0^r) = (g^{rt}, h^{rt})$ thus implying that $g^{srt} = h^{rt}$ or equivalently that $h = g^s$, meaning s is a valid solution to the DL oracle.

4   Threat Model

In this section, we present our model for cryptocurrency transactions, in which we view a transaction not as just transferring value from a sender to a recipient but as participants "re-distributing wealth" amongst themselves. Before presenting this model in Sect. 4.2, we first present the notion of an *updatable account* in Sect. 4.1, which is an extension of updatable public keys that associates them with a (hidden) balance; this is mainly done as a way to simplify notation in future sections. We then present the relevant notions of security in Sect. 4.3, focusing on *anonymity* (meaning no one can identify the "true" sender and recipient within the set of participants in a transaction) and *theft prevention* (meaning no one can steal the coins of other people or otherwise inflate their own wealth).

4.1   Updatable Accounts

To represent an *account* in a cryptocurrency, we use pairs $\mathsf{acct} = (\mathsf{pk}, \mathsf{com})$ of public keys, which act as the pseudonym for a user, and commitments, which represent the balance associated with that public key.

In more detail, each account carries a balance $\mathsf{bl} \in \mathcal{V}$, where $\mathcal{V} \subset \mathcal{M}$; i.e., the domain of values is a subset of the messages that can be committed to using Commit. To create a new account with initial balance $\mathsf{bl} \in \mathcal{V}$, one can run $(\mathsf{acct}, \mathsf{sk}) \xleftarrow{\$} \mathsf{GenAcct}(1^\kappa, \mathsf{bl})$, which internally runs $(\mathsf{pk}, \mathsf{sk}) \xleftarrow{\$} \mathsf{Gen}(1^\kappa)$ and $\mathsf{com} \xleftarrow{\$} \mathsf{Commit}_{\mathsf{pk}}(\mathsf{bl})$, sets $\mathsf{acct} = (\mathsf{pk}, \mathsf{com})$, and returns $(\mathsf{acct}, \mathsf{sk})$.

To verify that an account has a certain balance, it is necessary to be able to open a commitment using the secret key corresponding to pk. This also allows the owner of sk to open a commitment or prove statements about the committed message even without knowing the randomness used. We use the notation $\mathsf{VerifyCom}(\mathsf{pk}, \mathsf{com}, \mathsf{sk}, m)$, and require the commitment to be binding also with respect to this function; i.e., that no PPT adversary can output $(\mathsf{pk}, \mathsf{com}, \mathsf{sk}, m, \mathsf{sk}', m')$ with $m \neq m'$ but such that $\mathsf{VerifyCom}(\mathsf{pk}, \mathsf{com}, \mathsf{sk}, m) = \mathsf{VerifyCom}(\mathsf{pk}, \mathsf{com}, \mathsf{sk}', m') = 1$. With this algorithm in place, one can run $0/1 \leftarrow \mathsf{VerifyAcct}(\mathsf{acct}, (\mathsf{sk}, \mathsf{bl}))$, which parses $\mathsf{acct} = (\mathsf{pk}, \mathsf{com})$ and outputs 1 if $\mathsf{VerifyCom}(\mathsf{pk}, \mathsf{com}, (\mathsf{sk}, \mathsf{bl})) = 1$ and $\mathsf{bl} \in \mathcal{V}$ and 0 otherwise.

For an account $\mathsf{acct} = (\mathsf{pk}, \mathsf{com})$, observe that the output of $\mathsf{VerifyAcct}$ is agnostic to updates of the public key; i.e.,

$$\mathsf{VerifyAcct}((\mathsf{pk}, \mathsf{com}), (\mathsf{sk}, \mathsf{bl})) = \mathsf{VerifyAcct}((\mathsf{Update}(\mathsf{pk}), \mathsf{com}), (\mathsf{sk}, \mathsf{bl})).$$

Additionally, $\mathsf{VerifyAcct}$ is agnostic to re-randomizations of the commitment; i.e., $\mathsf{VerifyAcct}((\mathsf{pk}, \mathsf{com}), (\mathsf{sk}, \mathsf{bl})) = \mathsf{VerifyAcct}((\mathsf{pk}, \mathsf{com} \odot \mathsf{Commit}_{\mathsf{pk}}(0; r)), (\mathsf{sk}, \mathsf{bl}))$.

Thanks to these observations, we are able to "update" accounts using the following notation:

- $\{\mathsf{acct}'_i\}_{i=1}^n \xleftarrow{\$} \mathsf{UpdateAcct}(\{\mathsf{acct}_i, v_i\}_{i=1}^n; r_1, r_2)$ takes as input a set of accounts $\mathsf{acct}_i = (\mathsf{pk}_i, \mathsf{com}_i)$ and values v_i such that $|v_i| \in \mathcal{V}$, and outputs a new set of accounts $(\mathsf{acct}'_1, \ldots, \mathsf{acct}'_n)$ where $\mathsf{acct}'_i \xleftarrow{\$} (\mathsf{Update}(\mathsf{pk}; r_1), \mathsf{com} \odot \mathsf{Commit}_{\mathsf{pk}}(v_i; r_2))$.
- $0/1 \leftarrow \mathsf{VerifyUpdateAcct}(\{\mathsf{acct}'_i, \mathsf{acct}_i, v_i\}_{i=1}^n; r_1, r_2)$ outputs 1 if $\{\mathsf{acct}'_i\}_{i=1}^n = \mathsf{UpdateAcct}(\{\mathsf{acct}_i, v_i\}_{i=1}^n; r_1, r_2)$ and $|v_i| \in \mathcal{V}$, and 0 otherwise.

4.2   The Cryptocurrency Setting

Modeling the security of a cryptocurrency is a complex problem, as there are many different actors operating at different layers of the protocol: a user wishing to send some coins creates a transaction, which is then broadcast to their peers in a peer-to-peer network. Those peers in turn perform some cryptographic validation of the transaction, and if satisfied broadcast it to their peers. Eventually, it reaches a miner or validator, who engages in some form of consensus protocol to confirm the transaction into the blockchain.

For the sake of simplicity, we focus solely on the *transaction layer* of a cryptocurrency, and assume network-level or consensus-level attacks are out of scope; i.e., we assume that the system is free from eclipse attacks [17] or other de-anonymization attacks that depend on network-level information (such as IP addresses) and that an adversary is not sufficiently powerful to prevent honest transactions from being added to the blockchain or to add malicious transactions of their own.

Rather than use the traditional model of having a sender, in possession of some secret key and a coin, send this coin to a recipient, we instead consider a set of participants who want to *redistribute wealth* amongst themselves. This means we now model a transaction as taking place amongst a set of participants $\mathcal{P}$ who act as both the senders and the recipients in the transaction, and who each come in with some initial balance $\mathsf{bl}_{0,i}$ and end with some balance $\mathsf{bl}_{1,i}$.

This still captures the traditional model of keeping senders and recipients separate, because for a sender S sending one coin to a recipient R we can use $\mathcal{P} = (\mathsf{pk}_S, \mathsf{pk}_R)$, $\mathsf{bl}_0 = (1,0)$, and $\mathsf{bl}_1 = (0,1)$. The natural question, however, is who is required to authorize this transaction; for efficiency reasons we do not want every participant to have to do so, but to ensure that parties cannot simply steal each others' money we do need permission on behalf of the "true" senders. The simple way to provide both these properties is to require authorization only on behalf of the public keys whose associated balance has gone down; i.e., for every $\mathsf{pk}_i \in \mathcal{P}$ such that $\mathsf{bl}_{1,i} - \mathsf{bl}_{0,i} < 0$.

Again, this model fully captures the traditional model of senders and recipients, but crucially makes it easier to reason about cryptocurrencies designed to provide anonymity. More formally, a transaction layer for cryptocurrencies consists of (Setup, Trans, Verify), as defined below.

The setup algorithm state $\xleftarrow{\$}$ Setup(1^κ, **bl**) generates the initial state of the system. The vector **bl** represents the initial balance of the accounts in the system and it must be such that $\mathsf{bl}_i \in \mathcal{V}$ and $\sum_i \mathsf{bl}_i \in \mathcal{V}$. We assume that Setup runs $(\mathsf{acct}_i, \mathsf{sk}_i) \xleftarrow{\$} \mathsf{GenAcct}(1^\kappa, \mathsf{bl}_i)$ at some point, and that the state contains a set UTXO consisting of all accounts acct_i. All other algorithms take as input the (current) state even when omitted, and the state is updated in ways other than through these algorithms (e.g., by miners producing blocks at the network layer).

To create a transaction, a sender in possession of a secret key sk runs tx $\leftarrow$ Trans(sk, $\mathcal{P}$, A, v).[1] The vector of values $v \in \mathcal{V}$ represents the desired change in balance for each participant, meaning they should end up with $\mathsf{bl}_{1,i} = \mathsf{bl}_{0,i} + v_i$ (where $\mathsf{bl}_{0,i}$ is their initial balance according to state). In creating a transaction, the sender may want to achieve some degree of anonymity, meaning they want to hide the link between their accounts and those of the recipient. To this end, we introduce an anonymity set A, which consists of other accounts used to hide information about the sender. It is important that these accounts are "eligible" in some way (where this depends on the concrete system, but can mean for example that they have not yet spent their contents). If A is not explicitly

---

[1] For simplicity we consider a single sender but the notation can easily be generalized to allow for arbitrarily many.

specified, it is picked at random from the set of eligible accounts. We denote by
tx[inputs] = $\mathcal{P} \cup A$ the input accounts in a transaction, and by tx[outputs] the
output accounts.

Finally, 0/state ← Verify(state, tx) checks if a transaction is valid given the
current state. If so, it outputs an updated state, and if not it outputs 0.

We say a state is *valid* if it is output by Setup or if it was the output of
Verify(state′, tx) for a valid state′ and a transaction tx output by Trans. We say a
transaction layer *preserves value* if for any valid state′ $\neq \perp$ derived from a valid
state, ValueOf(state.UTXO) = ValueOf(state′.UTXO), where ValueOf computes
the number of coins associated with the UTXO set induced by a state.

4.3 Security

Intuitively, an anonymous cryptocurrency should provide *anonymity* for both the
sender and the recipient, meaning that even they cannot identify which accounts
belong to whom. From an integrity perspective, it is also important to guarantee
theft prevention, meaning an adversary can transfer value only from accounts for
which it knows the secret key (and therefore the adversary cannot reduce the
balance of the honest parties either).

Regardless of the goal, the basic outline of our security experiment is the
same, in order to capture the different ways an adversary can interact with
honest participants in the system. For example, the adversary can instruct honest
participants to engage in transactions, or form arbitrary (i.e., fully adversarial)
transactions itself, as long as they are valid.

Intuitively, the adversary begins by specifying the initial balances **bl** of all participants in the protocol. We continue this full control by allowing the adversary
to direct honest parties to make specific transactions (via **transact** queries), and
to inject fully malicious transactions in the system (via **verify** queries). It can
also learn the secret key for any account in the system (via **disclose** queries),
although here we must be careful to prevent "trivial" attacks resulting from these
disclosures in **challenge** queries (in which the adversary specifies two different
senders, recipients, and values, and tries to guess between transactions involving
them).

These trivial attacks include: (1) the adversary controls the secret key of one
or both of the senders; (2) the adversary controls the secret key of a recipient,
and (3) the adversary specified a sender who does not have enough funds to
complete the specified amount (meaning the output of Trans is $\perp$ in this case
but not the other). Formally, our game is defined as follows:

1. $b \xleftarrow{\$} \{0,1\}$;
2. $\mathbf{bl} \xleftarrow{\$} \mathcal{A}(1^\kappa)$;
3. state $\xleftarrow{\$}$ Setup$(1^\kappa, \mathbf{bl})$;
4. $b' \xleftarrow{\$} \mathcal{A}^{O(\cdot)}(\text{state})$.

Part of Setup involves running $(\text{acct}_i, \text{sk}_i) \xleftarrow{\$} \text{Gen}(1^\kappa, \text{bl}_i)$, and we assume that
this results in the values $(i, \text{acct}_i, \text{sk}_i, \text{bl}_i)$ being stored in memory available to
the oracle.

For several of the oracle queries, there is some *bookkeeping* required to update the keys and balances associated with these records. We define this bookkeeping subroutine with respect to a transaction tx and two sets honest and corrupt as follows: For every $\mathsf{acct}_j \in \mathsf{tx}[\mathsf{outputs}]$ identify the corresponding $\mathsf{acct}_i \in \mathsf{tx}[\mathsf{inputs}]$ such that $\mathsf{sk}_j = \mathsf{sk}_i$. For every such j, create a new record of the form $(j, \mathsf{acct}_j, \mathsf{sk}_i, \mathsf{bl}_i + v'_i)$, where v'_i is either (1) v_i if $i \in \mathcal{P}$ or (2) 0 if $i \in A$. Then, reset the value for every $\mathsf{acct}_i \in \mathsf{tx}[\mathsf{inputs}]$; i.e., save the record $(i, \mathsf{acct}_i, \mathsf{sk}_i, 0)$.

Finally, for every pair (i, j) as above: if $i \in$ honest add j to honest, else add j to corrupt.

Initialize honest to be the set of all indices i in memory, and corrupt to be the empty set. The oracle $O(\cdot)$ allows the following queries:

- (disclose, i): If $(i, \mathsf{acct}_i, \mathsf{sk}_i, \mathsf{bl}_i)$ was stored, call J the set of all j such that there is a record $(j, \mathsf{acct}_j, \mathsf{sk}_j, \mathsf{bl}_j)$ with $\mathsf{sk}_i = \mathsf{sk}_j$. Remove i and J from honest, add them to corrupt, and return $(\mathsf{sk}_i, \mathsf{bl}_i, J, \{\mathsf{bl}_j\}_{j \in J})$ to the adversary.
- (transact, $i, \mathcal{P}, A, \boldsymbol{v}$): If $(i, \mathsf{acct}_i, \mathsf{sk}_i, \mathsf{bl}_i)$ was not stored return $\bot$. Otherwise run tx $\xleftarrow{\$}$ Trans$(\mathsf{sk}_i, \mathcal{P}, A, \boldsymbol{v})$, and state$'$ $\leftarrow$ Verify(state, tx). If state$' \neq \bot$ update state = state$'$, run the bookkeeping for tx, and return tx.
- (verify, tx): run state$' \leftarrow$ Verify(state, tx). If state$' \neq \bot$ update state = state$'$, run the bookkeeping for tx, and return state$'$.
- (challenge, $b, (i_0, i_1, j_0, j_1, A, v_0, v_1)$): Let $A_0 = A_1 = A$. If (1) $i_0 \in$ corrupt or $i_1 \in$ corrupt, (2) $j_0 \in$ corrupt or $j_1 \in$ corrupt (except if $j_0 = j_1$ and $v_0 = v_1$), (3) $\mathsf{bl}_{i_0} < v_0$ or $\mathsf{bl}_{i_1} < v_1$, then halt and return 0 (i.e., the adversary lost the game). Otherwise, for $x \in \{0, 1\}$, if $i_0 \neq i_1$ add i_{1-x} to A_x, and if $j_0 \neq j_1$ add j_{1-x} to A_x. Now compute tx$_x \leftarrow$ Trans$(\mathsf{sk}_{i_x}, \{\mathsf{acct}_{i_x}, \mathsf{acct}_{j_x}\}, A_x, (-v_x, v_x))$. If Verify(state, tx$_x$) $= \bot$, then again we say the adversary lost the game. Otherwise, run the bookkeeping for tx$_b$.

After a **challenge** query, the oracle halts; i.e., it outputs $\bot$ as the response to all future queries.

In terms of the concrete security notions discussed above, we say that the adversary wins the *anonymity* game if $b' = b$ and the adversary did not lose the game as the result of some invalid query during the game. We define the *advantage* of the adversary as the probability that the adversary wins subtracted by $1/2$, and say that:

Definition 4. *Anonymity holds if no PPT $\mathcal{A}$ has non-negligible advantage in the* anonymity *game.*

Note that our definition of anonymity *does not* depend on the size of the anonymity set. Instead, our definition guarantees that, from the point of view of the adversary, a transaction is as likely to have been generated by any of the accounts in the input of the transaction (excluding those that the adversary owns or has corrupted).

We say that the adversary wins the *theft prevention* game if, as a result of any verify query: (1) there exists an account $j \in$ honest whose balance decreases or (2) the total wealth of the adversary increases; i.e., the sum of the balance of accounts in the set corrupt increases. (For this property, we could modify the game so that the adversary just outputs $\perp$ and does not need to make any challenge queries). Again, we say that:

Definition 5. *Theft prevention holds if no PPT $\mathcal{A}$ can win the* theft prevention game *with non-negligible probability.*

Note that theft prevention as defined above trivially implies protection from *double spending attacks*.

Finally, we address several seeming limitations in our definition, which have all been introduced for ease of notation and the sake of readability but which are not necessary for our construction. First, our challenge queries consider only a single recipient, but could be generalized to handle sets of recipients. Second, we do not consider adversarially generated keys (allowing the adversary only to corrupt honest keys), but we could capture this by changing the second step to allow the adversary to output a list of its own accounts. We would then have to process these accounts into records (in order to keep track of their balances) and restrict which keys could be used for which oracle queries; requiring, e.g., that transact only be used for non-adversarial keys. Finally, our current definition has the "IND-CCA1"-style requirement that after the first challenge query, the adversary cannot make any other queries. To generalize the definition to allow for this, the oracle would have to keep track of two balances bl_0 and bl_1 for each account after the challenge query, where bl_b represents the balance of each account in the "world" in which transaction tx_b was performed. This is necessary to prevent an additional type of trivial attack, in which the adversary made a transact query requiring the sender to transfer more than $\min(bl_0, bl_1)$: in one of the two worlds this would force the oracle to return $\perp$, which would trivially leak b. Again, all of these limitations were adopted to simplify presentation, but (as should be made clear in the next two sections) our construction would also satisfy the stronger definition relative to a modified game without these restrictions.

5   Our Quisquis Construction

5.1   Overview and Intuition

To get a sense of how Quisquis works, let's suppose that Alice wants to anonymously send 5 coins to Bob, and start with a strawman solution in which values are visible in the clear and associated with updatable public keys. To form a transaction, Alice identifies $n - 1$ unspent keys with exactly 5 coins associated with them. She then uses these keys, in combination with her own, as the input to the transaction. To form the output keys, she replaces her key with Bob's key, and updates all the other keys. Finally, she forms a ZK proof that she has created the output keys properly; i.e., that she knew the private key for any public keys that were replaced, and that she formed the other output keys by performing a valid update of the input ones. The final transaction consists of the lists of input and output keys, their associated values, and the ZK proof.

This solution allows Alice to use the other input keys as an anonymity set, but only in the restrictive setting in which she has the exact value she wants to send to Bob stored in one of her keys, and she can find multiple other keys with that same value. To address these issues, we first shift to the "re-distribution of wealth" model introduced in Sect. 4. Rather than replace her own key with Bob's key, she instead adds Bob's key to the list of input keys. If she picks two others keys pk_0 and pk_1 and forms $\mathcal{P} = (\mathsf{pk}_0, \mathsf{pk}_1, \mathsf{pk}_A, \mathsf{pk}_B)$, then even if she has 9 coins stored in her key she can still send Bob 5 coins by using $\boldsymbol{v} = (0, 0, -5, +5)$.

The problem with this new solution, of course, is that it has no anonymity: anyone can look at $\boldsymbol{v}$ and see who the real senders and recipients are. To hide these values, we switch to using the updatable accounts described in Sect. 4.1, which means including only commitments to the account balances. The main additional complexity is now in proving that the transaction has been formed correctly, and in particular proving that it does not take money away from anyone other than the real sender. Intuitively, Alice can do this by proving that for every output key, either she knows the secret key for the corresponding input key, or the balance corresponding to that key did not decrease; i.e., the difference between its balance and the balance of its input key is non-negative.

This also supports the case in which Alice wants to consolidate the coins associated with multiple account, as she can include these accounts in both the input and output lists but re-distribute her money so that it all ends up in one of them. This exposes an issue for efficiency, however, which is that once an account has a balance of 0 it is wasteful to leave it in the UTXO set. Thus, to "destroy" an output account, Alice can prove that its committed balance is 0, which signals to others to remove it from the UTXO set.

Conveniently, the technique of proving that a committed value is 0 can also be used to create a new account. This has a positive effect on Bob's anonymity (and communication overhead), as he can now send Alice a regular key once rather than providing a new account every time she wants to send him money. To use this key in the input list, Alice can first update it (to get a new random-looking key), generate a commitment relative to this public key (i.e., generate a new account for it), and prove that its committed balance is 0.

5.2 Transactions in Quisquis

Before describing the algorithms needed to form and verify transactions, we first describe how to instantiate the updatable accounts introduced in Sect. 4.1. Combining the commitment scheme from Sect. 2.3 and the UPK scheme from Sect. 3.2, we get accounts of the form $(\mathsf{pk}_i, \mathsf{com}_i) = ((g_i, g_i^{\mathsf{sk}}), (g_i^r, g^v g_i^{\mathsf{sk} \cdot r}))$. This already gives us most of the properties we need, and guarantees that $|\mathcal{V}| \ll |\mathcal{M}|$ as long as we use $\mathcal{V} = \{0, \ldots, V\}$, where V is an upper bound on the maximum possible number of coins in the system (e.g., the limit of $V = 2.1 \times 10^{15} < 2^{51}$

satoshis in Bitcoin, compared to $\mathcal{M} = \{0, \ldots, p-1\}$ for a 256-bit prime p in the commitment scheme). All it thus remains to show is that the owner of the secret key corresponding to $\mathsf{pk} = (g, h)$ can open the commitment. To do this, we can define the additional algorithm $\mathsf{VerifyCom}(\mathsf{pk}, \mathsf{com}, \mathsf{sk}, v)$ as parsing $\mathsf{com} = (c, d)$ and then checking that $\mathsf{VerifyKP}(\mathsf{pk}, \mathsf{sk}) = 1$ and $d = g^v \cdot c^{\mathsf{sk}}$. For every $(\mathsf{pk}, \mathsf{com})$ there exists exactly one pair (sk, v) for which $\mathsf{VerifyCom}$ outputs 1, so the commitment is unconditionally binding even with respect to this type of opening.

Setup On input 1^κ, Setup returns as state the output of Setup for the UPK scheme, and a list of all current accounts (which may be empty).

Trans As discussed in the overview, Quisquis allows a sender to "re-distribute" their wealth to one or more recipients, by including their accounts in both the input and output lists that comprise the transaction. In what follows we assume that transactions have a fixed number n of both inputs and outputs.

Suppose a transaction is meant to transfer v coins from a sender to a recipient. To hide the identity of the sender and recipient, the Trans algorithm picks an anonymity set A of size $n - 2$ uniformly at random from the set of all unspent transaction outputs, and creates a vector $\boldsymbol{v} = (v, -v, 0, \ldots, 0)$. It then updates all these accounts by running UpdateAcct. Intuitively, the properties of updatable accounts guarantee that the individual accounts that are generated as output of UpdateAcct cannot be tied to the input of the function. However, the ordering still reveals the link between the input and outputs. We thus simply present the input and output lists in some canonical (e.g., lexicographical) order. Because the updated keys are distributed uniformly at random, this can be thought of as applying a random permutation ψ to shuffle the updated accounts.

Finally, to ensure that malicious parties cannot steal funds from honest users, the transaction must contain a NIZK proof π that the output of the transaction has been computed following the protocol specification.

To summarize, $\mathsf{tx} \xleftarrow{\$} \mathsf{Trans}((s, \mathsf{sk}_s, \mathsf{bl}_s), \mathcal{P}, A, \boldsymbol{v})$ performs the following steps:

1. First, check that the input is valid by parsing $\mathcal{P} = \{\mathsf{acct}_1, \ldots, \mathsf{acct}_t\}$ and checking that $\mathsf{VerifyAcct}(\mathsf{acct}_s, \mathsf{sk}_s, \mathsf{bl}_s) = 1$. Then check that the vector $\boldsymbol{v}$ satisfies: (1) $\sum_i v_i = 0$, (2) $\forall i \neq s : v_i \in \mathcal{V}$ (i.e., is positive), (3) $-v_s \in \mathcal{V}$ and (4) $\mathsf{bl}_s + v_s \in \mathcal{V}$.
2. Let $\mathsf{inputs} = \mathcal{P} \cup A$ in some canonical order and $\boldsymbol{v}'$ be the permutation of $\boldsymbol{v}$ under the same order. Let $s^*, \mathcal{R}^*, A^*$ denote the indices of the respective accounts of the sender, the recipients, and the anonymity set in this list; i.e., it now holds that $-v'_{s^*} \in \mathcal{V}$, $v'_i \in \mathcal{V}$ $\forall i \in \mathcal{R}^*$ and $v'_i = 0$ $\forall i \in A^*$.
3. Let $\mathsf{outputs}$ be the output of $\mathsf{UpdateAcct}(\mathsf{inputs}, \boldsymbol{v}'; r)$ in some canonical order.
4. Let $\psi : [n] \to [n]$ be the implicit permutation mapping inputs into $\mathsf{outputs}$; i.e., such that accounts inputs_i and $\mathsf{outputs}_{\psi(i)}$ share the same secret key.
5. Form a zero-knowledge proof π of the relation $\mathsf{R}(x, w)$, where $x = (\mathsf{inputs}, \mathsf{outputs})$, $w = (\mathsf{sk}, \mathsf{bl}, \boldsymbol{v}', r = (r_1, r_2), \psi, s^*, \mathcal{R}^*, A^*)$, and $\mathsf{R}(x, w) = 1$ if for all $i \in [n], j = \psi(i)$, $\mathsf{acct}_i \in \mathsf{inputs}$, $\mathsf{acct}_j \in \mathsf{outputs}$:

$$\mathsf{VerifyUpdateAcct}(\mathsf{acct}_j, \mathsf{acct}_i, r, 0) = 1 \ \forall i \in A^*$$
$$\wedge \ (\mathsf{VerifyUpdateAcct}(\mathsf{acct}_j, \mathsf{acct}_i, r, v_i') = 1 \wedge v_i' \in \mathcal{V}) \ \forall i \in \mathcal{R}^*$$
$$\wedge \ \mathsf{VerifyUpdateAcct}(\mathsf{acct}_{\psi(s^*)}, \mathsf{acct}_{s^*}, r, v_{s^*}') = 1$$
$$\wedge \ \mathsf{VerifyAcct}(\mathsf{acct}_{\psi(s^*)}, \mathsf{sk}, \mathsf{bl} + v_{s^*}') = 1$$
$$\wedge \sum_i v_i' = 0.$$

Then the final transaction is $\mathsf{tx} = (\mathsf{inputs}, \mathsf{outputs}, \pi)$.

Due to the way transactions are generated, every address appears at most twice in Quisquis: once when it is created in the output of some transaction, and once when it appears as the input of some other transaction (regardless of whether it is the real sender or just an account added for anonymity). In particular, unlike in Monero the same account cannot be used as part of the anonymity set for two different transactions, since it will have been updated in the meantime and thus replaced in the UTXO set.

Verify The Verify algorithm ensures the validity of a transaction by checking that all the accounts in $\mathsf{tx}[\mathsf{inputs}]$ are considered unspent in the current state, and by running the verification algorithm for the NIZK argument.

Additionally, upon receiving a transaction in which one of their accounts was included in $\mathsf{tx}[\mathsf{inputs}]$, it is necessary for users to identify which (if any) of the accounts in outputs belongs to them. (If no such account appears in the inputs then they do not need to process the transaction further.) To do this, they first identify the secret key sk corresponding to their account in $\mathsf{tx}[\mathsf{inputs}]$. They then go through every $(\mathsf{pk}, \mathsf{com}) \in \mathsf{tx}[\mathsf{outputs}]$ and run $b \leftarrow \mathsf{VerifyKP}(\mathsf{pk}, \mathsf{sk})$. If $b = 1$, they replace their own existing record of that account with $\mathsf{acct} = (\mathsf{pk}, \mathsf{com})$.

The user should then figure out whether their address was an actual recipient of the transaction or whether it had only be used as part of the anonymity set. They can start by running $\mathsf{VerifyAcct}(\mathsf{acct}, \mathsf{sk}, \mathsf{bl}) = 1$, where bl was their balance before the transaction; if this passes, then their account was used as part of the anonymity set so their balance is unchanged. Otherwise, they need to find out the value v by which their balance was increased. For simplicity here we assume that the values v are small enough, say 32 bits (for comparison, the total number of satoshis that will ever exist is 2^{51}), so that computing v from g^v is computationally easy, and therefore the user can "brute force" their new account. Again, this is necessary only in the case of transactions that include their accounts as part of the input (and transactions creating new accounts); no other transactions can change the balance of a user's account.

The design can be easily extended for larger values of v: for instance, we can (1) require that senders communicate the value v_i to their recipients off-chain or (2) append to the transaction an encryption of v_i under the public key of the receiver, together with a proof that the encryption contains the correct value (using, e.g., a similar approach to Zether [10]).

Creating and Removing Accounts. The described scheme above supports the basic functionality of making anonymous payments, but as described in the overview in Sect. 5.1 it is possible to improve on the efficiency of this basic protocol. In particular, newly created accounts and fully spent accounts both have a (provable) balance of 0. Allowing users to create new accounts improves the overall communication overhead and anonymity of the system, since users can send one long-term key to potential senders rather than a new account every time (which would also reveal to the sender the transaction in which this account was created). Allowing users to destroy empty accounts reduces the storage overhead of the system, since other users do not have to keep track of accounts that have no contents left to spend.

We denote the respective algorithms used to perform creating and removing accounts by CreateAcct and DestroyAcct.

- acct $= (\mathsf{pk}', \mathsf{com}), \pi) \xleftarrow{\$} \mathsf{CreateAcct}(\mathsf{pk})$ is such that $\mathsf{pk}' \in [\mathsf{Update}(\mathsf{pk})]$, com $= \mathsf{Commit}_{\mathsf{pk}'}(0; r)$ for some r, and π is a ZK proof for the relation $R(x, w)$, where $x = (\mathsf{pk}', \mathsf{com})$, $w = r$, and $R(x, w) = 1$ if com $= \mathsf{Commit}_{\mathsf{pk}'}(0; r)$. Again, this algorithm can be run by anyone in possession of a public key for a user, which allows senders to send money to recipients without requiring their participation.
- $\pi \xleftarrow{\$} \mathsf{DestroyAcct}(\mathsf{sk}, \mathsf{acct})$ is such that π is a ZK proof for the relation $R(x, w)$, where $x = \mathsf{acct}$, $w = \mathsf{sk}$, and $R(x, w) = 1$ if $\mathsf{VerifyAcct}(\mathsf{acct}, (\mathsf{sk}, 0)) = 1$.

Proofs of this type can optionally be included in transactions, and have the effect that upon verification users remove the corresponding acct from the list of active accounts. The zero-knowledge proofs involved in both CreateAcct and DestroyAcct are standard proofs of relations between discrete logarithms, so we do not include descriptions of them here.

Mining Fees. As currently described, Quisquis does not provide any incentives for miners to include transactions, due to the lack of fees. More crucially, it assumes the total balance of the system is fixed during Setup, so does not capture the ability to mine new coins.

To add transaction fees to the Trans algorithm, we can add the fee f as an input and change the requirement on the vector v to be $f + \sum_i v_i = 0$. Assuming the fee is public (as it is in other privacy-enhanced currencies like Zcash), this does not add any complexity to the zero-knowledge proof. So, let $(\mathsf{tx}_1, \mathsf{f}_1, \ldots, \mathsf{tx}_m, \mathsf{f}_m)$ be a set of transaction that a miner wants to add to the blockchain. To collect the fees and add a block reward rwd, the miner can simply generate a new account $(\mathsf{acct}, \mathsf{sk}) \leftarrow \mathsf{GenAcct}(1^\kappa, \mathsf{rwd} + \sum_i \mathsf{f}_i)$ and a proof that the balance of this account is equal to the block reward plus the sum of fees present in the block. The initial balance is thus public, but as soon as it is used in any further transaction the usual anonymity guarantee is preserved.

Concurrent Transactions. Although it is somewhat out of scope of the core cryptographic design, we briefly discuss here how a cryptocurrency based on the Quisquis design might deal with concurrent transactions, in which two users both try to use the same account in their anonymity set at roughly the same time (and there is thus a non-empty intersection between the two tx[inputs]). Since each address can appear only once as input in Quisquis, this requires at least one of the two transactions to be rejected by the system. We propose here two simple approaches for dealing with this, although the probability of having such a collision could be quite low (depending on system parameters such as the frequency of transactions, the network latency, etc.).

The first heuristic is "reject and wait": if two conflicting transactions are received in the same time period, they are both rejected and the users are instructed to wait and attempt the transaction again. The second heuristic is "first come first serve": the transaction that is first received is approved and the second one is rejected. The sender of the second transaction is free to send a new transaction as soon as they want.

The first proposal might be better for anonymity, since – thanks to the waiting time – many (or even all) addresses in the original anonymity sets might have left the UTXO set (after being chosen as part of the anonymity set of other transactions) and been replaced by new random-looking accounts. The second proposal ensures lower latency, but might reduce the privacy of the second transaction: if all accounts in the intersection were part of the anonymity set, the sender might simply replace those and effectively run a transaction with a smaller anonymity set. On the other hand, if any actual sender (or receiver) of the transaction disappeared from the UTXO set, this would require the sender to use the new version of those accounts that was created in the tx[outputs] of the approved transaction.

5.3   Proofs of Security

Proof of Anonymity. The full proof of anonymity of Quisquis is given in the full version of the paper [13], but we sketch the main intuition here. Informally, we claim that any $\mathcal{A}$ that can determine b from tx can be used to break either the indistinguishability property of UPK, the hiding property of Commit, or the zero-knowledge property of the NIZK. That is, any $\mathcal{A}$ that can determine b can distinguish between tx_0 and tx_1. Since $tx_0[inputs] = tx_1[inputs]$ (by inspection), it must be the case that the adversary either distinguishes between the transactions based on the proof π or the set of accounts in outputs. The first option is ruled out due to the zero-knowledge property of π. To see why the adversary cannot distinguish based on outputs, note that in both cases outputs is obtained by updating all the accounts in inputs, and the only differences between $outputs_0$ and $outputs_1$ are (1) the amounts by which the accounts have been increased or decreased and (2) which accounts are included in $\mathcal{P}$ and which are included in A. Since the amounts are only present in committed form, we conclude that the adversary cannot distinguish based on (1) due to the hiding property of the commitment. Since all the accounts are updated (both those in $\mathcal{P}$ and in A), and they are then randomly permuted, the adversary cannot distinguish based on (2) either.

Proof of Theft Prevention. To win the theft prevention game, the adversary needs to submit a transaction tx that increases the total balance corresponding to the corrupted accounts or decreases the balance for the honest accounts. Intuitively, this can happen only in two ways: (1) if the adversary manages to transfer value from an honest account (to a corrupted account or to an "unspendable" account) and (2), if the adversary manages to transfer a value higher than the balance of a corrupted account. Due to the extractability of the zero-knowledge proof system, we know that the tx will be accepted only if the adversary has a valid witness. This means that: in case (1) we can use the adversary to compute a secret key sk for an honest account (thus breaking the unforgeability property of UPK); in case (2) we can use the adversary to compute an opening of a commitment with a balance different from the real one, thus breaking the binding property of the commitment scheme.

6   Instantiating the Zero-Knowledge Proof

In this section we will instantiate the zero-knowledge proof that inputs and outputs satisfy the relation described in the Trans algorithm. First consider the simplified case where Trans does not do any lexicographic ordering or any type of permutation of the public keys. Then a prover essentially has to prove that (1) accounts in outputs are proper updates of inputs, (2) the updates satisfy preservation of value, (3) balances in the recipient accounts do not decrease, and (4) the sender account in outputs contain a balance in $\mathcal{V}$. Properties (3) and (4) require a tool called *range proofs*. We choose to use the most efficient implementation of range proofs, which is the Bulletproofs of Bootle et al. [11]. The main requirement to use Bulletproofs is to have a public commitment key (g, h) such that the DL relation between them is unknown.

We now explain how to check properties (1) and (2). Let inputs have balances **bl**, and outputs have balances **bl′**. Let $v_i = \mathsf{bl}'_i - \mathsf{bl}_i$ be the change in value from inputs to outputs. Additionally, let the sender be inputs_1 and the recipients be $\mathsf{inputs}_2, \ldots, \mathsf{inputs}_t$.

To be able to easily verify that the update is done correctly, the prover creates accounts $\mathbf{acct}_\delta$ that contain values v. Since we need preservation of value, there needs to be a way to verify that $\sum_i v_i = 0$. To do this, recall that we can regard an account acct as two parts (pk, com) where pk is a UPK and com is a commitment to the balance. The idea is then to use the homomorphic property of the commitment. This is done by first creating $\mathbf{acct}_\epsilon$ that also contains values v but where $\mathsf{pk}_{\epsilon,i} = (g, h)$ for all i. (Hence $com_{\delta,i}$ and $com_{\epsilon,i}$ can be seen as two commitments of the same value under different public keys $\mathsf{pk}_{\delta,i}$ and $\mathsf{pk}_{\epsilon,i}$.) Then $\sum_i v_i = 0$ iff $\prod_i com_{\epsilon,i}$ is a commitment of 0 under public key (g, h). The values $\mathsf{acct}_{\epsilon,2}, \ldots, \mathsf{acct}_{\epsilon,t}$ will also be used to prove that the recipient's increase in values $v_2, \ldots, v_t$ are in $\mathcal{V}$.

Note however that the simplified case does not hide where the sender and recipient accounts are in both inputs and outputs. To get full anonymity, the input accounts are shuffled into a list inputs′ before the updates, then shuffled again after the updates to get the output accounts in an arbitrary order. The first shuffle uses a permutation so that the sender is always in position inputs'_1 and the recipients are $\mathsf{inputs}'_2, \ldots, \mathsf{inputs}'_t$, while the second shuffle uses a random permutation. This will help making the proof more efficient (otherwise, for every account in the transaction, we would have to prove the disjunction of the conditions for the sender and the recipients).

Table 1. Additional functions to perform a transaction.

Function	Description
CreateDelta	Creates a set of accounts that contains the difference (say v_i) between balances in the input and output accounts, and another set of accounts that also contains v_i but all with the global public key (g, h)
VerifyDelta	Verifies that accounts created using CreateDelta are consistent
VerifyNonNegative	Verifies that an account contains a balances in $\mathcal{V}$
UpdateDelta	Updates the input accounts by v_i, but with left half unchanged
VerifyUD	Verifies that UpdateDelta was performed correctly

6.1 The Auxiliary Functions

To realize the ideas above, we require some auxiliary functions defined as follows (see Table 1 for a summary).

CreateDelta($\{\mathsf{acct}_i\}_{i=1}^n, \{v_i\}_{i=1}^n$): Parse $\mathsf{acct}_i = (\mathsf{pk}_i, com_i)$. Sample $r_1, \ldots, r_{n-1}$ $\xleftarrow{\$} \mathbb{F}_p$ and set $r_n = -\sum_{i=1}^{n-1} r_i$. Set $\mathsf{acct}_{\delta,i} = (\mathsf{pk}_i, \mathsf{Commit}_{\mathsf{pk}_i}(v_i; r_i))$. Set $\mathsf{acct}_{\epsilon,i} = (g, h, \mathsf{Commit}_{(g,h)}(v_i; r_i))$. Output $(\{\mathsf{acct}_{\delta,i}\}_{i=1}^n, \{\mathsf{acct}_{\epsilon,i}\}_{i=1}^n), r)$.

VerifyDelta($\{\mathsf{acct}_{\delta,i}\}_{i=1}^n, \{\mathsf{acct}_{\epsilon,i}\}_{i=1}^n, v, r$): Parse $\mathsf{acct}_{\delta,i} = (\mathsf{pk}_i, com_i)$ and $\mathsf{acct}_{\epsilon,i}$ $= (\mathsf{pk}'_i, com'_i)$. If $\prod_{i=1}^n com'_i = (1, 1)$ and for all i, $com_i = \mathsf{Commit}_{\mathsf{pk}_i}(v_i; r_i) \wedge$ $\mathsf{acct}_{\epsilon,i} = (g, h, \mathsf{Commit}_{(g,h)}(v_i; r_i))$ output 1. Else output 0.

VerifyNonNegative(acct, v, r): If $\mathsf{acct} = (g, h, g^r, g^v h^r) \wedge v \in \mathcal{V}$ output 1. Else output 0.

UpdateDelta($\{\mathsf{acct}_i\}_{i=1}^n, \{\mathsf{acct}_{\delta,i}\}_{i=1}^n$): Parse $\mathsf{acct}_i = (\mathsf{pk}_i, com_i)$ and $\mathsf{acct}_{\delta,i} = (\mathsf{pk}'_i, com'_i)$. If $\mathsf{pk}_i = \mathsf{pk}'_i$ for all i output[2] $\{(\mathsf{pk}_i, com_i \cdot com'_i)\}_{i=1}^n$, else output $\perp$.

VerifyUD($\mathsf{acct}, \mathsf{acct}', \mathsf{acct}_\delta$): Parse $\mathsf{acct} = (\mathsf{pk}, com)$, $\mathsf{acct}' = (\mathsf{pk}', com')$ and $\mathsf{acct}_\delta = (\mathsf{pk}_\delta, com_\delta)$. Check that $\mathsf{pk} = \mathsf{pk}' = \mathsf{pk}_\delta \wedge com' = com \cdot com_\delta$.

---

[2] Note that if $\mathsf{acct} = (\mathsf{pk}, com)$ and $\mathsf{acct}_\delta = (\mathsf{pk}, \mathsf{Commit}_{\mathsf{pk}}(v; r)))$, then UpdateDelta($\mathsf{acct}, \mathsf{acct}_\delta$) = UpdateAcct($\mathsf{acct}, v; 1, r$).

6.2   The Proof System

Let (g, h) be a *global public key* output by the Setup algorithm, such that the DL relation between them is unknown. The NIZK system NIZK.Prove(x, w) performs the following:

1. Parse $x =$ (inputs, outputs), $w = ($sk, bl, $v, (u_1, u_2), \psi : [n] \to [n], s^*, \mathcal{R}^*, A^*)$. If $R(x, w) = 0$ abort;
2. Let ψ_1 be a permutation such that $\psi_1(s^*) = 1$, $\psi_1(\mathcal{R}^*) = [2, t]$ and $\psi_1(A^*) = [t + 1, n]$;
3. Sample $\tau_1 \xleftarrow{\$} \mathbb{F}_p^n$, $\rho_1 \xleftarrow{\$} \mathbb{F}_p$;
4. Set inputs$' =$ UpdateAcct$(\{$inputs$_{\psi_1(i)}, 0\}_i; (\tau_1, \rho_1))$;
5. Set the vector v' such that $v_i' = v_{\psi_1(i)}$;
6. Set $(\{$acct$_{\delta,i}\}, \{$acct$_{\epsilon,i}\}, r) \xleftarrow{\$}$ CreateDelta(inputs$', v')$;
7. Update outputs$' \leftarrow$ UpdateDelta(inputs$', \{$acct$_{\delta,i}\})$;
8. Let $\psi_2 = \psi_1^{-1} \circ \psi$, $\tau_{2,i} = \frac{u_{1,i}}{\tau_{1,\psi_2(i)}}$ and $\rho_2 = \frac{u_{2,i} - \rho_1}{\tau_{1,\psi_2(i)}} - r_{\psi_2(i)}$; (So that $\psi_1 \circ \psi_2 = \psi$ and outputs $=$ UpdateAcct$(\{$outputs$'_{\psi_2(i)}, 0\}_i; \tau_2, \rho_2)\})$.
9. Generate a ZK proof $\pi = ($inputs$'$, outputs$'$, acct$_\delta$, acct$_\epsilon$, $\pi_1, \pi_2, \pi_3)$ for the relation $R_1 \wedge R_2 \wedge R_3$, where

$$R_1 = \{(\text{inputs}, \text{inputs}', (\psi_1, \tau_1, \rho_1)) \mid$$
$$\text{VerifyUpdateAcct}(\{\text{inputs}_i', \text{inputs}_{\psi_1(i)}, 0\}_i; \tau_1, \rho_1) = 1\},$$
$$R_2 = \{((\text{inputs}', \text{outputs}', \text{acct}_\delta, \text{acct}_\epsilon), (\text{sk}, \text{bl}_{s^*}, v', r)) \mid$$
$$\text{VerifyUD}(\text{inputs}_i', \text{outputs}_i', \text{acct}_{\delta,i}) = 1 \quad \forall i$$
$$\wedge \text{VerifyUpdateAcct}(\text{inputs}_i', \text{outputs}_i', 0; 1, r_i) = 1 \ \forall i \in [t + 1, n]$$
$$\wedge \text{VerifyNonNegative}(\text{acct}_{\epsilon,i}, v_i', r_i) = 1 \quad \forall i \in [2, t]$$
$$\wedge \text{VerifyAcct}(\text{outputs}_1', (\text{sk}, \text{bl}_{s^*} + v_1')) = 1$$
$$\wedge \text{VerifyDelta}(\{\text{acct}_{\delta,i}\}, \{\text{acct}_{\epsilon,i}\}, v', r) = 1\},$$
$$R_3 = \{(\text{outputs}', \text{outputs}, (\psi_2, \tau_2, \rho_2)) \mid$$
$$\text{VerifyUpdateAcct}(\{\text{outputs}_i, \text{outputs}_{\psi_2(i)}', 0\}_i; \tau_2, \rho_2) = 1\}.$$

Instantiating the Shuffle Argument. The zero-knowledge argument of knowledge for R_1 and R_3 uses a shuffle argument $\Sigma_1 = \Sigma_{sh}(\psi_1)$, which is required to prove that inputs$'$ is a correct shuffle of inputs and $\Sigma_3 = \Sigma_{sh}(\psi_2)$, which is required to prove that outputs is a correct shuffle of outputs$'$.

Let (g, h) be the *global public key* output by the Setup algorithm, and let ck $= (\bar{g}, \bar{g}_1, \ldots, \bar{g}_n)$ be the commitment key of the extended Pedersen commitment scheme com$_{ck}(a; r) = \bar{g}^r \prod_i \bar{g}_i^{a_i}$. In the following, we just write this as com$(a; r)$.

Recall that an update of acct$_i = ($pk$_i, com_i)$ using randomness (τ_i, ρ_i) is acct$_j' = ($pk$_j', com_j') = ($pk$_i^{\tau_i}, com_i \cdot$ pk$_i^{\rho_i})$. The public key pk$_i$ is updated by just exponentiation, so its proof of correct shuffle is a slight modification of the Bayer-Groth [5] shuffle. For this we define the generalized commitments to a matrix $A = (a_1, \ldots, a_n) \in \mathbb{F}_p^{m \times n}$ to be the commitments of its n columns.

That is, $\text{com}(A; r) = (\text{com}(a_1; r_1), \ldots, \text{com}(a_n; r_n))$. Additionally, a Hadamard product of matrices A and B, denoted $C = A \circ B$, is simply the matrix such that $c_{ij} = a_{ij} b_{ij}$.

The shuffle argument uses the following sub-arguments [5]:

- The multi-exponentiation argument, π_{MExp}: Given a vector C' and a commitment C'_B, the prover shows knowledge of a witness $w = (b', r)$ such that $C'_B = \text{com}(b'; r)$, and for a fixed $T \in \mathbb{G}$, it holds that $\prod_{i=1}^{n} C_i'^{b'_i} = T$. In the shuffle argument, $T = \prod_{i=1}^{n} C_i^{x^i}$, where x is the second message of the protocol.
- The product argument, π_{prod}: Given a commitment C_A, the prover shows knowledge of a witness $w = (a, r)$ such that $C_A = \text{com}(a; r)$, and for a fixed $t \in \mathbb{F}_p$, it holds that $\prod_{i=1}^{n} a_i = t$. In the shuffle argument, $t = \prod_{i=1}^{n}(y \cdot i + x^i - z)$, where (y, z) is the fourth message of the protocol.
- The Hadamard product argument, π_{Had}: Given extended Pedersen commitments A, B, C, the prover shows knowledge of an opening to vectors a, b, c such that $a \circ b = c$.

A proof of correct shuffle for com_i uses the following invariant, provided we set all ρ_i to be the same value ρ. Let $\text{pk}_i = (g_i, h_i)$, $(G, H) = (\prod_{i=1}^{N} g_i^{X^i}, \prod_{i=1}^{N} h_i^{X^i})$ and $(G', H') = (G^\rho, H^\rho)$. For a random variable X, $\prod_{i=1}^{N}(com'_{\psi(i)})^{X^{\psi(i)}} = \prod_{i=1}^{N} com_i^{X^i} \cdot (G', H')$. Hence we can also use a multi-exponentiation argument (this time with $T = \prod_{i=1}^{n} com_i^{x^i} \cdot (G', H')$), with an additional proof of correct update Σ_{vu} for the tuple (G, H, G', H').

Note that using the same $\rho_i = \rho$ to update the com_i is secure under the indistinguishability of UPK and computational hiding of Commit. (An adversary that can distinguish if two accounts are updated using the same ρ, can be used to break DDH.)

The full shuffle argument Σ_{sh} is shown in Fig. 1.

The following lemma is similar to the one in [5], and the full proof is deferred to the full version of the paper [13].

Lemma 2. *Let the product argument π_{prod}, the Hadamard product argument π_{Had}, the verify update argument π_{vu} and the multi-exponentiation argument π_{MExp} be public-coin SHVZK arguments of knowledge. Then Σ_{sh} is a public-coin SHVZK argument of knowledge of (ψ, τ, ρ) such that $(\text{pk}'_i, com'_i) = (\text{pk}^{\tau_i}_{\psi(i)}, com_{\psi(i)} \cdot \text{pk}^\rho_{\psi(i)})$.*

Instantiating the Other Sub-arguments. To prove statements related to the function VerifyNonNegative we use Bulletproofs, which we denote by the argument $\Sigma_{range}(\text{acct}, v, r)$. VerifyAcct also uses Bulletproofs but since the sender may not know the randomness used to open his commitment (for example, if the account was previously updated by someone else), we need a separate argument $\Sigma_{range,sk}(\text{acct}, v, \text{sk})$. This argument first creates acct_ϵ, proves knowledge of (v, r) such that $\text{acct}_\epsilon = (g, h, \text{Commit}_{(g,h)}(v; r))$, then calls $\Sigma_{range}(\text{acct}_\epsilon, v, r)$.

The zero-knowledge argument of knowledge Σ_2 for the non-shuffle parts consists of the following sub-protocols:

1. Σ_{vud}: trivial check of VerifyUD.
2. Σ_{Com}: prover shows knowledge of v', r such that VerifyDelta $(\{\text{acct}_{\delta,i}\}), \{\text{acct}_{\epsilon,i}\}, v', r) = 1$.
3. Σ_{zero}^i: prover shows knowledge of r_i such that VerifyUpdateAcct(inputs$'_i$, outputs$'_i$, $0, (1, r_i)) = 1$.
4. Σ_{NN}: $(\bigwedge_{i=2}^{t+1} \Sigma_{range}(\text{acct}_{\delta,i}, v'_i, r_i)) \wedge (\bigwedge_{i=t+2}^{n} \Sigma_{zero}^i)$.

Σ_{sh} : a proof of shuffle of accounts **acct** into **acct'**

Prover (ψ, τ, ρ)	**Verifier**
Parse acct$_i$ = (pk$_i$, com$_i$)	Parse acct$_i$ = (pk$_i$, com$_i$)
$r, r', s, s' \xleftarrow{\$} \mathbb{F}_p^m$	Parse acct$'_i$ = (pk$'_i$, com$'_i$)
$a \leftarrow \{\psi(i)\}_{i=1}^N$	
$C_A \leftarrow$ XCom$(a; r)$	
$C_\tau \leftarrow$ XCom$(\tau; r')$	

$$\xrightarrow{\quad C_A, C_\tau \quad}$$

$$\xleftarrow{\quad x \quad} \qquad x \xleftarrow{\$} \mathbb{F}_p$$

$b \leftarrow \{x^{\psi(i)}\}_{i=1}^N$	
$b' \leftarrow \{x^{\psi(i)}/\tau_i\}_{i=1}^N$	
$C_B \leftarrow$ XCom$(b; s)$	
$C'_B \leftarrow$ XCom$(b'; s')$	

$$\xrightarrow{\quad C_B, C'_B, \pi_{Had} \quad} \qquad V(\pi_{Had}): b' \circ \tau \overset{?}{=} b$$

$$\xleftarrow{\quad y, z \quad} \qquad y, z \xleftarrow{\$} \mathbb{F}_p$$

$f \leftarrow ya + b$	$C_F \leftarrow C_A^y C_B$
$t \leftarrow yr + s$	$C_{-z} \leftarrow$ XCom$((-z, \ldots, -z); 0)$
$z \leftarrow (z, \ldots, z)$	$C_E \leftarrow C_F \cdot C_{-z}$
$e \leftarrow (f_1 - z, \ldots, f_n - z)$	
$(G, H) \leftarrow \prod_{i=1}^N \text{pk}_i^{x^i}$	$(G, H) \leftarrow \prod_{i=1}^N \text{pk}_i^{x^i}$

$$(G', H') \leftarrow \prod_{i=1}^N \text{pk}_i^{x^i \rho} \qquad \xrightarrow{\substack{\pi_{prod}, \pi_{vu}, \\ \pi_{MExp1}, \pi_{MExp2}}} \qquad V(\pi_{prod}): \prod_{i=1}^N e_i \overset{?}{=} \prod_{i=1}^N (y \cdot i + x^i - z)$$

$$C_E \leftarrow \text{XCom}(e; t) \qquad\qquad V(\pi_{vu}): (G, H, G', H') \text{ is a DDH tuple}$$

$$V(\pi_{MExp1}): \prod_{i=1}^N \text{pk}_i'^{b'_i} \overset{?}{=} \prod_{i=1}^N \text{pk}_i^{x^i}$$

$$V(\pi_{MExp2}): \prod_{i=1}^N \text{com}_i'^{b_i} \overset{?}{=} \prod_{i=1}^N \text{com}_i^{x^i} \cdot (G', H')$$

Fig. 1. The full shuffle argument Σ_{sh}. Here $V(\pi): x$ means that statement x should be verified using the argument π.

Hence $\Sigma_2 = \Sigma_{\text{vud}} \wedge \Sigma_{Com} \wedge \Sigma_{NN} \wedge \Sigma_{range,sk}(\text{outputs}'_1, \text{bl}_{s^*} + v'_1, \text{sk})$. The proof of the next lemma follows from the properties of AND-proofs, and is thus omitted.

Lemma 3. Σ_2 *is a public-coin SHVZK argument of knowledge of the relation* R_2.

The full SHVZK argument of knowledge for Quisquis is then $\Sigma := \Sigma_1 \wedge \Sigma_2 \wedge \Sigma_3$. The proof of the following theorem is deferred to the full version of the paper [13].

Theorem 1. Σ *is a public-coin SHVZK argument of knowledge of the relation* $R(x, w)$ *defined in Sect. 5.2.*

7 Performance

We now describe a prototype implementation of Quisquis, written in roughly 2000 lines of Go and interfaced with an existing Rust implementation for producing Bulletproofs,[3] to demonstrate that it is competitive in terms of both communication and computational costs.

As a reminder, transactions in Quisquis are made up of: (1) input and output account lists tx[inputs] and tx[outputs], (2) intermediate account lists inputs', outputs', $\{\text{acct}_{\delta,i}\}$ and $\{\text{acct}_{\epsilon,i}\}$, and (3) a NIZK $\Sigma = \Sigma_1 \wedge \Sigma_2 \wedge \Sigma_3$, with Σ_1 proving that a permutation has updated each of the accounts in tx[inputs] to the corresponding intermediate account, and Σ_3 similarly proving that tx[outputs] is an updated permutation of the set of intermediate accounts. Σ_2 is a combination of multiple NIZKs to prove that a number of conditions on the accounts and their balances are satisfied.

In our UPK construction, an account consists of four elements from $\mathbb{G}$. Using an elliptic curve at the 128-bit security level and with compressed points (i.e., in which points are represented just by the x-coordinate and the sign of the y-coordinate), each group element requires 33 bytes of communication (32 bytes for the x-coordinate and 1 bit for the sign), and each field element is 32 bytes.

The lists of accounts dominate the proof size for large anonymity set sizes. Since (1) and (2) are both lists of accounts of size n, and each account consists of 4 group elements, each transaction contains $24n$ group elements, or $792n$ bytes.

For Σ_1 and Σ_3, the Bayer-Groth shuffle that we use in Sect. 6 is parameterizable, and we have chosen the options that minimize communication. We thus implement the shuffle with communication complexity that grows proportionally to the square root of the size of the anonymity set. This means that it consists of $11\sqrt{n} + 7$ group elements and $5\sqrt{n} + 12$ field elements. Concretely then, each of these two proofs requires $352\sqrt{n}+224$ bytes for group elements, and $160\sqrt{n}+384$ for field elements, for a total of $512\sqrt{n} + 608$ bytes each, giving $1024\sqrt{n} + 1216$ bytes in total.

---

[3] https://github.com/dalek-cryptography/bulletproofs.

Table 2. The computation and communication complexity of the NIZKs in Quisquis, reported with various anonymity set sizes, and averaged over 20 seconds of runs.

$|A|$	Gen. (ms)	Verif. (ms)	Proof size	Proof size (bytes)
4	$124 \pm 4\%$	$25.6 \pm 3\%$	$122\mathbb{G} + 83\mathbb{F}_p$	6528
16	$471 \pm 4\%$	$71.6 \pm 3\%$	$244\mathbb{G} + 175\mathbb{F}_p$	13408
64	$2110 \pm 3\%$	$251 \pm 4\%$	$624\mathbb{G} + 503\mathbb{F}_p$	36064

Bulletproofs can be produced and verified in batches, leading to the resulting proofs growing only logarithmically with the size of the batch, rather than linearly. These proofs are then most efficient when batched in powers of two, and so we have chosen the anonymity set size to be both square and a power of two below. However, anonymity set sizes are not limited to these values. The proof size when using Bulletproofs for range proofs also grows depending on the size of the range, and this also must be a power of two. We have chosen $K = 64$ for $\mathcal{V} = [0, 2^K - 1]$.

Besides the $16n$ group elements used for lists of intermediate accounts, Σ_2 requires $6n + 38 + 2\log_2(t)$ group elements, and $6n + 15$ field elements. The total proof size is then $6n + 22\sqrt{n} + 52 + 2\log_2(t)$ group elements and $6n + 10\sqrt{n} + 39$ field elements.

Concretely, Table 2 shows the time to generate and verify the NIZK arguments in Quisquis with certain anonymity set sizes. These benchmarks were collected on a laptop with an Intel Core i7 2.8 GHz CPU and 16 GB of RAM, and demonstrate the overall practicality of Quisquis: proofs take 2.1 s to generate and comprise 36 kB in the worst case in which the size of the anonymity set is 64. We stress, however, that we do not expect users to end up using anonymity sets of anywhere near this size in a practical deployment of Quisquis, although we leave it as an interesting open problem to understand the effect different set sizes would have on the level of anonymity achieved by users.

8   Related Work and Comparisons

We provide a broad overview of related work, in terms of tumblers designed to provide anonymity, as well as a detailed comparison with the two solutions, Zcash and Monero, that are most related to our own. The results of our comparison are summarized in Table 3. The benchmarks in Table 3 were collected using a server with an Intel Core i7 3.5 GHz CPU and 32 GB of RAM, due to the Zcash client performing best when used with Linux, and due to the high RAM requirements of its prover. Both the prover and verifier in Quisquis and Monero are CPU rather than RAM bound, and so the additional RAM did not considerably change the proving and verification time, although optimizations may be possible.

There are several approaches that do not fit into the categories below, which we discuss now. First, Mimblewimble [15,32] is a cryptocurrency design that compresses the state of the blockchain via "cut-through" transactions; it thus

Table 3. The security properties and efficiency considerations for each privacy solution. For tumblers, the stated properties are for the best solutions, but they vary significantly among solutions. No tumblers satisfy plausible deniability, and all have relatively high transaction cost due to the required latency. Numbers are given for Monero with 2 newly created TXOs and a ring size 10, and Quisquis numbers are given for one sender, 3 receivers and 12 randomly selected accounts (giving a total size of 16). n is the number of participants in the transaction, and v is the bit-length of the largest value allowed in the system.

	Security			Efficiency				
	Anon.	Deniability	Theft prev	UTXO growth	tx size big-$\mathcal{O}$	kB	tx cost (ms) prover	verifier
Tumblers	yes*	no	yes*	non-monotonic	low - high		slow	
Zcash	yes	no*	yes	monotonic	1	0.29	21747	8.57
Monero	no	yes	yes	monotonic	$n + \log(v)$	2.71	982	46.3
Quisquis	yes	yes	yes	non-monotonic	$n + \log(v)$	13.4	471	71.6

achieves a goal similar to ours in providing a compact UTXO set. It also achieves a notion of privacy known as *transaction indistinguishability* [15], but it does not provide anonymity in the face of network-level attackers (who can still identify the senders and recipients in individual transactions). In this sense, Mimblewimble achieves anonymity only against "late-comer" attackers who see the data after it is published in the blockchain, so do not see individual transactions as they move around the network. In Quisquis the attacker is assumed to be able to see all individual transactions, so we can achieve anonymity even against attackers seeing all transactions at the network level. We view this as quite realistic given the high number of full nodes in existing cryptocurrencies. Further, the techniques used in Mimblewimble are in some sense complementary to Quisquis: if individual Quisquis transactions were able to be combined using the same techniques as Mimblewimble (meaning one block would contain a single "super-transaction" combining the inputs and outputs of all the individual transactions), then against the same late-comer adversary you could argue that the anonymity set would be bigger.

Second, after posting our paper online, we were made aware of Appecoin [21], a proposal for an anonymous e-cash system. While there are some similarities in the design of this system compared to ours, including the use of shuffles and updatable public keys, the presentation of Appecoin is very informal, which in turn makes it difficult to identify the extent to which it satisfies our desired security properties.

8.1 Tumblers

Solutions for tumblers are often split into two categories: centralized [8,16,38] and decentralized [7,23,24,35,36]. In terms of the former, the one that achieves the best security is arguably TumbleBit [16], which achieves anonymity and theft prevention assuming RSA and ECDSA are secure. The most naïve centralized solutions do not even achieve theft prevention (as a centralized mix can simply steal your coins rather than permute them), and none achieve plausible deniability. The mixing process is typically quite slow, either because participants must wait for others to join, or because multiple rounds of interaction with the tumbler are required.

In terms of decentralized solutions, the most common is Coinjoin [23], which has also given rise to the Dash cryptocurrency [1] and the coin mixing protocol ValueShuffle [35]. All of these solutions satisfy theft prevention, but none satisfy plausible deniability. The arguments for anonymity are not typically based on any cryptographic assumptions, and in some cases the protocols are not fully anonymous; e.g., ValueShuffle hides payment values but reveals which transaction outputs are unspent. One exception is Möbius [24], in which security is proven under the DDH assumption (in the random oracle model). Again, latency is often quite high due to the need to wait for others to join the mixing process, and for all participants to exchange messages.

8.2 Zcash

Zcash [6] is based on succinct zero-knowledge proofs (zk-SNARKs), which allow users to prove that a transaction is spending unspent shielded coins (i.e., coins that have already been deposited into a so-called shielded pool), without revealing which shielded coins they are. In terms of security, the anonymity set in Zcash is defined as all other coins that have been deposited into the pool. It also achieves theft prevention due to the soundness of the zero-knowledge proofs, but does not achieve plausible deniability, as all users opt in to the anonymity set by depositing their coins, and their transactions are performed independently of one another.

In terms of efficiency, since it is not known which shielded coins are being spent, no shielded coins can ever be removed from the UTXO set. The protocol mitigates this growth by storing information about shielded coins in a Merkle tree, meaning proofs grow in a logarithmic rather than a linear fashion with respect to the size of the UTXO set, but the growth of the set is still monotonic. It is relatively slow to generate Zcash transactions (https://speed.z.cash/), and they also require a large amount of RAM, although these numbers are expected to improve significantly in future releases [2].

Finally, in terms of cryptographic assumptions, despite recent advances [9], Zcash still requires a "trusted setup" to generate the common reference string used for the zk-SNARKs; otherwise, anyone with knowledge of its trapdoor can violate soundness and spend shielded coins that they do not rightfully own. Such structured reference strings are qualitatively different from a *common random string* (such as the one used in Quisquis), which can be generated using a random oracle, and instead require performing relatively cumbersome MPC-based "ceremonies". Additionally, all zk-SNARKs rely on strong (i.e., non-falsifiable and relatively untested) "knowledge-of-exponent"-type assumptions.

8.3   Monero

In Monero [31], senders form transactions by picking other unspent transaction outputs ("mix-ins") and forming a ring signature over them. Pairs of senders and recipients also strengthen the anonymity of this approach by using freshly generated *stealth addresses* every time they transact, meaning every address is used to receive coins only once. In terms of security, Monero satisfies both theft prevention (due to the unforgeability of the ring signature) and plausible deniability. For anonymity, however, it is known that selecting mix-ins uniformly at random can be used to distinguish the real input from the fake ones [27]. This not only means that a more complex algorithm is needed to generate the anonymity set inside the protocol but also that it is incompatible with our definition of anonymity, in which oracle queries may result in the selection of uniformly random UTXOs. Thus, while we do not rule out the option that Monero could be proved anonymous in a different model, the same anonymity set size does provide more anonymity in Quisquis (in which all keys appear only once) than in Monero (in which keys may be used and re-used in ways that leak information).

To illustrate the main conceptual difference between Monero and Quisquis, consider the following toy example of an intersection-style attack [20, 27]. Using a system in which accounts cannot be removed from the UTXO set, such as Monero, $acct_1$ transfers all its funds to $acct_4$ and uses $acct_2$ as its anonymity set. Then $acct_2$ transfers its funds to $acct_5$ using $acct_1$ as its anonymity set, and $acct_3$ transfers its funds to $acct_6$ using $acct_2$ as its anonymity set. As double-spending is not possible, anyone observing the blockchain can see that both $acct_1$ and $acct_2$ have already spent their contents at the time the last transaction was performed, so $acct_3$ must be the actual sender. Using Quisquis instead, all the accounts used as inputs would have been removed from the UTXO set and replaced by new random-looking accounts, meaning it would not be possible to use the same account twice in two different anonymity sets. Thus, such an attack could not be mounted. Furthermore, altruistic users in Quisquis could periodically send themselves money using large anonymity sets in order to "refresh" the UTXO set, in an attempt to ensure that the UTXO set has a relatively uniform distribution in terms of the age of the accounts (i.e., the time at which they were created) and thus evade attacks on Monero that are based on the differences in this distribution [27]. Again, such solutions do not work in Monero, as accounts always stay in the UTXO set.

With respect to efficiency, the UTXO set also grows monotonically, as it does in Zcash. Finally, in terms of assumptions, Monero makes the same ones as Quisquis: it requires DDH to be secure in the random oracle model.

9   Conclusions and Open Problems

In this paper we have identified and solved an open problem in anonymous cryptocurrencies; namely, that of a monotonically increasing UTXO set. We have introduced Quisquis, complete with an updatable public key system and accompanying NIZKs with low communication and computational complexity.

Quisquis allows users to achieve strong notions of anonymity and theft prevention, which we have presented with accompanying reductions to the DDH and DL assumptions. As the anonymity properties are achieved by each individual user's actions, transactions can be made anonymously without increased latency, and without strictly increasing the size of the UTXO set. While our NIZKs are already relatively efficient, we nevertheless leave as an interesting open problem the design of a special-purpose NIZK for improved communication efficiency.

Acknowledgements. Sarah Meiklejohn was supported in part by EPSRC Grant EP/N028104/1. Most of this work was done while the other three authors were working at Aarhus University and were supported by: the Concordium Blockhain Research Center, Aarhus University, Denmark; the Carlsberg Foundation under the Semper Ardens Research Project CF18-112 (BCM); the European Research Council (ERC) under the European Union's Horizon 2020 research and innovation programme under grant agreement No 803096 (SPEC); the Danish Independent Research Council under Grant-ID DFF-6108-00169 (FoCC); the European Union's Horizon 2020 research and innovation programme under grant agreement No 731583 (SODA).

References

1. Dash. https://www.dash.org/
2. What is Jubjub? https://z.cash/technology/jubjub.html
3. Androulaki, E., Karame, G.O., Roeschlin, M., Scherer, T., Capkun, S.: Evaluating user privacy in Bitcoin. In: Sadeghi, A.-R. (ed.) FC 2013. LNCS, vol. 7859, pp. 34–51. Springer, Heidelberg (2013). https://doi.org/10.1007/978-3-642-39884-1_4
4. Backes, M., Hanzlik, L., Kluczniak, K., Schneider, J.: Signatures with flexible public key: a unified approach to privacy-preserving signatures. IACR ePrint Archive, Report 2018/191. https://eprint.iacr.org/2018/191.pdf
5. Bayer, S., Groth, J.: Efficient zero-knowledge argument for correctness of a shuffle. In: Pointcheval, D., Johansson, T. (eds.) EUROCRYPT 2012. LNCS, vol. 7237, pp. 263–280. Springer, Heidelberg (2012). https://doi.org/10.1007/978-3-642-29011-4_17
6. Ben-Sasson, E., et al.: Zerocash: decentralized anonymous payments from Bitcoin. In: 2014 IEEE Symposium on Security and Privacy, Berkeley, CA, USA, 18–21 May 2014, pp. 459–474. IEEE Computer Society Press (2014)
7. Bissias, G., Ozisik, A.P., Levine, B.N., Liberatore, M.: Sybil-resistant mixing for Bitcoin. In: Proceedings of the 13th Workshop on Privacy in the Electronic Society, pp. 149–158. ACM (2014)
8. Bonneau, J., Narayanan, A., Miller, A., Clark, J., Kroll, J.A., Felten, E.W.: Mixcoin: anonymity for Bitcoin with accountable mixes. In: Christin, N., Safavi-Naini, R. (eds.) FC 2014. LNCS, vol. 8437, pp. 486–504. Springer, Heidelberg (2014). https://doi.org/10.1007/978-3-662-45472-5_31
9. Bowe, S., Gabizon, A., Green, M.: A multi-party protocol for constructing the public parameters of the Pinocchio zk-SNARK. In: Proceedings of the 5th Workshop on Bitcoin and Blockchain Research (2018)
10. Bünz, B., Agrawal, S., Zamani, M., Boneh, D.: Zether: towards privacy in a smart contract world. https://crypto.stanford.edu/~buenz/papers/zether.pdf

11. Bünz, B., Bootle, J., Boneh, D., Poelstra, A., Wuille, P., Maxwell, G.: Bullet-proofs: short proofs for confidential transactions and more. IACR Cryptology ePrint Archive 2017, 1066 (2017)
12. Delgado-Segura, S., Pérez-Solà, C., Navarro-Arribas, G., Herrera-Joancomartí, J.: Analysis of the Bitcoin UTXO set. In: Zohar, A., et al. (eds.) FC 2018. LNCS, vol. 10958, pp. 78–91. Springer, Heidelberg (2019). https://doi.org/10.1007/978-3-662-58820-8_6
13. Fauzi, P., Meiklejohn, S., Mercer, R., Orlandi, C.: Quisquis: a new design for anonymous cryptocurrencies. https://eprint.iacr.org/2018/990
14. Fleischhacker, N., Krupp, J., Malavolta, G., Schneider, J., Schröder, D., Simkin, M.: Efficient unlinkable sanitizable signatures from signatures with re-randomizable keys. In: Cheng, C.-M., Chung, K.-M., Persiano, G., Yang, B.-Y. (eds.) PKC 2016. LNCS, vol. 9614, pp. 301–330. Springer, Heidelberg (2016). https://doi.org/10.1007/978-3-662-49384-7_12
15. Fuchsbauer, G., Orrù, M., Seurin, Y.: Aggregate cash systems: a cryptographic investigation of mimblewimble. In: Ishai, Y., Rijmen, V. (eds.) EUROCRYPT 2019. LNCS, vol. 11476, pp. 657–689. Springer, Cham (2019). https://doi.org/10.1007/978-3-030-17653-2_22
16. Heilman, E., Alshenibr, L., Baldimtsi, F., Scafuro, A., Goldberg, S.: TumbleBit: an untrusted Bitcoin-compatible anonymous payment hub. In: Proceedings of NDSS 2017 (2017)
17. Heilman, E., Kendler, A., Zohar, A., Goldberg, S.: Eclipse attacks on Bitcoin's peer-to-peer network. In: Proceedings of the USENIX Security Symposium (2017)
18. Hinteregger, A., Haslhofer, B.: An empirical analysis of Monero cross-chain trace-ability. CoRR, abs/1812.02808 (2018)
19. Kappos, G., Yousaf, H., Maller, M., Mciklejohn, S.: An empirical analysis of anonymity in Zcash. In: Enck, W., Felt, A.P. (eds.) 27th USENIX Security Symposium, USENIX Security 2018, Baltimore, MD, USA, 15–17 August 2018, pp. 463–477. USENIX Association (2018)
20. Kumar, A., Fischer, C., Tople, S., Saxena, P.: A traceability analysis of Monero's blockchain. In: Foley, S.N., Gollmann, D., Snekkenes, E. (eds.) ESORICS 2017. LNCS, vol. 10493, pp. 153–173. Springer, Cham (2017). https://doi.org/10.1007/978-3-319-66399-9_9
21. Lerner, S.D.: AppeCoin: practical anonymous peer-to-peer e-cash system. https://bitslog.files.wordpress.com/2014/04/appecoin28.pdf
22. Malavolta, G., Schröder, D.: Efficient ring signatures in the standard model. In: Takagi, T., Peyrin, T. (eds.) ASIACRYPT 2017. LNCS, vol. 10625, pp. 128–157. Springer, Cham (2017). https://doi.org/10.1007/978-3-319-70697-9_5
23. Maxwell, G.: CoinJoin: Bitcoin privacy for the real world. In: Post on Bitcoin Forum (2013)
24. Meiklejohn, S., Mercer, R.: Möbius: trustless tumbling for transaction privacy. In: Proceedings on Privacy Enhancing Technologies (2018)
25. Meiklejohn, S., Orlandi, C.: Privacy-enhancing overlays in Bitcoin. In: Brenner, M., Christin, N., Johnson, B., Rohloff, K. (eds.) FC 2015. LNCS, vol. 8976, pp. 127–141. Springer, Heidelberg (2015). https://doi.org/10.1007/978-3-662-48051-9_10
26. Meiklejohn, S., et al.: A fistful of Bitcoins: characterizing payments among. men with no names. In: Proceedings of the 2013 Internet Measurement Conference, pp. 127–140. ACM (2013)
27. Miller, A., Möser, M., Lee, K., Narayanan, A.: An empirical analysis of linkability in the Monero blockchain. In: Proceedings on Privacy Enhancing Technologies (2018)

28. Moreno-Sanchez, P., Zafar, M.B., Kate, A.: Listening to whispers of Ripple: linking wallets and deanonymizing transactions in the Ripple network. In: Proceedings on Privacy Enhancing Technologies 2016, vol. 4, pp. 436–453 (2016)
29. Möser, M., Böhme, R., Breuker, D.: An inquiry into money laundering tools in the Bitcoin ecosystem. In: Proceedings of the APWG E-Crime Researchers Summit (2013)
30. Nakamoto, S.: Bitcoin: A Peer-to-Peer Electronic Cash System (2008). bitcoin.org/bitcoin.pdf
31. Noether, S., Mackenzie, A., et al.: Ring confidential transactions. Ledger 1, 1–18 (2016)
32. Poelstra, A.: Mimblewimble (2016). https://download.wpsoftware.net/bitcoin/wizardry/mimblewimble.pdf
33. Reid, F., Harrigan, M.: An analysis of anonymity in the Bitcoin system. In: Altshuler, Y., Elovici, Y., Cremers, A., Aharony, N., Pentland, A. (eds.) Security and Privacy in Social Networks, pp. 197–223. Springer, New York (2013)
34. Ron, D., Shamir, A.: Quantitative analysis of the Full Bitcoin Transaction Graph. In: Sadeghi, A.-R. (ed.) FC 2013. LNCS, vol. 7859, pp. 6–24. Springer, Heidelberg (2013). https://doi.org/10.1007/978-3-642-39884-1_2
35. Ruffing, T., Moreno-Sanchez, P.: ValueShuffle: mixing confidential transactions for comprehensive transaction privacy in Bitcoin. In: Brenner, M., et al. (eds.) FC 2017. LNCS, vol. 10323, pp. 133–154. Springer, Cham (2017). https://doi.org/10.1007/978-3-319-70278-0_8
36. Ruffing, T., Moreno-Sanchez, P., Kate, A.: CoinShuffle: practical decentralized coin mixing for Bitcoin. In: Kutyłowski, M., Vaidya, J. (eds.) ESORICS 2014. LNCS, vol. 8713, pp. 345–364. Springer, Cham (2014). https://doi.org/10.1007/978-3-319-11212-1_20
37. Spagnuolo, M., Maggi, F., Zanero, S.: BitIodine: extracting intelligence from the Bitcoin network. In: Christin, N., Safavi-Naini, R. (eds.) FC 2014. LNCS, vol. 8437, pp. 457–468. Springer, Heidelberg (2014). https://doi.org/10.1007/978-3-662-45472-5_29
38. Valenta, L., Rowan, B.: Blindcoin: blinded, accountable mixes for Bitcoin. In: Brenner, M., Christin, N., Johnson, B., Rohloff, K. (eds.) FC 2015. LNCS, vol. 8976, pp. 112–126. Springer, Heidelberg (2015). https://doi.org/10.1007/978-3-662-48051-9_9
39. Waters, B.R., Felten, E.W., Sahai, A.: Receiver anonymity via incomparable public keys. In: Jajodia, S., Atluri, V., Jaeger, T. (eds.) ACM CCS 2003, Washington D.C., USA, 27–30 October 2003, pp. 112–121. ACM Press (2003)
40. Yu, Z., Au, M.H., Yu, J., Yang, R., Xu, Q., Lau, W.F.: New empirical traceability analysis of CryptoNote-style blockchains. In: Goldberg, I., Moore, T. (eds.) Financial Cryptography and Data Security, FC 2019. LNCS, vol. 11598, pp. 133–149. Springer, Cham (2019). https://doi.org/10.1007/978-3-030-32101-7_9

Divisible E-Cash from Constrained Pseudo-Random Functions

Florian Bourse[1], David Pointcheval[2,3], and Olivier Sanders[1(✉)]

[1] Orange Labs, Applied Crypto Group, Cesson-Sévigné, France
Florian.Bourse@ens.fr , olivier.sanders@orange.com
[2] DIENS, Ecole normale supérieure, CNRS, PSL University, Paris, France
[3] INRIA, Paris, France

Abstract. Electronic cash (e-cash) is the digital analogue of regular cash which aims at preserving users' privacy. Following Chaum's seminal work, several new features were proposed for e-cash to address the practical issues of the original primitive. Among them, *divisibility* has proved very useful to enable efficient storage and spendings. Unfortunately, it is also very difficult to achieve and, to date, quite a few constructions exist, all of them relying on complex mechanisms that can only be instantiated in one specific setting. In addition security models are incomplete and proofs sometimes hand-wavy.

In this work, we first provide a complete security model for divisible e-cash, and we study the links with constrained pseudo-random functions (PRFs), a primitive recently formalized by Boneh and Waters. We exhibit two frameworks of divisible e-cash systems from constrained PRFs achieving some specific properties: either key homomorphism or delegability. We then formally prove these frameworks, and address two main issues in previous constructions: two essential security notions were either not considered at all or not fully proven. Indeed, we introduce the notion of *clearing*, which should guarantee that only the recipient of a transaction should be able to do the deposit, and we show the *exculpability*, that should prevent an honest user to be falsely accused, was wrong in most proofs of the previous constructions. Some can easily be repaired, but this is not the case for most complex settings such as constructions in the standard model. Consequently, we provide the first construction secure in the standard model, as a direct instantiation of our framework.

1 Introduction

Electronic payment systems offer high usage convenience to their users but at the cost of their privacy. Indeed, transaction data, such as payee's identity, date and location, leak sensitive information about the users, such as their whereabouts, their religious beliefs, their health status, etc.

However, secure e-payment and strong privacy are not incompatible, as shown by Chaum in 1982 [20] when he introduced the concept of electronic cash (*e-cash*). Informally, e-cash can be thought of as the digital analogue of regular cash with

© International Association for Cryptologic Research 2019
S. D. Galbraith and S. Moriai (Eds.): ASIACRYPT 2019, LNCS 11921, pp. 679–708, 2019.
https://doi.org/10.1007/978-3-030-34578-5_24

special focus on users' privacy. Such systems indeed consider three kinds of parties: the bank, the user and the merchant. The bank issues coins that can be withdrawn by users and then spent to merchants. Eventually, the latter deposit the coins on their account at the bank. Compared to other electronic payment systems, the benefit of e-cash systems is that the bank is unable to identify the author of a spending. More specifically, it can neither link a particular withdrawal—even if it knows the user's identity at this stage—to a spending nor link two spendings performed by the same user.

At first sight, this anonymity property might seem easy to achieve: one could simply envision a system where the bank would issue the same coin (more specifically, one coin for each possible denomination) to each user. Such a system would obviously be anonymous but it would also be insecure. Indeed, although e-cash aims at mimicking regular cash, there is an intrinsic difference between them: e-cash, as any electronic data, can easily be duplicated. This is a major issue because it means that a user could spend the same coin to different merchants. Of course, some hardware countermeasures (such as storing the coins on a secure element) can be used to mitigate the threat but they cannot completely remove it. Moreover, the prospect of having an endless (and untraceable) reserve of coins will constitute a strong incentive to attack this hardware whose robustness is not without limits.

To deter this bad behaviour, e-cash systems must therefore enable (1) detection of re-used coins and (2) identification of defrauders. Besides invalidating the trivial solution sketched above (a unique coin for each denomination) these requirements impose very strong constraints on e-cash systems: users should remain anonymous as long as they behave honestly while becoming traceable as soon as they begin overspending, from the first cent.

Chaum's idea, taken up by all subsequent works, was to associate each withdrawn coin with a unique identifier called a "serial number"[1]. The latter remains unknown to all parties, except the user, until the coin is spent. At this time, it becomes public and so can easily be compared to the set of all serial numbers of previously spent coins. A match then acts as a fraud alert for the bank which can then run a specific procedure to identify the cheater.

Unfortunately, by reproducing the features of regular cash, e-cash also reproduces its drawbacks, in particular the problem of paying the exact amount. Worse, as we explain below, the inherent limitations of e-cash compound this issue that becomes much harder to address in a digital setting. This has led cryptographers to propose a wide variety of solutions to mitigate the impact on user's experience. They include for example on-line e-cash, transferable e-cash or divisible e-cash.

---

[1] Actually, this specific terminology appeared later [21] but this notion is implicit in the Chaum's paper.

1.1 Related Work

On-line/Off-line Anonymous e-Cash. The original solution proposed by Chaum for anonymous payment was based on the concept of blind signature. This primitive, later formalized in [31,32], allows anyone to get a signature σ on a message m that is unknown to the signer. Moreover, the latter will be unable to link the pair (σ, m) to a specific issuance. Applying this idea to the payment context leads to the following e-cash system. A coin is a blind signature issued by a bank to a user during a withdrawal. To spend his coin, the user simply shows the signature to a merchant who is able to verify it using the bank's public key. Two cases may then appear. Either the e-cash system does not allow identification of defrauders, in which case the bank must be involved in the protocol to check that this coin has not already been spent. The resulting system is then referred to as *on-line* e-cash. Otherwise, the coin may be deposited later to the bank, leading to an *off-line* e-cash system. Obviously, the latter solution is preferable since it avoids a costly connection to the servers of the bank during the payment. In the following, we will only consider off-line e-cash systems.

Transferable vs. Divisible e-Cash. In theory, the problem of anonymous payment is thus solved by blind signatures for which several instantiations have been proposed (see *e.g.* [32]). However, as we mention above, it remains to address the problem of paying the exact amount, which becomes trickier in a digital setting. Indeed, let us consider a consumer that owns a coin whose denomination is €10 and that wants to pay €8.75. A first solution could be to contact his bank to exchange his coin against coins of smaller denominations but this would actually reintroduce the bank in the spending process and so would rather correspond to an on-line system. It then mainly remains two kinds of solutions: those where the merchant gives back change and those that only use coins of the smallest possible denomination (*e.g.* €0.01). They both gave rise to two main streams in e-cash: *transferable* e-cash and *compact/divisible* e-cash.

Let us go back to our example. At first sight, the simplest solution (inspired from regular cash) is the one where the merchant gives back change, by returning, for example, a coin of €0.05, one of €0.20 and one of €1. However, by receiving coins, the user technically becomes a merchant (in the e-cash terminology) which is not anonymous during deposit. Therefore, the only way to retain anonymity in this case is to ensure transferability of the coin, meaning that the user will be able to (anonymously) re-spend the received coins instead of depositing them. While this is a very attractive feature, it has unfortunately proved very hard to achieve. Worse, Chaum and Pedersen [22] have shown that a transferable coin necessarily grows in size after each spending. Intuitively, this is due to the fact that the coins must keep information about each of its owner to ensure identification of defrauders. In the same paper, Chaum and Pedersen also proved that some anonymity properties cannot be achieved in the presence of an unbounded adversary. Their results were later extended by Canard and Gouget [15] who proved that these properties were also unachievable under computational assumptions. More generally, identifying the anonymity properties that a transferable e-cash system can, and should, achieve has proved to be tricky [2,15].

All these negative results perhaps explain the small number of results on transferable e-cash, and quite recent constructions [2,6,17] are too complex for a large-scale deployment or rely on a very unconventional model [23]. In particular, none of them achieves optimality with respect to the size, meaning that the coin grows much faster than the theoretical pace identified by Chaum and Pedersen.

Now, let us consider our spending of € 8.75 in the case where all coins are of the smallest possible denomination. This means that the user no longer has a coin of € 10 but has 1000 coins of € 0.01. Such a system can handle any amount without change but must provide an efficient way to store and to spend hundreds of coins at once. A system offering efficient storage is called *compact* and a system supporting both efficient storage and spending is called *divisible*.

Anonymous Compact e-Cash. Anonymous compact e-cash was proposed by Camenisch, Hohenberger and Lysyanskaya [13] and was informally based on the following idea. Let N be the amount of a wallet withdrawn by a user (*i.e.* the wallet contains N coins that all have the same value). During a withdrawal, a user gets a certificate on some secret value s that will be used as a seed for a pseudo-random function (PRF) F, thus defining the serial numbers of the N coins as $F_s(i)$ for $i \in [1, N]$.

To spend the i-th coin, a user must then essentially reveal $F_s(i)$ and prove, in a zero-knowledge way, that it is well-formed, *i.e.* that (1) s has been certified and that (2) the serial number has been generated using F_s on an input belonging to the set $[1, N]$. All of these proofs can be efficiently instantiated in many settings. Anonymity follows from the zero-knowledge properties of the proofs and from the properties of the pseudo-random function, as it is hard to decide whether $F_s(i)$ and $F_s(j)$ have been generated under the same secret key s.

Unfortunately, compact e-cash only provides a partial answer to the practical issues of spendings: storage is very efficient but the coins must still be spent one by one, which quickly becomes cumbersome. An ultimate answer to this issue was actually provided by Okamoto and Ohta [29] and later named *divisible* e-cash. The core idea of divisible e-cash is that the serial numbers of a divisible coin[2] can be revealed by batches, leading to efficient spendings.

However, this is easier said than done, and it took 15 years to construct the first anonymous divisible e-cash system [14]. Moreover, the latter was more a proof of concept than a practical scheme, as pointed out in [1,16]. Although several improvements followed (*e.g.* [1,16,18,30]), the resulting constructions are still rather complex, which makes their analysis difficult. We highlight this issue by pointing out below a problem on exculpability that has been overlooked in the security proofs of these constructions.

---

[2] The terminology can be confusing here: the "divisible coin" considered by most of the papers corresponds to the "wallet" of a compact e-cash system. In particular, the divisible coin contains several coins that are all associated to a serial number.

1.2 A Major Issue with Exculpability in Previous Constructions

Intuition of the Problem. Among the natural properties expected from an e-cash system is the one, called *exculpability*, stating that a coin withdrawn by a user whose public key is upk* can only be spent by the latter. In particular this means that he cannot falsely be accused of double-spendings: in case of overspending detection, this user is necessarily guilty. All e-cash constructions enforce this property by requiring a signature (potentially a signature of knowledge) on the transaction under upk*. Intuitively, this seems enough: a transaction accusing an honest user of fraud should contain a signature (or more specifically a proof of knowledge of a signature) under upk* and so would imply a forgery. Actually, this argument is ubiquitous in previous papers[3] and leads to quite simple security proofs. It is explicitly stated in Section D.3 of the full version of [27] and in Section 4.6 of [16], and implicitly used in Section 6.3 of [18], in Section 6.2 of [30], and in the security proofs (page 22) of the full version of [13].

Unfortunately, this argument is not correct because of the complex identification process of e-cash systems, based on so-called double spending tags. Indeed, the public key upk* returned by the identification algorithm is not extracted from the signature itself, but from a complex formula involving several elements, such as PRF seeds, scalars, etc. An adversary might then select appropriate values that will lead this algorithm to output upk* while taking as input two transactions generated with different public keys. This scenario, that has not been taken into account in previous papers, invalidates their proofs[4] because, in such a case, the transactions do not contain a valid signature under upk*.

Concrete Example. To illustrate this problem, let us consider the lattice-based construction proposed by Libert *et al.* [27]. In this system, each user selects a short vector $\mathbf{e}$ and defines his public key as $\mathbf{F}.\mathbf{e}$ for some public matrix $\mathbf{F}$. Each coin withdrawn by this user is associated with two vectors $\mathbf{k}$ and $\mathbf{t}$. The former is used to generate the i-th serial number $y_S = \lfloor \mathbf{A}_i \cdot \mathbf{k} \rfloor_p$ for some public matrix $\mathbf{A}_i$ while the latter is used to generate the double-spending tag $y_T = \mathsf{upk} + \mathbf{H}(\mathbf{R}) \cdot \lfloor \mathbf{A}_i \cdot \mathbf{t} \rfloor_p$, where $\mathbf{H}(\mathbf{R})$ is a matrix derived from public information associated with the transaction $\mathbf{R}$.

If two transactions $\mathbf{R}$ and $\mathbf{R}'$ yield the same serial number, then one computes $y^* = (\mathbf{H}(\mathbf{R}) - \mathbf{H}(\mathbf{R}'))^{-1}(y_T - y_T')$ and returns $y_T - \mathbf{H}(\mathbf{R}) \cdot y^*$. One can note that this formula indeed returns a public key upk* if *both* transactions have been generated by the user upk* and tag $\mathbf{t}$, as y^* is then $\lfloor \mathbf{A}_i \cdot \mathbf{t} \rfloor_p$. However, there is no equivalence here, and an adversary might manage to generate $\mathbf{R}, \mathbf{R}', \mathbf{t}, \mathbf{t}', \mathsf{upk}, \mathsf{upk}'$ (in the exculpability game the adversary controls the bank, the merchants and all dishonest users) such that $\mathsf{upk}^* = y_T - \mathbf{H}(\mathbf{R}) \cdot (\mathbf{H}(\mathbf{R}) - \mathbf{H}(\mathbf{R}'))^{-1}(y_T - y_T')$.

---

[3] Our comment obviously only applies to papers that provide a security proof.

[4] We stress that the problem is located in the proofs and not in the definition of the exculpability property.

If we modify the original protocol, to ensure that collisions only occur when $\mathbf{t} = \mathbf{t}'$, the previous relation still gives us

$$\mathsf{upk}^* = \mathsf{upk} - \mathbf{H}(\mathbf{R}) \cdot (\mathbf{H}(\mathbf{R}) - \mathbf{H}(\mathbf{R}'))^{-1}(\mathsf{upk} - \mathsf{upk}')$$

from which it is not possible to conclude that $\mathsf{upk}^* = \mathsf{upk} = \mathsf{upk}'$. In particular, it does not seem possible to extract from these transactions a short vector $\mathbf{e}^*$ such that $\mathsf{upk}^* = \mathbf{F} \cdot \mathbf{e}^*$, which invalidates the original proof.

Discussion. This problem is not exclusive to lattice-based constructions but we note that the proofs can be fixed in the case where $\mathsf{upk} = g^x$ for some secret scalar x and where the transactions contain a signature of knowledge of the different secret values (including x). This is actually quite frequent in existing constructions (*e.g.* [13,14,16] and the ROM constructions of [18,19,30]).

Indeed, in such a case, the double-spending tag is of the form $\mathsf{T} = \mathsf{upk} \cdot F_s(i)^R$ where s is a seed, $i \in [1, N]$ is an integer, and R is derived from public information. In case of double-spending, there are two tags T and T' from which one can recover upk by computing $(\mathsf{T}^{R'}/(\mathsf{T}')^R)^{\frac{1}{R'-R}}$.

Here again, an adversary might generate $\mathsf{upk}, s, R, \mathsf{upk}', s', R'$ such that the corresponding tags T and T' satisfy $(\mathsf{T}^{R'}/(\mathsf{T}')^R)^{\frac{1}{R'-R}} = \mathsf{upk}^*$, for some honest public key upk^*. However, in this case, the reduction can recover the discrete logarithm of upk^* by extracting all the secret values from the proofs generated by the adversary. This means that exculpability can still be proven under the discrete logarithm assumption and so that the original proofs can easily be fixed by adding this remark.

Unfortunately, this patch is inherent to signatures of knowledge of discrete logarithms in the Random Oracle Model, and so cannot be applied to other settings (*e.g.* lattices [27]) or to standard model constructions [18,19,30]. In particular, this means that divisible e-cash secure in the standard model or even lattice-based compact e-cash is still an open problem.

1.3 Contributions

One can note that the above issue has remained undetected for more than a decade, whereas all compact/divisible e-cash systems are based on the same intuition. However, the latter has never been formalized. Intuition is necessary to design and understand a scheme but we must be very careful when it comes to complex primitives. This pleads for a more formal approach, where the common intuition are translated into a generic framework.

In addition, this lack of generic framework leads designers to create and combine several ad-hoc mechanisms, with complex security proofs that often rely on tailored computational assumptions. This stands in sharp contrast with a related primitive, group signature, whose foundations were studied by Bellare *et al.* [4,5] and for which very efficient constructions exist.

Two Generic Frameworks and Concrete Instantiations. In this work, we propose two generic frameworks that yield secure divisible e-cash systems from constrained PRFs, a well-known cryptographic primitive. For each framework, we identify the properties it must achieve and, so, we reduce the problem of constructing divisible e-cash systems to a simpler one: efficient instantiations of the building blocks. We additionally provide examples of instantiations to show that our frameworks are not artificial but can lead to practical schemes.

Our Approach: Constrained Pseudo-Random Functions. Starting from the work of Camenisch *et al.* [13] that defines the serial numbers as outputs of a PRF, we formalize the requirements on divisible e-cash systems as properties that must be achieved by the PRFs. Actually, the main requirement is that the serial numbers can be revealed by batches, which means that it must be possible to reveal some element k_S that (1) allows to compute $F_s(i) \; \forall i \in S \subset [1, N]$ and (2) does not provide any information on the other serial numbers, *i.e.* on the outputs of the PRF outside S. This exactly matches the definition of *constrained* PRF, a notion formalized in [10, 12, 26].

There are also several requirements that must implicitly be fulfilled by the *constrained key* k_S, for anonymity to hold, and namely unlinkability of the transactions: different constrained keys generated from the same master key must be unlinkable, which also requires k_S to hide any information on the subset S (besides its cardinality, which will represent the amount). All these notions were already defined in previous papers on constrained PRFs (*e.g.* [3,7,9]), although we only need here weaker versions of the original definitions.

Collision Resistance. Intuitively, unlinkability of k_S will ensure honest users' privacy. However, e-cash systems must also be able to deal with dishonest parties, including the bank itself. In such a case, the adversary has much more power than in usual PRF security games: it has a total control on the seeds and could use it to create collisions between serial numbers or worse, falsely accuse an honest user. To thwart such attacks, we need to introduce a new security property for constrained PRFs, that we call collision resistance. It requires that different keys (even chosen by the adversary) yield different outputs, similarly to the standard collision resistance notion for hash functions. We provide more details in Sect. 2.2.

Key Homomorphic vs. Delegable Constrained PRFs. We then investigate two different scenarios, leading to two different (but related) frameworks. In the former, we consider *key homomorphic* constrained PRF [3] whereas we use *delegatable* constrained PRF [26] in the latter. Interestingly, we note that all existing divisible e-cash systems can be associated with one of these frameworks, which brings two benefits. First, this means that it is possible to get, from existing systems, constrained PRFs (either key homomorphic or delegatable) that achieve all the properties we list above. We therefore believe that our results might be of independent interest outside e-cash since it draws attention on (implicit) constructions of constrained PRFs that might have been ignored. Second, it means that some of the constructions affected by the exculpability issue (see Sect. 1.2) could be fixed by using the same tricks we introduce in our frameworks.

Serial Numbers and Double Spending Tags. Once we have identified the sufficient properties for our PRFs, we explain how to use them to generically construct the serial numbers and the double spending tags. This is definitely the main contribution of the paper. We then describe how to combine these PRFs with very standard primitives, namely digital signatures, commitment schemes and NIZK proofs, to get a divisible e-cash system.

First Divisible e-Cash System Secure in the Standard Model. Finally, we provide detailed proofs for both frameworks to show that the security of the overall construction generically holds under the security of each of the building blocks. Concretely, this means that, for any setting, one can construct a secure divisible e-cash system by essentially designing a constrained PRF achieving some simple properties. To illustrate this point, we describe, by using our framework, the first divisible e-cash system secure in the standard model, since previous analyses in the standard model are all wrong, as explained above.

Several Security Issues. Another interesting outcome of our formalization process is that it highlights some security issues that have often been overlooked in previous papers.

First, there is the critical issue with exculpability, as discussed in Sect. 1.2.

Second, security models of e-cash systems only deal with the security of the users and the bank. We indeed note that (almost) no property related to the security of the merchant has ever been formalized. In particular, the ability of the merchants to deposit the electronic coins they received is not ensured by the e-cash scheme itself. For example, in most systems, nothing prevents the spender from depositing the coins he has just spent[5]: we define a new property, called *clearing*, that formalizes the security requirements for the merchants.

Eventually, in the withdrawal procedure, the coins secret values are traditionally generated collaboratively by the bank and the user. Our security analysis shows that this collaborative generation does not seem to provide any relevant benefit, at least for our frameworks.

1.4   Organization

We recall in Sect. 2.1 the notion of constrained pseudo-random functions and detail the security properties required in order to construct divisible e-cash systems in

---

[5] Identification of the spender is not possible in this case because the two transcripts received by the bank (the one sent by the spender and the one sent by the merchant) are exactly the same.

Sect. 2.2 (concrete instantiations of constrained PRFs can be found in the full version [11]). The syntax and the security model of divisible e-cash are described in Sect. 3. We provide, in Sect. 4, the intuition behind our two frameworks, however, due to space limitations, Sect. 5 only contains the formal description of our first framework, the second one being described in the full version [11]. The security analysis of our generic constructions is provided in the full version. The latter also contains a concrete instantiation of our framework along with an additional security notion for delegatable constrained PRFs.

2   Constrained Pseudo-Random Function

Our constructions of divisible e-cash systems will heavily rely on constrained pseudo-random functions [10,12,26] with special features that we present below. But first, we recall the syntax of this primitive.

2.1   Syntax

For sake of simplicity, our PRF $\mathcal{K} \times \mathcal{S} \to \mathcal{Y}$ will only be constrained on subsets of $\mathcal{S}$. We will then not consider the more general setting where it is constrained according to a circuit. Our PRF thus consists of the following five algorithms.

- $\mathtt{Setup}(1^\lambda, \{\mathcal{S}_i\}_{i=1}^n)$: On input a security parameter λ and a set of admissible subsets $\mathcal{S}_i \subset \mathcal{S}$, this algorithm outputs the public parameters pp that will be implicitly taken as inputs by all the following algorithms;
- $\mathtt{Keygen}()$: this algorithm outputs a master secret key $s \in \mathcal{K}$;
- $\mathtt{CKey}(s, \mathcal{X})$: On input the master key s and a set $\mathcal{X}$, this deterministic[6] algorithm outputs a constrained key $k_\mathcal{X} \in \mathcal{K}_\mathcal{X}$ or $\bot$;
- $\mathtt{Eval}(s, x)$: On input the master key s and an element $x \in \mathcal{S}$, this deterministic algorithm outputs a value $y \in \mathcal{Y}$;
- $\mathtt{CEval}(\mathcal{X}, k_\mathcal{X}, x)$: On input a set $\mathcal{X}$, a constrained key $k_\mathcal{X}$ and an element $x \in \mathcal{X}$, this deterministic algorithm outputs a value $y \in \mathcal{Y}$.

For conciseness, we will denote $\mathtt{CEval}(\mathcal{X}, k_\mathcal{X}, x)$ by $\mathtt{CEval}_\mathcal{X}(k_\mathcal{X}, x)$.

A constrained PRF is *correct* for a family of subsets $\{\mathcal{S}_i\}_{i=1}^n$ if, for all $\lambda \in \mathbb{N}$, $pp \leftarrow \mathtt{Setup}(1^\lambda, \{\mathcal{S}_i\}_{i=1}^n)$, $s \leftarrow \mathtt{Keygen}()$ and $x \in \mathcal{S}_i \subseteq \mathcal{S}$, we have, with overwhelming probability, $\mathtt{CEval}_{\mathcal{S}_i}(\mathtt{CKey}(s, \mathcal{S}_i), x) = \mathtt{Eval}(s, x)$. And this common value is $\mathrm{PRF}_s(x)$.

Definition 1. *A constrained PRF is key homomorphic [3,8] if:*

1. $\mathcal{Y}$, $\mathcal{K}$ *and* $\mathcal{K}_{\mathcal{S}_i}$ *are groups* $\forall i \in [1, n]$
2. $\forall i \in [1, n]$, $\mathtt{CEval}_{\mathcal{S}_i}(k_1 \cdot k_2, x) = \mathtt{CEval}_{\mathcal{S}_i}(k_1, x) \cdot \mathtt{CEval}_{\mathcal{S}_i}(k_2, x)$, $\forall k_1, k_2 \in \mathcal{K}_{\mathcal{S}_i}$ *and* $x \in \mathcal{S}_i$.
3. $\mathtt{CKey}(s_1 \cdot s_2, \mathcal{S}_i) = \mathtt{CKey}(s_1, \mathcal{S}_i) \cdot \mathtt{CKey}(s_2, \mathcal{S}_i)$, $\forall s_1, s_2 \in \mathcal{K}$ *and* $i \in [1, n]$

---

[6] Although the general definition in [10] allows randomized $\mathtt{CKey}$ algorithm, all our constructions will require this algorithm to be deterministic.

We use the multiplicative notation for our group operations, in $\mathcal{K}$ and $\mathcal{K}_{\mathcal{S}_i}$. As in [3], we require that the CKey algorithm, for any $\mathcal{S}_i$, is a group homomorphism from $\mathcal{K}$ into $\mathcal{K}_{\mathcal{S}_i}$.

Finally, some of our constructions will require the ability to derive a constrained key $k_{\mathcal{S}_i}$ from any key $k_{\mathcal{S}_j}$ such that $\mathcal{S}_i \subset \mathcal{S}_j$. This requires the following modifications of the syntax and of the correctness property.

Definition 2. *A constrained pseudo-random function is delegatable [26] if it additionally supports the following algorithm:*

- $\overline{\mathrm{CKey}}(k_{\mathcal{X}}, \mathcal{X}')$: *on input a constrained key $k_{\mathcal{X}} \in \mathcal{K}_{\mathcal{X}}$ and a set $\mathcal{X}' \subseteq \mathcal{X}$, this algorithm outputs a constrained key $k_{\mathcal{X}'} \in \mathcal{K}_{\mathcal{X}'}$ or $\bot$.*

To be *correct*, the delegatable constrained PRF must additionally satisfy, for a family of subsets $\{\mathcal{S}_i\}_{i=1}^n$, that, for all $\lambda \in \mathbb{N}$, $pp \leftarrow \mathrm{Setup}(1^\lambda, \{\mathcal{S}_i\}_{i=1}^n)$, $s \leftarrow \mathrm{Keygen}()$, $\mathcal{S}_i \subset \mathcal{S}_j \subseteq \mathcal{S}$, and $k_{\mathcal{S}_j} \leftarrow \mathrm{CKey}(s, \mathcal{S}_j)$, we have, with overwhelming probability, $\overline{\mathrm{CKey}}(k_{\mathcal{S}_j}, \mathcal{S}_i) = \mathrm{CKey}(s, \mathcal{S}_i)$.

2.2 Security Model

Our divisible e-cash constructions will use different types of constrained PRF, satisfying some of the following security requirements. Most of them have already been defined in previous works but we will need specific variants for some of them.

Pseudo-Randomness (PR). The first property one may expect from a constrained PRF is *pseudo-randomness*, which informally requires that an adversary, even given access to constrained keys, cannot distinguish the PRF evaluation from random, for a new point (not already queried and outside sets of known constrained keys). It is defined by $\mathrm{Exp}_{\mathcal{A}}^{pr-b}(1^\lambda, \{\mathcal{S}_i\}_{i=1}^n)$ in Fig. 1 where the adversary has access to the following oracles:

- $\mathcal{O}\mathrm{CKey}(\mathcal{X})$: on input a set $\mathcal{X}$, this algorithm returns $\mathrm{CKey}(s, \mathcal{X})$ if $\exists i \in [1, n]$ such that $\mathcal{X} = \mathcal{S}_i$ and $\bot$ otherwise.
- $\mathcal{O}\mathrm{Eval}(x)$: on input an element $x \in \mathcal{S}$, this algorithm returns $\mathrm{Eval}(s, x)$.

A constrained PRF is *pseudo-random* if $\mathrm{Adv}^{pr}(\mathcal{A}) = |\Pr[\mathrm{Exp}_{\mathcal{A}}^{pr-1}(1^\lambda, \{\mathcal{S}_i\}_{i=1}^n) = 1]$ - $\Pr[\mathrm{Exp}_{\mathcal{A}}^{pr-0}(1^\lambda, \{\mathcal{S}_i\}_{i=1}^n) = 1]|$ is negligible for any $\mathcal{A}$.

Key Pseudo-Randomness (KPR). We note that the previous definition only requires pseudo-randomness for the output of the PRF. As in [3] we extend this property to the constrained keys themselves, leading to a property that we call key pseudo-randomness. However, compared to [3], we additionally require some form of key privacy, in the sense of [26]. In particular, we need that constrained keys issued for subsets of the same size[7] should be indistinguishable.

Let F be a constrained PRF defined for a family of subsets $\{\mathcal{S}_i\}_{i=1}^n$ satisfying $\mathcal{K}_{\mathcal{S}_i} = \mathcal{K}_{\mathcal{S}_j} \ \forall i, j$ such that $|\mathcal{S}_i| = |\mathcal{S}_j|$. F is *key pseudo-random* if $\mathrm{Adv}^{kpr}(\mathcal{A}) =$

---

[7] We note that our privacy requirements are weaker than the ones of [7,9] since we allow the constrained keys to leak the size of the subsets.

$\mathrm{Exp}_{\mathcal{A}}^{pr-b}(1^{\lambda}, \{\mathcal{S}_i\}_{i=1}^{n})$ – Pseudo-Randomness

1. $pp \leftarrow \mathsf{Setup}(1^{\lambda}, \{\mathcal{S}_i\}_{i=1}^{n})$
2. $s \leftarrow \mathsf{Keygen}()$
3. $x \leftarrow \mathcal{A}^{\mathcal{O}\mathsf{CKey}, \mathcal{O}\mathsf{Eval}}(pp)$
4. $y_0 \leftarrow \mathsf{Eval}(s, x)$
5. $y_1 \xleftarrow{\$} \mathcal{Y}$
6. $b^* \leftarrow \mathcal{A}^{\mathcal{O}\mathsf{CKey}, \mathcal{O}\mathsf{Eval}}(pp, y_b)$
7. If $\mathcal{O}\mathsf{Eval}$ was queried on x, return 0
8. If $\mathcal{O}\mathsf{CKey}$ was queried on $\mathcal{X} \ni x$, return 0
9. Return b^*

$\mathrm{Exp}_{\mathcal{A}}^{kpr-b}(1^{\lambda}, \{\mathcal{S}_i\}_{i=1}^{n})$ – Key Pseudo-Randomness

1. $pp \leftarrow \mathsf{Setup}(1^{\lambda}, \{\mathcal{S}_i\}_{i=1}^{n})$
2. $s \leftarrow \mathsf{Keygen}()$
3. $i^* \leftarrow \mathcal{A}^{\mathcal{O}\mathsf{CKey}, \mathcal{O}\mathsf{Eval}}(pp)$
4. $k_0 \leftarrow \mathsf{CKey}(s, \mathcal{S}_{i^*})$
5. $k_1 \xleftarrow{\$} \mathcal{K}_{\mathcal{S}_{i^*}}$
6. $b^* \leftarrow \mathcal{A}^{\mathcal{O}\mathsf{CKey}, \mathcal{O}\mathsf{Eval}}(pp, k_b)$
7. If $\mathcal{O}\mathsf{Eval}$ was queried on $x \in \mathcal{S}_{i^*}$, return 0
8. If $\mathcal{O}\mathsf{CKey}$ was queried on $\mathcal{X}$ such that $\mathcal{X} \cap \mathcal{S}_{i^*} \neq \emptyset$, return 0
9. Return b^*

$\mathrm{Exp}_{\mathcal{A}}^{ckpr-b}(1^{\lambda}, \{\mathcal{S}_i\}_{i=1}^{n})$ – Combined Key Pseudo-Randomness

1. $pp_j \leftarrow F_j.\mathsf{Setup}(1^{\lambda}, \{\mathcal{S}_i\}_{i=1}^{n}), \forall j \in [1, t]$
2. $s \leftarrow F_1.\mathsf{Keygen}()$
3. $i^* \leftarrow \mathcal{A}^{\mathcal{O}\mathsf{CKey}, \mathcal{O}\mathsf{Eval}}(\{pp_j\}_{j=1}^{t})$
4. $(k_0^1, \ldots, k_0^t) \leftarrow (F_1.\mathsf{CKey}(s, \mathcal{S}_{i^*}), \ldots, F_t.\mathsf{CKey}(s, \mathcal{S}_{i^*}))$
5. $(k_1^1, \ldots, k_1^t) \xleftarrow{\$} \mathcal{K}_{\mathcal{S}_{i^*}}^t$
6. $b^* \leftarrow \mathcal{A}^{\mathcal{O}\mathsf{CKey}, \mathcal{O}\mathsf{Eval}}(\{pp_j\}_{j=1}^{t}, (k_b^1, \ldots, k_b^t))$
7. If $\mathcal{O}\mathsf{Eval}$ was queried on $x \in \mathcal{S}_{i^*}$, return 0
8. If $\mathcal{O}\mathsf{CKey}$ was queried on $\mathcal{X}$ such that $\mathcal{X} \cap \mathcal{S}_{i^*}$, return 0
9. Return b^*

Fig. 1. Pseudo-Randomness Games for Constrained Pseudo-Random Functions

$|\Pr[\mathrm{Exp}_{\mathcal{A}}^{kpr-1}(1^{\lambda}, \{\mathcal{S}_i\}_{i=1}^{n}) = 1]$ - $\Pr[\mathrm{Exp}_{\mathcal{A}}^{kpr-0}(1^{\lambda}, \{\mathcal{S}_i\}_{i=1}^{n}) = 1]|$ is negligible for any $\mathcal{A}$, where the game $\mathrm{Exp}_{\mathcal{A}}^{kpr-b}(1^{\lambda}, \{\mathcal{S}_i\}_{i=1}^{n})$ is defined in Fig. 1.

Combined Key Pseudo-Randomness (CKPR). In practice, divisible e-cash systems require multiple pseudo-random values, some acting as the unique identifier of the coin (the serial number) and some being used to mask the spender's identity. If F is key pseudo-random, a solution could be to split the constrained key $k_{\mathcal{S}_i} \leftarrow \mathsf{CKey}(s, \mathcal{S}_i)$ into several parts, each of them being used as pseudo-random values. Unfortunately, combining this solution with zero-knowledge proofs would be very complex. In our frameworks, we will follow a different approach and will generate several pseudo-random values by using different PRFs $F_1, \ldots, F_t$ evaluated on the same master key s and the same subset $\mathcal{S}_i$: Let $F_1 \ldots, F_t$ be constrained PRFs $\mathcal{K} \times \mathcal{S} \to \mathcal{Y}$ defined for the same family of subsets $\{\mathcal{S}_i\}_{i=1}^n$ satisfying $\mathcal{K}_{\mathcal{S}_i} = \mathcal{K}_{\mathcal{S}_j}$ $\forall i, j$ such that $|\mathcal{S}_i| = |\mathcal{S}_j|$. We say that the family $(F_1, \ldots, F_t)$ achieves combined key pseudo-randomness if $\mathtt{Adv}^{ckpr}(\mathcal{A}) = |\Pr[\mathtt{Exp}_{\mathcal{A}}^{ckpr-1}(1^\lambda, \{\mathcal{S}_i\}_{i=1}^n) = 1] - \Pr[\mathtt{Exp}_{\mathcal{A}}^{ckpr-0}(1^\lambda, \{\mathcal{S}_i\}_{i=1}^n) = 1]|$ is negligible for any $\mathcal{A}$, where the game $\mathtt{Exp}_{\mathcal{A}}^{ckpr-b}(1^\lambda, \{\mathcal{S}_i\}_{i=1}^n)$ is defined in Fig. 1.

This can be done very easily by constructing each F_i similarly but with different public parameters: let us assume that $F_1.\mathsf{CKey}(s, \mathcal{S}_i) = k_{\mathcal{S}_i}^1 = g_1^{\alpha_i \cdot s}$ $\forall i$ for some generator g_1 of $\mathcal{K}_{\mathcal{S}_i}$. We can define other PRFs $F_2, \ldots F_t$ with the same input spaces by setting $F_j.\mathsf{CKey}(s, \mathcal{S}_i) = k_{\mathcal{S}_i}^j = g_j^{\alpha_i \cdot s}$ for a different generator g_j. In such a case, we get t values $(k_{\mathcal{S}_i}^1, \ldots, k_{\mathcal{S}_i}^t)$ which are indistinguishable from a random element of $\mathcal{K}_{\mathcal{S}_i}^t$ assuming key pseudo-randomness of F_1 and the DDH assumption (see the full version [11] for more details).

Collision Resistance (CR). In our divisible e-cash constructions, the PRFs will mostly be used to generate serial numbers that act as unique identifiers of the coins. If a coin is spent twice (or more) the same serial number will appear in several transactions, which provides a very simple way to detect frauds. However, it is important to ensure that collisions between serial numbers only occur in such cases. Otherwise, this could lead to false alerts and even false accusations against an honest user.

At first sight, it might seem that this property is implied by pseudo-randomness. Unfortunately, this is not true in the context of e-cash where the adversary has total control of the master secret keys, contrarily to the adversary of the pseudo-randomness game. We therefore need to define a new property that we call collision resistance. Informally, it says that it should be hard to generate collisions between the outputs of the PRFs. However, some subtleties arise because of the different kinds of keys (secret master keys, constrained keys) that we consider here. We then define three variants of this property that are described in Fig. 2.

For $k \in \{1, 2, 3\}$, a constrained PRF achieves *collision resistance-k* if, for any $\mathcal{A}$, $\mathtt{Adv}^{cr-k}(\mathcal{A}) = \Pr[\mathtt{Exp}_{\mathcal{A}}^{cr-k}(1^\lambda, \{\mathcal{S}_i\}_{i=1}^n) = 1]$ is negligible. We provide in the full version [11] several examples of PRFs achieving these properties.

3   Divisible E-Cash

The syntax and the formal security model are drawn from [18, 30]. We nevertheless introduce several changes to make them more generic but also to add some specifications that were previously implicit only.

3.1   Syntax

A divisible e-cash system is defined by the following algorithms, that involve three types of entities, the bank $\mathcal{B}$, a user $\mathcal{U}$ and a merchant $\mathcal{M}$. Our model defines a unique value N for the divisible coin but it can easily be extended to support several different denominations.

Collision Resistance 1
$\text{Exp}_{\mathcal{A}}^{cr-1}(1^{\lambda}, \{\mathcal{S}_i\}_{i=1}^n)$

1. $pp \leftarrow \text{Setup}(1^{\lambda}, \{\mathcal{S}_i\}_{i=1}^n)$
2. $(s_1, s_2, x_1, x_2) \leftarrow \mathcal{A}(pp)$
3. If $(s_1, x_1) = (s_2, x_2)$, return 0
4. Return $\text{Eval}(s_1, x_1) = \text{Eval}(s_2, x_2)$

Collision Resistance 2
$\text{Exp}_{\mathcal{A}}^{cr-2}(1^{\lambda}, \{\mathcal{S}_i\}_{i=1}^n)$

1. $pp \leftarrow \text{Setup}(1^{\lambda}, \{\mathcal{S}_i\}_{i=1}^n)$
2. $(i, k_1, k_2, x) \leftarrow \mathcal{A}(pp)$
3. If $k_1 = k_2$, return 0
4. Return $\text{CEval}_{\mathcal{S}_i}(k_1, x) = \text{CEval}_{\mathcal{S}_i}(k_2, x)$

Collision Resistance 3
$\text{Exp}_{\mathcal{A}}^{cr-3}(1^{\lambda}, \{\mathcal{S}_i\}_{i=1}^n)$ (for Key Homomorphic Constrained PRFs only)

1. $pp \leftarrow \text{Setup}(1^{\lambda}, \{\mathcal{S}_i\}_{i=1}^n)$
2. $(i, j, k_i, k_j, x) \leftarrow \mathcal{A}(pp)$
3. If $i = j$, return 0
4. If $k_i = 1_{\mathcal{K}_{\mathcal{S}_i}} \vee k_j = 1_{\mathcal{K}_{\mathcal{S}_j}}$, return 0
5. Return $\text{CEval}_{\mathcal{S}_i}(k_i, x) = \text{CEval}_{\mathcal{S}_j}(k_j, x)$

Fig. 2. Collision Resistance Games for Constrained Pseudo-Random Functions

- $\text{Setup}(1^{\lambda}, N)$: On input a security parameter λ and an integer N, this probabilistic algorithm outputs the public parameters pp for divisible coins of global value N. We assume that pp are implicit to the other algorithms, and that they include λ and N. They are also given as an implicit input to the adversary, we will then omit them.
- $\text{BKeygen}()$: This probabilistic algorithm executed by the bank $\mathcal{B}$ outputs a key pair (bsk, bpk). It also sets L as an empty list, that will store all deposited coins. We assume that bsk contains bpk.
- $\text{Keygen}()$: This probabilistic algorithm executed by a user $\mathcal{U}$ (resp. a merchant $\mathcal{M}$) outputs a key pair (usk, upk) (resp. (msk, mpk)). We assume that usk (resp. msk) contains upk (resp. mpk).
- $\text{Withdraw}(\mathcal{B}(\text{bsk}, \text{upk}), \mathcal{U}(\text{usk}, \text{bpk}))$: This is an interactive protocol between the bank $\mathcal{B}$ and a user $\mathcal{U}$. At the end of this protocol, the user gets a divisible coin C of value N or outputs $\perp$ (in case of failure) while the bank stores the transcript of the protocol execution or outputs $\perp$.
- $\text{Spend}(\mathcal{U}(\text{usk}, C, \text{bpk}, V), \mathcal{M}(\text{msk}, \text{bpk}, \text{info}, V))$: This is an interactive protocol between a user $\mathcal{U}$ and a merchant $\mathcal{M}$. Here, info denotes a set of public information associated to the transaction, by the merchant, and V denotes the amount of this transaction. At the end of the protocol the merchant gets Z along with a proof of validity Π or outputs $\perp$. $\mathcal{U}$ then either updates C or outputs $\perp$.
- $\text{Deposit}(\mathcal{M}(\text{msk}, \text{bpk}, (V, \text{info}, Z, \Pi)), \mathcal{B}(\text{bsk}, L, \text{mpk}))$: This is an interactive protocol between a merchant $\mathcal{M}$ and the bank $\mathcal{B}$ where the former first sends a transcript (V, info, Z, Π) along with some additional data μ. $\mathcal{B}$ then checks (1) the validity of all these elements and (2) that this merchant has not already deposited a transcript associated with info. If condition (1) is not fulfilled, then $\mathcal{B}$ aborts and outputs $\perp$. If condition (2) is not fulfilled, then $\mathcal{B}$ returns another transcript $(V', \text{info}, Z', \Pi')$ along with the associated μ'. Otherwise, $\mathcal{B}$

recovers the V serial numbers $\mathtt{SN}_{i_0}, \ldots, \mathtt{SN}_{i_{V-1}}$[8] derived from Z and compares them to the set L of all serial numbers of previously spent coins. If there is a match for some index i_k, then $\mathcal{B}$ returns a transcript $(V', Z', \Pi', \mathsf{info}')$ such that $\mathtt{SN}_{i_k}$ is also a serial number derived from Z'. Else, $\mathcal{B}$ stores these new serial numbers in L and keeps a copy of $(V, \mathsf{info}, \mathsf{mpk}, Z, \Pi)$.

- $\mathtt{Identify}((V, \mathsf{info}, \mathsf{mpk}, Z, \Pi), (V', \mathsf{info}', \mathsf{mpk}', Z', \Pi'), \mathsf{bpk})$: On the wo transcripts, this deterministic algorithm outputs 0 if $\mathsf{info} = \mathsf{info}'$, if one of the transcripts is invalid, or if the serial numbers derived from these transcripts do not collide. Else it outputs a user's public key upk or $\bot$.
- $\mathtt{CheckDeposit}([(V, \mathsf{info}, \mathsf{mpk}, Z, \Pi), \mu], \mathsf{bpk})$: This deterministic algorithm outputs 1 if $[(V, \mathsf{info}, Z, \Pi), \mu]$ are valid elements deposited by a merchant whose public key is mpk and 0 otherwise.

Our model does not place restrictions on the values that can be spent nor on the size of a spending transcript. It is therefore more generic and in particular also fits compact e-cash systems where the serial numbers can only be revealed one by one.

3.2   Security Model

Existing security models essentially focus on the user's and the bank's interests. The former must indeed be able to spend their coins anonymously without being falsely accused of frauds while the latter must be able to detect frauds and identify the perpetrators. This is formally defined by three security properties in [18]: *anonymity* (user' spendings are anonymous, even with respect to the bank), *exculpability* (honest users cannot be falsely accused, even by the bank) and *traceability* (an author of overspending should be traced back).

However, all these notions (and the corresponding ones in previous papers) fail to capture an important security property for the merchant: he must always be able to clear his transactions, but also, he should be the only one able to deposit them. This is especially problematic for e-cash because users can reproduce the transcripts of their spendings. Designers of existing divisible e-cash systems seem to be more or less aware of this issue[9] because they usually attribute a signing key to the merchant. However, these systems do not specify the security properties expected from the corresponding signature scheme and most of them even do not specify which elements should be signed.

For completeness, we therefore add the property of *clearing* (only the recipient merchant can perform the deposit) to the above usual ones. All of them are defined in Fig. 3 and make use of the following oracles:

---

[8] We do not make any assumption on the indices $i_0, \ldots, i_{V-1}$, contrarily to some previous works that assume they are consecutive.

[9] The "correctness for merchant", informally defined in [1], is related to this issue. It ensures that the transcript deposited by an honest merchant will be accepted, even if the spender is dishonest and double-spends his coin. However, it only considers an honest bank and it does not consider situations where the transcript would be deposited by another entity. In particular, the scheme in [1] does not ensure that the merchant is the only one able to clear his coins.

- $\mathcal{O}\mathrm{Add}()$ is an oracle used by the adversary $\mathcal{A}$ to register a new honest user (resp. merchant). The oracle runs the Keygen algorithm, stores usk (resp. msk) and returns upk (resp. mpk) to $\mathcal{A}$. In this case, upk (resp. mpk) is said *honest*.
- $\mathcal{O}\mathrm{Corrupt}(\mathrm{upk}/\mathrm{mpk})$ is an oracle used by $\mathcal{A}$ to corrupt an honest user (resp. merchant) whose public key is upk (resp. mpk). The oracle then returns the corresponding secret key usk (resp. msk) to $\mathcal{A}$ along with the secret values of every coin withdrawn by this user. From now on, upk (resp. mpk) is said *corrupted*.
- $\mathcal{O}\mathrm{AddCorrupt}(\mathrm{upk}/\mathrm{mpk})$ is an oracle used by $\mathcal{A}$ to register a new corrupted user (resp. merchant) whose public key is upk (resp. mpk). In this case, upk (resp. mpk) is said *corrupted*. The adversary could use this oracle on a public key already registered (during a previous $\mathcal{O}\mathrm{Add}$ query) but for simplicity, we do not consider such case as it will gain nothing more than using the $\mathcal{O}\mathrm{Corrupt}$ oracle on the same public key.
- $\mathcal{O}\mathrm{Withdraw}_{\mathcal{U}}(\mathrm{upk})$ is an oracle that executes the user's side of the Withdraw protocol. This oracle will be used by $\mathcal{A}$ playing the role of the bank against the user with public key upk.
- $\mathcal{O}\mathrm{Withdraw}_{\mathcal{B}}(\mathrm{upk})$ is an oracle that executes the bank's side of the Withdraw protocol. This oracle will be used by $\mathcal{A}$ playing the role of a user whose public key is upk against the bank.
- $\mathcal{O}\mathrm{Spend}(\mathrm{upk}, V)$ is an oracle that executes the user's side of the Spend protocol for a value V. This oracle will be used by $\mathcal{A}$ playing the role of the merchant $\mathcal{M}$.
- $\mathcal{O}\mathrm{Receive}(\mathrm{mpk}, V)$ is an oracle that executes the merchant's side of the Spend protocol for a value V. This oracle will be used by $\mathcal{A}$ playing the role of a user.
- $\mathcal{O}\mathrm{Deposit}(\mathrm{mpk}, V, \mathrm{info})$ is an oracle that executes the merchant's side of the Deposit protocol for a transaction of amount V associated with the value info. This oracle cannot be queried on two inputs with the same value info. It will be used by $\mathcal{A}$ playing the role of the bank.

In the experiments, users are denoted by their public keys upk, c_{upk} denotes the amount already spent by user upk during $\mathcal{O}\mathrm{Spend}$ queries, m_{upk} the number of divisible coins that he has withdrawn and Tr_i the transcript $(V_i, \mathrm{info}_i, \mathrm{mpk}_i, Z_i, \Pi_i)$ for any $i \in \mathbb{N}$. This means that the total amount available by a user upk is $m_{\mathrm{upk}} \cdot N$. The number of coins withdrawn by all users during an experiment is denoted by m.

For sake of simplicity, we assume that all merchants are corrupted, and added through $\mathcal{O}\mathrm{AddCorrupt}$ queries, in the traceability, exculpability and anonymity experiments. We therefore do not need to add access to the $\mathcal{O}\mathrm{Receive}$ and $\mathcal{O}\mathrm{Deposit}$ oracles in the latter. We stress that this is not a restriction since the $\mathcal{O}\mathrm{AddCorrupt}$ oracle provides more power to the adversary than the $\mathcal{O}\mathrm{Add}$ and $\mathcal{O}\mathrm{Corrupt}$ ones. Similarly, we assume that the bank and all the users are corrupted in the clearing game and so do not provide access to the $\mathcal{O}\mathrm{Spend}$, $\mathcal{O}\mathrm{Withdraw}_{\mathcal{U}}$ and $\mathcal{O}\mathrm{Withdraw}_{\mathcal{B}}$ oracles in it.

$\mathrm{Exp}_{\mathcal{A}}^{tra}(1^\lambda, N)$ – Traceability Security Game

1. $pp \leftarrow \mathtt{Setup}(1^\lambda, N)$
2. $(\mathsf{bsk}, \mathsf{bpk}) \leftarrow \mathtt{BKeygen}()$
3. $\{(V_i, \mathsf{info}_i, \mathsf{mpk}_i, Z_i, \Pi_i)\}_{i=1}^{u} \xleftarrow{\$} \mathcal{A}^{\mathcal{O}\mathtt{Add}, \mathcal{O}\mathtt{Corrupt}, \mathcal{O}\mathtt{AddCorrupt}, \mathcal{O}\mathtt{Withdraw}_\mathcal{B}, \mathcal{O}\mathtt{Spend}}(\mathsf{bpk})$
4. If $\sum_{i=1}^{u} V_i > m \cdot N$ and $\forall i \neq j$, $\mathtt{Identify}(\mathsf{Tr}_i, \mathsf{Tr}_j, \mathsf{bpk}) = \perp$, then return 1
5. Return 0

$\mathrm{Exp}_{\mathcal{A}}^{excu}(1^\lambda, N)$ – Exculpability Security Game

1. $pp \leftarrow \mathtt{Setup}(1^\lambda, N)$
2. $\mathsf{bpk} \leftarrow \mathcal{A}()$
3. $[\mathsf{Tr}_1, \mathsf{Tr}_2] \leftarrow \mathcal{A}^{\mathcal{O}\mathtt{Add}, \mathcal{O}\mathtt{Corrupt}, \mathcal{O}\mathtt{AddCorrupt}, \mathcal{O}\mathtt{Withdraw}_\mathcal{U}, \mathcal{O}\mathtt{Spend}}()$
4. If $\mathtt{Identify}(\mathsf{Tr}_1, \mathsf{Tr}_2, \mathsf{bpk}) = \mathsf{upk}$ and upk not corrupted, then return 1
5. Return 0

$\mathrm{Exp}_{\mathcal{A}}^{anon-b}(1^\lambda, N)$ – Anonymity Security Game

1. $pp \leftarrow \mathtt{Setup}(1^\lambda, N)$
2. $\mathsf{bpk} \leftarrow \mathcal{A}()$
3. $(V, \mathsf{upk}_0, \mathsf{upk}_1, \mathsf{mpk}) \leftarrow \mathcal{A}^{\mathcal{O}\mathtt{Add}, \mathcal{O}\mathtt{Corrupt}, \mathcal{O}\mathtt{AddCorrupt}, \mathcal{O}\mathtt{Withdraw}_\mathcal{U}, \mathcal{O}\mathtt{Spend}}()$
4. If upk_i is not registered for $i \in \{0, 1\}$, then return 0
5. If $c_{\mathsf{upk}_i} > m_{\mathsf{upk}_i} \cdot N - V$ for $i \in \{0, 1\}$, then return 0
6. $(V, Z, \Pi, \mathsf{info}) \leftarrow \mathtt{Spend}(\mathcal{C}(\mathsf{usk}_b, C, \mathsf{mpk}, V), \mathcal{A}())$
7. $c_{\mathsf{upk}_{1-b}} \leftarrow c_{\mathsf{upk}_{1-b}} + V$
8. $b^* \leftarrow \mathcal{A}^{\mathcal{O}\mathtt{Add}, \mathcal{O}\mathtt{Corrupt}, \mathcal{O}\mathtt{AddCorrupt}, \mathcal{O}\mathtt{Withdraw}_\mathcal{U}, \mathcal{O}\mathtt{Spend}}()$
9. If upk_i has been corrupted for $i \in \{0, 1\}$, then return 0
10. Return $(b = b^*)$

$\mathrm{Exp}_{\mathcal{A}}^{clear}(1^\lambda, N)$ – Clearing Security Game

1. $pp \leftarrow \mathtt{Setup}(1^\lambda, N)$
2. $\mathsf{bpk} \leftarrow \mathcal{A}()$
3. $[(V, \mathsf{info}, \mathsf{mpk}, Z, \Pi), \mu] \leftarrow \mathcal{A}^{\mathcal{O}\mathtt{Add}, \mathcal{O}\mathtt{Corrupt}, \mathcal{O}\mathtt{AddCorrupt}, \mathcal{O}\mathtt{Receive}, \mathcal{O}\mathtt{Deposit}}()$
4. If $\mathtt{CheckDeposit}([(V, \mathsf{info}, \mathsf{mpk}, Z, \Pi), \mu], \mathsf{bpk}) = 0$, then return 0
5. If mpk is corrupted, then return 0
6. If $(\mathsf{mpk}, V, \mathsf{info})$ has been queried to $\mathcal{O}\mathtt{Deposit}$, then return 0
7. Return 1

Fig. 3. Security Games for Divisible E-Cash

Our clearing game ensures that no one can forge a valid deposit query from the merchant. This means in particular that the bank cannot rightfully refuse the deposit of an honest merchant (because it will not be able to provide a valid proof that the transcript has already been deposited) and that it cannot falsely accuse a merchant of trying to deposit the same transcript several times.

A divisible E-cash system is said to be *traceable*, *exculpable*, *anonymous*, and/or *clearable* if $\mathtt{Succ}^{tra}(\mathcal{A})$, $\mathtt{Succ}^{excu}(\mathcal{A})$, $\mathtt{Adv}^{anon}(\mathcal{A})$, and/or $\mathtt{Succ}^{clear}(\mathcal{A})$, are respectively negligible for any probabilistic polynomial adversary $\mathcal{A}$, where

$$\text{Succ}^{tra}(\mathcal{A}) = \Pr[\text{Exp}^{tra}_{\mathcal{A}}(1^{\lambda}, N) = 1] \quad \text{Succ}^{excu}(\mathcal{A}) = \Pr[\text{Exp}^{excu}_{\mathcal{A}}(1^{\lambda}, N) = 1]$$

$$\text{Succ}^{clear}(\mathcal{A}) = \Pr[\text{Exp}^{clear}_{\mathcal{A}}(1^{\lambda}, N) = 1]$$

$$\text{Adv}^{anon}(\mathcal{A}) = |\Pr[\text{Exp}^{anon-1}_{\mathcal{A}}(1^{\lambda}, N) = 1] - \Pr[\text{Exp}^{anon-0}_{\mathcal{A}}(1^{\lambda}, N) = 1]|$$

4 High-Level Description

Before introducing a generic framework for divisible e-cash, we focus on the heart of such systems, namely the construction of the serial numbers and of the double-spending tags.

Regarding the former, the fact that each serial number SN must look random has led designers to use pseudo-random functions (PRFs). More specifically, every anonymous divisible e-cash scheme defines SN_i as $F.\text{Eval}(s, i)$ where s is the master key and $i \in [1, N]$. However, to avoid a cost linear in the amount V it is necessary to provide a way to reveal these serial numbers by batches. Designers of divisible e-cash systems (*e.g.* [1,14,16,18,19,30]) have thus constructed pseudo-random functions with a special feature: given s and a subset $\mathcal{X} \subseteq [1, N]$, one can compute $k_{\mathcal{X}}$ allowing to evaluate the PRF only on the elements of $\mathcal{X}$. This matches the definition of constrained PRFs, as described above. To spend a value V, the user can now simply reveal a constrained key $k_{\mathcal{X}}$ for a set $\mathcal{X}$ of size V. However additional properties are required here to achieve anonymity. Indeed, informally, the constrained key must hide information on the spender (more specifically on the master secret key) and on the subset $\mathcal{X}^{10}$ itself. All these properties are captured by key pseudo-randomness that we defined in Sect. 2. Eventually, to avoid false positive in the fraud detection process, we will need the collision resistance properties defined in the same section.

Therefore, constructing divisible e-cash with efficient double-spending detections is roughly equivalent to constructing a key pseudo-random, collision resistant constrained PRF for subsets of $[1, N]$ that smoothly interacts with Non-Interactive Zero-Knowledge (NIZK) proofs. However, detection of double spending is not enough, it must also be possible to identify double spenders by using the additional information contained in the double-spending tag. This adds further requirements on the PRF and leads to two constructions that we present below.

4.1 Construction Using Key Homomorphism

Our first construction of double-spending tag is reminiscent of the techniques used by compact e-cash systems [13,27]. In these papers, the double spending tag T_i associated with SN_i is of the form $\text{ID} \cdot (F'.\text{Eval}(s', i))^R$, where ID is the "identity" of the spender (usually his public key), F' is a PRF seeded with a master secret key s' (note that we may have $F = F'$ or $s = s'$ but not both) and R is a public identifier of the transaction.

Intuitively, the idea behind this tag is that $(F'.\text{Eval}(s', i))^R$ will perfectly mask the user's identity as long as the latter does not overspend his coin. In

---

[10] Actually the size of $\mathcal{X}$ can leak as it corresponds to the public amount of the transaction.

case of double spendings, there will indeed be two tags $\mathrm{T}_i^{(1)}$ and $\mathrm{T}_i^{(2)}$ of the form $\mathrm{ID} \cdot (F'.\mathtt{Eval}(s',i))^{R_1}$ and $\mathrm{ID} \cdot (F'.\mathtt{Eval}(s',i))^{R_2}$. Therefore, by computing:

$$((\mathrm{T}_i^{(1)})^{R_2}/(\mathrm{T}_i^{(2)})^{R_1})^{1/(R_2-R_1)}$$

the bank can directly recover the identity ID of the defrauder. This idea was adapted in [18,19,30] to the context of divisible e-cash by replacing $F'.\mathtt{Eval}(s',i)$ with a key constrained to the appropriate subset.

However, we have explained in Sect. 1.2 that this process of identification is problematic and could lead to false accusations against honest user, thus breaking exculpability. Concretely, the problem arises from the fact that the above formula may output ID while involving tags $\mathrm{T}_i^{(1)}$ and $\mathrm{T}_i^{(2)}$ produced for different identities. Indeed, in the exculpability game, a malicious bank could cooperate with malicious users and merchants to select values ID_1, ID_2, R_1, R_2, s_1 and s_2 such that $((\mathrm{T}_i^{(1)})^{R_2}/(\mathrm{T}_i^{(2)})^{R_1})^{1/(R_2-R_1)} = ((\mathrm{ID}_1 \cdot (F'.\mathtt{Eval}(s_1,i_1))^{R_1})^{R_2}/(\mathrm{ID}_2 \cdot (F'.\mathtt{Eval}(s_2,i_2))^{R_2})^{R_1})^{1/(R_2-R_1)} = \mathrm{ID}$. This means that, in general, this tag construction cannot be used as it is.

To prevent this problem, our generic construction uses four PRFs, that we will denote by F_1, F_2, F_3 and F_4, defined for the same family of subsets $\{\mathcal{S}_i\}_{i=1}^n$ and sharing the same key space $\mathcal{K}$. We additionally require F_2, F_3 and F_4 to be key homomorphic.

Let $s \in \mathcal{K}$ be a secret master key and $\mathcal{S}_i$ be a subset of size V, the amount of the transaction. As previously[11], our first PRF will be used to reveal $k_{\mathcal{S}_i}^{(1)} \leftarrow F_1.\mathtt{CKey}(s,\mathcal{S}_i)$. Likewise, our third PRF will be used to generate an element of the form[12] $\mathrm{ID}^R \cdot k_{\mathcal{S}_i}^3$, with $k_{\mathcal{S}_i}^3 \leftarrow F_3.\mathtt{CKey}(s,\mathcal{S}_i)$. The novelty here is that these values will only constitute a part of the serial number and of the double spending tag. The other parts will be derived from $k_{\mathcal{S}_i}^{(2)} \leftarrow F_2.\mathtt{CKey}(s \cdot id, \mathcal{S}_i)$, where id is some element of $\mathcal{K}$ associated with the public identity ID, and from $\mathrm{ID} \cdot k_{\mathcal{S}_i}^4$ where $k_{\mathcal{S}_i}^4 \leftarrow F_4.\mathtt{CKey}(s,\mathcal{S}_i)$. More specifically,

$$\mathrm{SN}_j = F_1.\mathtt{CEval}_{\mathcal{S}_i}(k_{\mathcal{S}_i}^{(1)}, j)\|F_2.\mathtt{CEval}_{\mathcal{S}_i}(k_{\mathcal{S}_i}^{(2)}, j) \qquad \mathrm{T}_{\mathcal{S}_i} = (\mathrm{ID}^R \cdot k_{\mathcal{S}_i}^3, \mathrm{ID} \cdot k_{\mathcal{S}_i}^4).$$

Intuitively, the fact that the master secret key of F_2 depends on id will ensure that no collision can occur for different users, which thwarts the previous attack. Moreover, the first part of SN_j still ensures that collisions can only occur for spendings involving the same master key, evaluated on the same element $j \in \mathcal{S}$. The last element of the double-spending tag has a more technical purpose, it prevents identification errors in the case where the colliding serial numbers have been generated using different subsets (see Remark 3).

---

[11] For sake of clarity, we assume here that the elements associated with the users' identity live in the right spaces. Our formal definition will make use of suitable maps to ensure this fact.

[12] We need to apply the exponent R on the identity itself instead of the constrained key to rely on the correctness of $\mathtt{CEval}$, but the principle is the same.

Therefore, if two spendings with respective tags $T^{(1)}_{\mathcal{S}_{i_1}}$ and $T^{(2)}_{\mathcal{S}_{i_2}}$ lead to a collision, then we have:

$$T^{(1)}_{\mathcal{S}_{i_1}} = (\text{ID}^{R_1} \cdot k^3_{\mathcal{S}_{i_1}}, \text{ID} \cdot k^4_{\mathcal{S}_{i_1}}) \qquad T^{(2)}_{\mathcal{S}_{i_2}} = (\text{ID}^{R_2} \cdot k^3_{\mathcal{S}_{i_2}}, \text{ID} \cdot k^4_{\mathcal{S}_{i_2}})$$

with $j \in \mathcal{S}_{i_1} \cap \mathcal{S}_{i_2}$. If $\mathcal{S}_{i_1} = \mathcal{S}_{i_2} = \mathcal{S}_i$, we can compute:

$$F_3.\text{CEval}_{\mathcal{S}_i}(T^{(1)}_{\mathcal{S}_i}[1], j) = F_3.\text{CEval}_{\mathcal{S}_i}(\text{ID}^{R_1}, j) \cdot F_3.\text{CEval}_{\mathcal{S}_i}(k^3_{\mathcal{S}_i}, j)$$

$$F_3.\text{CEval}_{\mathcal{S}_i}(T^{(2)}_{\mathcal{S}_i}[1], j) = F_3.\text{CEval}_{\mathcal{S}_i}(\text{ID}^{R_2}, j) \cdot F_3.\text{CEval}_{\mathcal{S}_i}(k^3_{\mathcal{S}_i}, j)$$

Since $k^3_{\mathcal{S}_{i_1}}$ and $k^3_{\mathcal{S}_{i_2}}$ are derived from the same master key, correctness ensures that $F_3.\text{CEval}_{\mathcal{S}_i}(k^3_{\mathcal{S}_i}, j) = F_3.\text{CEval}_{\mathcal{S}_i}(k^3_{\mathcal{S}_i}, j)$. Therefore:

$$F_3.\text{CEval}_{\mathcal{S}_i}(T^{(2)}_{\mathcal{S}_i}[1], j) \cdot F_3.\text{CEval}_{\mathcal{S}_i}(T^{(1)}_{\mathcal{S}_i}[1], j)^{-1}$$
$$= F_3.\text{CEval}_{\mathcal{S}_i}(\text{ID}^{R_2}, j) \cdot F_3.\text{CEval}_{\mathcal{S}_i}(\text{ID}^{-R_1}, j)$$

The bank can then perform an exhaustive search on the set of public identities $\{\text{ID}_i\}$ until it gets a match. Identification of defrauders is then possible with a linear cost in the number of users of the system.

Now in the case where $\mathcal{S}_{i_1} \neq \mathcal{S}_{i_2}$, we have, for any identity ID^*:

$$F_4.\text{CEval}_{\mathcal{S}_{i_1}}(T^{(1)}_{\mathcal{S}_{i_1}}[2]/(\text{ID}^*), j) = F_4.\text{CEval}_{\mathcal{S}_{i_1}}(\text{ID}/(\text{ID}^*), j) \cdot F_4.\text{CEval}_{\mathcal{S}_{i_1}}(k^4_{\mathcal{S}_{i_1}}, j)$$

$$F_4.\text{CEval}_{\mathcal{S}_{i_2}}(T^{(1)}_{\mathcal{S}_{i_2}}[2]/(\text{ID}^*), j) = F_4.\text{CEval}_{\mathcal{S}_{i_2}}(\text{ID}/(\text{ID}^*), j) \cdot F_4.\text{CEval}_{\mathcal{S}_{i_2}}(k^4_{\mathcal{S}_{i_2}}, j)$$

Here again, $F_4.\text{CEval}_{\mathcal{S}_{i_1}}(k^4_{\mathcal{S}_{i_1}}, j) = F_4.\text{CEval}_{\mathcal{S}_{i_2}}(k^4_{\mathcal{S}_{i_2}}, j)$, therefore:

$$F_4.\text{CEval}_{\mathcal{S}_{i_1}}(T^{(1)}_{\mathcal{S}_{i_1}}[2]/(\text{ID}^*), j)/F_4.\text{CEval}_{\mathcal{S}_{i_2}}(T^{(1)}_{\mathcal{S}_{i_2}}[2]/(\text{ID}^*), j)$$
$$= F_4.\text{CEval}_{\mathcal{S}_{i_1}}(\text{ID}/(\text{ID}^*), j)/F_4.\text{CEval}_{\mathcal{S}_{i_2}}(\text{ID}/(\text{ID}^*), j)$$

and one can easily identify the case where $\text{ID}^* = \text{ID}$ since this it is the only one where the right member equals to $1_{\mathcal{Y}}$ if F_4 achieves collision resistance-3.

Remark 3. The use of two elements in the double-spending tag may seem surprising, in particular because the equality

$$F_3.\text{CEval}_{\mathcal{S}_{i_1}}(T^{(2)}_{\mathcal{S}_{i_2}}[1], j) \cdot F_3.\text{CEval}_{\mathcal{S}_{i_2}}(T^{(1)}_{\mathcal{S}_{i_2}}[1], j)^{-1}$$
$$= F_3.\text{CEval}_{\mathcal{S}_{i_1}}(\text{ID}^{R_2}, j) \cdot F_3.\text{CEval}_{\mathcal{S}_{i_2}}(\text{ID}^{-R_1}, j)$$

still holds for the right ID in the case where $\mathcal{S}_{i_1} \neq \mathcal{S}_{i_2}$. However, in this case, we cannot ensure that this equality *only* holds for ID, it might also work for other identities, leading to obvious identification issues.

4.2 Construction Using Delegation

Our second construction is inspired by what has been the main framework for divisible e-cash for many years (*e.g.* [14,16,28]). It makes use of a family of two delegatable PRFs (F_1, F_2) and two functions[13] (H, H') such that $H : \mathcal{K} \to \mathbb{G}$

---

[13] The requirements placed on these functions are specified in the full version [11].

and $H' : \mathcal{K}_{\mathcal{S}_i} \to \mathbb{G}$ for some group $\mathbb{G}$ (we here assume that $\mathcal{K}_{\mathcal{S}_i} = \mathcal{K}_{\mathcal{S}_j}$ for all $i, j \in [1, N]$). We assume that the subsets $\{\mathcal{S}_i\}$ of $[1, N]$ supported by the PRFs F_1 and F_2 satisfy the following requirement:

$$\mathcal{S}_i \cap \mathcal{S}_j \neq \emptyset \Rightarrow \mathcal{S}_i \subset \mathcal{S}_j \text{ or } \mathcal{S}_j \subset \mathcal{S}_i$$

Therefore, for each subset $\mathcal{S}_i \neq [1, N]$, it is possible to define the smallest subset containing strictly $\mathcal{S}_i$. Its index is given by a function D.

To spend a value V, a user whose coin secret key is s selects a subset $\mathcal{S}_i$ containing V elements and will reveal the following information:

1. $k_{\mathcal{S}_i}^{(1)} \leftarrow F_1.\mathsf{CKey}(s, \mathcal{S}_i)$
2. $k_{\mathcal{S}_i}^{(2)} \leftarrow \mathsf{upk} \cdot F_2.\mathsf{CKey}(s, \mathcal{S}_i)$
3. $\mathsf{T}_{\mathcal{S}_i} \leftarrow \mathsf{upk} \cdot H'(F_1.\mathsf{CKey}(s, \mathcal{S}_{D(\mathcal{S}_i)}))^R$

for some public element R. The first element will be used by the bank to derive the serial numbers $\mathsf{SN}_t \leftarrow F_1.\mathsf{CEval}_{\mathcal{S}_i}(k_{\mathcal{S}_i}^{(1)}, t) \ \forall t \in \mathcal{S}_i$. The second element prevents the problem we mention in Sect. 4.1: it will be used to discard collisions between spendings involving different users. Finally, the last element is the double-spending tag but the identification process is more subtle than in the previous case, as we explain below.

Let $(k_{\mathcal{S}_i}^{(1)}, k_{\mathcal{S}_i}^{(2)}, \mathsf{T}_{\mathcal{S}_i})$ and $(k_{\mathcal{S}_j}^{(1)}, k_{\mathcal{S}_j}^{(2)}, \mathsf{T}_{\mathcal{S}_j})$ be two spendings leading to a collision, i.e. such that there are $t_i \in \mathcal{S}_i$ and $t_j \in \mathcal{S}_j$ verifying the equation:

$$F_1.\mathsf{CEval}_{\mathcal{S}_i}(k_{\mathcal{S}_i}^{(1)}, t_i) = F_1.\mathsf{CEval}_{\mathcal{S}_j}(k_{\mathcal{S}_j}^{(1)}, t_j).$$

Collision resistance of F_1 implies that $t_i = t_j$ and that $k_{\mathcal{S}_i}^{(1)}$ and $k_{\mathcal{S}_j}^{(1)}$ were both derived from the same master secret key. Moreover, $t_i \in \mathcal{S}_i \cap \mathcal{S}_j \neq \emptyset$ which implies that $\mathcal{S}_i \subset \mathcal{S}_j$ or $\mathcal{S}_j \subset \mathcal{S}_i$. Let us assume that $\mathcal{S}_j \subset \mathcal{S}_i$. We then distinguish the two following cases.

- Case 1: $\mathcal{S}_j \subsetneq \mathcal{S}_i$, which implies that $\mathcal{S}_{D(\mathcal{S}_j)} \subset \mathcal{S}_i$. From $k_{\mathcal{S}_i}^{(1)}$, one can then compute $\mathsf{T}^* \leftarrow H'(F_1.\overline{\mathsf{CKey}}(k_{\mathcal{S}_i}^{(1)}, \mathcal{S}_{D(\mathcal{S}_j)}))$ and thus recover $\mathsf{upk} = \mathsf{T}_{\mathcal{S}_j}/(\mathsf{T}^*)^{R_i}$.
- Case 2: $\mathcal{S}_j = \mathcal{S}_i$. In such a case, $k_{\mathcal{S}_i}^{(2)} = k_{\mathcal{S}_j}^{(2)}$ if and only if both elements have been generated using the same public key upk. Therefore, one aborts if this equality does not hold. Else, one computes $\mathsf{upk} \leftarrow (\mathsf{T}_{\mathcal{S}_i}^{R_j}/\mathsf{T}_{\mathcal{S}_j}^{R_i})^{1/(R_j - R_i)}$.

4.3 Discussion

To our knowledge, all anonymous divisible e-cash systems can be associated with one of these frameworks. The main difference is that existing constructions require less PRFs but, as we explain in Sect. 1.2, this leads to a problem that has been overlooked in the proofs. Although some of them can be patched without adding new PRFs, we note that this patch is very specific to some constructions and so cannot be applied to our generic frameworks.

Starting from the seminal work of Canard and Gouget [14], several schemes [1,16,28]) implicitly followed the second framework[14] and so constructed (or re-used) delegatable PRFs satisfying the properties listed above. Unfortunately, the resulting PRFs do not interact nicely with NIZK, leading to quite complex constructions.

Recently, a series of papers [18,19,30] followed a different approach that actually matches our first framework. It is then possible to extract from these papers constrained key homomorphic PRFs that achieve key pseudo-randomness. Moreover, these PRFs interact smoothly with NIZK, even in the standard model, leading to very efficient constructions.

However, in practice, efficiency does not only depend on the compatibility with NIZK proofs. Divisible e-cash indeed achieves its ultimate goal when it allows the user to spend efficiently the V coins associated with a transaction of amount V. This means that the family of subsets $\{S_i\}$ supported by the PRF must be as rich and as diverse as possible. For decades, the constructions have only been compatible with intervals of the form $[1 + j \cdot 2^k, (j+1)2^k]$ due to the use of binary trees. It is only recently that Pointcheval, Sanders and Traoré [30] proposed a construction supporting *any* interval $[a, b] \subseteq [1, N]$. This led to the first constant-size divisible e-cash systems.

5   Our Framework

We now elaborate on the solutions sketched in the previous section to construct a full divisible e-cash system. We only consider here constructions based on key homomorphic constrained PRFs but describe those based on delegatable PRF in the full version [11].

5.1   Building Blocks

Our framework makes use of three standard cryptographic primitives, namely digital signature, commitment scheme and non-interactive zero-knowledge (NIZK) proofs that we recall below, along with their respective security properties.

$\mathrm{Exp}_{\mathcal{A}}^{\mathrm{euf-cma}}(1^{\lambda})$ – EUF-CMA security Game

1. $(\mathsf{sk}, \mathsf{pk}) \leftarrow \mathtt{Keygen}(1^{\lambda})$
2. $(m^*, \sigma^*) \leftarrow \mathcal{A}^{\mathcal{O}\mathtt{Sign}}(\mathsf{pk})$
3. If $\mathtt{Verify}(\mathsf{pk}, m^*, \sigma^*) = 0$ or $\mathcal{O}\mathtt{Sign}$ queried on m^*, then return 0
4. Return 1

Fig. 4. Security Game for Digital Signature

---

[14] We nevertheless note that the cut-and-choose technique used during withdrawal in [1] is very specific to this work and does not fit our framework.

Digital Signature. A digital signature scheme Σ is defined by three algorithms:

- Keygen(1^λ): on input a security parameter λ, this algorithm outputs a pair of signing and verification keys (sk, pk);
- Sign(sk, m): on input the signing key sk and a message m, this algorithm outputs a signature σ;
- Verify(pk, m, σ): on input the verification key pk, a message m and its alleged signature σ, this algorithm outputs 1 if σ is a valid signature on m under pk, and 0 otherwise.

The standard security notion for a signature scheme is *existential unforgeability under chosen message attacks* (EUF-CMA) [24]: it means that it is hard, even given access to a signing oracle, to output a valid pair (m, σ) for a message m never asked to the signing oracle. The formal definition is provided in Fig. 4 and makes use of an oracle $\mathcal{O}\text{Sign}$ that, on input a message m, returns Sign(sk, m). A signature scheme is EUF-CMA secure if $\Pr[\text{Exp}_{\mathcal{A}}^{\text{euf}-\text{cma}}(1^\lambda) = 1]$ is negligible for any $\mathcal{A}$.

Commitment Scheme. A commitment scheme Γ is defined by the following two algorithms:

- Keygen(1^λ): on input a security parameter λ, this algorithm outputs a commitment key ck that specifies a message space $\mathcal{M}$, a randomizer space $\mathcal{R}$ along with a commitment space $\mathcal{C}$;
- Commit(ck, m, r) : on input ck, an element $r \in \mathcal{R}$ and a message $m \in \mathcal{M}$, this algorithm returns a commitment $c \in \mathcal{C}$.

Informally, a commitment should be binded to the committed message, but still hiding the latter. This is formally defined by the games $\text{Exp}_{\mathcal{A}}^{\text{bind}}(1^\lambda)$ and $\text{Exp}_{\mathcal{A}}^{\text{hid}-b}(1^\lambda)$ of Fig. 5. A commitment scheme is binding if $\Pr[\text{Exp}_{\mathcal{A}}^{\text{bind}}(1^\lambda) = 1]$ is negligible, while it is hiding if $\Pr[\text{Exp}_{\mathcal{A}}^{\text{hid}-1}(1^\lambda) = 1] - \Pr[\text{Exp}_{\mathcal{A}}^{\text{hid}-0}(1^\lambda) = 1]$ is negligible.

Hiding Security Game $\text{Exp}_{\mathcal{A}}^{\text{hid}-b}(1^\lambda)$	Binding Security Game $\text{Exp}_{\mathcal{A}}^{\text{bind}}(1^\lambda)$
1. (ck) $\leftarrow$ Keygen(1^λ)	1. (ck) $\leftarrow$ Keygen(1^λ)
2. $m \leftarrow \mathcal{A}(\text{ck})$	2. $(m_0, m_1, r_0, r_1) \leftarrow \mathcal{A}(\text{ck})$
3. $r \xleftarrow{\$} \mathcal{R}$, $c_0 \leftarrow$ Commit(ck, m, r)	3. If Commit(ck, m_0, r_0) $\neq$ Commit(ck, m_1, r_1)
4. $c_1 \xleftarrow{\$} \mathcal{C}$	or $m_0 = m_1$, then return 0
5. $b^* \leftarrow \mathcal{A}^{\mathcal{O}\text{Sign}}(\text{ck}, c_b)$	4. Return 1
6. Return ($b = b^*$)	

Fig. 5. Security Game for Commitment Schemes

NIZK Proofs. Let R be an efficiently computable relation with triples $(\mathtt{crs}, \phi, w)$, where $\mathtt{crs}$ is called the *common reference string* and w is said to be a *witness* to the *instance* ϕ. A NIZK proof system is defined by the following three algorithms:

- $\mathtt{Setup}(1^\lambda)$: on input a security parameter λ, this algorithm outputs the common reference string $\mathtt{crs}$.
- $\mathtt{Prove}(\mathtt{crs}, w, \phi)$: on input a triple $(\mathtt{crs}, w, \phi) \in R$, this algorithm outputs a proof π.
- $\mathtt{Verify}(\mathtt{crs}, \phi, \pi)$: on input $\mathtt{crs}$, a proof π and an instance ϕ this algorithm outputs either 1 (accept) or 0 reject.

A NIZK proof is correct if the probability that $\mathtt{Verify}(\mathtt{crs}, \phi, \mathtt{Prove}(\mathtt{crs}, w, \phi))$ returns 0 is negligible for all $(\mathtt{crs}, w, \phi) \in R$. We will additionally require the properties of *zero-knowledge* and *extractability*. Both of them are defined in Fig. 6. Extractability requires the existence of an extractor $X_{\mathcal{A}}$ that takes as input the transcript $\mathtt{trans}_{\mathcal{A}}$ of the adversary $\mathcal{A}$. Zero-knowledge requires the existence of a simulator consisting of the algorithms $\mathtt{SimSetup}$ and $\mathtt{SimProve}$ that share state with each other. In the security experiment $\mathtt{Exp}_{\mathcal{A}}^{\mathtt{zk}-b}(1^\lambda)$, the adversary has access to the following oracle:

- $\mathcal{O}\mathtt{Prove}\text{-}b(w, \phi)$: on input (w, ϕ), this algorithm returns $\perp$ if $(\mathtt{crs}_b, w, \phi) \notin R$. Else, it returns $\mathtt{Prove}(\mathtt{crs}_b, w, \phi)$ if $b = 0$ and $\mathtt{SimProve}(\mathtt{crs}_b, \phi)$ otherwise.

A NIZK proof is zero-knowledge if $\Pr[\mathtt{Exp}_{\mathcal{A}}^{\mathtt{zk}-1}(1^\lambda)] - \Pr[\mathtt{Exp}_{\mathcal{A}}^{\mathtt{zk}-0}(1^\lambda)]$ is negligible. It is extractable if $\Pr[\mathtt{Exp}_{\mathcal{A}}^{\mathtt{ext}}(1^\lambda)]$ is negligible.

Zero-Knowledge Game $\mathtt{Exp}_{\mathcal{A}}^{\mathtt{zk}-b}(1^\lambda)$	Extractability Game $\mathtt{Exp}_{\mathcal{A}}^{\mathtt{ext}}(1^\lambda)$
1. $\mathtt{crs}_0 \leftarrow \mathtt{Setup}(1^\lambda)$	1. $\mathtt{crs} \leftarrow \mathtt{Setup}(1^\lambda)$
2. $\mathtt{crs}_1 \leftarrow \mathtt{SimSetup}(1^\lambda)$	2. $(\phi, \pi) \leftarrow \mathcal{A}(\mathtt{crs})$
3. $b^* \leftarrow \mathcal{A}^{\mathcal{O}\mathtt{Prove}-b}(\mathtt{crs}_b)$	3. $w \leftarrow X_{\mathcal{A}}(\mathtt{trans}_{\mathcal{A}})$
4. Return $(b = b^*)$	4. If $\mathtt{Verify}(\mathtt{crs}, \phi, \pi) = 0$ or $(\mathtt{crs}, w, \phi) \notin R$, then return 0
	5. Return 1

Fig. 6. Security Game for NIZK Proofs

5.2 Construction

Our construction makes use of a digital signature scheme Σ, a commitment scheme Γ and a NIZK proof system Π as described above. The difficulty here is to provide the description of a framework that encompasses very different settings such as cyclic groups or lattices. For example, the element $\mathtt{ID}^R$ of Sect. 4 that was involved in double-spending tags does not make sense in a lattice setting and would in practice be replaced by $R \cdot \mathtt{ID}$ where R is a matrix and $\mathtt{ID}$ is a vector.

To remain as generic as possible, we will then introduce several functions that will abstract the properties we need. In our example, we need that $\text{ID}^{R+R'} = \text{ID}^R \cdot \text{ID}^{R'}$ and that $(R + R') \cdot \text{ID} = R \cdot \text{ID} + R' \cdot \text{ID}$ and so will represent ID^R and $R \cdot \text{ID}$ by $G(\text{ID}, R)$ where G is a bilinear map (see Remark 5 for more details). Such functions make the description of our framework rather complex but we stress that they are actually very easy to instantiate. In particular, we emphasize that the following framework essentially formalises the high-level ideas described in Sect. 4 and does not significantly increase the practical complexity of our construction.

- Setup($1^\lambda, N$): To generate the public parameters pp, the algorithm first computes $\text{crs} \leftarrow \Pi.\text{Setup}(1^\lambda)$. It then selects four constrained PRFs F_1, F_2, F_3 and F_4 with the same master key space $\mathcal{K}$ and that support the same subsets $\mathcal{S}_1, \ldots, \mathcal{S}_n$ with $\mathcal{S}_i \subset [1, N] \; \forall i \in [1, n]$. For sake of simplicity, we assume that $\mathcal{K}_{\mathcal{S}_i} = \mathcal{K}_{\mathcal{S}_j} = \mathcal{K}_{\mathcal{S}}$ for all $i, j \in [1, n]$. F_2, F_3 and F_4 must additionally be key homomorphic. Finally, it selects a hash function $H : \{0,1\}^* \to \mathbb{G}$ for some group $\mathbb{G}$, two functions $G_1 : \{0,1\}^* \to \mathcal{K}$, $G_2 : \{0,1\}^* \to \mathcal{K}_{\mathcal{S}}$ along with a non degenerate bilinear map $G_3 : \mathcal{K}_{\mathcal{S}} \times \mathbb{G} \to \mathcal{K}_{\mathcal{S}}$ (see Remark 5). The public parameters pp are then set as $\text{crs}, F_1, F_2, F_3, F_4, H, G_1, G_2, G_3$.
- BKeygen(): The bank generates a commitment key $\text{ck} \leftarrow \Gamma.\text{Keygen}(1^\lambda)$ and a key pair $(\text{sk}_B, \text{pk}_B) \leftarrow \Sigma.\text{Keygen}(1^\lambda)$. It then sets bsk as sk_B and bpk as (hg, pk_B).
- Keygen(): The user (resp. the merchant) generates a signature key pair (usk, upk) (resp. (msk, mpk)) using $\Sigma.\text{Keygen}$.
- Withdraw($\mathcal{B}(\text{bsk}, \text{upk}), \mathcal{U}(\text{usk}, \text{bpk})$): To withdraw a divisible coin, the user first generates $s \leftarrow F_1.\text{Keygen}(1^\lambda, \{\mathcal{S}_i\}_{i=1}^n)$ and a random element r from the randomizer space $\mathcal{R}$ of Γ. It then sends $c \leftarrow \Gamma.\text{Commit}(\text{ck}, [s, \text{upk}], r)$ to the bank along with a signature $\tau_c \leftarrow \Sigma.\text{Sign}(\text{usk}, c)$.
  If τ_c is valid, the bank returns a signature $\sigma_c \leftarrow \Sigma.\text{Sign}(\text{sk}_B, c)$ to the user. The latter can then set its coin C as (c, s, r, σ_c).
- Spend($\mathcal{U}(\text{usk}, C, \text{bpk}, V), \mathcal{M}(\text{msk}, \text{bpk}, \text{info}, V)$): During a spending of amount V, the merchant first selects a string info that he never used before[15] and sends it to the user along with his public key mpk.
  The user then selects a subset $\mathcal{S}_i$ with $|\mathcal{S}_i| = V$ such that SN_j has never been revealed for all $j \in \mathcal{S}_i$, and computes $k_{\mathcal{S}_i}^{(1)} \leftarrow F_1.\text{CKey}(s, \mathcal{S}_i)$, $k_{\mathcal{S}_i}^{(2)} \leftarrow F_2.\text{CKey}(s \cdot G_1(\text{upk}), \mathcal{S}_i)$ and $\text{T}_{\mathcal{S}_i} \leftarrow (G_3(G_2(\text{upk}), H(\text{mpk}\|\text{info})) \cdot k_{\mathcal{S}_i}^{(3)}, G_2(\text{upk}) \cdot k_{\mathcal{S}_i}^{(4)})$ where $k_{\mathcal{S}_i}^{(3)} = F_3.\text{CKey}(s, \mathcal{S}_i)$ and $k_{\mathcal{S}_i}^{(4)} = F_4.\text{CKey}(s, \mathcal{S}_i)$.
  Finally, it generates a signature $\tau \leftarrow \Sigma.\text{Sign}(\text{usk}, (\text{mpk}, V, \text{info}, k_{\mathcal{S}_i}^{(1)}, k_{\mathcal{S}_i}^{(2)}, \text{T}_{\mathcal{S}_i}))$ along with a NIZK proof π of $(\text{upk}, s, c, r, \sigma_c, \mathcal{S}_i, \tau)$ such that:
  1. $\exists i^* \in [1, n] : \mathcal{S}_i = \mathcal{S}_{i^*} \wedge |\mathcal{S}_i| = V$
  2. $c = \Gamma.\text{Commit}(\text{ck}, [s, \text{upk}], r)$
  3. $1 = \Sigma.\text{Verify}(\text{pk}_B, c, \sigma_c)$

---

[15] This string can simply be a counter incremented by the merchant after each transaction, or include information that uniquely identifies the transaction such as the date and the hour.

4. $k_{\mathcal{S}_i}^{(1)} = F_1.\mathtt{CKey}(s, \mathcal{S}_i)$

5. $k_{\mathcal{S}_i}^{(2)} = F_2.\mathtt{CKey}(s \cdot G_1(\mathsf{upk}), \mathcal{S}_i)$

6. $\mathsf{T}_{\mathcal{S}_i} = (G_3(G_2(\mathsf{upk}), H(\mathsf{mpk}\|\mathsf{info})) \cdot F_3.\mathtt{CKey}(s, \mathcal{S}_i), G_2(\mathsf{upk}) \cdot F_4.\mathtt{CKey}(s, \mathcal{S}_i))$

7. $1 = \Sigma.\mathtt{Verify}(\mathsf{upk}, (\mathsf{mpk}, V, \mathsf{info}, k_{\mathcal{S}_i}^{(1)}, k_{\mathcal{S}_i}^{(2)}, \mathsf{T}_{\mathcal{S}_i}), \tau)$

The elements $(k_{\mathcal{S}_i}^{(1)}, k_{\mathcal{S}_i}^{(2)}, \mathsf{T}_{\mathcal{S}_i}, \pi)$ are then sent to the merchant who accepts them as a payment if π is valid.

- $\mathtt{Deposit}(\mathcal{M}(\mathsf{msk}, \mathsf{bpk}, (V, \mathsf{info}, k_{\mathcal{S}_i}^{(1)}, k_{\mathcal{S}_i}^{(2)}, \mathsf{T}_{\mathcal{S}_i}, \pi)), \mathcal{B}(\mathsf{bsk}, L, \mathsf{mpk}))$: To deposit a transaction, the merchant sends its transcript $\mathsf{Tr} \leftarrow (V, \mathsf{info}, k_{\mathcal{S}_i}^{(1)}, k_{\mathcal{S}_i}^{(2)}, \mathsf{T}_{\mathcal{S}_i}, \pi)$ along with a signature $\mu \leftarrow \Sigma.\mathtt{Sign}(\mathsf{msk}, \mathsf{Tr})$. The bank then checks that (1) the proof π is valid, (2) π proves knowledge of a signature on a tuple whose first coordinate is mpk, (3) $\Sigma.\mathtt{Verify}(\mathsf{mpk}, \mathsf{Tr}, \mu) = 1$ and (4) that this merchant has not previously deposited a transaction associated with info. If one of the first three conditions is not satisfied, then the bank returns $\bot$. If the last condition is not satisfied then the bank knows another transcript $(V', \mathsf{info}, k_{\mathcal{S}_j}^{(1)}, k_{\mathcal{S}_j}^{(2)}, \mathsf{T}_{\mathcal{S}_j}, \pi')$ along with a signature μ'. All these elements, along with $[\mathsf{Tr}, \mu]$ constitute a proof of double-deposit.

  Else, the bank recovers, for all $j \in \mathcal{S}_i$ (see Remark 6 below), the serial numbers $\mathsf{SN}_j \leftarrow F_1.\mathtt{CEval}_{\mathcal{S}_i}(k_{\mathcal{S}_i}^{(1)}, j)\|F_2.\mathtt{CEval}_{\mathcal{S}_i}(k_{\mathcal{S}_i}^{(2)}, j)$. It then distinguishes the following two cases:

  - $\exists j^* \in \mathcal{S}_i$ such that SN_{j^*} already belongs to L. In such a case, the bank recovers the first transcript $(V', \mathsf{info}', \mathsf{mpk}', k_{\mathcal{S}_{i'}}^{(1)}, k_{\mathcal{S}_{i'}}^{(2)}, \mathsf{T}_{\mathcal{S}_{i'}}, \pi')$ that yields this serial number and returns it along with Tr.

  - $\mathsf{SN}_j \notin L \; \forall j \in \mathcal{S}_i$, in which case the bank simply adds these serial numbers to L

- $\mathtt{Identify}((V, \mathsf{info}, \mathsf{mpk}, k_{\mathcal{S}_i}^{(1)}, k_{\mathcal{S}_i}^{(2)}, \mathsf{T}_{\mathcal{S}_i}, \pi), (V', \mathsf{info}', \mathsf{mpk}', k_{\mathcal{S}_j}^{(1)}, k_{\mathcal{S}_j}^{(2)}, \mathsf{T}_{\mathcal{S}_j}, \pi'),$
  $\mathsf{bpk})$: Given two transcripts, this algorithm first checks that (1) $\mathsf{mpk}\|\mathsf{info} \neq \mathsf{mpk}'\|\mathsf{info}'$ and (2) both proofs π and π' are valid. If one of these conditions is not satisfied, then it returns 0. Else, it checks that there is a collision between the serial numbers derived from these transcripts, $i.e.$ there are $x \in \mathcal{S}_i$ and $x' \in \mathcal{S}_j$ such that $F_1.\mathtt{CEval}_{\mathcal{S}_i}(k_{\mathcal{S}_i}^{(1)}, x)\|F_2.\mathtt{CEval}_{\mathcal{S}_i}(k_{\mathcal{S}_i}^{(2)}, x) = F_1.\mathtt{CEval}_{\mathcal{S}_j}(k_{\mathcal{S}_j}^{(1)}, x')\| F_2.\mathtt{CEval}_{\mathcal{S}_j}(k_{\mathcal{S}_j}^{(2)}, x')$. If there is no collision, it outputs 0.

  Else, it proceeds as in Sect. 4.1 to identify the defrauder. If $\mathsf{T}_{\mathcal{S}_i}[2] = \mathsf{T}_{\mathcal{S}_j}[2]$, it computes $R = H(\mathsf{mpk}\|\mathsf{info})$, $R' = H(\mathsf{mpk}'\|\mathsf{info}')$ along with

  $$F_3.\mathtt{CEval}_{\mathcal{S}_i}(\mathsf{T}_{\mathcal{S}_i}[1], x)/F_3.\mathtt{CEval}_{\mathcal{S}_j}(\mathsf{T}_{\mathcal{S}_j}[1], x')$$

  and $F_3.\mathtt{CEval}_{\mathcal{S}_i}(G_3(G_2(\mathsf{upk}), R), x)/F_3.\mathtt{CEval}_{\mathcal{S}_j}(G_3(G_2(\mathsf{upk}), R'), x)$ for all upk until it gets a match. It then returns the corresponding public key upk^* (or $\bot$ if the exhaustive search fails).

  Else, $\mathsf{T}_{\mathcal{S}_i}[2] \neq \mathsf{T}_{\mathcal{S}_j}[2]$ and it computes

  $$F_4.\mathtt{CEval}_{\mathcal{S}_i}(\mathsf{T}_{\mathcal{S}_i}[2]/G_2(\mathsf{upk}), x)/F_4.\mathtt{CEval}_{\mathcal{S}_j}(\mathsf{T}_{\mathcal{S}_{i_2}}[2]/G_2(\mathsf{upk}), x')$$

  for all public keys upk until it gets 1_y. It then returns the corresponding public key upk^* (or $\bot$ if the exhaustive search fails).

- CheckDeposit$([(V, \text{info}, \text{mpk}, k_{\mathcal{S}_i}^{(1)}, k_{\mathcal{S}_i}^{(2)}, \mathsf{T}_{\mathcal{S}_i}, \pi), \mu], \text{bpk})$: this algorithm checks that π is valid and that $1 = \Sigma.\text{Verify}(\text{mpk}, (V, \text{info}, k_{\mathcal{S}_i}^{(1)}, k_{\mathcal{S}_i}^{(2)}, \mathsf{T}_{\mathcal{S}_i}, \pi), \mu)$ in which case it outputs 1. Else, it returns 0.

Remark 4. An example of instantiation of our full construction, in the standard model, is provided in the full version [11] to assess the practical complexity of our framework. Nevertheless, we note that a spending essentially consists in generating 4 constrained keys along with a zero-knowledge proof that they have been correctly computed from a certified master key. In bilinear groups, such proofs can easily be produced in the random oracle model or by using Groth-Sahai proofs [25] if one selects an appropriate digital signature scheme for Σ, as illustrated in our full version where we show that the complexity of our framework is very similar to the one of (unsecure) schemes from the state-of-the-art. The case of lattices is more complex but we note that the proofs and the signature scheme required here are similar to those described in [27].

Remark 5. The only purpose of the functions G_1, G_2 and G_3 is to project the different elements of our system on the appropriate spaces, which ensures compatibility with most PRFs. As we illustrate on concrete examples in the full version [11], these functions are in practice very simple (for example G_2 is usually the identity function) and nicely interact with zero-knowledge proofs. In particular, our bilinear map G_3 can easily be instantiated in most settings. For example, when $\mathcal{K}_{\mathcal{S}}$ is a cyclic group of order p, we will simply have $\mathbb{G} = \mathbb{Z}_p$ and $G_3(x, y) = x^y$. Similarly, when $\mathcal{K}_{\mathcal{S}} = \mathbb{F}_q^n$, we will have $\mathbb{G} \subset \mathcal{M}_{m,n}$ and $G_3(x, A) = A \cdot x$.

We will also manage to make G_1 and G_2 injective in practice which means that the collision resistance will be trivially satisfied. We recall that the bilinear map G_3 is non degenerate if $G_3(x, y) = 1_{\mathcal{K}_{\mathcal{S}}}$ implies $x = 1_{\mathcal{K}_{\mathcal{S}}}$ or $y = 1_{\mathbb{G}}$.

Remark 6. Note that, even if the bank does not know the subset $\mathcal{S}_i$, it is always able to recover all the serial numbers $\mathsf{SN}_j \leftarrow \text{CEval}_{\mathcal{S}_i}(k_{\mathcal{S}_i}, j)$, for $j \in \mathcal{S}_i$. Indeed, it can generates the list L containing $\mathsf{SN}_k \leftarrow \text{CEval}_{\mathcal{S}}(k_{\mathcal{S}}, k)$, for all $\mathcal{S}$ containing V elements and $k \in \mathcal{S}$. Such a list contains the valid serial numbers (those for which $\mathcal{S} = \mathcal{S}_i$) and so can still be used to detect double-spendings. Moreover, due to the properties of PRF, the "invalid" serial numbers (those for which $\mathcal{S} \neq \mathcal{S}_j$) are random elements and so are unlikely to create false positives (collisions in the list L that are not due to double-spendings).

However, we stress that this is only a generic solution that works for any instantiation of our construction. In practice, it leads to quite complex deposits and so should be avoided, if possible. Actually, to our knowledge, it is only used in [18]. All other divisible e-cash systems manage to construct PRFs that can be evaluated on the elements of $\mathcal{S}_i$ without knowing $\mathcal{S}_i$. More specifically, theses PRFs are compatible with an algorithm $\overline{\text{CEval}}$ that takes as input a constrained key and the size of the corresponding subset and that outputs $\overline{\text{CEval}}(k_{\mathcal{S}_i}, |\mathcal{S}_i|) = \{\text{CEval}_{\mathcal{S}_i}(k_{\mathcal{S}_i}, x), \forall x \in \mathcal{S}_i\}$.

The security of our construction is stated by the following theorem, proven in the full version [11].

Theorem 7. *Our divisible e-cash system is*

- *traceable if F_1 and F_2 achieve collision resistance-1, Γ is computationally binding, Σ is EUF-CMA secure, Π is extractable, and G_1 is collision resistant.*
- *exculpable if Σ is EUF-CMA secure, Π is extractable, F_1 and F_2 achieve collision resistance-1, F_3 achieves collision resistance-2, F_4 achieves collision resistance-3 and H, G_1 and G_2 are collision resistant.*
- *clearable if Σ is EUF-CMA secure.*
- *anonymous if (F_1, F_2, F_3, F_4) achieves combined key pseudo-randomness, Γ is computationally hiding and Π is zero-knowledge.*

Remark 8. Most existing constructions require a collaborative generation of the coin secret values. Our framework can easily support this feature if Γ is homomorphic. In such a case, traceability no longer requires collision resistance for F_1 and F_2 because the randomness added by the bank (which is honest in this game) will make collisions very unlikely. Unfortunately, the collaborative generation has no effect on exculpability since both parties (the user and the bank) can be corrupted in this game. We therefore choose to simplify our withdrawal protocol by removing this step since we need collision resistance of F_1 and F_2 anyway.

6 Conclusion

Decades after their introduction, divisible e-cash systems are still remarkably hard to design, and even to analyse. Existing schemes are based on intricate mechanisms, tailored to very specific settings, and so can hardly be reproduced in different contexts. Moreover, such mechanisms often rely on ad-hoc computational problems whose intractability is hard to assess.

In this paper we introduce the first frameworks for divisible e-cash systems that only use constrained PRFs and very standard cryptographic primitives. We prove the security of our global constructions assuming that each of the building blocks achieve some properties that we identify.

Our work thus presents this complex primitive in a new light, highlighting its strong relations with constrained PRFs. More specifically, it shows that the bulk of the design of a divisible e-cash system is the construction of a constrained PRF with some specific features. We therefore hope that our results will encourage designers of constrained PRFs to add these features to their constructions, so as to implicitly define a new divisible e-cash scheme. We in particular believe that it is an important step towards a post-quantum divisible e-cash system.

Acknowledgements. We thank Benoît Libert for very helpful discussions on the exculpability issue of previous works. This work is supported in part by the European Union PROMETHEUS Project (Horizon 2020 Research and Innovation Program, Grant Agreement no. 780701) and the European Community's Seventh Framework Programme (FP7/2007-2013 Grant Agreement no. 339563 – CryptoCloud).

References

1. Au, M.H., Susilo, W., Mu, Y.: Practical anonymous divisible e-cash from bounded accumulators. In: Tsudik, G. (ed.) FC 2008. LNCS, vol. 5143, pp. 287–301. Springer, Heidelberg (2008). https://doi.org/10.1007/978-3-540-85230-8_26
2. Baldimtsi, F., Chase, M., Fuchsbauer, G., Kohlweiss, M.: Anonymous transferable e-cash. In: Katz, J. (ed.) PKC 2015. LNCS, vol. 9020, pp. 101–124. Springer, Heidelberg (2015). https://doi.org/10.1007/978-3-662-46447-2_5
3. Banerjee, A., Fuchsbauer, G., Peikert, C., Pietrzak, K., Stevens, S.: Key-homomorphic constrained pseudorandom functions. In: Dodis, Y., Nielsen, J.B. (eds.) TCC 2015. LNCS, vol. 9015, pp. 31–60. Springer, Heidelberg (2015). https://doi.org/10.1007/978-3-662-46497-7_2
4. Bellare, M., Micciancio, D., Warinschi, B.: Foundations of group signatures: formal definitions, simplified requirements, and a construction based on general assumptions. In: Biham, E. (ed.) EUROCRYPT 2003. LNCS, vol. 2656, pp. 614–629. Springer, Heidelberg (2003). https://doi.org/10.1007/3-540-39200-9_38
5. Bellare, M., Shi, H., Zhang, C.: Foundations of group signatures: the case of dynamic groups. In: Menezes, A. (ed.) CT-RSA 2005. LNCS, vol. 3376, pp. 136–153. Springer, Heidelberg (2005). https://doi.org/10.1007/978-3-540-30574-3_11
6. Blazy, O., Canard, S., Fuchsbauer, G., Gouget, A., Sibert, H., Traoré, J.: Achieving optimal anonymity in transferable e-cash with a judge. In: Nitaj, A., Pointcheval, D. (eds.) AFRICACRYPT 2011. LNCS, vol. 6737, pp. 206–223. Springer, Heidelberg (2011). https://doi.org/10.1007/978-3-642-21969-6_13
7. Boneh, D., Kim, S., Montgomery, H.: Private puncturable PRFs from standard lattice assumptions. In: Coron, J.-S., Nielsen, J.B. (eds.) EUROCRYPT 2017. LNCS, vol. 10210, pp. 415–445. Springer, Cham (2017). https://doi.org/10.1007/978-3-319-56620-7_15
8. Boneh, D., Lewi, K., Montgomery, H., Raghunathan, Λ.: Key homomorphic PRFs and their applications. In: Canetti, R., Garay, J.A. (eds.) CRYPTO 2013. LNCS, vol. 8042, pp. 410–428. Springer, Heidelberg (2013). https://doi.org/10.1007/978-3-642-40041-4_23
9. Boneh, D., Lewi, K., Wu, D.J.: Constraining pseudorandom functions privately. In: Fehr, S. (ed.) PKC 2017. LNCS, vol. 10175, pp. 494–524. Springer, Heidelberg (2017). https://doi.org/10.1007/978-3-662-54388-7_17
10. Boneh, D., Waters, B.: Constrained pseudorandom functions and their applications. In: Sako, K., Sarkar, P. (eds.) ASIACRYPT 2013. LNCS, vol. 8270, pp. 280–300. Springer, Heidelberg (2013). https://doi.org/10.1007/978-3-642-42045-0_15
11. Bourse, F., Pointcheval, D., Sanders, O.: Divisible e-cash from constrained pseudorandom functions. IACR Cryptology ePrint Archive, vol. 136 (2019)
12. Boyle, E., Goldwasser, S., Ivan, I.: Functional signatures and pseudorandom functions. In: Krawczyk, H. (ed.) PKC 2014. LNCS, vol. 8383, pp. 501–519. Springer, Heidelberg (2014). https://doi.org/10.1007/978-3-642-54631-0_29
13. Camenisch, J., Hohenberger, S., Lysyanskaya, A.: Compact e-cash. In: Cramer, R. (ed.) EUROCRYPT 2005. LNCS, vol. 3494, pp. 302–321. Springer, Heidelberg (2005). https://doi.org/10.1007/11426639_18
14. Canard, S., Gouget, A.: Divisible e-cash systems can be truly anonymous. In: Naor, M. (ed.) EUROCRYPT 2007. LNCS, vol. 4515, pp. 482–497. Springer, Heidelberg (2007). https://doi.org/10.1007/978-3-540-72540-4_28

15. Canard, S., Gouget, A.: Anonymity in transferable e-cash. In: Bellovin, S.M., Gennaro, R., Keromytis, A., Yung, M. (eds.) ACNS 2008. LNCS, vol. 5037, pp. 207–223. Springer, Heidelberg (2008). https://doi.org/10.1007/978-3-540-68914-0_13

16. Canard, S., Gouget, A.: Multiple denominations in e-cash with compact transaction data. In: Sion, R. (ed.) FC 2010. LNCS, vol. 6052, pp. 82–97. Springer, Heidelberg (2010). https://doi.org/10.1007/978-3-642-14577-3_9

17. Canard, S., Gouget, A., Traoré, J.: Improvement of efficiency in (unconditional) anonymous transferable e-cash. In: Tsudik, G. (ed.) FC 2008. LNCS, vol. 5143, pp. 202–214. Springer, Heidelberg (2008). https://doi.org/10.1007/978-3-540-85230-8_19

18. Canard, S., Pointcheval, D., Sanders, O., Traoré, J.: Divisible e-cash made practical. In: Katz, J. (ed.) PKC 2015. LNCS, vol. 9020, pp. 77–100. Springer, Heidelberg (2015). https://doi.org/10.1007/978-3-662-46447-2_4

19. Canard, S., Pointcheval, D., Sanders, O., Traoré, J.: Scalable divisible e-cash. In: Malkin, T., Kolesnikov, V., Lewko, A.B., Polychronakis, M. (eds.) ACNS 2015. LNCS, vol. 9092, pp. 287–306. Springer, Cham (2015). https://doi.org/10.1007/978-3-319-28166-7_14

20. Chaum, D.: Blind signatures for untraceable payments. In: Chaum, D., Rivest, R.L., Sherman, A.T. (eds.) Advances in Cryptology, pp. 199–203. Springer, Boston, MA (1983). https://doi.org/10.1007/978-1-4757-0602-4_18

21. Chaum, D., Fiat, A., Naor, M.: Untraceable electronic cash. In: Goldwasser, S. (ed.) CRYPTO 1988. LNCS, vol. 403, pp. 319–327. Springer, New York (1990). https://doi.org/10.1007/0-387-34799-2_25

22. Chaum, D., Pedersen, T.P.: Transferred cash grows in size. In: Rueppel, R.A. (ed.) EUROCRYPT 1992. LNCS, vol. 658, pp. 390–407. Springer, Heidelberg (1993). https://doi.org/10.1007/3-540-47555-9_32

23. Fuchsbauer, G., Pointcheval, D., Vergnaud, D.: Transferable constant-size fair e-cash. In: Garay, J.A., Miyaji, A., Otsuka, A. (eds.) CANS 2009. LNCS, vol. 5888, pp. 226–247. Springer, Heidelberg (2009). https://doi.org/10.1007/978-3-642-10433-6_15

24. Goldwasser, S., Micali, S., Rivest, R.L.: A digital signature scheme secure against adaptive chosen-message attacks. SIAM J. Comput. 17(2), 281–308 (1988)

25. Groth, J., Sahai, A.: Efficient non-interactive proof systems for bilinear groups. In: Smart, N. (ed.) EUROCRYPT 2008. LNCS, vol. 4965, pp. 415–432. Springer, Heidelberg (2008). https://doi.org/10.1007/978-3-540-78967-3_24

26. Kiayias, A., Papadopoulos, S., Triandopoulos, N., Zacharias, T.: Delegatable pseudorandom functions and applications. In: Sadeghi, A.-R., Gligor, V.D., Yung, M. (eds.) ACM CCS 13, pp. 669–684. ACM Press, November 2013

27. Libert, B., Ling, S., Nguyen, K., Wang, H.: Zero-knowledge arguments for lattice-based PRFs and applications to e-cash. In: Takagi, T., Peyrin, T. (eds.) ASIACRYPT 2017. LNCS, vol. 10626, pp. 304–335. Springer, Cham (2017). https://doi.org/10.1007/978-3-319-70700-6_11

28. Märtens, P.: Practical divisible e-cash. IACR Cryptology ePrint Archive 2015, 318 (2015)

29. Okamoto, T., Ohta, K.: Universal electronic cash. In: Feigenbaum, J. (ed.) CRYPTO 1991. LNCS, vol. 576, pp. 324–337. Springer, Heidelberg (1992). https://doi.org/10.1007/3-540-46766-1_27

30. Pointcheval, D., Sanders, O., Traoré, J.: Cut down the tree to achieve constant complexity in divisible e-cash. In: Fehr, S. (ed.) PKC 2017. LNCS, vol. 10174, pp. 61–90. Springer, Heidelberg (2017). https://doi.org/10.1007/978-3-662-54365-8_4

31. Pointcheval, D., Stern, J.: Provably secure blind signature schemes. In: Kim, K., Matsumoto, T. (eds.) ASIACRYPT 1996. LNCS, vol. 1163, pp. 252–265. Springer, Heidelberg (1996). https://doi.org/10.1007/BFb0034852
32. Pointcheval, D., Stern, J.: Security arguments for digital signatures and blind signatures. J. Cryptol. **13**(3), 361–396 (2000)

Author Index

Printed in the United States
By Bookmasters